the

AMERICANA ANNUAL

1981

GROLIER

AN ENCYCLOPEDIA OF THE EVENTS OF 1980

YEARBOOK OF THE ENCYCLOPEDIA AMERICANA

This annual has been prepared as a yearbook for general encyclopedias. It is also published as *Encyclopedia Year Book*.

© GROLIER INCORPORATED 1981

Copyright in Canada © by Grolier Limited

Library of Congress Catalog Card Number: 23-10041

ISBN: 0-7172-0212-7

ISSN: 0196-0180

Printed in the United States of America

Editor in Chief	EDWARD HUMPHREY
Executive Editor	JAMES E. CHURCHILL, JR.
Editor	JEFF HACKER
Art Director	ABBIE CARROLL WILSON
Assistant Editors	SAUNDRA FRANCE
	EDWARD M. KURDYLA, JR.
Copy Editor and Proofreader	VIRGINIA QUINN McCARTHY
Chief Indexer	JILL SCHULER
Indexer	SUSAN DEROMEDI
Staff Secretary	BARBARA L. NUNNERY
Photo Researcher	JANET C. BRAUNLE

MANUFACTURING DEPARTMENT

Vice-President and Director	HARRIET RIPINSKY
Senior Manufacturing Manager	WESLEY J. WARREN
Senior Production Manager	JOSEPH J. CORLETT
Production Assistant	CHRISTINE L. MATTA

• • • • • • • • • •

GROLIER INCORPORATED

Senior Vice-President, Publishing	HOWARD B. GRAHAM
Vice-President and Editorial Director	BERNARD S. CAYNE

CONTENTS

THE ALPHABETICAL SECTION

Separate entries on the continents, the major nations of the world, U.S. states, Canadian provinces, and chief cities will be found under their own alphabetically arranged headings.

CONTRIBUTORS

ADRIAN, CHARLES R., Professor of Political Science, University of California, Riverside; Coauthor, *Governing Urban America:* CALIFORNIA; LOS ANGELES

ALEXANDER, ROBERT J., Professor of Economics and Political Science, Rutgers University: ECUADOR; GUYANA; URUGUAY

ALLER, LAWRENCE H., Professor of Astronomy, University of California; Author, *Atoms, Stars, and Nebulae* and *Astrophysics, I and II;* ASTRONOMY

AMBRE, AGO, Economist, Bureau of Economic Analysis, U.S. Department of Commerce: INDUSTRIAL REVIEW

BALLINGER, RONALD B., Professor and Chairman, Department of History, Rhode Island College: BIOGRAPHY—*Robert Mugabe;* SOUTH AFRICA; ZIMBABWE

BARMASH, ISADORE, Financial Writer, *The New York Times;* Author, *The Chief Executives:* RETAILING

BECK, KAY, School of Urban Life, Georgia State University: GEORGIA

BEGLEY, SHARON, Associate Editor, *Newsweek:* GENETICS—*Gene Splicing*

BERGEN, DAN, Professor, Graduate Library School, University of Rhode Island: LIBRARIES

BERLIN, MICHAEL, Diplomatic Correspondent, *New York Post:* UNITED NATIONS

BEST, JOHN, Chief, *Canada World News,* Ottawa: NEW BRUNSWICK; PRINCE EDWARD ISLAND

BÖDVARSSON, HAUKUR, Coeditor, *News From Iceland:* ICELAND

BOLUS, JIM, Sportswriter, *The Louisville Times;* Author, *Run for the Roses:* SPORTS—*Horse Racing*

BOND, DONOVAN H., Professor of Journalism, West Virginia University: WEST VIRGINIA

BOULAY, HARVEY, Professor of Political Science, Boston University: BOSTON; MASSACHUSETTS

BOWERS, Q. DAVID, President, Bowers & Ruddy Galleries, Inc.; member, board of governors, American Numismatic Association: COINS AND COIN COLLECTING

BRADLEY, BILL, United States Senator from New Jersey: THE OLYMPICS/AN ARGUMENT FOR A PERMANENT SITE

BRAMMER, DANA B., Associate Director, Bureau of Governmental Research, University of Mississippi: MISSISSIPPI

BRANDHORST, L. CARL, Associate Professor of Geography, Oregon College of Education: OREGON

BRODIN, PIERRE E., Director of Studies, Lycée Français de New York: LITERATURE—*French;* OBITUARIES—*Jean-Paul Sartre*

BURKS, ARDATH W., Professor of Asian Studies, Rutgers University; Author, *Japan, Profile of a Postindustrial Power:* BIOGRAPHY—*Zenko Suzuki;* JAPAN

BUSH, GRAHAM W. A., Senior Lecturer in Political Studies, University of Auckland, New Zealand; Author, *Local Government & Politics in New Zealand:* NEW ZEALAND

BUTWELL, RICHARD, Vice-President for Academic Programs and Professor of Political Science, Murray State University, Murray, KY; Author, *Southeast Asia, a Political Introduction; U-Nu of Burma; Southeast Asia Today and Tomorrow; Foreign Policy and the Developing State:* ASIA; BURMA; CAMBODIA; LAOS; PHILIPPINES; VIETNAM

CAIRNS, JOHN C., Professor of History, University of Toronto: FRANCE

CALABRESE, MICHAEL, Program Manager, National Aeronautics and Space Administration: SPACE EXPLORATION (article written independent of NASA)

CALABRIA, PAT, Sports Department, *Newsday,* Long Island, NY: SPORTS—*Ice Hockey*

CAMMACK, PAUL, Glasgow University, Scotland: BOLIVIA

CANN, STAN, Consultant, *The Forum,* Fargo, ND: NORTH DAKOTA

CARLYLE-GORDGE, PETER, Manitoba Correspondent; *Maclean's* magazine: MANITOBA

CHALMERS, JOHN W., Concordia College, Edmonton, Alberta; Editor, *Alberta Diamond Jubilee Anthology:* ALBERTA

CLARKE, JAMES W., Department of Political Science, University of Arizona: ARIZONA

COCKRUM, E. LENDELL, Professor and Head, Department of Ecology and Evolutionary Biology, University of Arizona: ZOOLOGY

COLE, FRANCES E., CBS-TV Music Critic/Commentator: MUSIC—*Gospel Music*

COLE, GORDON H., Senior Staff Associate, George Meany Center for Labor Studies: BIOGRAPHY—*Lane Kirkland;* LABOR; OBITUARIES—*George Meany*

COLLINS, BOB, Sports Editor, *The Indianapolis Star:* SPORTS—*Auto Racing*

COMMANDAY, ROBERT, Music Critic, *San Francisco Chronicle:* MUSIC—*Classical*

CORLEW, ROBERT E., Dean, School of Liberal Arts, Middle Tennessee State University: TENNESSEE

CORNWELL, ELMER E., JR., Professor of Political Science, Brown University: RHODE ISLAND

CRONIN, THOMAS E., Professor and Political Scientist; Author, *The State of the Presidency;* Coauthor, *The Presidency Reappraised:* THE U.S. PRESIDENCY/THE OFFICE TODAY

CUNNIFF, JOHN, Business Analyst, The Associated Press; Author, *How to Stretch Your Dollar:* UNITED STATES—*Economy*

CUNNINGHAM, PEGGY, Staff Reporter, *News American,* Baltimore: MARYLAND

CURRIER, CHET, Financial Writer, *The Associated Press:* INTERNATIONAL TRADE AND FINANCE—*Gold and Silver;* STOCKS AND BONDS

CURTIS, L. PERRY, JR., Professor of History, Brown University: IRELAND

DANIELS, ROBERT V., Professor of History, University of Vermont: VERMONT

DARBY, JOSEPH W., III, Reporter, *Times-Picayune,* New Orleans: LOUISIANA

DE GREGORIO, GEORGE, Sports Department, *The New York Times:* THE OLYMPICS/THE XXII SUMMER GAMES; BIOGRAPHY—*John McEnroe, Juan Antonio Samaranch;* SPORTS—*Boxing, Swimming, Track, Yachting*

DELZELL, CHARLES F., Professor of History, Vanderbilt University; Author, *Italy in the Twentieth Century:* ITALY

DENNIS, LARRY, Senior Editor, *Golf Digest;* Coauthor, *How to Become a Complete Golfer:* SPORTS—*Golf*

DIETERICH, H. R., JR., Professor, History/American Studies, University of Wyoming, Laramie: WYOMING

DOBLER, CLIFFORD I., Professor Emeritus of Business Law, University of Idaho: IDAHO

DOLAN, PAUL, Professor of Political Science, University of Delaware; Coauthor, *Government of Delaware:* DELAWARE

DORPALEN, ANDREAS, Professor Emeritus of History, The Ohio State University: GERMANY

DRACHKOVITCH, MILORAD M., Senior Fellow, The Hoover Institute on War, Revolution, and Peace, Stanford University; Author, *U.S. Aid to Yugoslavia and Poland:* OBITUARIES—*Marshal Tito;* YUGOSLAVIA

DRIGGS, DON W., Chairman, Department of Political Science, University of Nevada: NEVADA

DUFF, ERNEST A., Professor of Political Science, Randolph-Macon Women's College; Author, *Agrarian Reform in Colombia:* COLOMBIA

DUFFY, HELEN, Art Critic and Curator to The Art Centre, Queen's University, Kingston, Ontario: CANADA—*The Arts*

DUROSKA, LUD, *The New York Times;* Author/editor, *Football Rules in Pictures; Great Pro Quarterbacks; Great Pro Running Backs:* SPORTS—*Football*

DURRENCE, J. LARRY, Department of History, Florida Southern College: FLORIDA

EDELMAN, MARIAN W., President, Children's Defense Fund: THE FAMILY/THE NEEDS OF CHILDREN

EINFRANK, AARON R., Free-lance Writer, Middle East Specialist: IRAN; IRAQ; THE THIRD WORLD

ELGIN, RICHARD, State Desk, *The Patriot, The Evening News,* and *The Sunday Patriot-News,* Harrisburg: PENNSYLVANIA

ELKINS, ANN M., Fashion Director, *Good Housekeeping Magazine:* FASHION

ENSTAD, ROBERT, Reporter, *Chicago Tribune:* CHICAGO; ILLINOIS

ETCHESON, WARREN W., Graduate School of Business Administration, University of Washington: WASHINGTON

EWEGEN, BOB, Editorial Writer, *The Denver Post:* COLORADO

FAGEN, M. D., Bell Telephone Laboratories (retired); Editor, *A History of Engineering and Science in the Bell System,* Vols I & II: COMMUNICATIONS TECHNOLOGY

FISHEL, JEFF, Professor of Government, The American University; Author, *Parties and Elections in an Anti-Party Age* and *Party and Opposition:* THE U.S. PRESIDENCY/JOHN ANDERSON AND THE THIRD PARTY MOVEMENT; BIOGRAPHY—*J. Anderson*

FOLEJEWSKI, ZBIGNIEW, Professor and Chairman, Department of Slavic Studies and Modern Languages, University of Ottawa: LITERATURE—*Soviet*

FRIIS, ERIK J., Editor-Publisher, *The Scandinavian-American Bulletin;* Author, *The American-Scandinavian Foundation 1910-1960: A Brief History:* DENMARK; FINLAND

GAILEY, HARRY A., Professor of History and Coordinator of African Studies, San Jose State University, California: CHAD; GHANA; LIBERIA; NIGERIA

GARFIELD, ROBERT, Associate Professor of History, Co-Director, Afro-American Studies Program, De Paul University, Chicago, IL; Editor, *Readings in World Civilizations:* KENYA; TANZANIA; UGANDA

GEIS, GILBERT, Professor, Program in Social Ecology, University of California, Irvine; Author, *Man, Crime, and Society:* CRIME; CRIME—HANDGUNS

GELMAN, ERIC, Reporter, *Newsweek* magazine: THE FAMILY/CHALLENGES TO TRADITION

GJESTER, THOR, Editor, *Økonomisk Revy,* Oslo: NORWAY

GLICKMAN, MARTY, Sports Announcer, Member of U.S. Olympic Team 1936: OBITUARIES—*Jesse Owens*

GOFF, COLIN, University of California, Irvine: CRIME—HANDGUNS

GOODMAN, DONALD, Associate Professor of Sociology, John Jay College of Criminal Justice, City University of New York: PRISONS

GORDON, MAYNARD M., Editor, *Motor News Analysis* and *The Imported Car Reports:* AUTOMOBILES

GORDON, MICHAEL, Staff Correspondent, *National Journal:* INTERNATIONAL TRADE AND FINANCE

GRAYSON, GEORGE W., Professor of Government, College of William and Mary: PORTUGAL; SPAIN

GREEN, MAUREEN, British Author and Journalist: GREAT BRITAIN—*The Arts;* LONDON

GRENIER, FERNAND, Director General, Télé-université, Université du Québec: QUEBEC

GROTH, ALEXANDER J., Professor of Political Science, University of California, Davis; Author, *People's Poland:* POLAND

GRUBERG, MARTIN, Professor of Political Science, University of Wisconsin, Oshkosh: CIVIL LIBERTIES AND CIVIL RIGHTS; LAW—*International;* OBITUARIES—*William O. Douglas*

GWERTZMAN, BERNARD, Diplomatic Correspondent, *The New York Times:* THE PERSIAN GULF/THE U.S. HOSTAGE CRISIS

HAKKARINEN, IDA, Graduate Research Assistant, Department of Meteorology, University of Maryland: METEOROLOGY—*The Weather Year*

HAND, SAMUEL B., Professor of History, University of Vermont: VERMONT

HARVEY, ROSS M., Assistant Director of Information, Government of the Northwest Territories: NORTHWEST TERRITORIES

HAYES, KIRBY M., Professor of Food Science and Nutrition, University of Massachusetts: FOOD

HEADY, EARL O., Distinguished Professor of Agricultural Economics, Iowa State University; Author, *Economics of Agricultural Production and Resource; Agricultural Policies Under Economic Development:* AGRICULTURE

HEBERLEIN, GREG, Sports Department, *Seattle Times:* BIOGRAPHY—*Larry Bird;* SPORTS—*Basketball*

HECHINGER, FRED M., President, The New York Times Company Foundation; Author, *The Big Red Schoolhouse;* Coauthor, *Teen-Age Tyranny* and *Growing Up in America:* EDUCATION—*The Changing Role of Testing*

HELMREICH, E. C., Thomas B. Reed Professor of History and Political Science, Bowdoin College, ME; Author, *The German Churches Under Hitler: Background, Struggle, and Epilogue:* AUSTRIA

HELMREICH, J. E., Professor of History and Dean of Instruction, Allegheny College, Meadville, PA; Author, *Belgium and Europe: A Study in Small Power Diplomacy:* LUXEMBOURG

HELMREICH, PAUL C., Professor of History, Wheaton College: SWITZERLAND

HELMS, ANDREA R. C., Associate Professor of Political Science, University of Alaska: ALASKA

HENDERSON, JIM, Sportswriter, *The Tampa Tribune, The Sporting News;* Former Publisher, *Annual Soccer Guide:* SPORTS—*Soccer*

HENRIKSEN, THOMAS H., National Fellow, Hoover Institution on War and Peace, Stanford University, CA; Author, *Mozambique: A History:* ANGOLA; ZAIRE

HIGHLAND, JOSEPH H., Chairman, Toxic Chemicals Program, Environmental Defense Fund; Coauthor, *Action for a Change: A Student Manual for Public Interest Organizing* and *Malignant Neglect:* HAZARDOUS WASTE/A PROBLEM FOR THE 1980s

HOGGART, SIMON, Political Correspondent, *The Guardian,* London; Author, *The Pact:* GREAT BRITAIN

HOOVER, HERBERT T., Professor of History, University of South Dakota: SOUTH DAKOTA

HOPKO, THE REV. THOMAS, Assistant Professor, St. Vladimir's Orthodox Theological Seminary, Crestwood, NY: RELIGION—*Orthodox Eastern*

HOWARD, HARRY N., Board of Governors, Middle East Institute, Washington, DC; Author, *Turkey, the Straits and U.S. Policy:* TURKEY

HOYT, CHARLES KING, AIA, Associate Editor, *Architectural Record;* Author, *Interior Spaces Designed by Architects; Public Municipal and Community Buildings; Buildings for Commerce and Industry:* ARCHITECTURE

HULBERT, DAN, *The New York Times:* NEW YORK; NEW YORK CITY; TELEVISION AND RADIO

HULL, RICHARD W., Associate Professor of African History, New York University; Author, *Modern Africa: Change and Continuity; African Cities and Towns Before the European Conquest:* AFRICA

HUME, ANDREW, Free-lance Writer/Photographer, Former Reporter, *The Whitehorse* (Yukon) *Star;* Author, *The Yukon:* YUKON

HUMMEL, RICK, Baseball Writer, *St. Louis Post-Dispatch:* SPORTS—*Baseball*

HUTH, JOHN F., JR., Reporter-columnist, *The Plain Dealer,* Cleveland: CLEVELAND; OHIO

JACKSON, LIVIA E. BITTON, Professor of Judaic Studies, Herbert H. Lehman College, City University of New York: Author, *Elli: Coming of Age in the Holocaust:* ISRAEL; RELIGION—*Judaism*

JAFFE, HERMAN J., Department of Anthropology, Brooklyn College, City University of New York: ANTHROPOLOGY

JEWELL, MALCOLM E., Professor of Political Science, University of Kentucky; Coauthor, *Kentucky Politics:* KENTUCKY

JOHNSON, JENNIFER, Librarian, Prairie History Room, Regina Public Library, Regina, Saskatchewan: SASKATCHEWAN

JOHNSON, WILLIAM OSCAR, Senior Writer, *Sports Illustrated:* THE OLYMPICS/TROUBLED GAMES

JOHNSTON, ROBERT L., Editor, *The Catholic Review,* newsweekly of the Baltimore Archdiocese: BIOGRAPHY— *The Rev. Robert F. Drinan;* RELIGION—*Roman Catholicism*

JOHNSTONE, J. K., Professor of English, University of Saskatchewan; Fellow of the Royal Society of Literature; Author, *The Bloomsbury Group:* LITERATURE—*English*

JONES, H. G., Curator, North Carolina Collection, University of North Carolina Library: NORTH CAROLINA

KARNES, THOMAS L., Professor and Chairman, Department of History, Arizona State University; Author, *Latin American Policy of the United States* and *Failure of Union: Central America 1824-1960:* CENTRAL AMERICA

KARSKI, JAN, Professor of Government, Georgetown University; Author, *Story of a Secret State:* BULGARIA; HUNGARY; RUMANIA

KASH, DON E., Professor, University of Oklahoma; Coauthor, *Our Energy Future: The Role of Research, Development, and Demonstration in Reaching a National Consensus on Energy Supply:* ENERGY

KEHR, ERNEST A., Stamp News Bureau; Author, *The Romance of Stamp Collecting:* STAMPS AND STAMP COLLECTING

KIMBALL, LORENZO, K., Professor of Political Science, University of Utah: UTAH

KIMBELL, CHARLES L., Supervisory Physical Scientist, United States Bureau of Mines: MINING

KING, PETER J., Associate Professor of History, Carleton University; ONTARIO; OTTAWA

KISSELGOFF, ANNA, Chief Dance Critic, *The New York Times:* DANCE

KOSAKI, RICHARD H., Professor of Political Science, University of Hawaii: HAWAII

LAI, CHUEN-YAN DAVID, Associate Professor of Geography, University of Victoria, B.C.: HONG KONG

LANDSBERG, H. E., Professor Emeritus, University of Maryland: METEOROLOGY

LARSEN, WILLIAM, Author, *Montague of Virginia, The Making of a Southern Progressive:* VIRGINIA

LAURENT, PIERRE-HENRI, Professor of History, Tufts University; Adjunct Professor of Diplomatic History, Fletcher School of Law and Diplomacy: BELGIUM

LAWRENCE, ROBERT M., Professor, Department of Political Science, Colorado State University; Author, *Arms Control and Disarmament: Practice and Promise* and *Nuclear Proliferation: Phase II:* MILITARY AFFAIRS; MILITARY AFFAIRS—*The Draft*

LEE, STEWART M., Professor and Chairman, Department of Economics and Business Administration, Geneva College, Beaver Falls, PA; Editor, *Newsletter,* American Council on Consumer Interests: CONSUMER AFFAIRS; UNITED STATES— *The Federal Trade Commission*

LEIDEN, CARL, Professor of History, University of Texas, Austin; Coauthor, *Politics/Middle East:* BANGLADESH; EGYPT; PAKISTAN

LEVITAN, SAR A., Director, Center for Social Policy Studies, George Washington University, Washington, DC; Coauthor, *Old Wars Remain Unfinished: The Veterans Benefit System:* VETERANS

LEVITT, MORRIS J., Professor, Graduate Department of Political Science, Howard University; Coauthor, *State and Local Government and Politics:* WASHINGTON, DC

LIDDLE, R. WILLIAM, Professor of Political Science, The Ohio State University; Author, *Political Participation in Modern Indonesia:* INDONESIA

LINDAHL, MAC, Harvard University: SWEDEN

LOBRON, BARBARA, Writer, Editor, Photographer: PHOTOGRAPHY

LORD, RODNEY, Economic Correspondent, *The Daily Telegraph,* London: GREAT BRITAIN—*Great Britain and the European Community;* GREAT BRITAIN—*The Economy*

LOTT, LEO B., Professor of Political Science, University of Montana; Author, *Venezuela and Paraguay: Political Modernity and Tradition in Conflict:* PARAGUAY; VENEZUELA

MABRY, DONALD J., Professor of History, Mississippi State University; Author, *Mexico's Acción Nacional:* MEXICO

MACAULAY, NEILL, Professor of History, University of Florida; Author, *The Prestes Column; The Sandino Affair; A Rebel in Cuba:* BRAZIL; LATIN AMERICA

McCORQUODALE, SUSAN, Associate Professor, Department of Political Science, Memorial University of Newfoundland: NEWFOUNDLAND

McDOUGALL, EDGAR J., JR., Assistant Professor in Finance, Member of the Center for Real Estate and Urban Economic Studies, University of Connecticut: HOUSING; HOUSING— *Condominiums*

McGILL, DAVID A., Professor of Ocean Science, U.S. Coast Guard Academy: OCEANOGRAPHY

MARCOPOULOS, GEORGE J., Associate Professor of History, Tufts University, Medford, MA: CYPRUS; GREECE

MATHEWS, THOMAS G., Research Professor, Institute of Caribbean Studies, University of Puerto Rico; Author, *Politics and Economics in the Caribbean* and *Puerto Rican Politics and the New Deal:* CARIBBEAN; PUERTO RICO; TRINIDAD & TOBAGO; VIRGIN ISLANDS

MEYER, EDWARD H., President and Chairman of the Board, Grey Advertising Inc.: ADVERTISING

MICHAELIS, PATRICIA, Curator of Manuscripts, Kansas State Historical Society: KANSAS

MILLER, JULIE ANN, Life Sciences Editor, *Science News:* BIOCHEMISTRY; MEDICINE AND HEALTH—*Interferon;* MICROBIOLOGY

MIRE, JOSEPH, Former Executive Director, National Institute for Labor Education: LABOR

MITCHELL, GARY, Professor of Physics, North Carolina University, Raleigh: PHYSICS

MONTVILLE, LEIGH, Sports Columnist, *The Boston Globe:* THE OLYMPICS/THE XIII WINTER GAMES; BIOGRAPHY—*Eric Heiden*

MORTON, DESMOND, Professor of History, Erindale College, University of Toronto; Author, *Ministers and Generals; The Canadian General; Social Democracy in Canada:* CANADA; CANADA—*The Year of the Referendum and the Constitution*

MULLINER, K., Southeast Asia Collection, Ohio University; Coeditor, *Southeast Asia, An Emerging Center of World Influence?:* MALAYSIA; SINGAPORE; THAILAND

MURPHY, ROBERT F., *The Hartford Courant:* CONNECTICUT

NADLER, PAUL S., Professor of Finance, Rutgers University; Author, *Commercial Banking in the Economy* and *Paul Nadler Writes About Banking:* BANKING

NAFTALIN, ARTHUR, Professor of Public Affairs, Hubert H. Humphrey Institute of Public Affairs, University of Minnesota: MINNESOTA

NOLAN, WILLIAM C., Professor of Political Science, Southern Arkansas University: ARKANSAS

NOVICKI, MARGARET A., Assistant Editor, *Africa Report,* The African-American Institute: ALGERIA; MOROCCO; SUDAN; TUNISIA

OCHSENWALD, WILLIAM L., Associate Professor of History, Virginia Polytechnic Institute; Author, *The Hijaz Railroad:* SAUDI ARABIA

OMENN, GILBERT S., Professor of Medicine, Division of Medical Genetics, University of Washington; Coeditor, *Genetics, Environment and Behavior: Implications for Educational Policy:* GENETICS

O'ROURKE, E. N., Horticulture Department, Louisiana State University: BOTANY; GARDENING AND HORTICULTURE

PALMER, NORMAN D., Professor of Political Science and South Asian Studies, University of Pennsylvania; Author, *Elections and Political Development: The South Asian Experience:* INDIA; SRI LANKA

PANO, NICHOLAS C., Associate Professor of History, Western Illinois University; Author, *The People's Republic of Albania:* ALBANIA

PARDES, HERBERT, Director, National Institute of Mental Health: MEDICINE AND HEALTH—*Mental Health*

PARKER, FRANKLIN, Benedum Professor of Education, West Virginia University; Author, *Battle of the Books, British Schools and Ours,* and *U.S. Higher Education: A Guide to Education Sources:* EDUCATION; OBITUARIES—*Jean Piaget*

PEARSON, NEALE J., Associate Professor of Political Science, Texas Tech University: CHILE; PERU

PERKINS, KENNETH J., Assistant Professor of History, University of South Carolina: PERSIAN GULF/ISLAM: HISTORY, CULTURE, AND FAITH; LIBYA

PIPPIN, LARRY L., Professor of Political Science, Elbert Covell College, University of the Pacific; Author, *The Remón Era:* ARGENTINA; BIOGRAPHY—*Adolfo Perez Esquivel*

PLATT, HERMANN K., Professor of History, St. Peter's College, Jersey City: NEW JERSEY

PLISCHKE, ELMER, Professor Emeritus, University of Maryland; Adjunct Professor, Gettysburg College; Author, *Modern Diplomacy: The Art and the Artisans* and *Conduct of American Diplomacy:* BIOGRAPHY—*Edmund S. Muskie;* UNITED STATES—*Foreign Affairs;* UNITED STATES—*Assistant to the President for National Security Affairs*

POPKIN, HENRY, Professor of English, State University of New York at Buffalo: THEATER

POULLADA, LEON B., Professor of Political Science, Northern Arizona University; Author, *Reform and Rebellion in Afghanistan:* AFGHANISTAN

PRITCHETT, C. HERMAN, Professor of Political Science, University of California, Santa Barbara; Author, *The Roosevelt Court* and *The American Constitution:* LAW—*The Supreme Court*

QUIRK, WILLIAM H., Former North American Editor, *Construction Industry International* magazine: ENGINEERING, CIVIL

RAGUSA, ISA, Research Art Historian, Department of Art and Archaeology, Princeton University: ART; ART—*The Picasso Exhibit*

RAYMOND, ELLSWORTH L., Professor of Politics (retired), New York University; Author, *Soviet Economic Progress and The Soviet State:* OBITUARIES—*Aleksei N. Kosygin; USSR*

REUNING, WINIFRED, Writer, Polar Programs, National Science Foundation: POLAR RESEARCH

RODRIGUEZ, ALFRED, Professor, Department of Modern and Classical Languages, University of New Mexico: LITERATURE—*Spanish and Spanish-American*

ROEDER, RICHARD B., Professor of History, Montana State University: MONTANA

ROSE, ERNST, Professor Emeritus, New York University; Author, *A History of German Literature:* LITERATURE—*German;* OBITUARIES—*Erich Fromme*

ROSENBERG, MORRIS, Travel Editor, *The Washington Post:* TRAVEL

ROSS, RUSSELL M., Professor of Political Science, University of Iowa; Author, *Government and Administration:* IOWA

ROTHSTEIN, MORTON, Professor of History, University of Wisconsin, Madison: SOCIAL WELFARE

ROWEN, HERBERT H., Professor, Rutgers University, New Brunswick, NJ; Editor, *The Low Countries in Early Modern Times: A Documentary History:* BIOGRAPHY—*Queen Beatrix;* THE NETHERLANDS

ROWLETT, RALPH M., Professor of Anthropology, University of Missouri; Coauthor, *Neolithic Levels on the Titelberg, Luxembourg:* ARCHAEOLOGY

RUFF, NORMAN J., Assistant Professor, University of Victoria: BRITISH COLUMBIA

SAKURAI, EMIKO, Professor, Department of East Asian Languages, University of Hawaii at Manoa: LITERATURE—*Japanese*

SALSINI, PAUL, State Editor, *The Milwaukee Journal:* WISCONSIN

SARRATT, WILLIAM A., Editor, *The Fish Boat;* FISHERIES

SAVAGE, DAVID, Lecturer, Department of English, Simon Fraser University: LITERATURE—*Canadian Literature in English*

SCHERER, RON, Business and Financial Correspondent, *The Christian Science Monitor:* BUSINESS AND CORPORATE AFFAIRS; BUSINESS AND CORPORATE AFFAIRS—*U.S. Oil Companies and the Issue of Profits*

SCHRIVER, EDWARD, University of Maine, Orono; Author, *Go Free: Antislavery, Maine 1833-1855:* MAINE

SCHROEDER, PATRICIA, U.S. Representative (D-CO), Member, House Armed Services Committee: WOMEN—*Women in the Military*

SCHROEDER, RICHARD C., Syndicated Writer on Foreign Affairs, Social Problems, and Legislation: REFUGEES

SCHWAB, PETER, Professor of Political Science, State University of New York at Purchase; Author, *Decision-Making in Ethiopia* and *Haile Selassie I:* ETHIOPIA

SCOTT, EUGENE L., Publisher and Founder, *Tennis Week;* Author, *Björn Borg: My Life & Game* and *Tennis Experience:* SPORTS—*Tennis*

SETH, R. P., Professor of Economics, Mount Saint Vincent University, Halifax: NOVA SCOTIA

SEYBOLD, PAUL G., Associate Professor of Chemistry, Wright State University, Dayton, OH: CHEMISTRY

SHINN, RINN-SUP, Senior Research Scientist, Foreign Area Studies, The American University, Washington, DC; Coauthor, *Area Handbook for North Korea* and *Area Handbook for South Korea:* KOREA

SHOGAN, ROBERT, National Political Correspondent, Washington Bureau, *Los Angeles Times;* Author, *A Question of Judgement* and *Promises to Keep:* THE U.S. PRESIDENCY/THE 1980 ELECTION; BIOGRAPHY—*George Bush, Jimmy Carter, Edward M. Kennedy, Walter Mondale, Ronald Reagan;* UNITED STATES—*Domestic Affairs, Reagan Cabinet*

SIEGEL, STANLEY E., Professor of History, University of Houston: Author, *A Political History of the Texas Republic, 1836-1845:* TEXAS

SIMMONS, MARC, Author, *New Mexico, A Bicentennial History:* NEW MEXICO

SLOAN, HENRY S., Associate Editor, *Current Biography:* BIOGRAPHY—*Jim Dale, Phil Donahue, Dan Rather, Meryl Streep;* OBITUARIES—*Jimmy Durante, Alfred Hitchcock, Alice Roosevelt Longworth, John McCormack, Mae West*

SPERA, DOMINIC, Associate Professor of Music, Indiana University; Author, *The Prestige Series—16 Original Compositions for Jazz Band:* MUSIC—*Jazz*

STENCEL, SANDRA, Managing Editor, *Editorial Research Reports:* WOMEN

STERN, JEROME H., Associate Professor of English, Florida State University: LITERATURE—*American*

STOKES, WILLIAM LEE, Professor, Department of Geology and Geophysics, University of Utah; Author, *Essentials of Earth History* and *Introduction to Geology:* GEOLOGY; GEOLOGY—*Mount St. Helens*

STOUDEMIRE, ROBERT H., Professor of Political Science, University of South Carolina: SOUTH CAROLINA

SYLVESTER, LORNA LUTES, Associate Editor, *Indiana Magazine of History,* Indiana University: INDIANA

TABORSKY, EDWARD, Professor of Government, University of Texas, Austin; Author, *Communism in Czechoslovakia, 1948-1960* and *Communist Penetration of the Third World:* CZECHOSLOVAKIA

TAFT, WILLIAM H., Professor of Journalism and Director of Graduate Studies, University of Missouri; Author, *American Journalism History:* PUBLISHING

TAN, CHESTER C., Professor of History, New York University; Author, *Chinese Political Thought in the 20th Century:* BIOGRAPHY—*Zhao Ziyang;* CHINA; TAIWAN

TAYLOR, WILLIAM L., Professor of History, Plymouth State College: NEW HAMPSHIRE

TESAR, JENNY, Free-lance Science Writer: MEDICINE AND HEALTH

THEISEN, CHARLES W., Assistant News Editor, *The Detroit News:* DETROIT; MICHIGAN

THOMAS, JAMES D., Professor, Department of Political Science and Center for Administrative and Policy Studies, The University of Alabama: ALABAMA

TOWNE, RUTH W., Professor of History, Northeast Missouri State University: MISSOURI

TSUNODA, WAKA, Free-lance Writer: CONSUMER AFFAIRS—THE FUNERAL INDUSTRY

TURNER, ARTHUR CAMPBELL, Professor of Political Science, University of California, Riverside; Author, *Tension Areas in World Affairs;* Coauthor, *Control of Foreign Relation:* THE PERSIAN GULF/THEATER OF WAR; BIOGRAPHY—*Abolhassan Bani-Sadr;* MIDDLE EAST; OBITUARIES—*Mohammed Reza Pahlavi;* THE YEMENS

UNDERWOOD, JOHN, Senior Writer, *Sports Illustrated;* Author, *The Death of An American Game* and *When in Doubt, Fire the Manager:* SPORTS—*The Crisis in College Athletics*

VALESIO, PAOLO, Professor of Italian, Yale University; Author, *Novantiqua; Rhetorics as a Contemporary Theory:* LITERATURE—*Italian*

VAN RIPER, PAUL P., Professor and Head, Department of Political Science, Texas A&M University: POSTAL SERVICE

VOGT, BILL, Senior Editor, *National Wildlife* and *International Wildlife* magazines; Author, *How to Build a Better Outdoors:* ENVIRONMENT

VOLSKY, GEORGE, Center for Advanced International Studies, University of Miami: CUBA

WALL, JAMES M., Editor, *The Christian Century;* Author, *Church and Cinema* and *Three European Directors:* RELIGION—*Protestantism*

WATTERS, ELSIE M., Director of Research, The Tax Foundation, Inc.: TAXATION

WEEKS, JEANNE G., Member, American Society of Interior Designers; Coauthor, *Fabrics for Interiors:* INTERIOR DESIGN

WEISMAN, CELIA B., Director, Yeshiva University Gerontological Institute; Author, *The Future is Now:* OLDER POPULATION

WEISS, JONATHAN M., Associate Professor of French, Department of Modern Languages, Colby College, Waterville ME: LITERATURE—*Canadian Literature in French*

WEISS, PAULETTE, Popular Music Editor, *Stereo Review:* MUSIC—*Popular;* OBITUARIES—*John Lennon;* RECORDINGS

WENTZ, RICHARD E., Chairman, Religious Studies Department, Arizona State University; Author, *Saga of the American Soul:* RELIGION—*Survey, Far Eastern*

WEST, DARRELL, Research Fellow, Indiana University: THE U.S. PRESIDENCY/JOHN ANDERSON—THIRD PARTY MOVEMENT; BIOGRAPHY—*J. ANDERSON*

WHITTINGHAM, ANTHONY, Business Editor, *Maclean's* magazine: CANADA—*The Economy*

WILLARD, F. NICHOLAS, Professor; JORDAN; LEBANON; SYRIA

WILLIAMS, DENNIS A., General Editor, *Newsweek:* BIOGRAPHY—*Vernon Jordan;* ETHNIC GROUPS

WILLIAMS, ERNEST W., JR., Professor of Transportation, Graduate School of Business, Columbia University; Author, *The Economics of Transportation and Logistics:* TRANSPORTATION

WILLIS, F. ROY, Professor of History, University of California, Davis; Author, *Italy Chooses Europe* and *France, Germany and the New Europe:* EUROPE

WOLF, WILLIAM, Film Commentator, *New York* magazine; Author, *The Marx Brothers* and *The Landmark Films/The Cinema and our Century:* MOTION PICTURES

WOOD, JOHN W., Professor of Political Science, University of Oklahoma: OKLAHOMA

WOODS, GEORGE A., Children's Book Editor, *The New York Times;* Author, *Vibrations* and *Catch a Killer:* LITERATURE—*Children's*

YOUNGER, R. M., Author, *Australia and the Australians, Australia's Great River* and *Australia! Australia! March to Nationhood:* AUSTRALIA; OCEANIA; VANUATU

ZABEL, ORVILLE H., Professor of History, Creighton University, Omaha: NEBRASKA

One week prior to the election, the League of Women Voters sponsored a televised presidential debate.

THE U.S. PRESIDENCY/

THE 1980 ELECTION

By Robert Shogan
National Political Correspondent, Washington Bureau
Los Angeles Times

The 1980 presidential campaign had moments of high drama and more moments of numbing tedium. But the word that was heard most often to describe the prolonged struggle for the White House was volatile. From start to finish the campaign was marked by a series of sharp shifts in the mood of the electorate which confounded the experts and repeatedly turned favorites into underdogs and vice versa. The culmination was a victory for the Republican nominee Ronald Reagan over Democratic President Jimmy Carter and Independent candidate John Anderson, by a lopsided margin unforeseen in the polls, along with stunning Republican gains in the Congress which gave the GOP control of the Senate for the first time since 1954.

With hindsight it was clear that this outcome was the result of widespread public dissatisfaction with Carter's management of the government, particularly economic affairs. However, the portents of Democratic defeat were often hard to discern amidst the baffling crosscurrents of the campaign.

Ted Kennedy and the Democratic Primaries. The surprises began on the Democratic side. Before the campaign for his party's nomination got under way Jimmy Carter seemed awash in a sea of troubles, and his standing in the polls had dropped below that of any other modern president. But the tide began to turn for the president, strangely enough as the result of a great national misfortune, the seizure of American hostages in the U.S. Embassy in Tehran on Nov. 4, 1979. Though Carter could do nothing to end the captivity of the hostages, many Americans found in his patient and resolute attitude a symbol of national unity, and rallied behind him.

After the hostages were seized Carter announced that he would not actively campaign until they were freed. This decision strengthened Carter politically, by cloaking him in the aura of the presidency, and disarmed his rivals, by making it hard to criticize him without appearing unpatriotic.

Moreover, by seeming to remain aloof from the political fray, while Vice-President Walter Mondale and other surrogates campaigned on his behalf, Carter focused attention on his principal challenger, Sen. Edward Kennedy of Massachusetts, to Kennedy's disadvantage.

As the heir to his brothers' political legacy, and the first choice of most Democrats in the precampaign polls, Kennedy had been heavily favored to defeat Carter and gain the nomination. But the formal announcement of his candidacy in November 1979 seemed to change the public's perception of his fitness for the presidency. A flood of stories in the press reminded the public of the episode at Chappaquiddick in 1969 in which a young woman passenger in Kennedy's car was killed under circumstances never fully explained. The publicity raised questions which Kennedy found difficult to answer, and put him on the defensive. And his performance on the campaign trail was compared to the glowing memories of his slain brothers, John and Robert, whose skills Edward Kennedy found difficult to match. Moreover, Kennedy, having supported most of Carter's presidential programs, had trouble defining clear differences with the incumbent to justify his candidacy.

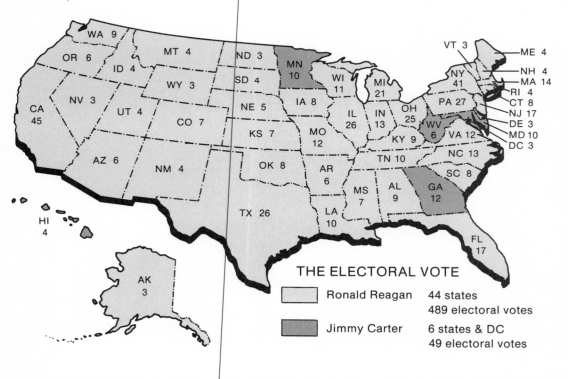

THE ELECTORAL VOTE

Ronald Reagan   44 states
489 electoral votes

Jimmy Carter   6 states & DC
49 electoral votes

"HI, THERE, THIS IS JIMMY CARTER CALLING. I REALLY WISH I COULD BE OUT THERE CAMPAIGNING AND MEETING WITH Y'ALL, BUT AS YOU KNOW I'M STUCK HERE IN THE DARN OL' ROSE GARDEN!"

Oliphant © "Washington Star"

Oliphant © "Washington Star"

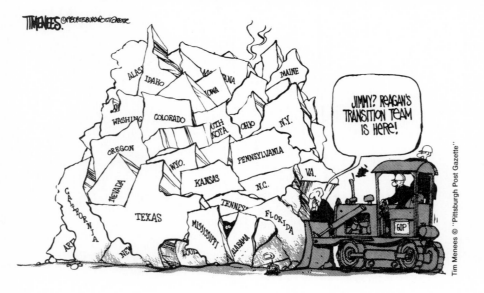

Tim Menees © "Pittsburgh Post Gazette"

Steve Liss, Liaison

Another challenge to Carter came from California Gov. Edmund G. Brown, Jr., who had run strongly in the 1976 Democratic primaries. But with most Democrats divided between Carter and Kennedy, little support was left for Brown.

The first real test of the campaign came in the Iowa precinct caucuses Jan. 21, 1980, in which Carter defeated Kennedy by a margin of two to one, while Brown abandoned his efforts to compete in the state. Carter followed up that success by winning the Maine caucuses and the New Hampshire primary in February, and on March 18 scored a smashing victory in the Illinois primary which seemed to make his nomination all but certain.

Brown, who ran a poor third in the New England primaries, dropped out of the race after another disappointing showing in the Wisconsin primary in April.

But Kennedy refused to quit. In a major speech at Georgetown University in January he sought to rally liberal support by more sharply defining the differences between himself and Carter. Kennedy called for the establishment of gasoline rationing to deal with the energy crisis, and for wage and price controls to curb inflation. He kept his candidacy alive by winning March primaries in his home state of Massachusetts, and then in New York and Connecticut. Though his prospects were slim Kennedy stayed in the race in large part for the sake of his political future. He repeatedly challenged Carter to debate the issues with him. And though Carter steadfastly refused, Kennedy's persistence earned him late primary victories in California and New Jersey.

Meanwhile the president was winning primaries steadily across the nation without leaving the White House. And his June victory in the Ohio primary, where he made his only official primary campaign appearance, assured his renomination.

Still, opposition to Carter persisted within his own party because of his continued low standing in the polls. As the Demo-
(Continued on page 17)

Both Massachusetts Sen. Edward M. Kennedy (above) and California Gov. Edmund G. Brown (below) challenged Jimmy Carter in the New Hampshire primary. The president won the primary with 49% of the vote and went on to gain renomination in August.

Matthew Naythons, Liaison

The Office Today

The term *president* has its roots in America's colonial past. A president was the officer who presided over provincial councils. Later the word was used to describe the presiding officer in the sessions of the Continental Congress and in the Congress established by the Articles of Confederation.

But the presidency as it is now understood was really a creation of the Constitutional Convention of 1787. The framers of the Constitution saw the need for a president who would be elected separately from Congress and who would not only preside over the executive branch of government but would also manage crises, direct the military in times of war, and serve as symbolic leader of the nation.

The original description of the job came about as a result of compromise. Some of the founding fathers wanted a presidency very close to a monarchy, with extensive powers and life tenure. Others, however, were distrustful of placing significant powers in the hands of one person and one office. Basically the fear of a monarchy growing up on American soil guided the design of the U.S. presidency. In a sense the founders were not exactly sure how much power they wanted in the presidency. But if they created an office with limited powers, they well knew that there would be an immediate problem. This was because George Washington, the most likely person to be the first president, was an especially influential person. The founders wanted a presidency that would stay clear of factions and parties, that would stay above the battle. A president, they decided, would enforce the laws passed by Congress, deal with foreign governments, and help the states put down disorders. They seemed to have in mind—and that is pretty much the way George Washington acted—that a president should be a temporarily elected king with substantial personal influence, acting above parties.

The delegates considered but rejected a collective or plural executive. They considered but rejected tenure for life, or even a seven-year term for the office. The term would be for four years, with presidents able to seek reelection.

Independent from the national legislature, a president nonetheless would share most of his powers with the Congress. Thus a president could nominate federal judges and department heads, but the Senate had to confirm such nominees. A president could negotiate treaties with foreign governments, but the Senate would then have to approve them by a two-thirds vote. A president could veto laws passed by Congress, but Congress could override his veto by a two-thirds vote of each chamber. The power to appropriate money was retained by Congress, as was the power to declare war. Perhaps the president's only truly unchecked, imperial power was his power to pardon persons convicted of federal crimes.

Plainly, the original conception of the office was one of limited powers, hemmed in by a complicated system of checks and balances. Even this relatively weak conception of the presidency worried some Americans in 1787. Without a recall or vote of no-confidence provision, a president could be removed from office only by an exceedingly difficult impeachment process. But most Americans were reassured by the fact that the highly esteemed General Washington was to be the first president.

The Growth of Presidential Power. The presidency has grown just as the country has grown and expanded. Indeed, there is a certain plasticity in the basic conception of the presidency and its powers. Whenever the nation is in trouble Americans gladly expand the president's leeway, allowing him more options and more flexibility to provide leadership. But when wars or depressions end and business returns to normal, so also the public tends to rein in the president and worry about whether the office has become imperial. At such times checks and balances are revitalized.

The exact dimensions of presidential power are largely the consequence of an incumbent's character and energy, combined with the overarching societal needs of the day. About every third president has been a power maximizer—enlarging the office so that he could better provide economic, military, or other kinds of leadership. Plainly, an office that was only vaguely defined on paper (Article II of the Constitution) gained new scope with accumulated traditions and with the cumulative legacy of some often brilliant achievements. The Civil War, the emergence of the United States as a world power, Theodore Roosevelt, Woodrow Wilson, Franklin D. Roosevelt, two world wars, the invention of the atomic bomb, and the Cold War all contributed to enlarging the presidency.

American presidents have been extending the limits of executive powers throughout U.S. history, but especially in the past 50 years. Congress, the courts, and the American people usually have approved of this. Whenever emergencies occur, Congress usually rushes to delegate rule-making discretion to the executive branch (example, the 1964 Gulf of Tonkin resolution). Congress is a splendid forum for registering the diversity of the nation's moods but it is ill-designed to provide quick action, particularly in foreign affairs. As the congressional power structure becomes more decentralized, the need for a single strong national crisis manager becomes even greater.

War and the danger of war have greatly expanded the role of presidents. The country has been involved in some 160 military interventions around the world, not to mention the Civil War, conflict with various Indian tribes, and occasional insurrections such as the Whiskey Rebellion in the 1790s. Some would say Americans have been a pugnacious people, obsessed with a sense of empire. The nation has certainly had its share of pugnacious presidents.

More recently the Cold War shattered any remaining nostalgia for once-cherished traditions against standing armies and entangling alliances. The combination of an enormous standing army, nuclear weapons, and the nation's Cold War commitments (to quote John F. Kennedy) to "pay any price, bear any burden, meet any hardship, support any friend or oppose any foe . . ." have ensured presidential dominance in national security matters.

Presidential power has also been increased by the vast growth of the national role in economic and domestic policy. Domestic policy responsibilities have contributed to the swelling of the White House staff, the federal budget, and the size of the federal bureaucracy. As of 1981, there is a White House staff of nearly 500 people, a federal budget of about $700,000,000,000, and a federal bureaucracy (combining civilians and military) of more than 5 million people. More people work for the federal establishment today than even lived in the United States in the 1780s. Another 13,500,000 civil servants work at the state, county, and city levels of government, many of them administering some kind of federal program, such as welfare assistance or environmental regulations.

Today, the increasing need for imported raw materials to fuel the economy continues to transform the presidency. The more interdependent the country's economy is with the economies of other nations, the more the chief executive needs to help negotiate multilateral economic arrangements. Plainly, the rise of OPEC (the Organization of Petroleum Exporting Countries) increased the job of the president as an energy planner and a manager of U.S. interests in the Middle East. The growing interdependence of world economies also makes the presidency more vulnerable to events beyond the incumbent's control. For when OPEC an-

nounces a price increase, for example, the effect is likely to add to U.S. inflation, and the president can react only after the fact.

Television doubtless has added to presidential influence and visibility. With access to primetime coverage whenever he wants it, the president can now take his case directly to the people. On the other hand, television is a great leveler—personal style is exaggerated and the president becomes just one more actor on the huge stage of dramatic world events. When things go wrong, presidents, in part because of their great visibility, become the scapegoats.

Do Americans Expect too Much of the Presidency? The presidency has been enlarged as well by popular expectations. The American public wants very much to believe in and trust its presidents. The public wants them to be forceful, decisive, and assertive. Sometimes Americans want the chief executive to do their job for them, such as with energy conservation. Presidents who do not use their formal powers actively and vigorously get condemned as weak and incompetent leaders. Nowadays the catalogue of what is expected from the president is large indeed:

Manage Crises: to exercise calm judgment in the midst of crises.

Set Priorities: to clarify the nation's interests and educate the public about what can and cannot be done.

Make Policy: to listen to the needs of the country and propose legislation to Congress.

SELLING SHORT

"We not only lack leadership. We also need someone to tell us what to do."

Recruit Personnel: to attract outstanding people to cabinet posts, ambassadorships, and advisory positions and to nominate qualified federal judges.

Prepare the Budget: to forecast U.S. fiscal needs and make crucial budgetary decisions.

Build Political Coalitions: to forge the needed party, legislative, and popular coalitions around policy goals.

Administer: to carry out faithfully and efficiently the laws passed by Congress and work with governors and mayors to make the federal system work effectively.

Plan: to serve as an early-warning system and look at problems from a long range and interdisciplinary perspective.

Renew the National Purpose: to radiate confidence in the political and economic systems, to justify U.S. commitments, to revitalize the democratic faith, and to encourage the forces for good that are at large in the country.

It is nearly impossible for presidents to perform at the level of the public's expectations. The description of the office is considerably greater than the resources that come with the job. John Steinbeck, the novelist, said it well when he wrote:

> We give the president more work than a man can do, more responsibility than a man should take, more pressure than a man can bear. We abuse him often and rarely praise him. We wear him out, use him up, eat him up . . . he is ours, and we exercise the right to destroy him.

Is the Presidency too Powerful or not Powerful Enough? The presidency is in fact constrained in many ways. In the wake of both Vietnam and Watergate, Congress and the courts have exercised greater checks on presidents. Recent presidents have found Congress more difficult to deal with because new reforms have dispersed power, especially in the House of Representatives. Moreover, brighter, better-educated, more independent-minded people are being elected to Congress. The large bureaucracies can also resist the president or undermine presidential initiatives. More aroused interest groups are both better equipped and more aggressive at making their views known. Thus environmentalists blocked the Alaska pipeline for several years. Oil interests have significantly altered some energy policies, and consumer interests have brought into being countless new regulations.

Most important, perhaps, the job of the president has been changed significantly by the fact that the U.S. economy is more dependent than ever on the importation of raw materials. This dependence on other nations has often been inflationary and has often made people upset with the need for central planning and coordination, and the attendant sacrifices. Presidents have become bearers of bad news, especially as the relative standard of living has declined.

For some years now many Americans think they have been misgoverned. Between November 1963 and January 1981, the United States has had six presidents. Americans respect the presidency but condemn the presidents. And there are repeated calls for fundamental constitutional, structural, and ideological changes.

Should the presidency be changed? Is a council of presidents, a co-presidency, or a single six-year-term presidency desired? Should some features of the parliamentary system be adopted? My own view is that the United States should strengthen the presidency in certain ways, but just as importantly other parts of the political system must be revitalized. Political parties should be renewed. Congress must strengthen its leadership capabilities. And perhaps more than anything else Americans need to be more realistic about how much leadership can come from any single individual.

Leadership in a society like that of the United States, a society that has long cherished decentralization and the dispersal of power, should emerge more from the middle or even bottom, up, and less from the top, down. While the nation requires all the leadership it can get from its presidents, it also needs to develop and nurture middle-level leadership, particularly in the nongovernmental and private sector.

What Else Can Be Done? Americans need to rally around and give support to presidents when they think the chief executives are right. They also should be a little more patient with their presidents; by too often forcing presidents to give instant solutions the public invites mindless bumper sticker slogans and gimmicky crash programs that fail to help. Americans need to realize, too, that presidents have to be shrewd politicians in order to balance competing interests. The presidency was clearly strained by the Watergate and Vietnam experiences. But it is a resilient office. The original job of the presidency has grown and yet the founding fathers wrote a marvelously flexible job description that is almost as appropriate today as it was when the nation was a struggling new republic. This flexibility plus the willingness of the American people to place confidence in effective presidents gives a president an enormous opportunity to serve the nation. Skepticism has its place, but fatalism saps the will. A premature attitude of self-defeat and cynicism toward the presidency set in during the 1970s. But this is likely to pass. The presidency will be what presidents and the American people want to make of it.

THOMAS E. CRONIN

Thomas E. Cronin is a political scientist. He is the author or coauthor of *The State of the Presidency, The Presidency Reappraised,* and a leading college text, *Government by the People.* He has worked as a White House aide, advised presidential candidates, and been a delegate to national conventions.

UPI   O'Halloran, "U.S. News and World Report"

cratic convention approached, a group of party leaders launched a drive for a so-called "open convention" by opposing a convention rule that would bind the delegates to vote for the candidates they had been elected to support in the primaries and caucuses. Blocking the rule would have freed the delegates to nominate someone besides Carter or Kennedy. But at the August convention in New York the Carter forces remained loyal to the president and adopted the delegate binding rule, thus ending the "open convention" drive. Carter was forced to make some concessions to Kennedy's liberal supporters on party platform planks and on the economy. But he succeeded in gaining the nomination, and also in winning Kennedy's endorsement of his candidacy.

As in 1976, the Democratic National Convention was held in New York City. Again, Carter-Mondale received the nomination. Ted Kennedy, who unsuccessfully sought an open convention, gave a key speech.

Dirck Halstead, Liaison

The GOP Primaries. The Republican contest for the presidential nomination had its share of turbulence, too. Ronald Reagan started out as the clear favorite. But his age—Reagan turned 69 on Feb. 6, 1980—and his conservative background raised questions about the viability of the former California governor's candidacy. Reagon faced a large field of contenders, including conservative Rep. Philip Crane of Illinois, moderate Rep. John Anderson, also of Illinois, Kansas Sen. Robert Dole, former Texas Gov. John B. Connally, Senate Minority Leader Howard Baker, and George Bush, former ambassador to the United Nations and Republican Party chairman. Though Bush was among the lesser known of these contenders he waged an intensive campaign in Iowa and scored an upset victory over Reagan in that state's party caucuses in January. The impetus of this surprising triumph made Bush the favorite in the contest for a time. But Reagan, on the

Dirck Halstead, Liaison

In February, the "Nashua (NH) Telegraph" sponsored a debate between Republican hopefuls Ronald Reagan and George Bush (right). When the former California governor insisted that the debate be opened to all GOP contenders and arrived at the debate with the other candidates (standing, left to right)—Anderson, Baker, Dole, and Crane—Bush suffered an embarrassment.

same day that he fired his campaign manager and other top aides, won an impressive victory over Bush in New Hampshire. The New Hampshire win and the regrouped forces led to a string of successes for Reagan across the country which ultimately eliminated all his opponents, including Bush. The former envoy did, however, win primaries in Pennsylvania and Michigan before being forced out of the race. Reagan had the advantage of being better known and also showed himself to be a more adroit campaigner.

The more liberal John Anderson had a number of differences with Reagan. Unlike Reagan, Anderson favored federal gun control, supported the Equal Rights Amendment (ERA), and backed President Carter's embargo on sales of grain to the Soviet Union. Anderson also proposed a 50-cent-per-gallon gasoline tax to conserve energy. His distinctive views and his eloquent oratory won him strong support in New England and in other areas of the country from moderate Republicans and from some independents and discontented Democrats as well. Anderson could not develop enough backing in his own party to have a serious chance for its nomination. But the favorable press attention given his candidacy encouraged him to seek the presidency as an independent, a decision officially announced on April 24. He later selected Patrick J. Lucey, former Democratic governor of Wisconsin, as his running mate.

With Anderson out of the way, Reagan went to the Republican convention in Detroit in July as the certain nominee of a united party. Bush's strong showing in the primaries and his appeal to moderates made him a logical choice for the vice-presidential nomination. And Reagan eventually selected him as running mate, after a futile effort to persuade former President Gerald Ford to join him on the ticket. Reagan emerged from the convention with a strongly conservative party platform that withdrew the party's previous support for the ERA amendment, and with a substantial lead over Jimmy Carter in the polls.

But the appearance of the party unity fostered at the Democratic convention helped reduce Reagan's advantage in the polls. And by Labor Day, the traditional start of the campaign, the two major party candidates were running about even in the polls, with Anderson trailing with about 15% of the vote.

Anderson posed a special problem for Carter. His strategists believed that most of Anderson's support was coming from potential Carter supporters and so they sought to squelch the Anderson candidacy. Toward this end, Carter supporters tried to block Anderson's access to the ballot in a number of states. These efforts were in vain, though, because Anderson eventually got his name on the ballot in all 50 states and the District of Columbia. Carter also declined to participate in a three-way debate with Anderson and Reagan, contending it was unfair for him to have to debate two Republicans. Anderson had to settle for a debate with Reagan which, despite the attention it gave him, did not help his candidacy. His support dropped steadily throughout the campaign as his backers realized he had no real chance of election. (*See* special article, page 25.)

The Campaign. Carter's campaign managers, concerned about the imperfections in the president's record, attempted to make Ronald Reagan the chief issue of the campaign and focus attention on the Republican nominee's alleged weaknesses. The president sought to depict his chief opponent as an extreme right-winger and as a threat to peace. He cited a number of bellicose statements on foreign affairs that Reagan had made in the past and particularly the Republican nominee's opposition to the Strategic Arms Limitations Treaty (Salt II). And Carter sought to rally

Chris Cross, Uniphoto

Detroit welcomed the GOP in mid-July. Convention delegates warmly received Nancy and Ronald Reagan at the Joe Louis Arena.

Michael Pettypool, Uniphoto

TOGETHER... A NEW BEGIN

The Republican choices, Ronald Reagan and George Bush, have given their acceptance speeches and are joined on the podium by Gerald Ford. The report that the former president would run as Reagan's mate had added some suspense to the convention.

Steve Liss, Liaison

union members, Jews, blacks, and other traditional Democratic constituencies to his cause.

Reagan's objective was to focus campaign debate on Carter's performance in office, particularly his inability to control inflation and to hold down unemployment. At the same time the Republican standard-bearer sought to broaden his constituency by appealing to blue-collar workers with his more conservative positions on social issues and his promise to stimulate the sagging national economy with an across-the-board cut in personal income tax rates.

He got off to a stumbling start. He made a clumsy attempt to link Carter to the Ku Klux Klan and got involved in discussing the validity of the theory of evolution and U.S. relations with Taiwan. Later on in the campaign he blamed trees for contributing to air pollution. All these comments served to distract attention from the main themes of his campaign. Eventually, however, the candidate became more disciplined, regained his footing, and concentrated on attacking Carter's handling of the economy.

With the outcome of the election still in doubt, the two major party candidates confronted each other in a nationally televised debate in Cleveland on October 28. Carter was by far the more aggressive of the two. He cited Reagan statements criticizing unemployment compensation and the minimum wage and repeatedly reminded viewers of Reagan's opposition to nuclear arms limitation treaties. But Reagan defended himself with poise and good humor, and his demeanor apparently reassured a good many undecided voters. At the same time Reagan hit hard at Carter's economic record. He pointed out that the "misery index," representing the combined rates of inflation and unemployment, was higher under Carter than it had been under his predecessor, Gerald Ford. And he drove his point home by suggesting that voters ask themselves in deciding whom to support: "Are you better off now than you were four years ago?" Public opinion polls showed that most viewers believed Reagan had won the debate. And this judgment seemed to give his candidacy momentum in the closing days of the campaign.

Photos Bruce Hoertel

After refusing to leave the White House to campaign during the primaries, President Carter worked hard for a second term. In fact, he introduced a new campaign format, outlining his views to small groups in selected areas across the country.

Then on November 2, the Sunday before election day, a final note of uncertainty was added. The Iranian parliament after much delay adopted conditions for release of the U.S. hostages. Carter broke off campaigning, returned to Washington to discuss the situation with his advisers, then issued a statement in which he called the action a positive development. But it was clear that the Iranian conditions would have to be discussed and studied for some time before the hostages would be freed. As the president returned to campaigning, some surveys suggested that the plight of the hostages had cost him support. Newspaper and television coverage on November 3, which marked the end of one year of captivity for the hostages, reminded voters of the long ordeal of the hostages and underlined the sense of national frustration over the episode.

The Results. At any rate the result, which most analysis had expected to be close, turned into a Reagan landslide. He took 51% of the popular vote to 41% for Carter, 7% for Anderson, and 1% for other independents. Reagan's margin in the electoral college was even more impressive, 489 to 49. Carter was able to carry only the District of Columbia and six states, his native Georgia, West Virginia, Maryland, Rhode Island, Mondale's home state of Minnesota, and Hawaii. He was the first elected president to be turned out of office since Republican Herbert Hoover in 1932.

An analysis of the vote based on surveys of voters as they left the polling booths illustrated the scope of Reagan's success. Not

Larry Downing, "Newsweek"

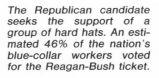

The Republican candidate seeks the support of a group of hard hats. An estimated 46% of the nation's blue-collar workers voted for the Reagan-Bush ticket.

Barr, Liaison

only did he hold on to traditional Republican voters among mid-dle-class white voters in the suburbs but he siphoned off substantial support from such normally Democratic constituencies as Catholics, blue-collar workers, and Jews. Only black voters stood by the president, giving him roughly the same margin of support—about 85%—he had won against President Gerald Ford in 1976.

Adding to the Republican jubilation were impressive gains they made in congressional and gubernatorial races. In the Senate the GOP captured a dozen Democratic seats, many of them previously held by liberal stalwarts, and gained control of that body. Among the vanquished liberal Democrats were Sen. George McGovern of South Dakota, his party's 1972 presidential nominee, who was beaten by Rep. James Abdnor; John Culver of Iowa, defeated by Rep. Charles Grassley; Sen. Birch Bayh of Indiana, who was replaced by Rep. Dan Quayle; Sen. Gaylord Nelson of Wisconsin, who was beaten by former Rep. Robert W. Kasten; and Sen. Frank Church of Idaho, beaten by Rep. Steven Symms.

Other defeated Democratic Senate incumbents were Warren Magnuson of Washington, defeated by Slade Gorton; Herman Talmadge of Georgia, beaten by Mack Mattingly; Sen. John Durkin of New Hampshire, replaced by Warren Rudman; and North Carolina Sen. Robert Morgan, who was beaten by John P. East. Most of the Republican victors were regarded as strong conservatives.

The Republican dominance of the Senate meant that a number of conservatives would replace liberals as head of key Senate committees. Sen. Strom Thurmond of South Carolina was in line to replace Sen. Edward Kennedy as Judiciary Committee chair-

Election night, 1980: Mr. and Mrs. Ronald Reagan triumphantly greet their supporters at a Los Angeles hotel. The president-elect called his landslide win a "humbling moment."

Fred Ward, Black Star

Surrounded by members of his family and his administration, Jimmy Carter concedes defeat at a Washington hotel at 9:50 EST. The president said: "I've not achieved all I set out to do, perhaps no one ever does, but we have faced the tough issues."

man; Utah Sen. Orrin Hatch was scheduled to head the Labor Committee instead of Sen. Harrison Williams of New Jersey; and Sen. Jesse Helms was expected to take over the Agriculture Committee from Talmadge.

Although the Democrats retained control of the House of Representatives, the Republicans also made significant inroads there. The GOP gained 33 seats, leaving the Democrats with 242 members to 192 Republicans. (Thomas M. Foglietta (PA), who ran as an independent, was expected to vote along Democratic lines.) Among the defeated Democrats were House Ways and Means Committee Chairman Al Ullman of Oregon and John Brademas of Indiana, the House Democratic whip.

In state races, the Republicans boosted the number of GOP governors from 19 to 23. The GOP took governorships away from the Democrats in Arkansas, where Frank White defeated incumbent Bill Clinton; North Dakota, where Allen I. Olsen defeated incumbent Arthur A. Link; Missouri, where Christopher Bond beat incumbent Joseph P. Teasdale; and Washington, where John Spellman was the victor.

The extent of the Republican victory indicated to some observers that Reagan's candidacy had forged a new political alignment replacing the traditional Democratic coalition which Franklin D. Roosevelt had forged in 1932 and which had dominated national politics ever since. But other analysts viewed the returns as simply a repudiation of the Democratic Party's management of the economy and contended that Reagan's hold on his 1980 support would depend on his ability to do better in dealing with inflation and unemployment. At any rate the many twists and turns in the 1980 campaign argued that any analysis of the portents of the vote should be tempered with caution.

John Anderson—Third Party Movement

The independent candidacy of John Anderson, a U.S. representative from Illinois since 1961, in the 1980 presidential contest, plus efforts of Libertarian Ed Clark and Citizens Party candidate Barry Commoner, among others, once again demonstrated the continuing vitality of third parties on the American political scene.

Like the flow and ebb of an ocean tide, third parties emerge for brief intervals and then frequently disappear or merge with a major party. According to Daniel Mazmanian, whose book, *Third Parties in Presidential Elections,* is the most authoritative source, ten parties have won significant portions of the presidential vote since 1828: the Anti-Masons in 1832 (8.0%); the Free Soilers in 1848 (10.1%); the American in 1856 (21.4%); the John Breckinridge Democratic and the Constitutional Union in 1860 (18.2% and 12.6%, respectively); the Populists in 1892 (8.5%); Theodore Roosevelt's Progressive Party and the Socialists in 1912 (27.4% and 6.0%, respectively); the Robert LaFollette Progressives in 1924 (16.6%), and the George C. Wallace American Independent in 1968 (13.5%). To these, one can add Anderson's independent candidacy in 1980 (6.6%).

Historically, four conditions appear to be associated with the emergence of third parties: a period of crisis politics in which there is severe national conflict over a few very important issues; the division of the electorate on these issues into an intense and estranged minority and a broad majority; rejection or avoidance of the minority position by both major parties so that the minority becomes alienated; and a political leader or group willing to exploit the situation by initiating a new party. Usually, all of these conditions must be present to produce a significant third-party vote. Often, major parties will absorb politically-active minorities rather than let voters be drawn to a third party. And in a crisis, there will be little leeway for a third party if the major parties take contrasting positions on important issues. So it was that during the Great Depression, no significant third-party vote emerged because, despite the economic crisis, the Democrats responded to popular discontent with innovative programs.

John Anderson's 1980 presidential campaign appears to represent a different kind of challenge than is usual in American politics. Typically, candidates bolt the major parties over emotional or ideological issues. For example, opposition to busing for purposes of racial segregation fueled the Wallace campaign of 1968. And, before that, slavery (1860), populism (1892), socialism (1912), and progressivism (1912 and 1924) were rallying points.

In contrast, Anderson embarked on his independent candidacy as a moderate, centrist candidate. Although Anderson had deeply-held beliefs, he did not emphasize issues at the fringe of the political spectrum. Rather he articulated mainstream and nonideological versions of fiscal conservatism and social liberalism. Consequently, his challenge to the two party system came from the center, not the extreme ends, of the political spectrum.

Perhaps more predictable than the emergence of significant third parties is their demise. No third party since 1828 has improved its share of the vote after the initial election. Generally, their decline is due to the adaptiveness of the major political parties. When a third party dis-

JOHN BRECKINRIDGE
Chicago Historical Society

THEODORE ROOSEVELT
Library of Congress

ROBERT LAFOLLETTE
Culver Service

plays a significant popular vote, one of the major parties usually shifts its position and absorbs the party's rhetoric and policy proposals. Subsequently, in the following election, disaffected voters face a choice between a third party with little chance for victory and a major party increasingly sympathetic to their views. So the weight of historic evidence is not encouraging for John Anderson if he were to attempt a second independent presidential effort sometime in the future.

Despite their periodic occurrence, critics often condemn third parties as threatening and disruptive. For one, they argue that third parties encourage political leaders to adopt extremist and uncompromising positions. Rather than having to appeal to a broadly-based electorate, these leaders use campaigns to incite the public and to disrupt the major parties. Critics claim that if third parties were to multiply, the nation's political system would deteriorate into a collection of unstable, narrowly-based parties unable to reach a consensus on overall government action.

The history of the American party system, however, does not support the notion of contagious growth of third parties. The rise of third parties has not produced a proliferation of par-

ties nor has it destroyed basic democratic institutions. Only in the elections of 1860 and 1912 has there occurred more than one significant minor party. And one can argue in these cases that the parties were more a result than a cause of political divisions.

Opponents of third parties also say they upset the nation's delicately-balanced electoral system and thereby thwart majority rule. These critics argue that third parties may prevent a majority of votes for any particular candidate. And depending on how the election contest would have ended if restricted to just two candidates, the third-party candidate may have altered the election outcome and thereby thwarted popular sentiment.

Considering past elections, the evidence at first appears to support this criticism. In the three-way contests of 1832, 1924, and 1980, when the winner won more than 50% of the popular vote, third parties did not prevent the formation of a popular majority. On the other hand, since victors won pluralities, not majorities, in 1848, 1856, 1860, 1892, 1912, and 1968, it is conceivable that the third-party vote may have changed the outcome.

One must consider several points in evaluating these latter presidential elections. First, it is

Steve Liss, Liaison

According to Illinois Rep. John Anderson, too many Americans were "disillusioned with the prospective choices" the Democratic and Republican parties were offering in the presidential race. To offer a "choice, of course, for the nation," the registered Republican decided to run as an independent. On November 4, he received 5,-719,437 votes, 6.61% of the total.

Representative Anderson presents his running-mate, Patrick J. Lucey, former Democratic governor of Wisconsin and ambassador to Mexico, to the nation. Mrs. Anderson (left) and Mrs. Lucey appear pleased with the selection.

UPI

essential to distinguish between the popular vote and the electoral college contest. While third parties have prevented popular majorities, they have never stopped a majority in the electoral college. So third parties have not played a kingmaker's role or forced an election into the House of Representatives. Second, information on the second choice of minor party voters in 1968 shows that the absence of George Wallace, former Alabama governor, probably would not have changed the election outcome. Although former Vice-President Richard Nixon defeated Sen. Hubert Humphrey by less than 1%, most Wallace supporters preferred Nixon over Humphrey, according to public opinion surveys. Third, analysts of other elections also conclude that removing the third-party challenger would change the election results "in only a very few instances." So third parties are less disruptive than often assumed.

Third parties also can serve a variety of positive roles. Unencumbered by the need to develop broad support, they often help dramatize minority positions on public policy questions. For example, when national leaders were unable to resolve the slavery issue, the Free Soil party forced debate of the topic in the 1848 election, as did their counterparts in 1856 and 1860. Three decades later, the Populists widened the political agenda to include key concerns of Western and Southern farmers. In 1912, the Socialists offered voters a fundamental choice on the questions of business and industry. And, in 1968, Governor Wallace spoke for a white minority anxious about busing, integration, and crime.

In addition, third parties expand the base of electoral politics. By appealing to constituencies uninvolved in conventional politics and largely ignored by the major parties, they add relevance for numerous Americans. The Wallace campaign appeared to have brought into politics a number of inactive voters from rural areas, many of whom were mistrustful of government and the nation's political institutions. Likewise, voter participation rose in the divisive contests of 1856 and 1860 (although it fell in some of the other election years).

Finally, third parties provide a reservoir of new ideas from which major party candidates can draw. While third parties have had mixed success in implementing their programs, many of their ideas have been incorporated into the platforms of the major parties and have implemented public policy. In 1856, the Republican Party incorporated the themes of slavery restriction and internal improvement from the Free Soil party of 1848 and 1852 and implemented them during the 1860s. Major portions of Roosevelt's New Deal programs rest on ideas raised previously by Populists, Socialists, and Progressives. And the Republicans, under Nixon in 1968 and 1972, undermined Wallace's political base by implementing his views on busing and crime. In sum, third parties help stabilize the political system by serving as a safety valve for dissidents and providing a source of innovation for the major parties.

See also Biography: John Anderson.

JEFF FISHEL, *Professor of Government*
The American University
DARRELL WEST, *Research Fellow*
Indiana University

An estimated 55% of the world's oil reserves are held by countries in the Persian Gulf area, making the waterway of extreme importance to the economies of industrial nations. Above: an Iranian refinery stands on the shore of the gulf.

The Persian Gulf/
Theater of War

BY ARTHUR CAMPBELL TURNER
Professor of Political Science
University of California, Riverside

The shores of the Persian Gulf are arid and inhospitable. The climate is one of the most disagreeable in the world. At first glance, it might seem unlikely to be of any special interest except to those who live there. This, however, has never been the case. Long before oil made the Persian Gulf an area of supreme interest to the whole world, its strategic setting for trade routes and the competing interests of various empires made it a center of political attention and a scene of constant naval and military activity.

Geography. The Persian Gulf is one of the several bodies of water that cut into the landmass of the Middle East and that have inevitably shaped the routes of commerce and war in Eurasia. Some of these gulfs or inland seas have significant "choke points," where the narrowness of access channels makes it easy to control or prohibit sea traffic. Among these are the Suez Canal, between the Red Sea and Mediterranean; the Dardanelles and Bosporus, linking the Black Sea and Mediterranean; the Strait of Bab el-Mandeb, connecting the Red Sea and Gulf of Aden (Arabian Ocean); and the Strait of Tiran, joining the Gulf of Aqaba and Red Sea. The Persian Gulf has what in today's world is probably the most significant choke point of all: the Strait of Hormuz, the only sea route between the Persian Gulf and the rest of the world's oceans.

The Persian Gulf lies between the landmasses of Iran (Persia) and the Arabian Peninsula, stretching 615 mi (990 km) in a northwest-southeast direction, from the mouth of the Shatt-al-Arab (confluence of the Tigris and Euphrates rivers) to the Strait of Hormuz. Its average width is slightly more than 200 mi (322 km), narrowing to 35 mi (56 km) at the strait. It is a shallow sea, seldom deeper than 300 ft (91 m). The few good harbors are all on either the Iranian side or the northern end. Thus, the great oil tankers that frequent the gulf are serviced mostly at island terminals or specially-built offshore structures. There is a considerable number of islands in the gulf, the largest being Bahrain off the coast of Saudi Arabia and Qatar.

Great Historic Route. Prior to the discovery of oil, the major products of the region—pearls, dates, and grain—were not of great importance. Other forms of economic activity were camel breeding, fishing, and, above all, seaborne trade. When opportunity offered, the latter shaded into piracy. What made the region important was its geographical location. Through the Middle Ages, the sea route up the gulf was the greatest highway of trade between the farther Orient and Europe. When Marco Polo journeyed to China in the 13th century, he used an overland route but returned by sea via the Persian Gulf. Over the centuries, trading cities rose and fell on the gulf. For several hundred years, the most

Map by Frank Senyk

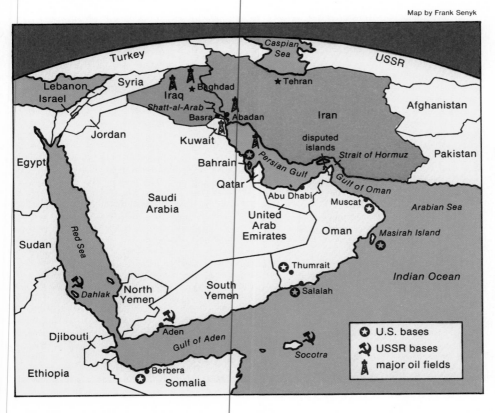

THE PERSIAN GULF AREA

important was Hormuz, near the present-day port of Bandar Abbas on the Iranian side of the strait.

Arrival of European Sea Power. Events in the gulf area in recent centuries have been shaped by the impact of European naval forces. The first European sea power to extend its grasp to the region was Portugal, which dominated the area for most of the 16th century; it held Hormuz from 1515 to 1622. There then ensued a period of rivalry among the French, the Dutch, and the British. By the 18th century, a British predominance was emerging in the gulf. This lasted until quite recently—until, in fact, 1971.

British Predominance, 1820–1971. The English East India Company carried on considerable trade in the Persian Gulf during the 18th century, using as a route to India the Tigris-Euphrates Valley and the gulf waterway. This route was made obsolete only by the opening of the Suez Canal in 1869. British hegemony lasted a century and a half and is generally dated from a treaty concluded in 1820 with the ruler of Bahrain and the tribal sheikhs of the Oman coast. Intended to combat piracy, the treaty gave to the British responsibility for the security of the Persian Gulf. There followed, in 1853, the more formal and general "Treaty of Maritime Peace in Perpetuity." In the 1850s, Britain also inaugurated a campaign against slavery in the gulf states.

The British assumption of control was a triumph of influence and prestige, backed by overwhelming sea power. Britain did not annex colonies, station forces on land, or assume direct rule anywhere in the area, though by 1900 it had become responsible for the foreign policy of the sheikhdoms. In 1899, the ruler of Kuwait,

An oil tanker passes through the Strait of Hormuz, the most strategic "choke point" between the gulf and the rest of the world.

alarmed by pressure from Turkey, entered into a similar agreement.

The system established by these treaties, rather oddly known as the "Trucial System," was one of the more respectable achievements of European imperialism. There was justification for the pride expressed by Lord Curzon, the viceroy of India, in a 1903 address to the Trucial sheikhs: "We found strife and have created order.... We have not seized or held your territory.... We opened the seas to the ships of all nations and enabled their flags to fly in peace."

British Withdrawal. The British imperial retreat from the gulf began in 1961, when Kuwait became fully independent. The crucial moment, however, which signaled the end of an era, came in 1968 when Britain announced that it would relinquish its imperial responsibilities in the gulf three years later. It was a curious decision, as it came precisely at a time when the gulf's oil was of more importance than ever to the West. Nor could it be justified on the ground that the British presence in the gulf area was highly costly. Indeed, it might well be argued that their presence provided valuable insurance for a very small premium. Various historians and experts on the Persian Gulf have maintained that the British decision to withdraw was both ill-considered and irresponsible.

In an effort to create a viable legatee of power, Great Britain sought to federate its nine protectorate states in the lower gulf. In 1971, the former Trucial Emirates became the United Arab Emirates, a federation of seven small states: Abu Dhabi, the largest; Dubai; Sharjah; Ajman; Umm al-Qaiwan; Ras al-Khaimah; and Fujairah. The other two British-protected states, Bahrain and Qatar, each chose to become independently sovereign.

Political Complexion. The coasts of the gulf have never been under the sovereignty of any one state. The Trucial System, the *Pax Britannica* as maintained in the Persian Gulf, was essentially a matter of relations with the rather minor political units of the

The withdrawal of British forces from Kuwait in 1961, above, marked the beginning of the end of a century-and-a-half of domination in the Persian Gulf. Ten years later, Great Britain fully relinquished its responsibilities in the region.

coast. It did not imply any domination of the power centers farther inland—the Persian Empire, the Wahabi rulers in Arabia, or the Ottoman power in Mesopotamia (Iraq), though after the collapse of the Ottoman Empire, Iraq did become a British Mandate (from 1920 to 1930).

At present, there are three large states with coastlines on the gulf—Iran, Iraq, and Saudi Arabia. There are five minor states, one of which is a composite structure. These are Kuwait, Bahrain, Qatar, Oman, and the United Arab Emirates.

The recent histories and current political attitudes of the eight gulf states show great diversity. But the minor states and one major state, Saudi Arabia, are, broadly speaking, traditional monarchies. They are conservative and, up to a point, pro-Western. The minor states of the gulf are indeed weak and vulnerable but have demonstrated a remarkable stability even in the face of the sometimes convulsive political developments of the 20th century. The Sabah family has ruled in Kuwait since 1756; Ahmad bin Said and his descendants have ruled in Oman since 1749; and the al-Khalifas have ruled in Bahrain since 1783. The Saudi family, the most notable monarchs of the Arab world, have ruled parts of Arabia since the 18th century, though their realm reached its present size only in the 1920s.

On the other hand, Iran and Iraq, combatants in the war that erupted in September 1980, are disruptive forces in the area. Both former monarchies, they now stand in sharp contrast to the conservative monarchies of the Persian Gulf and also to each other. Since the exile of Shah Mohammed Reza Pahlavi and the return of Ayatollah Ruhollah Khomeini in early 1979, Iran has been the seat of a Muslim theocracy. Iraq has gone through various radical regimes since the fall of the Hashemite monarchy in 1958 and is now ruled by the Baath party, champions of "Arab socialism."

Ethnic, religious, and political diversity among the nations of the Persian Gulf—indeed, of the whole Middle East—gives rise to frequent disagreements and conflicts. Even the Conference of Islamic States, with more than 40 member nations, is plagued by internal dissension. Seven nations boycotted an emergency meeting in January, below, in which "the Soviet military aggression" against Afghanistan was denounced and the latter country suspended.

Chip Hires, Liaison

Ethnic and religious division complicate the picture. All the gulf states except Iran are Arab, but Iran's population of approximately 36 million (half of them non-Persian) outnumbers all the other gulf states combined. Iraq, the next most populous country with a coastline on the gulf, has about 13 million persons. Many of the minor gulf states have more immigrants of non-Arab origin than they have native Arabs. There are also religious differences. Although all the gulf states are Islamic, Iranian Muslims and about half of Iraqi Muslims belong to the Shia sect, while the rest belong to the mainstream Sunni Islam.

Oil. It was the discovery of oil that turned the Persian Gulf from a poor into a fantastically rich region and made it of obsessive interest to the rest of the world. Iran began exporting oil just before World War I, Iraqi oil began to flow in the late 1920s, and Bahrain's followed suit in the early 1930s. The first oil was struck in Kuwait in 1938, but development did not begin until after World War II. Abu Dhabi and Dubai found oil in the 1950s, and Sharjah in 1972. The result of these discoveries was a boom in development unprecedented in world history, particularly after the seven great Western oil companies lost control of the pricing structure to the Arab producing countries in 1973 and after the formation of a cartel, the Organization of Petroleum Exporting Countries (OPEC). About 55% of the world's oil reserves are estimated to be in the Persian Gulf area, and the figure is expected to rise rather than decline in the coming years.

In 1976, before the convulsions in Iran and before the Iraqi-Iranian war, total Persian Gulf oil production was running at about 22 million barrels per day, or roughly 37% of world production. The latter figure still was fairly accurate in 1980. Decreases in world demand and increases in Saudi production made up for the declines in Iranian and Iraqi output. Of all the oil that goes

Apesteguy, Liaison

Oil and geopolitics have given the nations of southwest Asia new power and prestige in global affairs. The oil-rich gulf states have been able to buy sophisticated military equipment, such as U.S.-made F-15 fighter planes, left.

USAF

Golestan, Liaison

The outbreak of war between Iran and Iraq in September was dangerous to the world community both politically and economically. Oil installations were primary targets, and exports from these two major suppliers fell sharply.

into the stream of world trade (excluding that of the Soviet Union), approximately half comes from Persian Gulf sources, with by far the largest part going through the Strait of Hormuz. Western Europe is crucially dependent on Persian Gulf oil, the United States less so.

War in the Gulf. There was abundant reason for concern when, on September 22, after months of border clashes, Iraq launched a surprise attack on Iran. The advent of war was regarded by the world community as potentially disastrous. One U.S. newsmagazine lamented that "the nightmare, the conflict that had only been discussed as a worst-case scenario, was at hand." This was a natural reaction. Between them, Iran and Iraq supplied about 20% of gulf oil shipments, supplies that presumably would cease. The Strait of Hormuz might be closed, with incalculable consequences for Western Europe and the entire world. The Soviet Union, Iran's neighbor and the chief supplier of arms to Iraq, seemed to be presented with delicious and perhaps irresistible opportunities for intervention.

McCurry, Liaison

Causes of the War. It is all too easy to find exceedingly remote origins of the war. Iraqi President Saddam Hussein Takriti,
for example, alluded to the Battle of Qadisiya in the year 637,
when tribesmen out of Arabia defeated the Persian Empire and
ended oppressive Sassanid rule in the Tigris-Euphrates Valley.
Conflict between Arabs and Persians had indeed been frequent
through the centuries; the frontier has swung back and forth between them.

But these matters are remote. In fact, from 1975 until the fall
of the Pahlavi dynasty, relations between Iraq and the shah's
realm were unusually good. The Algiers Pact of 1975 was an
agreement genuinely advantageous to both sides. (The only losers
were the Kurds.) By that accord, Iran procured a shift of the
Shatt-al-Arab frontier from the Iranian side to the center of the
channel (the *thalweg*), while conceding that it would no longer harass Baghdad by supporting the Kurdish minority.

Apart from the revival of the two issues disposed of at Algiers,
there were at least three specific matters that contributed to the
outbreak of the Iraqi-Iranian conflict. One was the fact that Iran
has a large Arab minority, concentrated precisely where the oil
is—in Khuzestan province. Any ambitious ruler in Baghdad—and
Hussein is nothing if not ambitious—is bound to regard Khuzestan as *Iraq irredenta*. Second, the zealous Shia regime of the Ayatollah Khomeini presumably had some appeal to the Shia population of Iraq, often mistreated by the Sunni Baathist leaders in
Baghdad. Third, there was resentment in Iraq, on behalf of fellow
Arabs, at the shah's takeover in 1971 of three small islands in the
throat of the Strait of Hormuz claimed by some of the Trucial
states.

The war may thus be looked on as one of the innumerable disagreeable consequences of the fall of the shah—or, more re-

*With the Iranian army in dis-
array and the continuing
violence of Kurdish rebels,
Iraq's Hussein, below, felt it
was a good time to attack.*

Salhani, Liaison

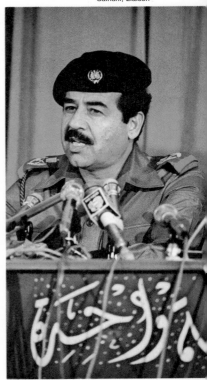

Abbas, Liaison

The Iranian armed forces, above, were plagued by a lack of unity and morale. Their Iraqi counterparts rallied behind Hussein but could not win an advantage.

J. Pavlovsky, Sygma

motely, of the British withdrawal. The shah's all-too-willing adoption (with the approval of the U.S. government) of the role of regional protector was an attempt to fill the British-created vacuum. With the shah gone and a chaotic Iran an easy mark, President Hussein no doubt found it an irresistible temptation to strike a blow against the detested Shia fundamentalists in Tehran. Iraq would emerge from a short, happy conflict as regional hegemon and leader of the Arab world. To the surprise of many, it did not turn out that way.

One Hundred Days of War. It would be uninteresting and unrewarding to follow chronologically the course of this unimpressive war. By the end of 1980, it had been in progress exactly 100 days and seemed as far as ever from either decision or conclusion. The initial impetus of the Iraqis' attack had enabled their forces to occupy a strip of Iranian territory along the border some 10 mi (16 km) wide, lay siege to Khorramshar and Abadan, and attack Ahwaz. But despite numerous claims of victory at these three sites, by year's end only Khorramshar seemed to be decisively in Iraqi hands, and by then the rainy season was beginning to limit the fighting.

The Dangers of Prophecy. The Iraqi-Iranian war proved to be a classic case study in the dangers of prophecy. Almost everything that the most respected commentators said about it during the first few days proved to be wrong. Many thought that it would be a formidable conflict in the style of the Egyptian-Israeli wars. Iraq and Iran are easily the leading military powers in the gulf area. They have the largest populations, as well as the largest and best-equipped armies and air forces. But the total forces actually employed by both sides was fairly small. Moreover, as a U.S. Pentagon officer was reported as saying, "This war is a case of the incompetent fighting the inept." Air forces were not used in support of ground operations as they should have been, and tanks were either misused or not used at all. In general, the conduct of the war testified to a total lack of experience in the military art. Experts noted that Iraq mysteriously failed to concentrate its forces in crucial areas, such as the passes through the Zagros Mountains. To cut the flow of oil from Khuzestan to Tehran would have been decisive, but it was not done. The exact objectives of the Iraqi military leadership remained unknown.

The expectation that Iraq would encounter a disorganized and crumbling Iran also proved fallacious. If anything, the war strengthened Iranian unity. Iranian defense, if not brilliant, at least caused the Iraqi attack to bog down by early December. Likewise, the prophecy that Iran would run out of supplies and spare parts proved wrong. It was adequately supplied by the Soviet Union, France, Libya, and Syria. France and the USSR also supplied Iraq.

The bombing of oil refineries, though at first ominous, ultimately appeared to have done less damage than initially reported. Like the rather random bombing of cities—sorties of one or two planes—it was an example of mutually destructive folly not likely to have decisive military significance. The bombing of the Iraqi capital of Baghdad was in sharp contrast to the mutual restraint exhibited by the much more professional combatants in the Egyptian-Israeli wars.

Oil and the War. The flow of oil from Iraq and Iran stopped immediately, but partial supply from Iraq resumed in November through pipelines to the Mediterranean. The impact on the outside world proved amazingly small. Reserves of oil were high, missing supplies were made good in part, and spot prices rose only slightly. France had to finance higher prices, but there was little trouble for others. Japanese oil stocks at year's end were what they had been in September. The oil exports of the other gulf states

McCurry, Liaison

The Soviet Union supplied helicopters and other materiel to both Iran and Iraq. The U.S. position is indicated by the cartoon below.

MacNelly, "Chicago Tribune," N.Y.T. Syndicate

were not subject to interference, and the Strait of Hormuz remained open. The mere potential for disaster evoked Western cooperation, with 50 warships from NATO powers in the area by November.

Inactivity of Minorities. The minority populations of Iran and Iraq did not behave as expected. Ayatollah Khomeini exhorted Shia Muslims in Iraq to rise up, but in vain, and the Kurds also were quiet. By the same token, Iraq derived no assistance at all from the Arabs of Khuzestan, who simply fled the fighting.

Lessons of the War. The war in the Persian Gulf between Iran and Iraq clearly established or reinforced three points. First, the unity of the Arab world once again proved to be a myth. The various governments again gave priority to their national interests over "Arab unity." Most Arab states supported Iraq in the war, but the radical states of Syria, Libya, and South Yemen sided with Iran.

Second, it was made clear that the conflict between Arab and Jew is not the only, and perhaps not even the most significant, conflict in the Middle East. Even were that perennial conflict solved, the region would still be far from peace and harmony.

Third, the impotence of the United Nations was laid bare. Even though it was a conflict not involving the major powers—who scrupulously refrained from choosing sides—the UN, and the General Assembly in particular, demonstrated extreme reluctance to deal with the very fact of the war. And yet, when fatigue shall have brought the combatants eventually to the point of negotiation, what is desperately needed are the services of a genuinely impartial arbitrator or organization to end a conflict of no possible advantage of either side or to the world at large. As 1980 came to an end, the Iraqi-Iranian war was still a real threat but a threat that had not—or at least had not yet—become a disaster.

Iranian Prime Minister Mohammed Ali Rajai addressed the United Nations Security Council on October 17 in its continuing debate on the Iran-Iraq war. The UN proved ineffectual in helping to resolve the dispute.

Pozarik, Liaison

A quiet scene at the U.S. embassy in Tehran belies the international furor caused by the hostage crisis.

THE PERSIAN GULF/

The U.S. Hostage Crisis

It began on a clear, crisp Sunday, Nov. 4, 1979, in the Iranian capital of Tehran.

Goaded by a fiery anti-American speech three days earlier by Iran's revolutionary spiritual leader, Ayatollah Ruhollah Khomeini, about 4,000 Iranian youths assembled at Tehran University and then marched on the U.S. embassy. The students and others demanded that ousted Shah Mohammed Reza Pahlavi, in a New York hospital for gallbladder surgery and treatment of lymphatic cancer, be returned to Iran with all his assets.

Within hours, several hundred of the protesters had forced their way into the embassy compound, seized control of the buildings, and taken hostage the approximately 60 diplomatic personnel inside.

U.S. Chargé d'Affaires L. Bruce Laingen, the senior American diplomat in Tehran, and two of his aides were at the Iranian foreign ministry when the violence broke out. Laingen, who maintained telephone contact with both the Americans under seige and the State Department in Washington, pleaded with Iranian Foreign Minister Ibrahim Yazdi for police protection. Although some security forces eventually arrived, they made no effort to intervene. Laingen was detained in the foreign ministry building with his aides.

The hostage crisis had begun.

The episode, which many American officials had expected to last only a few days, still had not been resolved by the end of 1980, nearly 14 months later.

The takeover of the embassy was an action without precedent in the annals of international relations. The detention of the hostages was the most frustrating foreign policy problem for U.S. President Jimmy Carter and probably contributed to his election loss in November 1980. It

39

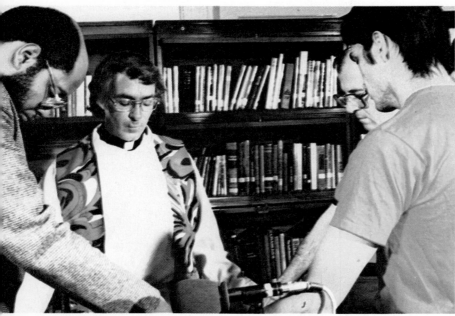

American clergymen were allowed to visit the hostages and reported that the ones they had seen appeared to be in good physical and mental health.

Liaison

created at least transitory rifts in the Western alliance over what course of action to pursue, and caused serious divisions in the Muslim world. Nowhere were the repercussions more severe than in Iran itself. The hostage crisis temporarily swung the balance of power to the radicals, but differences persisted between those seeking an accommodation with the West and those who regarded the isolation as a blessing. On the whole, the situation did make it more difficult for Iran's new revolutionary government to function smoothly.

The hostage crisis also made it harder for the United States and other concerned countries to react to the Soviet military intervention in Afghanistan. Theoretically, Iran and the United States should have stood together against the Russians, but the detention of the hostages made this impossible.

Paradoxically, the embassy takeover occurred at a time when the United States and Iranian governments seemed to be moving closer together. There was no question as to the truth of the revolutionaries' often-repeated claim of a virtual alliance between the United States and the former shah. But the Carter administration had made initial contacts with the government of Prime Minister Mehdi Bazargan, and plans were going ahead to supply Iran with some military spare parts.

In mid-October 1979, however, after months of pressure from former Secretary of State Henry Kissinger, banker David Rockefeller, and others to admit the shah into the United States, the Carter administration decided on "humanitarian grounds" to let him go to New York for specialized medical treatment.

Whatever the administration's humanitarian motives, they provided Iran's radicals, then engaged in a bitter political battle with the more moderate Bazargan government, a chance to build support by warning of a new U.S. conspiracy to place the shah back on his throne.

When it was informed of the shah's arrival in New York, the Bazargan government warned of grave consequences. Bazargan and Yazdi hastened their own political demise by meeting in Algiers with Zbigniew Brzezinski, Carter's national security adviser, on October 31. On November 1, in a preliminary demonstration, tens of thousands of Iranians marched on the embassy carrying banners that read "Give us the Shah" and shouting "Death to Carter, death to Americans."

American policy throughout the crisis vacillated between diplomatic efforts to persuade the Iranian authorities to release the hostages and punitive measures. U.S. actions were perceived by many to be influenced by the White House's sensitivity to election-year politics. The government's apparent inability to do anything about this direct challenge to U.S. power and what was perceived as an insult to the nation's honor, aroused deep anger among the American people. This produced, particularly in the early stages, a desire by the White House to be seen at all times as doing something to seek the hostages' release.

This strategy, in turn, appeared to play into the hands of the militants, who enjoyed the confrontation with the United States and appeared to relish the undivided attention of the rest of the world. American television, of course, also played its part by stirring up U.S. anger toward Iran and providing exposure to the militants.

For much of November and December 1979, the White House sought every available contact with Iranian authorities. Carter's own emissaries, former Attorney General Ramsey Clark and Senate staff aide William Miller, were refused entry into Iran even as their plane was on its way. Dozens of foreign governments, including some unfriendly to the United States, such as Libya, were asked to use their influence. Even the Palestine Liberation Organization (PLO), with which the United States had no dealings, sought to free the hostages. Neither the PLO nor any of the governments were at all successful.

On the punitive side, President Carter banned the import of Iranian oil; all Iranian assets in the United States were frozen; resident Iranian students with improper visas were threatened with deportation; the International Court of Justice in The Hague was asked to bring judgment against Iran; and naval task forces were sent into nearby waters.

At the beginning, Ayatollah Khomeini gave confusing signals as to his intentions. On November 19 and early November 20, with no advance warning, 13 of the hostages—all blacks and women—were released. At the same time, however, Khomeini said that because of the embassy's alleged espionage activities, the remaining diplomats "according to our laws, should be tried and punished." On November 20, the United States reminded Khomeini and the militants of its right to use force to free its citizens from illegal detention. Khomeini responded: "If the United States wants to attack us, we cannot restrain the students who are very emotional now, from blowing up the embassy. We will all be killed and the hostages will be killed."

On Jan. 29, 1980, U.S. and Canadian officials announced that six U.S. embassy employees who had fled the compound during the chaos of the November takeover were flown out of Iran the previous day. The six had shown up at the Canadian embassy, lived for three months in the residences of Canadian diplomats, and left the country with forged visas.

By early February 1980, it was evident that various intermediaries had failed to produce any movement toward the release of the rest of the hostages. A series of punitive measures—including denunciations by the UN Security Council—also accomplished nothing. Carter had told a group of U.S. Congressmen in January that he would "turn the screws a little tighter" to get the hostages returned. But having ruled out a direct frontal attack, the limited nature of the other measures persuaded Secretary of State Cyrus R. Vance to try a more concerted diplomatic probe.

What seemed to make this a propitious time was that Abolhassan Bani-Sadr had just been elected president of Iran. During his brief tenure as foreign minister in November, Bani-Sadr had worked through the United Nations to try to resolve the crisis and had made it known that he opposed holding the Americans.

UN Secretary General Kurt Waldheim volunteered his efforts. With Bani-Sadr he worked out a two-part solution: the UN would send a five-man panel to Iran to listen to its grievances against the shah and the United States and would prepare a report that would be sympathetic to Iran's concerns; meanwhile, the panel would visit the hostages and the Bani-Sadr government would take control of the Americans, preparing the way for their release.

But on February 23, the day the commission arrived in Tehran, Ayatollah Khomeini, whose

UPI

Six U.S. embassy employees who had escaped during the seizure of the complex were flown out of Iran Jan. 29, 1980, with the secret help of Canadian diplomats.

support for the two-tier plan had been assumed, issued a statement asserting that only the Iranian parliament could decide the hostages' fate. This seemed to undermine the efforts of the diplomats, since the parliament's election was still months away. Nevertheless, the commission went ahead with its task.

By early March, the Iranian government seemed ready to assume responsibility for the hostages. But Khomeini again intervened and blocked the move. The failure of the Iranians to carry out their part of the bargain irked and embarrassed the White House, which had to be concerned with the impact of the crisis on Carter's credibility with voters.

Beginning in the first week of April, the United States deliberately began to escalate the issue. Diplomatic relations with Iran were severed, and a series of economic sanctions were imposed. Allies were implored to do the same, and Iran was warned that unless the hostages were freed by mid-May, a naval blockade was possible. At the same time that these moves were being carried out in the public eye, however, Carter was secretly planning the most hazardous action in the crisis—the forcible rescue of the hostages.

Although the administration had repeatedly ruled out such a mission, it launched on the evening of April 24 a rescue operation involving a 90-man commando group, eight RH-53 helicopters, and six C-130 Hercules transport planes.

Called "Operation Blue Light," the two-day mission called for the shuttling of commandos in Iran by helicopter and the coordinated efforts of agents already in Tehran. The transport planes took off from Egypt, and the helicopters left from the *Nimitz* aircraft carrier in the Arabian Sea. All six planes arrived at the rendezvous point in the Iranian desert, but two helicopters had to turn back after developing mechanical problems. In the desert, a third helicopter developed a hydraulic problem, and the mission had to be aborted. Then during the pullout, one of the helicopters collided with a C-130 loaded with ammunition. The explosion killed eight men and injured five others.

The failure of the mission was the low point of the hostage crisis from the American point of view. In the eyes of the public and U.S. allies abroad, the operation seemed ill-prepared and overly cautious. Perhaps worst of all was the impression of Washington's irrationality. The attempted rescue hurt Carter politically, not the least because Secretary of State Vance, the administration's chief negotiator, resigned in opposition to the use of force.

With the naming of Edmund S. Muskie as the new secretary of state on April 29, Carter agreed to remove the hostage issue from public glare. Except for the unexpected return of one hostage, the seriously ill Richard Queen, on July 11, little was said about the hostage crisis for the rest of the spring and summer. The shah, who

Iranian troops examine the wreckage from the failed U.S. rescue attempt in April.

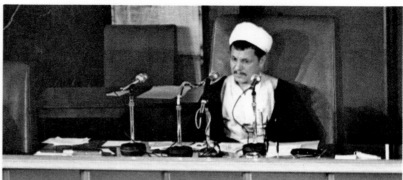

Prime Minister Mohammed Ali Rajai addresses the Iranian parliament on the hostage situation. Dominated by Islamic fundamentalists, the body took a hard line with respect to conditions for the hostages' release.

Liaison

had left the United States for Panama in December 1979 and moved on to Egypt in March 1980, died in Cairo on July 27. Meanwhile, Mohammed Ali Rajai had been named prime minister of the just-elected Iranian parliament. At the end of August, Muskie wrote Rajai suggesting the opening of a dialogue. The idea was denounced.

Then, on September 12, Ayatollah Khomeini issued a statement containing four conditions for the release of the remaining 52 hostages. These were made formal by the parliament on November 2, after considerable debate. The conditions were a pledge by the United States of nonintervention in Iran's affairs; the unfreezing of the more than $8,000,000,000 of Iran's assets in the United States; cancellation of all claims against Iran; and the confiscation and transfer to Iran of the shah's property.

There was widespread speculation that Iran's continuing isolation from the world community and the outbreak of war with Iraq made it eager to resolve the hostage crisis. Its demands, however, were difficult for the United States to meet. In its response to the Iranians, the Carter admin-

istration pointed out that while it was able to meet the nonintervention pledge and to unfreeze the frozen assets, it could not legally abrogate all claims against Iran or simply confiscate the shah's property. The discussions, held through Algerian intermediaries, began to be protracted. The next several weeks saw a series of proposals and counterproposals, with lengthy analysis and "study" of the various plans. Greetings from the hostages were broadcast to the United States at Christmas time, but their release still seemed remote. As another year came to an end, the 52 Americans were still in captivity.

Then, in the days immediately preceding the Jan. 20, 1981 inauguration of Ronald Reagan, the Carter administration negotiated a final agreement with the Iranians. Some of the frozen Iranian assets in the United States would be returned in exchange for the release of the hostages. On the day of the inaugural, Algerian planes left Tehran with 52 American citizens who had been held hostage for 444 days.

The waiting and the hoping were over.

BERNARD GWERTZMAN
Diplomatic Correspondent, "The New York Times"

Muslim pilgrims on their way to Mecca gather in a small town east of the holy city.

THE PERSIAN GULF/

ISLAM: The History, Culture, and Faith

The religion of Islam, which entered its fifteenth millennium in November 1980, originated in the Arabian Peninsula with the preachings of the Prophet Muhammad. Today the faith counts almost 800 million adherents throughout the world. Islam means submission to the will of God. The Muslim, or individual who makes such submission, attempts to live in conformity with the expression of that will, contained in the divine law, the *sharia.* This code not only defines a theological system but also provides guidelines for every aspect of a Muslim's behavior. Thus, Islam is more than a religion; it is a complete social, political, and economic system. That fact explains the increasing attention being paid to Islam as Muslim countries work toward defining their role in today's world.

Muhammad and the Koran. Muhammad was born in approximately 570 A.D. in Mecca, a prosperous Arabian commercial center and the site of important pagan shrines. A member neither of the aristocratic clans which profited most from the city's business and religious interests nor of the growing group of immigrants from the desert who barely survived on the fringes of Meccan society, Muhammad was a sensitive individual who was disturbed by the social problems that had accompanied the city's growth.

In 610, he experienced a revelation in which God, through the Angel Gabriel, conveyed to him a message for the Meccans. Other revelations continued until the end of Muhammad's life. These ultimately were collected in the *Koran,* the Islamic scriptures. The early revelations emphasized the principal tenets of Islam:

there is a single God, Allah, and Muhammad is His prophet; men should worship and obey Allah and act charitably toward their neighbors; and men will be held accountable for their acts on a Day of Judgment at the end of history. Similarities to Jewish and Christian beliefs are evident; indeed, the Koran indicates that God had delivered identical messages to Jews and Christians but that they had either misunderstood or distorted them. Muhammad was the final prophet, the Koran the final statement of God's will.

Some Meccans accepted Muhammad's teachings, but his attack on polytheism and criticism of materialism won him the enmity of most of the city's leaders. They brought such great pressure to bear on the Prophet that, in 622, Muhammad and his followers left Mecca and resettled in the agricultural oasis of Medina. In Medina the Muslims established a community in which the revelations were applied to social, economic, and political, as well as religious, life. The migration to Medina—the *hegira*—marks the official beginning of the religion. The hegira is the starting point of the Muslim calendar.

Until his death a decade later, Muhammad directed a campaign to convert the remainder of the peninsula to Islam. He was particularly interested in bringing Mecca into the Muslim fold. He had always insisted that the city's major shrine, the Kaaba, was a place of worship that should be dedicated to Allah. Through preaching, diplomacy, and the occasional use of force, the Muslims were successful, and by 632 most of Arabia, including Mecca, had accepted Islam.

The Five Pillars. The Kaaba became the scene of an annual Muslim pilgrimage—the *hajj*—which remains an important Islamic ritual. Obligatory once in a lifetime for all believers physically and financially capable of undertaking it, pilgrimage is one of the "Five Pillars of Islam"—practices that both reveal and strengthen a Muslim's faith. The other four pillars are reciting the *shahada,* the creed that "there is no God but Allah and Muhammad is His Prophet"; saying five daily prayers according to a set ritual called *salat; zakat,* giving alms for charitable and religious purposes; and fasting during the daylight hours of Ramadan, the ninth Muslim month.

The Law. After Muhammad's death in 632, an official called the *caliph,* or successor of the Prophet, led the Muslim community. The caliph issued administrative orders and supervised the government. He did not make laws regulating communal behavior, since the revelations had already done that. Instead, he ensured that the sharia was conscientiously observed. In addition to the Koran as a source of the law, *hadiths,* or stories about Muhammad's life, also serve as legal precedents.

Islam's emphasis on the law led to the development of a class of religious scholars—the *ulama*—who specialized in the study of the sharia. Within a few centuries, the ulama reached a consensus on the interpretation of all important legal points. The function of later ulama has been not to interpret the sharia themselves but to explain and comment on views previously agreed upon. While not clerics—Islam prides itself on the absence of priestly intermediaries in worship services, and the *imam,* or prayer leader, has no sacerdotal powers—the ulama have always been an influential force. Most prominent among them are *qadis,* or judges rendering decisions based on the sharia, and *muftis,* who serve as legal consultants.

Sectarianism. Muslim unity began to dissipate after Muhammad's death. The early caliphs, none of whom was from Muhammad's family, came to office because the elders of the community agreed that their piety and leadership qualified them for the position. Some Muslims, however, took exception to this approach. They believed that Muhammad's cousin and son-in-law, Ali, had enjoyed a unique relationship with the Prophet, that a charismatic quality had passed from Muhammad to Ali, and that only he and his descendants—who were also Muhammad's descendants—were worthy leaders of the Muslims.

Ali did become caliph in 656, but civil war punctuated his five-year rule, which ended with his assassination. Ali's sons were denied the caliphate, but supporters of the family's claims launched a struggle against the government. Called the *Shia,* or partisans of Ali, they accepted as rightful heads of Islam only Ali's heirs, whom they termed imams.

In addition to this political struggle, Shiism also stirred a religious controversy. Esoteric interpretations of the Koran supporting Shia claims were advanced, and the imam was said to possess a superior understanding of the Scriptures. This enabled him to formulate doctrine and assume powers far outstripping those of the caliph. Such challenges to the central Muslim authority could not be ignored, and the Shiites suffered persecutions that forced many of them to seek refuge in outlying areas of the Islamic world.

Just as the Shias had broken with the majority of orthodox Muslims—the Sunni—the Shiites themselves underwent fragmentation. Most Shiites acknowledged twelve imams, the last of whom disappeared in the late 9th century and, they believed, would someday return to preside over an era of peace, prosperity, and justice for the downtrodden followers of Ali. These "Twelvers" were prepared to await peacefully the return of the Hidden Imam. This assured their survival, and today they constitute the majority of Shia Muslims. More radical groups, differing with the "Twelvers" over the proper line of succession to the imam and insisting upon revolutions against governments they deemed illegitimate, caused greater problems for the caliphs but always remained minorities within the Shia movement.

One significant difference between Shia and Sunni Islam may be seen in the powers accorded the ulama. Shia *mujtahids* or religious interpreters, have retained the right, lost by their Sunni counterparts, to use their own powers of reason to form new interpretations of the law. Among the mujtahids there is a hierarchy predicated on study and acceptability by the community, at the top of which are officials called *ayatollahs.*

Islamic Culture. Despite these internal problems, the Muslim world experienced a cultural flowering from the 9th to the 14th centuries. The pace of expansion, which in the century after Muhammad had rapidly exposed Muslims to the Byzantine and Sassanian Empires, slowed considerably. Increasing commercial enterprises, however, soon brought Muslims into contact with India, East Asia, and Africa. Their willingness to learn from these divergent cultures and to combine that knowledge with uniquely Muslim ideas and customs was the basis of a truly great civilization.

Tremendous strides were made in such fields as medicine, astronomy, and agricultural science. Many Muslim ideas passed into Europe during and after the Crusades, challenging the Christian concept that the Muslim world was a land of barbarism. To the contrary, it was the interest of Muslim scholars in the literature of antiquity that preserved much classical Western writing during Europe's Dark Ages. In a very real sense, the Muslims helped make the Renaissance possible, for, as Europeans again became curious about their heritage, it was to Arabic translations of Greek and Roman authors that they turned for the most definitive renditions.

Following a disruptive period coinciding with the Mongol invasions of its heartlands, the Muslim world reached new political heights in the 16th century. The Ottoman Empire, a Turkish state whose ruler, the sultan, was also the caliph, took control of eastern Europe, the Anatolian Peninsula, and the Arab lands from the Fertile Crescent to the Nile Valley and across North Africa. In Persia, the Safavid dynasty ruled another empire, whose most striking feature was allegiance to Shia Islam as the state religion. The Mogul Empire, like the Ottoman Empire ruled by Turkish warriors, held sway in India and adjacent areas.

The very strength that allowed these entities to consolidate their positions imbued them with a self-confidence that contributed to their undoing. Convinced of their cultural, political, and religious superiority over the Christian world, they believed that they had nothing to learn from the West and isolated themselves from it. Their assessment might have been valid centuries earlier, but the European world was changing, and the Muslims' deliberate ignorance of it excluded them from sharing in the progress, particularly in technology, made during the Renaissance. Owing to its location, the Ottoman Empire was the first to suffer for its self-imposed seclusion, but the others also could not escape the rising power of Europe.

Modern Islam. Beginning in the late 1600s, territories which had been Muslim for centuries fell into European hands. Even in those parts of the Muslim world that retained their political freedom, foreigners exerted powerful social and economic influences. This experience dealt a severe blow to Muslim pride, for defeat at the hands of the infidel called into question the presumed superiority of Islam and the entire culture which derived from it.

Many Europeans argued that Islam was inherently backward, an assertion belied by Islamic history. Muslim intellectuals seeking to understand how their world order could have been so thoroughly shattered by the Christian West concluded that Islam became corrupted by superstitious and unorthodox practices creeping in over the centuries. This had weakened the whole political, social, and religious edifice, they contended, and had led to its collapse at the hands of Europe. They urged a return to the pure Islam of their ancestors, which would reinvigorate the faith and enable it to meet its challenges successfully. Such a reform movement emerged in the late 19th and 20th centuries, sometimes playing a role in nationalist causes by stressing the glories of the Muslim past and the need for Muslims to rule themselves according to norms which the colonial powers neither cared about nor understood.

After World War I, the Muslim states one by one regained their independence. Even then, however, few were comfortable with their relationship with the West. One devastating consequence of the years of European ascendancy was the enshrinement of the belief on the part of many Muslim rulers that, whatever the shortcomings of the Christian states, they were clearly more powerful than their own. Convinced that they could achieve similar power merely by recasting their own societies in the image of the West, they introduced industrial, agrarian, and even political schemes borrowed from Europe. Although great changes were effected, these innovations all too frequently were forced upon societies which were not ready for them and could not comprehend them. Too much changed too rapidly, as rulers attempted to achieve in a lifetime what in Europe had taken centuries. Many individuals were left adrift by this "progress," unable to retain their traditional way of life but ill-equipped or reluctant to enter the new one. The process of modernization continued to erode traditional societies even after their independence. In many respects the pace quickened as rulers sought to establish their credentials as heads of "advanced" states. The belittling of traditional values and ways of life—often closely linked with Islam—and their replacement by norms and practices imported from the West generated a feeling of resentment among those who believed they had not benefited from the transformations and those who questioned the assumption that Western ways were universally desirable. Frequently these were the same people.

The most recent manifestations of these attitudes have been the 1978 deposition of Shah Mohammed Reza Pahlavi of Iran, accused of allowing foreign interests to dominate his country to the detriment of its Muslim population, and his replacement with an avowedly Islamic revolutionary regime; the guerrilla war conducted by Muslim organizations in Afghanistan against the imposition of an alien, in this case Communist, ideology; and the upsurge in the demands of the Muslim Brotherhood and similar groups throughout the Middle East for the reinstatement of respect for fundamental Islamic values. The government of virtually every state in the Muslim world, including such secular ones as Egypt and such traditionally religious ones as Saudi Arabia, is devoting increasing attention to Islam.

If much of this activity appears extreme, it is because many Muslims feel the damage done to their culture during the centuries in which they were dominated by the West was so severe that only an initially extreme reaction can correct the situation. The results of the current Islamic revival may not be clear for years to come, but it is certain that Islamic values will play a formative role in shaping events in much of the non-Western world in the foreseeable future.

KENNETH J. PERKINS
University of South Carolina

Toxic chemicals seeping from the Love Canal in New York forced area residents to evacuate.

HAZARDOUS WASTE/ A PROBLEM FOR THE 1980s

By Joseph H. Highland
Chairman, Toxic Chemicals Program
Environmental Defense Fund

For a long time, virtually no one in the United States was concerned about the production or disposal of hazardous waste. As a society, Americans grew dependent on the products of the modern chemical industry and the benefits that they brought. Then they became aware that the manufacture of these products might foul the air and contaminate the water, but still the public paid little, if any, attention to the problems created by inadequate disposal.

Only during the past five years or so have Americans begun to realize the dimensions of the environmental and public health risks created by the improper disposal of toxic chemical wastes. Every day the problem seems to grow larger. Every month the federal government reports the discovery of additional hazardous waste disposal sites, and local residents and government officials voice concern over the potential health and environmental impact on surrounding areas. Today, Americans not only realize that past disposal practices have created great problems, many of which elude solutions, but they also have begun to recognize the degree of ignorance that still remains with respect to what should be done to prevent new problems in the future.

The problems of today are the result of decades of inaction. Industries that generated hazardous wastes devoted inadequate resources to ensure proper disposal. Government was silent, allowing disposal practices that resulted in widespread environmental contamination. Research efforts by both the government and private industry failed to address the development of proper disposal methods.

Even by 1980, the environmental and health impact of past disposal practices had not been evaluated fully, nor had a course been charted that would be certain to prevent new problems in the future. The challenge of the 1980s will be to assess the damage that has already occurred and to develop disposal procedures that will ensure that neither the environment nor human health is threatened.

Scope of the Problem. Each year, American industry generates more than 96,000,000,000 lbs (43 550 000 000 kg) of hazardous waste. This material is the byproduct of manufacturing processes that yield the virtually endless variety of products that is an integral part of current American life. Everything from the extraction of ores and minerals from the depths of the earth to the production of plastic novelty items involves the generation of a waste product. Whether the wastes pose a threat to public health and the environment depends on their chemical composition and the manner in which they are disposed of. Unless major steps are taken in the immediate future, there will be an increase of at least 30% in the yearly volume of new waste material by 1990.

Between 1950 and 1978, the 53 largest domestic chemical manufacturers in the United States estimated that they had produced 762 million T (691 million t) of hazardous and nonhazardous wastes at slightly more than 16,000 manufacturing facilities. The largest production of hazardous waste comes from the chemical and allied product industries, but a variety of other industries also contributes to the enormous quantities produced each year. (See Table 1.) Shockingly, the Environmental Protection Agency (EPA), the arm of the federal government responsible for protecting environmental quality, estimates that, until recently, as little

Table 1

U.S. Sources of Hazardous Waste

Source of Information: Environmental Protection Agency

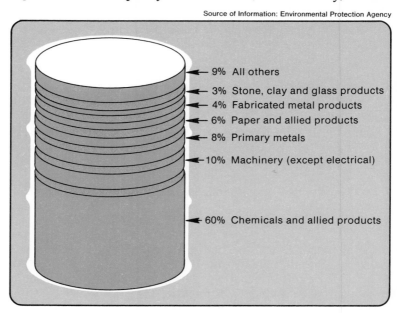

9% All others

3% Stone, clay and glass products

4% Fabricated metal products

6% Paper and allied products

8% Primary metals

10% Machinery (except electrical)

60% Chemicals and allied products

as 10% of all hazardous waste was disposed of properly. As a result, pesticides, toxic organic and inorganic chemicals, and radioactive wastes have escaped into the environment and caused widespread damage.

The past failure to regulate waste disposal properly is causing environmental and public health problems of staggering proportions. The EPA recently estimated that there are 52,000 hazardous waste dump sites across the United States. Of these, more than 12,000 pose a substantial and imminent threat to human health through contaminated groundwater, excessive radiation, or fire and explosion. The EPA continues to put out a monthly list of newly-found dump sites, and so the full magnitude of problems created by past disposal practices is not yet known. One estimate of the magnitude of the problem came from the Health and Scientific Research Committee of the U.S. Senate, which estimated that in 1980 more than 1.2 million Americans were exposed to highly or moderately serious health hazards from more than 200 dump sites that required immediate remedial work to prevent the hazards from taking their toll in the future.

The threat to the environment and public health occurs in many ways. The most typical problem is the contamination of groundwater—the waters that run below the earth's surface—which become contaminated with chemicals that have leached from disposal sites. These waters are a source of drinking water for more than 50% of U.S. residents—those who own their own wells or live in large metropolitan areas. The city of Memphis, TN, and towns on Long Island, NY, rely on underground water as a source of drinking water. Unlike surface waters—rivers, streams, and creeks—groundwater, once contaminated, is almost impossible to clean. Groundwater moves relatively slowly without the mixing that occurs in rapidly-moving streams and rivers. In addition, there is little opportunity for biological or chemical degradation of contaminants. Underground "plumes" of pollution can move great distances and pose a significant threat to human health if they enter a source of drinking water. Likewise, plumes of pollution may empty into surface waters and threaten the delicate ecosystems that depend on such bodies.

A recent nationwide survey of surface impoundments (pits, ponds, and lagoons) revealed that 50% of industrial impoundments are likely to contain hazardous substances. About 30%, or more than 8,000, of the industrial sites actually visited were found to be located above usable groundwater supplies and constructed on permeable soils. At more than half the sites investigated, the groundwater had been contaminated beyond EPA drinking water standards.

In addition to groundwater contamination, improperly disposed of wastes can threaten health and the environment in other ways. In Triana, AL, the health of a small, rural, relatively poor community was jeopardized by the leaching of hazardous pesticide wastes into a local river used by residents as a source of fish, a major staple in their diets. The residues of pesticides in the river "bioaccumulated" in the tissues of the fish and were passed along to town residents who ate them. The people of Triana are reported to have the highest body burden levels of DDT ever reported in the United States. Preliminary reports also associated extensive dental problems in children with exposure to DDT leached from the landfill.

Steve Aldridge
"Fayetteville Observer Times"

A roadside sign at Fort Bragg, NC, warns the public of PCB contamination. Careless dumping of the toxic chemical has contaminated more than 100 mi (161 km) of state roadways.

Chemicals stored at the waterfront warehouse of the Chemical Control Corp. in Elizabeth, NJ, exploded April 22. Toxic fumes from the chemical fire prompted the closing of schools in Elizabeth and nearby Staten Island, NY.

Air pollution from a landfill can also pose a threat to health and the environment. Many improperly disposed of chemicals are highly volatile and can be carried in the air to surrounding neighborhoods. Storm sewers that become contaminated can carry wastes far away from the original disposal site and contaminate rivers, streams, and soil. There are many ways in which chemicals can find their way into the environment and thereby threaten ecosystems and public health.

Love Canal. In 1980, a U.S. Congressional subcommittee reported that "the magnitude [of] the hazardous waste disposal problem cannot be overstated." Although the dumping of toxic waste has become the nation's number one environmental concern, it did not gain national attention until the alarming reports about the Love Canal area of Niagara Falls, NY, in the summer of 1978.

In 1892, William T. Love set out to fulfill his dream of developing a new industrial complex at Niagara Falls. Granted the right of eminent domain by the New York State legislature, Love planned to build a major new industrial city, using water power from the Niagara River. As part of the project, Love proposed the construction of a navigable canal between the upper and lower Niagara Rivers. Digging of the canal was begun in an area 7–8 mi (11–13 km) northeast of Niagara Falls but was halted when Love ran into financial difficulties.

The abandoned canal served for many years as a swimming hole for children. In 1947, the Hooker Chemical and Plastics Company purchased the canal and began using it as an industrial dump site. In 1953, after countless thousands of drums of toxic chemical waste and residue had been buried on the site, it was sold to the Niagara Falls Board of Education for one dollar. The board constructed an elementary school and playing field on part of the site, and sold the rest of it to a developer, who built hundreds of single-family homes on the periphery of the canal.

Chemicals began to surface in the following years, and in 1976, after six years of unusually heavy rains and snow, they began seeping through foundation walls into the basements of homes adjacent to the canal. In August 1978, the New York State Department of Health officially termed the Love Canal area "a grave and imminent peril" to the health of those living nearby. Pregnant women and children under the age of two were evacuated from the community, and the Department of Health began an investigation of residents' complaints of abnormal numbers of miscarriages, birth defects, cancer, and a variety of other illnesses. Studies performed by the Department of Health and independent investigators confirmed a high incidence of disease. Families adjacent to the canal were evacuated after findings of an increased incidence of miscarriage and birth defects. Additional investigations found an increased incidence of urinary tract and liver disease.

More than 200 different chemical compounds have been identified in the air, water, and soil around Love Canal. Many are known or suspected chemical carcinogens, mutagens, teratogens, or neurotoxins. More than half of the chemicals identified are process intermediates from various industrial processes and have no known toxicological properties.

In response to the widespread environmental contamination and the continuing migration of chemicals out of Love Canal, a cleanup plan was undertaken. The plan involved the installation of a subsurface tile drainage system designed to collect the wastes leaching out of the canal. A permanent pumping-collection system then was put into place. Any liquid wastes collected are treated with activated carbon, and the remaining effluent is disposed of through the local sewage system. A thick clay cap was put over the surface of the canal to prevent any further infiltration of rain water, and old river beds intersecting the canal were examined for the migration of toxic waste material. Scientists and engineers then began a detailed assessment of the success of the cleanup and the possible need for other measures.

Because of the widespread environmental pollution and adverse health effects, U.S. President Jimmy Carter declared a federal emergency, allowing members of the Love Canal community to relocate to new homes. Those families who own homes in the area could have them purchased by the government and be free to move away from the neighborhood. Those persons living in housing projects would be transferred to new accommodations outside the danger zone. The final disposition of area residences remained unclear. It is possible that the government would sell them to anyone willing to take part in revitalization efforts.

Other Instances. While the Love Canal is unique in terms of the media coverage it received, it is not unique in terms of the problems created by inadequate waste disposal. In Lowell, MA, for example, 1,000,000 gal (3 785 000 l) of mixed toxic waste in 15,000 rotting drums and tanks were discovered at a closed waste dump only a quarter of a mile (400 m) from inhabited homes. Among the wastes were flammable solvents, chlorinated hydro-

Leaking barrels of hazardous waste are found in dump sites and vacant lots all over the United States.

Marc Pokempner, Black Star

carbons, plating and etching wastes, and solvent distillation residue sludges. Spills and leaks had caused pollution of soil, groundwater, and air. Earlier, while the dump site was still active, improper discharges of untreated materials into sewers caused backups 1 mi (1.6 km) away and had created health problems for sewer workers and employees in neighboring firms. The waste dump operator, Silresim Company, had since gone bankrupt, and the state of Massachusetts was forced to appropriate $1.5 million to remove the wastes.

In Hardeman County, TN, 40 families near a rural landfill drank from wells polluted with such pesticides as endrin, dieldrin, aldrin, and heptachlor. From 1964 to 1972, the Velsicol Chemical Company had used a neighboring 300-acre (121-ha) site for shallow burial of 300,000 55-gal (208-l) drums of pesticide production residues. Residents complained of a wide variety of ailments, including liver and urinary tract problems, dizziness, nausea, and rashes.

Solving the Problem. Solutions to the hazardous waste disposal problem are not simple. Federal, state, and local governments, private industry, and local citizens groups have begun to address the problem, but their efforts are not coordinated under any one set of guidelines.

Two laws have been enacted, however, which provide a framework under which the problem is being addressed. The first law, entitled the Resource Conservation and Recovery Act (RCRA), was passed in 1976 with the explicit intent of providing federal regulation to ensure the proper and safe disposal of hazardous waste. In 1980, in the waning hours of the 96th Congress, a bill called "Superfund," which provides federal authority and money to resolve problems of existing dump sites, was enacted and signed into law by President Carter.

By law, the regulations implementing RCRA were to be promulgated by the federal EPA within 18 months after enactment of the bill, but major pieces still had not been promulgated four years after enactment. Several important sets of RCRA regula-

© 1980, Oliphant

tions that have been promulgated, however, went into effect in November 1980. Among the new measures was the creation of a "manifest" or tracking system, whereby accurate records would be kept of the types of waste generated, who transports them, and the ultimate disposal site. These regulations should be an effective step toward precluding indiscriminate dumping on vacant lots.

In addition, the new RCRA regulations provide the first definition by which industrial wastes can be classified as hazardous. But this vitally important section is very narrowly addressed, thereby excluding a number of dangerous wastes. The scheme relies almost exclusively on a listing mechanism, and the initial proposed list has shrunk from 103 to less than 70. And while the government also has established a limited testing program to determine the composition of certain wastes, the program has been heavily criticized for being scientifically invalid.

The next major regulations to be published by the federal government under RCRA will provide standards for the design of facilities receiving and ultimately disposing of hazardous waste products. Regulations specifying either design requirements or performance criteria for hazardous waste landfills, incinerators, and other facilities were expected to be promulgated during 1981.

While the direction of future disposal practices will be controlled by the RCRA program, the cleanup of existing dump sites, many of which are inactive and abandoned, will be addressed by the new Superfund legislation. The passage of Superfund was hailed by many as the first big step for the eventual cleanup of existing hazardous waste disposal sites.

Unlike many federal environmental laws, Superfund is not designed to establish a regulatory framework but rather to provide primarily financial resources to eliminate existing waste problems. Under Superfund, the EPA will be required to list in order of priority 400 dump sites where remedial cleanup is needed. Where the party responsible for the hazardous conditions can be determined, the federal government will have the authority to require it to do the necessary cleanup. If the party fails to do so, EPA may use assets of the fund to perform the cleanup and then through court action seek reimbursement. The responsible party may be liable for damages equaling three times the cleanup cost. Where a site is abandoned and no responsible party can be identified, the assets of the fund will be used to cover cleanup costs. The fund will be derived from contributions by both private industry and the federal treasury.

Superfund also provides federal money and authority to conduct research on health effects in communities near hazardous waste dump sites. The information not only will be made available to individual citizens who may have been affected, but may also be useful in establishing the cleanup priority list. In addition, funds will be made available to help residents who must move from their neighborhood, as happened in Love Canal, or who must obtain new sources of drinking water, as occurred in Toone, TN.

The enactments of Superfund and RCRA establish a framework for cleaning up after past mistakes and avoiding them in the future. But although the start has been made, much remains to be done. The United States is still a long way from understanding the full magnitude of the hazardous waste problem, and the 1980s will be a critical time to test the nation's commitment and concern.

Wide World Photos

A bag of dangerous chemical pentachlorophenol is placed in a container for sealing after being found at the bottom of the Mississippi River outlet at Shell Beach, LA. Divers searched for 25,000 lbs (11 340 kg) of the chemical for more than a week following the collision of two ships in July.

In the American family of the 1980's, men are taking on more domestic chores. Above, a father, together with his children, does the family grocery shopping.

The Family: Challenges to Tradition

By Eric Gelman
Reporter, *Newsweek*

The decades of the 1960s and 1970s saw many political and social upheavals in American life. Perhaps the most enduring of the movements born during those years is the Women's Movement, the liberation of women from compulsory participation in the traditional roles of mothering and homemaking. Along with a "revolution" in sexual values that has made sexual intimacy outside of marriage a recognized part of life for most American men and women, the Women's Liberation Movement has had a profound effect on the life of the family. Today, a woman no longer looks automatically to a man to provide financial support. She no longer needs the structure of marriage to legitimate her sexual relations. When she does marry, she may postpone or forgo having children in order to establish herself in a career; she may find that childbearing is not crucial to her identity as a woman; certainly she discovers that cooking and cleaning are not. If a couple does have children, both father and mother may find themselves facing competition from a host of outside forces—the conformist peer-pressure of their children's friends and classmates, television, and the expert opinions of professionals—when it comes to raising them. During 1980, at the outset of a new decade, in what the National Conference of Catholic Bishops named "Family Year," the family faced unprecedented challenges to its very survival.

In 1976, when campaigning Jimmy Carter first proposed a White House-sponsored Conference on Families aimed at exploring "specific ways we can better support and strengthen our families," he probably had no idea that he was inaugurating a controversy. The conference, held at three locations in 1980, became the focal point for a passionate debate between feminists and pro-family conservatives over a wide range of issues affecting the family, including abortion, homosexuality, day-care, and welfare. The fact that rival factions disagreed over the very definition of family is an indication of how controversial an issue the family has become. Is a family restricted to persons related by blood, marriage, and adoption, or does it include homosexual couples, unmarried live-togethers, and communal arrangements?

Concerns and Threats.   All could agree that the family, no matter how defined, is in trouble. In a Gallup poll taken in March 1980 specifically for the White House Conference, 45% of those questioned said that they believe family life has gotten worse since the mid-1960s. The importance of this discontent is thrown into relief by the finding of the poll that 61% of Americans rate the family as the most crucial aspect of their present lives. While Americans may be unhappy with the environment for family life, they are not discarding their belief in the family. Nearly half of the country's population says that their dream life still means marriage, children, and a career. A growing component of that group is the 33% of women who say they would like a full-time job outside the home, in addition to their own family.

The Gallup survey uncovered another surprising fact. The average American, as reflected in the poll, does not see abortion or homosexuality—two of the most loudly-debated issues—as the major threats to the family. Asked which factors were most inimical to family life, 63% decried the high cost of living, 60% named drug abuse, 59% alcohol abuse, 40% the decline of religious and moral values. Homosexuality appeared on only 13% of the lists. As to which problems burdened their own families,

More and more wives and mothers join the U.S. labor market. For many families it is economically necessary for the woman of the household to work at least part-time outside the home.

81% named the high cost of living, 53% cited energy costs, and 23% government policies. Despite all the hardships, most of those polled were optimistic. According to Gallup, 54% of Americans describe themselves as satisfied with the future facing their families.

It is helpful to remember that the family has always had to adjust to the forces of an evolving society. It has come a long way since the days of early America, when economic necessity was a binding force that worked to hold families intact. When most families were working farms, each member of the family had a specific role in the small, self-sufficient family economy. Children on the farm were assets, not financial liabilities. Not only was working life centered in the home, but education, health care, and religious training took place there, too. Some social scientists hypothesize that the rise of compulsory education was the first major blow to the primacy of the family. As the United States became urban and industrialized, the family's power to encompass the lives of its members diminished.

Recent Changes.   Against this background of long-term transformation, it is interesting to note some of the ways U.S. families changed in the 1970s. Today, only 13% of Americans live in what has been considered the typical nuclear family: breadwinning dad, homemaking mom, two or more kids. While a comparison of U.S. Census Bureau figures for 1970 and 1979 shows an increase of 3 million married couples—a 6.6% gain—the number of unmarried couples has leaped from 523,000 to 1.3 million—a stunning 157% jump. The people who do marry do so at an older age. The average age at first marriage for men has gone from 22.5 years in 1970 to 24.4 in 1979 and for women from 20.6 years to 22.1. Meanwhile, the number of married couples with children declined from 25.5 million to 24.6 million. Again, those who do have children have them later. In 1970, 56,-729 of the 1.4 million first-born children had mothers over 30; by 1978, an almost identical number of first-borns came into the world, and 104,212 of them had mothers over 30. There has been a 40% surge, from 8.2 million to 11.5 million, in the number of children living with one parent. Of those children, 90% were with their mothers. Among two-parent families, 4 million more children than in 1970 have both parents working outside the home. In fact, for the first time in history, the average school-age child has a mother with a paying job. Home itself has shrunk from 3.3 to 2.8 persons per household as the fertility rate dropped from 2.48 children per woman in 1970 to a ratio of 1.8 in 1978.

The typical Canadian family has changed, too. According to data released by Statistics Canada in 1980, Canadians are having fewer children, are earning more money as more women are joining the labor market, and are getting divorced and remarrying more often.

The Working Mother and Day-Care.   Despite the difficulties in arranging child care, 6 million mothers with children under six years of age now work outside the home. It is difficult to establish an accurate picture of their child-care arrangements. Sociologist Sheila B. Kamerman of Hunter College examined the statistics for 1976 and reported that about half of the nearly 10 million three- to five-year-olds were attending either nursery school or kindergarten; 1 million were in first grade; and 1.5

Occupations that were once limited to men are now opened to women too.

Bill Hubbel

million children were in day-care centers or family day-care programs. Today, there are 1.6 million slots for children in day-care programs, fewer than in 1945. Private day-care can be costly; subsidized day-care is scarce. By one count, there are 5.4 million children under six with working mothers, who must be looked after by nursery schools, relatives, or baby-sitters.

A 1978 survey of 10,000 working mothers by *Family Circle* magazine found that most preferred day-care centers for their children over other forms of care. Many in the survey said they wanted the care to be subsidized, but not controlled, by the federal government. But the survey also found that only 1 in 5 mothers who seek day-care finds openings for her children. The U.S. Congress has debated the day-care question furiously, but no legislation has been enacted. As of 1977, taxpaying parents have been able to claim a tax credit of $400 per child for child-care expenses, with a limit of two credits per family. One study showed that the typical range in yearly child-care costs is $1,500 to $2,500 per child. Many leaders of the women's movement list as their top priority for action such bread-and-butter issues as helping women manage both families and careers.

The cited statistics reflect a dramatic alteration in the fabric of society. Eli Ginzberg of the Columbia University School of Social Work describes the flood of women into the ranks of salaried workers as "the most outstanding phenomenon of our century." This tide is having a momentous impact on family life.

Many mothers simply do not participate in the raising of children the way their mothers did—that is, fully. Most mothers now have two jobs, working for wages and running the family. The logistical problems are legion. Preschool children need constant supervision; younger schoolgoers need to be picked up after school and watched on holidays and vacations. In ever-increasing numbers, parents rely on day-care centers, unpaid

For the working mother, child-care arrangements remain a major problem. Because of the lack of moderately-priced day-care facilities, many mothers must rely on the services of neighbors.

The Needs of Children

Although observation of the International Year of the Child (IYC) in 1979 increased public awareness of children's needs and provoked significant involvement within communities throughout the United States, it remained unclear how much of this interest would be channeled into ongoing efforts to achieve specific and critically needed gains for children.

Children remain the poorest age group in American society. More than one child in six is poor. An estimated 1,000,000 school-aged children still are not enrolled in school. About 800,-000 handicapped children lack the special services they need. And millions of black children still are denied a fair chance to grow up healthy, learn to read and write, and eventually obtain jobs. In the year after IYC, thousands of children were starving to death in some African and Asian nations.

Child Welfare. One major American accomplishment in 1980 was the passage of Public Law 96-272, the Adoption Assistance and Child Welfare Act of 1980, which was approved by Congress and signed into law by President Carter in June. The new legislation holds hope for some of the 500,000 children growing up without homes. For the first time, federal fiscal incentives will be directed away from costly out-of-home institutional and foster care for children and toward services that would prevent unnecessary placements, reunite children with their families, and ensure adoption when appropriate. The bill provides federal subsidies to assist in the adoption of foster children with mental, physical, or emotional handicaps and other special needs.

Child Care. In March 1980, after several years of study and debate, the U.S. Department of Health and Human Services issued final regulations governing its funding of day-care facilities. These regulations set forth minimum standards for staffing and safety. The standards were to go into effect in October 1980, but in June, the Senate voted to postpone implementation for yet another year. Attempts to expand child-care programs at the federal level were unsuccessful despite the growing number of working, single, and teenaged mothers.

Child Health. About 10 million children in the United States, or one in six, have no known regular source of health care. About 17 million have never been to a dentist. The major federal program to provide health care for poor children—the Early and Periodic Screening, Diagnosis, and Placement Program—screens only 2 million children out of the 13 million eligible; even fewer actually receive the treatment they need. Improvement and expansion of this program through passage of the Child Health Assurance Program (CHAP) was killed in Senate at year's end. CHAP would have extended preventive health-care coverage to another 1 to 5 million children and 220,000 pregnant mothers.

Housing Discrimination. In July 1980, the U.S. Department of Housing and Urban Development released a report on the growing problem of discrimination in rental housing against families with children. In 1974, 17% of rental units across the nation had a "no children" policy; by 1970, 26% had such a policy. Nearly half of the families with children surveyed in this study reported difficulties in finding a place to live. Earlier studies in several metropolitan areas found even more discrimination: as many as 70% of apartments in some major cities refused to accept children. Only a handful of states have laws prohibiting such discrimination.

Children and the Federal Budget. Children's programs did not fare well in the federal budget for fiscal year 1981. An estimated 14,000 children would have to be dropped from the Head Start program in 1981 because of insufficient funding. The Education for All Handicapped Children Act, Public Law 94-142, which guarantees a free appropriate public education for all handicapped children, is funded at less than one third the level authorized in the original legislation. Funds for Title I of the Elementary and Secondary Education Act of 1965, which provides remedial programs for low-achieving pupils in poor areas, are not keeping up with inflation.

The World's Children. The World Bank has estimated that 400 million children under the age of 10 do not get enough to eat. In many countries, more than 10% of the babies born each year die before they reach their first birthday; in some countries, as many as one in four dies.

In some less developed countries, many children receive no education at all. Except in the most developed Western nations, two thirds to three fourths of children do not attend school after age 11.

Child labor also is a major problem in some countries. The U.S. Department of Labor reports that in Mexico more than 1.5 million children 14 years old and younger work for a living. In Thailand, more than 975,000 children between the ages of 11 and 14 work. In India, about 16.5 million children between the ages of 5 and 14 work. The International Labor Organization estimates that worldwide there are 52 million children under age 15 who work; 80% are not paid.

Children don't vote. They don't lobby or make campaign contributions. If their needs are to be met, more public education and better organized efforts to pursue specific policy goals must be undertaken.

MARIAN WRIGHT EDELMAN
President, Children's Defense Fund

friends and relatives, and paid baby-sitters to care for their children while they are at work. A wide range of scholars—Urie Bronfenbrenner of Cornell, Alfred Kahn of Columbia, and Jerome Kagan of Harvard, for example—believes that no evidence has established that children with working mothers are more likely to develop personality problems than children whose mothers stay home. One study suggests that the more important factor in a child's development is how satisfied the mother is with her tasks. But Lee Salk, a child psychologist, has said that it is bad for children under three to be cared for outside the home. And Anti-ERA partisan Phyllis Schlafly proclaims, "there's no real substitute for the care of the real mother."

In the Gallup poll on families, parents asked for three things to make their career-family balancing act easier: flexible working hours (flextime or flexitime), sick leave to handle family members' illnesses, and a four-day workweek. As many as 17% of America's companies and 237 government agencies are now experimenting with flextime. The usual system calls for mandatory presence during a specified "core" portion of the workday and a minimum number of hours to be worked each week. In some cases, employees are permitted to vary the number of hours from week to week. Their freedom comes in choosing their hours of arrival and departure. Stanley Nollen of Georgetown University studied flextime and found that in some cases it allowed for better organization of work, improved morale and job satisfaction, and other benefits to both employer and employee. Nollen speculates that by the end of the 1980s, 30% of U.S. workers may be coming and going on flextime.

Flextime allows Dad to pick up the kids after school and frees working Mom to hold their hands through a scary dentist appointment. But it is not clear whether flextime means more time with the children. Halcy Bohen, a Georgetown University psychologist, examined two groups of U.S. Commerce Department workers, one on flextime and one on standard time. Flextime earned good marks in easing the conflicts between home and office responsibilities, but it did not create extra time for

"OPPOSITE WORK SHIFTS!"

Craig, Rothco Cartoons

either mothers or fathers to spend with their children. In addition, husbands with flexible hours showed no increased flexibility about their roles. Family responsibilities were the wife's priority. In fact, in all households across the United States, there are few signs that men and women are significantly altering the way household chores are performed. In many cases, men participate more than they used to in cooking, cleaning, and shopping, but overall, these tasks are still considered women's work. One study suggests that during 1965–75, men increased the time they spent on housework by only a few minutes a week.

Divorce.   With men and women caught in a whirlwind of social change and economic stress, the divorce rate pounded the stability of the family. Amitai Etzioni of George Washington University argues that society too readily accepts the epidemic of divorce. Writing in the *Journal of Current Social Issues,* he observes that when confronting a collapsing marriage people no longer ask "How can this marriage be saved?" Their first question now may be "Should this marriage be saved?" Where at one time the attitude was "stay together for the sake of the children," people may now feel that a child is better off in a happy but broken home than in an unhappy, unbroken one. This attitude contributes to people's willingness to abandon marriages that with hard work and sacrifice might be saved. Etzioni argues that the fad of self-fulfillment-seeking and the advent of quick, "no-fault" divorces have helped usher in the era of the disposable marriage. In 1979, there was one divorce for two marriages performed. In 1970, the ratio had been one to three.

After increasing at an average rate of 8% during the late 1960s and early 1970s, the divorce rate grew by a mere 1.5% from 1976 to 1977. However, the upward trend resumed in 1978, with the rate increasing from 5.0 per 1,000 population in 1977 to 5.2 in 1978—a 4% jump. And those who do divorce do not usually live out their lives in isolation; most marry a second, and some a third time. Thus, the "blended" family—regroupings of divorced people with children who marry each other—is becoming part of the American scene.

Economics.   While social forces shake up the families of America, the Carnegie Council on Children asserts that "the single most important factor that stacks the deck against tens of millions of American children is poverty." The council argues that not only does poverty contribute to the disintegration of families, but government programs and services provided to alleviate its effects may work against families, as well. The outstanding example is the fact that in many states, a family must show that the father is absent from the house to qualify for certain benefits.

Middle-class families have a hard time, too. In 1977 it was estimated that it cost a middle-class family of four in a Northeastern city more than $54,000 to raise a child to age 18. College costs would add thousands of dollars to the bill. Federal tax laws penalize married couples, especially when both partners earn similar amounts, in comparison with unmarried live-togethers. The rise of two-paycheck families may be setting a financial pace that is onerous for most one-breadwinner households to keep up with. Across the United States, families with two wage-earners had an average income of approximately $22,000 in 1979; the average for single-salary households was $16,000.

"As a nation, we are faced with serious problems both at home and abroad, and almost every one of those problems that we address has a direct effect on an individual family. The solutions we've worked out will either strengthen or weaken those families. . . ."

JIMMY CARTER
June 5, 1980

Photos White House Conference on Families

Alarmingly, one third of the single-paycheck families headed by women fell below the poverty level of $5,850 in 1979.

Financially strained families face more challenges than just balancing the checkbook and filling the grocery basket. Family togetherness may be difficult when Dad has to sacrifice weekends and vacation so he can do home repairs without hiring expensive workmen. Entertainment budgets, including costs for outings to restaurants and to the movies, are trimmed. The children may have to settle for nearby colleges to hold back housing and commuting costs; private college can be completely out of financial reach. The family dream house may remain a dream. Parents who take second jobs risk becoming strangers to their children. And parents under pressure are increasingly vulnerable to drug and alcohol abuse.

The White House Conference. When the shouting died down at the three sessions of the White House Conference on Families, the delegates found much they could agree upon. They roundly endorsed an assortment of resolutions, including ones calling for programs to combat drug and alcohol abuse, to examine the impact of government policies on the family, and to encourage businesses and government to allow adjustments in the workplace in order to accommodate workers with family duties. So despite the array of statistics that signal the plight of the family, most Americans seem ready to fight for its existence. One hopeful forecaster, University of Pennsylvania economist Richard Esterlin, speculates that the low birth rates of the 1960s will lead to a bullish job market for job seekers in the 1980s. The resulting fiscal well-being of those careerists should lead to higher birthrates; higher birthrates traditionally have meant lowered divorce rates. In short, bigger, happier families are to come. While few observers are as sanguine as Esterlin, even fewer can be heard predicting the demise of the family. For one thing, no one has come up with an improved system with which to replace it. So while the family may have to stretch and bend to accommodate the Americans of the future, it seems certain that it will survive.

Sessions of the White House Conference on Families were held in Baltimore, Minneapolis, and Los Angeles in June and July 1980. The conference was organized by President Jimmy Carter "to see how society can help American families." According to conference chairman Jim Guy Tucker (below), 37-year-old former Congressman from Arkansas, "the whole concept of the conference was to listen."

The first Olympics were held in 776 B.C. at Olympia, Greece. Nothing was more important to the Greeks than the quadrennial festival of sporting events and religious rites. Olympia was considered sacred ground. Wars were suspended, and a solemn peace—Ekecheiria—lasted for the duration of each Olympics.

THE OLYMPICS/
TROUBLED GAMES

By William Oscar Johnson

It was an almost cheerless XXII Olympics that took place in Moscow in the summer of 1980, a festival without festivity, games devoid of playfulness. A major reason for this air of bleakness was the boycott of the Games by dozens of Western nations, led by the United States, over the Soviet invasion of Afghanistan in December 1979. A total of 81 national teams appeared in Moscow to compete, while 62 countries with membership in the International Olympic Committee (IOC)—including West Germany, Canada, Japan, and China, as well as the United States—sent no athletes at all. (It must be pointed out that perhaps half of those that failed to send a team would not have competed under any circumstances—boycott or no boycott—simply because the caliber of their athletes did not meet Olympic standards.) Thus, the Moscow Games had gaping holes in the opening ceremonies, in which 16 participating nations refused to let their teams or flags go on parade, and hollow victories in almost every event from basketball without Americans to judo and gymnastics without Japanese. As one judo competitor from the tiny republic of San Marino said sadly of his competition: "It isn't the same without the Japanese. Even I have a chance here now."

Still, the boycott was not the only reason for the aura of joylessness that hung over the 1980 Games. Much of the atmosphere was generated by the strangely paranoid attitude of Soviet officialdom. Its defensiveness was evident in a pre-Olympic story in *Pravda,* the official government newspaper, which said that although Russia anticipated meeting most tourists with "friendship and benevolence," there were bound to be some bad apples who had come for reasons other than to support an Olympic team. "Muscovites are prepared for ideological opposition toward those who hope somehow to contaminate the atmosphere of athletic festival," the article said.

For fear of some unknown and unpredictable incident of terrorism, the entire city of Moscow was set off in penitentiary-like isolation for the Olympics, walled off not only from the rest of the world but from the rest of the Soviet Union itself. The town was densely packed with police and militia, as well as hundreds of plainclothes KGB agents, to guard against—what? Well, everything from bomb-filled suitcases to tourists passing out poisoned chewing gum, according to official warnings distributed to the citizenry before the Games began. As it turned out, the legions of security guards had little to do but rough up a couple of demonstrators in Red Square and prevent high-spirited gold medal-winners from running the traditional victory laps around the track in Lenin Stadium. Some 700,000 children of Moscow were sent out of town to avoid ideological contamination, as were most political dissidents, chronic alcoholics, petty criminals, prostitutes, and various "deleterious elements."

On the other hand, in order to bring in the greatest number of noncontaminated participants, the Soviets paid the travel expenses for many teams from relatively poor nations. Count Jean de Beaumont, a member of the IOC's executive board for many years, said icily, "Forty countries have been paid to come to Moscow. There are so many you get the feeling they are buying them to come."

The Moscow Olympics were, some said, a theatrical spectacle mounted in such a way as to screen from view the true atmosphere of oppression and unhappiness that pervades everyday Soviet life, a kind of Potemkin Olympics. Perhaps it was true. The Moscow Games were as unreal as any held since the modern revival of the Games in 1896. But by no means did that make them unique.

Strict security measures, such as those seen at Lake Placid in 1980, have become as much a symbol of the Games as the Olympic flame and five colored rings.

Photos Paul Sutton, Duomo

A Garden of Eden? In recent decades, certainly since the infamous though magnificent Nazi Olympics of 1936, all Olympic Games have bloomed in an atmosphere of artificiality, on an elaborate stage set that is meant by its producers to resemble some sort of Garden of Eden for athletes. Indeed, from their inception, the modern Olympics have been promoted by their most dedicated proponents in an atmosphere of unrealistic optimism and overblown boosterism. For example, Baron Pierre de Coubertin, the little French nobleman whose idea it was to revive the Games in 1896, once said, "The Olympic movement tends to bring together in a radiant union all the qualities which guide mankind to perfection." Henri de Baillet-Latour, a Belgian count who was president of the IOC at the time of the Berlin Olympics, tried to persuade Adolf Hitler that he should not attempt to use the Berlin Games as a public relations showcase for the new Germany. Said the count, "The Olympic Games are not held in Berlin, in Los Angeles, or in Amsterdam. When the five-circled Olympic flag is raised over a stadium, it becomes sacred Olympic territory and, theoretically and for all practical purposes, the Games are held in ancient Olympia. There *I* am the master." And Avery Brundage, the Chicago construction millionaire who served for 20 years as president of the IOC, at various times referred to the Olympic Games as 1) "a 20th-century religion," 2) "a ray of sunshine through clouds of racial animosity, religious bigotry, and political chicanery," and 3) "perhaps the greatest social force in the world . . . a revolt against 20th century materialism."

Sacred territory? A radiant union of mankind's perfection? A *religion?* This is blind bombast and idealistic balderdash. Anything that is expected to match such impossibly idealized dream-definitions can only fail in the harsh light of reality. And indeed, it is precisely because of these ludicrously overblown claims of divine inspiration and incipient purity that the Olympics seem so hopelessly flawed. They are a man-made institution, and they cannot escape the foibles and follies of the human condition.

Politics and the Boycott. The fact that the 1980 Games nearly turned to cinder in the heat of another East-West confron-

The excitement of the Winter Games in Lake Placid did not dissuade some visitors from opposing U.S. participation in the summer Olympics in Moscow.

John Swider

tation was widely taken as a sign that the Olympics are now on the brink of annihilation. It is true that the threat to these specific Games was a critical one. President Carter's determination to use American athletes as pawns in a game of international power chess and, in effect, to hold the Olympics hostage until the Soviets withdrew their 100,000-odd troops from Afghanistan was a bold though flawed idea whose success may be debated for years. Of course, no troops were withdrawn, and the Games did go on, after a fashion. Indeed, only history will judge whether Carter's tactics changed anything at all except the lives of several hundred would-be Olympians. Though most American athletes and the U.S. Olympic Committee (USOC) reluctantly went along with the boycott, Robert J. Kane, president of the USOC, stated concisely the doubts that may prevail for many years after the boycott: "The question we have," said Kane, "is whether the Olympic movement and the United States Olympic athlete are the kind of a weapon to use to whip the big bear, the weapon that is made of flesh and blood, the flesh and blood of our athletes." As the Moscow Games came to an end, President Carter invited the U.S. Olympic team to the White House, where he gave each of them a specially-struck, gold-plated medal and told them, "It is no exaggeration to say that you have done more to uphold the Olympic ideal than any other group of athletes in our history."

Whether Carter's boycott upheld or beat down the "Olympic ideal" is certainly open to debate. Lord Killanin, the outgoing IOC president, was predictably dark about the effect of Carter's injection of politics into the Games. "If we started to make political judgments about which nation is right and which is wrong, it would be the end of the Olympics," said Killanin. Of course, political judgments have for years been an inescapable element of the Olympics. In a book written almost 20 years ago, C. P. McIntosh said, "There are few governments in the world which do not now accept the political importance of success in international sport. Both global and local wars are likely to be suicidal ways of influencing people and winning support, and sport as a means of influence has assumed correspondingly greater political importance." And as Richard Mandell wrote in his book, *The Nazi Olympics,* "A trend that was strengthened by the results of the 1936 Olympics was to view athletes increasingly as national assets, procurable like fighter planes, submarines, or synthetic rubber factories. After 1936, a stable of athletes became necessary for a national standing."

And though the Russians protested self-righteously over the 1980 boycott of their Games, no nation has ever been more blatant—and more candid—in its use of the Olympics for self-serving political ends. A recent pamphlet, *Soviet Sport: Questions and Answers,* said with admirable forthrightness: "Whenever someone says that sport lies outside the framework of political relations, we feel their remark is not a serious one."

And as John Carlos, the U.S. gold-medal sprinter in the 1968 Mexico City Games who bowed his head and raised a black-gloved fist during the playing of his national anthem, said, "The Olympics is nothing but a full political scene—everything in world athletics is. It's country against country, ideology against ideology. The people you run for—the officials—overshadow you with their political ambitions, with the face they want *you* to put on your country."

The Associated Press

Misha the Bear was the official mascot of the 1980 Moscow Olympics. Signs and posters were put up around the city more than a year before the Games to generate enthusiasm among city residents. The celebration would be a showcase for the Soviet capital, and preparations were considered a national endeavor.

The 1976 Montreal Olympics were a financial disaster. The elaborate facilities built for the Games cost an estimated $1,500,000,000, more than five times the amount estimated when the city was named host. By the time of the next Olympics, cost overruns were still a taxpayer burden and sensitive political issue.

It is hard to believe that the Olympics are particularly threatened now by the cold pragmatism of politics. They have survived the same alleged depredation of politics for close to 50 years. There have been other boycotts. For example, 17 African nations refused to compete in 1976 in Montreal. The exclusion from Olympic membership of South Africa and Taiwan were blatant acts of political judgment perpetrated by the IOC itself. The shocking assassination of 11 Israelis at the 1972 Munich Games was politics at its bloodiest. The Tokyo Games of 1964 were openly planned as the post-World War II resurrection of Japan. In 1952, when the Russians emerged from behind the Iron Curtain for their first Olympic engagement since 1908, it was considered a clearcut political triumph for the West that the Americans won more medals than the Russians. Then, at Rome in 1960, when the Soviets won easily over the Americans, the pendulum of cold war ideology swung the other way.

No, it is unlikely that the boycott of 1980 has done any greater permanent damage to the Olympic Games than have the other political assaults that have pummeled them in the past.

Financial Burdens. Perhaps a greater threat to the future of the Games is the steadily rising cost of producing them, combined with a steadily declining interest on the part of cities—and nations—in doing so. The Olympics were, until recently, considered a truly valuable prize. Intense competition to host the Games preceded every IOC selection. Cities vied with each other to woo (or buy) the votes of IOC members. Detroit tried no fewer than seven separate times to become a host city. Douglas Roby, a longtime member of the IOC, recalled the methods of campaigning for the Games. "It's like courting a beautiful girl. People make all these subtle little approaches to the IOC, offer little gifts. The Japanese were past masters at this subtle approach, with really good-looking trinkets." The gifts got to be so expensive that they bordered on bribery, and a rule had to be passed forbidding any IOC mem-

Focus on Sports

ber from taking a present worth more than $100. Today the competition to host an Olympics is all but nil. When Lake Placid was given the Winter Games for 1980, it was the only town in the world that had even made a presentation. The IOC broke one of its strictest rules in order to allow the Los Angeles Olympic Organizing Committee to underwrite the 1984 Summer Games as a private corporation rather than insisting on a government guarantee. This breach of IOC law occurred because there was no other bidder in sight. Talk now is that the IOC will have to put off for a year or more the awarding of the 1988 Olympic sites—because no one wants to get involved.

Costs, of course, are a major reason. Little Lake Placid, which originally publicized a human-sized Games that would cost no more than $30 million, is now drowning in red ink after coming up with a Brobdingnagian-sized Olympics that cost $150 million. The billion-dollar debt after the Montreal Games is larger than the annual budget of many nations. The price of the Moscow Games will probably never be known.

In order to generate the massive treasuries necessary to finance an Olympics, the IOC and local sponsors are forced to depend more and more on huge amounts of cash from television. The American Broadcasting Company (ABC) bid some $265 million for rights and facilities to televise the 1984 Olympics. This is triple what the National Broadcasting Company (NBC) was to pay for televising the Moscow Games. It is estimated that despite the size of its bid, ABC will make a huge profit—perhaps more than $50 million—on the Los Angeles Games. But, in order to invest such an enormous amount of money, television blithely turns the beloved "sacred territory" of the Olympics into just another commercial selling ground, a dazzling backdrop to advertise shaving cream and steel-belted radial tires. Frederick S. Pierce, president of ABC television, spoke in typical hucksterese about the network's Olympic "buy." "The Olympics have impact value far be-

Billed as an "Olympics in Perspective," the Lake Placid Games nevertheless required construction of expensive athletic facilities, living quarters, and other buildings. Eight months after the end of competition, the first independent financial analysis showed a total operating loss of $4,366,029. Construction disputes were considered a major cause.

The Olympic Games have become a lucrative advertising vehicle.

yond an ordinary advertising vehicle. This goes far beyond a normal media buy in which an advertiser pays for reaching a given number of people. There is a great rub-off value in being associated with the Olympics, and we're confident that there are enough advertisers who will pay a premium for that."

Amateurism. The issue of amateurism, which once threatened the Olympics perhaps more than any other single element, is rarely heard of any more. A few years ago, Jack Kelly, then president of the Amateur Athletic Union (AAU), said, "Most of us are aware that as many as two thirds of the athletes signing the Olympic oath are committing perjury. What should concern us is the extent to which we damage the character of a young competitor by a code which has lost its relevance." The oath is still in effect, but no one speaks of perjury any more. Because of an IOC rule passed before the 1976 Games, athletes are allowed to receive "broken time payment," meaning that they can be reimbursed the money they would earn in a regular job if their time were not consumed in training. This rule has been stre-e-e-etched now to the point that every alpine skier who won a gold medal at Lake Placid was being paid well over $100,000 a year. So much for the old bugaboo of "amateurism"—and the Games go on.

The Future. Despite the troubles that have beset the modern Olympics at the beginning of the 1980s, it seems that they will somehow hobble onward, perhaps even to a centennial anniversary in 1996. They will have to be held at a permanent site, perhaps in Greece, or be moved to previous Olympic sites on a rotating basis, since a new location for each Olympiad seems out of the question. Politics and commercialization, chauvinism and professionalism will continue to assault the claims of purity that the aging curmudgeon-idealists of the IOC make for the Games. But like all things that survive to see another day, the Olympics will change to suit the times. They have done so in the past, and they almost certainly will in the future.

About the author: William Oscar Johnson is a Senior Writer for *Sports Illustrated* Magazine and is the author of numerous articles and books on the Olympics, including *All That Glitters Is Not Gold*—The Olympic Games (1972, G.P. Putnam's Sons).

An Argument for a Permanent Site

The Olympic Games were staged in ancient Greece for nearly 12 centuries with almost no intrusion by politics. Held in honor of Zeus, the Games were more than athletic competitions. They were Pan-Hellenic festivals, with contests in dance and choral poetry held on the plain of Olympia. Even wars were interrupted to assure that the quadrennial Olympic celebrations would take place.

But since their modern revival in 1896, the Olympics have been canceled three times because of world war and plagued repeatedly by nationalistic political rivalries. Now, after more than 60 countries boycotted the 1980 Games in Moscow to protest the Soviet Union's invasion of Afghanistan, major changes are urgently needed to make the modern Olympics more consistent with the ideals that inspired the original Greek festivals.

One immediate reform should be the establishment of a permanent site in Greece for the summer Olympics, as well as an appropriate home for the winter Games. Such action has been considered by the International Olympic Committee (IOC) as an alternative to the current system of moving the events to a different location every four years.

Under the present arrangement, the IOC chooses sites for the summer and winter Games several years in advance. Once the host countries are selected, it is their responsibility to provide all facilities and the bulk of the financing for the Games. In the past, these requirements have led almost invariably to excessive displays of nationalism by the host countries—including construction of extremely costly facilities seldom fully used after the Games. In the process, there also has been a shift in emphasis from the athletes themselves to the countries they represent and to gaining political mileage from symbolic "firsts," such as the first Games in Germany after World War II (Munich, 1972) or the first in a Communist country (Moscow, 1980).

Putting the summer Olympics permanently in Greece and the winter Games in their own home would help the Olympics become a strong institution rather than short-lived spectacles vulnerable to political or economic exploitation by temporary host countries and other nations. Given a stable, enduring setting, the Games could take on a special identity of their own, much like the celebrations of old.

A permanent site for the Olympics also could be coupled with an extension of the Games from two weeks to perhaps two or even three months. That would allow participants to get really to know one another and to share experiences that are generally impossible in the often politically-charged competitive environment of contemporary Olympiads.

In addition, the normal functions of the Olympic Village might be expanded to include cultural and artistic expressions from various parts of the world. Though the emphasis on sports would continue, the introduction of other activities would recognize the value of the whole person.

Naturally, important questions would have to be answered. How, for example, would the financial burden be borne? If there were financial benefits from the Games, how would they be shared? What governing body would control the Olympic site?

The government of Greece already has suggested some ways to proceed. It has proposed the formation of a politically neutral and militarily inviolable "Olympic State" in the area of the original site at Olympia. Under the Greek plan, this state would be under IOC jurisdiction, although sovereign territorial rights would remain with Greece. The Olympic Committee would install and own all facilities at the site. It also would be permitted to administer the Olympic area and to determine the terms of and conditions for entry. Greek law would apply within the area, but Greek military forces would not be allowed to enter under any circumstances.

The United States and all members of the IOC should study the Greek plan and any other alternatives that demonstrate a serious commitment to preserving the Olympic ideals.

In the future, other actions to make the Olympics less political should be considered. It might help to eliminate team sports, which can be tantamount to simulated war games. Team competition could take place apart from the Olympics. Another improvement would be a revision of the rules on eligibility, making skill the only standard, with no artificial distinctions such as amateurism. A third useful change might be to award a medal to all competitors and reserve gold medals only for those athletes who break Olympic records.

But above all, the reforms should be designed to reduce the causes of and opportunities for political conflict at the Games and to maximize attention on the participants.

If the right steps are taken soon enough, the modern Olympics still can achieve the goals that their founder, Pierre de Coubertin, set: to create "international respect and good will" and "construct a better and more peaceful world."

SEN. BILL BRADLEY

Senator Bradley (D-NJ) was a member of the U.S. Olympic basketball team in 1964.

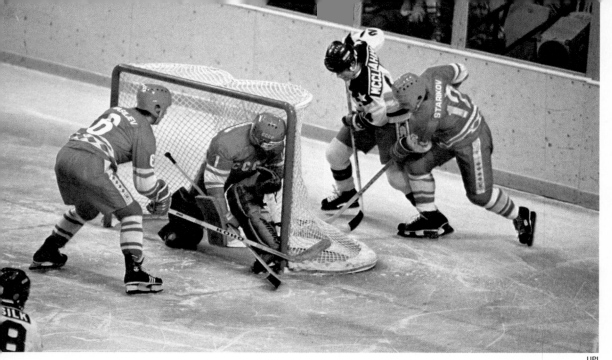

McClanahan (U.S.) and Starikov (USSR) battle for the puck as the Americans score a big win.

THE OLYMPICS/

The XIII Winter Games

The U.S. hockey team takes the gold medal and goalie Jim Craig wraps himself in an American flag.

The stranger came running onto the ice with an old American flag. Oddly enough, Jim Craig had noticed the stranger earlier, picking him out in the closing stages of the hockey game, one face in a sea of faces waving American flags. Now the stranger was in front of Craig, offering the flag. What to do? "I didn't know what to do," Craig explained later. "I didn't think about it at all. I just took the flag and put it around my shoulders."

The 22-year-old goaltender for the gold-medal-winning U.S. hockey team threw the flag around his shoulders the way an old woman puts on her shawl. The edges trailed a bit as he skated, dazed, bedlam all around him. His fat goalie's stick was in one hand. He was clumsy and smooth at the same time, burdened by his equipment, uplifted by the moment. He was a character from some Fourth of July pageant. He was the Statue of Liberty on skates. He was all of that and more, a living piece of Americana, a symbol of other, less confusing times. The flashbulbs popped everywhere. Jim Craig, the American flag, and the outstanding achievement of the young U.S. hockey team were the final, memorable pictures from the XIII Winter Olympics at Lake Placid, NY.

The U.S. hockey team became a larger and larger story during the 13 days of competition among 1,300 amateur athletes from 37 countries, held in the small Adirondack village. There were other stories that also made headlines—U.S.

speed skater Eric Heiden and his five gold medals, the skiing Wenzel family from small Liechtenstein, the parade of Russian gold medalists, the troubles of the Olympic organizers, the excellence of Swedish skier Ingemar Stenmark, the heartbreak of U.S. figure skaters Randy Gardner and Tai Babilonia—but none of them so unpredictable as the tale the U.S. hockey players spun.

"The Boys of Winter." The American team was the youngest in the Olympic hockey tournament. They were a collection of unknown recent college graduates. On the day the team began its work, even prior to the opening ceremonies, defenseman Bill Baker, with 27 seconds left, scored a goal to tie Sweden, 2–2. On the day the team ended its work, the final day of the Games, after it had beaten every team it had played, including the vaunted Russians in the semifinals, "The Boys of Winter" were a national obsession.

The 4–2 score of the final gold-medal win over Finland, a game played on a Sunday morning, was announced on U.S. airliners and the passengers stood up to applaud. People who never had watched a hockey game in their lives watched this one. President Jimmy Carter telephoned congratulations. Vice-President Walter Mondale watched in person. The crowd at the Olympic Ice Center spilled onto the street, waving American flags, singing patriotic songs.

"Were you surprised you won the gold medal?" goaltender Craig was asked in a gymnasium press conference in Lake Placid High School. "Would anyone in this room who is not surprised that we won the gold medal please put up his hand?" Craig asked in return. Not one hand was raised.

The major win for the U.S. team was a 4–3 upset over the Russians on Friday night, February 22. Winners not only of every Olympic title since 1964, but of every Olympic game they had played since 1968, the Russians were the odds-on choice to take the gold again. Their team basically was the same team that had beaten the National Hockey League All-Stars handily a year earlier in the three-game Challenge Cup series at New York's Madison Square Garden.

How did the young U.S. team stand a chance? It was not exactly the team of novices that it was made out to be—it was stocked with talent primarily from Minnesota and Massachusetts, the only two U.S. hockey hotbeds, and there had been a 60-plus game exhibition schedule in preparation for the Olympics—but it was a

IOC's Lord Killanin and the Swedish hockey team watch as the U.S. team basks in its triumph.
The Associated Press

much different team than the Russian team. There is no professional hockey in the USSR. The Russian players were the best players from an entire, hockey-playing country. They had played together, some of them, for years.

"I think the game could go two ways," U.S. captain Mike Eruzione from Winthrop, MA, predicted. "One is that the Russians come out and just blow us apart. The other is that we hang on. We hang on and hang on and then, at the end . . . well, anything can happen." Eruzione's second possibility was exactly what took place. The United States fell behind, 1–0, then tied the game. The United States fell behind, 2–1, then tied the game. They fell behind, 3–2, then tied the game. Less than ten minutes were left when Eruzione wound up with a pass, 25 feet (7.5 m) away from Russia's backup goalie Vladimir Myshkin. Eruzione shot. The puck flew past Myshkin. The U.S. hockey team "hung on" from there, with Craig stopping every shot that came at him.

"How do you explain it all?" U.S. coach Herb Brooks was asked. The Russians had outshot the Americans, 39–16. "Fate," Brooks replied.

Following the U.S. win, celebrations were held in restaurants and taverns across the country.

In the final game against Finland on Sunday, February 24, the United States fell behind, 2–1, but scored three times in the final period to capture the gold and begin a second round of celebrations. Russia captured the second-place silver medal. Sweden won the third-place bronze.

Mismanagement. The story that had threatened to dominate the Olympics, before the U.S. hockey team came along, involved confusion and mismanagement. Though the sign on Lake Placid's one main street read "Welcome World, We Made It," that was a long way from the truth during the first Olympic week. This resort town of 2,700 year-round residents and one traffic light simply could not handle the monster it had invited.

True, the Games were billed as "An Olympics in Perspective," a back-to-basics series of events that would "return the Games to the athletes." True, the Games had been held in Lake Placid in 1932 with a minimum of problems, but since that time the Games had grown considerably in every way. True, millions of dollars were spent on new facilities, including an Olympic Village for the athletes that would be transformed into a federal prison, but there still was only one major access road into the village and limited parking areas. The plan of the Lake Placid Olympic Organizing Committee (LPOOC) to control spectator traffic involved a system of parking lots as far as 30 miles (48 km) away from the village, with buses employed to ferry the visitors from one event to another. The plan fell apart, badly.

There were not enough buses. Many of the buses that were on hand were faulty. There were labor problems between American and Canadian bus drivers. The bus schedule sagged. The spectators waited. And waited some more. Many fans arrived at events two hours after the events were completed. Many were left, standing in the cold for two, three, and four hours after events had finished. Tickets, which cost from $15 to $60, were thrown away or, just as bad, could not be picked up. Ticket dispersal was another problem. Most of it was done through two offices, one in a trailer and another in a converted pharmacy.

Alpha, Zimmerman

A major transportation crisis, stemming from the use of ill-organized buses, marred the 1980 Lake Placid Games. Many spectators were forced to wait in the cold for hours for buses; others even missed the events for which they held expensive tickets.

Lake Placid headliners included: U.S. speed skater Eric Heiden, five gold medals; Canadian skier Stephen Podborski, a bronze in the down-hill; USSR figure skaters Mr. and Mrs. Zaitsev, a gold in the pairs.

Tony Duffy, Focus on Sports

Liechtenstein's Hanni Wenzel, winner of gold medals in the giant slalom and slalom and a silver in the downhill, as well as East Germany's Anett Poetzsch and Britain's Robin Cousins, who prevailed in the singles' figure skating, became familiar names during the 1980 Winter Games.

Steven Sutton, Duomo

Focus on Sports

On Saturday, February 16, New York Gov. Hugh Carey was forced to call a limited transportation emergency. He banned everyone but ticket-holders, officials, and local residents from the 15-mile (24 km) radius around Lake Placid. The Greyhound Bus Company was sent to the scene to realign the bus schedules. By February 18, the situation had changed considerably. By the end, the bus system finally worked. "The thing that amazed me was how patient the spectators were," said New York State Police Lieutenant Lee Hunt.

The Stars. The competition ran smoothly through all of the troubles, however, and the spectators who reached the competition sites were treated to some memorable performances. The 21-year-old Eric Heiden (*see also* Biography) not only became the first athlete to win five gold medals for individual competition in one Olympics but also set five Olympic records and one world record. Heiden's success put him in a special category, but there was a host of other individual stars.

Alpine skier Ingemar Stenmark was the supreme stylist on Whiteface Mountain, capturing the gold in both the slalom and giant slalom. Only the fact that the 23-year-old Swedish skiier did not enter the downhill kept him from equaling Jean-Claude Killy's sweep of the skiing golds in 1968. The downhill went to 21-year-old Leonhard Stock of Austria, a fairy-tale triumph, since he had been selected to his team only as an alternate.

Hanni Wenzel of Liechtenstein dominated the women's Alpine competition. She captured the slalom and giant slalom golds and a silver in the downhill, finishing second to Annemarie Moser-Proell of Austria. With Hanni's brother, Andreas, winning a silver in the giant slalom, the Wenzels alone pushed Liechtenstein into sixth place in the final medal standings.

Nikolai Zimyatov, a 24-year-old student, was the cross-country skiing standout. He captured three golds as the Soviet Union piled up medal after medal on the course at Mount Van Hoevenberg. No single performance in the Games could have been better than that of 29-year-old Anatoli Aljabiev, a lieutenant in the Red Army, who skied 20 kilometers and did not miss one shot at the 20 targets in the 20-kilometer biathlon. The Soviets, bolstered by their cross-country strength, won 10 gold medals at the Games, more than any other country. East Germany, which was top-heavy with winners in the luge and bobsled events, captured the most medals overall, 23.

Robin Cousins of Great Britain repeated countryman John Curry's 1976 win in the men's figure skating, but had to overtake East Germany's Jan Hoffmann in the final program to do it. Anett Poetzsch of East Germany defeated Linda Fratianne of the United States for the women's figure-skating gold. The Russian pair of Irina Rodnina and Aleksandr Zaitsev easily

The Associated Press

Cross-country skier Nikolai Zimyatov, a 24-year-old student, returned to the USSR with three golds.

won the gold after Americans Randy Gardner and Tai Babilonia were forced to withdraw when Gardner pulled a thigh muscle in practice.

Other noteworthy performances were turned in by American skier Phil Mahre, Canadian speed skater Gaetan Boucher, American figure skater Charlie Tickner, Canadian skier Steve Podborski, and American speed skaters Leah Poulos Mueller and Beth Heiden.

The narrowest defeat in the Games was suffered by sad Juha Mieto of Finland, who lost the 15 kilometer cross-country ski race by one one-hundredth of a second to Sweden's Tommy Wassberg. The most mysterious departure was made by world champion figure skater Vladimir Kovalev, who was sent home to the Soviet Union in a disciplinary move. The happiest losers were the 28 athletes from the People's Republic of China, a nation competing for the first time since the Communists took over mainland China in 1948.

The happiest winners were, of course, "The Boys of Winter." "I believe this is a dream that is never going to end," Jim Craig, the U.S. goaltender from North Easton, MA, said six months after the Winter Olympics had ended. "Maybe I'm wrong, but I think this is going to be something that people always are going to remember. I know they have, so far—my phone still hasn't stopped ringing."

LEIGH MONTVILLE

WINTER GAMES
FINAL MEDAL STANDINGS

Nation	Gold	Silver	Bronze	Nation	Gold	Silver	Bronze
Soviet Union	10	6	6	Great Britain	1	0	0
East Germany	9	7	7	West Germany	0	2	3
United States	6	4	2	Italy	0	2	0
Austria	3	2	2	Canada	0	1	1
Sweden	3	0	1	Hungary	0	1	0
Liechtenstein	2	2	0	Japan	0	1	0
Finland	1	5	3	Bulgaria	0	0	1
Norway	1	3	6	Czechoslovakia	0	0	1
The Netherlands	1	2	1	France	0	0	1
Switzerland	1	1	3				

	Gold Medalists	Silver Medalists	Bronze Medalists
Alpine Skiing			
Men's Downhill	Leonhard Stock, Austria	Peter Wirnsberger, Austria	S. Podborski, Canada
Men's Giant Slalom	Ingemar Stenmark, Sweden	A. Wenzel, Liechtenstein	Hans Enn, Austria
Men's Slalom	Ingemar Stenmark, Sweden	Phil Mahre, United States	J. Luethy, Switzerland
Women's Downhill	A. Moser-Proell, Austria	H. Wenzel, Liechtenstein	M.-T. Nadig, Switzerland
Women's Giant Slalom	H. Wenzel, Liechtenstein	Irene Epple, West Germany	Perrine Pelen, France
Women's Slalom	H. Wenzel, Liechteinstein	C. Kinshofer, West Germany	Erika Hess, Switzerland
Biathlon			
10-Kilometer Individual	F. Ullrich, East Germany	V. Alikin, Soviet Union	A. Aljabiev, Soviet Union
20-Kilometer Individual	A. Aljabiev, Soviet Union	F. Ullrich, East Germany	E. Rosch, East Germany
Relay	Soviet Union	East Germany	West Germany
Bobsled			
2-Man	Switzerland	East Germany	East Germany
4-Man	East Germany	Switzerland	East Germany
Figure Skating			
Pairs	Soviet Union	Soviet Union	East Germany
Men's Singles	Robin Cousins, Britain	J. Hoffmann, East Germany	C. Tickner, United States
Women's Singles	A. Poetzsch, East Germany	L. Fratianne, United States	D. Lurz, West Germany
Ice Dancing	Soviet Union	Hungary	Soviet Union
Ice Hockey			
	United States	Soviet Union	Sweden
Luge			
Men's Singles	B. Glass, East Germany	P. Hildgartner, Italy	A. Winkler, West Germany
Men's Doubles	East Germany	Italy	Austria
Women's Singles	Vera Zozulia, Soviet Union	M. Sollmann, East Germany	I. Amantova, Soviet Union
Nordic Skiing			
Men's 15-Kilometer	Thomas Wassberg, Sweden	Juha Mieto, Finland	Ove Aunli, Norway
Men's 30-Kilometer	N. Zimyatov, Soviet Union	Vasili Rochev, Soviet Union	Ivan Lebanov, Bulgaria
Men's 50-Kilometer	N. Zimyatov, Soviet Union	Juha Mieto, Finland	A. Zavjalov, Soviet Union
Men's Combined	U. Wehling, East Germany	Jouko Karjalainen, Finland	K. Winkler, East Germany
Men's 40-Kilometer Relay	Soviet Union	Norway	Finland
Men's 70-Meter Ski Jump	Anton Innauer, Austria	Hirokazu Yagi, Japan M. Deckert, East Germany (tie)	no medal
Men's 90-Meter Ski Jump	Jouko Tormanen, Finland	Hubert Neuper, Austria	Jari Puikkonen, Finland
Women's 5-Kilometer	R. Smetanina, Soviet Union	Hilkka Riihivuori, Finland	K. Jeriova, Czechoslovakia
Women's 10-Kilometer	B. Petzold, East Germany	Hilkka Riihivuori, Finland	Helena Takalo, Finland
Women's 20-Kilometer Relay	East Germany	Soviet Union	Norway
Speed Skating			
Men's 500 Meters	Eric Heiden, United States	Y. Kulikov, Soviet Union	L. De Boer, Netherlands
Men's 1,000 Meters	Eric Heiden, United States	Gaetan Boucher, Canada	Froede Roenning, Norway V. Lobanov, Soviet Union (tie)
Men's 1,500 Meters	Eric Heiden, United States	K. A. Stenshjemmet, Norway	Terje Andersen, Norway
Men's 5,000 Meters	Eric Heiden, United States	K. A. Stenshjemmet, Norway	Tom Erik Oxholm, Norway
Men's 10,000 Meters	Eric Heiden, United States	Piet Kleine, Netherlands	Tom Erik Oxholm, Norway
Women's 500 Meters	Karin Enke, East Germany	L. P. Mueller, United States	N. Petruseva, Soviet Union
Women's 1,000 Meters	N. Petruseva, Soviet Union	L. P. Mueller, United States	S. Albrecht, East Germany
Women's 1,500 Meters	A. Borckink, Netherlands	Ria Visser, Netherlands	S. Becker, East Germany
Women's 3,000 Meters	B. E. Jensen, Norway	S. Becker, East Germany	Beth Heiden, United States

Tony Duffy, Duomo

At the 1980 Summer Games, East Germans, led by Rica Reinisch, dominated women's swimming.

THE OLYMPICS/
The XXII Summer Games

Despite the U.S.-led boycott, the 1980 Summer Olympics at Moscow produced 36 world records and enough drama, controversy, and excitement to rival past Olympic Games.

On opening day, East German women swimmers, always strong in the Olympics, set the tone by breaking two world records, and for the first time a Russian, Sergei Fesenko, won a swimming gold medal. Fesenko took the 200-meter butterfly. On July 22, the third day of competition, Vladimir Salnikov, a 20-year-old freestyler, broke the 15-minute barrier in the 1,500-meter event, clocking 14 minutes 58.27 seconds and serving notice that the Russians had emerged as a power in swimming.

The 15-minute freestyle swimming barrier in the 1,500 was considered the equivalent of the 4-minute mile in track. Salnikov's time clipped an astonishing 4.13 seconds off the previous record set by Brian Goodell of the United States when he won the Olympic gold at Montreal in 1976. Salnikov went on to win gold medals in the 400 freestyle and the 800 freestyle relay.

East German women swimmers swept 11 gold medals. Rica Reinisch, a 15-year-old student from Dresden who captured three gold medals, was a standout.

In track and field, the glamour sport of the Games, a contingent of British athletes ignored the boycott by other Western nations, chose not to mix politics and sport, and competed on their own. Among them were Sebastian Coe and Steve Ovett, who had lowered Coe's world

record for the mile to 3:48.8 only weeks before the Olympics. Coe had set a world mark in the 1,000 (2:13.4) in the same meet at Oslo. Hopes were raised that they would compete in a showdown in the 800 and 1,500 runs at Moscow.

The hopes were realized. The 800 pitted Ovett and Coe for the first time in two years. Coe, who held the world record in the event, committed a tactical error by waiting too long to take up Ovett's challenge, and the 24-year-old Ovett outlasted the field to win in a slow time of 1:45.4; Coe finished second. The victory made Ovett the favorite to capture the 1,500, but the 23-year-old Coe redeemed himself with a strong performance, ending Ovett's three-year streak of 46 races without a loss at 1,500 and 800 distances. Other Britons fared well, too. Daley Thompson captured the decathlon with a score of 8,495 points, the second highest total in Olympic history, and Allan Wells of Scotland became the first Briton since 1924 to take the 100-meter dash.

Wladyslaw Kozakiewicz, a 26-year-old physical education teacher from Poland, set a world pole vault record of 18′ 11½″; Gerd Wessig, a 6′ 6″ East German, shattered the world mark in the high jump at 7′ 8¾″; and Yuri Sedykh of the Soviet Union threw the hammer for a world standard of 268′ 4″. Another East German, 21-year-old Lutz Dombrowski, became only the second man to break the 28′ long-jump barrier and only the third non-American in Olympic history to (*continued on page 81*)

Don Morely, Duomo

Highlights of the 1980 Summer Olympics included an exciting 800 track race in which Britain's Steve Ovett (279) defeated rival teammate Sebastian Coe (254); the eight-medal-winning performance, including a gold in the rings, of Soviet gymnast Aleksandr Dityatin; and Britain's Daley Thompson's high scoring victory in the decathlon.

Rich Clarkson, "Sports Illustrated"

Don Morely, Duomo

SUMMER GAMES

FINAL MEDAL STANDINGS

Country	Gold	Silver	Bronze	Country	Gold	Silver	Bronze
Soviet Union	80	70	47	Switzerland	2	0	0
East Germany	47	36	43	Spain	1	3	2
Bulgaria	8	16	16	Austria	1	3	1
Cuba	8	7	5	Greece	1	0	2
Italy	8	3	4	Belgium	1	0	0
Hungary	7	10	15	India	1	0	0
Rumania	6	6	13	Venezuela	1	0	0
France	6	5	3	Zimbabwe	1	0	0
Great Britain	5	7	9	North Korea	0	3	2
Poland	3	14	14	Mongolia	0	2	2
Sweden	3	3	6	Tanzania	0	2	0
Finland	3	1	4	Mexico	0	1	3
Yugoslavia	2	3	4	The Netherlands	0	1	3
Czechoslovakia	2	2	9	Ireland	0	1	1
Australia	2	2	5	Uganda	0	1	0
Denmark	2	1	2	Jamaica	0	0	3
Brazil	2	0	2	Guyana	0	0	1
Ethiopia	2	0	2	Lebanon	0	0	1

GOLD MEDALISTS

Archery

Men: Tomi Poikolainen, Finland
Women: Keto Losaberidze, Soviet Union

Basketball

Men: Yugoslavia
Women: Soviet Union

Boxing

Light Flyweight: Shamil Sabyrov, Soviet Union
Flyweight: Petar Lessov, Bulgaria
Bantamweight: Juan Hernandez, Cuba
Featherweight: Rudi Fink, East Germany
Lightweight: Angel Herrera, Cuba
Light Welterweight: Patrizio Oliva, Italy
Welterweight: Andres Aldama, Cuba
Light Middleweight: Armando Martinez, Cuba
Middleweight: José Gomez, Cuba
Light Heavyweight: Slobodan Kacar, Yugoslavia
Heavyweight: Téofilo Stevenson, Cuba

Canoeing

Men's 500-m Kayak Singles: Vladimir Parfenovich, Soviet Union
Men's 1,000-m Kayak Singles: Rudiger Helm, East Germany
Men's 500-m Kayak Pairs: Soviet Union
Men's 1,000-m Kayak Pairs: Soviet Union
Men's 1,000-m Kayak Fours: East Germany
Men's 500-m Canadian Singles: Sergei Postrekhin, Soviet Union
Men's 1,000-m Canadian Singles: Lubomir Lubenov, Bulgaria
Men's 500-m Canadian Pairs: Hungary
Men's 1,000-m Canadian Pairs: Rumania
Women's Kayak Singles: Birgit Fischer, East Germany
Women's Kayak Pairs: East Germany

Cycling

1,000-m Time Trial: Lothar Thoms, East Germany
1,000-m Sprint: Lutz Hesslich, East Germany
4,000-m Individual Pursuit: Robert Dill-Bundi, Switzerland
4,000-m Team Pursuit: Soviet Union
Individual Road Race: Sergei Soukhoroutchenkov, Soviet Union
Team Road Race: Soviet Union

Equestrian

3-Day Event: Federico Euro Roman, Italy
Team 3-Day Event: Soviet Union
Dressage: Elisabeth Theurer, Austria
Team Dressage: Soviet Union
Jumping: Jan Kowalczyk, Poland
Team Jumping: Soviet Union

Fencing

Men's Individual Foil: Vladimir Smirnov, Soviet Union
Men's Team Foil: France
Men's Individual Épée: Johan Harmenberg, Sweden
Men's Team Épée: France
Men's Individual Sabre: Viktor Krovopuskov, Soviet Union
Men's Team Sabre: Soviet Union
Women's Individual Foil: Pascale Trinquet, France
Women's Team Foil: France

Field Hockey

Men: India
Women: Zimbabwe

Gymnastics

Men's All-Around: Aleksandr Dityatin, Soviet Union
Men's Floor Exercises: Roland Bruckner, East Germany
Men's Horizontal Bars: Stoyan Deltchev, Bulgaria
Men's Long Horse: Nikolai Andrianov, Soviet Union
Men's Parallel Bars: Aleksandr Tkachyov, Soviet Union
Men's Rings: Aleksandr Dityatin, Soviet Union
Men's Side Horse: Zoltan Magyar, Hungary
Men's Team: Soviet Union
Women's All-Around: Yelena Davydova, Soviet Union
Women's Balance Beam: Nadia Comaneci, Rumania
Women's Floor Exercises: Nelli Kim, Soviet Union; Nadia Comaneci, Rumania (tie)
Women's Long Horse: N. Shaposhnikova, Soviet Union
Women's Uneven Bars: Maxi Gnauck, East Germany
Women's Team: Soviet Union

Handball

Men's: East Germany
Women's: Soviet Union

Judo

60 kg: Thierry Rey, France
65 kg: Nikolai Solodukhin, Soviet Union
71 kg: Ezio Gamba, Italy
78 kg: Shota Khabarell, Soviet Union
86 kg: Juerg Roethlisberger, Switzerland
95 kg: Robert Van De Walle, Belgium
Over 95 kg: Angelo Parisi, France
Open: Dietmar Lorenz, East Germany

Modern Pentathlon

Individual: Anatoly Starostin, Soviet Union
Team: Soviet Union

Rowing

Men's Single Sculls: Pertti Karppinen, Finland
Men's Double Sculls: East Germany

Rowing (continued)

Men's Quadruple Sculls: East Germany
Men's Coxed Pairs: East Germany
Men's Coxless Pairs: East Germany
Men's Coxed Fours: East Germany
Men's Coxless Fours: East Germany
Men's Eights: East Germany
Women's Single Sculls: Sanda Toma, Rumania
Women's Double Sculls: Soviet Union
Women's Quadruple Sculls: East Germany
Women's Coxless Pairs: East Germany
Women's Coxed Fours: East Germany
Women's Eights: East Germany

Shooting

Small Bore Rifle, Prone: Karoly Varga, Hungary
Small Bore Rifle, Three Positions: Viktor Vlasov, Soviet
Union
Trapshooting: Luciano Giovannetti, Italy
Skeetshooting: Hans Kjeld Rasmussen, Denmark
Free Pistol: Aleksandr Melentev, Soviet Union
Rapid-Fire Pistol: Corneliu Ion, Rumania
Moving Target: Igor Sokolov, Soviet Union

Soccer

Czechoslovakia

Swimming and Diving

Men's 100-m Backstroke: Bengt Baron, Sweden
Men's 200-m Backstroke: Sandor Wladar, Hungary
Men's 100-m Breaststroke: Duncan Goodhew, Great Britain
Men's 200-m Breaststroke: Robertas Zulpa, Soviet Union
Men's 100-m Butterfly: Par Arvidsson, Sweden
Men's 200-m Butterfly: Sergei Fesenko, Soviet Union
Men's 100-m Freestyle: Jorg Woithe, East Germany
Men's 200-m Freestyle: Sergei Kopliakov, Soviet Union
Men's 400-m Freestyle: Vladimir Salnikov, Soviet Union
Men's 1,500-m Freestyle: Vladimir Salnikov, Soviet Union
Men's 800-m Freestyle Relay: Soviet Union
Men's 400-m Individual Medley: Aleksandr Sidorenko,
Soviet Union
Men's 400-m Medley Relay: Australia
Men's Springboard Diving: A. Portnov, Soviet Union
Men's Platform Diving: Falk Hoffmann, East Germany
Women's 100-m Backstroke: Rica Reinisch, East Germany
Women's 200-m Backstroke: Rica Reinisch
Women's 100-m Breaststroke: Ute Geweniger, East Germany
Women's 200-m Breaststroke: Lina Kachushite, Soviet Union
Women's 100-m Butterfly: Caren Metschuck, East Germany
Women's 200-m Butterfly: Ines Geissler, East Germany
Women's 100-m Freestyle: Barbara Krause, East Germany
Women's 200-m Freestyle: Barbara Krause, East Germany
Women's 400-m Freestyle: Ines Diers, East Germany
Women's 800-m Freestyle: Michelle Ford, Australia
Women's 400-m Freestyle Relay: East Germany
Women's 400-m Individual Medley: Petra Schneider, East Germany
Women's 400-m Medley Relay: East Germany
Women's Springboard Diving: Irina Kalinina, Soviet Union
Women's Platform Diving: Martina Jaschke, East Germany

Track and Field

Men's 100-m: Allan Wells, Great Britain
Men's 200-m: Pietro Mennea, Italy
Men's 400-m: Viktor Markin, Soviet Union
Men's 800-m: Steve Ovett, Great Britain
Men's 1,500-m: Sebastian Coe, Great Britain
Men's 5,000-m: Miruts Yifter, Ethiopia
Men's 10,000-m: Miruts Yifter, Ethiopia
Men's Marathon: Waldemar Cierpinski, East Germany
Men's 110-m Hurdles: Thomas Munkelt, East Germany
Men's 400-m Hurdles: Volker Beck, East Germany
Men's 3,000-m Steeplechase: Bronislaw Malinowski, Poland

Track and Field (continued)

Men's 400-m Relay: Soviet Union
Men's 1,600-m Relay: Soviet Union
Men's 20-km Walk: Maurizio Damilano, Italy
Men's 50-km Walk: Hartwig Gauder, East Germany
Men's Decathlon: Daley Thompson, Great Britain
Men's High Jump: Gerd Wessig, East Germany
Men's Long Jump: Lutz Dombrowski, East Germany
Men's Triple Jump: Jaak Uudmae, Soviet Union
Men's Discus: Viktor Rashchupkin, Soviet Union
Men's Shot Put: Vladimir Kiselyov, Soviet Union
Men's Hammer Throw: Yuri Sedykh, Soviet Union
Men's Javelin: Dainis Kula, Soviet Union
Men's Pole Vault: Wladyslaw Kozakiewicz, Poland
Women's 100-m: Lyudmila Kondratyeva, Soviet Union
Women's 200-m: Baerbel Eckert Wockel, East Germany
Women's 400-m: Marita Koch, East Germany
Women's 800-m: Nadyezhda Olizarenko, Soviet Union
Women's 1,500-m: Tatyana Kazankina, Soviet Union
Women's 100-m Hurdles: Vera Komisova, Soviet Union
Women's 400-m Relay: East Germany
Women's 1,600-m Relay: Soviet Union
Women's Pentathlon: Nadyezhda Tkachenko, Soviet
Union
Women's High Jump: Sara Simeoni, Italy
Women's Long Jump: Tatyana Kolpakova, Soviet Union
Women's Discus: Evelin Jahl, East Germany
Women's Shot Put: Ilona Slupianek, East Germany
Women's Javelin: Maria Colon, Cuba

Volleyball

Men: Soviet Union
Women: Soviet Union

Water Polo

Soviet Union

Weight Lifting

Flyweight: Kanibek Osmanoliev, Soviet Union
Bantamweight: Daniel Nunez, Cuba
Featherweight: Viktor Mazin, Soviet Union
Lightweight: Yanko Roussev, Bulgaria
Middleweight: Assen Zlatev, Bulgaria
Light Heavyweight: Yurik Vardanyan, Soviet Union
Middle Heavyweight: Peter Baczako, Hungary
Heavyweight: Ota Zaremba, Czechoslovakia
Second Heavyweight: Leonid Taranenko, Soviet Union
Super Heavyweight: Sultan Rakhmanov, Soviet Union

Wrestling, Freestyle

Paperweight: Claudio Pollio, Italy
Flyweight: Anatoly Beloglazov, Soviet Union
Bantamweight: Sergei Beloglazov, Soviet Union
Featherweight: Magomedgasan Abushev, Soviet Union
Lightweight: Saipulla Absaidov, Soviet Union
Welterweight: Valentin Raitchev, Bulgaria
Middleweight: Ismail Abilov, Bulgaria
Light Heavyweight: Sanasar Oganesyan, Soviet Union
Heavyweight: Ilya Mate, Soviet Union
Super Heavyweight: Soslan Andiyev, Soviet Union

Wrestling, Greco-Roman

Paperweight: Zaksylik Ushkempirov, Soviet Union
Flyweight: Vakhtang Blagidze, Soviet Union
Bantamweight: Shamil Serikov, Soviet Union
Featherweight: Stilianos Migiakis, Greece
Lightweight: Stefan Rusu, Rumania
Welterweight: Ferenc Kocsis, Hungary
Middleweight: Gennady Korban, Soviet Union
Light Heavyweight: Norbert Nottny, Hungary
Heavyweight: Gheorghi Raikov, Bulgaria
Super Heavyweight: Aleksandr Kolchinski, Soviet Union

Yachting

470: Brazil
Finn: Finland
Flying Dutchman: Spain
Soling: Denmark
Star: Soviet Union
Tornado: Brazil

Jerry Cooke, "Sports Illustrated"

Don Morely, Duomo

Yelena Davydova of the USSR succeeded Rumania's Nadia Comaneci as all-around women's gymnast champ; Cuba's Téofilo Stevenson took his third gold in boxing.

win the event. He leaped 28¼", the longest in history at sea level. (The world record of 29′2½″ was set by the American Bob Beamon at high altitude in Mexico City in 1968.) Among the women, Nadyezhda Olizarenko of the Soviet Union was clearly the standout with a world mark of 1:53.5 in the 800-meter run.

Ethiopia's Miruts Yifter captured the 5,000- and 10,000-m runs, and in the steeplechase Bronislaw Malinowski of Poland beat Tanzania's Fibert Bayi, a former world record holder in the mile and 1,500. Bayi's silver medal was the first Olympic medal for his country.

The Soviet men's gymnastics team, in the absence of strong teams from the United States and Japan, easily won the gold medal. The spearhead was 22-year-old Aleksandr Dityatin, the world champion, who went on to take the all-around title, a gold in the rings, and a total of eight medals. It was the start of a duel for medals between the Soviets and East Germans that prompted some observers to comment that the two Eastern bloc nations were participating in a private Spartakiade. The Soviets harvested 80 gold medals and 197 overall; the East Germans won 47 gold and 126 overall.

In women's gymnastics, Nadia Comaneci of Rumania, who had excited the world with the precision that gave her seven perfect scores and three gold medals at Montreal, met with an un-

fortunate fall in the uneven parallel bars. That, and a scoring dispute in the final rotation in the balance-beam program, eventually cost her the all-around title. Yelena Davydova of the Soviet Union won the gold by less than one tenth of a point; Nadia was third. Miss Comaneci's coach became embroiled in a controversy over scoring, insisting that Nadia's score had been ordered lowered by a judge to ensure a gold-medal victory for the Soviets, who easily took the team title, also.

The Soviets, however, could not capture a gold medal in basketball. In the absence of the United States, the Soviet team was favored heavily to romp away with the title. Instead, they ran up against rugged opposition from the Italians and Yugoslavs and had to settle for a bronze. Yugoslavia emerged as the gold-medal winner.

Cubans dominated boxing, with Téofilo Stevenson, the heavyweight star, becoming the first boxer to win three straight Olympic gold medals. In weight lifting, Vasili Alekseyev, the defender billed for many years as "the world's strongest man" was upset in the final by Sultan Rakhmanov, a Ukrainian. Alekseyev, 37 years old and overweight at 357 pounds, failed in three attempts to lift 397 pounds in the snatch, and it cost him the title. Once a Soviet hero, he was booed by the crowd.

GEORGE DE GREGORIO

CHRONOLOGY

As 1980 begins, international attention centers on Afghanistan where Soviet troops and military equipment are lodged. Below, a Soviet tank moves through Kabul, the nation's capital.

JANUARY

3 In response to the Soviet invasion of Afghanistan begun in late 1979, U.S. President Jimmy Carter asks the U.S. Senate to delay its consideration of the Strategic Arms Limitation Treaty II.

A new 15-member civilian cabinet, headed by Francisco Sa Carneiro, takes the oath of office in Portugal.

4 President Carter announces that several steps, including a halt on the delivery of U.S. grain to Moscow, will be taken against the USSR because of its invasion of Afghanistan.

10 Egypt's President Anwar el-Sadat and Israel's Prime Minister Menahem Begin conclude a summit conference in Aswan, Egypt.

George Meany, president of the AFL–CIO from December 1955 until November 1979, dies in Washington, DC.

13 The USSR vetoes a U.S.-sponsored resolution in the UN Security Council that called for economic sanctions against Iran, part of an effort to obtain the release of Americans held hostage in Tehran since November 1979.

14 The UN General Assembly approves a resolution calling for the "immediate, unconditional, and total withdrawal of foreign troops" from Afghanistan. The USSR had vetoed a similar resolution in the Security Council on January 7.

Indira Gandhi is sworn in as prime minister of India following the victory of her party, Congress-I, in elections to the lower house of parliament on January 3 and 6.

U.S. Secretary of State Cyrus Vance indicates that the United States will boycott the 1980 Summer Olympics in Moscow if Soviet troops are not withdrawn from Afghanistan by mid-February.

16 In Boston, MA, scientists and officials from an international research organization based in Geneva, Switzerland, announce that human interferon, a natural virus-fighting substance, has been manufactured in the laboratory through gene splicing techniques.

19 William O. Douglas, associate justice of the U.S. Supreme Court from 1939 to 1975, dies at the age of 81.

20 The Pittsburgh Steelers defeat the Los Angeles Rams, 31–19, in professional football's Super Bowl XIV.

23 Delivering the State of the Union address, President Carter calls for the renewal of military draft registration and warns the Soviet Union that the United States will use "any means necessary, including military force," to repel an attack in the Persian Gulf.

25 The U.S. Bureau of Labor Statistics announces that the U.S. consumer price index rose by 13.3% in 1979, the highest annual increase in more than 30 years.

28 The Carter administration presents to Congress its budget for fiscal year 1981. Receipts are estimated at $600 billion and expenses at $615.8 billion.

29 Thirty-four Muslim nations meeting at the Conference of Islamic States in Islamabad, Pakistan, condemn the Soviet intervention in Afghanistan and suspend Afghanistan's membership in the Islamic organization.

U.S. and Canadian officials report that six American Embassy employees in Tehran, who have been hiding in diplomatic residences there for the past three months, were flown from Iran during the weekend of January 26–27. They carried forged Canadian passports. Earlier, Canada's External Affairs Minister Flora MacDonald announced that the Canadian embassy in Tehran was being closed.

UPI

Mrs. Indira Gandhi, prime minister of India from January 1966 to March 1977, is returned to office following parliamentary elections in early January.

Egypt and Israel open diplomatic missions in Tel Aviv and Cairo, respectively. At left, an Israeli worker fastens a bronze plaque to the gate of Israel's new embassy in Cairo.

UPI

FEBRUARY

Brian Willer

Pierre Elliott Trudeau's tenure as Canada's Opposition leader lasts only nine months. Following his Liberal Party's victory in February 18 elections, he is sworn in for a fourth term as prime minister on March 3.

3 Law enforcement authorities recapture the New Mexico State Penitentiary in Santa Fe, which had been seized by a group of rampaging inmates on February 2. At least 33 persons were killed and 89 were hospitalized during the rioting. Damage to the facility was extensive.

Details of an FBI bribery investigation involving congressmen and other public officials are published in several U.S. newspapers. According to the reports FBI agents had passed bribes to the officials while posing as Arab businessmen seeking political favors. On February 2, agents notified the principals in the "Abscam" (Arab scam) probe that they were under investigation.

4 Abolhassan Bani-Sadr, who had been elected president of the Islamic Republic of Iran on January 25, is formally installed in office by Ayatollah Ruhollah Khomeini.

5 China attends the opening of the 1980 session of the Conference of the Committee on Disarmament—the nation's first appearance at the conference since it was formed in 1962.

12 The Carter administration announces that it has ordered an amphibious assault force, including a Marine landing team, into the Arabian Sea during March to demonstrate American ability to project ground troops into the Persian Gulf area.

18 Parliamentary elections are held in Canada. The Liberal Party of Pierre Elliott Trudeau is returned to power with a majority government.

The United States resumes membership in the International Labor Organization, the UN agency from which it withdrew in 1977.

19 Ayatollah Ruhollah Khomeini designates President Abolhassan Bani-Sadr as supreme commander of Iran's military forces. Subsequently, the president formally accepts a five-member UN commission to investigate Iran's grievances against the deposed shah and U.S. intervention in Iran's internal affairs.

24 The XIII Winter Olympic Games end in Lake Placid, NY. Highlights of the Games include the gold-medal-winning performance of the U.S. hockey team and the five gold medals won by U.S. speed skater Eric Heiden.

26 Egypt and Israel exchange diplomatic ambassadors for the first time.

27 Kabul, Afghanistan, is reported to have returned to order following a general strike that began on February 21 in protest against the Soviet military presence. Some 200 civilians and an undetermined number of soldiers were killed during the upheaval. Martial law was declared on February 22.

Leftist guerrillas shoot their way into the Dominican Republic's embassy in Bogota, Colombia, and take as hostages several diplomats, including U.S. Ambassador Diego C. Asencio.

MARCH

3 President Carter states that the United States had erred March 1 in voting in favor of a UN Security Council resolution urging Israel to dismantle its settlements on the West Bank and Gaza Strip. The president attributes the mistake to a breakdown in communications.

Gen. Prem Tinsulanonda is chosen prime minister of Thailand, succeeding Kriangsak Chamanand, who resigned.

11 The UN inquiry commission that arrived in Iran on February 23 prepares to leave Tehran, having failed to negotiate the release of the American hostages held there.

Robert Mugabe is formally appointed prime minister of Zimbabwe (Rhodesia) following the victory of his party (the Zimbabwe African National Union) in February 27–29 elections for the House of Assembly. Earlier, he had designated Joshua Nkomo, a member of the rival Zimbabwe African People's Union, minister of home affairs.

14 President Carter announces a new anti-inflation program, which includes a $13 billion cut from the 1981 budget, an oil import conservation fee, and measures to curb consumer credit.

The crash of a Polish airliner during an attempted landing in Warsaw results in the death of 87 persons, including 22 members and officials of a U.S. amateur boxing team.

22 Fighting breaks out again between rival Muslim factions in Chad.

24 The deposed shah of Iran arrives in Egypt and is taken to a military hospital where he is to undergo an operation for the removal of an enlarged spleen. The shah left Panama one day before Iran's revolutionary government was to present to the Panamanian government a request for his extradition.

A floating platform in the North Sea oil field capsizes in rough seas on March 27. Heavy winds and high waves hamper rescue operations, and 123 persons die.

27 Mount St. Helens, a volcano in the Cascade Mountains of Washington that has been dormant for 123 years, begins to erupt.

A floating platform in the North Sea oil fields collapses in turbulent seas, causing the death of 123 persons.

29 The United States and Turkey sign an agreement in Ankara granting the United States the continued right to use an airbase, four intelligence-gathering installations, and seven communication stations in Turkey in exchange for military and economic assistance.

30 In San Salvador, El Salvador, bomb blasts, gunfire, and general panic cause a stampede during the funeral of Archbishop Oscar Arnulfo Romero, who was assassinated on March 24. Some 30 persons are killed.

APRIL

2 U.S. President Carter signs into law the Crude Oil Windfall Profits Tax of 1980.

The prime lending rate at several major U.S. banks rises to 20%.

4 Italian Prime Minister Francesco Cossiga announces the formation of a new coalition government, ending a three-week political crisis.

6 Some 7,000 persons seeking asylum and safe passage out of Cuba gather inside the Peruvian embassy in Havana. The crowd had been growing since April 1, when six Cubans crashed a bus through the embassy gates.

7 In response to a statement by Ayatollah Khomeini that the U.S. hostages in Tehran would be kept under control of the militants and not turned over to the government, the United States breaks diplomatic ties.

12 The House of Delegates of the U.S. Olympic Committee votes 1,604 to 797 in favor of a boycott of the Summer Olympic Games in Moscow.

Liberia's President William R. Tolbert, Jr., is killed in a predawn coup by army enlisted men. Master Sgt. Samuel K. Doe assumes power.

16 President Carter announces that the U.S. economy "has slowed and has probably entered a period of recession."

17 Zimbabwe (Rhodesia) officially becomes the independent nation of Zimbabwe, ending 90 years of British rule. Robert Mugabe is installed as the nation's first prime minister.

Edmund S. Muskie, Democratic senator from Maine since 1959, is the new secretary of state.

Photos UPI

The walkway of the Brooklyn Bridge is quite congested as workers are forced to walk or ride bicycles to their jobs during New York City's transit strike, April 1–10.

22 The 10th anniversary of Earth Day is celebrated.

24 Rep. John B. Anderson (R–IL) announces his independent candidacy for president of the United States.

25 President Carter announces that an overnight mission to rescue the U.S. hostages in Tehran had been aborted when one of the helicopters in the operation developed engine trouble. Two planes collided during the withdrawal from the staging area, and eight servicemen were killed.

27 The two-month occupation of the Dominican Republic's embassy in Bogota, Colombia, ends peacefully as left-wing guerrillas of the April 19 Movement release the remaining 18 hostages.

29 President Carter names Sen. Edmund S. Muskie (D–ME) secretary of state one day after accepting the resignation of Cyrus Vance. Vance resigned in disagreement with the president's decision to attempt the rescue mission in Iran.

30 The Iranian embassy in London is seized by five armed dissidents from Iran's Khuzistan province. In exchange for 20 hostages, they demand full autonomy for the region and an escape plane.

Queen Juliana of The Netherlands abdicates the throne, and Princess Beatrix is invested as the nation's sixth monarch.

Former U.S. Budget Director Bert Lance is acquitted by a federal jury in Atlanta, GA, of nine counts of bank fraud.

Netherlands' Princess Beatrix, with her husband, Prince Claus, at her side, becomes queen.

MAY

3 Genuine Risk, a filly, wins the Kentucky Derby.

4 Marshall Tito (Josip Broz), the 87-year-old president of Yugoslavia, dies in Ljubljana after a four-month illness.

5 British commandos storm the Iranian embassy in London after the body of a hostage is thrown to the street. The remaining 19 hostages are freed, and the Arab Iranian terrorists are either killed or arrested.

6 After pledging that the United States would "provide an open heart and open arms" to the thousands of Cuban refugees entering Florida since mid-April, President Carter declares a state of emergency in areas most affected by the influx and authorizes $10 million in relief funds.

8 George John Rallis is chosen prime minister of Greece, replacing Constantine Caramanlis, who was elected president May 5.

Photos UPI

Property damage is estimated at $100 million as racial rioting breaks out in Miami, FL, in mid-May.

9 At least 35 persons are killed as the 35,000-ton freighter *Summit Venture* hits a support pillar of the Sunshine Skyway Bridge at St. Petersburg, FL, and the bridge gives way.

10 The Chrysler Corp. Loan Guarantee Board approves $1,500,000,-000 in federal loan guarantees to the financially troubled car manufacturer.

14 Ugandan President Godfrey Binaisa is eased out of power by soldiers loyal to Chief of Staff Brig. Gen. David Oyite Ojok.

16 Japanese Prime Minister Masayoshi Ohira is voted out of office, as his Liberal Democratic Party (LDP) is defeated, 243 to 187, on a no-confidence motion in the lower chamber of parliament.

The Los Angeles Lakers capture the National Basketball Association (NBA) championship.

18 Mount St. Helens, a 9,677-ft (2 950-m) volcano in southwest Washington, erupts in a giant blast that devastates a 122-sq-mi (310-km^2) area. At least 22 persons are killed and 77 missing.

King Baudouin of Belgium swears in a new, six-party coalition government headed by Prime Minister Wilfried Martens.

19 Three days of racial rioting end in Miami, FL, after at least 15 persons are killed, 300 injured, and 1,000 arrested.

20 Voters in the province of Quebec reject separation from Canada, as they defeat a referendum on the sovereignty/association proposal of provincial Premier René Lévesque.

The government of South Korean Prime Minister Shin Hyon Hwack resigns "to take responsibility for failure to maintain domestic calm." The move comes one day after the proclamation of total martial law to quell antigovernment demonstrations throughout the country.

21 President Carter declares a state of emergency at the Love Canal in Niagara Falls, NY. A new study reports that 30% of the residents in the area, which for years had been used as a chemical dump site, had suffered chromosomal damage.

24 The New York Islanders win their first Stanley Cup.

27 Chinese Premier Hua Guofeng begins a four-day visit to Japan, the first ever by a Chinese head of government.

29 Black civil rights leader Vernon E. Jordan, Jr., National Urban League president, is shot and critically wounded in Fort Wayne.

30 The U.S. Commerce Department reports that the national index of leading economic indicators dropped by 4.8% in April, the largest monthly decrease on record.

UPI

The seal of the new U.S. Department of Education. The 13th Cabinet-level office officially began operations on May 4.

JUNE

1 Angry at delays in processing, some 200 Cuban refugees break through the gates of the Fort Chaffee, AR, military base and processing center. Forced back inside by Army troops, the refugees go on a rampage, burning barracks and setting fire to debris.

2 In defiance of President Carter's ban on travel to Iran, a ten-member delegation headed by former Attorney General Ramsey Clark arrives in Tehran for a three-day, Iranian-sponsored conference on U.S. "intervention in Iran."

Israeli extremists are blamed for a series of bombings in four West Bank cities. Several persons, including two Arab mayors who support the Palestine Liberation Organization (PLO), are seriously wounded.

6 The U.S. Labor Department announces that the national unemployment rate rose to 7.8% in May, an increase of 0.8% from April and the highest seasonally-adjusted monthly figure since November 1976.

The U.S. Senate overrides the president's veto of a resolution blocking a proposed fee on foreign oil. The action establishes as law a bill blocking the proposed imposition of a 10-cent-a-gallon duty at the gas pump. The House of Representatives had voted to override the veto on June 5.

12 Japan's Prime Minister Masayoshi Ohira, 70, dies of a heart attack in Tokyo ten days before scheduled parliamentary elections.

13 At the end of a two-day summit in Venice, Italy, the nine-member European Community (EC) issues an 11-point declaration urging self-determination for the PLO and calling for the PLO to be "associated with" negotiations for peace in the Middle East.

16 The U.S. Supreme Court rules, 5–4, that biological organisms can be patented under federal law (*Diamond v. Chakrabarty*).

20 The Carter administration announces that the majority of the 114,-000 Cubans and 15,000 Haitians who had arrived legally in the United States by boat in recent weeks would be allowed to remain for at least six months. With appropriate legislation by Congress, they could become permanent residents after two years.

22 In Japanese parliamentary elections, the ruling Liberal Democratic Party (LDP) wins a solid majority in both houses of the Diet.

23 Sanjay Gandhi, the son of India's Prime Minister Indira Gandhi and one of the nation's most powerful political figures, dies at age 33 in the crash of a small plane near New Delhi.

30 The U.S. Supreme Court rules, 5–4, that neither the federal government nor the individual states are required by the constitution to finance abortions for poor women.

UPI
Italy's Francesco Cossiga (left), Jimmy Carter, Britain's Margaret Thatcher, and Japan's Foreign Minister Saburo Okita attend Economic Summit Conference in Venice, Italy, in June.

Focus on Sports
On June 15, Jack Nicklaus wins his fourth U.S. Open golf tournament with a record total of 272.

JULY

1 President Carter signs into law the Motor Carrier Bill of 1980, deregulating the nation's interstate trucking industry.

"O Canada" is officially proclaimed Canada's national anthem.

2 President Carter signs a proclamation ordering four million young men born in 1960 and 1961 to register for the draft.

5 For the fifth consecutive time, Björn Borg of Sweden wins the men's tennis singles crown at Wimbledon. Earlier, Australia's Evonne Goolagong Cawley took the women's singles title.

Voters prepare to cast their ballots in June 22 parliamentary elections in Japan.

6 The bodies of 13 illegal aliens are found by policemen in an Arizona desert. Earlier a group of 14 illegal aliens (12 Salvadorans and 2 Mexicans suspected of smuggling) was rescued near death in Arizona's Organ Pipe National Monument.

10 After attending memorial services for Masayoshi Ohira, the late prime minister of Japan, President Carter and China's Prime Minister Hua Guofeng confer at Tokyo's Hotel Okura.

11 Following 250 days as a hostage at the U.S. embassy in Tehran, Richard I. Queen, a U.S. consular officer, is released for medical reasons on the orders of Ayatollah Ruhollah Khomeini.

17 Zenko Suzuki, who was chosen as leader of Japan's ruling Liberal Democratic Party on July 15, is elected prime minister of Japan.

At the Republican National Convention in Detroit, Ronald Reagan and George Bush accept nomination as the party's presidential and vice-presidential candidates.

18 After the armed forces take control of Bolivia, Gen. Luis García Meza, the nation's army commander, takes the presidential oath of office. Presidential elections on June 29 had failed to produce an outright victor.

24 The U.S. Senate establishes a nine-member committee, with Sen. Birch Bayh (D–IND) as chairman, to investigate the activities of Billy Carter, the president's brother, as an agent for Libya.

25 Canada's Prime Minister Trudeau and Alberta's Prime Minister Peter Lougheed conclude talks without agreement on how to share the benefits of domestic oil and gas production.

27 Mohammed Reza Pahlavi, the deposed shah of Iran, dies in Cairo.

28 Fernando Belaunde Terry is inaugurated president of Peru.

29 Ending a six-day special session, the UN General Assembly approves a resolution calling for the formation of a Palestinian state.

30 Israel's Knesset (Parliament) enacts a law reaffirming Jerusalem as the nation's capital. Israel had annexed the eastern section of the city after capturing it from Jordan in 1967.

Britain and France end 74 years of joint rule in the New Hebrides as the Pacific archipelago becomes the new nation of Vanuatu.

Detroit, MI, is pleased to host the 32d Republican National Convention, held July 14–17.

AUGUST

3 The XXII Summer Olympic Games end in Moscow. The United States, Canada, Japan, and West Germany were among nations that boycotted the Games.

4 In a 13,000-word White House report, President Carter declares "categorically" that his brother Billy had no effect at all on U.S. policy toward Libya.

5 One hundred ninety-one Iranians, held without charge in U.S. prisons while officials investigated possible immigration-law violations, are released. The group was arrested during a pro-Khomeini demonstration in Washington, July 27.

11 Hurricane Allen, which had caused at least 270 deaths and extreme damage in Haiti, other Caribbean areas, and Texas, dissipates over Mexico.

Iran's Parliament approves the nomination of Mohammed Ali Rajai as prime minister.

14 At the Democratic National Convention in New York City, President Jimmy Carter and Vice-President Walter Mondale are nominated for second terms. Sen. Edward M. Kennedy had withdrawn as a presidential candidate on August 11 after an attempt to permit convention delegates to vote freely, without regard to primary results, was defeated.

17 As fighting between Muslim and Hindu forces continues in the Indian state of Uttar Pradesh for the fifth consecutive day, rioting spreads to Kashmir, India's northernmost state.

19 A Lockheed L-1011 aircraft erupts in flames at the airport in Riyadh, Saudi Arabia, killing all 301 persons aboard.

20 With the United States abstaining, the UN Security Council passes a resolution urging the nations that maintain embassies in the city of Jerusalem to remove them.

21 Under an agreement signed today by representatives of Somalia and the United States, Somalia is to receive $151 million in U.S. military and economic aid over a two-year period, and the United States gains access to naval and air facilities at the port of Berbera, Somalia.

24 As a national crisis caused by strikes of at least 200,000 workers continues in Poland, Prime Minister Edward Babiuch and three other members of the ruling Politburo are dismissed. On August 22 a strikers' committee had presented the government with a series of demands, including political reforms and independent unions supervised by workers.

25 Third party presidential candidate John B. Anderson names Patrick J. Lucey, former governor of Wisconsin, as his running mate.

27 Retired Gen. Chun Doo Hwan is elected president of South Korea, succeeding Choi Kyu Hah who resigned on August 16.

Connolly, Liaison

In a large section of the United States, including the mid-Mississippi Valley, the Southwest, and the South, a long summer drought and record-high temperatures ruin farm crops and destroy livestock.

UPI

Polish strike leader Lech Walesa addresses workers at the Lenin shipyard gate in Gdansk as labor unrest leads to a crisis and major governmental changes.

SEPTEMBER

3 Most of Poland's striking laborers are back at work after the government accedes to their demands for the rights to strike and to form free, independent trade unions.

6 Polish Party Secretary Edward Gierek is replaced by party administrator Stanislaw Kania after reportedly suffering a heart ailment.

7 John McEnroe takes his second consecutive U.S. Open men's singles tennis title by defeating Björn Borg in five sets. Chris Evert Lloyd defeated Hana Mandlikova for the women's crown one day earlier.

10 At the end of a two-day meeting in Tripoli, Libyan head of state Muammar el-Qaddafi and Syrian President Hafez al-Assad issue a 14-point document proclaiming the merger of their two countries.

The Chinese National People's Congress accepts the September 7 resignation of Premier Hua Guofeng and his choice of Deputy Premier Zhao Ziyang as his successor. Hua remains Communist party chairman.

12 A six-man military junta headed by Gen. Kenan Evren takes control of Turkey in an apparently bloodless coup.

13 Canadian Prime Minister Pierre Elliott Trudeau and ten provincial premiers end six days of constitutional discussions without reaching any agreements.

17 Exiled Nicaraguan President Anastasio Somoza Debayle is brutally assassinated by gunmen in Asuncion, Paraguay.

19 A Titan 2 nuclear missile silo near Damascus, AR, is rocked by a fuel explosion that sends flames and debris 500 ft (152 m) in the air. Twenty-two Air Force personnel are injured, one of them fatally.

21 Presidential candidates Ronald Reagan and John Anderson engage in a nationally televised debate. President Carter refuses to participate.

22 A long-standing border dispute between Iran and Iraq erupts in open warfare, as both sides launch heavy air and artillery attacks against major cities and oil refineries. Both nations cut off valuable shipments of petroleum through the Persian Gulf.

Giansanti, Sygma

A soldier stands guard in downtown Ankara as the military takes control of the Turkish government.

In the urban battle-grounds of the Iran-Iraq war, which broke out in September, combatants are forced to erect make-shift protection points.

Golestan, Liaison

24 The U.S. Senate narrowly approves a June 19 executive order to sell 38 tons of enriched uranium to India.

25 A tentative agreement is reached in the 67-day-old strike against film studios and television networks by 60,000 members of the Screen Actors Guild and American Federation of Television and Radio Artists.

In the America's Cup yachting races off Newport, RI, the United States completes its 24th straight title defense as *Freedom,* skippered by Dennis Conner, defeats *Australia* in the fourth of five races.

27 A terrorist bomb explosion at Oktoberfest celebrations in Munich, West Germany, leaves 12 persons dead and 144 others injured.

Italy's coalition government of Prime Minister Francesco Cossiga resigns after a one-vote parliamentary defeat over economic policy.

OCTOBER

2 Rep. Michael J. Myers (D-PA), who on Aug. 31, 1980, was convicted of bribery and conspiracy in connection with the Abscam investigation, is expelled from the U.S. House of Representatives.

Canada's Prime Minister Trudeau calls Parliament into special session to consider a new constitution.

4 In the Gulf of Alaska, some 470 passengers and crew members safely flee the cruise ship *Prinsendam* as fire breaks out on the ocean liner.

5 The West German coalition government of Helmut Schmidt is returned to power in national elections. Parliamentary elections also are held in Portugal, and Prime Minister Francisco Sá Carneiro's Democratic Alliance emerges the winner.

8 The USSR and Syria sign a 20-year treaty of friendship.

10 A devastating earthquake strikes the northwestern Algerian city of El Asnam, killing thousands of persons.

11 Soviet cosmonauts Valery V. Ryumin and Leonid I. Popov conclude man's longest space mission, 185 days.

13 Adolfo Pérez Esquivel, a human rights activist in Latin America, is named winner of the Nobel Peace Prize.

The Cuban government announces a pardon for all Americans serving prison sentences in Cuba.

17 Iran's Premier Mohammad Ali Rajai addresses the UN Security Council.

18 A new four-party coalition government, headed by Arnaldo Forlani, is installed in Italy.

The Australian Liberal Party of Prime Minister Malcolm Fraser is reelected in national balloting.

21 The Philadelphia Phillies defeat the Kansas City Royals, 4 games to 2, to win baseball's World Series. Mike Schmidt is named most valuable player.

22 The United States and China sign a bilateral grain agreement.

French President Valéry Giscard d'Estaing concludes a four-day official visit to China.

In a referendum in South Korea, voters approve a new constitution.

23 Aleksei N. Kosygin resigns as prime minister of the USSR and is succeeded by his first deputy, Nikolai A. Tikhonov.

26 Israel's President Yitzhak Navon begins an official visit to Egypt.

27 The Cuban government releases 33 Americans from prison in Cuba.

28 U.S. presidential candidates Jimmy Carter and Ronald Reagan engage in a televised debate.

Saudi Arabia breaks diplomatic relations with Libya.

29 The Carter administration announces a federal budget deficit of $59,000,000,000 for fiscal year 1980.

In elections in Jamaica, Edward P. G. Seaga leads the Labor Party to victory.

The White House announces the nomination of A. W. Clausen, currently president and chief executive officer of the Bank of America, to succeed Robert McNamara as president of the World Bank.

Australian Information Service

In mid-October, Malcolm Fraser, 50, led the Australian Liberal Party to victory in parliamentary elections. The liberals held a majority of 23 seats in the House of Representatives but lost control of the Senate.

Elizabeth Marshall, Liaison

Edward P. G. Seaga (extreme right) campaigns prior to Jamaica's parliamentary elections. Seaga's Labor Party scored a major win, ending Michael Manley's experiment with socialism.

Voyager 1 spacecraft transmits photos of Saturn. The planet's rings appear quite uniform in color and sharply defined.

NASA

NOVEMBER

4 In U.S. elections, the Republican presidential candidate, Ronald Reagan, easily defeats the incumbent Democrat, Jimmy Carter; the Republican Party wins control of the U.S. Senate; and the Democratic Party retains control of the U.S. House of Representatives but with a reduced margin.

10 After the Polish Supreme Court rules in favor of the legal registration of independent trade unions, a national strike, scheduled for November 12, is called off.

Michael Foot, 67, is elected leader of Britain's Labour Party, succeeding James Callaghan, who resigned.

11 A 35-nation conference on European security, cooperation, and human rights opens in Madrid, Spain.

13 The New York Metropolitan Opera Company and its chorus reach a labor agreement, ending a strike that threatened to cancel the 1980–81 season.

14 President-elect Reagan names James A. Baker 3d and Edwin Meese 3d as his White House chief of staff and counselor to the president, respectively.

15 Pope John Paul II begins a five-day visit to West Germany.

17 Six members of the Ku Klux Klan and Nazi Party are acquitted by an all-white jury in Greensboro, NC, of charges of murdering five members of the Communist Workers Party at a 1979 anti-Klan rally.

19 Israeli Prime Minister Menahem Begin wins, 57-54, a parliamentary vote of confidence on economic policy.

20 Ten leaders of China's Cultural Revolution, including the so-called "Gang of Four," go on trial in Peking on charges of having persecuted officials, plotted to assassinate the late Chairman Mao Zedong, and planned "an armed rebellion in Shanghai."

The Dow Jones industrial average finishes the day above 1,000 for the first time in nearly four years.

21 Fire sweeps through the lower floors of the 26-story MGM Grand Hotel and casino in Las Vegas, NV, killing 84 persons.

23 A violent earthquake strikes southern Italy, leaving a reported 3,000 persons dead and 200,000 homeless.

25 Sugar Ray Leonard regains the WBC welterweight boxing championship as Roberto Durán concedes in the eighth round.

26 Syria and Jordan are reported to be massing troops on their common border. The buildup is said to be related to Syria's boycott of the 11th Arab League summit in Amman, November 25–27, and differences over the Iran-Iraq war, the PLO, and other issues.

DECEMBER

3 U.S. representatives Frank Thompson, Jr. (D–NJ) and John M. Murphy (D–NY) are found guilty on charges arising from Abscam.

4 Portuguese Premier Francisco Sá Carneiro, Defense Minister Adelino da Costa, and seven others are killed in a plane crash.

5 At an unscheduled meeting in Moscow, the Warsaw Pact nations express confidence that Poland will overcome its persisting labor unrest and pledge their "fraternal solidarity and support." The USSR continues to mobilize troops near the Polish border.

The United States suspends aid to El Salvador pending investigation of the murders of four American women, three of them nuns.

7 Gen. António Ramalho Eanes is reelected president of Portugal.

The ruling Kuomintang retains a large majority in Taiwan's first parliamentary elections since 1977.

8 Former Beatle John Lennon, 40, is shot and killed in New York City.

10 Syria and Jordan announce the pullback of border troops.

13 José Napoleon Duarte is named El Salvador's first civilian president in 49 years and leader of the ruling four-member junta.

Uganda's state election committee declares former President Milton Obote and his Uganda People's Congress the winners of the disputed December 10–11 elections.

16 The 96th U.S. Congress adjourns.

17 President Forbes Burnham of Guyana is declared the winner in elections described by foreign observers as replete with fraud.

18 Former Soviet Premier Aleksei N. Kosygin, 76, dies in Moscow.

19 In a continuing upward spiral of the corporate lending rate, most major U.S. banks raise the prime to 21.5%.

21 Iran demands $24,000,000,000 for the release of the 52 American hostages. U.S. Secretary of State Edmund S. Muskie calls the demand package "unreasonable."

24 The U.S. completes its reporting of the 1980 decennial census. The final national total is 226,504,825. Supreme Court Justice Potter Stewart temporarily suspends a lower court decision preventing the bureau from certifying its results.

27 Fifteen of the 52 American hostages in Iran are seen on television in the United States, raising to 41 the number who have appeared since Christmas Day.

28 Mexico terminates all fishing agreements with the United States after a continuing series of disputes.

Liaison

As 1980 ended, Alexander Haig, 56, was named secretary of state in the Reagan cabinet. The appointment caused controversy due to the former general's service in the Nixon White House.

President Jimmy Carter and Mrs. Carter welcome President-elect Ronald Reagan and Mrs. Reagan to the White House for their first post-election meeting, Nov. 20, 1980.

REVIEW OF THE YEAR

ACCIDENTS AND DISASTERS

AVIATION

Jan. 21—An Iran Air Boeing 727 crashes about 20 mi (32 km) from Tehran, killing 128 persons.

Feb. 22—Near Agra, India, an Indian Air Force plane catches fire on takeoff; 46 persons are killed.

March 14—A Polish jetliner crashes while attempting an emergency landing in Warsaw; all 87 persons aboard are killed, including 22 members and officials of a U.S. amateur boxing team.

March 14—A U.S. Air Force transport plane crashes in the Taurus Mountains north of Adana, Turkey; 18 persons are killed, all of whom are thought to be American military personnel.

April 12—In a landing approach at the Florianopolis, Brazil, airfield, a Transbrasil jetliner crashes during a tropical storm, killing 54 persons.

April 25—A chartered British jetliner crashes in the Canary Islands, killing 146 persons.

April 27—Lightning causes the crash of a Thai airliner near Bangkok, killing 40 persons.

June 28—An Italian DC-9 jetliner crashes in the Tyrrhenian Sea, 90 mi (147 km) southwest of Naples; all 81 persons on board are killed.

August 19—A Saudi Arabian Airlines jetliner catches fire and lands at the Riyadh, Saudi Arabia airport; all 301 persons aboard are killed.

August 26—An Indonesian Viscount turboprop airliner crashes about 20 mi (32 km) from the airport of Jakarta; 31 persons are killed.

Sept. 14—A Saudi Arabian Air Force transport plane catches fire and crashes in the desert near Medina, Saudi Arabia; 89 persons are killed.

Dec. 21—A Colombian jetliner explodes soon after takeoff from Ríohacha, Colombia, killing 69 persons.

EARTHQUAKES

Jan. 1—An earthquake shakes Portugal's Azores Islands, killing at least 52 persons.

May 18—Mount St. Helens, a Washington volcano, erupts. (*See* special report, page 248.)

Oct. 10—Two earthquakes strike northwestern Algeria, destroying most of the town of Al Asnam; 5,000 to 20,000 people are killed and at least 400,000 are homeless.

Nov. 23—An earthquake strikes southern Italy, particularly the provinces of Potenza, Naples, Salerno, and Avellino, killing some 3,000 people.

FIRES AND EXPLOSIONS

Jan. 1—During a New Year's Eve Lion's Club party, fire breaks out in a crowded social club near Chapais, Quebec, killing 44 persons.

May 20—In Kingston, Jamaica, fire breaks out in a two-story wooden home for the poor; 144 persons are dead and nine others are missing.

July 26—At Bradley Beach, NJ, 23 persons are killed in a fire in a four-story hotel for the elderly and mentally retarded.

August 14—An electrical fire in a Baghdad, Iraq, theater causes the deaths of 59 persons.

Oct. 2—Off the Saudi Arabian coast in the Persian Gulf, a blowout on an American-owned oil rig releases toxic gas, killing 19 men.

Oct. 4—Fire aboard the Dutch luxury cruise ship *Prinsendam* forces 470 passengers and crew members to abandon ship in the Gulf of Alaska.

Oct. 13—A gas-fired boiler in an Atlanta day-care nursery explodes, killing four preschool-age children and one adult.

Oct. 23—An explosion in an elementary school in Ortuella, Spain kills 64 people, mostly children.

Nov. 15–30—In five southern California counties a series of brush and timber fires kills five persons and destroys 86,-000 acres (34 830 ha).

Nov. 20—Fire destroys the four-story Kawaji Prince Hotel in Kawaji, Japan, killing 42 persons; three persons are missing.

Nov. 21—A fire in the MGM Grand Hotel in Las Vegas, NV, kills at least 84 persons; at least 500 are injured and some others are missing.

Dec. 4—Fire in the conference center of the Stouffer's Inn in Harrison, NY, leaves 26 persons dead.

LAND AND SEA TRANSPORTATION

April 20—An overcrowded ferry capsizes in a storm on the Padma River on the way to Dacca, Bangladesh; at least 230 persons are missing.

April 22—An oil tanker and inter-island ferry collide near the island of Maestre de Campo in the Philippines; 116 persons are dead.

May 7—A boat carrying a wedding party capsizes while crossing a river in the state of Gujarat, India; 50 persons are feared drowned.

May 9—A freighter ship, *Summit Venture*, strikes the Sunshine Skyway Bridge across Tampa Bay, St. Petersburg, FL, causing the collapse of a section of the bridge and the dropping of eight vehicles—including a bus—into the bay; at least 35 persons are killed.

June 5—A chartered bus on a mountain highway near Jasper, AR, slides down a steep embankment, killing 20 persons.

June 7—Near Empangeni, South Africa, a freight train and bus collide, killing at least 67 persons.

August 3—Northeast of Rio de Janeiro, 28 persons are killed when a bus collides with a truck.

August 19—A freight train and a passenger train collide near Torun, Poland, killing 62 persons.

August 22—A ferry—carrying cars, trucks, and a bus—sinks near Ciudad del Carmen, Mexico, drowning at least 50 persons.

Sept. 8—A boat on Nepal's Gandak River capsizes; 86 persons are missing.

Sept. 21—A bus plunges into an irrigation canal near Lahore, Pakistan, killing about 50 passengers.

Oct. 15—A bus falls into El Basurero gorge, 25 mi (40 km) north of Oaxaca, Mexico, killing 23 persons.

Oct. 30—Near Kanpur in northern India an express train crashes into the derailed cars of a freight train; 34 persons are killed.

Nov. 21—Near Vibo Valentia, Italy, two high-speed passenger trains strike a string of box cars that had become disconnected from a passing freight train, killing 26 persons.

STORMS AND FLOODS

Feb. 13–22—In a series of Pacific storms, floods and mudslides in the Los Angeles area, Palm Springs, San Diego, and Phoenix, AZ, cause the deaths of at least 31 persons.

March 1–2—Snowstorms cover the U.S. mid-Atlantic seaboard, depositing as much as 28 inches (71 cm) of snow and contributing to at least 36 deaths.

March 27–28—Heavy rains in eastern and western Turkey cause flooding, landslides, and collapsing houses and bridges; 75 persons are killed.

April 14—The Pearl and Leaf Rivers in Mississippi flood, while snow hits the Middle West; the storms kill at least nine persons.

April 14–21—Floods and landslides kill 70 persons in Peru's eastern Amazonian region.

July 20 (reported)–August 22—Seasonal rains and the accompanying flooding of the Ganges and other northern rivers cause the deaths of more than 1,100 persons in India; hardest hit is the state of Uttar Pradesh, with 661 deaths.

August 4–11—Hurricane Allen, with 185 mph (296 km/h) winds, strikes in the Caribbean, hitting Barbados, St. Lucia, Haiti, the Dominican Republic, Cuba, Jamaica, and moving into the Gulf of Mexico along Mexico's Yucatan Peninsula and the Texas coast; at least 272 persons are killed.

August 31—Flooding in Ibadan, Nigeria, following a 12-hour rainstorm kills at least 240 persons.

Sept. 8—Landslides in the Himalayas, set off by heavy rains, sweep down in the area of Darjeeling, India, killing 250 persons.

Sept. 17—More than 200 persons are killed in flash floods in the Indian state of Orissa.

Sept. 25—In a week of heavy rains in Caracas, Venezuela, mudslides and flooding cause the deaths of 20 persons and leave 1,000 others homeless.

Oct. 20–21—Flooding in northern and western Colombia causes the deaths of at least 40 persons.

Nov. 16–17—A snowstorm spreads from Texas to the northeast, dropping record snow for November and contributing to the deaths of 16 persons.

MISCELLANEOUS

Jan. 21—Bleachers at a bullring in Sincelejo, Colombia, collapse at the start of a bullfighting event, killing at least 222 persons.

March 27—An offshore platform, serving as a dormitory for oil workers, collapses in the North Sea oil fields, killing 123 men.

March 27—The cable of a mine-shaft elevator snaps, causing the elevator to plunge to the bottom of South Africa's Vaal Reefs gold mine; 31 miners are killed.

June 23–August 15—A major heat wave strikes the midwestern, southern, and southwestern United States; 1,265 heat-related deaths result.

July 6—Seventy persons are reported killed by a collapsed Chinese offshore oil drilling rig in the Bo Hai Gulf.

ADVERTISING

The economic recession of 1980 descended like a rainstorm on the U.S. advertising industry, further dampening growth in an already weakened economy. Advertisers spent 11% more during the year than in 1979, but the increase barely kept pace with the nation's tenacious double-digit inflation. As in any recession, consumers tightened their belts, changing life-styles and spending habits. In such times, sophisticated merchandisers understand the value of maintaining product awareness through advertising. However, the 1980 recession included some idiosyncrasies: new product introductions, usually the first to be reduced in hard times, actually increased in the first half of the year to 638, an all-time high. Another anomaly was the emergence of direct mail and specialty (ad-imprinted goods, such as ballpoint pens) advertising. Recession-induced cutbacks caused marketers to put more money in these "targeted" mediums, which deliver the message to a narrow audience.

Laws and Regulations. In May, the U.S. Congress passed a bill that effectively curbed the rule-making powers of the Federal Trade Commission (FTC), watchdog of the advertising industry. Major items in the FTC Improvements Act of 1980 include: 1) suspension through September 1982 of FTC authority to write rules against unfair advertising practices; 2) stipulation that a congressional veto by both houses will kill FTC rules before they take effect, thereby providing protection for corporate targets of the agency; and 3) reforms that would make the FTC's rule-making process less arbitrary. The beleaguered agency shelved a proposal that would have required fuller disclosure of the nutrient content of foods that claim to be "nutritious," "natural," or "organic." Finally, in a conciliatory gesture to the advertising industry, the FTC asked industry representatives for alternatives to its own stalled proposal that would have restricted television advertising aimed at children. In a joint statement, three major advertising trade associations refused to offer any suggestions and, in effect, told the FTC that current advertising for children does not require reforms. (*See also* special report, page 554.)

Media. Network competition for ratings supremacy in the 1979–80 season went down to the wire, but on the strength of several last-minute programming moves, CBS edged past ABC to win the prime time race by one tenth of a point. The intense competition resulted in increased program costs that, in turn, caused profits at all three networks to dip for the first time in many years. Adding to the networks' woes was an 11-week actors' strike, which forced the networks to air a patchwork schedule of movies, reruns, news, and sports in lieu of the traditional lineup of new fall shows. Cable and pay television continued to grow in 1980. Available data suggested that cable and pay television were significantly altering viewing patterns. During an average week, network stations received 83% of all viewing in homes that do not have cable television; in homes that do have cable, the networks' share dropped to 71%, and even lower in homes with pay television. In 1980, this new technology was further legitimized by the country's largest advertisers, who purchased time on cable television. Although the amount was still minimal compared with the advertising time bought on traditional broadcasting, cable television was building momentum as a viable advertising medium. Indeed, CBS and ABC—longtime foes of cable television—announced the formation of their own cable networks, scheduled to be operational in 1981.

Small-circulation special interest magazines continued to proliferate, while many larger publications found it increasingly difficult to maintain circulation. As a result of pressure from agencies and advertisers alike, these larger publications were forced to institute "floating" rate cards tied to short-term changes in circulation figures.

Volume. In 1980, advertisers increased media expenditures slightly to $55,300,000,000, a 10.8% increase from the previous year but only 2.4% greater than the 1979 gain. Nearly one third ($16,100,000,000) of the total went to newspaper advertising, a 10.3% increase over 1979. Total television outlays rose by 13.7% to $11,600,000,000, including $5,200,000,000 on network (up 15.5%) and $3,200,000,000 on national spot (up 14.3%) advertising. In terms of year-to-year gains, however, local television (up 14.3% to $3,200,000,000), direct mail (up 11.9% to $7,500,000), and business publication (up 6.3% to $1,700,000,000) were the big winners in 1980. The biggest losers in 1980, compared with 1979, were magazines (up 10.3% to $3,200,000,000), radio (up 8.8% to $3,700,000,000), and outdoor advertising ($600,000,000, no increase). Miscellaneous advertising, such as skywriting, rose by 9.2%, a healthy increase for this category.

Canada. With a growth rate of 11%, only slightly ahead of the nation's inflation rate, the Canadian advertising industry also showed the effects of the economic recession. The industry continued to regulate itself, establishing a task force to address the problem of sexual stereotyping in advertising. Media advertising rates increased by 11.4% overall, bringing $3,400,000,000 in spending. Newspapers accounted for the largest share with $1,100,000,000, 9% higher than in 1979. Television suffered from higher rates and tighter advertising budgets and increased by only 13%, to $565,000,000. Radio advertising, however, grew by 15% to $396,000,000, and magazines showed the strongest increase, up 21% to $121,000,000. Weekend supplement revenues of $36,000,000 rose by 7%, compared with 67% the year before.

EDWARD H. MEYER
Grey Advertising Inc.

The Afghan seat at the Conference of Islamic States, held in January 1980, is vacant. The organization suspended Afghanistan as a member in response to the Soviet invasion of the central Asian land.

UPI

AFGHANISTAN

The year 1980 was one of trauma and travail for Afghanistan. The massive Soviet invasion of December 1979 led to a popular uprising which grew ever more violent as 1980 progressed. More than 85,000 Red Army troops entered Afghanistan and soon were enmeshed in direct combat operations as the Afghan army was reduced by defections to the mujahidin (freedom fighters) and by desertions.

International Developments. The Soviet invasion of a nonaligned Third World country produced immediate worldwide reverberations. On Jan. 7, 1980, in the United Nations, the Security Council considered Resolution S/462 condemning the Soviet invasion and demanding immediate withdrawal. All members except East Germany voted in favor. The USSR, of course, vetoed it. In the General Assembly, where there is no veto, on January 15 Resolution ES/6-2 condemning the USSR passed by a resounding 104-vote majority, with 18 opposed and 18 abstentions. The USSR was supported only by its Eastern European satellites and its Third World client states. Following these UN actions all Western nations and Japan withdrew their ambassadors from Kabul. The Conference of Islamic States, held January 27–29, condemned the USSR for its invasion, demanded immediate withdrawal of Soviet troops from Afghanistan, and suspended Afghanistan as a member. It also decided to hold an extraordinary session in May to consider further action.

The USSR disregarded this international pressure. It claimed to be in Afghanistan legally pursuant to the Soviet-Afghan treaty of friendship signed on Dec. 5, 1978, under which Soviet intervention could be requested by the Afghan government. This claim ignored the fact that President Nur Mohammed Taraki's right to sign the treaty was questionable since he recently had seized power in a bloody coup in which Soviet complicity was suspected. Taraki himself had

been deposed and assassinated by Hafizullah Amin in September 1979 and there was no evidence that Amin had requested Soviet intervention. In fact there was considerable evidence to the contrary and the first action of the invading Soviets in December 1979 was to assassinate Amin and install a Soviet puppet, Babrak Karmal, in his place. Nevertheless, in all international forums the Soviets took the position that they were in Afghanistan legally to help the Afghan government repel invaders trained and equipped by Pakistan, China, the United States, and Israel.

American condemnation of the invasion went beyond the verbal chastisement of the international community. On Jan. 4, 1980, President Carter declared a grain embargo, banned exports to the USSR of sophisticated technology, curtailed Soviet fishing privileges in U.S. waters, delayed the opening of Soviet-American consular offices, and suggested a possible boycott of the Moscow Olympic Games. The president, who earlier decided to ask the Senate to delay consideration of SALT II, urged all countries to support these sanctions against the USSR. Carter also described the Soviet action as the most dangerous challenge to world peace since World War II and in his annual State of the Union Message on January 23 enunciated the Carter Doctrine, which specified that threats to the Persian Gulf region challenged the vital interests of the United States and would be met with force.

The American sanctions were only partially effective because they were not supported wholeheartedly by other countries or by American farmers. European allies felt the United States had overreacted, imperiling détente. A number of countries ignored the Olympic boycott and participated in the Summer Olympic Games in Moscow. American farmers opposed the grain embargo and were joined by some political leaders. Thus, American response was diluted and could not change the Soviet decision to occupy Afghanistan. The strong reaction in China to the invasion and the subsequent Chinese-American statements of closer cooperation with hints of military ties, combined with a visit to China in January by Defense Secretary Harold Brown, probably worried the Soviets far more than the condemnations of the international community.

Regional Developments. Within Afghanistan the Soviets soon experienced difficulties. Their hope that the new puppet Babrak Karmal government would be able to reconcile the Khalq and Parcham factions of the People's Democratic Party of Afghanistan (PDPA) was not fulfilled. Taraki and Amin had shattered the fragile party unity by purging Parcham members, including Karmal. The Soviets hoped that a reunited party would provide a stable government acceptable to the Afghan people and that popular insurgency would thus come to an end. They grossly underestimated the intensity of Afghan factionalism and the hatred of the Afghan people for the Communist invaders and their puppets.

The Khalqi faction bitterly opposed the new domination of Karmal's Parchamis and there were frequent partisan murders within the PDPA. Karmal's attempt to replace Khalqi army officers resulted in desertions of entire army units. Many joined the mujahidin, taking their Soviet weapons with them. The Afghan people rejected the Karmal government and the insurgency grew. Resistance was most intense and effective in the remote mountainous areas but even in large cities popular demonstrations became widespread. On several occasions Afghan troops and police refused to fire on the people and Soviet troops had to intervene, increasing popular hatred of the invaders. On at least one occasion in Kabul Soviet troops killed demonstrating school children, including young girls. In the countryside Soviet troops controlled only the large towns and main roads but were constantly under attack by bands of mujahidin who often controlled the countryside at night.

The growing insurgency was accompanied by a mass migration of refugees into Iran and Pakistan. Mostly women, children, and old men crossed the borders. By midsummer it was a flood of more than 1 million refugees that swept along the Pakistan border. This created serious economic and political problems for Pakistan, and had all the possibilities of becoming another Palestine situation. The problem was compounded by the establishment of mujahidin resistance headquarters in Peshawar near the Afghan border. The mujahidin groups were fragmented politically into factions ranging from extreme Muslim fundamentalists to secular socialists. The principal groups based in Pakistan were:

1. *Afghan National Liberation Front* led by Iman Seghbatullah Mujjaddedi, a well-known religious leader;

2. *Islamic Party* (Hizb-i-Islami) led by Gulbuddin Hekmatyar;

3. *National Front for the Islamic Revolution of Afghanistan* led by Sayed Ahmed Gailani;

4. *Jamaait-i-Islami Afghanistan* led by Burhanuddin Rabani;

5. *Islamic Party of Afghanistan* (Hizb-i-Islami-i-Afghanistan) led by Maulavi Mohammad Yunus Khales;

6. *Islamic Movement* (Harekat-Islami Afghanistan) led by Sheikh Mohammad Assef Mohseni; and

7. *Afghanistan Social Democratic Party* led by Mohammed Amin Wakman.

Various attempts during the year to unite these disparate groups failed. A temporary alliance was put together to represent the resistance at the Islamic Conference held in May. It was joined by all major groups except Hekmatyar's *Hizb-i-Islami*. The alliance, under the name of Islamic Alliance for the Liberation of Afghanistan, was headed by Ghulman Abdul Rasoul Sayaf and was given official status at the Islamic Conference by incorporating it into the official Iranian delegation. A further effort to achieve unity was made at the same time by convening a *Loya Jirgah* (Grand Tribal Assembly) in Peshawar. Although it is an ancient and revered institution, the Jirgah, attended by 916 chiefs, many coming from inside Afghanistan, failed in the attempt led by Mohammed Omar Babrakzai to organize a government in exile.

The presence of so many refugees and political resistance groups in Pakistan led to intense Soviet political pressure on that country and to frequent violations of Pakistani airspace by Soviet combat aircraft. Pakistan, fearing it might be next on the invasion list, asked the United States for assistance. The United States offered very limited military and economic aid because of Congressional resistance and India's opposition. In February a mission headed by National Security Adviser Zbigniew Brzezinski tried to explain the situation to Pakistan President Zia ul-Haq, who rejected the American offer as "peanuts" and decided it would merely provoke Soviet hostility without increasing Pakistan's security. Meantime, the intolerable burden of the Afghan refugees was somewhat lightened by American, international, and private aid. A substantial number of Afghan refugees also moved into Iran and some minor resistance groups were headquartered there. Despite the internal turmoil in Iran, Iranian leaders voiced support for the Afghan mujahidin and the Ayatollah Khomeini himself publicly and strongly condemned Soviet intervention.

Late 1980 Outlook. Soviet tactics and intentions had become clearer by the end of the year. In the first invasion wave Central Asian Muslim reservist troops were used extensively but soon were replaced by non-Asian regulars following a number of desertions and fraternization with the Afghan resistance. Initial Soviet military tactics featured heavy armored columns expecting to crush resistance by sheer weight of weaponry. By spring it was evident that these tactics had failed and that the Afghan army had become unreliable. The Soviets withdrew their heavy units amidst a barrage of propaganda announcing a partial withdrawal. But soon the heavy units were replaced by lighter combat formations supported by new armored helicopters. Although more effective this new approach still could not cope with the hit-and-run tactics of classic guerrilla warfare. The Soviets then resorted to massive reprisals against noncombatants, destruction of entire villages, crops, and livestock aimed at starving the resistance through a scorched earth policy. Experiments with chemical warfare, cluster bombs, new combat rifles, and other previously unknown weapons showed that the Soviets were using Afghanistan as a guinea pig for weapons testing. In addition the Soviets attempted to create tribal strife by infiltrating agents into the resistance groups and paying large bribes to dissident chiefs. More ominously, to prevent villagers from aiding the mujahidin, atrocities and massacres were committed. In one documented case in the village of Kerala, the entire population of 1,200 was machine gunned and buried with bulldozers. The Karmal government also offered amnesty to all "rebels" if they ceased resistance. By year's end all these tactics and ruses had failed. The harsh winter brought a lull in the fighting and doubts were expressed in some quarters whether the mujahidin could overcome arms and food shortages and survive to fight again in the spring. The principal com-

plaint of all mujahidin groups was that no country was supplying them with the arms they needed to combat the Soviets. Throughout the year the mujahidin had to rely almost exclusively on captured weapons or purchases of antiquated arms in the Pakistani bazaars. Behind the reluctance to supply effective weapons to the mujahidin seemed to lie a fear of Soviet reaction, a desire not to escalate the conflict, and a feeling that the mujahidin were too disunited and their cause hopeless.

This lack of confidence in the mujahidin resulted in a trend toward seeking a political rather than a military solution. Early in the year the British, with U.S. support, had suggested to the Soviets a plan for "neutralization" of Afghanistan. Later, in May, the Islamic Conference, while condemning the Soviet invasion, appointed a special committee consisting of the foreign ministers of Pakistan and Iran and the secretary general of the conference and charged them with seeking a political solution. The special committee met in Switzerland in June and invited all parties to attend. The USSR and the Karmal government declined. Only the mujahidin sent representatives. On June 22–23 at the economic summit meeting in Venice, the heads of the seven industrial countries, while again condemning the Soviet occupation, discussed possible political solutions. The same month, during a state visit in Belgrade, President Carter indicated he would support a political solution which would provide international security guarantees for the USSR and to a truly nonaligned Afghan government. The Soviets rejected all overtures

Although poorly equipped militarily, the freedom fighters managed to hold off the Soviets.

Steve McCurry, Liaison

Throughout the year, many Afghans took refuge in Iran. At right, Afghan students in Tehran stage a protest against Soviet intervention in their homeland.

for a political settlement, stating that their withdrawal was contingent on the cessation of all help to the mujahidin and the establishment of a secure Communist government in Kabul.

Parallel with these offers of a political settlement international pressure on the USSR to cease its aggressions in Afghanistan continued during the year. At a special meeting of NATO foreign and defense ministers in May, the Allies decided to bolster their defenses and the delegates made it clear this action was a direct response to Soviet aggression in Afghanistan. Later that month U.S. Secretary of State Edmund Muskie met with Foreign Minister Andrei Gromyko in Vienna and reiterated American opposition to the Soviet action in Afghanistan. In September demands for Soviet troop withdrawal were voiced by the participants at the 16-nation Asian and Pacific Commonwealth Nations conference in New Delhi. Even India reluctantly approved the resolution. In November the Soviets again were subjected to criticism from all the Western delegates to the Madrid conference reviewing the Helsinki accords.

In spite of this widespread international condemnation the USSR refused to budge from Afghanistan. In fact, by year's end it was evident that the Soviets were preparing for a long stay. Permanent barracks were being built. Logistical facilities were assuming an air of permanence. Domination of all Afghan government departments by Soviet advisers was clearly visible. The process of structuring the entire Afghan educational system along Communist ideological lines was well under way. Soviet combat units had for all intents and purposes replaced Afghan troops in the field and according to reports many Afghan units had been disarmed. The only remaining question was whether the Soviets would maintain present troop levels and dig in for a long and costly counterinsurgency war or whether they would try for a knockout blow involving dramatic escalation of force levels.

International opposition to the Soviet occupation was weakened by an extended debate between those who saw in the Soviet invasion part of a master plan to dominate the oil-rich Persian Gulf region and others who viewed the Soviet move as part of a defensive strategy against "encirclement." The future of the mujahidin resistance movement depended on the resolution of this debate. Most military experts had predicted that the invincible Red Army would crush the freedom fighters in a matter of weeks. But the Afghans refused to be overcome and with inferior weapons, mostly captured from Afghan troops or from the Soviets themselves, they fought the Red Army to a year-long stalemate. As 1980 came to a close the fierce and couragous resistance by the Afghans earned the world's admiration. It also caused most of the Third World countries to view the USSR in a new and far less favorable light. It bought precious time for the Western alliance to prepare its diplomatic counteroffensive and to build up its defense forces around the Persian Gulf region and became a significant factor in inhibiting other Soviet adventures.

LEON B. POULLADA
Northern Arizona University

AFGHANISTAN · Information Highlights

Official Name: Democratic Republic of Afghanistan.
Location: Central Asia.
Area: 250,000 sq mi (647 497 km²).
Population (1980 est.): 15,900,000.
Chief Cities (1980 est.): Kabul, the capital, 800,000; Kandahar, 230,000; Herat, 150,000.
Government: *Head of state and government,* Babrak Karmal, president and premier (took power Dec. 1979). *Policymaking body*—35-member Revolutionary Council.
Monetary Unit: Afghani (44.50 afghanis equal U.S.$1, Sept. 1980).
Manufactures (major products): Textiles, cement, carpets.
Agriculture (major products): Wheat, cotton, fruit and nuts, karakul pelts, wool, mutton.
GNP (1979 est., U.S.$): $2,900,000,000.
Foreign Trade (1979, U.S.$): *Imports,* $328,000,000; *exports,* $429,000,000.

AFRICA

For Africa, 1980 was a year of hope mixed with despair. The continent staggered with more than 4.2 million refugees, or 45% of the world's homeless, the highest number on any land mass. They were driven by cruel combinations of war, political repression, drought, and starvation. This human tragedy was most profoundly felt in Africa's Horn, where 1.5 million nomads fled Ethiopia's Ogaden region for Somalia in response to severe drought and a three-year war of attrition between Ethiopia and Somalia.

A new, crippling drought, reminiscent of the one in 1973, extended from Mauritania to the Nile and across the Horn. It triggered massive malnutrition and uncontrollable migration. By October, at least 12 million people, more than half of them children, suffered from famine in Somalia, Ethiopia, Uganda, and Djibouti, according to a United Nations Children's Fund report.

Political repression in Namibia (South-west Africa), Guinea, and Zaire forced tens of thousands to seek refuge in neighboring countries, straining their hosts' own food resources. To compound the problem, Africa has the world's highest population growth rates, exceeding 3.4% per year in several countries according to another UN study. Increasing numbers of formerly self-sufficient nations found themselves unable to meet their people's minimum caloric requirements and were forced to spend precious public revenue importing food from the West and in some cases from South Africa. Moreover, the escalating cost of imported oil contributed further to Africa's growing dependence on the outside world for its survival. By late October, 17 of the 26 countries facing severe food shortages were in Africa.

Simultaneously, most countries suffered deepening balance of payments deficits, negative growth rates, and mounting external debt owed to banks, corporations, and government agencies. In October the African Development Bank responded by shifting its aid priorities from development projects to stimulating food production. The World Bank and the International Monetary Fund (IMF) also pledged to assist members whose balance of payments problems were caused by higher oil prices. The World Bank would henceforth place greater emphasis on aid programs to countries lacking oil.

On the bright side of the energy coin, Africa's continuing search for uranium and oil led to significant discoveries in 1980. New uranium deposits were found in Zambia, Chad, Niger, and the Central African Republic. And there were important oil finds in Chad, Sudan, Gabon, and Madagascar. The Ivory Coast started producing its own oil.

But Africa groaned under the persistent problem of disease control. A viral disease, called Rift Valley fever, that devastates livestock and blinds humans, had spread the length of the continent. Immunization programs were grossly inadequate. There was also a greater incidence of malaria and rinderpest, particularly in Zimbabwe and southern Angola where guerrilla warfare prevented health teams from operating. Balanced against these outbreaks were successful efforts by UNESCO and UNICEF to control yellow fever, smallpox, and measles.

On the political front, 1980 witnessed peace and continuing war. In October Nigeria ended its first year under democratic civilian rule since 1966. Peace came to Zimbabwe, which became

Suhas, Photoreporters

A UN agency estimated that 12 million Africans were suffering from famine in 1980. Ugandans (left), living in the aftermath of the Idi Amin regime, particularly were affected.

an independent multiracial nation after seven years of debilitating civil war. However, racial violence increased in South Africa and Namibia, and war in Eritrea sputtered on. Also, war intensified in the Western Sahara and in the Ogaden.

A glimmer of hope and a sense of renewal was brought to Africa's approximately 53 million Roman Catholics with an 11-day tour by Pope John Paul II. John Paul addressed crushing throngs in Zaire, the Congo, Kenya, Ghana, Upper Volta, and the Ivory Coast and urged mass participation in political life.

WESTERN SAHARA: SLAVES, GUNS, AND PHOSPHATES

Mauritania's pro-Western President, Lt. Col. Mohammed Mahmoud Ould Luly, was overthrown in a January coup. His successor, Prime Minister Lt. Col. Mohammed Khouna Ould Haidala, proved less sympathetic to Morocco on the issue of Western Sahara and aligned his country more closely to the Polisario movement and the more radical Islamic nations. By abolishing the institution of slavery, he launched a social revolution in the caste-oriented country. For centuries, many desert Berbers had held Africans of sub-Saharan ancestry under conditions of benign servitude and had denied them full participation in the political and economic life of Mauritania.

In the Western Sahara, warfare escalated between the forces of Morocco's King Hassan II and guerrillas of the Polisario Front. In 1979, Mauritania relinquished all claims to the Western Sahara and withdrew from the war. The conflict soon strained Morocco's resources; and the United States, Hassan's traditional ally, agreed to resupply the kingdom with arms. For the United States, this represented a major foreign policy reversal. The Carter administration rationalized that greater military support would put Hassan in a stronger position to negotiate with Polisario and Algeria. Meanwhile, the Polisario Front, based in neighboring Algeria, received fresh shipments of Soviet-made weapons via Libya. Polisario is fighting for an independent Western Sahara. Both the United Nations and the Organization of African Unity (OAU) support its quest for the right of self-determination. The Western Sahara is a barren sparsely-populated though phosphate-rich former Spanish territory that was annexed by Morocco and Mauritania in 1975.

WEST AFRICA: MILITARY AND GREEN REVOLUTIONS

The political stability of West Africa was shaken on April 12, when, in Liberia, army enlisted men staged a predawn coup. President William R. Tolbert, Jr., was assassinated and replaced by a politically inexperienced 28-year-old master sergeant, Samuel K. Doe. Pennsylvania-sized Liberia, with 1.9 million people, had enjoyed political stability and civilian rule since its

Giansanti, Sygma

Dancers welcome John Paul II to Ghana. The pontiff spent May 2–10 in Africa, visiting 6 countries.

establishment as an independent republic in 1847. Tolbert's regime had been weakened in April 1979 by popular riots against food-price hikes which led to the killing of 40 demonstrators by government forces. The April 1980 coup was followed by treason trials and the execution by firing squad of many government officials.

In Guinea-Bissau, President Luiz de Almeida Cabria, who favored union with the Canary Islands, was overthrown in November. Upper Volta's president also was removed in a coup.

In Chad, a 14-year-old civil war intensified early in the year, with deepening French and Libyan involvement. Chad has been in a virtual state of war since its independence from France in 1960. It was initially a conflict between Christian and animist blacks in the south and northern Arab and Berber Muslims. The situation became more convoluted from 1979 after the ousting of President Félix Malloum, a Christian southerner, by two Muslim military figures. One of them, Goukouni Oueddei, emerged as president; the other, Hissène Habré, as defense minister. Together, they constituted a dyarchy. The power-sharing arrangement did not work and they resorted to fighting. Oueddei is closely aligned to Libya's radical ruler, Col. Muammar el-Qaddafi. Habré receives support from France. In October, under OAU auspices, representatives of the two Chadian leaders agreed on conditions for a cease-fire. The country remained deeply divided, and it was uncertain if the cease-

Fighting continued between the forces of Morocco's King Hassan and guerrillas of the Polisario Front, which is seeking an independent Western Sahara. Hassan's troops marched into the Western Sahara toward confrontation with the Polisario (left).

Spengler, Sygma

fire would endure. Fighting reportedly stopped in December.

By contrast, the process of economic, political, and ethnic unification in neighboring Nigeria accelerated. The federal relationship between the central government and the 19 states was strengthened under the moderate and pragmatic leadership of President Alhaji Shehu Shagari. To achieve self-sufficiency in food within five years, the Shagari regime launched an ambitious crash program in agricultural development, called the "Green Revolution." The government pledged to give major priority to the agricultural sector. The Green Revolution succeeds "Operation Feed the Nation," a similar program, initiated by the former military government, which failed.

Nigeria's booming economy is fueled primarily by its petroleum revenues. By midyear, oil accounted for 95% of the country's exports and 92% of the government's revenue. President Shagari visited the United States in October, amid growing disparity in trade between the two nations. The United States opened fiscal 1980 with a $7,200,000,000 trade deficit with Nigeria, larger than with any nation except Japan. A 1981 deficit of $11,000,000,000 was projected.

Nigerian-American educational and cultural ties were strengthened in 1980 with the arrival of more than 3,000 students for advanced studies in American universities. They complement nearly 30,000 Nigerian students presently in the United States. At the same time, an art exhibition entitled "Treasures of Ancient Nigeria: Legacy of 2000 Years" toured Detroit, San Francisco, New York, and Washington. It was highly acclaimed by Western art critics and was to go to Atlanta, New Orleans, Los Angeles, and Canada, as well as to the Soviet Union, Bulgaria, and Belgium. It was considered the most significant exhibition of Nigerian art to go on international tour and symbolizes a growing global recognition of Africa's rich artistic heritage.

The year 1980 also brought greater recognition of an ecological time bomb ticking away in Africa's tropical forests. The forests of the Ivory Coast are being depleted at the rate of 1.2 million acres (486 000 ha) a year. Deforestation already has led in Kenya and the Ivory Coast to soil impoverishment and erosion and, say some experts, to climatic changes. Wood is today a major export in the Ivory Coast and a major source of fuel in Kenya. But like most African countries, there was no government crash program of reforestation. In 1980, the Ivory Coast launched a huge reforestation campaign to replant 50,000 acres (20 250 ha) over a five-year period. It was expected to be a model for other African nations.

THE HORN OF AFRICA: AN EMPTY CORNUCOPIA

The war for the Ogaden, sputtering for two decades, heated up in 1980. Somalia increased its military support for the Western Somali Liberation Front, which since the mid-1960s has fought a guerrilla war to free the Ogaden and its Somali ethnic majority from Ethiopian rule. Somalia's President Mohammed Siad Barre is of Ogaden origin and would like to see the region annexed to Somalia. Ethiopia fears that this would encourage other provinces to secede and might lead to the disintegration of the nation. This war of attrition has led to enormous human suffering for the peoples of the Ogaden and has devastated the fragile economies of Ethiopia and Somalia. Foreign powers appear to be the only beneficiaries. Soviet and Cuban personnel, arms, and equipment, in Ethiopia since late 1977, have bolstered Ethiopian troops garrisoned in the Ogaden's major towns. Ethiopia's army of more than 200,000 men is black Africa's largest. They are pitted against nearly 22,000 guerrillas, operating from remote haunts. Though Ethiopia and Somalia have not officially declared war on each other, it is evident that the conflict centers on the two countries. Somalia, short on weapons and hard pressed to feed the Ogaden refugees, turned in 1980 to the United States for support.

EAST AFRICA: INTO THE MIDDLE EAST CAULDRON

Somalia approached the Carter administration at an opportune moment. With the deepening crisis in the Middle East, the western Indian Ocean began to assume greater strategic significance in the eyes of the West, particularly the United States. The United States reeled in fear and frustration from the seizure of American embassy officials by Iranian revolutionaries in Tehran and from the deteriorating political situation on the post-shah Persian Gulf. The overthrow of the pro-Western shah by a xenophobic Muslim theocracy left a power vacuum in the region. All approaches to the Gulf had to be protected and the Carter administration prepared to ask Congress for greater military and economic assistance to Kenya and Somalia in hopes of securing from those countries expanded access to ports and airfields. In January, President Carter boldly announced that the United States was prepared to employ military force, if necessary, to safeguard "vital" Western interests in the Persian Gulf. This so-called Carter Doctrine was a signal for a more aggressive policy in the western Indian Ocean. In the same month, American naval strength in that zone grew to 25 ships, including three aircraft carriers. American concerns for security in the Middle East and its sea approaches was heightened by the Soviet invasion of Afghanistan in December 1979. The Carter administration organized a Rapid Deployment Force (RDF), bolstered its naval and communications presence on Diego Garcia island off the East African coast, and sought access to facilities in Somalia and Kenya. The visit of Kenya President Daniel arap Moi to Washington in February opened the way for such access. Kenya decided to move militarily closer to the United States. In August, Somali President Siad Barre offered Carter a similar package of air and port facilities in return for sales of American arms and economic aid. The exchange, however, encountered stiff Congressional opposition, led by Rep. Stephen J. Solarz (D-NY) and the Congressional Black Caucus. Fears were expressed that the military equipment might be used in Somalia's war with Soviet-supplied Ethiopia. (*See also* feature article, page 28.)

In neighboring Uganda, the political situation steadily deteriorated as the landlocked, starving nation faced government paralysis. In a bloodless coup on May 11, President Godfrey L. Binaisa and his civilian administration were replaced by a six-member military commission. In June, Tanzanian President Julius Nyerere, whose army was still stationed in Uganda, convened a summit meeting in Arusha, Tanzania. It aimed to discuss the prospect of democratic elections for a new Ugandan government. Little was accomplished, because of strained relations among Tanzania, Kenya, and Uganda. Feuding among Uganda's political parties also impeded the quest for restoration. Former President Milton Obote and his Uganda People's Congress Party (UPC) were locked in a power struggle with three other parties, who fear UPC domination in the planned parliament. Elections were held in December and Obote's party emerged with a parliamentary majority. Although a commonwealth group observed the voting and called it fair, the defeated Democratic Party charged fraud. Nyerere welcomed the results and said that Obote's victory would lead to new East African cooperation.

CENTRAL AFRICA: DEBTS, DEVALUATIONS, DETENTIONS

Central Africa was a region of fragile political stability in the face of economic uncertainty. Angola's Marxist government survived the death in 1979 of its founder and president, Agostinho Neto, underwent a major administrative restructuring, and expanded its trade with Brazil and capitalist Western Europe. Angola's President José Eduardo dos Santos was most responsible for establishing economic contacts with the West. The country's stagnant economy was given a further boost with the reopening of the Benguela railway, for the first time since civil war began in 1975. Petroleum and other mineral exports to the United States continued, despite American refusal to grant diplomatic recognition until the removal of Cuba's military presence. Angola has argued that Soviet military equipment and Cubans are needed to protect the country's southern flank from persistent cross-border South African raids, emanating from Namibia, and to prosecute the civil war against South African–armed guerrillas under Jonas Savimbi's Union for the Total Independence of Angola (UNITA).

In Zaire, the Sese Seko Mobutu regime resisted IMF efforts to manage the country's mounting deficits and debt repayment problems. By midyear, Zaire was more than $6,400,000,000 in debt, inflation approached 200%, and real wages had fallen below 1910 levels. Several devaluations brought little improvement. Food imports from South Africa increased as the nation, with a deteriorating transportation infrastructure, found itself unable to feed itself. A major cabinet reshuffle in January was followed seven months later by the appointment of the able Nguza Karl-I-Bond as prime minister. Nevertheless, power remained firmly in President Mobutu's hands. In May, Amnesty International brought attention to gross human rights violations, especially arbitrary arrests, torture, and detentions without trial. Though some improvements followed, corruption continued.

Only Gabon showed signs of real economic growth. Per capita income rose to $4,713, as contrasted with a continent average of $490. Most of the wealth resulted from oil exports.

SOUTHERN AFRICA: FREEDOM AND TURMOIL

Zimbabwe's independence under black majority rule stands out as the year's major event in southern Africa. A cease-fire in January ended seven years of civil war between the Rhodesian government of Prime Minister Ian Smith and two guerrilla movements, the Zimbabwe African People's Union (ZAPU) and the Zimbabwe African National Union (ZANU), under the respective leaders, Joshua Nkomo and Robert Mugabe. Two months later, in an upset electoral victory, Mugabe's ZANU won 57 of 80 black seats in the 100-member legislature. Constitutionally, 20 seats are reserved for whites. But ZANU candidates won 63% of the 2.7 million black votes, giving them an overall legislative majority.

As prime minister, Mugabe was immediately confronted with the awesome tasks of national unification and reconstruction. From the start, the approach of this Marxist former guerrilla was conciliatory, pragmatic, and moderate. He appointed white and African opponents to a few cabinet posts and refused to follow his party's demands for the nationalization of all lands and businesses. He also reopened the borders with Zambia and Mozambique but continued to trade with South Africa. Great Britain on April 17 formally transferred sovereignty to the new multiracial regime.

Independence touched off a revolution of rising expectations among Africans, expressed in wildcat strikes for higher wages. In June, the government banned illegal industrial strikes in an effort to reduce the growing labor unrest. Workers grudgingly returned to their jobs. Mugabe also had to face growing violence from disaffected black nationalists, especially from within his own party, ZANU. His more radical wing accused him of moving too slowly in building a socialist state and of identifying too closely with local white interests. The situation was complicated in August when popular radical party leader, Manpower Planning and Development Minister Edgar Z. Tekere, was arrested and charged with murdering a white farm manager. (He was acquitted late in the year.) In addition, more than 22,000 former guerrillas remained in scattered camps, waiting impatiently to be resettled and retrained. By October, a growing number of them had resorted to raiding villages and farms for food and booty. As public security deteriorated, white emigration soared. The economic picture remained uncertain.

Neighboring South Africa was also rocked by labor unrest and economic uncertainty. The year opened with a crippling strike at Ford Motor Company's Port Elizabeth plant. Overnight, a black labor organizer, Thozamile Botha, became a national hero in the eyes of the nonwhite industrial workers. On June 1, the banned African National Congress (ANC) launched sabotage attacks on fuel installations. Black nationalists had

The new government of independent Zimbabwe consists of a president, premier, and 21-member cabinet.

Campbell, Sygma

Colorfully attired members of the South West Africa People's Organization (SWAPO), whose aim is an independent Namibia, attend a rally in Windhoek.

Wide World

thus damaged a multimillion-dollar symbol of white South Africa's desperate quest for energy self-sufficiency.

The easing of South Africa's labor laws in 1979 led to escalating black demands for higher wages and for wage parity with whites. By mid-June, more than 7,500 workers had struck 12 key industrial plants, in Durban, Port Elizabeth, and Cape Town. Weeks later, they were joined by 3,500 black municipal workers in Johannesburg, the commercial and mining center of the nation. Black workers everywhere were becoming increasingly frustrated and politicized, in part from the effects of inflation but also because their expectations had been lifted by the government's willingness to allow greater trade union activity. This unrest coincided with demonstrations and school boycotts by mixed-race and Indian students in Cape province.

At the heart of unrest in South Africa was an increasing impatience with white control over the economic and political destinies of the nonwhite majority. Blacks and mixed-race people refused in 1980 to consider any constitutional reform unless it provided for one-man-one-vote and African majority rule. No white political party in South Africa was prepared to go that far.

At the United Nations and the OAU, all eyes were on the continuing crisis in Namibia, a desolate, mineral-rich South African satellite containing about 800,000 blacks and 98,000 whites. Dirk Mudge, chairman of the Council of Ministers, rejected in August a Zimbabwe-style move toward independence from South Africa. Mudge, together with a clique of moderate black and mixed-race leaders, dominate the ruling Democratic Turnhalle Alliance (DTA).

South West Africa People's Organization (SWAPO) guerrillas under Sam Nujoma continued their struggle against South Africa and the DTA. In June, South African units swept into SWAPO bases in southern Angola, killing more than 200 persons. Efforts in September and October to arrange face-to-face talks between South Africa and SWAPO failed. The African front line states fear such discussions would only prolong minority rule. The Western powers, the OAU, and the UN have called for a cease-fire in the 15-year-old war, to be followed by UN-supervised elections. But South Africa is distrustful of the UN, which recognizes SWAPO as the authentic voice of Namibia. A UN conference was planned for early 1981.

In neighboring Botswana, democratic multiracial institutions were flourishing. Sir Seretse Khama, president of Botswana from independence in 1966, died of cancer in July. Vice-President Quett Masire was elected by the National Assembly to replace him. Masire was a close confidant of Khama's and it was expected that the mineral- and cattle-rich nation would continue to pursue a democratic course. Botswana is one of Africa's few multiparty democracies. But the landlocked nation must steer a delicate course between its black African neighbors and South Africa.

In Swaziland on July 22 ailing King Sobhuza II celebrated his 81st birthday and 59 years in power. Sobhuza's paternalistically authoritarian regime continued to cooperate closely with its neighbor, South Africa. However, efforts were under way to increase external trade through Mozambique port in order to lessen the nation's economic dependence on the South Africans.

RICHARD W. HULL, *New York University*

AGRICULTURE

Agriculture and food exports were central topics in international politics. Following crop shortfalls in the early 1970s, the Soviet Union stepped abruptly into the U.S. grain market. U.S. grain and food prices fluctuated widely as the Soviets alternated between large and small purchases. To prevent these wide price swings, the United States and the Soviet Union entered an agreement requiring them to buy at least 6 but no more than 8 million metric tons annually. This agreement expires in 1981. Due to short 1979 crops in the USSR and high production in the United States, the two countries agreed that the USSR might buy an additional 18.3 million metric tons in 1980. However, after the Soviet Union invaded Afghanistan, President Carter proclaimed a partial grain embargo in 1980. Under the embargo the USSR could buy its regularly scheduled quantity, but none of the additional 18.3 million tons.

The embargo's impact was hard to assess. As an alternative, the USSR made contracts for grain with Argentina and some other smaller grain exporters. Canada and Australia limited their exports to the Soviet Union. However, some other countries stepped up exports to the Soviet Union. While U.S. grain companies could not directly export to the USSR, grain companies in Europe could buy from the United States and transship to the Soviet Union. With these leakages in the international market, the grain embargo was less effective in imposing a food shortage on the Soviet Union than in providing a warning that the United States would strongly resist further Soviet imperialism.

The embargo was an important political topic in the United States. Upon declaration of the embargo, President Carter raised grain support prices to farmers and dispatched Secretary of Agriculture Bob Bergland to the corn belt to defuse farmers' ire over the embargo. Farmers initially accepted the embargo on a patriotic basis. However, as grain prices fell later, they generally voiced opinions against the embargo. By late spring, it was politically popular to be against the embargo. The GOP presidential candidate, Ronald Reagan, adopted such a stance.

Domestic Prices and Production. Grain prices in the United States declined considerably in the early part of 1980. This decline was due somewhat to the market psychology of the grain embargo. It also was due in some part to the 1979 record U.S. grain crop. The nation went into the 1979 autumn with good reserves of soil moisture and the potential for a large 1980 crop. However, extremely hot weather over the nation, especially in the South, caused crop prospects to decline as the growing season proceeded. Consequently, while it was still a large crop, 1980 U.S. grain production declined considerably from 1979 levels. The 1980 corn crop was 6.5 billion bushels, down by 16% from 1979. Wheat was 2.4 billion bushels, up 9.5% from 1979; soybeans were 1.8 billion bushels, down 19% from the 1979 record crop of 2.2 billion bushels.

The decline in production of coarse grains and pickup in export demand during the latter half of the year caused rather sharp increases in U.S. grain and livestock prices in the last half of 1980. Grain prices rose to the high levels of the 1970s and corn prices went over $3.00 per bushel for the first time since 1975.

Hog prices had been quite favorable for several years. Farmers increased pig farrowings accordingly. The increased number of hogs caused sharply reduced prices and profits for hogs in

USDA

Bob Bergland drives a tractor on a Maryland farm. During 1980, the U.S. secretary of agriculture had the task of explaining to American farmers President Carter's embargo on grain sales to the USSR.

early 1980. As hog numbers became more balanced with demand and as supplies of certain other meats declined, pork prices recovered to profitable levels in the latter part of the year. Beef prices remained high as a result of herd liquidation, earlier low cattle prices, and the small number of cattle on feed. Poultry prices increased rather sharply after a summer heat wave killed many chickens in the South.

Domestic Policies and Income. During July, the president ordered an increase in federal crop loan prices. Loan rates for 1980 wheat, corn, and soybeans were increased from $2.50 to $3.00, $2.10 to $2.25, and $4.50 to $5.02 per bushel for wheat, corn, and soybeans, respectively. One incentive was to get farmers to put more grain in storage and thus hold it off the market to improve prices.

All three major presidential candidates, Jimmy Carter, Ronald Reagan, and John Anderson paid homage to the family farm but none spelled out specific programs for it. Major new farm policy proposals would await the expiration in 1981 of the 1977 Farm Act.

While farmland prices slackened during a period of high interest rates in March and April, they continued to increase late in the year. The very high price of land hinders young people from entering the farming profession. The tendency toward fewer and larger farms thus is accentuated. With fewer but larger farms, country towns and rural communities are being impacted both economically and socially. Employment and business transactions decline, and human services decrease in number and quality. Concern over these ongoing structural changes caused Secretary of Agriculture Bergland to conduct a series of hearings across the nation. The findings of the hearings were to be used in formulating new agricultural proposals in 1981.

As 1980 closed, it appeared that net farm income would approximate $26,000,000,000. Under more favorable price and production conditions, 1979 net farm income was $31,000,000,000.

World Production and Trade. World grain production in the 1980 crop year was estimated at 1,430,000,000 metric tons, as compared with 1,400,000,000 metric tons in the previous crop year.

Europe was plagued by cold and damp weather during the entire summer. Yields of grains suffered accordingly. The Soviet Union had hoped to harvest a near-record 235 million metric tons of grain, but it appeared late in the year that the harvest would be no more than 200 million tons.

Abnormally dry weather in Canada began in 1979 and extended through the 1980 winter and spring. Rainfall was as much as 50% below normal in western Canada. Drought damage was expected to drop coarse grain production to 33.9 million metric tons, 5.6 million less than in 1978. Wheat production of 15.0 million metric tons,

UPI

Soybean prices plunge at the Chicago Board of Trade after news of the Soviet grain embargo.

24% less than the five-year average, was expected. Oilseed production was reduced about 40% by the poor weather. Because of high reserves, however, it was predicted that Canada would maintain its wheat exports at about normal levels.

Australia was the world's second largest wheat exporter in 1980. It has great potential for expanding its wheat exports. If world wheat demand and price continue to rise sharply, much land devoted to pasture can be shifted to wheat.

Japan's five-year surplus disposal program moved into its second year. Japan subsidized the export of about 850,000 metric tons of rice in reducing its surplus. Japan was scheduled to use 500,000 metric tons of rice as feed in 1980. This would reduce import demands for feed grains, especially corn and sorghum. Livestock production in Japan has been tending to slow down as a result of a slower rate of growth in real income, high grain prices, and depreciation in the value of the yen.

As a result of the U.S. embargo, the Soviet Union was probably able to import about only 34 million of the expected 37.5 million metric tons of grain. Year-end statistics showed some draw-down in livestock numbers. Hogs on state and collective farms were down about 600,000 head as compared with 1979. Sheep and goats were down about 2.6 million head, while cattle were up about 700,000 head. In its new plan for agriculture, Soviet grain production is to average from 238 million to 243 million metric tons per year during 1981–85, as compared with a record

237 million metric tons in 1978. The average during the five-year period 1975–80 was about 208 million tons.

Eastern European agricultural production plans ranged from no growth in East Germany to a 7.2% growth in Czechoslovakia. Hungary put special emphasis on increasing its exports. Except in Rumania, East European countries emphasized faster increases in grain production than in livestock production.

Shortages of feed grains and meat in Poland caused a large midsummer rise in meat and food prices. Polish workers, as they had in 1970 and 1976, resisted these meat-price increases by widespread strikes. They coupled their request for meat-price rollbacks with demands for independent worker unions, television time for church broadcasts, greater freedom of communication, and the release of dissidents from jails. After much political bickering, the worker demands were granted. The government's concessions were considered a great potential gain toward increased political power and freedom for the Polish people under a Communist system.

Other World Regions. China, which had tried to make each geographic segment and sometimes each collective farm self-sufficient, decided to encourage regional specialization. Attempts to expand soybean production continued although past efforts were not very successful. Farmers were given incentives to expand cotton areas. Attempts to increase livestock production continued, with emphasis on pork. Increased incomes from farm incentives and greater imports caused the demand for agricultural products to grow faster than crop production. Led by cotton and soybeans, agricultural imports reached records for the third consecutive year. Corn imports were down slightly, while wheat imports remained about constant.

Most Asian nations had good spring rainfall and appeared to have good, but not record, grain crops. India's wheat crop of about 31 million metric tons was 4 million less than the 1979 record. Rice production improved over 1979. India was to export about 200,000 metric tons of grain due to commitments.

Bangladesh's 1979–80 rice and wheat crops increased about 7% over 1978–79. The government was able to stabilize food supplies during 1978–80 by importing 2.2 million metric tons of grain. Because of a poor rice crop in 1979, South Korea imported $500 million of U.S. commodities. Thailand's rice exports in the early part of the year were at record levels. The Thai government limited rice exports in the last half of the year. The 1980 rice output in Indonesia, a country with a rapidly growing population and large grain imports, may exceed that of 1979 by 3% or more and attain a record level.

Food production in many West African countries may be below that of the early 1970s. At the same time, populations have grown rapidly. Extended droughts, unstable economic and political conditions, civil warfare, and increasing numbers of refugees have brought famine and nearly intolerable conditions to East Africa. Except for Ethiopia, all East African countries were importing corn for food in 1980. Even Zimbabwe, normally a corn exporter, contracted to import corn from South Africa. While Egypt's grain production increased slightly in 1979, it imported $3,500,000,000 worth of grain in 1980.

Inflation and related problems continued to plague countries of West Africa. Also, the increasing costs of imported oil depleted their foreign exchange reserves and substantially increased their cost of food imports.

Food-supply problems were widespread in southern and eastern Africa. Drought affected growing conditions in Zimbabwe, Zambia, Mozambique, Tanzania, Uganda, and Kenya, where grain supplies already were at low levels. A year of poor crops intensified the famine situation facing refugees from the Somali and Ogaden areas.

Early spring weather was somewhat unfavorable in Latin America. Hot midwinter weather curtailed Argentina's grain crop. However, Argentina was able to increase exports to the USSR from 1979 production. Rust sharply reduced Cuba's 1979–80 sugar crop. Sugar production in Central America was estimated to be down about 2% from a year earlier due to rust. Grain imports by Mexico rose sharply in 1980. Imports also rose in Central America, Peru, and Venezuela.

Because of expanded area and favorable weather, Brazil's production of corn, rice, and soybeans increased sharply. The early 1980 harvests of corn and rice were estimated at records of 19.7 million and 9.7 million metric tons, respectively. Soybeans production increased to a new high of 15.2 million tons. A strong expansion in exports of soybeans and soybean meals was expected. A shift of Argentine grain trade to the Soviet Union and civil disturbances disrupted usual trade patterns among Central American Common Market countries. U.S. exports to Latin America were up sharply from 1979. U.S. wheat exports, especially to Chile, Colombia, Peru, and Caribbean nations, were large. U.S. feed grain exports to Latin American countries also rose rapidly.

The Turkish wheat crop increased over the previous year. Consequently, greater exports should allow an improved balance of trade for the country. Imports of food products in Iran remain large. With cessation of U.S. food shipments, Iran's leading grain suppliers became Thailand, Australia, Argentina, and European nations. Israel, Jordan, and Lebanon had improved grain crops but the latter imported an estimated $75 million in grain from the United States. U.S. exports to Saudi Arabia increased over the previous year.

(1 metric ton = 1.102 short tons.)

EARL O. HEADY, *Iowa State University*

ALABAMA

Political landmarks were noted in Alabama during 1980.

Elections. In the presidential primary, President Jimmy Carter and former California Gov. Ronald Reagan won most of their respective party's delegates to the national nominating conventions. Carter officially opened his campaign for reelection with a Labor Day speech at Tuscumbia, in northwest Alabama.

Party primary elections were held early in September. The most notable contests involved the Republican nomination for representative to the U.S. Congress from the sixth district (Birmingham) and nominations by both parties for a seat in the U.S. Senate.

Alabama's sixth district had been represented since 1964 by Republican Congressman John H. Buchanan, Jr. Albert Lee Smith, Jr., challenged the veteran Congressman in the primary and won the Republican nomination. Smith went on to defeat Birmingham City Councilman W.B. "Pete" Clifford (D) in the general election.

Aspirants to the nomination for the Senate position, on the Democratic side, included incumbent Sen. Donald Stewart, who was serving the late Sen. James B. Allen's unexpired term, and Jim Folsom, Jr., a member of the state public utility regulatory commission and son of former Gov. James E. "Big Jim" Folsom. Stewart failed to attain a majority of the votes cast in the first primary and was forced into a run-off election against Folsom. In the run-off primary, held on September 23, Folsom defeated the incumbent senator. In the Republican primary for the Senate seat, former (Democratic) Congressman Armistead Selden, who had recently served as ambassador to New Zealand, faced retired Adm. Jeremiah Denton, of Mobile. Denton, a naval aviator in Vietnam and former prisoner of war, won the Republican nomination in the primary.

At the general election on November 4, Governor Reagan won Alabama's nine electoral votes and Admiral Denton became the first Republican elected to the U.S. Senate in recent Alabama history. Except for Senator Stewart and

Representative Buchanan, Alabama's Congressional delegation remained intact. In the House, the party balance remained at four Democrats and three Republicans, with the latter continuing to represent the major urban areas of Birmingham, Mobile, and Montgomery.

Judicial Appointments. President Carter nominated state Sen. U.W. Clemon and Tuskegee attorney Fred Gray to vacant judgeships on the northern and middle federal district courts. The Senate confirmed Clemon's appointment to the northern district court, and in July he apparently became Alabama's first black federal district judge. Gray's appointment met with complications in the Senate Judiciary Committee and he requested that the nomination be withdrawn. In September, Carter nominated Myron H. Thompson, a Dothan attorney with experience as an assistant attorney general of Alabama, for the position on the middle district court. The Senate quickly confirmed Thompson's appointment and he assumed the judgeship in October.

Also in October, Gov. Forrest (Fob) H. James, Jr., appointed Birmingham attorney Oscar W. Adams, Jr., to a vacancy on the Alabama Supreme Court. Justice Adams is the first black to serve on the state's highest court.

Court Decisions. In 1976 a federal district court ruled unconstitutional Mobile's commission form of government, with at-large elections, on the ground that it was racially discriminatory. The court ordered in its place a mayor-council form of government, with ward elections. In April, the U.S. Supreme Court reversed the order. The Supreme Court invalidated a major provision of Alabama's death penalty in June.

The case of Tommy Lee Hines, a mentally retarded black man convicted of rape, had precipitated a series of racial disturbances during 1978. In March 1980, Alabama's Court of Criminal Appeals ordered a new trial in the case. Later, however, Hines was found incompetent to stand trial and was committed to a mental institution.

JAMES D. THOMAS
The University of Alabama

ALABAMA · Information Highlights

Area: 51,609 sq mi (133 667 km²).

Population (Jan. 1980 est.): 3,791,000.

Chief Cities (1976 est.): Montgomery, the capital, 155,658; Birmingham, 280,544; Mobile, 201,594.

Government (1980): *Chief Officers*—governor, Forrest H. James, Jr. (D); lt. gov., George McMillan (D), *Legislature*—Senate, 35 members; House of Representatives, 105 members.

Education (1979–80): *Enrollment*—public elementary schools, 394,943 pupils; public secondary, 359,238; colleges and universities, 159,784 students. *Public school expenditures* (1978–79), $1,187,150,000 ($1,487 per pupil).

State Finances (fiscal year 1979): *Revenues,* $3,771,000,000; expenditures, $3,558,000,000.

Personal Income (1979): $26,240,000,000; per capita, $6,962.

Labor Force (May 1980): *Nonagricultural wage and salary earners,* 1,360,200; *unemployed,* 135,300 (8.3% of total force).

ALASKA

In an election runaway, Ronald Reagan and other Republican candidates for national office swept Alaska on November 4.

Politics. Incumbent Rep. Don Young (R) of Fort Yukon received nearly 90,000 votes to Kevin (Pat) Parnell's (D) 30,000. Reagan won more than twice as many votes as Jimmy Carter. Libertarian Ed Clark won close to 15,000 votes and ran third. The only close race was for the Senate seat once occupied by Mike Gravel (D). Former state Rep. Clark Gruening, grandson of the late Ernest Gruening, was defeated in the general election by Fairbanks banker Frank Murkowski (R). Murkowski would join Sen. Ted

Alaska's Sen. Stevens and Gov. Hammond, r, listen as Sen. Jackson, l, reviews the Alaska lands bill.

Stevens, who in December was elected majority whip.

The election did not seriously affect the state legislature. However, Fairbanks sent a second Libertarian, Kent Fanning, to join Dick Randolph in the state House. Fanning ranked third among six candidates elected from Fairbanks to the House. Randolph, who was reelected, had long supported the repeal of personal income taxes.

In August, voters narrowly approved creation of a statehood commission, which was charged with reviewing the state's role within the federal union. Widely viewed outside Alaska as a cover for secessionist sentiments, the commission was to examine the statehood act and its implementation and propose lawful changes, if they seem warranted.

State Income Tax Repeal. During 1980, the Alaska legislature passed legislation providing that Alaskan residents who paid state personal income taxes for three years were to be exempt from future income tax and that 1979 taxes would be refunded. Additionally, the legislature ordered that one half the earnings from the permanent fund be distributed to adult Alaskans on the basis of one dividend ($50.00) per year of residency retroactive to Jan. 1, 1959. These actions were challenged by Ronald and Penny Zobel, two-year residents of the state, as unconstitutional residential discrimination. Their argument

was upheld by the Alaska Supreme Court in the case of the income-tax repeal, but the court did not rule in respect to the permanent fund dividend. The Zobels sought and won a Supreme Court order suspending payment of dividends pending outcome of their appeal.

Following the Alaska Supreme Court's decision overturning income tax relief, the Alaska state legislature met in special session and repealed the state personal income-tax law.

Land Withdrawals. After the general election, conservationists in the U.S. Congress decided to seek immediate passage of a bill which they earlier had resisted. The so-called "Tsongas compromise" bill, whose passage by the Senate was

---

ALASKA • Information Highlights

Area: 586,412 sq mi (1 518 807 km²).
Population (Jan. 1980 est.): 405,000.
Chief Cities (1970 census): Juneau, the capital, 6,050; Anchorage, 48,081; Fairbanks, 14,771.
Government (1980): *Chief Officers*—governor, Jay S. Hammond (R); lt. gov., Terry Miller (R). *Legislature*—Senate, 20 members; House of Representatives, 40 members.
Education (1979–80): *Enrollment*—public elementary schools, 48,744 pupils; public secondary, 39,829; colleges and universities, 20,052. *Public school expenditures*, $386,403,000 ($4,261 per pupil).
State Finances (fiscal year 1979): *Revenues*, $1,699,-000,000; *expenditures*, $1,466,000,000.
Personal Income (1979): $4,555,000,000; per capita, $11,219.
Labor Force (May 1980): *Nonagricultural wage and salary earners*, 169,300; *unemployed*, 17,800 (9.4% of total force).

considered by many observers to have contributed to the downfall of Alaska's Sen. Mike Gravel (D), whether because he had failed to prevent its passage or because he had declined to support it along with Sen. Ted Stevens (R) and Gov. Jay Hammond (R). The law sets aside 104.3 million acres (42.2 million ha) of land, much of which will be perpetually preserved from development of renewable or nonrenewable resources: in wilderness areas, wildlife refuges, and in additional national parks and preserves. Among compromises which environmentalists had to accept were $40 million for roads and a considerable allocation for the timber industry in southeastern Alaska. In addition, 149,000 acres (60 000 ha) were excluded from the Misty Fjords to allow development of an important molybdenum deposit. The bill included a so-called "no-more" clause which strips the president of the authority to create national monuments by invoking the 1906 Antiquities Act without Congressional authorization.

Salmon Fishery Strike. For several weeks during the height of the salmon run, boats were idled in a dispute between fishermen and canneries over prices to be paid for the fish. What made the strike especially difficult was the fact that summer 1980 was a major season for salmon. Even with a late start, the catch approached record proportions.

Gas Line. Debate continued over construction of the gas line from Prudhoe Bay to the Midwest via the Alaska Highway. While there was a modest start-up of construction activity during the summer, there continued to be serious disagreement concerning the mode of construction and the proximity of the pipeline to the line transmitting crude oil to Valdez. State Pipeline Coordinator Dr. Charles Behlke expressed concern that the construction project not duplicate errors which led to collapse of the line and oil spills at Atigun Pass in 1979. Much concern was expressed that continued delays would nearly double the cost of construction.

ANDREA R. C. HELMS
University of Alaska, Fairbanks

ALBANIA

As the Albanian regime completed its planning for the 7th Five-Year Plan (1981–1985), it continued to strengthen economic ties with Yugoslavia, which replaced China as Albania's major trading partner.

Politics. In April, the Presidium of the People's Assembly announced several major cabinet changes. Premier Mehmet Shehu relinquished the post of defense minister to Maj. Gen. Kadri Hasbiu. Hasbiu's former post of interior minister was given to Fecor Shehu. Minister of Heavy Industry and Mining Xhafer Spahiu was replaced by Prokop Murra. Spahiu later was named secretary of the presidium of the People's Assembly. Minister of Light Industry and Food Kristaq

Dollaku was replaced by Esma Ulqinaku. In June, Rapo Dervishi was named to head the newly-created ministry of communal economy. The changes apparently were intended to improve the management of the economy and of the military.

In April elections for district and local legislators and judges, only 53 of 1,508,000 voters cast their ballots against regime-endorsed candidates. Government spokesmen called the results a demonstration of overwhelming support for the regime.

Foreign Relations. Despite the ideological differences between them, Albania and Yugoslavia continued to draw closer together. In July, the two countries signed a trade agreement for the years 1981–85. Under the terms of the agreement, the volume of trade between the signatories would total $720,000,000, a considerable increase over the $170,000,000 for the previous five years. Following the death of Yugoslav President Tito (Josip Broz) in May, Albania warned Moscow that it would come to the assistance of Yugoslavia in the event of an attack by the Soviet Union.

Tiranë strongly condemned the Soviet invasion of Afghanistan, terming it another manifestation of Moscow's desire to dominate Central Asia and the Middle East. Albania was equally critical of the buildup of Soviet troops for a possible invasion of Poland, but blamed the tense situation there on the concessions made by the Polish government to the labor movement.

Albania's relations with former ally China continued to deteriorate. Tiranë accused Peking of doing everything possible to provoke a confrontation of the "superpowers" in Europe. The Albanians described the trial of China's "Gang of Four" as a "Chinese comedy" by which the current leadership was attempting to "settle the score" with its erstwhile opponents.

Albania also displayed no inclination to improve its ties with the United States, West Germany, or Great Britain. It continued to champion the cause of the Iranian and Palestinian peoples in their "anti-imperialist struggles."

NICHOLAS C. PANO
Western Illinois University

——— **ALBANIA · Information Highlights** ———

Official Name: People's Socialist Republic of Albania.
Location: Southern Europe, Balkan peninsula.
Area: 11,100 sq mi (28 748 km²).
Population (1980 est.): 2,700,000.
Chief Cities (1975): Tiranë, the capital, 192,000; Shkodër, 62,400; Dürres, 60,000.
Government: *Head of state,* Haxhi Lleshi, president of the Presidium (took office 1953). *Head of government,* Maj. Gen. Mehmet Shehu, premier (took office 1954). *First secretary of the Albanian Party of Labor,* Enver Hoxha (took office 1941). *Legislature* (unicameral)—People's Assembly.
Monetary Unit: Lek (7 lekë equal U.S.$1, 1980—noncommercial rate).
Manufactures (major products): Textiles, timber, construction materials, fuels, semiprocessed minerals.
Agriculture (major products): Corn, sugar beets, wheat, cotton, grapes, potatoes, dairy products.

ALBERTA

In 1980, Alberta marked its 75th anniversary and saw a major crisis develop between the federal and provincial governments over revenue from the province's resources.

Government. In February federal elections, only two Liberals were elected west of Ontario; none in Alberta. As a result of the defeat of the Clark government, an almost-completed federal-provincial agreement on sharing of tax revenues from oil and natural-gas resources was not finalized. Growing Western alienation and confusion respecting further development of Alberta's oil sands and heavy oil deposits resulted. In late October, Canada's Prime Minister Pierre Elliott Trudeau announced a plan to more than double the federal share of oil and gas revenues. In response, provincial Premier Peter Lougheed announced that beginning in February 1981 Alberta would reduce oil and gas deliveries to eastern Canada by 15% over a nine-month period. Support for "Western separatism" showed disturbing popular interest.

Except in Calgary, most incumbent candidates were returned to office in triennial municipal elections in October.

Agriculture. Although forage crops in southern Alberta were adversely affected, widespread drought conditions had little impact on grain production. Wet fall weather delayed harvesting. It was, however, completed in October with some loss of grade. Total cereal production was above average; transportation to markets improved. Cattlemen continued to find financial returns unsatisfactory.

Industry, Business, and Transportation. Calgary and Edmonton experienced phenomenal levels of commercial and industrial construction. Residential building was hampered by high mortgage rates and remained sluggish. Rapid progress was made on Edmonton's Convention Center. Business activity continued buoyant.

Canadian National Railways became sole owner of Northern Alberta Railways. Pacific Western Airline's absorption of Transair proceeded easily. Time Air's takeover of Gateway Aviation gained it new Alberta routes. Calgary began its Light Rail Transit (LRT) system, and Edmonton started on the second leg of its LRT.

Labor. Unrest in public and private sectors exceeded 1979 levels. Unemployment was low.

Anniversary and Miscellaneous. To commemorate Alberta's 75th anniversary, festivals, exhibitions, and publications—not capital schemes which would entail subsequent operating costs—were emphasized. A new encyclopedia for free library distribution was planned.

Development continued on Kananaskis Provincial Park, west of Calgary. Edmonton was chosen as the site of the 1983 World Student Games. The Calgary Flames entered the National Hockey League, and the Edmonton Eskimos won their third consecutive Grey Cup.

JOHN W. CHALMERS, *Concordia College*

ALGERIA

By restructuring the political organs of the ruling National Liberation Front (FLN), President Benjedid Chadli consolidated control over the Algerian government in 1980. The president also launched a new five-year economic plan. Internal unrest by the Berber population presented his one-year-old regime with its most serious challenge. A gambit to boost the export price of liquefied natural gas (LNG) to a parity level with that of crude oil seemed to have failed. And in late October, Algeria's first president, Ahmed Ben Bella, was freed from house arrest.

Politics. Chadli undertook a number of reforms in party and state structures in 1980. A January cabinet reshuffle, in which the two posts of minister-counselor to the presidency were abolished, resulted in the enhancement of the role of the FLN.

A second reshuffle in July followed a June FLN party congress which invested Chadli with the right to designate politburo members. Representing all ruling factions, the politburo's membership was streamlined from 17 to 7, converting it to an advisory council.

Internal Security. Unrest within Algeria's Berber community over the government's Arabization policy erupted in April in the region of Kabylia. The Berbers, the country's largest minority, have been demanding official recognition of their language and culture, while government policy is to make Arabic Algeria's official language.

In April, student strikes and demonstrations over alleged suppression of Berber culture at the University of Tizi-Ouzou gained the support of the local population, who implemented a general strike. Rioting was put down by the security forces. A decision to try 24 people held responsible for the agitation prompted renewed unrest in May. In an effort to defuse the situation, authorities promoted a "democratic dialogue" among the differing language groups.

Economy and Foreign Affairs. Earlier in the year the FLN, in a major policy shift, reduced Algeria's dependence on Western revenue and aid and changed the focus to meeting basic needs by imposing drastic cuts in oil and LNG exports. The move scaled down industry's reliance on assistance from abroad.

Sonatrach, the state-owned oil and gas company, after raising its export price of oil in March and reducing its production and sales, began a campaign to renegotiate its LNG export contracts to align the price of gas with that of oil. By late August, however, the attempt appeared to have failed.

At the June FLN congress, a new five-year plan for the economy was unveiled, recognizing for the first time the importance of the private sector. Earnings from oil and gas exports would be channeled into industry, but some $33 million would be allocated to housing, education, and health. Food production was given a boost by a plan to allow private marketing of goods.

A major earthquake in October destroyed 80% of the town of El Asnam. Emergency aid from various governments poured in to assist in relief and rescue operations.

Foreign Minister Mohamed Benyahia's official visit to France in January to confer with President Valéry Giscard d'Estaing marked a significant thaw in relations between the two nations. Algeria continued to back the Polisario Front in the war in the Western Sahara, but did participate in September in an Organization of African Unity conference on the dispute, which failed to net results. Algeria also acted as an intermediary in the U.S.-Iran hostage crisis.

MARGARET A. NOVICKI, *"Africa Report"*
The African-American Institute

ANGOLA

Economic recovery and improved relations with Western nations existed alongside an increasingly violent border war with South African forces operating from Namibia (South-West Africa).

Domestic Affairs. The transition to the presidency of José Eduardo dos Santos in late 1979 was not only smooth but also marked by peace and order. The ruling *Movimento Popular de Libertação de Angola* (MPLA) has achieved a measure of stability; yet it underwent two cabinet reshuffles in 1980. But in the south its rival, the *União Nacional para Independência Total de Angola* (UNITA), continued to mount raids, which were intended to bolster UNITA's position in the proposed demilitarized zone between Angola and Namibia. The MPLA retaliated by executing several saboteurs.

Economy. Soaring oil revenues from Cabinda's offshore wells, rising world prices for diamonds, and expanding foreign investment accounted for a trade surplus, industrial revival, and large imports of food and machinery. Agriculture, especially in the state sector, continued to drop. Coffee production was down again, and sugar was being imported from Cuba. The *Jornal de Angola* blamed state-owned companies for congested ports and shortages of raw materials for industry. The Central Committee called for more private enterprise to overcome the "worrying financial and economic situation." War in the south damaged farming and commerce.

Foreign Affairs. South Africa increased the scope and intensity of its raids to include Angolan economic and industrial targets. June saw eight battalions cross the border in one strike. Luanda was supporting the South West African People's Organization (SWAPO) which contests Pretoria's control over Namibia. Although peace talks were held under UN auspices, Angola promised retaliation.

Washington still refused diplomatic recognition of the MPLA because of Cuban forces in Angola, but U.S. commercial links multiplied. Tension increased between Luanda and Lisbon when the MPLA nationalized Portuguese shares in the Diamang diamond company. Trade with France increased and OPEC gave aid. Economic relations with the Soviet bloc remained firm. Angola intended to sell oil to East Germany to offset losses from the Soviet Union.

See also AFRICA.

THOMAS H. HENRIKSEN
Hoover Institution on War,
Revolution and Peace

─────── **ANGOLA • Information Highlights** ───────

Official Name: People's Republic of Angola.
Location: Southwestern Africa.
Area: 481,351 sq. mi (1 246 700 km²).
Population (1980 est.): 6,700,000.
Chief Cities (1973 est.): Luanda, the capital, 540,000; Huambo, 89,000; Lobito, 74,000.
Government: *Head of state and government,* José Eduardo dos Santos, president (took office Sept. 1979).
Monetary Unit: Kwanza (46 kwanzas equal U.S.$1, Oct. 1980).
Manufactures (major products): Cement, textiles, fuel oil.
Agriculture (major products): Manioc, coffee, cotton, sisal, tobacco.
GNP Per Capita (1978 est., U.S.$): $300.

ANTHROPOLOGY

The year 1980 again brought new insights and new controversies in physical and cultural anthropology.

Language in Apes. The view that apes have the capacity for speech through the use of visual language symbols was challenged by Herbert S. Terrace and his colleagues at Columbia University. Working for a number of years with a chimpanzee named Nim, Terrace became disillusioned with his lack of progress in teaching the use of language symbols and suspected that there was more imitation on Nim's part than comprehension. After studying videotapes of other researchers, Terrace concluded that there is no evidence that apes can combine visual language symbols, whether of sign language or some other artificial language, to create new meanings. Apes apparently use symbols to satisfy the demands of their trainers in order to obtain a reward. The evidence that apes create sentences can, in each case, be explained by simpler, nonlinguistic processes, particularly the habit of imitating the utterances of teachers, Terrace maintained.

Other investigators, who have been teaching American Sign Language to great apes, insist that apes are capable of true speech. Among these investigators are R. Allen Gardner and his wife, who trained the well-known chimp Washoe; Roger Fouts, who worked with the Gardners and now is at the University of Oklahoma; and Francine Patterson of the Gorilla Foundation near Stanford, CA, who has been training the female gorilla Koko since 1972. Their work is said to have helped in the development of effective new methods for teaching severely retarded human beings.

Primate Ancestor. *Aegyptopithecus,* a monkey-like primate the size of a house cat, which roamed Africa 30 million years ago, was a common ancestor of humans and apes, according to Dr. Elwyn Simons, head of the Duke University Center for the Study of Primate Biology and History. The fossil primate was first identified by Dr. Simons in 1965, when it was found in the Fayum area of Egypt. Since 1977, more than two dozen skeletal fossils have been found at the original site. Dr. Simons' colleagues have confirmed his original identification and further described the form and its significance. Jaw fragments and teeth indicate sexual dimorphism, with males larger in size than females, and a vegetarian diet. The males competed for dominance, causing the formation of social groups. Skull fragments indicate that the creature was active in the daytime. The characteristics are similar to those of later primates whose descendants, some believe, led eventually to humans.

Fossils. More fossil footprints were discovered along the shore of Lake Turkana in northern Kenya. Anna K. Behrensmeyer and Leo F. LaPorte, coleaders of an expedition to study the geology of the region, found the fossils while digging a geological trench. The fossils, dated about 1.5 million years old, apparently were made by either *Homo erectus* or *Australopithecus africanus;* the case was stronger for the former, since its fossils had previously been found in the area. The newly discovered footprints were made by an individual between 5 and 5.5 ft (1.52 and 1.68 m) tall and weighing about 120 lbs (54.4 kg).

Unidentified Creature. At a conference of 200 anthropologists and paleontologists gathered in Peking in December 1979 to commemorate the 50th anniversary of the discovery of Peking Man, Zhou Guoxing, an anthropologist with the Peking Museum of Natural History, reported several sightings of a hairy anthropoid-like creature in the mountainous region of Shennogjia. Many footprints 12 to 16 inches (30.5 to 40.6 cm) were found. Feces, sometimes found beside the footprints and presumed to be from the creature, were analyzed and determined to be from neither a human nor a bear. Hair samples found on trees suggest it is some sort of primate. Zhou described the creature as about 6.5 ft (1.98 m) tall, with wavy red hair. Although it walks upright, its footprints indicate that it has a clumsy gait and no arch. Zhou suggested that it may be a descendant of *meganthropus,* a fossil primate with characteristics of both humans and apes.

Deaths. Two well-known anthropologists died during the year: Gene Weltfish, professor emeritus at Fairleigh Dickinson University and visiting professor at the New School for Social Research; and Gregory Bateson, the anthropologist and philosopher known and admired for his studies of simple societies and western culture.

HERMAN J. JAFFE
Brooklyn College, City University of New York

ARCHAEOLOGY

Laboratory and field work in both hemispheres during 1980 demonstrated that archaeological discoveries are an important source of information not only for anthropologists and historians but for other scientists, such as astronomers, zoologists, and botanists, as well.

EASTERN HEMISPHERE

Ice Age Mammals and Humans. The Soviet Mammoth Patrol saved from thawing a male of the species after it surfaced near the Yuribey River. Body tissues—blood, arteries, internal organs, marrow, skin, and hair—were recovered in good condition. Some of the cells were believed to be still alive and usable for experiments, including cloning. Meanwhile, biochemists at the University of California established the close genealogical relationship between the woolly mammoth and the elephant by isolating and studying the protein albumin from a 40,000-year-old baby mammoth found frozen in Siberia in 1977.

The oldest human artifacts yet found in Britain came to light in excavations by the British

Excavations near the Temple Mount in Jerusalem uncovered the ruins of what may have been part of the palace of King David.

Micha Bar-Am, NYT Pictures

Museum in a cave in the Mendip Hills near Cheddar, Somerset. Calcareous breccias from the Anglian Glaciation (Mindel time) contain flake tools and chipping debris of flints carried in from the Wiltshire Downs, 20 mi (32 km) away. An abundance of bison bones may reflect the diet of these prehistoric hunters. Also found were bones of an early form of water vole, deer, reptiles, and two species not previously known in Britain—the dhole hunting dog and now extinct European jaguar.

Lower Paleolithic Acheulean handaxes found in fluvial sediments nearly 7 m (23 ft) below unconsolidated sands show that during the Pleistocene, perhaps as late as 200,000 years ago, a major river drained the Kiseiba-Dungul Depression, and perhaps the Kharga Depression, into the Nile.

Food Production. Late Pleistocene (16,000 B.C.) hunters and plant gatherers of the Nile Valley used numerous grinding stones, as well as flint hunting implements, in their industry. Carbonized grains from their campfires were identified by U.S., Polish, and Egyptian researchers as barley. Some of the flints likely were sickleblades for harvesting the grain, which may have grown wild. Heavy use of barley helped establish conditions for the subsequent domestication of crops, a widespread process in southern Asia starting about 9,000 B.C.

Although the search for the beginning of food production occupies a major place in prehistoric archaeology, seldom do archaeologists find the remains of a single community in the transition from hunting and gathering to food production. However, on the Bolna River in east central Pakistan, an expedition found in lower level I the remains of a stone age people who hunted gazelles, goats, deer, and the *nilgai* antelope. The upper part of the level shows how they had learned from neighboring peoples to herd cattle, sheep, and goats.

Ancient Oriental Forts. A team from Chicago and Copenhagen, working in the soon-to-be-flooded Hamrin Basin in Northern Iraq, hit upon a circular fortress with a vaulted roof made of mud bricks. Dating from ca. 3,000 B.C., the roof manifests the oldest known use of the vaulted arch principle. Found partially intact, the mud-brick architecture dissolved when the basin was flooded by impounded waters later in the year. Stone implements, flint sickle blades, potsherds, and copper weapons lay inside the fort, which dominated an important trade route between Mesopotamia and more easterly lands.

Discoveries near the Temple Mount in Jerusalem included a sloping, five-story edifice which may have been part of the palace of King David and his son King Solomon. The huge, stepped, stone structure stood at least 15 m (50 ft) high. Well-constructed houses and a stone toilet date from the days of King Hezekiah, who lived some three centuries later (ca. 715–687 B.C.). Amid the finds lay a figurine of a nude, uncircumcised male with two pairs of arms. Israeli archaeologists concluded that the figurine was a cult figure, evidence that the ancient Hebraic ban on the veneration of graven images was neglected.

Clarifying the Classics. By inverting the long-known but enigmatic Nora Stele and Nora Fragment from Sardinia, F.M. Cross of Harvard University could read the Phoenician inscriptions thereon and date the monuments by comparing the shapes of letters with Phoenician material in the Near East. The text describes a battle, and the letters could be dated to the 9th century, thus pushing back by 200 years the known time of Phoenician entry into Sardinia.

After years of digging, archaeologists finally found the ancient coining mint in the Athenian Agora. Along with the mint building they unearthed more than 100 bronze coin blanks, basins, cisterns, and furnaces used in coinage from the 5th to the 1st centuries before Christ.

During their abortive campaign to conquer ancient Germanic tribesmen, the Romans built an extensive but short-lived camp at Oberaden in West Germany. Since the camp lasted only a few years, it had long been used as a discrete dating horizon by archaeologists. The trouble was that no one knew exactly when the camp was established. Tree-ring dating of a newly found, wooden well lining revealed that the camp was set up in A.D. 11.

Vikings and Their Neighbors. Near the 1977 finding site of an enormous gold Viking neck-ring, Danish archaeologists in 1980 excavated a triangular bronze fibula. The fibula bears the engraved likeness of a fierce figure with plaited beard and horned helmet.

Near Tipperary, Ireland, an amateur archaeologist found a treasure hidden from the Vikings about A.D. 900. Contained in a bronze cauldron were silver and gold beakers, a sieve, and platter.

WESTERN HEMISPHERE

Early Americans. Information about the Circum-Beringia Culture, the oldest in northwestern North America, was enhanced by finds at Putu on the north slope of the Brooks Range in Alaska. A charcoal sample provided a radiocarbon age of ca. 9,500 B.C. Other discoidal cores and ordinary sized blades were of mudstone, but two unequivocal Clovis-like fluted points of obsidian and chert confirmed the contemporaneity of this assemblage with the more southerly

A dagger of sunlight passing through an engraved sun symbol on the face of a cliff indicated the summer solstice to ancient Indians in New Mexico.

The Anasazi Project, Inc./Karl Kernberger

fluted-point hunters who otherwise had a different flint-working tradition.

A major discovery was made at Verde, Chile, in an environment which also preserved bone and wooden projectile points. Stone tools consisted of flakes and bifacial ovates. The most remarkable of these 15,000-year-old finds is a wooden sled, presumably used to haul the meat from mammoths.

Maya Production. A well-conceived project using sideways-looking synthetic aperture radar revealed drainage canals covering an area of 80,-000 km^2 but hidden by the rain forests of Guatemala and Belize. These canals, dug between 250 B.C. and A.D. 900, irrigated cornfields to feed an estimated 3 million Indians in an area marginally suited for agriculture.

A Classic Period (A.D. 700) stone artifact factory discovered in a Mayan city near Guatemala City mass produced jade artifacts and obsidian blades. Factory residue dumped over a retaining wall included broken blades and more than 5,-000 cores. The find gave archaeologists the best evidence yet of how the great demand for obsidian cutting tools was met.

Indian Cultivation. Impressions of actual ears of corn in pottery of the Moche Culture enabled M. E. Dunn of Vanderbilt University to identify 19 types of corn grown in Peru by A.D. 800. Ceramic figures showing medicine men treating illnesses with podcorn partially explain how the medical applications of this kind of primitive maize, ancestral to our corn but inferior as a food, helped keep it from becoming extinct.

Rescue archaeology performed by University of Illinois archaeologists over a 20-mile (32-km) stretch of Interstate 270 near Dupo, IL, uncovered a cemetery of more than 60 stone-box graves of the Mississippian Culture from late pre-Columbian times. Besides potsherds, stone points, and animal bones, habitation sites of these dead Indians produced two polished stone figurines. One of them, in reddish-brown bauxite imported from Arkansas or Alabama, shows an 8-inch (20-cm) tall woman hoeing. She wears only a backpack, ear spools, and a grimace, as she kneels on a snake with a feline head and a tail which divides into vines bearing gourds.

Solar Markers. Large stone slabs on the Fajada Butte in Chaco Canyon, NM, focus shafts of sunlight so that at the summer solstice a dagger of light passes through the middle of a spiral sun symbol engraved on the face of a cliff. At the December winter solstice, the two shafts embrace the sides of the symbol; at the equinoxes, the second shaft bisects a smaller version of the helical symbol to the left of the large spiral. Although the canyon is famous for the large ruins of the Anasazi-Pueblo Indians (A.D. 900 to 1300), differences in the sun symbolism as well as in the basic approach to solar watching made it unclear as to which Indians used the observatory.

RALPH M. ROWLETT
University of Missouri-Columbia

ARCHITECTURE

The year 1980 saw the consolidation of architectural concerns that seemed likely to remain important throughout the new decade: greater harmony with the surroundings of new construction; more reuse of existing construction; broader influences on the appearance of new construction (such as historic styles, nearby buildings, and regional tradition); and more development of energy conservation techniques. The various awards programs for excellence in architecture reflected these concerns.

AIA Awards. Of the 13 designs selected by the American Institute of Architects for the leading national awards, six made use of existing buildings, four were strict restorations, three were influenced heavily by historical styles, and most of the rest involved strong considerations of surroundings, regional character, and energy conservation. None were high-rise new construction; few were very large. The architects receiving these awards are considered to be among the most important in current design thought. The awards went to Caudill Rowlett Scott for the gleaming mirrored-glass Indiana Bell Telephone Switching Center in Columbus, IN; Anderson Notter Finegold, Inc. for the authentic restoration of the Market Square district in Newburyport, MA; Robert A.M. Stern for the artful reworking of a mid-20th-century townhouse in New York City; Frank Gehry for novel additions to his own house in Santa Monica; Holabird & Root for the strong new industrial forms of the Environmental Health Laboratory in St. Louis; Hugh Jacobsen for his immaculate restoration of the Arts and Industries Museum of the Smithsonian Institution in Washington; Hammel Green and Abrahamson, Inc. for combining new construction and technology with historical forms in the Colonial Church of Edina, MN; Goody, Clancy & Associates, Inc. for doing the same at Heaton Court housing for the elderly in Stockbridge, MA; Perry, Dean, Stahl & Rogers, Inc. for the adaptive and accurate restoration of Landmark Center in St. Paul; Wolf Associates Architects, Ltd. for the sleek new Southern Service Center for Equitable Life in Charlotte, NC; Ridgeway Ltd. for the carefully detailed restoration of the Biltmore Hotel in Los Angeles; Hawley & Peterson for the Qume Corporation's colorful offices and factory in San Jose, CA; and William Kessler & Associates, Inc. for the Wayne State University Health Care Institute/Detroit Receiving Hospital—Medical Center Concourse, a building that suggests a humane pleasant liveliness in an often dull building type.

Current Projects. The facts that none of the award-winning buildings was tall and that few were even large did not mean that architects were not working on designs for massive or high-rise construction—although possibly with some degree of personal reservation. In fact,

1980 began with starts on nonresidential construction in the United States worth $47,400,000,000. This construction was mostly office buildings (many of them large), and the pace was far ahead of the previous boom in the early 1970s. The greatly respected firm of I.M. Pei and Partners proceeded with work on the 49-story ARCO Oil & Gas Company's Dallas headquarters with its 1.4 million sq ft (130 064 m²) of space. I.M. Pei also proceeded with work on the massive $375-million convention center for New York City, and was involved in a similar project for downtown Miami.

Foreign architects made inroads in the United States. Australia's John Andrews International Ltd. won a competition against prominent U.S. architects for the go-ahead to design the headquarters of the International Telecommunications Satellite Organization in Washington, DC.

A great influx of foreign capital, led by funds from South America, made Miami among the most ambitious building centers worldwide and escalated plans for several billion dollars worth of mostly high-rise construction. Some of the foremost architectural firms in the United States were involved, including Hugh Stubbins (Dade County Administration Building), Philip Johnson (Dade County Cultural Center), and Skidmore, Owings and Merrill (several office buildings). At a conference sponsored by the South Florida chapter of the AIA on September 6, noted architects Charles Moore, Barton Myers, and Jacquelin Robertson criticized the lack of overall planning to interrelate the new construction, and warned that in their view the results could produce another anonymous new city like Houston or Los Angeles.

Architectural Conferences. Other conferences on the planning of cities stressed similarly strong beliefs in the need for more careful and thoughtful approaches. The Second International Conference on Urban Design, "Tools for Urban Design in a Period of Constraints and Opportunities," was held in September in Boston. It stressed the necessity for designers and government to work together. On a more self-critical note, the annual International Design Conference in Aspen, held in June, heard chairman and noted Israeli architect Moshe Safdie cite what is in his view a widening gap between design and social purpose. Architects Buckminster Fuller and George Nelson spoke respectively for a concept of a united planet and against Post-Modernism, the currently popular practice of incorporating historical styles into new designs.

Post-Modernism. Indeed, architects remained strongly divided on whether Post-Modernism is a totally new direction, a temporary fashion, or another stage of development in what had been done. As led by such architects as Robert A.M. Stern and Michael Graves, the movement ranges from such famous examples as Philip Johnson's ITT building and his Dade County Cultural

Luis Barragán, 78-year-old winner of the 1980 Pritzker Prize, designed Las Arboledas, a residential area near Mexico City, featuring a riding school with walled enclosures and a shoulder-high watering trough.

Center to Shozo Uchii's treasury for a Buddhist temple in Japan. The latter was awarded the annual R.S. Reynolds Memorial Award, and is a sensitive and imaginative interpretation of traditional forms with such modern materials as concrete and aluminum. In July, ground was broken for Michael Graves' Portland Public Service Building in Oregon. The design is the controversial, Post-Modern winner of a competition between it and other schemes that were more strictly Modern.

The Pritzker Prize of 1980 went to 78-year-old Luis Barragán of Mexico, who has always designed in a poetic way that is a combination of Modern and native Mexican. In their comments the Pritzker jury members stated: "For over half a century, his work has embodied the spirit of Mexico: austere spaces intensified by brilliant color, water, and the Islamic notion of successive garden spaces." The prize is administered and funded by the Hyatt Foundation as an annual event patterned after the Nobel Prize.

Energy Conservation. Although the recent shortage of fuel oil and the need for other forms of energy did not have a quickly perceivable impact on architecture, 1980 saw several energy-conservation breakthroughs. The AIA supported the U.S. Energy Department's strict Building Energy Performance Standards (BEPS) amid strong opposition from other construction interests. Herbert Epstein, the chief spokesman before Congress on BEPS and solar energy, received the 1980 Edward C. Kemper Award from the AIA. Owens-Corning Fiberglas Corporation awarded prizes to four teams of engineers and architects who had made significant contributions to energy conservation—mostly through

the use of solar collectors on their buildings, augmented by passive and mechanical measures. Architects Mitchell/Giurgola and Richard Thorp won a competition to design Australia's new parliament building in Canberra. The model which they submitted partially buries the facilities under the crest of a hill, and—while respecting the natural environment—would produce substantial energy savings.

Professional Standards. In the area of professional standards, 1980 was a year of voluntary strengthening and virtually involuntary weakening. The requirements for the issuance of national certificates leading to almost automatic licensing in any state (by the National Council of Architectural Registration Boards) were raised to make a professional degree from an accredited college program mandatory. But delegates to the annual national convention of the AIA voted, under pressure from the U.S. Justice Department, to make the previously mandatory Code of Ethics voluntary. Still, according to *Architectural Record* editor Walter Wagner, the weakening of wording from "shall" to "should" gave the institute the opportunity to reinsert many articles of the code lost in recent years because of its mandatory nature. These clauses involved such issues as advertising and replacing fellow professionals, when the latter are already under contract to a client. A survey of architects revealed that only 7% of all architectural firms were involved in the developmental role on the projects on which they worked. This situation existed despite pressure in the AIA that had led in 1978 to a lifting of restrictions against financial involvement.

CHARLES KING HOYT, *"Architectural Record"*

ARGENTINA

The issue of presidential succession in Argentina was resolved six months in advance of a scheduled 1981 inauguration. The regime turned its attention to a damaging human rights assessment, a rash of bank failures, and the equally important regulation of organized labor. Finding itself in an economic recession, Argentina was slow in responding to corrective measures. By broadening its relations with both China and the Soviet Union, Argentina encouraged the United States to reconsider its diplomatic "coolness" toward the Argentine government.

Government and Politics. A decision was readied by the ruling military junta on Oct. 3, 1980, to elevate former army commander Roberto E. Viola, a moderate, to the presidency in March 1981, for a three-year term. The junta decided to reduce presidential powers further, in part because of suspicion within the military over the extensive contacts maintained by Viola with the political and labor opponents of the four-year-old military regime. The junta decided to continue its support for the governmental reorganization plan issued in January by President Jorge R. Videla, which called for the elimination of Peronist and Marxist influence in Argentina prior to reviving national elections. The program also called for a free-market economy, reduced trade union influence, a strong conservative party, and a permanent "watchdog" role for the military over future civilian governments. The plan served as the basis for a dialogue between political party representatives and the military government regarding the resumption of legal activity by the parties. The Peronist movement, largest of the nation's political forces, was excluded from the dialogue.

When it decreed its long-awaited labor law in February, the military junta dealt an unprecedented blow to unionism and Peronist political activity. Anticipating the law, the labor press attempted, without success, to call a general strike late in 1979. The union leaders again failed to find popular support for their cause when, in February, they invited church leaders, management, and political parties to a protest meeting. By the end of the year, labor was expected to be operating under the new code, which eliminated the 59-year-old General Confederation of Labor, as well as closed and union shops. Political influence and economic power of the unions were severely curtailed under the new legislation. Peronist trade union leader Roberto Garcia, of the militant "group of 25," received several death threats before his home was bombed in July; he was kidnapped briefly, in August.

The Videla government rejected a report on human rights in Argentina, released in April by the Inter-American Human Rights Commission. According to the military junta, the commission failed adequately to assess the leftist, terrorist activities that produced the officially sanctioned repression in the 1970s. The report found the ruling junta and the military commanders directly responsible for thousands of deaths of record, as well as for unreported prisoners. In October, Adolfo Perez Esquivel, an Argentine human rights activist, was named the winner of the 1980 Nobel Peace Prize. (*See also* BIOGRAPHY.)

Economic Conditions. The always controversial policies of Economy Minister José Alfred Martínez de Hoz came under sharp attack in 1980 by farmers, businessmen, labor bosses, and politicians. The nation was pushed into recession by the anti-inflation measures Martinez had implemented. The economic situation was exacerbated by falling wages, high interest rates, declining exports, factory shutdowns, rising state deficits, and bank failures.

On March 28 the central bank ordered the closure of the Banco de Intercambio Regional, which contained more deposits than any other private bank in Argentina. On April 25 the central bank took over the Banco de los Andes, the largest commercial bank in the country. As the crisis spread, two other major institutions, the Banco Oddone and the Banco Internacional, were placed under central bank administration. The collapse of the largest banks in the nation was due to a rising number of bankruptcies in the industrial sector and an excessive number of bad debts. In order to restore confidence in the private banking system, the central bank in April and May lent 4,800,000,000,000 pesos ($2,600,-000,000) to the nation's crisis-ridden banking houses and financial companies, faced with collapse through capital flight. An official guarantee of all private bank deposits of up to 100 million pesos was reinstituted and the central bank had to spend more than $600 million, propping up the Argentine peso.

On November 1 the monthly devaluation rate of the peso against the dollar increased from 0.2 to 1%. A 1980 trade deficit of more than $2,-000,000,000 was expected. Inflation had reached an annual rate of 88% by September.

Foreign Relations. A concerted effort was made by Argentina to improve relations with the United States as the deputy foreign minister,

---

ARGENTINA · Information Highlights

Official Name: Republic of Argentina.
Location: Southern South America.
Area: 1,072,158 sq mi (2 776 889 km²).
Population (1980 est.): 27,100,000.
Chief Cities (1970 census): Buenos Aires, the capital, 2,-972,453; Córdoba, 781,565; Rosario, 750,455.
Government: *Head of state and government,* Jorge Videla, president (Roberto Eduardo Viola to take office March 1981). *Legislature*—Congress (dissolved March 24, 1976); Legislative Advisory Commission established.
Monetary Unit: New Peso (1,916.50 new pesos equal U.S.$1, Nov. 1980).
Manufactures (major products): Processed foods, motor vehicles, textiles, chemicals, metal and metal products, electrical appliances.
Agriculture (major products): Grains, oilseeds, livestock products.
GNP (1978 est., U.S.$): $45,000,000,000.
Foreign Trade (1978, U.S.$): *Imports,* $3,864,000,000; *exports,* $6,400,000,000.

Carlos Cavándoli, journeyed to Washington in November 1979 and again in February. Both Cavándoli and Economy Minister Martínez de Hoz went to the U.S. capital in May. Argentine authorities found support for their mission at the state and defense departments, where there was concern over expanding Argentine trade relations with the Soviet Union and China. Response to the Argentine initiative was complicated by official Argentine involvement in human rights abuses in that country. Also perplexing to Washington were Argentina's support for the incoming Bolivian military government, opposed by Washington, its sale of cereals to the USSR, and its "independent" nuclear policy.

Accords were signed with Brazil on the subjects of nuclear cooperation, hydroelectric exploitation, and economic cooperation during an exchange of presidential visits.

Full diplomatic relations with Great Britain were restored in February, after a four-year interruption. Discussions on the disputed Falkland Islands were resumed in April. Little progress was reported in the mediation by Pope John Paul II of the Beagle Canal dispute with Chile.

LARRY L. PIPPIN, *Elbert Covell College*
University of the Pacific

ARIZONA

The major issues and events of 1980 in Arizona were floods and water supply, illegal immigration, tax reform, the burro evacuation from the Grand Canyon, and the election.

Floods and Water Supply. Following heavy rain and snow in the Arizona high country in January and nine consecutive days of rain in the desert valleys, the Salt, Gila, and Verde rivers overflowed their banks and floodwaters swept through metropolitan Phoenix, reaching the highest levels since 1905. Thousands of homes and ranches in the floodplain were inundated as the raging torrents swept away automobiles, livestock, sewer lines, and bridges, forcing the evacuation of thousands of families. The high water also forced the closing of major bridges in Phoenix, causing unprecedented traffic jams. In the

––––––– ARIZONA • Information Highlights –––––––

Area: 113,909 sq mi (295 024 km²).
Population (Jan. 1980 est.): 2,495,000.
Chief Cities (1976 est.): Phoenix, the capital, 679,512; Tucson, 302,359; (1970 census): Scottsdale, 67,823.
Government (1980): *Chief Officers*—governor, Bruce Babbitt (D); secy. of state, Rose Mofford (D). *Legislature*—Senate, 30 members; House of Representatives, 60 members.
Education (1979–80): *Enrollment*—public elementary schools, 353,408 pupils; public secondary, 155,844; colleges and universities, 188,976 students. *Public school expenditures,* $958,021,000 ($1,548 per pupil).
State Finances (fiscal year 1979): *Revenues,* $2,817,000,000; *expenditures,* $2,288,000,000.
Personal Income (1979): $20,637,000,000; per capita, $8,423.
Labor Force (May 1980): *Nonagricultural wage and salary earners,* 1,003,100; *unemployed,* 68,900 (6.2% of total force).

wake of the flooding, land developers and their political spokesmen as well as flood victims called for the construction of another flood control dam on the scenic Verde River. Environmentalists and Apache Indians, whose Fort McDowell reservation lands would be sacrificed, rallied in opposition, advocating instead better-constructed bridges and more informed flood-plain management.

While floodwaters covered major portions of Phoenix, construction continued on the controversial Central Arizona Project which will bring Colorado River water east across the state to Tucson and the surrounding desert. At last, the state legislature, under strong pressure from U.S. Secretary of the Interior Cecil Andrus, adopted a code to regulate groundwater use, as water tables in the southern region of the state continued to decline from excessive agricultural use.

Illegal Immigration. Thirteen Salvadoran immigrants died of exposure in the desert heat when they became lost as they made their way north across the Mexican border. Steady streams of such illegal aliens contribute to growing ethnic-based tensions within the state.

Tax Reform. A special session of the state legislature enacted a major tax reform program that limits homeowner property taxes and imposes on local governments strict taxing and spending restrictions. In addition, the state's 4% sales tax on food was repealed. A major aim of the program was to restructure public school funding in order to equalize spending among school districts.

Burro Evacuation. In northern Arizona, a voluntary rescue operation was begun to remove wild burros from the Grand Canyon. This followed an announcement that the National Park Service planned to shoot the animals to halt their increasing destruction of the natural habitat.

The Election. Most Arizonans cast their votes for Ronald Reagan. The Republican received 61% of the vote, as compared with 28% for President Jimmy Carter, 9% for John Anderson, and 2% for Ed Clark. Sen. Barry Goldwater was returned to Washington after a surprisingly close win over William R. Schulz (D). He was joined in victory by incumbent Democratic Congressmen Morris K. Udall and Bob Stump, who survived the Republican onslaught, and Republicans Eldon Rudd and John Rhodes. Voters approved referenda to deregulate state transportation, raise legislative salaries from $6,000 to $15,000, and to establish a state-run lottery. A controversial property tax-limits proposition, similar to the one adopted earlier in California, was rejected.

JAMES W. CLARKE, *University of Arizona*

ARKANSAS

During 1980 Arkansas was burdened with inflation, rising utility rates, increasing unemployment, business failures, and fiscal shortages. The economic problems were intensified by farm

A Titan 2 nuclear missile silo was destroyed in an explosion near Damascus, AR, in September 1980.

losses resulting from the driest and hottest summer in the state's history. Part of Arkansas lost its rail transportation when the Rock Island went into bankruptcy.

The Election. Republicans made surprising gains in this usually Democratic state. Youthful Democratic Gov. Bill Clinton lost his bid for a second term to a political unknown, Frank D. White, who became the second Republican to be elected governor since 1874. In an aggressive and abrasive campaign, Frank White blamed the state's ills, including Cuban refugee disturbances at Fort Chaffee, the increase in the auto license fee, and the recession, on the state's Democratic leadership. White received a greater percentage (52%) of the vote than did Ronald Reagan who, with 48%, won the state's six presidential electoral votes. Republicans also retained two of the state's four seats in the U.S. House and made minor gains in the predominantly Democratic state legislature. Democratic Sen. Dale Bumpers easily won reelection. Voters rejected most referenda and initiative measures—decisively defeating, for the second time in ten years, a proposed document to replace the state constitution of 1874; a proposed amendment to permit the legislature to raise the 10% usury limit on interest rates; and, in Pulaski county, even the much-needed 3-mill road tax which must be ratified

each general election. However, voters overwhelmingly approved a 10% lid on increases in property tax revenues which will result from a court-ordered statewide property reassessment.

The Governor. The Clinton administration had difficulty in maintaining its credibility. Teachers received only a portion of a promised $1,200 pay raise. Revenue shortfalls required state employment and program cutbacks.

The Legislature. The state General Assembly was convened three times: once by the legislature to propose constitutional amendments, only to have the state supreme court declare unconstitutional the use of the extended session to propose amendments; and twice by the governor to distribute new revenues and to correct utility rate-setting procedures.

Local Governments. Both counties and cities, faced with inflation that outpaced revenue increases, cut programs, reduced pay increases, and laid off employees. School district revenues were trimmed when state grants to public schools were reduced and when the railroads, contesting in court the equity of their property tax assessments, refused to pay in full their property taxes. Teachers sued, or threatened to sue, school districts which cut salaries set by signed teacher contracts.

Race Relations. George Howard, Jr., of Pine Bluff became the first black federal district judge in Arkansas, and Mahlon A. Martin was the first black to become city manager of Little Rock. Some friction occurred when blacks in Helena and West Helena boycotted public schools over tracking policies and competency testing.

Missile Disaster. Serious concern developed in September when a fuel explosion occurred at an underground Titan 2 nuclear missile silo near Damascus. One member of the Air Force was killed and 22 were injured. Although 1,400 nearby residents were evacuated for a 12-hour period, the Defense Department said that no radiation leaks occurred. The slightly damaged warhead later was removed.

WILLIAM C. NOLAN
Southern Arkansas University

─────── **ARKANSAS · Information Highlights** ───────

Area: 53,104 sq mi (137 539 km²).
Population (Jan. 1980 est.): 2,190,000.
Chief Cities (1976 est.): Little Rock, the capital, 151,649; (1970 census): Fort Smith, 62,802.
Government (1980): *Chief Officers*—governor, Bill Clinton (D); lt. gov., Joe Purcell (D). *General Assembly*—Senate, 35 members; House of Representatives, 100 members.
Education (1979–80): *Enrollment*—public elementary schools, 241,210 pupils; public secondary, 211,915; colleges and universities, 74,701 students. *Public school expenditures* (1978–79), $618,246,000 ($1,158 per pupil).
State Finances (fiscal year 1979): *Revenues,* $1,968,000,000; *expenditures,* $1,897,000,000.
Personal Income (1979): $15,114,000,000; per capita, $6,933.
Labor Force (June 1980): *Nonagricultural wage and salary earners,* 747,600; *unemployed,* 80,000 (8.1% of total force).

ART

The central art figure of the year was indisputably Pablo Picasso. One year short of the centenary of Picasso's birth and as a spectacular wind-up to its own fiftieth anniversary celebration, the Museum of Modern Art (MoMA) in New York City devoted is entire gallery space to the comprehensive exhibition, "Picasso: A Retrospective" (*see* special report, page 130).

Numerous other anniversary exhibits were presented during the year. The New York Metropolitan Museum expanded its gallery space. Art auction houses likewise saw growth, as did California museums, which increasingly vied for attention.

The Picasso exhibition at MoMA was the latest in a series of "blockbusters" which have become economic necessities for museums, especially in the United States where there are no direct government subsidies. These popular exhibitions, drawing great numbers of visitors who ordinarily might not come to museums, are now multiplying nationally and internationally. Many years of planning, generous loan policies on the part of public and private collectors, and enormous expense are involved. The advantages of such exhibitions are that they bring in revenue from admissions and especially from the sales of books and other items. However, mounting criticism is heard regarding the possibility of damage to frequently transported works of art, and of inconvenience and disappointment to visitors who make trips to museums hoping to see absent works. Overcrowding at massive exhibitions, making viewing difficult, is also a concern.

Exhibits. In addition to Picasso, other artists were honored on the occasion of anniversaries. Louise Nevelson's 80th year was marked by shows at New York's Whitney Museum, which observed its 50th year, and at New York's Pace and Wildenstein galleries. At the Whitney four of Mrs. Nevelson's "environments"—sculptured walls of assembled pieces, carved, painted, or found, and dated from the 1950s and 1960s—were on exhibit. The Pace showed maquettes for her monumental metal sculpture and prints. Wildenstein displayed wood constructions and collages. In addition, a Nevelson giant steel sculpture was permanently installed on New York's Fifth Avenue. Sculptor Isamu Noguchi, 75 in November 1979, was honored by exhibitions at the Whitney Museum and at the Pace and Emmerich galleries. The Whitney show, a smaller version of one presented at the Minneapolis Art Museum in 1978, included stage sets and playground designs. The work displayed at the galleries demonstrated Noguchi's characteristic blend of Eastern and Western elements. The Spanish painter Salvador Dali, also 75 in 1979, was the subject of a major retrospective at the Centre Georges Pompidou in Paris. Although Dali—with his extraordinary fantasy and facile, realistic painting style—is the most popular painter in the Surrealist mode, it is his compatriot Joan Miró, also a Surrealist, who is considered the better painter. In fact, Miró has been called the greatest living painter. Two exhibitions were mounted on the occasion of Miró's 87th birthday. One, organized by the Hirshhorn Museum in Washington, consisted of paintings in American collections, and was shown also at the Albright-Knox Gallery in Buffalo. The second, "Joan Miró: The Development of a Sign Language," originated at Washington University in St. Louis, and later was moved to the University of Chicago. This exhibit went beyond painting to include works in other media. Finally, the German Expressionist painter Ernst Ludwig Kirchner, who died in 1938, was honored on the occasion of the centenary of his birth by a comprehensive survey of his work shown in museums in Berlin, Munich, Cologne, and Zurich. He was one of the most influential of the painters who worked outside the French ambience and was the founder of "Die Brücke," a society of artists. He was also featured at New York's Guggenheim Museum's autumn exhibition, "Expressionism: A German Intuition."

Belgium and the Netherlands provided interesting and lesser known material for American institutions. From Belgian collections the Brooklyn Museum assembled the show, "Belgian Art: 1880–1914." The exhibit presented a group of turn-of-the-century avant-garde painters, of whom only James Ensor is well known, who contributed especially to the Art Nouveau movement. Centered in the Pierpont Morgan Library's Stavelot triptych was a selection of Belgian Romanesque enamel and metal works of a much earlier period. Also at the Morgan Library an unusual show, "William and Mary and Their House: the Royal Collections, 1528–1979," was presented. The objects presented belong or once belonged to the Dutch royal family. Besides paintings and drawings by such great artists as Rembrandt, Van Dyck, Guercino, and Rubens, there were pieces of furniture, glass and metal vessels, and other objects collected for the private pleasure and use of the House of Orange.

At the Buten Museum in Philadelphia the collectors of Wedgwood pottery (most of whom are Americans—many of them Philadelphians) were treated to a series of eight events—seven exhibitions and a seminar—marking the birth of Josiah Wedgwood in 1730. The museum boasts some 10,000 examples of Wedgwood, the world's largest public collection.

In October, following five months at the British Museum earlier in 1980, the exhibition "The Vikings" opened at New York's Metropolitan Museum of Art. The show contained more than 550 exhibits and included some works not shown previously outside Scandinavia.

Noteworthy among art events in Europe was the show, "Florence and Tuscany of the Medicis and Sixteenth Century Europe." It was sponsored by the Council of Europe and was a type of exhibition occasionally mounted by member countries to illustrate a theme of cultural kinship and to honor European civilization. Various Renaissance palaces in Florence showed different aspects of the endeavors of the Medicis. The principal fame of the Medicis rests on their patronage of a number of the greatest Renaissance artists; in addition they sponsored scientific research, worldwide explorations, and classical studies and excavations, and commissioned works from artisans and craftsmen. Auxiliary expositions were arranged by the Region of Tuscany.

Metropolitan Museum Expansion. The Metropolitan Museum continued to expand, and in March the André Meyer Galleries of 19th-century European art were opened to the public. Occupying the top floor of the Michael C. Rockefeller wing to the south of the main part of the museum, the new installation is 24,000 sq ft (2 230 m^2). Thirteen rooms are arranged around a large central space subdivided by screens. Natural lighting, with harmful rays carefully eliminated, is used where possible, ending the recent trend toward windowless museums and permitting many paintings to be seen properly after years of distortion. The paintings are mainly French in origin. A welcome aid to the appreciation of the paintings is the addition of 19th-century sculpture in the installation. Also on view are the academic and salon pieces that were important to the art connoisseurs of the period.

At the opposite side of the Metropolitan, sections of the new American Wing were unveiled in June. One entire wall, facing New York's Central Park, is of glass. An interior glass-roofed garden court is the core around which three stories of painting, sculpture, and decorative arts, portraying American life since Colonial times, are gathered. Around the court, prized architectural elements, mostly from former buildings, have been built in. These include a glass and ceramic loggia designed by Louis Comfort Tiffany

for his own home, the facade of the Wall Street United States Assay Office dating from 1824, and a pair of stairways from Louis Sullivan's Chicago Stock Exchange. When the complete installation is ready (about 1982), it will include a row of period rooms, ranging from the 17th to the 20th century and ending with a complete room from a Frank Lloyd Wright house. The original American wing with its period rooms was opened in 1924 with only a fraction of the space now available. Hundreds of objects can now be seen for the first time by the general public, especially those works of folk art and 19th century painting and sculpture that had not previously been so well represented. One of the Metropolitan's most popular pieces, the 12 × 21' (4 × 6 m) canvas by Emanuel Leutze, depicting George Washington crossing the Delaware, has at last found a suitable and permanent display space.

California Museums. California museums are developing as serious rivals to the established Eastern institutions. While none can approximate the fabulous endowment enjoyed by the richest museum in the world, the Malibu museum founded by Paul Getty, museums in other cities forged ahead. San Francisco has undertaken a $2-million modernization of its Museum of Modern Art. This museum holds at least one big show annually and also participates in nearly all the major traveling exhibitions in the modern art field. In the same city the Palace of the Legion of Honor, which houses a comprehensive museum of French art, ranging from the 14th to the 20th century, reopened after renovation with a show titled "The Heritage of France." In Los Angeles the Museum of Contemporary Art, emphasizing the period after World War II, is scheduled to open in 1983; it promises to be the most important collection of that period in the United States. The Los Angeles County Museum of Art also planned to expand. The touring exhibition, "The Avant-garde in Russia, 1910–1930," was on view there from July until September 1980. At Pasadena's Museum of Modern Art,

A famous gilt bronze horse from the facade of the Basilica di San Marco in Venice was a focal point of "The Horses of San Marco" exhibit at New York City's Metropolitan Museum of Art.

It was a year of auctions! "Juliet and Her Nurse" by the 19th century British artist J. M. W. Turner, sold for $6.4 million. Mrs. Flora Whitney Miller (right) sold the work to benefit New York City's Whitney Museum.

taken over in 1974 by the millionaire Norton Simon in order to display his own collection of Old Masters, there was much dissatisfaction when a large group of contemporary paintings from the museum's original and permanent collection was sold at auction. It was observed that the Simon collection is only on loan and that the loss of the museum's paintings would be regretted in the future.

Other Museum News. The Corning, NY, Museum of Glass opened its new building. A peculiar structure, with a darkened tunnel winding around a core and with showcases along one side, it houses a unique collection of glass, dating from the Roman era to the 20th century. The museum was founded in 1951.

The Solomon R. Guggenheim Foundation took formal possession of the late Peggy Guggenheim's palazzo in Venice, along with her famous collection of modern art. In New York the Guggenheim Museum opened a new permanent display.

Loans from the Museum of Modern Art's collection, temporarily homeless, were on view at various U.S. and European art institutions.

The Gilbert Stuart portraits of George and Martha Washington—owned by the Boston Athenaeum since 1831—became the joint property of the Boston Museum of Fine Arts and the Smithsonian Institution. Each institution will pay a part of the purchase price and will have the privilege of hanging the portraits, alternating every three years.

Art Auction News. The long supremacy of London in the art auction field was seriously challenged by New York. Record after record was surpassed during several spectacular sales, and two major houses expanded their New York facilities. Sotheby Parke Bernet's sales throughout North America advanced by nearly $100 million over the 1979 figure, to a total of $247.7 million, of which about $222 million was registered in New York. At Christie's, sales doubled to $113 million, and at Phillips, Son & Neale the figures rose about 33% to $12.9 million. Most of these sales were in the fine arts, although jewelry

and such items as Tiffany lamps also accounted for the increases.

Sotheby's sold J.M.W. Turner's painting, "Juliet and Her Nurse," for a record $6.4 million in May. The amount surpassed the previous record at auction of $5.5 million for the Velásquez portrait of Juan Pareja, sold at Christie's in London in 1970. The Turner, actually a depiction of St. Mark's Square in Venice, was virtually unknown, having been displayed only once (in 1966 at the Museum of Modern Art) since its showing at the Royal Academy in 1836.

In May Henry Ford II's collection of ten Impressionist and modern paintings sold at Christie's for $18.3 million. Van Gogh's "Le Jardin du Poète, Arles" went for $5.2 million. Most of the purchasers were Japanese and West Germans; very few of the expensive paintings went to American museums. One that did was Paul Cézanne's "Paysan en Blouse Bleue," purchased for $3.9 million by the Kimbell Art Museum in Fort Worth.

Also in May, Sotheby auctioned the Edgar William and Bernice Chrysler Garbisch collection for $18.9 million, a record for a single-owner collection sold at auction in the United States. A Picasso, "Saltimbanque Seated with Arms Crossed," went for $3 million to the Bridgestone Museum of Fine Art in Tokyo. Valuable furniture, carpets, and porcelains from the Garbisch New York apartment were also sold, and at a separate sale the contents of their country home in Maryland were dispersed. Included were rare pieces of 18th century furniture and porcelains and bronzes. Not included was their unique collection of American naive paintings, which instead was donated to various museums.

At Christie's, the George R. Hann collection of Russian and Greek icons sold for a record $2.8 million. The highest price for a single icon was $170,000.

At Christie's of London, a Peter Paul Rubens painting, "Samson and Delilah," sold for $5.4 million, the third highest price ever paid at auction for an art work.

Isa Ragusa, *Princeton University*

The new American Wing of New York City's Metropolitan Museum of Art was opened June 11. It consists of a glass-enclosed sculpture garden and a three-floor structure built around the original American Wing.

The Whitney Museum of American Art paid $1 million for Jasper Johns' painting Three Flags. *It was believed to be the highest price ever paid for a work by a living artist.*

John Halaska, Photo Researchers

ART—SPECIAL REPORT:

The Picasso Exhibit

Pablo Picasso, the most famous and prolific artist of the 20th century, was celebrated anew in 1980. The exhibit "Picasso: A Retrospective" drew some 1.5 million visitors to New York City's Museum of Modern Art (MoMA) from May 22 to September 30. The largest such exhibit ever dedicated to a single artist, it contained nearly 1,000 art objects and took up MoMA's entire gallery space.

The show had pieces from all the media in which Picasso had experimented: painting, sculpture, ceramics, collage, drawing, printing, stage design, and costume design. About one third of the works had never been shown before in the United States, and 30 pieces had never been exhibited anywhere. (A similar but far smaller collection was shown at the Walker Art Center in Minneapolis in February.) Loans from public and private collections from such diverse places as Prague, Hiroshima, Düsseldorf, London, Lugano (Switzerland), and Barcelona, as well as from the Musée Picasso, scheduled to open in 1981 in the remodeled 18th century Maison Salé in Paris, rounded out MoMA's own splendid holdings. Last-minute political developments prevented scheduled loans from the Soviet Union.

The Musée Picasso will house the works chosen from Picasso's estate by the French government in lieu of taxes. Since many of the works had never left Picasso's studio (some were shown in 1979 in the Grand Palais in Paris), their presence in New York in the context of his complete oeuvre led to a reassessment of his entire career and of his influence and significance. Hitherto his Cubist works were considered his most important contribution; now it is evident that he continued to evolve and experiment throughout his life, inventing and changing styles with remarkable facility. His versatility was a model to other modern artists who were encouraged by his example to break from tradition. The paintings from his earliest period (on loan from the Barcelona Museum) surprised visitors in their complete adherence to the prevailing academic style, but immediately thereafter, he broke new ground.

An important feature of the show was the famous canvas "Guernica." The painting has hung at MoMA for many years but was to be removed permanently to the Prado in Madrid, in accordance with Picasso's wishes.

ISA RAGUSA
Princeton University

"*Picasso: A Retrospective,*" the most comprehensive collection of the artist's work ever shown, included nearly 1,000 objects in all the media into which he delved—painting, drawing, collage, printmaking, sculpture, theater and costume design, and ceramics. While this giant of modern art was perhaps most famous for his Blue, Rose, and Cubist Period paintings, the MoMA retrospective revealed his unique versatility and unbounded energy. On the following pages, courtesy of the Museum of Modern Art, is a small sampling of the work of Pablo Picasso (1881–1973).

"First Communion" *(Oil on canvas), 1896*

"The Harlequin's Family" *(Gouache and India ink), 1905*

"Self-Portrait" *(Oil on canvas), 1901*

"She-Goat" *(bronze), 1950*

"Mandolin and Clarinet" *(Construction of painted wood and pencil), 1914*

"Three Musicians" *(Oil on canvas), 1921*

Costume for the ballet ''Parade,'' 1917

''Man with Mandolin'' (Oil on canvas), 1911

''The Kiss'' (Oil on canvas), 1969

133

ASIA

War, which continued to rage in parts of Asia, concerned both neighbors and outside powers.

Continuing Conflicts. There were two major international conflicts: a growing war in Afghanistan and a declining one in Cambodia (Kampuchea). The Afghan battle was the more dangerous of the two because of the greater involvement of a big power (the USSR) and the concern of a larger portion of the world community (Muslim countries, major neighboring Asian lands, the United States, and Western European governments).

More than 100,000 Soviet troops were involved in the fighting between satellite President Babrak Karmal and a strong Muslim resistance movement to the communization of the country. The regular Afghan army virtually collapsed in the face of widespread popular and armed opposition, and the Kabul administration was kept in power by Soviet forces. Soviet defense of the increasingly isolated central government appeared to be greater even than the American protection of the South Vietnamese regimes in the 1960s; Afghanistan was becoming "Russia's Vietnam." Despite the dimensions of such a burden, the Soviet Union gave no evidence of any intention to evacuate the strategically important South Asian country. Direct Western aid to the Muslim rebels was largely nonexistent.

Strong international opposition to Moscow came from the 36 member-states of the Conference of Islamic States, which suspended Afghanistan from membership and condemned Soviet aggression against the country.

The scope of the fighting in Cambodia declined. This was the result of the growing, if far from complete, success of occupying Vietnamese troops who still could not defeat completely the remnant forces of the ousted Pol Pot. The latter regime was aided, in various ways, by China and neighboring Thailand. Efforts of UN Secretary General Kurt Waldheim to reduce the presence of Vietnamese troops in Cambodia failed. Isolated crossings of the Thai-Cambodian border by Vietnamese troops heightened tension along the frontier, unintentionally encouraging Thailand to accelerate arms purchases from the United States. Soviet advisers were reported to be with Vietnamese troops in Cambodia, but there was no direct Chinese or American participation in the war.

Recurring incidents along the Sino-Vietnamese frontier served as a reminder of persisting tensions between Peking and Hanoi but did not lead, as they did in 1979, to war between the two Communist neighbors.

New Leaders. Three East Asian lands—China, Japan, and South Korea—and one important Southeast Asian country, Thailand, got new leaders in 1980. In addition, a South Asian nation, India, saw a former leader return to power. Top-level political personnel changes in China were the result of major and continuing power shifts. The new leaders in the other Asian lands were only new faces—not architects or advocates of new policies.

Former leaders were both rehabilitated and downgraded in China. There were no giant pictures of the increasingly criticized Mao Zedong, who founded China's Communist government in 1949 and died in 1976, at the National People's Congress. Onetime President Liu Shaoqi, jailed by Mao, was honored posthumously during the year. Mao's successor as Communist party chairman, Hua Guofeng, who was also premier, stepped down as prime minister at the Congress—the result of the increasing influence of

Japanese officials in Kobe explain their latest technology to Hua Guofeng, the first Chinese head of government to visit Japan.

first deputy premier Deng Xiaoping. Taking Hua's place as premier was Deng's protégé, Zhao Ziyang. The accelerating de-emphasis and criticism of Mao and the continuing rise of the Deng faction represented major steps in the changing of the Chinese political guard that has followed Mao's death. They also reflected the legitimating of new policies in the areas of economic and technological change, worker incentives, international cooperation, and relations with the United States.

Japan's Prime Minister Masayoshi Ohira died in office in June, and his untimely passing was followed by the surprisingly strong showing of his Liberal-Democratic Party in scheduled elections later the same month. His successor, Zenko Suzuki, seemed to get off to a strong start in his new, unanticipated role of party and government leader.

The 1979 assassination of South Korean President Park Chung Hee set the stage for the meteoric rise of Chun Doo Hwan, an obscure general at the time of the slaying, to his country's presidency. Chun's political ascendency was the result of his military support but took place through the electoral college machinery created by Park to perpetuate his control of the nation.

When another soldier, Gen. Prem. Tinsulanonda, became Thailand's new premier in 1980, it was necessary for the Southeast Asian nation to change its laws so that the new leader could continue as military commander. The action reflected Prem's perceived need to keep his base of support among his fellow soldiers.

In India, Mrs. Indira Gandhi again took over as prime minister following her party's victory in January elections. Mrs. Gandhi's dream of having her son, Sanjay, succeed her ended when the airplane in which he was stunt-flying crashed, resulting in his death. In North Korea, longtime Communist President Kim Il Sung elevated his son (and presumed political heir) Kim Chong Il to the second most important post in the party.

Changing Courses. Both internal and foreign policy courses continued to be changed in China. Prior to 1980, China and the United States had emphasized the political aspects of their new relationship. However in 1980, economic relations assumed prime importance as Peking and Washington struck major agreements with respect to shipping, textiles, civil aviation, and consular services. Some 400 American companies were licensed to sell products of potential military as well as civilian use, including sophisticated computers, to China. The U.S. Congress also approved "most favored nation" trading status for the Chinese. Displaying apprehensiveness about the pro-Moscow posture of Prime Minister Gandhi since her return to office, the United States altered course with respect to India. The U.S. Senate reflected this concern by endorsing the sale of nuclear fuel to India. In addition, a $230 million U.S. missile sale to the Delhi government followed an even bigger ($1,600,000,-000) Soviet-Indian arms deal. Washington again was wooing the Indian government.

Internal Violence. Internal political violence, reflecting more serious tensions in some places than others, erupted across the map of Asia. The wave of urban terrorist bombings, beginning in August, in the Philippines represented a new opposition strategy to end the martial law administration of President Ferdinand E. Marcos. Intercommunal rioting in northeastern India, on the other hand, was the result of the still imperfect unity of the peoples of the world's second most populous country—33 years after independence. Local resistance to the intrusion of more skilled and culturally different Bengali "migrants" in the underdeveloped Assam area was fierce.

Violence also marred May state elections in India. Prime Minister Gandhi's Congress (I) Party gained control of the government in eight of the nine states. At least 59 persons, including nine candidates, died in the process.

Bloody antigovernment riots took place in several South Korean cities in May. Tension also mounted, but did not erupt into major violence, in Pakistan and Sri Lanka. Pakistan's President Zia ul-Haq further restricted the opposition and reduced the authority of civilian courts.

The USSR and the U.S. Moscow's stock rose and fell in Asia in 1980. The Soviet Union solidified its hold on Afghanistan but probably lost considerable influence elsewhere as a result of its bloody repression of dissidents in the South Asian Muslim land. Some 4,000 Soviet troops were reported at the former U.S. bases of Cam Ranh Bay, Danang, Bien Hoa, and Tan Son Nhut in Vietnam. And Soviet influence seemed to continue to increase in India and in support of Vietnam occupying Cambodia.

Soviet relations with China and Japan clearly declined in 1980. The 1950 Sino-Soviet friendship treaty was allowed to expire. Japan took very vocal exception to the towing of a disabled Soviet nuclear submarine through its territorial waters. Soviet ties with the five ASEAN (Association of Southeast Asian Nations) governments—Indonesia, the Philippines, Malaysia, Singapore, and especially Thailand—also took backward steps. This was caused by Moscow's support of Vietnam's occupation of Cambodia.

On the other hand, U.S. relations with almost all the Asian lands, especially China, improved. Japan, despite its dependence on Middle East oil and investments, strongly supported U.S. stands on Iran and Iraq. Even U.S.-Indian relations improved. But all the diplomacy did not erase the fact of de facto Soviet conquest of Afghanistan.

Natural Disaster. Nature took its toll in Asia in 1980. Severe drought afflicted Sri Lanka, while Nepal experienced its worst earthquake in two thirds of a century. Flood waters covered half the districts of acutely impoverished Bangladesh. Thousands died and more than 50 million persons were made homeless in flooding in India.

RICHARD BUTWELL, *Murray State University*

The Indochina War Plus Five

In the five years since the last U.S. troops left Indochina, Vietnam and the other nations of Southeast Asia have faced numerous problems—severe flooding, famine, disease, the plight of refugees, and even new military conflicts. However, perhaps the greatest challenge for the region has been the need completely to rebuild, economically as well as socially.

Matthew Naythons, Liaison

Dirck Halstead, Liaison

At left, Vietnamese orphans attend a school, organized especially for them. Above, workers dig out an irrigation canal on a state farm near Ho Chi Minh City (formerly Saigon). Below, an East German consultant aids in the rebuilding of a housing project in the North.

Dirck Halstead, Liaison

Photos Dirck Halstead, Liaison

General inefficiency turns cargo into junk at the Haiphong harbor. Nevertheless, new commercial activity is a key objective of the Communist regime. It depends heavily on the USSR for aid.

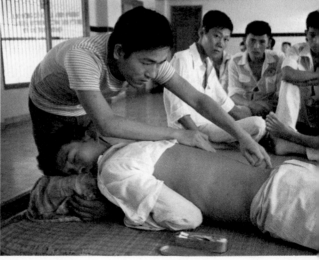

Although new cooperative factories (such as the one in photo, left) have been constructed, unskilled party loyalists have replaced experienced manpower in industrial areas of the South. This has led to a production decline. To overcome widespread drug addiction, rehabilitation centers have sprung up in Vietnam. Acupuncture (photo, above) is a common treatment for the drug addict.

ASTRONOMY

The findings of the various space probes were of prime interest in 1980. Early in the year, scientists particularly awaited the results of the Voyager probe, which reached Saturn in November and yielded more data than the earlier Pioneer probe. Exciting photos of the planet were transmitted. (*See also* SPACE EXPLORATION.)

Instruments. The Einstein X-ray satellite and the Multiple Mirror Telescope continued to provide exciting data. The United States launched the Solar Maximum Mission Observatory on February 14. An effort of unprecedented scale, which was to continue into 1981, the mission is intended to study solar flares and to cover the peak years of the solar cycle. The satellite employs six instruments to cover the solar spectrum from about 7000A to γ-rays involving solar flare emission up to 8MEV. The satellite also carries a device to measure total solar radiation to 0.1%. X-ray detectors are provided to (a) get good spatial and time resolution from incandescent gases (plasmas) the temperatures of which lie between 1.5 and 50×10^6 °K, (b) obtain two-dimensional pictures in six high-energy X-ray bands (thereby providing X-ray movies of flares), and (c) measure very hard X rays and their variations in times as short as 0.01 seconds.

Progress was made in the construction of the Space Telescope, which is scheduled to be launched as early as 1983. It will concentrate on visible and ultraviolet research. Large-sized ground-based telescopes in the 6-m to 10-m range have been proposed by a number of groups.

Eclipses. The February 16 total solar eclipse, visible in Southern Africa, India, Indonesia, and Western parts of the Philippines, was of interest because it occurred at an epoch of intense solar activity. An annular solar eclipse, visible in Hawaii, the West Indies, and other parts of the Americas, occurred August 10. There were three penumbral lunar eclipses, March 1, July 27, and August 26.

Comets. A very faint comet (Bowell), first detected outside the orbit of Jupiter, may become easily visible as it approaches the sun in April 1982. The most interesting comet of the year, Bradfield, was discovered Dec. 24, 1979, five days after it had passed closest to the sun. Its period is 307 years. Comet Bradfield was visible to the naked eye in January 1980 and then faded away. Studies of Bradfield's ultraviolet spectrum by the International Ultraviolet Explorer Satellite (IUE) confirmed that comets are dirty ice balls (a theory suggested by F. L. Whipple many years ago) and that polymers (e.g., H_2CO) rather than water ice may dominate.

Comets and asteroids may have played an important role in the history of the earth. Geological evidence shows that the transition from the Cretaceous to the Tertiary period was very abrupt, i.e., within 200 years. The sedimentary transition layer, about 5 mm thick, has a much higher iridium/silicon ratio than the earth's crust; in fact, the ratio is more akin to that found in stony meteorites. A supernova blast sufficient to account for that much iridium would produce detectable amounts of plutonium 244 (half-life of 80.5 million years); none has been found. An asteroid 10 km in diameter striking the earth

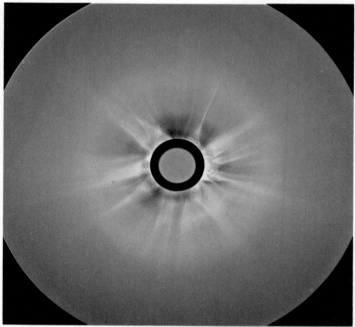

A total eclipse of the sun on February 16 was of special interest to astronomers, as it came at a time of intense solar activity. The symmetrical coronal streamers, which extended nearly two solar diameters from the limb of the sun, are typical of a corona at the peak of the sunspot cycle.

could produce enough dust to account for the layer and block out sunlight enough to affect life on earth severely. Alternately, a moderate-sized comet hitting the ocean could liberate great amounts of heat and noxious gases.

Venus. Studies by space probes have yielded much information about mysterious Venus. It appears to have no magnetic field; if one exists it is less than 5×10^{-5} that of the earth. The atmosphere is characterized by an orderly westward-blowing wind system whose speed varies markedly with elevation. Near the surface the speed is 2.2 m/sec; just below the clouds it is 50 m/sec, rising to 200 m/sec in the cloud layers themselves. In the upper atmosphere, the winds blow around Venus in four days, while the planet beneath rotates slowly once every 243 days. The radar altimeter in the Venus orbiter showed 60% of the surface to be a rather flat, gently rolling plain; 16% of the surface was depressed below the average radius of the planet, while 24% was above average. Maxwell Montes, a mountain that must be composed of low density material, towers 11 km above the plain. The planet's topography differs greatly from that of the earth.

Mars. The year saw the ending of the Viking I orbiter, which produced very detailed maps and stereo pictures of the planet. From such maps and photos, erosion estimates were made. Volcanic activity has resurfaced more than 40% of the planet. The red color of its surface, long attributed to iron rust, has defied interpretation in terms of any specific compound.

Jupiter. Theoretical attempts have been made to understand the Jovian atmosphere following the Voyager observations. In some respects, the behavior of bands and clouds can be understood in the framework of a scaled-up model of the earth's atmosphere, but in other respects, the turbulent motions suggest that Jupiter is more akin to a star. No satisfactory theory has been suggested to explain the Great Red Spot. The High Energy Astronomical Observatory-2 (HEAO-2) satellite, called the Einstein Observatory in honor of Albert Einstein, has detected X rays from electrons that spiral downward into the atmosphere from the magnetosphere. Particles trapped in the magnetosphere dissipate 3×10^{14} watts of energy. The ring of ionized sulfur around Jupiter (inferred from observations secured in 1975 in Israel) has been photographed with the 2.2-m Hawaiian telescope. It shows large temporal changes and has a radius of 400,-000 km. Three new satellites of Jupiter (1979 J1, J2, and J3) were confirmed from Voyager photographs. The last to be found, 1979 J3, is the fastest-known moon in the solar system and has a path similar to J1. J2 is the largest of the three objects.

Neptune, observed in the methane absorption feature, shows dark bands across the planetary equator. The bright areas probably correspond to clouds of methane ice crystals. No magnetic field has been found in this planet.

Stars. Although localized magnetic fields have been postulated in plage areas in stars like the sun, such fields have been detected only recently. Thus 70 Ophiuchi has a field of $2,000 \times 10^{-4}$T over 7 to 10% of its surface, while in ξ Boötes A, a field as large as $2,700 \times 10^{-4}$T covers about a third of the disk. In cooler, fainter, dwarf stars, magnetized areas cover greater percentages of the surface than they do in the sun.

Quasars. A multiple quasar (3, possibly 5, components with identical spectra) was discovered by a group of astronomers, led by Ray Weymann, at Steward Observatory in Arizona. The quasar is probably only a single object with images produced by a gravitational lens, possibly a black hole along the line of sight.

The wavelength ratio of optical and 21 cm lines in local sources and quasars in various regions of the sky is identical to an accuracy of better than 0.1%. Elfred Tubbs and Clarence Wolfe noted that this implies that the fine structure constant and gyromagnetic radius of the proton are the same in distant quasars at ancient epochs as here and now. They concluded that the laws governing electromagnetic, strong interaction, and other forces have been unchanged since the dawn of the universe.

LAWRENCE H. ALLER, *University of California*

AUSTRALIA

In a year in which both unemployment and union pressure for higher wages were constantly to the fore, the Liberal-National Country Party (L-NCP) coalition scored its third electoral victory in five years. Prime Minister Malcolm Fraser, 50, was presented with a 23-seat majority in the 125-seat House of Representatives but lost control of the Senate.

Before the election was announced, public opinion polls suggested an easy Fraser win. However, in a run-up to the October 18 election the Australian Labor Party (ALP), led by William G. ("Bill") Hayden, appeared to gain public favor, suggesting the possibility of an upset. The ALP had run an elaborate and caustic campaign to end Fraser's five-year tenure. Hayden attempted to exploit the unrelieved 6% unemployment and other economic and social issues. The L-NCP coalition was considered to offer a no-frills formula—"dull but responsible"—while ALP policy was described as "a cocktail of handout and take-aways designed almost blatantly to please the middle ground" together with a "Robin Hood approach to taxation."

The Political Fray. For much of the year more than the usual degree of political acrimony was evident. The ALP, struggling at the federal level to update both the party's relationship with the electorate and its own working structure, was riven by factionalism in Queensland and Victoria, and embarrassed by charges involving corruption and links with drug-related crime in New South Wales (NSW).

The coalition parties maintained amicable unity. NCP deputy leader Ian Sinclair was acquitted of charges brought by the NSW government over a family company's affairs and was restored by Fraser to the federal ministry.

Robert Hawke, former president of the Australian Council of Trade Unions, was elected to the House of Representatives and was widely talked of as a prospective leader of the parliamentary Labor party.

Economic Trends. Gross domestic product (GDP) was up by less than 3%, the inflation rate rose above 10% under the pressure of wage demands and higher oil prices, and average weekly earnings were almost 12% higher. Personal income tax rates were trimmed in July but the higher wage trend meant that tax collections rose overall. The money supply increased.

Export returns rose to record levels, with rural products showing the effect of good crop conditions and high prices (especially for wool, wheat, and sugar). The export rise led to a substantial trade surplus. Minerals were boosted by world price rises and buoyant production over a wide range of metals and coal. The coal industry felt the effects of a strike, however. Higher costs shaded profitability in the rural and mining sectors, while in manufacturing and commerce in general—where turnover was brisk—cost increases and a sharper bite from corporate taxes brought less favorable conditions. Many small businesses closed. Stock exchange prices rose to record levels. Investment from abroad was at higher than usual levels, and the Australian dollar was strong.

Automobile production fell to a ten-year low, though overall sales were sustained. Textile output was barely maintained. Elsewhere there was a marginal lift in manufacturing, a decline in farm production, and a solid increase in private dwelling construction in all states, except Victoria and Tasmania.

The "stay-put" budget presented in August held to the financial orthodoxy of recent years. Gross revenues were budgeted to rise 16.5% and gross outlays to increase 13.5%. Included was a 17.5% lift in defense spending to almost U.S.$4,000,000,000. The oil tax windfall allowed other taxes to be held. The budget was the first since 1973–74 to anticipate a domestic surplus.

Foreign Affairs and Defense. Fraser supported President Carter's stand against Soviet moves in Afghanistan by trimming grain sales to Moscow and by urging the national Olympic committee to boycott the Moscow Games. The latter request was rejected, however. In the Middle East crisis and the resulting build-up of U.S. strength in the Indian Ocean, Fraser agreed to allow U.S. B-52s to use northern Australian airfields as staging points; however, he decided against direct Australian participation in the multinational Persian Gulf force gathered in October.

As part of the augmented defense effort, the government agreed in principle to a new naval construction program and decided that a squadron of new fighter aircraft would be based in Darwin.

In March, Australian diplomats stationed in Southeast Asia and Foreign Minister Andrew Peacock reviewed general developments in the region and especially Australia's relations with the Association of Southeast Asian Nations (ASEAN). Recognition of the Pol Pot regime in Cambodia (Kampuchea) ended in October, after which Australia called for a phased withdrawal from Cambodia of Vietnamese forces. Australia took a leading part in developing the concept of a Pacific community in which the nations of the world's largest ocean would engage in closer consultation and more extensive cooperation. (See OCEANIA.)

National Projects. The new High Court building in Canberra was opened by Queen Elizabeth II in May. A plan for a new Parliament House, to be completed for the 1988 bicentennial, was unveiled. The design, expected to cost more than U.S.$500 million, visualizes a four-pronged structure set within the top of Canberra's central Capital Hill. Preliminary work on the site began with a ceremonial stone-laying by the prime minister.

A new railroad link between Adelaide and Alice Springs opened in October.

The year was seen as the opening of a decade of resource development. Among new resource undertakings were the Exxon-financed U.S.$1,300,000,000 Rundle shale-oil project in Queensland and a U.S.$6,000,000,000 natural gas project centered on the continental shelf off northwest Australia for which a consortium of energy groups signed an agreement with Western Australia's government. A major mining project associated with the Ranger uranium deposit in the Northern Territory was begun, and planning got under way for the large-scale liquefication of brown coal in Victoria as well as for refining facilities for bauxite and other minerals. Discovery of important deposits of a variety of minerals (including tantalite) was confirmed, and new coal and gas fields were announced.

——— AUSTRALIA · Information Highlights ———

Official Name: Commonwealth of Australia.
Location: Southwestern Pacific Ocean.
Area: 2,967,900 sq mi (7 686 861 km²).
Population (1980 est.): 14,600,000.
Chief Cities (1977 est.): Canberra, the capital, 228,040; Sydney, 3,121,800; Melbourne, 2,694,100.
Government: *Head of state,* Elizabeth II, queen; represented by Sir Zelman Cowen, governor general (took office Dec. 1977). *Head of government,* Malcolm Fraser, prime minister (took office Dec. 1975). *Legislature*—Parliament: Senate and House of Representatives.
Monetary Unit: Australian dollar (0.85 A. dollar equals U.S.$1, Oct. 1980).
Manufactures (major products): Motor vehicles, iron and steel, textiles, chemicals.
Agriculture (major products): Cereals, sugarcane, fruits, wine grapes, sheep, cattle, dairy products.
GNP (1979 est., U.S.$): $117,700,000,000.
Foreign Trade (Jan.-June 1980, U.S.$): *Imports,* $9,511,000,000; *exports,* $11,100,000,000.

The General Scene. A voluminous report on the impact and implications of technological change was endorsed by the government and well-received by the press. Some labor spokesmen attacked it as "shallow," however.

There was less foreign travel by Australians, and a strong increase in foreign visitors to Australia.

It was another good year for Australian films. *Breaker Morant,* starring Edward Woodward and Jack Thompson, was the most notable success of 1980. Robert Stigwood and Rupert Murdoch formed a new production company. The first commercially-operated FM stations opened in the main cities, while "multicultural" television was introduced by Sydney and Melbourne in October. The musical *Evita* opened in Adelaide, Perth, and Melbourne.

Investment in stamps intensified, and coin collectors pushed prices to new records. Public gambling reached new levels. Prospectors, using metal detectors, were reported to have found gold nuggets with values estimated from a few hundred dollars to one worth U.S.$1 million.

R. M. YOUNGER
Author, "Australia and the Australians"

AUSTRIA

A presidential election and the 25th anniversary of the nation's release from post–World War II Allied occupation were outstanding events of 1980 in Austria. The economy continued to be strong, with low rates of inflation and unemployment.

Politics. On May 18, Rudolf Kirschläger was reelected to a second six-year term as president, a largely ceremonial position in Austrian government. Not a member of any party, Kirschläger had been nominated by the ruling Social Democrats. The opposition People's Party, satisfied with his record, made no nomination. The Liberal Freedom Party named Wilfried Gredler, Austria's ambassador to China, and the neo-Nazi National Democratic Party nominated Norbert Burger. With 91.6% of the voters participating, Kirschläger received 79.9% of the vote, carrying all nine provinces; Gredler took 16.8%, Burger won 3.2%, and 7.3% of the ballots were declared invalid.

A June 15 referendum in Vorarlberg, Austria's westernmost province, produced a majority of 60% calling for the provincial government to start negotiations with the federal government for more autonomy, especially in financial matters. No significant changes resulted immediately.

Economy. The nation's economy grew by 5.2% in real terms in 1979, an unexpectedly strong performance. Labor productivity increased by 5.8%, while inflation stood at 3.7% and unemployment at 2%. By mid-1980, real economic growth stood at a surprising 5.5%, and the estimate of 3.5% for the whole year seemed certain

to be achieved. In June, employment reached a record high, as unemployment dropped to 1%. However, the estimated inflation rate was revised upward to approximately 6%. A trade deficit of 80,900,000,000 schillings was estimated for 1980, 27% higher than the 63,700,000,000 recorded in 1979.

Foreign Affairs. On March 13, Chancellor Bruno Kreisky announced that the Austrian government would formally recognize the Palestine Liberation Organization (PLO) representative to the Vienna-based United Nations agencies and would discuss with him matters concerning the Palestinian people and the PLO. Israel registered a sharp protest.

On May 16, the 25th anniversary celebration of the signing of the Austria State Treaty was held in Vienna. Representatives of the four occupying powers—France, the United States, the Soviet Union, and Great Britain—took part. While in Vienna, U.S. Secretary of State Edmund S. Muskie and Soviet Foreign Minister Andrei A. Gromyko held an important three-hour meeting, the first high-level U.S.-Soviet contact since the Soviet intervention in Afghanistan in December 1979.

Although Chancellor Kreisky had strongly condemned the Soviet military presence in Afghanistan, the Austrian Olympic Committee voted not to join the U.S.-led boycott of the Summer Olympic Games in Moscow.

As members of the Socialist International, Chancellor Kreisky, former Premier Olof Palme of Sweden, and Felipe Gonzalez, a Spanish socialist leader, made a fact-finding visit to Tehran May 25-28. On his return, Kreisky warned that the imposition of new sanctions against Iran would further delay the release of the U.S. hostages. The Austrian government, while condemning the seizure of the hostages, announced that as a neutral country it was unable to participate in any sanctions against Iran's new Islamic regime.

ERNST C. HELMREICH
Department of History
Bowdoin College

─────── **AUSTRIA · Information Highlights** ───────

Official Name: Republic of Austria.
Location: Central Europe.
Area: 32,376 sq. mi (83 853 km²).
Population (1980 est.): 7,500,000.
Chief Cities (1975 est.): Vienna, the capital, 1,650,000; Graz, 253,000; Linz, 207,000; Salzburg, 132,000.
Government: *Head of state,* Rudolf Kirschläger, president (took office July 1974). *Head of government,* Bruno Kreisky, chancellor (took office April 1970). *Legislature*—Federal Assembly: Federal Council and National Council.
Monetary Unit: Schilling (13.39 schillings equal U.S.$1, Oct. 1980).
Manufactures (major products): Iron and steel, chemicals, wool and cotton fabrics, fertilizers.
Agriculture (major products): Livestock, dairy products, grains, barley, oats, corn, sugar beets, potatoes.
GNP (1979 est., U.S.$): $56,500,000,000.
Foreign Trade (1979 est., U.S.$): *Imports,* $20,254,000,-000; *exports,* $15,483,000,000.

AUTOMOBILES

Caught with too many large cars and V-8 engines in a year of economic recession and sharply higher prices, the U.S. auto industry underwent a severe slump in 1980. Domestic car production in the first 10 months of 1980 declined 26.3% to 5,347,346 units, while output of trucks and buses suffered an even deeper setback—sliding 52.7% to 1,241,109 vehicles.

The Detroit-based motor vehicle manufacturers, facing falling consumer orders from the outset of the 1980-model year, found themselves compelled to institute a succession of price increases in order to offset escalating costs. All five domestic manufacturers lost money in 1980, and Chrysler Corp. was saved from bankruptcy by precedent-breaking federal loan guarantees. American Motors was rescued by increased cash infusions by its new equity partner, the French government-owned automaker Renault.

All U.S. producers except Volkswagen reduced car output substantially but the cutbacks were not of sufficient help to keep 1,643 new-car dealers from closing in the 1980-model year. The dealers were hurt by interest rates as high as 18%, which raised their inventory costs as well as made retail purchase installment payments more expensive. The average new-car price rose to $8,500 in the 1980-model year.

For January through October 1980, General Motors built 3,430,382 cars in the United States, a decline of 21.7% from the comparable 1979 pe-

riod; Ford Motor Co., 1,070,916 cars, down 40.9%; Chrysler Corp., 535,663, a drop of 32.1%; American Motors, 143,238, off 6.4%, and Volkswagen, 167,147, up 16.4%. Hardest hit by the 1980 slump were full-size and intermediate car models, as well as V-8 engines. V-8 installations dropped to 30% of 1980-model production from 58% of the 1979 models. For the first time, U.S. manufacturers built more cars with fuel-saving four-cylinder engines than V-8s, 2,371,152 to 2,-121,560. The remainder, 2,652,644, had six-cylinder engines.

The 1981 Models. Hopes for a sales upturn and profits restoration were pinned on two major new entries in the increasingly popular small-car segment of the market. Ford introduced redesigned subcompacts, the Ford Escort and Mercury Lynx, replacing the Pinto and Bobcat, respectively. Chrysler climaxed a yearlong brush with bankruptcy by announcing the restyled Plymouth Reliant and Dodge Aries in the compact segment, successors to the Volaré and Aspen, respectively.

Like GM's successful 1980 X-car compacts, both the Escort/Lynx and Aries/Reliant offered front-wheel drive and base four-cylinder engines. Front-wheel drive allowed expanded interior room, and the four-cylinder engines helped the manufacturers reach a federal fleet fuel average requirement that rose to 22 miles per gallon (35 km/g) on 1981 models.

Fuel efficiency proved the major objective throughout the domestic industry. Cadillac

The financial future of the Chrysler Corporation depends on the success of the new K cars, the Plymouth Reliant and the Dodge Aries. Company president Lee Iacocca personally introduced the line.

Tom Stathis, Liaison

pioneered with introduction of a "modulated displacement" V-8 engine which could run on four or six cylinders as needed. Oldsmobile stepped up production of V-8 diesel engines which it built for all GM cars, while Buick held its 1980 sales almost equal to 1979 with a unique V-6 engine.

The top three nameplate sellers were Chevrolet's smallest entries—the Chevette and Citation—plus the intermediate Oldsmobile Cutlass. AMC, the only U.S. maker with a four-wheel-drive car, added a subcompact SX/4 entry to its Eagle line. VW's Rabbit diesel car, now made in Pennsylvania, again led all domestic and import makes in the federal fuel ratings with averages ranging from 38 mpg (61 km/g) in the city to 56 mpg (90 km/g) on the highway.

The Imports. Sales of foreign-built cars exceeded the two million mark for 1980, reaching 2,057,711 through October. The rate of volume gain above 1979 was small, but the share of U.S. total new-car sales taken by the imports stood at a record 27.5% and sparked demands by Ford and the United Automobile Workers (UAW) to federal agencies for restraints either through quotas or tariffs. On November 10 the U.S. International Trade Commission rejected the Ford-UAW petition.

Japan's Toyota and Nissan (Datsun) agreed to reduce their U.S. shipments in the fourth quarter. Nissan announced plans to build a pickup truck assembly plant in Tennessee, while Japan's Honda began construction of a car manufacturing facility in Ohio.

MAYNARD M. GORDON
Editor, "Motor News Analysis"

WORLD MOTOR VEHICLE DATA, 1979

Country	Passenger Car Production	Truck and Bus Production	Motor Vehicle Registrations
Argentina	191,851	61,031	3,863,117
Australia	405,304	56,164	6,822,100
Austria	2,781	6,595	2,224,160
Belgium	278,259	36,738	3,272,274
Brazil	498,334	629,632	8,801,866
Canada	987,673	643,988	12,515,792
Czechoslovakia	182,090	49,697	2,318,110
France	3,220,394	393,064	20,258,500
East Germany	173,500	36,500	2,992,952
West Germany	3,932,556*	317,169	23,043,315
Hungary	—	13,814	994,000
India	29,233	72,044	1,637,620
Italy	1,480,991	151,167	18,311,980
Japan	6,175,771	3,459,775	34,120,734
Mexico	280,049	164,377	4,223,667
Netherlands	90,000	16,850	4,359,000
Poland	358,800	70,000	2,441,000
Portugal	—	259	1,102,500
Rumania	72,200	51,000	330,000
Spain	965,809	157,109	7,826,652
Sweden	296,540	58,280	3,041,638
Switzerland	—	1,464	2,218,443
United Kingdom	1,070,452	408,060	16,533,541
United States	8,433,662	3,046,331	148,777,965**
USSR	1,314,000	859,000	12,800,000
Yugoslavia	285,262	29,848	2,358,966
Total	30,725,511	10,789,956	380,020,258***

* Includes 274,896 microbuses. ** U.S. total includes 116,574,-999 cars and 32,202,966 trucks and buses. *** World total includes 297,360,995 cars and 82,659,263 trucks and buses.
Source: Motor Vehicle Manufacturers Association of the United States, Inc.

BANGLADESH

President Ziaur (Zia) Rahman remained firmly in control but was beset by constant low-level harassment by tribal rebels and by political strikes and work stoppages. In February, a general strike was urged by opposition groups in protesting a ruthless suppression of a prison riot in which three prisoners were killed. In the ensuing melée in Dacca, the capital, two more persons were killed and many wounded. In June the government executed five supporters of a former regime (sentenced to death in 1977 for murdering political opponents). The result was another strike and accompanying demonstrations.

But opposition to General Zia is not confined to Dacca or the cities. There is considerable unrest among the hill tribes to the southeast, near Chittagong. In September, for example, 17 people were killed in an attack on villages by the Shanti Bahini ("peaceful army"), a group of about 2,000 men acting as the guerrilla forces for the Chakma tribe (one of several Tibeto-Burman Buddhist tribes worrying about encroachments by the Muslim government of General Zia). These insurgents number about 500,000, and their unhappiness has produced a continuing problem for the government.

General Zia seems the tireless crusader for harder work (e.g., more food production) and reproductive constraints. Indeed these two items are the key to the viability of the country itself. The *Global 2000 Report to the President*, prepared for President Carter and released in 1980, estimated that Bangladesh's population would reach between 150 and 160 million by the year 2000, an increase of nearly 100% in 20 years. There seems little way that the country can sustain this increase in terms of food alone, saying nothing of the preservation of even the partially democratic political institutions it possesses. The political and cultural context in which the president is compelled to operate militate against any likely success.

Foreign Affairs. In August General Zia visited the UN where he argued that greater aid to poor nations should come from OPEC nations and the Eastern Bloc. Bangladesh condemned the USSR for moving into Afghanistan.

CARL LEIDEN, *The University of Texas*

——— **BANGLADESH · Information Highlights** ———
Official Name: People's Republic of Bangladesh.
Location: South Asia.
Area: 55,126 sq mi (142 776 km²).
Population (1980 est.): 90,600,000.
Chief Cities (1974 census): Dacca, the capital, 1,310,-972; Khulna, 436,000; Chittagong, 416,733.
Government: *Head of state,* Ziaur Rahman, president (took office April 1977). *Head of government,* Shah Azizur Rahman, prime minister (took office April 1979). *Legislature*—Parliament.
Monetary Unit: Taka (15.4 takas equal U.S.$1, Aug. 1980).
GNP Per Capita (1978 est., U.S.$): $90.
Foreign Trade (1978, U.S.$): *Imports,* $1,344,000,000; *exports,* $576,000,000.

BANKING

The year 1980 was momentous for U.S. banking. It witnessed the beginning of major deregulation of the industry, a short period of credit control, further steps toward interstate banking, and new, exciting technological experiments. The most significant legislation was the Depository Institutions Deregulation and Monetary Control Act. In time it should help accomplish the three major goals of promoting competition in financial markets, making monetary control more effective, and solving the problem of declining membership in the Federal Reserve System.

Legislation. Specifically the act, signed by President Carter on March 31, is important to the public because it authorized banks and thrift institutions throughout the nation to offer interest on checking accounts starting at the beginning of 1981. Until then only banks and thrift organizations in New England, New York, and New Jersey could offer this service to the public. Institutions in all other states were prohibited from paying interest on checking accounts. In addition, the interest rate ceilings that limit what financial institutions can pay the saver for his or her funds would be phased out over six years, so the public could earn competitive rates on savings in banks and thrift institutions throughout the land.

It further encouraged financial competition by authorizing savings and loan organizations to issue and extend credit on credit cards, to exercise trust powers, and to invest up to 20% of assets in consumer loans and various types of corporate debt. Savings banks were authorized to offer checking accounts to business and to place 5% of their assets in commercial loans.

As a price for this competition, however, the public was likely to pay more for banking service. The banks that were offering interest on checking (so-called NOW accounts) were setting high minimum balance requirements and stiff service charges on accounts that went below these levels in order to afford the higher cost of giving the public these new services and higher rates.

The new act removed the usury ceilings that many states had imposed on mortgage loans and on business and agricultural loans (of more than $25,000), and in general the public could expect to find that its financial markets would be changing to reward the saver with higher returns and charge the borrower more for his loans. The savers largely have been subsidizing borrowers during periods of inflation and high interest rates, but this should terminate slowly.

The new powers to pay higher rates on savings over time undoubtedly will make banks and savings institutions more competitive with money market funds. Such funds have grown to approximately $80,000,000,000 in size in the past few years, due to an inability of these deposit-taking institutions to offer rates competitive with those of the funds. All in all, the competition for the saver's dollar should intensify.

The second goal of the new legislation—making Federal Reserve credit control policy more effective—was tackled by imposing reserves on all transaction accounts and nonpersonal time accounts of all depository institutions. This means that credit unions, savings banks, savings and loan institutions, and nonmember banks will all have to keep reserves at the Fed. These requirements will be phased in over eight years.

Conversely, member banks will experience about a 43% reduction in aggregate reserve requirements. This should help solve the problem of banks leaving the Federal Reserve System due to the past inequity of reserve requirements. By making reserve requirements more uniform, the Congress hoped to make Federal Reserve policy more equitable and more effective in controlling business-cycle fluctuations, inflation, and unemployment.

During 1980, the need for smoother Federal Reserve policy became obvious, as interest rates skyrocketed to a 20% prime rate, plummeted to 10%, and then moved back up again. This made life difficult for all those dependent upon bank credit. The reason was the Federal Reserve's new emphasis on controlling the supply of money and letting the demand for funds determine interest rate levels. This step was taken as the Federal Reserve tried to restrict money supply to stem an inflation rate that reached a staggering 18% level.

The effort to control inflation also led to the invocation of the Credit Control Act of 1969 for a period of just under four months, in an effort to restrain the use of consumer credit. What was so significant was that the controls, with mandatory reserve requirements, were placed not just on banks and thrift institutions but also on all other consumer lenders, such as retailers and auto dealers. The experiment ended when the economy slowed; yet many felt that the government intervention in the credit allocation process was a major cause of the economy's extreme volatility during the year.

The year saw continued developments of interstate banking as banks and nonbanks alike tried to extend their services across the United States in every legal manner.

The efforts of major money center banks to lend and solicit funds nationally through finance company subsidiaries, credit card distribution, and broad solicitation of business continued to expand. And such companies as Sears Roebuck also talked about nationwide solicitation and lending of funds through credit cards and about the opportunity to save by paying an amount above the balance due with interest provided on the excess. The cash management account of Merrill Lynch continued to grow. It offered customers nationwide banking and money market rates on funds. Bankers in smaller and medium sized institutions expressed more fear for their future than ever before as they saw these expansive trends.

Another element of change was the beginning of experiments with "banking in the home." The plan is a program through which people can connect their telephones with their televison sets, see their bank balances, and then authorize any transactions they want. Bankers reported that this plan was a development of genuine importance because it could help lessen the dependence of customers on the writing and routing of the highly inefficient paper check.

The more banking can function through computer talking to computer without a need to move pieces of paper, the more efficient the industry will become. And many see the day approaching when bank service and the deposit and withdrawal of funds will be as automatic as the provision of electricity and water to the home. Most bankers concluded that by the end of the 1980s U.S. banks and bank service delivery systems will be radically different from what they were as the decade started.

See also UNITED STATES: Economy.

PAUL S. NADLER
Rutgers University

BELGIUM

In 1980, Belgium suffered the fall of two coalition governments—including the third in little more than a year—and in late October installed the 30th mixed ministry since World War II. The continuing crisis had three major components: economic, military-security, and constitutional.

Economy. The two governments of Prime Minister Wilfried Martens that failed in 1980 (April and October) experienced difficulties in convincing the six-party coalitions to approve Martens' plans to cut public spending. In the period 1974–80, government spending rose from 36% to 47%, with public borrowing steadily increasing to 7% of the gross national product. Martens argued that the nation was paying an enormous price for delaying the cuts. In particu-

lar, he cited rising interest rates; the highest unemployment rate, in excess of 11%, in the European Community (EC); and a severe decline—about 90% in the previous ten years—in foreign investments. The question of cuts in social security spending was directly related to government instability. Martens' Social Christian party and the Liberal Party advocated cuts based on their concern over the mounting public debt, but they were opposed by the Socialists.

Military. A general unwillingness to bear cuts in social services was related to a concurrent reduction in military spending. While Belgium had pledged its NATO allies that it would augment previous expenditures by 3%, the real increase was only about 1.5%. Austerity measures in the armed forces delayed renovations, limited flying time for pilots, and required the use of obsolete equipment. The Belgian role in NATO's long-term plans was the subject of controversy in two areas—its failure to buy radar reconnaissance planes (AWCS) for use in Europe and its wavering position on the stationing of new U.S. nuclear missiles on Belgian soil. Martens indicated that Belgium might be willing to deploy 48 cruise missiles, but he postponed a final decision until the completion of U.S.-Soviet negotiations on curbing such deployment. Meanwhile, the Belgian Socialist party, particularly its Flemish wing, took the lead in resisting military contributions to NATO and the housing of nuclear weapons in Belgium.

Constitutional Conflict. The long-running conflict over devolution continued to plague the bilingual, bicultural nation. Although constitutional revision created regional assemblies with exclusive authority in housing, town planning, employment, regional development, and water resources, the regionalization plan did not transfer jurisdiction in diplomatic or military affairs, transportation, justice, postal service, or telecommunications. The autonomy plan, which was passed in August, established parliaments for the 3.5 million French-speaking Walloons in southern Belgium and the 5.5 million Dutch-speaking Flemings to the north but made no accommodations for the future status of the 1 million inhabitants of bilingual Brussels. The Belgian variant of multiparty government made any further reform extremely difficult, primarily because all cabinets must have Flemish-Walloon equity in Liberal (conservative), Socialist, and Social Christian (centrist) groups. Constitutional changes necessary for devolution now would require the approval of the three militant regionalist parties.

Anniversary. Despite the government crisis, Belgium celebrated its 150th birthday in 1980. King Baudouin, who was reported to have heart ailments, and Queen Fabiola played the primary role in the anniversary celebrations held throughout the year.

PIERRE-HENRI LAURENT
Tufts University

BELGIUM • Information Highlights

Official Name: Kingdom of Belgium.
Location: Northwestern Europe.
Area: 11,781 sq mi (30 513 km²).
Population (1980 est.): 9,900,000.
Chief Cities (1978 est.): Brussels, the capital, 1,015,710; Liège, 224,136; Antwerp, 197,305.
Government: *Head of state,* Baudouin I, king (acceded 1951). *Head of government,* Wilfried Martens, prime minister (took office April 1979). *Legislature*—Parliament: Senate and Chamber of Representatives.
Monetary Unit: Franc (31.04 francs equal U.S.$1, Nov. 1980).
Manufactures (major products): Fabricated metal, iron and steel, coal, textiles, chemicals.
Agriculture (major products): Sugar beets, potatoes, grain, tobacco, vegetables, fruits, livestock.
GNP Per Capita (1978 est., U.S.$): $9,070.
Foreign Trade (1979, U.S.$, includes Luxembourg): *Imports,* $60,410,000,000; *exports,* $56,258,000,000.

BIOCHEMISTRY

Biochemists in 1980 produced pure human antibody from cells growing in the laboratory, moved genes between cells, and synthesized and described a natural substance involved in asthma and allergy. In addition, a food additive that never gets into the body from the digestive tract was proposed, and chemical variants of a brain hormone were entered into clinical trials as contraceptives for both sexes.

Pure Human Antibody. To unravel the complexities of the immune system, as well as to develop new vaccines, diagnostics, and medicines, scientists have long needed pure samples of antibody. The problem has been that the body naturally reacts to a foreign chemical or microorganism with a complex and unpredictable antibody mix. Several years ago, British scientists fused two types of mouse cells to create a line of laboratory-growing cells that produce large quantities of a single antibody. In August 1980 Lennart Olsson and Henry S. Kaplan of Stanford University reported that they had fused human cells into a hybrid cell that produces a pure human antibody. The Stanford researchers obtained human spleen cells, which make antibodies, from spleens removed in routine clinical evaluation of Hodgkin's disease patients. Each spleen cell was fused with a cancerous bone marrow cell, giving the hybrid the ability to reproduce repeatedly in the laboratory. In the first tests, the cells made antibody to the chemical 2-nitrochlorobenzene, which Hodgkin's disease patients receive in the course of their diagnostic tests.

Gene Manipulations. Genetic material from the human X chromosome has been moved into and reproduced in bacteria, Barbara R. Migeon and colleagues at Johns Hopkins University reported in August. The X chromosome is one of the two chromosomes that determine sex. Each cell in a woman's body contains two X chromosomes; each cell in a man's contains only one X and one smaller Y chromosome. The X chromosome carries the genes for such sex-linked diseases as hemophilia and Lesch-Nyhan syndrome. By using bacteria to make many copies of chromosome segments, scientists expect to be able to identify the genes responsible for more than 150 human hereditary diseases. The results might be used to identify women carrying single copies of defective genes and to determine the mechanism by which one X chromosome is inactivated in each cell of a woman's body.

The moving of genes into mouse cells exemplified two strategies of genetic engineering. A gene from a virus was placed in the newly fertilized egg of a mouse, and the egg was implanted in a foster mother. Francis H. Ruddle of Yale University found that in a few cases the gene had been reproduced along with the natural mouse genes and was distributed to cells of the newborn mouse. The experiment was a small step toward correction of human genetic diseases.

Cells that reproduce throughout the life of an animal provide another opportunity for genetic manipulations. Martin J. Cline of the University of California at Los Angeles added a gene to bone marrow cells taken from mice. Cline then introduced the altered cells into a mouse that had had its own bone marrow cells destroyed. The new cells populated the mouse's bone marrow and gave the mouse resistance to a drug, the trait provided by the added gene. In a controversial experiment, Cline applied gene therapy to two patients in Italy and Israel, inserting a copy of the human gene for the protein which the patients lacked. It was not immediately clear whether the procedure was beneficial.

New Birth Control. Clinical trials began in 1980 for a group of chemicals thought to have potential for birth control. The chemicals were modeled after a natural brain hormone called luteinizing hormone-releasing hormone which is important in both male and female reproduction, sexual development, and sexual behavior. One compound underwent separate clinical tests as a contraceptive for men and for women. The chemicals were selected from more than 1,000 compounds developed as potent, long-lasting hormones with very specific actions. Those now in clinical tests mimic the natural hormone. In 1980, Wylie Vale of the Salk Institute in San Diego also developed a chemical that powerfully opposes the hormone's actions. In animal tests, that "superantagonist" inhibited both ovulation and sperm production. Vale proposed that it also would be applicable to human contraception.

Novel Food Additive. A new concept in food additives reached the Food and Drug Administration in April 1980. Dynapol, a Palo Alto, CA, chemical specialty firm, presented for approval a food preservative that never enters the body beyond the digestive tract. Anoxomer is the name of the preservative, which contains the same active chemical groups as the common food antioxidant, BHT. The new molecule, however, is a branched structure and is too large to cross the intestinal lining into the body and too large for body enzymes to break down. The company continued work on a variety of food additives, including colorings and sweeteners, that are not absorbed by the intestines.

Promiscuous Chemical Defense. The scale insect *Dactylopius* contains a chemical called carminic acid, which protects it from being eaten by most insects. Thomas Eisner and colleagues at Cornell University discovered that the *Laetilia* caterpillar does feed on the scale insects. Not only does the caterpillar disregard carminic acid as a deterrent, but it also uses the chemical in its own defense. When the caterpillar is disturbed, it emits droplets containing a high concentration of the chemical. Eisner reported that during evolution the caterpillar managed to crash the scale's defensive chemical barrier and appropriate the weaponry for its own protection.

JULIE ANN MILLER, *"Science News"*

BIOGRAPHY

A selection of profiles of persons prominent in the news during 1980 appears on pages 147-158. The affiliation of the contributor is listed on pages 6-9. Included are sketches of:

ANDERSON, John Bayard

Once described as "the darkest of all possible darkhorses," John B. Anderson challenged conventional political wisdom in 1980 by becoming a serious presidential candidate. (*See* feature article, page 25.) Having served ten terms as a Republican U.S. representative from Illinois, Anderson at first sought the GOP nomination, pledging "to wear his wallet on the right and his heart on the left." Though he gained many admirers for his unconventional political style (symbolized by his campaign slogan, "The Anderson Difference") and willingness to speak frankly on controversial issues, Anderson in April 1980 concluded that his political future lay not in the Republican Party but in an independent candidacy. So he avoided the traditional party foundation and mounted what he called a "National Unity" campaign. Despite financial constraints and lack of support from elected public officials, Anderson garnered 6.6% of the general election vote, the best showing by an independent or third party candidate since 1968.

Background. John Bayard Anderson, the son of Swedish immigrants, was born in Rockford, IL, on Feb. 15, 1922. A star debater and valedictorian of his 1939 high school graduating class, Anderson entered the University of Illinois. After his graduation in 1942, he earned a J.D. degree from Illinois in 1946 and an LL.M. degree from Harvard Law School in 1949. Returning to Rockford, Anderson practiced law until 1952, when he began a two-and-a-half-year stint in West Germany as a foreign service officer. It was in Germany that he met and married his wife, Keke.

In 1956, having returned to law practice in Rockford, Anderson launched his political career by winning the office of state's attorney for Winnebago county. Four years later he was elected to Congress from Illinois' 16th district on a campaign platform that opposed "big government" and the expansion of Communism. During his first few terms, Anderson compiled a voting record that was hailed by right-wing groups as one of the most conservative in the House. And in moves he later repudiated, Anderson, a member of the Evangelical Free Church, introduced in 1961, 1963, and 1965 the so-called "Jesus Amendment," a constitutional amendment declaring that "This nation devoutly recognizes the authority and law of Jesus Christ, Saviour and Ruler of nations, through whom are bestowed the blessings of Almighty God."

The growing social and political ferment of the 1960s, however, led Anderson to rethink his political philosophy. In an action that exemplified his increasing moderation, Anderson gained national attention in 1968 by casting a crucial vote in favor of open housing legislation. With his growing credentials as a moderate, Anderson in 1969 assumed the chairmanship of the House Republican Conference, the third-ranking position among House Republicans. Thereafter he emerged as a leader of moderate and liberal Republicans. Although he generally supported the domestic programs of presidents Nixon and Ford, Anderson slowly began to adopt maverick positions as his party moved to the right. His disenchantment with the Watergate scandal led him to become one of the first Republicans to urge President Nixon to resign.

After facing a well-financed conservative challenger in the 1978 Republican primary for his House seat—the first primary challenge he faced in 18 years—Anderson decided that he had run his last race for Congress. Feeling that he would be too old to become a freshman senator but still wanting a platform for his ideas, Representative Anderson instead chose a long-shot race for the presidency. Although he lost the contest, he is likely to remain a highly visible and articulate gadfly in American public life.

JEFF FISHEL AND DARRELL WEST

Penelope Breese and Leif Skoogfors, Liaison

JOHN
ANDERSON

BANI-SADR, Abolhassan

Abolhassan Bani-Sadr, one of Iran's leading revolutionary theoreticians and a longtime friend and adviser to Ayatollah Ruhollah Khomeini, is said to have told the late Jean-Paul Sartre in 1965, "I shall be the first president of Iran." The man who at the age of 46 achieved this unlikely ambition is certainly one of the most energetic, able, and articulate leaders to have emerged from the Islamic revolution in Iran. His overwhelming victory in the country's first presidential election on Jan. 25, 1980 not only reflected the favor of Ayatollah Khomeini but also demonstrated wide support for his belief that economic independence is the key to the success of a classless, Islamic society.

An ardent nationalist, Bani-Sadr is critical of past U.S. involvement in Iran (despite opposing the holding of the American hostages in Tehran) and fearful of Soviet expansionism. An economist by training, he believes that the Iranian economy must be recast in accordance with traditional Islamic socialism. While his mild and casual manner, liking for European dress, and long residence in France have helped establish a reputation as a moderate, Bani-Sadr's basic attitudes are rooted in a strict Islamic upbringing.

Background. Born in 1933 at Hamadan (Ecbatana) in western Iran, Bani-Sadr is the son of a revered Shiite religious leader, Ayatollah Seyed Nasrollah Bani-Sadr. While a student at Tehran University, he took part in the nationalist anti-shah demonstrations of the early 1950s. During protests against the launching of the shah's "White Revolution" in 1963, Bani-Sadr was wounded and then imprisoned for four months. The next year he went into exile in France where he studied and taught at the Sorbonne. He was a tireless anti-shah propagandist, writing three books and numerous articles depicting Iran as the victim of foreign domination.

When the exiled Ayatollah Khomeini moved from Iraq to France in 1978, Bani-Sadr became his chief spokesman and closest associate. Less prickly than the ayatollah and adept in the use of the media, Bani-Sadr did much before and after the Iranian revolution to persuade the West to take a favorable view. As deputy prime minister of economics and finance in the new Islamic regime, he pushed for radical new policies, not all of which were adopted. He was appointed foreign minister Nov. 11, 1979, but served only 18 days before being ousted. As president, however, he effectively oversaw the nationalization of banks, insurance companies, and much private industry. As chief of Iran's military forces, his greatest test came with the outbreak of war with Iraq late in the year.

ARTHUR CAMPBELL TURNER

BEATRIX, QUEEN

When Beatrix was invested as queen of The Netherlands on April 30, 1980, she was greeted not only with the enthusiastic welcome of a large majority of the Dutch people but also with violent demonstrations outside the 15th-century Nieuwe Kerk (New Church) in Amsterdam where the ceremony was held. This combination of honor and trouble was characteristic both of current conditions in the nation and her personal history.

Background. Beatrix Wilhelmina Armgard of Orange-Nassau was born at Soestdijk Palace in Baarn on Jan. 31, 1938, the first child of then Princess Juliana and her husband, Prince Bernhard. She was taken to England after the German invasion of May 10, 1940, and then went immediately to Canada with her mother until the end of the war. She was named presumptive heir to the crown in 1948. (The constitutional law was changed on the occasion of her accession to provide that her eldest surviving heir would follow her without distinction of sex.) In this capacity she was named to the Council of State, the highest advisory body in the Dutch government, at the age of 18. Shortly thereafter she entered the University of Leiden, where for five years she studied law and associated subjects, nearly earning a doctorate. When it was announced that she was to marry a young German diplomat, Claus von Amsberg, there was considerable protest because of bitter memories of the German occupation and persecutions of World War

II. The marriage ceremony on March 10, 1966, in Amsterdam was marked by widespread and sometimes violent demonstrations. Prince Claus worked diligently to win over the Dutch people, acquiring Dutch nationality and learning to speak the language impeccably. The arrival of three sons assured the continuation of the royal line.

On the morning of April 30, 1980, Queen Juliana abdicated, and that afternoon Beatrix' investiture ceremony was held in Amsterdam. (There is no royal coronation under the Dutch constitution.) The ceremony was held despite bitter nearby street fighting between police and squatters and their sympathizers, who protested the city's housing shortage. (*See also* Netherlands.)

HERBERT H. ROWEN

BIRD, Larry

Larry Bird's long-awaited entry into the National Basketball Association (NBA) was not a disappointment. The 6'9" (2.06 m) forward from Indiana State University became the first NBA player since Wes Unseld (in 1969) to be named to the all-rookie and all-pro squads. Known to be a gifted passer with a deadly shot, Bird entered the league as a 22-year-old and promptly led the Boston Celtics to one of the most amazing turnarounds in league history. His steady and sometimes spectacular performance earned him rookie-of-the-year honors for the 1979–80 season.

The 1978–79 Celtics had won just 29 games and lost 53. But with Bird aboard and the hiring of a new coach, Bill Fitch, the Celtics rapidly erased the previous season's bad memories. Boston's 61–21 won-lost record in 1979–80 was the best in the NBA. Bird appeared in all 82 games as a season-long starter. His scoring average of 21.3 points per game led the Celtics and was 16th best in the NBA. He snared 10.4 rebounds per game, again best among the Celtics and 10th overall in the NBA.

Bird's long-range shooting ability was confirmed by his success from outside the new three-point circle, just less than 24 ft (7.32 m) from the basket. Bird made 40.6% of those attempts, third best in the NBA. His minutes-per-game average was a high 36, and he was disqualified for committing too many fouls only four times. He had a single-game scoring high of 45 points.

Larry Bird of the Boston Celtics

UPI

Background. Born Dec. 7, 1956, in French Lick, IN, the son of Georgia Bird became one of the most fabled collegiate athletes in decades. A star at Springs Valley High School, Bird enrolled at Indiana University but left soon after to attend the smaller Indiana State. While at ISU, Bird led the Sycamores to 81 victories and only 13 losses in three years.

At the same time that he was building his reputation as a deft passer and all-around team player, Bird was also a top scorer. In 94 college games, Bird scored 40 or more points 15 times, 30 or more points 49 times, and 20 or more 87 times. His highest one-game output was 49. He was voted the men's collegiate player of the year for his senior season, when he was the nation's second-leading scorer with a 28.6 average.

In Bird's final ISU season, the Sycamores won 29 straight games before losing the NCAA tournament final against Michigan State. Boston's first-round draftee the year before, Bird signed a 5-year contract for a reported $3.25 million, the highest ever for a National Basketball Association rookie.

GREG HEBERLEIN

BUSH, George

Throughout his political life George Bush has suffered setbacks and disappointments. But he has always rebounded as he did at the 1980 Republican National Convention when, after he failed to win the presidential nomination, Ronald Reagan picked him as his vice-presidential running mate. The career of the former Congressman from Texas continued to ascend as he was elected the nation's 43d vice-president on November 4.

Background. George Herbert Walker Bush was born June 12, 1924, in Milton, MA. His father, Prescott Bush, was an investment banker and later Republican senator from Connecticut, and young George was reared in affluence and with a sense of noblesse oblige. Bush attended Phillips Academy in Andover, MA, and Yale University from which he was graduated Phi Beta Kappa in 1948. He had interrupted his schooling during World War II to become a Navy pilot and was decorated with the Distinguished Flying Cross.

After Yale, Bush moved away from his native New England and out of his father's shadow to Texas, where he founded an oil drilling firm which ultimately made him wealthy in his own right. He also became active in politics in Texas, serving as a delegate at the 1964 Republican convention. He gained the 1964 GOP Senate nomination, but lost the November election. In 1966 Houston voters sent him to Congress where, during two terms, his voting record was generally conservative. He did, however, back environmental protection measures and vote for the 1968 Civil Rights Act.

After Bush lost another Senate race in 1970, President Richard Nixon appointed him ambassador to the United Nations and then chose him to be chairman of the Republican National Committee. As GOP chairman, Bush remained loyal to Nixon during the difficult days of the Watergate scandal.

Bush also served in the Ford administration, first as U.S. envoy to China and then as head of the scandal-ridden Central Intelligence Agency.

After the Democrats regained the White House in January 1977, Bush returned to private life and began planning his bid for the 1980 Republican presidential nomination. His long and diligent campaigning paid off in the Iowa caucuses in January. Bush scored a stunning upset victory over Ronald Reagan which vaulted him to the front of the Republican field.

Over the long campaign haul, though, Bush could not hold his advantage over Reagan and he bowed out of the race in May. But his spirited campaign and his strength among moderate Republicans made him Reagan's logical choice as running mate. His nomination as vice-president assured Bush that he would be a prominent figure in the Republican Party for years to come.

Bush and his wife, the former Barbara Pierce, whom he married in 1945, have four sons and a daughter.

ROBERT SHOGAN

UPI

U.S. Vice-President-elect George Bush

CARTER, Jimmy

When Jimmy Carter became the 39th president of the United States in January 1977 he was a relative unknown on the national scene. And although his actions as chief executive were subjected to intense scrutiny, in his fourth year in the White House he was still regarded as an ambiguous and enigmatic figure.

Opinion polls showed that most Americans admired him personally as a man of high integrity. But the surveys also indicated that many of Carter's fellow citizens questioned his competence to handle the problems facing him. This mixed impression stemmed in part from the harsh realities of the national condition—the unabating energy crisis, an economy plagued by inflation and recession, and growing threats to the U.S. position in international affairs.

But public uncertainty about the president also reflected the style and substance of his leadership. He lacked the oratorical skill or dramatic flair of some of his predecessors to inspire support for his policies. Moreover, Carter's critics complained, his conduct of his office fell far short of matching the bold promises of economic progress and government reform that he made as a candidate. In fact, one of Carter's major efforts in the White House was to diminish public expectations of the government. "Government cannot solve our problems," he declared in his 1978 State of the Union address. "It cannot set our goals; it cannot define our vision."

He called for self-reliance and sacrifice by the citizenry. Carter could point to some substantial achievements. In September 1978 he had helped engineer the Camp David accords between Israel and Egypt which ultimately led to the signing of a peace treaty between these two long-hostile nations. And he persuaded the Senate to ratify in April 1978 the Panama Canal Treaty under which the United States agreed to turn over the canal to Panama at the end of the century. But the Strategic Arms Limitation Treaty, which the United States and the Soviet Union agreed to in 1979, still languished in the Senate. And all of Carter's efforts in foreign policy were overshadowed in the public mind by anguish over the prolonged captivity of the U.S. hostages in Iran, an episode that raised questions about U.S. power and prestige abroad.

On the domestic side, the president could claim credit for pushing through a reform of the civil-service system, and for the creation of the two new cabinet departments of energy and education. But his promises of fundamental reforms in the welfare and income-tax systems remained to be kept, as did his pledge to establish a national health-insurance system. Unemployment dropped during Carter's first three years in the White House. But a raging inflation forced restrictions in monetary policy which contributed to one of the worst national recessions since World War II. Carter's energy program—phased decontrol of oil prices, an energy mobilization board, and government subsidies for developments of synthetic fuels—offered hope for the future. But for the present, the nation remained hostage to the will of the OPEC countries.

Carter's own sense of frustration at these developments was revealed in a dramatic speech to the nation in July 1979 which followed a so-called domestic summit conference at Camp David attended by more than 100 national leaders. The president warned Americans that they were going through "a moral and spiritual crisis," a sort of national "malaise," which he blamed largely on the unhealed wounds of Vietnam and Watergate. Then, striving to give his administration a new face, he fired four members of his cabinet and reorganized the White House staff under his closest personal aide, Hamilton Jordan.

These moves brought no immediate solution to the domestic problems that continued to plague Carter, nor did they improve immediately his standing in the polls. However, the president did receive unanticipated political help from developments overseas. The seizure of the hostages in Iran and the Soviet invasion of Afghanistan prompted many Americans to rally around their commander-in-chief. This patriotic reaction to international crises, combined with Carter's own skill at taking political advantage of the powers of incumbency, helped him to beat the challenges for the Democratic presidential nomination by California Gov. Edmund G. Brown, Jr., and Massachusetts Sen. Edward M. Kennedy. In spite of the advantages of incumbency, Carter was unable to convince the American public that he should be returned for a second presidential term. After his overwhelming defeat on November 4, the president indicated that he would return to his Plains, GA, home to write his memoirs.

Background. President Carter was born on a farm outside the small town of Plains, GA, on Oct. 1, 1924, the first of four children of James Earl Carter, Sr., and his wife Lillian. He was graduated from the U.S. Naval Academy in 1947 and served in the Navy until his father died in 1953. He then resigned, returned to Plains, and used the family farm to build a prosperous peanut business. After two terms in the Georgia Senate (1963–67), he was elected governor of the state in 1970. His victory over Gerald Ford in the 1976 presidential election made him the first chief executive from the Deep South since before the Civil War.

Jimmy Carter is married to the former Rosalynn Smith. They are the parents of three sons and a daughter.

ROBERT SHOGAN

DALE, Jim

The British actor, comedian, and song-and-dance man Jim Dale received a Tony award on June 8, 1980, for his performance in *Barnum*, the Broadway extravaganza which opened in April 1980. Dale was featured in the role of P. T. Barnum, the 19th-century master showman and amiable con man. *Barnum*—which depicts life as a circus—gave Dale free rein for his varied talents, including singing, dancing, clowning, juggling, and tight-rope walking. In preparation for the role, the actor read whatever books on Barnum he could find and toured the Barnum Museum in Bridgeport, CT. Regarding the show, Dale commented that, like Barnum, he wants "to enjoy life, to give excitement and magic to as many people as possible."

Since moving to the United States in 1974 to star as a roguish swashbuckler in Frank Dunlop's restaging of Molière's *Scapino* (for which Dale wrote the score), he has

UPI

Jim Dale, the star of "Barnum"

also appeared in three Walt Disney comedy films—*Pete's Dragon* (1977), *Hot Lead and Cold Feet* (1978), and *The Spaceman and King Arthur* (1979). Dale's activities also include a recent performance in a Connecticut production of Peter Nichols' burlesque comedy *Privates on Parade*.

Taking pride in the fact that he has never had an acting lesson, Dale reportedly has said: "The technique of acting is so simple, it's unbelievable. It's just being sincere, that's it."

Background. Jim Dale, whose name was originally Smith, was born on Aug. 15, 1935, in the town of Rothwell, England, the son of a steelworker. Encouraged by his parents in his urge to perform, he received ballet training from the time he was nine and made his debut as a solo comedian at Kettering in 1951. After a stint in the Royal Air Force, he worked as a pop singer, disc jockey, professional dancer, magician's assistant, and television-show host. Since 1963 he has appeared in a number of British films, including several in the "Carry On" comedy series. He also has made his mark as a songwriter, composing, among other hits, the Oscar-nominated title song of the film *Georgy Girl* (1966).

Dale's acting career was highlighted by performances at the Edinburgh Festival as Autolycus in *The Winter's Tale* (1966) and as Bottom in *A Midsummer Night's Dream* (1967). After being invited by Laurence Olivier in 1969 to join the Young Vic Company at Britain's National Theatre, Dale won plaudits for his performances in other Shakespearian roles and in Peter Nichols' satire *National Health* (1969).

Jim Dale, who lives in New York City, has four children.

HENRY S. SLOAN

DONAHUE, Phil

Convinced that "television's problem is not controversy but blandness" and that "you don't solve problems by repressing ideas," talk show host Phil Donahue has, since 1967, presented to his audiences no-holds-barred discussions of contemporary and often controversial topics. He has interviewed such diverse personalities as former Nazi Albert Speer, atheist Madalyn Murray O'Hair, Ku Klux Klan Grand Wizard David Duke, Yippie leader

Jerry Rubin, novelist Ayn Rand, Sen. Edward Kennedy, and First Lady Rosalynn Carter.

His Chicago-based program *Donahue*—winner of six national and two local Emmy awards—has been syndicated since 1976 by Multimedia Program Productions and is broadcast by more than 200 stations from coast to coast. In early 1980 it was the most widely watched syndicated television talk show in the United States. Since 1979 Donahue has also been a regular interviewer on NBC-TV's *Today* show. His autobiography, *Donahue: My Own Story* (1979), appeared on best-seller lists in 1980.

Background. The son of a furniture salesman, Phillip John Donahue was born in Cleveland, OH, on Dec. 21, 1935. Educated in Roman Catholic parochial schools, he attended the University of Notre Dame and was graduated with a B.B.A. in 1957. He worked summers at a local radio station and was hired for various radio and television assignments following graduation. In 1959 he joined station WHIO in Dayton as a newscaster/interviewer, a job that, from 1963 on, also involved producing and moderating a phone-in talk show, *Conversation Piece*. In November 1967 he began hosting his own morning interview program, *The Phil Donahue Show*, on Dayton's WLWD-TV. Unique among talk shows for its degree of audience involvement and the controversial nature of its subject matter, *The Phil Donahue Show* soon gained national popularity. Early programs included a debate between General Motors President Edward Cole and consumer advocate Ralph Nader and a series on prison conditions broadcast from Ohio State Penitentiary and a women's reformatory. In 1974 the program was transferred to Chicago station WGN-TV, and its name was shortened to *Donahue*.

Donahue considers himself a reformed male chauvinist who became an ardent champion of feminism and a "lapsed Catholic" who now believes that "organized religion has been very unfair to God." He has four sons and a daughter from his first marriage. In May 1980 he married actress Marlo Thomas.

HENRY S. SLOAN

DRINAN, The Rev. Robert F.

In May 1980, after almost ten years as a leading liberal in the U.S. Congress, Robert F. Drinan (D-MA), a Jesuit priest, abruptly and with considerable personal anguish cancelled plans to run for a sixth term in the House. His Jesuit superiors in Rome and Boston, acting on the "express wish" of Pope John Paul II, ordered him not to seek reelection. The 59-year-old priest, former dean of the law school at Boston College, accepted the Vatican decision "with regret and pain."

Like other Catholic clergy and religious who sought political office, Father Drinan for years had encountered stiff resistance from church authorities. Several bishops had denied priests permission to run for office; Father Drinan's political career was considered a significant exception to the church's general prohibition of clergy in politics. Since his accession, Pope John Paul consistently has voiced a hard line against clergy in politics. During his 1980 trip to Africa, the pope spoke directly against such involvement, terming politics a "proper field of action for the laity."

Expressing the belief that he had been chosen "to work for justice in America and peace throughout the world," objectives "recommended by the Second Vatican Council and all modern popes," Father Drinan described his years in Congress as his "most influential" as a priest. He claimed roles in many difficult problems confronting the nation, including the termination of the Vietnam war, the military draft, and mandatory retirement. As a member of the House Judiciary Committee, he played a central role in impeachment proceedings against President Nixon. He also participated in human rights missions in Latin America and the Soviet Union, served as a staunch supporter of Israel, and backed efforts to apply human rights criteria to the nation's dealings with dictatorships.

The Jesuit indicated that after his term expired in January 1981 he would continue to work for nuclear disarmament and the alleviation of world hunger, two issues he dealt with in Congress. "As a person of faith I must believe there is work for me . . . which somehow is more important than the work I leave," he said.

Background. Born in Boston, MA, on Nov. 15, 1920, Robert F. Drinan was graduated from Boston College in 1947. He later received law degrees from Georgetown University, Washington, DC, and a licentiate in sacred theology from the Gregorian University, Rome. Ordained in 1953, he was appointed assistant dean of the law school at Boston College in 1955 and dean a year later. He was elected to the 92d Congress in 1970 and to four succeeding Congresses from the 4th district in Massachusetts.

His writings include such books as *Religion, the Courts and Public Privacy* and *Democracy, Dissent and Disorder*.

ROBERT L. JOHNSTON

HEIDEN, Eric

The best description of the situation was given by a speed skater from Norway. "It's not exciting to be skating now," Froede Roenning complained, after collecting a third-place bronze medal in the 1,000-meter final at the XIII Winter Olympics in Lake Placid, NY. "The medals are delivered before the race." The entire sport belonged to one man, Eric Heiden.

The 21-year-old native of Madison, WI, captured all five gold medals for speed skating in the 1980 Games. He captured the shortest race, the 500-meter sprint, he captured the 10,000-meter endurance race, and he captured everything in between—the 1,000, 1,500, and 5,000. His performance was a record. No athlete in Olympics history—summer or winter—had won five individual gold medals in one Games.

There was only one moment of peril. Midway through the 1,500-meter race, he almost fell after catching his inside skate in a rut in the ice. He simply stopped his fall with his left hand and kept skating. His time for his final win, the 10,000, was 14:28.13; it knocked 6.20 seconds off the world record.

He was sometimes called "The Republic of Heiden" by headline writers. As such, he would have finished third in the gold-medal race behind the Soviet Union and East Germany. He would have beaten 34 countries, including the United States which won only one gold besides his.

Wearing the flashy gold spandex uniform of the U.S. skaters, just bigger than everyone else with his 29-inch (74-cm) thighs, and skating in his own country, he was in the spotlight from the beginning of the Olympics to the end. He laughed and called all the attention and the pressures "The Great Whoopee." "I didn't want anyone to set me up

The Rev. Robert F. Drinan
Franken, Liaision

on a pedestal," he said. "I just wanted to be relaxed and have a good time."

Introduced to the sport at the age of 13 and coached by former Olympian Dianne Holum, Eric is a product of the speed-skating program at West Allis, WI, the only artificial-ice track in the United States until the completion of the Olympic facilities. Although Heiden won the all-around World Championship in 1977, 1978, and 1979 and had taken the World Sprint Championship for the fourth consecutive time just prior to the Games, he was far from a national hero before the Olympics. He was a participant in a no-money sport in a country filled with big money sports. He had been attracted to the sport for its purity, one skater determining his own fate without relying on anyone else.

After finishing second in the 1980 all-around World Championship, two weeks after the Games, Eric Heiden indicated he would resign from competitive speed skating. His plans include cycling, hockey, a career in sports medicine, but no "commercial exploitation in which he would have the continual focus of the media."

LEIGH MONTVILLE

JORDAN, Vernon E., Jr.

Vernon Jordan had long since certified his position as the nation's most prominent black-rights spokesman. As president of the National Urban League, he helped lead the march for black equality from Southern highways into the more complex arenas of the political chamber and the corporate boardroom. In 1980, with a presidential campaign underway, he agitated to thrust the concerns of black and poor Americans into the political debate. After 1960s-style black rioting erupted in Miami, Jordan diagnosed the violence as a symptom of widespread despair that should not go unheeded. But just then, Jordan was silenced—almost permanently. He was attending an Urban League function in Fort Wayne, IN, when, in the early hours of May 29, he was shot in the back by an unknown assailant. Bullet fragments lodged inches from Jordan's spinal column, and he spent days in "very serious" condition before beginning a long, slow recovery. No arrests were made in the case, but FBI Director William Webster said in August that he believed it had been a political assassination attempt.

Vernon E. Jordan, Jr.
National Urban League

In September, Jordan returned to his post, vowing that he would "refuse to let the possibility of renewed violence stand in the way of my beliefs and my duties."

Background. Vernon Eulion Jordan, Jr., was born Aug. 15, 1935, in Atlanta, GA, the son of a postal supervisor and a caterer. He was graduated from DePauw University and Howard Law School. He began his civil-rights activities while working for Atlanta attorney Donald Hollowell, who sued to integrate the University of Georgia. Jordan himself literally paved the way for that integration in 1961 by personally leading the first black student, Charlayne Hunter, through a protesting white mob. Jordan later became Georgia state field secretary for the NAACP and director of the Southern Regional Council's Voter Education Project, for which he traveled extensively through the country registering black voters.

As the 1970s began, Jordan became executive director of the United Negro College Fund in New York. After Whitney M. Young, Jr., drowned in 1971, Jordan was tapped to head the Urban League. With his sophisticated style and background as both a fundraiser and grass-roots political organizer, he became an appropriate symbol for the black-rights movement. Often, he has remarked that the right to sit at a lunch counter is meaningless if one does not have the means to pay for the meal; jobs, he maintains, are the key to black progress. He has also preached constantly against what he calls "the new negativism" in the country that seeks to cut back on efforts to help the disadvantaged.

Jordan is married to the former Shirley M. Yarbrough. They are the parents of one daughter, Vickee.

DENNIS A. WILLIAMS

KENNEDY, Edward Moore

Sen. Edward Kennedy's defeat by Jimmy Carter in the contest for the 1980 Democratic presidential nomination was a stunning disappointment for his supporters, many of whom had longed for years for another Kennedy presidency. But Kennedy's grace in the face of adverse political pressures won him widespread respect. And with his liberal base of support still intact, he emerged from the campaign as a force to be reckoned with in the future.

Background. Edward Moore Kennedy was born in Boston on Feb. 22, 1932, the youngest child of Joseph Kennedy and his wife, Rose. Perhaps because he was the youngest child in a large family, as a young man he seemed to lack self-discipline and this occasionally caused him difficulty. As an undergraduate at Harvard he was suspended for allowing another student to take an examination for him.

Nevertheless he followed in the footsteps of his older brothers, John and Robert, and entered public life. After he was graduated from Harvard in 1956 and from the University of Virginia Law School in 1959, he was named assistant district attorney in Suffolk County, MA, in 1961. The following year, at the age of only 30, with the blessing of his brother John, who was then president, he ran for and won the U.S. Senate seat in Massachusetts that John Kennedy had held. In the Senate he has displayed a natural political flair, and a strong commitment to liberal causes, which together with his family name have helped him easily win reelection to the Senate three times.

But personal misfortune seemed to plague his life. Less than a year after he entered the Senate came the assassination of President Kennedy in November 1963, and less than five years after that, the assassination of Robert Kennedy. A 1964 airplane crash had left him with a back injury.

As the sole surviving brother, Edward "Teddy" Kennedy became the heir to his family's political dynasty. He moved quickly to establish himself by gaining election as Democratic Senate "whip," or assistant majority leader in 1969. But later that year Kennedy was involved in a strange and tragic auto accident on Chappaquiddick Island, MA, in which a young woman passenger in his car, Mary Jo Kopechne, was drowned. Although Kennedy was cleared of criminal responsibility for the death, he has never been able to explain fully the circumstances of that accident and the episode at Chappaquiddick has haunted his public life ever since.

Chappaquiddick ruled out a possible Kennedy presidential candidacy in 1972, and it also contributed to his decision not to run in 1976. Meanwhile, although he was defeated in his bid to remain Senate majority whip in 1971, his influence in the Senate increased. In January 1979 he became chairman of the Judiciary Committee. In November 1979, Kennedy, who had previously announced his intention to support Carter for reelection, announced that he would challenge the president, whose standing in the polls had been declining steadily.

Kennedy's candidacy revived questions about Chappaquiddick and Kennedy's character, which he had difficulty answering. And the hostage crisis in Iran prompted many voters to rally around Carter, who defeated Kennedy in a sufficient number of state primary and caucus campaigns to win renomination. Despite the steadily growing odds against him, Kennedy did not concede defeat until the Democratic convention met in New York City in August. Kennedy scored a personal triumph at the convention with a speech on the party platform which electrified the delegates. The Massachusetts senator subsequently endorsed Carter and campaigned for his reelection.

Kennedy, and his wife, the former Virginia Joan Bennett, have three children, Kara, Edward M., Jr., and Patrick Joseph.

ROBERT SHOGAN

KIRKLAND, Lane

(Joseph) Lane Kirkland, who was elected president of the AFL-CIO on Nov. 19, 1979, has broken the mold for the stereotyped U.S. labor leader. Kirkland is a soft-spoken Southerner and an intellectual with two academic degrees. More typical, perhaps, are his pragmatic and incisive opinions.

At the time of his selection as AFL-CIO president, Kirkland, a longtime protégé of his predecessor George Meany, pointed out that "everything that we (the union) have done and every program that we have undertaken, I think, has mine among the fingerprints on it."

In the first year of his presidency, the AFL-CIO altered course but slightly. Kirkland pressed for more aggressive organizing activity to enlist new union members and for the

AFL-CIO President Lane Kirkland

AFL-CIO

return to the AFL-CIO of the United Auto Workers and the Teamsters unions. If anything, Kirkland is tougher on management than his predecessor. He called the business community's support for the Senate filibuster against labor law reform in 1978 "class warfare."

As AFL-CIO president, Kirkland, an anti-Communist, seeks a larger voice in foreign affairs. He argues: "We have done our time in the field of international conflict; we have earned our scars and stripes; and we mean to be heard." Despite many reservations he developed the consensus position that enabled the AFL-CIO to support the SALT II treaty. He also began a campaign against free trade.

Background. Born in Camden, SC, March 12, 1922, Kirkland was graduated from the U.S. Merchant Marine Academy in 1942. He served through the remainder of World War II aboard merchant vessels. A licensed master mariner at the war's end, he entered Georgetown University's School of Foreign Service, from which he was graduated in 1948.

He joined the research staff of the American Federation of Labor, working as a speech writer and pension specialist. As such he wrote campaign speeches for Alben Barkley and Adlai E. Stevenson. In 1958 he moved to the International Union of Operating Engineers as research director. In two years he was back at the AFL-CIO as executive assistant to President George Meany, a post he held until his election as secretary-treasurer in 1969.

Kirkland's knowledge and skills have been recognized by the National Urban League, the Rockefeller Foundation, the Brookings Institution, and the Carnegie Endowment for International Peace, on whose boards he has served.

An avid gardener, a collector of modern paintings, a jazz buff, and a passable cook, Kirkland lives in a Washington suburb with his second wife, Irena, who survived Auschwitz, the Nazi prison camp. They take little part in the capital's cocktail and dinner circuit. He is the father of five grown daughters from his first marriage.

Kirkland still holds his membership in the International Organization of Masters, Mates and Pilots, which he joined as World War II ended.

GORDON H. COLE

McENROE, John Patrick, Jr.

John McEnroe, who won his second straight U.S. Open tennis title in September 1980, burst on the international tennis scene as an 18-year-old amateur in 1977. He was the first qualifier and the youngest player to reach the semifinals—against Jimmy Connors—at Wimbledon. McEnroe lost to Connors, but his showing was the start of a meteoric rise that has had few parallels in tennis. A left-hander with a devastating service, executed in an awkward motion that confuses opponents, McEnroe, who is 5'11" tall and weighs 165 pounds, has quick reflexes and amazing stamina. If McEnroe has a weakness it is a penchant for temper tantrums on the court. He will argue incessantly with officials about controversial calls and he will arouse fans not only to boo his behavior but to reward him with standing ovations as well.

He won the 1979 U.S. Open at the age of 20, defeating Vitas Gerulaitis in the final and becoming the youngest men's Open champion since Pancho Gonzales won in 1948.

In 1980, he and Björn Borg of Sweden, the No. 1 ranked player in the world, engaged in two of the most grueling championship matches on record—in the finals at Wimbledon and the Open. At Wimbledon the two went five sets and Borg emerged the winner after a 34-point tiebreaker in a duel many believed was the finest match ever played. At Flushing Meadows, NY, site of the Open, McEnroe, the defender who was seeded second to Borg, defeated the Swede in five breathtaking sets of the final. He took the court less than 24 hours after he had beaten Connors in another spine-tingling, five-set match in the semifinals.

Background. McEnroe was born on Feb. 16, 1959, in Wiesbaden, West Germany, where his father was in the Air Force. When John was 4 his family moved to Douglaston NY, where McEnroe grew up and still lives with his family.

His father, John McEnroe, Sr., a New York City lawyer, manages his son's career and financial affairs. His mother, Kay, is an avid fan, and his 14-year-old brother, Patrick, already has a ranking. His other brother, Mark, is a tennis buff, too.

John was graduated in 1977 from the Trinity School in New York, where he excelled in tennis, soccer, and basketball. He attended Stanford University, and after winning the NCAA tennis singles title as a freshman, turned pro in June 1978. In his first season he won $329,024 in prize money. In 1978 he was the youngest player since Jack Kramer in 1939 to compete for the United States in a Davis Cup final. His childhood tennis teacher was Harry Hopman, the well-known Australian Davis Cup coach of the 1950s. McEnroe is one of the most successful tournament doubles players in tennis, unusual for so high-ranking a performer. Since he dislikes practicing, he plays doubles to sharpen his game.

GEORGE DE GREGORIO

MONDALE, Walter

The U.S. vice-presidency is one of the most frustrating positions in government, and Walter P. Mondale, like every other vice-president, was sometimes uncomfortable in the role of permanent understudy. But Mondale probably got more satisfaction out of his job than have most of his 41 predecessors.

The reasons are to be found in Mondale's personality and background, and his relationship with Jimmy Carter, who twice chose him as his Democratic running mate. From his earliest days in Minnesota politics, as a protégé of the late Hubert Humphrey, Mondale learned to accept a subordinate role. His native caution and self-discipline helped him avoid public conflicts with President Carter and enabled him to find outlets for his experience and energies within the limitations of the job.

During 12 years in the U.S. Senate, from 1964 to 1976, Mondale attained a broad grasp of national and international issues and a practical understanding of the workings of the federal government. This experience was particularly useful to Jimmy Carter, who came to the presidential office as an outsider, unfamiliar with the ways of Washington. Equally valuable to Carter were Mondale's close ties to unions, blacks, and other liberal groups in the Democratic Party with whom Carter himself had trouble getting along.

Much of Mondale's work was shielded by the confidentiality of the White House, where he functioned as an adviser to the president on a host of problems, foreign and domestic. But there was also an important public dimension to his job. He traveled widely abroad as the president's personal representative. At home he frequently was the administration's spokesman, particularly in addressing liberal organizations, with which Mondale's liberal record as a senator usually gained him a sympathetic audience. On the campaign trail he was a workhorse. During Carter's battle for renomination, while the president restricted himself to the White House because of the Iranian hostage crisis, Mondale traveled 125,000 miles (200 000 km) and visited 36 states, where his liberal credentials helped offset the appeal of the president's principal challenger, Sen. Edward M. Kennedy. On November 4 the Carter-Mondale ticket was unsuccessful in its bid for reelection.

Background. Mondale, who was born in Ceylon, MN, on Jan. 5, 1928, entered politics as a campaign worker for Hubert Humphrey in 1948. Mondale's first public office was attorney general of Minnesota to which he was appointed in 1960. He and his wife, Joan, have two sons, Theodore and William, and a daughter, Eleanor Jane.

ROBERT SHOGAN

MUGABE, Robert

On April 18, 1980, Robert Mugabe officially was sworn in as the first prime minister of the newly independent state of Zimbabwe. As such, he became the leader of Africa's 50th independent state in the Organization of African Unity. This followed from his decisive victory in British-supervised elections six weeks earlier. His sweeping triumph, over both the white-Rhodesian-backed "internal settlement" party of Bishop Abel Muzorewa, and his own co-leader in the Patriotic Front guerrilla alliance, Joshua Nkomo, gave his Zimbabwe African National Union 57 of the 80 seats contested and 63% of the popular vote.

For Mugabe these events ended 20 years of participation in the struggle against discrimination and white supremacy in the former British colony. In the bitter and bloody seven-year guerrilla war his followers, operating from bases in Mozambique, had borne the main burden of the fighting. In consequence, and as a self-professed Marxist, he was regarded frequently as a radical extremist and the most militant and intractable of the nationalist leaders. In fact, since assuming office Mugabe has shown himself determined to subordinate his Marxism to the pressing problems he confronts. He has tempered ideology with a pragmatic recognition of the need to retain white skills and encourage a mixed economy, and has emphasized conciliation. And he has stressed not a one-party state but a commitment to work within the new constitution.

Background. Robert Gabriel Mugabe was born on Feb. 21, 1924, at Kutama, northwest of Salisbury. The son of a village carpenter, he was born into the majority Shona tribe and educated under the guidance of Roman Catholic missionaries who later arranged for him to attend Fort Hare University College in South Africa. He returned to teach at home, then spent four years in Ghana at the St. Mary Teacher Training College, Takoradi, 1956–60. There he met and married his Ghanaian-born wife, the former Sarah Haytron. He soon plunged into Southern Rhodesian nationalist politics, first as aide to Joshua Nkomo, then in 1963 to the Rev. N. Sithole and his new Shona-based rival organization. He said later that Nkomo was not committed to armed struggle.

In 1964 he was arrested for the third time and was detained for the next nine years. Released in 1974 with other leaders as a result of pressure from South Africa's John Vorster and his Southern Africa détente policy, he went briefly to Lusaka, Zambia, Dar es Salaam, Tanzania, and then to Maputo, Mozambique. There President Samora Machel permitted him to build up his own breakaway party and its guerrilla forces. He concluded a tactical alliance with Nkomo, the Patriotic Front, in 1976 in order to deal with a new diplomatic initiative by Prime Minister Ian Smith, U.S. Secretary Henry Kissinger, and British Foreign Secretary David Owen.

R. B. BALLINGER

MUSKIE, Edmund Sixtus

When Cyrus Vance resigned as U.S. secretary of state in the spring, President Carter turned to Edmund Sixtus Muskie, 66, as Vance's successor. Although Muskie had served on the Senate Foreign Relations Committee for six years, he was not regarded as an expert on external affairs. But he enjoyed other advantages, including long political experience at high levels, a reputation as one of the most respected members of Congress, and lofty political ambitions as Democratic vice-presidential candidate in 1968 and presidential contender in 1972.

Muskie also possessed important personal qualities essential to favorable relationships with the president, other Cabinet members, the assistant for national security affairs, and many foreign leaders. In recent years he had become a key congressional ally of the Carter administration. Known for his professional integrity, Muskie was acknowledged as conscientious, intelligent (Phi Beta Kappa), and thoughtful, as well as articulate and personally credible. He was regarded as tough-minded, with an appetite for debate and, despite his explosive temper, an instinct for timely compromise.

As secretary of state, Muskie's main concerns were developments in the Persian Gulf, especially the U.S. hostage crisis and the Iranian-Iraqi war; U.S. relations with its European allies; and overall U.S.-Soviet developments. Secretary of State Muskie represented the United States at the signing of an agreement with Canada to curb acid rain; addressed a special session of the UN General Assembly on the subject of international assistance; and met with

Soviet Foreign Minister Andrei Gromyko in Vienna in May. The secretary also campaigned for Carter's reelection.

In an interview following the November elections, the former Maine legislator said that he felt that the Soviet Union was seeking "a more stable, less confrontational relationship" with the United States. He also said that he expected changes in the conduct of U.S. foreign policy. According to Muskie, "the national security adviser ought not to have a press officer. And he ought not to give press backgrounders. He ought not to be dealing with representatives of foreign governments in an official way."

Background. Muskie's brief tenure as secretary of state capped a distinguished career in American politics that began in 1946. Son of a Polish immigrant tailor, he was born in Rumford, Maine, March 28, 1914. He was graduated from Bates College (B.A., 1936) and Cornell University (LL.B., 1939). Before entering politics, he practiced law in Maine, and during World War II he was commissioned in the U.S. Naval Reserve. Prior to 1958, when he became the first Democrat ever elected to the U.S. Senate from Maine, he served in the state's House of Representatives and as its governor.

During his 22 years on Capitol Hill he emerged as a member of the Senate's inner circle. He chaired various Senate committees and subcommittees, and became one of its leading environmentalists, sponsoring the Clean Air and the Water Quality acts. As chairman of the newly-created Senate Budget Committee, he made it a crucial link in the budgetary process.

ELMER PLISCHKE

PÉREZ ESQUIVEL, Adolfo

Adolfo Pérez Esquivel was awarded the Nobel Peace Prize for 1980. Since 1974, the Argentine human rights activist has headed a group called Peace and Justice Service. Based in Buenos Aires, the group assists those whose human, social, and economic rights have been violated, especially in Argentina, but also elsewhere in Latin America. In 1973 Pérez Esquivel formed the Ecumenical Movement of Peace and Justice, an organization backed by Catholics, Protestants, and others opposed to the violent confrontation of the political left and right in Argentina. An international campaign to pressure the United Nations into establishing a human rights commission was mounted by Pérez Esquivel in 1976.

Informed of his selection by the Norwegian Nobel Committee for having "shone a light in the darkness" of Argentina, Pérez Esquivel accepted the honor, recalling those in his Latin American movement who have worked diligently for peace and the rights of all. The Argentine was chosen from among 57 individuals and 14 organizations that had been nominated for the prize. He had been placed in nomination for the award by Mairead Corrigan and Betty Williams, Irish peace workers who won the prize in 1976. By winning the prize, Pérez Esquivel became the recipient of $212,000, as well as of a monthly pension equal to $5,-000. The pension was decreed for Argentine Nobel recipients by the military junta in Buenos Aires at a time (1977) when Argentine writer Jorge Luis Borges had been nominated for a Nobel award in literature. The ruling junta grudgingly responded to Pérez' recognition by claiming that his human rights activities abetted terrorism.

Pérez Esquivel promised to use his prize money to increase pressure on governments regarding human rights issues. The champion of nonviolent solutions to Argentine problems had expressed special concern for the disappeared persons, up to 20,000 in number, supposed victims of Argentine repression.

Background. A noted sculptor, Adolfo Pérez Esquivel was, until 1974, a professor of architecture. Born in Buenos Aires in 1931, he is married and has three children. He is a devout Roman Catholic and also a follower of the teachings of Mahatma Gandhi. Upon attempting to leave his country in 1977 to attend a human rights gathering in Europe, he was detained, imprisoned, and tortured. More than a year later he was released and placed under house arrest. Until September 1980, he had to report regularly to the police.

LARRY L. PIPPIN

RATHER, Dan

On Feb. 15, 1980, dynamic newscaster and investigative reporter Dan Rather was named anchorman and managing editor of the *CBS Evening News* effective early 1981, under a multimillion-dollar five-year contract. He succeeds Walter Cronkite, who asked to be relieved of day-to-day duties to concentrate on hard news and special assignments. Rather's appointment was preceded by several weeks of discussions during which the three major networks were vying for his services.

Since 1975, Dan Rather—who has won several Emmy awards—has served with Mike Wallace and Morley Safer, and later Harry Reasoner, as coanchorman of CBS's popular television newsmagazine *60 Minutes*. With an estimated Sunday evening viewing audience of some 40 million, the program was television's top-rated show in 1980.

Background. The son of an oil pipeline worker and a waitress, Dan Rather was born in Wharton, TX, on Oct. 31, 1931. His ambition to become a reporter dates back to his boyhood, when he attended local Democratic Party meetings with his father. At Sam Houston State College in Huntsville he lost out on a football scholarship but managed with the help of a journalism instructor to obtain a job as a sportscaster and writer for a local radio station. After he was graduated with a B.A. in 1953, Rather studied at the University of Houston and South Texas School of Law and served for a year as a journalism instructor at Sam Houston State. In the mid-1950s he joined the CBS radio affiliate in Houston, and toward the end of the decade he became director of news and public affairs with CBS's Houston television affiliate. He soon became nationally known for his skillful coverage of Hurricane Carla in 1961 and the John F. Kennedy assassination in 1963. Appointed CBS White House correspondent in 1964, Rather interrupted that assignment with a year as chief of the CBS London bureau and a stint on the battlefields of Vietnam before returning to Washington in 1966. As part of his coverage of the Johnson and Nixon administrations, Rather

TV newsman Dan Rather

UPI

traveled on presidential visits to the Middle East, the Soviet Union, and China; covered political conventions; and anchored dozens of news specials. But because of his outspokenness, he occasionally clashed with President Nixon and his advisers. Relieved of his White House duties in August 1974, he served as anchorman and correspondent for *CBS Reports* until his assignment to *60 Minutes* in late 1975.

Dan Rather collaborated with Gary Gates on the book *The Palace Guard* (1974), a chronicle of events surrounding the Watergate affair, and with Mickey Herskowitz on the autobiographical *The Camera Never Blinks* (1977).

He and his wife, Jean, who have a son and daughter in college, make their home on Manhattan's East Side.

HENRY S. SLOAN

REAGAN, Ronald Wilson

The selection of Ronald Reagan as the Republican Party's 1980 presidential candidate underlined two major trends in national politics which have contributed greatly to Reagan's political success. One is the increasing domination of the electoral process by television, a medium which Reagan's experience as an actor has enabled him to exploit brilliantly. The other is the growing strength of the conservative movement, for which Reagan has long been a principal national spokesman.

Background. Ronald Wilson Reagan was born on Feb. 6, 1911, in the village of Tampico, IL, and grew up in Dixon IL, a town of about 12,000. His father, a shoe salesman, struggled most of the time to make a living. Reagan, the younger of two sons, worked part-time and during the summer to earn spending money. But Reagan has happy memories of his boyhood. And the rugged individualism, optimism, emphasis on home and family, and other small town Midwestern values of his youth shaped his outlook on life and provided the basis for his political creed.

Reagan's first job after he was graduated from Eureka College, near Peoria, in 1932, was as a radio sports announcer. But his ambition was to be an actor. And in 1937 he made his way to Hollywood where he started a motion-picture career that was to last 20 years. Most of the more than 50 films he made were undistinguished. Probably his best remembered role is as the ill-fated Notre Dame football star George Gipp in the movie biography of Knute Rockne.

Reagan, who served in the Army during World War II, started his political life as a liberal Democrat. He was an ardent supporter of Franklin D. Roosevelt, and for a number of years was a leader of the Screen Actors Guild. But in the 1950s Reagan's political outlook became more conservative as the times changed and, some critics have suggested, as his own wealth increased. His new views became evident when, as a spokesman for General Electric Co., he toured the country addressing the company's employees on the virtues of free enterprise and the excesses of big government.

In 1964 Reagan delivered a televised fund raising appeal on behalf of GOP presidential candidate Barry Goldwater which won the admiration of conservatives throughout the country. The speech also impressed California Republican leaders and paved Reagan's way to the GOP gubernatorial nomination in 1966. In his first attempt to seek elective office Reagan defeated incumbent Democratic Gov. Edmund G. (Pat) Brown by nearly a million votes. And in 1970, despite the difficulties of governing the nation's largest state, Reagan won reelection handily.

Reagan's performance during his eight years as governor was more pragmatic than his conservative campaign rhetoric had suggested it would be. During his tenure the state's hitherto regressive tax structure became more progressive, and he pushed through welfare-reform legislation which, while it reduced the welfare case load, significantly boosted payments to the neediest recipients.

Critics complained that Reagan took too little interest in day-to-day operations of the statehouse, preferring to delegate authority to his appointees. But his two-term administration was free of any major scandal, and his overall record of governing was respectable enough to give him credibility as a presidential candidate.

Reagan's first attempt to win the Republican presidential nomination, in 1968, was too little and too late to overtake Richard Nixon, who became the party's candidate and gained the presidency. Reagan tried again in 1976. But his challenge to President Gerald Ford failed chiefly because most Republicans rallied around the incumbent.

His strong showing in defeat, though, made Reagan the early front-runner in the 1980 GOP presidential competition. The chief obstacle facing him was his age; Reagan turned 69 just before the crucial New Hampshire primary. But his victory in that contest, and his vigorous campaigning there and elsewhere against a large field of younger opponents erased doubts about his stamina and endurance. Reagan's skill as a campaigner and his faithful base of conservative support assured him of his party's nomination weeks before the national convention in Detroit in July. His inexperience in foreign policy posed problems for Reagan as a candidate and as a potential president, and so did some of his conservative views. But his choice of George Bush, who appealed to moderate voters, as his running mate demonstrated that though Reagan is a conservative at heart he has a practical political mind. On November 4 the American electorate decided to give the Reagan-Bush ticket a chance to lead the United States.

Reagan has four children, Maureen and an adopted son, Michael, from his first marriage to the actress Jane Wyman, and Patricia and Ronald from his present marriage to the former Nancy Davis.

ROBERT SHOGAN

U.S. President-elect Ronald Reagan

Michael Evans, Liaison

SAMARANCH, Juan Antonio

Three days before the Summer Olympics opened in Moscow on July 19, 1980, and the day before his 60th birthday, Juan Antonio Samaranch, Spain's ambassador to the Soviet Union, was elected president of the International Olympic Committee (IOC). ''When I take my post,'' Samaranch said upon his election, ''I cannot be a diplomat any longer. I will be a diplomat the IOC way.''

He was alluding to the major task he would confront as he began his tenure——healing the rift caused by the boycott, led by the United States, of the Moscow Games. He would have to bring the international sports community back into harmony in time to preside in 1984 over the Winter Games at Sarajevo, Yugoslavia, and the Summer Games at Los Angeles. ''I am going to follow the path that Lord Killanin has already embarked on and I hope with the collaboration of my colleagues . . . to preserve the unity of the Olympic movement,'' he said prior to taking office.

Known for his quiet, serious, and business-like manner, Samaranch won many friends during 14 years as an IOC member. He served as vice-president, chief of protocol (responsible for organizing meetings and ceremonial functions), and chairman of the press commission. His diplomatic position in Moscow made him a link between IOC and the Soviets during the planning of the 1980 Olympics. This link increased his stature among his colleagues and helped foster the strong support he received for his election from the Eastern, African, and Latin American nations. He was chosen on the first ballot, becoming the first Spaniard to be elected to the top post of the 86-member body since it was founded in 1894. His term runs for eight years.

Background. In 1977, Samaranch became the first Spanish ambassador to the Soviet Union since 1939. He says little in public, but has been sought often for advice. He speaks French and English fluently. His interest in contemporary art is well-known.

His first association with sport came when he served as president of the Spanish Roller Skating Federation, a sport not on the Olympic program.

He is married and the father of two children.

GEORGE DE GREGORIO

STREEP, Meryl

A versatile actress, equally adept at playing ingenues and senior citizens, Meryl Streep received the best supporting actress award of the Academy of Motion Picture Arts and Sciences on April 14, 1980 for her performance in the divorce drama *Kramer Vs. Kramer* (1979). Miss Streep, who catapulted to stardom on the stage, in films, and on television within a short period of time, also appeared in 1979 in the films *Manhattan* and *The Seduction of Joe Tynan*. Her laurels for that year included honors from the National Board of Review and the New York Film Critics, as well as the Golden Globe and Los Angeles Film Critics awards. Earlier, she had won an Emmy for her portrayal of the Roman Catholic wife of a Jew during the Nazi era in the television miniseries *Holocaust* (1978) and had earned critical acclaim for her stage performances, beginning in 1975, in productions of the New York Shakespeare Festival, the Phoenix Theater, and other ensembles.

Late in 1980, Miss Streep also appeared in a New York stage production of the musical *Alice in Concert.*

Background. The daughter of a pharmaceutical company executive, Mary Louise Streep—who acquired the name Meryl as a child—was born in Summit, NJ, on June 22, 1949. She began taking voice lessons at 12, and starred in several musical comedies at her high school. Following drama studies at Vassar College and a stint with a theatrical company in Vermont, she entered the Yale Drama School, and appeared in a variety of roles at the Yale Repertory Theatre under Robert Brustein's direction.

Armed with a master of fine arts degree from Yale, Miss Streep went to New York in 1975 and auditioned for New York Shakespeare Festival director Joseph Papp, who cast her in a revival of Sir Arthur Wing Pinero's *Trelawny of ''the Wells''* and later engaged her for summer productions of Shakespeare's *Henry V, Measure for Measure,* and *The Taming of the Shrew.* Additional New York stage productions in which she appeared were *27 Wagons Full of Cotton, A Memory of Two Mondays, The Cherry Orchard,* and *Happy End.* On television, Miss Streep won acclaim in the dramatic special *The Deadliest Season* (1977). Other of her film credits include *Julia* (1977), her film debut, and *The Deer Hunter* (1978).

Meryl Streep lives in New York City with her husband, sculptor Donald Gummer, and their son, Henry.

HENRY S. SLOAN

UPI

Meryl Streep and her Oscar

SUZUKI, Zenko

Few in the majority Liberal Democratic Party (LDP) of Japan saw Zenko Suzuki as a possible prime minister until the summer of 1980, when a deadlock developed among faction leaders following the party's election victory of June 22. The compromise choice for president of the LDP, it had been decided, would come from the faction of the late Masayoshi Ohira because he was belatedly recognized (after his death on June 12, 1980) as having sacrificed his life in an effort to unite the party. Suzuki was selected as the president of the LPD, and as such was elected by a special Diet session to become Japan's 15th postwar prime minister on July 17, 1980.

Known as Zennin Zenko (''Zenko the Good Fellow''), Suzuki displays a rough, inarticulate demeanor, but he has won the trust of conservatives and has made few enemies. His strength lies in the characteristically Japanese penchant for quiet human relations behind the scenes in advising others, settling party disputes, and reaching a consensus.

Background. Born on Jan. 11, 1911, into a fishing family of Yamada, Iwate prefecture, Suzuki was graduated in 1935 from the Imperial Fisheries Institute. He once organized a national fisheries workers' union. After World War II, in April 1947, he was first elected to the Diet as a member of the Japan Socialist Party (JSP). In 1949 he left the JSP to run as a member of the Liberal Party, a conservative group that combined with the Democratic Party in 1955 to form the LDP, which has dominated Japanese politics ever since. Suzuki has been elected to the (lower) House of Representatives fourteen times.

As an associate of Ohira, Suzuki rose slowly but steadily in the LDP. In 1960 he first entered the cabinet as Minister of Posts and Telecommunications. Later he served as chief cabinet secretary and held the portfolios of welfare and agriculture. He has been chairman of the executive council of the LDP nine times.

The family of the new prime minister includes his wife, Sachi, whom he married in 1939; one son; and three daughters.

ARDATH W. BURKS

TIKHONOV, Nikolai Aleksandrovich

A longtime friend of President Leonid Brezhnev, 75-year-old Nikolai A. Tikhonov was appointed the new prime minister of the Soviet Union upon the resignation of Aleksei Kosygin on Oct. 23, 1980. An economic organizer from the Ukraine, Tikhonov had served as Kosygin's first deputy since 1976 and had become a full member of the Politburo as recently as November 1979. Although Kosygin, 76, had suffered a severe heart attack in 1979, his resignation came as somewhat of a surprise. But because he had resigned in good standing and Tikhonov had been carrying out many of his responsibilities anyway, the new prime minister was not expected to institute major changes in policy. A thin, gray-haired man who speaks with a Ukrainian accent, Tikhonov was not widely known either to the Soviet public or the international community.

Background. Nikolai Aleksandrovich Tikhonov was born in Kharov, the Ukraine, on May 1, 1905. He was graduated from the Metallurgical Institute in Dniepropetrovsk in 1930 and worked his way up to workshop foreman and eventually plant manager. He first met Leonid Brezhnev in the late 1930s and then again in the late 1940s, when Brezhnev served as first secretary of the Dniepropetrovsk committee. Like others in the so-called ''Dniepropetrovsk group,'' Tikhonov benefited from Brezhnev's rise in the party. He became a deputy minister in 1955; deputy chairman of the State Economic Council in 1960; and deputy chairman of the State Planning Committee in 1963. Shortly after Brezhnev became president and party leader in 1965, Tikhonov was named a deputy prime minister. He is identified with heavy industry and related economic planning.

JEFF HACKER

WALESA, Lech

At midyear an unemployed electrician, Lech Walesa, 37, by the end of 1980 had become one of the most powerful men in Poland. By scaling the gates of the strikebound Lenin shipyard at Gdansk in August, Walesa embodied the defiance that led to the creation of the only independent labor union in the Communist world, called Solidarity. (*See* POLAND.) As head of the federated union, Walesa led the successful negotiations with Polish government officials and rallied his fellow workers to stand up to the pressure and veiled threats from the Soviet Union. The short, heavily mustachioed father of six became a folk hero to his countrymen and a recognizable world figure.

Background. Born in the village of Popow, between Warsaw and Gdansk, during the Nazi occupation in World War II, Walesa attended a state vocational school in the nearby town of Lipno. He became a labor leader at the Lenin Shipyards during the bloody food price riots of 1970. In 1976, as a delegate to the government-sponsored trade union, he was fired for drawing up a list of worker grievances. Working in a machine repair shop, he helped found the Baltic Free Trade Unions Movement, a predecessor of Solidarity, in 1978. Twice more before August 1980, he was fired from jobs for labor agitation. On Aug. 14, 1980, when he scaled the gate of the Lenin Shipyard, he took the helm of the angry strike movement.

A devout Roman Catholic, Walesa always wears on his left lapel a picture of the Black Madonna of Czestochowa, Poland's patron and a symbol of Polish nationalism. Aides carry a wood-and-silver crucifix to be prominently displayed wherever he speaks. Reportedly well-groomed, polite, and soft-spoken in negotiations with government leaders, he also is known sometimes to pressure the rank and file into agreeing with him.

His unionizing efforts have brought him a salary roughly equal to that of a shipyard worker—$330 a month—which allowed him to move with his wife, Miroslawa, and children from a drab, two-room flat in Gdansk to a new six-room suburban apartment.

JEFF HACKER

Polish labor leader Lech Walesa
Bulka, Liaison

ZHAO, Ziyang

On Sept. 10, 1980, the National People's Congress of China elected 61-year-old Zhao Ziyang as the new prime minister, replacing Hua Guofeng. A practical bureaucrat with proven administrative ability, Zhao was chosen to lead China's drive toward modernization.

With the support of party leader Deng Xiaoping, who at age 76 was anxious to install a new, progressive leadership, Zhao had risen rapidly in the Communist hierarchy. Serving in relative obscurity as government and party leader in Sichuan, China's largest province, Zhao was summoned to Peking in January 1980 to take charge of the day-to-day work of the government as a deputy prime minister. In February, he was elected one of seven members of the Politburo's Standing Committee, China's highest decision-making body. His ascension to the prime ministership was considered a rarity because he had served in the provinces rather than in the central government and played no major role in party politics.

Background. Zhao Ziyang was born of a landlord family in 1919 in Huaxian district in Henan province. He joined the Young Communist League in 1932 and became a party member six years later. Before the Communists came to power in 1949, Zhao served as party secretary for the Nanyang district committee in southwestern Henan. In 1950, he worked in the Communist party's South China sub-bureau in Guangdong province and became the first secretary there in 1965. A protégé of Tao Zhu, a high-ranking party leader, Zhao was purged by the Red Guard in 1967 when Tao was disgraced for obstructing the Cultural Revolution. Rehabilitated, Zhao returned to Guangdong in 1972 as party chief. Three years later, he was transferred to Sichuan to be its first secretary.

It was in the late 1970s that his economic reorganization in Sichuan attracted the attention of the central leadership. By granting autonomous authority to factories and expanding privately cultivated land, he brought increases in industrial and agricultural production while reducing unemployment. Rescued from bankruptcy, Sichuan became the economic model for other provinces. For Zhao, decentralized management, incentives for workers, and promotion of productive forces became the three essentials of economic development.

CHESTER C. TAN

Armed guards make sure no one enters San Andres University in La Paz in the tense aftermath of the July 17 military coup. The new junta faced violent resistance.

BOLIVIA

On June 29, 1980, Bolivians went to the polls for the third time in three years to elect a president. Because none of the candidates won an outright majority of the vote, the final decision would be made by Congress one month later. But before the process could be brought to fruition, the armed forces seized control of the country, ousting interim President Lydia Gueiler Tejada and bringing to power army commander Gen. Luis García Meza Tejada, her cousin.

Elections and Coup. The interim government of President Gueiler, established in November 1979, seemed weak from the start. Gueiler was unable to keep García Meza and other allies of former President Natusch Busch from maintaining and strengthening their hold on the army. In addition, the harsh economic policies imposed in December 1979, including a devaluation of the peso and a sharp rise in bus fares and gasoline prices, provoked widespread protests, led by the national trade union organization, the COB.

Elections were announced for June 1980, and tensions began to mount. Rumors of a coup by García Meza intensified in mid-April, when he returned to the position of commander-in-chief of the armed forces, a post he had held during the brief presidency of Natusch Busch. Although García Meza and labor leader Juan Lechin Oquendo signed a pact pledging to respect an outright winner in the election, the United States made it clear that military intervention would be met by economic sanctions. The campaign was also marked by an assassination attempt against President Gueiler by the commander of the palace guard and two assassination efforts against Jaime Paz Zamora, the vice-presidential candidate of the Democratic Popular Union (UDP).

As expected, none of the 13 candidates won the 50% majority needed for outright victory. Former President Hernan Siles Zuazo of the UDP emerged with a substantial plurality, 34%, followed by Paz Estenssoro (18%), right-wing Hugo Banzer Suarez (14%), and Socialist Party leader Marcelo Quiroga Santa Cruz (7%). With Siles Zuazo sure to win confirmation in Congress, the armed forces seized control of the government on July 17. The following day, García Meza was appointed head of a three-man junta.

The takeover was met with widespread resistance. In a gun battle at COB headquarters in La Paz, Quiroga was killed and Lechin arrested. Workers in the tin- and zinc-mining district of Santa Ana clashed with military forces until bombed into submission. Resistance even began to appear in the ranks of the military. Subsequent months saw a campaign of arrest and torture by the junta to consolidate power.

Foreign Affairs and Economy. International condemnation of the coup was swift and severe. García Meza was subjected to an international economic blockade, a withdrawal of military and economic aid by the United States, and strong criticism from the Andean Pact countries and the European Parliament. In August, U.S. Sen. Dennis DeConcini (D-NM) revealed information linking García Mesa with the smuggling of cocaine to the United States.

Foreign and domestic opposition to the new government only worsened a rapidly deteriorating economy. Falling tin prices and oil production added to García Meza's problems, and at year's end he was forced to hold emergency talks with the International Monetary Fund (IMF).

PAUL CAMMACK
University of Glasgow (Scotland)

BOLIVIA · Information Highlights

Official Name: Republic of Bolivia.
Location: West-central South America.
Area: 424,164 sq mi (1 098 585 km²).
Population (1980 est.): 5,300,000.
Chief Cities (1976 census): Sucre, the legal capital, 63,-259; La Paz, the actual capital, 654,713; Santa Cruz de la Sierra, 255,568; Cochabamba, 204,414.
Government: *Head of state and government,* Gen. Luis García Meza Tejada, head of military junta (took power July 1980). *Legislature*—Congress: Senate and Chamber of Deputies.
Monetary Unit: Peso (25 pesos equal U.S.$1, Dec. 1980).
Manufactures (major products): Textiles, cottage industry goods, cement, tin, petroleum.
Agriculture (major products): Potatoes, corn, sugarcane, cassava, cotton, barley, rice, wheat, coffee, bananas.
GNP (1979 est., U.S.$): $4,700,000,000.
Foreign Trade (1979, U.S.$): *Imports,* $1,011,000,000; *exports,* $777,000,000.

BOSTON

Founded in 1630 on a marshy spit of land in Massachusetts Bay, the city of Boston celebrated its 350th birthday in 1980. Over the centuries, Boston has grown into a unique and complex mix of neighborhoods, ethnic groups, cultural styles, and institutions of business, trade, and government. "Jubilee 350," held from May to September 1980, was a program of festivities honoring the many facets and rich heritage of life in the city.

In July, 17th-century Boston was represented by exhibits in the city Common sponsored by area museums and historic sites. The rise of the city as a major port in the 18th and 19th centuries was commemorated by a visit of the "tall ships" May 30-June 4; in a repeat of their visit during national bicentennial celebrations in 1976, more than 40 large sailing ships anchored in Boston harbor. The many ethnic groups who first swelled Boston's population and shaped its culture in the 19th century were honored during August with a series of theater, dance, and music performances on an outdoor stage set up at City Hall.

September 12 to 21 was declared Boston Week to commemorate the founding of the original town on Sept. 17, 1630. The events included a reception for the Lord Mayor of Boston, England, and for British and American descendants of the original settlers; the opening of a permanent exhibit on Boston architecture; the opening of time capsules sealed in 1880 and 1930; and the dedication of two statues of a legendary political figure, former congressman, governor, and five-time mayor, James Michael Curley.

A special committee selected 350 citizens to be honored as "Grand Bostonians." The 350 included not only persons well-known in education, business, and cultural life, but also a large number nominated by neighborhood groups in recognition of local services which might not be known city-wide. A ball for the Grand Bostonians was held September 30 under four huge tents set up in historic Copley Square.

The final event of the jubilee was the "Great Cities of the World" conference held September 21–27. Representatives from 30 cities around the world participated. The theme of the meeting was "cities as places for people," focusing on the problems of and accomplishments in urban revitalization, the future of sea and river ports, and the refurbishing of historic buildings and older districts for new uses.

Continuing Problems. For all its historic uniqueness, Boston continued to be troubled by such typically urban problems as racial tension, disputes over school desegregation, strikes by municipal workers, and a rise in property taxes. These and other conflicts pointed up the fiscal and social pressures under which the city operates. The solution to these long-term problems will determine to a great extent whether Bostonians will be able to regard their city as a good place to live at its quadricentennial in 2030.

HARVEY BOULAY, *Boston University*

BOTANY

Current research in the biological sciences has made it increasingly difficult to categorize knowledge in the traditionally-defined areas of botany, zoology, biochemistry, microbiology, or genetics. Much of the research conducted in university botany departments and reported in botany journals in 1980 fell under the heading of molecular biology. The 1980 U.S. Supreme Court decision that biological organisms created in the laboratory can be patented under federal law (*Diamond v. Chakrabarty*) generated as much interest and as much new research in botany as it did in other fields of biology.

Cell and tissue culture techniques were employed in a wide range of studies of the basic genetics and physiology of plants. These methods also offer the promise of obtaining a variety of rare materials for experimental use on crops. The first plant steroid with growth-regulating properties was isolated and identified after three years of exacting work. This plant steroid, a compound found in the pollen of the rape plant, was named brassinolide. A few milligrams were isolated from 500 lbs (227 kg) of pollen. Identification of the chemical structure allowed scientists to synthesize similar compounds with a degree of growth-regulating activity; synthesis, it is hoped, will provide sufficient amounts for further testing on plants. The use of microorganisms or cell cultures to produce the natural compound is a possible alternate approach.

The worldwide energy shortage has revitalized interest in plant exploration and made botanists more conscious of possible new uses for plants. In 1980, considerable work was underway on the use of plant materials as sources of methane and alcohol. Some plants contain substances, such as latex, that can be refined into gasoline substitutes. Cooperative work by university and industrial researchers was in progress to determine the feasibility of producing hydrocarbons from plants on land not suited to food crops. Some of the plants showing promise are native or introduced xerophytic types that grow in arid areas of the southwest United States. The caper spurge (*Euphorbia lathyris*) shows promise as a source of fuel stocks, while jojoba (*Simmondsia chinensis*) produces seeds rich in a liquid wax with many properties of sperm whale oil.

Reports continued to appear on the successful regeneration of entire plants from dedifferentiated cells of various plant organs. The list of responsive genera and species continued to grow, supporting the thesis of totipotency in all plant cells.

EDMUND N. O'ROURKE
Department of Horticulture
Louisiana State University

BRAZIL

The political liberalization program of President João Baptista Figueiredo stayed on track in 1980 despite labor union militancy, right-wing terrorism, and an inflation rate of more than 100%. President Figueiredo visited Argentina in May, effecting a rapprochement between South America's two most powerful nations, and Pope John Paul II went to Brazil for a 12-day visit.

New Political Parties. In accordance with legislation enacted in 1979, newly-authorized political parties scrambled to sign up members in the first months of 1980. The old groupings—the pro-government National Renovation Alliance (ARENA) and the opposition Brazilian Democratic Movement (MDB)—were dissolved, as the law required formal political organizations to be designated as parties. Hoping to preserve the broad opposition coalition, many former members of the MDB reunited in the Party of the Brazilian Democratic Movement (PMDB). However, much of the working-class support for the old MDB went to the various labor parties: the Labor Party (PT), the Brazilian Labor Party (PTB), and the Democratic Labor Party (PTD). A similar split occurred on the government side, with some business and banking interests shunning the official Democratic Social Party (PDS) and promoting the Popular Party (PP).

When congress met in March for the first time under the new system, 226 deputies and 37 senators, an absolute majority in both houses, registered under the PDS label. Ninety deputies and 17 senators chose the PMDB, while 69 deputies and six senators went with the PP. Of the labor parties, only the PT, the party of metalworkers leader Luís Inácio da Silva (Lula), managed to sign up a senator; the PT also claimed five deputies, more than any other labor party.

By law, no party was allowed to identify itself with a single social class. This provision ensured the continued illegality of the Brazilian Communist Party (PCB), the professed vanguard of the proletariat. Within the PCB, a long-simmering dispute culminated in April with the ouster of hardline Secretary General Luís Carlos Prestes, leader of the party since 1935. His replacement, Giocondo Dias, sought to give the party a democratic and reformist image.

Metalworkers' Strike. In the industrial suburbs of São Paulo, 250,000 metalworkers went on strike April 1, demanding higher wages, job security, and union shop stewards on factory floors. A court decision favoring the union on the wage issue was ignored by union chief Lula, who insisted that all worker demands had to be met before they would return to work. The government declared the strike illegal and moved against the strikers in massive force. Troops occupied factories and working-class neighborhoods, arrested Lula and other union leaders, and roughed up striking workers and their sympathizers. In the hope of preventing a bloodbath, opposition politicians, religious leaders, and communists urged moderation on both sides.

Although President Figueiredo declared his determination to avoid violence, some of his troop commanders seemed eager to wipe out the troublesome metalworkers' union. In the end, however, reason prevailed. On May 11, after 41 days of confrontation, the strikers returned to work without achieving their demands of job security and shop stewards. Lula and his colleagues were released from jail, but the image of the union leader was somewhat tarnished while that of the president was enhanced. The government's willingness to approve wage increases based on productivity, while standing firm on other issues, discouraged further disruption.

Despite outbreaks of right-wing terrorism during the labor crisis, President Figueiredo resisted the demands of government hardliners for press censorship and other repressive measures. His policy of *abertura*—opening—remained intact. Congressional, state, and municipal elections were scheduled for 1982. The previously appointive offices of governor and senator were made elective.

Papal Visit. The pilgrimage of Pope John Paul II was the longest papal trip outside Italy in modern times and the first ever to Brazil, the world's most populous Catholic country. His arrival on June 30 was preceded by maneuvering within the Brazilian hierarchy to influence the pontiff's itinerary. Proponents of the "social gospel" wanted him to visit city slums and impoverished rural areas and to approve at least implicitly their social and political activism. Conservatives, recalling John Paul's condemnation of "liberation theology" during his 1979 visit to Mexico, hoped the pope would steer clear of politically sensitive areas and order Brazilian clergymen to confine their activities to matters of faith and morals. Neither faction was entirely satisfied. The pope toured some slums and reaffirmed the Church's concern for the poor. He drew his largest crowd, about one million persons, in São Paulo, where the clergy was closely identified with striking metalworkers. But the pontiff also reminded Brazilian churchmen that

---
BRAZIL • Information Highlights

Official Name: Federative Republic of Brazil.
Location: Eastern South America.
Area: 3,286,478 square miles (8 511 965 km²).
Population (1980 est.): 122,000,000.
Chief Cities (1975 est.): Brasília, the capital, 763,254; São Paulo, 7,198,608; Rio de Janeiro, 4,857,716; Belo Horizonte, 1,557,464.
Government: *Head of state and government,* João Baptista Figueiredo, president (took office March 1979). *Legislature*—National Congress: Federal Senate and Chamber of Deputies.
Monetary Unit: New Cruzeiro (58.38 n. cruzeiros equal U.S.$1, Oct. 1980).
Manufactures (major products): Steel, chemicals, petrochemicals, machinery, consumer goods.
Agriculture (major products): Coffee, rice, beef, corn, milk, sugarcane, soybeans, cacao.
GNP Per Capita (1978 est., U.S.$): $1,570.
Foreign Trade (1979 est., U.S.$): *Imports,* $19,804,000,-000; *exports,* $15,250,000,000.

their main concern should be the spiritual, not material, welfare of the people.

Economy. In 1980, Brazil experienced the worst inflation—more than 100%—in its history. The cruzeiro, already diminished by massive devaluations in 1979, lost about half its foreign-exchange value in 1980. The nation's foreign debt rose from $50,000,000,000 to nearly $60,000,000,000, a record for any country. Brazil's "economic czar," Planning Minister Antônio Delfim Neto, scurried among the financial capitals of the world to arrange new loan commitments. Despite Brazil's severe economic difficulties, however, the consensus among world bankers seemed to be that it was basically a good risk.

By the end of the year there was renewed optimism, as Brazil's trade gap narrowed. Manufactured and agricultural exports were up sharply, offsetting the increased cost of imported petroleum. In a giant step toward reducing the country's dependence on petroleum, more than 100,000 completely alcohol-powered vehicles rolled off Brazilian assembly lines. A nationwide network of service stations selling fuel alcohol at a price set 35% below that of gasoline went into operation.

Rapprochement with Argentina. Brazil's main trading partner in Latin America was its traditional geopolitical rival, Argentina. The rivalry gave way to cooperation as President Figueiredo journeyed to Buenos Aires in May. Figueiredo and Argentine President Jorge Rafael Videla concluded agreements on a wide range of issues, including cooperation in the development of nuclear energy and the manufacture and exchange of arms.

NEILL MACAULAY, *University of Florida*

BRITISH COLUMBIA

Energy resources and intergovernmental relations were areas of special attention in British Columbia in 1980.

The Economy. While depreciation of the Canadian dollar increased British Columbia's penetration of markets outside North America, slow economic growth in the United States reduced shipments to the province's primary market. Higher prices for such commodities as lumber underlay increases in the dollar value of exports, but natural gas exports dropped significantly. The development of northeastern provincial coal reserves continued to be central to the government's economic development strategy. In February, a new blueprint for the conservation and development of energy was announced, and in response to a legislative inquiry, a seven-year moratorium was put on uranium mining. The British Columbia Resources Investment Corporation (BCRIC) was again the focus of controversy because of the terms of its takeover bid for Kaiser Resources Ltd., the country's largest coal producer. BCRIC earlier had entered the forest industry by obtaining a 14% interest in MacMil-lan Bloedel Ltd. In June, the publicly-owned Ocean Falls newsprint mill ceased operations.

Budget. The new minister of finance, Hugh Curtis, introduced a balanced budget with a total expenditure of (C.) $6,152,800,000. This included statutory appropriations of $250,000,000 and a withdrawal from revenue surpluses of $353,200,000. Financing was provided for the first year of the previously promised Denticare scheme, a five-year forest management program, and measures for energy conservation and development.

Legislation. The Legislative Assembly approved bills providing for a new utilities commission with jurisdiction over all energy matters; for extended municipal voting rights to non-resident tenants; for new family and child services; for coverage of farm workers and domestics under labor employment standards; and for timber and tree farm licenses. Confirmation also was given for the sharing of natural gas revenues with the Fort Nelson Indian Band. Determined opposition to proposed restrictions on the indexing of government employee pension plans and holiday shopping regulations led to their withdrawal and subsequent modification. Charges of interference with the 1978 Eckardt Report on electoral boundaries prompted an investigation by the attorney general. A government inquiry into the handling of election expenses by the Social Credit party during the 1979 general election found that there had been no breach of the Elections Act.

Intergovernmental Relations. While federal aid for the expanded Roberts Bank Coal port and the new Prince Rupert-Ridley Island grain and coal facilities was announced during the year, the financing of rail links to provincial coal reserves generated considerable tension between British Columbia and the federal government. Stronger ties with Alberta were signaled by joint meetings of the two provincial cabinets and their mutual alarm at a federal energy excise tax. In December, British Columbia decided to withhold payment of the tax. The provincial energy minister called the new levy illegal.

NORMAN J. RUFF, *University of Victoria*

— BRITISH COLUMBIA • Information Highlights —

Area: 366,255 sq mi (948 600 km²).
Population (1980 est.): 2,626,400.
Chief Cities (1976 census): Victoria, the capital, 62,551; Vancouver, 410,188.
Government (1980): *Chief Officers*—lt. gov., Henry Bell-Irving; premier, William R. Bennett (Social Credit party); chief justice, Court of Appeal, Nathaniel T. Nemetz; Supreme Court, Allan McEachern. *Legislature*—Legislative Assembly, 57 members.
Education (1979–80 est.): *Enrollment*—public elementary and secondary schools, 513,870 pupils; private schools, 23,950; Indian (federal) schools, 2,715; postsecondary, 47,960 students.
Public Finance (1980–81 est.): $5,800,000,000 balanced budget.
Personal Income (average weekly salary, May 1980): $356.95.
Unemployment Rate (July 1980, seasonally adjusted): 6.6%.
(All monetary figures are in Canadian dollars.)

BULGARIA

Still the Soviet Union's most faithful ally, Bulgaria in 1980 sought new trade contacts with the West to help reverse its poor economic performance of the previous year. At the same time, the Communist party remained the sole repository of political power, and Todor Zhivkov, the first secretary of the party and president of the State Council, criticized the United States for providing military assistance to neighboring Turkey, meddling in the Balkans, and trying to exploit political instability in the region.

Domestic Affairs. At the February meeting of the National Council of the Fatherland, Zhivkov praised Bulgaria for its achievements; supported recent price increases for consumer goods; called for higher labor productivity; advocated détente; severely criticized the United States for its "dangerous" foreign policy; applauded the Soviet Union for its "assistance" to Afghanistan; and advised NATO countries to keep in mind that "God is high and America is far away."

Simultaneously with the Polish workers' upheaval in September, Minister of Interior Dimitar Stoyanov inaugurated a campaign against the "ideological assaults of imperialism."

In June, the Council of Ministers announced that the "List of State Secrets" henceforth would include data on the economy and defense.

Economy and Foreign Trade. Available information indicated that Bulgaria's 1979 growth rate, balance of trade, and expansion of industry and agriculture did not reach expected levels. Western economists believed that inflation was about four times the official figure of 4.5%.

About half of the country's $16,000,000,000 in foreign trade in 1979 was with the Soviet Union and another 30% with Soviet-bloc countries. Still, exports to Western industrialized nations increased by 70% that year and imports by 11%. In 1980, Bulgaria took further steps to promote commerce with the West. In March, it enacted a new law that for the first time allowed foreign companies to set up joint ventures with Bulgarian firms on Bulgarian soil.

JAN KARSKI, *Georgetown University*

―――――― BULGARIA • Information Highlights ――――――

Official Name: People's Republic of Bulgaria.
Location: Southeastern Europe.
Area: 42,758 sq mi (110 743 km²).
Population (1980 est.): 8,900,000.
Chief Cities (1978 est.): Sofia, the capital, 1,059,206; Plovdiv, 332,899; Varna, 278,827.
Government: *Head of state,* Todor Zhivkov, president of the State Council and first secretary of the Communist party (took office July 1971). *Head of government,* Stanko Todorov, chairman of the Council of Ministers (took office July 1971).
Monetary Unit: Lev (0.85 lev equals U.S.$1, June 1980).
Manufactures (major products): Processed agricultural products, electric power, crude steel.
Agriculture (major products): Grain, tobacco, fruits, vegetables, livestock.
GNP (1979 est., U.S.$): $34,800,000,000.
Foreign Trade (1979 est., U.S.$): *Imports,* $8,514,000,-000; *exports,* $8,869,000,000.

BURMA

President Ne Win sought reconciliation with various onetime rivals in an apparent effort to avoid a succession struggle when his rule ends.

Politics. The key move in the 69-year-old president's strategy was the return from exile in India of former Premier U Nu, 73, in July. Nu was ousted by then Gen. Ne Win in 1962. Following four years' detention, he fled abroad to lead an insurgency against Ne Win before accepting exile in India to engage in Buddhist meditation. Nu's return to Burma was at Ne Win's invitation, and the former premier kept his promise to continue his religious studies.

In May, Ne Win pardoned political offenders, inviting the return of all exiles; 700 such expatriates returned without harm. Approximately 5,000 political prisoners, including many onetime insurrectionists, were released.

Internal Security. Burma's several-sided insurgencies, which involved different ethnic minorities as well as Chinese-aided Communists, continued to keep most of the country's armed forces in the field. One third of the Burmese governmental budget was spent on fighting insurgents. The army may have had as many as 5,000 casualties in the first eight months of 1980.

Economy. The gross national product increased 5.6%. Real growth in agriculture, backbone of the economy, was 4.8%. For the fourth straight year, Burma had a budget surplus. Foreign trade increased dramatically.

Foreign Relations. Burma continued to move cautiously away from its previously unyielding posture of isolation. After an interruption of 17 years in Burmese-U.S. aid relations, Burma accepted a two-year, $5 million U.S. aid contribution to improve primary health care. The Ne Win government also cultivated improved relations with the five non-Communist Association of Southeast Asian Nations (ASEAN) governments, especially neighboring Thailand. The Burmese strategy shift was a reaction to Soviet endorsement of Vietnam's military occupation of Cambodia and continued Chinese aid to antigovernment rebels in Burma.

RICHARD BUTWELL, *Murray State University*

―――――― BURMA • Information Highlights ――――――

Official Name: Socialist Republic of the Union of Burma.
Location: Southeast Asia.
Area: 261,218 sq mi (676 555 km²).
Population (1980 est.): 34,400,000.
Chief Cities (1975 est.): Rangoon, the capital, 2,100,000; Mandalay, 417,000; Moulmein, 202,000.
Government: *Head of state,* U Ne Win, president (took office March 1974). *Head of government,* U Maung Maung Kha, prime minister (took office March 1977). *Legislature* (unicameral)—People's Assembly.
Monetary Unit: Kyat (6.50 kyats equal U.S.$1, July 1980).
Manufactures (major products): Agricultural products, textiles, wood and its products, refined petroleum.
Agriculture (major products): Rice, jute, sesame, ground nuts, tobacco, cotton, pulses, sugarcane, corn.
GNP Per Capita (1978 est., U.S.$): $150.
Foreign Trade (1979 est., U.S.$): *Imports,* $319,000,000; *exports,* $363,000,000.

BUSINESS AND CORPORATE AFFAIRS

The long-expected recession finally hit most U.S. businesses in 1980. Fortunately for the economy, the recession was short-lived.

Corporate Profits. Corporate profits nosedived, bankruptcies rose, and some major industries stayed alive only because of government support. In spite of the downturn, which began in March and ended in September, inflation remained a problem, as it headed toward an annual rate of 12–13%.

In the first quarter of 1980, corporate profits were deceptively strong, posting an average gain of 15% over the first quarter of 1979. When adjusted for inflation, however, profits were basically unchanged. Analysts pointed out that inventory profits represented 25% of pre-tax earnings, a rate not seen since 1974.

Second quarter profits fell, as corporations found themselves in the throes of the recession. Executives began cost-cutting in the expectation of even more difficult times in the third quarter, when profits dropped by 3% compared with the third quarter of 1979. Although sales rose by 12%, profit margins sagged. Predictions for fourth quarter profits were not high in spite of a rebound in economic activity during September. Merchants expected a mediocre Christmas, and business spending on capital projects lagged.

The Strong and the Weak. Mining, railroads, stock brokerage, oil, and banking had the strongest performances among U.S. industries during 1980, while automobiles, steel, airlines, and savings and loans were among the weakest.

The automobile companies began 1980 with a modest recovery from the doldrums of 1979. However, the consumer splurge was only temporary, and by the spring, showrooms for the Big Three were empty in spite of $500 rebates offered to consumers. By the end of the second quarter, the industry's combined losses had amounted to nearly $2,000,000,000, and some analysts were predicting a total loss of more than $4,000,000,000 for the year. Chrysler stayed afloat only after it received a $1,500,000,000 loan guarantee from the government and raised another $2,000,000,000 from private sources. American Motors was bailed out by Renault, which bought a majority share in the company. And General Motors sold Terex, a subsidiary, for $325 million to a German company to raise cash. In an effort to capitalize on the public's shift to smaller cars, American manufacturers brought out new lines of subcompacts, raised prices more for existing small cars than for full-size cars, and lobbied Congress to adopt quotas on Japanese imports. (*See* AUTOMOBILES.)

At General Motors, chairman and chief executive officer Thomas A. Murphy retired, and Roger B. Smith, an executive vice president of financial operations, was elected to replace him.

The recession severely stymied the steel companies, as well. U.S. Steel filed an "anti-dumping" suit against most of the major European steel manufacturers. By September, the government announced that it would offer new protection to the U.S. companies, who quickly raised their prices. In an effort to raise cash, U.S. Steel sold its Universal Atlas Cement subsidiary to a German company for more than $100 million.

The deregulation of the airline industry brought increased competition on the most profitable routes, which, combined with the recession, hurt the financial health of the industry. Braniff responded by selling 15 of its most fuel-efficient planes to American Airlines, while Pan Am sold its New York City headquarters to the Metropolitan Life Insurance Co.

Deregulation and high fuel costs meant a consolidation of the railroad industry. Proposed mergers included the Southern Pacific and Santa Fe railroads; Southern Railway and Norfolk & Western; and Union Pacific and Missouri Pacific and Western Pacific. Chessie System and Seaboard Coast Line merged to form CSX Corp.

The telecommunications industry also began to prepare for deregulation. In August, American Telephone and Telegraph (AT&T) announced a sweeping reorganization to establish two separate subsidiaries, one that would compete head-on with such companies as Xerox and IBM in computers and office equipment, and one that would provide its traditional communication services. Two months earlier, AT&T lost a record $1,800,000,000 antitrust suit to MCI, a provider of long-distance telephone service, for deliberately interfering with its growth.

The recession did not spare the department stores either. E. J. Korvettes, a well-known discount store, went into bankruptcy, and Montgomery Ward, a subsidiary of Mobil, was ex-

Chairman William T. Seawell of Pan Am announces a merger with National Airlines in January.

UPI

pected to post a sizable loss by year's end. Sears Roebuck, the nation's largest retailer, posted only a $12 million profit on $7,400,000,000 in sales for the first six months. (*See* RETAILING.)

Another consumer-oriented company, Procter & Gamble, took a $75 million writedown of its investment after introducing Rely tampons, which were cited by the government for inducing a high incidence of toxic shock syndrome.

A new industry, genetics, sprang to life with the offering of a new stock issue by Genentech, which raised $35 million for capital spending.

Earnings growth slowed in the computer industry, as production problems cut into profitability. With IBM reducing main frame prices because of increased efficiencies, most of the industry had to work hard to keep up. Home computers grew in popularity, with Tandy Corporation and Apple Computers capturing a major part of the market.

See also INDUSTRIAL REVIEW; UNITED STATES: The Economy.

RON SCHERER
"The Christian Science Monitor"

BUSINESS AND CORPORATE AFFAIRS—SPECIAL REPORT:

U.S. Oil Companies and the Issue of Profits

In spite of significant nationwide conservation and the enactment of a windfall profits tax, U.S. oil company profits continued to soar in 1980. In spite of abundant reserves and a decline in expensive imported crude, the price of a gallon of gas continued to rise. The American consumer asked why. The questions of what constitutes a "fair profit" and the role of oil companies in future energy development were heatedly debated.

In the first quarter, oil company profits showed an average gain of 91%, while the major producers—such as Conoco, Exxon, Mobil, and Texaco—doubled their earnings. The big first-quarter gains were partly explained by the decontrol of crude oil prices and the fact that the windfall profits tax was effective in only one month of the quarter. Also, markets remained relatively tight, as companies continued to buy oil in case of cutoffs of supply. Gasoline prices rose as crude prices increased. OPEC countries continued to raise prices, sensing that consumer nations would pay more.

In the second quarter, oil profits again mushroomed. Exxon reported a 60% increase in operating earnings, Gulf 62%, Shell and Texaco 47%, and Mobil 70%. However, demand was beginning to slacken, as the impact of recession worked its way to U.S. tanks. Consumer demand decreased by about 10% compared with the previous year.

With the memory of 1979 gas lines fresh in the minds of consumers, the reports of oil company profits created a furor. The companies were accused of profiteering, and some consumer groups called for a return to crude oil price controls. The oil companies replied that their net profit margins on a gallon of gasoline had remained about the same, and they defended their high profits on the grounds that reinvestment costs remained high. Indeed, the companies raised their levels of capital spending on new oil projects in each quarter of the year. Important initiatives also were taken in the development of alternate energy sources.

By the third quarter, the momentum of the increases had begun to wane. An oversupply of 2.5 million barrels per day on the world market, tighter margins, higher prices charged by Saudi Arabia, and worldwide recession had their effect. Exxon and Standard Oil of Ohio reported gains of 18% over the third quarter of 1979, other companies reported more modest gains, and Gulf reported a 41% decline. Fourth quarter earnings were not expected to be much better, although the cutoff of oil from Iran and Iraq again tightened the market. The weakness of the world economy held down demand for petroleum products and kept pressure off oil prices.

Since 1973, crude oil prices had been subject to price controls that depended on the quality of the oil and when it was discovered. For example, newly discovered oil in 1979 sold for $32 per barrel, whereas oil discovered much earlier sold for $5.94 per barrel. On Jan. 1, 1980, these controls were lifted, and profits were bolstered. In return for the total decontrol of oil prices by October 1981, which the companies said would boost exploration, Congress also passed the windfall profits tax.

The windfall profits tax, which went into effect on March 1, 1980, is a levy on the production of all crude oil based on the difference between the selling price and a quarterly-adjusted base price of about $12.81 per barrel. The major companies pay a 70% tax on that difference, while independent operators are subject to a 50% rate for their first 1,000 barrels per day. The tax also affects oil that is newly discovered, heavy, or produced through expensive tertiary methods.

Despite the profits tax, oil companies were expected to enjoy real benefits from the decontrol of prices. Some analysts estimated that the average selling price would be $36.93 per barrel by 1983, with a net profit to the companies of $26.32 per barrel (up from $13.02 in 1979). And so long as consumers had to face higher prices and short supplies at the gas pump, U.S. oil companies would remain under attack.

RON SCHERER

CALIFORNIA

In the November 1980 elections, the nationwide Republican sweep that sent a Californian to the White House also was reflected in changes in the state's congressional delegation. California increased its lead as the nation's most populous state and would gain two additional seats in the U.S. Congress. The budget adopted for fiscal 1981 was the largest in history, but the increase was less than the rate of inflation. The state suffered from floods in the spring and fires in the autumn, but there were no damaging earthquakes. After a 20-year battle, the Peripheral Canal around the delta of two major rivers finally was approved by the state legislature, and the controversial New Melones Dam was at last ordered filled.

Elections. There were few surprises in the November elections. Former Gov. Ronald Reagan won the 45 electors from his home state, receiving 53% of the popular vote. President Jimmy Carter received 36% of the vote and John Anderson 9%. Voter turnout was low.

Sen. Alan Cranston (D) easily won reelection with 59% of the vote, over Paul Gann (R), co-author of "Proposition 13," who received 37%.

California Republicans made a net gain of three seats in the U.S. House of Representatives, leaving the Democrats with 22 congressmen to 21 for the Republicans. Of the Democratic losses, only that of the veteran Lionel Van Deerlin of San Diego came as a real surprise.

Democrats retained majorities in both houses of the state legislature. However, intraparty leadership fights were under way in both houses.

Gov. Edmund G. (Jerry) Brown, Jr., was an early candidate for the Democratic presidential nomination, but his campaign seemed never to be taken seriously, not even in California. He withdrew from the race after the Wisconsin primary April 1, having secured only one pledged delegate. Brown received little attention at the convention, where he endorsed Mr. Carter.

Census. Preliminary census reports indicated that California has a population of more than 22 million, about 25% larger than the second most populous state, New York. As a result of the increase, it was expected to gain two seats in Congress, increasing its delegation to 45. The legislature was expected to become more conservative, though the party balance would not necessarily change. Suburbs, small cities, and the southern part of the state would gain in representation at the expense of Los Angeles, Oakland, and San Francisco.

Courts. Late in the year, the California Supreme Court sustained (4-3) the state's death penalty statute, clearing legal obstacles to the first execution in the state since 1967.

In May, Justice Paul Halvonik of the State Court of Appeal, California's second highest tribunal, resigned after being charged with a variety of offenses involving the growing and possession of marijuana.

Weather. Floods and fires brought death and vast property damage to the state. Heavy rains throughout February caused serious flooding. More than 25 persons were killed and 5,000 driven from their homes; property damage exceeded $250 million. In November, brushfires in southern counties burned more than 400 homes

The Louise M. Davies Symphony Hall, home of the San Francisco Symphony, opened in 1980.

and caused property damage of more than $200 million.

Legislature. The state budget of $24,030,000,-000 was signed by the governor, but it was not sent to him until a record 31 days after the constitutional deadline and 16 days into the new fiscal year. Republicans in the Senate held out in a dispute over cost-of-living increases for welfare recipients. In all, 1,445 bills were passed, but there was no agreement on a motor vehicle inspection program, without which federal highway and sewerage aid programs might be cut off.

Several bills to provide for low- and middle-income housing were passed. Another would change the emphasis of bilingual education to help foreign language students learn English as quickly as possible. Several industries were given tax breaks, and inheritance tax rates were cut, but the governor vetoed a bill to index the income tax to offset the effects of inflation.

Consumer protection measures had little success during the session, but credit card firms were authorized to increase their interest rates. Governor Brown's proposal for a three-year program to retrain persons with obsolescent skills failed to pass.

Probably the most important legislation adopted in 1980 provided for a $5,100,000,000 expansion of the California Water Project, approximately doubling the amount of water to be transferred from northern California to southern California. A Peripheral Canal around the delta of the San Joaquin and Sacramento rivers will be built from south of Sacramento to the enormous state-owned pumps at Tracy, which will pull the water into the California Aqueduct. The proposed canal will be 43 miles (69 km) long and 400 ft (122 m) wide. The whole project will include four hydroelectric plants and six reservoirs. It is expected to take 20 years to complete.

Miscellaneous. In a change of policy, U.S. Secretary of the Interior Cecil D. Andrus announced in March that leasing of additional oil drilling acreage in California waters would be a top priority for five years.

The way at last seemed to be cleared for the filling of the long-completed New Melones Dam

----

—————— **CALIFORNIA • Information Highlights** ——————

Area: 158,693 sq mi (411 015 km²).
Population (Jan. 1980 est.): 22,925,000.
Chief Cities (1976 est.): Sacramento, the capital, 262,-305; Los Angeles, 2,743,994; San Francisco, 663,-478.
Government (1980): Chief Officers—governor, Edmund G. Brown, Jr. (D); lt. gov., Mike Curb (R). Legislature—Senate, 40 members; Assembly, 80 members.
Education (1979–80): Enrollment—public elementary schools, 2,729,523 pupils; public secondary, 1,318,-027; colleges and universities, 1,698,668 students. Public school expenditures, $9,548,400,000.
State Finances (fiscal year 1979): Revenues, $31,058,-000,000; expenditures, $28,319,000,000.
Personal Income (1979): $228,017,000,000; per capita, $10,047.
Labor Force (May 1980): Nonagricultural wage and salary earners, 9,803,800; unemployed, 734,900 (6.6% of total force).

----

on the Stanislaus River. Despite opposition by environmentalists and white-water rafting buffs, Congress exempted the river from the National Wild and Scenic Rivers Act.

In April, all state laws regulating nuclear power plants were overturned by a U.S. District court, which held that the national government has sole jurisdiction over the production and control of such energy.

See also LOS ANGELES.

CHARLES R. ADRIAN
University of California, Riverside

CAMBODIA

Cambodia's evolution as an ever more dependent Vietnamese satellite proceeded in 1980. Famine conditions diminished and the "Khmer Rouge" guerrilla resistance in the western part of the country persisted.

Continuing Resistance. Although peace prevailed in most of the country, the Pol Pot-led remnant forces of the once ruling Khmer Rouge continued to hold off the better equipped Vietnamese occupying troops in the Cardamon mountains area of western Cambodia near the border with Thailand. Of the 200,000 Vietnamese forces in the country, 100,000 were engaged in the fighting with the Khmer Rouge, who were supported by their own former foes, the revived right-wing "Khmer Serei." The Vietnamese invaders, who swiftly conquered most of the country in early 1979 and installed the puppet Heng Samrin government in Phnom Penh, were bogged down in a costly stalemate with 30,000 Communist and non-Communist guerrillas two years after they entered the country.

Not only was there no end in sight to the Vietnamese-Khmer Rouge war in western Cambodia, but the anti-Vietnamese forces also escalated their attacks in other parts of the country. The latter posed no threat to the de facto Vietnamese occupation or the Heng Samrin satellite regime, but it was a measure of the depth of dislike of the Vietnamese invaders throughout the country. Significantly, no Cambodian troops were involved in the war with the Khmer Rouge.

The Vietnamese-Khmer Rouge war spilled over into Thailand at midyear, when Vietnamese troops crossed the tense western Cambodian frontier on June 23 to engage in direct combat with Thai forces. Earlier, Vietnam repeatedly had accused the Thais of violating the Cambodian border to aid the adversary Khmer Rouge and Khmer Serei. The conflict, which ended in a matter of days, appeared to be a warning to the Bangkok government against continued intervention—in the form of supplies or other aid—in the fighting.

Vietnam's solution to the Thai government's expressed fear that its security was endangered by the war in Cambodia was a proposed demilitarized zone inclusive of both sides of the Thai-Cambodian border and direct Bangkok-Phnom

Penh talks. Thailand, however, saw no need for demilitarization of its side of the frontier and would not legitimize the Heng Samrin regime by talks with it.

Politics. The Heng Samrin regime continued nominally to administer most of the country, but neither Heng Samrin nor his government were the real rulers of the land. Heng Samrin himself was a figurehead political leader. The real power in the government was Pen Sovan, defense minister, secretary general of the Cambodian Communist Party, and chief liaison with the occupying Vietnamese forces. However, there was no doubt that major decisions for Cambodia were made in Hanoi and conveyed to Phnom Penh through military channels.

The fact of continued Khmer Rouge resistance in the West was not a reflection of popular yearning for a restoration of the ousted—and brutal—Pol Pot regime, which governed Cambodia from April 1975 to early 1979. Disliked though the occupying Vietnamese were, the greatest fear of most Cambodians was unquestionably the return of the extraordinarily hated Pol Pot and the Khmer Rouge, who engaged in mass slaughter of their countrymen when they were in power. Although political arrests and even personal disappearances continued in Cambodia in 1980, they did not resemble at all the widespread killings of the Pol Pot era.

In an effort to improve its image internationally, if not internally, the Khmer Rouge made a superficial political change in 1980. Pol Pot stepped aside as prime minister of his "government"—which still represented Cambodia in the United Nations. He was succeeded by Khieu Samphan, who also retained his post as "head of state." Pol Pot remained, however, commander-in-chief of the Khmer Rouge military forces.

Economy. The threat of famine largely disappeared in most of Cambodia. There was still a serious food shortage—particularly of rice—and refugees continued to flee westward to the Thai border in search of food. However, refugees in 1980 were not, for the most part, the walking skeletons of the previous year. And by year's end, most of the country's population was probably getting enough to eat—albeit largely corn, which is not so popular as rice with Cambodians. Nutritionally, however, the Cambodian diet still was not generally an adequate one.

A major effort was made in 1980 to plant enough rice to return the country to the level of self-sufficiency which it possessed before civil war erupted at the start of the 1970s. Only 70% of the area due to be planted actually was brought under cultivation, however, since 300 000 t (330,-000 T) of rice seeds were supplied by Western agencies and 10 000 t (11,000 T) by Vietnam.

The country's continuing economic recovery was indicated by a fivefold increase in Phnom Penh's population from the reduced level of 100,-000 to which it had fallen under Pol Pot, reactivation of 63 of 100 of the capital city's factories, and the reappearance of money and postage stamps.

Foreign Relations. Cambodia still required international food aid, however, and a 59-nation UN conference pledged $116 million in such help. The United States criticized Vietnam and the USSR for their nonparticipation in the conference. An additional $200 million in aid was promised by 51 nations at the UN in November.

The UN General Assembly, which voted to continue to seat the Pol Pot delegation in October, subsequently supported—97–23 (with 22 abstentions)—a motion for withdrawal of Vietnamese troops from Cambodia introduced by the five Association of Southeast Asian Nations (ASEAN) governments—Indonesia, the Philippines, Thailand, Malaysia, and Singapore. India recognized the Heng Samrin government, but no other non-Communist country did so.

Khmer Rouge Premier Khieu Samphan paid a state visit to China. The trip was reflective of Peking's continuing support of the anti-Vietnamese guerrilla forces.

RICHARD BUTWELL
Murray State University

Khieu Samphan is the new leader of the Khmer Rouge government, which is recognized by the UN.

UPI

--- **CAMBODIA · Information Highlights** ---

Official Name: Democratic Kampuchea.
Location: Southeast Asia.
Area: 69,898 sq mi (181 035 km²).
Population (1980 est.): 6,000,000.
Chief City (1979 est.): Phnom Penh, the capital, 200,000.
Government: *Head of state and government,* Heng Samrin, president of People's Revolutionary Council (took office Jan. 1979).
Monetary Unit: Riel.
Manufactures (major products): Textiles, cement, paper products.
Agriculture (major products): Rice, rubber, sugarcane.

CANADA

For most Canadians, 1980 was a year of conflict and anxiety. The winter election ended with the return of a Liberal government. Pierre Elliott Trudeau used his new mandate to impose his own ideas on constitutional reform (*see* special report, page 172) and on the control of Canada's energy resources. While Quebec voters exorcised the specter of imminent separation, the prime minister's policies helped revive the threat in Western Canada. Amid the noise of political indignation, ordinary Canadians struggled with soaring interest rates, a prairie drought, continued inflation, and the worst recession since 1962.

The Election. On February 18, Canadians restored to power the leader and party they had rejected nine months before. Voters gave 146 seats and 43.9% of their support to Pierre Elliott Trudeau's Liberals (L), cut Joe Clark's Progressive Conservatives (PC) to 103 seats and 33.0% of the vote, and boosted Ed Broadbent's New Democrats (NDP) to 32 seats and 19.8% of popular support. It was the left-wing party's best showing ever. The remaining 3.3% of the vote was divided among the Social Credit and other parties.

The winter campaign, the first since 1891, gave cynics plenty of ammunition. Polls predicting a Liberal victory altered hardly at all during two months of campaigning. Cheered on by most of Canada's business leaders and English-language dailies, Clark and his Minister of Finance, John Crosbie, preached the doctrine of "short-term pain for long-term gain" in defense of their 18¢-a-gallon excise tax on gasoline. Voters preferred to worry about high interest rates, Clark's apparent submission to Alberta Premier Peter Lougheed, and the young government's alleged confusion over the publicly-owned oil company, Petrocan. The Liberals read the polls, avoided trouble, and waited for Joe Clark's unpopularity to win them the election. Their own leader was effectively "low-bridged." The articulate but abrasive Trudeau made few appearances, avoided chance encounters with journalists or voters, and refused every format for a television debate with Clark and Broadbent. Late in the campaign, outflanking the NDP in Ontario, Trudeau emerged in a new guise as a nationalist, promising 50% Canadian ownership of the petrochemical industry by 1990. As for the New Democrats, they campaigned for a national industrial strategy, a bigger role for Petrocan, and an end to erosion of Canada's federally funded health insurance system.

The February 18 outcome confirmed Canada's dangerously regional voting pattern. Liberals won in Atlantic Canada, took all but one of Quebec's seats (eliminating an exhausted Social Credit party), and took all but 43 of Ontario's 95 seats, hurting both the Conservatives and the NDP. The sweep ended there. Beyond the Manitoba border, Trudeau found only two more supporters, both from Winnipeg. The rest of the region gave 51 seats to Joe Clark and 27 to the NDP.

The Government. By agreement, the Liberal leader resumed power on March 3. Ignoring Ed Broadbent's suggestion that he add seats to Parliament on a basis of proportional representation, gaining Liberals from the West in return for Conservatives from Quebec, Trudeau chose his Western cabinet ministers largely from the appointed Senate. His new government had 32 ministers, 2 of them women and 14 of them new faces in the cabinet. A former minister, Jeanne Sauvé, became speaker of the 32nd Parliament. Meanwhile, Joe Clark, widely blamed for the Conservative defeat, rallied his party and prepared for a February 1981 review of his leadership.

The new Liberal administration faced a host of problems, some of them inherited from its own previous term in office. A five-year search for a new fighter aircraft ended on April 10 when McDonnell-Douglas won a C$4,000,000,000 contract for 137 F-18A Hornets, largely on the promise of an industrial benefits package estimated at C$3,260,000,000, much of it to be spent in Quebec. The loser, General Dynamics, enlivened the Quebec referendum campaign by claims that its deal would have done far more for the French-speaking province.

A new issue was Canada's response to Soviet aggression in Afghanistan. The Clark government had supported Washington's Moscow Olympic boycott strategy; the Trudeau government reluctantly followed suit. Despite obvious embarrassment as the previous Olympic host in 1976, the government on April 22 advised Canadian athletes to stay home from the Moscow games. Four days later the Canadian Olympic Committee voted in support of the government's decision. Embargoes on cultural and educational exchanges and on sales of wheat and technical products were confirmed. Western farmers were promised compensation.

Making a Living. While the government and most Canadian politicians spent the spring coaxing Quebeckers to reject sovereignty-association, other Canadians struggled with more mundane preoccupations. Two elections had not settled energy prices, curbed a federal deficit estimated at C$14,000,000,000 in 1980, or stabilized the Canadian dollar. Interest rate increases had hurt Joe Clark's reelection hopes. By March 27, the Bank of Canada rate reached 15.49% and chartered banks took the cue to go far higher. The Canadian dollar slumped to U.S.$0.836. By summer, rates had eased to 10% but serious damage had been done to small companies and investment plans.

Ontario, once the complacent, wealthy heartland of Canada, shared with the United States the harshest impact of the recession. As home for 90% of Canada's automotive industry, Ontario

The 32nd Parliament takes over in Canada. Montreal's Jeanne Sauvé, the first woman to be chosen speaker of the House of Commons, is escorted to her seat by Prime Minister Pierre Elliott Trudeau and Opposition leader Joe Clark (left).

suffered the tribulations of other North American auto manufacturers. Ontario pressure persuaded the Trudeau government against its better judgment to extend $200 million in loan guarantees to a wobbly Chrysler Canada Ltd. In return, Chrysler promised $950 million in new Canadian investment and a work force of 15,900 by 1984.

For all their energy boom and minimal unemployment, Westerners experienced their own brand of economic disaster in 1980. An unseasonably mild winter made electioneering easier but it presaged a serious spring drought. Grain farmers, already hurt by Canada's under-capitalized grain-handling system, faced reduced yields and quality. The cattle industry, emerging from a period of low prices and rebuilding its herds, faced parched grazing land and zooming feed prices. Ottawa's hesitant response to the problems was added to a growing list of prairie grievances. When farmers put off equipment purchases, their decisions hit Canada's debt-ridden farm machinery giant, Massey-Ferguson. As the big multinational staggered toward bankruptcy, Ottawa weighed the dangers of another Chrysler-style rescue for one of the country's few major multinational corporations.

Around the troubled giants, a host of smaller companies collapsed, leaving aging workers to face a grim future. One such company, Houdaille Industries in Oshawa, shut down in October by its new Florida-based owners, hit the headlines when hitherto unmilitant workers occupied the plant and demanded parity with office workers. The tactics brought a richer offer but no reprieve from a shutdown. When the Canadian Labor Congress met in Winnipeg in May, 2,500 delegates grimly urged greater solidarity on its 2.3 million affiliated members and pleaded, like the NDP, for a job-creating industrial strategy. Ontario's Conservative government considered the economic climate and prudently deferred its planned election until the spring of 1981.

Edmonton v. Ottawa. Having refused Joe Clark a firm or favorable oil-price deal during nine months of Conservative rule, Alberta's Premier Peter Lougheed was in no mood to give Pierre Elliott Trudeau what he had denied a fellow Albertan. For his part, having promised Canadians cheaper oil than the Clark government, the new federal prime minister also lacked bargaining room. By year's end, the energy minister, Marc Lalonde, boasted that he had kept oil price increases to C$3.50 a barrel, not the planned C$4.00. It was a Pyrrhic victory.

For Alberta and its neighbor, Saskatchewan, resources are a political as well as an economic issue. Both prairie provinces wrestled control of their natural resources away from Ottawa in the 1920s. Both hold bitter memories of misery and destitution during the depression years of the 1930s. Alberta may be committed to free-wheeling capitalism while Saskatchewan's political tradition is social democratic, but both Lougheed and his more soft-spoken neighboring premier, Allan Blakeney, believe that wealth from depleting energy resources must be used to give the prairie region a diversified industrial economy.

Ottawa sees it differently. Since 1973, when OPEC sent oil prices soaring, the Trudeau government has tried to protect the less affluent Atlantic provinces and Quebec from the full impact of world prices. A multibillion dollar subsidy program has held down fuel and gas prices while imports from Latin America and the Middle East have increased steadily in cost and quantity.

Meanwhile, Ottawa insisted that the Western provinces hold their energy prices to the costs of production and replacement. The result has been bitter political conflict.

Since any federal budget depends on an oil-pricing agreement, both Prime Minister Trudeau and Energy Minister Marc Lalonde made repeated pilgrimages to Edmonton and Premier Lougheed and his energy minister, Merv Leitch, traveled to Ottawa. Apart from Ontario, consumer provinces cheerfully left the struggle to Ottawa, and several became beneficiaries of loans from Alberta's C$7,000,000,000 Heritage Fund, built from oil royalties. Lougheed insisted on moving the price of Alberta's oil to at least 75% of the OPEC level; the Trudeau government insisted that the Canadian economy could not afford a price within C$10 a barrel of the Alberta demand. At stake was C$16,000,000,000 per year.

Both sides had weapons. Ottawa had proven legislative power to act in what it defined as a national emergency. Alberta could stall two C$8,000,000,000 oil sands projects at Fort McMurray and Cold Lake vital to Canada's hopes for energy self-sufficiency by the end of the 1980s. Approval would come, Lougheed warned on March 16, only when Alberta got "a fair commercial relationship." Ottawa's threat to tax natural gas exports as well as the oil outflow to help find cash for growing fuel subsidies for Eastern Canada brought a furious response from both British Columbia and Alberta. It would be "a declaration of war," Lougheed warned.

The National Energy Policy. Such a tax did not come. Instead, on the strength of feeble promises from President Jimmy Carter and the U.S. Congress that the United States would complete the 5,000-mi (8 000 km) Alaska natural gas pipeline, the Trudeau government approved a C$1,600,-000,000 "pre-build" of the Canadian section. While the NDP warned that the decision broke the law and sacrificed Canadian gas at low prices, Alberta should have been placated. Also, Ottawa did not interfere when the Lougheed government, on August 1, imposed a unilateral oil price increase of C$2 a barrel. Still, by late 1980, there was no Ottawa-Edmonton agreement and there was no budget.

On October 28, Trudeau's finance minister, Allan MacEachen, finally delivered his government's budget. Dire warnings that the revenue-hungry government would end indexing of taxable income and other middle-income tax shelters proved groundless. As in an earlier mini-budget in April, MacEachen's measures hurt only smokers, drinkers, and profit-makers. The real surprise came with the unveiling of a dramatic new national energy policy. It was, as it confessed, "a fundamental departure, in many instances, from the current policy environment." Trudeau's belated election promise of 50% Canadian ownership had not been forgotten after all. Unilaterally, the government would set an oil price that would double in four years and quadruple by 1990. An ownership tax collected at the gas pumps would allow Petrocan to increase Canadian ownership from 30 to 50% of the industry. An incentive would favor companies 50% Canadian-owned and even more generously if Canadians owned 75%. Meanwhile, as prices rose, Ottawa insisted on 24% of the take, not 10%, while the company share would drop from 45% to 33%. Since Western provinces opposed an export tax on natural gas, the Trudeau government substituted a 10% excise tax on all gas. Western needs for industrial capital would be met from a C$4,000,000,000 development fund.

In the winter campaign, Trudeau had warned that he would return to office for as little as 18 months. He would do what was right, not popular. Lalonde, his closest lieutenant, had accused his own party of losing direction before its 1979 defeat. They had kicked a hornet's nest with the national energy policy, enraging the West, provincial governments, multinational oil companies, and even Canada's own vulnerable private-sector energy companies. In a pretaped speech, Premier Lougheed claimed that Ottawa "without negotiation and without agreement simply walked into our homes and occupied the living room." Approval of the big oil sands plants stayed frozen. Alberta would cut its energy exports to Eastern Canada by 15%, 10% of Canadian consumption.

(Continued on page 174)

THE CANADIAN MINISTRY
(According to precedence, December 1980)

Pierre Elliott Trudeau, prime minister
Allan Joseph MacEachen, deputy prime minister and minister of finance
Jean-Luc Pepin, minister of transport
Jean Chrétien, minister of justice; minister of state for social development
John Munro, minister of Indian Affairs and northern development
H.A. (Bud) Olson, minister of state for economic development; Senate house leader
Herb Gray, minister of industry, trade and commerce
Eugene Whelan, minister of agriculture
André Ouellet, minister of consumer and corporate affairs; postmaster general
Marc Lalonde, minister of energy, mines and resources
Ray Perrault, leader of the government in the Senate
Roméo LeBlanc, minister of fisheries and oceans
John Roberts, minister of state for science and technology; minister of the environment
Monique Bégin, minister of national health and welfare
Jean-Jacques Blais, minister of supply and services
Francis Fox, secretary of state; minister of communications
Gilles Lamontagne, minister of national defence; acting minister of veterans affairs
Pierre De Bane, minister of regional economic expansion
Hazen Argue, minister of state for the wheat board
Gerald Regan, minister of labour
Mark MacGuigan, secretary of state for external affairs
Robert Kaplan, solicitor general
James Fleming, minister of state for multiculturalism
William Rompkey, minister of national revenue
Pierre Bussières, minister of state in the department of finance
Charles Lapointe, minister of state for small business
Ed Lumley, minister of state for trade
Yvon Pinard, president of the Privy Council; government house leader
Donald Johnston, president of the treasury board
Lloyd Axworthy, minister of employment and immigration; minister of state for the status of women
Paul Cosgrove, minister of public works
Judy Erola, minister of state for mines

The Year of the Referendum and the Constitution

In 1980, Quebeckers refused to seek "sovereignty-association," Ottawa stopped waiting for unanimity on a new constitution, and Canadians looked forward with mixed feelings to the prospect of having their own fundamental law after 113 years of the British North America Act.

The Referendum. Elected in 1976, René Lévesque's Parti Québécois (PQ) government had promised a referendum to test support for its pro-independence ideas. After delays for two federal elections, the date was set for May 20, 1980. Elaborate rules obliged rival sides to join "Yes" or "No" committees, restricted spending, and banned outside interference.

On March 4, the National Assembly began a week-long session to debate the referendum question. While Parti Québécois supporters delivered polished nationalist speeches to a television audience, Claude Ryan's Liberal opposition denounced the lengthy question as "vicious, dishonest, and unacceptable in its present form." The words put to Quebec voters by a vote of 68–37 described the PQ idea more clearly than most of its proponents:

> The government of Quebec has made public its proposal to negotiate a new agreement with the rest of Canada, based on the equality of nations. This agreement would enable Quebec to acquire exclusive powers to make its own laws, levy taxes, and establish relations abroad—in other words, sovereignty—and at the same time, to maintain with Canada an economic association including a common currency. No change in political status resulting from these negotiations will be effected without approval by the people through another referendum. On these terms do you give the government of Quebec the mandate to negotiate the proposed agreement between Quebec and Canada?

Though federalist sympathizers, particularly in Ottawa, questioned the quality of Claude Ryan's austere leadership, his "No" campaign picked up steam. He was helped by Lise Payette, a PQ cabinet minister who accused federalist women of being "Yvettes"—a reference to a deferential figure in Quebec children's books. Other provincial premiers rejected René Lévesque's boast that Canadians would "negotiate on their knees" if Quebeckers voted Yes. Prime Minister Trudeau and federal ministers reminded Quebec voters that they stood to lose billions of dollars in equalization grants and oil price subsidies. On May 20 a nervous Canada waited while 88% of Quebec voters passed judgment on Confederation: 1,485,761 (40.44%) voted Yes, 2,187,991

(59.56%) voted No. The referendum carried in only 16 of 110 provincial constituencies and failed narrowly even among the 80% of Quebec voters whose mother tongue is French.

During the campaign, federalists had promised Quebec major constitutional reforms, mainly in the direction of more provincial powers. The pace was set by Ryan's own policy paper, *A New Canadian Federation,* calling for a much bigger provincial say in communications, taxation, and foreign relations, ending Ottawa's residual power over "peace, order, and good government" and proposing a provincially-appointed federal council to veto any measure that impinged on provincial rights. As chief defender of federalism, Ryan met little criticism of his proposals outside Quebec and some provincial premiers and academics welcomed his views. The return to power of Pierre Elliott Trudeau ended Ryan's claim to be the major voice of Quebec Liberalism and guaranteed a stronger defense of Ottawa's national role. Equally committed to constitutional reform, Trudeau's direction was very different from that of Ryan or Joe Clark's "community of communities." Ottawa's commitment was apparent immediately. Still tired from referendum campaigning, Justice Minister Jean Chrétien made a whirlwind tour of provincial capitals. He found a new eagerness for action, as well as all the old attitudes. Alberta insisted that setting an oil price came first. Newfoundland, excited by deep-sea oil finds, demanded full control of offshore resources. Coastal provinces (except Nova Scotia) wanted to control fisheries. Only Ontario would join Ottawa in trying to protect the economically troubled central provinces. Under Lévesque, Quebec, Ontario's normal ally, was not interested in protecting any aspect of Confederation. On May 27, Marc Lalonde, minister of energy, gave notice of Ottawa's tough stand when he told the Canadian Manufacturers' Association: "We defeated those who wanted political sovereignty with economic association. We did not carry out this difficult battle to get economic sovereignty with political association."

Chrétien's preparations helped bring the prime minister and ten premiers together in Ottawa on June 9 to agree on twelve items, from resource ownership and family law to the composition of the new upper house and Supreme Court, on which agreement might be possible. Failure to agree, Trudeau warned, would have serious consequences. A committee of provincial representatives, chaired by Chrétien and Saskatchewan's attorney general, Roy Romanow, spent much of the summer in week-long meetings in Montreal, Toronto, Vancouver, and Ottawa, seeking that agreement. None was found.

The differences were predictable. Manitoba's Premier Sterling Lyon and Saskatchewan's Allan Blakeney opposed entrenching rights on the ground that it encouraged appointed judges to make political decisions. Alberta's Peter Lougheed and Newfoundland's Brian Peckford refused to compromise on claims to control every aspect of natural resources. Coastal provinces disagreed on control of fisheries. René Lévesque insisted that any preamble refer to Canada as "nations," not as a "nation" and that the right to self-determination—shorthand for unilateral separation—be incorporated.

As a result, when Trudeau and the ten premiers opened their widely heralded conference in Ottawa on September 8, the possibility of compromise had vanished. Armed with poll results suggesting strong support for most of his constitutional stands, the prime minister encouraged the impression that the provincial leaders were self-seeking opportunists. Only Ontario's William Davis stood solidly behind Trudeau, while Saskatchewan's Blakeney sought in vain to play a mediating role. A leaked federal document suggested that the atmosphere of confrontation may well have been part of a Trudeau game plan. With provincial premiers looking selfish, particularly to people in regions where the Liberal Party had gained its majority on February 18, the prime minister felt free to act unilaterally on his own constitutional priorities, entrenching civil and linguistic rights, confirming the key central government role in equalization of provincial wealth, and establishing an amending formula for a Canadian constitution that safeguarded Quebec and Ontario.

The Trudeau constitutional package, settled by mid-September and unveiled to Parliament which was summoned on October 6, included patriation of the British North America Act from Westminster to become the Canada Act; a choice of amending formulas to be settled either unanimously or by referendum; a guarantee of equalization across Canada; and a charter of rights and freedoms carefully designed not to alienate the prime minister's current and potential allies. Language rights did not, for example, extend to immigrants. Quebec and Manitoba would be bound by official bilingualism; New Brunswick, which wanted bilingualism, and Ontario, which did not, could be exempt. Minority education rights extended only "where numbers warrant." Fundamental freedoms would be subject to "generally accepted" community standards. Mobility was guaranteed to people, not to capital or trade, allowing provinces to continue to restrict land ownership to residents or even to legislate local hiring preferences.

Unilateral action defied every Canadian constitutional precedent, and angered even Quebec's erstwhile federalist spokesman, Claude Ryan. The prime minister counted on widespread exasperation with delay, the evident impossibility of gaining provincial unanimity, and the fact that Britain's parliament had never even questioned any would-be amendment to the British North America Act endorsed by both houses of the Canadian parliament. Moving quickly meant imposing closure on the House of Commons, reducing committee sessions—when the Canadian public had their first and only chance to give their opinions—to less than a month, and hurrying forward in hopes that the deed would be done before any court challenge or public uproar could interfere.

The government, which was engaged in bitter battle with much of the West and Newfoundland over its energy policies, relied on its parliamentary majority for victory. New Democrats, who originally backed the Trudeau package because of a concession to Saskatchewan on resource taxation, began to have second thoughts.

Early December polls showed most Canadians, particularly in the West, opposed to the constitutional package and the government's unilateral approach. Belated extension of the parliamentary debate only encouraged Joe Clark and the opposition critics. Challenges in the courts and uneasiness in Britain fueled speculation that Mr. Trudeau might settle for patriation and an amending formula, leaving Canadians to adopt their own charter of rights and freedoms.

DESMOND MORTON

Canada Press

Trudeau and Peter Lougheed disagreed on the distribution of wealth from Canada's natural resources.

Across the West, separatist groups, once an untidy collection of fringe groups, began boasting of having such defecting Conservatives as Richard Collver, former Saskatchewan opposition leader, and Carl Nickle, an oil millionaire and former member of parliament, as leaders. Mass rallies showed more curiosity and unfocused anger than organization but separation was a palpable force in Western Canada by the end of 1980. It would be fed as oil exploration companies fled to the more profitable environment of Ronald Reagan's United States.

Lalonde predicted a six-month uproar from the oil companies, longer if his government showed any sign of weakening. He insisted that multinationals had met 90% of their exploration and development costs through tax concessions and grants and even under the new rules, both Canadian and foreign energy investors could count on better terms than they got from Britain, Norway, Australia, or Mexico. The government may not have appreciated that the immediate panic—with a 13% collapse in the value of energy shares on the Toronto Stock Exchange—hurt weaker Canadian companies more than multinationals.

International Relations. The Trudeau government's new energy policy also ensured a sour end to a difficult year for Canadian-U.S. relations. It had begun much better, with news on January 29 that Ambassador Kenneth Taylor had engineered the escape of six Americans from Islamic revolutionaries in Tehran. The outpouring of appreciation by Americans failed to ease any of the sources of friction between the two countries. A tuna fishery treaty ended a costly dispute on the Pacific coast but 1979 agreements on the Atlantic scallop fishery remained stuck in the U.S. Senate. The Garrison diversion project, with its threat to Manitoba's environment, limped toward completion. Both countries blamed each other for acid rain but eastern Canadian lakes continued to die from added sulphuric acid content while U.S. Republican politicians campaigned for heavier reliance on coal. An agreement to control acid rain was signed, however.

Canada sought relief from its U.S. connection in a wider world. The new fighter plane and slightly stronger defense forces were designed to enhance Canada's standing in NATO. Ottawa welcomed the visit of Mexico's President José López Portillo as part of a renewed search for broader North American contacts and discovered that Mexican officials drove a hard bargain in exchanging their oil for Canadian technical and agricultural products. At the Venice summit of the seven most industrialized Western nations, Trudeau represented Canada and, as host for the 1981 summit, spent ten days in November visiting the Middle East and lecturing Arab leaders on their duty to the impoverished Third World. Since business remained Canada's main business in world affairs, by year's end Canada had lifted its ban on new wheat deals with the Soviet Union. The United States, Ottawa complained, had moved in on Canada's other major wheat customer, China.

People. During 1980, thanks to pertinacious New Democrats in the Ontario legislature, Canadians began to discover more about themselves from government-funded surveys. Ontarians found that most of them favored film censorship and opposed official bilingualism. So, by no coincidence, did their provincial government. In Ottawa, both the Clark and Trudeau governments were shown to have shaped their policies on polls. Canadians favored constitutional reform, legally entrenched rights, and minority education by a ratio of three to one though less than half still firmly insisted on Queen Elizabeth as head of state. Further polling showed that 70% of Albertans were willing to share their natural resources—at a fair price.

Former Supreme Court Justice Emmett Hall, directed by the Clark government to report on the national Medicare scheme he had helped design, submitted his findings in August. The report denounced British Columbia, Ontario, and Alberta for still collecting premiums, condemned doctors who billed over the official fee schedule, and proposed that rates be set by compulsory arbitration. The offending provinces rejected the denunciation and the Canadian Medical Association's leaders threatened to form a union if Hall's suggestions were adopted.

Canada's most famous patient of 1980 was a 22-year old university student from Port Coquitlam, B.C. On April 12, Terry Fox began his marathon of hope from St. John's, Nfld. By September 2, the one-legged victim of bone cancer had run halfway across Canada to the outskirts of Thunder Bay when he discovered that cancer had attacked his lungs. He flew home for a new struggle but Canadians, humbled and deeply moved by Fox's courage, poured $12.5 million into the research funds of the Cancer Society.

DESMOND MORTON
Erindale College, University of Toronto

--- **CANADA · Information Highlights** ---

Official Name: Canada.
Location: Northern North America.
Area: 3,851,809 sq mi (9 976 185 km^2).
Population (1980 est.): 24,000,000.
Chief Cities (1980 met. est.): Ottawa, the capital, 726,-400; Toronto, 2,856,500; Montreal, 2,823,000.
Government: *Head of state,* Elizabeth II, queen; represented by Edward Schreyer, governor-general (took office Jan. 22, 1979). *Head of government,* Pierre Elliott Trudeau, prime minister (took office March 1980). *Legislature*—Parliament: Senate and House of Commons.
Monetary Unit: Canadian dollar (1.1863 dollars equal U.S.$1, Nov. 1980).
Manufactures (major products): Motor vehicles and parts, fish and forest products, petroleum and natural gas, processed and unprocessed minerals.
Agriculture (major products): Wheat, livestock and meat, feedgrains, oilseeds, dairy products, tobacco, fruits and vegetables.
GNP (1979 est., U.S.$): $224,400,000,000.
Foreign Trade (1979, U.S.$): *Imports,* $52,230,000,000; *exports,* $55,336,000,000.

THE ECONOMY

The performance of the Canadian economy in 1980 was almost universally poor. National output and, along with it, productivity, declined, while both inflation and unemployment increased. By almost all indicators, 1980 was Canada's weakest economic year in more than two decades.

The year began with Canada, along with the United States and other Organization for Economic Development (OECD) countries, awaiting the long-expected recession. In Canada's case, the downturn started in the first quarter with a decline of 2.2% in real gross national product (GNP). As Canada's economy is particularly sensitive to foreign trade, the deepening recession beginning in the second quarter among Canada's main trading partners, particularly the United States, sustained Canada's dim overall performance throughout the year. This led to an overall year-to-year decline in GNP of an estimated full one percent.

In addition to the impact of external circumstances, the Canadian economy also was affected adversely by internal structural weaknesses and by a series of internal political events. Two federal elections within nine months brought about significant changes in federal economic policy. The short-lived Progressive Conservative government steered a course of firm monetarism, deficit reduction, and sharply higher domestic energy pricing. The Conservatives' policies were reversed in large measure by the return of the federal Liberals under Prime Minister Pierre Trudeau. This change, combined with the uncertainty generated by the May Quebec independence referendum and subsequent confrontations between the federal and provincial governments over proposals to redraft Canada's constitution, made 1980 an unsettled and unhappy year. In addition, the nation's major economic stumbling block—oil prices and energy policies in general—had a seriously distorting impact on Canada's economic stability.

Following lockstep with U.S. monetarist initiatives, Canada's federal bank maintained high interest rates throughout most of 1980. Though the Bank of Canada moves were intended primarily to stabilize Canadian currency in international markets (the Canadian dollar ranged between U.S. $0.85 and $0.87 during the year), the resulting downward pressure on internal demand for money also succeeded in retarding internal economic growth. A declining auto industry played a central role in the slump. Greater labor participation but slower job creation saw unemployment rise moderately from 7.5% in 1979 to 7.8% in July 1980. Similarly, inflation, measured by the Consumer Price Index, broke the 10% barrier in 1980, up from 9.1% in 1979. Wages, up an estimated 10% in 1980, showed a fractional decline in real terms. The worst casualty of the recession was residential construction, which saw housing starts decline to a 15-year low. Both exports and imports declined by about 3% in 1980.

Forecasters called for an end to the recession by midyear 1981. However, the November federal budget, which raised the specter of sweeping nationalism within Canada's energy sector, could bring about a broader withdrawal of capital—both indigenous and foreign—from Canadian markets and further retard recovery.

ANTHONY WHITTINGHAM
Business Editor, "Maclean's" Magazine

THE ARTS

Canada—a country with a federal form of government, with highly individual provinces jealous of their local power, and with two main cultural traditions (English and French) which it seeks to unite—generates a strong documentary interest in all aspects of the arts. Historians, museum curators, critics, and publishers continually probe what has been called Canada's cultural explosion, trying to delineate the problems of the Canadian national identity. The prevailing inequities among various regions create difficult economic issues which are aggravated by an uneven distribution of natural resources and wealth. Canada's cultural institutions, agencies, and organizations, and the artists who give them their raison d'être, reflect a diversity of ethnic regional characteristics which the Canada Council has respected and supported since it was founded in 1957. In May 1980, an independent study on the question of government cultural policy was launched by the Canadian Conference of the Arts (CCA), the national nongovernmental advocate for the arts. In August, Communications Minister Francis Fox announced that a government study group appointed in 1978 has been raised to the status of public inquiry. Backed by a $2.6 million budget, the cultural areas to be studied by the 15-member committee include visual and performing arts, heritage (museums and historical sites), cultural industries such as book and magazine publishing, musical recordings, films, broadcasting, the National Library and Archives, international cultural relations, and the respective roles of the federal cultural agency and the government.

Visual Arts. According to statistics released in August, Canada's principal museums and the public and university-affiliated art galleries spent 57% more on exhibitions in 1979 than in 1978. About 85% of the total operating revenues came from government grants. Of the $17 million raised for capital purposes in 1979, $10.5 million came from the private sector. Attendance increased by 1.1 million. These figures indicate that the substantial cuts in government support for the arts in 1978 did not have the crippling effect that had been feared.

For its centennial year the National Gallery's exhibition program evoked a sense of the museum's multiplicity of interests and resources.

The exhibition "To Found a National Gallery: The Royal Canadian Academy of Arts 1880–1913" that opened March 6 in Ottawa examined the period before the National Gallery was incorporated by Act of Parliament which placed it under a board of trustees. Nationwide tribute was paid to the academy's pioneer members who, by donating diploma works in their chosen professions, formed the nucleus of the gallery's permanent collections. "Pluralities 1980," a multi-media cross section of contemporary Canadian art which opened at the gallery July 5, was followed by the spectacular major exhibition of paintings, drawings, and prints of Anthony Van Dyck (1599–1641).

At the 1980 Venice Biennale, Canada's exhibition, "Canada Video," was in keeping with the show's theme "Art Systems Opposed to Accepted Art." Thirteen artists, all under age 35, represented the nation at the *Eleventh Biennale de Paris* held in September.

Under the sponsorship of *Artmagazine* and in collaboration with the Professional Art Dealer's Association, the first international art fair, "Toronto 80," took place on July 4–7.

Performing Arts. Drama, music, opera, dance, and film festivals alternated among classical, educational, and popular themes. These ranged from the plebeian "It's showtime, folks!" at oil-rich Alberta's $3-million summer extravaganza (400 performances in 300 communities over three months) to budget-conscious regional art and craft fairs; from fund-raising dinners for symphony orchestras to discussion forums complementing university-sponsored theater or concerts. Season tickets for opera, concerts, and ballet sell out before the box office opens.

The year's Stratford Festival, the last under artistic director Robin Phillips, who resigned, presented 15 plays. Festival highlights included Peter Ustinov repeating his acclaimed performance as King Lear and Maggie Smith in Anton Chekhov's *The Seagull*, Edna O'Brien's *Virginia,* and Shakespeare's *Much Ado about Nothing*. *Titus Andronicus* evoked the bloody tragedy of the Roman Empire's last days and *Foxfire* (adapted by Susan Cooper and Hume Cronyn) depicted the last years of an Appalachian mountain woman. There were no Canadian plays.

In Scotland, the 1980 Edinburgh International Festival welcomed Canada as a major participant. Edinburgh's twin city, Vancouver, BC, sent the National Arts Centre Theater Company, the Mendelssohn choir, and the Canadian Brass quintet, among other Fringe Festival shows, as well as John Gray's virtuoso play *Billy Bishop Goes to War* and two major Canadian art exhibitions—"The Legacy," traditional and contemporary artifacts by British Columbia Indians, and paintings by the late Jack Bush, Canada's celebrated abstract painter.

The National Ballet of Canada was invited to the 30th anniversary of the Carter Barron Amphitheater in Washington, DC. Star roles were danced by Karin Kain, Veronica Tennant, Frank Augustyn, and Peter Schaufuss. The company's fall season presented the world premiere of Brian MacDonald's ballet "Newcomers" and Ann Ditchburn's "Mad Shadows," a work based on a novel by Quebec writer Marie-Claire Blais.

The Canadian Opera Company began its 30th year with James McCracken appearing as Otello, followed by the Canadian premiere of Alban Berg's *Lulu* and Joan Sutherland's appearance in *Norma*. At Place des Arts on October 8, the newly-formed Opéra de Montréal presented *Tosca*. Sung in Italian (with Canadian soprano Nicole Lorange as Floria Tosca), the operatic presentation was the musical event of the year.

In French Canada, Radio Québec added ten minutes of cultural news to its daily evening news program.

Motion Pictures. A substantial number of the 55 English-language movies produced in Canada in 1979 may never reach the screen, regardless of artistic merit. The Canadian film industry was not endangered by lack of generous funding but by overproduction and failure to break into the international mass market. At the Cannes Film Festival in May, the Canadian Film Development Corporation (CFDC) watched its promotion campaign, "Great pictures—Canada's got them," turn into a bitter joke. Only two feature films, *The Handyman*, directed by Quebec's Micheline Lanctôt, and *Mr. Patman*, directed by John Guillermin, met with a favorable press. *Mr. Patman* followed the unfortunate routine pattern of disguising the Canadian background. CFDC issued a warning in the autumn that it would no longer support films which pass off Canadian cities as American. In contrast, the superb French-Canadian film *Les Bons Debarras* (The Rejects), directed by Francis Mankiewicz, gained enormously by its setting of a small rural community in Quebec.

The cause célèbre in Canada was the Ontario Board of Censorship's decision to withhold approval for the release of *The Tin Drum,* the 1980 winner of the Academy Award for best foreign film, unless specific cuts were made. *The Tin Drum* was shown uncut in all other provinces.

The National Film Board of Canada continued to win international awards for its work in film animation. Eugene Fedorenko's *Every Child* received the Oscar at the 52d annual Academy Awards (short films animation category). Among other award-winning entries at international festivals three films were especially noteworthy: Jean-Thomas Bédard's *Chairmen,* Caroline Leaf and Veronica Soul's *Interview*, and Norma Bailey's *The Performer*. The Canadian Film Institute sponsored the third biannual Ottawa International Animated Film Festival at the National Arts Centre in August. A sizable portion of festival time was devoted to video and computer animation.

HELEN DUFFY, *Art Critic and Curator*

CARIBBEAN

One of the most powerful hurricanes in memory brought destruction and further economic difficulty to the islands of the Caribbean in 1980. Civil unrest, a growing refugee problem, and a political shift to the right were other noteworthy developments of the year.

Storms and the Economy. With winds of up to 185 mi (298 km) per hour, hurricane Allen caused some 270 deaths and a total of almost $500 million in property damage and agricultural losses. The first hurricane of the 1980 season, Allen struck a glancing blow at Barbados on August 4 and tore into the Caribbean by passing over the Windward Islands of St. Lucia and St. Vincent. Blowing well to the south of Puerto Rico, it assumed a northerly course and hit the southwestern peninsula of Haiti. With more than 220 deaths, property damage estimated at more than $200 million, and complete destruction of the country's coffee crops—its major source of income—Haiti was hardest hit by the storm. The powerful winds then passed the northern coast of Jamaica, damaging resort areas but sparing heavily populated areas, and proceeded between Cuba and the Yucatan Peninsula into the Gulf of Mexico.

The banana industries of St. Lucia and St. Vincent were ruined. In October, the latter island announced a $4.9 million grant from the United Nations Development Program, mostly provided by Sweden. Canada agreed to furnish three fishing boats to replace those destroyed by the storm. Although the rest of the season saw the expected number of hurricanes, the islands were spared further destruction.

The Caribbean, however, was still feeling the effects of 1979 hurricanes David and Frederic. Combined with the effects of Allen in 1980, the economic outlook was anything but encouraging. Speaking in Washington in June, the World Bank vice president in charge of Latin America and the Caribbean, Nicolas Ardito, warned that in spite of all good efforts, the Caribbean was faced with seriously worsening economic difficulties. Sharply declining trade and a worsening balance of payments deficit made financial needs even greater than anticipated in most countries.

In response to the growing economic problems of the area and concerned with the political status of some of the newly independent states, U.S. President Jimmy Carter helped organize the Central America-Caribbean Action Group to reverse the negative financial trend. Headed by Gov. Bob Graham of Florida and composed of leading U.S. and Latin American businessmen, the group aimed to stimulate the flow of nongovernment economic resources to the Caribbean.

Politics and Unrest. Elections around the Caribbean appeared to reverse the trend toward the left of previous years. Every contest saw the defeat of leftist parties and the success of conservatives. On Dominica, where a moderate leftist government had taken over after allegations of corruption forced Prime Minister Patrick John out of office in 1979, elections finally were held on July 21, 1980. The Dominican Freedom Party headed by Maria Eugenia Charles easily defeated the Democratic Labor Party of acting Prime Minister Oliver Seraphine, taking 17 of 21 seats in the bicameral parliament.

After a surprise call for elections only one month after independence, Prime Minister Milton Cato of St. Vincent defied a challenge from the left and won 11 of the 13 parliamentary seats contested on Dec. 5, 1979. Shortly after the election, a Rastafarian group sought to take over Union Island—one of the Grenadines dependencies of St. Vincent—but were quickly captured and jailed.

Conservative victories also were registered in Antigua and Barbados and in St. Kitts-Nevis. In Grenada, where Prime Minister Maurice Bishop was firmly in control of a pro-Castro government and giving no signs of holding an election, a "war alert" was declared after an unsuccessful assassination attempt on June 19. A bomb explosion by political opponents left three persons killed and 21 injured, but Bishop escaped unharmed.

In Jamaica, the moderate democratic Jamaica Labor Party led by Harvard University-trained sociologist Edward P. G. Seaga defeated the radically pro-Castro government of Prime Minister Michael W. Manley in a landslide election victory October 30. The campaign had been marred by outbreaks of violence that left untold numbers of Jamaicans dead or wounded. The country also was in dire economic straits. When Seaga took office on November 1, the Bank of Jamaica was completely out of foreign exchange.

The same adverse economic and social conditions that affected the English-speaking Windward and Leeward islands also were felt in the French islands of Guadeloupe and Martinique. The results were widespread general strikes and organized expressions of political discontent. France countered the unrest with verbal denunciations of Cuban influence and a mobilization of armed guards.

In September 1980, after more than a year of deliberation, the United States finally appointed Sally Shelton, who already held the post of U.S. ambassador to Barbados, as the nation's ambassador to St. Lucia's leftist government.

Refugees. The political status and resettlement rights of tens of thousands of Cuban and Haitian boat people was a thorny diplomatic issue and a persistent concern throughout the year. Many were admitted into the United States, but thousands of others were left at sea with no food and no place to land. (*See* REFUGEES.)

See also TRINIDAD AND TOBAGO.

THOMAS MATHEWS
University of Puerto Rico

CENTRAL AMERICA

Except in Costa Rica, bitter polarization characterized political developments in much of Central America in 1980.

Costa Rica. Tentative figures projected that the cost of living in Costa Rica was rising dangerously and that the rate of economic growth continued to decline. Only a lack of unity within the labor movement prevented a general strike in March. Many workers received 8 to 10% raises the next month, but insisted they needed more. By autumn the trade balance had become so unfavorable that the government of President Rodrigo Carazo Odio found it necessary to introduce severe measures to reduce imports and the outflow of capital while increasing exports. Importers complained of trade losses, and labor, contending that the measures had the effect of devaluating the colon, asked for additional wage increases. Energy costs, which threatened to double those of 1979, and import restrictions by Nicaragua aggravated the economic picture. More hopeful signs could be found in the largest coffee crop in the nation's history and the export of rice for the first time.

President Carazo Odio found time to express his dissatisfaction with the Communist world. He accused the USSR of using fifth columnists to "create mischief" all over Central America, and he forced the recall of several foreign agents. And while defending himself against charges of being "soft" on Nicaragua's Sandinists, he was appealing to Cuba to release thousands of persons who sought exile. Costa Rica, which does not have full diplomatic relations with Cuba, felt

National Guardsmen stand guard in El Salvador after the assassination of Archbishop Romero.

UPI

it could permanently support only a few hundred Cubans, but was willing to give temporary asylum to thousands prior to their resettlement elsewhere in America in the face of Fidel Castro's fluctuating policies.

El Salvador. If at all possible the right and left in El Salvador had pulled themselves even farther apart in 1980, and violence and assassination continued to be the order of the day. In January 100,000 persons marched in demonstration against the government, and 20 were killed in the ensuing battle. Banks were nationalized, and millions of dollars fled the nation. Members of a teachers union seized hostages in the ministry of education and even the church split over politics. A national tragedy for which no one took blame was the March assassination of the Archbishop Oscar Arnulfo Romero while he celebrated mass. Once moderate, the archbishop had become increasingly critical of the government. But the shocked nation continued on its path of self-destruction. Some 40 persons died in a panic caused by gunfire at his funeral.

The government could not control either the guerrillas or the paramilitary, and the violence continued. Foreigners were no longer immune. Officers of the Organization of American States (OAS) were held hostage for several weeks. The South African ambassador was kidnapped, held, and believed to be dead. Many embassies closed. The U.S. embassy functioned under a virtual state of siege. The desperate state of many Salvadoreans was dramatized by the July death in the Arizona desert of 13 men, women, and children who had paid large sums to smugglers to gain entry into the United States. The Mexican embassy issued Salvadoreans 500 visas a day, and the Honduras government estimated that 10,000 Salvadoreans had fled into Honduras.

Twenty persons were reported killed November 29, as fighting broke out in San Salvador after the abduction and murder of six prominent leftist leaders. On December 4, the bodies of four American women, three of them nuns, were found near the nation's capital. The United States suspended aid to the junta for two weeks pending an investigation of the murders.

In the hope that a restructuring of the government would put an end to the bloodshed, José Napoleon Duarte was named president on December 13, and Col. Jaime Abdul Gutierrez, another junta member, was named vice-president and commander in chief of the armed forces.

Guatemala. As in El Salvador, civil war by assassination continued unmoderated in Guatemala. University of San Carlos administrators blamed government-supported rightists for the killing of more than 100 student leaders and faculty members alone. (Soldiers are not permitted on the campus.) In turn, the various leftist groups argued policy with one another and resorted to bombings, as well as selective assassinations that included scores of soldiers. In January 39 persons were killed by a bomb thrown at police during an occupation of the Spanish embassy. Between the uprisings of guerrillas and the attacks of private armies it was estimated that 20,000 Guatemalans were killed during a 20-year period. Until 1980 most of the struggle bypassed the Indians who constitute more than one half the population, but the Indians increasingly have concluded that they have a stake in the struggle too, and have begun to join the guerrillas. The major result was attacks by the army upon previously untouched villages far from the urban heart of the nation. Neither side seemed to be giving serious attention to trying to solve the problems that brought Guatemala to this state. Vice-President Francisco Villagrán Kramer made several unsuccessful attempts at labor mediation, then, apparently fearing assassination for protesting his government's repressive policies, resigned from the government while in Washington. He was replaced by Col. Oscar Mendoza Azurdia. In October the foreign minister claimed that there was no longer a single political prisoner in Guatemala, yet in the same week 25 tortured bodies were found in one location.

In the midst of all the terror the petroleum industry flourished. A joint venture called "Petromaya" was able to export modest amounts of oil and promised much more. The government also reiterated its usual claims regarding Belize, and later reached agreement with Great Britain and the United States regarding Belize's future.

Honduras. In April Hondurans turned out in large numbers to select an assembly, which after drawing up a new constitution could be empowered to end the military rule which began in December 1972. The Liberal Party won, narrowly and surprisingly, but did not have a clear majority in the new body because of third party votes. The losing Nationalists were supported by the ruling junta. Washington was pleased with the results because of the assumption that the Liberals would be more willing to resolve the outstanding problems with neighboring El Salvador. These matters include the unsettled border questions left from the 1969 Soccer War and the activities of guerrillas and arms smugglers in those poorly policed border areas.

In July the junta formally turned over the government to the newly-elected Constitutional Assembly. Gen. Policarpo Paz Garcia was to remain provisional president until April 1981 elections.

Meanwhile, the junta had attempted to revive the 1972 land reform program which had collapsed from its own corruption. Hoping to encourage more reform and prevent the violence found elsewhere in Central America, the United States doubled its Honduran aid program to some $59 million. Most of the assistance, which was welcomed by the junta, was aimed at rural health, housing, and sanitation improvements.

OAS mediation resulted in an October agreement for a future El Salvador-Honduras treaty.

No Central American nation could be considered well off in 1980, but Honduras could boast of the greatest economic growth in the region. Much of it stemmed from the first Swiss loan to Central America (going into rural development), Inter-American Development Bank loans for a new palm oil industry, and a vast road program for the lumber industry. Less fortunate was the spread of "roja," a leaf disease threatening the invaluable coffee crop, which since 1977 has been the nation's chief export.

Nicaragua. In July the nation celebrated the first anniversary of the overthrow of the long-lived Somoza regime, but the new government had little time to spend boasting of its progress. With help from abroad most people were now being fed again, but rebuilding would take many years. The foreign debt exceeded $1,000,000,000, there was much unemployment, and society was torn by the many excesses committed by armed men cast adrift by the civil war of 1978–79. Observers considered the government's philosophy to be experimental socialism, leaving businessmen uncertain of how to plan. Lack of experience in government led to cabinet shufflings that also left their mark. Gradually Sandinists seemed to be taking over most of the positions in the ruling junta as well as in the lawmaking council of state. Among those leaving the government was Violeta Barrios de Chamorro, whose family had long opposed Somoza and who owned the paper, *La Prensa.* Businessmen asked for and received an end to expropriations and a state of emergency but obviously feared a resumption. The appointment of a few moderates to important positions seemed to have opened the way for a $75-million credit from the United States. Trials of former Somozistas began with government promises that no one would be executed. In September, while it sought the extradition of former President Anastasio Somoza

Debayle himself, he was suddenly assassinated in Asunción, Paraguay, by reported Argentine guerrillas. Nicaragua celebrated the death as a holiday but still could do little to obtain the return of millions of dollars in assets believed hidden by Somoza around the world.

An unexpected source of friction to the government was the behavior of peasants in the Atlantic coastal region. A kind of separatism was developing among the blacks and Indians, many of whom speak no Spanish and fear the Cuban teachers and doctors working among them as threatening their religious and political principles. To compensate, the government made its first real attempt to integrate the region into the nation.

Panama. Much of the turbulence over the Canal disappeared in 1980 as most Panamanians accepted the new status. In accordance with the treaty, the Panama Canal Commission met in June for the first time, with five American and four Panamanian members. In 1990 the relationship will be reversed. In 1980 Panama could earn more than $70 million, a figure in excess of the little republic's total returns from the canal in the previous six decades.

That the recent bitterness over the treaty may not really be of importance is evidenced by the increasingly accepted conviction that the waterway is too small to accommodate today's tankers. A consortium of Japanese firms expressed an interest in building a sea-level route paralleling the current one, and totally within Panama's borders. The situation was dramatized by an accident to a tanker, threatening the waters of Gatún Lake. It was the worst wreck in the canal's history.

Panama's economic picture brightened in 1980. Continual expansion in banking made it clear that the nation was the financial capital of Latin America, and surveys indicated that Cerro Colorado might be one of the largest copper mountains in the world, only awaiting the solution of logistical and ecological problems. The government received nearly $100 million in international loans, much of it for highways, and in October announced plans to purchase two communications subsidiaries of I.T.T. Organized labor held a general strike in January, alleging that much of the economic progress was at labor's expense.

President Aristides Royo visited Costa Rica in February. The two nations announced agreements to attack some of their common problems including border disputes, maritime limits, and trade.

THOMAS L. KARNES
Arizona State University

CHAD

The civil war that ravaged Chad for 14 years resumed in March 1980. The conflict, which originally pitted the Muslim Berbers of the north against the politically dominant Bantu of the south, had deteriorated into a power struggle among factions loyal to one powerful leader. Serious fighting, which had ousted President Félix Malloum in 1979, was ended by a truce and the third coalition government of that year.

The new president was Goukouni Oueddei and the defense minister was Hissène Habré. Both men are northerners and were once allies in the struggle against the south, but they became political rivals in 1980. Other important members of this unstable coalition were Vice-President Wadal Abdelkader Kamougue, a southerner, and Foreign Minister Acyl Ahmat Aghbach. Each of these men maintained his own army. Peace among the factions was to be aided by peacekeeping forces from other African states and by the 1,200-man French force already in the capital of Ndjamena. Congolese units arrived on January 18 and forces from Guinea and Benin were scheduled to arrive later. The truce was violated before their arrival when Oueddei's and Habré's armies clashed in the capital on March 22. Both groups used rockets and artillery. Within three days the death toll reached 700 persons. On March 24, 400 whites, including all U.S. Embassy personnel, were evacuated by the French Air Force. French and Congolese units stayed clear of the fighting. The Congo removed its troops on March 30. The French withdrew theirs, beginning on April 27.

The International Red Cross and concerned African governments attempted to stop the war, but to no avail. Five separate cease-fire agreements were violated by midyear. The last, arranged with the personal intervention of Togo's President Gnassingbe Eyadema, lasted only 18 hours. After intense fighting broke out again late in the year, Libyan troops, supporting Oueddei, entered Chad and forced Habré to flee to Cameroon. Habré then signed another cease-fire agreement.

The economy of Chad, never healthy, was in shambles. Large sections of Ndjamena were destroyed and its population, normally more than 500,000, had fallen to 150,000. Chad's refugees continued to pour into Cameroon and Nigeria.

HARRY A. GAILEY, *San Jose State University*

CHAD • Information Highlights

Official Name: Republic of Chad.
Location: North-central Africa.
Area: 496,000 sq mi (1 284 634 km^2).
Population (1980 est.): 4,500,000.
Chief Cities (1979 est.): Ndjamena, the capital, 303,000; Moundou, 66,000; Sarh, 65,000.
Government: *Head of state and government,* Gen. Goukouni Oueddei, president of transitional Government of National Unity (Nov. 1979).
Monetary Unit: CFA franc (208 CFA francs equal U.S.$1, Aug. 1980).
Manufactures (major products): Flour, beer, refined sugar, cotton textiles.
Agriculture (major products): Wheat, rice, cotton, yams, manioc, groundnuts.
GNP Per Capita (1978 est., U.S.$): $140.
Foreign Trade (1976, U.S.$): *Imports,* $118,000,000; *exports,* $59,000,000.

CHEMISTRY

In 1980 public attention in chemistry focused on problems related to storing and disposing of toxic chemical wastes. With less notice, advances came in the technologies of solar cells and photographic films, splitting of water molecules by light, and the theory of nuclear transformations.

Toxic Chemicals. Chemical waste disposal has been called the number one environmental problem in the United States. According to the Environmental Protection Agency (EPA), the United States produces about 60 million metric tons of hazardous chemical wastes each year, and only a tenth of that amount is properly disposed of. The problem was highlighted in April when a toxic waste storage site in Elizabeth, NJ, with 25,000 drums of chemicals, exploded and burned. Because of dangerous fumes, local schools were closed and residents were urged to stay indoors. Less spectacular, but in the long range more alarming, was the growing realization that many public and private groundwater supplies are being contaminated by toxic chemicals as a result of seepage from storage sites, illegal dumping, and pesticides sprayed on fields. The EPA estimates that as many as 2,000 dump sites in the nation pose potentially serious problems. In May the EPA released a long-awaited and extensive set of regulations on the handling of hazardous wastes.

Controversy about Hooker Chemical's Love Canal site in Niagara Falls, NY, where more than 21,000 metric tons of chemicals were disposed of in 1947–53, continued to simmer. An EPA-sponsored study in May indicated apparent chromosomal abnormalities in some area residents. Later, several reports strongly criticized the scientific merits of the chromosome study and earlier health studies, pointing in particular to lack of adequate controls. Congress spent the final days of its lame duck session considering means of controlling toxic waste and a bill passed. (*See also* feature article, page 47.)

Technology. Among the year's technological advances were thin film solar cells developed by workers at the University of Delaware and Boeing Aerospace Company. The Boeing cell uses copper indium selenide/cadmium sulfide layers and the Delaware cell copper sulfide/cadmium sulfide. Although displaying only modest 9–10% efficiencies in converting light to electricity, the thin cells may be cheaply produced, an important aim in solar conversion. A new black-and-white photographic film developed by researchers at the Ilford division of Ciba-Geigy Corporation utilizes dyes to form its negative, allowing recovery of the film's silver. Each year about 60 million ounces (2.3 million kg) of silver are consumed in photography, and rising silver prices have sparked a search for ways to recover the metal. The new film is expensive, but promises fine-grain images with high speed. Research continues on batteries to drive electric vehicles, but a practical alternative to the lead-acid battery remains elusive. In June, Gulf & Western scientists announced a new zinc/chlorine battery with high energy density, constructed largely from low-cost materials.

Research. Splitting of water by light to yield hydrogen and oxygen has long been a goal of photochemists. Michael Grätzel and his coworkers in Lausanne, Switzerland, devised a system with special catalysts that carries out this process with high efficiency. The catalytic material consists of platinum and ruthenium dioxide deposited on titanium dioxide. A notable feature of the system is that it is effective over long periods, with hydrogen production undiminished after two days of irradiation.

Nuclear chemists have thus far been frustrated in their attempts to create superheavy elements, with atomic numbers greater than 106, although theories predict that some such elements may be relatively stable. In 1980 hopes turned to "transfer reactions," in which one nucleus transfers a portion of its nucleons to another nucleus during a collision. Traditionally it has been believed that colliding nuclei should combine totally to form a compound nucleus, but Darleane Hoffman and colleagues from Los Alamos Labs, New Mexico, observed that partial combinations occur in certain reactions. The transfer mechanism holds out hope for producing some of the superheavy elements.

Scientists at Lawrence Berkeley Labs in California reported development of new compounds capable of specifically binding and transporting plutonium. These compounds can help remove this radioactive element from persons accidentally contaminated, and may also prove useful in treating nuclear wastes. Researchers at the Naval Research Laboratory and Case Western Reserve University have synthesized phthalocyanine polymers capable of conducting electricity. Adding iodine to phthalocyanine chromium fluoride polymers increases conductivity a billion-fold.

Computers are playing an increasing role in chemistry. On the experimental side, more and more instruments are being combined with mini- and micro-computers, both to run the instruments and to analyze the data collected. And theoretical calculations on computers are becoming more sophisticated and useful. Calculations are aiding in the design of new drugs and photographic sensitizing dyes, and in predicting whether certain chemicals may cause cancer. Prime advantages of the calculations are that they are rapid and do not require costly and time-consuming syntheses of the substances.

Indicative of continuing activity in synthetic chemistry, in August Chemical Abstracts Service recorded the 5 millionth chemical in its computer registry, and continued to add 6,000 new substances weekly.

See also GENETICS; PRIZES AND AWARDS.

PAUL G. SEYBOLD
Wright State University

CHICAGO

Chicagoans, accustomed to a "city that works," won't soon forget 1980. The topsy-turvy year began with a bankrupt public school system and payless paydays for Chicago's 46,000 teachers and other school-system employees. Other complications during the year included a firemen's strike and a preliminary census report of declining population. The record number of new office buildings, hotels, and apartments being constructed in the downtown area provided one bright spot for Chicago's citizens.

Crisis in the Public Schools. Years of financial mismanagement brought the Chicago Board of Education to its knees before less than half the school year was completed. It was only through the advancement to the school system of millions of dollars in state funds, as well as an initial education budget cutback of $60 million, that order was restored. During the crisis, the school superintendent and the entire school board resigned, and teachers went on a week's strike.

Firemen's Strike. In another crisis Chicago firemen, for the first time in history, went on strike for three weeks in a contract dispute. Their union president Frank Muscare was jailed, and the union was fined $40,000 a day for calling an illegal strike. Mayor Jane Byrne vowed that the striking firemen would "never again work for the Chicago Fire Department, never."

However, after the firemen voted to return to work, Muscare was freed from jail, the fines were dropped, and the firemen returned to their stations.

U.S. Census Data. Preliminary census data, released in August, showed that the "second city" had dropped to third place, behind New York and Los Angeles, in population. City officials maintained that there was an undercount and that when the official figures were released in 1981, Chicago would maintain its second position with about 3 million people. The Bureau of the Census preliminary figures showed that Chicago had lost 644,072 residents during the 1970s, a dramatic drop of 19.1%, and more than double the decline between 1950 and 1970.

The exodus was attributed primarily to white families fleeing to suburban areas. For the first time blacks and Hispanics comprised more than half of the city's population.

The Mayor. For Mayor Byrne, 1980 was a year of setbacks. Public confidence in her administration remained low, and when she led the traditional St. Patrick's Day parade, she was booed by some spectators. Her efforts to be a "political kingmaker" by winning support in Chicago and Illinois for the presidential aspirations of Sen. Edward Kennedy (D-MA) fell flat. She spent less than a day at the Democratic National Convention in New York City.

ROBERT ENSTAD, *"Chicago Tribune"*

In frigid temperatures, striking firemen wait to see a visiting senator, Edward M. Kennedy.

UPI

CHILE

The nation's most important political event of 1980 was a September 11 plebiscite that ostensibly favored the continuation in power of Gen. Augusto Pinochet Ugarte until 1989. Prices increased, but unemployment dropped.

Plebiscite. While 67.06% of 6,268,652 voters cast "yes" ballots in the referendum held on the seventh anniversary of the overthrow of President Salvador Allende, both Roman Catholic and Christian Democratic leaders denied the validity of the referendum, which lumped together a vote for a new constitution, Pinochet's continuation in office, and the assignment to him of greater powers of office. The new constitution provided for a Senate of nine members appointed by the current and past Chilean presidents, and two members from each electoral district except for Santiago, which would have six appointed senators. The Chamber of Deputies would have 120 members elected by direct popular vote in 1989 and could be dissolved by the president one time during its six-year term of office. The new constitution also provided that those accused of terrorist crimes would be judged by military tribunals and not the civil courts.

On August 27, former President Eduardo Frei Montalva (1964–70) called for the immediate formation of a transition government—including military participation—to replace the regime, which has been in power since 1973. More than 8,000 persons attending Frei's speech marched through the streets shouting slogans against General Pinochet and his government. Further opposition came from Gen. Gustavo Leigh Guzman, a former junta member, who said he would vote against the constitution and Pinochet's continued rule. Other opposition leaders complained that citizens should not be required to respond to more than one issue with a single answer, and that they were denied access to television while the government spent an estimated $44,000 per day on TV ads alone, as well as thousands more on billboard and newspaper advertising. Further, voters had to affix their signatures and be fingerprinted next to their names on new voting registers which also contained the numbers of their ballots. Even the pro-regime daily *El Mercurio* admitted there was no real alternative to the government package.

Opposition to the government was manifested in other ways during the year. Progovernment candidates won only about 32% of the vote in April elections at the University of Chile, not much better than in April 1979. The Movimiento de Izquierda Revolucionaria (MIR), headed by Andres Pascal Allende, nephew of the late president, seized the flag on which the oath of independence was taken in 1821, attacked three banks on April 12, and on July 15 assassinated Lt. Col. Roger Vergara Campos, director of the army intelligence school.

Cardinal Raúl Silva Henríquez canceled his traditional May Day Mass at the last moment after officials hinted they could not take responsibility for any violence that might occur. Enrique Alvear, the Auxiliary Bishop of Santiago, and four other senior priests were stopped and searched by intelligence agents after meeting with textile leaders on May Day.

In April and June, the government confined more than 500 persons for varying lengths of time for organizing or attending forbidden political meetings. On August 12, the government announced that 20 policemen belonging to the Avengers of Martyrs Command had been arrested and would be tried for the kidnapping and torture of students.

Diplomatic relations with the Philippines were strained severely when President Ferdinand Marcos refused to see Pinochet, who was in the Fiji Islands on March 22. The general was on his way to the Philippines, Hong Kong, and Tahiti in an effort to improve Chile's image and presence in the South Pacific. Following the snub, the general cut short his trip. Relations with Peru also continued tense.

Economy. The Chilean peso remained stable at 39 to U.S. $1.00. Copper prices also remained above October 1979 levels of 90 cents a pound, reaching a high of $1.03 per pound in December–January following the outbreak of tension on the Iraqi–Iranian border. These high prices, along with increased industrial output and productivity, contributed to a reduction of unemployment to 12% in 1980. It was 19.1% in August 1976.

Higher prices for the 75% of oil needs that Chile imports plus a 63.2% increase in imported machinery and transportation equipment fueled inflation, which was estimated to reach 30% in 1980, slightly lower than 1979 but about the same as the 1978 rate. Bank interest rates remained high—around 40%—discouraging domestic private investment but encouraging foreign investment, from which the limits on profits repatriated abroad were removed.

NEALE J. PEARSON
Texas Tech University

CHILE · Information Highlights

Official Name: Republic of Chile.
Location: Southwestern coast of South America.
Area: 292,257 sq mi (756 945 km^2).
Population (1980 est.): 11,300,000.
Chief Cities (1978 met. est.): Santiago, the capital, 3,448,700; Valparaiso, 248,200; Viña del Mar, 362,100.
Government: *Head of state and government,* Gen. Augusto Pinochet Ugarte, president (took power Sept. 1973). *Legislature*—Congress (dissolved Sept. 1973).
Monetary Unit: Peso (39.00 pesos equal U.S.$1, Nov. 1980).
Manufactures (major products): Small manufactures, refinery products.
Agriculture (major products): Wheat, rice, oats, barley, fruits, vegetables, corn, sugar beets, beans, wine, livestock.
GNP Per Capita (1978 est., U.S.$): $1,410.
Foreign Trade (1979, U.S.$): *Imports,* $4,219,000,000; *exports,* $3,766,000,000.

At the Chinese National People's Congress in September, three new deputy prime ministers—(left to right) Yang Jingren, Zhang Aiping, and Huang Hua—were named.

CHINA

The year 1980 brought significant changes in the leadership of the People's Republic of China. Deng Xiaoping, the powerful deputy premier, succeeded in removing his rivals and placing his trusted associates in key positions. With the appointment in September of his protégé Zhao Ziyang to replace Hua Guofeng as premier, Deng's dominance in the government was indisputable.

Important changes also were adopted to advance the economy. The principles of management autonomy, material incentive, development of productive forces, and correlation between production and market demands were extended to both industry and agriculture.

Fear of Soviet expansion remained the central element in China's foreign policy. Greater cooperation with the United States, friendship with Japan, and confrontation with Vietnam all were directed against Soviet expansionism.

DOMESTIC AFFAIRS

Leadership. Deng Xiaoping had only the title of deputy premier—and he gave that up in September—but his ascendancy over Premier and Chairman of the Chinese Communist Party Hua Guofeng never was in doubt. In February, Deng removed from the Politburo four of his formidable enemies who were closely associated with Hua: Wang Dongxing, former chief bodyguard of Mao Zedong; Wu De, former mayor of Peking; Ji Dengkui, deputy prime minister; and Chen Xilian, former commander of the Peking military region. Deng then appointed his own followers to the key positions: Hu Yaobang as secretary general of the Chinese Communist Party and Zhao Ziyang as deputy prime minister

to take charge of the "day-to-day work" of the government. Both were elected into the Standing Committee of the Politburo, the powerful ruling organ of the party. The functions of Hua Guofeng were substantially curtailed. After he failed to appear at a Central Committee reception for the nation's highest officials on New Year's Day, 1981, there were reports that Hua had been dropped entirely from the Chinese leadership. On January 3, Deng took over Hua's function as head of the party's Military Commission, which controls the Chinese armed forces.

The People's Congress. The National People's Congress, China's legislative body, met from August 30 to September 10 and adopted far-reaching changes in leadership as well as social and economic policy. It elected Zhao Ziyang premier, replacing Hua Guofeng, who retained his titular post as chairman of the Communist Party. On the principle that officials should not hold both party and government posts at the same time, it accepted the resignation of seven deputy prime ministers—including Deng—and appointed three new ones: Foreign Minister Huang Hua, 67; Zhang Aiping, 70, an army deputy chief of staff; and Yang Jingren, 62, who headed the Nationalities Affairs Commission. The change was a triumph for Deng, who remained a deputy chairman of the party and retained his ultimate control. Deng had installed a new team of leaders to carry out his policies and to ensure an orderly succession when he retired.

Other actions taken during the final session included the following: abolishing Article 45 of the Constitution, which had established the "four freedoms to speak out freely, air views fully, hold great debates," and write wall posters criticizing official policies; raising by two years the minimum age for marriage to 22 for men and 20 for women; levying a 33% tax on foreign companies participating in joint ventures in China; and instituting the country's first income tax, but only for resident foreigners and some artists and writers.

Denigration of Mao. Mao Zedong, the late party chairman, was subjected to more and more direct attacks as the Deng group rose to power. They called Mao's paternal type of rule a remnant of feudalism and regarded the Cultural Revolution as an appalling calamity. Mao's misdirection, said Hu Yao-bang, the new secretary general of the party, was "the cause of great misfortunes for the party and the people."

Mao's economic policies were denounced as unsuitable to modern times. The Dazhai agricultural brigade in Shanxi province, which had been regarded by Mao as a model for agricultural production, now was pronounced a failure.

The denigration of Mao Zedong took another form in the rehabilitation of Liu Shaoqi, the onetime chief of state who was purged by Mao during the Cultural Revolution.

Gang of Four Trial. The celebrated Gang of Four and six other defendants went on trial November 20 in Peking. The defendants were charged with "48 specific offenses" during the Cultural Revolution and up to the 1976 death of Mao. Among these were attempting to overthrow the state, plotting to assassinate Mao, and persecuting to death more than 34,000 officials and other persons. The trial ended on December 29, with the prosecutor demanding the death sentence for Jiang Qing, Mao's widow, and severe punishment for another gang member, Zhang Chunqiao. The eight others confessed most of the charges and pleaded for leniency. Sentences were expected to be handed down in early 1981.

Discipline and Rejuvenation. The government found its functionaries unable to carry out many of its newer programs. Remnants of the Cultural Revolution were a resisting force, especially at the local level. These officials were suspicious of the new leadership and, having gone through many changes and restorations, became, as one Communist leader put it, "inert in thought and action," afraid of taking initiatives, and overly protective of their jobs. To rejuvenate the administration, Peking decided to retire aging officials and tighten up discipline. Government agencies, schools, and factories were instructed to select and appoint to leading posts young, talented people who had distinguished themselves "in practical work." Officials were forbidden to use their positions to seek special treatment for their relatives.

Military Development. On May 18, Peking announced that it had successfully launched its first intercontinental ballistic missile into an area south of Kiribati in the South Pacific. From a launching site in northern China, the missile traveled about 6,000 miles (9 656 km) before landing in the target area. The rocket was said to be capable of carrying a nuclear warhead with a destructive power of 5 to 20 megatons.

At the same time, China was still lacking in conventional weapons. Much of its arsenal was out of date, particularly fighter planes and warships, and it was badly in need of sophisticated equipment. But with the military budget cut by $2,000,000,000 in 1980, defense procurement was necessarily limited and military modernization a slow process.

Tibet. In 1980, Peking adopted a series of measures to improve the economy and social conditions of Tibet, one of China's five autonomous regions. Rigid controls imposed during the Cultural Revolution were to be relaxed, and the Chinese Communists in Tibet were ordered to end such "incorrect tendencies," as factionalism, favoritism, waste of state funds, and enjoyment of special privileges. Tibetan peasants were to be freed from taxes for two years, and more Tibetans were to serve in the local governments.

Peking indicated that it would welcome the return of the Dalai Lama, Tibet's spiritual leader who had fled to India in 1959 after an abortive uprising. Though he sent delegations to visit Tibet, the exiled leader had no plans to return to his country.

Economy. China's program of economic modernization, which called for rapid development in industry and agriculture, had been criticized for its overestimation of natural resources. The critics contended that plans for "too fast, too much growth" would only lead to disaster. In September, the People's Congress affirmed the importance of economic growth over political ideology but took a more moderate approach toward the former, which was set at 5% for the year.

Peking undertook a number of economic experiments which led to far-reaching changes. Autonomy was granted to factories, which were to retain part of their profits and sell directly to other enterprises any produce above quota. Factories in nonessential industries were allowed to set their own prices, to increase worker bonuses, and to dismiss employees found unsatisfactory. The new policy was to pay workers according to productivity and to let market demand determine the production of goods in daily use. These experiments, first introduced in Sichuan province by Zhao Ziyang, then first party secretary of the province, had proven highly successful. Output had increased and more jobs had been created for the unemployed.

In agriculture, as well, peasants were allowed greater individual initiative. Work points were changed to reflect more accurately what they actually accomplished. The amount of land to be privately cultivated was increased, and production teams were allowed to determine what crops to grow.

Light and Heavy Industry. Economic policy during the year appeared to stress light industry over heavy industry. The intended growth rate for light industry was raised, especially in textiles. Ambitious production goals for iron, steel,

Grain is poured into new silos at the Guzhuang Commune in Xinghua county, China's leading grain-producing region. By planting three grain crops a year, China hoped to become more self-reliant in agriculture, and through the increased yields, control prices.

UPI

coal, and oil were put off. Light industry required less capital and would help improve the living conditions of the people, which remained generally poor.

Living Conditions. Urban workers earned an average of $39 a month, while peasants took home much less. Unemployment in the cities was estimated at 20 million. Adding to the hardship was rising inflation, which had reached 5.8% in 1979. To cope with the situation, Peking increased production of food and consumer goods and expedited construction of housing. At the same time, it intensified its efforts to reduce the population growth to 1% per year. Various rewards and privileges were offered to families with not more than one child.

Foreign Trade. China's exports rose by 36% and imports by 7.8% in the first half of 1980, compared with the same period a year earlier. The increase in exports was attributed to better quality, greater variety, and improved packing of goods. While imports of rolled steel and other metals declined, purchases of foreign technology, fully operating plants, and materials for light industry increased.

China was admitted to the International Monetary Fund (IMF) in April and to the World Bank in May. The new associations entitled it to loans that would help advance imports and long-term development projects.

FOREIGN AFFAIRS

United States. The Soviet Union's intervention and continued military presence in Afghanistan spurred the United States to strengthen its relations with China. On Jan. 5, 1980, U.S. Secretary of Defense Harold Brown arrived in Peking for an eight-day visit. During his stay, Brown called for "parallel responses" to the world situation and "wider cooperation on secu-

rity matters" between the two countries. A Sino-American security relationship, he said, was "beginning to emerge," and if a third party should threaten the "shared interest" of the two countries, "we can respond with complementary actions in the field of defense as well as diplomacy."

The Chinese welcomed the American move. Deputy Premier Deng Xiaoping told Secretary Brown that the two countries "should do something in a down-to-earth way so as to defend world peace against hegemonism."

The United States, however, did not plan to sell weapons to Peking, though it would increase exports of technology to help China's military industry. On January 8, Brown announced that the United States would sell China a ground station for receiving information from the Landsat satellite. In May, Chinese Deputy Premier Geng Biao visited the United States to discuss the possible purchase of American military equipment. The Carter Administration agreed that U.S. companies would sell to China a variety of military support equipment, including radar, aircraft, computers, and communication apparatus.

Progress also was made in commercial relations. On February 1, China was extended most-favored-nation trade status, under which the United States would no longer charge duties higher than those demanded of other nations. The Soviet Union had sought to receive, but was not granted, such status. On September 17, China and the United States signed trade pacts covering civil aviation, shipping, textile trade, and consular services. The agreements represented a major development in the commercial relations between the two countries.

President Carter met Chinese Premier Hua Guofeng on July 10 in Tokyo, where they attended a memorial service for Masayoshi Ohira, the late Japanese prime minister. The two leaders conferred for more than an hour. Speaking on Japanese television after the talk, President Carter suggested that the growing Sino-American friendship would "minimize the threat of the Soviet military build up," which had been "exemplified most vividly" by the Russian intervention in Afghanistan and "support of the Vietnamese invasion" of Cambodia.

Peking was more than a little apprehensive about Ronald Reagan, the Republican candidate for U.S. president. In one campaign speech, Reagan called for giving "official status" to relations between the United States and Taiwan. On August 20, the Republican vice-presidential candidate, George Bush, visited China to convince its leaders that Reagan had no intention of changing established relations between the two countries. Peking did not seem convinced.

Europe. To check Soviet influence, Peking continued to develop ties with the Scandinavian countries. In June, Foreign Minister Huang Hua visited Sweden, Norway, and Denmark, holding talks with the prime ministers and foreign secretaries of all three countries. Huang's journey was immediately denounced by the Soviet press as a scheme to disrupt Soviet relations with northern Europe.

President Valéry Giscard d'Estaing of France was well received when he arrived in China in October, but during his stay differences of opinion emerged on some issues. Peking was displeased with France's emphasis on détente and its condemnation of the ousted Pol Pot regime of Cambodia. But the Chinese agreed to buy from France an 1,800-megawatt nuclear power plant at the cost of about $1,600,000,000.

Soviet Union. China considered the Soviet Union a serious threat to its security. The Soviet strategy, as seen by Peking, was to encircle China by massing armed forces on its northern border and establishing powerful bases in Vietnam to the south. Peking sent representatives to countries all over the world to alert them to the Soviet threat. China also joined the United States in boycotting the Moscow summer Olympic Games to protest the Soviet intervention in Afghanistan. To accentuate its condemnation,

— **COMMUNIST CHINA · Information Highlights** —

Official Name: People's Republic of China.
Location: Central part of eastern Asia.
Area: 3,705,396 sq mi (9 596 976 km²).
Population (1980 est.): 975,000,000.
Chief Cities (1980 est.): Peking, the capital, 8,500,000; Shanghai, 12,000,000; Tianjin, 7,200,000.
Government: *Chairman of the Chinese Communist Party,* Hua Guofeng (took office Oct. 1976). *Head of government,* Zhao Ziyang, premier (took office Sept. 1980); Deng Xiaoping, senior deputy premier. *Legislature* (unicameral)—National People's Congress.
Monetary Unit: Yuan (1.50 yuan equal U.S.$1, June 1980—noncommercial rate).
Manufactures (major products): Iron and steel, coal, machinery, cotton textiles, light industrial products.
Agriculture (major products): Rice, wheat, corn, millet, cotton, sweet potatoes.
GNP Per Capita (1978 est., U.S.$): $460.

Peking canceled talks with the Soviet Union on improvement of relations.

Japan. Premier Hua Guofeng arrived in Tokyo on May 27 for a six-day visit with Japanese leaders. He urged Japan to cooperate with China in checking Soviet aggression. Moscow, he said, was planning to use Vietnam and Cambodia as springboards to the Strait of Malacca and thereby extend its dominance from the Indian Ocean to the Pacific.

Sino-Japanese trade had grown rapidly since 1972, when diplomatic relations between the two countries were normalized. In 1980, China was the world's seventh largest importer of Japanese products and the tenth largest exporter to Japan. Peking sent Chinese students to Japan to learn advanced technology and expertise in the fields of economic management and production control. Joint ventures were established, and Japanese companies assisted in Chinese projects on port and harbor development and the construction of railroads and hydro-electric power stations. A number of Japanese banks, including the Export-Import Bank, agreed to provide huge loans for developing China's oil and coal resources and financing Japan's export contracts.

Southeast Asia. Viewing the Vietnamese as "the Cubans of the Orient," Peking continued its efforts to prevent Vietnam from gaining control of Southeast Asia in partnership with the Soviet Union. In 1979, China had attacked the neighboring country "to teach it a lesson." In early 1980, there were reports that Peking was considering teaching Vietnam another lesson. But the Chinese decided against it, attempting instead to mobilize international pressure and encourage regional resistance to Vietnamese aggression. As sporadic fighting continued along the Chinese-Vietnamese border, peace talks between the two countries collapsed. On September 23, China rejected Hanoi's proposal to resume negotiations. The Vietnamese insincerity, said Peking, was reflected not only in its persisting hostility toward China but by its aggression throughout Indochina, particularly against Cambodia.

In Cambodia, Peking provided arms and medicine to rebellious guerrillas fighting the Vietnamese-supported regime in Phnom Penh. It also promoted insurgency against the Vietnamese-dominated government of Laos and offered assistance to Thailand in the eventuality of an attack by Vietnam.

Afghanistan and Pakistan. After the Soviet intervention in Afghanistan, Peking shipped small arms, by way of Pakistan, to Afghan insurgents fighting Soviet troops. China also increased its military aid to Pakistan, with which it maintained good relations. China's role in bolstering Pakistan against Soviet pressure became even more important after Islamabad rejected a U.S. offer of $400 million in aid.

See also TAIWAN (Republic of China).

CHESTER C. TAN
New York University

CITIES AND URBAN AFFAIRS

As the United States moved into the 1980s, its cities and urban areas found themselves caught in the crossfire of a number of significant changes—population shifts, changing life-styles, uncertain national and regional economies, inflation and eroding fiscal strength, rising energy costs, and public disenchantment with government. While many of these changes offer opportunities for reshaping and recycling the nation's cities, they also present new and difficult obstacles to improving the quality of life in urban areas large and small.

Census. Preliminary and final figures for the 1980 U.S. decennial census confirmed not only the steady growth of the American population but also a shift out of older and larger central cities into suburban and more rural communities. A decrease in the size of families and a decline in the number of persons per dwelling unit were other important changes in American living patterns revealed by the census.

The census did create controversy in several major cities, however, as New York, Chicago, Detroit, Philadelphia, and Newark (NJ) filed lawsuits against the Census Bureau for undercounting, especially of poor minorities. Dozens of other cities that stood to lose congressional representation and federal aid as a result of the alleged undercount supported the suits.

Campaign Promises and National Priorities. The three major candidates for the U.S. presidency actively sought the support of mayors and other urban leaders across the country. Proposals and promises for aid, renewal and development, job programs, and housing were presented and debated among and even within the parties. In June, candidates Jimmy Carter, Ronald Reagan, and John Anderson all visited the United States Conference of Mayors in Seattle, and in August they each addressed the annual conference of the National Urban League in New York.

One of the more far-reaching proposals was made by unsuccessful Democratic hopeful Sen. Edward Kennedy (MA), who called for some $12,000,000,000 in federal spending to create more than 800,000 jobs. As on other issues, Kennedy was no less vehement in his attacks on the urban policies of President Carter than were the Republican candidates and Independent John Anderson. In his initial budget proposal for fiscal 1981, presented to Congress January 28, President Carter sought a five-year extension of revenue sharing to states and localities, maintaining the current $6,860,000,000 spending level. (Congress in December barred revenue sharing to states, limiting payments to $4,600,000,000 annually to local governments for a three-year period.) The revised budget sent to Congress March 31, however, called for spending cuts that John Gunther, executive director of the Conference of Mayors, said "yield a minus sign for the nation's cities."

Although candidate Carter did offer an economic renewal plan with billions of dollars to go to urban areas and also vowed to relieve welfare and Medicaid costs, Ronald Reagan's conservative philosophy of limited government and economic restraint apparently was more in tune with the national sentiment. For example, the ninth annual Harris Poll for the Advisory Commission on Intergovernmental Relations showed that, unlike previous years, citizens placed more confidence in their local government than they did in their state and federal governments. The commission reported that government in general has become so overloaded that its workability and flexibility are critically endangered. It has become a system noted for intergovernmental bickering, administrative inefficiency, countless and costly federal mandates on states and local governments, and a bewildering array of grant-in-aid programs that diffuse responsibility and accountability of government officials and distort local priorities. What is needed during the Reagan administration and throughout the 1980s is a reclarification of responsibilities at all levels and a true partnership of federal, state, and local government.

President-elect Reagan's appointee for secretary of Housing and Urban Development (HUD), Samuel Riley Pierce, Jr., a 58-year-old black attorney from New York City, stated that his goal would be "to streamline that department so that the people will get the best they can for the amount of money that we can give the programs."

Problems and Solutions. As part of its 350th birthday celebration, Boston, MA (see page 160) held the "Great Cities of the World" conference September 21–27. Chief executives of some 30 cities throughout the world attended the meetings and events, and agreed that they had many problems in common but that potential solutions are diverse.

In the United States, the many thousands of mayors, city and town council members, and other elected officials whose responsibility it is to govern America's vast array of communities see a number of immediate as well as longer-range priorities for meeting the challenges of the 1980s. Among these are rebuilding the national economy in such a way as to restore economic growth, control inflation, and promote full employment; renewing efforts to protect and enhance the urban environment and meet human needs by improving air and water quality, providing better housing and job opportunities for all, and developing adequate transportation systems and facilities; and launching the much-needed reform of the tangled system of federal, state, and local government. Clarifying responsibilities at all levels of government and the private sector may well be one of the most significant challenges facing U.S. cities and urban areas during the 1980s.

(See articles on individual cities.)

CIVIL LIBERTIES AND CIVIL RIGHTS

A divided and unpredictable Supreme Court, racial turmoil in several major cities, and serious disagreements over the rights of Cuban refugees, Iranian students, criminal defendants, and other groups made 1980 an unsteady year for civil liberties in the United States

Minority Rights. The long, hot summers of racial turmoil in the 1960s were echoed in 1980 in Chattanooga, TN, Birmingham, AL, Philadelphia, PA, and several cities in Florida, as ghetto blacks reacted to what they felt was a double standard in the criminal justice system. Whites accused of violent crimes against blacks, they felt, were dealt with gently, while black defendants in general received stiff penalties.

In *Fullilove v. Klutznick,* the Supreme Court again considered whether a program based on preferential treatment by race is constitutional. Its decision upheld a law requiring certain federal contractors to reserve at least 10% of their business for minority-owned firms.

In a case affecting black voters, the high court overturned a finding by two lower courts that Mobile's (AL) black population was denied equal protection by an at-large voting system for the city commissioners (*Mobile v. Bolden*).

Legislation strengthening a 1968 federal statute prohibiting discrimination in the sale or rental of housing slowly was making its way through Congress. It was passed by the House of Representatives in June.

Alien Rights. In response to the Iranian hostage crisis (*see* feature article, page 39), U.S. President Carter ordered the identification of all Iranians in the United States and the deportation of those found in violation of their immigration status. More than 1,500 of the approximately 56,000 Iranian students in the country were forced to leave. Those who remained faced reprisals by local governments and private parties. Mississippi imposed a $4,000 nonresident fee on students "from a nation not having diplomatic relations with the United States or against whom the United States has economic sanctions." A federal district court prohibited implementation of the law, holding that it violated the students' 14th Amendment rights to due process. The New Mexico State University Board of Regents voted to bar Iranian students from the school, but a federal judge issued an injunction.

The arrival of more than 120,000 refugees from Cuba created a dilemma for the U.S. government. With the nation in an economic recession, it was feared that the Cubans would become a burden and a focus of taxpayer animosity. Boat people from Haiti were not welcomed as generously as the Cubans. They faced expulsion until a judge ordered the Immigration and Naturalization Service to reconsider.

Defendants' Rights. The Supreme Court had a mixed record in the area of defendants' rights. It barred warrantless arrests in the home and defined more broadly the kind of police interrogation that oversteps constitutional safeguards against self-incrimination and the guarantee of right to counsel. However, the court also expanded admissibility of illegally-obtained evidence by allowing the prosecution to use such evidence to impeach a defendant's false answers in cross-examination.

Nearly 100 prosecutors from 23 of the 38 states with capital punishment laws met for a three-day strategy session aimed at finding ways to remove legal roadblocks to execution of prisoners. Another Georgia death sentence was reversed by the Supreme Court, which held that "there is no principled way to distinguish this case, in which the death penalty was imposed, from the many cases in which it was not."

The right of access to criminal trials by the press was affirmed by the court, while in Congress, a bill protecting the press and other third parties from surprise searches by police looking for evidence of crimes committed by others cleared the House Judiciary Committee.

Women's Rights. A three-judge District Court panel declared that the military draft registration law violated the Fifth Amendment because it discriminated against men by excluding women. The next day, however, Supreme Court Justice William Brennan overruled the lower tribunal and registration began as scheduled.

By a 5–4 vote, the Supreme Court decreed that the federal government did not have to pay for abortions sought by women on welfare (*Harris v. McRae, Williams v. Zbaraz*).

The Equal Rights Amendment (ERA) teetered on the brink of defeat. Not a single state legislature had voted for ratification since January 1977, and it appeared doubtful that the amendment would win the final three states necessary for ratification by the June 1982 deadline.

The Right to Sue Governments. In several cases, the Supreme Court chipped away at the immunity of government officials from suits by private citizens. A welfare recipient could challenge state computation of benefits; a federal prisoner could sue prison officials for inadequate medical treatment; a court-appointed defense lawyer could be sued by his indigent client for malpractice; a public official sued for civil rights violations had the burden of proving good faith; and state judges could be sued for actions enforcing a disciplinary code for lawyers.

Freedom of Religion. Both federal and state governments faced objections from mainline religious groups when they sought to investigate possibly fraudulent activities of religious cults. Efforts by the Internal Revenue Service to remove tax-exempt status from religious schools that racially discriminate in admissions were thwarted.

See also ETHNIC GROUPS; LAW—U.S. SUPREME COURT; REFUGEES; WOMEN.

MARTIN GRUBERG
University of Wisconsin-Oshkosh

CLEVELAND

As a result of its 1978 default on bank loans, Cleveland's City Hall remained $10 million in debt to eight banks as 1981 approached. But it was developing a program through which the banks would roll over the defaulted notes and refinance another $25 million in short-term obligations. The negotiations were proceeding under the administration of Mayor George V. Voinovich, who defeated Mayor Dennis J. Kucinich in November 1979.

Early in 1980 Voinovich accepted a bid from 80 company executives who studied the city's operations and finances and found that previous administrations had wasted millions of tax dollars annually. The study uncovered overstaffing and excessive absenteeism, uncollected traffic violation fees and utility bills, and losses on city-owned parking lots and a lakefront airport. The executives recommended 650 changes which they said could save $37 million annually. Voinovich promised to put many of the changes into effect immediately. In addition, greater tax revenues were cited as a must, and a key part of Mayor Voinovich's recovery program became a proposed 0.5% increase in the municipal income tax, to 2%. This plan was rejected by the voters in November.

Public Schools. Following a two-week delay, Cleveland's 120 schools opened relatively quietly on September 29. The 1979 busing program was expanded. Two months earlier U.S. District Judge Frank J. Battisti had stripped the school system's top officials of desegregation authority, found them and Board of Education members in civil contempt of court, and assailed their failure to carry out desegregation moves faster. The action, reportedly unprecedented in such cases, was based, the judge said, on noncompliance in routine tasks but especially was due to failure in developing court-ordered educational improvements despite four years of warnings.

In early August, Battisti appointed Dr. Donald A. Waldrop, former Cincinnati school superintendent, desegregation administrator. The Justice Department had described the desegregation offices as suffering from "pervasive maladministration." Waldrop promptly transferred 75 desegregation-staff members.

An order by Judge Battisti in late September found the Ohio Department of Education equally responsible, with Cleveland, for illegal segregation of minority pupils.

The 1979–80 school year was also beset by a teachers' strike from Oct. 18, 1979, to after the Christmas holidays. The teachers settled for a 10% wage raise, and classes continued into July.

Census. The possibility that Cleveland no longer is Ohio's largest city was raised with an August release of preliminary census figures. The incomplete results gave the lake city 532,660, to 545,934 for Columbus.

JOHN F. HUTH, JR., *"The Plain Dealer"*

COINS AND COIN COLLECTING

During January and February 1980 the price of silver crossed the $50-per-ounce mark and the price of gold rose to close to $1,000 per ounce. This speculation had an effect on the rare coin market. Some people who cashed in silver coins, gold jewelry, silverware, and the like for considerable profit spent the proceeds on rare issues.

The activity in metals caused some problems. In January the U.S. Bureau of the Mint discontinued the sale of 40% silver bicentennial proof sets as rising silver prices forced the bullion value of the set above the $12 asking price.

In February the General Services Administration opened a new ordering period for the remainder of its horde of Carson City silver dollars, mainly minted in the 1880s and held by the U.S. Treasury Department since. More than 500,000 collectors and others wrote to the order processing office in San Francisco, completely swamping the facilities.

In March the second part of the Garrett Collection sale, sold at public auction for The Johns Hopkins University by Bowers & Ruddy Galleries of Los Angeles, saw many world record prices established, including $400,000 for an 1804 silver dollar, the highest price paid for a silver coin. In November 1979, a 1787 Brasher gold doubloon from the same sale had fetched $725,000, a world record price for any coin. The Garrett sale results fueled an increased interest in coins. As a result many older issues doubled and tripled in price. By autumn 1980 the market had become calmer.

In Chicago in May the Rare Coin Company of America sold the unique 1870-S half-dime for $425,000. The private sale set a world record.

The Susan B. Anthony dollar, released in 1979, continued to attract negative comments. Mint Director Stella B. Hackel mentioned that design and format changes for the coin were being considered.

In July the government offered gold medals of one ounce and one-half ounce weight to the public at current bullion prices, to be adjusted daily, plus a nominal minting and distribution charge. It was expected that public interest would be strong. Earlier there had been intense interest in the Krugerrands of South Africa, the Maple Leaf gold coins of Canada, and other issues. The U.S. medals, which do not have the status of coins, bore the portraits of the contralto Marian Anderson and the painter Grant Wood. The public was largely apathetic, however.

In October South Africa introduced fractional parts of the Krugerrand, including one weighing just one-tenth of an ounce, to attract additional buyer interest.

The American Numismatic Association held its annual convention in Cincinnati, OH, in August. More than 10,000 persons attended.

Q. DAVID BOWERS
Bowers & Ruddy Galleries, Inc.

COLOMBIA

The year 1980 saw increasing use of violence by both government and antigovernment forces in the impasse between the entrenched elite and its opponents. The most visible manifestation of the deteriorating situation was the taking of hostages at the Embassy of the Dominican Republic on February 27 and the subsequent two-month siege by Colombian security forces. Among the hostages, most of whom were foreign diplomats, was U.S. Ambassador Diego Asencio. The Colombian economy had a mixed year, with most of its gains coming from high world prices for coffee, the country's major official export, and from the illegal traffic in marijuana sent to the United States. Perhaps because of the internal security problems and the government's hardline approach to dissenters, mostly from the left, Colombian foreign policy during 1980 veered sharply away from a nonaligned position and became more oriented toward the developed capitalist nations.

Politics. Both internal dissent and general apathy increased during 1980. The great mass of the Colombian electorate seemed unwilling to take a position either in support of the government's increased anti-insurgency measures or in support of the organized opposition groups operating clandestinely in the countryside. In by-elections March 9 to fill 8,617 municipal council seats and 406 departmental (state) legislative seats, less than 25% of Colombia's 13.8 million voters went to the polls. The massive abstention occurred in spite of efforts by President Julio César Turbay Ayala to make the elections a national referendum on his government's handling of the siege at the Dominican Republic Embassy and of the larger question of opposition to the government. Turbay's Liberal Party gained a majority of both council and legislative seats. The Liberals took 1.8 million votes; 1.1 million went to the Conservative Party. The left opposition, grouped loosely in the Democratic Front (Frente Democrático), also suffered defeat. Having called for an outpouring of support for its criticism of the government, the Frente received less than 200,000 votes. A big winner was Regina Betancourt de Liski, a self-proclaimed witch, who was elected to two municipal council seats (Bogotá and Medellin) and two state assemblies. Betancourt campaigned on a platform of health, money, and love, with a broom as her campaign symbol.

During 1980, the government took a tougher stand against Colombia's guerrilla movements—the Armed Colombian Revolutionary Front (FARC), the 19th of April Movement (M-19), and the Worker's Self-Defense Movement (MAO). In May, the second in command of FARC, Jorge Caballero Cartagena, was killed in an ambush, and one of the founders of MAO was captured by secret police. Both the FARC and M-19 retaliated with ambushes of army patrols and assassinations of politicians. On June 16, President Turbay announced a limited amnesty for the guerrillas. The move apparently was calculated to drive a wedge between the guerrillas and their nonviolent supporters. A report by Amnesty International in April documented more than 600 cases of torture, political murder, and persecution of opposition leaders. The report added fuel to the controversy over the government's handling of the insurgency situation.

Economy. The gross national product (GNP) climbed from $27,500,000,000 in 1979 to $32,200,000,000 in 1980, a 5% increase at constant prices. Per capita GNP rose from $1,025 to $1,161 at current prices. However, the Consumer Price Index rose from 129.8 in December 1979 to 149.6 in June, an annual rate of more than 30%. By June, the floating peso had dropped from 44 per U.S. dollar to 47.20. Foreign exchange reserves reached a record high of $4,600,000,000 during the year, spurred by record earnings from coffee exports and marijuana sales to the United States estimated at $3,000,000,000. Colombia's three-year development plan was made public on May 30. It called for an investment of $22,000,000,000, mainly in hydroelectric power, transportation, water supply, and communications.

Embassy Siege. A diplomatic party at the Dominican Republic Embassy on the night of February 27 was interrupted by members of the Marcos Zambrano commando group of the M-19. The 16 guerrillas stormed the embassy and took 45 hostages, including the U.S. ambassador and the papal nuncio. The Zambrano group took its name from a companion who had been tortured and killed by the military two weeks earlier. The M-19 and the government negotiated over terms of release of the hostages, until Cuban President Fidel Castro offered the guerrillas asylum on March 18. After another month of demands and counterdemands, the guerrillas and the hostages were flown to Cuba. The remaining 12 captives—others had been freed at various stages of the negotiating—were released on April 27 in Havana. Both the M-19 and the

---
COLOMBIA • Information Highlights

Official Name: Republic of Colombia.
Location: Northwest South America.
Area: 439,737 sq mi (1 138 914 km²).
Population (1980 est.): 26,700,000.
Chief Cities (1979 est.): Bogotá, the capital, 4,055,909; Medellín, 1,506,661; Cali, 1,316,137.
Government: *Head of state and government,* Julio César Turbay Ayala, president (took office Aug. 1978). *Legislature*—Congress: Senate and Chamber of Representatives.
Monetary Unit: Peso (49.90 pesos equal U.S.$1, Dec. 1980).
Manufactures (major products): Textiles, beverages, processed food, clothing and footwear, chemicals, metal products, cement.
Agriculture (major products): Coffee, bananas, rice, cotton, sugarcane, tobacco, corn, plantains, flowers
GNP (1980 est., U.S.$): $32,200,000,000.
Foreign Trade (1979, U.S.$): *Imports,* $4,437,000,000; *exports,* $3,381,000,000.

government claimed victory in the siege, which was marked by restraint on both sides. The two military officers accused of torturing and killing Zambrano were acquitted by a military court-martial in August.

Foreign Affairs. Colombia's long opposition to a UN Security Council seat for Cuba paid off in January, when neither nation was able to gain the two-thirds General Assembly vote necessary for election. As a compromise, Mexico was elected to the contested seat. In a related move the next month, the Colombian ambassador to Cuba was recalled, in what was described by the foreign office as a "routine transfer." Also in February, Colombia announced a temporary suspension of beef sales to the Soviet Union, apparently acceding to U.S. pressure.

Colombian relations with neighboring Venezuela remained cool during the year, with border disputes and Venezuela's continuing refusal to buy Colombian beef the major irritants. Colombia appeared to move closer to the United States on a number of issues. Its handling of the hostage situation at the Dominican Embassy drew praise from U.S. officials, and its efforts to curtail marijuana production and exports to the United States were commended by U.S. Ambassador Asencio.

ERNEST A. DUFF
Department of Political Science
Randolph-Macon Women's College

COLORADO

National and international trends in natural resources continued as the chief driving forces for change in Colorado in 1980. State residents were jolted when Clifton Garvin, chairman of Exxon, suggested that there might be an 8 million-barrel-a-day-oil shale industry by 2010. Such production would make Colorado a rival to Saudi Arabia in energy, add 1.5 million residents in sparsely populated Western Colorado, and impose severe strains on the state's environment and water supplies.

Of more immediate concern was Congressional approval of President Carter's synthetic fuels plan, setting a production goal of 500,000 barrels of "synfuels" a day by 1987. Colorado's Democratic Gov. Richard Lamm used the advancing state of oil shale development to underscore his demands that the state take a more active role in controlling its growth. But the state legislature, controlled by Republicans, often challenged Lamm's policies. GOP critics particularly flailed his "human settlements policies," which they saw as a back-door attempt to establish statewide land-use controls in Colorado. Lamm finally withdrew the policies.

The legislature, however, responded to the onrush of development by voting an exception to Colorado's 7% ceiling on overall annual state budget increases. The exception would permit an additional $100 million to be spent developing Colorado water resources and maintaining overworked highways.

Elections. Natural resources also affected the state elections. Ronald Reagan swamped Jimmy Carter by 55% to 31.6%, with John Anderson winning 11%, and minor candidates splitting the remaining 2.4%. Carter had infuriated Coloradans by attempting to kill several Western water projects.

But incumbent Democratic U.S. Sen. Gary Hart narrowly won a second term over GOP challenger Mary Estill Buchanan, Colorado's secretary of state. Democrats kept their 3-2 edge in the U.S. House of Representatives by re-electing incumbents Patricia Schroeder, Timothy Wirth, and Raymond Kogovsek. Republican incumbent Kenneth Kramer was joined by Republican newcomer Hank Brown, who replaced retiring GOP Rep. James Johnson.

The Republicans kept firm control of the legislature, adding one House seat for a 39-26 edge and keeping a 22-13 Senate majority. The GOP failed in an ambitious effort to "veto-proof" the legislature against Lamm by winning two-thirds majorities in each chamber. Lamm's term expires in 1982.

Denver and Miscellaneous. Downtown Denver's skyscraper boom continued and was augmented by a $57 million project to create a downtown pedestrian and mass transit mall underwritten by the Regional Transportation District. But Denver's hopes of someday approaching New York cultural standards came to one rueful parallel when a bitter strike by members of the Denver Symphony Orchestra delayed the season's opening until December 4.

After 85 years of independent ownership, *The Denver Post,* with the state's largest combined newspaper circulation, was sold to the Times Mirror Co. in a complicated deal worth about $84 million.

The University of Colorado football team turned in its worst-ever season, 1-10, and students protested when they were forced to pay higher fees to cover athletic department deficits.

BOB EWEGEN
"The Denver Post"

——— **COLORADO • Information Highlights** ———

Area: 104,247 sq mi (270 000 km²).
Population (Jan. 1980 est.): 2,816,000.
Chief Cities (1976 est.): Denver, the capital, 479,513; Colorado Springs, 180,821; Pueblo, 103,918.
Government (1980): *Chief Officers*—governor, Richard D. Lamm (D); lt. gov., Nancy Dick (D). *General Assembly*—Senate, 35 members; House of Representatives, 65 members.
Education (1979–80): *Enrollment*—public elementary schools, 305,776 pupils; public secondary, 244,751; colleges and universities, 156,100 students. *Public school expenditures,* $1,383,941,000 ($2,267 per pupil).
State Finance (fiscal year 1979): *Revenues,* $3,050,000,-000; *expenditures,* $2,518,000,000.
Personal Income (1979): $25,285,000,000; per capita, $9,122.
Labor Force (June 1980): *Nonagricultural wage and salary earners,* 1,259,700; *unemployed,* 88,700 (6.0% of total force).

COMMUNICATION TECHNOLOGY

The major advances in communication technology during 1980 took place in lightwave and satellite communication systems; in the arrangement of telephone, data, and video terminals for a wide spectrum of new information services available for home or business use; in a proliferation of systems in which the digital computer is closely integrated with communication apparatus; and in the widening use of more versatile and complex microelectronics to provide increasingly sophisticated circuitry at lower cost and with enhanced reliability.

Lightwave Systems.   Lightwave systems have wide application in the communications field because of their high capacity, long spacing between repeaters (amplifiers), use of small-diameter cable made up of optical fibers, and freedom from electrical interference.

In 1980, the Bell system announced plans to construct the world's longest lightwave telecommunication system, extending 611 mi (983 km) and linking the Washington, New York, and Boston metropolitan areas. Up to 80,000 simultaneous telephone calls will be carried on pulses of light over hair-thin strands of highly purified glass fibers made into a cable about 0.5 inch (1.27 cm) in diameter. Voice, data, and video signals will be carried in digital format. The first section was scheduled for completion in 1983.

At Lake Placid, NY, during the Winter Olympics, a lightwave system, linking the telephone switching office, ski areas, and the broadcast center, helped carry voice communications and television coverage of the Games. A lightwave telecommunication system 2.5 mi (4 km) long, linking computers of the New York Telephone Company, was put into service for transmission of high-speed digital data at 44 million bits per second. Bell Canada installed its first commercial lightwave system, the FA-1, connecting a satellite earth station and a terrestrial microwave tower, both near Ottawa, Ontario.

The world's first long-wavelength (1.3 microns) optical fiber system was put into operation in Sacramento, CA, as a modification of an older, shorter-wavelength (.83 micron) experimental installation 2.7 mi (4.3 km) long, linking two central offices of the Pacific Telephone Company. The longer-wavelength system uses light-emitting diodes (LEDs) as light sources and indium-gallium-arsenide PIN diodes as receivers. The new system requires fewer amplifiers, has greater reliability, and is simpler than its laser-powered predecessor.

High-Capacity Mobile Radio Systems.   Extensive in-use testing of the Bell System's new Advanced Mobile Phone Service was continued in the Chicago area. The system utilizes new technology that multiplies by several hundred times the number of mobile telephones that can be served in a given area. The area is divided into cells, each with its own transmitters and receivers.

As a car containing the mobile phone moves from cell to cell through the area, electronic switching changes transmitter frequencies, automatically tunes the receiver, and connects mobile calls to the rest of the telephone network.

New Services.   Technological advances toward end-to-end, digital, stored-program-controlled communications networks were made during the year, making many new services possible. One example is a Voice Storage System installed by Bell of Pennsylvania in the Philadelphia area. Using electronic switching in conjunction with special data processors and multiple high-capacity memory disks for information storage, call-answering and advance-calling services are available to the telephone user. The first of these stores phone messages at the central office when a customer is not home and plays them back at the customer's request. The second records a customer's message and automatically transmits it via the telephone network to a designated party at a specified time.

A wide range of new technology has become available for bringing textual and graphic information into the home or business office by telephone lines, video cable, or broadcast television receivers or on special viewing screens. The capacity of such systems is limited only by the storage capability of the central computer. In the United States, Britain, France, Canada, and Japan, systems with such names as Teletext, Viewdata, Prestel, and Antiope are being tested for commercial market value and user interest.

Experiments with electronic mail multiplied throughout the year. The U.S. Postal Service initiated a pilot system for international electronic mail—Intelpost—by which a standard business letter can be scanned and transmitted in six seconds. International Telephone and Telegraph (ITT) introduced Faxpax, a store-and-forward electronic mail service. Telemail was announced by GTE Telenet, a subsidiary of General Telephone and Electronics Corp. The 3M Corporation and Electronic Communications Systems, Inc. installed their first Voice Message System (VMS), which uses digital techniques for voice conversion to electronic mail.

Microelectronics.   The merging of communications and computer technologies continued through the year. The basis for the rapid evolution of new systems and new capabilities is the transistor principle, embodied in its modern form—microelectronics. One example is the MAC-4 "computer on a chip," which contains 30,000 solid-state circuit elements in logic array, input-output, and other configurations on a 1-cm square of silicon. Another tiny chip, a Digital Signal Processor, is capable of making one million calculations per second. Echo cancelers, developed by Bell Laboratories and RCA, have solved the troublesome problem of echoes on long telephone circuits.

M.D. FAGEN
Formerly, Bell Telephone Laboratories

Connecticut's U.S. Senate race pitted Rep. Christopher J. Dodd (left) against James L. Buckley. The 36-year-old three-term Congressman defeated the former senator from New York.

CONNECTICUT

Gov. Ella T. Grasso's illness, state fiscal problems, a municipal corruption scandal, the finding of a final berth for a historic submarine, and election-year politics made headlines in Connecticut during 1980.

Mrs. Grasso underwent surgery on April 3 for ovarian cancer. While she was hospitalized in November for phlebitis, cancer was found in her liver, and chemotherapy was begun. On December 4, Governor Grasso announced her resignation, effective Dec. 31, 1980, when Lt. Gov. William A. O'Neill would assume the office.

The Legislature. The General Assembly set a precedent in balancing the 1980–81 state budget of $2,700,000,000 by making Connecticut the first state to tax the gross receipts of major oil companies that do business in the state. The annual 2% tax was expected to raise $60 million. Affected oil companies said that they would pass the cost on to their consumers. The legislature also raised the sales and use tax to 7.5% from 7%, to help plug a $160-million revenue gap in the budget. Also passed by the legislature was a law which reinstated the death penalty for such offenses as rape-murder and multiple murder during the commission of a single crime.

Elections. Republican presidential candidate Ronald Reagan easily won Connecticut's eight presidential electoral votes in the November 4 election. Republicans also won a second of the state's six congressional seats when former state senator Lawrence J. DeNardis took the Third District congressional seat held for 22 years by Democrat Robert N. Giaimo, who did not run.

U.S. Rep. Christopher J. Dodd, a Democrat and son of the late U.S. Sen. Thomas J. Dodd, won the Senate seat vacated by Democrat Abraham A. Ribicoff. Dodd defeated James L. Buckley, who represented New York in the Senate from 1971–77 as a Conservative-Republican. If Buckley had won he would have been the first senator to represent two states at different times.

Municipal Scandal. On November 10, New Britain Detective Sgt. George F. Sahadi was sentenced to a term of 5½ to 11 years in prison and fined $15,000, after conviction on bribery and conspiracy charges stemming from the rigging of civil service promotion test results in New Britain. Sahadi's sentence was the severest given so far in the scandal that has seen 24 persons arrested, including a former fire chief who went to jail for seven months in 1980. Sahadi said he would appeal his conviction.

The Nautilus. In November President Jimmy Carter signed a bill appropriating $1.93 million for the preparation of a permanent berth on the Thames River in Groton for the decommissioned *USS Nautilus,* the world's first nuclear-powered submarine. The *Nautilus* will be berthed a short distance from the Electric Boat shipyard from which it was launched in January 1954.

Census. A preliminary analysis of the 1980 census figures showed a total state population of 3,096,951, 2% higher than the 1970 figure but

--- **CONNECTICUT · Information Highlights** ---

Area: 5,009 sq mi (12 973 km²).
Population (1980 census, preliminary count): 3,096,951.
Chief Cities (1976 est.): Hartford, the capital, 134,957; Bridgeport, 139,552; New Haven, 124,583.
Government (1980): *Chief Officers*—governor, Ella T. Grasso (D); lt. gov., William A. O'Neill (D). *General Assembly*—Senate, 36 members; House of Representatives, 151 members.
Education (1979–80): *Enrollment*—public elementary schools, 377,762 pupils; public secondary, 188,872; colleges and universities, 156,067 students. *Public school expenditures,* $1,346,300,000 ($2,187 per pupil).
State Finances (fiscal year 1979): *Revenues,* $3,173,-000,000; *expenditures,* $2,963,000,000.
Personal Income (1979): $31,553,000,000; per capita, $10,129.
Labor Force (May 1980): *Nonagricultural wage and salary earners,* 1,415,000; *unemployed,* 80,800 (5.0% of total force).

lower than the state Department of Health Services' 1979 population estimate of 3,168,540.

Other News. Imperial Wizard Bill Wilkinson of the Louisiana-based Invisible Empire of the Ku Klux Klan went to Connecticut in May and September to recruit members and burn crosses.

The Hartford Civic Center Coliseum reopened February 6, after the installation of a new roof. The original roof collapsed Jan. 18, 1978, under the weight of ice and water. The sports center, home of the National Hockey League's Hartford Whalers, was empty when the roof caved in.

Annhurst College, a 39-year-old coeducational Catholic liberal arts institution in Woodstock, closed its doors in May because of declining enrollment and debt.

Unemployment in mid-September was reported at 6.4% compared with the national rate of 7.5%.

A gift from the late Katharine Ordway of Weston to the Yale University Art Gallery of nearly 200 works of modern art valued at more than $4 million was announced in November. Another $2 million was provided for maintenance and housing of the art.

ROBERT F. MURPHY, *"The Hartford Courant"*

CONSUMER AFFAIRS

The U.S. consumer did not fare well in 1980. Faced with prices that rose with dismaying regularity, and a lack of protective legislation in Congress, consumers found some support in the creation by President Carter of a Consumer Affairs Council.

The Presidential Campaign. Consumerism was not a significant part of the 1980 presidential campaign. The differences among the candidates centered primarily on government regulation of business. President Carter, having failed to persuade Congress to fulfill his 1976 campaign pledge to create an agency for consumer advocacy, continued to support increased consumer protection, appointing a number of consumer activists to key government positions. Ronald Reagan vehemently attacked what he believed to be over-regulation of business by government, while John Anderson was more supportive of the consumer position. Both the Consumer Federation of America and consumer advocate Ralph Nader supported President Carter as the best Candidate for consumers, although Nader said that his choice was "on the basis of picking the least of the worst."

Government Consumer Action. Scant consumer legislative activity took place during the year. A potentially significant curb on government regulation of business was established with the passage of the Federal Trade Commission Improvement Act of 1980, which allows a two-house veto of trade regulation rules promulgated by the Federal Trade Commission (FTC). (*See also* special report, page 554.)

Under an executive order issued by President Carter, a Consumer Affairs Council was established in 1980. The order stipulated that consumer representatives be appointed in 35 federal agencies, giving each agency a high-level consumer representative reporting directly to the head of the agency. All appointees are members of the council, which has been chaired by Esther Peterson, Special Assistant to the President for Consumer Affairs.

National Consumer Education Week. President Carter issued a proclamation designating Oct. 5–11, 1980, as National Consumer Education Week. Many activities emphasizing the importance of consumer education took place in schools, colleges, and communities nationwide. In issuing the proclamation the president stressed the need for well-informed consumers in a free economy and the vital role that government, schools, labor unions, consumer organizations, and business can play in meeting this challenge.

Inflation. Consumers continued to be shocked by constantly rising prices for goods and services as the marketplace experienced another year of double-digit inflation. Little moderation in the rate of inflation was predicted for 1981.

Protectionism. The economic plight of the steel and automobile industries, particularly with regard to competition from imports, poses a potential problem for consumers. During 1980 forces in the automobile industry pressed for import curbs on Japanese cars. If the movement toward government protection continues, consumers may be affected by higher automobile prices and a possible shortage of foreign cars.

Bankruptcies. With double-digit inflation, recession, and increasing unemployment, the number of nonbusiness bankruptcies soared to 355,000 in fiscal 1980. This figure topped the 224,354 nonbusiness bankruptcies filed during the 1974–75 recession. Contributing to the upsurge was the Bankruptcy Reform Act of 1978, the first major revision of the federal bankruptcy laws since 1938, which provides greater protection for those in financial trouble and makes it easier to file a bankruptcy petition.

Canada. A Quebec law banning commercials aimed at children under age 13 went into effect in 1980. Officials began work on guidelines to specify which commercials are directed primarily at children. (A similar regulation, proposed by the FTC, was rejected by the U.S. Congress in 1980.)

About 100 Canadian grocery stores that went metric in a pilot program during the summer of 1979 returned to the Imperial system in 1980 after consumer opposition prompted the government to halt metrication plans until at least 1981. About 200 stores in the pilot program have scorned reconversion, however, and have elected to remain a metric "island."

STEWART M. LEE
Geneva College

The Funeral Industry

Along with the utilitarian automobile, basic foods, plain weddings, and the simpler life generally, the dignified but simpler funeral has become a trend in American culture. A growing number of people are now looking for less elaborate and less expensive alternatives to the traditional funeral, which, according to the Federated Funeral Directors of America, cost on the average $2,475 in 1979. In so doing, some say, Americans are merely returning to the way things used to be. Until the end of the 19th century, the elaborate funeral was rare in the United States, and even today religious leaders maintain a preference for simplicity. "The Protestant Christian religion has a certain tendency to simplify and even to minimize the funeral as a ritual," says Donald W. Shriver, Jr., president of Union Theological Seminary. Jewish and Roman Catholic leaders also insist that the funeral should be a religious rite rather than an earthly production.

Despite the teachings of religious leaders, the funeral has been an elaborate and expensive affair, with undertakers embalming and beautifying the corpse, displaying it in a luxurious casket, and transporting it in great ceremony to a cemetery for burial. The undertaker, whose job once was to make a coffin and bury the dead, has become the funeral director, the orchestrator of the entire process, as well as the self-appointed "grief counselor." Critics claim this type of funeral was foisted on the public by undertakers.

Interest in the funeral industry has been rising since Jessica Mitford's 1963 exposé, *The American Way of Death,* which pointed to the needless expense to and exploitation of the deceased's emotionally vulnerable family. Statistics document the recent trend toward the less expensive funeral. The Cremation Association of North America reports that in 1975 there were 123,918 cremations, 6.55% of all deaths in the United States. By 1979, the total had risen to 179,393 or 9.42%. "It's the fastest growing segment of the death business," says Thomas B. Weber, Ph.D., president of the Telophase Society of America. Telophase, a direct disposition company, is a commercial competitor to the traditional undertaker. Begun in San Diego in 1970, it performed nearly 2,000 cremations in California alone in 1980. The average fee was $250. Telophase now has over 40,000 members in California, Washington, and Oregon. Weber observes that "the greater the education and economic standing the more likely the choice for cremation." He traces the increased interest in simple funerals to at least the early 1970s, when his society was founded. "We like to think that we were in the vanguard of this trend," he says. He acknowledges that a more recent rise in interest followed a Federal Trade Commission (FTC) investigation into the funeral industry. In addition, an unusual ally, inflation, has encouraged the simple funeral movement. A Chicago undertaker has noted that it used to be that people went to funeral homes and "just ordered what they wanted and thought about the cost later." Now a lot of people "shop around and compare costs," and ask such pertinent questions as "Do we need a real fancy casket?"

Other factors contributing to the trend include loosened religious commitments, the fact that many families are scattered across the country, and more open discussion of the subject of death. According to psychologist Mary Ann Watson, there is a "growing willingness among people generally to discuss issues of death, to confront family members who are dying, and not seeing death as a taboo subject."

Acting on complaints, the FTC determined that about $6,400,000,000 a year is spent in burying the dead, involving 50,000 licensed funeral directors and embalmers and more than 20,000 funeral homes. In 1975, the FTC proposed a rule that would, among other things, have prohibited undertakers from embalming the corpse without family permission. The commission also sought to require funeral homes to quote prices. Its proposals ran into opposition, however, most prominently from the National Funeral Directors Association, which, the FTC noted, spent more than $500,000 in opposing its measures. In 1979, the commission tentatively approved a modified version of the recommendations, but the House of Representatives then passed an amendment prohibiting the FTC from regulating the industry. In 1980 both the House and Senate passed an alternative that in effect restricts rather than prohibits FTC regulation. Stymied, the FTC was considering in late 1980 how to proceed. (*See also* page 554.)

Meanwhile, people are pressing ahead in their search for better alternatives to the funeral. Some are forming memorial societies. The Continental Association of Funeral and Memorial Societies, a Washington (DC)-based, nonprofit organization, formed in 1973 and representing 175 societies, has seen membership grow by about 10 societies each year. The societies do not sell merchandise or services but help members arrange inexpensive funerals with cooperating undertakers or act as information centers on funeral arrangements. Cremations cost from $250 to $500, depending upon the area of the country. Simple burials without embalming, cosmetology, and viewing, and in a basic casket that might even be made of pressed cardboard, cost somewhat more.

WAKA TSUNODA

CRIME

Escalating crime rates and a report on nationwide fear of crime dominated U.S. criminal news in 1980.

Election Campaign. Silence about crime on the part of the three major presidential candidates in 1980 was an unexpected development. Since 1964, presidential candidates have vied with each other to impress the electorate with proposals for dealing effectively with crime. The sudden shift in 1980 may have been due to a continuing rise in U.S. crime rates, despite the proclamations and promises of earlier presidents. Candidates no longer appeared willing to hobble themselves with campaign promises to control crime in the face of overwhelming evidence that they would not be able to do so.

Public Opinion. The neglect of the issue of crime by the presidential candidates was counterpointed by evidence that the threat of crime badly frightens a large number of American citizens. The Figgie Report on Fear of Crime, a survey based on 1,047 interviews conducted throughout the nation, was released in September. The report, named for its sponsor, concluded that "fear of criminals is slowly paralyzing American society." According to the results of the survey, four out of every ten Americans feel unsafe in their everyday environments, and one in four is afraid to venture into familiar neighborhood places. Six of ten respondents indicated that they dress plainly in order to avoid attracting the attention of criminals. More than half reported that they possess guns for self-protection.

The survey also queried Americans concerning appropriate methods for dealing with criminals. Eight of ten respondents said that they do not think that prison rehabilitates criminals and

60% favored the death penalty for murderers. Almost half supported sterilization of habitual criminals. Support for the police was strong. Eighty-four percent of the persons surveyed had "high confidence" in the police, and slightly more than half would be willing to pay higher taxes to hire more law enforcement officers.

Crime Statistics. Statistics on U.S. criminal activity, issued annually by the FBI, showed sizable rises for 1979 in the number of major offenses known to the police. The 21,456 murders committed during the year constituted an increase of 7.8% from the previous 12 months. Southern states reported the highest regional murder rates. There were more murders in December than in any other month, and males constituted three out of every four murder victims. The use of firearms for murder decreased slightly, from 66% in 1975 to 63% in 1979. Romantic triangles and arguments over money or property continued to be the predominant motives for murder.

The number of robberies increased by 12% from the previous year. Aggravated assaults were up 10.1%, while burglaries rose 6.3%, larceny-theft, 9.9%, and motor-vehicle theft, 10.6%. Among major crimes, rape showed the largest increase, jumping 13.2% to a total of 75,989 cases in 1979. (The increase in the number of rapes that became known to the police may reflect a growing tendency of women to report such offenses, rather than an actual increase in rapes. Law reforms mitigating the harassment that formerly accompanied the filing of rape reports may encourage more victims to contact police.) The FBI reported that the rate of arrests for forcible rape had improved, up 9% from the previous year.

Crime again increased during the first six months of 1980, according to FBI statistics re-

Authorities in Atlanta, GA, conducted an intensive investigation and imposed a curfew after it became known that more than 12 black children were missing or killed in the city during a 16-month period.

Howard ("Buddy") Jacobson, shown here with his attorney, Otto Fusco (right), was the subject of a worldwide search after he walked out of a New York jail May 31. The former horse trainer, who was convicted of second degree murder in New York in 1979, was arrested in California six weeks later.

UPI

leased in October 1980. Serious crime rose 10% over this period; robbery, with an increase of 13%, had the greatest increase of the violent crimes.

Arson. By dictate of the U.S. Congress, the FBI added the offense of arson to its list of major crimes for which detailed nationwide statistics are collected. Arson is defined in the FBI statistical enumeration as "any willful burning or attempt to burn, with or without intent to defraud, a dwelling house, public building, motor vehicle or aircraft, personal property of another, etc." Only fires determined through investigation to have been willfully or maliciously set are classified as arson, with fires of suspicious or unknown origin excluded from the tabulations. During the year, reports on arson were received from police agencies representing 61% of the country's population; the agencies listed a total of 77,147 arson cases.

A breakdown of the numbers shows that fixed structures, primarily single occupancy dwellings, accounted for 57% of the reported arson cases. Mobile structures, such as motor vehicles, trailers, airplanes, and boats, were involved in 24% of the episodes, while property, such as crops, timber, fences, and signs, accounted for the remaining 19% of the cases. The monetary value of property damaged by the reported arsons exceeded $500 million—the average loss per incident was $7,465. When industrial or manufacturing structures were the target of arson, the loss averaged $49,769 per offense.

The FBI reported that 19,800 persons were arrested during the year for arson crimes. Almost half of these persons were under the age of 18 and 73% were younger than 25. Males comprised 89% of the arson offenders apprehended.

Criminologists generally distinguish two major forms of arson. First, there are those offenses committed by persons who are believed to be emotionally disturbed, and who see the deliberate burning of another person's house or property as a means of obtaining revenge for real or imagined wrongs against them. These are the offenders who may be caught when they stand by in the crowd to watch the conflagration that they have produced. Fires also are deliberately set by persons who seek to defraud insurance companies. Some individuals make a business of setting such fires for those who hire them for this purpose. At other times, hard-pressed businessmen, perhaps caught with an inventory of goods that they cannot sell, will resort to burning their own establishment in order to recoup their costs.

Crime in the Schools. Research probes during the year provided details about crimes that take place in U.S. schools. Writing in *The Public Interest,* a scholarly journal, Jackson Toby of Rutgers University noted that such crime is more prominent in junior high schools than in senior high schools. The question: "In the previous month did anyone physically attack and hurt you?" found 8% of junior high school students and 4% of senior high school students in urban areas answering in the affirmative. In suburban areas, the figures for assaults were somewhat lower (7.2% for junior high school pupils, and 3% for students in high schools), with students in rural schools reporting similar rates. Eight percent of the pupils in big-city junior high schools told interviewers that they had remained at home some time during the previous month because they thought that they might be hurt or otherwise harmed at school.

CRIME—SPECIAL REPORT:

Handguns

It is conservatively estimated that about 50 million handguns are owned by private citizens in the United States today. Such ownership is believed to have increased dramatically during the 1970s. In that time period, the percentage of handguns owned relative to all weapons in the possession of private citizens jumped from 32% to 42%. The increase was said to result from a growing citizen fear of violent crime, as well as from the easy availability, low cost, and small size of handguns. Though fear of crime may underlie the acquisition of handguns by private persons, most of those who are killed by use of the guns are not depredators or strangers. Instead, the victims are more likely to be family members or friends who are shot during quarrels or other emotional outbursts.

Handguns were employed in 49% of the 19,-555 homicides reported in the United States in 1978, the latest year for which figures are available. Eight percent of these homicides were attributed to shotguns and 19% to cuttings and stabbings. Handguns also were employed more than any other weapon in armed robberies and aggravated assaults. And approximately 13% of suicide victims used handguns to kill themselves.

There are in the United States more than 20,-000 statutes and ordinances regulating the acquisition, ownership, and transportation of handguns. Federal legislation includes the 1968 Gun Control Act, enforced by the Bureau of Alcohol, Tobacco, and Firearms of the Treasury Department. In 1980 Congress considered expanding the act by barring the importation of replacement parts for handguns known as "Saturday night specials." Another proposed amendment would stipulate that sales of handguns between private parties be conducted through a licensed gun dealer in order to establish a public record of the transfer. About half of all gun sales are currently carried out privately.

Most state laws are less stringent than the proposed federal requirements. California, for example, in a typical state law, provides a one-year penalty for possession of a handgun by a person who has been convicted of a felony or who suffers from drug addiction. Anyone else over 18, except those declared mentally ill, can purchase a handgun by completing a form and waiting two weeks to pick up the gun.

New York and Massachusetts, on the other hand, have enacted tough handgun control laws. New York City police report that there are some 2 million handguns in the city alone and that 882 persons were murdered by handguns in 1979. According to the city's police, fewer than 10% of those arrested for carrying guns received sentences. In part, those statistics led New York State in 1980 to enact the "toughest handgun law in the country." As a result of the legislation, possession of a loaded, unlicensed gun in public places carries a mandatory minimum one-year sentence. Illegal sale or possession of more than 20 guns may result in a 25-year sentence. One to seven years is the penalty for handgun possession, even if the weapon is not loaded, if the person has been convicted of a felony or a Class A misdemeanor during the previous five years.

The Bartley-Fox gun control law went into effect in Massachusetts in 1975. It decrees a mandatory one-year term for carrying a firearm outside a home or place of business without a permit. A study by the National Institute of Justice in 1980 reported that gun-related crimes in Massachusetts have dropped since 1975, but that assaults involving other weapons have increased. In Boston, there was a 55% drop in homicides involving guns, compared with a 23% decrease in those urban areas being used for comparison purposes.

Jamaica has the most stringent gun control laws in the world. Private ownership of any type of weapon has been barred there since 1974. Law enforcement officers have the right to stop and search any person or any vehicle as well as to enter any dwelling if they believe that firearms or ammunition are to be found. Offenders against the Jamaican gun act are not entitled to bail. They appear before a special "gun court," which has the right to imprison them for an indeterminate period in a "gun stockade." The rate of crime involving firearms is said to have dropped in Jamaica during the first three months following enactment of the new law, but to have risen dramatically since then.

In Switzerland, virtually all men are considered permanent members of the armed forces and are required to keep an assault rifle, submachine gun, or handgun as well as a supply of ammunition in their residences. Nonetheless, compared with other Western nations, the rate of crimes of violence and crimes against property in Switzerland is exceptionally low.

Debate in the United States regarding gun control is often deeply bitter. Opponents of controls insist that all citizens have the constitutional right to possess weapons. "Guns don't kill, people do" is the rallying call of the National Rifle Association (N.R.A.). The N.R.A. has an effective political lobby and tends to be treated gingerly by officeholders, even if they oppose its position. Proponents of strong gun control cite the harms they believe result from unchecked gun ownership and maintain that strictly-enforced laws against such ownership would decrease crime and improve the quality of life in the United States.

GILBERT GEIS and COLIN GOFF

The view that "outsiders" come into the schools and commit crimes was found to be largely a myth, as was the idea that older students prey upon younger ones. Depredators were discovered to be about the same age as their victims.

Public school crime, according to Toby, seriously interferes with the learning climate. Moreover, some children who might lend additional stability to the classroom are sent to private schools by their concerned parents. A greater involvement of parents as paid school aides, Toby believes, could appreciably reduce school crime rates. He advocates more extensive use of expulsion procedures for "the small percentage of violent students who have proved that they cannot be controlled by anyone." Expelled students would remain eligible for home instruction and for enrollment in alternative schools. Toby also suggests the inauguration of restitutive sanctions, under which students who commit crimes at school would be allowed to atone for their behavior by performing such tasks as school cleanup.

Computer Crime. The increasing use of computers throughout American society has produced ingenious new forms of criminal behavior, according to reports issued in 1980. Robert Campbell, president of the Advanced Information Management Corporation, claimed that only 1% of all computer crimes are detected, and

As crime against children at school increased, various U.S. communities established "parent patrols."
Bill Anderson, Monkmeyer

that only one in 22,000 such crimes is successfully prosecuted.

Major offenders included a federal worker who used a computer to issue $500,000 in fraudulent welfare checks and then programmed the computer to erase the records of the bogus claims, and a computer consultant who defrauded a west coast bank by surreptitiously authorizing the transfer of $10.2 million from bank funds to his own account. A Wall Street computer analyst programmed a machine to sell nonexistent securities through fictitious accounts and pocketed $832,000 before the fraud was accidentally discovered. The assistant chief of the FBI's white-collar crimes section noted that a major problem in combating computer crime is the reluctance of corporations to admit that they have been taken. By late 1980, 11 states had enacted new laws to deal with computer crime, but Congress failed to enact federal legislation on the subject.

Soviet Crime. The doctrines of Communism maintain that crime is a capitalistic phenomenon that will disappear in a truly socialist society, where people will have no reason to violate the law. But this utopian ideal continues to evade authorities in the Soviet Union. Recent reports indicated that high levels of alcoholism, crowded living conditions, and a growing number of broken homes in the USSR all contribute to what is labeled as "hooliganism." The crimes, generally committed by youths, include public disorderliness, assault and vandalism, and intimidation of passersby by gang members. Cities such as Moscow and Leningrad still are considered to be safer than most American urban areas, but the number of police on patrol in these jurisdictions visibly increased during the year, and citizens were being enrolled as auxiliary law enforcement officers to help guard the nation's inner city districts.

Capital Punishment. Debate arose during the year over the ethics of having doctors inject with legal drugs criminals who have been sentenced to death. Four states—Idaho, New Mexico, Oklahoma, and Texas—recently have enacted laws mandating this method of execution. It is maintained by some that execution by drug injection provides a more dignified death than hanging, gassing, shooting, or electrocution, the usual methods employed in the United States.

Two Harvard medical school professors maintained that for a doctor to take part in such an execution would constitute "a corruption and exploitation of the healing profession's role in society." But other physicians noted that doctors can kill in wartime and in self-defense, and maintained that participation in capital punishment should be left to the conscience of the individual doctor. No executions by drug injection occurred in 1980, but they are likely to take place in the near future.

GILBERT GEIS
University of California, Irvine

CUBA

On Dec. 27, 1979, Cuban President Fidel Castro delivered an unusually frank speech at the annual session of the National Assembly of People's Power, the country's one-party parliament. After describing the country's economic and social problems, and announcing broad changes but "without traumas," the president concluded: "We are sailing in a sea of difficulties . . . and the shore is far away."

At the close of 1980, the Cuban ship of state continued to flounder in an ocean of troubles. None of the problems mentioned by President Castro one year earlier had been solved and new ones appeared on the horizon. Cuba lost friends abroad, its international prestige declined, and Havana viewed with foreboding the prospect of a Reagan administration in Washington.

Not since 1970, when the failure to produce 10 million metric tons (10.92 million T) of sugar caused major economic dislocations and widespread discontent, were so many problems disclosed by the government. The 1980 cane harvest, the mainstay of the economy, was affected by a fungus called "roya" and the total sugar production was estimated at 6.8 million t (7.4 million T), 1.2 million t (1.3 million T) less than in 1979. The 1979–80 tobacco harvest was almost a total loss because of blue mold, a plant disease. Cuba lost $150 million in cigar exports as all cigar factories were closed for six months.

Cubans were working as little as possible, General of the Army Raul Castro, Cuba's number two leader, indicated. Agricultural laborers worked about four hours a day and were, in collusion with their foremen, "falsifying production records," he said, adding that a similar situation existed elsewhere, "generating justified irritation on the part of broad sectors of the population."

In January, the Cuban regime carried out its most sweeping governmental reorganization in 20 years. Four ministries and six independent agencies, a quarter of all governmental bodies, were eliminated. About 100 cabinet and subcabinet officials were dismissed or reappointed. President Castro gave himself more authority than ever, taking "direct" supervision of the ministries of the Armed Forces, Interior, Culture, and Public Health. But the reorganization appeared to be largely cosmetic. After several months, most of the officials dismissed because of incompetence were reassigned to other jobs in equally important economic departments.

The government did not expect, or promise, economic miracles as a result of the reorganization. Lacking foreign exchange to buy raw materials in the West, scores of factories had to reduce operations, causing what President Castro called a "provisional reduction in the labor force." A new salary scale, the first change since 1963, was introduced. The scale was tied to "job efficiency." A worker's monthly salary was raised from $109 to $124, and that of a service employee from $94 to $110. Managers' salaries were increased from $365 to $598. At the same time, Havana announced an increase in prices for certain foods and consumer goods, which continued to be strictly rationed.

Soviet assistance was estimated at between $8 and $10 million daily. At the end of 1980, Cuba and the Soviet Union signed a $45,000,000,000 trade agreement for the 1981–85 period which also confirmed Moscow's leading role in the Cuban economy through the year 2000. The Soviet Union pledged to ship to Cuba 61 million t (66.6 million T) of oil, about 15% more than in the preceding five-year period. Cuban deliveries of sugar, nickel, and other goods were to be maintained essentially at the same level, while Havana was promised more Soviet products. In 1980, the Cuban government allowed peasants to sell surplus products on free markets, which had been prohibited. Previously outlawed, private service sector activities were also permitted on a small scale.

Widespread discontent over shortages and stifling governmental bureaucracy were probably intensified by contacts with Cuban refugees in the United States who were allowed to visit their homeland. Such voyages were curtailed at the end of 1980. What amounted to a peaceful invasion in one year of almost 100,000 exiles, bringing presents and goods their relatives and friends had not seen in two decades, had given many Cubans a foretaste of the consumer society and a desire to leave the island.

Thus, early in April, when the government in a minor dispute with the Peruvian ambassador in Havana withdrew guards from his embassy, 10,000 Cubans crashed into the embassy grounds seeking political asylum. Three weeks later, realizing that its miscalculation had given it a black eye internationally, Cuba opened the port of Mariel for those wishing to leave the country, calling them "scum, parasites, vagabonds and lumpen." For six weeks the Mariel sealift was allowed by Washington. (*See also* REFUGEES.)

In September, Cuba returned to the United States two hijackers who two days earlier had forced a U.S. plane to fly to Havana, thus reducing a rash of hijackings to Cuba. In October,

---

CUBA · Information Highlights

Official Name: Republic of Cuba.
Location: Caribbean Sea.
Area: 42,823 sq mi (110 912 km^2).
Population (1980 est): 10,000,000.
Chief Cities (Dec. 1978): Havana, the capital, 1,986,500; Santiago de Cuba, 333,600; Camagüey, 236,500.
Government: *Head of state and government*, Fidel Castro Ruz, president (took office under a new constitution, Dec. 1976). *Legislature* (unicameral)—National Assembly of People's Power.
Monetary Unit: Peso (0.72 peso equals U.S. $1, 1980—noncommercial rate).
Manufactures (major products): Refined sugar, metals.
Agriculture (major products): Sugar, tobacco, rice, coffee, beans, meat, vegetables, tropical fruits.
GNP (1978 est., U.S.$): $12,500,000,000.
Foreign Trade (1978, U.S.$): *Imports*, $4,687,000,000; *exports*, $4,456,000,000.

In October a group of Americans just released from Cuban prisons prepare to fly home. Most of the Americans had been jailed for illegally entering Cuban territory.

UPI

Havana unilaterally pardoned all of its 33 American prisoners.

For Fidel Castro 1980 was the first full year of his presidency of the organization of nonaligned countries, but it proved to be less than a happy tenure of office. Principally because of the Soviet invasion of Afghanistan, which Havana supported, albeit belatedly, Cuba was thwarted in January by disaffected third world countries from becoming a member of the UN Security Council. In October it again gave up its battle for that seat. Internal problems prevented President Castro from attending the funeral of Yugoslavia's Tito. These same tensions were seen as the main reason why Cuban jets sank a Bahamian patrol boat and why Havana later tried to bully the Nassau government.

The election defeat of Jamaican Prime Minister Michael Manley, Castro's best friend in the Caribbean, left Havana on good terms with only the tiny island of Grenada. The Havana regime exchanged bitter diplomatic notes with Costa Rica, Peru, and Venezuela, alienating many Latin politicians previously its friends. Castro tried to maintain good relations with both Iran and Iraq and to mediate their conflict. He said it was folly for two nonaligned nations to fight each other since such war was only helping "imperialist enemies."

GEORGE VOLSKY, *University of Miami*

CYPRUS

In 1980, Cyprus celebrated the 20th anniversary of its independence from Great Britain amid the same tensions and uncertainties that have existed there since the 1974 invasion by Turkey.

Under President Spyros Kyprianou, a Greek Cypriot, the central government at Nicosia insisted that it was the only legitimate regime for the entire island. Meanwhile, Turkish Cypriots massed in the northern occupied territories remained separate under the name of the "Turkish Federated State of Cyprus," led by its president,

Rauf Denktaş. How to bring together the Greek Cypriots, comprising about 80% of the population, and the Turkish Cypriots, comprising some 18%, remained a seemingly insolvable puzzle. The UN maintained the peacekeeping force that had been on the island for 16 years.

Intercommunal Talks. Formal discussions between the Greek Cypriots and the Turkish Cypriots, which had broken down in June 1979, were resumed Aug. 9, 1980, in Nicosia. The talks were held, as they had been previously, under the sponsorship of UN Secretary General Kurt Waldheim. The first session dealt with preliminary issues, and the substantive issue of an overall island government was broached in mid-September. Each side immediately accused the other of intransigence. While he favored the discussions in principle, Archbishop Chrysostomos, head of the self-governing Greek Orthodox Church of Cyprus, publicly expressed his dislike of the way they were constituted.

Opposition to Kyprianou. While the Turkish Cypriots seemed closely united around Denktaş, President Kyprianou came under increasing criticism from his own people. The Cyprus Communist Party (AKEL) withdrew its support, and the right-wing Democratic Rally, led by former acting president Glavkos Clerides, was in constant opposition. In October, Alecos Michaelides,

——————— CYPRUS • Information Highlights ———————

Official Name: Republic of Cyprus.
Location: Eastern Mediterranean.
Area: 3,572 sq mi (9 251 km²).
Population (1980 est.): 600,000.
Chief Cities (1978 est.): Nicosia, the capital, 121,500; Limassol, 102,400.
Government: *Head of state and government,* Spyros Kyprianou, president (took office Aug. 1977). *Legislature*—House of Representatives.
Monetary Unit: Pound (0.34825 pound equals U.S. $1, Aug. 1980).
Manufactures (major products): Processed foods, asbestos, cement.
Agriculture (major products): Potatoes, grapes, citrus fruits, wheat, barley, carobs, livestock.
GNP Per Capita (1978 est., U.S.$): $2,110.
Foreign Trade (1979, U.S.$): Imports, $1,001,000,000; exports, $456,000,000.

speaker of the Cyprus House of Representatives, left Clerides' Democratic Party and formed the New Democratic Party. Enough deputies followed him to reduce significantly Kyprianou's influence in the legislative body.

Cyprus and Greece. The reentry of Greece into the military wing of NATO on Oct. 20, 1980, further complicated matters for Kyprianou. Greece's withdrawal in 1974 had been a protest against Turkey's invasion of Cyprus. Its reentry before the problems caused by the invasion had been solved disquieted many Greek Cypriots. Although Kyprianou tried to appear moderate after the Greek government's decision, the Cyprus House of Representatives expressed its unease to Greece's parliament. On October 26, Archbiship Chrysostomos harshly criticized the Greek government for its attitude toward Cyprus generally and for returning to NATO's military wing before a Cyprus settlement.

Independence Celebration. The 20th anniversary of independence from Great Britain was celebrated on October 1. In official statements and celebration speeches, the government emphasized that Cyprus was still a single, sovereign state—albeit territorially divided—and that reconciliation between Greek and Turkish Cypriots was a realistic goal.

GEORGE J. MARCOPOULOS, *Tufts University*

CZECHOSLOVAKIA

Developments in Czechoslovakia during 1980 followed very much the pattern of 1979. The performance of the economy remained lackluster, and dissident voices continued to be heard despite police harassment.

Economy. Although the midyear report of the Statistical Office claimed that Czechoslovakia's economy "evolved in conformity with the main intentions embodied in the operative state plan for 1980," it conceded that more than 50% of all industrial enterprises and more than 80% of construction firms failed to meet the prescribed quality criteria. While food supplies were said to be "balanced on the whole," many sectors of consumer goods production were listed as being unable to meet demand. The number of apartments built in the first half of 1980 was even lower than in the first half of 1979. Nor did preliminary estimates of agricultural production appear to be encouraging, especially in the crucial livestock sector. The average wage rose by a mere 2% over the first half of 1979.

In an effort to revive the stagnating economy, the government adopted in March a massive "Set of Measures to Improve the System of Planned Management of the National Economy after 1980." Among other things, the plan called for a gradual increase in wholesale prices, greater pay differential based on quality of work, curtailment of state subsidies, and reinforcement of economic controls. In April, the Presidium of the ruling Communist Party of Czechoslovakia

(KSC) issued a follow-up resolution calling for a "comprehensive assessment" of managerial cadres to replace "those leading workers who are incapable of coping with their tasks" and who "tend to seek alibis for their failings."

Repression of Human Rights. The government's concern over the continued activities of the Charter 77 and other dissident groups was greatly increased by the labor crisis in neighboring Poland. In an effort to minimize the impact of the dissident community in Czechoslovakia, the regime of President and Party Secretary Gustav Husák stepped up repressive measures. In March and April, the police broke up several scholarly lectures in the private apartments of various dissidents, detained many of the participants, and deported those of foreign citizenship. In September, the police rounded up for interrogation some 30 of the most prominent human rights activists. The dissidents were questioned about a solidarity message that the Charter 77 group had sent to the striking Polish workers and about a document on violations of human rights in Czechoslovakia that they were preparing for the European conference on security and human rights scheduled for later in the year in Madrid. In May, President Husák proclaimed an amnesty to mark the 35th anniversary of Czechoslovakia's liberation from Nazi rule, but it did not extend to persons deemed guilty of political offenses.

Antireligious Campaign. Religious repression also worsened in 1980. Antireligious propaganda increased and became more strident. Admissions to the country's theological institutions were sharply curtailed. The depleted ranks of the clergy were further reduced by forced premature retirements. Five of the six existing bishoprics continued to be without properly appointed bishops.

Husák Reelected. In May, Czechoslovakia's National Assembly elected Gustav Husák to a second five-year term as president.

EDWARD TABORSKY
University of Texas at Austin

— CZECHOSLOVAKIA • Information Highlights —

Official Name: Czechoslovak Socialist Republic.
Location: East-central Europe.
Area: 49,374 sq mi (127 879 km^2).
Population (1980 est.): 15,400,000.
Chief Cities (Dec. 1978): Prague, the capital, 1,188,573; Brno, 369,028. Bratislava, 367,743.
Government: *Head of state,* Gustav Husák, president (took office 1975). *Head of government,* Lubomir Strougal, premier (took office 1970). *Communist party secretary-general,* Gustav Husák (took office 1969). *Legislature*—Federal Assembly: Chamber of Nations and Chamber of the People.
Monetary Unit: Koruna (10.44 koruny equal U.S.$1, 1980—noncommercial rate).
Manufactures (major products): Machinery and equipment, iron and steel products, textiles, motor vehicles, footwear.
Agriculture (major products): Sugar beets, potatoes, wheat, corn, barley, livestock, dairy products.
GNP (1979 est., U.S.$): $85,400,000,000.
Foreign Trade (1979, U.S.$): *Imports,* $14,262,000,000; *exports,* $13,198,000,000.

DANCE

American dance was on a creative upswing in 1980 after a relative lull in recent years. Many fine works received their premieres during the season, and several new choreographers gained prominence. New dancers arrived on the ballet scene, both from abroad and from a generation of extremely talented American teenagers. Fewer major ballet companies toured the United States than in the past. The accent was on the home product.

The Joffrey Ballet returned to New York City with a full repertory season, the first such season it could afford in its home base since the 1978 financial pinch.

After celebrating its 40th anniversary with a gala that paid tribute to its founding patron, Lucia Chase, American Ballet Theatre entered a new era with a new administration. Mikhail Baryshnikov became the company's artistic director, succeeding Miss Chase and Oliver Smith. Although this transition appeared smooth, on the eve of its first season under Baryshnikov, the company dismissed Gelsey Kirkland and Patrick Bissell, two leading dancers, for failing to attend a dress rehearsal for an opening at the Kennedy Center.

The Ballet Season. The New York City Ballet produced an unusually large number of premieres. George Balanchine's ballet, "Robert Schumann's 'Davidsbündlertänze'" had an unwieldy title but was hailed as a masterpiece. Among the four couples onstage, one pair symbolized the composer, Schumann, and his wife, Clara. Yet the ballet transcended its historical references. Never literal, its greatness was found in its meditation on love, life, and death.

Another new neo-Romantic ballet by Balanchine was the Gabriel Fauré "Ballade." The other City Ballet premieres were Peter Martins' trio to Igor Stravinsky, "Eight Easy Pieces," and his ensemble ballet to Carl Nielsen, "Lille Suite"; and Jerome Robbins' "Rondo" to Mozart and "Suite of Dances," an excerpt refashioned from the Robbins "Dybbuk." Two new Balanchine ballets were reworkings of choreography created for opera troupes: "Le Bourgeois Gentilhomme" and "Walpurgisnacht Ballet." "Fancy Free," created in 1944 for Ballet Theatre, entered the City Ballet repertory for the first time.

The Joffrey Ballet presented 11 new productions in New York. The new ballets were Laura Dean's "Night," with the women spinning on toe; Gerald Arpino's "Epode" and "Celebration"; Choo San Goh's "Helena"; Robert Joffrey's "Postcards"; and Moses Pendleton's "Relâche," a recreation of a celebrated avantgarde theater piece originally done in Paris in 1924.

The Joffrey presented company premieres of works originally created elsewhere, such as Sir Frederick Ashton's "Illuminations," Glen Tetley's "Mythical Hunters," Goh's "Momentum," and Marjorie Mussman's "Random Dances" (both first done for Joffrey II), and Jiri Kylian's "Return to the Strange Land." With 17 new dancers in a company of 39, the Joffrey appeared at a stronger technical level than ever.

The American Ballet Theatre's major premiere was Natalia Makarova's version of Marius Petipa's full-length 1877 ballet, "La Bayadère." It was staged as an opera-house spectacular, with highly acclaimed sets by PierLuigi Samaritani.

Various pas de deux and Daniel Levans' "Concert Waltzes" made up the other premieres until Baryshnikov took over. At the Kennedy Center, Ballet Theatre presented the first American production of Ashton's "Les Rendezvous,"

The New York City Ballet presented George Balanchine's critically acclaimed ''Robert Schumann's Davidsbündlertänze,'' featuring (l-r) Heather Watts, Peter Martins, Ib Andersen, and Sara Leland.

excerpts from "Raymonda," and Balanchine's "Prodigal Son."

Among American Ballet Theatre's new members were Alexander Godunov, formerly of the Bolshoi, and the French dancer, Magali Messac.

William Forsythe, an American working in Stuttgart, confirmed his talent with the Expressionist-style "Time Cycle," given by the new Contemporary Ballet Company. Another new troupe, Makarova and Company, headed by Natalia Makarova and Anthony Dowell, ended a four-week run with an uncertain future after a poor reception. The Mercury Ballet attracted a specialized audience because of its focus on British ballets of the 1930s.

The Eliot Feld Ballet presented three new ballets by Eliot Feld: "Anatomic Balm," to ragtime; "Scenes for the Theater," to an Aaron Copland score; and "Circa," to Paul Hindemith. The choreography of "Circa" centered on Richard Fein as an archaic athlete.

Dance Theater of Harlem did Glen Tetley's "Greening," Marius Petipa's "Paquita," and Act II of "Swan Lake."

Among other major ballet events was the start of the Brooklyn Academy of Music's "Ballet America" series which presented companies from outside New York. In Chicago, the Royal Danish Ballet performed works from its Bournonville Festival. In New York, Roland Petit's Ballet National de Marseille, with Zizi Jeanmaire, presented Petit's "The Bat," his French-farce version of "Coppélia," and his "Marcel Proust Remembered." Rudolf Nureyev and Galina and Valery Panov danced in Panov's "The Idiot" with the Berlin Ballet. Nureyev danced with Ghislaine Thesmar and the Boston Ballet in the 1832 Filippo Taglioni version of "La Sylphide," as reconstructed by Pierre Lacotte.

"New" Names in Dance. One of the most visible dancers in the City Ballet was Ib Andersen who, like Martins and Adam Lüders, came from the Royal Danish Ballet. Andersen quickly adapted his pure classical dancing to the City Ballet's nondramatic style and danced more than 20 roles in his first year.

In the fall, Balanchine surprised all by casting 16-year-old Darci Kistler in numerous major roles. A corps member since the spring, Miss Kistler performed with total confidence and proved a sensation with the public.

Also typical of the very promising young dancers who emerged in 1980 was 16-year-old Nancy Raffa, who took on 19th-century ballerina roles with perfect aplomb when she appeared on a program with Natalia Makarova and with two other Russian defectors, Leonid and Valentina Kozlov. Susan Jaffe, 18, made her debut with Ballet Theatre by filling in for the dismissed Gelsey Kirkland.

Other names to remember were those of three French dancers who appeared in New York—Patrick Dupond, Jean-Charles Gil, and Denys Ganio. One dancer thrust forward by

Photo by Herbert Migdoll, Courtesy The Joffrey Ballet

Lynne Chervony, Tom Mossbrucker, Valmai Roberts, Luis Perez star in the Joffrey's new "Night."

publicity was Ron Reagan, the son of the president-elect, a hardworking member of Joffrey II, the Joffrey Ballet's junior company.

Modern Dance. Rudolf Nureyev was seen with Martha Graham's company at the Metropolitan Opera House. Miss Graham presented the new "Frescoes" and "Judith" and a major revival, "Episodes." Another highlight in modern dance was Paul Taylor's "Le Sacre du Printemps (the Rehearsal)" which used a two-piano version of the Igor Stravinsky score for a comic detective-story plot, intercut with scenes from a dance rehearsal.

Twyla Tharp took an innovative step with "When We Were Very Young," a dance-play with text by Thomas Babe, presented on Broadway. Other Tharp premieres were "Brahms' Paganini," "Ocean's Motion," and a revised "Deuce Coupe." Merce Cunningham's premieres were "Duets" and "Locale." Alvin Ailey's new "Phases," to jazz, was a hit for his company, which also presented Kathryn Posin's "Later That Day" and Ulysses Dove's "Inside."

The modern dance season featured the José Limón and Murray Louis companies and such new faces on the experimental scene as Molissa Fenley, Johanna Boyce, Charles Moulton, and Jim Self. Liz Thompson was the new director of the Jacob's Pillow Dance Festival.

ANNA KISSELGOFF, *"The New York Times"*

DELAWARE

In the November elections Gov. Pierre S. duPont, IV (R) was returned to office with a majority of 72% of the vote. Michael N. Castle (R) was chosen lieutenant-governor. Delaware was in the Republican column for president with 47% for Reagan, 45% for Carter, and 7% for Anderson. Thomas B. Evans, Jr. (R), the incumbent member of the U.S. House of Representatives, received 62% of the two-party vote. In other statewide elections, Thomas R. Carper (D) was returned as state treasurer; T. W. Spruance (R) was chosen state auditor; and D. H. Elliott (R) was selected to be insurance commissioner. The state House of Representatives was captured by the Republicans, 25-16. The state Senate remained Democratic, 12-9. In populous New Castle county, R. T. Collins (R) was elected county executive. W. T. McLaughlin (D) was returned as mayor of Wilmington, the state's largest city. The Democrats retained control of the county councils in each of the state's three counties. Over 80% of the eligible voters cast ballots.

The proposed constitutional amendment to permit initiative and referendum was defeated. The amendment to increase the terms of state treasurer and state auditor from two to four years passed.

Economy. The economy experienced a marked decline in 1980. The jobless rate was near 8%, with the Chrysler assembly plant in Newark contributing decidedly to the number of unemployed. The total employed, however, reached a new high.

There were some gains in business construction but housing starts were down 32% compared with 1979, and overall housing production slipped 8% in the same period. Retail sales showed a slight decrease. General cargo clearing the Port of Wilmington was down 10%, but both dry and wet bulk showed increases of up to 40%. Cash farm income increased from $260,536,000 in 1979 to $323,247,000 in 1980. Total farms in Delaware numbered approximately 3,400, a slight decrease from 1979.

Schools. Public school enrollment showed a decrease of 5%; private schools had an increase

---
DELAWARE • Information Highlights

Area: 2,057 sq mi (5 328 km²).
Population (Jan. 1980 est.): 582,000.
Chief Cities (1970 census): Dover, the capital, 17,488; Wilmington, 80,386; Newark, 21,078.
Government (1980): *Chief Officers*—governor, Pierre S. duPont IV (R). *General Assembly*—Senate, 21 members; House of Representatives, 41 members.
Education (1979-80): *Enrollment*—public elementary schools, 50,247; public secondary, 53,787; colleges and universities, 32,308 students. Public school expenditures, $265,270,000 ($2,327 per pupil).
State Finances (fiscal year 1979): *Revenues,* $869,000,-000; *expenditures,* $762,000,000.
Personal Income (1979): $5,428,000,000; per capita, $9,327.
Labor Force (May 1980): *Nonagricultural wage and salary earners,* 259,500; *unemployed,* 16,800 (6.0% of total force).

---

of close to 7%. Forced busing between suburban New Castle and Wilmington produced problems of student discipline. Suburban resentment over busing was manifested by a resounding rejection of a referendum to increase school taxes in the integrated district of northern New Castle county. The pace of so-called "white flight" from the public schools seemed to be slowing.

Government. The state continued to supply local communities with funds for repair of local roads although the state Department of Transportation has the responsibility for all public roads in the state. The total state budget for fiscal 1981 was $633,721,400, an increase of about 14% over fiscal 1980. During 1980 a constitutional amendment was passed requiring that state expenses stay within 98% of anticipated revenue. The total state debt as of September 1980 was $528,510,000.

Wilmington. Hercules, Inc., second largest chemical company in the state, decided to remain in the city and planned to erect a large office building to house its home office.

PAUL DOLAN, *University of Delaware*

DENMARK

Anker Jørgensen's Social Democratic minority cabinet continued to struggle against the intractable problems that have faced Denmark since the end of World War II, namely, inflation, unemployment, lagging production, heavy taxes—the highest of any European Community member—and an unfavorable trade balance. Jørgensen's efforts had been foreshadowed in his somber speech made at the opening of the 1979-80 session of Parliament on Nov. 6, 1979, in which he promised to do everything possible to alleviate these conditions.

The government followed up, in late December 1979, with a 5% devaluation of the currency, a step, however, which did not seem to have much effect. In April the cabinet unveiled a new economic crisis plan, involving new taxes and fees. The plan was to produce about 5,000,000,-000 kroner in extra fees for the national treasury, and 6,000,000,000 kroner were to be trimmed from the national budget.

Denmark became involved in developments in Iran. In February, the Danish government offered to handle Canadian interests in Iran, to have the Danish embassy act as a Canadian consulate, and to take charge of the Canadian embassy premises and property. The Danish people solidly condemned Iran for taking American hostages. In May the Danish government decided to institute sanctions against Iran, cutting off all exports, except food and medicines.

The term "Denmarkization" gained currency throughout Europe and the United States. It was applied to a situation in which a country does not carry its full and proper burden as regards outlays for the common NATO defense. It was thought that such designation was a bit unfair in

Copenhagen, Denmark's capital, hosted the 1980 United Nations conference of women. Some 1,000 delegates from 136 nations attended.

Tatiner, Liaison

the case of Denmark. It was true that Denmark had indicated its inability to raise its 1981 defense budget the 3% called for in excess of inflationary increases, but it was pointed out that Denmark was not the only nation to fall short of the 3% NATO request. As for the plans of storing NATO military supplies in Denmark and Norway, there was an indication of willingness to accept NATO depots, except for missiles with nuclear warheads, on Danish soil.

In June the fisheries zone around Greenland was extended to 200 nautical miles (370 km) except vis-à-vis Canada and Iceland, where a center line was adopted. This step affected the fisheries zones already announced by Iceland and by Norway around the Arctic island of Jan Mayen. Denmark maintained that Jan Mayen, a practically uninhabited island, should not serve as the base for the establishment of 200-mile fisheries zones, while Norway was willing to negotiate a center line between Greenland and Jan Mayen. Iceland protested the Danish action, maintaining that a small Icelandic island off the west coast should serve as the base for drawing a new line.

The two last weeks of July were marked by the UN conference of women meeting in Copenhagen. The 1,183 delegates elected as its pres-

ident Lise Østergaard, Danish minister of cultural affairs. (*See also* WOMEN.)

ERIK J. FRIIS
Editor, "The Scandinavian-American Bulletin"

DETROIT

A depressed economy, high unemployment, and cutbacks in public services plagued Detroit during 1980. However, the Republican National Convention boosted the city's image, and urban renewal progressed in older areas of Detroit.

Economy. The auto industry, battling sluggish sales, lost a record $1,500,000,000 during the second quarter of the year. Thirty-five percent of the industry's work force was laid off, and unemployment in Detroit was 14.6% in July.

City Services. Tax income fell below anticipated amounts, and Detroit ended the 1979–80 fiscal year with an $85.5-million deficit and expected a $135-million deficit in 1980–81. Moody's Investors Service and Standard & Poor's Corporation lowered their ratings of the city's bonds below investment grade, an action which raised interest rates.

To reduce deficits, 690 of Detroit's 4,895 policemen were laid off on September 5. The layoffs affected all officers hired after June 1975, most of whom were blacks and women. The action was criticized as destructive of affirmative action efforts.

City employees went on strike from July 1 until July 12, halting bus service and garbage collection.

Schools. Detroit voters bucked a statewide trend against higher taxes, to approve a 3.5 mill tax increase. The increase avoided the layoff of 840 of 9,000 teachers.

Urban Renewal. Washington Boulevard, a downtown thoroughfare once known as Detroit's "street of fashion," was rebuilt as a mall. Construction of "phase two" of the downtown Renaissance Center—two smaller office buildings modeled on the original circular towers—was

---
DENMARK · Information Highlights

Official Name: Kingdom of Denmark.
Location: Northwest Europe.
Area: 16,631 sq mi (43 074 km²).
Population (1980 est.): 5,100,000.
Chief Cities (1979 est.): Copenhagen, the capital, 1,244,-741; Aarhus, 245,174; Odense, 167,952.
Government: *Head of state,* Margrethe II, queen (acceded Jan. 1972). *Head of government,* Anker Jørgensen, prime minister (took office Feb. 1975). *Legislature* (unicameral)—Folketing.
Monetary Unit: Krone (5.90 kroner equal U.S.$1, Nov. 1980).
Manufactures (major products): Industrial and construction equipment, furniture, textiles, processed foods.
Agriculture (major products): Grains, sugar beets, dairy products, livestock.
GNP Per Capita (1978 est., U.S.$): $9,920.
Foreign Trade (1979, U.S.$): *Imports,* $18,450,000,000; *exports,* $14,506,000,000.

begun. General Motors Corporation completed the first stage of a multi-million-dollar program to rehabilitate a residential area near its world headquarters.

Census. Preliminary census results showed a sharp drop in Detroit's population. The city successfully filed suit in federal court to force the Census Bureau to add an estimate of uncounted residents to the actual count. At stake were a Congressional seat and federal funding.

Miscellaneous News. The *Detroit Free Press* was shut down July 13 by a Teamsters Union strike. *The Detroit News* subsequently printed a "joint edition" which carried the mastheads of both newspapers from July 15 until July 25, when the *Free Press* resumed publication.

Despite the fact that the four-day GOP convention (July 14–18) did not produce the economic boom that many had expected, Detroiters hailed the convention as evidence of the city's rebirth.

John Cardinal Dearden (72), Roman Catholic archbishop of Detroit since 1959, resigned.

CHARLES THEISEN, *"The Detroit News"*

ECUADOR

In 1980, Ecuador continued to be governed by the democratic administration of President Jaime Roldós Aguilera, elected the year before. The country's political status was perhaps best reflected by the assessment of Freedom House, the New York-based human rights watchdog, which relisted the country in its select "free" category.

Politics. Political maneuvering continued between President Roldós and Assad Bucaram, president of Congress and the effective head of Roldós' own Concentration of Popular Forces (CFP). By April, Roldós had vetoed 48 of the 70 bills sent to him by the Bucaram-controlled Congress.

The feud finally resulted in a showdown and at least a temporary victory for President Roldós. On April 11, Roldós announced his intention to submit to popular referendum a constitutional amendment allowing the president to dissolve Congress and call new elections at least once during his five-year term. The move brought the

---
ECUADOR • Information Highlights

Official Name: Republic of Ecuador.
Location: Northwest South America.
Area: 104,506 sq mi (270 669 km²).
Population (1980 est.): 8,000,000.
Chief Cities (1974): Quito, the capital, 557,113; Guayaquil, 814,064.
Government: *Head of state and government,* Jaime Roldós Aguilera, president (took office Aug. 1979). *Legislature* (unicameral)—Congress.
Monetary Unit: Sucre (28.10 sucres equal U.S. $1, Nov. 1980).
Manufactures (major products): Food products, textiles, light consumer goods, light industrial goods.
Agriculture (major products): Bananas, coffee, cacao, rice, corn, sugar, livestock.
GNP (1978 est., U.S.$): $7,000,000,000.
Foreign Trade (1978, U.S.$): *Imports,* $1,627,000,000; *exports,* $1,494,000,000.

defection from Bucaram of a number of CFP members of Congress and a realignment in the legislature giving a majority to the president. The new congressional majority included not only dissident CFP members but also representatives of the moderate-left Izquierda Democratica and the Christian Democrats. As a result, President Roldós announced the suspension of his referendum plans on May 19.

The first test of the new majority was the defeat (33-27) on June 3 of Bucaram's attempt to impeach Minister of Interior Carlos Feraud Blum. On August 10, Bucaram was replaced as president of Congress by Raul Baca Carbo, a leader of Izquierda Democratica.

The year in politics was also marked by outbreaks of violence. On September 1, Conservative Party deputy Ezequiel Calvijo, who had been strongly denounced by members of his own party for voting with the new majority to reorganize the congressional leadership, was shot and seriously wounded. On September 30, former President Otto Arosemena shot and wounded another Conservative deputy, Pablo Davalos Dillon, during a debate in Congress.

Economy. Ecuador's economic picture was mixed in 1980. Increases in the price of oil by OPEC, to which Ecuador belongs, brought an increase in oil revenues of almost 66% during the first six months of the year. Overall exports were almost 50% higher in value. The carrying capacity of the government oil tanker fleet was significantly increased, effecting major savings in foreign exchange. But despite these gains, the state oil company announced that it would face bankruptcy because of its inability to retain sufficient revenue to pay both current expenses and development requirements.

The rate of inflation surpassed 20% during the year, and the large foreign debt accumulated by the previous military regime necessitated the rescheduling of much of the debt on a longer-term basis.

The difficult economic situation provoked several strikes and political demonstrations during the year. In February, a student demonstration against price increases resulted in two students being killed by the police. In June, striking oil workers occupied the oil refinery at Esmeraldas before their dispute was settled. In August, urban transport workers staged a walkout to protest gasoline price hikes.

Foreign Affairs. In July, President Roldós joined with the presidents of Venezuela, Peru, and Colombia in denouncing the military coup in Bolivia. In September, the presidents of Colombia, Costa Rica, Panama, and Venezuela met with Roldós in Quito and signed agreements "to consolidate democracy in Latin America."

Ecuador announced in January that it was extending diplomatic recognition to the People's Republic of China, and in February that it was recognizing Albania.

ROBERT J. ALEXANDER, *Rutgers University*

EDUCATION

In 1980, striking U.S. teachers worried about job security as enrollments continued to fall and schools closed; Chicago schools narrowly averted financial disaster; controversy continued over prayers in public schools and over bilingual education; and private university faculty unions felt threatened.

Internationally, the United States warily eyed Soviet math and science advances, the People's Republic of China continued its education catchup by increasing advanced study abroad, and student eruptions in South Korea illustrated growing world urban youth discontent.

THE UNITED STATES

Teachers' Strikes. In September, some 30,000 teachers in nine states and Puerto Rico went on strike, affecting nearly 600,000 students. Teachers demanded higher salaries, cost of living increases, smaller classes, and more class preparation time. A new demand for 1980 was job security, once assured to tenured teachers but now threatened by school closings and teacher dismissals resulting from declining birth rates, recession, and inflation.

Teacher Attitude and Competency. A July 3 National Education Association (NEA) poll found 35% of the 2,165 NEA teachers polled (out of the nearly 2.2 million U.S. teachers) dissatisfied with their jobs; 41% said they would not become teachers if they could start over again (up from 32% in a similar 1979 poll). The report noted that the 133,500 prospective teachers who graduated in 1979 entered a market with only 74,750 job openings in the public schools.

A teacher competency report by the American Association of School Administrators said that 85–95% of U.S. teachers are performing their jobs adequately. It suggested rewarding good teachers with bonuses (opposed by teacher unions as giving administrators excessive power and leading to favoritism), eliminating or reducing nonteaching duties, and making in-service training more practical than theoretical. Observers note that teachers have been buffeted by changing educational trends: the open classroom and child-dominated schools in the 1960s, the back-to-basics movement in the late 1970s, and teacher competency tests in 1980.

Chicago Schools Crisis. Financial problems, segregation, a high dropout rate, and a two-week teachers' strike plagued Chicago's school system, third largest in the nation (after New York and Los Angeles). In January, the insolvent Chicago school board failed to meet payrolls for its 453,-000-student school system, precipitating a 25,000-teacher strike which ended February 11 with a $60 million budget cut, bank loans, and some teacher and teacher aide layoffs.

Chicago also has a more than 50% high school dropout rate, higher than New York City's 45%.

On September 24 Chicago's school board agreed to use various desegregation strategies in 1981–82, thus ending several years' conflict with the federal government over the extent of school desegregation and legal remedies.

School Prayer. Sharply divided U.S. House Judiciary Subcommittee hearings were held in July and August on a Senate-passed bill (51–40) to abolish federal court jurisdiction over state laws on voluntary prayer in public schools. The bill, introduced by U.S. Sen. Jesse Helms (R-NC), attempted to reverse the 1963 U.S. Supreme Court decision prohibiting formal prayers in public schools. Supporting the Helms bill were conservative politicians and evangelical clergy, whose political influence is growing among fundamentalist followers. Opponents included civil liberties unions, the American Jewish Congress, and the National Council of Churches. A proprayer plank in the Republican presidential-election platform encouraged proponents, who believe school prayer will reverse what they view as recent moral decay. They cited a Gallup poll indicating that 76% of those polled want voluntary prayers in schools. Opponents contended that school prayers violate the constitutional rights of those who belong to minority religions or who have no religion. They felt that the Helms bill, if passed, would be challenged as unconstitutional. Meanwhile, a growing number of states approved prayers in the school. In Massachusetts, one of about a dozen states with such laws, the Supreme Judicial Court on March 13 struck down the state law allowing voluntary prayer in public schools. Bottled up in subcommittee at year's end, the Helms bill was expected to come up in the 1981 Congress.

Foreign Language Decline. A decline in foreign language studies was criticized by the November 1979 report of the President's Commission on Foreign Language and International Studies. Only 15% of high school students take a foreign language (24% in 1965). Of these only 1 out of 20 studies beyond the first year of French, German, or Russian. And only 8% of colleges and universities require a foreign language for graduation (34% in 1966).

Bilingual Education. The new cabinet-level Department of Education, inaugurated May 4, ended bilingual education hearings in six cities on September 18. Federal proposals on how to integrate into public schools the estimated 3.5 million children whose primary language is not English (70% of these are Hispanics) require identifying these children by interviews and tests, placing them in bilingual classes, and teaching them subjects in the home language while introducing more material in English. When revised after the hearings, federal regulations will replace 1975 guidelines, which followed a 1974 U.S. Supreme Court interpretation of the Civil Rights Act of 1964 mandating bilingual education. Only 60% of children eligible for bilingual education currently receive it.

Those who want the proposed regulations to be more inclusive complain because a class must be below the 9th grade, and have at least 25 eligible children of the same language background; because parents allegedly will not be involved; because test scores will allegedly be too high for entrance and too low for exit; and because children who are limited in both English and their home language are neglected. While they endorse bilingual education, eight major educational organizations prefer local school districts to choose among various approaches. Critics fear that the 2–5-year minimum-maximum bilingual education period will foster Spanish as the official second language and cause national divisiveness. Others object to local school districts paying two thirds of the estimated $591 million program cost, while the federal government will pay only one third.

Yeshiva University Faculty Union Case. On February 20 the U.S. Supreme Court decided 5–4 that Yeshiva University's full-time faculty had such authority over academic matters and institutional policies that they were managers rather than employees and hence that their union, formed in 1973, cannot bargain collectively under the National Labor Relations Act (NLRA). The decision applied specifically to Yeshiva, a private New York City university, but the result was to slow down—if not stop—collective bargaining activities of private higher education faculty unions. Before year-end, more than a dozen private universities had refused to bargain with their faculty unions.

Of U.S. public higher education institutions, 380 campuses are unionized (251 of these are two-year community colleges). But since some 25 states prohibit collective bargaining at state- or city-supported colleges or universities, unionizers have looked to the 1,660 private higher institutions, only 80 of which are unionized.

In his dissent, Justice William J. Brennan, Jr., said that the Yeshiva faculty did not align itself with the administration or it would not have tried to unionize and that the court's majority did not understand how universities work. The chief unionizing organizations agreed. Taking the lead, the American Association of University Professors (AAUP), working with the NEA and the American Federation of Teachers (AFT), began readying several test cases to overturn the Supreme Court Yeshiva decision. Congressman Frank Thompson, Jr. (D-NJ), introduced a bill in June, drafted by the AAUP, to amend the NLRA higher education provisions. Many believe it unfair and unconstitutional to deny faculty the right to unionize, bargain, and strike.

Education of Illegal Aliens. Illegal alien children entered Texas public schools in September. On July 21 a federal judge struck down a 1975 Texas law prohibiting state funds to educate the estimated 20,000–100,000 illegal alien children in the state. On September 9, U.S. Supreme Court Justice Lewis F. Powell upheld the decision. Opponents were concerned about the burden to taxpayers, particularly near the Mexican border.

Desegregation. On May 15, the U.S. Justice Department filed suit to order cross-district desegregation of 23 school systems in the Houston, TX, metropolitan area. The suit, the first of its kind ever filed by the Justice Department, sought to revise a 1967 lawsuit that did not encompass schools in suburban areas surrounding the city.

In a related case in St. Louis, MO, a federal judge on May 21 ordered that suburban school districts be included in that city's desegregation plan. The plan, which went into effect in the fall of 1980, originally included only city schools.

Increased Funding. In October, President Carter signed a group of education bills mandating enlarged elementary and secondary school programs and expenditures of $48,000,000,000 over five years for student loans and grants.

Enrollment Down, Costs Up. Elementary and secondary school enrollment declined for the fifth consecutive year while higher education enrollments reached an all-time high. School statistics for 1980–81 (1979–80 in parentheses) were:

Enrollments, kindergarten through grade 8: 31,200,000, −1.3%, with projected decline to mid-1980s (31,600,000); high school: 14,900,000, −2.6%, with projected decline through the 1980s (15,300,000); higher: 11,700,000, +0.85%, with projected decrease 1981–90 (11,600,000); total: 57,800,000, −1.2% (58,500,000). The total was 5.7% below the 1975 record high of 61,300,000.

Education directly involved 61,400,000 (62,-000,000) persons, or nearly 30% of the total population. Expenditures were: public elementary and secondary schools, $103,500,000,000 ($92,-100,000,000); nonpublic elementary and secondary, $12,800,000,000 ($10,600,000,000); public higher education, $43,900,000,000 ($39,300,000,-000); nonpublic higher education, $21,100,000,-000 ($18,700,000,000), a total of $181,300,000,-000 ($160,700,000,000), or 7% of the 1979 gross national product. Expenditure estimates for 1981–82: public schools and colleges, $147,000,-000,000; private schools and colleges, $34,000,-000,000. Federal grants for all educational purposes, $24,400,000,000 (three-fold increase since 1970, $8,700,000,000).

Number of teachers, elementary and secondary, 2,500,000 (same); higher, 830,000 (820,000), total, 3,330,000 (including 300,000 administrators and other staff).

Graduates, high school, 3,100,000 (3,150,-000), with over 3,000,000 expected in 1981 (high school graduate peak in 1977 was 3,161,000); bachelor's degree, 952,000 (950,000); first professional degrees, 70,000 (68,000); master's, 316,000 (330,000); doctorates, 33,000 (same).

INTERNATIONAL

USSR. An analysis of U.S.-USSR educational systems prepared for the National Science Foundation (NSF) in March implies that the United States is in a threatened position because too few talented American youths are exposed to advanced math, physics, and chemistry. Key findings include: from kindergarten to 6th grade, Soviet schools teach considerably more math than the United States, which offers slightly more science; relatively few U.S. secondary school students but all Soviet secondary school students take a curriculum oriented to science and math; Soviet specialized secondary schools (the United States has no equivalent) turn out more than 1 million graduates in technical-applied skills annually; in 1976, the USSR graduated six times as many engineers as the United States, a substantial edge, even allowing for weaker Soviet university training; at the end of the 8th grade, Soviet students have had eight years of math, three years of physics, two years of chemistry, and five years of foreign language training; in contrast, more than half the U.S. high schools require only one math course for graduation and very few require physics.

The report says that the first eight years of Soviet schools ensure science and math mastery. Their goal is to give the economy a strong scientific-technical base and to have more technically oriented military recruits, an advantage traditionally held by American armed forces.

Schools in the Soviet Union's non-Russian Republics are flawed by low quality, large classes, inadequately trained teachers, and poor laboratory equipment. But Soviet education's major flaw is excessive specialization: of 480 higher education specialties, 200 are in industrial engineering alone. Soviet leadership has recognized and is correcting this weakness. The report concludes that the math and science effort is paying off for the USSR and that the United States cannot afford to allow large numbers of its students to remain ignorant of math and science.

Echoing the above report was a separate NSF survey on math and science in Eastern Europe. Survey director Izaak Wirszup told the prestigious Academy of Education that the Soviet's decade-long effort to upgrade math and science has resulted in "quantitative and qualitative gains without equal in the history of education." He said that the same arithmetic taught during eight years in U.S. schools was taught in the first three years in Soviet schools, that geometry taught in U.S. 9th grade is taught in the Soviet 6th grade, that 105,000 U.S. students take 1 year of high school calculus while more than 5 million Soviet students study two years of calculus. However, some Academy members felt that Soviet educational claims were exaggerated.

People's Republic of China. The appointment of an American resident of Peking, Sidney Rittenberg, as adviser to the Chinese Academy of Social Science was announced March 17. The report indicated that he would aid U.S.–China academic exchanges at the Academy, a major academic research institute. The 58-year-old Rittenberg, who spent 16 years in Chinese prisons after going there in 1945 as an Army Judge Ad-

vocate interpreter, is one of several longtime American expatriates recently appointed to advise Chinese government agencies.

About 85% of the 2,400 Chinese now studying in the United States are graduate students. About 1,000 are on Chinese government-sponsored programs (the rest have government permission for their arrangements with American institutions) and 1,000 more are expected in the United States in 1980–81. In contrast, only 175 Americans will be studying in China. Deputy Prime Minister Deng Xiaoping's son, a Peking University physicist, was among Chinese scholars studying at the University of Rochester in 1980. The temporary outflow of university teachers and researchers is causing a shortage; since May 1 the Chinese have required case-by-case discussion of those above the rank of associate professor who desire to go abroad.

Compared with those of other Communist countries, U.S.–China exchanges are loosely structured, disproportionate in numbers, with little concern for reciprocity. Chinese research and study are linked to national objectives of modernization. Some U.S. scholars are engaged in transferring to their Chinese hosts knowledge in natural science, public health, and other fields. Most others study politically safe topics (ancient history or archaeology) rather than critical aspects of Chinese politics, party and government organization, foreign policy decision-making, nationalities policy, and similar sensitive topics. Surmising that U.S. scholars in China have acquiesced to Peking's political constraints, some observers would prefer more realistic academic reciprocity to gain a greater understanding of China.

Discontented Youth. The most violent protests in 30 years rocked South Korea in May, causing the closing of its 85 colleges and universities for several months and the strengthening of military rule. Incited by various socio-political repressions, hundreds of thousands of students, kept from their campuses by martial law, temporarily seized the city of Kwangju.

The South Korea student eruption appeared to be linked to a spreading third-world phenomenon of discontented youth. Iran's anti-shah revolution began when half the population was under age 17 and when Tehran was bursting with dissident students and the unemployed. South African eruptions in 1980 (the most widespread since Soweto in 1976) were precipitated by black students, most of them under age 15, ostensibly wanting to improve educational opportunity, but also frustrated by political repression and an economic downturn.

The discontent is not confined to the third world. In May, Zurich youth groups rioted when authorities voted to restore an old opera house in the city. The youths were enraged because their request for an alternative culture center had not been given precedence.

FRANKLIN PARKER, *West Virginia University*

Mimi Forsyth, Monkmeyer

EDUCATION—SPECIAL REPORT:

The Changing Role of Testing

Testing has always been a delicate issue in American education. Advocates warn that without testing society would stagnate in a morass of mediocrity; opponents of testing say that tests discriminate against the outsider, the poor, and the disadvantaged.

Two opposing trends are evident in the United States as the 1980s begin. On the one hand, triggered by widespread alarm over a decline in achievement (particularly in reading and writing), there is a nationwide movement toward minimum competency tests as a prerequisite for high school graduation. On the other, there are mounting pressures against the use of such standardized yardsticks as the Scholastic Aptitude Test (SAT) as a determining factor of college admission, particularly admission to prestigious schools.

"Truth-in-testing" Legislation. Reflecting the anti-test movement, legislators are increasingly interested in the enactment of laws, under the label of "truth in testing," which will provide student access to the tests taken and will compel testmakers to publish the questions after the tests have been administered. The first "truth-in-testing" laws were enacted in California (1978) and New York (1979). Initial hearings have been held in the U.S. Congress to consider federal legislation.

Under the New York law, anyone who has taken a standardized admissions test for postsecondary or professional school is entitled to request a copy of the questions, his or her an-

swers, and a correct-answer key. Similar bills have been introduced in 20 other states.

While spokesmen for the testing industry say they are sympathetic to the general aims of such legislation, they warn that full disclosure of every test question and answer would make it nearly impossible, and certainly very costly, to prepare nationwide tests of high quality. Nevertheless, the College Entrance Examination Board, which administers the SATs, has announced a voluntary policy outside New York State which will allow students to see their answer sheets, but not the actual questions, thus dealing with the issue of wrong scoring without continually exposing the tests to public scrutiny.

The Discrimination Factor. A more fundamental ideological issue was raised by the Ralph Nader consumer organization in a critical report on the Educational Testing Service, the organization that constructs the SATs and other national standardized tests. The Nader critique attacked college admissions tests on the basis that the tests are imperfect predictors of success in college and favor the children of the rich, assuring them a place in prestigious educational institutions, while discriminating against the poor.

Historically, such a claim was demonstrably true. The fact is that in the past children of wealthy families had easy, almost automatic, access to elite colleges and universities. Graduation from a selective prep school all but assured admission to a prestigious university traditionally associated with that school. For the most part, children of minorities were kept out, generally on the basis of subjective admissions criteria.

It was largely in answer to complaints about such discriminatory practices that the College Board introduced objective tests in 1926. Statistics indicate that the occurrence of these tests initially paralleled less discriminatory admissions policies by institutions. Moreover, college admissions officers were eager to have a means by which they could compare the transcripts provided by some 20,000 widely-diverse high schools.

In the 1960s, however, civil-rights spokesmen raised a new question: were these tests, however unintentionally, biased against the cultural background of such minorities as blacks and Hispanics? Considerable research and corrective effort subsequently went into making the tests culturally and racially objective.

The Advance Preparation Factor. In the view of some critics, these reforms failed to come to grips with one crucial matter—the extent to which students could prepare, or cram, for the tests in order to raise their scores. In an effort to protect the integrity of the tests, the testmakers originally argued that the SATs measured innate aptitude and thus were not affected by special preparation. They strongly advised against cramming and coaching.

In recent years, the testmakers' claim has been effectively challenged and proven exaggerated, if not downright false. National chains of coaching schools have demonstrated considerable success in helping students master at least the technique of test-taking. The evidence, supported by a study by the Federal Trade Commission, was sufficiently persuasive to move the testmakers and the College Board to revise their original stand. They now offer specific guides to students on how to prepare for the tests.

Competency Tests. The issue of minimum competency tests (already introduced in 36 states) differs greatly from that of the college-admission tests. There is a general consensus on the need for competency, at least in the basic skills, for any person who expects to function in the modern world and to compete in the job market. Nor is there any doubt that a high school diploma ought to certify that the recipient has mastered those fundamental skills. What remains open to controversy, however, is the timing of such tests. Is it fair, opponents ask, to block a youth's graduation on the basis of a minimum competency test administered in the junior or senior year, when it is too late to make up for lost time? Should not the schools be responsible for preventing such failure? In other words, could not tests be used more effectively as diagnostic instruments able to expose weaknesses early in the pupils' school career, rather than as end-of-the-line hurdles which cause them to falter?

Conflict among Educators. The educational community itself is sharply divided. The Na-

tional Education Association (NEA), which represents well over one million teachers, has taken a militant stand against virtually all standardized testing as well as against state or federally mandated competency tests. On the other hand, the smaller American Federation of Teachers (AFT), an affiliate of the AFL-CIO, has generally supported tests as a necessary aid to effective schooling. It has opposed "truth-in-testing" legislation because of the need constantly to create new test questions, a process that is costly and that will eventually invalidate the use of the tests as a comparative measure of quality. The goal, the AFT maintains, should be to work on the elimination of the tests' imperfections and ambiguities, not to scuttle the tests. On the matter of competency testing, the AFT reports that its own poll of teachers showed that 41% approved, 38% were neutral, and only 21% responded unfavorably.

The Future of Standardized Testing. A realistic view of higher education in the years ahead suggests that the SATs as a factor in college admissions are on the way to becoming less important, as other determinants such as a declining birthrate and a diminished applicant pool force colleges to be less selective. The relatively low student interest in the new disclosure rights available to them may be indicative of an increased lack of competition. Only 4.5% of those who have taken the SATs since New York's "truth-in-testing" law went into effect have requested information from the Educational Testing Service. On the other hand, 21% of those who took the Law School Admissions Test availed themselves of the right of full disclosure, thus illustrating the relationship of intense competition to student inquiry. As long as there are more candidates than desirable institutions or fields of study in which to place them, unsuccessful applicants are likely to blame the tests for their failure to gain acceptance. They will seek support from political mentors and consumer advocates who are willing to foster a rebellion against the testing process.

The basic dilemma remains unsolved and perhaps insoluble. On the one hand, there is the need for quality controls which implies selection of those able to live up to standards set by an institution or by ultimate job requirements. On the other, there is legitimate concern that the sorting process may protect those already privileged and exclude those less fortunate.

Present American sentiment suggests the likelihood of compromise. Access to higher education remains a strong commitment, but there is also a growing realization, reinforced by the United States' new difficulties in worldwide competition for markets and ideas, that a valueless democracy becomes dangerously vulnerable. Many of the signposts point to a continued use of tests, but increasingly as instruments to diagnose pupil deficiencies.

FRED M. HECHINGER

EGYPT

Rather quietly, Egypt and Anwar el-Sadat, its president, celebrated in September 1980 the tenth anniversary of Sadat's rule. Sadat's tenth year (and a bit of the eleventh) encompassed a complex series of events both domestic and international. Normalization of relations with Israel continued, although the "autonomy" talks were stalled. U.S. aid was immense, but domestic prosperity continued elusive.

Domestic Affairs. Domestic affairs in Egypt generally relate to political survival first and then to periodic attempts to patch up the economy. International pressures always infringe upon these areas, and the prevailing poverty and expanding population endanger economic planning. The above is a fair description of Egypt in 1980.

Anwar el-Sadat was continually under pressure throughout the year. His continuing efforts to dismantle what remains of the old Nasserite authoritarianism encountered many snags. Sadat has wanted at least the trappings of democracy; the *sine qua non* of this is an opposition party. Sadat began encouraging the Socialist Labor Party on that note in 1978 in contrast to his own National Democratic Party (NDP); by 1980 Sadat was skirmishing with opposition leadership with all the traditional weapons, including censorship and denunciations. To Sadat such parties had crossed the fine line between opposition and obstruction. Exiled former Gen. Saad Eddin al-Shazli, headquartered in Syria, claimed to head up a government in exile opposed to Sadat.

In May, Sadat pulled one of his usual rabbits from the hat in the form of a national referendum regarding changes in the Egyptian constitution of 1971. In effect, the referendum, if approved, would have made Sadat president indefinitely (although not without the formality of elections every six years) and also would have put on record that Islam was the proper source of all legislation. The referendum passed with 98.96% of the vote.

A current joke in Cairo was that Sadat, flushed with this victory and eager to help his friend U.S. President Jimmy Carter, offered to lend his campaign manager to President Carter. The joke ended with Sadat winning the American presidency by a landslide.

Also in May Sadat announced that he was assuming "broadened powers." This was hardly as significant as he made it out to be since his powers invariably are what he defines them to be, but it gave him an opportunity to reshuffle aides and ministers. In September Sadat's NDP won all 140 seats for a new advisory tier called the Consultative Council, ostensibly organized to advise the government. The council is not the parliament nor a substitute for it: the parliament remains.

For many it was not easy eating in Egypt in 1980. In February a shortage of cheap bread occasioned government warnings and intervention. The standard bread for the Egyptian poor has been an unleavened flat brown bread about the size and shape of a salad plate. It costs—heavily subsidized—less than one cent. Bakers were accused of investing some of the subsidized flour in the baking of more fancy breads and pastry.

A U.S. UH-60 Black Hawk troop-carrying helicopter participates in a U.S.-Egyptian military exercise.

UPI

Prices of flour (bread), sugar, cooking oil, and kerosene are the traditional bellwethers of economic distress in Egypt and Sadat is very sensitive to this. In September Sadat declared a ban of a month on the slaughter of local animals and the sale of meat. The ban was intended to control prices. At the time meat was averaging $2.30 a pound in Cairo and eggs about $1.50 a dozen (although they usually are sold singly). Egypt's per capita income is only about $400 a year.

Efforts to control the population have been unsuccessful. It is estimated that there will be 70 million Egyptians by the year 2000; the 1960 population was 30 million. Egypt lives on foreign aid, whether from the Arab world or from the United States. Increased revenues from the Suez Canal—a tunnel under the canal was completed in 1980—and from the sale of petroleum have helped, but economic problems remain. And unfortunately there is a limit to Nile waters and usable land. The future, as Sadat knows only too well, is gloomy.

Foreign Affairs. Egypt, the first country to which the shah of Iran flew when he left Iran in early 1979, proved to be his final resting place. After being hounded from one country to another (including the United States for surgery, occasioning the seizure of hostages in Iran) he finally returned to Egypt, where he died at the age of 60 on July 27. He was given a state funeral by Sadat, but only former President Richard Nixon and former King Constantine of Greece attended. On October 31 the late shah's son, Crown Prince Riza, then in Egypt, assumed the title of shah. Sadat's gestures toward the shah and his family benefited the United States but further isolated Sadat in the Arab world. Although Syria and Libya, very much the enemies of Egypt, were supportive of Iran in its war with Iraq, Egypt was no friendlier with Iraq or its ally Jordan.

Indeed, relations with the Arab world have meant uncertainty for Sadat. The peace treaty with Israel was greeted with dismay and anger among many Arab states; the Arab League, long headquartered in Cairo, moved to Tunis. Oman, Somalia, and the Sudan have remained, if in low

key, supportive of Egypt. In spite of their rhetoric, Saudi Arabia and probably Morocco were not pressing Egypt very hard. Libya, Syria, and Iraq denounced Egypt strongly. But all of this must be put in the context of Arab politics. The Iraqi invasion of Iran, to some degree at least, represented an attempt by Saddam Hussein, Iraq's leader, to have Iraq supplant Egypt as the leading Arab state. But Egyptian leadership was on a back burner and would eventually reassert itself.

An important part of Egypt's 1980 efforts in foreign policy hinged on its relations with Israel. Normalization between the two states proceeded, if slowly. The old economic boycott against Israel was abolished legally in February, although in practical terms it already had been abandoned. Ambassadors officially were exchanged. Commercial air communications were established. A state visit to Egypt by the Israeli president occurred in October.

But the Palestinian question remained the stumbling block. Although Israel agreed to discuss and negotiate with Egypt the future of the Palestinians, the Begin government in fact did not move from its "autonomy" formula, which would mean something short of independence for Palestinians on the West Bank or in Gaza. Moreover a deliberate Israeli move to change its capital to Jerusalem, although unimplemented, was hardly in the spirit of Camp David. By the autumn of 1980 both the Israelis and Egyptians were awaiting the outcome of the U.S. elections. Both supported President Carter to varying degrees, although some Israelis were convinced that Ronald Reagan would further their interests better than Carter. To sum up, the "talks" on the Palestinian issue resulted in very little progress in 1980.

Egyptian relations with the United States were strong and productive. Huge amounts of economic aid and substantial military aid flowed to Egypt. The American and Egyptian armies undertook several joint maneuvers and the question of American military forces being stationed on Egyptian soil was discussed sufficiently often to cause the ghosts of both David Ben-Gurion and Gamal Abdel Nasser to jump about with anxiety. In fact the rumors in the Middle East were that an Egyptian-U.S. military alliance would call the tune from Libya to the Persian Gulf. Although it was uncertain whether it ever would materialize, there was enough evidence to support a belief in its strong possibility. Sadat also expected the United States to pressure the Israelis into more concessions.

During the year a threat to Blue Nile waters came from Ethiopia. In June, Sadat responded by saying that Egypt would be forced to maintain the flow of water in the Nile. He reinforced his nation's border with Libya and warned its leader, Colonel Qaddafi, against adventurism.

See also MIDDLE EAST.

CARL LEIDEN, *University of Texas*

—————— **EGYPT · Information Highlights** ——————

Official Name: Arab Republic of Egypt.
Location: Northeastern Africa.
Area: 386,660 sq mi (1 001 449 km²).
Population (1980 est.): 42,100,000.
Chief Cities (Nov. 1976 est.): Cairo, the capital, 5,084,-463; Alexandria, 2,318,655; El Giza, 1,246,713.
Government: *Head of state,* Anwar el-Sadat, president (reelected for second six-year term, Sept. 1976). *Head of government,* Moustafa Khalil, prime minister (took office June 1979). *Legislature* (unicameral)—People's Assembly.
Monetary Unit: Pound (0.69 pound equals U.S.$1, Nov. 1980).
Manufactures (major products): Textiles, processed foods, tobacco, chemicals, fertilizer, petroleum and petroleum products.
Agriculture (major products): Cotton, rice, wheat, corn.
GNP Per Capita (1978 est., U.S.$): $400.
Foreign Trade (1979, U.S.$): Imports, $3,837,000,000; exports, $1,840,000,000.

ENERGY

The unpredictability of the world's energy system was illustrated once again in 1980. The oil shortage that existed in the summer of 1979 became an oil glut through most of 1980. At year-end, however, shortage once again threatened when war broke out between Iran and Iraq, causing a cessation of their oil exports.

Three developments caused the oil surplus that characterized 1980. They were a 65% increase in world oil prices, a worldwide economic recession, and an increase in production by non-members of the Organization of Petroleum Exporting Countries (OPEC). Overall, non-Communist countries reduced their oil consumption during 1980 by approximately 2 million barrels a day, or roughly 4%. Total U.S. energy consumption in 1980 was down by an estimated 3%. Most striking was an estimated 8% reduction in gasoline consumption. With gasoline costing as much as $1.30 a gallon, Americans were both driving less and buying more fuel-efficient automobiles.

The key domestic energy problem remained oil imports, which averaged 7 million barrels per day during the year, more than a million barrels a day less than in 1979. Imports, however, cost the United States some $20,000,000,000 more in 1980 than they did in 1979, for a total of $87,-000,000,000. These expenditures reflect an increase in the average price per barrel of imported oil from $22.00 in 1979 to $33.50 in 1980.

Two optimistic trends continued during 1980. First, significant progress was made in substituting other fuels, particularly coal, for petroleum liquids. Second, real progress was made in energy conservation. In this latter connection, there was clear evidence that the United States had reconfigured its energy-economy relationship so that economic growth could occur more rapidly than energy consumption. The proportion of that change can be seen in the fact that since 1973 Americans have learned to produce $1 of gross national product (GNP) with 10% less energy.

Domestic energy production also offered some reason for optimism. Overall domestic energy production was up by approximately 4%. Coal increased by more than 11%, and therefore represented the lion's share of the overall energy production increase. The rapid increase in price for both oil and gas resulted in an acceleration of domestic drilling to the highest level in history. One result was that domestic production of oil and gas in 1980 was maintained at roughly the same level as in 1979.

World Oil Production and Use. The rapid rise in world oil prices during the year reflected decisions made by OPEC, rather than an oil shortage. In fact, because of reduced demand, OPEC production was at a five-year low of roughly 27 million barrels per day. Even with lower OPEC deliveries, world production exceeded consumption by 2 to 3 million barrels per day for most of the year. Increased storage by consumer nations, however, absorbed the surplus. Oil in storage was at the highest level in history.

Saudi Arabia's influence on world oil policy increased with the surplus. The Saudis' stated goal was to ensure stable pricing. During 1980, OPEC prices ranged from a low of $28 per barrel for Saudi crude, to a high of $37 per barrel for crude from the so-called "price hawks." To maintain a downward pressure on prices, the Saudis continued to produce at a level of 9.5 million barrels per day or 1 million barrels per day more than their desired production level. At an OPEC meeting in September 1980, the Saudis agreed to increase their price to $30 per barrel, but refused to reduce production even though it was the stated goal of OPEC to decrease production by 10% to maintain upward pressure on prices. The Saudi position was that OPEC prices should be pegged to world inflation rates. It was the Saudi view that a pricing structure tied to inflation would provide the basis for a stable, predictable world oil pricing structure.

The Saudi commitment to stable pricing was demonstrated once again with the outbreak of war between Iraq and Iran. Prior to the war, Iraq and Iran were exporting over 3 million barrels per day, or slightly more than the amount of world oil surplus. With the cutoff of Iraqi-Iranian exports, the Saudis indicated they would increase production by nearly 1 million barrels per day and encourage other OPEC nations to follow similar policies.

The impact of the war nonetheless threatened to cause shortage and uncertainty over the longer term. Each of the warring countries directed its military action against the other's oil refining and transportation facilities. Outside experts believed it would be, at best, months and maybe years after the war ended before the two nations could return to prewar production levels. Perhaps more disturbing, the attacks on oil processing facilities broke an unwritten agreement that oil facilities would be left alone in regional conflicts.

The war made the Strait of Hormuz, the narrow entrance to the Persian Gulf, a topic of dinner-table conversation around the world. Nearly a third of the non-Communist world's oil passes through this strait. Should the strait be closed, it would sever the energy lifeline of the consuming nations. (*See also* feature article, page 28.)

Although the ever-increasing price of oil has had serious impact on the industrialized nations, the impact has been even more serious for less developed nations. The International Monetary Fund (IMF) estimated that oil price increases which occurred between 1978 and 1980 had cost oil-importing, less developed countries an additional $35,000,000,000 in 1980. Oil price increases were threatening the development plans for many less developed countries. Such countries as Brazil and India were spending well over

50% of their hard currency, money they raised from export sales, on oil. Robert McNamara, who was retiring as president of the World Bank, saw rising energy costs to the less developed nations as a major contributor to future world instability.

Two non–Middle Eastern countries, Nigeria and Mexico, stood out as examples of the hope and opportunity that come with sudden new oil wealth. Perhaps the most striking consequence of this wealth is their sudden rise in international stature. Nigeria is now the second largest supplier of oil to the United States (after Saudi Arabia). Nigerian oil exports to the United States were expected to exceed total imports from the United States by $11,000,000,000 in 1980. On a visit to the United States, Nigeria's President Alhaji Shehu Shagari was quite explicit in stating his country's intention to use its oil leverage to induce increased United States opposition to South Africa's apartheid policies.

Mexico's continued discovery of huge new oil and gas fields now gives it reserves nearly equal those of the United States. Unlike the United States, however, all estimates project continued major new discoveries for Mexico. Clearly, the new oil riches have allowed the Mexicans to deal on a more nearly equal basis with the United States. The size of Mexican oil finds was imprinted on the minds of Americans by a massive well blowout in the Bay of Campeche. The blowout from Ixtoc I continued for about ten months and ultimately oil spread several hundred miles, fouling beaches as far away as Padre Island off the coast of Texas. During the early days of the blowout, estimates of oil being lost ranged from 20,000 to 50,000 barrels per day. By comparison, a good well off the U.S. coast will produce 1,000 barrels per day.

In summary, by the end of 1980 rising oil prices were clearly driving worldwide inflation and an associated worldwide recession. The world's financial system was being severely stressed by the fact that oil exporters had an estimated income over expenditures surplus of more than $100,000,000,000. Finally, war between Iraq and Iran threatened another period of oil shortage and renewed upward pressure on prices in 1981.

Domestic Developments. The fact that domestic crude oil and natural gas production held steady during 1980 was the result of governmental actions taken in 1978–79. Specifically, both oil and natural gas prices were being gradually deregulated, and the higher prices were stimulating vigorous exploration activities. Although reliable data for the year were not available at the time this article was written, most estimates suggested the nation may have found nearly as much new oil as it produced in 1980. In the case of natural gas, more resources were found than were produced. This was at odds with most of the 1970s when production consistently outstripped discovery. The 1980 experience, how-

A tanker (left) is loaded in the Bay of Campeche, Mexico. The nation continues to discover new oil.

ever, offers only very limited reason for optimism. Most of the additions to the nation's reserves came from the discovery of small fields or because higher prices allowed the use of techniques for enhancing recovery from known fields. Because federal price regulations had for years held gas prices to a level much lower than oil, when judged on an equivalent energy basis, substantial quantities of known gas were not being produced prior to the beginning of deregulation. Most experts, therefore, believe the gas production potential of the nation is much more optimistic than is the oil potential.

The only real hope for a significant increase in domestic crude oil production rests on finding giant new fields such as the 10,000,000,000-barrel discovery on the North Slope of Alaska. In the decade since the North Slope find, no similar reserves have been proven. Opportunities for major new finds exist in three areas: the Outer Continental Shelf, Alaska, and the western Overthrust Belt which runs along a line north and south from the Utah-Wyoming border.

The major landowner in these three high-potential areas is the federal government. In a speech late in the year, a vice-president of Shell Oil Company estimated that 70% of the remaining oil and gas to be found in the United States was on federal land. The combination of an oil and gas shortage plus the potential on federal lands caused the industry to make increased federal leasing a central energy issue during 1980.

The energy industry mounted a major campaign against what it called the "lockup" of federal resources. The focal point of debate over "lockup" was a Carter administration-backed bill to set policy for the long-term use of federally owned lands in Alaska. Congress enacted an Alaska Lands Bill during its lame-duck session in 1980. Central to the debate, which had been going on since the mid-1970s, was how much of and in what way the federal lands in Alaska would be made available for energy and mineral development. Debate over the bill has represented a particularly acrimonious example of the decade-long struggle between environmental and development interests. It appeared that substantial mineral leasing and exploration would take place in Alaska during the 1980s. (*See also* ALASKA.)

Similarly, 1980 represented a major turning point in energy development on the Outer Continental Shelf (OCS) and on federal lands onshore. Secretary of the Interior Cecil Andrus issued a five-year lease schedule for the OCS which included lease sales in every high-potential basin around the United States. Further, leases were being let in ever-deeper waters out on the continental slope. In parallel, both the quantity of leases and the rate of drilling for oil and gas on onshore federal lands accelerated during 1980. If giant oil fields are to be found on federal lands, it appears they will be found during the 1980s.

Even under the most optimistic assumptions, however, no one argued that the United States could meet its liquid fuel needs from new oil discoveries. The need for more liquid fuels increased pressures for leasing more federal coal, oil shale, and tar sands resources. During 1979 the secretary of the interior had implemented a new leasing program for coal on federal lands, bringing to an end a moratorium on leasing that had lasted for more than a decade. This new program was put into effect in 1980 and was to lead to the first lease sale in January 1981.

In 1974, the federal government leased four oil shale tracts under a prototype program. The purpose of the program was to learn how best to manage the development of this new energy industry. In 1980, the first test production occurred under the prototype program. Under the pressure of the energy crisis, the secretary of the interior in 1980 mandated that four more prototype oil shale leases be let and that planning begin on a permanent leasing program.

Legislation was introduced in 1980 that would facilitate the leasing of tar sands. These new leasing initiatives were intimately linked to the passage by Congress of two major pieces of energy legislation, the windfall profits tax on oil and the establishment of a Synthetic Fuels Corporation.

The Synthetic Fuels Corporation was established for the purpose of ensuring the rapid development of a commercial synthetic fuels industry. The stated national goal is to have a production capability of 500,000 barrels per day of crude oil equivalent by 1987 and 2 million

Exxon is developing a coal liquefaction process at a plant in Baytown, TX.

Exxon Corporation

barrels per day by 1992. The second figure represents roughly 30% of today's imports.

The new corporation has the authority to commit $88,000,000,000 by 1992. This effort will focus primarily on synfuels from coal, oil shale, and tar sands. Something of the measure of the effort involved can be seen by noting that the production goals will require 40 huge plants costing approximately $2,000,000,000 each. Assuming it takes 6 years to complete a plant, one new project will have to be started every 2 or 3 months from 1981 through 1986.

Each coal synthetic plant will require a mine capable of producing from 5 to 7 million t a year. Each oil shale plant will require a mine capable of producing 25 million t per year. At present there are no mines in the United States of a size similar to those needed to feed an oil shale synfuels plant. It is this need for huge quantities of resources that is driving the accelerated federal leasing.

In addition to synfuels from coal, oil shale, and tar sands, the government initiated a separate $1,500,000,000 program to turn various forms of vegetation (biomass) into fuel. This program will probably use corn as its major source of biomass. The primary fuel produced by this biomass synfuels program will be alcohol. Expectations are that the alcohol will be mixed with gasoline to increase the quantity of gasohol used in the future.

Much of the funding for the federal synfuels program is expected to come from the windfall profits tax. This tax was the focus of a bitter debate in Congress. It was expected to raise $227,-000,000,000 during the 1980s. The tax is designed to ensure that the federal treasury will receive a substantial portion of the revenue difference between the value of presently producing wells that have regulated prices and the world price. The goal of the government policy is to raise the price of oil to consumers to create an economic incentive for them to save energy while at the same time ensuring that the oil companies do not receive all of the windfall profits coming from this change in government policy. During 1979, domestic oil prices were controlled in three categories or tiers. The lower-tier controlled price was from $5.00 to $6.71 per barrel, and the upper-tier controlled price was from $11.60 to $14.00 per barrel. Under the new tax legislation, the government takes in tax 70% of the difference between the regulated lower-tier price and the decontrolled price of roughly $35 per barrel. The tax percentage for middle-tier oil is 60%, and for the upper tier it is 30%.

One major piece of the administration's energy legislation, the proposed Energy Mobilization Board, was defeated. Under this legislation, the board would have designated 12 priority energy projects a year on which it could have cut red tape. The purpose was to ensure that government regulations did not slow down the nation's effort to respond to the energy crisis. Doubtless many of the designated projects would have been synfuels facilities. Opposition by the various energy-producing states was one element in the defeat of the Energy Mobilization Board legislation. The states opposed giving the federal government authority to bypass their regulations. Another element in the defeat was opposition by environmental protection interests who were fearful that many of the protections built into federal regulations in the 1970s would be bypassed in responding to the energy crisis.

No significant progress was made during the year in resolving the issue blocking continued development of conventional nuclear energy. The legacy of the nuclear accident at Three Mile Island continued to impede nuclear energy development. By the end of the year, the problems associated with finding a disposal site for nuclear wastes generated in cleaning up Three Mile Island had only served to underline the general problem of nuclear waste disposal. Until the disposal problem is solved, the future of nuclear fission will be at best uncertain.

At the same time that the nation continued to resist increased use of fission nuclear power plants, the Congress made a major commitment to the development of nuclear fusion as a future source of power. Late in September, with little fanfare, Congress approved a bill intended to accelerate the invention of a fusion reactor. Fusion energy uses a component of water as the fuel for a process that parallels the operation of the sun. Although fusion energy is entirely unproven as a commercial power source, its potential as an inexpensive, inexhaustible way to produce power was enough to carry the day with Congress. Under the new initiative, which may cost more than $20,000,000,000, a power-producing reactor could be available by the year 2000. Clearly, the 1980 fusion legislation reflected a striking new initiative in the nuclear area.

The U.S. commitment to solar energy as a future energy source remained strong during 1980. Congress was expected to add 10% to solar research and development for 1981, bringing those activities to about $650 million. With the exception of the program for developing synthetic fuels from biomass and solar space and water heating, however, commercial solar energy production technologies are all still long-term options.

Overall, 1980 was a year of real progress on the energy front. The United States made progress on energy conservation and it took major steps toward making new energy sources available. None of this progress, however, changes the fact that the nation will be critically dependent upon oil imports for more than the next decade. The great danger remains a major interruption of exports by OPEC. As yet no one has proposed how the nation can effectively deal with such interruptions. The 1980s, then, remain a hazardous period for the United States.

DON E. KASH, *University of Oklahoma*

ENGINEERING, CIVIL

The design and construction of bridges, canals, dams, and tunnels continued steadily in the United States and throughout the world in 1980.

BRIDGES

United States. When the Columbia River bridge opens in 1983, it will complete the I-205 bypass east of Portland, OR, and Vancouver, BC, thus easing traffic around the two cities. The river separating Oregon and Washington is now crossed by twin three-lane bridges with lift spans. The new $170-million project will consist of two pairs of twin structures separated by a 1,200-ft (366-m) stretch of embankment across Government Island. The crossing from the Oregon shore to the island is 3,140 ft (957 m). From the island to the Washington shore, the crossing is 7,460 ft (2 274 m). Each of the twin structures will carry four traffic lanes supported by prestressed concrete trapezoidal box girders. Over the channel the main span will be 600 ft (183 m) long, with a vertical clearance of 145 ft (44 m).

New bridges also are being built to connect mainland Florida with Key West, 130 mi (209 km) south. The new structures will replace 45-year-old deteriorating concrete bridges. Both the old and new crossings are two lanes wide. Built in 1912 for the railroad, the original line spanned 39 islands and included 30 mi (48 km) of bridges. The crossing was so damaged by a hurricane in 1935 that the rail line was abandoned. The state of Florida bought the property and rebuilt the crossing into a two-lane highway with 44 bridges linking the islands. One of the longest bridges over open water will be the 2.3-mi (3.7-km) Long Key Bridge, connecting Long Key and Conch Key. The concrete box girder segmental construction is expected to cost $15.3 million. Spans will be 118 ft (36 m) long, each consisting of six large segments and a smaller one over the pier. The bridge will have 103 spans and is scheduled for completion in 1981. The cost of the entire project is estimated at $175 million.

Austria. A prestressed 2,800-ft (853-m), twin-cell concrete girder bridge was completed in 1980 over the Danube River at Vienna. Started in 1978, the new structure replaces the Reichsbrücke crossing that collapsed in 1976. It consists of 10 spans varying in length from 179 to 556 ft (55 to 169 m). The bridge carries six traffic lanes on the upper deck, with a rail transit track within each of its two cells. Pedestrian and bicycle paths cantilever out from the sides.

Australia. In 1980, construction was started in Brisbane on a high-level crossing over the Brisbane River. The mile-long (1.6-km), six-lane, prestressed concrete box girder structure will have an 853-ft (260-m) main span of record length, with 180-ft (55-m) vertical clearance. The single box girder will be 40 ft (12 m) wide with cantilever wings to carry the 72-ft- (22-m-) wide deck. The bridge is scheduled for completion in 1985 at a cost of $55 million.

CANALS

Argentina. The Rio Negro Province in Argentina is being enriched by a 115-mi (185-km) canal irrigating northern Patagonia. Work on the $18-million, concrete-lined canal began in 1976 and was completed in 1980. It takes water from the Negro River at Choele, carries it to Pomona, and continues southeasterly to the south Atlantic coastal city of San Antonio Oeste. The land along the new water route is irrigated for agricultural purposes and to provide watering places for cattle.

Sudan. The 200-mi (322-km) Jonglei Canal is being built to drain the Sudd, a vast pestilential swamp in the Upper Nile area of Sudan. Egypt and Sudan are dividing the cost of the $250-million project and will share the water. Some 5,200,000,000 cu yd (4 000 000 000 m³) of water a year will be brought to northern Sudan. Originating in Lake Victoria, the Nile River spreads out over a 40,000-sq mi (103 600-km²) marshy plain near the town of Bor in southern Sudan. The canal will channel the flow of water northward to a point near Malakal, where it will join the White Nile. The additional fresh water brought to the Egyptian boundary via the Blue Nile will help provide food for Egypt and the entire Arab world. The French builders plan to open the canal in 1984.

DAMS

United States. About 22 mi (35 km) southwest of Denver, a concrete arch dam is being built on the South Platte River to supply water to the mile-high capital of Colorado. Strontia Springs Dam, a major part of the city's $180-million Foothills water supply project, will add 125 million gal (473 million L) per day to the present 495 mgd (1 874 million L per day) capacity. Scheduled for completion in 1982, the double-curved arch structure will be 290 ft (88 m) high, 630 ft (192 m) long, and 31 ft (9 m) wide at the base, tapering to 10 ft (3 m) at the crest. The dam impounds a reservoir 1.7 mi (2.7 km) long.

China. For about ten years, the People's Republic of China has been building Gezhouba Dam on the Chang Jiang (Yangtze River) to provide hydroelectric power, flood control, and aid for navigation. The concrete gravity structure, 8,400 ft (2 560 m) long and 230 ft (70 m) high, is scheduled for completion in 1985, but initial production of power is expected in 1982. This first dam on the Chang Jiang is located near Yichang, Hubei province, and will back up water for 62 mi (100 km).

Brazil. Upstream from Belem, at the mouth of the Amazon River, Tucurui Dam will provide Brazil with a major source of electric power. The concrete gravity structure lies about 185 mi (298 km) south of Belem, across the Tocantins River basin. Started in 1977, the concrete portion of the dam is 279 ft (85 m) high and nearly 1 mi (1.6 km) long, including spillway and powerhouse. It contains 6.8 million cu yd (5.2 million m^3) of concrete. With flanking rock and earth embankments, the barrier will stretch 5.5 mi (8.9 km) across the valley. The dam will form a lake extending 5 mi (8 km) upstream. The first-phase powerhouse, expected to go on stream in 1983, will have a 4,000 Mw capacity.

Ecuador. High in the Andes Mountains, about 60 mi (97 km) from Cuenca, Ecuador is taming the Paute River with the Amaluza concrete arch dam, 560 ft (171 m) high and 1,300 ft (396 m) long. The highest of its type in South America, the dam will tap the hydro potential of the river. Work on the $120-million dam started in 1977; the powerhouse is scheduled to come on stream in 1982.

TUNNELS

United States. Philadelphia is undertaking a complex subway project in the heart of its downtown business area. The 1.7 mi-(2.7 km) tunnel is a cut-and-cover operation that goes as deep as 70 ft (21 m) below ground level and will accommodate two-, three- and four-barrel tunnels with a maximum width of 125 ft (38 m). On a course parallel to Market Street, it will pass over one existing subway line and go under another. Several buildings are being underpinned, including the city hall at Broad Street. Known as the Center City Commuter Connection (CCCC), the line will link the former Penn Central suburban station with the 90-year-old Reading Railroad terminal, which has been declared an historic landmark. The line also joins Amtrak's main 30th Street station and a new rail line to the Philadelphia International Airport. The tunnel will bring 500 mi (805 km) of commuter lines into a single system. Due for completion in 1984, the CCCC will cost more than $300 million.

Work on the Fort McHenry Tunnel beneath inner Baltimore Harbor began in 1980 under a $436-million contract. This last gap in Interstate-95 in Maryland will pass under the northwest branch of the Patapsco River. A pair of four-lane, 8,800-ft (2 682-m) tunnels, of which 5,-400 ft (1 646 m) are subaqueous, will carry eight lanes of traffic. It will be the widest sunken tube tunnel in the United States. Steel segments will be 350 ft (107 m) long, 82.5 ft (25 m) wide, and 42 ft (13 m) high. With its concrete lining, each segment weighs 35,000 T (31 752 t). The tunnel will be part of an eight-mi (13-km) bypass south of Baltimore. The estimated $1,000,000,000 project is scheduled for completion in 1985.

Germany. West Berlin is adding a 2-mi (3.2-km) section of subway to extend a double-track tunnel from Olympic Station to Spandau, a western suburb. The $245 million improvement includes a 290-ft (88-m) sunken tube section 70 ft (21 m) below the level of the Havel River. To cope with the high water table and poor soil, the subway has two ft- (1.6 m-) thick reinforced concrete floor, walls, and roof. When the section opens in 1984, West Berlin will have more than 60 mi (97 km) of subway.

WILLIAM H. QUIRK
Construction Consultant

ENVIRONMENT

In 1980, the world's environmental situation and prospects for the next 20 years were graphically described in *Global 2000,* a report prepared by the U.S. State Department and the president's Council on Environmental Quality. As expected, the report predicted continued environmental deterioration unless international conservation efforts can be stepped up dramatically. Appropriately, another document released during the year outlined ways of dealing with global environmental problems: the *World Conservation Strategy,* prepared by the International Union for Conservation of Nature and Natural Resources (IUCN), the United Nations Environment Programme (UNEP), and the World Wildlife Fund (WWF). In the United States, 1980 brought new concern about toxic substances in the environment and disposal of hazardous wastes, and a strong commitment to protect fragile coastal areas and wetlands.

GLOBAL 2000

The *Global 2000* report was the outcome of President Jimmy Carter's May 23, 1977, Environmental Message to Congress, in which he called for an interagency study of the "probable changes in the world's population, natural resources, and environment through the end of the century." The resulting three-volume study was released July 24, 1980. "If present trends continue," the report begins, "the world in 2000 will be more crowded, more polluted, less stable ecologically and more vulnerable to disruption than the world we live in now. . . . Barring revolutionary advances in technology, life for most people on earth will be more precarious in 2000 than it is now—unless the nations of the world act decisively to alter current trends."

Population. The report projects a world population increase of more than 50%, reaching a total of more than 6,000,000,000 by 2000, as compared with 4,000,000,000 in 1975.

Food. Food production could increase by 90% over 1970 levels, the report says, but the poorer nations would receive a disproportionately small share of the benefits and consequently would face severe famine.

Natural Resources. If present trends continue, the report projects massive depletion of forests, traditional fisheries, and other renewable resources. Fossil fuels would become scarce before satisfactory alternatives could be developed, and the demand for water would at least double in nearly half the countries in the world.

Species Extinction. Because of pollution, development, and deforestation, the report projects a reduction in genetic diversity. The result could be the extinction of one fifth of all the world's plant and animal species.

The Challenge. "It is important to understand that the conditions the report projects are by no means inevitable," said President Carter when *Global 2000* was released. "In fact, its projections can and should be timely warnings which will alert the nations of the world to the need for vigorous, determined action, at both the national and international levels." The president named Gus Speth, chairman of the Council on Environmental Quality, to head a new Task Force on Global Resources and Environment. The mission of this cabinet-level task force was to make recommendations for action on the most pressing environmental problems.

Mixed Reactions. Some critics claimed that in some areas, such as energy, the report used outdated figures to make its projections. Others questioned apparent contradictions, such as the projection of tremendous increases in development and food production, along with losses in cropland due to desertification and soil erosion. "The report is correct in emphasizing that the world faces decades of difficulties and some of its sections are well done," said Philip H. Abelson, editor of *Science,* a publication of the American Association for the Advancement of Science. "But outdated materials and inaccuracies detract from its value."

WORLD CONSERVATION STRATEGY

The *World Conservation Strategy,* issued by IUCN, UNEP, and WWF, is a framework for coordinated global, regional, and national action by governments, international organizations, and private interests for well-managed economic development and conservation. The strategy calls for the design and enforcement of sound conservation laws, ecologically safe development, environmental planning, and increased education in the field of conservation management. The document places special emphasis on the "Global Commons": the open ocean, the atmosphere, and Antarctica, areas in which international cooperation is urgently needed to ensure ecological well-being. UN Secretary General Kurt Waldheim said that the strategy "has resulted in an unprecedented degree of agreement on what should be done to ensure the proper management and optimal use of the world's living resources. . . ."

OTHER WORLD DEVELOPMENTS

Law of the Sea. After seven years of negotiating, 150 nations appeared close to agreeing on a comprehensive law of the sea. At a July meeting in Geneva, delegates tentatively agreed to protocols governing navigation and fishing in international waters. Still to be resolved were differences over seabed mining. Pressure for an early signing was intensified when both houses of the U.S. Congress agreed to allow American companies to begin exploring the seabed and to begin mining operations by 1988.

Whales. A U.S.-backed move to ban commercial harvests of whales, which have become imperiled, was defeated at the July 1980 meeting of the International Whaling Commission in Brighton, England. But the commission did approve a 14,500 great whale quota for the 1980–81 season—a 9.2% decrease from 1979–80. The commission also agreed to a total ban on the taking of killer whales by factory ships. In addition, the United States was allowed major responsibility for administering the subsistence hunting of bowhead whales by Eskimos. The decisions reached in 1980, said U.S. Whaling Commissioner Richard A. Frank, "follow a pattern

Wide World

The tenth anniversary of Earth Day was celebrated April 23. A massive outdoor street fair on the Avenue of the Americas marked the occasion in New York City.

that will make it uneconomical for whaling nations to continue their operations."

Acid Rain. In August, the United States and Canada agreed to establish an international task force to study the impact of airborne sulfur and nitrogen oxides which fall to earth as "acid rain." The fallout, from industrial emissions, causes lakes to become too acid to support fishlife. In June 1981, the two countries are scheduled to begin negotiating a formal plan of action to deal with the problem.

U.S. DEVELOPMENTS

Environmental constraints on economic development and toxic pollutants in groundwater were major issues in 1980, and the U.S. government began a crackdown on the illegal wildlife trade.

Hazards to Health. Despite progress in cleaning up polluted air and water, it became more apparent than ever that Americans are being exposed to increasing amounts of hazardous substances. A Congressional report released in September listed 2,100 unlined chemical depositories located above usable groundwater and noted 300 incidents in which subsurface water supplies in the United States had been contaminated. (*See* feature article, page 47.)

Nuclear Energy. During the week of March 24–30, around the country thousands of opponents of nuclear power held marches and demonstrations to mark the first anniversary of the Three Mile Island incident near Harrisburg, PA. On September 23, voters in Maine rejected a ballot measure that would have shut down a 7½-year-old nuclear power plant and banned construction of others. In November, less restrictive antinuclear initiatives appeared on the ballots of several other states, including Montana, South Dakota, and Washington.

The Year of the Coast. A coalition of environmental groups called the Coast Alliance designated 1980 as "The Year of the Coast." The purpose was to generate public and governmental interest in protecting fragile coastline and wetlands. The effort was launched in the wake of reports that more than 40% of the wetlands along the coastline of the lower 48 states have been destroyed, and that within a decade, more than 75% of the U.S. population may be living in the coastal belt. The U.S. Congress passed the Coastal Zone Management Improvement Act, which created incentives for the individual states to develop their own coastal protection plans.

Resource Priorities. Because of the United States' increased energy and economic needs, conflicts increased over priorities in the use of natural resources. In May, the Public Service Company of Colorado and the Riverside Irrigation District sued the U.S. Army Corps of Engineers in a Colorado federal court after the corps denied them a condition-free permit to build a dam and reservoir on Wildcat Creek, a tributary of the South Platte River. The corps had refused the permit after being advised by the U.S. Fish and Wildlife Service that the dam could have adverse effects on the habitat of the endangered whooping crane. In June, the U.S. Supreme Court handed down a landmark decision involving rights to federally subsidized irrigation water in California's Imperial Valley. In its decision, the court said that farms of any size could qualify for the subsidized water. Previously there had been a 160-acre (65-ha) maximum limit.

Park Problems. Threats to the natural and cultural resources of the 326-unit National Park System were described in the U.S. National Park Service's 1980 "State of the Parks" message to Congress. The report identified seven major "threat categories": aesthetic degradation, air pollution, physical removal of resources, exotic encroachment (of feral hogs and burros, unnatural weather and fires, and seismic blasting), physical impact of visitors, water pollution and quantity changes, and such park operations as trails and visitor facilities. More than half of the 4,000 examples given in the report came from sources external to the parks: industrial and commercial development projects on adjacent lands, air pollution, and urban encroachment. The major threats inside the parks were attributed to expanded visitor use, which went from 135 million visits in 1960 to 282 million in 1979.

Wildlife. In August, a government crackdown on the smuggling of endangered species resulted in the largest court case of its kind in history. A federal grand jury in Miami indicted four men and six corporations for illegally importing into the United States 45 T (41 t) of meat from endangered sea turtles. Officials estimated that about 7,500 endangered Pacific (olive) Ridley sea turtles were slaughtered in Mexico to obtain the meat, which was seized at a Miami airport. U.S. Fish and Wildlife officials estimate that illegal wildlife trade conducted by "well-organized, large-scale operators" amounts to as much as $100 million a year.

Wildlife restoration efforts continued in 1980 with mixed results. In March, a large-scale investigation of declining populations of Atlantic Coast striped bass was begun. State and federal agencies and private researchers hope to determine the cause of the decline and to make recommendations for efforts to reverse the trend. There was some progress toward creating a western flock of whooping cranes using eggs hatched on the nests of greater sandhill cranes, a related species. Eleven of 15 whoopers hatched in this fashion returned to summering grounds in the Rocky Mountains. In California, an effort to save the California condor from extinction was called off. The $1.25 million plan involved live-trapping the birds and then breeding them in captivity. However, the plan was halted when one condor died while researchers were handling it.

See also Zoology.

BILL VOGT, *"National Wildlife" and "International Wildlife" Magazines*

ETHIOPIA

In 1980 Ethiopia became embroiled in the politics of the Horn of Africa, successfully sought foreign aid, and continued its war against domestic insurgents.

Ethiopia and the Horn of Africa. The United States in 1980 reacted to the Soviet naval presence in the Indian Ocean and to the 1979 Soviet invasion of Afghanistan. Agreements were signed between the United States and Oman and Kenya in April 1980, and with Somalia on August 21, permitting the United States access to air and naval bases. In mid-July the U.S. task force in the Indian Ocean was increased to 24; the Soviet fleet there numbered 25. The Soviets established an anchorage in the Dahlak Islands in the Red Sea and also were reported to be seeking a base in the Seychelles, a group of islands in the Indian Ocean. Beginning in February 1980, Ethiopia warned the United States that its agreements and its naval presence could "lead to an Ethiopian invasion" of Somalia. On August 27 Somalia claimed it had been attacked by Ethiopian jets. Additional claims were made in late September. Ethiopia denied the attacks.

Civil War. In September Ethiopia launched another major offensive against guerrillas in Tigre and Eritrea provinces. Some 40,000 Ethiopian troops together with Cuban and Soviet advisers were said to be involved. Earlier, in April, Sudan had closed its borders to Eritrean guerrillas. The secessionist forces in Eritrea, reeling from continuous Ethiopian successes, stated in April that they were prepared to enter into negotiations with Ethiopia over the issue of self-determination.

Refugees. The United Nations maintained that 1.2 million Ethiopians had fled the Ogaden and were living in Somalia, while the Sudan was harboring 150,000 refugees who had fled from Eritrea. Drought and famine throughout Ethiopia added to the migration that was primarily caused by continuous warfare.

Diplomatic Activity. On January 14, Ethiopia voted against the UN General Assembly resolution calling for the removal of foreign troops from Afghanistan. The resolution passed. The European Common Market agreed to extend $250 million in economic aid to Ethiopia to 1985, while West Germany and Sweden agreed to undisclosed commitments of aid. In 1980 the United States provided $30 million in humanitarian aid, and the Soviet bloc granted $100 million in nonmilitary aid.

Human Rights. The U.S. State Department's fourth annual report on human rights released in February indicated that summary executions, arbitrary arrests, and arrests for political reasons were continuing in Ethiopia.

Domestic Politics. In February two members of the ruling military council, the Dergue, were purged for corruption, and a third was charged with "fronting for the Central Intelligence Agency (CIA)." In July four military officers were ordered executed after being accused of conspiring with the CIA to overthrow the Ethiopian government. In June, the first congress of the Commission for Organizing the Party of the Working People of Ethiopia (COPWE) met to begin the process of creating a vanguard political party for Ethiopia.

Sports. At the 1980 Summer Olympics Miruts Yifter, an Ethiopian runner, won the gold medal in the 5,000- and 10,000-meter races.

PETER SCHWAB
State University of New York at Purchase

Miruts Yifter (191) brings glory to Ethiopia as he wins the 5,000- and 10,000-meter Olympic races.
Tony Duffy, Duomo

--- **ETHIOPIA · Information Highlights** ---

Official Name: Ethiopia.
Location: Eastern Africa.
Area: 471,778 sq mi (1 221 905 km²).
Population (1980 est.): 32,600,000.
Chief Cities (1977 est.): Addis Ababa, the capital, 1,104,500; Asmara, 352,700.
Government: *Head of state and government,* Mengistu Haile Mariam, chairman of the Provisional Military Administrative Committee (took office Feb. 1977).
Monetary Unit: Birr (2.07 birrs equal U.S.$1, July 1980).
Manufactures (major products): Processed foods, textiles, cement, building materials, hydroelectric power.
Agriculture (major products): Cereals, coffee, pulses, oilseeds, hides, skins, meat.
GNP (1979 est., U.S.$): $3,000,000,000.
Foreign Trade (1979 est., U.S.$): *Imports,* $576,000,000; *exports,* $423,000,000.

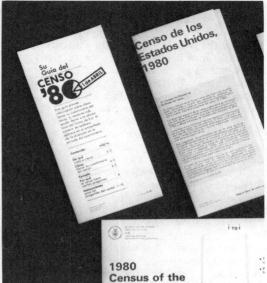

Photos U.S. Bureau of the Census

To assist in the counting of members of minority groups, a problem during the 1980 U.S. census year, census forms were printed in Spanish and English.

ETHNIC GROUPS

In 1980, America's ethnic minorities became the focus of a prolonged controversy regarding the United States census. The problem was basic—and extremely complicated: just how many members of minority groups are there? The answer would affect their political representation and the funds and services they would receive from the government.

The presidential and congressional elections also proved to be a critical juncture for minorities as conservative Ronald Reagan led the Republican Party to control of the U.S. Senate for the first time since 1954. As a result, many of the liberal social programs engineered by the Democrats seemed likely to be de-emphasized or eliminated. Minorities feared, rightly or not, that much of the progress they had made with the help of those programs might be curtailed.

The year also brought some completely unforeseen ethnic upheavals. In the spring, a flood of Cuban refugees swelled the already growing number of Hispanics in the United States, strained services and emotions in several localities, and threatened temporarily to undermine U.S. refugee policy. Only weeks later, blacks rioted in Miami in the worst urban disorders in a dozen years, suggesting a renewal of the kind of despair and frustration that most Americans considered a thing of the past.

The Census. The U.S. government went to great lengths to persuade U.S. residents to comply with the April 1 census, a count-off on which a host of federal formulas would be based until 1990. But, for perhaps the first time in the na-

tion's history, there was strident debate over how the census should deal with illegal aliens, untold millions of whom had stolen into the country since 1970. Most of the illegals were Hispanic, and Hispanic leaders insisted they should be counted like everyone else. The Constitution, they argued, made no provision for legal status in requiring that a count be made of everyone in the country. Since most of the illegal aliens were here to stay, advocates said, the localities in which they lived should get their full share of government largess.

Opponents contended that counting illegals would unfairly skew legislative apportionment on the basis of persons who were not citizens and could not even vote. A group called the Federation for American Immigration Reform, joined by 28 members of the U.S. Congress, sued to have illegal aliens omitted from the census. The suit was dismissed.

Hispanic groups then made concerted appeals of their own to make sure illegal aliens, who normally avoid dealings with the government, stood up to be counted. The Census Bureau hired Spanish-speaking census takers so that Hispanics, both citizens and aliens, might be more likely to respond. The bureau also upgraded its efforts to reach blacks in big-city ghettos, who reportedly were missed in significant numbers in 1970, when the census was last taken. But according to some, that was not enough. Hispanics in Chicago sued the government, claiming that they had not been accurately counted. Several large cities, including New York, Detroit, Philadelphia, and Baltimore, also sued, charging that an undercount of minorities there would cause the cities to lose Congressional representatives and federal aid. In September, a federal judge ruling in the Detroit case declared the census void, pending an adjustment in the count of blacks and Hispanics. Census officials balked at the decision, but U.S. Supreme Court Justice Potter Stewart temporarily suspended the lower court ruling December 24, allowing the bureau to certify its results.

The Election. In 1976, black voters overwhelmingly supported Jimmy Carter for president, and according to some analyses contributed his margin of victory in a very close election. In 1980, blacks were somewhat less enthusiastic in their support of incumbent Carter, but still they cast their lot with him in more nearly solid numbers than did any other significant voting bloc. The reason for that die-hard loyalty was clear: Ronald Reagan had long espoused positions that were anathema to blacks and other minorities. For his part, Reagan conscientiously sought black support during the campaign. He addressed the National Urban League's annual conference, visited New York's South Bronx, and won the endorsement of the Rev. Ralph Abernathy, onetime aid to Martin Luther King, Jr.

Yet by mid-November some blacks' fears seemed grounded in reality. The lame-duck Congress nearly voted to bar the Justice Department from pursuing school-desegregation cases if that action might result in court-ordered busing. Reagan, saying that he was "heart and soul" in favor of civil rights, endorsed the busing ban. Although busing was not a uniformly favored desegregation remedy among blacks, the congressional vote struck many as a signal of a marked conservative shift in government. Since Reagan, as well as many new members of Congress, had won election by promising to limit government spending, minorities feared that the new administration would seek a reduction in several social programs such as food stamps and Medicaid on which they often must depend.

Cuban Refugees. Early in April, Fidel Castro removed the Cuban guard from the Peruvian embassy in Havana, thereby allowing disenchanted Cuban citizens to seek asylum there. That action, intended to rid the country of a few malcontents, quickly backfired as 10,000 Cubans crowded into the embassy. Seeking to turn an embarrassment into an advantage, Castro then announced that anyone who wanted to leave Cuba could. Within days, Cuban refugees who had already settled in the United States began flocking to Key West, FL, where they hired boats bound for Cuba to fetch long-separated relatives.

The ragtag sealift, soon dubbed the "freedom flotilla," was an unprecedented event that caused problems for the U.S. government from the start. The Carter administration declared the operation illegal, but it continued to grow daily. Within a few weeks, Carter said that the United States would welcome the Cuban newcomers

with "open hearts and open arms," and in fact government agencies were already heavily involved in processing procedures. But as the numbers swelled to tens of thousands with no end in sight, the administration again seemed to switch signals, announcing that boats bringing the Cubans into the United States would be seized and that the Cubans themselves would be considered illegal aliens, not refugees. One problem was that just weeks before the sealift began, a new refugee law went into effect. Prompted largely by the influx of Indochinese refugees in 1979, it set new limits and processes for admitting people into the United States. The unexpected arrival of the Cuban "boat people" threatened to make a shambles of that policy. Finally, the government reached a compromise that allowed the Cubans to remain in the country as parolees for a period of time, after which they could apply for American citizenship.

But in the interim, the Cuban tide created a slew of difficulties. Large numbers settled in Miami, where they had relatives among the 500,000 earlier immigrants who had transformed that once-fading resort into a center of Latin American commerce and tourism. The newcomers, though, were less skilled and educated than their middle-class predecessors and soon strained local services and provoked resentment from Anglos.

Those who did not settle in Miami were herded into four hastily set-up refugee camps at military bases in Florida, Arkansas, Pennsylvania, and Wisconsin. With the massive help of volunteer agencies, more than 110,000 of the Cubans were resettled with friends and sponsors around the country. But months after the sealift began, more than 10,000 were still languishing in the camps, many of them single young men, juveniles, or "undesirables" like convicts and mental patients whom Castro had forced to leave during the mass exodus. By the end of the year, all the remaining refugees had been consolidated in one camp at Fort Chaffee, AR. Resettlement officials acknowledged that as many as 5,000 could become indefinite wards of the government.

Riots. Miami bore the brunt of another crisis as blacks there engaged in a three-day riot in May that was a throwback to the urban conflagrations of the 1960s. The violence came immediately after an all-white jury acquitted four white Miami-area policemen charged with the 1979 beating death of black insurance salesman Arthur McDuffie. That surprising verdict came after a long series of alleged police abuses of blacks in Miami, aggravating frustration over high black unemployment in a booming Miami economy and enforcing a feeling that recent Cuban immigrants were given favorable treatment. The riot, concentrated in the Liberty City neighborhood, left 18 people dead and 400 injured and resulted in tens of millions of dollars in property damage.

During the summer, a routine arrest in Liberty City sparked renewed violence, with armed black youths holding policemen at bay for hours. Tampa and Orlando, FL, were also the scenes of racial unrest, and in Chattanooga, TN, blacks rioted for three nights after two Ku Klux Klansmen were acquitted of shooting four black women.

The Jordan Shooting. In the aftermath of the first Miami riot, National Urban League president Vernon Jordan (*See also* BIOGRAPHY), perhaps the country's foremost civil rights spokesman, in a May 28 address to the Urban League chapter of Fort Wayne, IN, denounced the violence and warned America to take heed of black frustration. Hours later, Jordan himself was the victim of violence. Returning to his motel after midnight, Jordan was gunned down by an unseen assailant. Several officials, including President Carter and later FBI director William Webster, speculated that the attack was a racial assassination attempt. Tensions in Fort Wayne and around the United States ran high for several days before calm prevailed. Jordan eventually recovered, but his attacker remained at large.

Later in the year, police arrested an admitted white racist for the murder of two black men in Salt Lake City, UT. Officials in other cities had speculated that that crime might have been linked to a series of other sniper killings of blacks around the country—a pattern which, along with unsolved killings in Buffalo, NY, and Atlanta, GA, caused considerable trepidation in black communities. The FBI had also sought the Salt Lake City suspect for questioning in connection with the Jordan case.

Native Americans. Throughout the year, the St. Regis Mohawk reservation in upstate New York was the scene of an unusual siege that reflected basic tensions within a people whose status in the United States has always been ambiguous at best. One faction of Mohawks, who call themselves traditionalists, opposed the government-recognized tribal leadership and favored a return to an agriculture-based economy and autonomy from the U.S. government. In 1979, an armed group of traditionalists occupied a corner of the St. Regis reservation and held it for more than a year despite attempts by tribal authorities to vanquish them. At one point, in June, the long stalemate produced an armed confrontation, with the competing factions facing each other across a highway that runs through the reservation. State police officers moved in to reimpose a tenuous peace, but the basic conflict remained unresolved.

That internal dispute also prevented final approval of a land-claims settlement that was negotiated among Mohawk tribal officials, the state of New York, and the U.S. Department of the Interior. Under the proposed settlement, the Mohawks would relinquish claims on New York State territory in exchange for an allotment of

Gary Guisinger, "The New York Times"

In 1980 the U.S. Congress and the state of Maine ratified a pact with the Passamaquoddy Indians. Timber remains the tribe's sole source of income.

9,750 acres (3 949 ha) and $6 million in federal funds.

Two other long-standing Native American land claims were settled. The U.S. Supreme Court ruled that the government must pay the Sioux $17.5 million plus $105 million in interest (5% annually since 1877) for the seizure of South Dakota's Black Hills. The area, sacred to the Sioux, had been deeded to them in the 1868 Treaty of Fort Laramie, but when gold was discovered there the government had reclaimed the territory for $6 million in subsistence payments. The state of Maine and the U.S. Congress also ratified the previously negotiated settlement with the Passamaquoddy, Maliseet, and Penobscot Indians, in which the tribes agreed to surrender their claim to nearly two thirds of the state in return for a $27-million federal trust and $54.5 million with which to buy 300,000 acres (121 500 ha) of forest land.

Affirmative Action. Following the path marked by the Bakke and Weber cases, the Supreme Court made another ruling in favor of affirmative action devices that grant preferential treatment to minorities to compensate for past discrimination. In *Fullilove v. Klutznick,* the court upheld a congressional decision to set aside 10% in public works construction contracts for minority-owned companies.

DENNIS A. WILLIAMS, *"Newsweek"*

EUROPE

For Europeans, 1980 was yet another year of gloom. In Western Europe, high oil prices—driven even higher by the cessation of supplies from warring Iran and Iraq—led to increases in inflation and unemployment. Economic difficulties in turn caused bitter social and political unrest. In Eastern Europe, discontent with economic conditions resulted in massive strikes by Polish workers for better pay and the right to organize independent trade unions. The disquiet in Western Europe was further increased by a sense of insecurity relating to both external and internal affairs. The power of the Communist military alliance appeared to be increasing in relation to that of the North Atlantic Treaty Organization (NATO), giving the Soviet Union the confidence to ignore condemnation by the Western allies and many Third World countries of its military intervention in Afghanistan. Internally, acts of violence by extreme leftists, regional autonomists, and political assassins were augmented by a resurgence of terrorism from the extreme right.

Continuing Recession. Rises in the price of oil remained the primary cause of European inflation. In June, the Organization of Petroleum Exporting Countries (OPEC) set the average price of one barrel at $32—almost double that of the previous year—and several of its members planned to limit production. These actions seriously threatened the balance of payments of all European countries, and determined efforts were made to reduce dependence on oil. All European nations raised gasoline prices, and many encouraged a return to the use of coal. France led the way in expansion of nuclear plants, which were expected to produce 70% of that country's electricity by the year 1990. Even ecologically-minded Sweden in a nationwide referendum endorsed the construction of nuclear reactors. Energy conservation was one of the main topics of discussion at an economic summit meeting held in Venice in June. U.S. President Jimmy Carter and the heads of the six leading non-Communist industrial powers (Canada, Japan, Britain, France, Italy, and West Germany) agreed to double coal production by 1990 and to increase nuclear energy supplies. They also promised to reduce inflation by cutting government spending and avoiding protectionism. At a time when economic recession was causing a decline in U.S. oil consumption, and world oil production was running 2.5 million barrels a day above consumption, these measures helped preserve a glut in supply. It was a temporary respite. The outbreak of war between Iran and Iraq in mid-September renewed the threat of oil shortages. Both nations suspended exports. The cutting off of Iran's small exports affected only Spain and Rumania among the European powers, but the loss of Iraq's exports—3.2 million barrels a day, representing 11% of OPEC

production—was more serious. France, the principal European importer, was especially hard hit. Even more unsettling, however, was the prospect that the war would interrupt European supplies from Saudi Arabia and other Persian Gulf countries. Industrial production would be seriously affected even in such prospering nations as West Germany, which had an inflation rate of only 5% and an unemployment figure of about one million. In the economically weaker countries, such as Great Britain (more than 15% inflation and 2 million unemployed), the consequences would be disastrous.

Throughout Western Europe, the difficult economic conditions provoked political unrest. In Britain, where Conservative Prime Minister Margaret Thatcher had been elected in 1979 on a platform of reduced state intervention and tight monetary controls, government programs were failing. As hundreds of companies collapsed into bankruptcy, only infighting among factions of the Labour party prevented a massive shift of support away from the Conservative government. In Italy, where inflation reached 22%, unemployment climbed to almost 8%, and labor strikes halted many services, the seven-month-old government of Christian Democrat Prime Minister Francesco Cossiga was overthrown in March by its own Socialist allies. Cossiga's reaction, however, was to reform his center-left government without Communist support, ending an experiment in Communist-Christian Democratic collaboration that began in 1976. The new three-party coalition, in turn, resigned in September. Discontent in Portugal, where one quarter of the work force was unemployed, further polarized that country. In national elections in December 1979, the Communist party grew at the expense of the Socialists, who were blamed for the economic chaos; but a center-right coalition gained a slight majority on a platform of reduced agricultural collectivization and more limited nationalization of industry. The greatest chaos, however, occurred in Turkey, where some 5,000 persons had been killed by acts of terrorism in the previous two years and where the two perennial rivals for power, Prime Minister Süleyman Demirel of the Republican People's Party and opposition leader Bülent Ecevit of the Justice Party, seemed equally incapable of handling the country's problems. In September, the army, headed by Gen. Kenan Evren, seized control of the government, arrested the leading politicians as well as thousands of suspected terrorists, and set up a military junta to restore order and economic progress. West Germany, with the lowest inflation and unemployment rates in the West, was the principal exception to the pattern of political turmoil. In a hard-fought election campaign, Social Democratic Chancellor Helmut Schmidt was returned to power in October with an increased majority over the Christian-Democratic challengers. As in Portugal, the real gainer in the West German election was the moderate

Seeking to avoid a break with the Soviet Union over its continued military presence in Afghanistan, French President Valéry Giscard d'Estaing (second from right) *met with Soviet President Leonid Brezhnev* (seated second from left) *for five hours of secret talks May 10 near Warsaw, Poland.*

Alain Mignan, Liaison

right, the Free Democratic Party. The success of the moderate right in those two countries suggested a revival of business-oriented parties in Western Europe.

Economic and Political Discontent in Eastern Europe. Eastern Europe first felt the impact of the oil crisis in 1975, when the Soviet Union, which supplied 80% of that area's oil, raised to the world level its export prices on raw materials. Other factors worsening the crisis were poor grain harvests in the Soviet Union in 1979 and 1980, an excessive burden of debts to Western countries, and a continuing decline in labor productivity. In 1979–80, almost every East European country failed to achieve the goals of its five-year plan, and increases in official prices, especially for foodstuffs, were greater even than inflation in the West. Although there were large-scale strikes in Rumania and occasional work stoppages in East Germany, it was only in Poland, the least repressive of the East European states, that worker actions forced changes in government policy. In July, a sharp rise in meat prices prompted strikes at the Gdansk shipyards which, by September, spread to more than 500,-000 workers. With the economy paralyzed, the government capitulated and promised not only higher pay and better food supplies but the right to organize independent trade unions. First Secretary of the Communist party Edward Gierek was swept from power and replaced by a reputed hard-liner, Stanislaw Kania. At year's end, it was uncertain whether the new government would honor all aspects of its agreement.

Growing Tension Between the Blocs. The Soviet Union's reluctance to intervene in the Polish crisis was due in part to the extent of its military commitment in Afghanistan. Since December 1979, it had maintained a force of almost 100,000 to suppress resistance to its imposition of a puppet Communist government. The embarrassment of the U.S.-led boycott of the Olympic Games in Moscow failed to influence Soviet policy in Afghanistan. Many European observers attributed its rigidity to the growing disparity in strength between the NATO forces and those of the Communist Warsaw Pact powers. With the SS-20 Missile and the Backfire Bomber, the Soviet Union possessed intermediate-range weapons directly threatening to Western Europe. In reaction to the threat, the West European powers agreed to the installation of American Pershing II mobile missiles and the ground-launched Cruise Missile. In conventional forces, however, NATO lagged behind the Warsaw Pact powers; it had 16,000 fewer tanks, 2,600 fewer tactical aircraft, and 140,000 fewer ground troops.

The tension between the blocs was apparent at the 35-nation East-West conference on human rights and cooperation in Europe, which opened in Madrid on November 11. There was an immediate deadlock on an overall agenda, and differences over the 1975 Helsinki accords, Afghanistan, and human rights created pessimism that any meaningful agreements would be reached.

Terrorism. Assassinations of former political leaders grew more numerous, especially in Paris, where twelve Mideastern political refugees were assassinated in 1979–80. The Irish Republican Army (IRA) continued its terrorist campaign for the unification of Ireland, murdering more than 60 people. The extreme left remained active in Italy, where two organizations, the Red Brigade and the First Line, competed in their attacks on leading officials. Yet it was the resurgence of the extreme right throughout Europe that most shocked the public. A bomb explosion at the Great Synagogue in Paris killed four people; in Munich, 13 persons were killed at an Oktoberfest celebration; and, in the worst incident of all, a bomb placed in a Bologna railroad station left 81 persons dead and 160 others injured. The indiscriminate carnage provoked great public anger, but little prospect of a reduction of politically-motivated violence could be seen.

See also individual country articles.

F. ROY WILLIS
University of California, Davis

UPI

The braid-trimmed jacket, jabot-trimmed blouse, and velvet skirt exemplified the Hapsburg look.

FASHION

Ruffles and flourishes, Hapsburg splendor and Victorian innocence, "preppy" Eastern Establishment classics, the Indian look versus the Cowboy look, tropical flora and fauna, pants, sweaters, shoulder and hip focus, rising hemlines and lowering heels—these were the major elements of fashion in 1980. Designers began the year in a traditional mood. Prep school classics such as kilts, shetland sweaters, button-down shirts worn with blazers, penny loafers, and patterned knee socks were the backbone of their collections. However, as the year progressed designers shifted from these conservative stylings to indulge themselves in glamour and fantasy. Manufacturers and retailers, looking for a stimulus to excite a reluctant, recession-conscious consumer, encouraged the change. While still stressing investment fashion, newness and change were heavily promoted.

The Silhouette. Overall, the silhouette was eased and fuller. In coats and dresses the fitted reefer and body conscious chemise of 1979 were replaced by wider tent or smock shapes. The skirts of 1980 were flared, gathered, pleated, and full or half circles; jackets were square and boxy or cocoon-like blousons. The shoulder was wider and heightened with padding, sleeve tucks, gathers, or ruffles. To balance the shoulder, the hip became a focal point and was accentuated by dropped waistlines, hip ties, bands, or yokes. Peplums on dresses, coats, tunics, and jackets also appeared.

Major Fashion Features. The ruffle was the single most omnipresent detail in fashion. Ruffles in every width and fabric appeared on virtually every item of apparel. Pinafore ruffles replaced or accompanied sleeves on sweaters, blouses, and dresses. Tiers of ruffles fell from the lowered waistlines of dresses, and both fur and cloth coats featured flounced hems or capelets of ruffles. Narrow ruffled collars and lapel edges adorned suit jackets, and blouses were lavished with frills, ruffs, and jabots. Ruffled trims ran up the legs of pants or across shoulders and down sleeves like the dorsal fin of some prehistoric animal. They even appeared on handbags and gloves, and as shoe trimmings.

While the ruffle was the fashion detail of 1980, the most celebrated trend was toward pants. In every shape, length, and width, pants eclipsed skirts in major American and European collections. From chino camp shorts and madras bermudas to linen and gauze bloomers and jersey pantaloons, the variety of styles in pants was overwhelming. Conservative looks included safari shorts, man-tailored trousers, and culottes; more adventurous versions were knickers, jodhpurs, zouaves, clam diggers, capris, and harem pants. All of the styles could be found in a variety of fabrics for day and evening wear.

Designer jeans, an important trend in previous years, had evolved into celebrity jeans, with socialites, models, sports figures, hair dressers, and country/western singers lending their names and collecting royalties in a rapidly growing, highly competitive market area. Jumpsuits, an offshoot of the pants emphasis, were a heavily promoted junior fashion item.

Although Western wear was still popular, and boutiques featuring ten gallon hats, fancy boots, and rodeo wear were springing up in major American and European cities, it was more "in" to be Indian in 1980. The beaded, soft glove-leather moccasin replaced the running shoe on fashionable feet in Paris and New York. Feathers adorned jewelry and hair ornaments. Other popular accessory items included liquid silver and bead necklaces, kachina doll pendants, braided lariats, tomahawk and tribal motif pins, and beaded belts. Bags trimmed with fringe and saddle stitchery, shoes, boots, gloves, squaw skirts, deerskin jackets, and Navaho skirts were seen on city streets.

In contrast to 1979's intense colors, 1980's fashion palette was muted. Clear but soft floral-tinted pastels and deep jewel tones were customary. However, the most important colors by far were black and white, used singly or together in checks, stripes, plaids, and prints. Black and white were also the basis for two romantic trends—Victorian innocence and Hapsburg elegance. Virginal white organdy and lawn and batiste type fabrics—detailed with smocking, tucks,

embroidery, and lace—created summer's garden party dresses. In suits, coats, and evening separates, rich black velvets, meltons, and brocades were encrusted with braid, beads, passementerie, frogs, and tassels to duplicate the splendors of Austro-Hungarian elegance. The return of the "little black dress," in crepe or satin for evening, and the concept of "winter white," in fall dresses of jersey and sweater knits of cashmere and angora blends, were revivals of two fashion ideas of former years that reinforced the importance of black and white as major fashion colors.

The sweater-as-art trend of 1979 sparked a general return to knits. The variety of sweater dressing seemed infinite and ranged from classic shetlands to the art sweaters, with their intricate patterns or pictures. Stitches ranged from lacy pointelle to bulky cables. There were sweater dresses, coats, jackets, and suits in fine gauges of patterned, tweeded, or slubbed yarns. There were slim shapes, full bubbles, ribs, and ruffles. There was also the "skimp," a mini dress or elongated tunic—the choice being left to the adventuresome spirit of the customer.

Sweater dressing also renewed interest in many knit fabrics which, for a number of years, had been out of favor. Jerseys, interlocks, and double knits—some incorporating stretch yarns for comfort and stability—were beginning to surface at every level of the sportswear and dress market.

The squared shoulder and dropped waistline were features of 1980's fashion silhouette.

Presenting a look of romantic Victorian innocence, the frilly lace blouse was a fashion staple of 1980.

Photos UPI

Photos Giorgio Armani

The bomber jacket and bold geometrically-patterned sweaters were part of the male fashion scene of 1980.

Accessories. Accessories followed the trends in apparel. Knits were represented by snug caps, floppy berets, and shaped scarves in a multitude of yarns, patterns, and textures. "Preppy" dressers took to pearls, bow ties, the head band, Bermuda bags, circle pins, madras or regimental striped belts, argyle or cabled knee socks, and white piqué or lace collars. Victorian touches included white or pale hosiery, cameo pins, flowers, ribbon sashes, and straw boaters. The Hapsburg influence was evident in feather-trimmed Tyrolean fedoras, bold and ornate gemstone or bead jewelry, drop earrings, paisley shawls, fur boas, snoods and elaborate hair ornaments, and dark textured hose.

The one accessory all of these trends shared was the low-heeled shoe. Styled as a pump with bow or cockade ornament, as a ballet slipper, or a strapped Mary Jane, it could sport a wafer-thin flat heel or one gracefully shaped and up to two inches in height. In suede, kidskin, fabric, or patent leather, it was the perfect shoe for any look, day or evening. It also owed much of its popularity, no doubt, to the fact that it was comfortable.

Coming Trends. Intimations of new trends came at the end of 1980 in the resort collections that are traditionally a sounding board for spring fashion notes. Here hemlines inched up to the top of the knee and higher. Mini skirts appeared even in active sportswear's conservative lines. Vivid color prints featured tropical flora and fauna. Blossoms of hibiscus, orchid, and frangipani vied for fashion favor with parrots, cockatoos, flamingos, tigers, and leopards. Brightly colored snakeskin was a primary material for shoe and handbag designers, while exotic wrappings such as sarongs, pareus and dhotis inspired many designer looks.

Menswear. In menswear, the overall silhouette was changed little. Shoulder squared a bit, lapels narrowed, shirt collars lengthened and were buttoned down, and a slender, relaxed fit was still the standard. Special suit fabrics included Prince of Wales plaids and stripes for day and velvet for evening. Soft suedes and leathers or textured knits were used for the casual jackets that replaced the blazer.

The outdoor look had camping or "lumberjack" overtones—with checked or plaid flannel shirts, down vests, hunting caps, and lug-bottomed tie boots as accompaniments to jeans or corduroy pants.

New in menswear, however, was the increased use of colors not traditional in men's fashions, such as emerald, jade, scarlet, curry, gold, and royal blue. These high colors were most obvious in accessories and sportswear separates. Corduroy and poplin slacks, baseball and bowling jackets, and polo and sportshirts took on these high shades. Sweaters, a strong menswear category, glowed in these brights and in vivid geometric, striped, or argyle patterns. Scarves, ties, hosiery, and handkerchiefs were the colorful accents for classic tweeds and flannels.

Outerwear featured jackets and full-length coats of quilted down, as well as wool to poplin reversible rain or shine coats. Bomber jackets and Olympics-inspired ski jackets made a change from the duffel coat.

Fashion seemed to be moving away from the safe classics into a new creativity and excitement.

ANN M. ELKINS
"Good Housekeeping Magazine"

FINLAND

Local Finnish elections, which were held on Oct. 19–20, 1980, were the high-point of a year without many important political developments.

Political Affairs. The greatest advances were registered by the Social Democrats who won 25.6% of the vote, increasing their share of the vote by 1.6% over the last local elections. The opposition National Union Party gained 23% of the vote, a new record for a conservative party, while the Center Party advanced by 1.3% to end up with 18.7% of the vote. The biggest loser was the Democratic Union for the Finnish People, an amalgam of Communists and leftist socialists. Its share of the vote was reduced by 1.2%, to a low of 16.7%. A number of smaller parties, with the exception of the Swedish People's Party, suffered reverses.

On September 3, President Urho K. Kekkonen, who has held office since 1956, celebrated his 80th birthday. The occasion was a time for tribute to a man who more than any other has set his stamp on Finnish foreign and domestic policies since World War II. Although Kekkonen's term would not expire until 1984, there already was much talk among the country's politicians that he should be renominated for another term. The chairmen of the Conservative, Communist, and the Center parties were quoted to the effect that they would support him again. The president, meanwhile, was suffering from poor health.

Foreign Affairs. Finland abstained when the UN General Assembly on January 14 approved a resolution condemning Soviet intervention in Afghanistan. The Finnish representative at the UN pointed out that his nation refrains from taking a position in disputes between the great powers.

Economic Affairs. An ongoing debate between the government and agricultural interests came to an end in March, with the government agreeing to an adjustment of 1,100,000,000 Finnmarks of the income on the part of Finland's agricultural interests. Thus, the price of agricultural products rose by about 10%, while the income of farmers was to be increased by 19%. At the same

UPI

Urho Kekkonen, Finland's president since 1956, celebrated his 80th birthday in September 1980.

time the Central Bank devalued the currency by 2%.

The year also showed a growing deficit in the trade balance and little progress in combating inflation and unemployment. A number of strikes, especially a shipping strike in the spring, hurt the economy.

Nuclear Power. Finland opened its fourth nuclear power station in the fall, at Lovisa. The nuclear reactor was built in the Soviet Union and is to produce 420 megawatts of electricity. A Finnish Gallup poll taken earlier in the year showed that 44% of the population was opposed to nuclear power, 26% was in favor, and 30% did not voice an opinion.

ERIK J. FRIIS
Editor, "The Scandinavian-American Bulletin"

FINLAND · Information Highlights

Official Name: Republic of Finland.
Location: Northern Europe.
Area: 130,129 sq mi (337 032 km²).
Population (1980 est.): 4,800,000.
Chief Cities (1978 est.): Helsinki, the capital, 484,879; Tampere, 165,519; Turku, 164,586.
Government: *Head of state,* Urho Kaleva Kekkonen, president (elected Feb. 1978 for 5th term). *Head of government,* Mauno Koivisto, prime minister (took office May 1979). *Legislature* (unicameral)—Eduskunta.
Monetary Unit: Markka, or Finnish mark (3.90 markkaa equal U.S.$1, Dec. 1980).
Manufactures (major products): Timber and forest products, machinery, ships, clothing, transportation equipment, appliances.
Agriculture (major products): Dairy products, wheat and other grains, livestock products.
GNP (1979 est., U.S.$): $40,900,000,000.
Foreign Trade (1979, U.S.$): *Imports,* $11,400,000,000; *exports,* $11,175,000,000.

FISHERIES

After a few relatively fat years following a crisis in the mid-1970s, caused primarily by the fuel shortage of the time, the U.S. commercial fishing industry fell victim to a far more serious crisis in 1980.

Again the most potent contributing factor was fuel, but this time it was a matter of cost rather than supply. Diesel fuel prices have increased by more than 700% since 1973. This development naturally has adversely affected all fuel-using industries, but fishing, a particularly ravenous fuel-intensive industry because of the extremely high power requirements of dragging trawls, has suffered inordinately.

To make matters worse, demand and, hence, prices fell in 1980 as inventories built up and high interest rates made for cautious buying of fishery products and fishing vessels alike. U.S. fishermen complained bitterly of their inability to compete with imports from countries that subsidize their fisheries. For example, Mexico, the largest importer of shrimp into the United States, was making diesel fuel available to Mexican fishermen for 17 cents a gallon, while U.S. fishermen were paying more than 90 cents a gallon.

As a result, many boat owners in the U.S. shrimp fishery, the nation's most valuable, were unable to meet operating expenses. Ironically, even with boat payments to cope with, they found that they lost less money keeping their boats tied up than they did sending them out.

Although the shrimp fishery was the hardest hit, other fisheries had their share of problems due to the year's adverse economic conditions. The first half of the year brought strikes for higher prices by New England groundfish and Alaskan salmon fishermen, and despite good catches New England lobster fishermen found profits elusive. They attributed the unattractive market conditions to imports of low-priced lobsters from Canada.

The East Coast scallop fishery, which for the last few years has been remarkably lucrative and consequently has attracted a growing number of boats, suffered from a scarcity of resource. The U.S. tuna fleet, unable to cope with tightening federal regulations restricting porpoise mortality (porpoise are often taken in tuna nets), continued to dwindle. Five more tuna "superseiners" were transferred from U.S. to Mexican registry in 1980.

Until the 1980 crisis arose, the U.S. fishing industry had been in a generally healthy condition since passage of the Fishery Conservation and Management Act of 1976, commonly referred to as the 200-mile-limit law since, among other things, it established a 200-mile fishing conservation zone in which foreign fishing is regulated. From 1975 to 1979 the value of the U.S. catch increased from $977 million to $2,200,000,-000, and for the same period the value of exports increased from $305 million to more than $1,-000,000,000. Still, however, U.S. imports of fishery products are three times the value of its exports.

The increased landings of recent years have brought the United States up to fourth place (behind Japan, the USSR, and mainland China) in world fish production. It ranked sixth in 1976.

Record landings of more than 6,200,000,000 lbs (2 810 000 000 kg) in 1979 notwithstanding, it was in the closing months of that year that the U.S. fishing industry became alarmed at its bleak outlook. In the early months of 1980 boat owners and processors, who were either losing money or operating marginally at best, began looking for means to avert disaster.

A number of industry leaders, many of them historically opposed to federal assistance programs, called a meeting in Washington to plead for some sort of government help. They were given no hope of receiving any sort of direct subsidies, but at subsequent meetings in September and October they were able to take their problems directly to Secretary of Commerce Philip Klutznick. They received a commitment for a closer, more effective relationship with the Department of Commerce.

Late in the year, Congress considered legislation to aid the industry.

WILLIAM A. SARRATT, *Editor, "The Fish Boat"*

FLORIDA

Politics dominated the spotlight during most of the 1980 presidential election year. Refugees, racial violence, tragedy at sea, and tax reform were also major events.

Politics. President Jimmy Carter began his climb to the White House in 1976 with an impressive victory in Florida's presidential preference primary, and he attempted to duplicate that strategy in 1980. He started off with a victory over Sen. Edward Kennedy in the primary; however, the economy and the Cuban refugee problem undermined his support in the state. Ronald Reagan, who easily captured the Republican primary, won over many of the traditionally Democratic voters in South Florida and the panhandle on his way to victory in November.

While Reagan's victory was no surprise, it was surprising that Republican Paula Hawkins was elected to the U.S. Senate, defeating Democrat Bill Gunter, the state insurance commissioner and former Congressman. Hawkins' victory may have occurred in part because of splits within the Democrat Party, but there were more subtle reasons. Voters also gave the Republicans one additional U.S. Congressional seat and eight more seats in the legislature. Apparently the indictment of Republican Congressman Richard Kelly after the Abscam investigation did not hurt the party. Kelly, who was on trial as 1980 ended, was defeated in the Republican primary by Bill McCollum, who went on to victory in November.

Refugees. A flotilla of boats of all sizes and descriptions ferried approximately 125,000 Cubans and 9,000 Haitian refugees to South Florida between April and September. Miami and Dade County especially suffered severe economic and social stresses from this influx. Intense criticism of the Carter administration resulted when Carter welcomed the refugees, but failed to act quickly to help local and state officials deal with the acute problems, other than to begin moving some Cubans to Eglin Field in north Florida. In October President Carter signed legislation providing for federal grants to states to aid refugees. Deep resentment was created in Dade County and was reflected by the passage of a referendum in November against bilingualism. (*See also* REFUGEES.)

Republican Paula Haw-kins, 53-year-old con-sumer advocate, con-ducts a successful campaign for a seat in the U.S. Senate.

Linda Grotke, "Herald Tribune," Sarasota

Miami Riot. The worst racial riot in Florida's history took place in Miami. Three days of riot-ing, beginning on May 17, left 18 persons dead, 400 injured, and property damage estimated at $100 million. Approximately 4,000 persons were left jobless by the destruction.

The immediate cause of the rioting was the acquittal of four white policemen accused of beating to death a black Miami businessman. Blacks also were angry because a popular black educator had been arrested on charges of misus-ing public funds, and others were upset over the refugee situation. They charged that government officials were ignoring black unemployment while they labored hard to find jobs for Cubans. Some black leaders across the country called the U.S. refugee policy racist because Cubans were being welcomed while Haitians were being sent back home.

The legislature passed an $11 million aid package for job training and economic assistance to Miami's riot-torn black community. Federal aid also was promised.

Tragedy at Sea. Tampa Bay was the scene of two major tragedies in 1980. On January 28, the Coast Guard buoy tender *Blackthorn* collided with a tanker. There was virtually no warning for the crew of the *Blackthorn* and 23 men died when it quickly sank. Less than four months later, during a rain squall, the ship *Summit Ven-ture* struck one span of the Sunshine Skyway bridge, causing 1,360 ft (378 m) of the span to topple into the bay. Thirty-five persons died as their vehicles plunged into the water.

Tax Reform. Floridians promoted tax relief programs again in 1980. Efforts were concen-trated on the issue of increasing the homestead exemption in order to reduce the taxes of home owners. In March voters approved a constitu-tional amendment increasing the homestead ex-emption for school taxes from $5,000 to $25,000. Voters approved another measure in November that raised the exemption for nonschool taxes to $15,000 in 1980, $20,000 in 1981, and $25,000 in 1982 and thereafter. The potential tax savings were reduced, however, when property apprais-ers were ordered to appraise property at the rate of 100% of face value. Most county appraisers had been using a 70% rate.

Drug Traffic. Reacting to the increasing flow of drugs into south Florida and increased violence involving the "cocaine-cowboys" of Miami, Gov. Robert Graham called a special session of the legislature to get its approval for a statewide grand jury to investigate the problem. New state laws have increased the penalties for drug smug-gling.

J. LARRY DURRENCE
Florida Southern College

───── **FLORIDA** • Information Highlights ─────

Area: 58,560 sq mi (151 670 km²).
Population (Jan. 1980 est.): 8,981,000.
Chief Cities (1970 census): Tallahassee, the capital, 72,-586; (1976 est.): Jacksonville, 532,346; Miami, 354,-993.
Government (1980): *Chief Officers*—governor, Robert Graham (D); lt. gov., Wayne Mixson (D). *Legislature*—Senate, 40 members; House of Representatives, 120 members.
Education (1978–79): *Enrollment*—public elementary schools, 776,607 pupils; public secondary, 737,212; (1979–80): colleges and universities, 395,233 stu-dents. *Public school expenditures,* $3,207,000,000.
State Finances (fiscal year 1979): Revenues, $7,286,-000,000; *expenditures,* $6,462,000,000.
Personal Income (1979): $75,713,000,000; per capita, $8,546.
Labor Force (June 1980): *Total labor force,* 3,985,000; *unemployed,* 263,100 (6.6%).

FOOD

In 1980, the world was affected by shortages of different crops in different geographical areas. Problems with weather, crop yields, water, farming supplies, and availability of money were of prime concern. As the population of the world increases, pressure for food also increases in certain areas. With this pressure come shortages, higher costs for imported foods, and increased problems in distribution. Overall in 1980, world tensions and wars, droughts, crop failures or reductions, and political maneuverings created food supply problems and shortages in many parts of the world.

Supply. Weather vagaries, such as droughts and floods, affected crop yields and disrupted distribution schedules. Although food comes from animal, plant, and water origins, the overall measure of food supply usually is related to the grain harvests reaped in the major nations. Storms, heat, and drought played an extensive role in the U.S. harvest. In the Southwest, heat and drought wilted crops, killed millions of chickens, and reduced cattle herds. To the north, wheat and cattle were deeply affected by drought. Durum wheat, the prime ingredient of pasta, was expected to yield only 90 million bushels out of an expected 150 million bushels. The durum wheat region of Canada was also affected. In corn, a crop that feeds cattle, hogs, and poultry, the expectation was that the U.S. crop would be 16% less than the record harvest of 1979. Normally, a smaller corn crop influences the price of beef, pork, chicken, eggs, milk, and cheese, as well as the amount of exports. Losses in both crops and animals were widespread.

In the Caribbean and Mexico, a series of violent hurricanes destroyed millions of dollars of crops destined for home consumption and export and damaged growing areas that will take years to recover.

Twenty-three of the world's 29 countries labeled by the UN's Food and Agriculture Organization (FAO) as suffering from abnormal food shortages are in Africa. Many of these are in East Africa, where drought and human failings have combined to create an almost insoluble food crisis that has resulted in starvation and malnutrition for millions. Even emergency food donations and relief aid have failed to improve the nutritional lot of Africa's 470 million people.

In Europe and the Soviet Union, weather proved to be a limiting factor. While the Soviet grain crop was expected to exceed 1979's total of 179 million metric tons, it would be below the 1978 record harvest of 237 million metric tons. Weather reduced the yield of fruits, vegetables, milk, and meat, but chickens and eggs showed an increase. However, distribution, storage, and price increases were proving to be serious problems. In Poland, a government program increasing prices of meat helped precipitate work stoppages and strikes.

In other world areas, food aid in Thailand and Cambodia was headed by the International Committee of the Red Cross, UNICEF, and the UN World Food Program. Problems with food supplies falling into the wrong hands rather than helping hungry civilians threatened relief efforts late in the year, but reports indicated that the massive international effort averted mass starvation. In Cuba, the 1980 sugar harvest was affected by a series of agricultural plagues and adverse weather conditions. The harvest was expected to be about 6.8 million metric tons. Indications were that the Castro regime would be forced to import sugar from nearby sources.

Inflation. In all parts of the world food prices were boosted by inflation-creating strikes, boycotts, and threats of more starvation. In China, an effort was under way to control prices by increasing the number of crops of grain. By planting three grain crops a year, China hoped to become more self-reliant in agriculture, and through the increased yields, control prices. However, the need for additional farm labor was expected to slow or reduce other projects, such as the public health campaign against schistosomiasis (a parasitic infection). In late summer, President Carter announced a $670 million credit guarantee to permit Poland to purchase U.S. farm commodities. This was the largest amount ever awarded to a single country, and would be used by Poland to buy some 4 million metric tons of feed grains, wheat, and soybeans in the 1980–81 marketing year. This plus other aid from the USSR followed upon increased meat and food prices in Poland, and resultant workers' strikes.

In the United States, inflation, drought, and heat combined to increase grocery prices at the greatest rate in more than five years. It was expected that food prices would inflate at an annual rate of between 9 and 13% in 1980. In the midst of the summer heat wave, poultry prices jumped 23.5%, with beef rising 7.4% at wholesale, and pork 13.7%. Increases in costs of fuel, fertilizer, and other production items caused net income for many farmers to fall in 1980. To aid grain farmers, President Carter in July ordered a boost in federal price support loan rates. This action was expected to increase retail food prices slightly but would enable farmers to survive the cost-price squeeze.

The Industry. The year brought changes in terms of food regulations, studies and reports on food quality, and consumer values. The use of nitrites in cured meats was allowed to continue. Nitrites became suspect in 1978 when an extensive study showed that sodium nitrite fed rats increased the rate of lymphatic cancer. Since an estimated 7% of the food supply, with an annual market value of $12,500,000,000, uses nitrites, the U.S. Food and Drug Administration (FDA) and the Department of Agriculture (USDA) commissioned a special study to review the 1978 findings. This independent study concluded that there was insufficient evidence to link sodium nitrite with cancer. Nitrites not only aid in preserving the color and flavor of hot dogs, bologna, bacon, and ham but prevent growth of botulin, a deadly toxin. To ensure that their use is safe, the National Academy of Sciences was to carry out an extended review of the safety of nitrite, nitrate, and nitrosamines. In related action, the U.S. Court of Appeals ruled that prior sanction did exist for the use of sodium nitrite, thus preventing the meat preservative from being considered a food additive subject to the restrictions of the 1958 Food Additives Amendment.

A bill was enacted extending the moratorium preventing the FDA from banning the use of saccharin until June 30, 1981. Studies by highly regarded research organizations found the connection between saccharin and bladder cancer to be negative.

Within the food-processing industry, changes and developments related to inflation and consumer desires were evolving. A study of the baking industry showed that the staple white bread is losing its leading spot to wheat, rye, and other specialty breads. Reasons for the change were vague, although nutritional interests appeared to have an influence. Inflation kept alive the consumer's interest in generic products, generally lower-priced products bearing no brand names. A 1980 survey showed that 43% of all supermarkets now offer generics and are increasing their selection of such items. Many firms were directing new product development toward better, less wasteful use of raw products or toward the food-service field. Meat products made by flaking and forming, or by cutting and forming, appeared; fabricated or restructured cuts of steak (beef), lamb, pork, and veal joined seafood items prepared in this manner. Many such cuts are made from less expensive or previously rejected portions and resemble the original, except that composition in terms of fat and lean can be more accurately controlled. Other new food items include imitation cheeses, specialty foods for microwave heating, frozen catfish, and health snacks.

The Federal Trade Commission (FTC) announced in October a definition for "natural" foods. It states that "a food is natural if it contains no synthetic or artificial ingredients and has had no more processing than generally can be done in a home kitchen." The definition excluded some familiar foods formerly advertised as natural. In the report, the FTC indicated that characterizing a food as natural implies superiority over foods that do not have the description, but also added that the term "natural" has been applied to foods which run the gamut of processing. Overall, the standard should reduce the use of claims based on the word "natural," and aid consumers in making better food choices.

Nutrition. The results of a long awaited USDA food consumption survey, comparing the period of spring 1965 with that of spring 1977,

Andrew Partos

An official definition of "natural" foods, which remain popular, was issued by the FTC in 1980.

were released. Preliminary data indicated that Americans did alter their diets in the 12-year period. The 1977–78 survey used 15,000 households for basic sampling, and an additional 15,000 households for supplemental research. Major changes in dietary habits showed an approximate 10% decline in the level of food energy available to households, reflecting decreases in fat, carbohydrate, and protein consumption. With the exception of calcium, most vitamin and mineral intake rose.

In a controversial issue of diets, major government and private agencies became entangled in a long-lasting, unsettled area of recommendations. Early in the year, the then Department of Health, Education, and Welfare (HEW) and the USDA released joint dietary guidelines similar to earlier ones released by the Surgeon General and the Senate Select Committee on Human Nutrition. These guidelines suggested that consumers should eat a variety of foods; maintain ideal weight; eat food with adequate fiber and starch; avoid excessive sugar; reduce intake of saturated fat, cholesterol, and sodium; and consume alcohol in moderation, if at all. Within several months, the Food and Nutrition Board of the National Academy of Sciences issued a report, "Toward Healthful Diets." The report took issue with the HEW-USDA guidelines, primarily on the value of reducing cholesterol and fat consumption. The net result of the debate was that a healthy diet for all was yet to be defined.

KIRBY M. HAYES
University of Massachusetts

During talks with West German Chancellor Helmut Schmidt (left) in July, French President Valéry Giscard d'Estaing emphasized the need to end the "self-effacement of Europe in the world."

Francolon, Liaison

FRANCE

Politically, 1980 was a relatively quiet year, as President Valéry Giscard d'Estaing looked toward reelection in 1981 despite allegations of scandal. A rash of anti-Semitism, the testing of controversial new weapons and defense systems, a blockade by striking fishermen, and measures to curb rapidly escalating street crime were major issues. Events in the Middle East and the Persian Gulf and relations with European neighbors, the United States, and the USSR were the focus of attention in foreign affairs.

DOMESTIC AFFAIRS

Inching toward the political center and aloof from accusations of impropriety made against himself, his family, and his friends, Giscard enjoyed popular approval and fully expected reelection to a new seven-year term in the spring of 1981. Content to retain much-criticized Prime Minister Raymond Barre as his lightning rod on the domestic front, Giscard ostensibly filled his days with foreign policy and diplomacy by visitation. Jacques Chirac, mayor of Paris and president of the Gaullist opposition party, the Rassemblement pour la République (RPR), severely criticized government policies and still loomed as a challenger of Giscard and his Union pour la Démocratie Française (UDF) in 1981. But Chirac's own drift toward the center displeased Gaullist purists in the RPR, prompting another party member, Michel Debré, to declare his candidacy on June 30. The split was expected to benefit Giscard.

The left also showed little hope of unity. Shattered by the Communists in 1978, the Union of the Left was just a memory. Among the Socialists, party leader François Mitterrand was confronted by a dissident movement led by 49-year-old Michel Rocard. By year's end, however,

Mitterrand had declared his candidacy and Rocard had stepped back.

Led by hard-line Secretary-General Georges Marchais, the Communist Party (PCF) held its course. During a visit to Moscow in early January—his first since 1974—Marchais endorsed the Soviet invasion of Afghanistan and completed what many regarded as the party's return to a pro-Soviet stance. He was criticized for undermining Eurocommunism, as both the Italian and Spanish Communist parties had condemned the Soviet intervention, but Marchais ignored the attacks. In March, the magazine L'Express printed the photocopy of an alleged German document which proved that Marchais had remained voluntarily in Germany after his forced labor at the Messerschmidt aircraft factory in Augsburg. Marchais denounced the document as "a crude forgery," German authorities declared it authentic, but its precise import was uncertain. Simultaneously, the weekly Le Nouvel Observateur claimed that Marchais had been a Soviet agent before joining the party in 1947. Prior to the accusations, 63% of the French said that they would accept a Communist in the cabinet and 21% could countenance a Communist as president. Subsequently, polls showed 49% and 14%, respectively. Nevertheless, on October 12 the PCF nominated Marchais as its presidential candidate.

Giscard's effort to broaden the base of his support was evidenced by the July 31 naming of Robert Fabre, once president of the Radicals of the Left, to the office of ombudsman. In the triennial partial elections to the Senate on September 28, the Socialists gained 9 seats, to become the largest group; the RPR gained 6; Giscard's UDF gained 2; and the Communists remained unchanged.

Scandals. In April, the satirical weekly Le Canard Enchainé published documents that renewed a scandal regarding the 1977 murder of former Gaullist cabinet minister Jean de Broglie. The documents suggested that Giscard's close friend and then Interior Minister Michel Poniatowski concealed or failed to act on information regarding de Broglie's impending murder. Poniatowski denied the charges, but with the Socialists demanding his impeachment, he testified before a parliamentary commission on July 24. The story eventually faded away. During the year, *Canard* also published details of allegedly indiscreet and profitable stock-market operations by Giscard's wife, as well as a telephone interview in which former Emperor Bokassa I of the Central African Empire alleged that Giscard had taken his wife as a mistress and certified that he had given diamonds to Giscard and two members of his family. On February 7, the appeals court ended *Canard*'s six-year lawsuit against the government for an abortive attempt to bug its offices. In November, the government began contempt-of-court proceedings against *Le Monde,* France's most distinguished daily newspaper, for a series of articles accusing the regime of having manipulated several court decisions.

Strikes and Protest. The country was hurt by strikes throughout the year. Dockworkers staged a one-day strike on March 20. On May 13, the leftist CGT and CFDT union confederations staged nationwide strikes to protest government changes in the national health service whereby patients would pay between 5% and 12% of treatment costs. Through May and June, activities in the energy and transport sectors were interrupted by labor unrest. Turkish garment workers in Paris began a lengthy hunger strike in February, demanding regularization of their status. Led by village mayors, opponents of the four nuclear energy plants planned for the Plogoff area in Brittany battled police and federal troops from January through March. On March 19, 50,000 Parisians marched through city streets to demonstrate against government plans for a drastic reduction in the number of teaching positions in the school system. Students demonstrated May 13-14 against government regulations to keep marginal foreign students out of French universities.

The most publicized strike was by the nation's fishermen. Demanding larger government fuel subsidies, larger crews, and rises in the price of fish, they set up a blockade of France's major ports and brought maritime commerce to a virtual halt in late August. The blockade finally was broken at several Atlantic and Mediterranean ports by naval tugboats using water cannons and tear gas. Concessions were made by both the government and fishermen, and the strike ended by mid-September.

Terrorism and Anti-Semitism. Kidnappings, bombings, and strikes by Corsican nationalists occurred in Ajaccio, Corte, Nice, and other towns. On April 22, Giscard promised higher investment, better education and agricultural support, and improved communications for the is-

land, but ruled out independence. The moderate Union of the Corsican People asked only for autonomy. On May 13, the State Security Court handed down four- to eight-year sentences to Corsican National Liberation Front militants for a series of bombings in 1979.

On February 24, the Paris office of Aeroflot, the Soviet airline, was firebombed. On March 18, the French Ministry of Cooperation was machine-gunned, reportedly in protest against African policies. On April 5 and 9, the Toulouse offices of the Data Systems and Honeywell companies were bombed. On May 12, the Palais de Justice in Paris was bombed. Seven cleaning women were wounded in a June 12 bombing at Orly airport. The École Militaire in Paris was machine-gunned on September 19. While responsibility for many of these acts was claimed by the rightist Direct Action Group, it was less clear who was responsible for the February 1 murder of former Labor and Education Minister Joseph Fontanet.

In response to the spreading crime problem, the National Assembly approved (265-205) a tough criminal code revision on June 25. The legislation, called the Security and Freedom Act, expanded police powers, increased minimum sentences for certain crimes, and introduced machinery akin to habeas corpus in the United States, whereby arrested persons are brought before a judge within three days. In another measure on September 13, the government outlawed the extremist right-wing Federation of National and European Action (FANE).

Anti-Semitism was a festering problem, as Jewish schools and synagogues were repeatedly attacked. A bomb explosion on October 3 outside Paris' largest synagogue on rue Copernic killed four persons and seriously injured ten others. Massive demonstrations were held all over France to protest the violence and what was regarded as anti-Semitic government policy. Five days after the Paris bombing and amid loud accusations of the government's aloofness and lack of responsiveness, Giscard appeared on national television to announce a series of measures to combat anti-Semitism. Still, the regime was held morally suspect, and some reactionary violence ensued. (*See* RELIGION—Judaism.)

Economy. In 1980, the rate of inflation surpassed 13%, unemployment reached 1.5 million, and worker purchasing power dropped by 1.3%. The year 1979 showed a trade deficit of $2,600,-000,000, largely because of expensive oil imports. On April 12, the government announced its target for sources of energy in 1990: 30% from oil, 20% from coal and gas, 30% from nuclear, and 10% each from solar and hydroelectric. On September 3, Prime Minister Barre promised new measures to boost exports, construction, and household spending. The government would raise school allowances for low-income families, provide bonuses to pensioners, and increase the minimum wage. The 1981 budget, presented on

September 10, called for expenditures of $147,-700,000,000, a 16% increase over 1980, with targets of a 10.5% inflation rate, a 7.1% deficit, and a growth rate of 1.6%. The eighth five-year plan (1981-85) was designed to stimulate high technology sectors (nuclear power, aerospace, telecommunications, and computers), encourage larger families, and make agriculture more competitive outside the European Community (EC). Work on the controversial Super-Phoenix, the world's first commercial-sized fast-breeder nuclear reactor, continued at Creys Malville, south of Lyons. It was expected to be ready by 1983.

Defense. An 18% increase in military spending was budgeted for 1981, with outlays for several new weapons and defense systems tested in 1980. On March 24, a 50-kiloton device was exploded on Mururoa atoll. On June 26, Giscard announced that France had developed and tested a prototype neutron bomb warhead and would be ready to make a decision on production in two or three years. The RPR, the Socialists, and Communists opposed building it, however, with only the Socialists approving more research. In addition, Giscard indicated that France's strategic land-based missile system would be made mobile, evidently for the protection of all western Europe. Two 32,000-ton nuclear carriers would replace the existing *Foch* and *Clemenceau* in the 1990s. The moves to strenghten France's arsenal reflected not only immense technological and industrial strength, but a sense of a decline in U.S. power.

Empire. Disturbances in overseas departments and territories indicated that decolonization had perhaps not ended. A general strike paralyzed St. Pierre and Miquelon March 12-22, with gendarmes being flown in to aid the local police. Groups in Martinique and Guadeloupe, evidently backed by Cuba, threatened the Europeans. The Organization of African Unity encouraged La Réunion to seek independence. Madagascar demanded restitution of the strategically significant Iles Glorieuses in the Mozambique Strait. France and Great Britain, withdrawing from joint rule in the New Hebrides, had to send in paratroops and marines to quell an internal secessionist movement before the July 30 independence ceremony.

FOREIGN POLICY

Giscard was sharply criticized by Spain and Portugal for maintaining that no new members should be admitted to the EC until problems caused by the previous admissions were resolved. The French feared agricultural competition and a new influx of Iberian workers. Spanish trucks entering France during the summer were attacked by farmers, and Spain complained that France was harboring Basque separatists.

The agricultural quarrel with Great Britain continued, although a compromise was being worked out by which British contributions to the EC would be cut by about $2,000,000,000 in return for higher farm prices, settlement of fishing disputes, and more sharing of North Sea oil. Despite a September 1979 ruling by the European Court of Justice, France continued to restrict imports of British lamb. In Gaullist fashion, RPR leader Chirac demanded that Britain observe the rules or quit the EC, while it was France that actually was defying the law. Plans for private construction of the long-delayed English Channel train tunnel, at a cost of $1,700,-000,000 continued.

At their semiannual meeting in Paris in early February, Giscard and West German Chancellor Helmut Schmidt declared that the Soviet intervention in Afghanistan was "unacceptable" and called on the USSR to withdraw its forces. During a five-day state visit to West Germany July 7-11, the first by a French head of state since 1962, Giscard exhorted the two nations to dedicate themselves to ending the "self-effacement of Europe in the world."

Despite its reproof of the USSR for events in Afghanistan, France decided on May 13 not to join the boycott of the Moscow Summer Olympics. Soviet Foreign Minister Andrei A. Gromyko visited Paris for two days in late April and

Lambert, Liaison

French naval tugboats used water cannons to break a blockade set up during the summer by striking fishermen.

Giscard reviews troops in the United Arab Emirates during a March tour of the Persian Gulf states.

gave no hint of conciliation or concession on the Afghanistan situation. Giscard's dramatic rendezvous with Soviet President Leonid Brezhnev in Warsaw on May 19 achieved nothing beyond a vague proposal for a 1981 world summit. Great Britain, Germany, and the United States complained that they had not been informed of the Warsaw meeting until the last minute.

During a ten-day visit to the Middle East in March, Giscard formally endorsed the Palestine cause and the Palestine Liberation Organization (PLO) as its agent. The announcement occasioned a giant pro-Israel rally in Paris, attended by Mitterrand and parliamentarians from Gi-

scard's own party, on April 27. Giscard also shored up relations with Jordan and Saudi Arabia, continued selling nuclear equipment to Iraq, avoided public criticism of Iran, and assumed a neutral state in the Iran-Iraq war.

Fighting off Libyan-backed insurgents, Tunisia welcomed French supplies and military advisers. On February 4, the French embassy in Tripoli was burned, apparently in response to that support. France withdrew its troops from war-torn Chad in late April and, at the request of Mauritania, withdrew from the western Sahara in May.

On a state visit to India, January 26-28, Giscard signed agreements to import Indian coal and to provide French mining technology. During a state visit to China in October, Giscard and Chairman Hua Guofeng agreed on policies in the Middle East and Asia.

In Franco-American relations, 1980 was another year of acerbic reproaches. Neo-Gaullist efforts to assert French leadership in Europe and to assert its independence from what it regarded as a shaky American sphere of influence exacerbated Giscard's poor relations with U.S. President Jimmy Carter. Giscard's meeting with Brezhnev in May brought a round of unpleasant recriminations, perhaps mostly for domestic consumption. If the French were prickly and quick to snap, it was because they felt the Americans were. unable to view the world through eyes other than their own.

JOHN C. CAIRNS, *University of Toronto*

─────── **FRANCE • Information Highlights** ───────

Official Name: French Republic.
Location: Western Europe.
Area: 211,207 sq mi (547 026 km^2).
Population (1980 est.): 53,600,000.
Chief Cities (1975 census): Paris, the capital, 2,299,830; Marseille, 908,600; Lyon, 456,716; Toulouse, 373,-796.
Government: *Head of state,* Valéry Giscard d'Estaing, president (took office May 1974). *Chief minister,* Raymond Barre, prime minister (took office Aug. 1976). *Legislature*—Parliament: Senate and National Assembly.
Monetary Unit: Franc (4.44 francs equal U.S.$1, Nov. 1980).
Manufactures (major products): Chemicals, automobiles, processed foods, iron and steel, aircraft, textiles, clothing.
Agriculture (major products): Cereals, feed grains, livestock and dairy products, wine, fruits, vegetables.
GNP (1979 est., U.S.$): $566,000,000,000.
Foreign Trade (1979, U.S.$): *Imports,* $106,944,000,-000; *exports,* $98,059,000,000.

Mia et Klaus/Valen Photos

The world's major horticultural traditions were represented at Floralies 1980, a floral exhibition held from May 31 to September 1 in Montreal. Twelve countries and four Canadian provinces had displays.

GARDENING AND HORTICULTURE

The workshops and reports at the 77th annual meeting of the American Society for Horticultural Science at the University of Colorado in Fort Collins, July 27–Aug. 1, 1980, were indicative of current interests in horticulture. Among the topics covered were fruit setting and development; the use of municipal wastes for horticultural crops; food quality; the effects of plant growth regulators; water usage; mechanization; utilization of germ plasm; integrated pest management; the use of statistics in horticultural science; tissue culture applications; and the efficient use of energy. Enthusiasts welcomed the announcement of the 1980 All-America winners.

Energy and Inflation. Greenhouse growers were painfully conscious of limited energy supplies and rising inflation, as they continued to experience increases in the cost of heating, supplies, and transportation. Many supplies, including some fertilizers, are based on petroleum feedstocks and reflect the double effects of rising oil costs and general economic inflation. Not surprisingly, much effort is being made to conserve energy and increase productivity. Double-plastic film coverings for greenhouses, the sealing of glass laps, thermal blankets to cover crops at night, and the use of "split night temperatures"—in which crops are kept at growing temperature for only part of the night—are effective in reducing energy costs. The use of movable benches instead of walkways, high intensity lights in dark weather, increased carbon dioxide

levels, and fast-growing crops can significantly increase production.

Because of rising heating costs, plants that require lower forcing temperatures are becoming increasingly more profitable, and horticulturists are working on new crops with that characteristic. Meanwhile, the development of new cultivars and breeding techniques allows some of the old favorites—such as calceolaria, cineraria, and even cyclamen—to be grown from seed to marketable stage in only seven months. And tissue culture laboratories are offering plants of many new species and cultivars developed through the application of aseptic culture techniques to the rapid multiplication of plants.

New Tool. Work on the identification of basic plant material has been assisted by a new tool. The scanning electron microscope has allowed researchers to identify unique features in the "micro-landscape" of plant surfaces. Various microscopic features appear to offer a means of plant "fingerprinting." A grant from the Horticultural Research Institute supports work in this area at the USDA Nursery Crops Research Center in Delaware, OH.

All-America Selections. The All-America winners in the annual and vegetable plant categories were: the marigold Janie, zinnia Peter Pan Flame, verbena Sangria, ornamental pepper Holiday Time, and squash Summer Gold Rush F_1.

The All-America Rose Selections (AARS) again were given in the three major classifications—hybrid tea, grandiflora, and floribunda. Bing Crosby, the hybrid tea, was developed by

Ollie Weeks of Ontario, CA, who won his fifth AARS honor. The heavy-petaled, mildly fragrant rose has brilliant persimmon orange flowers with a slightly fluorescent glow. The bushes grow to about 5 ft (1.53 m) with above-average disease resistance.

White Lightning, the award-winning grandiflora, was bred by Herbert C. Swim, another past honoree. It was the first white grandiflora to win an AARS, although its ruffled flowers are sometimes edged with a slight pink blush. White Lightning has long, pointed buds, a long blooming season, and a citrus-like fragrance.

Marina, the top floribunda, has nonfading coral-orange blooms with red and gold tones. They are lightly fragrant, high-centered, and borne in profusion. The bush has a marked resistance to disease and few thorns. Marina is larger than traditional floribundas and does well as a greenhouse rose. It was the fourth prize-winner in six years for German hybridizer Reimer Kordes.

EDMUND N. O'ROURKE
Louisiana State University

GENETICS

Genetic research in 1980 continued to show dramatic progress. There was new, surprising information in an ever-wider array of living organisms on the dynamic structure of genes and chromosomes; on the role of methylation of deoxyribonucleic acid (DNA) in the regulation of gene activity; on techniques for inserting purified genes or chromosomes into cells; on inherited factors in immune functions, cancer risk, and neurological disorders; and on the interaction of environmental agents and genes.

Media coverage of scientific, industrial, and political developments made genetics a household word. The dominating theme was the interaction of genetics and the environment. There was the continuing question of the health hazards of radiation exposures. There was increasing evidence that toxic chemicals lie in wait at thousands of dump sites throughout the United States, the most publicized being the Love Canal at Niagara Falls, NY. (*See* feature article, page 47.) There was great care taken to protect workers and the public, as chemical, pharmaceutical, and agricultural companies utilized genetic manipulations to produce ethylene oxide, insulin, growth hormone, interferon, and vaccine against foot and mouth disease.

Nobel Prizes. Nobel Prizes in 1980 went to six distinguished scientists for their work in genetic research. The prize in physiology and medicine was shared by Baruj Benacerraf of Harvard Medical School for his work on immune response (IR) genes and by George Snell of The Jackson Laboratory, Bar Harbor, ME, and Jean Dausset of Paris, France, for their work in mice and humans on genes that determine the cell surface histocompatibility antigens. Their immunogenetic discoveries form the basis for successful transplants of skin, kidneys, and other organs. Histocompatibility antigens, probably via linked IR genes, are associated with altered susceptibility or resistance to specific infections, autoimmune diseases, allergies, and possibly certain cancers. The Nobel Prize in Chemistry was shared by Paul Berg of Stanford University, for development of recombinant DNA techniques, and Walter Gilbert of Harvard University and Frederick Sanger of Cambridge University, England, for methods of rapid sequencing of the DNA of specific genes. Sanger won the prize previously for his pioneering work on sequencing of proteins (insulin).

Agriculture. Agricultural crops are being threatened by the increasing salinity and acidity of soils, and rising cost of fertilizers, and greater competition for water. Tools of modern genetics are being employed to permit growth in adverse environmental conditions, improve efficiency of photosynthesis, and eliminate the need for fertilizer through association with nitrogen-fixing bacteria (Rhizobium) or blue-green algae (Azolla) or by the insertion of genes for nitrogen fixation. In tobacco and other dicotyledonous plants, crown gall tumors are induced upon infection with the soil bacterium *Agrobacterium tumefaciens.* Tumor-producing bacterial plasmid DNA is transferred and integrated into the plant cell DNA; reversal of tumor growth is associated with loss of foreign DNA. Such plasmids may serve as vehicles for inserting other, more desirable genes into plants.

Jumping Genes. The insertion of plasmid genes is probably analogous to the newly-discovered capacity of certain gene segments to transpose themselves from one chromosome site to another. Transposable "jumping" genes play a crucial role in differentiation, especially in cells that produce specific antibodies. They probably also account for unstable mutations, described long ago in maize, fruitflies, and bacteria.

Environment. Rapid in vitro screening assays for carcinogenicity of chemicals have been developed, using bacteria or cultured mammalian cells in which specific mutation rates can be quantitated. Coincubation with liver enzymes converts the chemical from an environmental procarcinogen to its activated form. There is a high correlation between mutagenic effects and tumor production in animal bioassays. Mutagenic and carcinogenic effects can result from various actions on DNA, including direct chemical adducts and altered nucleotide precursor concentrations. Monitoring of human cells for mutagenic effects is now done with assays for specific mutations, including hemoglobin mutants in red blood cells, and the examination of chromosomes in blood or sperm cells for breaks, rearrangements, or increased sister chromatid exchange.

GILBERT S. OMENN, *University of Washington*

Recombinant DNA

To scientists it is known as "the construction of biologically functional bacterial plasmids in vitro." In laymen's terms it means the creation of new forms of life. By stitching genes from one organism into those of another, biologists have triggered a scientific revolution which has already brought far-reaching consequences—and controversies—in medicine, pharmaceutics, agriculture, environmental science, and a host of other industries. The new technology is recombinant DNA (deoxyribonucleic acid)—or gene splicing.

Gene splicing involves the manipulation of DNA, the chemical twisted into a double helix that contains genes, the blueprints for life. Genes, simply segments of DNA, encode the protein products of a cell, such as insulin in a pancreas cell or hemoglobin in a blood cell. By implanting a gene in a bacterium, scientists can make the microbe also produce these proteins. And since bacteria divide and reproduce themselves and their genes as often as three times an hour, scientists soon have a tiny farm for growing genes.

The Technique. There are many recipes for recombinant DNA, but most are variations on the same basic steps. First, scientists must get the gene they want. Starting with a cell that makes the protein coded by the gene, they identify and isolate the messenger RNA (ribonucleic acid) for that protein. (Messenger RNA is a single-stranded copy of DNA; it carries DNA's code to sites in the cell that manufacture protein.) They then add to the mRNA an enzyme called reverse

transcriptase, which reverses the usual DNA-makes-RNA scheme and makes DNA from the messenger. This DNA is then spliced into a circular bit of DNA from a bacterium. The circular bit, called a plasmid, exists independently from the bacterium's chromosomes. The resulting hybrid is reintroduced into the bacterium, which is then mixed with nutrients in a fermentation vat. The bacterium divides and replicates, with every division yielding more patchwork genes. If the gene is stitched in near an "on-off" gene in the plasmid, the gene can be turned on to make whatever protein it codes for.

Dangers and Precautions. One hitch in this scheme is the unknown hazard of recombinant organisms. When scientists first discovered how to make them, they feared that the new genes might prove pathogenic. There were visions of monstrous hybrids escaping from the laboratory and causing epidemics of disease and mutation. Therefore, in 1974, researchers imposed a moratorium on their work. The moratorium lasted until 1976, when the National Institutes of Health (NIH) adopted safety guidelines. Stipulating that the recombinant organisms must be physically and biologically contained, the guidelines—and further study—convinced biologists that the work was safer than they had thought. Billions of bacteria with recombined genes were grown without any problems; pathogenicity proved much less likely to develop than it seemed at first. The scientists' favorite bacteria for gene splicing, *Escherichia coli* (*E. coli*), come in a weakened strain which could not exist out-

Drawing by Frank Senyk

*How Gene
Splicing Works:*

1) A plasmid (DNA ring) is isolated from a bacterium. 2) An enzyme is added; it cuts the plasmid at specific cleavage sites. 3) Genes from a foreign DNA molecule are cut with the same enzyme. 4) The foreign DNA is spliced into the plasmid; it fits the cleavage sites exactly. 5) The recombinant DNA plasmid is reinserted in the bacterium, which divides and replicates itself.

side the laboratory even if it did manage to escape. And the viruses spliced into *E. coli* may be safer inside the bacteria than outside. Still, scientists worry that research that is safe in a laboratory may not be safe once it is scaled up to commercial levels. Although the recombinant DNA industry has a perfect safety record, both the Food and Drug Administration and the Occupational Safety and Health Administration are trying to come up with regulatory policies.

In 1980, the gene splicing industry was given a boost by two important decisions. First, the NIH relaxed its guidelines so that experiments using weakened *E. coli* were required to follow only the standard microbiological precautions—such as decontaminating material before throwing it out and keeping food out of the lab. Second, the U.S. Supreme Court ruled, 5–4, that new forms of life are eligible for patent protection (*Diamond v. Chakrabarty*). More than 100 genetic hybrids were awaiting patent approval. These two rulings cleared the way for research unhindered by cumbersome regulations or the need to guard trade secrets.

Commercial Research and Application. Five companies are setting the pace in the genetics industry. Genentech Corp., in South San Francisco, CA, boasts the most triumphs in gene splicing. In 1977 it induced bacteria to make the brain hormone somatostatin, which may prove valuable in the treatment of diabetes and acute pancreatitis. In 1978 it did the same with human insulin (which is now being tested in human patients), and has since scored successes with human growth hormone, interferon, and thymosin (which stimulates the immune system and may help combat brain cancer). At Cetus Corp., in Berkeley, CA, work in gene splicing has yielded impressive results in pharmaceuticals, food, and industrial chemicals, including the promise of a new organism that makes alcohol from manioc. Biogen S.A., in Geneva, Switzerland, hit the front pages in 1980 when it induced bacteria to produce interferon. Biogen is also pursuing work with serum albumin. Genex Corp., in Rockville, MD, concentrates on industrial chemicals. Bethesda Research Labs, also in Rockville, used recombinant DNA to synthesize an amino acid, opening the possibility of making food in bacteria.

All told, recombinant DNA attracted some $200 million in private capital in 1980. Financial analysts predicted the kitty would top $1,900,000,000 by 1985.

Still on the commercial horizon in 1980 were vaccines. If bacteria can be engineered to produce proteins on the outer coat of a disease-causing virus, these proteins could be injected into patients to trigger the immune response. Since the whole virus would not be injected, as it is in conventional vaccines, the virus could not replicate in the body and cause disease. Biogen is attempting to make vaccines for malaria and for foot-and-mouth disease.

Although the headlines have so far gone to pharmaceuticals, analysts say the most important use of DNA technology will come in the chemicals industry. There are plans for stitching genes into bacteria to produce ethylene glycol (antifreeze) or to oxidize minerals, making the rocks soluble and the metals they contain more easily mined. Microbes might even be used to make plastic out of sugar instead of petroleum, thereby reducing industry's dependence on oil.

Basic Scientific Research. The challenge for the purely scientific researcher—as opposed to the commercial technologist—lies in using bacteria as copiers for genes, so that, with enough copies, they can determine how genes work. The guiding question is how they are regulated—how they turn on and off. Every cell in an organism has the same set of genes, yet not all are expressed; for instance, eye cells don't express insulin genes. With recombinant DNA, scientists can isolate not just the gene but also the regulatory sequences. In 1980, they discovered that the control site of a viral gene can either repress or activate the gene, depending on how it interacts with a repressor protein. If the protein sits on one side of the control region, near the gene, it blocks the transcribing enzyme from reaching the gene to make the RNA messenger. The gene stays off. But if the repressor sits on the other side of the control region, the enzyme can reach the gene and transcribe it into RNA.

The most important theoretical breakthrough to result from recombinant DNA research was the 1977 discovery that genes of higher organisms come in pieces. In other words, while an RNA copy is made of a whole stretch of DNA sequences, an unexpected step intervenes before the messenger travels to the protein-manufacturing site. Some of the RNA gets snipped out by enzymes, leaving pieces of the original gene, which are subsequently glued back together by other enzymes. These "introns"—nonexpressed chunks of DNA that get cut out and discarded—were a total shock to molecular biologists, who still don't quite know what to make of them.

Cloning genes in bacteria has also enabled scientists to crack some of the mysteries of genetic disease. Using recombinant DNA to clone genes for globin, for example, researchers found that thalessemia, a blood disorder, arises from just a single change in the gene for beta globin. Similarly, by cloning genes of tumor viruses, scientists are seeing how such agents induce cancer and are getting clues as to how natural carcinogens might do the same.

The gene stitchers have only begun their revolution. If the first few years of research are any indication, recombinant DNA will be as important to industry as the transistor and as exciting for science as the double helix itself.

See also MEDICINE AND HEALTH: Interferon.
SHARON BEGLEY
"Newsweek"

GEOLOGY

The most dramatic geologic event of 1980 was the eruption in southwestern Washington of Mount St. Helens, one of a chain of 15 large volcanoes that have been building in the Cascade Mountain Range in the western United States over a period of 50 million years. (*See* special report, page 248.) Also during the year, important new information on cloud-shrouded Venus was obtained by radar imagery transmitted by the Pioneer Venus spacecraft; new data regarding plate tectonics were discussed; plans were advanced for the Ocean Margin Drilling program; and a devastating earthquake killed thousands in Algeria.

Planetary Geology. As a result of the Pioneer Venus spacecraft flight, scientists were able to prepare a contour map of almost all of Venus. The planet is similar to other solid bodies of the solar system. Continent-sized features, including great rift valleys and mountains higher than Everest, were charted. Two thirds of the surface are a great planet-circling plain. Lower tracts, which are potential ocean basins, make up about 16% of the surface, and two great highland areas supporting lofty nonlinear mountains, thought to be volcanic, rise above the general level. The entire surface is pocked by craters of all sizes like those of Mercury and the moon. In contrast to the multifractured earth, the crust of Venus appears to be static. Geologic activity capable of creating major topographic features may have ceased 2,000,000,000 years ago.

Update of Plate Tectonics. The concept that the outer shell of the Earth consists of a half-dozen interlocking plates of brittle rock moving on a plastic substratum has had phenomenal success in explaining worldwide geological conditions and processes. The moving lithospheric plates interact in various complex ways to generate heightened geologic activity along mutual contacts. The long-term consequence has been an almost complete reorganization of the major geographic features of the globe within the past 200 million years. Although the movements of the major continents have been fairly well charted, it is now realized that minor chunks and slivers, called microcontinents by some, have also shifted from one place to another in lively and unexpected fashion.

In a September meeting, 57 specialists discussed the exotic blocks that seem to have accreted to form western North America. These are variously referred to as microplates or tectonostratigraphic terranes. There is general agreement that at least 15, perhaps as many as 25, individual blocks, each separated from its neighbors by great faults and made up of its own distinctive rock types and structures, have contributed to making up the western margin of the continent, including practically all of Alaska. Among the best documented are pieces collectively known as Wrangellia that are embedded in southwest Alaska, southwest British Columbia, and southeast Washington. These blocks contain fossils of Triassic age. They are judged to have originated 5° to 10° south of the equator in warm tropical climates and to have drifted north to fuse with North America in the Cretaceous Period.

Similar events may have built eastern North America, including the entire Appalachian chain. Some believe that repeated collisions with other land masses, including Africa, have driven a number of relatively thin plates westward onto North America where they now appear as discrete belts making up the Coastal Plain, Pied-

A major earthquake, registering 6.8 on the Richter scale, struck southern Italy, including the cities of Naples and Salerno in November. The quake, the worst one to hit Italy since 1908, killed nearly 3,-000 persons. A worldwide relief effort to aid the victims was conducted.

mont, and Blue Ridge provinces. This action continued from 550 million to 270 million years ago and resulted in a doubling of the thickness of continental rocks. Optimists argue that rocks below the displaced sedimentary blanket may contain great stores of hydrocarbons.

Deep Drilling Programs. Plans to taper off the eminently successful Deep Sea Drilling Project (DSDP) in 1981 and to terminate it in 1982 were finalized. Scheduled to replace DSDP is the Ocean Margin Drilling program (OMD). Details of the project were discussed in 1980, and it was generally agreed that problems of active and passive continental margins, oceanic crust near continents, and paleoenvironmental reconstructions of marginal marine situations justify a change in emphasis. The potential economic value of mineral resources of the shelf areas has led governmental and commercial interests to agree to share OMD costs.

Tentative plans are to restrict OMD drilling to depths between the continental margin and 6,-500 ft (2 000 m). This leaves shallower areas, where many operations have been carried out, to commercial exploration. *Glomar Challenger,* the vessel from which the DSDP drilling has been done, is not considered capable of supporting the OMD project. The larger, more sophisticated, former "spy ship," *Glomar Explorer,* is to be adapted for the project.

Disasters. A sharp earthquake, Richter magnitude 7.5, broke a relatively long respite from major tremors, and practically destroyed the Algerian city of El Asnam and surrounding villages October 10. Five thousand to 20,000 persons were killed and at least 400,000 were rendered homeless. The city is located on a major seismic fault and suffered severe earthquake damage on Sept. 9, 1954, when 1,600 persons were killed. Following the October quake, serious consideration was given to relocating the city.

On November 23 an earthquake, registering 6.8 on the Richter scale, shook southern Italy, killing nearly 3,000 persons.

The U.S. Geological Survey released *When the Earth Moves,* a film on natural hazards. Focusing on volcanic eruptions, earthquakes, subsidence, landslides, swelling soils, flooding, and glacial outbursts, the film emphasizes how people can avoid or moderate natural hazards.

Field Discoveries. Traditional outdoor searches turned up interesting finds. Although first reported in 1977, fossil evidence of organized life forms 3,500,000,000 years old were confirmed in 1980. Specimens, discovered in western Australia, include microbes and finely banded stromatolites, structures formed by growth and metabolic activity of primitive algae. These specimens not only extend the known span of life backward by 400 to 500 million years but also prove that sophisticated means of reproduction, food-getting (photosynthesis), and adaptation to environment were in existence at an unexpectedly early age.

Siccoli, Liaison

In El Asnam, Algeria, on October 10, an earthquake killed thousands of persons, left many homeless, and severely damaged buildings it did not destroy.

Likewise in Australia gold nuggets of fabulous size were unearthed. One, weighing nearly 60 lbs (27 kg) and found by use of a metal detector in Victoria, had a current value of about $1.3 million. Fossilized bones of a giant bird, related to the condor, with an estimated wingspread of 25 ft (7.6 m), were unearthed in Argentina.

Organizations. The International Geological Congress, held every four years, assembled in Paris, July 7–17, 1980. In addition to the usual technical topics the congress focused a great deal of attention on economic and political matters. Faced with energy shortages and economic difficulties, many countries are hoping that earth-science research will turn up substantial supplies of petroleum, natural gas, and minerals. A special session on the continental margins, an explorational frontier, was of interest. The French government announced plans to increase funds for research in earth science and to lower dependence on oil from 60 to 30% by 1990.

Another indication of economic influences on geological science was the announcement that the American Association of Petroleum Geologists had 25,000 members in 1980. The association's widely read monthly bulletin reports on activities, discoveries, and new geological ideas throughout the world.

WILLIAM LEE STOKES
University of Utah

Mount St. Helens in Washington is part of a chain of volcanoes, stretching from Canada to California.

GEOLOGY—SPECIAL REPORT:

Mount St. Helens

At precisely 8:32 A.M. Pacific time May 18, 1980, Americans were made aware of an environmental hazard that few had thought about or anticipated. Mount St. Helens in southwestern Washington had blown its top in a spectacular and destructive volcanic eruption. The event was described as mammoth, awesome, and cataclysmic. The mountain, once a scenic, forested, snow-capped cone, became a scene of ugly desolation that has been referred to as "an unpredictable foe."

The event was not entirely unheralded. An eruption in the mid-1800s, at a time when the region was almost uninhabited, is known but poorly documented. Geologists of the U.S. Geological Survey have been studying the Cascade Range in a comprehensive way for several decades, and in 1978 they characterized Mount St. Helens as "probably the volcano most likely to endanger people and property in the western United States." Minor earthquakes of between 3.0 and 4.5 Richter magnitude began to shake the area March 20 and continued until March 27, at which time steam began to be emitted more or less continually and often with considerable force. This continued until the major May 18 blast. The most ominous preeruption event was a rapid swelling of the upper north summit area. This was detected April 23, and is sus-

pected of having started after the March eruptions. The area moved upward as much as 5 ft (1.52 m) per day to a maximum of about 560 ft (170 m).

The bulge eventually reached what appeared to be near a state of gravitational instability and a warning was issued that it might break loose. The break did occur, but not as had been expected. Three almost simultaneous events are recorded. An earthquake of magnitude 5 shook the mountain, the unstable bulge broke away, and several explosive blasts of hot gas and rock were ejected. Rocks in the landslide mass were instantly pulverized by a laterally directed blast and the resulting slurry of broken volcanic rock and mud moved swiftly northward, chiefly down existing drainage ways. Immediately after the lateral blast a great cloud of steam and ash was expelled vertically from the summit, creating an awesome plume 10 mi (16 km) high. It was estimated that the flank eruption contributed about .5 cu mi (2 km³) of material and that the airborne ash had a volume of .25 cu mi (1.1 km³). Erupted material was about the same in volume as that produced by the famous eruption of Mount Vesuvius that destroyed the Roman cities of Pompeii and Herculaneum in 79 A.D.

More distant effects ranged from practical devastation to mere irritation. The northward-

Tom Zimberoff, Sygma

At precisely 8:32 A.M., Pacific time May 18, Mount St. Helens erupted for the first time since 1857. Several more eruptions followed during the year. The U.S. Army (above) was brought in to look for bodies and to assess the damage to the surrounding area.

UPI

directed blast of heated gas was of hurricane velocity and blew down all trees (chiefly large conifers) within approximately 5 mi (8 km) of the north flank of the mountain. For another 5–6 mi (8–9.6 km) beyond, most of the trees were blown down and still farther away, the trees, although still standing, were scorched and killed. Needless to say, animal life in these zones was practically eliminated.

The landslide swept the lower northern slope of the mountain, rushed into and across Spirit Lake, and had force enough to continue about 13 mi (21 km) down the North Fork of the Toutle River, filling it to a depth of 200 ft (60 m). Ensuing flows of volcanic debris, fed directly from the breached cone, raised the outlet of Spirit Lake by about 300 ft (90 m) and the water level by 115–148 ft (35–45 m). The valley of the North Fork was eventually filled to a depth of 200–300 ft (60–90 m) with a chaotic mass of landslide blocks, trees, volcanic debris, and chunks of ice.

A new and larger Spirit Lake was formed, and uncounted smaller lakes on dammed tributaries.

The airborne ash was carried generally northeastward and fell in decreasing amounts ranging from 3.2 inches (8 cm) on the immediate flanks, to 1 inch (2.5 cm) at Yakima, to slightly less at Spokane. Traces were found as far away as west central Montana. Particles reaching the stratosphere were detected throughout the Northern Hemisphere.

Mount St. Helens is one of a chain of 15 almost evenly spaced volcanoes extending from Mount Garibaldi in British Columbia to Lassen Peak in northern California. Volcanic activity, both destructive and constructive, has been almost continuous along this chain for the past 50 million years. Eight of the present great cones have erupted in the past 200 years but, excluding Mount St. Helens, only Mount Lassen, northern California, in the 20th century. Mount St. Helens is known to have significant peculiarities; it is

Tom Zimberoff, Sygma

The eruption of Mount St. Helens sent volcanic ash and gases into the air and caused severe mudslides and avalanches. Helicopters played a big part in the relief efforts.

UPI

Although many trees were destroyed, much of the fallen timber would be used for construction purposes.

relatively young and most of the present cone has been produced in the past 500 years.

Material erupted by volcanoes is popularly thought to originate deep within the earth. This is generally true, but the Mount St. Helens eruptions ejected chiefly material derived from the cone itself, including surficial soil and shattered glacial ice. The great May 18 explosion almost certainly resulted from release of steam. Eruptions such as this—related to underground water—are called phreatic. Analyses of ash and gas from Mount St. Helens enhance this interpretation. Rock types of the original cone are identifiable, and the emitted gases, chlorine, sulfur dioxide, and small traces of fluorine, are easily derived from such material. Geologists feel that the phreatic eruptions may well be followed by expulsion of material from much deeper (magmatic) sources. If this appears, it will be of different composition and the ash will be composed chiefly of sharp-sided shards that are the walls of collapsed bubbles. Among the more ominous predictions regarding Mount St. Helens activity was that deep-seated magma would move upward to produce hotter and more violent eruptions in the future.

By mid-November, the impact of the eruptions of Mount St. Helens was judged to be not so serious as expected. Nevertheless, 34 persons were killed and 28 were missing and presumed dead. By midyear, 220,000 acres (89 000 ha) of timberland were affected, with a loss of $695 million; crops, chiefly barley and wheat, suffered $260 million damage; $270 million would be required to repair roads, bridges, and sewer systems; and an estimated $44 million was to be spent to dredge the ship channel in the Columbia River. Other damages, variously evaluated, relate to wildlife (especially fish), buildings and homes, temporary business shutdowns, and job losses. Total monetary damage was estimated at $2,700,000,000. In July the U.S. Congress appropriated $951 million in disaster relief.

The May 18 eruption was followed by lesser ones on May 25, June 12, July 22, August 7, and October 16 and 17. These produced substantial ash fall over populous southwest Washington and northwest Oregon. Between eruptions lava rose in the crater to create domes with crusts that were distended and split by pressure from below. Clouds of dust and steam hung over the summit area and earthquakes shook the area almost continuously. The situation was ominous and no optimistic predictions were being made.

The picture was not entirely bleak, however. The blanket of ash proved to be more of a nuisance than a hazard. Although possibly 1 million persons inhaled irritating amounts of ash, it was chemically inert, nontoxic, nonradioactive, and generally no more dangerous than ordinary windblown silt. For some types of soil it is a beneficial additive. There was a bumper crop of hops, and the apple harvest, even in dust-sprinkled orchards, was good. The yield from some wheat fields increased by as much as 33% over 1979. Experts claimed that the ash curbed a threatened grasshopper plague in northern Idaho. The tourist industry, while temporarily depressed, may eventually surge as the curious flock to the scene. Enterprising residents offered bottled and packaged ash as souvenirs and, by covering the W on their license plates, were advertising their state as *ashington*.

WILLIAM LEE STOKES

GEORGIA

Politics, crime, the Bert Lance trial, and the opening of Atlanta's new international airport complex attracted the attention of Georgians in 1980.

Politics. Despite denouncement by the Senate for mishandling of funds, Herman Talmadge defeated Lt. Gov. Zell Miller in a hotly contested primary race, but the four-term senator was defeated by his Republican challenger, Mack Mattingly, in the general election. President Jimmy Carter, as anticipated, carried his home state in the presidential race.

Crime. The mysterious slayings and disappearances of 15 Atlanta children baffled criminal experts as thousands joined search parties to uncover clues related to the crimes.

Convicted murderer Jack Potts made headlines when he twice appealed his death sentence and then dropped his appeals. U.S. District Court Judge O'Kelley denied Potts' second petition, but the 5th circuit granted him a stay of execution. The U.S. Supreme Court in an 8-0 decision upheld the stay, and a three-judge panel of the 5th Circuit was appointed to rule on the legality of O'Kelley's decision.

Lance Trial. Bert Lance, former director of the Office of Management and Budget, along with two codefendants was named in an indictment alleging bank fraud and conspiracy to obtain funds illegally. After a 16-week trial, a jury of six men and six women found the defendants not guilty of all but three counts on which they could not reach a unanimous verdict. The Justice Department later dismissed the remaining bank fraud charges.

Airport Terminal. The William B. Hartsfield Atlanta International Airport's $500 million midfield terminal opened in September. With 138 gates and occupying an area of 378 acres (153 ha), it is the world's largest terminal.

Day-Care Center Tragedy. An explosion at a public housing day-care center in Atlanta took the lives of four children and one teacher. In the aftermath city officials worked feverishly to head off rumors that the explosion had been set deliberately by an extremist group with a vendetta against blacks. The officials were concerned about the recent slayings of black Atlanta children. After full-scale investigations, however, it was concluded that a boiler exploded because of improper maintainence and wiring of an electrically-triggered gas cutoff valve. The Atlanta Housing Authority, which is responsible for maintenance of the center, disputed the findings.

Legislation. A Public Service Reform bill which would expand the staff of the Public Service Commission (PSC) but also limit the PSC's discretion in several technical areas of rate-making was filibustered to death. A bill requiring public schools to teach the biblical theory of creation along with the theory of evolution was debated at length but defeated by the Assembly. Georgia's legal drinking age was raised from 18 to 19, excluding 18 year olds actively serving in the military.

Five years of hard lobbying and some last-minute pressure from the White House netted Georgia's pro-equal rights amendment (ERA) forces only one additional vote as the Senate soundly defeated the ERA.

Gov. George Busbee failed in two attempts to pass legislation dealing with gun registration and background checks of potential purchasers of handguns. The therapeutic use of marijuana for cancer and glaucoma patients was signed into law, while a right-to-die bill was defeated in both houses.

KAY BECK
Georgia State University

Georgia resident Billy Carter, the president's younger brother, was forced to register as a foreign agent as a result of his dealings with the government of Libya. His activities received wide media attention and were the subject of a Senate investigation. No charges were filed against Billy, however.

UPI

GEORGIA • Information Highlights

Area: 58,876 sq mi (152 489 km²).
Population (Jan. 1980 est.): 5,140,000.
Chief Cities (1976 est.): Atlanta, the capital, 425,666; Columbus, 162,599; Macon, 121,898.
Government (1980): *Chief Officers*—governor, George D. Busbee (D); lt. gov., Zell Miller (D). *General Assembly*—Senate, 56 members; House of Representatives, 180 members.
Education (1979-80): *Enrollment*—public elementary schools, 656,743 pupils; public secondary, 421,713; colleges and universities, 178,017 students.
State Finances (fiscal year 1979): *Revenues,* $4,605,-000,000; *expenditures,* $4,347,000,000.
Personal Income (1979): $39,044,000,000; per capita, $7,630.
Labor Force (June 1980): *Nonagricultural wage and salary earners,* 2,124,500; *unemployed,* 184,600 (7.6% of total force).

Mourners pay their respects to 13 persons killed by a bomb explosion at the Oktoberfest in Munich.

GERMANY

Relations between the Federal Republic of Germany (West Germany) and the German Democratic Republic (East Germany or DDR) remained stable during the greater part of 1980. Both sides repeatedly stated their interest in establishing closer ties but attached different meanings to that objective. While the Federal Republic hoped for closer human and cultural contracts in addition to increased trade, the DDR wished to limit the new ties to trade alone.

A continuing irritant in inter-German relations was the question of a separate DDR citizenship. West Germany refused to acknowledge a separate citizenship on the grounds that East and West Germany still were one nation. However, Bonn ceased treating every East German who entered the Federal Republic as automatically a West German citizen and began doing so only at the person's request. The DDR found the new arrangement equally unacceptable and continued to insist on recognition as a completely separate state with a citizenship of its own.

Interstate trade continued to expand, with the DDR once again attaining a slight export surplus. A five-year transportation agreement was concluded in April, providing for improvements in road, rail, and water links between West Berlin and West Germany.

Although both sides wished to shield their mutual contact from the effects of deteriorating U.S.-USSR relations, they could not ignore the Soviet intervention in Afghanistan and the nationwide strikes in Poland. Both events led to the further postponement of a long-planned meeting between West Germany's Chancellor Helmut Schmidt and Erich Honecker, the head of East Germany's (Communist) Socialist Unity party.

In the wake of the Polish labor crisis during the summer and early autumn, East-West German relations worsened sharply. The turning point actually came after the October election victory of the Schmidt government, which the DDR government, by its own admission, did not wish to jeopardize. East Berlin charged Bonn with instigating the Polish strikes and seeking to overthrow the East German government. To reduce the number of West German visitors, who were regarded as fuelers of political discontent, the East German government required all foreign visitors to convert the equivalent of $14 per day into the DDR mark, as against $7 previously. Honecker also renewed his demand for the recognition of DDR citizenship and for normal diplomatic relations, including the exchange of ambassadors.

The West German government rejected these demands as contrary to a treaty the two states had signed in 1973. It also dismissed the various charges as completely unfounded. Yet so as not to preclude the modification or even the cancellation of the new conditions by East Berlin, Bonn abstained from any immediate retaliation and did not impose any economic sanctions. It merely suspended further talks on joint transportation and energy projects and warned that it might not renew existing interest-free credits when they expire in 1982. Meanwhile, a group of 25 West German banks granted Poland nearly $1,000,000,000 in credits to tide that country over its economic and foreign currency problems.

FEDERAL REPUBLIC OF GERMANY
(West Germany)

Elections for the 497-seat *Bundestag* (lower house) on October 5 produced a substantial victory for the governing coalition parties, the Social Democratic Party (SPD) and Free Democratic Party (FDP). The chief gainer was the FDP, which increased its delegation from 39 to 53 seats; the SPD won only four additional seats, raising its delegation to 218. The opposition parties, the Christian Democratic Union (CDU) and its Bavarian offshoot, the Christian Social Union (CSU), lost 17 seats, with their combined delegation declining to 226 seats. The outcome was a personal triumph for Chancellor Schmidt. Many Christian Democrats who did not support the opposition candidate, the feisty CSU minister-president of Bavaria, Franz Josef Strauss, but did not wish to vote for Schmidt's left-of-center SPD, cast their ballots for the middle-of-the-road FDP to keep the chancellor in office.

The election campaign was unusually aggressive. A special nonpartisan commission was appointed to stop distortions and vilifications but it was unable to raise the level of debate. Despite the sometimes vicious attacks from both sides, the outcome of the election was a foregone conclusion. The opposition could not make a convincing case against either the domestic or foreign policies of the Schmidt government. Perhaps more accurately, Strauss himself was no match for Schmidt, as the elections seemed to revolve more around the characters of the two men than their policies.

The Chancellor. Helmut Schmidt continued to dominate the political stage in West Germany during 1980. A man of keen intelligence and wide experience in government—he had been finance minister and defense minister in previous governments—Schmidt was instrumental in bringing economic strength and international status to West Germany during his six years as chancellor. At the same time, Schmidt was careful to stress that West Germany did not seek world power but owed its new strength to economic stability, a determination to ease East-West tensions, and a desire to provide aid and guidance to alleviate the world's economic trou-

Supporters of chancellory candidate Franz Josef Strauss show their enthusiasm at a campaign rally.

Alain Mingam, Liaison

Regis Bossu, Sygma

"Security for Germany" was a theme of the successful reelection campaign of Chancellor Helmut Schmidt.

bles. With the help of his foreign minister, Hans Dietrich Genscher, Schmidt was largely successful in these efforts and was rewarded with an easy election victory.

State Elections. Schmidt's success had been foreshadowed in the spring state elections in Baden-Wuerttemberg, Saarland, and North Rhine-Westphalia. The SPD, but not the FDP, scored gains at the expense of the CDU. In Baden-Wuerttemberg, the new Ecology Party, called the Greens, won 6 seats. Because of internal dissension, however, its attraction quickly subsided, and the party won no seats in the federal elections.

Radicalism. Also unsuccessful in the West German federal elections were the nation's radical parties. The neo-Nazi National Democratic Party (NDP), for example, called for an end to the influx of foreigners—a serious issue in the Federal Republic—but did not win a single seat.

Political extremism, however, was not dead. Leftist radicals blew up a planning office in West Berlin to protest the city's urban renewal plans. In Frankfurt and West Berlin, they organized riots in front of American libraries. And in Bremen, an antiwar demonstration escalated into bloody clashes with the police at a public swearing-in ceremony for army recruits.

Right-wing extremists also were involved in arson, bombings, and beatings. Sizable arms caches were discovered in several of their homes and meeting places. At Munich's Oktoberfest celebration, 13 persons were killed and 214 others injured in a bomb explosion believed to have been set off by a right-wing student radical, Gundolf Köhler. There were recurrent complaints in Bavaria that rightist radicals were being treated with undue leniency by law enforcement authorities.

The Economy. While still among the strongest in the world, the West German economy hovered on the brink of difficulty for much of the year. Unemployment wavered between 3.5 and 5%. The inflation rate, after a rise to 6% in May, dropped to 5.5% by September; however, it would have been almost twice as high if it had been computed according to the U.S. method.

─── **WEST GERMANY · Information Highlights** ───

Official Name: Federal Republic of Germany.
Location: North-central Europe.
Area: 97,883 sq mi (253 517 km^2). West Berlin, 186 sq mi (481 km^2).
Population (1980 est.): 61,100,000.
Chief Cities (1978 est.): Bonn, the capital, 285,100; Hamburg, 1,664,300; Munich, 1,297,000.
Government: *Head of state,* Karl Carstens, president (took office July 1979). *Head of government,* Helmut Schmidt, federal chancellor (took office May 1974).
Legislature—Parliament: Bundesrat and Bundestag.
Monetary Unit: Deutsche mark (1.90 d. marks equal U.S.$1, Oct. 1980).
Manufactures (major products): Iron, steel, coal, cement, chemicals, machinery, ships, vehicles.
Agriculture (major products): Grains, potatoes, sugar beets, meat and dairy products.
GNP (1979 est., U.S.$): $761,000,000,000.
Foreign Trade (Jan.-June 1980, U.S.$): *Imports,* $95,976,000,000; *exports,* $98,431,000,000.

West Germany spent nearly twice as much for foreign oil as it did in 1979, despite a 5% drop in imports. Other imports, especially of Japanese cars, continued to rise, as did payments to the European Community (EC) and remittances by foreign workers to their homelands. Similarly, tourism abroad continued at its usual large volume. In the face of these expenditures, an 11% increase in exports could not redress the balance of payments. The ministry of economics predicted a payments deficit of $15,000,000,000 for the year.

Social Conditions. The presence of some four million foreign workers—mainly Turks, Yugoslavs, Italians, and Greeks—created serious tensions. Concentrated in major industrial centers and shunned by the West German population, they clung to their native customs and cultures and remained unintegrated into their German environment. The Turks, moreover, developed a new Islamic militancy that increased the uneasiness of the Germans. In March, the government took steps to facilitate integration: the waiting period for naturalization was reduced from 10 to 6 years; special courses were to be set up to train foreign school dropouts in various trades; social services for non-citizens would be expanded; and schools introduced special classes for non-German-speaking students.

While the influx of new foreign workers had been stopped some years earlier, foreigners asking for political asylum continued to enter the Federal Republic. Many of these, however, were not bona fide refugees and often came with forged papers. Measures were taken to bar fraudulent claimants at the point of entry, and only 10% of the new arrivals were granted asylum. Since the right to political asylum is an actionable constitutional right, expulsion often was possible only after prolonged judicial procedures. Right-wing extremists fanned the fires of this controversy even further by harassing the refugees. In August, they hurled explosives into a building in Hamburg that housed Vietnamese boat people, killing two and wounding several others.

The West German population continued to decrease, though more slowly (0.2%) than in previous years. Defense Minister Hans Apel warned that because of the drastic decline in the birth rate during the previous ten years there would be a shortage of draft-age men by 1988.

Foreign Affairs. Growing East-West tensions, fueled by the Soviet intervention in Afghanistan, dominated Bonn's foreign policy. The government reaffirmed its close ties with the United States and joined the boycott of the Moscow Olympic Games. On the other hand, it rejected economic sanctions against the USSR as ineffective.

West Germany backed the North Atlantic Treaty Organization (NATO) decision of De-

Apesteguy, Liaison

Chancellor Schmidt met with Soviet President Leonid Brezhnev (right) in Moscow, June 30–July 1, to discuss the Afghanistan situation and possible arms limitations.

cember 1979 to deploy medium-range missiles in Western Europe to counter the growing nuclear capabilities of the Soviet Union. However, it also continued to call for new arms limitations talks with Moscow, hoping to reverse the NATO decision in return for a reduction of the Soviet nuclear potential. In June, Chancellor Schmidt met with Soviet President Leonid Brezhnev in Moscow. The talks did not produce any concrete results, but Schmidt later suggested that arms talks might be resumed.

Despite mutual concerns in regard to the Soviet Union, West German relations with the United States were not without problems. Chancellor Schmidt felt that he was not adequately consulted on American moves affecting West Germany. He insisted that it would be counterproductive to press Moscow too hard on Afghanistan. Bonn also feared that a further deterioration of U.S.-Soviet relations might strain West German ties with East Germany and other socialist states, jeopardizing the repatriation of ethnic Germans from those countries.

Since West Germany obtains the largest part of its oil from the Middle East, it followed developments there with growing concern. In the escalating Persian Gulf crisis, Bonn again allied itself with the United States but made clear that it would not participate in any military action.

In September, the West German ambassador to the United Nations, Rüdiger von Wechmar, was elected president of the General Assembly. West Germans rejoiced in Wechmar's election, considering it a recognition of their country's growing importance.

GERMAN DEMOCRATIC REPUBLIC
(East Germany)

East Germans followed the West German election campaign with keen interest. They felt that the reelection of Helmut Schmidt would allow relations with the Federal Republic to remain relatively stable, while a Strauss victory might lead to new difficulties. However, as soon as Schmidt's reelection was assured, the East German government began charging Bonn with imperialist and subversive designs and issued its new, restrictive currency regulations. There were indications that these steps were part of an overall Soviet-bloc drive, in response to the Polish strikes, to check Western influences.

Internally, the government announced new police initiatives against counterrevolutionary and antisocialist elements. These warnings stood in sharp contrast to the relaxation of pressure against dissidents earlier in the year. At that time, publication of works by authors expelled from the East German Writers Union had been resumed, and one critic of the regime, novelist Stephan Hermlin, had even received the Fatherlandic Order of Merit.

Religion. In preparation for the 500th anniversary of the birth of Martin Luther in 1983, a "Luther Committee of the DDR" was set up.

Erich Honecker assumed the honorary chairmanship of the organization. His wife, Margot, the minister of education, was named a member, along with representatives of political parties, universities, and other official organizations. Church representatives, however, were to serve merely in an advisory capacity. Luther, the German Protestant reformer, was to be celebrated as a bourgeois revolutionary who helped undermine the feudal order and pave the way for the rise of the bourgeoisie.

Church-state relations were generally untroubled. In September, a synod was held near Leipzig, with the state providing assistance in technical matters. Church officials and clergymen were admitted into the state pension system, and a leading sociologist, Rudi Weidig, declared at a congress of East German sociologists that a religious person, too, could make useful contributions to a socialist society. It remained to be seen how the new internal security policies would affect the government's attitude toward the churches. There was never any question, however, as to the priority of Marxist-Leninist principles.

Economy. Despite inflationary pressures, prices for essential goods and services—such as basic foodstuffs, rents, and utilities—remained low. Prices for other goods, however, continued to rise. The lack of foreign currency created shortages in both consumer and capital goods. There was increased recycling of used materials, and prices for scrap metal doubled. The DDR expected recycling to meet 12% of its raw material needs by 1985.

Because of the scarcity of oil, efforts were made to use lignite, the one raw material of which the DDR has ample supplies, as a replacement wherever possible. In addition, the maximum speed for cars was reduced to 50 mph (80 km/h). Visitors from other socialist countries were barred from buying gas except with special government-issued coupons. Westerners still could buy as much as they wished with hard Western currency.

—— EAST GERMANY · Information Highlights ——

Official Name: German Democratic Republic.
Location: North-central Europe.
Area: 41,768 sq mi (108 179 km^2).
Population (1980 est.): 16,700,000.
Chief Cities (1978 est.): East Berlin, the capital, 1,128,-983; Leipzig, 563,980; Dresden, 514,508.
Government: *Head of state,* Erich Honecker, Chairman of the Council of State. *Head of government,* Willi Stoph, chairman of the Council of Ministers Presidium. *First secretary of the Socialist Unity (Communist) party,* Erich Honecker (took office 1971). *Legislature* (unicameral)—Volkskammer (People's Chamber).
Monetary Unit: DDR mark (1.77 DDR marks equal U.S.$1, June 1980—noncommercial rate).
Manufactures (major products): Electrical and precision engineering products, fishing vesels, steel, machinery, chemicals.
Agriculture (major products): Grains, fruits and vegetables, meat and dairy products.
GNP (1979 est., U.S.$): $75,300,000,000.
Foreign Trade (1979 est., U.S.$): *Imports,* $16,214,000,-000; *exports,* $15,063,000,000.

Crime Rate. The continuing shortages in various commodities accounted in part for an increasing crime rate. The increase was especially marked for such offenses as theft, fraud, and embezzlement. Bribery also became more widespread, as money was paid to obtain scarce apartments or other goods and services in short supply. While these developments caused growing concern, it was pointed out that the East German crime rate was still only one sixth that of West Germany.

Foreign Policy. At first siding with the Islamic government of Iran in its capture and detention of U.S. diplomatic personnel, East Berlin soon changed its position and called for the release of the hostages. Special security measures were taken for the protection of the U.S. embassy in East Berlin. The DDR was anxious to show its goodwill on other occasions, as well. At international congresses and exhibitions, East German spokesmen stressed the need for close economic cooperation to preserve world peace.

On the other hand, First Secretary Honecker also made it clear that the DDR would not allow Poland to leave the socialist camp. In a speech to party activists in October, he warned that the Polish workers wished to "liquidate socialism, not to make it more humane." He implied that the Soviet bloc would intervene should the Polish Communist regime be threatened.

Throughout the year, the DDR provided economic and military aid to Marxist and other leftist governments in Africa. East German advisers were active in Ethiopia, Angola, Mozambique, and the Congo. Other experts assisted national liberation movements in South Africa and Namibia (South-west Africa). By aiding these causes, East Berlin acted in keeping with the Marxist-Leninist understanding of "peaceful coexistence" among Marxist and non-Marxist countries. By that definition, however, peaceful coexistence did not preclude support of national liberation movements which are part of the international class struggle.

WEST BERLIN

For the first time in several years, the economy of West Berlin gave promise of some improvement. Two leading car manufacturers, West Germany's Bayerische Motoren-Werke and the West German branch of the Ford Motor Company, set up new plants in the city which were expected to provide some 2,000 new jobs. The International Congress Center, opened in April 1979, hosted some 160 congresses and conferences with more than 100,000 participants during its first year.

In the October federal elections, West Berlin chose its 22 deputies to the *Bundestag.* Because of the special status of the city, however, the 22 deputies are chosen not by the people but by the West Berlin parliament, and their voting rights in the *Bundestag* extend only to matters directly affecting the city. Eleven Christian Democrats, 10 Social Democrats, and 1 Free Democrat were elected.

Railroad Strike. In September, West Berlin found itself caught in a potentially serious East-West controversy. The city's rail services, linking it to eastern and western Europe, are run by the East German railway administration. Apparently inspired by the strikes in Poland, some 500 of the 3,500 West Berlin railroad workers went on strike, demanding wages comparable to those of West German railroaders, which were 30% higher. They also called for the formation of a free trade union. Fearful of trouble, neither the West Berlin government nor Allied military authorities in the city, who still have some supervisory rights, wanted to intervene. The city merely set up an emergency air and bus service. After only a few days, however, railroad police, recruited by the East Germans largely from West Berlin's Socialist Unity party, drove the strikers from most of the installations they had occupied, and the strike collapsed.

ANDREAS DORPALEN
The Ohio State University

UPI

West Berliners line up at a bus station, as a strike by rail workers in September restricted transportation between the divided city and West Germany.

GHANA

President Hilla Limann's civil government, which assumed control from the Armed Forces Revolutionary Council (AFRC) in September 1979, weathered a number of major economic problems without serious challenge from either the Army or political rivals.

Economy. The economy improved only slightly. Inflation and low world prices for cocoa, Ghana's major export, handicapped the government and created general labor unrest. The unemployment rate in the cities stood at 20%. The minimum wage was 4 cedis ($1.45) per day, which would buy less than .5 lb (.25 kg) of fish or three eggs. The economic situation was made worse by the shortage of many staples in the urban areas, although farmers complained of the lack of transport to carry their crops to market.

Strikes were endemic throughout the country. The most serious was that of workers of the Industrial Holding Corporation whose representatives invaded parliament in June. There was also a strike at Ghana Airways and by the food handlers and sanitation workers at the University of Ghana. The former crippled the already marginal airline; the latter closed the university. There was a chronic shortage of spare auto parts and the railway needed an estimated 6 million cedis' ($2.2 million) worth of replacements. Imports of petroleum products remained high, costing more than 15% of Ghana's export earnings. Ghana's petroleum production at Saltpond, which by agreement was sent to the United States, fell by one third to only 2,000 barrels per day. President Limann reiterated that Ghana's economic ills would take years to solve and refused to consider devaluation of the cedi. Short term deficits were met by borrowing, as was some agricultural and rural development. Foreign advisers were consulted on improving the industrial sector. An agreement was reached with Rumania for an agro-industrial complex at Brong-Ahafo, and discussions were conducted with Nigeria about joint exploitation of bauxite reserves.

Politics. President Limann's People's National Party controlled enough seats in parliament to assure that his conservative approach to Ghana's problems would be supported. Despite a call from some opponents to resign, there was no serious threat to the new government. Limann's chief opponent, Victor Owusu of the Popular Front Party, wary of the army, did little to embarrass the president. There was a brief crisis in the north, where 27 people were killed in Wa in a dispute over the chieftaincy and police were dispatched to deal with striking workers of the Industrial Holding Corporation. The most serious potential threat to stability, further intervention by the armed forces, was not in evidence during the year. Flight Lt. Jerry Rawlings, the popular leader of the AFRC, retired and chose to remain generally in the background except to

Stan Sherer

Sparsely stocked shelves in a government supplied store indicate Ghana's lack of consumer goods.

help celebrate the first anniversary of civilian rule. Some members of government demanded that army officers swear allegiance to the government rather than the state, and there was criticism, fueled by Amnesty International's report, of the summary trials conducted by the AFRC. Rawlings and the army might be silent but President Limann, his supporters, and his detractors knew of their presence and the implicit demands that the civil government solve Ghana's problems or risk another military coup.

Foreign Affairs. President Limann was not particularly active in international affairs except in the economic sphere, where he sought better relations with the United States, Upper Volta, Nigeria, and Rumania. He paid a state visit to Sierra Leone in April, where he reiterated Ghana's support of the Organization for African Unity (OAU) and promised cooperation with his neighbors and hostility toward South Africa.

The visit of Pope John Paul II to help celebrate Catholicism's centenary in Ghana was a major event. The pope arrived in Accra on May 8, met with government leaders and the Archbishop of Canterbury, and then flew to Kumasi. His motorcade was greeted by an estimated 1 million persons and he received a ceremonial welcome from the king of the Ashanti.

HARRY A. GAILEY
San Jose State University

───── **GHANA · Information Highlights** ─────

Official Name: Republic of Ghana.
Location: West Africa.
Area: 92,100 square miles (238 538 km²).
Population (1980 est.): 11,700,000.
Chief Cities (1973 est.): Accra, the capital, 848,800; Kumasi, 249,000.
Government: *Head of state and government,* Hilla Limann, president (took office Sept. 1979). *Legislature*—Constituent Assembly.
Monetary Unit: New cedi (2.75 new cedis equal U.S.$1, July 1980).
Manufactures (major products): Minerals, lumber, cement, aluminum.
Agriculture (major products): Corn, manioc, coconuts, cocoa beans, sugarcane.
GNP (1978 est., U.S.$): $10,800,000,000.
Foreign Trade (1977 est., U.S.$): *Imports,* $1,398,000,-000; *exports,* $965,000,000.

Britain's Conservative leaders, including Mrs. Thatcher, attend the party's annual conference.

GREAT BRITAIN

It was another exceedingly difficult year for Great Britain. The country faced the worst recession since the 1930s, and the Conservative government of Margaret Thatcher, in its first full year, was under intense pressure from both friends and opponents to moderate its policies.

Mrs. Thatcher, a disciple of the U.S. economist Milton Friedman, had surrounded herself with economic ministers, all of whom were keen monetarists. They saw their principal task as squeezing inflation out of the economy, a goal which was to override all other considerations, including employment and business confidence.

Unfortunately, the unpleasant side effects of the cure proved far worse than the government or its advisers had predicted, and by the end of the year there were few hopeful signs that the cure was likely to prove effective. Owing in part to miscalculations by the Bank of England, the country's central bank, the amount of money in circulation remained far higher than had been hoped for or foreseen. The minimum lending (prime) rate was raised to 17% in the hope of persuading industry to borrow less. The move failed since companies required the loans to remain solvent, while the high interest rate merely added to the nation's considerable problems.

The Economic Scene. Thanks to oil from the North Sea, now flowing in abundance, Britain retained an excellent balance-of-payments surplus, one of the very few bright spots in an oth-

erwise uniformly gloomy picture. But North Sea oil had another side effect: it pushed the pound sterling up to artificially high rates of exchange. By the end of the year the pound had reached about U.S.$2.40, and business interests complained that this was making their products far too expensive in foreign markets. The high pound also sucked in imports from abroad, adding yet another burden to the load being carried by British business.

By the end of the year industrialists were in open revolt. The Confederation of British Industry, a normally cautious body which had worked hard and paid well for the election of the Conservative government in 1979, spent its entire annual conference complaining about the effects of government policies, and its chairman went so far as to demand a "bare knuckle" fight to persuade Mrs. Thatcher to change her program.

Worst of all, unemployment continued to rise at a dizzying rate, going over the 2 million mark during the summer, the worst figures since the Great Depression. Most of the jobs lost were in the manufacturing industry, the traditional source of Britain's economic strength.

The sheer numbers of unemployed, roughly 8% of the working population, and more than 10% in some badly affected areas, not only cost an enormous amount of money in relief payments, but represented a huge and incalculable loss of output. It also raised anxious queries about what became known as the "social fabric," the consensus which holds a country together. There were fears that the unemployed might turn to crime and violence to try to solve their problems or at least withdraw their support from a government which, while democratically elected, had done little to help them. However, in spite of these fears, there was no clear sign that violence was on the increase, although fighting and dangerous scenes remained an unpleasant feature of some football matches. Fans of the England soccer squad behaved in a particularly violent manner in Turin, during a match against Italy.

People began to realize that high unemployment might be a feature of British life for many years and began to plan for the future. One wealthy restaurant owner in Bath experimentally offered unemployed people £10 ($24) a day to study the best ways of using their time, by going to art galleries, plays, and museums.

The Political Scene. Surprisingly, given the Conservatives' traditions, some party ministers began to display open disloyalty. The Conservatives always have insisted on silent and loyal support for the party. Mrs. Thatcher's position was made all the more difficult by doubts over her policies expressed by former Conservative prime ministers. Edward Heath, her predecessor as party leader, always had been skeptical of her abilities, but Harold Macmillan, perhaps the best-loved and most respected of Britain's living former prime ministers, was a more surprising and damaging defection. Sir Harold Wilson, the former Labour premier, forecast that the Conservatives would ditch Mrs. Thatcher as their leader within three years. Opinion polls showed her policies to be losing support fairly consistently throughout the year.

She herself insisted that there would be no change. She told the annual Conservative conference: "The lady's not for turning." Nevertheless, observers noted a number of shifts of direction in response to the serious economic crises the country appeared to be facing. For example, the government, which had renounced all attempts to control wages, preferring to leave that to the free market economy, attempted to hold wage rises among public employees to 6%, well below the rate of inflation.

Inflation had fallen from about 22% at midyear to a more hopeful but still too high 15% by year's end.

Ministers, or at least those who remained loyal both in public and private, still insisted that the policy was essential for the long-term economic health of the nation, and that it would be pursued to the bitter end. As the situation worsened, and as those who were suffering began to protest more loudly—thanks in part to a reinvigorated Labour opposition—Mrs. Thatcher's economic dream seemed depressingly far away.

The Labour Party had a traumatic year. For some time the party, which by late 1980 had formed the British government for 18 of the 35 years since the end of World War II, has been a battleground between Left and Right. The left wing, openly socialist in its ideals, has been gaining ground on the social democratic right, which is much more dubious about the benefits of state intervention and which tends to look with admiration at West Germany's Social Democratic Party (SPD). At the party conference the Left scored several significant constitutional victories over the Right. Most left-wing party members would work to transfer power from the usually rightist members of Parliament to the more left-wing grass-roots constituency workers. Their greatest triumph was in removing from the members of Parliament (MPs) the sole right to choose the party's leader.

The last election of a leader in which the MPs did have the sole right of choice came in November 1980 after a weary James Callaghan had announced his resignation. Callaghan had been a popular and not unsuccessful prime minister from April 1976 to May 1979, but was tired of holding together a fractious and ungrateful party. The choice of successor boiled down to two: the right-wing former Chancellor of the Exchequer Denis Healey and the more leftist deputy leader Michael Foot. Foot's victory on the second ballot, by 139 votes to 129, was surprising because he originally had been unwilling to stand. He won largely because the MPs felt he stood the best chance of uniting the dangerously frangible party and partly because of his own personal charm and intellectual ability.

But his election undoubtedly marked a strong leftward move in British politics. Foot is, for example, a strong opponent of nuclear weap-

(Continued on page 263)

Michael Foot, 67-year-old former journalist, is the new leader of Britain's Labour Party.

Liaison

Britain and the European Community

The politics of the European Community (EC) were dominated in the first half of 1980 by the question of Britain's contribution to the Community budget. After a protracted negotiating battle the issue was settled, at least temporarily, in early June. But there were a number of ways in which the significance of the episode, both for the Community as a whole and for Britain's relationships within the Community, transcended its immediate impact on EC business.

In the first place, it again raised doubts about how enthusiastic a member of the Community Britain is. The country rejected the opportunity to become a founding member in 1957. It was not until 1971 that Edward Heath succeeded in making a place for Britain in the Community. Since the beginning of Britain's formal membership in the EC in January 1973, successive governments have attempted to redefine the nation's relationship with its European partners. In 1975 Harold Wilson renegotiated the terms of membership, and a referendum was held in which Britain voted to remain in the Community; and in 1979–80 Margaret Thatcher fought a hard battle over Britain's budget contribution.

Prime Minister Thatcher, in contrast to the preceding Labour government, made it plain that her administration unequivocally supports Community membership. But her tactics at the negotiating table were much tougher. By threatening to veto fundamental Community decisions, such as the annual farm-price structure, she set new standards as to the degree of disruption that can be employed to further the interests of individual members.

Mrs. Thatcher and Lord Carrington outline their position regarding Britain and the EC budget.

Alain Mignam, Liaison

UNITED KINGDOM

For the Community the episode again emphasized the inherent imbalance of a joint budget which is three quarters devoted to supporting a single industry, agriculture. The determination to change this balance is increasing at varying speeds among all members. However, by late 1980, there was no sign of an imminent agreement on a radical change of direction.

The text for Mrs. Thatcher's budget renegotiation was set out in the Conservative Party election manifesto in 1979. "National payments into the budget," said the Manifesto, "should be more closely related to ability to pay." As an industrial nation with a relatively small agricultural sector, Britain was bound to lose out from a budget which was largely devoted to supporting the incomes of farmers. The problem was compounded by the relatively high proportion of Britain's imports traditionally coming from outside the Community and by the relative decline of the British economy. With 16% of the Community's gross national product, Britain faced gross contributions of 20.5% and receipts of only 9.5%. The prospects were that these trends would move more against Britain in the future.

Initial talks culminated in an offer at the European summit meeting in Dublin in November 1979 to reduce Britain's prospective net payments of £1,080,000,000 by £350,000,000 in 1980. Mrs. Thatcher had already said publicly that she was aiming at budget balance, in other words net payments of nil, and dismissed the offer as only "a third of a loaf."

By the time of the Luxembourg summit in late April 1980, Britain's partners were prepared to consider a reduction of about £750,000,000, more than double their initial offer. To the evident surprise of other European leaders, Mrs. Thatcher rejected this offer, too. It was not until the foreign ministers' meeting in Brussels at the end of May that agreement was reached on a similar reduction plan. Mrs. Thatcher accepted the proposal on June 2. The accepted plan provided for a formula of budget cuts over a three-year period unless and until the entire system is revised. In exchange Britain accepted higher farm prices.

Under the agreed formula a more generous abatement of gross contributions will contribute one third of the reduction and additional European subventions to British public spending programs the other two thirds. If Britain's net budget contribution turns out larger than expected, the EC will bear three quarters of the excess. In the longer term, there was hope that the European Council would resolve the underlying problem of the budgetary emphasis on agriculture.

RODNEY LORD

ons, which rapidly was becoming a central issue in British politics. In July the government announced that it would buy the U.S. Trident missile system as Britain's own nuclear deterrent, as well as agreeing to station U.S. cruise missiles on British soil. The fevered debate which followed led to a sudden and startling revival of the moribund Campaign for Nuclear Disarmament, which held many well-attended rallies.

Foot is also an opponent of Britain's membership in the European Common Market, an institution increasingly unpopular in the United Kingdom. Mrs. Thatcher spent the best part of a year attempting to reduce Britain's contribution to the Common Market budget which, in 1979, was more than £1,000,000,000 ($2,400,000,000) over the country's receipts. Finally, through dogged persistence, she and her ministers persuaded the other EC countries to reduce Britain's contribution by about £710 million ($1,704,000,000). The compromise was accepted, but the British people remained deeply unhappy about the Common Market. (*See* special report, page 262.)

The Diplomatic Scene. The most dramatic event in the British year was the rescue in May of hostages held in the Iranian embassy, London, by dissident terrorists from Arabistan. After five days during which six armed terrorists had held the hostages, the building was stormed by members of the Army's top secret Special Air Service, a commando group formed in World War II and more recently used in Northern Ireland. All but two of the 20 hostages were saved and five of their six attackers were killed in the brilliantly executed operation. One of the dead hostages had been shot and his body was thrown into the street; the other was believed to have been killed prior to the attack. The government hoped that the lessons of this success would not be lost on other terrorist groups, such as the Irish Republican Army and various Palestinian organizations, which had in the past used London as a battleground.

Swift diplomatic moves had to be made to repair relations with Saudi Arabia following the television showing of a film, *Death of a Princess,* about the execution of a Saudi princess and her lover for adultery. The program possibly may have exaggerated the true story, but many Britons were exceedingly unhappy about the virtual apology offered by Lord Carrington, the foreign secretary. He expressed "deep regret."

The government pleaded with British Olympic athletes to join in the boycott of the Summer Games in Moscow, but with little success. A number of teams, including the riding and fencing squads, did withdraw, but the bulk of the participants arrived in Moscow and took part.

Following two days of talks in April, Lord Carrington and his Spanish counterpart, Marce-

UPI

In the spring, terrorists from Arabistan held 20 persons hostage in the Iranian embassy in London. Fire broke out when a British commando group stormed the building in a successful rescue effort.

POLICE

lino Orega, agreed that direct communications between Spain and Gibraltar should be restored.

Unrest. Fears of racial conflagration were stirred by a serious riot in the St. Paul's area of the normally peaceful historic city of Bristol. Some 19 policemen were injured in fighting which broke out after an attempted arrest at a largely black eating place. Though there were widespread predictions of further violence, none occurred, and even the annual Notting Hill Carnival in London—the scene of grave violence in 1976—was entirely peaceable.

In Northern Ireland, the level of violence remained lower than in some past years. Once again about six times as many people were killed in traffic accidents in the province as died in the fighting. However, ministers faced a hunger strike in the notorious "H-block" of the Maze prison, near Belfast, where most people convicted of terrorist crimes are held. The prisoners wanted so-called "political status" and hence privileges not granted to other convicts. It was feared that the hunger strike and any subsequent deaths might trigger further violence. In the meantime the British government seemed incapable of finding any political solution to the province's troubles, though it continued to withdraw British troops at a steady rate as the number of people murdered decreased.

The Royal Family. Speculation remained high about the marriage intentions of 32-year-old Prince Charles, heir to the throne. Every woman he escorted was subject to intense investigation by the newspapers and broadcasting networks. By the end of the year, the excitement had centered on a 19-year-old teacher, Lady Diana Spencer, the soft-spoken and attractive daughter of an earl. It was learned that Charles' younger sister, Princess Anne, and her husband, Mark Phillips, were expecting their second child. The Queen Mother celebrated her 80th birthday, and Queen Elizabeth traveled to Australia and several Mediterranean nations.

Other Domestic News. A great British institution, the *Times of London,* was threatened with permanent closure when its Canadian owners, the Thompson Organisation, Ltd., announced that they intended to sell it or close it down in March 1981. The same applied to the *Sunday Times,* a quite separate newspaper which the Thompson group also owns. Since 1967 losses on the two titles had, thanks to union action and loss of production, mounted to more than £70 million ($168 million) and the Thompson Organisation was prepared to lose no more. There was a shortage of buyers, partly because of labor problems, partly because of the *Times'* dwindling sales.

The Rt. Rev. Robert Runcie was installed officially as the 102d archbishop of Canterbury. It was announced that Pope John Paul II would visit Britain in 1982.

Heart transplants were revived, and all but two patients at the hospitals in London and Cambridge where the operations were carried out had survived until the fall at least. In April, 146 people were killed when a British plane crashed into a mountain in the Spanish holiday resort of Tenerife, the Canary Islands.

SIMON HOGGART, *"The Guardian," London*

GREAT BRITAIN · Information Highlights

Official Name: United Kingdom of Great Britain and Northern Ireland.
Location: Island, western Europe.
Area: 94,250 sq mi (244 108 km²).
Population (1980 est.): 55,800,000.
Chief Cities (1976 est.): London, the capital, 7,028,200; Birmingham, 1,058,800; Glasgow, 856,012; Liverpool, 539,700.
Government: *Head of state,* Elizabeth II, queen (acceded Feb. 1952). *Head of government,* Margaret Thatcher, prime minister (took office May 1979). *Legislature*—Parliament: House of Lords and House of Commons.
Monetary Unit: Pound (0.4258 pound equals U.S.$1, Dec. 1980).
Manufactures (major products): Metal products, motor vehicles, aircraft, textiles, chemicals.
Agriculture (major products): Wheat, barley, oats, potatoes, livestock, livestock products.
GNP (1979 est., U.S.$): $381,300,000,000.
Foreign Trade (1979, U.S.$): *Imports,* $102,969,000,000; *exports,* $91,030,000,000.

UPI

Queen Mother Elizabeth and her grandson, Prince Charles, ride in an open coach to St. Paul's Cathedral for a thanksgiving service in honor of her 80th birthday.

UPI

Rapidly increasing unemployment brought demonstrations against the government's monetary policies.

THE ECONOMY

The British Conservative government's policy of squeezing out inflation by means of a strict monetary policy began to work in 1980, but at the cost of a rapid increase in unemployment. Economic activity, which began the year still reasonably buoyant, ended in deep recession.

Gross domestic product, which grew by about 1.75% in 1979, ended 1980 nearly 3% lower. The main factor behind the slump was a rapid rundown of inventories. The Bank of England's Minimum Lending Rate was raised in November 1979 to a record 17% and stayed at that level until the following June when it was reduced by 1%. This imposed a heavy penalty on carrying high stocks of raw materials and finished goods while at the same time an unexpectedly strong sterling exchange rate reduced exporters' profits. By the final quarter the average value of the pound against other major currencies had risen 12%, partly because of North Sea oil and a current account surplus and partly because of the attraction of high interest rates to foreigners.

As a result of falling activity there was a very rapid rise in unemployment. The numbers out of work increased considerably faster than would have been suggested by the experience of previous recessions and by the final quarter the number of registered unemployed had reached 9.3% of the work force by mid-December.

During the first half of the year inflation continued to rise from 17.2% at the end of the previous year to a peak of 21.9% in May. About 3.5% of the increase reflected a steep increase in the Value Added Tax, which dropped out of the annual comparison in July. At the same time there was a rapid underlying rise in prices largely as a result of oil price increases and high pay settlements, particularly in the public sector. During the second half of the year the recession discouraged companies from raising prices and the underlying level of inflation fell back to below 10%, producing a year-on-year figure in the final quarter of 15–16%, considerably lower than the government's forecast. Inflation slowed in spite of a more rapid increase in the money supply than intended. The government's policy continued to be directed toward cuts in public expenditure and a conservative fiscal balance.

The balance of payments also defied the government's expectations by finishing the year in strong surplus rather than in the expected large deficit. Exports held up longer than forecast in the face of falling competitiveness while the recession reduced the level of imports.

See also INTERNATIONAL TRADE AND FINANCE; LABOR.

RODNEY LORD, *"The Daily Telegraph," London*

THE ARTS

Against a background of deepening economic recession, administrators and innovators of the arts in Great Britain had to shape their plans more skillfully in 1980 and seek private as well as basic Arts Council patronage. For the first time the Royal Shakespeare Company acquired corporate sponsors for several of its productions and for a national tour of small towns. However, financial uncertainties did not seem to have depressed artistic vitality. The year brought sharp surprises, spectacular flops, and unexpected successes. For some presentations—such as the National Theatre's *Amadeus*—tickets were almost impossible to get; for other events audiences were reportedly less willing to fill houses. Despite cutbacks, there appeared to be no recession in quality.

Theater. Two defiantly extravagant dramatic amalgams were presented by the Royal Shakespeare Company (RSC). Early in 1980, John Barton directed *The Greeks,* a mammoth cycle of the plays of Euripides, Aeschylus, and Sophocles, interspersed with events from Homer. Each nine-hour showing was spread over three evenings. Entirely different, but received with something like ecstasy by the London critics, was the RSC's stage version, over two evenings, of Charles Dickens' *Nicholas Nickleby,* skillfully adapted by Donald Edgar.

Excellent Shakespearean productions were presented by both the National Theatre and the RSC. The productions included the National Theatre's *Othello,* with Paul Scofield, and the RSC's *Hamlet,* with Michael Pennington, and *Timon of Athens,* with Richard Pasco. However, top honors for originality went to Richard Eyre's production of *Hamlet* at the Royal Court Theatre, with Jonathan Pryce as Hamlet. Pryce, hailed in the role as "the Hamlet of his generation" and "Hamlet without the ghost," played Hamlet's scenes with the ghost as a mentally deranged conversation with himself.

The commercial theater sustained notable flops, while the "fringe" flourished. In the field of musicals a lavish production of *On the Twentieth Century* folded after four months, but a "fringe" revival of *Pal Joey* made it to the West End, London's major commercial theater district. The year welcomed new plays from Alan Ayckbourn, Alan Bennett, and Howard Brenton. Michael Frayn's *Make and Break* moved into the West End from the Lyric Hammersmith, and Ronald Harwood's *The Dresser* arrived from the Royal Exchange, Manchester. Also applauded was the appearance of the play *Funny Turns* by Victoria Wood.

A significant move was made toward the end of 1980. Director Peter Gill, who started the new Riverside Studios and directed notable productions there, including a tough *Julius Caesar* in 1980, was invited to join the National Theatre under the stewardship of Sir Peter Hall.

Music. Financial cutbacks in 1980 cast some gloom in the music world. The British Broadcasting Corporation (BBC), the largest employer of musicians in Britain, decided to close down five orchestras, including the large Scottish Symphony orchestra. This move provoked a dispute with the Musicians Union which caused the promenade concerts, an historic and popular summer event, to lose the first week of their season. After negotiations, the BBC decided not to disband the Scottish Symphony orchestra or the Northern Ireland orchestra, but merely three light music orchestras. The strike then ended. Overall, audience numbers at concerts were down, and proposals to increase ticket prices were under discussion.

Despite the unpredictable financial picture, there was no lack of audiences for some of the year's major operatic events. At the Edinburgh Festival, the Scottish Opera opened to general acclaim with Alban Berg's *Wozzeck,* and the Royal Opera at Covent Garden mounted a magnificent *Lucrezia Borgia,* with Joan Sutherland. The English National Opera presented Josephine Barstow in *Fidelio* and a rarely done George Frederick Handel work, *Julius Caesar.* At the Glyndebourne Festival Opera, an exquisite *Entführung aus dem Serail* opened the season, although *Der Rosenkavalier,* featuring Felicity Lott as an excellent Octavian, provoked disappointed reactions to the chocolate-box sets and costumes of French designer Erté.

Dance. The year opened with a series of linked productions throughout London under the title of "Dance Umbrella." Featuring soloists and small groups from the United States and Canada, the productions stirred interest in contemporary dance. BBC television designated June "Dance Month" and showed a wide range of performers and choreographers at work in master classes. As well as reviving old favorites like "Romeo and Juliet," with Margot Fonteyn and Rudolf Nureyev, and securing a first broadcast direct from the Kirov Theatre in Leningrad of Marius Petipa's "Raymonda," the BBC also presented "post modern" choreographers from New York. At the Royal Ballet two top choreographers produced new works—Frederick Ashton's "Rhapsody" for Lesley Collier and Mikhail Baryshnikov, and Kenneth MacMillan's "Gloria," with music by Francis Poulenc.

Fine Arts. Included in 1980's successful major art shows were the British Museum's comprehensive archaeological exhibition "The Vikings" and the Royal Academy of Art's huge "Post-Impressionism" exhibition. An enormous success with the younger generation was the Tate Gallery's Salvador Dali exhibition, which attracted more than 250,000 visitors.

The Tate Gallery had an eventful year—art historian Alan Bowness became the director in January, and the Barbara Hepworth sculpture gallery in St. Ives was accepted as an extension.

Maureen Green, *Author and Journalist*

On May 5, the National Assembly of Greece elected Prime Minister Constantine Caramanlis to a five-year term as president of the republic. Three days later, the ruling New Democracy Party chose George John Rallis as the new premier.

GREECE

The election of Prime Minister Constantine Caramanlis as president, the naming of his successor, and controversy over the nation's role in the North Atlantic Treaty Organization (NATO) highlighted the year 1980 in Greece.

Elections. Prime Minister Caramanlis, whose New Democracy Party held a parliamentary majority, was elected president of Greece on the third and final ballot in parliament on May 5. The 73-year-old Caramanlis, who guided Greece back to democracy after the collapse of the military dictatorship in 1974, took the oath of office on May 15. He succeeded Constantine Tsatsos. Following Caramanlis' resignation from the office of prime minister, the New Democracy Party surprised political observers by electing (88 to 84) Foreign Minister George J. Rallis as the new prime minister over Defense Minister Evangelos Averoff-Tositsas. Although rumors abounded that Averoff would form his own party, he remained as defense minister in the new cabinet. Rallis, scion of a longtime politically active family and himself once a royalist, indicated his devotion to the current republican system and generally followed the policies previously implemented by Caramanlis.

The chief parliamentary opposition, the Panhellenic Socialist Union (PASOK), led by Andreas Papandreou, refused to participate in the presidential balloting, hoping to force national elections earlier than November 1981, as scheduled.

NATO and the American Bases. Prime Minister Rallis and the new foreign minister, Constantine Mitsotakis, made strenuous efforts to bring Greece back into the military wing of NATO. Greece withdrew from the military aspects of NATO in 1974, after the Turkish invasion of Cyprus led to a strain between Greece and other NATO members. Greece had sought to return since 1976, but the Turkish government had blocked the attempt. Rallis emphasized that Greece's reentry was directly related to the signing of a new accord for the continued existence of four strategically important U.S. bases in Greece. The issue became important domestically, because Papandreou and PASOK had built up anti-American and anti-New Democracy sentiment by calling for a full withdrawal of Greece from NATO. With the help of NATO Supreme Commander Gen. Bernard W. Rogers, Rallis and Mitsotakis came to an understanding with the military government that had come to power in Turkey in September. On October 20, Greece was reintegrated into NATO's military wing. Negotiation on a new agreement regarding the U.S. bases began the following week.

Constantine II. A socialist call for the expropriation of former King Constantine II's private holdings was resisted by the government on the grounds that his status did not deprive him of the personal property rights held by all Greeks. Constantine and Queen Anne-Marie were present at the July funeral of the ousted shah of Iran, Mohammed Reza Pahlavi, in Cairo.

Economy. A high rate of inflation—approximately 25%—eroded popular support for the New Democracy party despite measures to soften the impact. Early in the year, the government set voluntary import curbs and a partial freeze on prices and profits. A balance of payments deficit and an inability to attract significant new foreign investments added to Greece's financial difficulties.

GEORGE J. MARCOPOULOS, *Tufts University*

GREECE · Information Highlights

Official Name: Hellenic Republic.
Location: Southeastern Europe.
Area: 50,961 square miles (131 990 km²).
Population (1980 est.): 9,600,000.
Chief Cities (1971 census): Athens, the capital, 867,023; Salonika, 345,799; Piraeus, 187,458.
Government: *Head of state,* Constantine Caramanlis, president (took office May 1980). *Head of government,* George J. Rallis, prime minister (took office May 1980). *Legislature*—Parliament.
Monetary Unit: Drachma (42.95 drachmas equal U.S.$1, Oct. 1980).
Manufactures (major products): Food products, textiles, metals, chemicals, electrical goods, cement, glass.
Agriculture (major products): Grains, citrus fruits, grapes, vegetables, olives and olive oil, tobacco, cotton, livestock, and dairy products.
GNP (1978 est., U.S.$): $32,500,000,000.
Foreign Trade (Jan.-March 1980, U.S.$): *Imports,* $2,-147,000,000; *exports,* $1,162,000,000.

Liaison

Forbes Burnham is Guyana's first president with executive powers but was accused of election fraud.

GUYANA

The year 1980 was one of political and economic crisis for Guyana.

Politics. During the first months of the year, the government of Prime Minister Forbes Burnham prepared for the trial of Walter Rodney and two other leaders of a new opposition party, the Working People's Alliance (WPA). The three were charged with having burned the headquarters of the governing People's National Congress on July 11, 1979. Just before the trial, 16 other WPA members were arrested for plotting to overthrow the government. Six were accused of treason, a charge that had not been used in Guyana since 1823.

Observers from several international human rights groups were present for the opening of the Rodney trial in early June. The proceedings, however, would never come to fruition. On June 13, Rodney was murdered, the victim of a bomb explosion in his car.

Rodney's murder brought protests from political leaders in many parts of the world, and

some 30,000 people participated in the funeral procession. And although the reaction to .the murder did not immediately endanger the Burnham government, political unrest continued.

Despite criticisms of its human rights record and its mounting political problems, the Burnham administration was not hampered in its plans to change the Guyana constitution. The document was approved, and parliament elected Burnham as Guyana's first president with executive powers. Taking office October 6, Burnham named Ptolemy Reid as prime minister, an office now with limited power. In December 17 national elections, Burnham got 76% of the votes to defeat opposition candidate Dr. Cheddi B. Jagan, but an international team of observers said the election was replete with fraud and intimidation of voters.

Economy. Inflation, a decline in the gross national product (GNP), and a severe balance of payments deficit continued to plague the economy. In spite of political protests, however, Burnham sought and reached agreement with the International Monetary Fund (IMF) and World Bank to help resolve these difficulties. On July 25, the two organizations approved loans to Guyana totaling $133 million. In return, Guyana agreed to a wide range of austerity measures. The loans included $5 million for a feasibility study of a major hydroelectric and irrigation project in central Guyana. Also in July, the government received a loan of four million pounds from Lloyd's Bank for several smaller development projects.

ROBERT J. ALEXANDER
Rutgers University

GUYANA · Information Highlights

Official Name: Cooperative Republic of Guyana.
Location: Northeast coast of South America.
Area: 83,000 sq mi (214 970 km²).
Population (1980 est.): 900,000.
Chief City (1976 est.): Georgetown, the capital, 205,000 (met. area).
Government: *Head of state*, Lynden Forbes Burnham, president (took office Oct. 1980). *Head of government*, Ptolemy Reid, prime minister (took office Oct. 1980). *Legislature* (unicameral)—National Assembly.
Monetary Unit: Guyana dollar (2.55 G. dollars equal U.S.$1, Aug. 1980).
Manufactures (major products): bauxite, wood products.
Agriculture (major products): sugar, rice, coconuts.
GNP (1978 est., U.S.$): $470,000,000.
Foreign Trade (1978, U.S.$): *Imports,* $279,000,000; *exports,* $289,000,000.

HAWAII

Federal and local elections highlighted the year 1980 in Hawaii.

Government and Politics. The 1980 elections saw no major surprises, as the Democrats continued to dominate. Although Hawaii was one of the six states won by President Carter, the margin of victory was a slim 5,767 votes. Both Democratic incumbents in the U.S. House of Representatives—Cecil Heftel and Daniel Akaka—won reelection, as did Sen. Daniel Inouye. The Democrats also retained control of the state legislature, with a 17 to 8 margin in the Senate and a 39 to 12 edge in the House. In her first try for elective office, former state Director of Budget and Finance Eileen Anderson, 52, narrowly defeated incumbent Mayor Frank Fasi in the September 20 Democratic primary and went on to become the first woman mayor of the city and county of Honolulu.

Of special significance was the election of the first board of trustees for the newly-created Office of Hawaiian Affairs. Mandated by constitutional amendments adopted in 1978, the agency would provide and coordinate services for persons of Hawaiian ancestry. Only voters of Hawaiian extraction were allowed to vote, and nine trustees were elected from a field of 90 candidates.

Several referendum items also were on the ballot. State constitutional amendments imposing more rigid standards for the adoption of future constitutional amendments were ratified, but amendments to the Honolulu city charter calling for a change in council representation were defeated. Voters in the County of Kauai rejected by a 2-to-1 margin resort development in a specified area, but the legal effect of the vote remained unclear.

Economy. The Hawaiian economy continued to show steady growth, but much of the gain was due to inflation. Sugar and pineapple fetched high prices, and defense spending in the islands remained stable. Tourism, Hawaii's major industry, did not grow so rapidly as in previous years, and an increase in air fares created concern over a slowdown in the industry. Related to the concern were worries over Hawaii's growing crime problem. Much publicity was given to the incidence of crime against tourists, particularly those from Japan and Canada. While tourism was expected to continue as Hawaii's major industry, public debate over its adverse social and environmental effects likely would continue.

Population. Preliminary estimates of the 1980 census indicated a 25% increase in the state's population from 1970 to 1980. While approximately 79% of the population resided on the island of Oahu, larger growth was recorded on the outlying islands. The counties of Maui and Hawaii had increases of slightly more than 50%.

The 1980s. In 1981, the Hawaiian legislature would consider an official government plan to help guide the future growth of the state. In a state largely dependent on imported oil, more attention would be paid to the development of alternate energy sources. Renewed interest in the welfare of native Hawaiians already was complemented by a growing awareness of a "Pacific community"—the idea that Hawaii should work more closely with its neighbors to promote the welfare of Oceanian peoples.

RICHARD H. KOSAKI, *University of Hawaii*

――――――― **HAWAII · Information Highlights** ―――――――

Area: 6,450 sq mi (16 706 km²).
Population (Jan. 1980 est.): 920,000.
Chief Cities (1970 census): Honolulu, the capital, 324,-871; Kailua, 33,783; Kaneohe, 29,903; Hilo, 26,353; Waipahu, 22,798.
Government (1980): *Chief Officers*—governor, George R. Ariyoshi (D); lt. gov., Jean Sadako King (D). *Legislature*—Senate, 25 members; House of Representatives, 51 members.
Education (1979–80): *Enrollment*—public elementary schools, 89,115 pupils; public secondary, 79,545; colleges and universities, 47,204 students. *Public school expenditures*, $269,418,000 ($1,556 per pupil).
State Finances (fiscal year 1979): *Revenues*, $1,670,-000,000; *expenditures*, $1,524,000,000.
Personal Income (1979): $8,356,000,000; per capita, $9,223.
Labor Force (May 1980): *Nonagricultural wage and salary earners*, 408,700; *unemployed*, 17,400 (4.4% of total force).

HONG KONG

Increasing economic ties with China augured prosperity for Hong Kong's future. The British colony joined the U.S.-led boycott of the Summer Olympic Games in Moscow and the economic sanctions against Iran. A merger of the Hong Kong stock exchanges and a large influx of immigrants were other significant developments.

Economy. In the first half of the year, Hong Kong's exports increased by 33%, imports by 35%, and reexports by 44%, compared with the same period in 1979. Hong Kong's container port at Kwai Chung became the world's third largest after New York and Rotterdam, and a second terminal was being considered. Airborne merchandise in 1979 increased by 41% over 1978, and a $350 million study was conducted for a replacement airport at Chek Lap Kok.

In March, Hong Kong became the first entity besides the founding nations in Europe and America to link up with the Society for Worldwide Interbank Financial Telecommunications (SWIFT). After three years of negotiations, an agreement was announced in May for the merger of Hong Kong's four stock exchanges. However, the Unified Stock Exchange of Hong Kong Ltd. was not expected to begin functioning for three years. Gold prices soared in January, and the Hong Kong Commodity Exchange operated a gold futures market later in the year.

Nearly 2.5 million tourists visited Hong Kong during the year, representing a 10% increase over 1979.

Joint Ventures. In February, China signed with a Hong Kong company to operate the first passenger bus service between the People's Republic and Hong Kong; in April, it signed with another company to establish a rock crushing plant at Woo Shek Koo quarry; in May, to build a flour mill at Shekou; and in June, with Cathay Pacific Airways to operate scheduled air service between Hong Kong and Shanghai. A second Lo Wu Bridge linking Hong Kong with Shenzhen was expected to be completed by February 1981. With a guaranteed supply of coal from China, the Hong Kong Electric Company planned to spend $400 million on a conversion program to allow the use of coal for 80% of its output by 1984. In July, China Merchants Steam Navigation gave a contract to Hong Kong's Cable and Wireless Co. for the installation of a telephone exchange and microwave communications network between Hong Kong and Shenzhen.

Immigration. Between January and July, Hong Kong accepted some 27,000 legal immigrants from China and 36,000 illegal immigrants from China and elsewhere. To cope with the problem, Gov. Murray MacLehose announced a new policy on October 23. Authorities were empowered to arrest and repatriate all illegal immigrants.

CHUEN-YAN DAVID LAI
University of Victoria, British Columbia

HOUSING

The housing market in 1980 was the worst since the major housing recession of 1975. Production and existing home sales were down sharply from 1979. The construction of single-family homes was down 50% and the sale of existing homes was down 25%. Worldwide, the housing shortage in the developing nations remained acute. President-elect Reagan named Samuel R. Pierce, Jr., as secretary of Housing and Urban Development.

THE UNITED STATES

The decline in the housing market in 1980 was related directly to the rise in mortgage interest rates. The housing market actually began to decline in October 1979. By January 1980, existing homes sales were at an annual rate of 3.2 million units, down sharply from the 1979 sales of about 3.7 million units. During January, mortgage interest rates for single-family homes were generally in the 11.5-12.5% range. Spring usually signals the start of the active months of the housing market. However, spring 1980 was a resounding "dud." Interest rates rose to the 14-16% range, and home sales were down to an annual rate of less than 2.5 million units. Housing production also was down dramatically, from 1979 levels of 1.2 million units to about .6 million units.

Housing specialists agreed that the demand for housing was strong. The problem was that prospective buyers could not afford to buy a home when the only financing available was at record high interest rates. The monthly payment to amortize a $60,000 mortgage at 10% annual interest over a 30-year period is $526.54. If the interest rate increases to 12.5% the payment increases to $640.35 per month. When interest rates are 15%, as they were in April and May, the payment is $758.67 per month. Many homeowners could not afford the payments on the homes they currently own if their payments were based on high interest rates. Several studies demonstrated this fact and concluded that the average American can no longer afford the average American home.

High interest rates usually mean unhappy voters. Since 1980 was an election year most economists expected presidential action to ease interest rates. The rates appeared to peak in March and April, and by June were down to the 12% range. The 12% rate was unbelievably high in a historical sense and at any other time a rate that high would have driven away home buyers in droves. However, when compared with the 15% rate of March, the 12% rate did not look so bad. The housing market showed an underlying strength and rebounded sharply. By the end of the summer, existing homes sales had returned to the respectable level of about 3.0 million units. New construction did not rebound so sharply. Many builders were afraid of starting homes because unsold units might be carried by the builder throughout the winter. Another reason for fewer starts was that by the autumn there were fewer builders. Some analysts estimated that one of four builders who were in business in 1979 was no longer in business in 1980. Those still in business were extremely cautious about the future. To help improve the housing situation federal legislation was enacted.

In a Rose Garden ceremony on October 8, President Jimmy Carter signed into law the Housing and Community Development Bill of 1980. This act expanded by 30% federal aid to low-income and moderate-income housing programs. The legislation also revised Federal Housing Administration (FHA) mortgage rates and gave some protection to condominium and cooperative owners. Also on October 8, the president named an advisory committee on housing prospects for the 1980s, with Robert C. Weaver, former secretary of Housing and Urban Development, as head.

NEW HOUSING UNITS STARTED

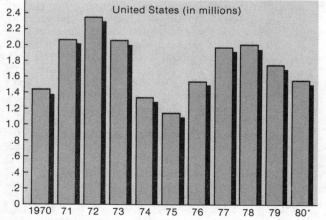

United States (in millions)

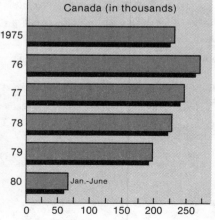

Canada (in thousands)

Sources: Bureau of the Census, Department of Commerce; Statistics Canada

*preliminary, seasonally adjusted

Condominiums

The term condominium describes a certain type of housing ownership and not a particular type of property. The condominium form of ownership provides for the complete ownership of a particular unit of a multi-unit property and an undivided share in the common areas of the property. The particular unit may be an apartment-type unit in a high-rise building, one-half of a duplex, a lot in a mobile-home park, or a spot in a camp ground. The common areas, in which the unit owner has an undivided share, include those parts of the property that many owners will use, such as parking lots, hallways, elevators, and the grounds surrounding the building. Such common areas may also include swimming pools, tennis courts, recreation rooms, and other amenities. Unit owners are responsible for the upkeep of the interior of their own units and must contribute to a general fund for the upkeep of the common areas.

Many people confuse condominiums with cooperative apartments. The cooperative apartment is owned by the tenants of the apartment complex. The tenants own a portion of the entire property, similar to the undivided interest that condominium owners have in their common areas. The basic difference between co-ops and condos is that the condominium owner actually owns a particular unit. The cooperative owner does not own the unit in which he or she lives. The ownership is a share, similar to the shares of stock in a corporation, in the entire building and not in one unit. The obvious advantages of owning one particular unit have contributed to the current popularity of condominiums.

Condominium ownership now constitutes an increasing share of the housing market. The typical condominium buyers are single, between 25 and 35 years of age, or "empty nesters," married couples whose children no longer live at home. Both of these groups are increasing in size. Because of rising property prices and the limited amount of land that is readily accessible to downtown areas, more developers are turning to condominiums. Many areas are experiencing a conversion-to-condo boom, as rental apartments, especially in downtown areas, are being converted at a rapid rate. According to a study released in 1980 by the Department of Housing and Urban Development, 19.3% of the nation's rental housing is suitable for conversion to condominiums. In fact, the condo-conversion craze has been so widespread recently that some cities have enacted and others have considered legislation to protect the rental-housing market by controlling the number of condo conversions.

Many home buyers have become attracted to the condominium life-style. The chores normally associated with home ownership, such as yard care and snow removal, are paid for by the condominium association. Most condominiums also offer facilities for leisure activities. Through shared ownership, the unit owner can enjoy tennis courts, swimming pools, and other facilities that he or she could not afford to own solely.

The condominium may also offer significant financial advantages over single-family homes or apartments. More condominium units than single-family homes can be built on a parcel of land. More units mean a lower land cost for each unit. The developer can further reduce the costs per unit by concentrating the units in one area and reducing the costs of roads, sewer lines, and water mains. Therefore, the condominium is within the price range of many people who cannot afford single-family homes.

There are also certain tax advantages to owning a condominium rather than renting an apartment. The condominium owner is allowed to reduce taxable income by the amount of interest paid on the mortgage loan that finances the unit and by the amount of land-property taxes paid each year. These savings can be quite significant and may reduce the cost of owning a condominium to approximately the amount it would cost to rent a similar unit. For example, the buyer of a $70,000 condominium who financed the purchase with a $56,000 loan at 12% interest would pay approximately $760 per month in mortgage payments, association charges, property taxes, and insurance. (The monthly cost of $760 assumes a 30-year mortgage and a common charge of about $50 per month.) The tax advantages of ownership would reduce that cost to $485 per month (assuming a 40% tax bracket).

One of the major advantages to the condominium owner is the appreciation in value of the condominium unit. Inflation and the demand for real estate have caused prices to rise. In some areas the increases have been dramatic. However, even modest rates of increase in value may cause dramatic increases in the owner's equity. If the price of a $70,000 condominium were to increase at a modest 8% per year, then in seven years the unit would be worth $120,000. In that time the owner's equity would have increased from $14,000 to $59,000, a four-fold increase, or 23% per year, compounded annually.

Condominiums are not for everyone. Many people dislike the rules and regulations that are part of the condominium life-style. The condominium unit cannot be expanded or the exterior modified without approval of the condominium association. The life-style and the regulations which provide security and greater opportunity for social activity for some are unnecessarily restrictive and limiting to others.

EDGAR J. MCDOUGALL, JR.

Business viewed Ronald Reagan's landslide victory in the presidential race as a positive sign. However, by November, interest rates had climbed back to the spring levels of about 15% and the housing market was ending the year with a "thud." Existing home sales for the year were approximately 2.6 million units and single-family housing starts were approximately .7 million units. The year 1980 would be remembered as one of the worst years for housing since World War II.

The Outlook. The housing market should rebound sharply in 1981. As 1980 ended, Ronald Reagan seemed ready to fight inflation through tax cuts and reduced government spending rather than through a tight money supply and higher interest rates. What remained to be seen was how effective the president's policies would be in the short term and if those policies could be enacted with a Democrat-controlled House of Representatives.

The long-run prospects for the housing market remained very good. The sun belt states were growing rapidly. Labor and land costs were lower in those states than in other parts of the United States so that people could buy "more house" for the money they received from selling their homes in the North. Many prospective home buyers would have adequate funds for a down payment because of the equity in their previous home. All the market really needed was a sustained period of fairly low interest rates and the housing boom would return.

A Different Market. The new housing produced in the 1980s should be quite different from the traditional American home. Units should be smaller, more energy efficient, and part of planned developments rather than the traditional single-family subdivision of detached houses on individual lots. Households should have fewer members and demand less space. Family size has been declining since the mid-1960s. According to the National Association of Realtors, four out of five of the households formed during the 1980s will consist of one or two persons. By 1990 the size of the average household is expected to be 2.5 persons. The number of households should continue to increase. Much of the construction should be one-or two-bedroom condominium units. (*See* special report, page 271).

Financing. The high interest rates of 1980 caused lenders and borrowers to seek new methods of financing. Lenders always have had the problem of making long-term loans based on current information. Once the loan is made, the interest rate is fixed over the term of the loan and that term is typically 25 to 30 years. If interest rates go up, the lender is unable to raise the rate and the borrower receives an unexpected benefit. To protect themselves, lenders began to offer loans with rates that vary with the market interest rates. If rates go down, the borrower benefits. If rates go up, the lender benefits. Generally the variable rate loans were offered at rates .75%-2% below the current fixed rate.

Some lenders were attempting to benefit from the increase in housing values through equity participation loans. The borrower was offered the loan at an exceptionally good interest rate, such as 8% when market rates are 13%. However, if the borrower were to sell the home, a certain portion of the equity (the sale price minus the loan balance) would go to the lender. The idea is that receiving a portion of the equity allows the lender to benefit from the increase in home prices, and the lower interest rate makes homes affordable to more persons.

Some home buyers attempted to avoid the high interest rates of new loans by assuming the existing loans on the homes they were buying. The existing loans were made in earlier years when interest rates were appreciably lower. Lenders typically do not like new owners assuming old loans because the lender cannot charge the current higher rate. Many mortgages have an acceleration clause which prohibits the new buyer from obtaining the old loan at the old rate. However, landmark court cases in California and Florida have voided, at least temporarily, the acceleration clauses. If interest rates remain high, then court cases should arise in many more states.

WORLDWIDE

Canada. The housing slump in Canada was even worse than in the United States. Mortgage interest rates in Canada reached as high as 20%. Inflation also was high, so the Canadian home buyer was confronted with higher prices and expensive loans to finance the higher prices. Analysts were not optimistic about a quick turnaround in the Canadian market. Several of the very large Canadian real estate development companies appeared to think the grass might be greener on the other side of the border. They entered the U.S. market and were engaged in large projects in the United States.

South America. Housing shortages still were a pressing problem throughout South America. The housing in many areas is poor and the density is great, which causes serious sanitation and social problems. Attempting to raise the quality of housing may reduce the quantity of housing. For example, Buenos Aires, Argentina, instituted a new stricter building code and city plan. The result was that there was a 50% drop in building construction in 1980 compared with 1979.

Soviet Union. The Soviet Union entered the 1980s with plans to upgrade the quality and aesthetics of its mass-produced housing. Soviet housing often has been criticized for poor quality and monotony. New plans would emphasize a greater sensitivity to aesthetics. Higher quality construction should mean lower maintenance costs and longer lives for housing units.

EDGAR T. McDOUGALL, JR.
University of Connecticut

HUNGARY

A close examination of the country's economic problems and a reshuffling of the government hierarchy highlighted the 12th Congress of the Hungarian Socialist Workers' Party, March 24–28, 1980.

Domestic Affairs. Addressing the 764 delegates at the Congress, First Secretary János Kádár acknowledged that the country's rate of inflation was nearly 20% in 1979 and that real incomes had risen by only 9% since 1975, instead of the promised 25%. The gross national product increased by only 1.5% in 1979, instead of the planned 3–4%. Instead of rising by 3-4% as planned, industrial production fell by 1.8% in the first part of 1980. Kádár called for greater efficiency in production and greater response to international demand. He advocated the shutting down of noncompetitive enterprises, flexibility in management and pricing, and support for small enterprises and agriculture.

At the congress, Kádár also announced social policies to be incorporated in the Sixth Five-Year Plan (1981-85). Included were a five-day work week, an improved service sector, a large-scale housing program, higher family allowances, and an increase in pensions.

At the end of the congress, five of the 15 Politburo members and one fourth of the party's Central Committee were replaced. The Politburo was reduced to 13 members, and the new Central Committee members tended to be younger and better educated than those who had been dropped.

In June, elections were held for the 352-seat National Assembly, as well as for 59,270 seats in local councils. Double candidacies were allowed in 15 parliamentary districts. Of 7,809,000 eligible voters, 97% went to the polls. Of those, 99.3% cast their ballots for candidates of the Patriotic People's Front. Some 210 incumbent deputies were renominated and reelected. Kádár received 99.8% of the vote in his constituency.

The labor unrest in Poland, which received more media coverage in Hungary than in most other Eastern European countries, had a minor effect on domestic affairs. Jozsef Timmer, secretary of the National Trade Unions, called for greater "autonomy" for his organization.

Foreign Affairs and Trade. At the party congress, First Secretary Kádár praised the Soviet Union and reaffirmed his country's loyalty. He blamed "reactionary circles" for the conflict in Afghanistan, criticized China for aggression, but refrained from direct criticism of the United States.

To increase competition and flexibility in foreign trade, a new import-export company, Generalimex, was formed. At the end of 1979, The Central European Bank (CEB)—in which the Hungarian National Bank holds a 34% interest—was opened. The first of its kind in Eastern Europe, CEB's ownership is shared by Italian, West German, Austrian, French, and Japanese banks. A few months later, a branch of the National City Bank of Minneapolis was opened in Budapest.

According to official statistics, more than 9,-845,000 tourists visited Hungary in 1979.

JAN KARSKI, *Georgetown University*

ICELAND

Ending a government crisis that began with the general elections of December 1979, Gunnar Thoroddsen, deputy chairman of the right-of-center Independence Party (IP), announced a new—and rather peculiar—coalition government in February 1980. Thoroddsen's initiatives were in direct defiance of an IP Althing (parliament) caucus. His desertion led to speculation as to how the IP, Iceland's strongest party for half a century, would be affected. All but five of the IP members of parliament opposed the government, as did the Social Democrats. Joining the coalition were the centrist Progressive Party and the left-wing People's Alliance. The new government was expected to command 32 votes in the 60-seat Althing.

On June 30, Vigdís Finnbogadóttir, a leftist opponent of Iceland's membership in NATO, won a dramatic four-way election race for the

─────── HUNGARY • Information Highlights ───────

Offical Name: Hungarian People's Republic.
Location: East-central Europe.
Area: 35,920 sq mi (93 033 km²).
Population (1980 est.): 10,800,000.
Chief Cities (1979 est.): Budapest, the capital, 2,093,187; Miskolc, 210,948; Debrecen, 199,742.
Government: *Head of state,* Pál Losonczi, chairman of the presidential council (took office April 1967). *Head of government,* György Lázár, premier (took office 1975). First secretary of the Hungarian Socialist Workers' party, János Kádár (took office 1956). *Legislature* (unicameral)—National Assembly.
Monetary Unit: Forint (20.31 forints equal U.S.$1, 1980, noncommercial rate).
Manufactures (major products): Iron and steel, pharmaceuticals, textiles, transportation equipment.
Agriculture (major products): Corn, wheat, potatoes, sugar beets, fruits.
GNP (1979 est., U.S.$): $41,900,000,000.
Foreign Trade (1979, U.S.$): *Imports,* $8,674,000,000; *exports,* $7,938,000,000.

─────── ICELAND • Information Highlights ───────

Official Name: Republic of Iceland.
Location: North Atlantic Ocean.
Area: 39,709 sq mi (102 846 km²).
Population (1980 est.): 228,000.
Chief Cities (Dec. 1978): Reykjavik, the capital, 83,376; Kópavogur, 13,269; Akureyri, 12,889.
Government: *Head of state,* Vigdís Finnbogadóttir, president (took office Aug. 1980). *Head of government,* Gunnar Thoroddsen, prime minister (took office Feb. 1980). *Legislature*—Althing: Upper House and Lower House.
Monetary Unit: Króna (540 krónur equal U.S.$1, Oct. 1980).
Manufactures (major products): Fish products, aluminum.
Agriculture (major products): Hay, potatoes, turnips, meat and dairy products.
GNP Per Capita (1978 est., U.S.$): $8,320.
Foreign Trade (1979, U.S.$): *Imports,* $824,000,000; *exports,* $781,000,000.

presidency of the republic. Although the post is largely ceremonial, Finnbogadóttir received extensive international publicity for becoming Iceland's first woman head of state.

Economy. The joint policy declaration by the governing coalition gave top priority to reducing inflation, which had increased by about 60% over 1979. Full employment, a traditional commitment in Icelandic politics, also was emphasized. The solid popular backing for Thoroddsen's cabinet began to wane in the autumn, however, largely because of its lack of success in curbing inflation. Wages and prices rose steadily, despite the docility of organized labor, a carry-over from the tenure of the left-of-center coalition government of Ólafur Jóhannesson.

Icelandair reeled from losses on its U.S.-Luxembourg routes, and an intense controversy broke out over the carrier's request for government assistance. The economy continued to rely heavily on foreign credit, and the burden of agricultural subsidies was the subject of an acrimonious public debate.

Fisheries. Catches were generally good in 1980, but the industry as a whole suffered from a grave cost squeeze despite relatively high export values. The take of cod was headed beyond 400-000 t (441,014T), far more than marine biologists had suggested. Capelin fishing was under strict controls, while the recovery of the south Iceland herring stock permitted an enlarged take. A long-standing dispute with Norway over fishing rights near Jan Mayen faded after a compromise solution was reached.

Energy. The skyrocketing cost of imported petroleum products, still coming largely from the Soviet Union but with prices conforming to Rotterdam spot-market quotations, spurred domestic energy development. Work on a new hydroelectric station in the south progressed on schedule. The northwest region, whose geothermal potential is minimal, was given access to the expanding national power grid. There was renewed drilling for steam for the geothermal power plant at Krafla in the north; three volcanic eruptions near the site in 1980 left the installation intact.

HAUKUR BÖDVARSSON, *"News From Iceland"*

IDAHO

Volcanic ash and politics were the big events in Idaho in 1980.

Volcano. The May 18th eruption of Mount St. Helens, 200 mi (320 km) to the west in Washington, deposited a layer of ash as deep as 4 inches (10 cm) in the center of a 150-mi (240-km)-wide swath in northern Idaho. A heavy rain four days later helped stabilize the ash, but during heavy windstorms unplowed fields and forests (evergreen trees retain their needles for two years) still supply ash that increases particulate levels far above Environmental Protection Agency standards.

Politics. Idaho voters defied a national low vote trend when 80% of registered voters cast a record-breaking 439,678 ballots.

A strident Senate campaign between four-term incumbent Frank Church (D), chairman of the Foreign Relations Committee, and Congressman Steve Symms (R) was won narrowly by Symms. In the Senate campaign more than $3 million was spent by the candidates and more then $250,000 by other groups, a rate exceeding $7 for each vote cast.

Rep. George Hansen (R) held his first district seat against a challenge by Diane Bilyeu (D). State Sen. Larry Craig (R) defeated Glenn Nichols (D) for the seat vacated by Symms. Republicans increased their 19-16 margin in the state Senate to 23-12, and their 50-20 House margin to 56-14.

Two constitutional amendments were approved. One allows initiatives to be voted on every two years instead of the four previously required. The other allows nonprofit church-owned health facilities to use tax exempt bonds to finance construction.

Economy. The summer was cold and wet. By mid-July more than double the normal rain had fallen. Cereal crop yields set records. Potato harvest declined 8% due to a decrease in acres planted. Prices, more than twice 1979's and caused by decreased national output, indicated profits for farmers.

Lumbering, Idaho's second largest industry, was hard hit. High interest rates substantially reduced home building. One major lumber producer reported that earnings had fallen 41%. Other business earnings were also down.

Legislature. The 1980 session lasted 84 days. The Senate adjourned early but was forced back when the House refused to consent. The legislature increased appropriations 13.5% to $405.8 million, but declining revenues forced Gov. John V. Evans (D) to hold back 3.85% of the appropriations. The session also passed bills to freeze, for the third consecutive year, the amount local governments may spend; gave homeowners a 20% exemption from taxes on their homes; established minimum flows for some streams; or-

------------ **IDAHO • Information Highlights** ------------

Area: 83,557 sq mi (216 413 km²).
Population (Jan. 1980 est.): 917,000.
Chief Cities (1976 est.): Boise, the capital, 102,915; (1970 census): Pocatello, 40,036; Idaho Falls, 35,776.
Government (1980): *Chief Officers*—governor, John V. Evans (D); lt. gov., Philip E. Batt (R). *Legislature*—Senate, 35 members; House of Representatives, 70 members.
Education (1979–80): *Enrollment*—public elementary schools, 110,782; public secondary, 91,976; colleges and universities, 40,661 students. *Public school expenditures,* $328,328,000 ($1,475 per pupil).
State Finances (fiscal year 1979): *Revenues,* $995,000,-000; *expenditures,* $891,000,000.
Personal Income (1979): $6,852,000,000; per capita, $7,571.
Labor Force (June 1980): *Total labor force* 436,600; *unemployed,* 36,200 (8.3% of total force).

ganized a Court of Appeals; set conditions regulating leasing of mobile homes; exempted the speculative portion of the value of farm lands from taxation; and limited state expenditures to 5⅓% of total personal income.

It failed to pass bills mandating jail sentences for drunk driving, higher truck and auto fees to facilitate road repair, local option taxing plans, and a constitutional amendment favoring the Sagebrush Rebellion (a plan to transfer federal lands to states and private owners).

CLIFFORD DOBLER, *University of Idaho*

ILLINOIS

Politics and political figures dominated the news during much of 1980.

William J. Scott, the state's popular attorney general, saw both his personal and political life turn to shambles almost overnight. On March 19 a federal jury convicted Scott, 54, of tax fraud for understating his 1972 income by $22,153. The verdict followed a ten-week trial in which federal prosecutors tracked Scott's lavish spending, world travels, and philandering over a four-year-period—a time during which Scott said he was tending the store as state attorney general.

Coincidentally, the jury's finding came one day after the Republican primary election in which Scott was seeking to become the Republican candidate for the U.S. Senate seat being vacated by Sen. Adlai E. Stevenson. Scott, who had been favored to win the primary, lost. Scott later was sentenced to one year and a day in federal prison and was forced to resign as attorney general, a post to which he was elected in 1968. He maintained that he would eventually be vindicated on his appeal.

Elections. Scott lost the Republican primary to Lt. Gov. Dave O'Neal, who was defeated in November by Illinois Secretary of State Alan Dixon, one of the state's more popular Democrats.

Illinoisans felt honored to have their state known as the home of the newly-elected president, Ronald Reagan, the first native son to be elected to the office. Reagan was born in a second-floor flat over the First National Bank in the village of Tampico, IL, on Feb. 6, 1911. The Reagan family lived in several Illinois communities, including Chicago, before settling in Dixon, a relatively small farming and manufacturing community, when the future president was nine years old. Reagan calls Dixon his "hometown."

Like most of the rest of the nation, Illinois voters chose Reagan over President Carter and kept up a tradition since 1920—broken only in 1976—of voting for the winner. Reagan's margin of victory over Carter was 51 to 42%, roughly the same as his national margin. Republicans also won back control of the Illinois house.

Although Illinois Gov. James R. Thompson said the state chose Reagan because voters would not reward Carter for "four years of failure," Illinois voters apparently voted their pocketbooks. Unemployment in the state reached 9.8% in July, the highest since the state started keeping records during the great depression. In addition, adverse farming conditions caused the state's farmers to have a poor year.

Illinois voters decided in a "citizens referendum" to reduce the size of the Illinois House from 177 members to 118, effective in 1983. The margin of victory for the referendum was two to one. The electorate also voted out the 110-year-old system of cumulative voting—a system that confused many voters and gave each legislative district three House members in the General Assembly.

Illinois legislators worked hard to defeat the "cutback" referendum, arguing that it would reduce minority representation and would not save taxpayers' money. Proponents argued that Illinois had the second-largest House in the country and that the legislative process was cumbersome. They said the 118 new single-representative districts would be "good for the citizens, rather than just good for the politicians."

Agriculture. Illinois farmers were hurt in 1980 by spring storms that were followed by scorching, dry weather and insects during the summer months. The U.S. Department of Agriculture estimated that Illinois farmers would produce 19% less corn and 13% less soybeans than in 1979. The state ranks first in soybean production and second in corn.

Seventy-nine Illinois counties, most of them in the southern portion of the state, were declared disaster areas as a result of the heavy rains and hot weather. In those counties, corn yields dipped to 20 bushels per acre, compared with a statewide average of 100 bushels per acre. Losses for the farmers totaled tens of millions of dollars.

ERA. Illinois legislators, for the seventh time in eight years, again refused to ratify the Equal Rights Amendment. The vote fell five votes short in the Illinois House, despite a concerted drive by Gov. James R. Thompson and Chicago Mayor Jane Byrne to win ratification.

ROBERT ENSTAD, *"Chicago Tribune"*

─────── **ILLINOIS • Information Highlights** ───────

Area: 56,400 sq mi (146 076 km²).

Population (Jan. 1980 est.): 11,234,000.

Chief Cities (1970 census): Springfield, the capital, 91,-753; (1976 est.): Chicago, 3,074,084; Rockford, 141,-358.

Government (1980): *Chief Officers*—governor, James R. Thompson (R); lt. gov., David C. O'Neal (R). *General Assembly*—Senate, 59 members; House of Representatives, 177 members.

Education (1979–80): *Enrollment*—public elementary schools, 1,367,133 pupils; public secondary, 676,-106; colleges and universities, 612,916 students. *Public school expenditures*, $4,315,892,000 ($1,937 per pupil).

State Finances (fiscal year 1979): *Revenues*, $11,202,-000,000; *expenditures*, $10,418,000,000.

Personal Income (1979): $110,032,000,000; per capita, $9,799.

Labor Force (June 1980): *Total labor force*, 5,493,500; *unemployed*, 504,700 (9.2% of total force).

Residents of Lucknow, the capital of Uttar Pradesh, wade through floodwater in late July. The floods in northern India left more than 400 persons dead and an estimated 10 million homeless.

UPI

INDIA

After a period of political confusion in late 1979, former Prime Minister Indira Gandhi regained firm control of India in January 1980 with a landslide victory in the nation's seventh general election and with a strong showing in May by her Congress (I) Party in state assembly elections. Her position was adversely affected, however, by the death of her son, Sanjay, in a June plane crash, and by widespread violence, especially in the troubled northeast and Uttar Pradesh. After "deterioration in almost every sector of the economy" in the fiscal year 1979–80, the economic situation began to improve. But inflation, uncertainty about planning, and drought and floods of unusual severity adversely affected the economy. The year was a very active one in foreign policy, with Mrs. Gandhi meeting numerous heads of state during two trips abroad. India was visited by an unusually large number of foreign leaders, and two major international conferences were held in New Delhi. India's official reaction to the Soviet invasion of Afghanistan in December 1979 provoked considerable criticism and bewilderment, both at home and abroad.

Politics. The Janata party, which had been in power since India's sixth general elections in March 1977, was shattered by internal dissension in 1979, and its remnants were no match for Mrs. Gandhi's Congress (I) in the seventh general elections, held on Jan. 3 and 6, 1980. Six national parties and 4,626 candidates contested the elections, in which 196 million Indians—55.49% of the eligible voters—participated. Although the

Congress (I) got only 42.56% of the vote, it won 350 of the 542 seats in the Lok Sabha (lower house of parliament). The rump Janata, consisting mostly of members of the former Jana Sangh party, got 18.97% of the vote but only 32 seats. The Lok Dal, an outgrowth of Janata led by former Prime Minister Charan Singh, won 41 seats. The Communist Party-Marxist (CPI-M) took 35 seats (27 from West Bengal); the Tamil Nadu-based Dravida Munnetra Kazhagam (DMK), 16 seats; the Congress (U), 13 seats; and the pro-Soviet Communist Party of India (CPI), 11 seats. Congress (I) won a majority of seats in all but two major states—West Bengal, where the CPI-M-led left front won 31 of 41 seats, and Kerala, where it won only 5 of 20. It scored almost a clean sweep in Andhra Pradesh, Gujarat, Himachal Pradesh, Karnataka, Orissa, and the Punjab. Because of the unsettled situation in Assam, voting was held in only 2 of the state's 14 parliamentary constituencies. Of the 416 members of the previous Lok Sabha who sought reelection, only 149 were successful. About half the members of the new Lok Sabha were newcomers.

In elections to the state assembly in Kerala, held only two weeks after the national elections, a left front headed by the CPI-M won almost twice as many seats as a right front led by the Congress (I), even though Mrs. Gandhi campaigned for two days in that state.

On January 14, Mrs. Gandhi was sworn in as prime minister, along with 14 other cabinet ministers and 7 ministers of state. Key appointments were those of R. Venkataraman as minister of finance and P. V. Narasimha Rao as minister of external affairs.

When Congress (I) returned to power in January, the party controlled only 7 of the 22 state governments. In subsequent weeks it gained control of 3 more states—Haryana, Himachal Pradesh, and Karnataka—as a result of defections and party-switching. Then, on February 17, on the instructions of Prime Minister Gandhi, the president dismissed the governments of, and called for new assembly elections in, 9 states controlled by the opposition—Bihar, Gujarat, Madhya Pradesh, Maharashtra, Orissa, the Punjab, Rajasthan, Tamil Nadu, and Uttar Pradesh. In elections to the state assemblies of these states on May 28 and 31, the Congress (I) won control of all except Tamil Nadu, where the local DMK got a majority of the 234 seats and the Congress (I) only 30.

The Janata again underwent a split in March, when former Minister of Defense Jagjivan Ram and his followers left the party, and still another in April, when former Jana Sangh members formed a new party called the Bharatiya Janata. The Lok Dal split apart in April, when Raj Narain broke away to revive the Janata party (Secular). During the same month, a pro-Congress (I) section of the CPI, mostly followers of veteran Communist S. A. Dange, who had resigned as chairman of the CPI in November 1979, formed the All-India Communist party.

In the January national elections, Prime Minister Gandhi's controversial son, Sanjay, was elected to the Lok Sabha for the first time. He became his mother's chief confidant and adviser, a role he had also played during the emergency of 1975–77. Many observers believed that he was being groomed as Mrs. Gandhi's successor, thus perpetuating the Nehru "dynasty." But Mrs. Gandhi suffered a personal tragedy and the Indian political scene was substantially changed when, on June 23, Sanjay was killed in the crash of a light plane that he was piloting.

On April 14, an assassination attempt in New Delhi nearly took Prime Minister Gandhi's own life. A knife thrown by a man standing in a crowd outside the parliament building only narrowly missed her.

Unrest. In spite of the reestablishment of a strong central government, law and order deteriorated alarmingly throughout the country, with a sharp increase in communal rioting and other violent crimes. Political tension and violence were most serious in the troubled northeast, especially in Assam and Tripura. In Assam, a ten-month movement against non-Assamese (mainly Bengalis from Bangladesh or West Bengal), forced the closing of schools and colleges and the postponement of elections in most constituencies, paralyzed operations at some of the country's major oil facilities, and blocked the flow of crude oil to refineries in Bihar. Units of the Indian army were sent into the state. Many persons were killed and hundreds arrested. Tripura was the scene of the worst ethnic warfare since India's independence in 1947, with more

than 400 deaths. In June, the government rushed in troops to put down riots stemming from efforts by natives to expel thousands of Bengali immigrants from Bangladesh. Communal violence also was common in other parts of India, especially Bihar, Gujarat, and Uttar Pradesh. In August, more than 100 people were killed in fighting between Hindus and Muslims in Moradabad, Uttar Pradesh.

Citing the troubled internal situation, the central government and many of the state governments assumed extraordinary powers. In September, a new national security ordinance was issued, empowering the central government "to detain any person if it is necessary to prevent him from acting in any manner prejudicial to the defense of India or to the security of the nation." Opposition leaders condemned the ordinance as a revival of the hated Maintenance of Internal Security Act, which Mrs. Gandhi's government invoked during the emergency of 1975–77.

Economy. The fiscal year 1979–80 was a difficult one for the Indian economy. The gross national product declined by 3%. Industrial production was only 0.8% less than in 1978–79, but agricultural production declined by about 10%, mainly because of widespread drought. Inflation

Sanjay Gandhi, the politically powerful son of the prime minister, died in a plane crash in June.

UPI

increased alarmingly to 16.7%. Sharp increases in oil prices added to a large balance of payments deficit. Costs of imports increased by about 25%, whereas export earnings rose by only 8%. Foreign exchange reserves declined for the first time in several years. The overall budget deficit was nearly 80% higher than in 1978–79.

In presenting the budget for 1980–81 to parliament on June 18, Finance Minister Venkataraman said that the main task was to arrest the deterioration in the economy. Total expenditures were estimated at Rs. 274,670,000,000, including Rs. 73,400,000,000 from the central government for the annual plan outlay. The deficit was estimated at a staggering Rs. 16,400,000,000—eight times that of the previous fiscal year. The budget included provisions for Rs. 30,940,000,000 for assistance to the Indian states, Rs. 1,500,000,000 for drought relief, and Rs. 3,400,000,000 for a massive national rural development program.

In July, the Aid India Consortium pledged a total amount of $3,400,000,000 for the fiscal year 1980–81, approximately the same as the pledge in the previous year. World Bank commitments to India in 1980 reached the record figure of $1,-625,000,000.

In 1980, the main task of a thoroughly reorganized Planning Commission was to prepare the long-delayed Sixth Five-Year Plan. While the plan was officially launched in April, the draft framework was approved by the National Development Council only in late August. It envisioned an outlay of Rs. 900,000,000,000 during 1980–85, which would require about Rs. 9,375,-000,000 in additional taxes, reduced budgetary subsidies, and substantial external aid. A target of 5% in overall growth was set—4% in agricultural production and 8–9.5% in industrial production. Broad objectives included the expansion of employment opportunities and the removal of poverty.

In spite of drought and erratic monsoon rains, food grain production in 1980–81 gave promise of reaching between 132 and 135 million tons, substantially higher than in 1979–80 but only slightly higher than in 1978–79. By the end of the year, there were other encouraging signs of at least a partial recovery from the economic setback of 1979–80.

Foreign Policy. Mrs. Gandhi became prime minister only about two weeks after the Soviet invasion of Afghanistan in December 1979. She obviously did not share U.S. President Jimmy Carter's assessment that this was the most serious threat to world peace since World War II. Even before Gandhi's election, India's representative to the United Nations expressed what presumably were her views, when he accepted the Soviet explanation that it had been invited to send troops into Afghanistan and that its move was a reaction to hostile actions against Afghanistan by unspecified "foreign powers." Mrs. Gandhi seemed to be more concerned with the U.S. offer of military and economic aid to Pakistan—which

President Zia ul-Haq eventually refused—than with the Soviet actions in and threats from Afghanistan. But she repeatedly stated that she was opposed to intervention in any country, and apparently she did urge the Soviet leaders to withdraw their troops from Afghanistan at the earliest possible time. Her position on this issue provoked considerable criticism, in India and elsewhere, but it was consistent with her overall foreign policy and with India's heavy dependence on and close ties with the Soviet Union.

State Visits. During 1980, Prime Minister Gandhi met numerous world leaders, both in India and during two trips abroad. Many heads of state went to India for two major international conferences. From January 21 to February 9, the third general conference of the United Nations International Development Organization (UNIDO) was held in New Delhi. It was attended by more than 1,000 delegates from 84 countries and about 45 UN organizations. Among the participants were UN Secretary General Kurt Waldheim, Austrian Chancellor Bruno Kreisky, and President Ziaur Rahman of Bangladesh. From September 4 to 8, the second regional conference of the Commonwealth heads of government in the Asian-Pacific region—"the first Commonwealth Summit in India," as Mrs. Gandhi described it—brought the presidents and prime ministers of 15 countries to New Delhi. Among the other heads of state who visited India in 1980 were the presidents of Cyprus, France, the Maldives, Seychelles, Sri Lanka, Zaire, and Zambia; the kings of Nepal and Bhutan; and the emir of Kuwait.

In April, Prime Minister Gandhi went to Salisbury to represent India at Zimbabwe's independence ceremonies. While in Salisbury, she met many prominent world leaders, including the presidents of Bangladesh, Tanzania, and Pakistan, and the foreign ministers of the United Kingdom and the People's Republic of China. During a May trip to Belgrade for the funeral of the late Yugoslav President Josip Broz (Tito), she met an even more impressive group of world leaders: Chinese Premier Hua Guofeng, Soviet President Leonid Brezhnev, East German President Erich Honecker, President Saddam Hussein Takeiti of Iraq, British Prime Minister Margaret Thatcher, Japanese Prime Minister Masayoshi Ohira. She met with Brezhnev again during his highly publicized visit in mid-December.

Indian Foreign Minister P. V. Narashima Rao also traveled extensively in 1980. In May, he went on a four-day official visit to Moscow. In New York during August and September, he addressed the Special Session on Economic Cooperation and Development of the United Nations (UN) General Assembly, as well as the inaugural meeting of the ministers of the "Group of 77," and the 35th regular session of the UN General Assembly.

In two highly controversial diplomatic moves, India accorded full diplomatic recogni-

PLO leader Yasir Arafat is met in New Delhi by Prime Minister Gandhi in late March, a week after India granted full diplomatic recognition to his organization.

UPI

tion to the Palestine Liberation Organization (PLO) in March—after which PLO leader Yasir Arafat was officially welcomed—and to the government of Cambodia (Kampuchea), headed by Heng Samrin, in July.

United States. The biggest contention between India and the United States in 1980 was over the very sensitive issue of nuclear fuel. The Carter administration was embarrassed by the conflict between a 1963 agreement to supply enriched uranium for the atomic power plant at Tarapur, near Bombay, and the 1978 Nuclear Nonproliferation Act, which permitted the United States to sell nuclear fuel only to countries complying with the terms of the international Nuclear Nonproliferation Treaty of 1968. India had not signed the 1968 treaty, and while it accepted international inspection of the Tarapur plant, it would not permit inspection of its other reactors. In spite of a unanimous recommendation by the Nuclear Regulatory Commission against the further shipment of enriched uranium to India, President Carter decided to authorize the shipment of an additional 39 tons. The U.S. House of

Representatives voted overwhelmingly against the president's decision, but on September 24 the Senate upheld it by a vote of 48 to 46. The outcome helped to improve Indo-American relations at a time of special U.S. concern over southern Asia, but President Carter was widely criticized in the United States for risking the spread of nuclear weapons.

India strongly protested a variety of U.S. moves which, it alleged, adversely affected trade between the two countries. In 1979 Indo-U.S. trade reached about $2,000,000,000. Charges of unfair and discriminatory treatment of Indian exports were quieted in October, when the United States withdrew the countervailing duties it had imposed three months earlier on imports of Indian textiles.

In October, the United States agreed to sell India $230 million worth of antitank missiles and mountain warfare artillery. This was the first major purchase of U.S. arms by India in more than a decade.

In August, K. R. Narayanan, a veteran Indian diplomat who had been ambassador to Thailand, Turkey, and the People's Republic of China, was nominated as the New Indian ambassador to the United States. He assumed charge of the Indian Embassy in Washington a few weeks later, after a lapse of nearly 18 months since the departure of his predecessor, Nani Palkhivala.

In 1980, three subcommissions of the U.S.-India Joint Commission held meetings—the fifth meeting of the Economic and Commerical Subcommission in March, the sixth meeting of the Subcommission on Education and Culture in April, and the first meeting of the Subcommission on Agriculture in September. All three sessions were reported to be particularly fruitful.

NORMAN D. PALMER
University of Pennsylvania

INDIA • Information Highlights

Official Name: Republic of India.
Location: South Asia.
Area: 1,269,346 sq mi (3 287 606 km²).
Population (1980 est.): 676,200,000.
Chief Cities (1971 est.): New Delhi, the capital, 3,600,-000; Bombay, 6,000,000; Calcutta, 3,200,000.
Government: *Head of state,* Neelam Sanjiva Reddy, president (took office July 1977). *Head of government,* Indira Gandhi, prime minister (took office January 1980). *Legislature*—Parliament: Rajya Sabha (Council of States) and Lok Sabha (House of the People).
Monetary Unit: Rupee (7.69 rupees equal U.S.$1, Oct. 1980).
Manufactures (major products): Textiles, processed food, steel, machinery, transport equipment, cement.
Agriculture (major products): Rice, pulses, oilseeds, cotton, jute, tea, wheat.
GNP (1979 est., U.S.$): $96,000,000,000.
Foreign Trade (1979 est., U.S.$): *Imports,* $8,427,000,-000; *exports,* $6,702,000,000.

Dan Quayle, 33-year-old Republican, prepares to move from the U.S. House of Representatives to the U.S. Senate. The former newspaper executive defeated three-term incumbent Birch Bayh in a highly publicized race.

Wide World

INDIANA

Indiana was in the forefront of the Republican Party landslide in the 1980 state and national elections. The legislature's 30-day, alternate-year "short session" was both busy and productive.

Election. Republicans dominated the elections in Indiana. Ronald Reagan carried 85 of the state's 92 counties to defeat President Jimmy Carter by almost 400,000 votes. The most significant Republican victory was that of Dan Quayle over three-term Democratic Sen. Birch Bayh in a campaign reminiscent of Bayh's victory over Homer E. Capehart in 1962. Also significant was the defeat of 22-year-veteran Congressman John Brademas of South Bend, Democratic party whip in the House of Representatives. Democrats did retain six of Indiana's eleven congressional seats.

With the election of Robert D. Orr, Republicans retained control of the governorship for the fourth straight term, and all other state offices also went to Republicans. Democrats lost no key leaders in the state legislature, but Republicans substantially increased their hold on both houses. Although narrowly reelected to his seat in the General Assembly, state Sen. Martin Edwards, under federal indictment for bribery and conspiracy, relinquished his position as president pro tem to fellow Republican Robert J. Garton.

Legislature. The Indiana legislature repealed the unpopular vehicle safety inspection law, refused to mandate vehicle emission control testing despite possible loss of $100 million in federal highway funds, and outlined a major reorganization of state transportation reponsibilities. Lawmakers provided judges and juries with a new verdict, "guilty but mentally ill," which carries the same sentence as if the defendant were found

guilty, and finally appropriated funds to administer the two-year-old crime victim assistance program. Energy-related legislation included a law encouraging coal desulfurization and gasification and offering state income tax credits for installation of solar and other alternative energy systems in homes and businesses.

The legislature reluctantly authorized a $39 million loan to the financially troubled Chrysler corporation. The approximately 15,000 Indiana jobs at stake overrode the legislators' distaste for further government intervention in the free enterprise system, but Chrysler's plans to close or sell several plants in the state, despite the loan, angered Gov. Otis R. Bowen and the General Assembly. After a bitter four-year fight the legislature enacted a new highway funding bill that replaced the 8-cent-a-gallon excise tax on gasoline with an 8% charge.

Budget. Lawmakers approved a $70 million supplement to the biennial $9,200,000,000 budget passed during the preceding legislative ses-

─────── **INDIANA • Information Highlights** ───────

Area: 36,291 sq mi (93 994 km²).
Population (Jan. 1980 est.): 5,422,000.
Chief Cities (1976 est.): Indianapolis, the capital, 708,-867; Fort Wayne, 183,039; Gary, 163,675; Evansville, 133,609.
Government (1980): *Chief Officers*—governor, Otis R. Bowen (R); lt. gov., Robert D. Orr (R). *General Assembly*—Senate, 50 members; House of Representatives, 100 members.
Education (1979–80): *Enrollment*—public elementary schools, 563,117 pupils; public secondary, 520,709; colleges and universities, 228,397 students. *Public school expenditures,* $1,904,674,000 ($1,615 per pupil).
State Finances (fiscal year 1979): *Revenues,* $4,612,-000,000; *expenditures,* $4,089,000,000.
Personal Income (1979): $46,279,000,000; per capita, $8,570.
Labor Force (May 1980): *Nonagricultural wage and salary earners,* 2,232,700; *unemployed,* 278,900 (10.5% of total force).

sion. Approximately $50 million of the supplement was an "11% model" inflation adjustment for teachers, university personnel, and state employees. A so-called "fail-safe" budget measure that would have allowed the previous spending program to continue if any legislature failed to enact an appropriations bill did not pass.

Legal. Indiana made legal history in 1980 when for the first time an automaker faced criminal rather than civil charges in deaths resulting from a car crash. The state's penal code allows criminal charges against individuals or corporations whose failure to take responsible action constitutes reckless behavior. After a two-week trial Ford Motor Company was acquitted of reckless homicide—due to improper and unsafe gas tank placement—in the deaths of three young women whose Pinto exploded in flames when struck from the rear.

Other. Unemployment figures in several Hoosier cities were among the highest in the nation. Indiana's population grew at a rate of 3.9% in the 1970s, less than half the national average of 8.3%.

LORNA LUTES SYLVESTER, *Indiana University*

INDONESIA

The most noteworthy political event in Indonesia during 1980 was the submission to parliament in May of a petition signed by 50 nationally prominent political figures attacking President Suharto. Angered by a parliamentary walkout, the president had charged Muslim and other critics with opposition to the state philosophy of Panca Sila (five principles of belief—in God, nationalism, humanism, democracy, and social justice). The petitioners responded that Suharto was dangerously polarizing the country. The government reacted quickly, prohibiting any newspaper discussion of the issue, withdrawing use of government facilities from the petitioners, and threatening the leading critics with arrest.

The department of education made a determined effort to remove university students—who played a prominent role in every major political crisis in the 15 years of Suharto's New Order government—from the political arena. In an attempt to prevent future agitation, the minister of education moved to replace elected student councils with appointed "student coordinating bodies." The new regulations were accepted quietly on all but the most prestigious campuses. The minister also angered Muslims by carrying out a threat to deny government subsidies to Muslim schools refusing to conform to the new school calendar, under which the Islamic fasting month is no longer a school holiday.

A more positive aspect of the president's political strategy was the military development policy begun in 1978 by the new minister of defense, Gen. Mohammad Jusuf. In 1980, there were major equipment purchases, further improvements in military pay scales and living conditions, and a higher degree of battle-readiness. In September, a new civic action program to restore a close relationship between the army and the people was implemented.

Foreign Affairs. In 1980, Indonesia maintained its close relationship with the United States and other non-Communist industrialized powers. Within the region, it appeared to be moving closer to the position of its fellow members of the Association of Southeast Asian Nations (ASEAN), that Vietnam is a greater threat to regional security than China. In particular, the Indonesian government increasingly echoed Thailand's anxiety about the presence of Vietnamese troops near the Thai border. A simplified naturalization program for Chinese residents was perhaps another sign of movement toward recognition of the People's Republic.

Coverage in the foreign press of mistreatment and malnutrition of refugees again made East Timor an international issue. A former Portuguese colony, East Timor was occupied by Indonesia in 1975. Despite an intense American-aided effort, Indonesian armed forces remained unable to suppress guerrilla attacks by Timorese nationalists.

Economy. Macroeconomic indicators were favorable in 1980. Inflation, a serious problem after the November 1978 devaluation of the rupiah, was brought under control. However, inflationary pressures were again felt after the government's announcement in May of substantial price increases for domestic oil and electricity. The balance of payments position was strong, principally as a result of three increases in oil export prices. The 1979–80 state budget rose by about 25% in real terms.

The distribution of economic benefits remained the crucial issue in Indonesia's political economy. The government's major policy initiative in this area was an improved set of regulations giving preference to indigenous (as against domestic Chinese) businessmen in the competition for government contracts.

R. WILLIAM LIDDLE
The Ohio State University

─── **INDONESIA • Information Highlights** ───

Official Name: Republic of Indonesia.
Location: Southeast Asia.
Area: 735,432 sq mi (1 904 769 km²).
Population (1980 est.): 144,300,000.
Chief Cities: (1974 est.): Jakarta, the capital, 5,000,000; Surabaya, 2,000,000; Bandung, 2,000,000; Medan, 1,000,000.
Government: *Head of state and government,* Suharto, president (took office for third 5-year term March 1978). *Legislature* (unicameral)—People's Consultative Assembly.
Monetary Unit: Rupiah (625 rupiahs equal U.S.$1, Nov. 1980).
Manufactures (major products): Textiles, food and beverages, light manufactures, cement, fertilizer.
Agriculture (major products): Rice, rubber, cassava, copra, coffee, soybeans, palm oil, tea.
GNP Per Capita (1978 est., U.S.$): $360.
Foreign Trade (1979, U.S.$): *Imports,* $7,225,000,000; *exports,* $15,578,000,000.

INDUSTRIAL REVIEW

Industrial production declined in most countries in 1980. The drop was especially pronounced in the United States, reflecting a brief but sharp recession that was followed by weak recovery. Basic and heavy industries, including autos, were hit hard. Every major auto producing country but Japan and Italy suffered setbacks.

Overall U.S. Trends. U.S. industrial production showed little change in the first quarter of 1980, plummeted in the second, dropped a little further in the third, and began recovering in the fourth. For all of 1980, the Federal Reserve Board's (FRB) preliminary data indicated a drop of about 4%, in sharp contrast to the 4.4% gain registered by the FRB index of industrial production for 1979. It was the worst setback since 1975.

The brunt of the decline was borne by manufacturing, where output dropped well over 5%, compared with a 4.6% increase in 1979. The drop was especially sharp in durable goods output—7.5% in contrast to a 4.7% gain in 1979. Utilities increased their output by almost 2%, and mining production climbed 5.5%, spurred by a nearly 10% increase in oil and gas extraction.

Bright spots were few in the 1980 manufacturing record. Railroad equipment production showed the best gain—nearly 10%, but even that was anemic compared with the nearly 40% gain posted for 1979. Aircraft and parts production increased almost 6%, about one third as much as it did in 1979. Output of agricultural chemicals increased a little more than 5%, slightly bettering the gain of the preceding year. Production of communication equipment also increased 5%, a slowdown from the 13% increase in 1979. The production of ordnance rose 3.5%, up from the 2% growth the year before. Tobacco products rolled up a nearly 2% gain, reversing the 0.4% decline of 1979. Food products production increased about 1%, just about one fourth of the preceding year's gain. Printing and publishing turnout was up a little above 1%, down from the 4.3% gain of 1979. Metalworking machinery production increased barely 1%, following a 10% growth the year before. Office and service equipment was up almost 5%, compared with a 6.8% growth in 1979.

At the head of the list of production declines was the output of trucks, buses, and trailers, with a drop of 46% that came on top of a 1979 decline of 13%. Automobile production declined 25%, following a 9% reduction. Iron and steel output fell by more than 20%, compared with a 0.3% decrease in 1979. Nonferrous metals dropped 15%, compared with a nearly 3% growth. The production of mobile homes plunged 21% after a fractional gain in 1979. The production of tires slumped 22%, following a 4% drop in the preceding year. The output of lumber and wood products dropped 15%, after a slight gain in 1979. Production of furniture and fixtures dropped 9%, after a growth of 3.6% in 1979. Stone, clay, and glass products had a 12% falloff, following a 4.4% gain. Fabricated metal products were down 10%, reversing the 5% growth of 1979. Farm equipment output fell off 18%, in contrast to the 9% increase in the preceding year.

Declines were widespread among the electrical machinery categories. The group had an overall decline of 3.5% after a nearly 11% growth. Household appliances had a 9% drop, and television and radio output went down 12%. Instrument production decreased almost 2%, reflecting a 4% decline in consumer-oriented products, while equipment instruments had a meager 0.5% increase, following a 7% increase in 1979. Chemicals had an overall decline of more than 7%, a reversal of its 7% growth in 1979. Output of synthetic materials dropped 12%, in sharp contrast to the 11% gain shown for the preceding year. Basic chemicals dropped almost 5%, after a 5.6% increase. Paint production declined by more than 2% after a 3.4% increase in 1979.

Consumer products manufacturers turned out an increasing volume of goods with a practical appeal, such as energy-saving quartz heaters. But there was no shortage of gadgets, either. Among them was one for TV addicts that at the touch of a button turns down the sound so that the viewer can answer the telephone and still watch the picture. There was much talk about increasing the use of robots in manufacturing operations. About 3,200 robots were estimated to be in place at year-end, a good many of them in the auto industry.

U.S. Expenditures. Despite the decline in activity, business investment came through 1980 relatively unscathed. Spending for new plant and equipment by U.S. business reached $294,300,-000,000 in 1980, 8.8% above 1979. However, if price increases, which are likely to be about 9% for capital investment, are factored out, then the 1980 record represents no increase at all. The figures are not adjusted for inflation.

Manufacturing industries raised their expenditures for new plant and equipment 16.4% in 1980, to $114,900,000,000. Producers of nondurable goods hiked their spending by 19%, to $56,-700,000,000. Durables producers invested $58,-300,000,000, an increase of 14%. Mining firms' capital spending came to $13,500,000,000, a 4.4% increase. Transportation companies cut their outlays to $12,000,000,000, a 3% drop. Public utilities' capital investment amounted to $34,-600,000,000, a mere 1.9% higher than in 1979.

Among nondurable manufacturers, petroleum firms reported a 25% increase in capital expenditures, followed by the paper industry with 21%, and chemicals with 18%. Food-beverage producers reported an increase of 11%, and textiles, 7%. Rubber producers showed an 18% reduction.

The largest increases in capital spending among durables producers were for aircraft,

30%; electrical machinery, 29%; and nonferrous metals, 28%. Motor vehicle, nonelectrical machinery, and iron and steel producers reported increases of about 9%. Small declines were registered for fabricated metals and stone-clay-glass producers.

U.S. Production. Passenger car production in the United States dropped 25% in 1980. Even the spate of new small-car entries failed to raise the year's total much above 6.3 million units. That was the lowest since 1961. Truck rollout slowed to 1.6 million units, a fall of 46%. It was the smallest truck turnout since 1967.

While domestic auto production reeled under the impact of the recession and severe credit restraints, imports racked up a record volume of 2.4 million. They claimed a record 27% of the U.S. auto market in 1980.

Despite its financial troubles, Chrysler managed to score a first for domestic automakers: its Omni "Miser" achieved a 50 mpg (80 km/g) highway estimate rating. But the K-cars, although they were looked upon as the firm's hope for recovery, did not do so well as expected. Their production was shut down for the month of December.

The production of recreational vehicles (RV) took another tumble in 1980, 35%, after dropping 40% in 1979 to 307,000 units. RV manufacturers sought to overcome the effects of high fuel prices by redesigning their products.

The American steel industry poured 108 million T (98 million t) of the raw metal in 1980, a steep drop of 20% from the year before. The industry utilized 72% of its production capacity, sharply below its capacity utilization rate of 87% in 1979. While the demand was slack for most product lines, the outstanding exception was the demand for steel tubes and pipes that the oil industry needs for its rapidly growing exploration and development program. Domestic steelmakers cannot produce enough "oil country" goods, and foreign firms supplied about 25% of the steel products bought by the U.S. oil industry.

An indication of the boom in oil drilling activity was suggested by the number of drilling rigs operating each week in 1980: 2,800. That was almost 30% more than in 1979, and surpassed the previous record of nearly 2,700 set in 1956. The number of oil and gas wells completed in 1980 was about 60,000, topping the 58,000 record also set in 1956.

Energy production moved ahead as crude oil output increased about 1% to more than 3,000,-000,000 barrels. Natural gas production increased by 3%. Coal production increased 7% to 825 million T (748 million t). That performance disappointed the industry in view of the fact that oil now costs nearly four times more than the equivalent energy from coal. While export demand was up substantially, the conversion of the country's stationary combustion industries to coal from oil was relatively slow. A major block has been the resistance to compromise air-quality standards which often are stricter at the state level than federal standards. Another factor is financial. Public utility commissions can deny utilities rate increases to pay for the conversion to coal. At the same time, they can allow utilities to pass through to consumers the increases in the price of oil.

About two thirds of the U.S. coal came from surface mines in 1980, a reversal of the produc-

Quartz heaters and food processors were popular products with the American consumer of 1980.

Markel/Nutone Division

Cuisinart

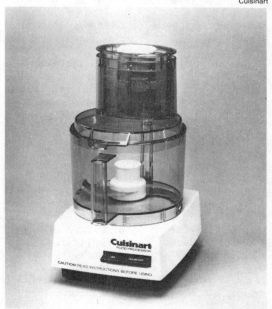

tion pattern of 1970 when underground mines supplied 56% of the fuel. Much of the mining activity has shifted West, where about 30% of the coal was produced in 1980, up sharply from the meager 7% share a decade ago. As most of the Western mines are not unionized, the percentage of total production mined by union members dropped from 70% in 1970 to 45% in 1980.

The depressed home construction activity depressed the output of a wide variety of durables, including residential central air conditioners. Their shipments dropped to 1.7 million units in the first nine months of 1980, 20% under the same 1979 period. The extreme heat of the 1980 summer was not enough to overcome the high interest rates and economic jitters as far as room air conditioners were concerned. Their shipments for the first nine months were 2.8 million, about 15% below the like 1979 period.

The short but steep recession, combined with high cost of fuel and worries about its availability, also hurt leisure products such as outboard motors. The recession was the major factor in quashing bicycle manufacturer's hopes of cashing in again on the fuel situation.

The demand for the products of the aerospace industry held up fairly well. One of the bright spots was the demand for helicopters, with about 1,300 civilian units turned out in 1980, up 25% from 1979. There was some softening of demand for large transport planes, and single-engine aircraft took an unexpected dive of 35%, as production dropped to 8,500 units.

Foreign Trends. Industrial production in major developed countries was generally stronger than in the United States throughout 1980. While the U.S. industrial production index at year-end 1980 was 4.4% below its 1979 level, the index for Japan stood 5.7% above 1979. Canadian production was off 3%. There was no significant change in industrial production in Italy and West Germany. There was a 5% decline in France, and steep cuts also were registered in the United Kingdom, 9.4%, and the Netherlands, down 8.8%.

Motor vehicle production declined 10% worldwide, led by the sharp plunge in the United States. Canadian auto output dropped 16%, to 835,000 units, the lowest since 1967, and truck production was cut by 13%, to 517,000.

The world output of cars, trucks, and buses was estimated at 24.4 million for the first ten months of 1980, compared with 27.1 million for the like period in 1979. The output in Japan was up 18%, to more than 10 million units. Production gains also were listed by Spain, a relatively small producer, 8%, and Italy, 12%. Output was down 17% in the United Kingdom, 7% in West Germany, and nearly 4% in France.

Steel production in the European Community (EC) in the first nine months of 1980 was down 5% from the comparable period the year before. Production for the fourth quarter of 1980 was cut to a level 14% below the same 1979 period, according to a plan under the EC steel treaty. As in the United States, the European steel plants were showing signs of old age. The EC steel industry was on the way to trim its production capacity by 25 million t (27.6 million T) by 1985. Steelmaking capacity was declining slightly in the United States, remaining stable in Japan, and expanding moderately in Spain, Portugal, Greece, and Turkey. Canada was the only developed country building a new integrated steel mill.

Oil production did not change much, despite the conflict between Iraq and Iran that by year-end had virtually stopped both countries' combined output of 5 million barrels a day, 80% of which normally was exported. As other oil producers, such as Saudi Arabia, boosted their liftings, the world oil output still came to about 63,-000,000,000 barrels, just about level with the year before. Consumption cuts in the developed countries helped ease the pressure on supplies. By year-end 1980, for example, the U.S. imports of petroleum had dropped by 20%.

The auto slump affected the world's tiremakers as well. The shift to longer-lasting radials and smaller cars was stunting market growth. European producers have cut their capacity 25% since 1975, and are being squeezed further by heavy imports from Japan and the East bloc. U.S. producers have been closing their plants on the continent as well as in the United States where they have a hard time dealing with foreign competition and higher energy costs. The industry's work force has dropped 30% in five years, and employees in some plants have accepted pay cuts to help make the plants economically viable. The U.S. tire-making capacity has shrunk 20% since 1975.

Production of semiconductors was brisk in 1980, with U.S. manufacturers in the lead and the Japanese expanding rapidly. The demand for chips for use in microprocessors in automobiles, sophisticated machine tools, some 250 different kinds of toys, and in instruments of all kinds, not to mention computing applications, grew apace in 1980. American manufacturers held 60% of the semiconductor market in Europe, and the Japanese were pushing for 5%.

Industrial production in the Soviet Union apparently fell short of the 4.5% gain planned for 1980. Indications were that the increase was a little better than the 3.4% registered for 1979. That itself was short of the planned growth of 5.7%. Soviet industry is hampered by labor shortages, lagging technology, and bureaucratic bottlenecks, all of which work a special hardship on the production of consumer goods. As for energy production, the country is the largest oil producer in the world. It produced just about 600 million t (600 million T) in 1980, a bit less than the planned target of 606 million t (670 million T). Steel production was expected to reach the 1980 target of 165 million t (182 million T).

AGO AMBRE, *U.S. Department of Commerce*

INTERIOR DESIGN

There are people who collect for pleasure and people who hoard for simple acquisition. In recent years, however, a new breed of antique-hunter has emerged—the investment collector, an individual or corporation which, during times of inflation, puts money into tangible objects. These are objects which, for reasons of scarcity, age, or esthetics, are expected to appreciate in value.

The *Wall Street Journal* declared that stamps, coins, art, and antiques are the most profitable hedges against inflation. The June 1980 issue of *House and Garden* magazine devoted major editorial coverage to collecting for investment.

High on the list of profitable investment are decorative arts objects. Fine palace or mosque Oriental rugs have long been prized by museums and wealthy collectors for their beauty and fine weave and because each is a unique work of art. Oriental rugs of lesser value were popular among the middle class, who coveted them not only for their value but for social cachet. The fashion waned during the late 1920s. Now, again, even the smaller, more primitive, hand-made nomad or village rugs and kilims (slit- or flat-weave rugs from Asia Minor) are being coveted and purchased at auction at rapidly rising prices. An example is a Turkish Kashkai purchased in 1978 for $4,000 and resold in late 1979 for $30,000.

American folk art—coverlets, samplers, patchwork quilts, primitive art; furniture of lesser craftsmen; American Indian artifacts, ceramics, rugs, and baskets—has become the focus of collectors, who have recognized the intrinsic value of such objects.

Corporations go about the acquisition process in a number of ways: on the advice of an art consultant, dealer, or gallery, or through an architectural or interior design firm. Large interior design firms, such as ISD Incorporated, are hiring art and antique experts for their own staffs or as outside consultants.

Several reputable antique rug dealers have developed acquisition plans for corporations as once they did for wealthy patrons. The dealers amass collections of quality rugs to fit designated areas.

More and more of the smaller interior design firms send representatives to auctions and antique markets to buy choice pieces, thereby acquiring esthetic control and the ability to fit objects into preconceived design schemes.

What the collecting rush is doing to interior decoration is not difficult to comprehend. Individuals and interior designers are finding interesting ways to accommodate varieties of objects and unusual forms—woven or otherwise—in the design scheme. Art objects and carpets have a tendency to become focal points, and in the case of rugs to dominate both color and pattern schemes. In effect, the handling of such numbers

Fine oriental rugs adorn the offices of Shawmut Corporation in Boston.
Ezra Stoller, Courtesy of Architect's Collaborative

Jaime Ardiles-Arce, Courtesy of ISD Inc.

A 19th-century Mandarin robe hangs in the Stamford, CT, headquarters of Xerox Corporation.

and types of objects poses a considerable challenge, and the solutions must be imaginative. In the case of corporate organizations, the decorative result is humanizing.

Offices. Through its art program, the Xerox Corporation has addressed itself to the office of the future and demonstrated its concern for humanity. The program is so important to Xerox that its design/art consultant, Joseph Rosen of ISD, approached the gathering of art and its placement in the new Xerox headquarters in Stamford, CT, as a separate case study above and beyond the problems of the space plan.

The art includes not only such sculpture as a large-scale David Lee Brown piece—a series of polished stainless steel rectangular elements formed into an angel wing hanging in the multi-story-high lobby atrium—but smaller sculptured stone and marble pieces as well. The latter are placed on upright, painted, wooden pedestals. Textured tapestries and wall hangings, including an antique, hand-embroidered Chinese coat, are mounted as paintings. Spectacular in its size is the multi-plane fiberwork sculpture by Gertrude Knobel that hangs and curves in space in the four-story-high cafeteria atrium.

In Boston, the Shawmut Corporation, named after an American Indian tribe, displays Indian artifacts—carvings, rugs, and ceramics—in specially designed architectural niches or on pedestals. In its offices at One Federal Street, the design firm, Architect's Collaborative, used a fine

collection of Oriental rugs as a color and pattern focus.

Designers Sylvia Owens and Nancy Hertsfeld adroitly and discreetly incorporated a collection of paintings into the interior scheme for the Bedminster, NJ, headquarters of AT&T Long Lines.

Residences. Individuals are inclined to be more personal in acquiring valuable art and craft objects for their home. Because collecting is so personal, an empathy and sense of trust must prevail between the individual and his interior designer.

The Serge Gagaris of Connecticut collect folk art because ". . . until recently primitives were not well thought of. Now all young, up-and-coming collectors are interested." Using no interior designer, they put together a joyous display of weathervanes, samplers, quilts, ceramics, glassware, and primitive portraits. The objects are on floors, walls, tops of tables and cabinets, and in cases.

Quite the opposite is the refined, understated display of Orientalia in the Honolulu home of the Adrian Zechas, whose designer, Jun Alday, devised well-lighted architectural niches and stands for larger pieces of furniture and sculpture. Paintings and framed textiles are hung on walls, and ceramics and small sculpture are displayed in cases.

JEANNE WEEKS
American Society of Interior Designers

INTERNATIONAL TRADE AND FINANCE

The year 1980 was a period of severe strain in international trade and global financial relations. Just the year before, the United States and 99 other nations completed and signed a long-sought multilateral trade agreement that reduced tariffs by about one third and curtailed the use of nontariff barriers to trade. However, despite this treaty and a general consensus among world leaders that protectionism would fuel inflation and frustrate economic growth, major trade disputes simmered in a number of key areas, including automobiles and steel. Trade relations were also strained by Mideast and East-West politics as the United States called upon its West European allies and Japan to impose economic sanctions against Iran and to observe a partial grain and technology trade ban against the Soviet Union. Additionally, the United States and West European countries, particularly France, were locked in a dispute over the use of government subsidized credits and loan guarantees to foreign buyers that threatened to lead to an escalation of credit competition. Finally, efforts to bridge the rift between developing and Western industrialized nations were only mildly successful, as developing countries continued to criticize sharply Western trade and foreign aid policies.

Inflation and Growth. Underlying much of this disharmony in trade relations were increasing inflation and sagging growth rates. In a report that characterized the world economic situation as "rather grim," the International Monetary Fund (IMF) stated that inflation in industrialized countries was expected to reach 9.5% in 1980 and to recede to 8.5% in 1981. This, the report observed, compares with an annual price rise of about 4% from 1962 to 1972. To a large extent, the rise in the inflation rate in 1980 reflected the oil price hikes of 1979, an inflationary stimulus which is likely to persist. A 1980 report by the World Bank, for instance, projected that oil would be priced at $78.30 per barrel in 1990—$40.85 per barrel in 1980 dollars. In 1980 dollars, the price of oil per barrel would reach $35.10 in 1985, according to the report. The 1980 price of imported oil was approximately $33 per barrel.

Recession in industrialized nations also led to the shrinkage of some export markets, hurting growth. The Bank of America, for example, predicted that the growth rate of West European economies would drop to 1.6% in 1980, down from 3% in 1979. "The economic growth of countries that performed well in 1979 and 1980, such as Japan and (West) Germany, will slow until mid-1981," the bank reported.

Though it was in a stronger position than other U.S. trading partners, Japan suffered a decline in its growth rate. According to the United States-Japan Trade Council, Japan's growth for the first two quarters of 1980 averaged 4.9%, a full percentage point below the growth rate that Japan posted in 1979. The decline, the trade group reported, was largely due to sluggish consumer spending in Japan. Fortunately for Japan, a huge supply of stockpiled oil and effective energy policies helped prevent the Japanese growth rate from slipping further.

An expanding U.S. trade deficit with Japan also indicated that the demand for Japanese exports remained strong. According to the U.S. Commerce Department, that deficit reached $7,450,000,000 for the first nine months of 1980, compared with a trade gap of $6,600,000,000 for a similar period in 1979. As this deficit grew, Japanese exports to the United States increased by 17.3%.

For its part, the United States endured several quarters of stagnant growth and another sizable annual trade deficit. The Commerce Department reported that the deficit was $7,600,000,000 at the end of the second quarter. During that quarter, the dollar also depreciated 13% against the Japanese yen, 12% against the Swiss franc and 9% against the West German mark and the French franc.

Trade Patterns. Some economists saw the United States trade deficit as an indication that U.S. competitiveness was waning. A study by the U.S. Department of Labor noted that, with the exception of aircraft and power generators, the top 20 American exports have garnered a shrinking share of the world market between 1963 and 1977. U.S. farm equipment, which once commanded 40% of the world market, for example, dropped to 25% of that market.

More optimistic observers pointed out that U.S. agricultural exports remained strong and may reach a record $40,000,000,000 in 1980 despite the imposition of the grain embargo against the Soviet Union. Moreover, they pointed out, while the Labor Department study recorded a $30,200,000,000 deficit in consumer goods for 1979, that same report noted a $17,900,000,000 surplus in agricultural commodities and a $32,600,000,000 surplus in capital goods.

Many Washington policymakers called for measures to further strengthen U.S. export competitiveness. President Carter submitted a 250-page report to Congress that called for tax relief for U.S. citizens abroad, strong support for the Export-Import Bank, the "elimination of uncertainties" in the Foreign Corrupt Practices Act, and the creation of export trading companies, among other measures. Of these steps, the establishment of export trading firms received the most support. In September the Senate, by a vote of 77–0, approved legislation that would allow banks to invest in export trading companies. Presently, banks are not allowed to make such investments—a prohibition that is designed to prevent banks from taking risks that could result in business losses and from using the extension of credit as a business weapon.

(*Continued on page 290*)

O.K... YOU'VE SETTLED ON THE $27 DIAMOND, AND YOU'VE PICKED OUT A MODEST GOLD SETTING... THAT WILL BE $1,627, PLEASE...

JEWELER

Wright, "The Providence Journal-Bulletin"

INTERNATIONAL TRADE AND FINANCE—SPECIAL REPORT:

Gold and Silver

On March 21, 1980, millions of television-watchers in the United States and abroad learned that big trouble had struck a wealthy Texas family. The fictional oil tycoon J.R. Ewing of *Dallas* had been shot. On that same Friday evening, though almost no one knew it, a decidedly nonfictional crisis was brewing for the Ewings' real-life Dallas counterparts, the billionaire Hunt Brothers.

In the television melodrama, J.R. was to recover from his wounds and eventually confront his attacker. Similarly, none of the featured players in what became known as the "Hunt-silver debacle" suffered much permanent harm. But in those last days of March, the Hunts, along with a major Wall Street firm and U.S. securities and commodities markets, came perilously close to financial disaster.

From the early 1970s on, the Hunts had been amassing a mountain of silver holdings in one of the grandest investment plans in economic history. When the market turned against them in the first three months of 1980, that mountain very nearly collapsed on them and on countless others who had been attracted into the game.

The allure of silver and its precious-metals companion, gold, stemmed from a long series of economic calamities. Starting in 1973, with the rise to power of the Organization of Petroleum Exporting Countries, oil prices quadrupled, then tripled again. Shock waves of inflation hit the industrial nations of the West. Currency markets

swung wildly back and forth, with their anchor, the U.S. dollar, no longer holding against the tide. Stock prices in New York and in other financial capitals fell. Bonds and conventional bank savings accounts quickly lost their appeal as inflation drained their purchasing power. So investors everywhere began to turn to the oldest stores of value they could find—gold and silver.

Gold, pegged at $35 to $40 an ounce in the late 1960s, climbed to $200 by the end of 1974; $500 by late 1979; then $600, $700, and $800 in a matter of days thereafter. Silver, which over the years had acquired a reputation as "the poor man's gold," lagged behind until 1979, when it began the year at $6 an ounce. Within the next 12 months, it made up for lost time by soaring past $50.

The precious-metals craze that had begun among a handful of maverick doomsayers and their followers now reached into millions of American homes. People combed their attics and closets for old tea sets, jewelry, grandmothers' wedding silver—anything they might use to cash in on the boom. Just as suddenly, an entire industry of dealers in gold-and-silver-for-cash (some of them scrupulous, others anything but) materialized to accommodate the sellers. "Goodbye, old silverware, hello, new refrigerator!" exclaimed one commercial that flooded the airwaves in the New York City area.

While all this excitement was mounting, however, prices of gold and silver quietly started changing direction and heading downward. There were several reasons for this turnabout. Included were the facts that credit had been tightened significantly in the United States and alert investors began to sense the approach of a recession which would temporarily diminish inflation fears. Even more important, authorities in the commodities business were acting to curb speculation in the silver market. On January 8, the New York Commodity Exchange (Comex), the world's largest silver market, took the drastic step of limiting trading in silver. Within the next couple of months, the number of silver contracts outstanding on the Comex fell by more than half. This created what is known in the trade as a "thin" market, with fewer and fewer participants. Thin markets are notoriously unstable, and in short order the silver market became unstable indeed.

Gold was sliding back toward the $500 mark; silver was falling even faster. The latter stabilized for a short time in the $20–$30 range. Then, on March 26, it tumbled $4.40 in a single day to $15.80 an ounce.

Up to that point, the Hunts' role in all that was happening had received scant public attention. Nelson Bunker Hunt, W. Herbert Hunt, and the other children of the late, legendary oilman H. L. Hunt, always had shunned publicity. They were known only vaguely to most of the public as the owners of one of the largest private fortunes in the United States. The press had to settle for its own rough estimates of their wealth. There were the family-owned Placid Oil Co., coal lands, vast real estate holdings from Florida to Anchorage, cattle and thoroughbred horses, a string of pizza restaurants, and the Kansas City Chiefs football team. And there was perhaps their biggest investment of all, many millions of ounces of silver with a market value well into the billions of dollars at the peak.

In accumulating silver, Bunker and Herbert Hunt had used a tool employed by nearly all commodity traders—margin, or loans backed by the commodity itself as collateral. When all goes well, margin enables a trader to increase his profits enormously. When the market goes the wrong way, however, it can put him in a deep hole.

That was precisely where the Hunts found themselves in the waning days of March when their principal commodities broker, the national investment firm of Bache Halsey Stuart Shields, asked them for more collateral on their loans. This "margin call," for more than $100 million, was not the first the Hunts had ever received. But it was the first they did not answer.

Wall Street's ever-active rumor mills were quick to pick up word of the developing crisis. Talk that Bache might face a capital squeeze prompted the Securities and Exchange Commission (SEC) to halt trading in the stock of its parent company, Bache Group, on the afternoon of Thursday, March 27. The entire stock market plummeted in what one broker described as a "classic panic," then rallied again just before the close. The Dow Jones industrial average, down more than 25 points at a five-year low as of 3:30 P.M., wound up with only a 2.14 loss when the closing gong sounded a half hour later.

Silver, meanwhile, continued its free-fall decline, losing another $5 to $10.80. As the business day closed on "Silver Thursday," many a Wall Street executive and government regulator was still hard at work, seeking ways to avoid an even worse situation when Friday, the 28th, arrived.

The next morning, they got a huge assist from the silver market, which steadied and then even edged upward a bit. In that climate, Bache and the Hunts' other brokers were able to feed silver out to willing buyers, and thus start covering the unpaid debt. After that, order was swiftly restored. Bache stock resumed trading the next week at prices above the $8 level to which it fell on March 27. The Hunts, with the help of a $1,100,000,000 bank loan secured by many of their diverse assets, settled up their silver debts. In a few weeks' time, stock prices were back in a runaway bull market that was to continue for most of the year. (*See also* STOCKS AND BONDS.)

Though Bache drew heavy criticism from others in the securities industry for putting so many of its eggs in a single basket, it also emerged unscathed. For the fiscal year that ended on July 31, 1980, the company reported earnings of $26.72 million, by far the largest in its 101-year history. In its annual report, the firm referred only briefly to the silver crisis, promising its holders that steps had been taken to "improve credit policy, supervision, and control."

The Commodity Futures Trading Commission, the regulatory body which also was criticized for being slow to act in the months before Silver Thursday, began putting together new rules aimed at preventing a repeat performance.

As the year passed, gold and silver prices gradually recovered. By autumn, the precious-metals markets turned uncharacteristically dull, with gold hovering slightly above $600 an ounce and silver in the neighborhood of $18 to $20.

And the Hunt Brothers? Well, the affair left them saddled with a $1,100,000,000 debt. A Congressional committee called them on the carpet for a series of hearings. And in a rare interview in *Fortune* magazine, they complained bitterly that they were the victims, not the villains, in the whole affair. In changing the rules of the silver market in January, the Hunts charged, many of the directors of the Commodity Exchange had acted unfairly and for their own personal profit.

It was evident, nevertheless, that the Hunts still were not quite a charity case. They retained 63 million ounces of silver on which, for all the market's wild swings, they showed a net paper profit. By *Fortune*'s calculations, the brothers remained "around $8,000,000,000 from the poorhouse."

CHET CURRIER

The day after the Senate vote, the Commerce Department's International Trade Administration released a staff study reporting that five of the largest U.S. exporters accounted for 17% of total U.S. exports. Robert E. Herzstein, Commerce undersecretary for international trade, said that the study "underscored the need for passage of the export trading company legislation."

Other responses to the problems of slow growth and recession were less constructive and led to strain in U.S., West European, and Japanese relations. On March 21, the U.S. Steel Corp. filed antidumping complaints at the International Trade Commission (ITC) and Commerce Department, covering five years of steel imports from France, Belgium, Luxembourg, Italy, Great Britain, West Germany, and the Netherlands. In essence, the complaints alleged that 16 producers in these nations had sold their steel in the United States at less than their home market prices. Three fourths of the $1,500,000,000 worth of European steel imported to the United States in 1979, the complaints allege, were "dumped" in this manner.

At the time the complaints were filed, the Commerce Department suspended the three-year-old trigger-price mechanism designed to protect the domestic steel industry from price-cutting foreign competition. The Carter administration explained that the trigger-price mechanism, which marks imports below a set price as candidates for possible antidumping investigations, was intended as a substitute for dumping complaints filed by U.S. producers.

For his part, Viscount Etienne Davignon, the European Community's industrial affairs commissioner said the complaints could result in a trade war. Before the ITC could issue a ruling on the case a deal was struck. U.S. Steel withdrew its complaints. The trigger-price mechanism was restored at a level that was 12.5% higher. According to the Carter administration's steel aid plan, announced on September 30, the trigger-price mechanism would be in place for up to five years and then would be abandoned. That plan also called for special tax breaks and amendments to the Clean Air Act that would delay in certain cases steel industry compliance with environmental standards.

Trade war fears, however, were expressed once again when the ITC took up a petition by the United Auto Workers and the Ford Motor Co. that asked that tariffs or import quotas be applied to Japanese cars and trucks. Some $6,300,000,000 worth of Japanese vehicles were imported in 1979. The UAW asked that imports of passenger vehicles be restricted to 1975–76 levels and that duties on these cars be raised from 2.9 to 20%. The Federal Trade Commission (FTC) stated that imposing the quotas requested by the UAW and Ford would cost consumers from $3,000,000,000 to $5,000,000,000 and that the proposed tariff increases would cost $5,600,000,000

to $6,600,000,000. On November 10, by a 3–2 vote, the ITC ruled that the importing of Japanese cars was not a "substantial cause" of injury to the American automotive industry. Although all commissioners agreed that the industry had suffered and that sales had plunged 30% since 1978, a majority of commissioners found that the recession and a shift of consumer preference in favor of small cars were the principal causes of the industry's ills. After the ruling, the UAW and Ford appealed to Congress. On December 2 the House alone adopted a resolution that authorized the president to negotiate and enforce import restrictions on Japanese vehicles.

Other trade disputes in 1980 involved the imposition of economic sanctions against the Soviet Union. In November, the Treasury Department imposed a ban on certain alloy steel products made by Creusot-Loire, a French firm. The department said that the action was taken because the company uses nickel from Cuba. But observers noted that the ban closely followed the firm's decision to build a steel plant south of Moscow. Originally, Armco Inc. and the Nippon Steel Co. of Japan had contracted jointly to build that plant, but that deal was blocked by the Carter administration's trade bans against the USSR.

The U.S.-EC. The United States and the European Community (EC) also were at odds over the use of government-subsidized loans to foreign buyers. Although the heads of state at the Venice economic summit had agreed to raise these loans closer to market levels, the United States complained that the EC offer to raise the floor on interest rates by 1% for loans to industrialized nations and 0.6% for loans to poor countries did not go far enough. C. Fred Bergsten, assistant treasury secretary for international affairs, said France was most opposed to increasing the interest rate floors further. France's policy of "mixing" foreign aid and credits also was criticized by U.S. officials.

Socialist Nations. Socialist countries also had little to cheer about. Poland, which carried a debt burden to Western banks and governments of an estimated $24,000,000,000, appealed for $8–12,000,000,000 more of Western aid and low-interest credit to compensate for a stagnating economy that resulted in food shortages. A report by the National Foreign Assessment Center of the Central Intelligence Agency (CIA) also noted that the Soviet Union shared the West's worries over sagging growth. The Soviet GNP growth rate for 1978 and 1979, it reported, was 2.1%, "the lowest for any two-year period since World War II." The center stated that the growth rate might improve slightly in 1980 but would probably fall short of 3%.

On the plus side, the Soviet Union's fortunes were strengthened by high gold prices. The USSR, the center's report added, "could earn $5,000,000,000 just by selling out of current production at $500 per ounce." The prospect of increased Soviet-West European energy trade, particularly in natural gas, also brightened the picture. In 1979 the Soviet Union supplied about 10% of the total West European gas consumption and about 7% to 8% of that region's total oil consumption.

Still, the stagnating Soviet oil production was expected to limit that nation's foreign exchange receipts. Additionally, the Soviet's poor harvest of 185 million t (200 million T), the second disappointing harvest in a row, along with the U.S. declared grained embargo, placed more burdens on its centrally planned economy, though the precise impact of the embargo was a matter of debate. After the Soviet invasion of Afghanistan, President Carter on January 4 stipulated that the United States would not sell the Soviet Union any more grain than the 8 million t (8.8 million T) guaranteed annually under the five-year U.S.-Soviet grain agreement.

Despite the embargo, agricultural officials conceded that the Soviet Union succeeded in importing a record 31 million t (34 million T) of grain during the marketing year that ended on June 30. Large quantities of grain were purchased from other suppliers, including Argentina, with whom the Soviets signed a new five-year grain agreement. U.S. Agriculture Department officials said, however, that much of this grain was purchased at as much as $40–50 per ton above the world price and that the Soviet grain requirements were so great that there was still a shortfall of 8–9 million t (8.8–9.9 million T) for the fourth year of the U.S.-Soviet grain agreement.

Third World. One thing that was not debatable was the plight of developing nations that imported oil. The IMF predicted that the current account deficit of non-oil-producing developing nations would jump from $63,000,000,000 to $78,000,000,000. Meanwhile, the petrodollar surplus of oil producers was forecast to rise from $68,000,000,000 in 1979 to $115,000,000,000 in 1980.

These developments added to the already sizable debt burden of developing countries. The World Bank figured the overseas debt of developing nations at $376,000,000,000 in 1980, up from $142,000,000,000 in 1974. As a partial remedy, the World Bank proposed increasing its lending by $8,000,000,000 between 1980 and 1985 so that oil-importing developing countries would undertake projects to explore for and produce oil. Lending on this scale, the Bank said, could boost production in these Third World nations from 2 million barrels a day to between 3,-600,000,000 and 4,800,000,000 barrels a day by 1990.

Other proposals to aid the Third World were presented in a report on North-South relations by an independent commission headed by former West German Chancellor Willy Brandt. That report suggested increasing bilateral aid to $30,000,000,000 a year by 1985 and expanding lending to Third World nations by $50–60,000,-000,000 over a five-year period. The report's supporters stressed the importance of Third World markets to industrialized nations and called for the creation of a World Development Fund. But the suggestions failed to win widespread support.

Some progress on North-South issues was made when developing and industrialized nations wrapped up the final negotiations on June 28 on a Common Fund to stabilize commodity prices. That agreement provides for $750 million to maintain buffer stocks of commodities and to support research on ways to expand developing country commodity exports. Though that agreement was billed as one of the United Nations' greatest achievements, the Common Fund was a far cry from the $6,000,000,000 fund that developing nations initially demanded. Apart from the West, China's decision to join the IMF and the World Bank worried some Third World countries, who feared that China's development needs would divert funds from other developing nations.

MICHAEL R. GORDON, *"National Journal"*

IOWA

The Iowa General Assembly met for 104 days. With the Republicans in control of both the Senate (28R-22D) and the House (56R-44D), the status of the state treasury became the major concern of the session.

Legislation. The first bill to be enacted in 1980 allowed legislators and all elected public officials in the state to accept gifts. The final measure to be approved increased the benefits that may be received by the approximately 132,000 public employees covered by the Iowa Public Employees Retirement System.

Gasohol's tax-free status was changed, with a five-cent-per-gallon tax levied as of July 1, 1980. In an attempt to protect the falling surplus in the Iowa treasury, the phaseout of personal property tax was stopped for one year. The action saved about $3.8 million. The increased indexing of the state personal income tax system also was ceased as of July 1, 1980, as the state treasury did not have the required $60 million balance. In other economy actions the legislature refused to approve a proposed additional 2% wage increase for state employees. State capital improvements of more than $18 million likewise were shelved because of economy. The legislature put a 6% limit on valuation increases of commercial real estate.

Longer and heavier trucks on Iowa's highways were authorized and speeding fines were increased.

The revised formula for computing state aid to public schools will slow the increase in aid paid by the state and will probably require about a $12 million increase in property taxes within local school districts. The state ceilings on home mortgage loans and on business and personal loans were removed. The legislation also increased from 18% to 21% the rates that may be charged on various types of credit purchases but did not change the rate of interest that may be charged on revolving charge accounts.

Among the few appropriation increases was an added $1 million allocated to the $5 million previously granted to soil conservation projects underwritten by the state.

Gov. Robert D. Ray, having cut back on his appropriation recommendations in the 1980 legislative session, still found it necessary in August to require all state agencies to reduce expenditures by 3.6% of their budget allocations.

Economy. Unemployment in 1980 in Iowa reached a four-year high, with more than 91,200 persons drawing unemployment compensation. August unemployment was 6.2% of the work force.

Corn production was 109 bushels per acre and totaled 1,440,000,000 bushels. Soybeans were 37 bushels per acre and totaled 305 million bushels. Iowa ranked first in both soybeans and corn production.

After suffering a minidrought in July, the state had more rainfall in August than in any previous August in weather reporting history.

Elections. In the U.S. Senate race, Sen. John Culver (D) was beaten by Congressman Charles Grassley (R). Incumbents in all six Congressional districts, except Grassley's third, were reelected. In the third, Cooper Evans (R) defeated Lynn Cutler (D). The Iowa legislature in 1981 will have 29 Republicans and 21 Democrats in the Senate and 58 Republicans and 42 Democrats in the House.

The Iowa voters rejected an amendment to the state constitution that would have granted equal rights to women and also voted against holding a constitutional convention.

Other. The Iowa state penitentiary at Fort Madison, the oldest state penal institution west of the Mississippi, was under investigation by the federal court for not meeting standards.

Secretary of State Melvin Synhorst resigned after serving 30 years.

RUSSELL M. ROSS, *University of Iowa*

———— IOWA • Information Highlights ————

Area: 56,290 sq mi (145 791 km²).
Population (Jan. 1980 est.): 2,910,000.
Chief Cities (1976 est.): Des Moines, the capital, 195,405; Cedar Rapids, 108,684; Davenport, 101,459.
Government (1980): *Chief Officers*—governor, Robert D. Ray (R); lt. gov., Terry E. Branstad (R). *General Assembly*—Senate, 50 members; House of Representatives, 100 members.
Education (1979–80): *Enrollment*—public elementary schools, 285,948 pupils; public secondary, 262,369; colleges and universities, 132,599 students. *Public school expenditures,* $1,344,955,000 ($2,304 per pupil).
State Finances (fiscal year 1979): *Revenues,* $3,056,000,000; *expenditures,* $3,011,000,000.
Personal Income (1979): $25,455,000,000; *per capita,* $8,772.
Labor Force (June 1980): *Nonagricultural wage and salary earners,* 1,107,000; *unemployed* (August 1980), 91,200 (6.2% of total force).

IRAN

The situation in Iran was so bad in 1980 that the invasion by Iraq in September (*see* feature article, page 28) at first had a positive impact in tending to create unity in order to meet the foreign threat. But by December, this aura of unity was fast vanishing as a result of the resumption and intensification of internal political rivalries.

During the first eight months of the year, the chaos which characterized the Islamic revolution in 1979 continued in full force. The Ayatollah Ruhollah Khomeini could unleash terror, but he could not bring it under control. It was impossible to keep track of the executions and imprisonments of opponents and alleged opponents of the revolution. For the semiliterate mullahs (clergy) who were running the ad hoc revolutionary tribunals, human rights was not a concept applicable to Iran. Government administration and the economy deteriorated even further. With Iran's armed forces thrown into disarray by purges and executions, it was no wonder that Iraq chose this time to settle old scores.

Elections. In January, Abolhassan Bani-Sadr won a landslide victory in the presidential elections, getting more than 70% of the vote. His election seemed to bode well for the cause of moderation. The new president, although a longtime supporter of Khomeini, was educated in the West and is a moderate with slightly leftist views on how the government and the economy should be run. (*See* BIOGRAPHY.) Bani-Sadr, like then Foreign Minister Sadegh Ghotbzadeh, was opposed to the seizing of the American hostages and favored their release. The president spoke out against the rule of the mullahs. He was particularly sharp in condemning the summary executions and torture of prisoners. Bani-Sadr hoped to be president of a state ruled by law and not religious fanaticism. His problem was that in Iran there was a difference between being president and wielding real power.

Hardline Islamic fundamentalists led by the Ayatollah Mohammud Beheshti, the head of the supreme court, controlled most of the organs of government and much of the information media. They were unwilling to give up their theocratic rule to the secular Bani-Sadr and could summon mobs of hundreds of thousands to make their point whenever anyone dared to contradict them. The hardliners were diametrically opposed to Bani-Sadr on the hostage issue, even demanding that the hostages be put on trial for spying.

The hardliners showed their power in the parliamentary elections of March and May, when Beheshti's Islamic Republican Party won control of the new legislature (*Majlis*). Khomeini had advised voters that when in doubt as to whom to vote for, they should consult a mullah.

Bani-Sadr had wanted to nominate one of his moderate followers as prime minister and thereby be in a position to control the operations

Ayatollah Ruhollah Khomeini (second from left) casts his ballot in the March 14 elections for the Islamic National Assembly. Ahmad Khomeini (front, black clothes), the religious leader's son, assists in the voting.

of government ministries. But the Beheshti-dominated parliament would not go along and in August chose a Muslim fundamentalist, Mohammed Ali Rajai, as prime minister. The president did veto Rajai's cabinet selections on the grounds of incompetence, and several cabinet posts were left vacant. But despite Bani-Sadr's opposition, the cabinet that was approved by parliament in September was Beheshti's creation. Bani-Sadr and Rajai were soon in open conflict, and the Rajai government had other problems, as well. The new minister of justice, Ebrahim Ahadi, resigned at year's end, saying he had no control over the judicial system, particularly the various ad hoc revolutionary courts.

Supreme power under the constitution rests with the country's religious leader, Ayatollah Khomeini. But the 80-year-old Khomeini remained mostly in seclusion in the holy city Qum and failed to act decisively in political affairs, no doubt because of his poor health and traditional lack of concern for secular matters. Khomeini did seem to be tilting in favor of Ayatollah Beheshti but not enough to eliminate Bani-Sadr

---
IRAN • Information Highlights

Official Name: Islamic Republic of Iran.
Location: Southwest Asia.
Area: 636,300 sq mi (1 648 000 km²).
Population (1980 est.): 38,500,000.
Chief Cities (1976 census): Tehran, the capital, 4,496,-159 (met. area); Isfahan, 671,825; Meshed, 670,180.
Government: *Head of state,* Abolhassan Bani-Sadr, president (took office Feb. 1980). *Head of government.* Mohammed Ali Rajai, premier (took office Aug. 1980). *Legislature* (unicameral)—Parliament.
Monetary Unit: Rial (70.35 rials equal U.S.$1, Sept. 1980).
Manufactures (major products): Petrochemicals, textiles, cement, processed foods, steel, aluminum.
Agriculture (major products): Wheat, rice, barley.
GNP (1978 est., U.S.$): $76,100,000,000.
Foreign Trade (1979, U.S.$): *Imports,* $7,261,000,000; *exports,* $19,000,000,000.

from the scene. Khomeini's son, Hojatolislam Ahmad Khomeini, was the only person with full access to the all-powerful leader and was generally credited with maintaining the delicate balance that kept Bani-Sadr from being completely eliminated from the political scene in the first half of the year. An offer by Bani-Sadr to resign was rejected by the elder Khomeini.

Turmoil. The revolutionary courts were not only condemning to death and imprisonment supporters of former Shah Mohammed Reza Pahlavi. Charges against the accused ranged from counterrevolutionary behavior and spying to drug pushing, prostitution, and homosexuality. The Robespierre of Iranian terror was the Islamic "hanging judge" Sadegh Khalkhali, who by midyear had handed down more than 400 death sentences. Khalkhali had special responsibility for the antinarcotics campaign. The universities were purged of students and faculty whom the mullahs considered antagonistic to their rule. Women's rights had no place in Khomeini's Islamic Republic, with strict female dress codes being enforced and some women being deprived of jobs they had held under the shah. Criticism was unwelcome. Former foreign minister Ghotbzadeh was temporarily imprisoned in November for criticizing the fundamentalists and was released only after Bani-Sadr appealed to Ayatollah Khomeini. In the streets of Tehran, gangs of Muslim fanatics called Hezbolahi (Party of God) attacked leftists and other dissidents. Christian institutions, particularly ones run by missionaries, were harassed, and in some cases, the missionaries were arrested. At least one Jew was executed for alleged links with Israel. In August, the only Jew in parliament was expelled on the same grounds.

Opposition. The regime announced in July that it had smashed an attempted coup by members of the armed forces, and more than 60 persons were executed in subsequent weeks. Iran's minorities were especially restive. There was full-scale war in Kurdistan, where Iranian forces had to contend with both invading Iraqi forces and Kurdish rebels. Unrest also continued in Azerbaijan despite appeals by the region's spiritual leader, Ayatollah Shariat Madari, to avoid clashes with Revolutionary Guards and other supporters of the Khomeini regime. In the oil-rich province of Khuzestan, ethnic Arabs were in revolt against the Persian-dominated Tehran regime, resulting in the sabotage of several oil installations. Khuzestan also was the scene of the heaviest fighting between Iranian and Iraqi forces, and citizens of the province were executed for collaborating with the invaders.

In January, the government said that it had smashed a guerrilla group known as Forghan (Koran Fighters) which had launched an assassination campaign against Khomeini's associates. But Forghan claimed responsibility for the unsuccessful assassination attempt against Public Prosecutor Ayatollah Abdul Karim Mosavi-Ardabili in Tehran on December 23. Also in December, leftist groups staged demonstrations in a number of Iranian cities, during which Khomeini's picture was burned publicly.

Economy. Even before the Iraqi invasion in September, Iran was plagued by shortages of food and fuel. Inflation was estimated at 50%. Factories reportedly were operating at less than half of their capacity. Oil exports had fallen to less than one million barrels a day (from more than six million during the shah's era) and they came to a virtual halt with the outbreak of war. Gold and foreign currency reserves dwindled, while the trade deficit mounted. Bani-Sadr estimated that economic sanctions by the United States and its allies (because of the hostage issue) were forcing Iran to pay between 20 and 25% more for imports. But the real problem was the inability of the clergy to run the economy.

The war with Iraq made matters much worse. There was serious damage to the country's oil and petrochemical installations, with the major producing center at Abadan especially hard hit. At year's end, the government announced that one million Iranians had been left homeless by the war. Shipment of goods through the Persian Gulf was limited because of the possibility of Iraqi air attacks. The Tehran government did work out an agreement with the Soviet Union for the transshipment of goods across Soviet territory. Negotiations with Moscow for the export of Iranian natural gas, which had been halted in a price dispute, also were begun. Ties with Moscow were somewhat strained, however, when on December 27 Afghan exiles in Tehran broke into the Soviet embassy compound to protest the Soviet invasion of their country. Iranian authorities prevented anything like the takeover of the U.S. embassy in November 1979. Moscow had warned that it would not tolerate such an act.

Impact of the War. The Iraqi invasion at first proved beneficial to Bani-Sadr's political fortunes. The president condemned the fundamentalists for creating the chaos that made Iran ripe for an attack. On December 7, after Bani-Sadr attacked him for judicial irregularities, Judge Khalkhali resigned as head of the antinarcotics campaign. As commander-in-chief of the armed forces and charged with organizing the Iranian defense effort, Bani-Sadr was in the spotlight. Despite initial military setbacks, morale in Tehran was high, and the president was given high marks for dealing so well with a very difficult situation. One of his most difficult tasks was to get Khomeini's Revolutionary Guards to cooperate with the regular army, and he was constantly at the war front trying to build morale and unity. By the end of the year, however, Bani-Sadr had come under attack by the Beheshti-led fundamentalists for not doing enough to drive out the invaders. The president's popularity as a war leader apparently had made the fundamentalists jealous, and they were out to discredit him at all costs.

Polarization. There was growing evidence of polarization between left and right. Two years of rule by the mullahs had neutralized the small but once-influential middle class. What remained was an Islamic fundamentalist faction on the right and increasingly assertive groups on the left. Although the fundamentalists could play the religious card to get the support of the illiterate masses, the leftists were better organized.

The two main leftist groups were the Fedayeen (People's Fighters), a secular Marxist organization, and the Muja Hadeen (People's Freedom Fighters), an Islamic Marxist organization. The two groups had to operate underground because of strong condemnations by Khomeini, but both are capable of more extensive guerrilla operations than they engaged in during 1980.

The Iranian Communist Party—known as the Tudeh—is small and highly organized. It is controlled by Moscow and can be expected to follow the orders of the Kremlin. The Tudeh operates in the open, thanks to its public support of Khomeini.

In 1980, the Islamic Republic of Iran was held together primarily by the prestige and charisma of Ayatollah Khomeini. His likely successor, the Ayatollah Hossein Ali Montazeri, does not have Khomeini's popular support, and in the event of Khomeini's death, a full-scale civil war is not out of the question.

AARON R. EINFRANK, *Free-lance writer*

IRAQ

Prior to the outbreak of war between Iraq and Iran in September (*see* feature article, page 28), Iraqi President Saddam Hussein seemed to have the domestic situation well under control in both the political and economic spheres. Hussein, who assumed full power in July 1979, was still faced with problems, but Iraq under his rule was enjoying a stability and prosperity unparalleled in the modern history of the country.

Elections. The 43-year-old president was so confident that he invited the international press to come to normally-secretive Baghdad to witness the June 20 parliamentary elections, Iraq's first since the fall of the monarchy in 1958. An estimated six million Iraqis voted for some 840 candidates seeking four-year terms in the 250-seat assembly. Women voted for the first time in general elections, and nearly a dozen women candidates won seats.

However, the election was run by Hussein's ruling Baath (Arab Socialist) Party, which has been in power since 1968, and there was no real opposition in the new parliament. Moreover, parliamentary legislation requires the approval of the Baath's Revolutionary Command Council (RCC), headed by Hussein and dominated by his cronies and relatives. The RCC can dissolve the parliament at will. Nevertheless, the exercise in simulated parliamentary democracy was impressive. The elections were marred by only one event—unidentified terrorists were killed by Iraqi security forces after storming the British Embassy in Baghdad the day before—and the state-controlled press described the balloting as a "major victory for democracy."

In September, Hussein again resorted to the electoral process by allowing the first elections in Iraq's autonomous Kurdistan region, the scene of bloody revolts by Kurds against the Baghdad government. Some 700,000 Kurds elected 50 representatives from 194 candidates running for the region's legislative assembly. Although there were unrest and fighting in Kurdistan throughout the year, the mere fact that Hussein was able to stage a rather efficiently-run (albeit rigged) election seemed to substantiate government claims that progress was being made in placating the Kurds.

Tight Control. Despite the veneer of parliamentarianism, Hussein headed a tightly-controlled police state. In its 1980 report, Amnesty International, the human rights watchdog agency, protested the upsurge of executions and imprisonments.

IRAQ • Information Highlights

Official Name: Republic of Iraq.
Location: Southwest Asia.
Area: 169,284 sq mi (438 446 km²).
Population (1980 est.): 13,200,000.
Chief Cities (1970 est.): Baghdad, the capital, 2,183,800 (met. area); Basra, 370,900; Mosul, 293,100.
Government: Head of state and government, Saddam Hussein Takriti, president (took office July 1979).
Monetary Unit: Dinar (0.2953 dinar equals U.S.$1, Aug. 1980).
Manufactures (major products): Leather, consumer goods.
Agriculture (major products): Barley, wheat, dates, vegetables, cotton.
GNP (1979 est., U.S.$): $21,400,000,000.
Foreign Trade (1978, U.S.$): Imports, $4,213,000,000; exports, $11,064,000,000.

Iraqis must have a license even to own a typewriter, which probably explains the lack of a notable underground literature, and the import of foreign publications is strictly controlled.

Shiites. Although the Hussein regime is dominated by Sunnis, it is estimated that between 50% and 60% of the country's population are Shiites. In 1980, as in the previous year, some Iraqi Shiites were extremely partial to the Islamic revolution being staged by Iran's Shiite leader, the Ayatollah Ruhollah Khomeini. In fact, one of the causes of the Iran-Iraq war was Khomeini's attempt to export his Shiite revolution to Iraq and his calls for the overthrow of Hussein.

In the first six months of 1980, Hussein staged a massive crackdown on Iraqi Shiites. As Amnesty International pointed out, arrests and executions of Shiites were common. Among those executed was the Iraqi Shiite leader, the Ayatollah Mohammed Bakr-Sadr. Shiite officers were purged from the armed forces, and in April, the Baghdad government announced it was expelling ethnic Iranians.

Opposition. Exile groups opposed to Hussein were operating in both Syria and Iran. These groups included dissident Baathists, Kurds, Shiites, and Communists. Despite Iraq's Treaty of Friendship and Cooperation with the Soviet Union, the Iraqi Communist Party remained underground, with most of its leadership in Moscow. Aside from occasional assassination attempts on Hussein's associates and the terrorist attack on the British Embassy, Iraq's security forces had a successful year in keeping domestic order.

Economy. The key to Hussein's political future appeared to be the economy. Because of Iraq's vast oil supplies, the standard of living is high compared with the rest of the Middle East. Prior to the outbreak of war, the country was exporting 3.5 million barrels of oil per day, making it the second largest Arab exporter, after Saudi Arabia. Gold and foreign currency reserves were at a high level. The 1980 budget allocated $17,800,000,000 for various development programs, an increase of $6,600,000,000 over the 1979 level. Hussein looked to the Western nations, including the United States, for new technology. The Soviet Union was no longer a major source of civilian goods, falling well behind the United States. American-made tractors were replacing Soviet-built machines. Western Europe and the United States also provided equipment and know-how for the petrochemical industry and for the ambitious power-irrigation projects on the Tigris and Euphrates rivers. But in a long-term attempt to lessen Iraq's reliance on foreign technicians, the government sent many of its young to study abroad.

One of Hussein's pet projects, the country's ambitious nuclear development program, was being aided by France. Baghdad said that the nuclear reactors would be used for peaceful purposes, but Israel claimed that Hussein was trying to develop nuclear weapons.

Consequences of the War. A major question raised by the war was whether Iraq's economic success could continue. Many of the foreign technicians, including the French nuclear experts at the reactor project outside Baghdad, fled when the fighting started. (The nuclear project was bombed, but the reactors were reported undamaged.) And with Iraq's Persian Gulf ports blockaded by the Iranian navy, the government had to rely on the transshipment of goods by truck from Jordan. The government went out of its way to make sure that the shops remained full, and Iraq's socialist economy made it possible to keep prices low despite the war.

Since oil could not be sent through the gulf, Iraq had only its pipelines to the Mediterranean for exporting its major commodity. It was not clear just how much oil was getting through. The pipelines were either subject to attack by terrorists and the Iranian air force or controlled by Syria. On several occasions in the past, Syria has blocked the flow of Iraqi oil.

At year's end, it appeared that Hussein had to get the economy operating at its previous level to avoid adverse political consequences. The first essential step was to bring the war to a successful conclusion.

AARON R. EINFRANK, *Free-lance writer*

IRELAND

While the Northern Irish conflict continued to embroil Irish political life, the government made clear its opposition to terrorism. Prime Minister Charles Haughey adopted a moderate position with regard to reunification of north and south, insisting that a peaceful solution was "the first political priority" of his administration. At the annual conference of the ruling Fianna Fail party on February 16, Haughey called for cooperation between the British and Irish governments in order to end "the tragedy of the North" and to create a united Ireland. Only a "joint initiative" from both Dublin and London, he added, would bring about this goal.

In May, Haughey traveled to London for talks on the issue with British Prime Minister Margaret Thatcher, who returned the visit in December. At a Fianna Fail rally in Cork on July 27, the Irish premier spoke out strongly against terrorism, denouncing the Northern Irish Aid Committee (NORAID), the Irish National Caucus, and other extremist groups in the United States providing support to the Irish Republican Army (IRA). Haughey appealed to all Americans who care about Ireland not to give money to these organizations. He also issued orders to increase the number and strength of army security patrols along the border with Northern Ireland.

The government's moderate approach to the dispute was put to the test in a parliamentary by-election in northwest Donegal on November 6. Haughey's policy was challenged by an independent Fianna Fail candidate, Patrick Kelly, who took a harder line toward the north. With the premier's strong support, however, the official Fianna Fail candidate, Clement Coughlan, won decisively; Kelly finished a distant third.

Foreign Affairs. In international relations, Ireland pursued a policy of peace and arms limitation, largely under the auspices of the United Nations. The government refused to support the U.S.-sponsored boycott of the summer Olympic Games in Moscow. In mid-April, three Irish soldiers in the UN peace-keeping force (UNIFIL) in Lebanon were killed. When a leader of the Lebanese Christian militia accused the Irish troops of favoring PLO guerrillas in their sector, Irish Minister of Foreign Affairs Brian Lenihan denied the charge but added that the Palestinians had a right to "self-determination."

Economy. Inflationary pressures, caused primarily by higher energy costs, dominated the economic scene. Some economists expressed concern over heavy government borrowing, which increased the amount of interest paid to overseas lenders. There also was worry over a decline of about 11% in domestic investment, compared with 1979. The 1980 budget, introduced by Finance Minister Michael O'Kennedy in February, called for higher taxes, notably on alcoholic beverages, cigarettes, and petroleum products. The proposed taxes drove the price of a gallon of gas to $2.70 and a pint of beer to $1.26. The value added tax (VAT) was raised from 20% to 25%. The increases were intended to generate enough revenue to lower the total national deficit from $2,100,000,000 to $1,900,000,000. Although wage and salary earners, especially married ones, received modest income tax relief, the proposed indirect taxes were expected to curb consumer spending by more than 15%. The decline in real incomes was expected to be close to that of industrial output—between 2% and 2.5%. The volume of exported goods, on the other hand, increased by almost 7% over 1979.

L. PERRY CURTIS, JR.
Brown University

─────── **IRELAND • Information Highlights** ───────

Official Name: Republic of Ireland.
Location: Island in the eastern North Atlantic Ocean.
Area: 27,136 sq mi (70 282 km²).
Population (1980 est.): 3,300,000.
Chief Cities (1979 est.): Dublin, the capital, 543,563; Cork, 138,092; Limerick, 60,769.
Government: *Head of state,* Patrick J. Hillery, president (took office Nov. 1976). *Head of government,* Charles J. Haughey, prime minister (took office Dec. 1979). *Legislature*—Parliament: House of Representatives (Dáil Éireann) and Senate (Seanad Éireann).
Monetary Unit: Pound (0.5203 pound equals U.S.$1, Dec. 1980).
Manufactures (major products): Processed foods, textiles, construction materials, machinery, chemicals.
Agriculture (major products): Cattle, dairy products, wheat, potatoes, barley, sugar beets, turnips, hay.
GNP Per Capita (1978 est., U.S.$): $3,470.
Foreign Trade (1979, U.S.$): *Imports,* $9,858,000,000; *exports,* $7,175,000,000.

Israeli President Yitzhak Navon (center foreground) and Egyptian President Anwar el-Sadat (right) listen to their countries' national anthems upon Navon's arrival in Cairo for five days of talks and sightseeing in late October.

Wide World

ISRAEL

The year 1980 was another critical one for the State of Israel. The country was plagued with soaring inflation and confronted by domestic political crises, Arab terrorism, and mounting international pressure to give up territories basic to its defense.

As the year began, two issues occupied the center of attention. One was the normalization of relations with Egypt, and the other was negotiations for autonomy in Judea, Samaria, and Gaza, regions occupied by Israel during the six-day war in June 1967.

Ties with Egypt. The opening of the Egyptian-Israeli border on January 27 was followed by the exchange of ambassadors one month later and the first commercial air flight between Cairo and Tel Aviv on March 3. Newspapers and magazines were exchanged, and postal and telephone communications were established. In April, Israel and Egypt concluded an agreement on land and sea transportation, and the first Israeli freighter docked at Alexandria in July, beginning biweekly cargo service between the two countries. After repeated Israeli complaints of Egyptian foot-dragging in the normalization process, the Egyptians agreed to speed up procedures for granting visas to Israelis and to open the El Arish border point to commercial traffic. The overland shipment of freight was expected to reduce costs and stimulate trade between the two countries. In October, Israeli President Yitzhak Navon visited Cairo at the invitation of Egyptian President Anwar el-Sadat, and the two leaders agreed on an eight-point program to expedite normalization. Included in the program were additional El-Al (Israeli airline) flights to Cairo (raising the number to four per week, as compared with two per week by Nefertiti, the Egyptian airline); mutual agricultural and commercial exhibitions; and a visit to Israel by an Egyptian cultural delegation.

Autonomy Talks. A wide gap in interpretations of the 1978 Camp David peace accords made for repeated breakdowns in the negotiations on autonomy in Judea, Samaria, and Gaza. Egypt insisted on broad powers for the autonomous body, which eventually would lead to self-determination. Israel, on the other hand, was determined to restrict autonomy to administrative and public services, thereby precluding the establishment of a Palestinian state. Other major points of contention were the establishment of Jewish settlements in these territories and the status of Jerusalem, neither of which is mentioned in the Camp David accords. While Egypt regarded the Jewish settlements as illegal and insisted that East Jerusalem be linked to the autonomy scheme, Israel considered the settlements indispensable to its security and the status of Jerusalem nonnegotiable. In April, the Egyp-

297

tian parliament passed a resolution stating that East Jerusalem is an Arab territory. But in July, the Knesset (Israeli parliament) overwhelmingly passed a bill declaring that "undivided" Jerusalem is the capital of Israel.

World reaction to the "Jerusalem Bill" was vehement. Egyptian President Sadat suspended the autonomy talks for the fourth time in the year. The UN Security Council denounced Israel and urged all nations with embassies in Jerusalem to remove them. A UN General Assembly resolution directed Israel to withdraw from all occupied territories, including East Jerusalem. Saudi Arabia called for a "holy war" against Israel. All 13 nations with embassies in Jerusalem moved them to Tel Aviv. But in a gesture of spiritual support for the Jerusalem Bill, more than 1,000 evangelical Christians gathered in Jerusalem in October to establish a "Christian Embassy" there.

Terrorism. Arab terrorist activity triggered a round of retaliatory moves by Israel, which in turn brought more Arab violence. The murder in Hebron of a yeshiva (religious school) student in February was followed by the sniper shooting of an Israeli soldier in Bethlehem, an attack on a kibbutz nursery in Galilee in April, and the massacre of six worshippers in Hebron in May. The killing of three Israelis during the Palestinian attack on kibbutz Misgav Am on April 7 prompted a raid by Israeli army units into southern Lebanon two days later. It was the largest military operation by Israel north of the Litani River since 1978. In a countermove, terrorists fired rockets toward the Israeli border and set off bombs in public parks, marketplaces, bus stops, and gas stations. Following the Hebron massacre in May, the Israeli government ordered the deportation of a religious judge and the mayors of Hebron and Halhul, two towns on the West Bank. A month later, bomb explosions in four cities in Judea and Samaria maimed the mayors of Nablus and Ramallah and blinded an Israeli explosives expert.

Politics. In March, Yitzhak Shamir was appointed foreign minister, a post that Prime Minister Begin had held since December 1979. Two

months later, another political crisis was precipitated when Defense Minister Ezer Weizman resigned in protest against cuts in defense spending. To fill the post, the prime minister undertook a cabinet reshuffle. When none of his appointments was approved by the Knesset, however, he assumed the defense post himself. After a mild heart attack in July, Begin resumed his dual responsibility with vigor.

Prime Minister Begin's most serious political challenge came in mid-November, after the release of inflation figures for the previous month, while Begin was on a trip to the United States. Begin rushed home to face no-confidence motions by three opposition parties over the country's worsening economic problems. Two of Begin's former cabinet ministers, Moshe Dayan (foreign) and Ezer Weizman (defense) voted against him, but Begin survived the motion, 57 to 54. Days later, Weizman was ousted from Begin's Herut Party for his vote against the government. His expulsion left the governing coalition without a parliamentary majority.

In March, the country mourned the passing of Yigal Allon, a leader of Labor Zionism, a hero of Israel's war of independence, and a former deputy premier. In July, the first kidnap-murder case in Israel's history shocked the nation. Although Israel does not have a capital punishment law (except for Nazi war crimes), the courts were considering the imposition of the death penalty.

Economy. The transfer to Egypt of the Alma oil fields on the Gulf of Suez created grave economic hardships for Israel. Unlike the Abu Rodeis fields, the oil there was discovered and developed at great expense to Israel. Experts had predicted that the Alma fields would have made Israel self-sufficient in one to three years. The replacement of this oil with expensive imports, combined with the high cost of evacuating air bases in the Sinai and redeploying them in the Negev, burdened Israel's economy. The gradual removal of government subsidies for food staples drastically accelerated an already high inflation rate. The 11% increase in October that almost toppled the Begin government brought the annual rate to a staggering 138%. To generate new respect for the currency, the government replaced the pound with a new monetary unit—the shekel. One shekel equaled ten pounds.

In August, the cabinet approved a $700 million plan for a canal between the Mediterranean and the Dead Sea. A waterfall created by the difference in altitude between the Mediterranean coast and the Dead Sea region would power a hydroelectric plant. The canal would provide cooling lakes for a nuclear plant to be built in the Negev Desert, and supply energy for nearby factories. The proposed power plant was expected to supply 10% of Israel's electrical power by the year 1990.

LIVIA E. BITTON JACKSON
Herbert H. Lehman College, CUNY

ISRAEL • Information Highlights

Official Name: State of Israel.
Location: Southwest Asia.
Area: 7,848 sq mi (20 326 km²).
Population (1980 est.): 3,900,000.
Chief Cities (1979 est.): Jerusalem, the capital, 386,600; Tel Aviv-Jaffa, 339,800; Haifa, 229,000.
Government: *Head of state,* Yitzhak Navon, president (took office May 1978). *Head of government,* Menahem Begin, premier (took office June 1977). *Legislature* (unicameral)—Knesset.
Monetary Unit: Shekel (6.34 shekels equal U.S.$1, Nov. 1980).
Manufactures (major products): Processed foods, textiles, metal products.
Agriculture (major products): Wheat, hay, citrus fruits, dairy products, cotton.
GNP Per Capita (1978 est. U.S.$): $4,120.
Foreign Trade (1979, U.S.$): *Imports,* $7,471,000,000; *exports,* $4,553,000,000.

ITALY

Italy experienced an upsurge of terrorism and economic troubles in 1980, but greater political stability seemed likely after the Socialist Party decided to enter a center-left government.

The economic difficulties, political maneuvering, and acts of terrorism all paled, however, in comparison with the devastation caused by an earthquake—the strongest in the country's history—in southern Italy on November 23. Worst hit were the provinces of Naples, Salerno, Potenza, and Avellino. According to the government, 97 municipalities suffered serious damage. By the time the aftershocks had ceased and the rubble had been examined, more than 3,000 persons were reported dead and some 200,000 left homeless. In the days following the tragedy, the government came under criticism for a poorly organized and inadequately supplied relief effort. The Communist Party even called for an ouster of the cabinet.

POLITICS

Terrorism. The year began with a sharp increase in assassinations and other acts of terrorism. On January 6, Piersanti Mattarella, the Christian Democratic president of Sicily's regional government, was killed, and in ensuing weeks, numerous politicians, magistrates, police officials, journalists, and industrialists also were murdered. In some cases the extreme left claimed responsibility, and in others the extreme right.

In February, parliament voted 522 to 50 in favor of an emergency law under which a person charged with subversion or terrorism might be kept in jail without trial for 12 years. The law also gave police the power to search homes without warrants, conduct wiretaps, and hold a suspected terrorist for 24 hours without informing anyone.

A crackdown against leftist Red Brigades in Turin in April led to the arrest of Fabrizio Peci, who revealed the internal structure of that terrorist group. He also confessed to having played a part in the 1978 kidnapping and murder of former Prime Minister Aldo Moro.

The nation's most significant terrorist trial since the 1978 proceedings against Renato Curcio ended June 22 with the sentencing of Corrado Alunni, a leader of the leftist Front Line organization, to 29 years in prison for leading a Milan jailbreak in April. By midsummer, some 700 left-wing and 260 right-wing radicals were in jail on charges of terrorism.

Italy's worst atrocity since World War II occurred on August 2, when 84 people were killed and 200 injured in a bomb explosion at the Bologna railway station. Right-wing extremists were thought to be responsible, but no rational motive was adduced for the crime.

Cossiga Government. The year began with a three-party coalition headed by Christian Democrat Francesco Cossiga in power. The cabinet comprised 16 Christian Democrat, 4 Social Democrat, 2 Liberal, and 2 uncommitted ministers.

In February, the Christian Democrats held their national congress and reverted to a tough anti-Communist stance by approving a declaration opposing Communist participation in the government under any circumstances. The vote was a defeat for outgoing Party Secretary Benigno Zaccagnini and former Prime Minister Giulio Andreotti, both of whom advocated a more flexible position. Flaminio Piccoli, a strong anti-Communist, was elected party secretary.

The fall of the Cossiga government became almost inevitable after the Christian Democrats ruled out new negotiations with the Communists. Bettino Craxi, the ambitious leader of the Socialist Party, decided to provoke the crisis in the hope of becoming the first non-Christian Democratic prime minister since 1945. On March 19, the Socialists announced that they would join with the Communists in active parliamentary opposition, and the Cossiga government was forced to resign.

The crisis ended on April 4 with the formation of a new center-left coalition, again headed by Cossiga. The new coalition included Cossiga's own Christian Democrats, Socialists, and Republicans. It was the first time since 1974 that the Socialist Party was included in a government.

The "Marco Affair." At the end of May, Prime Minister Cossiga faced a new crisis. He was threatened with impeachment when charges were made that he had told a fellow party official, Carlo Donat-Cattin, that his son, Marco, was wanted as a terrorist. A recently arrested member of the Front Line, Roberto Sandalo, told police in Turin that the younger Donat-Cattin left the country when his father heard from Cossiga that he was about to be arrested.

A special parliamentary commission dismissed the accusation against Prime Minister Cossiga by a vote of 11 to 9, but Communist Party leader Enrico Berlinguer called for impeachment proceedings. Berlinguer was backed by the Social Democratic, Liberal, Radical, and neo-Fascist Social Movement parties. On June 12, parliament voted in favor of impeachment proceedings, but these were delayed until midsummer. On July 27, parliament met in joint session and voted by secret ballot (535 to 370) to absolve the premier of complicity in the flight of the suspected terrorist. Three days later, the Cossiga government won another vote of confidence in the Chamber of Deputies on a Communist challenge to its court reform policy.

Regional Elections. The Christian Democrats also were cheered by slight gains at the expense of the Communists in regional and municipal elections June 8. The Christian Democrats received 36.8% of the vote, a gain of 1.5% over similar local elections in 1975. The Communists polled 31.5%, a loss of 1.9%. The Socialist Party

Arnaldo Forlani (left) is sworn in as prime minister by President Sandro Pertini (right), October 18.

improved its standing by 2.8%, polling 12.7% of the vote. The Christian Democrats won control of Piedmont, which the Communists had dominated, and Latium. But the Communists retained their hold on ten regional capitals, as well as 38 of 40 provincial capitals. Their chief losses came in the south.

Failure of Cossiga's "Economic Package." By midsummer, there was growing awareness among politicians and trade unionists that economic problems again were becoming critical. On July 2, therefore, the Cossiga government presented to parliament a new "economic package." Designed to curb inflation—running at an annual rate of 20%—shore up the lira, and reduce the foreign payments deficit, the plan provided for five new nuclear reactors to reduce dependence on imported oil; called for a reduction in social security and health taxes paid by employers, instead shifting the burden to the government; provided for a 0.5% increase in indirect taxes on industrial wages; and slated about $3,-000,000,000 of the income for development in southern Italy and aid to troubled industries. However, the package did not call for any modification of the highly inflationary system of wage indexation.

The plan faced opposition in parliament, especially from the Communists. On September 27, the six-month-old Cossiga government was defeated (298-297) in a vote of confidence and again forced to resign. At least 30 of the government's supporters deserted the coalition in the secret vote, which came just 20 minutes after the government had won a confidence motion by 65 votes in open balloting. The defectors were presumed to be left-wing Christian Democrats and left-wing Socialists who were angry at Cossiga and Craxi and favored overtures to the Communists. The defeat of the Cossiga government came just as the economy faced a major strike by automotive workers at Fiat.

Forlani Government. On October 18, Arnaldo Forlani, president of the Christian Democratic party since March and a former foreign minister, brought an end to the political crisis by forming a new government. It was the 40th administration in post-World War II Italy. The four-party coalition included 14 Christian Democrats, 7 Socialists, 3 Social Democrats, and 3 Republicans. It held a 90-seat majority in the Chamber. Foreign Minister Emilio Colombo was one of the Christian Democratic ministers who retained his post, and the Socialist Party was reassigned the defense ministry.

The Forlani government was expected to present an economic program similar to the one defeated in September, but it was not expected to devalue the lira to boost exports.

Craxi's "Third Force." In the autumn, Socialist Party leader Bettino Craxi, the new power broker in Italian politics, speeded up his plans to forge a new political bloc that would break down the polarization of Christian Democrats and Communists. At a meeting of the party's Central Committee in October, Craxi made the entire

Socialist leadership resign and persuaded it to elect a directorate in which he would have a much larger majority. Next he signed a pact with Social Democratic Party leader Pietro Longo, whereby the two parties agreed to cooperate within a greater "democratic socialist" alliance. Then he sought to woo the small Radical Party of Marco Pannella; if the Radicals agreed to join with Craxi, the new bloc would comprise 19% of the electorate.

Communist Party. Enrico Berlinguer, leader of the Communist Party, continued to take a critical line toward the Kremlin. He and other party leaders strongly condemned the Soviet aggression in Afghanistan. In April, Berlinguer made a 10-day visit to the People's Republic of China and North Korea. After a 15-year breach, the Italian and Chinese Communist parties normalized relations. During the same month, the Italian Communists boycotted a Kremlin-sponsored meeting of Communist parties in Paris.

ECONOMY

After two years of growth, surpluses in the balance of payments, and a stable lira, Italy's economic situation deteriorated in 1980. Economic growth dropped to less than 4%, compared with 4.9% in 1979. Inflation pushed above the 20% mark. By midyear, unemployment had risen to 7.8%. Energy consumption was up sharply over 1979, causing the balance of payments to go into the red. Government spending was out of control. On September 28, the Central Bank's lending rate went up from 15% to 16½%.

Fiat Strike. In mid-September, Fiat, the nation's major automobile manufacturer, announced that until 1982 it would have to trim production by 20% because of foreign competition and reduced demand. The cutback would mean the dismissal of 14,000 workers, an action without precedent in postwar Italy. The normally cautious unions reacted by calling an indefinite strike. Whereas strikes in Italy normally last only a few hours, the Fiat walkout lasted 35 days—the longest in a major industry since World War II. Some observers maintained that the unions overestimated their strength.

――――――― **ITALY · Information Highlights** ―――――――

Official Name: Italian Republic.
Location: Southern Europe.
Area: 116,318 sq mi (301 264 km^2).
Population (1980 est.): 57,200,000.
Chief Cities (Dec. 1978): Rome, the capital, 2,914,640; Milan, 1,693,351; Naples 1,225,377; Turin, 1,172,482.
Government: *Head of state,* Sandro Pertini, president (took office July 1978). *Head of government,* Arnaldo Forlani, prime minister (took office Oct. 1980). *Legislature*—Parliament: Senate and Chamber of Deputies.
Monetary Unit: Lira (911.50 lire equal U.S.$1, Nov. 1980).
Manufactures (major products): Automobiles, machinery, chemicals, textiles, shoes.
Agriculture (major products): Wheat, rice, corn, fruits, vegetables.
GNP (1979 est., U.S.$): $317,000,000,000.
Foreign Trade (1979, U.S.$): *Imports,* $77,970,000,000; *exports,* $72,242,000,000.

The Communist Party also was accused of going too far. Berlinguer told workers at the gates of the main Fiat plant in Turin that his party would support them "morally and materially" if they occupied the plant. After years of moderation and restraint, the Communists shocked much of the country with their inflammatory rhetoric. To the surprise of many, a back-to-work movement developed. On October 15, some 30,000 workers marched through the streets of Turin in defiance of the union leaders.

Two days later, the strike was settled on terms that were generally favorable to Fiat. There would be no outright dismissals, but 23,000 workers would be suspended for at least 15 months. The state would pay some 93% of their salaries. The setback for the unions was regarded as a possible landmark in Italy's postwar industrial labor relations.

Alfa Romeo-Nissan Deal. On September 21, the government approved plans for Alfa Romeo, the troubled, state-owned auto maker, to set up a joint venture with the Nissan Motor Company of Japan. The two companies would jointly finance an assembly plant at Naples that by 1984 would produce 60,000 cars annually. The decision was made despite strong objections from Fiat.

Financial Scandals. In March, the biggest banking scandal in modern Italian history erupted with the resignation of a cabinet minister and the arrest of 38 members of the banking establishment. Italcasse, the central savings institute, had been the target of the probe. In November, a $2,200,000,000 tax evasion scandal involving oil imports put strains on the government.

FOREIGN AFFAIRS

In January, Premier Cossiga visited Washington where he expressed support for U.S. policies regarding Iran and the Soviet Union.

Italy held the rotating presidency of the European Community (EC) during the first half of 1980. Amid tight security, Venice was the site for a meeting of EC leaders in mid-June. A week later, Venice also hosted the annual meeting of the heads of governments of the major industrial democracies.

En route to the latter meeting, U.S. President Jimmy Carter stopped in Rome for a state visit. Italian leaders agreed with him that Soviet aggression in Afghanistan was a threat to peace and an obstacle to détente. But Italy, along with most EC countries, did not go along with the U.S.-led boycott of the Summer Olympic Games in Moscow.

Although Italy continued to support NATO's deployment of medium-range nuclear missiles in Europe, Rome failed to meet the targeted increase in defense spending of at least 3% per year above the rate of inflation, as agreed to by NATO members. In the autumn, NATO used its base in Naples to conduct naval exercises in the Mediterranean.

CHARLES F. DELZELL, *Vanderbilt University*

JAPAN

As one of the advanced industrial nations, Japan both enjoyed the advantages and suffered the disadvantages of interdependence in a tumultuous world. Once again the country was represented at a meeting of the industrial democracies, the June 1980 summit in Venice. Japan joined with the six other participating nations in condemning the Soviet invasion of Afghanistan and in calling on Iran to release the 52 U.S. hostages being held in Tehran.

The escalation of the Iran-Iraq war in October threatened one of Japan's lifelines—the Strait of Hormuz, through which flows about 70% of the nation's imported oil. Despite a deterioration of more than $25,000,000,000 in Japan's current account since the record balance of payments surplus of $12,000,000,000 in fiscal 1978, Tokyo felt pressure to reduce exports, especially of automobiles, to both the United States and Western Europe.

At home, the majority Liberal-Democratic Party (LDP) survived the challenges posed by the death of Prime Minister Masayoshi Ohira and an unprecedented dual election, both in June. The LDP emerged with a comfortable majority in the Diet (parliament) and with a new, little-known president, Zenko Suzuki, who in July became Japan's 15th postwar prime minister. (*See* BIOGRAPHY.)

International Affairs

Increasingly, sometimes reluctantly, Japan found itself identifying with the strategic concerns of the United States and the People's Republic of China, specifically the need to face a Soviet military buildup in Asia. The Soviet Union in turn denounced American and Chinese efforts as attempts to arouse "anti-Soviet tendencies" in Tokyo's policies.

Japan's other major concerns were directed to troubled areas in nearby Asia. Tokyo worried about Vietnam's intentions in Southeast Asia. The Japanese public expressed increasing alarm at the attempts of the military dictatorship in South Korea to suppress dissident opinion.

Relations with the United States. Although Japan's foreign affairs revolved largely around the Tokyo-Washington security axis, Japanese-American trade relations caused concern in both capitals. In May alone, for example, Toyota Motors reported that its auto exports had increased by more than 50% (as compared with May 1979) to a record monthly total of 163,114 units. Nissan (producer of Datsuns) increased its exports to a monthly total of 131,030 units, 40% more than in the corresponding month of the previous year. In July, Japanese auto production registered an all-time monthly high of more than 1 million units. The flood of cars, coupled with widespread unemployment in the U.S. automobile industry, led United Auto Workers (UAW) President Donald Fraser, while in Tokyo in February, to warn the Japanese of import quotas. At working-level meetings held in Washington April 7–9, delegates of the two governments agreed not to make a political issue of the problem. It was not a major item on the agenda for talks between Prime Minister Ohira and U.S. President Jimmy Carter in Washington on May 1. On May 20, however, the U.S. Customs Service decided to raise duties on imported truck cab-chassis units, a move Tokyo protested.

One of the responses by the Japanese was a series of decisions to build cars in the United States. Honda was already established in Ohio. On April 9, Nissan announced plans to build

Japan's vast export of small cars was a sore point in relations with the United States.

small trucks in the United States. In October in Tokyo, Ford Vice-President Louis Ross reported that a "final selection" of a subcompact car to be jointly produced with Toyota would be made by the end of the year. In Washington in September, Foreign Minister Masayoshi Ito assured U.S. union leaders and congressmen that Japanese auto imports would decline in the last quarter as new American compacts appeared.

Meanwhile, Japan lent whatever support it could muster to its American ally. When U.S. Defense Secretary Harold Brown stopped in Tokyo on January 14 on his way home from Peking, he pointedly suggested that Japan could contribute to security in Southwest Asia by providing increased economic assistance to Pakistan. He also expressed hope that, in the wake of the Soviet invasion of Afghanistan, Japan would increase its expenditures on defense. On May 1, Prime Minister Ohira, in Washington on the first leg of a North American tour, assured President Carter of Japan's cooperation in resolving the Afghan and Iranian issues. Ohira did, however, urge Carter to exercise restraint in handling the hostage problem. Carter in turn joined world leaders in paying final respects to the prime minister at his official funeral held in Tokyo, July 9. The next day, in a televised interview with Japanese media before meeting with Chinese Premier Hua Guofeng, the president urged Japan to join in U.S. and Chinese plans to offset Soviet military threats in Asia.

After the new Suzuki government was formed, Foreign Minister Ito held talks in Washington on September 19 with U.S. Secretary of State Edmund Muskie, Defense Secretary Brown, and National Security Adviser Zbigniew Brzezinski. He assured them and congressional leaders of Japan's intention to boost defense spending to 1% of the nation's gross national product (GNP).

With the election of Ronald Reagan in November, Prime Minister Suzuki announced his desire to visit Washington in March or April 1981. In Tokyo on August 19, Reagan's vice-presidential running mate, George Bush, had told Suzuki that a Republican administration would continue to recognize the importance of U.S.–Japanese relations. He added that Reagan had "no intention of turning the clock back," by pursuing a policy of two Chinas.

On a lighter note, New York City Mayor Edward Koch visited Gov. Shunichi Suzuki of Tokyo in late February to commemorate the 20th anniversary of the sister-city relationship between the two metropolises.

Relations with the USSR. In his address to the 91st Diet session on January 25, Prime Minister Ohira condemned the Soviet invasion of Afghanistan and promised that Japan would take "appropriate measures" to press for a withdrawal. Relations between Tokyo and Moscow took a turn for the worse on February 8, when a district prosecutor in Tokyo indicted for espio-

nage two active officers and a retired major general of Japan's Self-Defense Forces (SDF). The defendants were charged with passing classified information about China to Col. Yuri Kozlov of the Soviet Embassy in Tokyo. The colonel and his wife had departed Japan on January 19.

In his speech, Prime Minister Ohira also called attention to the military threat posed by the USSR in Japan's "northern territories." These were the southern Kuril islands, claimed by Japan and occupied by the Soviets since World War II. On March 5, in the Diet, Defense Agency Director Kichizo Hosoda pointed to the strengthening of Soviet forces, development of missiles, and presence of the Kiev-class aircraft carrier *Minsk* on or at the island of Shikotan. On September 16, at the UN General Assembly in New York, Foreign Minister Ito called on Moscow to withdraw its forces and return the territories. "Unfortunately, however," Ito added, "because the question regarding the northern territories still remains unresolved, we have not yet concluded a peace treaty."

Relations with China. In his first policy speech to the Diet on October 3, Prime Minister Suzuki pledged to further "relations of peace and friendship" with China. The extension of peaceful relations earlier had included the first visit to Japan by a Chinese premier, May 28 to June 1. In addition to witnessing the signing of a scientific cooperation agreement between Peking and Tokyo, Hua Guofeng was quoted as saying that Japan needed a higher defense capability. "The matter is up to the Japanese themselves to decide," he added.

In Tokyo again on July 10 for the Ohira funeral and his first meeting with President Carter, Hua promised to continue efforts to promote closer relations among China, Japan, the United States, and the nations of Western Europe.

In Peking on September 3, Hua Guofeng formally introduced his successor, Deputy Premier Zhao Ziyang, to visiting Foreign Minister Ito.

Relations with Neighbors in Asia. In October, foreign ministry officials pressed the Republic of Korea for the full text of a verdict rendered in Seoul on September 17, sentencing to death the dissident leader Kim Dae Jung. The two governments had agreed in 1973 to disregard all of Kim's political activities in Japan before he was kidnapped from a Tokyo hotel and removed to Seoul. But the Korean military court judged that Kim had violated Korean law by continuing antigovernment activities as chairman of Hanmingdon, a Tokyo-based organization of Korean residents in Japan. Japanese observers linked the Kim case with what they saw as increasingly authoritarian trends under Korean Gen. Chon Doo Hwan.

On July 2, then Foreign Minister Saburo Okita threw Japan's support behind the Association of Southeast Asian Nations (ASEAN), denouncing Vietnam's intrusion into the territory of Thailand. In October, Prime Minister Suzuki announced his intention to visit members of ASEAN in January 1981. Suzuki planned to stop in the Philippines, Indonesia, Singapore, Malaysia, and Thailand.

Domestic Affairs

The majority LDP, which early in the year fully expected to be forced to share power in a coalition government, made a remarkable comeback during the second half of 1980. In May, public opinion polls revealed that two out of every three Japanese did not support the Ohira government. By late September, the new LDP administration of Zenko Suzuki enjoyed an approval rate of 58.3%, according to the Japan Public Opinion Survey Board.

Party Politics and Elections. As a result of the previous general election in October 1979, the Ohira-led LDP held the slimmest possible majorities in both the lower House of Representatives and the upper House of Councillors. Japanese interviewed in opinion surveys cited inflation, oil supply, and defense policy as major issues.

On May 19, Prime Minister Ohira exercised his constitutional privilege of dissolving the lower house, just seven months after it had been organized. His action followed by three days the surprise passage of a vote of no-confidence. The vote was made possible by the rebellion of 69 LDP members, who simply remained absent during the crucial test. The triennial election for the House of Councillors had been scheduled for June 29, but for convenience Ohira set both elections for June 22.

On June 12, however, as a result of his strenuous activities abroad and the political crisis at home, Prime Minister Ohira died of a heart attack. The incumbent administration, headed by Chief Cabinet Secretary Masayoshi Ito, continued in office until the Diet could select a new prime minister following the elections of June 22.

Both because of the unusual dual election and the sympathy stimulated by Ohira's death, there was a high voter turnout. This came as a boon to the LDP, which sharply increased its share of the popular vote to almost 45%. The party won a comfortable majority in the lower house: 284 LDP representatives, plus two conservative independents, for a total of 286 out of 511 seats. Prior to the election it had held only 258 seats. Among opposition parties, the Japan Socialist Party (JSP) remained level at 107 seats; but the Komeito, 33 seats, the Democratic Socialists (DSP), 32, and the Japan Communists (JCP), 29, all lost seats. Results of voting for half the seats in the 252-seat House of Councillors showed the LDP gaining 11 seats, for a total of 135.

Ohira's death also shocked the squabbling LDP factions into unity, and they soon settled on a backstage compromiser, Zenko Suzuki, to be party president. On July 17, a special Diet session named him prime minister. Suzuki announced that the slogan of the LDP henceforth would be "Harmony and Unity." In characteristic fashion, Suzuki chose a cabinet that recognized the delicate balance among powerful faction leaders. Masayoshi Ito took up the foreign affairs portfolio. In a show of party unity, three

Funeral rites for Prime Minister Masayoshi Ohira were attended by representatives of 112 nations.

Sipa Press, Black Star

At the November convention of the ruling Liberal Democratic Party, Prime Minister Zenko Suzuki was formally elected party president for the next two years.

LDP faction leaders accepted government posts: Yasuhiro Nakasone headed the administrative management agency; Toshio Komoto headed the economic planning agency; and Ichiro Nakagawa directed the science and technology agency.

Economy. Prime Minister Suzuki inherited a stubborn recession coinciding with inflation, which in February the Bank of Japan labeled a crisis. On February 19, Bank Governor Haruo Maekawa raised the official discount rate one percentage point to 7.25% per annum. By mid-1980 the rate reached a record 8.25%.

By the end of the year, however, there were signs of improvement. In October, the Research Institute of National Economy forecast a real growth rate of 6% in both fiscal 1981 and fiscal 1982, as compared with 4.6% projected for fiscal 1980. In August, the unemployment rate stood at 2.09% (a total of 1.5 million persons), down 0.1% from the year before. An annual inflation rate of 7.9% was expected for fiscal 1980. Japan's wholesale price index for the first ten days of October dropped by 0.5% (as compared with September) to a level of 133.3 (1975=100). Early in November, the Bank of Japan indicated that it was considering the lowering of the discount rate.

Despite the encouraging signs, the government moved with caution. Earlier in the year, the cabinet had submitted to the Diet a budget of 42,600,000,000,000 yen, including the smallest increase in expenditures in two decades. In his October 3 policy speech, Prime Minister Suzuki told the Diet that his administration still relied on borrowing for one third of its revenue. He announced a decision to cut bond issues by 1,000,000,000,000 yen in fiscal 1980, and another 2,000,000,000,000 yen in the fiscal 1981 budget. Japan's GNP for the fiscal year 1979–80 totaled 224,800,000,000,000 yen.

Defense. Certainly one of the reasons for Japan's remarkable growth in the post-treaty period was the relatively low proportion of GNP spent on defense. In the early postwar period, there had been a revulsion in public opinion against the military, a bias that was at first encouraged by the Allied (chiefly U.S.) occupation. Indeed, Americans were partly responsible for incorporation into Japan's new constitution (1947) of the celebrated article 9, which foreswore "the threat or use of force" as a means of settling disputes.

In the post-treaty era, conservative LDP-led governments successively argued that the article by no means relinquished Japan's inherent right of self-defense. The argument was implemented by the creation of the Self-Defense Forces (SDF), which in 1980 was still for defensive purposes only. So-called "progressive" opposition groups regularly argued that the SDF—as well as U.S. air and naval bases located in Japan under the Tokyo-Washington security treaty—

—— **JAPAN · Information Highlights** ——

Official Name: Japan.
Location: East Asia.
Area: 147,470 sq mi (381 947 km²).
Population (1980 est.): 116,194,900.
Chief Cities (1978 est.): Tokyo, the capital, 8,493,804; Yokohama, 2,729,433; Osaka, 2,700,303; Nagoya, 2,086,118.
Government: *Head of state,* Hirohito, emperor (acceded Dec. 1926). *Head of government,* Zenko Suzuki, prime minister (took office July 1980). *Legislature*—Diet: House of Councillors and House of Representatives.
Monetary Unit: Yen (210.60 yen equal U.S.$1, Nov. 1980).
Manufactures (major products): Machinery and equipment, metals and metal products, textiles, automobiles, chemicals, electrical and electronic equipment.
Agriculture (major products): Rice, vegetables, fruits, milk, meat, natural silk.
GNP (1979 est., U.S.$): $1,091,000,000,000.
Foreign Trade (1979, U.S.$): *Imports,* $110,670,000,-000; *exports,* $103,045,000,000.

violated the no-war constitution. Meanwhile, public opinion steadily shifted toward a realistic view of the security issue. An opinion survey in 1979 revealed that a record 86% of respondents believed that the SDF was necessary.

With the waning of American power in the Western Pacific, increase of Soviet strength in the area, and occurrence of numerous flashpoints in Korea, Southeast Asia, and the Middle East, Japanese concern over security issues grew rapidly in 1980. In October, Foreign Minister Ito publicly expressed Japan's concern over escalation of the Iran-Iraq war, the possible closure of the Strait of Hormuz, and constitutional limitations on the use of force components overseas. On October 21, Defense Agency Director Joji Omura forthrightly informed the Diet that the government might give "serious consideration to the defense of the sea lanes" in order to secure the nation's oil supply. Earlier, another defense official had touched on the most sensitive issue—nuclear weapons—insisting that under the constitution Japan is able to possess nuclear arms, but only for self-defense.

There were, of course, limitations on the scope of the debate. No prime minister has dared to abandon Japan's famous nonnuclear policies: the nation will not possess, will not construct, and will not knowingly allow in its territory, nuclear weapons. Prime Minister Suzuki sought to

Sadaharu Oh, the Babe Ruth of Japanese baseball, retired after 21 years with the Tokyo Yomiuri Giants.

Focus On Sports

mollify the opposition in an upper house budget committee by stating that he would not propose an amendment to the peace constitution. But government spokesmen persisted in the somewhat confusing position that it is constitutional for Japan to engage in UN peacekeeping endeavors so long as the SDF does not engage in military action.

Society. Japanese media commented on several significant demographic developments in the nation. As of the end of March, the total population was estimated at 116,194,900, a rise of only about 900,000 (or 0.8%) from the year before. According to the Tokyo Metropolitan Government, the population of the capital prefecture on Jan. 1, 1980, stood at about 11.6 million, down by some 8,000 (0.07%) from the year before. It was the first decrease in postwar history. The capital-prefecture continued to have the largest population in Japan, however, followed by the urban-prefecture of Osaka (8.5 million), Kanagawa (6.8 million, including Yokohama), and Aichi (6.2 million, including Nagoya).

As early as 1979, observers had pointed to a phenomenon referred to as "the graying of Japan." By September 1979, the number of Japanese over the age of 65 had topped 10 million (8.9% of the total) for the first time. One year later, the total had reached 10,630,000. Projections indicated that the percentage of aged would exceed 10% in 1985, reach 15.5% in 2005, and pass 18.8% by 2020. Meanwhile, according to a Tokyo Education Board survey, the total number of primary school pupils was expected to drop sharply to about 610,000 by 1993. In 1979, the number hit a peak of some 1,030,000 because of the postwar "baby boom." These population trends held profound implications for public policy in Japan.

For example, three leading commercial banks—Fuji, Sumitomo, and Mitsubishi—announced an extension of the traditional retirement age from 55 to 60. These firms followed similar decisions by Japan Air Lines and the world's largest steel complex, Nippon Steel. Political leaders prepared for demands of increased social security by an aging population.

In the realm of sports, to which many Japanese are addicted, the residents of Nagoya hoped to invite the Olympic summer games to their city in 1988. In October, however, Vice-Minister of Finance Takashi Tanaka reported that the Japanese people were not eager to tender the invitation if doing so were to mean towering expenditures and tax increases.

In October, at the end of the baseball season, Sadaharu Oh announced his retirement at the age of 40. Playing 21 years with one team, the Tokyo Yomiuri Giants, Oh hit a record 868 home runs, compared with 714 by Babe Ruth and 755 by Hank Aaron.

ARDATH W. BURKS
Professor of Asian Studies
Rutgers University

JORDAN

Jordan's King Hussein saw his best-laid plans for a unified "Arab alternative" to the Egyptian-Israeli peace process frustrated early in 1980 and hopelessly complicated by divisions in the Arab world after the outbreak of the Iraq-Iran war in September. Relations with neighboring Syria grew especially strained, with a massive border conflict nearly breaking out late in the year. (*See* Syria.)

Arab Alternative. Hussein's consistent refusal to join the Camp David peace process led several Arab oil states and the conservative wing of the Palestine Liberation Organization (PLO) to enlist his support in countering the Egyptian-Israeli negotiations on Palestinian autonomy.

After a March meeting with PLO representatives, Hussein was authorized to propose a joint Palestinian-Jordanian delegation during his April 17 visit to the United States. But when it was announced that Israeli Prime Minister Menahem Begin and Egyptian President Anwar el-Sadat would visit Washington in late March to work out differences in their negotiations, Hussein canceled his visit on the grounds that it would tend to associate him with the Camp David peace process. Hussein declared that he was "horrified" at the U.S. inability to stand up against Israeli pressure.

Basically, Hussein continued to find support for his demands of a total Israeli withdrawal to its 1967 borders, autonomy and self-determination for Palestinians living on the West Bank, and an Arab Jerusalem under Arab sovereignty. But when he advocated this position at an Arab Summit meeting in Tunis early in April, it drew strong criticism from Syria and the other members of the so-called "Steadfastness Front." Hussein called for an end to divisiveness at a late November conference of the Arab League in Amman, but Syria, Libya, Algeria, Lebanon, South Yemen, and the PLO were not in attendance.

Europe and the United States. Frustrated by the inability of the Arabs to agree on a unified position, Hussein expressed his support for a European plan for Palestinian self-determination.

UPI

King Hussein and his American-born queen, Noor, made an official visit to the United States in June.

The plan was based on an amendment to UN Security Council Resolution 242.

King Hussein met with President Carter in Washington, June 17–18, and resisted entreaties to join the Israeli-Egyptian negotiations. The next day, Hussein repeated an earlier warning that if the United States continued to back Israel, it risked losing all its support in the Arab world. The Carter administration announced the sale of 100 advanced M-60 tanks to Jordan.

Iraq-Iran War. Substantive proposals regarding the Palestinian situation ended with the Iraqi invasion of Iran on September 22. The next day, Hussein declared his complete support for Iraqi President Saddam Hussein. He called on the Arab world to back Iraq in "defending its dear homeland and national soil." Iraq had given Jordan nearly $300 million in outright grants and soft-term loans during the year, and Jordan became the first Arab state to provide material assistance for Iraq's war effort. After a visit to Baghdad October 4–5, Hussein ordered all transport vehicles in the country mobilized to carry food and supplies to Iraq; made the port city of Aqaba available to Iraqi ships; and put two of its airfields at the disposal of Iraqi aircraft.

Prime Ministership. On July 3, Prime Minister Abdul Hamid Sharaf, King Hussein's top foreign policy strategist and close adviser, died of a heart attack at age 41. Kassem al-Rimawi, who was appointed the new prime minister the same day, resigned on August 28. Rimawi was replaced by Mudar Badran, who had held the post from November 1976 to December 1979.

F. NICHOLAS WILLARD

JORDAN · Information Highlights

Official Name: Hashemite Kingdom of Jordan.
Location: Southwest Asia.
Area: 37,738 sq mi (97 740 km^2).
Population (1980 est.): 3,200,000.
Chief Cities (Nov. 1979): Amman, the capital, 648,587; Zarqa, 215,687; Irbid, 112,954.
Government: *Head of state,* Hussein ibn Talal, king (acceded Aug. 1952). *Head of government,* Mudar Badran, prime minister (took office Aug. 1980). *Legislature*—National Consultative Assembly.
Monetary Unit: Dinar (0.2950 dinar equals U.S.$1, Nov. 1980).
Manufactures (major products): Cement, phosphate, petroleum products.
Agriculture (major products): Wheat, fruits, olive oil, vegetables.
GNP (1979 est., U.S.$): $2,690,000,000.
Foreign Trade (1979, U.S.$): *Imports,* $1,949,000,000; *exports,* $402,000,000.

Although unsuccessful in his bid to win the Republican presidential nomination, Kansas Sen. Robert Dole was reelected easily. Later, President-elect Reagan named the senator's wife, Elizabeth H. Dole, assistant to the president for public liaison.

Dennis Brack, Black Star

KANSAS

Although the national recession led to layoffs in the state aircraft, automotive, and related industries, the Kansas economy remained relatively stable during 1980. The state's unemployment rate was one of the lowest in the nation and the per capita income of residents increased approximately 15%. The state also ranked among the leaders in aircraft and wheat production.

Weather. Kansas, along with the rest of the Midwest, experienced excessive heat and a drought that lasted from the middle of June to the first week in August. Record high temperatures were recorded with regularity throughout the state and more than 70 deaths in Kansas were attributed to the heat. The news media cautioned the public to be aware of the symptoms of heat exhaustion and heat stroke, while volunteer groups provided emergency centers for those lacking air conditioning.

Agriculture. The heat also affected the agricultural industry. Fortunately for the wheat harvest, that crop's critical growing period was past by the time the heat wave began. The total wheat yield of 414.8 million bushels surpassed the previous high set in 1979 by approximately 1%. The yield per acre dropped to 34 bushels, below the record high of 38 bushels per acre, also set in 1979. The wheat crop was harvested from 12.2 million acres (4 941 000 ha).

The weather conditions, however, damaged the crops harvested in the fall. The yield from the corn crop was 105.6 million bushels, down 39% from 1979's total. The soybean harvest totaled 54% less than the 1979 crop, while the milo crop was estimated at 44% less than the year before. It was estimated that 50 to 60% of these three row crops, grown extensively in central and eastern Kansas, was damaged by the prolonged drought and excessive heat. The cash loss was estimated at more than $300 million. Hay production was down approximately one third and pasture conditions were well below normal. Disaster designations were requested for 37 of the state's 105 counties.

Legislation. The major issues of the 1980 Kansas legislative session dealt with money. A school aid bill that could raise property taxes by $73

KANSAS • Information Highlights

Area: 82,264 sq mi (213 064 km²).
Population (Jan. 1980 est.): 2,380,000.
Chief Cities (1979 est.): Topeka, the capital, 141,236; Wichita, 261,001; Kansas City, 170,252; Overland Park, 81,271.
Government (1980): *Chief Officers*—governor, John Carlin (D); lt. gov., Paul V. Dugan (D). *Legislature*—Senate, 40 members; House of Representatives, 125 members.
Education (1979–80): *Enrollment*—public elementary schools, 225,312; public secondary, 197,612; colleges and universities, 133,360 students. *Public school expenditures*, $973,403,000 ($2,226 per pupil).
State Finances (fiscal year 1979): *Revenues*, $2,178,-000,000; *expenditures*, $2,012,000,000.
Personal Income (1979): $21,873,000,000; per capita, $9,233.
Labor Force (June 1980): *Nonagricultural wage and salary earners*, 953,700; *unemployed*, 61,500 (4.9% of total force).

million was passed in spite of efforts to draw upon the sales tax for increased funding of legislation. The legislature also approved a constitutional amendment allowing for the pass-through of federal funds for internal improvements to be placed on the general election ballot in November. The Kansas constitution prohibited the use of state money, including federal funds once they reached the state, for internal improvements. (The electorate approved the amendment in November.) A floating lid on home loan interest rates was approved. The legislature failed to pass measures to increase highway funds.

Election. Kansas held its first presidential primary on April 1, 1980. Approximately 450,000 people, 40% of the registered voters, participated in the election. Ronald Reagan received 63% of the Republican vote, while Jimmy Carter defeated Edward Kennedy 56% to 32%.

In the general election in November, Ronald Reagan was victorious over President Carter. Sen. Robert Dole defeated his Democratic challenger, John Simpson, by a comfortable margin. Retiring congressman Keith Sebelius was succeeded by one of his staff members, Pat Roberts. In the other congressional districts, the incumbents—Republicans Jim Jeffries, Larry Winn, and Robert Whittaker and Democrat Dan Glickman—were reelected.

PATRICIA A. MICHAELIS
Kansas State Historical Society

KENTUCKY

Kentucky joined much of the rest of the country in voting for Ronald Reagan. The Republican gained the state's electoral votes by winning 49% of the vote by a margin of less than 18,000 votes—a smaller margin than in most states he carried. Reagan did particularly well in rural areas and relatively poorly in metropolitan areas. There was no change in the congressional delegation.

Legislative Session. Newly inaugurated Gov. John Y. Brown chose not to play the dominant role in legislative affairs traditional for Kentucky's governors. He did not try to select legislative leaders and offered a limited program to the 1980 session of the General Assembly. He did, however, exert his influence on some of the major legislative issues.

The governor emphasized the need for economic development, and the legislature authorized $100 million in revenue bonds for industrial development and $300 million in highway bonds. The governor took an important part in a compromise revision of the workmen's compensation law designed to lower the high rates in Kentucky by limiting the duration of benefits to those partially injured. Despite the governor's support, the teacher organizations failed once again to win passage of a professional negotiations bill. The legislature adopted a constitutional amendment, which would be on the ballot in 1981, to permit a second consecutive term for state constitutional officers. If approved, the amendment could affect Governor Brown's political future.

Both the governor and the General Assembly participated in shaping a two-year $9,500,000,-000 budget, which gave priority to energy, development, and salary increases to state employees and teachers to meet inflationary pressures. To deal with a serious shortage of road funds, the gasoline tax was tied to the price of gasoline, which should lead to long-term increases in revenue. The scope of the severance tax was also extended.

The Recession. The budget adopted by the 1980 legislature was precariously balanced, and it soon became evident that the effects of the national recession in Kentucky would destroy that balance by sharply reducing revenues. Early in the 1980–81 fiscal year the governor ordered most agencies in the state to make substantial reductions in spending for the year, and plans were under way to extend the reductions into the second year of the biennial budget.

Most new capital construction was halted and, although salaries were not cut, most jobs were frozen in agencies and institutions. State universities and colleges were particularly hard hit by the reductions.

Meanwhile, local governments and school boards were coping with the consequences of a law passed in 1979 that placed a 4% limit on increases of local property taxes, unless voters approved a higher rate. Given public attitudes toward taxes, few localities sought such permission.

The recession affected all of the state, but it was felt particularly in Louisville, where thousands of workers were laid off in automobile, appliance, and other factories. In addition, a summer drought, particularly serious in the western part of the state, reduced crop yields, cut farmers' income, and contributed to the reduction in state tax revenues.

MALCOLM E. JEWELL
University of Kentucky

KENTUCKY • Information Highlights

Area: 40,395 sq mi (104 623 km²).

Population (Jan. 1980 est.): 3,547,000.

Chief Cities (1970 census): Frankfort, the capital, 21,902; Covington, 52,535; (1976 est.): Louisville, 330,011; Lexington, 188,744.

Government (1980): *Chief Officers*—governor, John Y. Brown (D); lt. gov., Martha Lane Collins (D). *General Assembly*—Senate, 38 members; House of Representatives, 100 members.

Education (1979–80): *Enrollment*—public elementary schools, 435,874 pupils; public secondary, 241,249; colleges and universities, 135,179 students. *Public school expenditures*, $906,410,000 ($1,196 per pupil).

State Finances (fiscal year 1979): *Revenues*, $3,842,-000,000; *expenditures*, $3,880,000,000.

Personal Income (1979): $26,066,000,000; per capita, $7,390.

Labor Force (May 1980): *Nonagricultural wage and salary earners*, 1,229,100; *unemployed*, 101,500 (6.4% of total force).

Kenya's President Daniel arap Moi visited President Carter at the White House in February 1980.

KENYA

Continuing economic problems, political unrest, and a more active foreign policy were the highlights of 1980 developments in Kenya.

Economy. The rapid increase in world oil prices almost crippled the Kenyan economy. Nearly one third of all Kenyan foreign exchange had to go to pay for the nation's oil imports, resulting in severe cuts in financing for schools, roads, and electrification, and a virtual scrapping of the 1979–1983 Development Plan. The nearly 12 million barrels of oil imported (which provided Kenya with 80% of its total energy) was creating an estimated trade deficit of $500 million for 1980 and probably an equal amount for each of the next five years.

To worsen economic matters, rains and a poor world market cut Kenya's coffee and tea earnings by nearly 40%. Since these two crops represent almost 60% of the country's earnings, the loss, plus the huge oil bill, created severe problems for the government in trying to provide services for a population growing by some 3% a year. Except for a 36¢-per-gallon increase (to $2.16) in the gasoline prices, the government took few austerity measures to meet the crisis. Only Western loans and grants of $400 million kept Kenya economically afloat in 1980.

Politics. Economic difficulties were reflected in massive personnel changes within the government as a result of elections held in November 1979. Half of the 158 members of the National Assembly were defeated (though all candidates belonged to the sole party, KANU), including seven Cabinet ministers. As a result, the Cabinet was enlarged to 26 ministers, 13 of them newcomers, which gave President Daniel arap Moi a younger and more vigorous administration.

Foreign Affairs. President Moi greatly modified Kenya's low foreign-policy profile in 1980. Moving closer to the West as a result of events in the Mideast and East Africa, Moi agreed to expanded United States use of Kenyan facilities for military purposes. The United States was given port and supply rights in Mombasa, and negotiations for a permanent U.S. base continued. In exchange, the United States gave Kenya some $40 million in aid, plus 105,000 T (94 500 t) of food. Details of the agreement were discussed by President Jimmy Carter and President Moi during the latter's February 1980 visit to Washington. The Kenyan president also visited Britain and West Germany in February in an effort to obtain increased economic aid.

In view of Kenya's oil problems, Moi had visited Saudi Arabia in late 1979. The Saudis pledged continued (though high-priced) oil for Kenya, and the latter promised to increase its export of meat and dairy products to Arabia.

Kenya continued to have trouble with its East African neighbors. Chaos in Uganda threatened to flood Kenya with refugees, and as a result, the Kenya-Uganda border was closed, and thousands of Ugandans already in Kenya were forcibly repatriated. Many of the refugees had been accused of murder, robbery, and other crimes, as well as of using Kenya as a staging area for factions involved in Uganda's internal upheavals. Kenya and Tanzania continued to quarrel over assets of the defunct East African Common Services Commission and over their differing economic policies and foreign orientations. As a result, Kenya's border with Tanzania was also sealed in January 1980. Meetings between Presidents Moi and Julius Nyerere failed to resolve any of the issues involved.

ROBERT GARFIELD, *DePaul University*

--- **KENYA · Information Highlights** ---

Official Name: Republic of Kenya.
Location: East Coast of Africa.
Area: 224,961 sq mi (582 649 km^2).
Population (1980 est.): 15,900,000.
Chief Cities (1978 est.): Nairobi, the capital, 786,000; Mombasa, 374,000.
Government: *Head of state and government,* Daniel arap Moi, president (took office Oct. 1978). *Legislature* (unicameral)—National Assembly.
Monetary Unit: Kenya shilling (7.45 shillings equal U.S.$1, July 1980).
Manufactures (major products): Petroleum products, cement, beer.
Agriculture (major products): Corn, wheat, rice, sugarcane, coffee, tea, sisal.
GNP (1979 est., U.S.$): $6,300,000,000.
Foreign Trade (1979 est., U.S.$): *Imports,* $1,535,000,-000; *exports,* $1,062,000,000.

KOREA

The year 1980 was truly eventful for the two Koreas. In the Republic of Korea (ROK—South Korea), the political crisis which began in October 1979 led to the birth of a Fifth Republic in October 1980. Gen. Chun Doo Hwan became president. In the Democratic People's Republic of Korea (DPRK—North Korea), Kim Chong Il publicly emerged as heir apparent to President Kim Il Sung. Stability and continuity seemed assured for Seoul and Pyongyang, at least in the short run.

SOUTH KOREA

Politics. Independent public opinion surveys, disclosed in January, showed an overwhelming majority favoring reduced presidential powers, direct presidential election, and full freedom of the press. In February, 687 persons, including former opposition leader and presidential candidate Kim Dae Jung, were rehabilitated politically. Early in the year, expectations for political freedom were rising, although coupled with concern and uncertainty. This was because of mounting student unrest, an unprecedented wave of labor strikes for wage increases, and factional infighting among leaders of both the majority Democratic Republican Party (DRP) and the opposition New Democratic Party (NDP). Students demanded an end to martial law, the removal of army strongman Chun Doo Hwan from key intelligence posts, and a speedy democratization under a new constitution.

On May 18, General Chun and his military backers intervened. The generals tightened martial law; banned political activities and labor strikes; ordered universities closed; imposed censorship; and arrested hundreds of persons, including politicians (among them, Kim Dae Jung and former Premier Kim Jong Pil), student leaders, human rights activists, academics, and dissidents. On May 19, a student-led civil uprising erupted in Kwangju, a regional stronghold of Kim Dae Jung. The nine-day disturbance, ended by the intervention of paratroopers and tanks, cost at least 250 lives. On May 31, a Special Committee for National Security Measures was formed as a de facto shadow government with Chun as chairman of its standing committee. With a virtually free hand, the generals began reshaping the political structure by purging "corrupt" politicians and government officials. Some leading public figures agreed to leave politics rather than defy the military. Kim Dae Jung, however, was tried and convicted on charges of sedition in connection with the Kwangju uprising and was sentenced to death in September.

Chun's assumption of power was backed by younger officers with hard-line, nationalist views. Amid a "draft Chun" movement, President Choi Kyu Hah abruptly resigned in August. On August 27, Chun was elected as Choi's successor by a rubber-stamp electoral college formed under the 1972 constitution. A new cabinet was sworn in with Nam Duck Woo, a technocrat, as prime minister.

A draft constitution, prepared by the government in secrecy, was approved in a referendum and published in October as the basic charter of the Fifth Republic. It provided for a single seven-year term for the president, who would be chosen indirectly by an electoral college in February 1981. All existing parties and the National Assembly were dissolved under the charter; a Legislative Council for National Security was appointed as an interim legislature. Its first bill, passed in November, was a Political Renovation Act under which 835 "tainted" public figures were summarily banned from politics until June 1988. Also in November, news organizations were ordered reorganized, giving the government tighter control of the media. Political activities resumed in November, and many political parties had been formed by year-end. The group

In May in the South Korean city of Kwangju, student demonstrations against the extension of martial law led to general insurrection and the death of some 250 persons. The military was called in to restore order.

With his wife at his side, Gen. Chun Doo Hwan becomes president of the Fifth Republic of (South) Korea.

Neveu, Liaison

backing Chun organized a Democratic Justice party.

The government sought in earnest to improve South Korea's tarnished international image. Among the steps taken was the renaming of the controversial Korean Central Intelligence Agency (KCIA) as the Agency for National Security Planning (NSP), effective January 1981. Another was the release of Kim Chi Ha, a renowned poet and one of South Korea's best-known political prisoners, from his 20-year imprisonment, on the eve of U.S. Defense Secretary Harold Brown's arrival in Seoul on December 12. According to a midyear Gallup Poll, 63% of U.S. respondents regarded South Korea's human rights conditions unfavorably. A total of 51% expressed opposition to U.S. defense of South Korea even in the event of a North Korean invasion. Only 38% favored defending Seoul.

Economy. For the first time since 1956, the economy showed a negative growth rate, −5.7%. (The year's target was +3%). GNP per capita declined to $1,533 (at current prices). Exports and imports were $17,200,000,000 and $21,700,-000,000, respectively. The recession was blamed on the political turbulence since Park Chung

Hee's assassination and its uncertain effect on investment; continuing high inflation; deflationary measures and a sharp drop in domestic demand for goods and services; soaring prices of imported oil ($6,500,000,000) and other raw materials; and arbitrary government controls over the financial system. In January, the *won* currency was devalued to boost exports against the U.S. dollar, and interest rates were hiked for commercial loans.

The government sought to remedy its economic problems by instituting long-delayed reforms in the areas of industry, agriculture, finance, energy, and marketing. It proposed to establish "a rational economic order" based on a private enterprise market system with fewer government controls and backed by "burden-sharing" labor-management cooperation.

Foreign Policy and Defense. South Korea's relations with the United States and Japan were strained. Both Washington and Tokyo shared a widely held belief that the trial of Kim Dae Jung was politically contrived. In December, U.S. Defense Secretary Brown flew to Seoul to express U.S. concern for Kim and to reemphasize the crucial point that American commitment to Seoul stemmed not merely from a shared interest in security but also from a shared devotion to universal human values.

While Washington worried over the setback to democratization, Japan showed more concern for Kim's personal fate. Prime Minister Zenko Suzuki stated in September and again in November that if Kim were executed, Japan might have to cut its economic and technological aid to Seoul and might also pursue closer links with North Korea. This triggered a virulent anti-Japanese campaign in South Korea.

The government continued to bolster its defense posture. In 1980 Seoul earmarked $4,200,-000,000 for defense, as compared with Pyongyang's $1,400,000,000. In March, a war game was staged jointly with the United States to dem-

─────── **South Korea • Information Highlights** ───────

Official Name: Republic of Korea.
Location: Northeastern Asia.
Area: 38,022 sq mi (98 477 km²).
Population (July 1980): 37,589,100.
Chief Cities (July 1980): Seoul, the capital, 8,450,000; Pusan, 3,100,000.
Government: *Head of state,* Chun Doo Hwan, president (took office Sept. 1980). *Head of government,* Nam Duck Woo, prime minister (took office Sept. 1980). *Legislature*—Legislative Council for National Security (interim and appointed).
Monetary Unit: Won (661 won equal U.S. $1, Dec. 1980).
Manufactures (major products): Textiles, clothing, electronic equipment, petrochemicals, plywood, processed foods, metal products.
Agriculture (major products): Rice, barley, wheat, soybeans, sweet potatoes, fish, livestock.
GNP Per Capita (1980 est., U.S.$): $1,533.
Foreign Trade (1980, U.S.$): *Imports,* $21,700,000,000; *exports,* $17,200,000,000.

onstrate a combined defensive capability against possible North Korean attacks. The 51-day exercise, dubbed "Team Spirit '80," involved 150,000 men from both sides.

NORTH KOREA

The Sixth Congress and Kim Chong Il. The Sixth Congress of the ruling Korean Workers party (KWP) was held October 10–14 in Pyongyang and was presided over by General Secretary Kim Il Sung. A significant event of the congress, the first in ten years, was the formal confirmation of Kim Chong Il, President Kim's 40-year-old son, as the second most powerful figure in the DPRK and, for all practical purposes, heir apparent to his father. Only Kim Il Sung and Kim Chong Il held positions in all three major party organs elected at the end of the congress—the five-member Standing Committee of the Political Bureau, the 10-member Secretariat, and the 19-member Military Commission. In the 248-member Party Central Committee, technocrats outnumbered other groups, and nearly 60% of the members were new.

Equally noteworthy at the congress was Kim Il Sung's proposal for the establishment of a Democratic Confederal Republic of Korea (DCRK) as a neutral, nonaligned state. The DCRK would no longer be "a transitional step" toward unification but would itself be regarded as the "unified state" of North and South Korea. The two "regional" governments of North and South Korea would be run by a central governing body—the supreme confederal assembly and its standing committee, composed of equal numbers of representatives from both sides.

The unified state would respect the "regional autonomy" of both sides, with neither one attempting to impose its ideas and policies on the other. The ten-point unification program called for, among other things, multifaceted coopera-

tion, a "single combined national army" on a cost-sharing basis, the repeal of all treaties and agreements each side had signed with other countries, a "permanent peace and nuclear-free zone" on the Korean peninsula, and the continued guarantee of "the capital invested by other nations in South Korea prior to unification."

At the congress, Kim also disclosed ten "prospective" economic production goals to be attained by the end of the 1980s. These were 100,-000,000,000 kilowatts of electricity; 120 000 000 t (132,304,000 T) of coal; 15 000 000 t (16,538,000 T) of steel; 1 500 000 t (1,654,000 T) of nonferrous metals; 20 000 000 t (22,050,000 T) of cement; 7 000 000 t (7,718,000 T) of chemical fertilizers; 1 500 000 000 m (1,640,300,000 yds) of fabrics; 5 000 000 t (5,513,000 T) of fishery products; 15 000 000 t (16,538,000 T) of grain; and approximately 300 000 ha (750,000 acres) of reclaimed tideland.

Economic Performance. Production goals for 1980, it was declared, were attained "more than a month ahead of schedule." Total industrial output rose by 17% over 1979, but grain output remained the same as in the previous year—9 000 000 t (9,923,000 T). Shortages in fuel, power, and raw materials for the metal and chemical industries continued. Emphasis still was given to boosting coal and ore output, developing new technology, and improving transportation.

The economy appeared to have partially recovered from the recession of the mid-1970s, but the need for foreign currency was still acute, and expanded exports remained a major goal. Nonetheless, Kim Il Sung was sanguine about the future of the economy. The per capita national income in 1979 was announced as $1,920.

Inter-Korean Relations. In January, the DPRK called South Korea by its official name for the first time in proposing premier-level contact. In

Neveu, Liaison

A South Korean local market. For the first time in nearly 25 years, the nation's economy declined in 1980.

North Korea's President Kim Il Sung welcomes Enrico Berlinguer, general secretary of the Italian Communist Party, to Pyongyang.

Fornaciari, Liaison

accepting the overture, the ROK reciprocated by calling North Korea by its formal name—also for the first time. In February, preparatory talks opened at Panmunjom.

Through August, the two sides met ten times and agreed on several procedural and technical matters but were unable to decide on the agenda for the premiers' conference because of deep-seated mutual distrust. In September, Pyongyang suspended the talks, because of an alleged South Korean policy of "fascism, confrontation, and division."

Foreign Policy. In July, Kim Il Sung told visiting U.S. Rep. Stephen Solarz (D-NY) that he would welcome cultural, scholarly, journalistic, and other exchanges with the United States even before diplomatic normalization. Solarz, the first U.S. congressman to visit the north, disclosed that Kim also repeated his demand for a peace pact with the United States and for the withdrawal of all American troops from South Korea. In September, Tom Reston, former U.S. deputy assistant secretary of state for public affairs (until June 1980), visited Pyongyang as a

"free-lance correspondent." Also in September, Kim told a visiting group of Japanese lawmakers that he would cancel his mutual security pacts with the Soviet Union and China in exchange for a peace pact with the United States. In November, a senior member of the Academy of Social Sciences told a visiting scholar from Washington that North Korea would enter into scholarly exchange with the United States on a bilateral "reciprocal invitation" basis.

Favorable prospects were on the horizon for increased contacts with Japan. In June, Pyongyang informed the UN-affiliated International Civil Aviation Organization of its readiness to permit Japanese and Chinese civil aircraft to fly over its airspace so as to shorten the flight time between Tokyo and Peking. In July, the East Asia Trade Research Board was formed by prominent Japanese businessmen and industrialists to promote expanded trade with North Korea. In September, a group of Japanese legislators proposed "a memorandum trade formula" similar to the one Japan and China had followed so successfully before their diplomatic normalization.

North Korea showed active interest in the development of the nonaligned movement as an antiwar and peace force. The interest was especially apparent after the death in May of Yugoslav President Tito (Josip Broz), possibly reflecting Kim's wish to gain recognition as leader of the nonaligned movement. In October, Iraq severed diplomatic ties with North Korea because of the latter's alleged supply of medicine and arms to Iran. Pyongyang's official position regarding the Iran-Iraq war was one of neutrality and noninvolvement.

RINN-SUP SHINN
Foreign Area Studies
The American University

NORTH KOREA · Information Highlights

Official Name: Democratic People's Republic of Korea.
Location: Northeastern Asia.
Area: 46,540 sq mi (120 538 km²).
Population (July 1980 est.): 19,050,000.
Chief Cities (July 1980 est.): Pyongyang, the capital, 1,-445,000; Hamhung, 780,000.
Government: *Head of state,* Kim Il Sung, president (nominally since Dec. 1972; actually in power since May 1948). *Head of government,* Li Jong Ok, premier (took office Dec. 1977). *Legislature* (unicameral)—Supreme People's Assembly. The Korean Workers (Communist) Party: General Secretary, Kim Il Sung.
Monetary Unit: Won (1.6 won equal U.S.$1, Nov. 1980).
Manufactures (major products): Cement, coke, pig iron, ferroalloys, textiles, fertilizers.
Agriculture (major products): Rice, corn, potatoes, barley, millet, soybeans, livestock, fish.
GNP (1980 est., U.S.$): $11,000,000,000.

LABOR

American labor voted its dissatisfactions with the U.S. economy in the November election.

UNITED STATES

Ronald Reagan, the president-elect, was the only former national president of a labor union ever to be nominated for the U.S. presidency by a major political party. He had served six years (1947–52, 1959–60) as president of the Screen Actors Guild, an AFL-CIO union. Nonetheless, in the 1980 campaign he had formal support from only two unions, the Teamsters and the National Maritime Union, AFL-CIO. Three unions—Machinists, Government Employees, and Firefighters—declared neutrality in the presidential campaign.

The AFL-CIO and most of its 98 other unions endorsed the Carter-Mondale ticket, collected funds to support it, mounted telephone banks, rang doorbells, distributed literature, and helped get out the vote on election day. The union effort in the 1980 campaign was the most extensive in the AFL-CIO's political history. Its committees on political education tried to convince union members that Mr. Reagan had changed his views since his early years as union actor to become the champion of management and the hero of the anti-union right wing.

Despite these efforts, more union members are believed to have voted for Ronald Reagan than for any Republican presidential nominee since Dwight Eisenhower.

Defeated with Jimmy Carter were many of labor's friends in both the U.S. Senate and House of Representatives. Like so many voters, wage earners were frustrated by the government's inability to cope with rising prices and rising unemployment in a recession aggravated by imports. Layoffs were widespread, especially in construction, automobile, steel, and rubber industries.

Employment. The unemployment rate hovered between 7% and 8% of the labor force. This meant that more than 20 million Americans suffered the indignities of joblessness sometime during the year. Eight million were out of work in October; 97.2 million were employed.

Prices. Rising prices continued to eat into workers' purchasing power. In September the Consumer Price Index was 12.7% higher than a year earlier.

Wages. With few exceptions, earnings failed to keep pace with prices. Real spendable income, after tax deductions and Social Security contributions, declined 6.5% over the 12 months ending in September. At midyear the Labor Department announced: "Real hourly compensation now stands at the same level as in the third quarter of 1972." Weekly earnings of nonsupervisory employees averaged $240.77 in October.

Settlements. Collective bargaining settlements for the first six months covered 1,350,000 work-ers. Wage adjustments averaged 8.5%. In May, the Council on Wage and Price Stability replaced the 7% standard for allowable wage increases with a flexible guideline ranging from 7.7 to 9.5%.

Two settlements were benchmarks in labor-management relations. In March, the United Steelworkers and Newport News Shipbuilding Co. of Virginia signed their first contract covering 15,500 workers in the traditionally anti-union South. The pact ended a three-year struggle by the union.

In October, after 17 years of hostilities, the J.P. Stevens textile company signed with the Amalgamated Clothing and Textile Workers for 3,500 of its employees in seven Southern mills. The union called off its consumer boycott of Stevens products.

Several unions voluntarily made wage concessions to avoid plant closings and to save jobs. They included the Auto Workers at Chrysler, Steelworkers at Wheeling-Pittsburgh Corp., Rubber Workers at Uniroyal, and Airline Pilots and Machinists at the Braniff International Corp.

Strikes. A total of 3,984 strikes occurred in the first eight months of 1980. The only year since 1970 with fewer strikes in the first nine months was 1978 when there were 3,675. In all, 1,442,000 workers were involved.

Major strikes involved 30,000 employees in the copper industry, 30,000 motion picture and

Douglas Fraser is the first union leader to be elected to the board of a U.S. business corporation.

UPI

television actors and musicians, and 9,000 San Francisco hotel employees.

Codetermination. On May 13, UAW President Douglas A. Fraser became the first union leader to be elected to the board of directors of a U.S. business corporation. In being chosen as one of the directors of Chrysler Corp., he got more than 98% of the shareholder votes. The vote supported the recommendation of chairman Lee A. Iacocca.

A new contract between the UAW and American Motors will put a union representative on that corporation's board of directors.

AFL-CIO Leadership. The changing of the guard at the AFL-CIO after 24 years of George Meany's presidency was smooth. Lane Kirkland, who took over following Meany's death in January, had been AFL-CIO secretary-treasurer for ten years and a principal in policymaking. A few innovations were notable.

For the first time a woman was named to the executive council. There always has been one black on the council but no woman had ever qualified under the old policy limiting each of the 33 vice-presidencies to one top officer of an affiliated union. The first woman vice-president is Joyce Miller, a vice-president of the Amalgamated Clothing and Textile Workers Union. Ms. Miller is also president of the Coalition of Labor Union Women (CLUW) which had been campaigning for female representation on the coun-

cil. About 39% of the members of U.S. unions are women.

For the first time, a woman was picked to head a staff department at AFL-CIO headquarters. She is Dorothy Shields, director of the Education Department.

Three unaffiliated unions—the Teamsters with nearly 2 million members, the Auto Workers with 1.5 million, and the United Mine Workers with 300,000—began to participate in the AFL-CIO's weekly meetings on legislative issues. However, efforts to bring these unions back into the national labor center were unsuccessful.

The AFL-CIO had increased influence on national economic and social policies under the national accord that Kirkland negotiated with the Carter administration in 1979. In May, the executive council reaffirmed that accord.

Already a full partner with management on the Council on Wage and Price Stability, labor got equal status with business and government on a new 15-member Economic Revitalization Board. President Carter picked Kirkland and Irving S. Shapiro, chairman of E.I. duPont de Nemours & Co., as cochairmen. The board's task was to develop a long-range program of industrial renewal, including modernization of industrial plants and equipment and retraining of workers.

The government's plan for renewal of the steel industry was announced in September as an important first step in reindustrialization. It provides for import limitations, tax breaks on investment for retooling, additional unemployment benefits for workers, a $300 million federal fund for retraining and relocating employees laid off because of new technology and plant closings, and $600 million for research and development.

On its own, the AFL-CIO began encouraging its affiliates to press for the investment of union-negotiated pension funds in job-creating reindustrialization projects in unionized industries.

ILO. In February, the United States rejoined the International Labor Organization, a branch of the United Nations. The United States had withdrawn in November 1977 on the ground that the agency had become "politicized" and was continually attacking the United States and its allies while avoiding any criticism of Communist nations. The reaffiliation was approved by a U.S. Review Committee composed of representatives of the AFL-CIO, the U.S. Chamber of Commerce, and the U.S. departments of state and labor.

Health and Safety. By executive order, President Carter authorized the Occupational Safety and Health Administration (OSHA) to inspect federal workplaces, directed government agencies to establish labor-management safety committees, and, for help in identifying hazards, gave federal employees access to the National Institute for Occupational Safety and Health.

L. Kirkland congratulates Joyce Miller, the first woman named to the AFL-CIO's executive council.
UPI

INTERNATIONAL

Canada. Canadians had the same familiar difficulties with unemployment and inflation. In June unemployment was reported at 7.8% of the labor force, compared with 7.4% in June 1979. The Consumer Price Index jumped 10.1% between June 1979 and June 1980. By September it was advancing at the rate of 10.7%. Wage adjustments averaged 8.6% from June to June, a 1.4% drop in purchasing power. Later adjustments averaged 10.2%.

For the first quarter, work stoppages resulted in the loss of 2,430,000 workdays, compared with 1,685,000 lost in the same period of 1979.

The largest strike in Canadian history occurred in October when 55,000 members of the Public Service Alliance withheld their services for nearly two weeks. Mail was disrupted when postal workers respected the picket lines. The settlement included 25% salary increases spread over two years. A strike by bank employees against the Imperial Bank of Commerce brought quick recognition of the union when all Canadian unions threatened to withdraw their funds, estimated at more than $800 million.

A 1980 official report showed that 39% of Canadian workers are union members, most belonging to unions affiliated with the Canadian Labour Congress (CLC), which claims 2.5 million members. However, U.S.-based building trades unions with locals in Canada began withholding per capita dues payments from the CLC in a dispute over an autonomous Quebec building trades union. The dispute cut the CLC's income more than 20%.

In June, a new union was formed for 30,000 oil and petro-chemical workers. The group formerly was part of the U.S. Oil, Chemical and Atomic Workers (OCAW). The new union would continue to share in the OCAW strike fund and participate in its health and safety program. The CLC's relationship with Ottawa improved after Pierre Trudeau's Liberal Party returned to power in February. In that election, the CLC-supported New Democratic Party won its biggest popular vote ever with nearly 20% of the vote. The New Democratic Party has 32 members in Parliament as a result.

Great Britain. By September, the annual inflation rate in Great Britain was 16.7%. About 8.3% of the labor force were out of work. For the first time since the 1930s more than 2 million were unemployed.

Prime Minister Margaret Thatcher's government cut public expenditures for education, health care, social services, subsidies to industry, and cash flow to nationalized industries. To "restore the balance in industrial relations" the government introduced in Parliament an employment bill. It would make available public funds for unions agreeing to use secret ballots on votes to strike, on amendments to union rules, and on the elections of union officers. The bill would re-quire an 80% majority for a closed shop and limit secondary picketing. British unions opposed both the government's economic policies and its employment bill.

To develop a positive alternative to the Conservatives' program, the British unions launched a campaign for economic and social advance. A massive London demonstration in March was followed by a Day of Action, a general strike, May 14. The latter drew few supporters even from the 13 million members of the Trade Union Congress (TUC).

The Labour Party, a close ally of the unions, was in disarray because of an internal struggle for control between left and right wings. With support from the trade unions, Michael Foot replaced James Callaghan as Labour Party leader in November.

A 13-week strike at the state-owned British Steel Corp. ended with a 17% wage adjustment, equal to the inflation rate, as recommended by a committee of inquiry. Another 13-week strike at British Leyland produced only a modest settlement, but a strike in the television industry lasting 75 days brought a record salary increase.

Sweden. Sweden's model of peaceful industrial relations, which had freed the country from industrial strife since early in the century, shattered in May. For the first time since 1909, unions and management failed to reach agreement in their annual wage negotiations. A strike by 105,000 members of the national union federation (LO) was followed by a lockout of 563,000 workers on orders of the employers' federation (SAF). Another 300,000 were idled because of the work stoppages. The conflict lasted from May 1 to May 11, costing Sweden more than 4 million workdays. The settlement, a wage increase of 6.8% for the private sector, 7.3% for public employees, came about through the intervention of a government-appointed arbitrator.

A new law provides Swedish workers with parental leave or shortened hours of work to allow them more time with their families. A National Parents Insurance Scheme pays child-care allowances for 12 months if either parent stays home.

Federal Republic of Germany. West Germany's unemployment in the second quarter was 3.4% of the labor force. The Consumer Price Index for the same quarter rose at a rate of 3.8%, jumping to more than 5% in the third quarter.

Workers' earnings rose about 6.5%. The settlement for the metalworking industry, usually the pattern-setter, amounted to 6.8%, with larger increases for those in the lower wage brackets.

The metalworkers lost a bitter struggle to cut the workweek from 40 to 35 hours. Instead they settled for a six-week annual paid vacation to be realized in steps by 1984.

Italy. A confrontation between labor and management in the auto industry was settled in October. It started when Fiat announced plans to lay off 22,000 of its 114,000 employees because

Fornaciari, Liaison

In Italy, a labor-management dispute at Fiat was settled with the aid of the government.

of declining sales, need to improve productivity and shop discipline, and the need to reduce absenteeism and terrorism. Strikers blocked Fiat's factory gates. They were supported by an eight-hour general strike. The settlement, reached with the assistance of the minister of labor, forbids mass dismissals, limits layoffs, and freezes hiring. It allows a force reduction through retirements and resignations. Laid-off workers received 93% of their normal pay for one month.

Italy's Consumer Price Index in September was 21.2% above the level of one year earlier. Unemployment in July was 7.9% of the labor force.

Japan. Labor's spring offensive, the annual negotiations between unions and management, produced a wage settlement of 6.74%, slightly higher than the 1979 increase of 6%.

Inflation picked up some speed in Japan during 1980. After an increase of only 3.4% in the Consumer Price Index between 1978 and 1979, the increase jumped to 8.7% by August 1980. Unemployment in July was only 2% of the labor force, slightly less than in 1979. Another effort was begun to unify the fractured labor movement. The six industry-wide union federations in the private sector were considering a merger proposal.

Poland. A wave of strikes, led by the shipyard workers at Gdansk, swept Poland in August. A 17-day walkout involving more than 100,000 workers ended when the Communist government formally recognized an independent labor movement, acknowledged the right of Polish workers to strike, and made other historic concessions.

The result was the formation of a new Polish labor federation, Solidarity, with an estimated 10 million members. The old Communist-dominated labor organization, a branch of the government, was displaced in most areas. The new union passed a critical test in October when it carried out a successful one-hour strike to protest the government's delay in carrying out its August agreement.

In November the Polish supreme court overruled a lower court which had insisted that the "leading role" of the Communist Party be included in the charter of the new union. Also overturned was lower court language limiting the right to strike. By way of compromise, Solidarity leaders agreed to acknowledge the party's supremacy in the Polish state. At the year's end the workers' organization was consolidating its newfound strength, preparing for conflicts over issues on access to the media, wage rates, and labor legislation.

In the United States and throughout the free world, union members raised funds and declared their support of the Polish workers' cause, knowing that previous strikes in East European Communist countries were suppressed by military intervention; the imprisonment, exile, or death of strike leaders; and wholesale dismissals of striking workers.

GORDON H. COLE and JOSEPH MIRE

LAOS

The Communist rulers of Laos tightened their grip on the country in 1980. Such action reflected new signs of discontent with the strongly Vietnam-influenced Vientiane regime.

Politics. Political repression persisted and probably increased as tension mounted along the frontiers of landlocked Laos. Amnesty International quoted former non-Communist Premier Souvanna Phouma, now an adviser to the Communist government of Laos, as stating that there were still 10,000–15,000 former soldiers, police officials, and public servants of his old regime in "political re-education" camps—nearly five years after their original detention.

Approximately 500 officials, soldiers, students, and previously undetained participants in the pre-Communist government were arrested in October. The Communist regime claimed that the detainees were involved in a plot against the government by pro-China sympathizers—indicating a continuing link between internal and external politics in Laos.

A major result of the continuing political repression—and equally persistent economic difficulties—was the flow of refugees from the country. More than 115,000 refugees from Laos were in Thailand at midyear.

Scattered antigovernment groups continued to harass, but not threaten, the government. Hmong (Meo) hill tribesmen were particular objects of government military action.

Economy. Laos, which is not self-sufficient in foodstuffs, ordinarily has met many of its consumer and other needs by means of imports through Thailand. Such imports were increasing at the year's start. This had the effect of slowing government control over the whole economy and of encouraging private shops dealing largely in goods from Thailand. A Thai ban on such trade in midyear had a dramatic effect on the already weak Laotian economy. Because of the halt in imports, the price of certain types of rice doubled and gasoline had to be rationed. Consequently, some domestic air flights had to be canceled. Other commodities were also in short supply, and prices in general rose. A number of government projects—dependent on materials imported through Thailand—were postponed.

LAOS · Information Highlights

Official Name: Lao People's Democratic Republic.
Location: Southeast Asia.
Area: 91,429 sq mi (236 800 km²).
Population (1980 est.): 3,700,000.
Chief Cities (1973 census): Vientiane, the capital, 176,-637; Savannakhet, 50,690.
Government: *Head of state*, Prince Souphanouvong, president. *Head of government*, Kaysone Phomvihane, prime minister. *Legislature* (unicameral)—National Congress of People's Representatives.
Monetary Unit: Liberation kip (400 liberation kips equal U.S.$1, 1980).
Manufactures (major products): Tin, lumber.
Agriculture (major products): Rice, corn, coffee, cotton, tobacco.
GNP (1978 est., U.S.$): $260,000,000.

Electricity from hydroelectric power plants, financed by international lending agencies, earned a large portion of the foreign exchange needed to pay for the country's imports. Laos gained one third of its foreign money from power sales to neighboring Thailand.

Foreign Relations. An incident on the Mekong River separating Laos from Thailand caused the Thais to close the 870-mi (1 400-km) border between the two countries. A Thai naval officer was killed on June 15 by gunfire from Laos, and the Thais kept the frontier with Laos closed until August 28. The Thai ban on trade with Laos was part of the same boycott.

The Thai action partly reflected frustration over their failure to deal successfully with the problem of the presence of Vietnamese troops in adjacent Cambodia. Such troops crossed over the border into Thailand. The ban on trade with Laos, however, had the undesired effect of increasing Laos' economic dependence on Vietnam. There were 40,000 Vietnamese troops still in Laos, a satellite of Vietnam, at year-end.

U.S.-Laotian relations failed to improve. Vientiane persisted in its noncooperation regarding Americans missing in the Indochina war as well as in its slavish support of Vietnamese-Soviet diplomacy in the area.

RICHARD BUTWELL, *Murray State University*

LATIN AMERICA

Major developments in Latin America in 1980 included a bloody military coup in Bolivia, a return to civilian rule in Peru, a heated election campaign in Jamaica, and continued violence in El Salvador. The year also saw a growing commitment to monetarist, free-market doctrines.

Bolivian Coup. The Bolivian presidential election in June produced a plurality of about 38% for Hernán Siles Zuazo, a moderate leftist; centrist and rightist candidates trailed with 20% and 16%, respectively. The likelihood that congress would certify Siles as president-elect prompted military elements, led by Gen. Luis García Meza Tejada, to seize power in July and arrest incumbent President Lydia Gueiler Tejada. Dozens of leftists were summarily executed by the new rulers, but Siles managed to escape to the United States. Armed resistance to the new military regime by miners and other Siles partisans continued in the Bolivian countryside for weeks.

The United States denounced the coup, as did Bolivia's partners in the Andean Group—Venezuela, Colombia, Ecuador, and Peru. The new government received diplomatic support from an odd assortment of nations, including Argentina, Brazil, Egypt, Israel, the Soviet Union, and East Germany. Adding to the ideological confusion about the García Meza regime were charges that the general and his cohorts were heavily involved in illegal drug trafficking.

Peruvian Elections. Fernando Belaúnde Terry, the former president of Peru ousted in a 1968 military coup, regained the presidency in May 1980 elections. Twelve years of military rule ended in July, as Gen. Francisco Morales Bermúdez relinquished the presidency to Belaúnde.

A new economic course for Peru was charted by Belaúnde's prime minister, Manuel Ulloa, who doubled as economy minister. Ulloa proposed to lower import duties, reduce subsidies to Peruvian industry, and encourage foreign investment. This caused consternation among other members of the Andean Group, whose pact for economic integration and development emphasizes regional tariff barriers and restrictions on foreign capital. Peru's call for revisions in the pact was reminiscent of a similar move by Chile before it withdrew from the group in 1976.

Chilean Constitution. While Peru seemed to be following the lead of Chile in economic policy, the two countries moved in opposite directions politically. The military rulers of Chile produced a constitution designed to legitimize their authoritarian regime and permit Gen. Augusto Pinochet Ugarte to remain president until 1997. Opposition to the new constitution was widespread, ranging from Communists to Catholic churchmen. A plebiscite on the constitution was scheduled for September. Christian Democrat opponents of ratification were allowed to hold rallies but were denied access to the press and broadcast media. The official results of the referendum showed 4,203,615 votes in favor of the constitution and 1,891,332 opposed.

Argentina and Brazil. In Argentina, a changing of the guard was announced in October. Gen. Jorge Rafael Videla would hand over the presidency to Gen. Roberto Viola in 1981. Like Videla before him, Viola was "elected" to a three-year term by his military colleagues. Videla, in his last year in office, worked out a rapprochement with Brazil, Argentina's traditional rival in South America. The two countries agreed to cooperate in a number of sensitive areas, including the manufacture of armaments and the development of nuclear energy.

Market forces were given freer rein as the Argentine government slashed subsidies to industry and lowered import tariffs. Import-substitute manufacturers were hard hit, and some banks failed. Increased export earnings allowed the government to continue gradually reducing the rate of growth in the money supply. Brazil, which unlike Argentina had to import virtually all its petroleum, saw its inflation rate soar to more than 100% in 1980. Despite economic troubles, political liberalization continued.

Turmoil in Central America. The attention of much of Latin America was fixed on tiny El Salvador. Oil-rich Venezuela supported the military-Christian Democrat junta, while equally oil-rich Mexico sympathized with the Revolutionary Democratic Front waging guerrilla warfare against the regime. The United States openly furnished arms to the junta, while Cuba was charged with secretly supplying the guerrillas.

The archbishop of San Salvador, a critic of the junta, was shot dead in March while saying mass. Following the assassination, which the left and right blamed on each other, the violence intensified not only in the capital but also in the countryside, where guerrillas sought to sabotage the government's land reform program. The junta seemed to gain the upper hand, but continuing violence forced a reorganization.

Guatemala was also wracked by leftist terrorism and government repression in 1980, though on a lesser scale than El Salvador. Vice-President Francisco Villagrán Kramer resigned in September, accusing President Romeo Lucas García of condoning "political murders."

Nicaragua was relatively peaceful in 1980, as the Sandinista government strove to consolidate its control of the country while placating the private sector, the U.S. government, and the foreign bankers who had lent vast sums to the government of deposed dictator Anastasio Somoza. After coming to terms with the bankers and convincing the U.S. government that it was not fomenting insurrection in other countries, Nicaragua received a $75 million aid package from the United States. The money was released shortly before the September assassination of the exiled Somoza in Paraguay. Nicaragua disclaimed responsibility for the act.

Cuban Exodus. The death in April of a Cuban guard who was trying to prevent dissidents from entering the Peruvian embassy in Havana prompted Cuban President Fidel Castro to remove all guards from the embassy. This led to a rush onto embassy grounds of 10,000 refugee-seeking Cubans. Castro then declared that all Cubans who wished to leave the island were free to emigrate to any country that would accept them. For those desiring to go to the United States, Castro designated the port of Mariel, about 100 miles (161 km) from Key West, FL, as the point of departure. During the summer, about 125,000 Cubans, including convicted criminals and mental patients, were transported, mostly in small private boats, to the United States. The operation was halted in September as a result of a U.S.–Cuban understanding.

Jamaica Elections. Castro's cordial relationship with Jamaican Prime Minister Michael Manley was an issue in Jamaican elections in October. The opposition Jamaica Labor Party (JLP), led by Edward Seaga, accused Manley and his People's National Party (PNP) of trying to turn Jamaica into "another Cuba." The JLP blamed the PNP for Jamaica's sagging economy and rising crime rate, while government supporters accused the opposition of joining the U.S. Central Intelligence Agency (CIA) in a campaign to "destabilize" the country. When the votes were counted, the more moderate Seaga had won in a landslide.

NEILL MACAULAY, *University of Florida*

LAW

During its 1979–80 term, the U.S. Supreme Court decided a number of emotionally charged cases but continued to defy attempts to label it liberal or conservative, activist or restrained. The International Court of Justice, meanwhile, was unwavering in its condemnation of the seizure and detention of U.S. embassy personnel in Iran.

U.S. SUPREME COURT

Headline actions by the Burger Court included a ruling that Congress can authorize affirmative action to redress past racial discrimination, a holding that the First Amendment protects public right of access to criminal trials, and several decisions expanding the opportunity to bring suit for the protection of civil rights. The court also upheld a congressional ban on federal funds for abortion, extended patent protection to new forms of life created in the laboratory, approved an at-large election system that had kept blacks off a city council, and allowed life imprisonment for the theft of $229.11.

Because of sharp divisions among the justices and the absence of strong leadership, the court tended to act through pluralities rather than majorities. Rulings were increasingly diluted or clouded by concurring or dissenting opinions. The number of signed opinions (132) was about the same as in the preceding term (130), but the ratio of nonunanimous decisions rose from 64% to 74%, and the number of dissenting votes from 233 to 267. There were twenty-six 5-to-4 decisions and thirty-five with 3 dissents. Of the 21 per curiam decisions, only 4 were unanimous.

Justice William Rehnquist, the most conservative member, had the most dissents with 44, closely followed by the court's two liberals, William Brennan (42) and Thurgood Marshall (41). Chief Justice Warren Burger modified his usual conservative stance by his votes in affirmative ac-

tion and First Amendment cases; he also had the fewest dissents (17). Potter Stewart (26), Lewis Powell (20), Byron White (21), and Harry Blackmun (25) maintained centrist positions. John Paul Stevens (34) remained rather unpredictable.

The term was also marked by the publication of a sensationalized and overdrawn exposure of the court's inner workings. In their best-selling book *The Brethren,* investigative reporters Bob Woodward and Scott Armstrong presented the chief justice as incompetent and the court's decisions as being arrived at by a bargaining process in which law clerks played a dominant role.

Major Decisions. In its most controversial ruling, the court upheld the authority of Congress to refuse federal funds for abortions, even if needed to preserve the health of indigent women. The constitutional right to abortion had been established by the court in 1973, and under Medicaid, Congress pays for almost all other medical expenses. But the court ruled (5–4) that a constitutional right to abortion does not require federal subsidization (*Harris v. McRae, Williams v. Zbaraz*).

Broadly endorsing the power of Congress to use its spending power to remedy past racial discrimination, the court upheld (6–3) a federal public works program in which 10% of funds was reserved for minority contractors. This was the court's first explicit endorsement of federal benefits based on race (*Fullilove v. Klutznick*).

In a decision of great potential for "genetic engineering" the court held that scientists or companies may obtain patents on living microorganisms manufactured in their laboratories. The government had contended that a living thing cannot be patented, but the court concluded (5–4) that a research scientist has the legal right to patent a new organism that is the product of human ingenuity (*Diamond v. Chakrabarty*).

Clarifying the right of public access to trials—which had been uncertain since a 1979

Uniphoto

Outside the Supreme Court, women demonstrate against a ruling that neither the federal government nor the states are constitutionally required to fund abortions for the poor.

UPI

The court upheld a Texas law under which Bill Rummel received a life sentence for stealing $229.11.

ruling that pre-trial hearings could be closed—the court held (7–1) that the public and press have a First Amendment right to attend criminal trials and that this right can be restricted only under very limited circumstances (*Richmond Newspapers v. Virginia*).

The court ruled (5–4) that a Texas "habitual offender" law providing an automatic life term for anyone convicted of three separate felonies (in this case three thefts totaling $229.11) did not constitute cruel and unusual punishment (*Rummel v. Estelle*). A dissent by Justice Powell charged that the sentence "would be viewed as unjust by virtually every layman and lawyer."

First Amendment. The court upheld (6–3) the breach of contract conviction of Frank Snepp, a former CIA agent who, in violation of his conditions of employment, wrote a book about the CIA in Vietnam without submitting it to the agency for clearance. The book revealed no classified information, but royalties were ordered surrendered to the government (*Snepp v. U.S.*).

Although the court previously had denied a First Amendment right of access to shopping centers for the peaceful circulation of petitions, it unanimously upheld the California supreme court, which had based such a right on the state constitution (*PruneYard Shopping Center v. Robins*).

Extending previous support for the free speech rights of corporations, the court ruled in two New York cases that public utilities have the right to include promotional advertising and public policy statements with their bills (*First National Bank of Boston v. Bellotti, Consolidated Edison v. Public Service Commission*). However, military regulations requiring members of the armed forces to get the permission of their commanding officers before circulating petitions on military bases were upheld (*Brown v. Glines, Secretary of the Navy v. Huff*).

In a challenge to political patronage, the court held that public employees cannot ordinarily be dismissed solely on the basis of political party affiliation (*Branti v. Finkel*).

The court held unconstitutional a local ordinance barring door-to-door solicitation by charities which could not prove that at least 75% of the money collected would go directly to charitable purposes (*Village of Schaumberg v. Citizens for a Better Environment*).

Equal Protection. The court decided two election discrimination cases. The Mobile (AL) system for electing its city council at large, which had prevented the election of any blacks, was upheld for lack of proof that the system was adopted for the specific purpose of discrimination (*City of Mobile v. Bolden*). But in the other case, the court ruled that the 1965 Voting Rights Act prohibits changes in electoral procedures that have a discriminatory effect, whether or not there is a discriminatory intent (*City of Rome v. U.S.*).

The court let stand a lower court decision requiring extensive school busing between the city of Wilmington (DE) and eleven surrounding school districts (*Delaware State Board v. Evans*) and declined to hear three challenges to the latest desegregation orders for the Dallas (TX) school system (*Estes v. Dallas NAACP*). However, it affirmed a lower court ban on any form of interdistrict desegregation for Atlanta area schools (*Armour v. Nix*).

In a sex discrimination case, the court ruled that treating widows and widowers differently with regard to the death benefits of their spouses violates equal protection (*Wengler v. Druggists Mutual Insurance Co.*).

Criminal Prosecutions. In spite of the Burger Court's hard-line reputation, several of its decisions were favorable to defendants' claims. In an unexpected extension of the Fourth Amendment, it ruled that police may not, except in an emergency, enter a person's home to make an arrest without first obtaining a warrant (*Payton v. New York*). Police who entered a tavern with a warrant to search the establishment and the bartender were not authorized by the warrant to search anyone else who happened to be on the premises (*Ybarra v. Illinois*). On the other hand, the court reversed a 20-year-old precedent in holding that a defendant may challenge the legality of a search only if the materials seized are in a location where there is a legitimate expectation of privacy (*U.S. v. Salvucci*). The court also held that use of a "drug courier profile" by federal agents to stop suspicious airline passengers and submit them to questioning does not violate the Fourth Amendment (*U.S. v. Mendenhall*).

The exclusionary rule, under attack by some justices, was narrowly interpreted to hold that illegally seized evidence can be introduced by the prosecution to discredit a defendant's testimony on cross-examination (*U.S. v. Havens*). Also, evidence seized illegally from a third party can be used against a criminal defendant, since the seizure did not violate the latter's constitutional rights (*U.S. v. Payner*).

Imposing a new limit on undercover tactics of police, the court reversed a criminal conviction because the FBI had developed key evidence by placing a paid informant in the jail cell where the defendant was being held before trial (*U.S. v. Henry*). In a sharp limitation on the long-established marital privilege under which husbands and wives have been barred from testifying against each other, the court ruled that a person asked by prosecutors to testify against his or her spouse may elect to do so (*Trammel v. U.S.*).

The Miranda rule was more strictly interpreted to forbid indirect police interrogation of suspects by the use of words or actions reasonably likely to elicit an incriminating response, but in this case the majority ruled that no interrogation had occurred (*Rhode Island v. Innis*).

A Georgia death sentence was overturned because the crime was not sufficiently horrible to justify the sentence (*Godfrey v. Georgia*). And a Texas death sentence was reversed because the prosecution had been allowed to keep off the jury all persons whose beliefs about capital punishment would affect their deliberations (*Adams v. Texas*).

In a civil rights suit by the parents of a girl murdered by a man released on parole five months earlier, the court held that states can give parole officers absolute immunity from liability for their decisions (*Martinez v. California*).

Economic Issues. Holding that the Occupational Safety and Health Administration (OSHA) was empowered to guarantee "safe" but not "risk free" workplaces, the court ruled (5–4) that OSHA had exceeded its authority by setting overly strict standards limiting workers' exposure to benzene, a cancer-causing material (*Industrial Union Department v. American Petroleum Institute*). But a company cannot fire or discipline workers who refuse to carry out tasks they reasonably believe may lead to death or serious injury (*Whirlpool Corporation v. Marshall*).

A nationwide labor union cannot be held financially responsible for wildcat strikes by its members unless there is proof that the union's leaders were directly involved (*Carbon Fuel Co. v. United Mine Workers*). In a serious blow to unionization of college faculties, the court ruled (5–4) that professors at private universities are "managerial" employees whose efforts to unionize are not protected by federal labor laws (*National Labor Relations Board v. Yeshiva University*).

The court unanimously held that an "open space" ordinance limiting development of private property for environmental reasons does not constitute a "taking" of the property under the Fifth Amendment, but it left open the question of damages (*Agins v. City of Tiburon*).

Real estate firms and boards in the same area who agree to fix commissions may be sued for price fixing under federal antitrust laws (*McLain v. Real Estate Board of New Orleans*). California's state-enforced system of producer-set minimum wine prices for retail sales within the state was likewise held to violate antitrust laws (*California Retail Liquor Dealers v. Midcal Aluminum*).

In two cases, the court held that states can levy corporate income taxes on major international oil companies based on total corporate income rather than on in-state operations (*Exxon v. Wisconsin, Mobil Oil v. Vermont*). The commerce clause of the federal constitution forbids states from barring out-of-state banks from competing locally for various kinds of bank-related business (*Lewis v. BT Investment Managers*).

Other Decisions. Former Secretary of State Henry Kissinger won his fight to prevent public disclosure under the Freedom of Information Act of the transcripts of telephone conversations conducted from his White House and State Department offices (*Kissinger v. Reporters Committee*). The court upheld the federal law providing for public financing of major party presidential campaigns, dismissing Republican Party complaints that the law unfairly favors incumbents and labor-backed candidates and infringes freedom of speech. The law bars private fund-raising by the presidential nominee who accepts public financing (*Republican National Committee v. FEC*). The court ordered the federal government to pay $122.5 million to eight Sioux Indian tribes as compensation for the illegal seizure of the Black Hills of South Dakota in 1877 (*U.S. v. Sioux Nation of Indians*).

Several decisions facilitated damage suits against the government for violations of civil rights. The Eighth Amendment prohibition against cruel and unusual punishment, the court held, gives federal prisoners or their survivors a right based directly on the constitution to bring suits for damages against prison officials on charges of mistreatment (*Carlson v. Green*). In a decision involving Maine's computation of welfare benefits, the court held that the Civil Rights Act of 1871 permits private citizens to sue state officials whenever a state policy violates a federal law (*Maine v. Thiboutot*). Local governments are not entitled to base their defense in civil rights suits on the claim that employees acted in good faith or unintentionally violated civil rights (*Owen v. City of Independence*).

C. HERMAN PRITCHETT
University of California, Santa Barbara

INTERNATIONAL LAW

The Iranian hostage drama overshadowed other international law developments in 1980. After six years of bargaining, the International Law of the Seas Conference was on the verge of a draft treaty.

Iran. Among the avenues pursued by the United States to secure the release of the 53 U.S. embassy personnel taken hostage in Tehran in November 1979 was the pleading of its case before the International Court of Justice in The Hague. Then in mid-December, after only days of deliberation, the court issued a provisional order that, pending final judgment, the embassy should immediately be given back and the hostages released. Iran maintained that the court had no authority to take cognizance of the case. It neither filed pleadings nor was represented in the hearings and made no submission on its behalf. The court admonished both states not to "take any action which (might) aggravate the tension between the two countries or render the dispute more difficult of solution."

In May 1980, the 15-member court unanimously decided that Iran must immediately release all U.S. diplomatic personnel and other U.S. nationals being held under unlawful detention. The six-point decision also called for the return of all American property, warned Iran against putting the hostages on trial, held it responsible for violating international law, and required that it pay reparations to the United States.

According to international law, the host government is responsible for securing the release of any foreign diplomatic hostages taken within its borders. In its May decision, the World Court held that the militants who had taken over the embassy had become agents of the Iranian government and that the latter was internationally responsible for the act.

At the same time, the United States was reproved for its rescue attempt one month earlier. The court criticized it for undermining respect for the judicial process. International lawyers debated whether the U.S. effort had any legality under international law as a "humanitarian intervention." Others said that the United States should have waited a reasonable amount of time to see if compliance with appeals by the World Court or other international channels would be forthcoming from Iran. The UN Charter authorizes appeal to the Security Council "if any party to a case fails to perform the obligations incumbent upon it under a judgment rendered by the Court." If the Security Council fails to act, recourse to the General Assembly is available.

Law of the Seas. The ninth session of the United Nations Conference on the Law of the Seas (UNCLOS) was held in March and April in New York and July and August in Geneva. The chaos of conflicting claims of sovereignty at last appeared to be giving way to an internationally approved formula. There were improved prospects for consensus on such matters as the definition of the continental shelf and 200-mile (370-km) exclusive zone and a voting formula for the proposed Sea Bed Authority. Further negotiations were necessary, but a treaty was expected by early 1981.

Under permits from the proposed International Sea Bed Authority, an initial five to eight sites would be opened for mining metallic nodules. A major defect of the plan, according to the prospective mining countries, is that there is no "grandfather" clause guaranteeing the right to continue operations begun before the treaty is ratified and goes into effect. The extractors would have to agree to share technological, nonproprietary information. Part of the income from the mining of nodules would be distributed by the authority to all countries as their share in the "common heritage of mankind." The United States pressed for a voting formula that would give due weight to the economic interests of industrial states. Eastern European countries favored a geographic area veto. Developing countries opposed any system that would include a veto right.

Still to be worked out was a proposal for having coastal countries share with the international community part of the revenue derived from exploiting petroleum and other resources from areas of the continental shelf more than 200 miles from shore. There also was no agreement on how to delimit maritime boundaries between states situated opposite one another across a narrow body of water or adjacent to one another across the same coastline.

Other Sea Issues. Although the United States and Canada agreed in 1979 to a fishing and boundary treaty, opposition by fishermen in New England stalled ratification by the U.S. Senate in 1980. In the absence of an agreement, fishermen from both countries engaged in overfishing and sought to depress market prices. In apparent retaliation for U.S. heel-dragging, Canada voted against a moratorium on sperm whaling sought by the United States and the International Whaling Commission.

Another dispute led to a "tuna war" between the United States and Mexico. Mexico, claiming a 200-mile coastal zone, seized U.S. fishing vessels for trespassing its territorial waters. In retaliation, the United States halted imports of Mexican tuna.

Not all the news in 1980, however, involved disputes. Seventeen Mediterranean nations agreed on a treaty to clean up that polluted sea. Longtime enemies, Arabs and Israelis, Greeks and Turks, recognized their common interest in restoring the Mediterranean.

See also feature article on the Iranian hostage crisis (page 40).

MARTIN GRUBERG
University of Wisconsin, Oshkosh

LEBANON

For the sixth consecutive year, neither the government nor the armed forces of Lebanon were capable of halting the vicious cycle of anarchy and fighting among Muslim leftist, Christian rightist, and Palestinian factions. In 1980, the internecine strife threatened to plunge the country into a civil war with potentially far more serious consequences than the bitter fighting of 1975–76. President Elias Sarkis found himself virtually powerless to restore peace, as events were controlled by Christian militiamen, Palestinian guerrillas, Syrian peacekeeping forces, and the Israeli-Free Lebanon alliance in the south.

Peace Efforts. On February 4, Syrian President Hafez al-Assad announced that 5,000 Beirut-based Syrian troops would be withdrawn from the city, prompting immediate fears that major outbreaks of fighting between rival Muslim and Christian militias would follow. The move, never fully implemented, was taken by Sarkis as a prod to speed up efforts to end factional strife.

Sarkis and Prime Minister Selim al-Hoss began a series of meetings intended to head off a renewal of fighting and thus deny Israel a pretext for carrying out its February 7 threat to intervene on the side of the Christians. A month-long exchange of Syrian and Israeli military alerts increased tensions and gave impetus to the government discussions.

On March 5, Sarkis revealed a 14-point plan for national unity based on the return of authority to the central government and the return of Lebanese sovereignty to the Israeli-controlled Free Lebanon enclave. It rejected, however, the permanent settlement of Palestinians on Lebanese soil. The rejection was a victory for the Christian right, as the Palestinians were blamed for the decade-long string of Israeli attacks on Lebanese territory.

When the government plan proved to offer no basis for unifying Lebanon's diverse factions, Hoss, in frustration, offered his resignation on June 7. Sarkis, asking Hoss to carry on until a new prime minister was named, turned his attention to reuniting Christian groups.

The Christian Factor. Despite Sarkis' efforts, fighting among the rival forces of former President Camille Chamoun, former President Suleiman Franjieh, and Phalangist Party leader Pierre Gemayel reached a bloody watershed in July and renewed the threat of a Christian partition of northern Lebanon.

In a sustained and well-planned assault July 7–8, Phalangist forces led by Gemayel's son, Bashir, demolished Chamoun's National Liberal Party (NLP) militia, seizing 11 party offices, its two main garrisons, and four tanks. With Chamoun conceding defeat, the well-organized, 10,-000-troop Phalangist Khatab militia became the dominant Christian power.

The Phalangist consolidation of power also raised fears that Geyamel would call for a unified offensive against Palestinian guerrilla strongholds in the south. That the offensive did not materialize was fortunate for all, as it threatened to spark a regional conflict in which the Israelis would have supported the Phalangists and the Syrians undoubtedly would have been drawn in to back the Palestinians.

More Fighting and Free Lebanon. Sarkis reacted quickly to the Phalangist ascendancy, accepting Hoss' month-old resignation on July 16 and appointing veteran politician Takieddin Solh to the post on July 20. Sarkis revealed that he would instruct Solh to form an "activist" cabinet made up of leaders from the rival militias, both Muslim and Christian.

The following week, however, the growing Iraqi-Iranian conflict spilled into Lebanon, as fighting broke out east of Beirut between pro-Iraqi and pro-Iranian gunmen. The pro-Iranian forces, Shiite Muslim followers of Ayatollah Ruhollah Khomeini, fought viciously, leaving 14 dead by July 27. The tension caused by the Muslim fighting led to the failure of Solh's attempt to form a government. Hoss retained a caretaker role until October 25, when a new prime minister, former Minister of Justice Chafiq al-Wazan, announced the formation of a 22-member cabinet.

A large-scale Israeli raid into Lebanon on August 19, the most significant of several summer attacks on Palestinian guerrilla targets, exacerbated Sarkis' position and reemphasized Lebanon's role as a pawn in the greater Arab-Israeli conflict. The Israelis launched the attack through the 60-mi (97-km) long and 5-mi (8-km) deep "Free Lebanon" enclave, which had been controlled by former Lebanese Army officer Major Saad Haddad since the Israelis turned it over to him following their withdrawal of invasion forces in 1978.

Sarkis remained powerless to force Haddad to recognize the authority of the central government, and Haddad, an avowed enemy of the Palestinians, continued to allow Israel to operate freely on Lebanese soil in return for full financial and military backing. As long as that situation exists, the Free Lebanon enclave is a threat to the nation's security.

F. NICHOLAS WILLARD

─────── **LEBANON · Information Highlights** ───────

Official Name: Republic of Lebanon.
Location: Southwest Asia.
Area: 4,000 sq mi (10 360 km^2).
Population (1980 est.): 3,200,000.
Chief Cities (1974 est.): Beirut, the capital, 1,000,000; Tripoli, 128,000.
Government: *Head of state,* Elias Sarkis, president (took office Sept. 1976). *Head of government,* Chafiq al-Wazan, prime minister (took office Oct. 1980). *Legislature* (unicameral)—National Assembly.
Monetary Unit: Lebanese pound (3.51 pounds equal U.S. $1, Nov. 1980).
Manufactures (major products): Petroleum products, lumber, cement.
Agriculture (major products): Fruits, wheat, corn, barley, potatoes, olives, onions, tobacco.
GNP (1977 est., U.S.$): $2,900,000,000.

LIBERIA

The resentment of the continued domination by Americo-Liberians noted in the Monrovia food riots of 1979 caused the violent overthrow of the government of President William R. Tolbert, Jr., on April 12.

Liberia was an example of black imperialism—the minority descendents of American freed slaves had dominated the interior Africans for over a century. The True Whig Party of President William Tubman had begun to loosen its control over the Africans beginning in the 1940s. His successor, President Tolbert, who took office in 1971, continued the slow process of sharing a small portion of the new wealth of the country with the African majority. Criticism of the oligarchy and its corruption increased in the 1970s, culminating in the riots of 1979.

The chief opponent of the regime was Baccus Matthews, leader of the Progressive People's Party, who was arrested and jailed on March 9 on charges of treason. This act convinced the enlisted men of the army that a takeover of the government was required. Led by Master Sgt. Samuel K. Doe, army units took control of Monrovia on April 12. President Tolbert and 27 other government officials were killed and their bodies thrown into a common grave. Doe charged the civilians with rampant corruption and continuous failure to act properly.

Hundreds of persons were arrested. Five-member military courts tried some of the most influential members of Tolbert's government and on April 22, 13 officials, including the chief justice, the foreign minister, and the late president's brother, Frank Tolbert, were machine-gunned in front of a festive crowd. Doe promised to seek out all who were guilty of corruption and deal with them harshly. However, there was such a great international outcry over the executions that on April 29, he announced a suspension of the killings.

Three days before, the 133-year-old Constitution was suspended. All legislative and executive powers were vested in a 17-member People's Redemption Council. Matthews, released from prison earlier, became foreign minister. Doe at

first had great difficulty with foreign relations due to the ferocity of his coup. On May 28, he was refused admission to the West African Economic Community conference in Togo. On June 14, Liberian troops stormed the French Embassy and seized the former president's eldest son, Adolphus Tolbert, who had been granted asylum. The French protested and recalled their envoy. By midyear Doe had modified his actions. The growing acceptance of the new regime was signaled by Liberia's presence at the Organization of African Unity (OAU) conference in Sierra Leone in July.

HARRY A. GAILEY, *San Jose State University*

LIBRARIES

During 1980 librarians, information scientists, and citizens alike sought the implementation of the resolutions emanating from 1979's White House Conference on Library and Information Services. In the main, they met with some initial success, but there was at least one prominent setback.

White House Conference Resolutions. In May 1980 the Department of Health, Education, and Welfare (HEW) was divided into a Department of Health and Human Services and a Department of Education. A significant conference resolution had called for the creation within the Department of Education of an Assistant Secretary for Library and Information Services. Instead, the Secretary of Education, Shirley Hufstedler, established an Office of Libraries and Learning Technologies, headed by a deputy assistant secretary under the assistant secretary for educational research and improvement. At the confirmation hearings of F. James Rutherford, former New York University professor and an assistant director of the National Science Foundation, as the assistant secretary, Rhode Island's Sen. Claiborne Pell, a strong supporter of library development, urged that the sector be renamed the Office for Educational Research and Improvement and for Libraries. The senator's plea was unheeded, and librarians could draw comfort only from the fact that their interests were positioned somewhat higher in the federal bureaucratic structure than had been the case in HEW.

Another important conference recommendation was the adoption of a National Library and Information Services Bill to replace the Library Services and Construction Act which expires in 1982. In May 1979 a "study bill," the National Library Bill (S-1124), was introduced before the U.S. Senate. The bill called for the creation of a national library agency with a director and governing board, substantially increased federal support of public library service, and coordination of the work of various types of libraries and information centers. The White House Conference resolution on National Library and Information Services endorsed "the general principles, goals, and objectives" of this legislation. However, many librarians had reservations about the bill, largely because it was to fund only public libraries while calling for national library agency coordination of all types of libraries. Nevertheless, the Washington office of the American Library Association (ALA) and the association's Committee on Legislation worked actively during 1980 to persuade Congress to conduct full hearings on the National Library Bill.

The National Commission on Libraries and Information Science (NCLIS) announced a variety of actions in the spring of 1980 aimed at the realization of White House Conference objectives. Beginning in July 1980, the staff of the National Commission and the Library of Congress embarked on a study of federal library services and resources. The study was expected to provide proposals for the improved coordination of federal library and information services so as to satisfy local, state, regional, and national needs. Alphonse Trezza left his post as the executive director of the NCLIS on June 30, 1980, in order to head this study. Responding to other concerns expressed during the White House Conference, the National Commission established an International Relations Planning Group, an Ad Hoc Committee on Postal Services to Libraries, a Task Force on the Role of the Special Library in a National Network Program, a Cultural Minorities Advisory Committee, and a Task Force on Community Information and Referral Service.

Networking Information. During the spring of 1980, the Ohio College Library Center (OCLC) determined that it would not, after a previous announcement to the contrary, restrict non-member access to the bibliographic records in its computerized database. In the summer, the Research Libraries Information Network (RLIN) of the Research Libraries Group and the Washington Library Network (WLN) began a project aimed at the creation of a telecommunications link between their two records files. More long range in character was a study, ongoing during the first half of 1980, by Battelle-Columbus Laboratories on the feasibility of connecting the OCLC, the RLIN, and the WLN. The linkage could result in the demise of competitive pricing of bibliographic services and the advent of homogeneous pricing.

The Library of Congress. On April 24, 1980, the 180th birthday of the Library of Congress, the $160-million James Madison Memorial Building was dedicated. This newest addition to the library effectively doubles its storage and office space. With the naming of the old main building for Thomas Jefferson and of the annex thereto for John Adams, all three buildings of the library bear the names of U.S. presidents.

American Library Association. The 99th annual conference of the ALA was held in New York, June 28–July 4, 1980. Peggy Sullivan, assistant commissioner for extension services of the Chi-

cago Public Library, presided. In a late 1979 mail ballot, the membership of the association increased personal dues by 43%, effective Jan. 1, 1980. On April 30, 1980, the association's executive board celebrated the topping off of the Huron Plaza, a new headquarters facility in Chicago. The ALA again sponsored National Library Week, April 13–19, 1980, employing as its theme, "America's Greatest Bargain . . . The Library." The association accredited, for the first time under its 1972 standards, the master's degree program in the Department of Library Science at Ball State University (Muncie, IN) and the School of Library Service at the University of Southern Mississippi (Hattiesburg, MS).

ALA members mourned the death of Louis Round Wilson, 104-year-old former director of the School of Library Science at the University of North Carolina in Chapel Hill and dean of the Graduate Library School at the University of Chicago.

The ALA cancelled the 1980 Soviet-American seminar on libraries, protesting developments in the Andrei Sakharov case and the Soviet invasion of Afghanistan.

International Library Activities. The 46th Council Meeting of the International Federation of Library Associations and Institutions convened in Manila, Aug. 18–23, 1980. The meeting, the organization's first in an undeveloped country, reflected some diminution of Anglo-Scandinavian dominance within the organization and an increasing influence of Third World nations. The federation obtained funding from the Council on Library Resources to support its substantial effort in the areas of international copyright and library materials conservation.

The Canadian Library Association's annual conference was held in Vancouver, June 11–17,

---

Major Library Awards of 1980

Beta Phi Mu Award for distinguished service to education for librarianship: Virginia Lacy Jones, dean, School of Library and Information Studies, Atlanta University

Randolph J. Caldecott Medal for distinction in picture book illustration: Barbara Cooney, *Ox-Cart Man*

Melvil Dewey Medal for creative professional achievement of a high order: Robert D. Stueart, dean and professor, Graduate School of Library and Information Science, Simmons College

Grolier Foundation Award for unusual contribution to the stimulation and guidance of reading by children and young people: Mabel Williams, Highstown (NJ) Public Library, formerly, New York Public Library

Joseph W. Lippincott Award for distinguished service to the profession of librarianship: E. J. Josey, Chief of the Bureau of Specialist Library Services, New York State Department of Education

John Newbery Medal for the most distinguished contribution to children's literature: Joan W. Blos, *A Gathering of Days*

Ralph R. Shaw Award for outstanding contribution to library literature: Rhea Rubin, director, Regional Library for the Blind and Physically Handicapped, Salem, OR, for her books, *Using Bibliotherapy: A Guide to Theory and Practice* and *A Bibliotherapy Sourcebook*

Laura Ingalls Wilder Award for longstanding contributions to children's literature: Theodor S. Geisel (Dr. Seuss)

H. W. Wilson Company Periodical Award: *PLA Bulletin*, published by the Pennsylvania Library Association

1980. A theme day devoted to "Libraries, Librarians, and Power: Developing Strategies" was held. Alan H. MacDonald, director of libraries at the University of Calgary, took over as president.

DAN BERGEN, *Graduate Library School*
University of Rhode Island, Kingston

LIBYA

Libyan head of state Muammar el-Qaddafi remained in the forefront of Middle Eastern radical leadership by his outspoken denunciation of the Egyptian-Israeli peace process, his consummation of Libya's merger with Syria, and his support for the new Islamic government of Iran in its war with Iraq. On the domestic front, however, Qaddafi encountered political opposition which caused disturbances not only in Libya, but in Europe as well. Meanwhile, Libyan oil revenues rose in 1980, despite a marked decline in production.

Foreign Affairs. Libya showed its opposition to the negotiations mandated in the 1978 Camp David accord by hosting an April meeting of the "rejectionist" states. In Tripoli, it joined with Syria, Algeria, South Yemen, and the Palestine Liberation Organization (PLO) in pledging continued opposition to the Egyptian-Israeli détente, the establishment of closer ties with the Soviet Union, and the coordination of propaganda efforts.

Colonel Qaddafi criticized moderate leaders throughout the Middle East, reserving especially harsh attacks for his closest neighbors. Angered by Egyptian President Anwar el-Sadat's relations with Israel and also by Sadat's admission onto Egyptian soil of the exiled shah of Iran, Qaddafi gave open support to Egyptian exiles seeking Sadat's overthrow. Fighting at the Libyan-Egyptian border was reported throughout the year.

Libya's western neighbor, Tunisia, accused the Qaddafi regime of complicity in a guerrilla attack on the city of Gafsa in January. Its government charged that the raiders had been trained in and supported by Libya and that the mission was part of a concerted effort to undermine the government of President-for-Life Habib Bourguiba. Libya denied any involvement in the Gafsa affair, although it did express sympathy with the goals of the attackers and repeated its opposition to the policies of the Bourguiba government.

Distressed by the lack of a unified, militant Arab approach to Israel, Qaddafi celebrated the 11th anniversary of the Libyan revolution on September 1 by calling for a merger between his nation and Syria. Syrian President Hafez al-Assad accepted the proposal one day later, and a proclamation was made on September 10. The union was a culmination of Libyan efforts, begun in 1973, to join with other Arab states in forging a united front against Israel. Although details of the plan remained to be worked out, the merger envisioned a unified congress and executive for the new entity. The 14-point proclamation invited other Arab states to join the union.

When fighting erupted between Iran and Iraq in the fall, both Syria and Libya supported the Iranian revolutionary government. Their support predominantly took the form of verbal backing for the regime of Ayatollah Ruhollah Khomeini, but there was speculation that Libya may have transferred arms and other material to the hard-pressed Iranian army and air force.

The dealings with Libya of Billy Carter, brother of U.S. President Jimmy Carter, led to controversy and a congressional investigation. (*See* UNITED STATES.)

Domestic Affairs. Rumors of internal political problems persisted throughout the year. Repeated reports of an army mutiny in Tobruk were denied by the authorities, but large numbers of Libyans were believed to have been arrested for this and other antiregime activities. Libyan political quarrels spilled over into Europe and the United States, as Qaddafi demanded that Libyan exiles return home or face assassination. When several Libyan activists were murdered in Great Britain and the United States, Libyan diplomatic officials were expelled from London, Washington, and Rome.

Oil continued to constitute Libya's major source of revenue, although production declined. In the late 1970s, production had peaked at just over two million barrels per day, but by late 1980 it had dropped to a low of only 1.4 million barrels per day. The rising price of oil, however, guaranteed that Libyan earnings would actually rise by about 25% over 1979, reaching $20,000,-000,000. The main reason for the decrease in output was the difficulty of selling Libyan crude. Low in sulphur and therefore quite expensive, it did not fare well in a glutted market. Much of the revenue was, as in the past, channeled into major industrialization and social projects.

KENNETH J. PERKINS
University of South Carolina

───────── **LIBYA · Information Highlights** ─────────

Official Name: Socialist People's Libyan Arab *Jamahiriya* ("state of the masses").
Location: North Africa.
Area: 679,360 sq mi (1 759 540 km²).
Population (1980 est.): 3,000,000.
Chief Cities (1975 est.): Tripoli, the capital, 295,000; Benghazi, 190,000.
Government: *Head of state,* Muammar el-Qaddafi, secretary general of the General People's Congress (took office 1969). *Head of government,* Abdullah Obeidi, chairman of the General Popular Committee. *Legislature*—General People's Congress (met initially Nov. 1976).
Monetary Unit: Dinar (0.296 dinar equals U.S.$1, Aug. 1980).
Manufactures (major products): Crude petroleum, processed foods, textiles, paper products.
Agriculture (major products): Wheat, barley, dates, olives, peanuts, citrus fruits, livestock.
GNP Per Capita (1978 est., U.S.$): $6,910.
Foreign Trade (Jan.-June 1979, U.S.$): *Imports,* $2,514,-000,000; *exports,* $6,275,000,000.

LITERATURE

Czesław Miłosz, a 69-year-old Polish poet and novelist who emigrated to the United States in 1960, was the recipient of the 1980 Nobel Prize for Literature. In its October 9 citation, the Swedish Academy said that Miłosz "with uncompromising clearsightedness, voices man's exposed condition in a world of severe conflicts. His writing is many-voiced and dramatic, insistent and provocative. He is an author of great importance—captivating and arresting."

A professor of Slavic languages at the University of California at Berkeley, Miłosz was active in the Polish resistance in German-occupied Warsaw in World War II. He served in the postwar Communist government for four years but fled to Paris in 1951. The humble, gray-haired poet has lived a solitary, somewhat secluded life since his arrival in the United States. The theme of exile appears throughout his work, which includes *Bell in Winter* (1978), a collection of poems; *Selected Poems* (1973); *The Usurpers* (1955), a novel; *Native Realm: A Search for Self-Definition* (1968), his autobiography; and numerous essays and translations.

Reviews of the major literatures follow.

American Literature

In 1980, economic trends and tax rulings were clear threats to the health of American literature. The increased centralization of the book industry and the decline of independent publishing meant that serious authors had fewer outlets. In the competition for profits, fine writers suffered from a lack of promotion and had smaller returns. Meanwhile, huge amounts were spent on "blockbusters." The paperback rights to Judith Krantz's potboiler *Princess Daisy* were bought for $3.2 million, leaving little money for more worthy books that promised only a modest return. A ruling by the U.S. Internal Revenue Service that books in inventory are taxable made it more expensive for publishers to keep books in print. Quality writers, who depend on the sale of their works over many years, were adversely affected.

The stormy 30-year history of the National Book Awards ended with the establishment of The American Book Awards (TABA) by a newly-formed academy of literary associations. The new awards immediately brought criticism that the many categories, entry fees, voting procedures, and presentation ceremonies lent themselves more to commercial promotion than to rewarding literary excellence. Many writers criticized the awards; Norman Mailer, Philip Roth, and William Styron refused their nominations. The academy argued that it sought to represent the tastes of general readers.

On May 1, the Academy of the American Book Awards announced 34 prizewinners out of

Wide World

Czesław Miłosz was awarded the Nobel Prize in Literature for his "insistent and provocative" poetry.

147 nominations. A highlight of the awards ceremony was the presentation of the 13th annual National Medal of Literature to 71-year-old Southern novelist and short-story writer Eudora Welty. The later appearance of *The Collected Stories of Eudora Welty* was a major literary event of the year.

In October, the TABA board announced that in 1981 the number of prize categories would be reduced to 17 and that nominees and winners would be chosen by small panels of judges instead of 2,000 booksellers, publishers, librarians, critics, and authors. (*See* PRIZES AND AWARDS.)

Novels. Although a number of interesting novels appeared during the year, none excited universal praise. Walker Percy's *The Second Coming,* a continuation of the story of Will Barrett begun in *The Last Gentleman* (1966), was fairly well received. Barrett, a wealthy widower, seeks meaning for his comfortable but oddly empty life. After a near-fatal descent into a cave in an experiment to find God, Barrett discovers love in the mentally ill daughter of his former girl friend.

Percy further enriched American literature with his discovery of John Kennedy Toole's *A*

Confederacy of Dunces. Toole, who was unable to find a publisher for his manuscript, committed suicide in 1969. Set in New Orleans, the book is a slapstick, philosophical story about a charmingly pompous, horribly overweight man who is in love with the Middle Ages. Tyrannized into getting a job by his tippling mother, he spends most of the book as a hot dog vendor in the French Quarter, eating his profits and innocently being drawn into underworld life while inveighing against the decadence of the modern world.

William Maxwell's *So Long, See You Tomorrow* is both a personal memoir and a stunningly evocative tragedy of American rural life. A love affair between a farm woman and her husband's best friend ends with the husband killing his friend and himself. There are no villains. Despite their goodness and strength, the woman and her lover are left helpless by their emotions and are led to their fate purely by circumstance. Lillian Hellman's brief *Maybe* similarly interweaves fact and fiction, as she tells the story of a friend named Sarah whom she knew for 40 years.

E. L. Doctorow's stylistically ambitious *Loon Lake* tells of a man named Joe who rises from obscurity to wealth during the Great Depression of the 1930s. Joe's many escapades as a worker, traveler, and lover allow Doctorow to portray the struggles of the poor and the antics of the rich. Mary Lee Settle's *The Scapegoat,* the fourth novel in her "Beulah Quintet," is a moving study of a coal miners' strike in West Virginia. It dramatically portrays both owners and workers trapped by economic pressures and social forces that frustrate the individual will. Another novel of political unrest, Marge Piercy's *Vida,* follows American radicals who went underground in the early 1970s.

Joyce Carol Oates' Gothic *Bellefleur* traces an upstate New York family over seven strange generations. The complex plot, numerous characters, and weird occurrences are brilliantly interwoven. Oates invokes the supernatural to suggest the genuine mysteriousness of life. John Gardner's *Freddy's Book* begins like a Gothic novel, with a house inhabited by a bitter old professor and his cloistered, overgrown son, but ends up as a fairy-tale about the Devil and Swedish knights.

Thomas Berger's *Neighbors* tells of a family almost driven to madness by the bizarre behavior of a couple down the street. Ann Beattie also deals with suburbia in *Falling in Place,* an acute observation of the various kinds of unhappiness in a middle-aged husband, his trapped wife, young mistress, and unsettled children.

In *The Bleeding Heart,* Marilyn French continues her inquiry into the complex and unhappy relationships of men and women. Written as an 18th-century novel in the manner of *Tom Jones* and *Fanny Hill,* Erica Jong's exuberant *Fanny* is at once a high adventure and an intellectual and erotic discourse on various subjects. Judith Rossner's *Emmeline* recreates the life of a 19th-century New England mill girl.

Hilma Wolitzer's *Hearts* is about a 13-year-old girl and her young mother who discover each other as they drive across America. William Kotzwinkle's *Jack in the Box* deals nostalgically with growing up in the 1940s. Tom Robbins' *Still Life with Woodpecker* is a zany love story.

Promising first novels were Anne Lamott's *Hard Laughter,* Anne Arensberg's *Sister Wolf,* Burke Davis III's *Dwelling Place,* and Philip Caputo's *Horn of Africa.*

Short Stories. Ella Leffland's reputation as a short-story writer was enhanced by *Last Courtesies,* stories written over the previous 20 years. Stuart Dybek's vital *Childhood and Other Neighborhoods* focuses on growing up in Chicago. Joanne Greenberg's *High Crimes and Misdemeanors* centers on the American West. Martha Gellhorn brings together three tragic stories of colonialism in her admirable *The Weather in Africa.* Patricia Zelver was warmly praised for *A*

Courtesy, Dutton

Joyce Carol Oates' *"Bellefleur"* is a Gothic novel with a complex plot and evocations of the supernatural.

Man of Middle Age, in which she uses both European and American settings. Paul Theroux's *World's End* cleverly dramatizes the ironies of human nature around the world. Laura Furman evokes the significance of ordinary events in *The Glass House.* Difficult to describe but often brilliant are the satiric, penetrating sketches in Woody Allen's *Side Effects* and George W. S. Trow's *Bullies.* Truman Capote's *Music for Chameleons* again proved that he is a master of social observation. The volume contains six stories, a novella—"Handcarved Coffins," which claims to be a nonfictional account of a crime—and seven penetrating "Conversational Portraits."

Poetry. James Merrill's *Scripts for the Pageant* concludes the major poem begun with the *Book of Ephraim* (1976) and *Mirabell: Books of Number* (1978). Recording a series of ouija board sessions with the author's friend, David Jackson, the poem speaks in different voices ranging from playful to profound in raising the deepest questions about life and death. Robert Penn Warren's *Being Here: Poetry 1977–1980* proves his continued strength as an eloquent and moving poet. America's political condition is addressed in Frederick Seidel's *Sunrise.*

Relationships and emotions are treated sensitively in Marilyn Hacker's *Taking Notice,* June Jordan's *Passion,* and Marge Piercy's angry *The Moon Is Always Female.* The direct language of Mark Strand's *Selected Poems* gives them a quiet, enduring power. Howard Nemerov's *Sentences* ranges from philosophical speculation to thoughts on domestic chores. Nature is particularly well observed in Wendell Berry's *A Part* and Mary Cheever's *The Need for Chocolate.* Galway Kinnell's mastery of technique is clear in his moving *Mortal Acts, Mortal Words.* Eugene O'Neill's verse is collected in *Poems 1912–1944.*

Literary History and Criticism. Because of Vladimir Nabokov's unique personality and literary sensibilities, his course in modern literature at Cornell University became legendary. Collected in *Lectures on Literature,* Nabokov's discourses examined authors ranging from Jane Austen to James Joyce in search of the magic that creates art.

Although radical new methods of literary criticism are constantly being formulated, William H. Pritchard's *Lives of the Modern Poets* proves the value of a traditional approach. He selects nine poets from Thomas Hardy to William Carlos Williams and explicates their work by examining their lives and other writings. Helen Vendler's perceptive *Part of Nature, Part of Us* deals with more contemporary poets, such as A. R. Ammons, Frank O'Hara, and Robert Lowell.

The poet speaks for himself in Robert Penn Warren's *Talking: Interviews 1950–1978.* Randall Jarrell's essays, *Kipling, Auden & Co.,* prove that he was a sensitive critic as well as an important poet.

When he died in 1965, the eminent critic R. P. Blackmur left a major manuscript. Now edited by Veronica Makowsky, *Henry Adams* is a thoughtful meditation on the life and works of a key figure in American intellectual history. Henry Miller's spirited defense of D. H. Lawrence written during the 1930s, *The World of Lawrence,* gives insight into both men. Malcolm Cowley's *The Dream of the Golden Mountains* is a personal account of the turbulent 1930s. That decade is also recalled in Leon Edel's edition of Edmund Wilson's notebooks and diaries, *The Thirties.* The World War II diaries and letters of Anne Morrow Lindbergh appear as *War Within and Without.* Paul Fussell's *Abroad: British Travel Writing Between the Wars* reveals much about the cultural crises of modern England. Richard King's *A Southern Renaissance* argues that the rise of the South in American literature after 1930 can be explained in terms of the writers' relation to the family.

The *Arna Bontemps-Langston Hughes Letters 1925–1967* chronicles their difficulties as serious black writers. In *The Wayward and the Seeking,* Darvin Turner selects works by Jean Toomer, the mysterious author of *Cane* (1923) who lived as a white man for many years. Matthew J. Bruccoli edited *The Correspondence of F. Scott Fitzgerald.* The late Martha Foley's *The Story of Story Magazine,* edited by Jay Neugeboren, describes the birth and growth of that prize-winning journal.

Lionel Trilling's *Speaking of Literature and Society* completes the 12-volume edition of his essays. Mary McCarthy continues to be provocative in her collection *Ideas and the Novel.* Susan Sontag's *Under the Sign of Saturn* includes her remembrances of Paul Goodman and Roland Barthes. John Simon bemoans the vulgarization of the English language in *Paradigms Lost.*

Michael Kreyling's *Eudora Welty's Achievement of Order,* Frank Doggett's *Wallace Stevens: The Making of the Poem,* and George Hunt's *John Updike and the Three Secret Things* explicate these important writers. Walter Kaufmann discusses the seminal modern philosophers, Friedrich Nietzsche, Martin Heidegger, and Martin Buber in *Discovering the Mind.*

History and Biography. James R. Mellow's evocative *Nathaniel Hawthorne In His Times* recreates the cultural life of the mid-1800s, in which the United States produced its greatest literary figures. Madelon Bedell's *The Alcotts* looks at a literary family that included Louisa May Alcott (*Little Women,* 1868) and her father, the transcendentalist thinker and author Amos Bronson Alcott. David Heymann's *American Aristocracy* bridges a full century in a study of the remarkable poets of the Lowell family, James Russell, Amy, and Robert. Justin Kaplan's *Walt Whitman* vividly and judiciously tells the life of the great American poet.

One of the most problematic American writers is revealed in Townsend Ludington's *John*

JUSTICE	AGE AT APPOINTMENT	PRESIDENT	APPOINTED	RESIGNED
Hugo L. Black	51	Roosevelt	1937	1971
William O. Douglas	40	Roosevelt	1939	1975
Earl Warren	62	Eisenhower	1953	1969
John M. Harlan	55	Eisenhower	1954	1971
William J. Brennan, Jr.	50	Eisenhower	1956	—
Potter Stewart	43	Eisenhower	1958	—
Byron R. White	44	Kennedy	1962	—
Abe Fortas	55	Johnson	1965	1969
Thurgood Marshall	59	Johnson	1967	—
Warren E. Burger	61	Nixon	1969	—
Harry A. Blackmun	61	Nixon	1970	—
Lewis F. Powell, Jr.	64	Nixon	1971	—
William H. Rehnquist	47	Nixon	1971	—
John Paul Stevens	55	Ford	1975	—

Two Washington journalists created a stir with the publication of "The Brethren," an inside look at the justices and workings of the U.S. Supreme Court.

Courtesy Simon and Schuster

Dos Passos. Addison Gayle's sympathetic *Richard Wright* uses documents released under the U.S. Freedom of Information Act to reveal the government's harassment of Wright during his years abroad. The poet and longtime poetry editor of *The New Yorker* magazine, Louise Bogan, was too self-effacing to write an autobiography; but her life is lovingly reconstructed through personal papers in Ruth Limmer's *Journey Around My Room.*

Ian Watt's *Conrad in the Nineteenth Century* is a learned and penetrating study of one of the most complex modern writers. Peter Stansky and William Abrahams' *Orwell: The Transformation* begins a multivolume biography with an examination of the five-year period that culminated in George Orwell's participation in the Spanish Civil War.

Merle Miller uses the subject's own words as much as possible in *Lyndon: An Oral Biography.* Ronald Steel's *Walter Lippmann and the American Century* tells of the influential columnist whose career spanned the presidencies of Woodrow Wilson to Lyndon Johnson.

Techniques of literary scholarship are sometimes used by historians to examine important texts of the past. Sacvan Bercovitch's *The American Jeremiad* argues that the Puritan sermon created a rhetorical form that still influences contemporary secular society. The intellectual backgrounds of James Madison, Alexander Hamilton, and the Federalist Papers are analyzed in Garry Wills' *Explaining America.* Patricia J. Tracy's *Jonathan Edwards, Pastor* is a study of that complex religious figure.

Several important historians turned their attention from presidents and treaties to the daily life of the people. Carl Bridenbaugh focuses on a single community in *Jamestown 1544–1699.* James Thomas Flexner's *States Dyckman: American Loyalist* studies some unobtrusive Tories of the American Revolution. E. Digby Baltzell's *Puritan Boston and Quaker Philadelphia* speculates on the reasons for the significant cultural differences between the upper classes of those cities. In *Small Town America,* Richard Lingeman looks at the village from New England to the Far West and its effects on America. Gwendolyn Wright's *Moralism and the Modern Home* shows how changes in domestic architecture reveal cultural conflict and family values at the turn of the century.

Carl N. Degler's ambitious *At Odds* discusses the role of women and the family since the American Revolution. Mary Beth Norton's *Liberty's Daughters* argues that women, encouraged to political and intellectual activism during the revolutionary period, were subsequently suppressed. Several fine essays on women's history are collected in Nancy F. Cott's and Elizabeth H. Pleck's *A Heritage of Her Own.*

Robert Nisbet's *History of the Idea of Progress* argues that the concept of progress is pervasive in the history of Western thought and that current doubts manifest a profound cultural crisis. Richard Sennett's provocative *Authority* discusses America's paradoxical attraction to and resentment of power.

General. *American Dreams: Lost & Found* is another illuminating series of Studs Terkel interviews with Americans of all classes. Malcolm Cowley's *The View From 80* is a graceful essay on aging. Stephen Jay Gould's lively science essays appear in *The Panda's Thumb.* George B. Schaller's *Stones of Silence* shows how man's inroads destroy nature's delicate balance.

Deaths. Henry Miller, the controversial author who helped liberate the novel from censorship, died at 88. The poets Muriel Rukeyser and James Wright also died during the year. (*See* Obituaries.)

Jerome H. Stern, *Florida State University*

Children's Literature

Economic stresses were apparent in children's book publishing in the United States during 1980. Library sales diminished, while prices for quality books increased sharply. More publishers turned to mass-market merchandising of "nonbooks"—calendars, novelty items, punchouts, and pop-ups. Stories from the movies *Star Wars* and *The Empire Strikes Back* were among the most popular sellers.

Individual title production in the United States was estimated at 1,700, approximately the same as in the previous year. There were handsome, newly-illustrated editions of such classics as *Hansel and Gretel, East of the Sun and West of the Moon, The Fisherman and His Wife, The Wind in the Willows,* and *Peter Pan.* New works of distinction, however, were difficult to find.

The American Library Association's (ALA) John Newbery Medal for the most distinguished contribution to American children's literature went to Joan W. Blos for *A Gathering of Days: A New England Girl's Journal, 1830–32,* a skillfully woven, fictional account of a farm girl's life. Mrs. Blos also received The American Book Award (formerly the National Book Award) for children's literature for the same book. The ALA's Randolph Caldecott Medal for the most distinguished picture book was awarded to Barbara Cooney for her work in Donald Hall's *Ox-Cart Man,* depicting the life of a 19th-century New Hampshire farm family. T. A Dyer won the Child Study Children's Book Committee Award for *The Whipman Is Watching,* about three American Indian children torn between tradition and modern society.

Perhaps the outstanding book of the year was Paul Fleischman's *The Half-a-Moon Inn,* A haunting tale for 10-to-14 year olds in which a mute boy, lost in a blizzard, stumbles into a bewitched inn where he is held prisoner by a cruel proprietor.

For the picture book audience (ages 3 to 7), the most noteworthy books were *Louis the Fish* by Arthur Yorinks and Richard Egielski, the story of a butcher who happily turns into a fish; William Steig's *Gorky Rises,* the tale of a frog who becomes airborne after drinking a magic potion; James Stevenson's *Howard,* about a duck who winters in New York City; John Goodall's *Paddy's New Hat,* a wordless account of an accident-prone pig who becomes a hero; M. B. Goffstein's *An Artist,* offering a brief, descriptive portrait of the creative act; Alice and Martin Provensen's *The Golden Serpent,* a wry fable about a wise man and a boy solving a mystery for a king; and Edward and James Marshall's *Space Case,* an amusing story about a U.F.O. being mistaken for a Halloween prankster.

For children between 6 and 10, the best books were *Anno's Italy* by Mitsumasa Anno, a panoramic journey featuring elements of art and architecture, folklore, and fairy tales, as well as stories from the Old and New Testaments; Mildred Pitts Walter's *Ty's One-Man Band,* illustrated by Margot Tomes, about the performance of a one-legged itinerant musician; Jack Prelutsky's *The Headless Horseman Rides Tonight,* a dozen verse portraits of demonic beings, with properly spooky illustrations by Arnold Lobel; and *Fables,* with twenty original tales written and illustrated by Arnold Lobel.

In the 9-to-12 category, the most outstanding books were Lee Harding's *The Fallen Spaceman,* in which a giant spacesuit runs out of control, endangering the lives of an alien being and a human trapped inside; Judy Blume's *Superfudge,* the story of a sixth grader's problems with a younger brother and a new baby in the family; John Reynolds Gardiner's *Stone Fox,* the story of a 10-year-old boy's dogsled race against a giant Indian; Jane Langton's *The Fledgling,* a fantasy about a young girl's friendship with a wild goose; Betsy Byars' *The Night Swimmers,* a story about the daughter of a country and western singer who takes care of her two young brothers; and Scott O'Dell's *Sarah Bishop,* a story, based on fact, of a young girl hiding from the British in the Westchester wilderness during the American Revolution.

Among the year's best novels for teenagers were Paula Fox's *A Place Apart,* a finely honed, first-person account of a 13-year-old girl's search for order and security in her changing world; Katherine Paterson's *Jacob Have I Loved,* about the rivalry between twin sisters living on a small island in Chesapeake Bay during World War II; Zibby Oneal's *The Language of Goldfish,* a compassionate profile of a 13-year-old girl's mental and emotional breakdown; Stanley Kiesel's *The War Between the Pitiful Teachers and the Splendid Kids,* a devastating satire featuring all-out combat between students and faculty; Paul Zindel's sequel to *The Pigman, The Pigman's Legacy,* in which two teenagers befriend a belligerent old man; Jan Slepian's *The Alfred Summer,* about four handicapped children working together to build a rowboat; and David Macaulay's *Unbuilding,* a satiric, step-by-step account of the dismantling of the Empire State Building.

In the area of nonfiction for teenagers, there were excellent biographies of such persons as Alexander Calder, Joseph de Veuster, the Belgian priest known as Father Damien—who worked among lepers on the island of Molokai—Margaret Bourke-White, and John Brown. Especially praiseworthy were William Jaspersohn's *The Ballpark,* a textual and photographic behind-the-scenes tour of the Boston Red Sox' Fenway Park; Paxton Davis' *Three Days,* a superb, short account of the battle of Gettysburg seen through the eyes of Gen. Robert E. Lee; and Francine Jacobs' *Fire Snake,* an account of the building of the Uganda Railway in East Africa.

GEORGE A. WOODS
Children's Book Editor
"The New York Times"

Canadian Literature: English

Books by three of the country's top writers—Hugh MacLennan, Mordecai Richler, and Pierre Berton—made 1980 a vintage year in Canadian literature. A number of books about federal and provincial rights and the Canadian constitution reflected current political concerns.

Nonfiction. Pierre Berton's *The Invasion of Canada, 1812-1813* is the first of two volumes on the War of 1812. The popular and prolific Berton again demonstrates his ability to present history in accurate and readable prose.

Among many new books about Canada's constitutional problems were Norman L. Nicholson's *The Boundaries of the Canadian Constitution; Keeping Canada Together,* by Norman Penner, et al; and *Canada Challenged: the Viability of Confederation,* edited by R. B. Byers and Robert W. Redford.

John Sawatsky's *Men in the Shadow: the RCMP Security Service* is an often critical look at the methods of the famous police force.

In *Spreading Time,* senior Canadian poet Earle Birney describes the turmoil and growth of Canadian poetry between 1904 and 1949.

In *Growing Up Stupid Under the Union Jack,* Austin Clark describes one year of his life in Barbados. Frank H. Epp's *The Israelis: Portrait of a People in Conflict* is based on a series of interviews.

John Bracken: a Political Biography, by John Kendle, is a balanced study of the man who was premier of Manitoba for 20 years and who led the federal conservatives for five years. *The Great Scot* is Joseph Schull's biography of big, bluff Donald Gordon, chairman and president of the Canadian National Railways from 1950 to 1966. *Laurier: His Life and World* is Richard Clipp's study of the great Canadian prime minister. Len Coates' *Villeneuve!* tells of Canada's leading racing driver, Gilles Villeneuve, with exciting photographs by Allan de la Plante. *James G. Endicott: Rebel out of China,* by his son, Stephen Endicott, tells of the elder Endicott's years as a United Church missionary in China.

Barbara Amiel, already renowned for her beauty and her career as a broadcaster, tells her own life story and articulates her right-wing beliefs in *Confessions.* William Kurelek's *Someone With Me* is his posthumously-released autobiography. Kurelek, a well-known painter, survived four years in an insane asylum and credits his recovery to a religious awakening.

Dieppe 1942, by Ronald Atkin, is a well-written account of that World War II battle. *Vakil Abad, Iran: a Survivor's Story* is Richard Savin's frightening account of his more than two years in the shah's Vakil Abad prison. In *Rough Road to the North,* Jim Christy describes the building of the Alaska Highway.

Poetry. *The Love Poems of Irving Layton* brings together some of the best verse from Layton's 40 years of writing. Robin Skelton's *Landmarks* is a series of poems on Vancouver Island. George Bowering's latest volume, *Another Mouth,* consists mainly of short poems. *The Collected Poems of Raymond Souster, Volume I* covers the years 1940–55. *East of Myloona,* by Andrew Suknaski, is a book of poems about the North, illustrated with drawings by the author. *Signs Against an Empty Sky* is the fine first volume of Steve Hume.

Fiction. Hugh MacLennan's first novel in 13 years, *Voices in Time,* is set in the future. The narrative describes the end of contemporary civilization and the emergence of a new, more cruel society, the "Third Bureaucracy." An underlying theme is the survival of the human spirit. With this book, MacLennan, whose previous works include the critically acclaimed *Barometer Rising,* about the 1917 Halifax explosion, adds new luster to his reputation as a writer.

Mordecai Richler's *Joshua Then and Now* is a biting, lively book that brings out Richler's best. Joshua, a Jewish sports commentator, knocks down the metaphorical walls of a modern Jericho—Westmount, a bastion of wealthy, English-

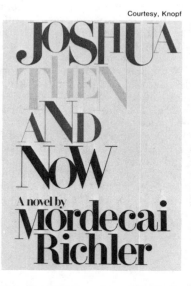

Courtesy, Little, Brown & Co.

Courtesy, Knopf

Pierre Berton's first of two volumes on the War of 1812 and a new novel by Mordecai Richler helped make 1980 a vintage year in Canadian English literature.

speaking Montrealers—by marrying a senator's daughter.

Former federal cabinet minister Judy La-Marsh's *A Right Honourable Lady* is about a woman prime minister of Canada caught in a vicious political power struggle. In *The Charcoal Burners,* a suspense story, poet Susan Musgrave successfully mixes death and humor. Joy Carroll's *Pride Court* is a sequel to her very popular *Proud Blood.*

Sylvia Fraser's *The Emperor's Virgin* is set in the violent and licentious times of the Roman Emperor Domitian. *Odd's End,* by Tim Wynn-Jones, is a thriller about a psychopath. Jane Rule's *Contract with the World* traces the tangled lives and loves of some unusual characters. *Five Hundred Keys,* a first novel by Michael Carin, is about smuggling hashish from Morocco to Canada. Silver Donald Cameron's *Dragon Lady* is an exciting story of international intrigue.

Rudy Wiebe's *The Mad Trapper* tells in fictional form the story of Albert Johnson, who killed two policemen in the Arctic. Roy MacGregor's *Shorelines* is an account, in the form of a novel, of the mysterious death of painter Tom Thompson.

Peter McLaren's *Cries from the Corridor* powerfully indicts the school system in a poor Toronto neighborhood. Short story writer Shirley Faessler's *Everything in the Window* is about a Jewish girl married to a gentile in Toronto. Hugh Hood again demonstrates his mastery of the short story in a collection titled *None Genuine Without This Signature.*

Kowalski's Last Chance, by Leo Simpson, features a small-town Ontario policeman who discovers that the suspected bank robber he has captured is a leprechaun. John Metcalf's *General Ludd* satirizes the Canadian literary establishment.

DAVID SAVAGE, *Simon Fraser University*

Canadian Literature: Quebec

In the province of Quebec, 1980 was the year of the referendum on sovereignty-association. (*See* special report, page 172.) The literary community played an active role in the debate, with most of it favoring the *oui.* The poet Paul Chamberland wrote an impassioned plea called *Terre souveraine,* and the essayist Pierre Vadeboncoeur published a convincing piece under the appropriate title *To Be or Not to Be....* The winter issue of the review *Possibles* contained statements, essays, and poems from 27 authors in support of political independence. But despite these and other efforts, the referendum was defeated, causing disappointment among many Quebec intellectuals and literati.

Novels and Short Stories. After a silence of five years, Anne Hébert published a new novel, *Héloïse,* in which she tells in concise, almost arid prose a haunting adventure about vampires living in the Paris *métro.* On a less gory note, Michel Tremblay published the second volume of his *Chroniques du Plateau Mont-Royal;* the new work is a further imaginary exploration of his youth, entitled *Thérèse et Pierrette à l'école des Saints-Anges.* The prolific but somewhat uneven Marie-Claire Blais brought out her fourteenth novel, *Le Sourd dans la ville;* this stream of consciousness story about women made miserable by men won the Governor General's Prize for fiction by a Canadian author in French. Other important fictional works of 1980 included a sensitive portrait of young brothers by Claude Jasmin (*La Sablière*); a new adventure novel by the recipient of the Prix David, Yves Thériault (*La Quête de l'ourse*) and two new works by Roch Carrier, *Les Fleurs vivent-elles ailleurs que sur la terre?* and *La Céleste bicyclette* (a play), both of which enter the realm of the metaphysical. Finally, Gérard Bessette published two new works: a novel entitled *Le Semestre,* which tells the reflections of a professor about to retire, and a collection of short stories called *La Garden party de Christophine,* which demonstrates that the author is an excellent story teller as well as an introspective and incisive intellectual.

Theater. A number of established dramatists continued to expand and enrich their repertory in 1980. Jean-Claude Germain published *Mamours et conjugat,* a comic but serious exploration of the myths and realities of sex. Germain also produced a new play, *Les Nuits de l'Individa,* a sequel to an earlier work about a showwoman. Michel Garneau's *Nasopodes et autres bêtes merveilleuses* was well received as an avant-garde, poetic spectacle. But Michel Tremblay's new play, *L'Impromptu d'Outremont,* had little success; critics found this bourgeois comedy far inferior to Tremblay's earlier works.

Poetry. Two of Quebec's most important poets were in the news during the year. Paul-Marie Lapointe brought out two volumes titled *Ecritures,* poems which refer to themselves and constitute a kind of game. Gaston Miron's poetry was finally translated into English (*The Agonized Life*). Miron, silent since 1975, began writing again; he published a series of bittersweet love poems, *Femme sans fin,* in the summer 1980 issue of *Possibles.* Other poetry of note included Gilbert Langevin's *Le Fou solidaire,* Cécile Cloutier's *Chaleuils,* and Georges Dor's fourth volume of *Poèmes et chansons.*

Criticism. Two highly intelligent and sensitive critics, André Brochu and Gilles Marcotte, published an epistolary exchange with insights into the literary world of France and Quebec (*La Littérature et le reste*). Jean-Cléo Godin and Laurent Mailhot put out an excellent introduction to modern theater (*Théâtre québécois II*), and Gabrielle Poulin did the same for the modern novel (*Roman du pays 1968–79*). Insightful new studies of individual authors include Pierre L'Hérault's *Jacques Ferron, cartographe de l'imaginaire,* and Pierre Nepveu's study of three modern poets, titled *Les Mots à l'écoute.*

JONATHAN M. WEISS, *Colby College*

English Literature

The year 1980 was a particularly good one for English literature, with important new works by major authors, especially novelists. However, it also saw the demise of three English novelists—Olivia Manning, Barbara Pym, and Sir Charles Percy Snow.

In a series of novels entitled *The Fortunes of War,* Olivia Manning described the lives of British civilians and soldiers in the Balkan and Mediterranean theaters of World War II. The last of these novels, *The Sum of Things,* was published after her death. Barbara Pym's nine novels were concerned mainly with the lives of single women. The last of them, *A Few Green Leaves,* published posthumously, deals with loneliness and approaching death.

C. P. Snow's lifework included 25 books of fiction and nonfiction, five plays, and numerous articles. His major work was *Strangers and Brothers,* a series of 11 novels. While his works focused mainly on aspects of English society, Snow, a trained physicist, also emphasized the kinship of art and science. (*See* OBITUARIES.)

Fiction. Another posthumous novel published in 1980 was John Cowper Powys' *After My Fashion,* written in 1920 and set in the United States and England. Because it is autobiographical, Powys apparently did not want to publish the book during his lifetime. The central characters, Richard Storm and Elise Angel, are based on Powys and his friend, Isadora Duncan.

Kingsley Amis' new novel, *Russian Hide-and-Seek,* is set in the 21st century. Russians occupy Great Britain, having taken it over in a war. An insurrection is planned, but fails.

Times are also bad in Anthony Burgess' *Earthly Powers,* but they are contemporary times. Writers and other historical figures of the 20th century appear in this novel, which poses timely moral and theological questions. A priest in Chicago saves a boy's life by faith-healing.

Later, the priest becomes pope and the boy becomes the leader of a cult reminiscent of Jim Jones' People's Temple in Jonestown, Guyana.

Iris Murdoch's *Nuns and Soldiers* and Graham Greene's *Doctor Fischer of Geneva or The Bomb Party* are also moral tales. Murdoch portrays the vices and virtues among her characters after the death of one of their husbands. Greene's wealthy Dr. Fischer humiliates his guests, who are willing to accept abuse in exchange for gifts. Finally, he has them play a game in which they may receive either money or a bomb.

The characters in Margaret Drabble's *The Middle Ground* and Angus Wilson's *Setting the World on Fire* are middle-class Londoners. Drabble's central character is a journalist who must cope with her profession, an abortion, and her responsibilities to friends. Wilson's main characters, two brothers, live in Westminster's only remaining house with a park and garden. The novel is largely unadorned, consisting mainly of dialogue, memories, and the thoughts of its characters. Wilson's style and his characterization of the two brothers reflects the architecture of the house, Palladian and baroque.

William Golding won the 1980 Booker Prize for his novel, *Rites of Passage.* Set in the early 19th century, the novel recounts a passenger ship voyage to Australia. The trip is recorded in the diary of a confident, well-to-do young man and in an unfinished letter written by a humble clergyman. The clergyman, humiliated by the officers and crew of the ship as it crosses the equator and by his own actions later, dies of shame.

Beryl Bainbridge's *Winter Garden* is about a visit to Russia by two women, artists who have been invited as official guests, and the two men who accompany them.

Other significant novels of 1980 were Stan Barstow's *A Brother's Tale;* Stanley Middleton's *The Other Side;* Paul Bailey's *Old Soldiers;* John le Carré's *Smiley's People;* Thomas Hinde's *Day-*

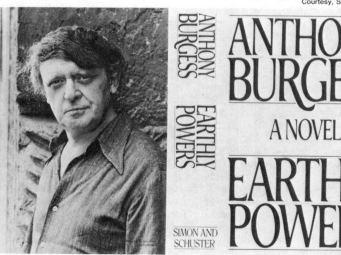

In "Earthly Powers," on which he worked for nearly ten years, Anthony Burgess uses his two main characters to explore timely issues of religion and the morality of power.

mare; Doris Lessing's *The Marriages Between Zones Three, Four, and Five;* A. N. Wilson's *The Healing Art;* David Lodge's *How Far Can You Go?* Richard Adams' *The Girl in a Swing;* Fay Weldon's *Puffball;* Gordon Giles' *Ambrose's Vision;* Peter Redgrove's *The Beekeeper;* and Penelope Shuttle's *The Mirror of the Giant.*

Notable collections of short stories were Kingsley Amis' *Collected Short Stories;* William Trevor's *Other People's Worlds;* Nadine Gordimer's *A Soldier's Embrace;* Elaine Feinstein's *The Silent Areas;* J. I. M. Stewart's *Our England Is a Garden;* Elspeth Davie's *The Night of the Funny Hats;* and Sam McBratney's *Lagan Valley Details.*

Nonfiction. In *Ways of Escape,* Graham Greene reprints the introductions to the collected edition of his works and links them with comments about his experiences in various parts of the world, including Vietnam, Cuba, and Haiti, from which many of his novels are drawn.

A. C. Benson, a schoolmaster at Eton, Fellow of Magdalene College at Cambridge University, and a popular novelist, began to keep a diary in 1897. By the time he died in 1925, the diary had grown to 180 volumes. In *On the Edge of Paradise,* David Newsome includes excerpts of Benson's acute observations about himself, his students, and his colleagues.

Montague Summers was a priest of the Church of England and, later, of the Church of Rome, a scholar of Restoration drama and the Gothic novel, and the author of *The History of Witchcraft and Demonology* and other books on the supernatural. He finished his autobiography shortly before his death in 1948, but it was not published until 1980, as *The Galanty Show,* edited by Brocard Sewell.

Two important collections of letters that appeared in 1980 were *Dai Greatcoat: A Self-Portrait of David Jones in His Letters,* edited by René Hague, and *The Letters of Evelyn Waugh,* 850 correspondences selected by Mark Amory.

Among new biographies were the first volume of James Lees-Milne's *Harold Nicolson;* Mary Moorman's life of her father, *George Macaulay Trevelyan;* Barbara Strachey's *Remarkable Relations: The Story of the Logan Pearsall Smith Family;* Sean Day-Lewis' *C. Day Lewis: An English Literary Life;* Charles Osborne's *W. H. Auden: The Life of a Poet;* John Lehmann's *Rupert Brooke: His Life and Legend;* Peter Kavanagh's *Sacred Keeper: A Biography of Patrick Kavanagh;* Alan Jenkin's *Stephen Potter: Inventor of Gamesmanship;* William Walsh's *F. R. Leavis;* Frances Spalding's *Roger Fry: Art and Life;* and Paul Levy's *Moore: G. E. Moore and the Cambridge Apostles.*

Significant among new works of literary history and criticism were Blake Morrison's *The Movement: English Poetry and Fiction in the 1950s;* Marilyn Butler's *Peacock Displayed: A Satirist in His Context;* Morine Krissdottir's *John Cowper Powys and the Magical Quest;* Barbara

Fisher's *Joyce Cary: The Writer and His Theme;* Peter Faulkner's *Angus Wilson, Mimic and Moralist;* and Richard Todd's *Iris Murdoch: The Shakespeare Interest.*

Poetry. Vernon Scannell, W. S. Graham, Patricia Beer, Gavin Ewart, Robert Garioch, and Ted Hughes all published important new poetry collections.

Scannell's versification in *New and Collected Poems 1950–1980* is formal, the tone conversational. As the poet observes incidents of everyday life and recalls his experiences as a soldier and a boxer, the reader is drawn by his monosyllabic wording and seemingly transparent meanings into associations and feelings that pierce the surface.

W. S. Graham's *Collected Poems* displays the author's constant concern with language, vision, and man's role in the universe. The style of the early poems in the book is orotund and abstract. In the later poems, the bardic tone is gentler, the diction simpler, and the concrete images more frequent.

Patricia Beer's dry and economical *Selected Poems* reveals aspects of a disciplined but sympathetic personality developing from childhood to middle age. An awareness of death affects the feeling and thought of the collection.

As the title of his book, *The Collected Ewart 1933–1980,* suggests, Gavin Ewart has cast himself in the character of a poet. With a thirst for experience, especially the erotic, he appears to toss his poems off easily, if not carelessly. Compassion and cynicism vie in this energetic verse.

Although some of his *Collected Poems* are written in standard English, Robert Garioch is most at home in a colloquial Scots dialect. Cannily critical of a world that has little time for regional traditions, Garioch responds with quiet wit and a vibrant demonstration that Scots is indeed a living language.

The first poems in Ted Hughes' *Moortown* are also regional, rooted in the soil of Hughes' Devonshire farm. The next group of poems includes acute descriptions of people, and the collection ends with two mythic, visionary works, "Prometheus on His Crag" and "Adam and the Sacred Nine."

The work of Ulster poets since 1960 is surveyed in Frank Ormsby's anthology, *Poets From the North of Ireland.* Books published by Northern Irish poets in 1980 include Norris Leslie's *Kites in Spring;* William Peskett's *Survivors;* Michael Longley's *The Echo Gate;* and Tom Paulin's *The Strange Museum.*

Other important poetry collections were C. H. Sisson's *Exactions;* Kathleen Raine's *The Oracle in the Heart;* Robert Conquest's *Forays;* John Silkin's *The Psalms and Their Spoils;* Norman MacCaig's *The Equal Skies;* Roy Fuller's *The Reign of Sparrows;* Geoffrey Grigson's *History of Him,* and D. J. Enright's *The Oxford Book of Contemporary Verse.*

J. K. JOHNSTONE, *University of Saskatchewan*

French Literature

The French literary world mourned the passing of 66-year-old novelist and former diplomat Romain Gary, who died in Paris Dec. 2, 1980, apparently of a self-inflicted gunshot wound. (*See* OBITUARIES.) His novel *Les Cerfs Volantes* (The Kites) appeared earlier in the year. Three other well-known authors also died in 1980: Maurice Genevoix, dean and former *secrétaire perpétuel* of the French Academy; Pascal Jardin, a 46-year-old novelist and screenwriter; and Max-Pol Fouchet, poet, critic, essayist, and founder of the literary review *Fontaine*.

Fiction. The *Grand Prix du Roman de l'Académie Française* was awarded to Henri Coulonges for *L'Adieu à la femme sauvage* (Farewell to the Distraught Woman), a moving novel about a young widow and her 12-year-old daughter, both traumatized by the bombing of Dresden in 1945. Other novels well received by the public were *Les lits à une place* (The Single Beds), a tale in praise of solitude, and Zöe Oldenbourg's *La Joie Souffrance* (Joy-Suffering), a realistic fresco of the life of Russian émigrés in Paris between World War I and World War II. French colonial Africa inspired the best-selling *Fort Saganne,* by Louis Gardel.

Love furnished, as usual, the theme of a good many novels, including Christine Arnothy's *Toutes les chances plus une* (All the Chances, Plus One); Jean Freustié's *La dernière donne* (The Last Deal); Geneviève Dormann's *Fleur de péché* (Flower of Sin); and Simone Arèse's light and amusing *Mado*.

Novels of adventure and suspense were, as in preceding years, very much appreciated by the general public. The most popular were *Le Retournement* (The Turnabout) and the trilogy *Les Humeurs de la mer,* by the prolific Vladimir Volkoff; *Le Cinquième cavalier* (The Fifth Horseman), by Dominique Lapierre and Larry Collins; and *Money,* a "financial Western" by Paul Loup Sulitzer.

In addition to Romain Gary, three other major writers published new novels in 1980: *Désert,* by Jean Marie Le Clézio; *L'Angoise du roi Salomon* (King Solomon's Anguish), by Emile Ajar; and *La Parodie* (The Parody), by Henry-François Rey.

Finally, an ambitious, exuberant, romantic novel by a younger, very promising writer, was *Fin de Siècle* (End of the Century), which was well received by most of the critics.

Nonfiction. Two of the best nonfiction works of 1980 were Jacques Lacarrière's *Le Pays sous l'écorce* (The Country Behind Bars), a kind of rediscovery of the world through observation of plants and animals, and Elizabeth Badinter's *L'Amour en plus* (Added Love), a remarkable, though unorthodox, history of maternal love from the 17th to the 20th century.

Among the many volumes of memoirs published in 1980, the most notable were the late Maurice Genevoix's *Trente mille jours* (Thirty-thousand Days); Henri Vincenot's *Mémoires d'un enfant du rail* (Memoirs of a Railroad Child); and two volumes about Charles de Gaulle, Olivier Guichard's *Mon Général* and Maurice Schumann's *Un certain dix-huit juin.* Outstanding biographies were *Talleyrand,* by André Castelot, and *Balzac,* by Maurice Bardéche.

Other words deserving special mention were Vincent Descombes' exhaustive *L'Inconscient malgré lui: 45 ans de philosophie française* (The Unconscious in Spite of Itself: 45 Years of French Philosophy); and the humorous, satiric *Propos secrets* (Secret Talks), by *enfant terrible* Roger Peyrefitte, who reveals some of the scandals and secrets of French society and government during the Fifth Republic.

Poetry. A major event was the publication of Eugène Guillevic's *Autres* (Others), a collection of his laconic, humorous poems, fables, and short dialogues. The year also saw the publication of a series of revealing conversations with Guillevic, entitled *Vivre en Poésie* (To Live in Poetry). Four noteworthy collections by promising younger poets came out in 1980: *La branche la lumière* (The Branch, The Light) by Jean Luc Peurot; *L'or suspect* (Suspect Gold) by Jean Marie Pedron; *Entrevoir* (Perceive) by Paul de Roux; and *Leçons des ténèbres* (Lessons from Darkness) by Jean-Pierre Colombi.

PIERRE E. BRODIN
Lycée Français de New York

German Literature

The West German literature of 1980 could be described as a literature of uncertainty. While the older writers enjoyed the German Federal Republic's jealously guarded freedom of expression, the younger ones felt uneasy about their state and their society.

Fiction. An older writer like Horst Bienek, in *Zeit ohne Glocken,* could detach himself from the prewar past, and Hermann Lenz, in *Konstantinsallee,* could poetically analyze the painful transition from the Hitler debacle to the new democracy. Günter Grass (*Kopfgeburten*) was even able to treat the present humorously.

However, for younger authors even a conditional acceptance of existence proved too difficult, and they confined themselves to raising questions. This assessment holds true for Bruno Hillebrand, Peter Handke, Gert Janke, and even ambitious Matthias Mander (*Der Kasuar*). The surrealism of Herbert Rosendorfer (*Das Messingherz*) and the sturdy Swiss realism of Adolf Muschg (*Noch ein Wunsch*) appealed only to special groups.

Nonfiction. Two noteworthy autobiographies were published. Hans Leip, the octogenarian author of *Lilli Marleen,* contributed *Das Tanzrad,* and Elias Canetti produced *Die Fackel im Ohr.*

In the final volume of Theodor Schieder's *Handbuch der Europäischen Geschichte,* Europe's loss of prestige since World War I was addressed. Special episodes of recent history were elucidated by Felix Hirsch (*Stresemann*), Edmund Theil (*Rommels verheizte Armee*), Helmuth Spaeter (*Die Brandenburger*), and Paul Carell and Günter Böddeker (*Die Gefangenen*). Scholars and journalists interested in the non-European world wrote excellent general works on China (Willy Kraus, *Wirtschaftliche Entwicklung und sozialer Wandel in der Volksrepublik China*), Indochina (Peter Scholl-Latour, *Der Tod im Reisfeld*), Africa (Dieter Rösner, *Das Ringen um Afrika*), and the developing countries (Ferdinand Otto Miksche, *Bis 2000*).

In the sociological field, Walter Wannenmacher's *Der zerdachte Staat* and Winfried Schlaffke's *Abseits-Die Alternativen* were important additions. A new encyclopedia of the fairy tale was begun by Kurt Ranke.

A heated psychoanalytic controversy was brought on by the Vienna journalist Karin Oberholzer's *Gespräche mit dem Wolfsmann*. Even more doubtful appeared Richard Fester's feminist theses in *Weib und Macht*. Johannes Irmscher's *Lexikon der Antike* was a most biased Marxist treatment of antiquity.

Poetry. Although the general public's attention was not to be counted on, German poets brought out a number of interesting collections. Their themes reached from the conservative Lutheranism of Arnim Juhre (*Wir stehn auf dünner Erdenhaut*) to the unsentimental love lyrics of Christoph Meckel (*Säure*); from the pronounced leftism of Peter Rümkorf (*Haltbar bis ans Ende*) to the radical introspection of Karin Kiwus (*Angenommen später*) and Jürgen Becker (*In der verbleibenden Zeit*).

Drama. The only noteworthy new dramas were Thomas Bernhard's *Weltverbesserer* and Ernst Jandl's *Aus der Fremde*. Rolf Hochhuth's latest dramatic editorial, *Juristen,* was disappointing, and performances of posthumous plays by Else Lasker-Schüler and Marieluise Fleissner did not enhance the repertory.

East Germany. Christa Wolf, a prominent writer from East Germany, was awarded the 1980 Georg Buechner Prize of the [West] German Academy for Language and Poetry. Meanwhile, her East German fellow authors continued to produce more or less subservient works. Their plays, which the theaters were directed to favor, attracted only limited audiences, and talk of a theatrical crisis was common.

ERNST ROSE
Author, "A History of German Literature"

Italian Literature

By 1980, it was widely recognized that the writing of Italian poetry had become more lively and original than the production of prose. One reason may be that fiction—no matter how abstract or experimental—requires a more explicit stand relative to, or at least in acknowledgment of, current social developments and political events. Poetry does not carry so clear a referential requirement. With Italian intellectuals under pressure to conform with the conservative political establishment of the Christian Democratic regime and with the pieties and constraints of the left-wing cultural establishment, it is not surprising that the literature has become vastly elliptical and metaphoric, without clear links to the contemporary social structure. Because fiction writing in Italy today requires a greater effort at, and perhaps is more criticized for, nonconformism, poetry has fared much better.

The pressures of the political and cultural establishments may help explain why the dramatic changes in contemporary Italian society, such as the proliferation of terrorist violence and the alarming increase in heroin addiction, have yet to be treated in any scholarly work or serious fictional mode. In 1980, they were left to book-length journalistic compilations.

While the contemporary Italian novel in general is stubbornly persistent, diligent, traditional—and ultimately out of focus and somewhat irrelevant—the art of short story writing, once a glory of Italian literature, seemed on the verge of demise. Recent efforts in the genre by old-fashioned narrators tended to prove, rather than disprove, the point.

There were, to be sure, noteworthy new works of fiction and some signs of a renewal. Italian writers outside Italy, such as the Mexico-based Carlo Coccioloi, who until recent times were largely ignored, became the subject of serious critical attention in Italy. Another highlight abroad was the first translation into English of the 1954 *Fiabe Italiane* (Italian Fables) by Italo Calvino, one of Italy's most respected living writers.

Meanwhile, poetry did have its own problems. The obsession with public performance, which again had its peak in summer readings at Rome's Piazza di Siena, seemed to manifest a growing lack of discernment of the best serious work being done. Another fashionable vehicle, the anthology of contemporary works, was beset by the arbitrariness and categorization of many selections, reflecting the narrow preoccupations of critical coteries.

In contrast to the flux and transition in creative writing were the richness, depth, and variety of themes in scholarly essays and books in the humanities. These ranged from studies in ancient philosophy—such as the posthumously published *Eraclito* (Heraclitus), the third book in Giorgio Colli's series *La sapienza greca* (Greek Thought)—to histories of film and theater—such as a two-volume documentation of the work of director Luchino Visconti. Especially lively was the revival of scholarly work and debate in the field of religious studies. In addition to straightforward theological treatises, there were new historical and sociological explorations.

PAOLO VALESIO
Yale University

Japanese Literature

The year 1980 saw publication of numerous books dealing with World War II and with the Edo Period (1603–1868) but fewer works related to the centuries preceding it. A shift of interest from Japan's distant past to more recent history and toward greater internationalism was apparent in all genres.

Fiction. Japanese fiction in 1980 was more cosmopolitan than ever, with many characters and plots set in faraway locales. Reiko Mori's *Mokkinbaado no iru Machi* (A Town with Mockingbirds), winner of the 1980 Akutagawa Prize, describes the lonely lives of Japanese war brides in a small American town. Masaaki Tachihara's *Kiro* (Homebound) tells of an art dealer's wanderings in Europe, while Yasushi Inoue's *Ryūsa* (The Desert) is a romantic tale about an archaeologist who marries a concert pianist in Paris and travels to ancient ruins in Asia and the Middle East. Shūsaku Endō's *Samurai* recounts the journey of Japanese envoy Tsunenaga Hasekura to Rome in 1613 and its tragic aftermath. Counter to the trend was the highly acclaimed *Dōjidai Geemu* (A Contemporary Game) by Kenzaburō Ōe, in which the protagonist returns to the myths and history of his village to criticize Japanese values.

Nonfiction. The Ōyake Sōichi Nonfiction Prize was awarded to a newcomer, Fumiko Halloran, for her reportage on the U.S. capital, *Washington no Machi kara*. In literary history and criticism, the most outstanding new contributions were Shūichi Katō's *Nihonbungakushi Josetsu Ge,* which traces the development of Japanese literature from 1568 to the present, and Hajime Shinoda's *Nihon no Gendai Shōsetsu* (Contemporary Japanese Fiction). One of the year's most compelling works was *Shikeishū no Kiroku* (A Record of Condemned Criminals) by Otohiko Kaga, who had won a prize in 1979 for a novel about men on death row. The new book is a study by a prison psychiatrist of 145 men awaiting execution.

Poetry. The new decade started with impressive gains in status and number of women poets. Women dominated the poetry scene, publishing excellent new collections, critical biographies of women poets, and numerous poetry magazines of their own, and receiving a large number of prizes. Major poetry magazines praised their achievements in featured articles and special issues. The increasing popularity of tanka and haiku had some critics worried about the inevitable decline in quality or even the disappearance of professional poets.

Drama. The 1980 season saw the production of several brilliant comedies. Hisashi Inoue, who received the 1980 Yomiuri Literature Award for a 1979 comedy, *Kobayashi Issa,* presented another hilarious play, *Iihatoobo no Gekiressha* (Drama-train of Iihatoobo), based on the life of poet Kenji Miyazawa. Kansei Komatsu's comical play about Tokyo policemen, *Shisatu Yūgi* (The Stabbing Game), and Sugako Hashida's farce *Rikon* (Divorce) were also well received.

EMIKO SAKURAI, *University of Hawaii*

Soviet Literature

One of the issues that continued to loom large on the Soviet literary scene in 1980 was the phenomenon of the so-called "village prose" (*derevenskaia proza*).

The preoccupation of many writers with aspects of rural life steeped in peasant tradition, religion, individualism, and the instinct for private ownership was heatedly debated when the doctrine of Socialist Realism was introduced in the early 1930s. It was officially proclaimed that works expressing these rural sentiments were reactionary and anti-revolutionary. The social command to writers was to produce works glorifying collectivization and a new type of literary hero, the kolkhoz worker. During and after World War II the issue remained relatively dormant, as the majority of works were devoted to themes associated with the war experience. However, the dichotomy between individualism and collectivism and the attachment to the traditional values of country life never totally ceased to exist. Over the years, more and more writers, especially those of the younger generation, touched upon some of the private, individual aspects of Soviet rural life. During the 1970s, the number of stories and novels emphasizing these officially nonexistent aspects of country life increased markedly. One of the most talented writers of this genre, V. Shukshin, attained a tremendous popularity. In 1980, his *Rasskazy* (Stories) was published in a mass edition of more than a million copies. However, other writers of this genre, such as Rasputin, Soloukhin, and Abramov, have been criticized for their lack of a correct social perspective.

Apparently the issue caused some official concern, as efforts were made to channel the stream of village prose in the right direction. In 1980, a number of articles in leading periodicals praised the freshness and vigor of some village prose authors, but expressed hope that they would find a broader, more "civic-minded" perspective and not lose sight of the social and political reality in which the real hero must be the collective. Stronger warnings were heard in a "Round Table" discussion among writers, editors, and political leaders published in the New Year edition of the *Literary Gazette*. At the end of the discussion, Oleg Poptsov, editor of the powerful journal *Agriculture,* suggested to Soviet writers that they reread party documents on the subject. Works during the year provided evidence that his advice was taken to heart. In a "documentary novel," *Rasskazhi pole* (Tell us, Field), Fedor Morgun paints an ideologically "correct" picture of Soviet country life—an agricultural collective in which there is no room for "obsolete" sentiments; actual party documents are included. Anatol Anaiev's *Gody bez voiny* (Years without War) is similar in ideological emphasis.

Siberia continued to fascinate many writers in the same way as the American West fascinated many U.S. artists. In *Strogovy* (The Strogovs), Georgi Markov follows the beginning of the revolutionary movement in a Siberian village. M.D. Sergeev's novel *Sviazi vremeni* (Ties of Time) also takes place in Siberia, and the entire March issue of the periodical *Soviet Literature* is devoted to the region.

An important event in poetry was the long-awaited publication of a selection by Anna Akhmatova in the prestigious *Biblioteka Poeta* (Poet's Library). Of contemporary poets, Robert Rozhdzhestvenskii had published a two-volume edition of collected works, and Yevgeni Yevtushenko had two volumes published, *Svarka vzryvom* (Welding by Exploding) and *Doroga ukhodiashchaia vdal'* (The Road Leading into Distance).

ZBIGNIEW FOLEJEWSKI, *University of Ottawa*

Spanish and Spanish-American Literature

The fourth annual Cervantes Prize, one of the Hispanic world's most prestigious prizes for literature, was awarded to both Jorge Luis Borges, the patriarch of Spanish-American letters, and Gerardo Diego, one of the last surviving members of Spain's poetic Generation of 1927.

Fiction. Major novelists whose works were published during 1980 included Juan Goytisolo (*Makbara*); the Cuban Guillermo Cabrera Infante (*La Habana para un infante difunto*); Francisco Umbral (*Los helechos arborescentes*); the Chilean José Donoso (*El lugar sin límites*); Ramón Sender (*La mirada inmóvil*); the Mexican Carlos Fuentes (*Una familia lejana*); and Juan Benet (*Saúl ante Samuel*).

Significant prize-winning novels were the Uruguayan Juan Carlos Onetti's *Dejemos hablar al viento* (Spain's National Critic's Prize); the poetess Carmen Conde's *Soy la madre* (Ateneo de Sevilla Prize); Juan Ruiz Rico's *Ejercicios para romper una muñeca* (Eulalio Ferrer Prize); and Juana Trulla's *Una mujer* (Círculo Mercantil de Almería Prize).

Other noteworthy novels that appeared included Manuel Vicente's *Angeles o neófitos;* Luis Berenguer's posthumous *Tamatea, novia del otoño;* the Ecuadorian Pedro Jorge Vera's dictator novel, *El pueblo soy yo;* Montserrat Roig's feminist *Ramona, adiós;* Gabriel García Badell's *Nuevo auto de fe;* Feranando Savater's *Criaturas del aire;* and works by the new novelists Elena Santiago (*Acidos días*) and Raúl Ruiz (*El tirano de Taormina*).

Important short-story collections published included the playwright Lauro Olmo's *Golfos de bien,* the Peruvian Carlos Eduardo Zavaleta's *Un día en muchas partes del mundo,* and José Fernández Santos' *A orillas de una vieja dama.*

Nonfiction. Significant essay collections published during 1980 were Miguel Delibes' *Mis amigas las truchas;* the Cuban Alejo Carpentier's *Bajo el signo de Cibeles,* edited by Julio Rodríguez Puértolas; the Argentinian Ernesto Sábato's *Apologías y rechazos;* and Fernando Díaz-Plaja's edition of *Si mi pluma valiera tu pistola.*

Important scholarly publications included Benito Varela Jácome's *Alas, 'Clarín';* the Uruguayan Nelson Martínez Díaz' *Diccionario privado de Mariano José de Larra;* William H. Shoemaker's *La crítica literaria de Galdós;* Diego Martínez Torron's *Variables poéticas de Octavio Paz;* Rafael Martínez Nadal's *Cuatro lecciones sobre Federico García Lorca;* Juan Ignacio Ferreras' *Fundamentos de sociología de la literatura;* and Bernard Sese's *Antonio Machado.*

Poetry. The most significant poetic publication was José Bergamín's *Poesías casi completas,* which, although belated, served to add another important name to the list of the lyrical Generation of 1927. Other major poetic works included Ramón de Garciasol's *Memoria amarga de la paz de España* and *Segunda selección de mis poemas;* Gloria Fuertes' *Historia de gloria, amor, humor y desamor;* Alfonso Canales' *El puerto;* Gabino-Alejandro Carriedo's *Nuevo Compuesto, descompuesto viejo;* José Agustín Goytisolo's *Los pasos del cazador* and *Salmos al viento;* Rafael Montesinos' collected verse, *Poesía, 1944–1979;* Justo Jorge Padrón's *Otesmita;* and Angel Gonzalez' *Poemas.*

Major prizes for poetry were awarded to the Costa Rican poet Laureano Albán for *Herencia del otoño* (Adonais Prize) and to the established poet Luis Rosales for *Diario de una resurrección* (National Critic's Award).

Other significant poetic publications were Antonio Porpetta's *La huella en la ceniza,* Clara Janes' *Antología personal,* Lázaro Santana's *Las aves,* the Argentinian Ricardo Aduriz' *Torre del homenaje,* Miguel Fernández' *Las flores de Paracelso,* Angel García López' *Auto de fe,* Joaquín Galán's *Ni el desorden del fuego,* Octavio Uña's *Castilla, plaza mayor de soledades,* Antonio Hernández' *Metaory,* and Santiago Castelo's *Memorial de ausencias.* Impressive young poets whose work appeared were Miguel Angel Molinero (*Venir de lejos*) and the Argentinian Jorge Sánchez Aguilar (*Tierra sin mal*).

Theater. Major prizes awarded for theater were the Juan Ruiz de Alarcón Prize, won by the Mexican playwright Maruxa Vilalta for *Historia de él;* and the Lope de Vega Prize, awarded to Marcial Suárez Fernández for *Dios está lejos.*

Noteworthy were theatrical collections published by major dramatists. These included Francisco Nieva's *Malditos sean Coronada y sus hijos,* edited by Antonio González; the first volume of Fernando Arrabal's *Obras Completas;* and Alfonso Sastre's important *Teatro político.*

ALFRED RODRIGUEZ
The University of New Mexico

LONDON

Environmental concerns were evident in London during 1980. The city also witnessed some traditional royal pageantry, in honor of the 80th birthday of Queen Elizabeth, the Queen Mother; a rebuff for property speculators and promoters of high-rise office blocks; a move toward more careful thought regarding the preservation of the character of London; and the election of Col. Ronald Gardner-Thorpe, 63-year-old underwriting member of Lloyd's of London and former soldier, as Lord Mayor.

Proposed Construction. After a six-month inquiry, Minister for the Environment Michael Heseltine rejected all six planning applications for the Coin Street site on the south bank of the Thames near Blackfriars Bridge. To almost universal approval, Heseltine rejected, as well, the planning application of European Ferries Ltd. to build a 500-ft- (152-m-) high green glass tower on the downstream side of Vauxhall Bridge. The proposed "green giant" had aroused keen protest from citizens determined to preserve the banks of the river Thames from what seemed visual ruin.

Covent Garden. Lively national and international approval, however, surrounded the opening in June of the elegantly restored market buildings of Covent Garden. The buildings, which for years had housed London's fruit and vegetable markets, were transformed into a thriving collection of specialty shops, restaurants, and pubs. Around the piazza, which is still dominated by St. Paul's Covent Garden, a church designed by architect Inigo Jones in the 17th century, people now browse in bookshops

that were once banana warehouses, or sniff old English perfumes where flowers were originally sold. The London Transport Museum opened an exhibit of old buses, trains, and tram cars in the renovated Victorian cast iron and glass building that had been built by William Cubitt in 1871 to house the Flower Market.

The Council of Europe chose the revitalized Covent Garden area as an outstanding example of life returning to an inner city.

MAUREEN GREEN, *Author and Journalist*

LOS ANGELES

In 1980, Los Angeles became the second largest city in the United States, as it gained slightly in population and Chicago continued its decade-long sharp decline. In September, the city began a year-long celebration of the 200th anniversary of its founding.

Politics. Mayor Tom Bradley was an early supporter of the reelection bid of President Jimmy Carter. In October, Bradley announced that he would run for a third four-year term in 1981.

Education. After a difficult 15-month search, the University of Southern California chose a new president, James H. Zumberge, 56, a geologist and former head of Southern Methodist University (Dallas, TX). The great educational conflict of the year, however, was over the means by which to integrate the public school system. The school board was badly divided, but a majority of members favored an all-voluntary approach. After long conflict, a Superior Court judge put his own compulsory plan into effect.

Local Government. Four former officials of the dissolved city-county antipoverty agency were indicted by a federal grand jury in August on various charges involving alleged kickbacks, embezzlement, and bribery. By late in the year the city still had not formed a new agency, although Los Angeles County had.

Electrical workers in the city's vast Department of Water and Power struck in August but were back on the job in five days. The settlement was expected to set a pattern for other city employees.

In urban renewal, Bunker Hill Towers, originally built to attract middle-class suburbanites back into the city, were made into condominiums with an average unit price of $163,900.

Sports. The Los Angeles Lakers won the 1979–80 National Basketball Association (NBA) championship. UCLA and USC both were banned from competing in the Rose Bowl after being found guilty of various recruiting and academic violations. After many years of dissatisfaction, the Los Angeles Rams of the National Football League (NFL) moved from the Los Angeles Coliseum to Anaheim Stadium in Orange County.

CHARLES R. ADRIAN
University of California, Riverside

Covent Garden's 150-year-old market hall was transformed into a three-level shopping complex.
UPI

LOUISIANA

Sen. Russell Long (D) and seven of the state's eight representatives were returned to Congress by the voters. Reelected were Reps. Robert Livingston (R), first district; Lindy Boggs (D), second; W. J. "Billy" Tauzin (D), third; Jerry Huckaby (D), fifth; Henson Moore (R), sixth; John Breaux (D), seventh; and Gillis Long (D), eighth. In the fourth district newcomer Charles "Buddy" Roemer III (D) ousted Claude "Buddy" Leach, who was acquitted of charges of vote-buying that stemmed from his 1978 election, but still faced trial for allegedly accepting illegal campaign contributions. Some 35 persons were convicted of buying votes in Leach's 1978 election. Representative Tauzin had previously won a special election to fill the seat vacated by David Treen, who in 1979 was the first Republican to be elected governor since Reconstruction.

The Legislature. Several of Governor Treen's programs were passed by the heavily Democratic legislature, but he was forced into a struggle with powerful state Senate leaders over the annual capital outlay bill. Although the state's fiscal year spending was a record $5,200,000,000, Treen vetoed several spending measures which he said amounted to pork barrel projects. Senate leaders contended the projects were needed and it would be better to fund them now, before inflation made them more expensive.

Among Treen's programs approved, however, were a reform bill to weed out incompetent teachers, reforms of election laws and the process through which the state spends money on new projects, a record $100 million state income tax cut, and a 9.7% teachers' pay raise. A bill regulating abortions also was enacted. The administration held up action on a measure that would ban strikes by the state's public employees.

Scandals. New political scandals surfaced in Louisiana. In addition to Representative Leach's case, former state Agricultural Commissioner Gil Dozier was convicted of extortion and racketeering and was sentenced to ten years in prison and fined $25,000. The sentence was the stiffest given a Louisiana official since the historic Louisiana scandals broke in the late 1930s, following the Huey Long era.

Louisiana was one of the focuses of the FBI's "Brilab" (bribery and labor) investigation. Five persons, including alleged rackets boss Carlos Marcello of New Orleans, were indicted by a federal grand jury. Others indicted were Charles E. Roemer II, who was the top administrative assistant to former Gov. Edwin Edwards; Aubrey W. Young, who had held several minor state posts; New Orleans attorney Vincent Marinello; and Washington, DC, lobbyist I. Irving Davidson. The men faced trial early in 1981 for allegedly taking part in a scheme to obtain public insurance contracts through bribery and kickbacks. In their investigation, FBI agents posed as insurance agents. Others named as being investigated but not indicted were former Governor Edwards and several of the gubernatorial candidates of 1979, including former Lt. Gov. James E. Fitzmorris. Defense lawyers claimed that the federal officials investigating the case leaked details to local news media. As the year ended, a federal judge was studying grand jury transcripts to determine whether the news stories influenced the jury's proceedings and whether the reporters should be subpoenaed to testify about their sources.

New Orleans. A growing concern with crime and, toward the end of the year, tension between police and blacks troubled New Orleans. During the year, several tourists and residents were murdered in the city's tourist areas, including the historic French Quarter and the Louisiana Superdome grounds, prompting some officials to express concern for the city's image. Tourism is second only to the port among New Orleans' industries. Late in the year, a policeman was found shot to death in his squad car in a heavily black area. A few days later, police killed two men and a woman in the neighborhood, saying the men were suspects in the officer's murder. Blacks said the three were murdered by police and threatened marches and boycotts, but police said all three persons had fired at police first. Police chief James Parsons resigned shortly afterward, and in December a sniper fired from an all black housing project into a police building. No one was injured.

Geology-Weather. An unusual geological phenomenon occurred late in the year when an oil well punctured a giant salt mine dome near New Iberia, causing a lake to drain into the underground mine and some nearby tropical gardens, one of the area's major tourist attractions, to collapse. Drilling rigs were sucked into the ground.

JOSEPH W. DARBY III
"The Times-Picayune," New Orleans

LOUISIANA · Information Highlights

Area: 48,523 sq mi (125 675 km^2).

Population (Jan. 1980 est.): 4,055,000.

Chief Cities (1976 est.): Baton Rouge, the capital, 302,-236; New Orleans, 580,959; Shreveport, 187,583.

Government (1980): *Chief officers*—governor, David Treen (R); lt. gov., Bobby Freeman (D). *Legislature*—Senate, 39 members; House of Representatives, 105 members.

Education (1979–80): *Enrollment*—public elementary schools, 555,095 pupils; public secondary, 245,340; colleges and universities, 153,812 students. *Public school expenditures*, $1,449,700,000 ($1,669 per pupil).

State Finances (fiscal year 1979): *Revenues*, $4,589,-000,000; *expenditures*, $4,123,000,000.

Personal Income (1979): $30,467,000,000; per capita, $7,583.

Labor Force (June 1980): *Nonagricultural wage and salary earners*, 1,530,900; *unemployed*, 130,800 (7.6% of total force).

LUXEMBOURG

In 1980, the leaders of Luxembourg continued their campaign to make the duchy the permanent seat of the expanded European Parliament. A new building capable of accommodating the larger number of deputies was completed in the spring. In September 1980, it housed the first session of the 410-member body. (Previously there were only 198 deputies.) Competition for the assembly remained strong; Strasbourg, France, the alternate host city, and Brussels also bid for the permanent site. Loss of the parliament and its secretariat, which together employ some 5,000 Luxembourgers, would be a blow to the prestige and economy of the duchy.

On Jan. 1, 1980, Foreign Minister Gaston Thorn, a former prime minister and a three-time chairman of the European Community (EC) Council of Ministers, took over as president of the EC Commission.

Luxembourg also sought to establish itself as the logical site for an eventual EC central bank. It already is the home of the EC Investment Bank. The duchy is negotiating new double taxation agreements with other nations to strengthen its position as a financial capital. Banking provided more than two thirds of Luxembourg's corporate tax receipts in 1979 and nearly as many jobs as the EC institutions.

Employment in the steel sector fell in 1980, as ARBED, the chief producer group, followed its plan of reducing the payroll by 1,600 workers by 1983. Despite recession in the steel, synthetic fiber, and construction industries, however, unemployment was nearly nonexistent. Some 48% of the labor force was employed in government or the delivery of services, 46% in industry and commerce, and 6% in agriculture. The estimated economic growth rate for 1979 was 3.2%, while the inflation rate of 5% for that year was one of the lowest in Europe.

J. E. Helmreich, *Allegheny College*

─── **LUXEMBOURG · Information Highlights** ───

Official Name: Grand Duchy of Luxembourg.
Location: Western Europe.
Area: 999 sq mi (2 586 km²).
Population (1980 est.): 400,000
Chief Cities (1977 est.): Luxembourg, the capital, 76,500; Esch-sur-Alzette, 26,200; Differdange, 17,300.
Government: *Head of state,* Jean, grand duke (acceded 1964). *Head of government,* Pierre Werner, prime minister (took office July 1979). *Legislature* (unicameral)—Chamber of Deputies.
Monetary Unit: Franc (28.78 francs equal U.S.$1, Aug. 1980).
Manufactures (major products): Steel, rubber products, synthetic fibers.
Agriculture (major products): Grains, potatoes, livestock, dairy products.
GNP Per Capita (1978 est., U.S.$): $10,410.
Foreign Trade (1979, U.S.$, includes Belgium): *Imports,* $60,410,000,000; *exports,* $56,258,000,000.

MAINE

National and state elections captured the Maine spotlight in 1980.

Politics. The state partially followed national trends. At the national level, Ronald Reagan won over President Jimmy Carter. Two Republicans, Olympia Snowe and David Emery, were returned to the U.S. House of Representatives. On the state level, the national trends were resisted and a Democratic majority was elected to the state legislature: 84 Democrats and 67 Republicans in the House and 16 Democrats and 17 Republicans in the Senate.

On the five referendum questions, the voters approved issuing bonds to make school buildings more energy efficient, to deal with legislative apportionment, to regularize dates for state referenda, and to make changes in the appointment of probate judges. A bond issue to improve the efficiency of the buildings in the state court system was rejected.

Earlier in September a referendum was forced by antinuclear forces aimed at closing the Maine Yankee Atomic Power Plant. Petitioners had gathered enough signatures to call the continued operation of the plant into question. The opponents of nuclear power pointed to its dangers: radiation, toxic wastes, the impossibility of evacuation in case of an accident, and the dangerous long-term health effects. Central Maine Power Company and its allies pointed to the positive accomplishments of nuclear power and the decided possibility of even higher electric rates were Maine Yankee to close. The economic arguments of the proponents were particularly telling in light of high inflation. The result was a victory for nuclear advocates by a margin of 3 to 2. The opponents of nuclear power said, however, that this was not their last attempt to rid the state of nuclear energy. In a poll taken by the University of Maine during the debate, it was evident that a majority of people, while not wishing to close Maine Yankee, did not want any more nuclear plants built in the state.

After President Carter named Sen. Edmund S. Muskie (*see* Biography) secretary of state, Gov. Joseph E. Brennan named District Judge George J. Mitchell to fill out the term.

Smuggling. Drug smuggling continued to plague the coast of Maine. In October, 34 T (31 t) of marijuana were seized and 23 people were arrested on an estate in Stonington. Prior to the smuggling operation, the smugglers had purchased the estate in this coastal community for

─── **MAINE · Information Highlights** ───

Area: 33,215 sq mi (86 027 km²).
Population (Jan. 1980 est.): 1,100,000.
Chief Cities (1970 census): Augusta, the capital, 21,945; Portland, 65,116; Lewiston, 41,779; Bangor, 33,168.
Government (1980): *Chief Officer*—governor, Joseph E. Brennan (D). *Legislature*—Senate, 33 members; House of Representatives, 151 members.
Education (1979–80): *Enrollment*—public elementary schools, 155,882 pupils; public secondary, 71,941; colleges and universities, 42,912 students. *Public school expenditures,* $434,000,000 ($1,740 per pupil).
State Finances (fiscal year 1979): *Revenues,* $1,234,000,000; *expenditures,* $1,183,000,000.
Personal Income (1979): $7,722,000,000; per capita, $7,039.
Labor Force (May 1980): *Nonagricultural wage and salary earners,* 415,900; *unemployed,* 35,200 (7.1% of total force).

several hundred thousand dollars. Apparently some of those arrested were members of the Zion Coptic Church, a Florida-based cult which employs the drug in its ceremonies.

Other Issues. Another unsettling problem is the plight of Aroostook county potato farmers. Canadian potatoes have been imported into Maine and New England and sold at prices the Aroostook farmers cannot meet. As an act of frustration, some farmers drove their potato-filled trucks to the Maine-Canada border and then dumped their cargoes in the roads at the border stations. Their behavior was aimed at attracting both state and federal attention to their difficulties. Similar clashes have occurred with Maine woodsmen who resent the hiring of Canadian woodsmen to work at rates lower than those paid to local laborers.

Two situations of some importance were ameliorated during the year. The Indian Land Claims dispute finally was settled. Congress passed legislation which was signed by President Carter approving about $81 million to be employed by the Maine Indians to buy land from private owners and to provide a trust fund for the benefit of the Indians. Through the efforts of both sides and Congress, the cloud over the titles of much Maine land was lifted.

The second situation was the continued operation of Loring Air Force Base in Limestone. It was not closed as had been feared, but its usefulness may be challenged again by the Reagan administration.

Longley. Former Gov. James B. Longley, who was elected as an independent and served from 1975–79, died of cancer in August.

EDWARD SCHRIVER
University of Maine, Orono

MALAYSIA

Earnings from oil, tin, rubber, and oil palm increased. Ethnic tensions over the government's policies continued.

Politics. The National Front government, led by the Malay-based United Malays National Organization (UMNO), was shocked by a large peasant protest January 23 which became a riot in Alor Setar, capital of the predominantly Malay rice-growing state of Kedah. The protest was against a coupon system to increase peasant revenue and savings. Inadequate implementation was blamed by the government and the program was quickly revised.

Blame also was placed on the opposition Islamic Party. A subversive Holy Army was uncovered by the government and a number of Islamic Party leaders were detained. Shortly afterward UMNO won a parliamentary by-election in an Islamic Party stronghold in Kedah.

Central to government concern was the New Economic Policy aimed at redressing the economic imbalance between indigenous peoples (primarily Malay) and the immigrant Chinese and Indians. On the Malay side there is suspicion that not enough is being done, despite preferences in education and employment.

The issue surfaced within the ruling party in the midyear election for president of the UMNO Youth. Harun Idris, who was serving a six-year prison term for corruption but is seen as a champion of Malay privilege, narrowly was defeated by the incumbent Suhaimi Datuk Kamaruddin, his nephew. The winner was backed strongly by the UMNO leadership.

Non-Malays fear that Malay advancement is coming at their expense. Both Chinese and Indian parties within the National Front were challenged as to their ability to defend the interests of their ethnic constituents. Despite turbulent debates and ongoing tensions, the National Front emerged intact.

The resource-rich East Malaysian states of Sabah and Sarawak remained the scenes of internal party struggles. However, the political skills of Prime Minister Hussein bin Dato Onn apparently defused much of the secession talk of previous years.

Defense. Substantial steps were taken to increase Malaysian military capacity. Previously directed toward counterinsurgency, new programs aimed at preparing for conventional warfare. A new airbase was to be constructed in the northeast peninsular state of Kelantan.

Internal Security. Although not ignoring Vietnam, Malaysia's major concern remained guerrilla remnants of the Malayan Communist Party active on the Thai border. To counter the threat the government has severe internal security laws. Early in the year, a number of persons were executed for possession of firearms. More positively, noted scholar and socialist, Syed Husin Ali, was freed after almost six years of detention.

Foreign Affairs. Seeking to transform Southeast Asia into a zone of peace and neutrality, the government softened criticisms of Vietnam but followed other members of the Association of Southeast Asian Nations (ASEAN) in decrying Vietnamese aggression. Cooperation with Thailand in controlling their mutual border was disrupted when Malaysian military forces were accused of killing innocent Thais.

K. MULLINER, *Ohio University*

MALAYSIA · Information Highlights

Official Name: Malaysia.
Location: Southeast Asia.
Area: 127,315 sq mi (239 746 km²).
Population (1980 est.): 14,000,000.
Chief Cities (1975 est.): Kuala Lumpur, the capital, 500,-000; George Town, 280,000; Ipoh, 255,000.
Government: *Head of state,* Sultan Ahmad Shah (took office April 1979). *Head of government,* Hussein bin Dato Onn, prime minister (took office Jan. 1976). *Legislature*—Parliament: Dewan Negara (Senate) and Dewan Ra'ayat (House of Representatives).
Monetary Unit: Ringgit (Malaysian dollar) (2.14 ringgits equal U.S.$1, Aug. 1980).
Manufactures (major products): Steel, tin, automobiles, electronic equipment.
Agriculture (major products): Rubber, palm oil, pepper.
GNP (1978 est., U.S.$): $14,900,000,000.

MANITOBA

A continuing population decline helped create a gloomy economic climate, which in turn affected politics and the arts in the province.

Economy. In 1980, migration from the province continued at a rate of more than 3,000 per year. By July 1, the population had fallen to 1,-028,700, compared with 1,031,900 a year earlier. Most of those who left went to the resource-rich provinces of Alberta, Saskatchewan, and British Columbia. The depressed economy was reflected in a bleak real estate market, a predicted government deficit of $200 million, and poor retail sales. Statistics Canada reported that growths in public and private investment, retailing, mineral production, and employment lagged behind those of all other provinces. In the private sector, real estate, furniture, and electronics firms went bankrupt. The 90-year-old *Winnipeg Tribune,* with a circulation of 106,000, was closed in August, putting 365 full-time staff out of work and giving the Thomson-owned *Winnipeg Free Press* a daily newspaper monopoly. The thrice-weekly *Winnipeg Sun* was founded.

In brighter economic news, business boomed at the $24-million Winnipeg Convention Centre, which saw a 32% increase in bookings. Tentative plans to expand the center were announced. Manitoba Hydro reported hydroelectric exports of about $100 million. Canada's first gasohol plant was established at Minnedosa by Mohawk Oil of Calgary, and the federal government announced in late October that $20 million would be spent on an energy research facility at Winnipeg. In mid-April, CanWest Capital Corporation of Winnipeg paid $100 million to buy the Gambles-MacLeod-Steadman chain of stores from owners Gambles-Skogmo of Minneapolis. In October, CanWest resold the three Winnipeg Gambles stores to Zellers of Montreal, owned by the Hudson's Bay Company.

Politics. An October civic election saw Winnipeg Mayor Bill Norris returned to office, beating his closest opponent, Al Golden, by a margin of more than 2-to-1. Provincially, public pressure forced Premier Sterling Lyon to back away from plans to sell publicly owned McKenzie-Steele-Briggs, a Brandon seed company. The Conservative government was bitterly attacked by the opposition New Democratic Party for its poor handling of the economy and its negative attitude to public investment. The opposition, led by lawyer Howard Pawley, began to gear up for an election, expected in 1981.

Arts. The gloomy economic picture extended to the Winnipeg Symphony Orchestra, which saw its accumulated deficit rise to $700,000. In July, provincial trustees were appointed to run the symphony's affairs. Manager Tony d'Amato was fired, and Maestro Piero Gamba, music director for nine years, quit in October. At the Royal Winnipeg Ballet, which ended the season with a $240,000 surplus, ticket sales were up by 40%. At the Manitoba Theatre Centre, artistic director Arif Hasnain was replaced by Richard Ouzounian.

PETER CARLYLE-GORDGE
Manitoba Correspondent, "Macleans" Magazine

MARYLAND

Maryland struggled with economic problems in 1980. When the mild winter gave way to a hot, dry summer, severe crop damage qualified many agricultural areas for disaster status.

Previous state budget surpluses evaporated and Gov. Harry Hughes came in for considerable public criticism when, as Maryland motorists reduced gasoline use, he suggested raising the gas tax. He quickly dropped the idea.

The Economy. The management of McCormick and Co., a Baltimore tea, food, and spice company, turned back a takeover offer by the Swiss drug maker, Sandoz, Ltd., refusing $37 a share when McCormick's stock was priced at $22. A group of shareholders prepared a lawsuit over the company's use of $13 million to buy out Sandoz's 4.8% interest.

Although the state's unemployment rate was lower than the national average, an estimated 150,000 Marylanders were out of work. In September, when the Social Security Administration headquarters near Baltimore offered 75 unskilled jobs paying as little as $7,210 a year, more than 25,000 people—most of them young blacks—stood in line in order to be included in a lottery which selected 225 to be interviewed.

Bethlehem Steel Co. laid off some 3,500 workers for most of the year, a third of the 10,-700 it furloughed nationally. And General Motors laid off nearly 2,000 of more than 4,000 employees at its Baltimore-area mid-size car and light truck assembly plants.

Not all the economic news was bad. GM started a $500 million plant improvement and expansion program aimed at producing a front-wheel drive car for the 1983 model year.

Radiation. At the Baltimore Gas and Electric Company's Calvert Cliffs nuclear-generating plant, there were at least five low-level radiation

---

MANITOBA • Information Highlights

Area: 251,000 sq mi (650 090 km²).
Population (July 1980 est.): 1,028,700.
Chief City (1976 census): Winnipeg, the capital, 560,874.
Government (1980): *Chief Officers*—lt. gov., Francis L. Jobin; premier, Sterling R. Lyon (Progressive Conservative); chief justice, Court of Appeal, Samuel Freedman; Court of Queen's Bench, A. S. Dewar. *Legislature*—Legislative Assembly, 57 members.
Education (1979–80 est.): *Enrollment:* public elementary and secondary schools, 212,400; private schools, 8,-230; Indian (federal) schools, 8,025; post-secondary, 21,150 students. *Total expenditures,* $758,265,000.
Public Finance (1980–81 est.): *Revenues,* $1,900,000,-000; *expenditures,* $2,000,000,000.
Personal Income (average weekly salary, May 1980): $278.35.
Unemployment Rate (July 1980, seasonally adjusted): 5.4%.
(All monetary figures are in Canadian dollars.)

leaks during the year, although officials said they caused no health hazard.

Census. The U.S. Census showed that Maryland's population grew during the 1970s by 5.7%, compared with the national rate of 8.3%. Growth was greatest in suburbs barely within commuting distance of such employment centers as Baltimore and Washington, DC, while slower growth occurred in closer suburbs. Many cities lost population.

Baltimore officials expressed dismay that preliminary census figures set the city's population at 737,557, far below the 1970 total of 905,759. The 1980 figure was revised to 783,320 but appeared subject to further revision in light of a federal judge's order to adjust population figures for Detroit.

Baltimore. So-called "blue" laws were changed to allow department stores in Baltimore and surrounding counties to open on the four Sundays before Christmas. The Baltimore City Council spent months trying to hammer out an acceptable rent-control ordinance after one was adopted in the November 1979 election but voided by court action a short time later.

A homosexual rights bill was defeated unexpectedly in the Baltimore City Council, partly because of pressure from Roman Catholic Archbishop William Borders. It had been designed to ban discrimination in employment, public accommodations, health, and welfare.

A 60-year-old Baltimore county man was acquitted of shooting one teenager to death and wounding another who had been throwing snowballs at his house. The jury ruled he acted in self-defense after he testified about the years of harassment he suffered at the hands of young neighbors.

Elections. Although he failed to attend the first League of Women Voters debate September 21 in Baltimore, Jimmy Carter carried the Maryland presidential vote. Sen. Charles McC. Mathias, Jr., and seven of the state's eight representatives were reelected. A newcomer, Royden Dyson (R), won the House seat in the first district.

------ **MARYLAND · Information Highlights** ------

Area: 10,577 sq mi (27 394 km^2).
Population (Jan. 1980 est.): 4,153,000.
Chief Cities (1970 census): Annapolis, the capital, 30,-095; Rockville, 41,821; Hagerstown, 35,862; (1976 est.): Baltimore, 827,439.
Government (1980): *Chief Officers*—governor, Harry Hughes (D); lt. gov., Samuel W. Bogley (D). *General Assembly*—Senate, 47 members; House of Delegates, 141 members.
Education (1979–80): *Enrollment*—public elementary schools, 386,661 pupils; public secondary, 391,064; colleges and universities, 218,745 students. *Public school expenditures,* $1,701,417,000 ($2,057 per pupil).
State Finances (fiscal year 1979): *Revenues,* $4,977,-000,000; *expenditures,* $4,678,000,000.
Personal Income (1979): $38,706,000,000; per capita, $9,3331.
Labor Force (May 1980): *Nonagricultural wage and salary earners,* 1,639,900; *unemployed,* 150,900 (6.1% of total force).

Mandel. The U.S. Parole Commission said former Maryland Gov. Marvin Mandel, serving three years in a Florida prison camp for political corruption, would be released in May 1982, two years after beginning his sentence.

PEGGY CUNNINGHAM
"The News American," Baltimore

MASSACHUSETTS

Interest in electoral politics dominated events in the Bay State in 1980 even more than usual.

Elections. For the first time since 1956, the state's 14 electoral votes went to the Republican presidential candidate. Independent candidate John Anderson won a larger share of the vote (14%) than in any other state. Political sparks flew earlier in the year, when state Democrats split ranks over the presidential candidacy of Sen. Edward M. Kennedy. Conservative Gov. Edward J. King (D) was an early supporter of President Carter.

Seven of the state's 12 U.S. representatives had either token opposition or none at all. Four other House contests, however, attracted national attention. In the sixth district, first-term Rep. Nicholas Mavroulas fended off a strong challenge from Republican Thomas Trimarco. In the tenth district, Margaret Heckler, the only woman and one of only two Republicans in the state's congressional delegation, defeated Democrat Robert McCarthy.

Two other House races attracted national attention because of the injection into the campaigns of the controversial abortion issue. In the Democratic primary in the fifth district, first-term incumbent James Shannon faced strong opposition from conservative Robert Hatem. In the fourth district, State Representative Barney Frank, a liberal, faced Arthur Clark, the mayor of Waltham. (The seat was contested after church authorities prevented Rep. Robert Drinan, the only priest in the U.S. House, from seeking reelection.) The week before the primaries, Humberto Cardinal Medeiros, archbishop of Boston, circulated a "pastoral letter" urging Catholics to vote against candidates favoring government funding of abortions. The timing of the letter and its obvious tragets—Shannon and Frank—created a furor. In the primaries, however, both Shannon and Frank won party nominations and in November were elected to Congress.

Tax Cut Proposal. Another issue attracting intense interest was a referendum mandating a ceiling on local property taxes. The proposal would limit property taxes to 2½% of the "average fair market value" of real estate in each community. Opponents of the measure argued that poorer cities and towns would lose millions of dollars in revenue. Proponents pointed to the refusal of the state legislature to enact any of several tax reduction schemes proposed in recent years. "Proposition 2½," as it came to be known,

A tall ships exhibition highlighted celebrations of Boston's 350th birthday.

was passed by an overwhelming 2-to-1 margin, and municipal officials scrambled to sort out its implications. Because the referendum enacted a general law as opposed to a constitutional amendment, there were demands for the legislature to revise or repeal the act. The proposition promised continuing controversy during 1981.

Investigating Commission. Reports of widespread corruption in the awarding of state contracts for construction of public buildings led to the formation of an independent investigating commission. The commission heard evidence documenting questionable and illegal practices in the relationships between some state officials and architectural and construction firms. The investigation led to the indictment of several former political figures.

— MASSACHUSETTS • Information Highlights —

Area: 8,257 sq mi (21 386 km²).

Population (Jan. 1980 est.): 5,771,000.

Chief Cities (1976 est.): Boston, the capital, 618,250; Worcester, 168,619; Springfield, 167,577.

Government (1980): *Chief Officers*—governor, Edward J. King (D); lt. gov., Thomas P. O'Neill III (D). *General Court*—Senate, 40 members; House of Representatives, 160 members.

Education (1979–80): *Enrollment*—public elementary schools, 682,752 pupils; public secondary, 348,983; colleges and universities, 396,267 students. *Public school expenditures,* $2,607,960,000 ($2,347 per pupil).

State Finances (fiscal year 1979): *Revenues,* $6,824,-000,000; *expenditures,* $6,377,000,000.

Personal Income (1979): $51,303,000,000; per capita, $8,893.

Labor Force (June 1980): *Total labor force,* 2,893,900; *unemployed,* 191,500 (6.6% of total force).

MBTA Problems. Controversy surrounded the Massachusetts Bay Transportation Authority (MBTA), the state's major public transit facility. On June 9, Governor King fired MBTA Chairman Robert Foster, whom he had appointed to the post in 1979, and replaced him with Secretary of Transportation Barry Locke. Locke, however, became embroiled in a battle with the MBTA Advisory Board (which represents the 53 cities and towns served by the authority) over funding of a large deficit. In October, Locke's position was further complicated when the state attorney general ruled that he was holding the post illegally because he had never been confirmed by the advisory board. The MBTA fiscal crisis continued to deepen as the year ended.

Death Penalty Ruled Out. In a major decision on October 28, the Massachusetts Supreme Judicial Court struck down a law passed the previous year establishing capital punishment for certain crimes. The court found the death penalty "impermissably cruel" under the state constitution, casting doubt on the legality of any future capital punishment legislation.

Higher Education Reorganization. In June, a law was passed which sharply changed the governance of the state public higher education system. The legislation eliminated independent boards of trustees at three institutions and created a "superboard" of 15 regents with authority over the 10-campus state college system and the 15-campus community college system.

See also BOSTON.

HARVEY BOULAY, *Boston University*

MEDICINE AND HEALTH

The year in medicine and health saw continuing research into the causes and treatment of cancer; a scare over the apparent association between toxic shock syndrome (TSS) and the use of tampons; a new technique that offers hope for some infertile women; development of a method for transferring disease immunity from one person to another; important technological developments in diagnostic radiology; new treatments for rheumatoid arthritis; and several new reports on nutrition and drug abuse.

Perhaps the year's most exciting news involved recombinant DNA, or gene-splicing, research. This area offered enormous hope for revolutionary changes in the understanding, prevention, and treatment of disease. (*See* special report, page 244.) The public's concern over the medical effects of environmental problems continued to grow. Contradictory scientific studies were issued on the seriousness of the health problems caused by toxic wastes leaking from the Love Canal at Niagara Falls, NY. (*See* feature article, page 47.) Similarly, a debate raged over the health effects of radioactive leaks from the damaged nuclear facility at Three Mile Island, PA. There was no doubt, however, as to the effects of the summer heat wave across the United States. More than 1,260 deaths were attributed to the high temperatures.

Cancer. New studies have confirmed earlier data that linked heavily chlorinated drinking water and cancer. Chlorine is added to water supplies to kill bacteria and to bleach out undesirable brown colors. Scientists believe that the chlorine reacts with substances in the water to form trihalomethanes, compounds that cause cancer in laboratory animals. According to Dr. Robert Harris of the U.S. Council on Environmental Quality, drinking chlorinated water appears to increase a person's chances of getting gastro-intestinal cancer by 50 to 100%. As a result of such studies, alternate methods of disinfection have begun to replace chlorination in water treatment plants.

In February 1980, the American Cancer Society revised its checkup recommendations for cancer of the cervix, breast, lung, colon, and rectum. The changes were based on updated information on how the diseases develop, as well as on the effectiveness, cost, and risk of the tests. Its recommendation that asymptomatic women do not need Pap smear screenings for cervical cancer more than once every three years drew fire from the American College of Obstetricians and Gynecologists, which continued to support the recommendation of yearly examinations. At a National Institutes of Health (NIH) conference, a compromise recommendation of rescreening at 1- to 3-year intervals was reached. Sexually active women should be tested more frequently than others.

According to Dr. Norman F. Boyd of the Ontario Cancer Institute, breast cancer patients who are overweight have a "significantly reduced" chance of survival compared with patients of normal weight. Boyd's report supported the theory that hormones play an important role in the development and course of breast cancer, since it is known that obesity causes a variety of changes in a person's hormonal status.

Two studies published in 1980 supported earlier research that tetrahydrocannabinol (THC), the active ingredient in marijuana, helps combat nausea in cancer chemotherapy patients. The drug seems to be much more effective in younger patients than in older patients. "Younger people—especially those with previous exposure—tolerate it very well," said Dr. Charles G. Moertel of the Mayo Clinic. In June, the U.S. Food and Drug Administration's (FDA) Oncologic Drugs Advisory Committee voted to recommend wide distribution of THC. It suggested that the drug might help some 50,000 chemotherapy patients.

Gynecology. A ten-year study of more than 16,000 women indicated that "in a population of young, adult, white, middle-class women, the risks of oral contraceptive use appear to be negligible." No increased risk of cancers of the ovary, uterus, or breast was found. Smokers who use birth control pills have an increased risk of chronic heart disease. The study also concluded that oral contraceptives produce an increased, though reversible, risk of high blood pressure. The pill also seems to protect against fibrocystic breast disease.

Scientists at the National Institute of Child Health and Human Development described a new technique that offers hope to women who are unable to conceive because of blocked fallopian tubes. The technique involves removing an egg cell from the ovary with a hollow needle. The egg is placed at the juncture of the fallopian tube and the uterus, thereby bypassing the blocked passageway. The technique, which had not yet been tried in humans, produced five successful pregnancies in monkeys without adverse consequences.

Fibrocystic Breast Disease. Dr. Robert S. London of The Johns Hopkins University School of Medicine reported that vitamin E is effective in treating fibrocystic breast disease. He indicated that dosages of 600 IU of vitamin E per day for 8 weeks relieved symptoms in a majority of the patients tested and resulted in a regression of the disease in some patients. Fibrocystic disease is characterized by liquid-filled cysts in the breast. These often cause pain or tenderness, particularly just before menstruation. Up to 20% of American women have the disease. At least some types of fibrocystic breast disease increase the risk of breast cancer.

Dr. John Peter Minton of The Ohio State University College of Medicine has been successful in treating fibrocystic breast disease by changing his patients' diets. He forbids patients to consume coffee, tea, cola, or chocolate. These contain methylated xanthines, such as caffeine, which Minton maintains interfere with the action of the enzyme phosphodiesterase. The result is stimulated growth of breast tissue and increased metabolism, culminating in the formation of fibrous tissue and fluid. Minton likewise forbids patients to smoke, since nicotine also stimulates breast tissue growth, though in a different way.

Infectious Diseases. Women who use tampons are the main victims of toxic shock syndrome, an acute illness characterized by high fever, vomiting, diarrhea, and a dramatic drop in blood pressure. By late 1980, more than 400 cases of TSS had been recorded in the United States; 40 of these cases were fatal. However, the Federal Center for Disease Control estimated that the actual number of cases is about 2,000 per year. Of the recorded cases, 96% were women; of these, 95% were menstruating when stricken, and almost all were using tampons. The illness appeared to be caused by the bacterium *Staphylococcus aureus*. Researchers are trying to identify

A microbe created by Dr. Ananda Chakrabarty was declared patentable by the U.S. Supreme Court.

UPI

the specific toxin that causes TSS and to develop ways to prevent and cure the illness.

A cluster of 57 cases of Kawasaki disease was reported in Massachusetts. The disease, whose cause remained unknown, usually affects children under the age of 5. It is characterized by acute fever, and cardiovascular complications may occur. The death rate is between 0.5 and 2.8%. Since 1974, when Kawasaki disease was first recognized in the United States, more than 650 cases have been recorded. Earlier clusters occurred in New York City, Rochester, NY, and Los Angeles County. Some investigators feel that the disease is more severe in North America than in Japan, where it was first described. However, it is possible that only the more serious cases are correctly diagnosed in North America.

Researchers at the University of Arkansas showed that it is possible to transfer disease immunity from one person to another. They worked with transfer factor, a protein in white blood cells that protects people from contracting more than once such diseases as mumps and measles. The researchers injected transfer factor into one group of children and a placebo into a second group. Of 15 children in the placebo group who were accidentally exposed to chicken pox, 13 contracted the disease. Of 16 children who received transfer factor and then came in contact with chicken pox, only one became ill.

The first large-scale trial of a new hepatitis B vaccine showed it to be 96% effective in eliciting antibodies and 92.3% effective in protecting high-risk individuals against viral liver disease. The highly purified, inactivated vaccine was developed at the Merck Institute for Therapeutic Research.

Rheumatoid Arthritis. Many rheumatoid arthritis patients get relief from the disease by taking intramuscular injections of gold. Smith-Kline has developed an oral medication called auranofin that contains 29% gold. Two of three trial studies reported significant improvement in patients receiving 6 mg (.01 grains) of auranofin daily. In the third study, about half the patients were helped by the drug, but others had to stop taking the drug because of toxic side effects.

Physicians at Dudley Road Hospital in Birmingham, England, reported that sulfasalazine, a drug composed in part of an aspirin-like compound, is useful in treating rheumatoid arthritis. The physicians theorized that sulfasalazine's usefulness is related to its antibacterial properties and not to its aspirin-like component.

Drug Abuse. The National Institute on Alcohol Abuse and Alcoholism recommended that pregnant women abstain from drinking. Some physicians expressed hope that the advice would not become public policy, feeling that the warning is exaggerated. Although research has indicated a firm connection between heavy drinking and birth defects, there is little evidence that light or moderate drinking affects the fetus.

(*continued on page 352*)

Interferon

Hailed as a potential cure for diseases ranging from the common cold to cancer, the natural drug interferon has been the subject of extensive and costly research which in 1980 created a wave of optimism in the medical community. Although only a few hundred patients have actually received a dose, the development of new techniques for making the rare material, as well as increased funding for research efforts, made large clinical trials seem imminent.

Discovered in 1957 by virologists Alick Isaacs and Jean Lindenmann, interferon is a chemical produced by animal cells infected with a virus. It stimulates neighboring cells to produce compounds to protect against viral infection. It is the reason a person suffering from one viral infection rarely succumbs to another.

The possibility that interferon might be a panacea for viral infections appealed to scientists immediately, but practical difficulties severely limited their research. Cells make only tiny amounts of the substance, and that meager production must be stimulated by either a virus or, as scientists later learned, certain chemicals. An additional problem is that to be effective in clinical treatment, the interferon must come from human cells. The material is exceedingly difficult and enormously expensive to obtain. Most interferon used in recent experiments has come from a laboratory of the Finnish Red Cross in Helsinki, but the American Cancer Society (ACS) has been able to buy only enough to treat half the patients it intended. And although the drug appears to be effective against certain viral diseases, its scarcity and high cost have made routine treatment out of the question.

Still, the promise of interferon in the treatment of cancer has been steadily heightened by important breakthroughs in fundamental research. In the early 1970s, after 10 years of full-time study, Finnish virologist Kari Cantell devised a reliable method to obtain a small amount of interferon from white blood cells. Although the process yields a material that is only 1% interferon, it remains the most successful and widely used method. In 1972, Hans Strander at the Karolinska Institute in Stockholm found that interferon improved the survival rate among 44 patients having a rare and deadly form of bone cancer called osteogenic sarcoma. Smaller studies have indicated that interferon is effective against some cases of breast cancer, cancer of the lymph glands, and a second type of bone cancer, multiple myeloma.

In July 1978, the ACS announced the largest series of clinical trials of interferon ever conducted. It earmarked $2 million for the purchase of enough interferon to treat 150 patients. Ten U.S. hospitals and universities were chosen to test four kinds of cancer—breast cancer, non-Hodgkin's lymphoma, multiple myeloma and melanoma, and aggressive skin cancer. The first reports on those tests were released May 28, 1980. The results indicated that interferon had an anticancer effect but that its success did not equal that reported in earlier studies. The ACS suggested that impaired potency of one or two shipments of interferon that had been freeze-dried instead of liquid frozen may have contributed to the somewhat disappointing results.

The findings of the ACS study underscored how much work still needs to be done. Exactly how interferon fights cancer is still unclear. It seems to slow the growth of cells by inhibiting their division and to boost the activity of the body's natural defense system. Preliminary indications are that interferon causes fewer and less distressing side effects than many cancer drugs, but physicians still need to determine the best dosages and treatment schedules, whether one type of interferon works better than the others, and whether some groups of patients are more responsive than others.

Several recent developments were expected to result in more abundant supplies of interferon for research. At least ten U.S. firms (and others in Europe and Japan) have invested an estimated total of $150 million in production. The ACS, the Interferon Foundation of Houston, and the National Institutes of Health (NIH) have together budgeted more than $20 million for experiments with the treatment.

In 1980, British scientists announced the first technique for substantially purifying interferon without destroying its activity. They found an antibody which will bind only interferon from white blood cells. With that antibody, they can concentrate it 5,000-fold in a single step.

The exact chemical makeup of two of the three known types of human interferon was reported in 1980. Each interferon molecule has sugar groups attached to a string of about 150 amino acids, the basic units of all proteins. Scientists determined the sequence of those amino acids. The length of the molecule makes its laboratory synthesis impractical, but chemical synthesis of a segment may be feasible.

Gene splicing continued to be the most promising source of interferon. Several groups of researchers in 1980 reported the transfer of the appropriate genetic material into bacteria. The bacterial cells, which can be grown in large quantities, have made a protein that seems to be identical to the amino acid chain of human interferon. One company predicted the bacterial production for clinical use during 1981.

See also GENETICS: Recombinant DNA.

JULIE ANN MILLER

New research also challenged the widely held belief that malnutrition is the primary cause of brain damage in alcoholics. Until recently, said Dr. Don Walker of the University of Florida College of Medicine, many people believed "that as long as I take vitamins and eat steak, I can drink all I want." Walker and his associates kept alcohol-imbibing rats on well-balanced diets. Despite good nutrition, the rats showed a 20% loss in brain cells.

One of the newest forms of drug abuse, smoking freebase cocaine, "appears to be extremely hazardous and carries substantial risk of accidents and toxic reactions," said Dr. Ron Siegel of the University of California at Los Angeles (UCLA). To obtain freebase cocaine, the salts and cutting agents in street cocaine are removed chemically, a potentially hazardous process that involves heating flammable solvents. Smoking freebase coke results in a brief but intense high. This is followed by depression, restlessness, and a craving for more cocaine. According to Siegel, smokers become compulsive and unable to control dosage, thereby increasing the risk of overdose. Withdrawal is difficult and is characterized by both physical and mental problems.

Radiology. Technological developments such as positron emission tomography, nuclear magnetic resonance, digital electron radiography, and nuclear medicine cameras hooked to computerized data-processing equipment have fueled a revolution in diagnostic radiology that began with computerized axial tomography (CAT). The new technology is resulting in more noninvasive examination procedures, sparing many patients hospital confinement and surgery.

Varicocele, a varicose condition of the veins in the spermatic cord, is the most common cause of male infertility. Radiologists at Johns Hopkins described a nonsurgical method of treatment that involves the use of silicone balloons to occlude the testicular vein. They reported that the technique resulted in a 50% pregnancy rate in spouses.

Needle biopsy of lesions in the lungs using X-Ray methods was 96.5% accurate in a series of 400 patients. The procedure spared 191 of the patients open chest surgery or other diagnostic procedures, according to radiologist Jack L. Westcott of Hartford (CT) Hospital. The use of small, 20-gauge needles "has practically eliminated the risk of major hemorrhage, and deep as well as superficial lesions of the lung may be approached safely," he said.

Dr. Morris J. Wizenberg of the University of Oklahoma Hospital reported that radiation offers the possibility of cure to the 60 to 70% of men with cancer of the prostate who do not have distant metastasis (spread) of the cancer. The cure rate approaches 100% in patients with very early prostatic cancer.

(*See also* FOOD.)

JENNY TESAR
Science and Medical Writer

Mental Health

The Mental Health Systems Act of 1980 (P.L. 96-398), was enacted October 7 to improve the availability and appropriateness of community-based mental helth care. The law emphasizes services for chronic mentally ill persons, children, the elderly, minorities, and others lacking access to care. Programs to prevent mental illness, protect patients' civil and constitutional rights, and to link more closely mental health with general health care are authorized to begin in October 1981.

An estimated 1.7 million people with chronic mental illness were the focus of a national action plan prepared by the U.S. Department of Health and Human Services. The plan proposed improved financial and social supports.

Basic Research. Neuroscientific advances continued to be made in studies of the brain and behavior. U. S. scientists at several sites developed a technique, Positron Emission Transaxial Tomography (PETT), that yields computer-generated pictures of biochemical activity in the brain. PETT offers improved diagnostic capabilities and further understanding of the brain.

Investigators at the Addiction Research Foundation in Palo Alto, CA, identified and isolated the latest in a line of morphinelike substances, endorphins, that occur naturally in the brain. Named "dynorphin," the agent is estimated to be 200 times more potent than morphine. The discovery represents a major step forward in attempts to synthesize an effective, nonaddictive painkiller.

Clinical Research. Sleep came under renewed scrutiny for clues to patterns of normal behavior as well as clinical disorders. To determine natural biological and biochemical cycles, researchers at Montefiore Hospital in New York City allowed subjects to sleep and wake at will, without such routinized cues as dawn, darkness, and mealtimes. Subjects typically adjusted to a 25-hour "day."

National Institute of Mental Health (NIMH) researchers found that manipulating the normal sleep patterns of clinically depressed patients results in temporary relief of depression, a finding that implicates biological rhythms in this incapacitating and widespread disorder.

Treatment. Increasing public and scientific interest in the effectiveness of treatments for mental illness was answered in part by a University of Colorado review of nearly 500 studies on the outcome of psychotherapy. There was clear evidence that patients benefited substantially from various psychosocial therapies.

Drug treatment of manic-depressive illness advanced with the NIMH finding that carbamazepine, an anticonvulsant drug used in the treatment of nonpsychiatric disorders, is effective in helping depressed patients.

HERBERT PARDES
National Institute of Mental Health

METEOROLOGY

In the 20 years since the 1960 launching of the first successful weather satellite, Tiros I, meteorological data gathering from space has advanced from 25% global coverage to twice-daily, high-resolution, total weather intelligence. Weather satellites provide data on cloud images, atmospheric and surface temperatures, extent of snow and ice cover, and substantial information on large-scale wind fields. Geostationary satellites permit systematic surveillance of even small storm systems every half hour. Satellite observations, combined with conventional surface and radar data, are a significant help in predicting flash floods. The intensity of tropical storms has been successfully gauged from satellite determinations of surface pressure and wind speed. And a successful scheme for forecasting 24-hour changes in maximum wind speeds also has been developed.

Global Weather. Satellites played a crucial role in the success of the first Global Atmospheric Research Program (GARP). The largest international meteorological project ever undertaken, GARP was fully set up in 1979 and has continued to provide a complete view of world weather. The data, which have become important to meteorological researchers, include equatorial wind information gathered by 313 constant level balloons floating at 14 km (8.7 mi). Nine international airlines used a new system of aircraft-to-satellite data relay (ASDAR) for hundreds of additional upper air observations, supplemented by data gathered in remote regions by 17 NASA airplanes.

The most successful part of the experiment was the use of drifting weather buoys, which obtained for the first time adequate weather information from the oceans of the southern hemisphere. The 2 m- (6.6 ft-) long, torpedo-shaped fiberglass buoys are powered by solar panels. Satellites collect the data and fix the position of a buoy within 1 km (.6 mi). Twenty-one buoys were deployed in the Arctic and 15 in the Weddell Sea in the Antarctic. The new information from these buoys immediately improved the accuracy of weather forecasting in Canada and Norway. More accurate forecasts for Australia led to the continuation of the floating buoys in the southern oceans.

Severe Storms. Doppler radar, now a common tool in tornado detection, revealed that wind speeds in a tornado are somewhat lower than estimated earlier. They are typically 40 to 60 meters per second (90–135 mph) and rarely exceed 120 m/sec (269 mph). The tornado vortex was observed to grow down from a thundercloud as a result of a buoyant updraft, usually in the southwest quadrant of the storm. The observation was verified by laboratory simulations in which a stream of fine bubbles released from a tube in the bottom of a vessel of water formed a vortex at the surface and fell to the bottom.

Cloud Physics. Doppler radar, coupled with surface and balloon observations, revealed the fine structure of cyclonic cloud systems in the Pacific Northwest. Updraft zones in warm sectors with vertical speeds of 60 cm (2 ft) per second create thick clouds with ice crystals in the upper zone, where 20% of the precipitation forms. These seed the cloud layers below 5 km (3.1 mi), where 80% of the precipitation originates. The rain cells have banded structures resembling miniature squall lines near the warm front. In the cold frontal zone there are narrow lines of updrafts, moving at 1–3 m/sec (3.3–9.8 ft/sec), which are 1 to 5 km (.6 to 3.1 mi) wide. A surge band at the leading edge of the front, updrafts and downdrafts, and steady production of ice crystals cause heavy precipitation. Lines of convective clouds form post-frontal rain bands.

Atmospheric Electricity. Cloud-to-ground lightning strokes in storms that produce tornadoes intensify after the tornado lifts off the ground. In the 60-minute lifetime of such a storm in Oklahoma, a rate of 3 ground strokes per minute, with a peak of 8 per minute, was noted. The greatest average lightning density to ground—6 per km^2 per year—occurs in south-central Florida. Most areas in the United States average between 2 and 3 strokes per km^2 per year.

The global atmospheric field is a big closed circuit with thunderstorms as the major generator and electrical current flowing through the ionosphere and back down to the ground in fair weather areas. The current is stronger in regions of higher ionization. Thus, mountain ranges, with higher ionization because of cosmic rays in the upper air, receive about 20% of the global current. The whole field is modulated by the stream of electric particles from the sun, known as solar wind, which moves at speeds from 300 to 600 km (186 to 373 mi) per second. As the speed of solar wind decreases, the electric potential in the ionosphere rises; as it increases, the electric potential declines. Solar wind therefore affects the fair weather electric current, and some meteorologists hypothesize that it might influence thunderstorm frequency.

Meteorologists also discovered that the correlation between solar and terrestrial temperatures is better when based upon the umbra (dark center) of sunspots rather than on their surrounding light, the conventional base. The higher this ratio, the warmer the northern hemisphere.

A cavity radiometer on the satellite Nimbus 7 obtained the first daily values of solar energy received by the earth above the atmosphere. The mean value during a six-month interval was 1,-376 watts per square meter, with the variation ranging only three watts per square meter and a day-to-day variability of .05%. Other satellite data of the earth's energy flux now permit meteorologists to obtain the globe's energy budget on a daily basis.

H. E. LANDSBERG, *University of Maryland*

The Weather Year

December 1979–February 1980. The winter of 1979–80 in the United States did not match its two predecessors in severity of temperature anomalies. The Southwest, the northern Plains, and the Great Lakes regions averaged warmer temperatures than expected. Precipitation tended to be very heavy in the Southwest and above average in most of the West. The northeastern part of the country, however, experienced a "snow drought," with some regions receiving less than half the expected amount of precipitation.

Most of western Europe experienced a mild and rainy winter. Seasonal average temperatures were up to 7 °F (4 °C) warmer than expected in portions of West Germany, Austria, and Czechoslovakia. The Saint Bernard Pass in Switzerland recorded its highest December temperatures (44 °F; 7 °C) in 100 years. Precipitation in many areas of the continent was as much as 200% above average. Severe storms wracked southern Italy in mid-December. Venice reported its worst flooding since 1966. Several countries in southeastern Eurasia encountered harsh winter weather conditions. Snow fell south of Amman, Jordan, for the first time in 60 years. In Turkey, temperatures fell as low as −31 °F (−35 °C). Yugoslavia suffered through its worst winter in a decade, with heavy snowfalls in January causing avalanches.

March–May. Spring was excessively wet over the southeastern United States and extremely dry in the northern Plains states. Seasonal average temperatures were 4 °F (2 °C) more than expected in the Northeast, southeastern Florida, and Pacific Northwest. Positive anomalies of 7 °–11 °F (4 °–6 °C) were recorded in the northern Plains, combining with the lack of moisture to damage newly-planted crops. Seasonal temperatures throughout the rest of the continent were slightly below average.

The prevalent storm track remained near its wintertime position, across the southeastern Ohio Valley. Heavy precipitation fell in a broad band throughout the South for all of March. As the month ended, a severe snowstorm battered the High Plains and eastern Rocky Mountains. During April, the northern Great Plains received less than half the expected amount of precipitation, while the South had an overabundance of rainfall. Fifty-six tornadoes were reported through the central Mississippi Valley, affecting parts of 13 states. From April 20–22, the north central United States registered record high temperatures, but the warmth was short-lived. May continued the precipitation pattern of the previous two months. Numerous severe thunderstorms and tornadoes occurred throughout the Texas Panhandle and Ohio Valley during the last week of May. At least 44 tornadoes were sighted on May 29, but few injuries were reported.

Spring was cold and wet in most of southeastern Europe and western Soviet Union. Monthly average temperatures were 4 °–5 °F (2 °–3 °C) below expected levels. March was somewhat wetter than average in most parts of northwestern Europe, but this trend reversed dramatically in the next two months.

The southern coastal provinces of China received excessive rainfall during each month of spring. In the western provinces of Canada, by contrast, dry, warm spring weather brought the worst incidence of forest fires in 25 years. Large areas of Australia were affected by serious drought during the first half of the Southern Hemisphere autumn, with southeastern Australia particularly hard hit.

June–August. The most notable weather event of the summer was the intense, record-breaking heat wave which began in the south central Plains and spread to the Southeastern United States. Seasonal average temperatures were higher than expected throughout the entire continent, with the exception of the Pacific Northwest. In the center of the heat wave area, seasonal temperatures were 6 °–8 °F (3 °–4 °C) above average. Precipitation was as much as 50% below average along much of the East Coast, the northern Plains, and the intermountain region. Severe drought conditions were present in central Missouri and Arkansas, north central Texas, and western Oklahoma.

The great heat wave of 1980 began in Texas during the last week of June. Afternoon temperatures surpassed the 100 °F (38 °C) mark in many locations. In July, the heat wave encompassed most of the country east of the Rockies. The Ohio Valley and the mid-Atlantic states consistently recorded daily maximum temperatures in excess of 90 °F (32 °C). The heat did not abate in August. Warmer than average conditions prevailed from the Southwest to the northern Mississippi Valley and eastward to the Atlantic. Precipitation was scarce, with only half the average amount of rain falling over the southern Plains, the South and Southeast, and the Eastern Seaboard. After a record 42 consecutive days of 100 °F temperatures or above, Dallas–Fort Worth (TX) finally failed to reach the century mark on August 4. As the summer came to a close, the oven-like conditions in the center of the nation persisted. The dry, hot weather had directly caused some 1,200 deaths, millions of dollars of bridge and roadway damage, and losses in poultry and livestock running into billions of dollars.

On August 10, Hurricane Allen struck the southern coast of Texas, dumping up to 14 inches (36 cm) of rain on the region. The 9- to 15-ft (3- to 5-m) storm surge caused widespread flooding from Corpus Christi to Brownsville. The storm took the lives of 275 persons on its journey through the Caribbean from the Lesser Antilles. At its greatest intensity, Allen had sustained winds of 180 mph (290 km/h) and a central barometric pressure of 26.55 inches (899 mb). It ranked as one of the most powerful storms ever to threaten the U.S. mainland. The actual destruction, however, was much less than the potential for catastrophe.

In contrast to the extreme heat in the United States, much of Europe experienced a cloudy, cool, and wet summer. Early in June, rains of 1.5 inches (3.8 cm) effectively ended the two-month drought in Great Britain. France had its coldest summer in nearly 25 years. At midseason, rainfall in Germany was 130% above average.

September–November. Most of the United States experienced above average temperatures in September. Precipitation remained light throughout the Great Plains, the mid-Atlantic region, and southern New England. Heavier than average rain fell in a narrow band from west Texas to the coast of South Carolina. A cold front swept southward from Canada into the central United States at the end of the month, decisively ending the summer-long heat wave in that region. The first two weeks of October saw record high temperatures in the West and below average temperatures in the East. Stagnant air and high temperatures combined with automotive exhaust to produce a serious air pollution episode in the Los Angeles basin. As the month ended, colder air encompassed all of the nation with the exception of the desert Southwest. Alaska experienced a rather warm October, while temperatures in Hawaii were near average values. The first snowstorm of autumn developed in the lee of the Rocky Mountains during the last week of October. Portions of Iowa and Nebraska were blanketed with up to 7 inches (18 cm) of snow on October 27.

Wet weather posed problems in other parts of the world. Tropical storm Ruth, reported to be the strongest to affect Southeast Asia in 30 years, devastated central Vietnam in mid-September. Persistent cloudy, cool, and showery weather in October hampered harvesting operations in the eastern USSR. Three weeks of storminess in the same month produced widespread flooding in Italy, France, and Austria and heavy snows in the Alps. Flooding caused by Typhoon Wynne struck Japan in the middle of October, resulting in severe highway and housing damage.

In the Southern Hemisphere, heavy rains in parts of Brazil and Argentina caused some local flooding, while Australian grasslands continued to suffer from a severe lack of precipitation.

IDA HAKKARINEN

MEXICO

President José López Portillo's announcement of a new foreign policy overshadowed the news that in 1980 Mexico became the fifth largest oil producer in the world. The economy boomed in spite of severe droughts and high inflation.

Politics. Domestic politics were relatively quiet in this nonfederal election year. Communist Party deputies entered Congress for the first time in decades and enlivened debates in that usually docile body. In February, leftist protesters held the Danish and Belgian embassies in Mexico City for four days until ejected by unarmed policewomen. During the same month, the Mexican ambassador was held hostage for several days in Bogota, Colombia. In an effort to improve relations with student radicals, López Portillo released 4,000 young people from prison, where they had been held on minor drug charges.

Thousands of workers went on strike during the year, while thousands of others staged political protests. López Portillo reaffirmed his belief in the right to strike but warned that political strikes would be subject to political solutions.

Early in the year, exposés by the newspaper *ABC* of official corruption in Tijuana and elsewhere in the Baja prompted labor and political leaders to close the paper. In September, the appointment of the president's 27-year-old son as undersecretary of planning and budget brought protests. Government plans for a national identification card caused concern among civil libertarians.

Presidential politics had an unusual twist. U.S. presidential candidates and their supporters traveled to Mexico to gain the support of Mexican-Americans. Even though the Mexican presidential election would not be held until 1982, speculation about the government's candidate began to circulate in September.

Energy. Mexico became the fifth largest oil-producing nation with daily production of 2.3 million barrels (scheduled to be 2.7 million in 1981). López Portillo announced that proven reserves stood at more than 60,000,000,000 barrels, an increase of more than 20%. Oil exports, primarily to the United States, earned more than $12,000,000,000, as Mexico raised its prices in tandem with OPEC. Natural gas exports to the United States (300 million cu ft per day) were repriced at $4.47 per thousand cu ft in an agreement signed by both nations in March. The Ixtoc I well, which had been polluting the Texas shore for almost a year, was finally capped in March. The government raised gasoline prices late in the year but kept them far below prices paid in the United States. Investments in electricity generation raised the nation's total installed capacity to 14 million kilowatts.

Economic Performance. In spite of severe droughts and high inflation, the economy boomed for the second straight year. The gross domestic product was expected to increase by 8% in real terms. In the first half of the year, manufacturing output increased by 6% but could not meet demand. Harvests of oily seeds increased by 34%. Droughts reduced grain harvests by 18%, however, forcing Mexico to import some 10 million t (valued at $2,000,000,000) from the United States. Agricultural exports earned $750,000,000 more than the cost of agricultural imports. The commercial balance of payments deficit through June was $887 million, but this was 25% less than in the same period of 1979. Tourism brought 4.2 million visits (up by 4%) and $1,680,000,000 in revenue, while border transactions earned $5,200,000,000. Steel production reached almost 7 million t, cement 5.2 million, and fertilizers 2.7 million. The fishing yield sur-

UPI

The Avenue of the Reform in Mexico City is engulfed by dense smog, a growing problem in Latin America's most populated metropolis.

passed one million t. Inflation, fueled by petroleum earnings and insufficient domestic supply, threatened to surpass 30%.

Economic Policy. President López Portillo continued his efforts to give Mexico a planned, balanced economy with strong incentives for the private sector. The new Global Plan of Development brought together prior plans for labor, agriculture, and industrial programs. The federal budget was increased by 33% to $72,400,000,000. Investment expenditures rose by 35.5% to $15,200,000,000, with priority given to transportation, warehouses and ports, rural production, and social welfare. Rural investment was scheduled to double in an effort to reduce dependency on imports. Commercial investment was doubled. Administrative expenses were decreased by 6%, while more funds were directed to state and local governments. Financial policy was designed to stimulate domestic savings and channel capital to the productive sectors of the economy.

Deficit spending meant that Mexico had to borrow $7,800,000,000 from abroad, but foreign indebtedness ($32,000,000,000) was only 2.3% of gross domestic product. International reserves stood at almost $6,200,000,000. A large tax cut reduced revenues by $458 million. This was offset in part by the institution of a 6% added value tax, which raised the yield from indirect taxes by 34%.

Social Conditions. The government took several steps to protect citizens against inflation, shortages, and population growth. Wages of federal employees were increased by 25%, pensions by 37.5%, and teachers' salaries by $25 per month. Minimum wages were increased almost as much as the inflation rate, while labor unions demanded increases of 25%–50%. With the new Mexican Alimentary System, the government raised subsidies on consumer items, joined agricultural producers as a partner, and launched a campaign to ensure that citizens would be adequately fed with Mexican products. The government set the goal of reducing unemployment from 8.5% to 5.5% by 1982. Through continuing family planning efforts, the population growth rate was brought down to 2.9%, significant be-

cause the nation's 68 million people would be more than 100 million in twenty years.

Foreign Policy. In a major departure from past policy, Mexico decided to become active in Central American and Caribbean affairs and to support liberal and leftist movements in the region. In January, President López Portillo visited Nicaragua, where he announced increased support for the revolutionary junta there. Mexico provided material aid, as well as advice on renegotiating downward Nicaragua's foreign debt. Mexico called for an inter-American task force to help with the reconstruction of war-torn Nicaragua.

Consistent with the World Energy Plan it proposed at the United Nations in 1979, Mexico tried to set an example for providing aid to poorer countries. It signed an agreement with Venezuela to guarantee petroleum supplies—beginning at 160,000 barrels a day—to countries in the Caribbean region and to finance 30% of the purchases at 4% interest. In addition, they planned to grant 20-year loans at 2% for energy projects.

Mexico and Cuba established visibly closer ties during the year. With the support of Cuba, Mexico became a nonpermanent member of the UN Security Council in January. In July, López Portillo received a rousing welcome in Havana, where he supported Cuba's demand for U.S. withdrawal from the Guantanamo naval base. Elsewhere in the region, Mexico supported the leftist governments of Jamaica and Panama, while shunning the U.S.-backed militaristic governments of El Salvador and Guatemala.

Mexican attention to the Caribbean region was welcomed by the United States, since Mexico would offset Cuban influence in an area of the world in which the United States remained unpopular. Mexico had many of the same goals as the United States and was disturbed by the region's instability, a potential threat to Mexican resources and domestic political stability. Mexican friendliness to Cuba gave López Portillo's conservative government greater credibility among leftists at home and abroad.

Mexican-U.S. relations improved during the year, despite the new thrust of Mexican foreign policy and minor disputes between the two countries. By a new treaty, Mexico received 25,000 sq mi (40 233 km²) of potentially oil-rich territory in the Gulf of Mexico, while the United States received 18,000 sq mi (28 968 km²) of Pacific waters, rich in fish. In July, U.S. tuna boats fishing inside Mexican territorial waters were seized by the government. In retaliation, the United States prohibited imports of Mexican tuna. In his State of the Nation address in September, President López Portillo spoke warmly of relations with the United States while stressing that Mexico would continue to follow an independent foreign policy.

DONALD J. MABRY
Mississippi State University

───────── **MEXICO • Information Highlights** ─────────

Official Name: The United Mexican States.
Location: Southern North America.
Area: 761,602 sq mi (1 972 549 km²).
Population (1980 est.): 68,200,000.
Chief Cities (1977 est.): Mexico City, the capital, 8,785,236; Guadalajara, 1,724,656; Monterrey, 1,041,565.
Government: *Head of state and government,* José López Portillo, president (took office Dec. 1976). *Legislature*—Congress: Senate and Chamber of Deputies.
Monetary Unit: Peso (23.10 pesos equal U.S.$1, Nov. 1980).
Manufactures (major products): Processed foods, chemicals, basic metals and metal products, petroleum products.
Agriculture (major products): Corn, cotton, sugarcane, wheat, coffee.
GNP (1978 est., U.S.$): $91,000,000,000.
Foreign Trade (1979, U.S.$): *Imports,* $11,829,000,000; *exports,* $8,768,000,000.

MICHIGAN

Michigan's economy plunged sharply during 1980 on the heels of a declining auto industry. The state's unemployment rate was close to 1930s depression levels, and the number of residents receiving public aid was the highest on record.

Economy. The auto industry, Michigan's largest employer, reported losses of $3,700,000,000 for the first nine months of the year, its worst financial performance in history. The unemployment rate stayed at double digit levels most of the year. Flint, the state's third largest city and heavily dependent on General Motors Corp., had the nation's highest unemployment, with a high of 25.5% in midsummer.

Chrysler Corp. was threatened with bankruptcy and the state loaned the firm $150 million as part of a package to entice the U.S. government to provide Chrysler with $1,500,000,000 in federal loan guarantees.

More than 800,000 persons were receiving public aid of some kind and the state reduced benefits in an effort to keep its welfare funds solvent.

State Budget. With revenues reduced in the depressed economy, Gov. William G. Milliken cut spending sharply. Nine hundred state employees were laid off and in November the governor urged the legislature to approve further reductions, including laying off 1,000 additional workers. The cuts were designed to slash more than $1,000,000,000 from the state's original $4,900,000,000 budget.

The reduction of state aid to cities and schools had a ripple effect. School districts and the state's public universities reduced their teaching staffs. One, Oakland University, froze enrollment. Cost-cutting efforts by cities included the layoffs of 690 police officers in Detroit, 15% of the city's force.

Election. Voters rejected seven ballot proposals in the November 4 election, including three separate proposals to limit the state's taxing powers. The most popular measure, the so-called Tisch Amendment to the state constitution, which would have slashed property taxes more

UPI

Unemployed Detroiters apply for their benefits. Michigan's unemployment rate was quite high.

than half and required 60% voter approval of any new taxes, failed by a 4–3 margin. One result was that legislative leaders said they would make property-tax relief a top priority in 1981. Voters also rejected a proposal to reduce Michigan's legal drinking age from 21 to 19.

Republicans gained six seats in the state House of Representatives but failed to make a major dent in the Democratic majority, 64–46.

Schools. Tax proposals were defeated in 180 local school districts, forcing budget cuts and layoffs. Strikes delayed school openings in 19 districts, affecting 94,000 students.

Pigeon River. A ten-year controversy over gas and oil development rights in the Pigeon River State Forest ended with agreement between Shell Oil Co. and environmentalists who had halted drilling through court action. The agreement allows Shell to drill in the southern third of the 83,000-acre (33 615-ha) forest but imposes a time limit on oil and gas production.

Storm. Ten southern Michigan counties were declared disaster areas after a July 15–16 storm. The declaration enabled residents to apply for federal aid. The storm caused an estimated $180 million damage.

Cancer. A series of articles in *The Detroit News* focused attention on high rates of cancer among auto company wood pattern makers and assembly line workers. Separate studies by medical researchers confirmed an unusual incidence. In November, the United Auto Workers union began gathering death certificates from every auto plant in the country in an effort to document work place hazards.

See also Detroit.

CHARLES THEISEN, *"The Detroit News"*

MICHIGAN • Information Highlights

Area: 58,216 sq mi (150 779 km²).
Population (Jan. 1980 est.): 9,233,000.
Chief Cities (1976 est.): Lansing, the capital, 126,071; Detroit, 1,314,206; Grand Rapids, 185,558.
Government (1980): *Chief Officer*—governor, William G. Milliken (R). *Legislature*—Senate, 38 members; House of Representatives, 110 members.
Education (1979–80): *Enrollment*—public elementary schools, 1,222,830 pupils; public secondary, 637,668; colleges and universities, 503,839 students. *Public school expenditures,* $4,231,609,000.
State Finances (fiscal year 1979): *Revenues,* $11,449,000,000; *expenditures,* $10,507,000,000.
Personal Income (1979): $86,572,000,000; per capita, $9,403.
Labor Force (May 1980): *Nonagricultural wage and salary earners,* 3,426,800; *unemployed,* 607,100 (14.0% of total force).

357

MICROBIOLOGY

In 1980, the U.S. Supreme Court allowed patent protection for laboratory-created organisms. Advances in genetic engineering research enabled more animal genes to be transferred into bacterial cells. New vaccines and drugs for several human diseases were developed, as was a bacterial treatment for a tree disease. And a fungus was considered for a meat substitute.

Patent Approval. Live microorganisms are appropriate subjects for a patent so long as they are products of human ingenuity, the Supreme Court ruled in *Diamond v. Chakrabarty*. The decision settled a case begun in 1972, when a patent examiner rejected an application from General Electric Co. for a bacterium, which it called *Pseudomoma Originesa,* that can break down crude oil. The patent examiner had claimed that living organisms (except plants, which already were permitted patents under a special Congressional act) could not be patented.

The 1980 decision had great commercial importance because it offered patent protection for the microorganisms being developed with new techniques of genetic engineering. Although private companies already were working with genetically altered bacteria and viruses, while protecting their research as trade secrets, the patent decision was considered a boost to that rapidly growing field. The Supreme Court ruled that the relevant distinction in patent law falls between products of nature and human inventions, not between living and inanimate things.

Recombinant DNA Research. Genetically engineered bacteria became the source of a growing list of desirable substances in 1980, although none reached the market. The most intriguing advance was bacterial production of interferon, an antiviral material made by animal cells. Small amounts of interferon derived from human blood cells had given promising results in preliminary clinical tests on cancers. (*See also* SPECIAL REPORT, page 351).

Bacteria also were genetically altered to make them produce an enzyme that is used clinically to dissolve blood clots in lungs. Abbott Laboratories in North Chicago announced that urokinase, the first human enzyme to be produced by genetic engineering techniques, dissolves blood clots in laboratory tests as effectively as enzyme isolated from kidney cells or from urine. Large amounts of a single amino acid also were produced by genetically engineered bacteria. The altered bacteria turned out 20 to 50 times the normal amount of proline. That amino acid is used as a supplement to livestock feed and also is administered with other amino acids in clinical intravenous feeding. Scientists at the Bethesda (MD) Research Laboratories, where the work was performed, said they also will apply the method to other amino acids. In research at the University of California at San Francisco, geneticists altered bacteria to make

them produce the mouse version of a pain-countering chemical, beta-endorphin. That compound is naturally produced by mammalian pituitary glands and is considered a potential drug for treating schizophrenia and depression.

Diseases. Among the important medical advances of 1980 was the development of two safer, more effective, and less painful vaccines against rabies. One vaccine, produced from viruses grown in laboratory cultures of human cells, was approved by the Food and Drug Administration (FDA). The vaccine is injected into the patient's arm instead of into the abdomen. Five injections, rather than the conventional 23, provide immunity with fewer side effects than the previous treatment. Other research produced a highly purified rabies vaccine from a modification of the prevalent duck egg technique.

Another advance was the discovery of a drug to cure snail fever, or schistosomiasis, which affects up to 300 million people around the world. The drug, called amoscanate, was originally developed to treat hookworm. In animal tests, Ernest Bueding of Johns Hopkins University coupled amoscanate with the antibiotic erythromycin. Bueding predicted the drug combination will be more than 90% effective in clinical use against snail fever.

A potential cure for the common cold resulted from a systematic, persistent investigation at Lilly Research Laboratories in Indianapolis. By gradually modifying a family of compounds, Charles J. Paget and colleagues developed chemicals that fight rhinoviruses, the viruses that cause colds. The most effective chemical, called Enviroxime, protected cells growing in the laboratory against infection by more than 60 different cold-causing viruses, poliovirus, and other related viruses.

Bacteria for Elms. A bacterium was found that can protect elm trees from Dutch elm disease. Gary Strobel at Montana State University discovered that a bacterium normally found on leaves of wheat, barley, and oats can counter the fungus that causes the disease. Bacteria injected into infected trees stopped the disease, took up residence there, and allowed the tree to grow around its wound.

Fungi as Food. A British company received permission to place a novel food on the market. It is a meat substitute made by processing fungal filaments. Although several microorganisms already are grown and processed to provide protein supplements to animal feed, the new product, called mycoprotein, would be the first to be used for human consumption. Mycoprotein from a pilot plant, which produced 100 tons per annum, was fed to generations of laboratory animals without ill effects; it passed several short-term tests on human volunteers. The pressing question remaining for the company, Ranks Hovis McDougall, is whether anyone will buy what it is calling the "nylon of the food trade."

JULIE ANN MILLER, *"Science News"*

Zehdi Labib Terzi (left), the PLO's observer of the United Nations, and Farouk Kaddoumi, the head of the group's political department, hold a press conference July 29 after the General Assembly voted for a resolution calling for an independent Palestinian state and the withdrawal of Israel from Arab lands. During 1980, the PLO seemed to gain support outside the Middle East while losing support within the region.

UPI

MIDDLE EAST

Compared with previous years, 1980 was not, on the whole, one of major new trends and developments in the Middle East. Although it did see the outbreak of war between Iran and Iraq (*see* feature article, page 28), the year was marked by the continuation and working out of trends and circumstances that had their beginnings before calendar 1980. It was also a year of some confusion and uncertainties. Events sometimes seemed to work at cross-purposes, and the general lines of development were difficult to discern.

Aftermaths. There have been three major events in recent years that brought in their train momentous consequences. Most developments in the Middle East in 1980 might be regarded as the aftermath of one or more of those events. The first, and still possibly the key, development in recent years in the region was the Egyptian-Israeli peace treaty of March 1979—itself the outcome of the historic Camp David meeting the previous fall. Attempts to implement the peace treaty provided one of the cliff-hanging dramas of the year. Second was the fall of Shah Mohammed Reza Pahlavi of Iran in January 1979, which had a whole series of complicated consequences, including the seizure of the U.S. embassy in Tehran and the taking hostage of more than 60 embassy personnel. (*See* feature article, page 39.) Third was the Soviet invasion and takeover of Afghanistan in December 1979, which gave reason for gloomy forebodings in the West and led to reassessments of policy by nations of the Middle East.

Difficulties in Implementing the Treaty. The 1979 treaty between Israel and Egypt contained a good many ambiguities and expedient silences on the most difficult issues. In 1980, efforts to resolve these remaining difficulties continued. The negotiations were not particularly successful, however, on the central issue of how much and what kind of "autonomy" (the word used in the treaty) West Bank and Gaza Palestinians would enjoy in the future. The principals in the negotiations were the same three men—Israeli Prime Minister Menahem Begin, Egyptian President Anwar el-Sadat, and U.S. President Jimmy Carter—who had reached the agreements of 1978 and 1979, but they did not produce any astounding breakthroughs in 1980. This may have been due, in part, to their preoccupations and uncertainties regarding the crisis in Iran and the forthcoming U.S. presidential election. After November 4, no new American initiatives were expected until President-elect Ronald Reagan took office. But the real and underlying reasons for the lack of an agreement were substantive. The easy questions had all been resolved in the 1979 treaty. What remained were the intractable ones, the hard kernel of the problem.

Moreover, the Israeli perception—perhaps accurate—was that the Egyptian attitude on Palestinian autonomy had hardened and that both Egypt and the United States were now expecting Israel to make further concessions which would imperil its security. Israel resisted U.S. pressures for a "speedy" settlement, called for (in the U.S. view) by the concurrent crises in Iran and Afghanistan. Israel regarded those developments as irrelevant to its own security problems. Egypt's more demanding attitude seemed to stem from a reluctance to distance itself further from the rest of the Arab world, a likely consequence of any settlement of the Palestinian issue acceptable to Israel.

Negotiations Suspended. Begin and Sadat held their ninth summit meeting, Jan. 7–10, 1980, in Aswan, Egypt. Over the next few months, a series of meetings brought together Egyptian and Israeli negotiators in a variety of places (including The Netherlands in late February), but no real progress was made. Both the United States and Egypt were unhappy with the Israeli policy of continuing to establish settlements on the

West Bank. In an embarrassing foul-up, the United States on March 1 voted in the UN Security Council to condemn the Israeli settlement policy. Two days later, President Carter admitted that the vote was cast "in error" and was the result of a "failure in communication" between the state department and the UN delegation. Carter held talks on the deadlock with Sadat in Washington, April 8–9, and with Begin the following week. On May 8, Sadat called for a suspension of the negotiations, on May 14 agreed to their resumption, and the next day again asked for suspension, citing the "formidable gap" between the Egyptian and Israeli positions. The original deadline for conclusion of the talks, May 26, came and went. On June 9, U.S. pressure resulted in an agreement by both sides to resume the talks, which began again in Cairo, July 13–15. The occasion was marred by conflicting statements outside the conference room on the future status of Jerusalem. In the Israeli view—never concealed at Camp David or elsewhere—"undivided" Jerusalem is simply part of Israel, and its status is nonnegotiable; in the Egyptian view, the city is a negotiable aspect of the whole West Bank question. The Israeli position was reaffirmed in a law passed by the Knesset (parliament) on July 30 making undivided Jerusalem the nation's capital. On August 9, Sadat asked for indefinite suspension of the talks. U.S. efforts through special envoy Sol Linowitz in September brought the possibility of a new three-way summit, but by year's end nothing substantial had materialized. In December, the Begin government yielded to U.S. pressure and shelved a proposal to annex the Golan Heights area on the Syrian border.

Normal Diplomatic Relations. The abortive negotiations on Palestinian autonomy stood in contrast to the low-key establishment of normal relations between Egypt and Israel early in the year. The establishment of full diplomatic contact brought an end to the state of war that had persisted since the founding of Israel in 1948. With both sides having agreed to authorize a single land route between them and having consented to other technical arrangements, the Egyptian-Israeli border was formally opened on January 27. On February 5, Egypt passed a law ending its participation in the Arab economic boycott of Israel. Israel set up an embassy in Cairo on February 18, and Egypt established an embassy in Tel Aviv on February 21; the two ambassadors took up residence on February 26. These moves, while they did not imply the end of problems or mutual recriminations—as the rest of the year showed clearly enough—at least symbolized the reasonable hope that the generation-long era of Israeli-Egyptian conflict was at an end. Yitzhak Navon became the first Israeli president to visit any Arab country when he began a five-day visit to Egypt on October 26. The visit went well and seemed to augur well for the future. After Navon left, Sadat expressed the view that the Iran-Iraq war had created a dangerous situation in the Middle East, and that Egypt and Israel were obligated to accelerate their peace talks.

The Jordanian Option. One proposal that was widely discussed in 1980 and which many regard as a way out of the impasse is the so-called "Jordanian option." The ingenious plan even enjoys the support of Israel's opposition Labor Party, in particular of Chaim Herzog, its leader. Briefly stated, the compromise would hand over heavily-populated Arab West Bank areas to Jordanian sovereignty, while areas vital to Israel's security, such as the strip along the Jordan river, would be retained by Israel. Champions of the Jordanian solution point out that 80% of the Palestinian Arabs are by law Jordanian citizens, with Jordanian passports. They point also to the care with which Jordan's King Hussein, who ruled the West Bank areas from 1948 to 1967, has maintained his links with the area. West Bank territories still are represented in the Jordanian parliament, and King Hussein still pays the salaries of Jordanian civil servants on the West Bank. Israel and Jordan both maintain unofficial diplomatic ties.

The Jordanian solution is, of course, anathema to the Palestine Liberation Organization (PLO). But the very existence of the Jordanian monarchy is threatened by the PLO, whereas Israel poses no such threat. The PLO in 1980 appeared to be gathering more and more support outside the Middle East—from the European

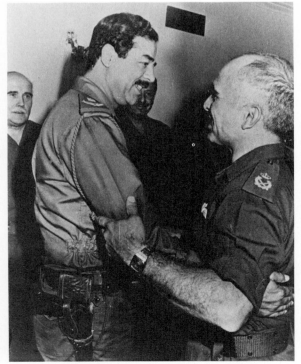

King Hussein of Jordan (right) met with Iraqi President Saddam Hussein in Baghdad, October 4 and 5.

Alain Mingam, Liaison

Common Market, for example—while at the same time it was losing support within the region. Few established governments in the Middle East truly viewed the PLO with favor. The PLO's anti-Iraq line in the war with Iran and its failure to attend the Arab summit in Amman on November 25 were in opposition to Saudi Arabia and Kuwait, its principal paymasters.

Iran. The fall of Shah Mohammad Reza Pahlavi in 1979 and his replacement by perfervid theological revolutionaries was the second major event of recent years whose consequences were still working themselves out in 1980. The whole year was overshadowed by the continued detention in Iran of 52 kidnapped U.S. citizens. The apparent disorganization of the Iranian government and the talent of Iranian leader Ayatollah Ruhollah Khomeini for verbal abuse were probably the stimuli which led Iraqi President Saddam Hussein to seek resolution of assorted grievances against Iran by launching a military attack in late September. Thus began an inconclusive conflict which was still in progress at year's end.

Afghanistan. The Soviet invasion of Afghanistan on Dec. 27, 1979 was rapidly followed by the takeover of major cities, the assumption of control over main routes between the two countries, and a reconstruction of Afghan society, including the legal system, to conform with Soviet ideology. The Soviets were far from successful, however, in stamping out opposition. Their troops continued to encounter ambushes and sporadic fighting. It was estimated that the Soviets suffered between 1,000 and 2,000 casualties in attempting to suppress a vigorous and independent people.

The situation in Afghanistan had various worldwide ramifications. Within the context of the Middle East, its important consequences were twofold. It made the United States ready to play a more positive role abroad, even if it involved some risk. Secondly, it made the governments of the region, confronted by the overt Soviet threat to their security, consider using American help to bolster their own continued independence and safety.

U.S. Policy. The strongest statement of the new forward thrust of U.S. policy in the Middle East was a declaration by President Carter in his State of the Union message on January 23:

> "Let our position be absolutely clear . . . : an attempt by any outside force to gain control of the Persian Gulf region will be regarded as an assault on the vital interest of the United States, and such an assault will be repelled by any means necessary, including military force."

That the United States might achieve the means to implement such a policy became more credible as the months passed. On April 21, it was announced that basic military and economic agreements had been reached with Oman and Kenya, providing access to air and naval bases in those two countries. Specific agreement with Oman was reached on June 4, whereby the facilities would be upgraded at U.S. expense beginning late in the year. On August 21, a similar pact was signed with Somalia. Another significant development was the ending of a period of bad relations with Turkey when, on January 9, the two countries initialed an agreement providing for continuing U.S. use of 24 bases in Turkey to monitor Soviet missile launches and troop movements. On March 1, the U.S. Army set up the headquarters organization for a new command known as the Rapid Deployment Joint Task Force, the key element in a new strategy envisaging the possibility of moving a task force rapidly into the Middle East. A trial run of such a maneuver was conducted with Egyptian cooperation in November. In October, during the Iraq-Iran war, President Carter sent four AWAC (command and radar) planes to Saudi Arabia to bolster its defenses. This led to a breach between Saudi Arabia and radical Libya, which gave diplomatic and military support to Iran.

Conclusions: A Cautious Optimism. The Middle East continued to be a scene of considerable disorder and instability. Actual war raged between Iraq and Iran, as well as, at a lower level of violence, between Ethiopia and Somalia in Ogaden province. The precarious civil peace in Lebanon was threatening again to disintegrate. There were troop concentrations on both sides of the Syrian-Jordanian border for some ten days at the end of November, but the crisis passed. Several Middle Eastern governments (notably Syria, Iraq, and Iran) are shaky and could easily disappear in revolution. Turkey—where a military takeover in September ended a long period of increasing terrorism and disorder—was probably the only country in the area which looked a great deal more stable at the end of the year than at the beginning.

Nevertheless, some potentially dangerous developments did not come to pass, and, broadly considered, the year did not see any real worsening of Middle Eastern affairs. There were enough hopeful elements in the situation to justify a cautious optimism. Perhaps the most auspicious elements were the renewed readiness of the United States to play an assertive role and the acceptance of that role by countries chastened by blatant Soviet expansionism.

In the last days of the year, former U.S. Secretary of State Henry Kissinger returned to the scene of earlier diplomatic efforts when he embarked on a two-week fact-finding tour of the Middle East on behalf of President-elect Reagan. And in a Christmas message to the incoming American leader, Egyptian President Sadat expressed his confidence that the new U.S. president would play a "positive and energetic" role in the Middle East.

(*See* articles on individual countries.)

ARTHUR CAMPBELL TURNER
University of California, Riverside

MILITARY AFFAIRS

The election of Ronald Reagan as U.S. president, and the resultant replacement of President Jimmy Carter's military and arms control advisers with those selected by the president-elect, were potentially the most important 1980 events in the area of military affairs. A related occurrence was a series of Republican victories in Senate races which resulted in the control of that body moving to the Republicans for the first time in a quarter of a century. The switch to majority status enabled the Republicans to assume all the committee chairmanships in the Senate. The most important of these in terms of likely effects upon military policy were the replacement of Frank Church (ID) as chairman of the Foreign Relations Committee by Charles Percy (IL) and the replacement of Armed Services Committee Chairman John Stennis (MS) by John Tower of Texas.

The new Reagan teams of top defense advisers in the executive branch included Caspar Weinberger, who replaced Harold Brown as the secretary of defense, and Frank C. Carlucci, who replaced W. Graham Claytor as the deputy secretary of defense. Both appointments were approved by the Senate. By Inauguration Day, the new president had not yet named the new secretaries of the Army, Navy, and Air Force. The director of the National Security Council is Richard Allen, replacing Zbigniew Brzezinski.

Beyond changes in personnel brought to Washington by Ronald Reagan, the president-elect brought new perspectives on military affairs which differed sharply from those of the Carter administration. Chief among these was the oft-expressed belief that much of the trouble in international relations is caused by the Soviet Union and other Communist states. An associated view was the charge by Reagan that President Carter contributed to Soviet adventurism by permitting a dangerous decline in the military capacity of the United States.

During the presidential campaign, Reagan repeatedly voiced his belief that peace results from the United States being so prepared for war that a potential aggressor would perceive the gains from aggression as being far outweighed by the costs which would be imposed by the United States. Congruent with this perspective was Reagan's announced plan substantially to increase U.S. military capacity across the board in order to deter war if possible, or fight it successfully if that were to become necessary.

In dramatic contrast to President Carter, Ronald Reagan promised in the campaign that if elected he would make sure the arms control treaty, Strategic Arms Limitation Treaty II (SALT II), would never go into force. Instead, the former California governor stated that it was his intention to negotiate a new treaty (SALT III) with the Soviets. In pursuit of a new treaty Reagan indicated that it would be his objective to increase the strength of the U.S. strategic nuclear forces so that future negotiations with the Soviets could be conducted from a position of American superiority.

In still another departure from the Carter military philosophy, Reagan stated his belief in the theory of "linkage." According to this view SALT negotiations ought to be linked to acceptable Soviet behavior in other areas of concern to the United States. In contrast, the Carter administration's operating principle was that SALT was so important that negotiations should be conducted with the Soviets despite the fact that Moscow often was engaged elsewhere in activity the United States opposed.

Until the new Reagan administration could clearly establish its agenda for the SALT III negotiations, the president-elect indicated he wished some kind of moratorium on strategic building as an interim policy.

Former President Richard Nixon, who did not play a direct role in the 1980 Reagan campaign, published *The Real War* in 1980. The book echoed the concerns voiced by the Republican presidential candidate regarding the threat from the Soviet Union and the appropriate military counters by the United States. The former chief executive argues that the Soviet Union has never swerved from the policy of world conquest. Nixon contends that the danger from the Soviets is greater now because the Carter administration did not keep up American military strength. Nixon's advice to his country, and the new president, is to commence an impressive

Caspar Weinberger, 63, a lawyer and former member of the Nixon and Ford administrations, is named secretary of defense by the president-elect.

UPI

A Sea Sparrow III surface-to-air missile is fired from the amphibious command ship "USS Mount Whitney" during special NATO exercises in the North Atlantic.

military buildup and to be willing to confront the Soviets militarily when Moscow appears to be on the march.

The MAD Dispute. The incoming administration inherited a doctrinal dispute which had been under study for nearly a decade. The question was whether the United States should configure its strategic forces according to the MAD (mutual assured destruction) concept of only being able to retaliate to a Soviet attack with the destruction of Soviet cities, or to alter the strategic forces to give a president the flexibility to engage in limited nuclear war as an alternative to total destruction. Limited nuclear war would involve the targeting of selected and specific military targets not colocated with Soviet urban centers. The argument in favor of moving from a MAD doctrine was that it is preferable for an American president to have the option of engaging in limited nuclear war.

In August the Carter administration announced that the Pentagon was moving ahead with redesigning the strategic forces to permit their use in limited nuclear war as a response to less than all-out Soviet attacks. Carter's critics claimed the move was more cosmetic than substantive, a step taken in the heat of the presidential campaign.

The MX Controversy. One of the most controversial major weapons systems ever considered for deployment by the United States was even more hotly debated in 1980. The system is termed the MX (for missile, experimental). The new missile represents a significant improvement in accuracy, reliability, and size over the currently deployed Minuteman ICBM. For example, the MX weighs 192,000 lbs (86 976 kg) as compared with the Minuteman weight of 78,000 lbs (35 334 kg). In contrast to the Minuteman's three warheads of 170 kilotons each, the MX carries ten warheads of either 350 or 500 kilotons each. (The two atomic bombs dropped in World War II were rated beteen 12 and 15 kilotons of TNT equivalent.) In spite of opposition by some Democrats, President Carter supported the development of the MX. The Republican platform did, too. Reagan, however, expressed some doubts about its deployment.

According to Pentagon strategists there are three reasons for the development of the MX and the partial replacement by it of the Minuteman force. Generally believed to be the most important is the necessity to offset the eroding survivability of the Minuteman with a new missile which cannot be destroyed before launching by a Soviet first strike. The loss of Minuteman survivability is due to the increased accuracy, size, and reliability of the current generation of Soviet ICBMs targeted against U.S. missiles. By employing mobility and concealment it is believed that the MX will be much more survivable in case of a Soviet attack. The second reason given for the MX is the need to reestablish the balance in nuclear destructiveness, which currently favors the Soviets because of their large number of higher-yield warheads. The third reason given by MX proponents is to obtain the accuracy necessary to ensure that any target in the Soviet Union can be destroyed.

The deployment mode for the MX envisions 200 missiles being shuttled among 4,600 shelters (23 shelters for each MX) in order to confuse the Soviets as to which shelters are housing the missiles. A transporter vehicle would carry the missile and its erector-launcher along an individual main road to any of the 23 shelters which would be at the termini of 23 branch roads. The transporter vehicle would slide the missile and erector-launcher into a shelter while shielding the operation from overhead by Soviet satellites. In 1980 the planned road system was changed from an oval "race track" configuration to a linear pattern. The transporter vehicle would have some capability to "dash" the missile and erector-launcher from one shelter to another during the 30 minutes it would take for a Soviet warhead to traverse the distance from its firing point to the United States. It is theoretically possible for Soviet reconnaissance to determine which shelters hold missiles by measuring the difference in mass between the empty and the occupied shelters. To counter this possibility the Air Force planned to place an object in each empty shelter with the same mass as the missile and the launcher-erector. The devices are termed mass simulators.

The 200 MX missiles and the 4,600 shelters and connecting roads are to be built in a number of valleys in southern Nevada and Utah. This projected basing pattern has created considerable opposition from citizens of the two states. Those opposed to the MX cite concern about the potential damage to the fragile desert environment which might result from what could be the largest construction project in U.S. history. Others fear that the influx of MX project construction workers and their families would create serious socioeconomic impacts upon the small towns of the MX deployment region.

Local fears were soothed to some extent by the government's issue of an environmental impact statement which concluded that the damage to the environment would be manageable, and that the socioeconomic impacts could be handled by the local population. Both the environmental fears and those about socioeconomic impacts were compounded by the possibility that the MX deployment area may also be the site for substantial energy development in the 1980s.

In 1980 many of those who call themselves arms controllers strenuously opposed deployment of the MX. Their basic line of argument was that construction of the missile would be perceived by Soviet leaders as a very threatening move. This was because the extreme accuracy of the MX, coupled with the large number of high-yield warheads, would make the system appear to be a first-strike force—a force which the United States could use to destroy the Soviet ICBMs which are the bulk of Moscow's nuclear retaliatory force. Arms controllers point out that this is a situation the Soviets cannot accept without taking some kind of compensatory action which could be viewed as threatening by the United States. Such a situation was described by Robert McNamara, secretary of defense in the 1960s, as an action-reaction syndrome. This would be a circumstance in which the two superpowers would endlessly compete with each other in trying to obtain an advantage, with neither Washington nor Moscow obtaining greater security.

MX opponents contended that there exists a number of means to preserve the survivability of the Minuteman force which would not appear so threatening to the Soviets as the MX deployment. One alternative would be to negotiate an agreement requiring the Soviets to keep their ICBMs at a level too low to threaten the Minuteman survivability. Another possibility would be to construct antiballistic missiles (ABMs) to protect the Minuteman from Soviet warheads. This option is complicated by the need to renegotiate the ABM treaty between Washington and Moscow which limits both countries to only 200 ABM launchers each. A third alternative to the MX would be to deploy SUM (shallow underwater mobile) vehicles. These would be small submarines that would operate in the waters off the two coastlines and in the Gulf of Mexico. Opponents of the MX argued that the SUMs would be survivable and their smaller SLBMs would be less of a first strike threat to Moscow.

The Rapid Deployment Force. In March President Carter announced the formation of the Rapid Deployment Force (RDF). Its mission was to interject U.S. military forces into any trouble spot in the Middle East. In theory the RDF was to be drawn from some 200,000 troops which are normally assigned to three Army and one Marine divisions, and several smaller elite units. Some questioned whether the units earmarked for the RDF were combat ready. It also was questionable whether the United States possessed the numbers and kinds of aircraft needed to fly the RDF to the Middle East.

The Budget. The Reagan administration was inheriting a Carter defense budget of $157,000,000,000. The incoming Armed Services Committee chairman, Sen. John Tower, stated that an extra $3,000,000,000 was needed immediately. Thereafter, Tower stated, the budget should increase some 9% to 13% above the inflation rate.

Soviet Activity. The Soviet Union did not stand still in the area of military affairs during 1980. The most impressive efforts were observed in regard to continued expansion of the Soviet Navy. In the fall it was learned that Moscow had launched the largest submarine ever built. It was the first of what was expected to be a number of Typhoon-class boats nearly the size of the U.S. aircraft carrier *Yorktown.* The Typhoon-class submarines have 20 tubes for firing SLBMs. The Soviets also launched two new submarines capable of firing cruise missiles while submerged.

In late 1980 the Soviet Union was operating four aircraft carriers which are small in comparison to such U.S. super carriers as the *Nimitz* and *Eisenhower*. However, intelligence reports indicated that Moscow had laid the keel of an aircraft carrier the size of the largest U.S. ships.

Trying to establish accurately the true military threat from the Soviet Union, and then to utilize U.S. resources properly to counter the threat, became for president-elect Reagan, as it had been for his predecessors, one of the most important tasks.

ROBERT M. LAWRENCE
Colorado State University

The first day of renewed draft registration brings out the pickets in front of the main post office in New York City.

MILITARY AFFAIRS—SPECIAL REPORT:

The Draft

The summer of 1980 marked the first time since 1975 that the U.S. government required young men to register for a possible draft into the armed forces. Failure to comply was made a felony, punishable by up to five years in prison, and a $10,000 fine.

In asking the Congress to approve an additional $10 million for fiscal 1980 to gear up registration machinery, President Carter stated that he saw no immediate requirement to move beyond registration to a draft. However, doubters accused the president of planning to use registration as a first step in an evolutionary process that would culminate in a draft sometime after the fall 1980 presidential election. Some charged that with registration and a draft the government would be more inclined to intervene militarily in what Washington could view as deteriorating political situations overseas.

Those supporting registration cited several reasons for it. One was the argument that in a hostile and unpredictable world it would be a prudent step to have men already registered in case there developed a need to call them quickly into service. Supporters stated their belief that registration would communicate to U.S. allies, most of which, except for England and Japan, employ some type of national conscription, that the United States is serious about meeting its military commitments. It was also contended, with references to the Soviet invasion of Afghanistan, that registration would demonstrate to the USSR, where 18-year-olds are drafted, the resolve of the United States to make unpopular decisions if necessary for security interests.

The registration procedures mandated by Congress are a phased process. In July, young men born in 1960 and 1961 were required to register, giving name, date of birth, current and permanent address, telephone number, and social security number. Men born in 1962 were required to register in January 1981. Afterward men will be required to register 30 days before or after their 18th birthday.

Resumption of registration was accomplished in the midst of legal uncertainty and political opposition. Several days before registration was to begin, a three-judge panel in Philadelphia declared the law establishing registration unconstitutional on the grounds that it excluded women. One day later Supreme Court Associate Justice William F. Brennan, Jr., overruled the lower tribunal and registration began as scheduled. Justice Brennan explained his action by stating that failure to proceed with registration could result in problems for national military and foreign policies. He noted that at a later date the entire Supreme Court could decide upon the constitutionality of the law.

The constitutional question of whether women should be registered, and later possibly drafted into the military service, is a murky one fraught with emotion. Favoring the treatment of women equally with men in the military context are those who argue that equal rights for women would be a hollow concept if the military segment of society is excluded. Persons taking this view note that elsewhere, Israel and Vietnam for example, women serve in military support roles, as well as in combat.

Those opposing registration of women state that combat is no place for women. It is argued that inequality in certain facets of military life does not imply inequality in the other areas of society. Military men point out that women are less able to perform some military tasks, such as hand-to-hand combat, than are men. Further, military men suggest that the presence of women in combat could jeopardize the accomplishment of the mission as men put protecting women before accomplishment of given objective. (*See also* WOMEN: Women in the Military.)

A month after registration began, Bernard Rostker, director of the Selective Service System, announced that approximately 93% of the 19- and 20-year-olds eligible for registration had signed up as required by the law.

ROBERT M. LAWRENCE

MINING

The overall pattern of worldwide mineral industry activity in 1980 was one of increased exploration, production, processing, trade, and consumption. However, mining areas affected by international and/or internal warfare suffered significant downturns. The Iran-Iraq war, which began in September, devastated those nations' petroleum and natural-gas production facilities, virtually assuring that their productive activities were at a standstill through year-end. In the case of Iran, the war heightened an already badly deteriorated economic situation, where almost all mineral industry activity had been curtailed severely. Afghanistan's limited mineral industry, chiefly natural gas for export to the Soviet Union and coal for local consumption, suffered substantially as a result of the civil war and the Soviet incursion. In Africa, industrial activity turned upward in Zimbabwe (Rhodesia) as the establishment of a new government ended guerrilla warfare and international sanctions which had combined to restrict mineral industry activities. In the Western Sahara area, formally controlled by Morocco, however, the area's sole mineral activity, phosphate rock output, remained at a standstill.

Value of World Output. Value of world crude mineral output in 1980 was estimated at $211,-700,000,000 (constant 1973 dollars), compared with $201,300,000,000 for 1979 and $191,400,-000,000 for 1978. (Figures have been revised downward from those published previously.) The United States and the USSR were in close contention for first rank in terms of value of output, with each accounting for nearly 20% of the total, far ahead of China, Canada, and Venezuela, each with 5 to 6% of the total. Iran, which formerly had ranked with the latter group, registered a sharp downturn.

Ferrous Ores and Metals. Preliminary information suggested that 1980 world iron ore output was about on a par with the 1979 level of 910 million t, approaching, but not exceeding, the historic high of 913 million t of 1974. Similarly, manganese ore output apparently was only slightly above the 24.4-million-t level of 1979, but chromite output seemingly reached a new record high of about 9.8 million t.

The pattern of growth rates among ferrous ore producers of China and the Communist countries of Europe relatively greater than among market economy nation producers was evidently disrupted in the latter part of 1979 and in 1980. Many output targets projected by the Communist nations were not met, while Western producers seemed to be recovering from the 1977–78 slump.

World steel output in 1980 was estimated to be of the order of 745 million t, just slightly above the 739-million-t level of 1979, with the USSR, United States, Japan, West Germany, and China, in that order, remaining the leading producers and together accounting for nearly two thirds of the world total.

Nonferrous Ores and Metals. Incomplete returns suggested that world output of virtually all major nonferrous ores and metals exceeded that of 1979. Estimates for 1980 (in million metric tons) include: aluminum—14.5; bauxite—88.4; copper (mine output)—7.6; copper (refined including secondary)—8.9; lead (mine output)—3.5; lead (smelter including secondary)—5.5; nickel (mine output)—0.7; tin (mine and smelter)— 0.26; titanium ores (ilmenite, rutile, and titaniferous slag)—4.7; zinc (mine output)—6.0; zinc (smelter including secondary)—6.2.

Precious Metals. The early months of 1980 saw the price of gold soar to a new all-time high, topping $800 per troy ounce, as the result of a combination of falling value of U.S. currency, speculative buying, and a variety of international political events. As the Soviet Union moved significant quantities of gold into Western markets and as Iran and Iraq began disposing of gold to finance their war, there was a decline in the gold price. The still exceedingly high prices led to a substantial cutback in jewelers' consumption of gold so that demand for the yellow metal fell as the price advanced, and world output in 1980 was believed to be little higher than the 38.9 million ounces of 1979.

Prices for the other precious metals—silver, platinum, and the related metals of the platinum group—also grew far out of proportion to levels anticipated on the basis of normal supply-demand relationships.

Fertilizer Materials. The world's ever-growing food requirements apparently drove output of the main mineral-based fertilizer materials to new record highs in 1980. Incomplete 1980 returns indicated that phosphate rock output topped the 1979 historic high of 126.8 million t; that production of potash (K_2O equivalent basis) exceeded the 26.3 million t of 1979; and that nitrogen output (measured in terms of nitrogen content of ammonia) surpassed the 70.5-million-t mark set in 1979.

Other Trends. World asbestos output apparently advanced over the 1979 level of nearly 5.3 million t in response to higher demand for insulation materials occasioned by the ever-higher costs of energy, and despite questions raised regarding possible environmental hazards. World cement output apparently reached a level of 920-940 million t, exceeding the 885 million t level of 1979. World gypsum output in 1980 approached 78 million t, a level higher than that of both 1978 and 1979. Natural diamond output apparently exceeded 40 million carats in 1980, slightly ahead of the 1979 level, with output in Zaire exceeding that of the USSR. The world sulfur industry, which had suffered from an over-supply situation, enjoyed better market conditions in 1980, and it was expected that total output would exceed 56 million t.

CHARLES L. KIMBELL, *U.S. Bureau of Mines*

U.S. Vice-President Walter F. Mondale addresses Democratic-Farmer-Labor supporters in his native Minnesota after the election results were in. His wife, Joan, is at his side for the concession.

Wide World

MINNESOTA

Despite the continuing sharp rise in energy costs and soaring interest rates, Minnesota enjoyed a stable and profitable year in 1980.

Agriculture. The state escaped the severe drought that plagued other sections of the nation. Yields of corn, wheat, and sunflower—the state's leading crops—were good, though they did not reach record levels. Farm prices slumped badly during the early part of the year but by autumn had recovered substantially. In April, hogs were selling at a low of $28.50 per hundredweight; by October, the price had reached $47.70. The state continued its upward climb in hog production, becoming the third largest producer behind Iowa and Illinois.

Employment. Although Minnesota's unemployment rate increased in 1980, it remained below the national average. In September, the state's unemployment rate was 5.6%, compared with the national rate of 7.1%. In the Twin Cities, unemployment stood at an even 5%.

Urban Redevelopment. The downtown areas of Minneapolis and St. Paul underwent extensive redevelopment. In Minneapolis, $600 million of new construction was in progress, while projects costing $200 million were under way in St. Paul.

In November, St. Paul voters considered a proposal for construction of a downtown people mover. Backers of the $150-million internal distribution system believed it would alleviate traffic congestion and stimulate further development. Although 80% of the cost would have been financed by federal money, voters saw it as unnecessary and rejected the proposal by a 3-to-1 margin.

Politics. Ordinarily a national bellwether, Minnesota bucked the national trend in the No-

vember elections, casting its ten electoral votes for the Carter-Mondale ticket and strengthening the Democratic-Farmer-Labor (DFL) majority in the state legislature. But the Republicans did pick up one U.S. congressional seat, giving them a 5-to-3 margin in the state's delegation. Seven incumbent representatives (four Republicans and three Democrats) won reelection. The sixth district seat of retiring Rep. Richard Nolan (D) was won by St. Cloud newspaper publisher Vin Weber (R). At year's end, the major political question on the minds of Minnesotans was the future of native son Vice-President Walter F. Mondale.

State Government. State finance was a riches to rags story. In 1979, the state had a bulging surplus; the state legislature voted to index the state income tax and reduce rates, forgoing $770 million in revenue for the 1979–81 biennium. In August 1980, however, a severe revenue shortfall forced Republican Gov. Albert H. Quie to order a cut of $195 million in state expenditures. Quie blamed the problem on the "Carter recession," while the DFL claimed it was due to poor planning on the governor's part.

Constitutional Amendments. In the November election, Minnesota voters turned down by a narrow margin a constitutional amendment that would have allowed for initiatives and referenda, a move strongly supported by Governor Quie. Although the amendment received a majority of votes on the issue, it did not obtain the necessary majority in terms of the total number of votes cast in the election. Also defeated were amendments that would have moved responsibility for legislative and congressional reapportionment from the legislature to an independent bipartisan commission and eliminated a 5% interest limit on bonds issued for highway construction.

Charter Amendments. Minneapolis voters extended the city's mayoral term from two to four years. St. Paul voters switched from at-large elections to ward elections for members of the city council.

ARTHUR NAFTALIN
University of Minnesota

MISSISSIPPI

An extremely close presidential contest that attracted visits from both major candidates, a legislative session responsive to the proposals of a newly inaugurated governor, a summer of record-breaking heat, and an economic downturn of significant proportions were events of major importance to Mississippians in 1980.

Elections. More than 63% of Mississippi's estimated 1.4 million registered voters participated in the November 4 presidential election. Electors pledged to former California Gov. Ronald Reagan (R) narrowly defeated those pledged to incumbent President Jimmy Carter (D) to capture the state's seven electoral votes. Of the record 893,000 popular votes cast, 49.4% went to Reagan, while 48.1% went to Carter. The remaining 2.5% was split among electors pledged to four other candidates, including Independent John Anderson (1.3%). The victory was a particularly significant one for the Republican Party since it was achieved in the face of both heavy black voting and active campaigning by Democratic Gov. William F. Winter.

All five incumbent U.S. representatives (three Democrats and two Republicans) won reelection, but only Democrat G. V. Montgomery went unchallenged. The election of a Republican-controlled U.S. Senate not only cost John C. Stennis (D) his chairmanship of the Armed Services Committee but also denied him the chance to become president pro tempore.

The Legislature. The first legislature elected entirely from single-member districts was perhaps less reform-minded than had been anticipated. Much of Governor Winter's legislative program was adopted, however, including the consolidation of various planning and policy-making agencies into a Mississippi Energy and Transportation Board, the reorganization of the State Board of Health, the transfer of the functions of the Office of Motor Vehicle Comptroller into the State Tax Commission, the strengthening of hazardous waste laws, and the enactment of a low-interest home mortgage program financed by tax-exempt revenue bonds. Perhaps the most significant action of the session was the passage of legislation aimed at bringing about the equalization of property tax assessments statewide.

Heat Wave. A severe heat wave which covered Mississippi during much of the summer of 1980 claimed the lives of at least 61 persons, most of whom were poor and elderly. The deaths were especially regrettable since a number of them likely could have been prevented if fear of prowlers had not caused many of the victims to keep their doors and windows closed tightly. Record-high, three-digit temperatures, coupled with a prolonged drought, killed crops and poultry throughout much of the state, prompting officials to seek federal assistance for farmers.

The Economy. Continuing inflation, lagging housing construction, relatively high unemployment, and reduced consumer spending characterized the state's economy for much of the year. By late summer, however, there were indications that the recession was easing and that a slow recovery was under way. Nonetheless, the mood remained cautious as the year ended.

For the first time in several years, it was reported that Mississippi's already-low per capita income slipped as a relative proportion of the national figure.

Other Events. Two major obstacles to continued construction of the Tennessee-Tombigbee Waterway were overcome with the passage of a $212 million Congressional appropriation bill in the summer and the dismissal of a U.S. district court suit in October. When the Pearl River threatened to repeat its spring 1979 rampage, Jackson city officials reacted quickly and effectively.

DANA B. BRAMMER
The University of Mississippi

─────── **MISSISSIPPI · Information Highlights** ───────

Area: 47,716 sq mi (123 584 km²).
Population (Jan. 1980 est.): 2,418,000.
Chief Cities (1976 est.): Jackson, the capital, 188,205; (1970 census): Biloxi, 48,486; Meridian, 45,083.
Government (1980): *Chief Officer*—governor, William F. Winter (D). *Legislature*—Senate, 52 members; House of Representatives, 122 members.
Education (1979–80): *Enrollment*—public elementary schools, 262,301; public secondary, 219,738; colleges and universities, 100,272 students. *Public school expenditures,* $701,000,000 ($1,348 per pupil).
State Finances (fiscal year 1979): *Revenues,* $2,598,-000,000; *expenditures,* $2,367,000,000.
Personal Income (1979): $15,007,000,000; per capita, $6,178.
Labor Force (May 1980): *Nonagricultural wage and salary earners,* 830,500; *unemployed,* 70,800 (6.9% of total force).

Jimmy Carter addresses a town meeting at Truman High School in Independence. Although the president made several campaign stops in Missouri, Ronald Reagan carried the state in the November election.

UPI

MISSOURI

In keeping with the national trend, Missouri gave its 12 electoral votes to Republican Ronald Reagan. Since 1904 Missouri has failed only once to support the presidential winner.

Politics. It was by no means a Republican landslide as Democrat Thomas Eagleton won his bid for a third term in the U.S. Senate despite the efforts of the National Conservative Political Action Committee which had targeted him for defeat. Missouri Republicans, however, did pick up two seats in the U.S. House of Representatives, giving them four to the Democrats' six. Wendell Bailey, a Republican, was elected from the eighth district to replace 20-year veteran Richard Ichord, who did not seek another term, and Bill Emerson defeated incumbent Democrat Bill Burlison in the tenth district. All other incumbent representatives were reelected.

The most exciting state race pitted former Gov. Christopher Bond (R) against Democratic Gov. Joseph P. Teasdale, who ousted Bond from the governorship in 1976. This time Bond was victorious with 53% of the vote. Bond spent roughly $2 million and Teasdale $3 million to make it the most expensive gubernatorial race in the state's history. Teasdale hammered at his 1976 theme that Bond was a rich man who cared nothing about the poor and elderly. Bond retaliated with the assertion that Teasdale would say anything to be elected and then would fail as before to deliver on his promises.

As governor, Teasdale had displayed little facility for administration, but he had a knack for recognizing an issue that had the potential for popular appeal and tying it to his banner. Two such issues appeared in the summer of 1980. One was the attempt of businesses engaged in the burial of hazardous waste to establish dumps in three places in northeast Missouri. The second developed over Teasdale's response to a prolonged heat wave. During many days of July temperatures soared above 100°F (38°C).

As the heat-related deaths in the state climbed to more than 300 for the highest total of any state in the union, the governor ordered units of the National Guard to make door-to-door checks in St. Louis and Kansas City to locate elderly persons living alone in nonair-conditioned rooms. Fans were placed in such units, and persons displaying heat stroke symptoms were moved to hospitals. Next, Teasdale called a special session of the legislature to consider a tougher law against illegal dumping of hazardous waste and a "cool-aid" bill to reimburse poor people over 65 for the additional utility costs occasioned by the prolonged heat.

Legislative leaders in Teasdale's own party were less than enthusiastic, noting that the questions could have been handled better when the Assembly convened in January and that the ses-

---

MISSOURI • Information Highlights

Area: 69,686 sq mi (180 487 km²).
Population (Jan. 1980 est.): 4,891,000.
Chief Cities (1970 census): Jefferson City, the capital, 32,407; (1976 est.): St. Louis, 519,345; Kansas City, 458,251.
Government (1980): *Chief Officers*—governor, Joseph P. Teasdale (D); lt. gov., William C. Phelps (R). *General Assembly*—Senate, 34 members; House of Representatives, 163 members.
Education (1979-80): *Enrollment*—public elementary schools, 481,360 pupils; public secondary, 391,573; colleges and universities, 222,046 students. *Public school expenditures,* $1,539,243,000.
State Finances (fiscal year 1979): *Revenues,* $3,821,-000,000; *expenditures,* $3,337,000,000.
Personal Income (1979): $40,155,000,000; per capita, $8,251.
Labor Force (June 1980): *Nonagricultural wage and salary earners,* 1,986,400; *unemployed,* 184,000 (7.7% of total force).

sion imposed an additional burden on members who faced challenges for their seats. While the legislators deliberated in Jefferson City, their opponents campaigned.

In other races, the Democratic speaker of the Missouri House of Representatives, Kenneth J. Rothman, was elected lieutenant governor, and the Democrats also retained the office of state treasurer, as Melvin E. Carnahan of Rolla replaced James Spainhower who was ineligible to succeed himself. James C. Kirkpatrick was an easy victor over his Republican opponent for his fifth term as secretary of state. Republican John Ashcroft was reelected as attorney general. Both houses of the General Assembly continued to have large Democratic majorities.

Two constitutional amendments on the November 4 ballot sparked considerable interest. One that mandated a tax and spending lid passed by a vote of 995,817 to 803,885, despite charges that it would impede state services and that its provisions were so complicated as to be unworkable. The other controversial amendment would have prohibited the construction of nuclear power facilities until there was a guaranteed method of handling the resultant waste. This proposition was defeated.

Legislation. The second session of the 80th General Assembly which adjourned April 30 enacted a bill containing longer penalties for convicted rapists, but feminists and prosecutors alike viewed the measure with mixed reactions. Repeal of the inheritance tax on estates worth less than $175,000 and an adult abuse bill passed, but legislation of laetrile was defeated. Treatment standards for mental patients were modernized.

RUTH W. TOWNE
Northeast Missouri State University

MONTANA

Elections, the metals industry, coal taxes, and natural phenomena made news in 1980.

Elections. The elections both followed and departed from the national pattern. Ronald Reagan overwhelmed Jimmy Carter. Republicans picked up enough seats to gain control of both houses of the legislature, the first time in many years that one of the parties has been able to do so. However, Lt. Gov. Ted Schwinden, after defeating incumbent Gov. Thomas Judge in the primary, easily defeated his Republican opponent Jack Ramirez in the race for governor. Voters also reelected the two incumbents, a Democrat and a Republican, to the U.S. House of Representatives; filled four seats on the state supreme court; and approved a constitutional amendment removing some restriction on the confidentiality of documents of the Judicial Standards Commission.

Initiatives banning disposal of radioactive wastes, increasing the disclosure requirements on money spent by lobbyists, and requiring adjustment of income tax rates to inflation were approved. An initiative requiring refundable deposits on beverage containers was rejected by the voters.

The Metals Industry. The metals industry was disrupted by a strike which began on July 1. Before the strike ended late in the fall, approximately half the strikers were without jobs. On September 29 the Anaconda Copper Company shocked the state with an announcement that it was closing its smelter in Anaconda and its refinery in Great Falls, creating a loss of about 1,000 jobs in the former city and 500 in the latter.

Coal Tax. The constitutionality of Montana's coal severance tax, the highest in the nation, was upheld when the state supreme court unanimously sustained a state district court ruling. The eleven utilities and three coal mining companies opposing the tax asked the U.S. Supreme Court to review the case. Bills in the U.S. Congress which would place a ceiling on state taxes on coal taken from federally owned land have not passed.

Railroad. Efforts of public officials and citizen groups to keep the Milwaukee railroad alive proved unsuccessful as trustees for the bankrupt firm cut trains west of Miles City, dismantled spur lines, and sold trackage in the center portion of the state to the Burlington Northern. Meanwhile, the state's attorney general filed antitrust actions against the Burlington Northern for conspiring to eliminate the Milwaukee.

Nature. Mount St. Helens' May 18 eruption deposited ash across much of Montana and disrupted normal routines in the western portion of the state, but subsequent eruptions caused only minor inconvenience. While the western half of the state experienced abnormally large rainfalls, the eastern part of the state, where grain growers already were upset by President Carter's grain embargo against the USSR, suffered the severest drought in decades. Very poor crop yields, range fires, and soil erosion resulted.

The Department of Natural Resources and Conservation began implementing the Water Adjudication Act as amended by the 1979 legislature. It was hoped that all water claims would be clarified by Jan. 1, 1982.

RICHARD B. ROEDER, *Montana State University*

MONTANA · Information Highlights

Area: 147,138 sq mi (381 087 km²).
Population (Jan. 1980 est.): 793,000.
Chief Cities (1970 census): Helena, the capital, 22,557; Billings, 61,581; Great Falls, 60,091.
Government (1980): *Chief Officers*—governor, Thomas L. Judge (D); lt. gov., Ted Schwinden (D). *Legislature*—Senate, 50 members; House of Representatives, 100 members.
Education (1979–80): *Enrollment*—public elementary schools, 105,735 pupils; public secondary, 52,473; colleges and universities, 31,906 students.
State Finances (fiscal year 1979): *Revenues,* $1,006,-000,000; *expenditures,* $901,000,000.
Personal Income (1979): $6,040,000,000; per capita, $7,684.
Labor Force (June 1980): *Nonagricultural wage and salary earners,* 291,000; *unemployed,* 23,600 (6.0% of total force).

MOROCCO

The Moroccan government's domestic and foreign policies in 1980 were dictated by its continued involvement in the five-year-long war in the Western Sahara. King Hassan's stepping up of military activities in the war met stiff opposition by the Algerian-backed Polisario Front, and mounting defense expenditures continued to tax the deteriorating economy. Efforts at diplomatic settlement of the war were rebuffed by the Hassan government.

Sahara War. The Moroccan government's campaign to gain control of the disputed Sahara took a more aggressive turn in late 1979 and 1980, with the launching of two major military offensives. "Operation Ouhoud" began in November 1979 to push Polisario forces back into Algeria. While Ouhoud met with little resistance, the second offensive, "Zellagha," begun in March, suffered a major setback at Polisario's hands in southern Morocco. In the Tighzert region of the Ouarkziz mountains, up to 2,000 Moroccan soldiers were killed in the largest confrontation in the war.

Fierce battles continued to be fought throughout 1980 and the Polisario was successful in launching attacks into southern Morocco. While the war continued on the ground, activities at the diplomatic level in 1980 brought no closer the prospect for a peaceful resolution of the conflict.

The Organization of African Unity (OAU) summit meeting in Freetown, Sierra Leone, in July witnessed a near diplomatic triumph for the Polisario when a majority of members recognized its government, the Saharan Arab Democratic Republic, as the legitimate representative of the Sahara people. But Morocco was able to forestall its admission into the OAU by gaining support of other member states who threatened to walk out.

To avert a schism in the organization, Morocco and the other parties to the dispute, Algeria, Polisario, and Mauritania, agreed to attend a meeting chaired by the OAU ad hoc committee on the war. Although the first face-to-face meet-

Anwar Hussein

King Hassan and Queen Elizabeth dine in Moroccan style during the monarch's Mediterranean tour.

ing of all parties took place in September, Morocco remained intransigent by refusing to accept the terms of the peace plan—a cease-fire by December 1980 and a fair and general referendum in the Sahara.

Economy. A deteriorating economy strained by a $1.5 million-per-day expenditure on the war, showed few signs of improvement in 1980. Operating under an austerity budget with a $6,000,000,000 public external debt, the government concentrated its public investment in boosting agricultural production and natural resource exploitation.

Although Morocco is the world's largest exporter of phosphates, its oil import bill alone outstripped declining revenues from phosphate production. One of the world's richest mines at Bou Craa in the Western Sahara stopped production in the summer because of stepped-up Polisario sabotage. One means of raising government revenues was the imposition of a national "solidarity tax." With defense spending absorbing 20% of Morocco's gross national product (GNP) under the 1980 budget, there was little hope that the gloomy economic outlook would improve.

Sporadic strikes by students and building, transport, manufacturing, and phosphate workers continued throughout 1980. The main opposition party, the Socialist Union of Popular Forces, continued to denounce government economic policies and boycotted a referendum in May on parliamentary terms of office.

MARGARET A. NOVICKI, *"Africa Report"*
The African-American Institute

MOROCCO · Information Highlights

Official Name: Kingdom of Morocco.
Location: Northwest Africa.
Area: 180,602 sq mi (467 759 km²).
Population (1980 est.): 21,000,000.
Chief Cities (1973 est.): Rabat, the capital, 385,000; Casablanca, 2,000,000; Marrakesh, 330,000; Fez, 322,000.
Government: *Head of state,* Hassan II, king (acceded 1961). *Head of government,* Maati Bouabid, prime minister (took office March 1979).
Monetary Unit: Dirham (3.86 dirhams equal U.S.$1, Aug. 1980).
Manufactures (major products): Coal, electric power, phosphates, iron ore, lead, zinc.
Agriculture (major products): Barley, wheat, citrus fruit, sugar beets, grapes.
GNP (1979 est., U.S.$): $15,200,000,000.
Foreign Trade (1979 est., U.S.$): *Imports,* $3,807,000,000; *exports,* $1,872,000,000.

Warner Brothers

Robert Duvall (right) won critical raves for his performance as a Marine pilot in "The Great Santini."

MOTION PICTURES

Whatever might be said against the autocratic policies of the Hollywood moguls of yesteryear, their reigns were marked by a strong personal touch and identification with their films, as well as a love of moviemaking. In the past decade the tendency of the film business to be increasingly dominated by conglomerates with extensive holdings in other areas of business has resulted in stronger emphasis on the balance sheet. The pressure to show a profit to banks and stockholders has made it more difficult for film people with offbeat ideas to induce producers to take risks. Management upheavals, power struggles, and rising costs have rendered executive positions even more unsafe than usual.

This growing inflexibility was dramatically manifested in several symptomatic instances during 1980. *The Great Santini,* produced by Orion and distributed by Warner Bros., became a cause célèbre. The film was tested according to usual patterns, but there was little initial public response. The prospect of opening it for the scrutiny of New York critics was abandoned, and quick ancillary sales were made to cable television's Home Box Office and to American Airlines. But director-screenwriter Lewis John Carlino refused to give up, and when money was raised independently to open the film in New York, Orion finally agreed to foot the bill for advertising and promotion. *The Great Santini,* a drama about an aging Marine Corps pilot and the rigid values he imposes on himself and on his family, won rave reviews—particularly for the performance of Robert Duvall. A film that was almost buried got another chance and appeared to be headed for a profitable future.

Producer-director Richard Rush battled for nine years to have his unusual film *The Stunt Man* made and released. Every major studio had turned it down. Finally Rush convinced the independent Melvin Simon Productions to make the picture, but no releasing company would accept it for distribution. Rush took his film to festivals and arranged for test bookings. Despite successful business in Seattle and other trial cities, the distributors still feared it would flop. Finally, after Rush was able to open the picture in ten Los Angeles theaters to vast box office business, Twentieth Century-Fox, which had turned it down before, agreed to distribute it.

Airplane, a spoof on such films as *Airport,* turned out to be a summer hit. Jim Abrahams, David Zucker, and Jerry Zucker, the directors and writers, finally convinced Paramount to produce the comedy following its rejection by other studios that were leery of the low-key cast chosen by the filmmakers for the purpose of keeping the film's satirical tone.

372

Others have been less fortunate in getting their films released. Director Robert Altman was bitter about the fate of *Health,* his spoof on the political system as seen through electioneering at a Florida health organization convention. Despite Altman's stature, Twentieth Century-Fox claimed that it had found response too negative in test situations to give Altman the advertising-backed distribution he wanted. With costs of newspaper and television ads skyrocketing, unless a studio has an enormous investment in a film, it may be more economical to write off a problem film than to invest further. Altman charged that the film was shelved because of a change of management at Fox.

Some of the films in which the studios did invest heavily met with cool public response. Notorious examples included *1941, Can't Stop the Music,* and *Xanadu. Heaven's Gate,* Michael Cimino's lavish western that had soared over budget to about $36 million, in November was withdrawn from exhibition, following severe panning by film critics. However, the success of other blockbuster attempts, such as *The Empire Strikes Back* (the *Star Wars* sequel), kept alive the big-picture mentality and consequently diminished the chances of small, offbeat films.

The Actor's Strike. The Screen Actors Guild, joined by the American Federation of Television and Radio Artists, undertook what turned out to be the longest strike in its history. At issue was the development of a basic formula for sharing in the revenues the industry is expected to reap as the home-video market broadens. The industry capitulated early on the principle of sharing, but bargaining persisted on the percentages. The figures settled on were 4.5% of revenues from video cassettes and disks after the first 100,000 sales, and 4.5% of the gross for pay-television programs after ten days of play. The walkout lasted from July 21 until October 23, setting back the production of many movies and delaying fall television programming. Actors and actresses generally refused to go on film promotional tours or to give interviews until the strike was settled.

Foreign Influence. Most Americans have never seen a foreign language film, and yet the work of directors from abroad has had a profound influence on American filmmakers. Some of the masters whose works have been studied and emulated had new films out in 1980 that again illustrated their command of the medium. Japanese director Akira Kurosawa, acknowledged as a major influence on their work by Francis Ford Coppola (*The Godfather* films and *Apocalypse Now*) and George Lucas (*Star Wars*), won new acclaim with *Kagemusha—The Shadow Warrior,* an impressive epic of warring samurai clans in 16th century Japan. French "New Wave" director Jean-Luc Godard, whose 1960s pictures, such as *Breathless,* ushered in cinematic techniques now taken for granted, presented his bold, fragmented study of relationships, *Every Man for Himself.* François Truffaut, another influential "New Wave" director, was lauded for *The Last Metro.*

Of all the foreign directors, Sweden's Ingmar Bergman has achieved the greatest international reputation. Bergman unveiled two new films. His made-in-Germany feature, *From the Life of the Marionettes,* is a disturbing probe of violent feelings that explode in an unlikely direction. He

Yoda, a two-foot creature voiced by Frank Oz, and sacred-mission seeker Luke Skywalker (Mark Hamill) converse in this scene from "The Empire Strikes Back," the blockbuster sequel of "Star Wars."

also made *Fårö Document 1979,* a study of inhabitants on the Baltic isle of Fårö, where he maintains a home. Bergman agreed to visit New York, Chicago, and Los Angeles as part of a series of Scandinavian film weeks. His purpose was to boost the films of lesser-known Scandinavian directors. However, at the last moment he cabled notice of his withdrawal, asserting that the distributor of *From the Life of the Marionettes* had, without his knowledge, tied the film opening to his visit, and that in keeping with his principle of not becoming involved in the promotion of his own work, he could not lend himself to such plans.

The strength of German films continued to manifest itself, particularly through such films as Volker Schlöndorff's *The Tin Drum* and the work of Rainer Werner Fassbinder, Germany's most prolific director.

The New York Film Festival showcased three Polish films, a timely choice considering the position Poland occupied in the headlines as a result of the workers' revolt. *The Constant Factor, Orchestra Conductor,* and *Camera Buff* all indicated a vibrant level of filmmaking and a forthrightness in attacking problems inherent in contemporary Polish life.

Meanwhile, Australian films gained further recognition among critics and showed promise in the marketplace. The foremost examples were *The Chant of Jimmie Blacksmith,* which dramatized exploitation of aborigines and a rampage of retaliatory violence, and *My Brilliant Career,* which told of a farm girl struggling to become a writer and to establish her dignity as a woman.

Bye-Bye Brazil, a comedy examining the lives of an itinerant troupe of entertainers against the background of a changing nation, gave evidence of Brazil's expanding film industry.

American Directors. Some critics hailed Woody Allen's *Stardust Memories* as another superior achievement; others chastised him for making a film that was mean-spirited and complaining. Allen took his latest comedy to bitter satirical extremes. Structured along the lines of Federico Fellini's *8½,* Allen's comic lament concerned a director who attends a weekend retrospective of his films. The films within the film were used by Allen as devices for plunging into facets of the director's life, past and present. The portrait that emerged was that of an unhappy and frustrated director who questions the standard of values that brings him so much adulation and who worries about the pain and suffering in the world.

Claudia Weill, who came to public attention in 1978 with an independent, low-budget feature *Girl Friends,* directed *It's My Turn,* with Jill Clayburgh. The film was released in the fall. Although Weill demonstrated that she could work in a slick, mass-appeal vein, she adhered to an intimate theme involving a woman math professor trying to find her way between conflicting career and personal relationship problems.

A symbolic saga, "The Tin Drum" chronicled a German family's experiences from ca. 1900 through 1945.

New World Films

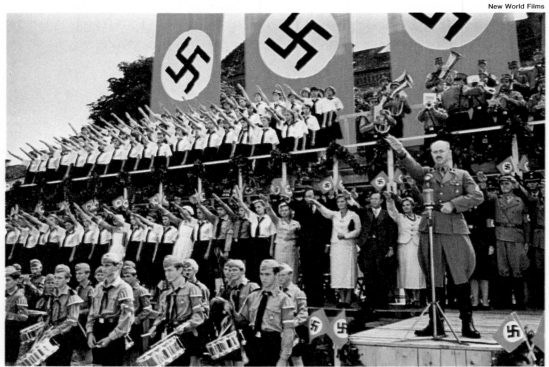

Sissy Spacek (left) and Mary Tyler Moore (above) sparkled in "Coal Miner's Daughter" and "Ordinary People."

The Museum of Modern Art's New Directors/New Film series in New York showcased the work of John Sayles, whose *The Return of the Secaucus Seven* revived memories of the 1960s and forecast a promising career for Sayles. Another director in the limelight was David Lynch for *The Elephant Man*. His previous *Eraserhead* had been a cult film on the midnight show circuit.

Actor Robert Redford demonstrated that he has talent behind the camera as well as in front of it. His *Ordinary People* became one of the year's hits, and it assured Redford of further directorial opportunities.

Imaginative films by several veteran directors were released during 1980. Robert Altman, turning to a comic strip hero, filmed *Popeye*. The picture starred Robin Williams as the spinach eater and Shelley Duvall as the beanpole girlfriend Olive Oyl. John Huston presented *Wise Blood*, Flannery O'Connor's gallows humor story about Southern street-corner preachers. (Huston was honored by the Film Society of Lincoln Center at its annual gala.) Martin Scorsese cast brilliant Robert DeNiro as former boxer Jake LaMotta in *Raging Bull*. Sidney Lumet's *Just Tell Me What You Want* gave Alan King an opportunity for a bravura performance as a tycoon trying to hold on to his mistress, played engagingly by Ali MacGraw. Although it did not have a long theater run, the film is a stylish, often hilarious comedy that should show up in Lumet retrospectives. Stanley Kubrick delved into the horror genre with *The Shining*, an accomplished film that nevertheless did not catch on with critics or the public. William Friedkin drew sharp criticism for the violence in *Cruising*, which also became controversial because it was picketed by gay activists. The trend toward violence was further illustrated by *Dressed to Kill*, Brian DePalma's flashy murder mystery, and by a spate of horror cheapies.

Star Performances. Gena Rowlands gave one of the toughest characterizations in memory as a moll who protects a child from the mob in her husband John Cassavetes' film *Gloria*. In *Resurrection* Ellen Burstyn lent dimension and credibility to the character of a woman who has an auto accident and discovers she has acquired the power to heal. Jane Fonda, Dolly Parton, and Lily Tomlin struck a blow for the rights of office women in *Nine to Five*. Sissy Spacek brilliantly portrayed country singer Loretta Lynn in *Coal Miner's Daughter*. In *Melvin and Howard* Mary Steenburgen gave an impressive performance. Sally Field won an Oscar for *Norma Rae*, and Meryl Streep won the best supporting actress Oscar for *Kramer vs. Kramer*. Among the men, Dustin Hoffman won his first Oscar for *Kramer vs. Kramer*. Donald Sutherland was outstanding as the troubled father in *Ordinary People*.

Deaths. Filmdom lost Sir Alfred Hitchcock, one of its greatest directors. Hitchcock left a legacy of thrillers that not only entertained millions but taught other directors how to use the medium creatively through visual emphasis rather than dialogue.

British comedian Peter Sellers bequeathed to the film world a scrapbook of hilarious characters with an assortment of accents. His death came after his triumph in *Being There* and after the subsequent release of the far less gratifying *The Fiendish Plot of Dr. Fu Manchu*. (*See also* OBITUARIES.)

WILLIAM WOLF, *Film Commentator*
"New York Magazine"

The film "Airplane," a spoof of disaster-type thrillers like the "Airport" movies, was a 1980 summer hit.

MOTION PICTURES 1980

AIRPLANE. Written and directed by Jim Abrahams, David Zucker, and Jerry Zucker. With Lloyd Bridges, Peter Graves.

AMERICAN GIGOLO. Written and directed by Paul Schrader. With Richard Gere, Lauren Hutton.

BLOOD FEUD. Written and directed by Lina Wertmuller. With Sophia Loren, Marcello Mastroianni, Giancarlo Giannini.

THE BLUE LAGOON. Director, Randal Kleiser; screenplay by Douglas Day Stewart. With Brooke Shields, Christopher Atkins.

THE BLUES BROTHERS. Director, John Landis; screenplay by Dan Aykroyd and Mr. Landis. With John Belushi, Dan Aykroyd.

MY BODYGUARD. Director, Tony Bill; screenplay by Alan Ormsby. With Chris Makepeace, Ruth Gordon, Martin Mull, John Houseman.

BRUBAKER. Director, Stuart Rosenberg; screenplay by W. D. Richter. With Robert Redford, Jane Alexander.

CALIGULA. Produced by Bob Guccione and Franco Rossellini. With Malcolm McDowell, Peter O'Toole, John Gielgud, Helen Mirren.

THE CHANGELING. Director, Peter Medak; screenplay by William Gray and Diana Maddox. With George C. Scott, Trish Van Devere, Melvyn Douglas.

THE CHANT OF JIMMIE BLACKSMITH. Written and directed by Fred Schepisi. With Tommy Lewis, Freddy Reynolds.

COAL MINER'S DAUGHTER. Director, Michael Apted; screenplay by Tom Rickman. With Sissy Spacek, Tommy Lee Jones.

THE COMPETITION. Written and directed by Joel Oliansky. With Richard Dreyfuss, Amy Irving.

CRUISING. Written and directed by William Friedkin. With Al Pacino.

DIVINE MADNESS. Director, Michael Ritchie; screenplay by Jerry Blatt, Bette Midler, Bruce Vilanch. With Bette Midler.

DRESSED TO KILL. Written and directed by Brian De Palma. With Michael Caine, Angie Dickinson.

EBOLI. Director, Francesco Rosi; screenplay by Mr. Rosi, Tonino Guerra, and Raffaele La Capria. With Gian Maria Volonte, Irene Papas.

THE ELEPHANT MAN. Director, David Lynch; screenplay by Christopher DeVore, Eric Bergren, and Mr. Lynch. With Anthony Hopkins, John Hurt, Anne Bancroft, John Gielgud, Wendy Hiller.

THE EMPIRE STRIKES BACK. Director, Irvin Kershner; screenplay by Leigh Brackett and Lawrence Kasdan, story by George Lucas. With Mark Hamill, Carrie Fisher, Harrison Ford, Billy Dee Williams.

EVERY MAN FOR HIMSELF. Director, Jean-Luc Godard; screenplay by Jean-Claude Carrière and Anne-Marie Miéville. With Isabelle Huppert, Jacques Dutronc, Nathalie Baye.

FAME. Director, Alan Parker; screenplay by Christopher Gore. With Debbie Allen, Anne Meara.

THE FIENDISH PLOT OF DR. FU MANCHU. Director, Piers Haggard; screenplay by Jim Moloney and Rudy Dochtermann. With Peter Sellers, Sid Caesar.

THE FOG. Director, John Carpenter; screenplay by Mr. Carpenter and Debra Hill. With Adrienne Barbeau, Janet Leigh, Hal Holbrook.

FROM THE LIFE OF THE MARIONETTES. Written and directed by Ingmar Bergman. With Robert Atzorn, Christine Bucheggerm, Martin Benrath.

THE GETTING OF WISDOM. Director, Bruce Beresford; screenplay by Eleanor Witcombe. With Susannah Fowle.

GLORIA. Written and directed by John Cassavetes. With Gena Rowlands, John Adames, Buck Henry.

THE GREAT SANTINI. Written and directed by Lewis John Carlino. With Robert Duvall, Blythe Danner.

HEART BEAT. Written and directed by John Byrum. With Nick Nolte, Sissy Spacek, John Heard.

HIDE IN PLAIN SIGHT. Director, James Caan; screenplay by Spencer Eastman. With James Caan, Jill Eikenberry.

HONEYSUCKLE ROSE. Director, Jerry Schatzberg; screenplay by Carol Sobieski, William D. Wittliff, and John Binder. With Willie Nelson.

HOPSCOTCH. Director, Ronald Neame; screenplay by Brian Garfield and Bryan Forbes. With Walter Matthau, Glenda Jackson.

THE HUMAN FACTOR. Director, Otto Preminger; screenplay by Tom Stoppard. With Richard Attenborough, John Gielgud, Nicol Williamson.

IN EINEM JAHR MIT 13 MONDEN (In a Year of 13 Moons). Written and directed by Rainer Werner Fassbinder. With Volker Spengler.

In a scene from "The Shining," Jack Nicholson, left, is surrounded by specters of the Overlook Hotel.

IT'S MY TURN. Director, Claudia Weill; screenplay by Eleanor Bergstein. With Jill Clayburgh, Michael Douglas, Charles Grodin.

JUST TELL ME WHAT YOU WANT. Director, Sidney Lumet; screenplay by Jay Presson Allen. With Ali MacGraw, Alan King.

KAGEMUSHA—THE SHADOW WARRIOR. Director, Akira Kurosawa; screenplay by Mr. Kurosawa and Masato Ide. With Tatsuya Nakadai.

THE KIDNAPPING OF THE PRESIDENT. Director, George Mendeluk; screenplay by Richard Murphy. With William Shatner, Hal Holbrook, Van Johnson.

THE LAST MARRIED COUPLE IN AMERICA. Director, Gilbert Cates; screenplay by John Herman Shaner. With George Segal, Natalie Wood.

LITTLE DARLINGS. Director, Ronald F. Maxwell; screenplay by Kimi Peck and Dalene Young. With Tatum O'Neal, Kristy McNichol.

LITTLE MISS MARKER. Written and directed by Walter Bernstein. With Walter Matthau, Julie Andrews.

THE LONG RIDERS. Director, Walter Hill; screenplay by Bill Bryden, Steven Phillip Smith, Stacy Keach, James Keach. With David Carradine, Keith Carradine, Robert Carradine, James Keach, Stacy Keach, Dennis Quaid, Randy Quaid, Christopher Guest, Nicholas Guest, James Whitmore, Jr.

MELVIN AND HOWARD. Director, Jonathan Demme; screenplay by Bo Goldman. With Jason Robards, Paul Le Mat, Mary Steenburgen.

MY BRILLIANT CAREER. Director, Gillian Armstrong; screenplay by Eleanor Witcombe. With Judy Davis.

NIJINSKY. Director, Herbert Ross; screenplay by Hugh Wheeler. With Alan Bates, George de la Peña, Leslie Browne.

NINE TO FIVE. Director, Colin Higgins; screenplay by Mr. Higgins and Patricia Resnick. With Jane Fonda, Lily Tomlin, Dolly Parton, Dabney Coleman.

ONE AND ONE. Directors, Erland Josephson, Sven Nykvist, and Ingrid Thulin; screenplay by Mr. Josephson. With Ingrid Thulin, Erland Josephson.

ORDINARY PEOPLE. Director, Robert Redford; screenplay by Alvin Sargent. With Donald Sutherland, Mary Tyler Moore, Judd Hirsch, Timothy Hutton.

THE OUTSIDER. Written and directed by Tony Luraschi. With Craig Wasson, Sterling Hayden.

POPEYE. Director, Robert Altman; screenplay by Jules Feiffer. With Robin Williams, Shelley Duvall, Paul Dooley, Ray Walston, Paul L. Smith.

PRIVATE BENJAMIN. Director, Howard Zieff; screenplay by Nancy Meyers, Charles Shyer, and Harvey Miller. With Goldie Hawn, Eileen Brennan.

RAGING BULL. Director, Martin Scorsese; screenplay by P. Schrader, M. Martin. With Robert De Niro.

RESURRECTION. Director, Daniel Petrie; screenplay by Lewis John Carlino. With Ellen Burstyn.

ROUGH CUT. Director, Donald Siegel; screenplay by Francis Burns. With Burt Reynolds, Lesley-Anne Down, David Niven.

SEEMS LIKE OLD TIMES. Director, Jay Sandrich; screenplay by Neil Simon. With Goldie Hawn, Chevy Chase, Charles Grodin.

SERIAL. Director, Bill Persky; screenplay by Rich Eustis, and Michael Elias. With Martin Mull, Tuesday Weld, Sally Kellerman, Bill Macy.

THE SHINING. Director, Stanley Kubrick; screenplay by Mr. Kubrick and Diane Johnson. With Jack Nicholson, Shelley Duvall, Danny Lloyd.

SIMON. Written and directed by Marshall Brickman. With Alan Arkin, Madeline Kahn.

SMOKEY AND THE BANDIT II. Director, Hal Needham; screenplay by Jerry Belson and Brock Yates. With Burt Reynolds, Jackie Gleason, Sally Field.

STARDUST MEMORIES. Written and directed by Woody Allen. With Woody Allen, Charlotte Rampling, Jessica Harper, Marie-Christine Barrault.

THE STUNT MAN. Written and directed by Richard Rush. With Peter O'Toole.

THE THIRD GENERATION. Written and directed by Rainer Werner Fassbinder. With Eddie Constantine, Bulle Ogier.

THE TIN DRUM. Director, Volker Schlöndorff; screenplay by Jean-Claude Carrière, Mr. Schlöndorff, and Franz Seitz. With David Bennent.

TOM HORN. Director, William Wiard; screenplay by Thomas McGuane and Bud Shrake. With Steve McQueen, Linda Evans, Slim Pickens.

URBAN COWBOY. Director, James Bridges; screenplay by Mr. Bridges and Aaron Latham. With John Travolta, Debra Winger.

WILLIE AND PHIL. Written and directed by Paul Mazursky. With Margot Kidder, Ray Sharkey, Michael Ontkean.

WISE BLOOD. Director, John Huston; screenplay by Benedict Fitzgerald. With Ned Beatty, Brad Dourif.

XANADU. Director, Robert Greenwald; screenplay by Richard Christian Danus and Marc Reid Rubel. With Olivia Newton-John, Gene Kelly.

A strike by the chorus at the New York Metropolitan Opera leads members of the orchestra to offer free outdoor concerts. The strike delayed the opening of the 1980–81 season until December.

MUSIC

Classical

In 1980, many separate currents in music began drawing together into more distinct but fewer trends. In the slow-changing world of classical music, with its broad and disparate public and high performance costs, there were clear indications that audiences, performers, and composers were accepting new music as a normal part of the repertory.

New Music. In the United States, this movement was symbolized by the widespread observance of milestone birthday anniversaries of composers who were major pioneers of new music. Aaron Copland's 80th birthday was celebrated November 14 by the National Symphony at the J. F. Kennedy Center, Washington, DC. Samuel Barber's 70th birthday on March 9 was observed with concerts at the Curtis Institute of Music where he both studied and taught. William Schuman, composer-in-residence at the Aspen Music Festival (Colorado), was honored there on his 70th birthday, August 4. Numerous performances of these composers' works throughout the United States during 1980 signi-

fied popular recognition of the modern creative tradition in American music.

In a related occurrence, symphony subscription and other regular series music programs showed a marked increase in 20th century works, including more by younger American composers. A more responsive public also was reported. One major reason was the more moderate compositional approach—a trend toward working with materials from earlier idioms, if not actual parody and quotation, and a new feeling for tonality. Contemporary European composers who were given premieres were Witold Lutosławski (the National Symphony, January; the St. Louis Symphony, April) and Krzysztof Penderecki (his *Second* or *"Christmas" Symphony*, New York Philharmonic, May 1).

Among the Americans, David Del Tredici continued his success with a restrospective style. He won the 1980 Pulitzer Prize for Music for his *In Memory of a Summer Day* (commissioned and performed on April 14 by the St. Louis Symphony). The composition was part of Del Tredici's Alice-in-Wonderland cycle of symphonic and chamber pieces begun in 1968 when he turned to a simpler tonal style. By 1980, his *Final Alice* (1976) had had 40 performances by 11 orchestras. Another new and nostalgic "Alice" work was *Happy Voices,* premiered by the San Francisco Symphony, Edo de Waart conducting, at the opening of its Louise M. Davies Symphony Hall on September 16.

The premiere of John Harbison's *Piano Concerto* was played on May 12 with the American Composers Orchestra; on September 28, the work was given the third annual Kennedy Center Friedheim Award. The work showed a strong and original assimilation of the major idioms in a rather romantic though not nostalgic manner. Other orchestral premieres included Alberto Ginastera's *Iubilum: Celebración Sinfonica* (Buenos Aires, April 11); William Schuman's *Three Colloquies* for French Horn and Orchestra (the New York Philharmonic, January 24); and Mark Neikrug's *Eternity's Sunrise* (New York Philharmonic, November 20).

A generally "softer" manner in composition was observed at specialized festivals such as the Colorado Music Festival (Boulder). A more accepting attitude by the public was also noted at the New Music America festival (nine days of predominantly avant-garde works, Minneapolis) in June. One example of lingering experimentalism at the New Music America festival was Richard Lerman's *Travelon,* the amplification of the spokes, chains, and brakes of 30 bicycles being ridden simultaneously. Of the tenth Annual International Electro-Acoustical Musical Festival in Bourges, France (18 concerts, June 1–6), one summary gave higher marks to the technology demonstrated than to the musicianship.

The International Society of Contemporary Music's World Music Days during July offered 52 compositions (chosen by an international jury from 365 submitted scores) in ten concerts held in three cities and one kibbutz in Israel. The concerts' repertoire included three compositions by Americans Jonathan D. Kramer, Norman Dinerstein, and Brian Fennelly. At the Donaueschingen (West Germany) Festival's Music Days (ten programs, October 17–19), a pattern was observed of conciliation of the listener without condescension. It was a move away from the aesthetics of dramatic violence and toward the poetic approach. *Con alcune licenze* (for 18 instruments) by Thomas Pernes of Austria was singled out for its expressive qualities and originality. The milder trend was noted even in the newest music of Karlheinz Stockhausen, performed two weeks later in Berlin.

Opera. The premieres of the truly large operas took place in Europe. At the June 18 opening of Gottfried von Einem's *Jesu Hochzeit* at the Vienna Festival, there were public demonstrations because of its subject matter—the mystical union of Jesus, representing life, with a female Death. Also on religious grounds, John Taverner's *Thérèse* (based on the autobiography of St. Thérèse) drew heavy criticism when it premiered at London's Royal Opera House, Covent Garden, on March 12. At the Holland Festival, June 1–23, two important new works were Jan van Gilse's *Thijl,* based on the oppression of Flanders during the 80-Years' War, and Karlheinz Stockhausen's *Michaels Heimkehr,* Act II of a massive trilogy, *Donnerstag.*

In connection with the Mannheim Opera's 200th anniversary, Giselher Klebe's *Der Juengste Tag* (Doomsday), a 12-tone score on a libretto about a 1938 Austrian train wreck, was produced. A work based on yet another disaster, *The Sinking of the Titanic* by Wilhelm Dieter Seibert, was sent from Berlin's Deutsche Opera as part of a sister-city tribute to Los Angeles' 200th anniversary.

Among notable revivals in Europe were two works by Ernst Krenek in celebration of the Austrian-American composer's 80th year. On June 3, the Vienna Festival produced his *Jonny spielt auf,* the controversial jazz opera of 1927. In August, the Salzburg Festival offered a concert performance of Krenek's *Karl V* of 1933. (The major Krenek observance was at the Styrian Autumn Festival, Graz, Austria, October 23–26.)

In the United States, new operas were produced primarily by smaller, regional companies. One of the important productions was John Eaton's *The Cry of Clytaemnestra,* a one-act

Conductor and composer John Williams succeeds the late Arthur Fiedler as Boston Pops conductor.

Steve Liss, Liaison

work which premiered at Indiana University on March 12. Its electronic/orchestral score was highly praised, but Patrick Creagh's libretto was criticized. Coincident with a Kurt Weill renaissance, the New York City Opera on March 20 introduced his *Silverlake,* a new version of a piece which was originally—in its only other staging, in 1930—a play with music. It was not well-received by music critics, and neither was the company's American trilogy project which opened on October 9—Jan Bach's *The Student from Salamanca,* Thomas Pasatieri's *Before Breakfast,* and Stanley Silverman's *Madame Adare.*

Modern premieres of neglected early operas continued to play a major part in the American as well as the European opera scenes. These included George Frederick Handel's *Radimisto* (February 16) at the Kennedy Center and Antonio Vivaldi's *Orlando Furioso,* given by the Dallas Civic Opera on November 28, with Marilyn Horne in a starring role. There were performances of scholarly reconstructions. One was Antonio de Almeida's restoration of Jacques Offenbach's *Les Contes d'Hoffmann,* which drew on 1,500 pages of manuscript that de Almeida had discovered; it was performed by the Greater Miami Opera on January 14. Another was Giuseppe Verdi's *The Force of Destiny* in Andrew Porter's new translation. The production used the complete original score of 1862 and the 1869 production and design books in its U.S. premiere staged at the University of California, Irvine, on April 22.

During August a 74-member troupe from the Peking Opera company performed at the Metropolitan Opera House in New York. The performances were the first of a 12-week, 10-city tour for the troupe. Despite an unadorned, rather severe set, spectacular effects were produced through colorful facial makeup, lavish costumes, and daring acrobatics.

Economic Events. The biggest news stories, however, were economic in nature. The Metropolitan Opera's season was canceled on September 29 due to difficulties in negotiating some of the 17 labor union contracts which had expired. After compromises, especially in the orchestra's demand for a four-performance week, the season was reconstructed. The season began on December 10 with a concert performance of Gustav Mahler's Symphony No. 2, *Resurrection.* On December 12, a new production of the three-act version of Alban Berg's *Lulu* (completed in 1979 and premiered in Paris) was performed.

The economic downturn was reflected in the Chicago Lyric Opera's reduction of its season from seven productions to five, and in serious financial problems of the Royal Opera House, Covent Garden. The British Broadcasting Company (BBC), the world's largest patron of live classical music, in order to save money cut the number of musicians in its employ by disbanding three light music orchestras. The BBC had earlier attempted to close down the large Scottish Symphony orchestra, but this move provoked a Musicians Union dispute. After negotiations the Scottish Symphony was not disbanded. (*See also*

As outdoor opera gains in popularity, the Houston Grand Opera presents "Madam Butterfly."

Jim Caldwell, Courtesy, Houston Grand Opera

Photos Opera Theatre of Saint Louis

The Opera Theatre of Saint Louis' outdoor season included "The Magic Flute" (left) and "The Turn of the Screw."

GREAT BRITAIN: The Arts.) The Detroit Symphony's budget had to be reduced severely because of setbacks in the automobile industry and the high spending policies of the music director, Antal Dorati. Dorati quit in protest but reconsidered, deferring his resignation until after 1981, when he will become Conductor Laureate.

San Francisco was one of few communities which substantially increased musical activities. The San Francisco Opera announced a new festival of international grand opera beginning with 27 performances of five productions (June 12–July 19, 1981) and formed its own independent 67-member orchestra, the city's third major contract orchestra.

Louise M. Davies Symphony Hall. The San Francisco Symphony's activities were expanded when the orchestra exchanged its home at the War Memorial Opera House (where the orchestra shared space with the San Francisco Opera) for the Louise M. Davies Symphony Hall. The new house makes possible a full-length concert schedule for the orchestra. The September 16 inauguration of the $27.5 million structure, with its distinctive "wraparound" interior design, attracted national attention. Its acoustics drew tentative criticism. Portions of the building and the "tuning" process could not be completed by its opening date because strikes had interrupted construction.

Prizes and Anniversaries. Alison Deane of New York won the piano competition, and John Clayton (Los Angeles) and Marcus Thompson (New York) won the string competition of the National Black Music Colloquium and Competition at the Kennedy Center on January 20. In Tel Aviv, Gregory Allen of Austin, TX, won the third annual Artur Rubinstein International Piano Competition. Kathleen Winkler won the Carl Nielsen International Violin Competition in Odense, Denmark. Gregory Fulkerson, violinist from Louisville, KY, won the Kennedy Center/Rockefeller Foundation competition for excellence in American music performance. Leonard Bernstein and Leontyne Price (along with James Cagney, Agnes de Mille, and Lynn Fontanne) were recipients of the 1980 Kennedy Center Awards.

The centennial season of the St. Louis Symphony, postponed from 1979 because of an orchestra strike, began on September 13. The Boston Symphony began its centennial season on September 25 with Leonard Bernstein's *Fanfare*, the first of 12 commemorative commissions. For the University of Southern California's centennial, musical works were commissioned from six faculty composers. Carnegie Hall prepared for its 90th birthday celebration, which will fall on May 5, 1981. It was also the 15th anniversary of the founding of the National Endowment for the Arts. The federal organization in that time has awarded $1,000,000,000 in 40,000 grants, and has been a major factor in drawing increased private support for the arts. For 1980, $14 million was allocated to music, an increase of $1.7 million over 1979.

ROBERT COMMANDAY
Music Critic, "San Francisco Chronicle"

An enthusiastic crowd enjoys the Newport Jazz Festival.

Jazz

The jazz scene of 1980 saw a slight increase in national and a substantial increase in international jazz festivals and concerts. Important talents included young and old alike, from Europe's Stephane Grappelli to Nieis-Henning Orsted Pederson to Terumasa Hino. Mel Torme presented three concerts at Carnegie Hall in the spring. In Canada on the occasion of Alberta's 75th anniversary, the province subsidized a week-long jazz festival in Edmonton.

Charlie Parker Tributes. The phrase "Bird Lives," found new meaning in 1980, as the jazz establishment paid tribute to Charlie Parker, the alto sax virtuoso who died in 1955. From the Newport Jazz Festival's opener, "Year of the Bird," to the Chicago Jazz Festival's "Charlie Parker's Birthday," performances all over the world were dedicated to Mr. Parker and honored his musical legacy.

Women in Jazz. The third annual Women's Jazz Festival was held in Kansas City. The festival, an outgrowth of Clark Terry's All Girl Jazz Band performances at the 1976 Wichita Jazz Festival, was one of the many varied and successful women's jazz activities. Other such concerts were New York's third annual "Salute to Women in Jazz" concert series and the "Blues is a Woman" concert of the Newport Jazz Festival.

Big Bands. In 1980 a larger number of big bands were working than at any time since the big band heyday of the 1940s. Besides the established name bands (of Buddy Rich, Woody Herman, Count Basie, Duke Ellington, etc.), many new and important local big jazz bands were performing, including those of Mel Lewis in New York, Rodger Pemberton in Chicago, Baron Von Olen in Indianapolis, the Blue Wisp 16-piece group in Cincinnati, the Dallas Jazz Orchestra in Dallas, and Bill Berry in Los Angeles.

Jazz Recordings. Due to the unpredictable economics of the recording industry, only music considered able to command great public interest was recorded. The reaction to this trend in the jazz world was two-fold—jazz artists produced their own albums and jazz drifted unnoticed out of the pop top-40 list.

In 1980 Miles Davis (the master of timing) broke a five-year recording hiatus with the album *Circle in the Round.* Although it contained fine cuts of previously recorded work, it was less than a critical success.

Awards. Winners in the 28th annual International Jazz Critics Poll included: Record of the year, Air, *Air Lore;* Reissue of the year, Charles Mingus, *Mingus at Antibes;* Big band, Toshiko Akiyoshi/Lew Tabackin; Jazz group, Art Ensemble of Chicago; Alto sax, Art Pepper; Tenor sax, Sonny Rollins; Baritone sax, Pepper Adams; Trumpet, Dizzy Gillespie; Trombone, Albert Mangelsdorf. Drum category winner Max Roach was also the 50th inductee into the *Downbeat* Hall of Fame.

DOMINIC SPERA, *Indiana University*

MUSIC—SPECIAL REPORT:
Gospel Music

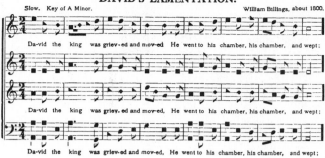

DAVID'S LAMENTATION.

Slow. Key of A Minor. William Billings, about 1800.

Da-vid the king was griev-ed and mov-ed He went to his chamber, his chamber, and wept;

Da-vid the king was griev-ed and mov-ed, He went to his chamber, his chamber, and wept;

Da-vid the king was griev-ed and mov-ed, He went to his chamber, his chamber, and wept;

Sacred Harp Publishing

Early gospel songbooks featured the shaped musical note.

Gospel music, which had its beginnings in the early 18th century, during 1980 was in the midst of resurgence. Throughout the year, gospel music performances took place in churches, concert halls, night clubs, and the Broadway theater, and were broadcast on television and radio. Within the music industry in 1979 there were 98 recording companies exclusively handling gospel music, 226 radio stations devoted to full-time gospel programming, 480 gospel groups performing at least three times weekly, and 131 publishing companies dealing entirely with gospel products. These figures were expected to increase during 1980.

Dove Awards, the gospel music industry's highest honor, have been given to worthy recipients since 1969. Outstanding figures of the modern gospel movement have included the Reverend James Cleveland, pastor of the Los Angeles Cornerstone Institutional Baptist Church and known as the King of Black Gospel; the late Clara Ward; Eva Mae Lefevre; Brook Speer; Aretha Franklin; Jimmy Dean; and the late Mahalia Jackson. Important groups are the Dixie Hummingbirds, as well as the Imperials and The Blackwood Brothers, the members of which were presented with Grammy Awards in 1980.

History. A product of the "Great Awakening" of 1735 and the religious revival movements that spread from New England to Kentucky, impelled by such famed preachers as Jonathan Edwards, gospel music was created by common people out of a sincere need for involvement and communication with God. Following the appearance of early singing schools (including the first black singing school in Newport, RI), the first gospel songbook was published in 1798. A unique feature of the book was that the musical notes were written out in shaped notation rather than in the universally familiar round notes.

PTL Network

Jim Bakker (right) is host of the PTL Club, a Christian-talk/variety TV show, featuring the PTL Singers (below), gospel-music performers.

PTL Network

383

Broadway theater's "Your Arms Too Short to Box with God" is a gospel music celebration of the Bible's "Book of St. Matthew." With music and lyrics by gospel soloist Alex Bradford, the musical concludes with a tribute to past gospel greats, Mahalia Jackson, Clara Ward, and Bradford (who died in 1978).

Max Eisen

Gospel tunes became widely popular by the 19th century through the all-denominational camp meetings. In 1869, the Jubilee Singers, a group of black men and women, toured the United States and Europe with their "spiritual songs." Traveling for seven years and earning $150,000 to help found Fisk University, they ushered in the first commercial gospel music era.

Gospel music in the 20th century gained worldwide recognition. Small professional groups that began traveling and recording in the 1920s and 1930s helped to advance the "golden period of gospel music" (1945–1960).

Gospel soloist Marion Williams is famous for her rhythmic, improvisational style.

David Gahr

Style. The enslavement and segregation of the Negro in America were responsible for the development of gospel music in two separate styles. The white gospel style, with its straightforward melody, often sentimental text, and lively tempo, had its roots in American and British folk songs. The black gospel style began with the first shipload of African slaves who landed in the United States in 1619. In the New World the Africans were attracted by European harmony and melody and soon combined characteristics of British and American folk hymns with their African song styles. The black gospel style incorporated a more improvised, richer melodic line over a strong beat; vigorous, intricate rhythmic patterns; and much syncopation. Delivered in a freer "preachin'/hollerin'" manner, black gospel music eventually influenced such modern forms as jazz, blues, soul, popular ballad, country/western, rock'n'roll, and rock.

Both black and white gospel styles were known by a variety of names, including gospel hymns, Sunday school songs, evangelical hymns, shout songs, jubilee songs, inspirational hymns, and Jesus rock songs. Whatever the name, they were based on religious or spiritual themes which often inspired spontaneous participation—dancing, shouting, clapping hands, and stamping feet—by the listeners. The songs were made up of simple, catchy melodic lines with repeated phrases, combined with lyrics that told a story.

In the past few decades such performers as Mahalia Jackson, Thomas A. Dorsey, Andrae Crouch, Bud Howell, and Shannon Williams have successfully integrated the black and white gospel styles.

FRANCES E. COLE

Popular

Perhaps the most significant development in popular music in 1980 was the new breadth of mainstream contemporary taste. In the past, new pop-music trends had started as underground movements (as rock did in the mid-1950s) and then had spread gaining mass popularity or perhaps had remained an isolated cult. In 1980 underground trends did not blend readily into the mainstream but remained separate currents that added to the flow. The year offered what appeared to be a glut of resurgences. There was renewed activity in rhythm & blues, in both traditional and contemporary country, and in "heavy metal" and "soft" rock. Broadway flourished, and the big band sound returned, as did the blues, reggae, and rockabilly. The murder of former Beatle John Lennon, who had an overwhelming effect on pop music, was a major loss. (*See* OBITUARIES, page 413.)

Popular music activity was vigorous and healthy in 1980, but the recording and broadcast industries did not enjoy a similar success. The economic slump that had hit in 1979 loosened the industries' firm hold on the great mass of consumers. In the scramble to regain that hold, they discovered the difficulty of relating to consumers as large collective units (as they formerly had been able to do). Radio stations frantically switched formats to aid in attracting suddenly elusive high ratings. Perhaps the most extreme case was WRVR-FM in New York. Overnight, the station replaced its all-jazz broadcasts with a 24-hour-a-day country-music format. In general AM radio moved toward all-talk formats while FM radio went toward all-music frameworks. In the recording industry, major companies began to lose their customers to the smaller recording companies that provided more varied musical fare.

New Wave also found a cozy niche in small rock-disco clubs. Performers like the B-52's sold substantial quantities of their disks through the word of mouth generated at these clubs, which were 500 strong and growing throughout the United States. This new and informal marketing means undermined the accepted belief that radio air-play time was the only means to pop commercial success. The clubs, true outgrowths of the music scene of 1980, featured videotape performances, as well as live acts, and almost any music with a good beat for dancing.

The following for 1970s-style disco generally shrank, although the music maintained advocates in some urban centers, most of Middle America, and Europe. In 1980 its greatest strength was developing in Latin America.

Black music of all types—from the rhythmic soul of the Jacksons and Spinners to the punk-funk of Parliament, Funkadelic, and myriad spinoffs—surged up in disco's wake.

Country music, second only to rock in the mass enthusiasm that it generated, was broadcast everywhere along the radio dial. The strong success of the film *Urban Cowboy* and increased television exposure brought new performers like Eddie Rabbitt and Lacy J. Dalton before the public. The annual International Fan Fair, in its ninth year, drew record-breaking crowds, and Nashville's music industry labored to change the image of the city from that of the Hillbilly Capital to the Pop-Music Capital.

Rock's huge, multiple-act stadium concerts moved toward extinction. Not only had they become too expensive, but they had become dangerous as well. Eleven people were killed in a crush at a Who concert in Cincinnati in 1979.

Some individual rock acts still drew enormous crowds. In September, Elton John's free concert in New York's Central Park drew more than 400,000 fans. The rock star had made his first U.S. appearance in Los Angeles about ten years before. The sold-out concerts of Pink Floyd, given in early 1980, were theatrical extravaganzas based on their concept album *The Wall.* Bruce Springsteen's fall tour generated massive excitement. Established rock groups like Yes and Jethro Tull survived major personnel changes, but the sudden death of drummer John Bonham left undecided the fate of the internationally popular Led Zeppelin.

Bob Marley's brand of reggae continued to be popular. British groups like the Police and the Specials brought Caribbean-derived ska rhythms to the United States. Also from Britain came a "heavy-metal" rock revival. Australian AC/DC and native American Ted Nugent bashed their way into the hearts of teenagers.

Bob Dylan, one of pop music's enduring performers, brought out his album *Saved.*

The Broadway musical theater's *Evita, Barnum,* and *A Day in Hollywood/A Night in the Ukraine* took numerous Tony awards. The Gower Champion musical, *42nd Street,* which opened after the 1980 Tony awards, recreated traditional Broadway razzle-dazzle.

Some pop performers took fascinating side trips from their traditional career fortes. Linda Ronstadt sang in a New York production of Gilbert and Sullivan's *The Pirates of Penzance* and David Bowie appeared on Broadway in *The Elephant Man.*

The movie and television activities of several pop stars increased dramatically in 1980. Blondie's Deborah Harry, Aretha Franklin, and Dolly Parton all appeared in motion pictures. *One-Trick Pony,* a film written by and starring Paul Simon, presented an especially sensitive view of the new stresses on pop performers. The film deals with a rock performer who must adjust to turning 40. Deborah Harry and David Bowie, with their flair for theater, appeared destined for success in the blossoming home-video market medium. In 1980, several pop artists were already involved with the production of video performances, notably Todd Rundgren, Al Kooper, the Boomtown Rats, and Marty Balin.

PAULETTE WEISS, *"Stereo Review"*

NATIONS OF THE WORLD

A PROFILE AND SYNOPSIS OF MAJOR 1980 DEVELOPMENTS

Nation, Region	Population in millions[1]	Capital	Area Sq mi (km^2)	Head of State/Government[2]
Bahamas, Caribbean	0.2	Nassau	5,382 (13 939)	Lynden O. Pindling, prime minister

Eight Cuban MiG-19 fighter planes sank a patrol boat of the Royal Bahamas Defense Force as it was towing two impounded Cuban fishing vessels within territorial waters, May 10. Four crew members were killed. Cuban authorities said the attack was a mistake. On November 13, 102 Haitian refugees stranded on Cayo Lobos Island for 40 days were herded aboard a ship by Bahamian police and returned to Haiti.

| **Bahrain,** W. Asia | 0.4 | Manama | 258 (668) | Isa ibn Salman, emir
Khalifa ibn Salman, prime minister |

French President Valéry Giscard d'Estaing visited Bahrain during his tour of the Persian Gulf states, March 1–10. The U.S. attempt to rescue the hostages in Iran sparked demonstrations in Bahrain on April 26; the demonstrators protested the alleged use of airfields in Bahrain by U.S. aircraft.

| **Barbados,** Caribbean | 0.3 | Bridgetown | 166 (430) | John M.G. Adams, prime minister |

Hurricane Allen struck Barbados on August 4, causing major damage.

| **Benin,** W. Africa | 3.6 | Porto-Novo | 43,484 (112 622) | Mathieu Kérékou, president |

| **Bhutan,** S. Asia | 1.3 | Thimphu | 18,000 (40 000) | Jigme Singhye Wangchuk, king |

| **Botswana,** S. Africa | 0.8 | Gaborone | 231,805 (600 372) | Quett Masire, president |

Sir Seretse Khama, the president of Botswana since it gained independence from Great Britain in 1966, died of cancer on July 13. Vice-President and Minister of Finance and Planning Quett Masire, a close confidant of Sir Seretse, was elected by the National Assembly to replace him on July 18.

| **Burundi,** E. Africa | 4.5 | Bujumbura | 10,747 (27 835) | Jean-Baptiste Bagaza, president |

| **Cameroon,** Cen. Africa | 8.5 | Yaoundé | 183,569 (475 442) | Amadou Ahidjo, president |

President Amadou Ahidjo was reelected to a fifth consecutive five-year term on April 5. In his opening speech to the third congress of the Cameroon National Party, February 13–17, at which he was nominated, unanimously, Ahidjo denied charges by self-exiled opponents of his regime and by Amnesty International of widespread human rights violations.

| **Cape Verde,** W. Africa | 0.3 | Cidade de Praia | 1,557 (4 033) | Aristides Maria Pereira, president |

The national assembly in early September approved a constitution to replace the provisional laws which had governed the country since it gained independence in 1975. The constitution calls for the election of a president by the national assembly for a five-year term and the nomination of a prime minister by the legislative body, and abolishes the death penalty and life imprisonment. The overthrow of Guinea-Bissau President Luis de Almeida Cabral in November ended his plan to unify Guinea-Bissau and the Cape Verde Islands. U.S. Vice-President Walter Mondale visited in July.

| **Central African Republic,** Cen. Africa | 2.2 | Bangui | 240,535 (622 984) | David Dacko, president |

President David Dacko began 1980 by adopting increasingly repressive measures to tighten his control, such as the outlawing of all strikes for the duration of the year. In March, he created the Central African Democratic Union (UDC) and traveled to France, where he was assured of substantial aid. Later in the month, he dismissed Justice Minister François Gueret. In early July, he dissolved the Government of Public Salvation, formed after the 1979 coup against Emperor Bokassa. He then enlarged the cabinet from 14 to 22 members. In late August, he dismissed two unpopular cabinet ministers, Vice-President Henri Maidou and Prime Minister Christian Bernard Ayandlo. And in December, court officials announced that former Emperor Bokassa would be tried in absentia for alleged atrocities during his rule.

| **Comoros,** E. Africa | 0.3 | Moroni | 838 (2 171) | Ahmed Abdallah, president |

After the formal resignation of the cabinet on July 7, President Ahmed Abdallah reappointed Prime Minister Salim Ben Ali on July 12. A revised cabinet was announced the same day.

| **Congo,** Cen. Africa | 1.6 | Brazzaville | 132,047 (342 000) | Mobutu Sese Seko, president |

Tensions with Zaire increased in January over the movement of Zairians into the Congo at the Congo River border. The conflict had begun with the Congo's deportation of Zairians allegedly living illegally in Brazzaville. In mid-February, the government denied reports that it was sheltering Zairian rebels who planned to launch an invasion of Zaire. In August, sharp increases in the Congo's oil production were predicted for the following two years.

| **Djibouti,** E. Africa | 0.4 | Djibouti | 8,494 (22 000) | Hassan Gouled, president
B. G. Hamadou, prime minister |

The Information Center on Djibouti, an opposition group based in France, maintained in March that the government had arrested bureaucrats and young military personnel "on the pretense of an attempt on the life of a military security officer" and further alleged that the government was guilty of "poor treatment" of the prisoners. In December, Kenyan President Daniel arap Moi and Ethiopian leader Lt. Col. Mengistu Haile Mariam urged Somalia to renounce its claims to territories in their countries and Djibouti.

| **Dominica,** Caribbean | 0.1 | Roseau | 289 (749) | Mary Eugenia Charles, president |

In February, President Fred DeGazon, who had fled to Great Britain in 1979, and Acting President Jenner Armour resigned, and former magistrate Aurelius Marie was appointed president. Pressure for a general election resulted in nationwide balloting July 21, which brought a landslide victory to the opposition Dominica Freedom Party (DFP). Mary Eugenia Charles, leader of the DFP, became the first woman prime minister of a Caribbean country.

---

* Independent nations not covered separately or under Central America (pages 98–592). [1]1980 estimates. [2]As of Dec. 31, 1980.

Nation, Region	Population in millions[1]	Capital	Area Sq mi (km²)	Head of State/Government[2]
Dominican Republic, Caribbean	5.4	Santo Domingo	18,818 (48 739)	Antonio Guzmán, president

The Dominican Republic embassy in Bogotá, Colombia and some 60 diplomatic personnel were seized by members of the Colombian left-wing guerrilla organization M-19, on February 27. The siege ended without bloodshed on April 27, when the terrorists were flown to Cuba with 12 remaining hostages, who were set free.

Equatorial Guinea, Cen. Africa	0.4	Malabo	10,831 (28 051)	Teodoro Obiang Mbasogo, president

Despite aid agreements with Spain and France, the country's hopes for economic recovery were imperiled by widespread poverty, disease, and the legacy of former dictator Macias Nguema.

Fiji, Oceania	0.6	Suva	7,095 (18 376)	Ratu Sir Kamisese Mara, prime minister

Chilean President Augusto Pinochet encountered hostile demonstrations in Fiji on March 23, at the beginning of what was to be an 11-day Asian tour. On May 19, Australia announced plans for an undersea telephone cable linking itself, Norfolk Island, Fiji, Hawaii, and Canada.

Gabon, Cen. Africa	0.6	Libreville	103,346 (267 667)	Albert-Bernard Bongo, president

President Albert-Bernard Bongo was reelected to another seven-year term Dec. 30, 1979. In legislative elections in early February 1980, candidates proposed by Bongo's Gabonese Democratic Party (GDP) won overwhelming popular support. Prime Minister Léon Mébiame announced a cabinet reorganization February 28; the new body comprised 28 members.

Gambia, W. Africa	0.6	Banjul	4,361 (11 295)	Sir Dawda K. Jawara, president

A revision of the tax structure and an increase of the minimum wage by nearly 30% were among the initiatives taken by the government to bolster the economy. On November 1, at the request of President Jawara, Senegalese troops arrived in Banjul to protect Gambia from invasion by Libya.

Grenada, Caribbean	0.1	St. George's	133 (344)	Maurice Bishop, prime minister

Grenada was placed on "war alert" June 20 after an assassination attempt on Prime Minister Maurice Bishop the day before. A bomb explosion under a podium where Bishop and other government officials were standing killed three persons and wounded 22.

Guinea, W. Africa	5.0	Conakry	94,926 (245 857)	Ahmed Sékou Touré, president

The 210 deputies to the new Popular National Assembly were elected in late January. President Touré survived an assassination attempt May 14.

Guinea-Bissau, W. Africa	0.6	Bissau	13,948 (36 925)	João Bernardo Vieira, leader, Council of the Revolution

On November 14, President Luis de Almeida Cabral was deposed and put under house arrest in a coup by João Bernardo Vieira, leader of the new Council of the Revolution. Vieira had opposed Cabral's plan to unite the country with Cape Verde.

Haiti, Caribbean	5.8	Port-au-Prince	10,714 (27 750)	Jean-Claude Duvalier, president

In an effort to consolidate further his autocratic rule, President Duvalier overhauled his cabinet April 26, for the second time in five months. His marriage to Michelle Bennett on May 27 was estimated to have cost the impoverished country up to $5 million. Nearly all of the country's coffee crop, its major source of income, was destroyed by Hurricane Allen on August 5. Haitian refugee "boat people" arrived in Florida in record numbers during the first part of the year.

Ivory Coast, W. Africa	8.0	Abidjan	124,503 (322 462)	Félix Houphouët-Boigny, president

President Félix Houphouët-Boigny ran unopposed and was reelected to a five-year term in October. Nationwide parliamentary elections were held November 9 for the first time since the Ivory Coast became independent in 1960. At the September congress of the ruling Democratic Party, Philippe Yacé, the president's apparent designated successor, was dismissed as secretary general.

Jamaica, Caribbean	2.2 (See CARIBBEAN, page 177.)	Kingston	4,244 (10 991)	Edward P.G. Seaga, prime minister

Kiribati, Oceania	0.056	Bairiki	331 (861)	Iremia Tabai, president

After celebrating its first year of independence on July 12, Kiribati was one of the beneficiaries of an agreement signed July 24 by Australia and New Zealand giving better access to commercial markets.

Kuwait, W. Asia	1.3	Kuwait City	6,880 (17 818)	Jabir al-Ahmad al-Sabah, emir Saad al-Abdullah al-Sabah, prime minister

Kuwait joined with other OPEC members in instituting substantial increases in the price of oil. It continued to enjoy the world's highest per capita income despite a 25% cut in oil production, to 1.5 million barrels a day, beginning April 1. Kuwait joined Saudi Arabia in freezing assets to the Wold Bank in protest against that body's decision to deny the PLO observer status in September meetings. Iraq was reported to have stationed war planes in Kuwait for use in its conflict with Iran. On November 12 and 16, Iranian planes bombed Kuwait border posts on the Iraqi frontier. To offset losses caused by that war, Kuwait and the other major Arab oil-producing states increased their exports.

Lesotho, S. Africa	1.3	Maseru	11,720 (30 355)	Moshoeshoe II, king Leabua Jonathan, prime minister

In an effort to quell increasingly violent opposition, Prime Minister Jonathan offered amnesty to members of the banned Basotho Congress Party, but guerrilla activity continued.

Liechtenstein, Cen. Europe	0.024	Vaduz	62 (160)	Francis Joseph II, prince Hans Brunhart, premier

At the 1980 Winter games in Lake Placid, NY, skier Hanni Wenzel won Liechtenstein its first two gold medals in Olympic history, as well as a silver.

Madagascar, E. Africa	8.7	Antananarivo	226,656 (587 041)	Didier Ratsiraka, president

Just days after stating that rising costs of imported oil had helped create serious economic difficulties, President Didier Ratsiraka announced in January that oil had been discovered. On February 28, he announced that an attempt to disrupt the nation's food supplies had been foiled.

Nation, Region	Population in millions[1]	Capital	Area Sq mi (km²)	Head of State/Government[2]
Malawi, E. Africa	6.1	Lilongwe	45,747 (118 484)	Hastings Kamuzu Banda, president

Despite extensive development aid, including $19 million by the UN Development Program in 1980 alone, and a rising per capita income, Malawi remained one of the world's poorest nations.

Maldives, S. Asia	0.1	Malé	115 (298)	Maumoon Abdul Gayyoom, president
Mali, W. Africa	6.6	Bamako	478,767 (1 240 000)	Moussa Traoré, president

Teacher strikes, student unrest, insufficient rainfall, energy shortages, skyrocketing fuel prices, and overall economic malaise left President Moussa Traoré with serious problems. On August 2, he announced a reorganization of the government, including the appointment of five new ministers.

Malta, S. Europe	0.3	Valletta	121 (313)	Anton Buttigieg, president Dominic Mintoff, prime minister

On August 28, the Maltese government expelled 50 Libyan military advisers in a dispute over offshore oil exploration rights. Libya had warned an Italian oil rig that it was operating in Libyan waters, to which Malta objected.

Mauritania, W. Africa	1.6	Nouakchott	397,950 (1 030 700)	Mohammed Khouna Ould Haidala, president and prime minister

In Mauritania's third coup d'etat since mid-1978, President Mohammed Mahmud Ould Luly was removed from office January 4 and replaced by Prime Minister Mohammed Khouna Ould Haidala. The new president reshuffled his cabinet in April and in July announced the abolition of slavery.

Mauritius, E. Africa	0.9	Port Louis	790 (2 045)	Sir Seewoosagur Ramgoolam, prime minister

Armed with a resolution passed at the Organization of African Unity (OAU) summit in July, Mauritius demanded that the island of Diego Garcia, an important U.S. military base but owned by Great Britain, be turned over to it. Prime Minister Ramgoolam took the demand to Britain but was refused.

Monaco, S. Europe	0.025	Monaco-Ville	0.73 (1.89)	Rainier III, prince

The two-year marriage of Princess Caroline and Philippe Junot ended in divorce October 9.

Mongolia E. Asia	1.7	Ulan Bator	604,247 (1 565 000)	Yumjaagin Tsedenbal, president Jambyn Batmönh, prime minister
Mozambique, E. Africa	10.3	Maputo	302,330 (783 030)	Samora Machel, president

The end of the war in Zimbabwe enabled president Samora Machel to concentrate on reconstructing a troubled economy, establishing stronger international ties—especially with the West—and reaffirming political control. In a major policy speech on March 18, he announced a radical change in economic policy, whereby private enterprise would assume a significantly larger role.

Nauru, Oceania	0.007	Nauru	8 (21)	Hammer de Roburt, president
Nepal, S. Asia	14.0	Katmandu	55,304 (141 577)	Birendra Bir Bikram, king

In Nepal's first nationwide election in 22 years, voters rejected the introduction of a multiparty system and chose to retain the modified version of a partyless system called panchayat. King Birendra, who wields almost unlimited power in this system, reaffirmed his commitment to constitutional reforms.

Niger, W. Africa	5.5.	Niamey	489,191 (1 267 000)	Seny Kountché, president

Commemorating the sixth anniversary of the army's seizure of power in June, President Seyni Kountché announced the release from custody of former President Hamini Diori and the leader of the banned Sawaba Party, Djibo Bakary. In a move regarded as a step toward democratization, Kountché set up a special advisory commission on national economic, social, and political issues.

Oman, W. Asia	0.9	Muscat	82,029 (212 457)	Qabus ibn Said, sultan

On June 4, the United States and Oman reached an agreement giving U.S. military planes and ships access to airfields and ports in Oman in exchange for economic and military assistance. U.S. planes stopped in Oman on their April mission to rescue the hostages in Iran.

Papua-New Guinea, Oceania	3.2	Port Moresby	178,704 (462 840)	Julius Chan, prime minister

The government of Prime Minister Michael Somare lost a vote of confidence March 11 and was succeeded immediately by that of Julius Chan, leader of the opposition People's Progress Party. An outbreak of malaria was reported in May. On August 11, about 100 troops from Papua-New Guinea put down a secessionist movement on Espiritu Santo, the largest island in the Vanuatu group.

Qatar, W. Asia	0.2	Doha	4,402 (11 400)	Khalifa bin Hamad al-Thani, emir
Rwanda, E. Africa	5.1	Kigali	10,169 (26 338)	Juvénal Habyarimana, president

President Habyarimana in April removed the secretary-general of the cabinet and the chief of security, leaving only two military men in the 16-member cabinet which came to power in 1973. A $3.5 million pesticide refinery, expected to employ 5,000 families, was opened in Ruhengeri.

Saint Lucia, Caribbean	0.1	Castries	238 (616)	Boswell Williams, acting governor-general Allan F. Louisy, prime minister

Sir Allen Montgomery Lewis took a preretirement leave from the governorship-general in February and was replaced by Boswell Williams, whose nomination caused a serious political conflict. Hurricane Allen killed a reported 16 persons and caused extensive damage on August 4.

Saint Vincent and the Grenadines, Caribbean	0.1	Kingstown	150 (389)	Sydney Douglas Gun-Munro, governor-general Robert Milton Cato, prime minister

The state of emergency declared in December 1979 following an uprising on Union Island organized by members of the Rastafarian cult was lifted on May 16, 1980. St. Vincent and the Grenadines was admitted as the 154th member of the United Nations on September 16.

Nation, Region	Population in millions[1]	Capital	Area Sq mi (km²)	Head of State/Government[2]
San Marino, S. Europe	0.02	San Marino	24 (61)	Co-regents selected semiannually
São Tomé and Príncipe, W. Africa	0.1	São Tomé	374 (964)	Mañuel Pinto da Costa, president and prime minister

At midyear, President Mañuel Pinto da Costa dismissed Prime Minister Miguel Trovoada and assumed the duties of the post himself, then reshuffled the government.

Senegal, W. Africa	5.7	Dakar	75,750 (196 192)	Abdou Diouf, president

After adopting a more activist foreign policy, permitting the establishment of several new political parties, and instituting major reforms in the agricultural sector, 74-year-old President Léopold S. Senghor, who had led Senegal since its independence from France 20 years earlier, announced his resignation Dec. 31, 1980. Prime Minister Abdou Diouf was sworn in as president the next day.

Seychelles, E. Africa	0.1	Victoria	108 (280)	F. Albert René, president

The Seychelles slowly returned to normal after the discovery of a coup attempt and declaration of a state of emergency in November 1979. On Aug. 1, 1980, the curfew imposed on the main island of Mahe was lifted. The Seychelles were admitted to the World Bank in September.

Sierra Leone, W. Africa	3.5	Freetown	27,699 (71 740)	Siaka P. Stevens, president

Sierra Leone hosted the 1980 Organization of African Unity (OAU) summit conference in July. At the conclusion, President Siaka Stevens assumed the chairmanship of the OAU for one year.

Solomon Islands, Oceania	0.2	Honiara	11,500 (29 785)	Peter Kenilorea, prime minister

In legislative elections August 6, none of the three political parties won a clear majority, giving independent members effective control of parliament. Although about two thirds of the members of the previous parliament were defeated, the new body reelected Prime Minister Peter Kenilorea.

Somalia, E. Africa	3.6	Mogadishu	246,201 (637 657)	Mohammed Siad Barre, president

The conflict in Ethiopia's Ogaden region intensified during the first months of the year. Ethiopia and Kenya issued a joint communiqué in March—and again in December—against arming Somalia because of its "expansionist policies," but on April 21 the United States signed an agreement for U.S. military access to Somalian facilities in exchange for military aid. As the war continued in the spring and summer, refugees streamed into Somalia. On August 27, the government reported that Ethiopian forces had crossed the border into Somalia, but Addis Ababa denied the charge. On October 20, President Mohammed Siad Barre declared a state of emergency to put down dissidents.

Surinam, S. America	0.4	Paramaribo	63,037 (163 265)	Henk R. Chin A Sen, president and prime minister

On February 25, army sergeants staged a predawn coup that toppled the government of Prime Minister Henck A. E. Arron. Henk R. Chin A Sen was chosen to head a civilian government under supervision of a national military council. In early May, 300 mercenaries entering Surinam from French Guiana to overthrow the new government were captured. In yet another coup, President Johan Ferrier was ousted August 13 and replaced by Chin, apparently at the request of the military command.

Swaziland, S. Africa	0.6	Mbabane	6,704 (17 363)	Sobhuza II, king

King Sobhuza II continued his harsh treatment of political opponents begun in 1973. The crackdown caused increasing concern to international human rights organizations.

Togo, W. Africa	2.5	Lomé	21,622 (56 000)	Gnassingbe Eyadéma, president

After being reelected in December 1979 under a new constitution, President Gnassingbe Eyadéma declared the Third Republic on Jan. 13, 1980, the 13th anniversary of his accession to power. To mark the occasion, he freed 34 political prisoners and 200 criminals.

Tonga, Oceania	0.1	Nuku'alofa	270 (699)	Taufa'ahau Tupou IV, king Prince Tu'ipelehake, prime minister
Tuvalu, Oceania	0.01	Funafuti	9.5 (25)	Toalipi Lauti, prime minister

Tonga and Tuvalu both signed an agreement with Australia and New Zealand providing better access to the latters' commercial markets.

United Arab Emirates, W. Asia	0.8	Abu Dhabi	32,278 (83 600)	Zaid ibn Sultan al-Nuhayan, president Rashid ibn Said al-Maktum, prime minister

Conflict in the Persian Gulf made the UAE a center of attention. (See feature article, page 28.) French President d'Estaing visited in early March, and a nuclear cooperation agreement was signed.

Upper Volta, W. Africa	6.9	Ouagadougou	105,869 (274 200)	Saye Zerbo, president

After mounting political and economic problems, President Sangoulé Lamizana was overthrown in a bloodless military coup on November 25. Col. Saye Zerbo, head of the armed forces, took control. A confrontation between the government and opposition had occurred in September over a teachers strike. Upper Volta's two main exports, cattle and cash crops, were severely damaged by drought.

Vatican City, S. Europe	0.001	Vatican City	0.17 (0.44)	John Paul II, pope
Western Samoa, Oceania	0.2	Apia	1,097 (2 841)	Malietoa Tanumafili II, head of state Tupuola Taisi Efi, prime minister
Zambia, E. Africa	5.8	Lusaka	290,585 (752 614)	Kenneth D. Kaunda, president

President Kenneth D. Kaunda faced growing political and social unrest. In mid-April he threatened to curtail freedom of the press and take action against private dissenters. To curb mounting labor unrest, the government in June banned industrial strikes. Then, on October 27, Kaunda announced that security forces had foiled a plot supported by South Africa to overthrow the government. In foreign affairs, Zambia hosted an April conference attended by nine African nations to formulate a plan to reduce their economic dependence on South Africa.

NEBRASKA

Natural disasters, reduced crops, a busy legislative session, two elections, and the University of Nebraska football team (which won the Sun Bowl on December 27) claimed the attention of Nebraskans in 1980. The state income tax was reduced to 15%, retroactive to Jan. 1, 1980.

Natural Disasters. In June a devastating tornado hit Nebraska's third largest city, Grand Island. Damage was estimated at more than $100 million and many persons were injured but, miraculously, only 5 were killed. A thunderstorm caused an airliner crash, killing 12 persons. Hailstorms damaged autos, buildings, and crops. A summer drought further damaged crops and the Farmers Home Administration declared 82 of Nebraska's 93 counties disaster areas.

Agriculture. Except for wheat, major grain crops—corn, grain sorghum, and soybeans—had reduced yields because of drought and heat. Farm prices were higher than in 1979, but both farm production costs and land prices also continued to rise in 1980.

Legislature and State Government. A busy legislative session increased gasoline taxes, aid to dependent children, homestead exemptions for the elderly, state aid to schools, the legal usury rate (to 16%), and the food tax rebate. It banned the use of studded tires, outlawed drug paraphernalia, and raised the legal drinking age to 20. It also passed a compromise energy act and increased personal property tax reimbursement. Long-range legislation was passed to revitalize branch rail lines and to allow cooperation with other states in developing Missouri River barge traffic. The legislature failed to remove the controversial property tax lid to support Omaha and Nebraska City schools and again did not pass effective legislation protecting water and land resources.

The legislature and Gov. Charles Thone, with his ever-ready veto, limited the increase in the state's operating budget to slightly above 7%.

Elections. Only 40% of those eligible voted in the May primary. Presidential preferences were Carter (D) and Reagan (R). Incumbent Representatives Douglas Bereuter and Virginia Smith,

------ NEBRASKA · Information Highlights ------

Area: 77,227 sq mi (200 018 km²).
Population (Jan. 1980 est.): 1,578,000.
Chief Cities (1976 est.): Lincoln, the capital, 164,035; Omaha, 371,012; (1970 census): Grand Island, 31,-269; Hastings, 23,580.
Government (1980): *Chief Officers*—governor, Charles Thone (R); lt. gov., Roland A. Luedtke (R). *Legislature* (unicameral)—49 members (nonpartisan).
Education (1979-80): *Enrollment*—public elementary schools, 153,476 pupils; public secondary, 133,812; colleges and universities, 86,446 students. *Public school expenditures*, $551,045,000 ($1,931 per pupil).
State Finances (fiscal year 1979): *Revenues*, $1,334,-000,000; *expenditures*, $1,250,000,000.
Personal Income (1979): $13,668,000,000; per capita, $8,684.
Labor Force (June 1980): *Nonagricultural wage and salary earners*, 634,200; *unemployed*, 33,700 (4.2% of total force).

both Republicans, were renominated easily. Leading vote-getters to replace retiring John Cavanaugh were Richard Fellman (D) and Hal Daub (R). Voters rejected a controversial amendment aimed at increasing legislators' salaries.

In the November general election about 75% of those eligible voted. Reagan received 66% of the vote to Carter's 26%. Republican candidates for the House easily defeated their Democratic opponents.

Voters approved constitutional amendments to broaden powers to discipline judges and to provide additional tax advantages for energy saving projects. They rejected amendments that would have corrected gerrymandering of supreme court districts and a controversial proposal to authorize the legislature to finance "a thorough and efficient system of common schools."

ORVILLE H. ZABEL, *Creighton University*

NETHERLANDS

While celebrating the enthronement of a new queen, The Netherlands found itself grappling with increasing economic difficulties and recurrent street disorders in the capital city of Amsterdam. The future of Holland's welfare state, one of the most advanced in the world, was jeopardized by mounting inflation and the halt of economic growth.

Unrest. The underlying tensions of Dutch society were evidenced by the violent street riots that took place during the inauguration of Queen Beatrix in Amsterdam on April 30. (*See* BIOGRAPHY.) Queen Juliana had abdicated the throne one day earlier, after a 32-year reign marked by an extraordinary rise in Dutch prosperity but marred by conflicts within and concerning her family. The elaborate accession ceremony (there is no royal coronation in The Netherlands) was held at the Royal Palace on the Dam in Amsterdam. Outside, rioters surged up to within a block of the palace before being held off by police lines. The demonstrators called for government programs to provide housing, especially for young adults in Amsterdam, both by new construction and requisition of vacant buildings. Only two months before, on March 3, squatters occupying an empty office building in the museum district fought a fierce street battle with police, and army tanks were brought in to help take down their barricades. The squatters remained in possession of the disputed building, however, which eventually was bought by the city for conversion to private housing. There was renewed rioting in August and September, when other buildings held by squatters were cleared by special mobile units of the national police force. Then again in October, fighting broke out when the final section of the new Amsterdam subway, constructed despite much local opposition, was opened.

The investiture of Princess Beatrix as queen of The Netherlands on April 30 was marred by rioting in the streets of Amsterdam. The demonstrators protested the cost of the ceremonies in light of the city's housing needs.

Postel, Liaison

Politics. The troubles in Amsterdam, however, had little impact on national politics, which centered on the States General (parliament) in The Hague. The government of Premier Andreas van Agt held a thin majority formed by the three religious parties combined in the Christian Democratic Appeal (CDA) and the Liberal party (VVD). But the handling of the nation's mounting economic problems brought sharp criticism not only from the opposition parties—principally the Labor Party (PvdA) and the Progressives (D'66)—but also from within the ranks of the religious parties. The merger in October of the three historic religious parties into the CDA ended more than a century of separate representation for Catholics and Protestants and presumably strengthened the government's position in the national election scheduled for the spring of 1981. The merger also indicated a weakening of the religious-ideological "pillars" (*zuilen*) of Dutch social and political life. The presentation of a new national budget in September, which called for mild reductions in public expenditures, personal income, and living standards, unleashed a fierce debate. Yet both the Labor Party and the Progressives recognized the severity of the economic situation and endeavored to maintain the minimum wage level and social welfare payments and to increase tax burdens on the wealthy. Despite the Labor Party's vigorous criticism, the principal government party, the CDA, held open the possibility of a coalition with the PvdA after the elections. Their cooperation would renew the political alliance that had governed The Netherlands for most of the postwar years.

Foreign Affairs. The government's position in international relations was made more difficult by the unwillingness of the States General to finance the 3% expansion of national defense outlays called for by NATO and by a strong movement opposing the installation of new nuclear weapons in the country. The traditional openness of the Netherlands to those seeking refuge

from oppression was called into question by problems with immigrants from Surinam, the former Dutch colony in South America, as well as "guest workers" from Turkey, Morocco, and other Mediterranean countries. There was debate over the national policy of fostering the cultural identity of the new immigrants, who tended to live in separate communities without fully integrating into Dutch customs and attitudes.

Economy. The export-oriented Dutch economy faced mounting problems during a period of worldwide recession. Although their only important raw material was natural gas, the Dutch had achieved a very high standard of living since World War II. Rotterdam continued to be Europe's busiest port, but Dutch industry, coping with both high taxes and high wages, tended to fall behind competitors in Europe and elsewhere. Business failures rose in frequency and began to threaten some of the largest employers, but the government became more reluctant to provide grants or loans. Unemployment rose to almost 300,000. Legislation permitting the government to curb wage increases through 1981 brought strikes and a mass demonstration by the country's largest union federation, the FNV, in March. Taxes were unusually high because of

---

NETHERLANDS • Information Highlights

Official Name: Kingdom of the Netherlands.
Location: Northwestern Europe.
Area: 13,054 sq mi (33 811 km²).
Population (1980 est.): 14,100,000.
Chief Cities (1979 est.): Amsterdam, the capital, 718,577; Rotterdam, 582,396; The Hague, 458,242.
Government: *Head of state,* Beatrix, queen (acceded May 1980). *Head of government,* Andreas van Agt, prime minister (took office Dec. 1977). *Legislature*—States General: First Chamber and Second Chamber.
Monetary Unit: Guilder (2.13 guilders equal U.S.$1, Dec. 1980).
Manufactures (major products): Metals, textiles, chemicals, electronic equipment.
Agriculture (major products): Sugar beets, wheat, barley, fruits, potatoes, oats, flax, bulbs, flowers, meat and dairy products.
GNP (1979 est., U.S.$): $151,300,000,000.
Foreign Trade (1979, U.S.$): *Imports,* $67,284,000,000; *exports,* $63,667,000,000.

the high level of social welfare expenditures. A rate of inflation in excess of 10% made the government reluctant to indulge in further deficit financing.

HERBERT H. ROWEN, *Rutgers University*

NEVADA

The November general election, Question 6, decreasing state revenues, and dissension on the state Supreme Court were subjects of importance to Nevadans in 1980. On November 21, at least 84 persons were killed in a tragic fire at Las Vegas' MGM Grand Hotel.

The Elections. In the presidential primary in May, Ronald Reagan (who easily had won the 1976 primary also) swamped George Bush. On the Democratic side, President Jimmy Carter led with 37.5% of the vote, Sen. Edward Kennedy polled 29%, and "none of these" received 33.5%.

In the November election Nevada gave its three electoral votes to its neighbor Ronald Reagan. Nevadans continued their tradition of split-ticket voting as Sen. Paul Laxalt, Reagan's national campaign chairman, easily defeated former state senator Mary Gojack, while Democratic Congressman Jim Santini was returned for a fourth term. Although there were some changes in the makeup of the state legislature, the party membership remained the same, with the Democrats retaining a 15-5 margin in the Senate and a 26-14 majority in the Assembly.

The ballot issue that received the greatest attention was Question 6, the tax-cutting amendment that was the twin of California's Proposition 13. The initiative measure, which had to be passed a second time to be effective, had received the support of 80% of the voters in 1978. However, an October media campaign, highlighted by a television commercial featuring joint pleading against the amendment by Republican Gov. Robert List and former Democratic Gov. Grant Sawyer, proved to be very effective. Question 6 was soundly defeated, as 58% of the voters cast their ballots against it.

Eight of the counties, including Washoe (Reno), had a nonbinding advisory referendum regarding the construction of MX missile sites in Nevada. The voters in all eight counties decisively voted "no" on the question.

Economy. Gambling tax revenues, which account for about half of the state's General Fund revenues, increased by 15% for the 1979–80 fiscal year. However, the closing of some Reno casinos due to poor business, the partial shutdown after a bombing of Harvey's at Lake Tahoe, the temporary closing of the Aladdin Hotel in Las Vegas because of charges of mobster influence, and the increase in travel costs led to an increase of only 7.8% in gaming revenue for the first quarter (July–September) of the 1980–1981 fiscal year. With revenues increasing at a rate substantially below the inflation rate, the belief of some gaming authorities that Nevada's principal industry is "recession-proof" was challenged.

Revenue from the state sales tax, the other major source of income for the General Fund, increased only 3% for the 1979–80 fiscal year over that of 1978–79. However, the two years were not comparable, as the legislature and the voters eliminated the sales tax on food as of July 1, 1979. The state's unemployment rate, which had declined to 4.9% in March, rose to a high of 7% in September.

Supreme Court. The state's highest court was rocked by dissension that led the Commission on Judicial Discipline to investigate charges against four of the five justices. The commission dismissed all the charges, but infighting continued, and some legislators threatened to act on the matter during the 1981 legislative session.

DON W. DRIGGS, *University of Nevada, Reno*

Sen. Paul Laxalt (R), Ronald Reagan's national campaign chairman, was elected to a second term.
U.S. Senate

NEVADA • Information Highlights

Area: 110,540 sq mi (286 299 km²).
Population (Jan. 1980 est.): 722,000.
Chief Cities (1970 census): Carson City, the capital, 15,-468; Reno, 72,863; (1976 est.): Las Vegas, 153,553.
Government (1980): *Chief Officers*—governor, Robert List (R); lt. gov., Myron E. Levitt (D). *Legislature*—Senate, 20 members; Assembly, 40 members.
Education (1979–80): *Enrollment*—public elementary schools, 77,427 pupils; public secondary, 70,307; colleges and universities, 35,935 students. *Public school expenditures,* $331,422,000 ($1,997 per pupil).
State Finances (fiscal year 1979): *Revenues,* $1,059,-000,000; *expenditures,* $862,000,000.
Personal Income (1979): $7,386,000,000; per capita, $10,521.
Labor Force (May 1980): *Nonagricultural wage and salary earners,* 398,600; *unemployed,* 20,100 (5.4% of total force).

NEW BRUNSWICK

A major dredging project on the Miramichi River, which will enable the province to handle larger ships, obtained federal government backing. In the federal election, New Brunswick went Liberal.

Deepening the Miramichi. A project sought by northeastern New Brunswick for more than two decades—dredging the Miramichi River to increase its ship-carrying capacity—gained federal cabinet approval in September. Work was planned to begin in 1981. The project, expected to cost $13 million, would enable ocean-going ships with a 25-ft (7.5-m) draft to use the river, placing the Miramichi on a par with the St. Lawrence Seaway.

School Holiday. A three-week, unscheduled holiday for New Brunswick's schoolchildren ended April 28 with settlement of a strike by 3,-000 nonteaching school workers. On April 23 a new two-year contract, calling for basic wage increases, had been signed in Fredericton by the provincial government and the Canadian Union of Public Employees. The strike closed all but 18 of the province's 465 schools.

Fiscal. Finance Minister Fernand Dubé unveiled a $1,700,000,000 budget in the legislature March 25. The controversial user fees for hospital admissions, emergency and outpatient services—introduced in 1979—were abolished.

The Elections. In the February 18 federal election, New Brunswick fell in with the national Liberal tide, electing seven Liberal members to the House of Commons and only three Conservatives. In the 1979 election, Liberals had won six seats and Conservatives four.

Among those elected was Roméo LeBlanc (Westmorland-Kent), who subsequently returned to Prime Minister Trudeau's cabinet as minister of fisheries and oceans.

Energy Agreement. An $11.25 million agreement to develop renewable energy projects and conservation technologies in New Brunswick was signed by representatives of the provincial and federal governments on January 16.

JOHN BEST, *Canada World News*

NEWFOUNDLAND

Like most other Canadians, Newfoundlanders watched in disbelief as the six-month-old Conservative government of Joe Clark was defeated in December 1979. The victory of the Liberal Party and Pierre Elliott Trudeau in February 1980 elections ended a brief hope for federal accommodation in the resource issues troubling the provincial government. It also meant the defeat of the only New Democrat ever elected to the House of Commons from Newfoundland and a return to the established representation pattern of five Liberals and two Conservatives.

Internally, nothing seemed to shake the strength of the Conservatives. The Liberals, on the other hand, faced their third leadership convention in three years on Oct. 31, 1980. The candidate chosen to replace Don Jamieson was Len Sterling, a 42-year-old insurance executive. The party came out of convention united but in an ambivalent position regarding support for federal constitutional amendment proposals.

Much of 1980 was taken up with federal-provincial conferences on the Constitution. The chief proposals of the Progressive Conservative government of Brian Peckford were for complete provincial control of offshore oil and minerals; concurrent jurisdiction in the fisheries; and the right to move electricity freely from Labrador across Quebec. The federal minister of fisheries and oceans, Roméo LeBlanc, remained adamant that federal management of resources from the "water to the table" was the only scheme that could work. At year's end, the federal government had made it clear that no substantial alteration in the division of powers was possible.

With so much of the government's energy concentrated on the Constitution, there was little time for other matters. The 1980–81 provincial budget called for total expenditures of $1,500,-000,000 and increases in cigarette and corporate income taxes. In February, provincial Minister of Mines and Energy Leo Barry announced the creation of an Offshore Petroleum Impact Committee to advise on all matters of Newfoundland's expected boom.

SUSAN MCCORQUODALE
Memorial University of Newfoundland

NEW HAMPSHIRE

In New Hampshire, as in most of the nation, politics and the state of the economy received most of the attention during 1980. In the February 26 primary, voters gave Ronald Reagan 49.8% of the ballots cast and runner-up George Bush 22.9%. The Democratic slate elicited much interest because of Edward Kennedy's challenge to Jimmy Carter. Carter received 47.6% of the vote to 37.7% for Kennedy and 9.7% for Jerry Brown.

On the state political scene, two contests dominated the news: the rematch between Gov. Hugh Gallen (D) and former Gov. Meldrim Thomson, Jr. (R) and the Senatorial contest between incumbent John Durkin (D) and former state Attorney General Warren Rudman (R). Gallen and Thomson fought a rather acrimonious campaign in which Gallen used as an effective issue Thomson's membership on the board of directors of the ultraconservative John Birch Society. Both "took the pledge" to oppose any broad-based taxes. On November 4 it became clear that New Hampshire voters were as independent-minded as they are often portrayed. Reagan easily won the state's electoral votes; Gallen, bucking the Republican sweep, overwhelmed Thomson 226,436 to 156,178; and in a close Senate race, Rudman defeated Durkin. Each party won a seat in the House of Representatives. The 1980 election may have brought Thomson's colorful political career to a close.

Economy. The national economic malaise affected New Hampshire less than many states, but was evident. A virtually snowless winter permitted only 10 of the state's 22 ski areas to open. This followed the disastrous summer of 1979 when gasoline shortages caused a major drop in tourism. In contrast to the poor winter, the summer of 1980 was one of the best on record for tourism, with revenues up 30–50% over 1979.

Economic growth slowed, as was evident in the general decline in housing construction coupled with high interest rates of 16–17%. Unemployment remained well below the national level as indicated by the July-August unemployment figures of 5.0% and 4.2%, compared with a 7.8% and 7.6% rate nationally.

Census. Since 1970 the state's population has risen 24.6%, 737,681 to 918,827. Most of the growth occurred in the southern half of the state and included cities as well as towns. While most towns added less than 50% to their population, a few had excessive growth; Londonderry and Merrimack expanded a staggering 153% and 80%, respectively. Such growth is attributed to the lack of any broad-based taxes, the life style, and the rural environment.

In other matters, a $15 million fire destroyed the grandstand of Rockingham Park, a Salem racetrack. The state received $5 million annually from the track and the loss of revenue had serious ramifications for an already tight state budget. Of significance also were the inauguration of rail passenger service between Concord and Boston, the problems of hazardous waste disposal, and the impact of acid rain on the environment.

New Hampshire appeared robust and healthy as the 1980s began and its citizens seemed confident about the future. Since New Hampshire generally has supported the conservative view, the movement of the nation's political pendulum to the right was seen as confirmation of that view.

WILLIAM L. TAYLOR, *Plymouth State College*

NEW JERSEY

The integrity of the New Jersey Casino Commission and the ethics of a number of leading state political leaders were called into question by the FBI's Abscam investigation, in which bribes were allegedly accepted in order to further the American business interests of a mythical Arab sheikh.

Abscam. Among the New Jersey figures involved in the Abscam investigation were Sen. Harrison Williams, Congressman Frank Thompson, Jr., state Sen. Joseph Maressa, and Angelo Errichetti, mayor of Camden. They were accused of using their influence to obtain favors for their client from the vice-president of the

---

NEW HAMPSHIRE · Information Highlights

Area: 9,304 sq mi (24 097 km²).
Population (1980): 918,827.
Chief Cities (1970 census): Concord, the capital, 30,022; Manchester, 87,754; Nashua, 55,820; Portsmouth, 25,717.
Government (1980): *Chief Officer*—governor, Hugh J. Gallen (D). *General Court*—Senate, 24 members; *House of Representatives,* 400 members.
Education (1979–80): *Enrollment*—public elementary schools, 96,939 pupils; public secondary, 73,607; colleges and universities, 42,112 students. *Public school expenditures,* $323,860,000 ($1,776 per pupil).
State Finances (fiscal year 1979): *Revenues,* $840,000,-000; *expenditures,* $784,000,000.
Personal Income (1979): $7,407,000,000; per capita, $8,351.
Labor Force (May 1980): *Nonagricultural wage and salary earners,* 381,400; *unemployed,* 19,100 (4.1% of total force).

NEW JERSEY · Information Highlights

Area: 7,836 sq mi (20 295 km²).
Population (Jan. 1980 est.): 7,334,000.
Chief Cities (1970 census): Trenton, the capital, 104,638; (1976 est.): Newark, 331,495; Jersey City, 239,998.
Government (1980): *Chief Officer*—governor, Brendan T. Byrne (D). *Legislature*—Senate, 40 members; General Assembly, 80 members.
Education (1979–80): *Enrollment*—public elementary schools, 797,879 pupils; public secondary, 489,930; colleges and universities, 312,460 students. *Public school expenditures,* $3,356,000,000 ($2,385 per pupil).
State Finances (fiscal year 1979): *Revenues,* $7,881,-000,000; *expenditures,* $7,718,000,000.
Personal Income (1979): $71,461,000,000; per capita, $9,747.
Labor Force (May 1980): *Nonagricultural wage and salary earners,* 3,047,500; *unemployed,* 289,400 (8.1% of total force).

Casino Commission, Kenneth MacDonald. Evidence was gathered by FBI undercover agents using hidden videotape machines that showed cash being exchanged between the defendants and the supposed representatives of the sheikh. Although the Abscam inquiry was conducted in a number of states, attention was especially centered on New Jersey, and indictments were brought against all of the above persons. Following a three-week trial late in the year, a jury found Thompson guilty of conspiracy to defraud and bribery.

Early in the year MacDonald resigned as Casino Commission vice-president, and much pressure was put on Gov. Brendan Byrne to institute comprehensive reforms in the commission's structure and functions. A bill was introduced in the legislature which, among other things, would have made all the commissioners, not just the chairman, full-time; required the chairman, Joseph P. Lordi, to resign and serve as a regular commissioner; and forbade state employees to accept positions with the Atlantic City casinos until they had been retired for at least two years. The last provision aroused much controversy on the grounds that it discriminated against state employees. Governor Byrne initially supported the bill, which was passed in the latter part of the legislative session, but changed his mind and refused to sign it after many protests were registered over its discriminatory features.

The Elections. Abscam's political repercussions were revealed in the November elections when Rep. Frank Thompson, who had served in Congress since January 1955, was defeated, largely on account of his indictment. New Jersey was considered one of the pivotal states in the presidential election. Throughout the campaign polls showed it leaning toward Governor Reagan, although not solidly in his column. Both Reagan and President Carter visited the state many times, seeking support from the urban blue col-

lar workers in Hudson and Essex counties. In September Reagan held a large rally at Liberty Park in Jersey City and in the final weeks of the campaign Carter made three stopovers. In the election itself Governor Reagan easily won New Jersey's 17 electoral votes.

No statewide offices were contested. However, Republicans made a strong showing in the congressional elections, picking up 2 seats and thus holding 7 to the Democrats' 8. In addition to Thompson, Andrew Maguire, a three-term incumbent, lost his seat.

Drought. The worst drought since the mid-1960s developed in northern New Jersey in the summer and autumn. In late September Governor Byrne ordered mandatory water rationing in more than 100 communities in the northeastern counties, as the reservoirs of the Hackensack Water Company, the major supplier for the region, were far below normal capacity. Compliance with the rationing was spotty since enforcement depended largely on voluntary cooperation. Efforts were made to pump water from New York City through the Holland Tunnel to relieve Jersey City, but they were only moderately successful.

VHF Television. In November the Federal Communications Commission opened the way for New York City's WOR-TV outlet to move to New Jersey, in an attempt to give the state its first VHF television channel.

HERMANN K. PLATT
Saint Peter's College

NEW MEXICO

In 1980 New Mexicans faced a troubling year. Revelation that the athletic department of the University of New Mexico, Albuquerque, had committed serious violations of NCAA regulations created a scandal that gained nationwide attention. A disastrous prison riot proved to be one of the worst in history.

New Jersey Congressman Frank Thompson, Jr. (D) and Mrs. Thompson leave federal court following his conviction in an Abscam case.

Election. On November 4, New Mexico joined with the majority of states and delivered its electoral votes to Ronald Reagan. In a narrow victory, Rep. Manuel Lujan (R) won a seventh term representing the first district. Joe Skeen (R), in a write-in bid, managed to win the seat vacated by the August death of Rep. Harold Runnels (D) in the second district. He defeated David King (D).

Crime. Early in the morning of February 2, inmates of the New Mexico State Penitentiary, south of Santa Fe, seized control of the institution. In a bloody day-and-a-half rampage, 33 persons were tortured and killed by fellow prisoners and 12 guards were held hostage. Fires destroyed several buildings, causing millions of dollars worth of damage. Gov. Bruce King remained on the scene throughout the uprising. National Guard troops prevented any escapes.

In the aftermath of the affair, the state legislature appropriated $82 million for prison riot-related expenses. Warden Jerry Griffin and Corrections Secretary Adolph Saenz resigned. The state also faced protracted legal proceedings brought by families of slain inmates.

Energy and Environment. Controversy continued over the proposed use of a site near Carlsbad as the nation's first federal storage area for weapons-grade low-level nuclear waste generated by defense work. Early in October, President Carter signed an appropriations bill earmarking $20 million for fieldwork on the project.

Navajo Indians living in the vicinity of Crownpoint demanded a halt to uranium mining there. Opposition was based on fears over health hazards and depletion of water resources.

Plans by large corporations to begin geothermal development in the Jemez Mountains northwest of Albuquerque drew strong fire from area residents, including Pueblo Indians. They charged that a proposal to construct ultimately 60 to 80 geothermal plants would, among other things, pollute the air, contaminate streams, interfere with recreational land use, and desecrate sacred Indian religious sites.

Meanwhile, scientists at nearby Los Alamos Scientific Laboratory for the first time succeeded in generating electricity from hot, dry rocks, a geothermal process in which water is injected below the earth's surface, heated upon contact with the rocks, and then recovered to serve as an energy source.

Health. The state experienced 13 cases of plague, which included three fatalities. Four of the cases were of the severe pneumonic form of the disease, representing a significant increase over previous years. Public health officials expressed concern for the future.

Science. On October 10, scientists and federal officials met near Socorro to dedicate the world's largest telescope. The $78 million system, the Very Large Array, is composed of 27 dish-shaped antennae.

MARC SIMMONS
Author, "New Mexico, A History"

NEW YORK

The conflict at the center of the 1980 presidential campaign was played out on a smaller scale in the race for U.S. senator from New York, as Alfonse D'Amato, a conservative outside the Republican Party mainstream, defeated U.S. Rep. Elizabeth Holtzman, a noted liberal Democrat. Although Holtzman's support was split by 76-year-old incumbent Jacob Javits, who was forced to run on the Liberal Party ticket, the election signaled an end to the state's tradition of liberal Republicanism and an endorsement of D'Amato's favorite themes—reduced government spending, stronger defense, and right-to-life.

In the presidential race, Ronald Reagan won the state's 41 electoral votes with a surprising 47% of the popular vote; President Carter took 44% and John Anderson 7.5%. Republicans picked up four more of the state's 39 seats in Congress, raising their total to 17. Party alignment in the state legislature remained unchanged. Democrats retained an 86–64 majority in the Assembly, and Republicans held a 35–25 edge in the Senate.

Business and Finance. Gov. Hugh Carey called a special session of the state assembly to propose legislation designed to stimulate economic growth. Included was a bill, passed November 21, that eliminated state limits on interest rates for unpaid balances on credit cards. The legislation was intended—but failed—to keep Citicorp credit card operations in the state. As part of New York's effort to stem the flow of jobs out of the state, maximum income taxes were lowered to 10% in 1980. Having reached a maximum of 15% in 1976, the tax decreased at a rate second only to California, with Proposition 13.

Unemployment remained high in New York City and rural areas, but in such medium-sized towns as Poughkeepsie, Binghampton, Utica, and White Plains, the transfer of corporate offices from other states brightened the economic picture.

─── **NEW MEXICO · Information Highlights** ───

Area: 121,666 sq mi (315 115 km²).

Population (Jan. 1980 est.): 1,255,000.

Chief Cities (1970 census): Santa Fe, the capital, 41,167; Las Cruces, 37,857; Roswell, 33,908; (1976 est.): Albuquerque, 284,617.

Government (1980): *Chief Officers*—governor, Bruce King (D); lt. gov., Roberto A. Mondragon (D). *Legislature*—Senate, 42 members; House of Representatives, 70 members.

Education (1979–80): *Enrollment*—public elementary schools, 144,934 pupils; public secondary, 130,638; colleges and universities, 56,189 students. *Public school expenditures,* $632,735,000 ($1,838 per pupil).

State Finances (fiscal year 1979): *Revenues,* $1,847,-000,000; *expenditures,* $1,578,000,000.

Personal Income (1979): $9,383,000,000; per capita, $7,560.

Labor Force (June 1980): *Nonagricultural wage and salary earners,* 477,700; *unemployed,* 45,100 (8.1% of total force).

New York senatorial candidates Elizabeth Holtzman (D), the incumbent Jacob Javits (who ran as a Liberal), and Alfonse D'Amato (R) engage in a videotaped debate. In November, voters chose the 43-year-old Republican.

Fred R. Conrad, The New York Times

Energy and Environment. In a February 12 address, President Carter designated West Valley in upstate New York as one of three possible sites for storage of spent fuel from U.S. and foreign nuclear reactors until technology is developed to reprocess the fuel safely. Meanwhile, the president committed the federal government to paying 90% of the cost of cleaning up radioactive wastes at the inactive West Valley reactor.

A $1,200,000,000 national "superfund" for cleaning up toxic chemical wastes in such areas as the Love Canal near Niagara Falls was passed by the U.S. Congress. The state also filed a second suit for $635 million against the Hooker Chemical Corp. for allegedly dumping some 21,-000 tons of chemicals in the Love Canal between 1942 and 1953.

Crime. On June 13, Governor Carey signed what he called "the toughest handgun law in the country." The legislation required a mandatory jail term of one year for most persons convicted of carrying an unlicensed handgun.

A favorite cover story for many tabloids in 1980 was the fatal shooting of Dr. Herman Tarnower, author of the best-selling *The Complete Scarsdale Medical Diet*, at his home in the exclusive New York City suburb of Scarsdale.

─────── **NEW YORK • Information Highlights** ───────

Area: 49,576 sq mi (128 402 km²).
Population (Jan. 1980 est.): 17,579,000.
Chief Cities (1976 est.): Albany, the capital, 109,196; New York, 7,422,831; Buffalo, 400,234; Rochester, 262,766.
Government (1980): *Chief Officers*—governor, Hugh L. Carey (D); lt. gov., Mario M. Cuomo (D). *Legislature*—Senate, 60 members; Assembly, 150 members.
Education (1979–80): *Enrollment*—public elementary schools, 1,439,734 pupils; public secondary, 1,505,-955; colleges and universities, 970,168 students. *Public school expenditures,* $9,068,000,000.
State Finances (fiscal year 1979): *Revenues,* $25,181,-000,000; *expenditures,* $22,708,000,000.
Personal Income (1979): $160,662,000,000; per capita, $9,104.
Labor Force (June 1980): *Total labor force,* 8,002,600; *unemployed,* 565,100 (7.1% of total force).

Charged with the March shooting was Jean S. Harris, the 56-year-old headmistress of the Madeira School for Girls in Virginia, who police said had been romantically involved with the 69-year-old bachelor.

Sports. For the 20,000 visitors to the XIII Olympic Winter Games in Lake Placid, reactions ranged from elation—as the U.S. ice hockey team won a surprise gold medal—to misery—as a chaotic bus shuttle system left many exposed to bitter cold temperatures for hours. But the prologue, and possibly the epilogue, to the mid-February competition was not on the slopes but in the courtroom. State courts denied Taiwan the right to compete under the name of the Republic of China, as the mainland People's Republic of China entered Olympic competition for the first time since the Communist takeover in 1949. And when the snow had finally settled, the Lake Placid Olympic Organizing Committee reported an $8 million debt and threatened to file for bankruptcy unless it received additional government aid. Congress turned down the committee's plea in December.

People. Hugh Carey, entering his sixth year as governor, had often proven himself able to step gingerly through allegations of improprieties without extensive political damage. On November 11, Carey backed away from a confrontation with Dr. Philip D'Arigo, a Scarsdale dentist who had bought land adjacent to the governor's home on Shelter Island and planned to build a house obstructing his view of an inlet. The governor ordered the state to seize the land but relented when Dr. D'Arigo appeared on national television to air his complaint.

Abbie Hoffman, the 1960s Yippie leader who dropped out of sight in 1974 after jumping bail on a cocaine possession charge, resurfaced in New York City on September 4. The 43-year-old fugitive had been living under the name of Barry Freed in the upstate town of Fineview.

DAN HULBERT, *"The New York Times"*

NEW YORK CITY

Buoyed by his city's role as host to the Democratic National Convention and by a 59% popularity rating in a September poll by *The New York Times,* Edward I. Koch completed his third year as mayor a happier, if no less controversial, man. The mayor had come under heavy fire from blacks and Hispanics over the closing of Harlem's Sydenham Hospital earlier in the year. And a surprising $334 million surplus in revenues for fiscal 1980 did not solve the problem of how the city would close a $1,200,000,000 budget gap for 1981 and return to full financial health.

Business and Labor. Seeking to break the domination of financial futures by the Chicago Board of Trade and the Chicago Mercantile Exchange, the city opened its own New York Futures Exchange (NYFE) on August 7.

A resurgence of the tourist industry continued to boost commerce and brought a spate of construction of new luxury hotels: the Harley, the $100-million Helmsley Place, and the 1,400-room Grand Hyatt. The old Royal Manhattan in the slowly recovering area around Times Square was lavishly refurbished and renamed the Milford Plaza.

A costly transit strike shut down the city's subways, buses, and ferries for the first 11 days of April, but the system's 5.4 million daily riders weathered the storm well. So many of them rode bicycles that the mayor had permanent bike lanes constructed, only to tear them up when they fell into disuse in the fall.

International Affairs. New York's cosmopolitan character continued to make it an arena for many of the world's conflicts. A diplomat attached to the Cuban Mission to the United Nations, Garcia Rodriguez, was shot and killed September 11 while driving to his office through the borough of Queens. He was the first UN official to be assassinated in New York since the organization was founded in 1945.

On August 2, 192 Iranians who had been arrested following demonstrations in Washington against the Islamic regime of Ayatollah Ruhollah Khomeini were taken to federal detention centers in New York City and in the upstate town of Otisville. Their release August 5 was decried by some immigration officials who said that the Iranians' credentials had not been properly checked.

Crime. The city's crime problem was highlighted by the December 10 murder of former Beatle John Lennon outside the Dakota apartments on Manhattan's fashionable Central Park West. The following Sunday, December 16, at least 100,000 persons gathered in nearby Central Park for commemorative ceremonies. Earlier in the year, on March 14, Allard K. Lowenstein, a former congressman from New York and a major anti-Vietnam War spokesman, was slain in his downtown law office.

After a month-long, highly-publicized search, police arrested a young stagehand at the Metropolitan Opera House for the July 23 murder of 31-year-old violinist Helen Hagnes, whose body had been found in an air shaft.

Arts and Entertainment. Between May 12 and 16, the art and antique houses of Sotheby Parke Bernet and Christie, Mansion, and Woods set several records by auctioning $55.8 million in works of art, including Vincent Van Gogh's *Le Jardin du Poète, Arles* for $5.2 million, the highest price ever paid for a single work. On June 11, the new American wing of the Metropolitan Museum of Art was opened. (*See* ART.)

On Broadway, *Barnum* with Jim Dale and *Evita* divided most of the 1980 Tony awards for musicals. The Vivian Beaumont Theater at Lincoln Center, dark for more than two years, reopened with an ambitious slate of straight dramas. (*See* THEATER.)

People. An August 7 visit to the desolate South Bronx by Mother Teresa, the Roman Catholic nun who was awarded the 1979 Nobel Peace Prize for her work among the destitute of Calcutta, and demonstrations at the Charlotte Street site where President Jimmy Carter once had promised aid for the area, underscored the almost catastrophic poverty of this section of the city.

Rosie Ruiz, a 26-year-old Manhattanite, became the butt of many jokes when her "victory" in the Boston Marathon and her 24th-place finish in April's New York Marathon (which qualified her for Boston) were invalidated after it was discovered that she did not run the entire race.

Mayor Koch, whose continued bluntness and contentiousness made him a hero in the eyes of

John Lennon and wife, Yoko Ono, had lived quietly in Manhattan before his murder there December 10.
UPI

some New Yorkers and a despot in the eyes of others, won a court case on June 6 against a San Diego physician, Navvin Gordon, who had pelted him with an egg during a 1979 demonstration against the closing of municipal hospitals. Gordon was sentenced to 30 days in prison and fined $1,000.

DAN HULBERT, *"The New York Times"*

NEW ZEALAND

During 1980, New Zealand remained locked in a battle with inflation, mounting unemployment, and a heavy deficit in overseas transactions.

Economy. Inflation, which ran at 16.5% for calendar 1979, soared to a new record of 18.4% for the fiscal year ending March 31, 1980. Food prices jumped by 25%. A current external deficit of almost $500 million was recorded. Under the controlled float system, the value of the New Zealand dollar slipped regularly. A net migration outflow of 22,300 persons almost matched the natural increase in population. By September, more than 60,000 persons (6% of the work force) were unemployed or in special programs.

A budget introduced in July endeavored to hold economic activity stable in the face of a downturn in the major industrial economies. It incorporated a 4% general wage hike, extra taxes on luxuries, the imposition of a 5% internal air travel tax, and sharp rises in postal charges. An internal deficit of $1,260,000,000 and an increase of 18.2% in government spending were forecast. The emphasis in economic policy was on combating inflation by encouraging a greater measure of competition rather than by imposing price controls.

Foreign Affairs. Prime Minister Robert Muldoon made four major trips during the year. On a tour of the ASEAN nations, Muldoon held discussions on regional security, while in June he participated in Paris talks on European Community (EC) prices for sheepmeat. Later in the year, the EC announced a new policy to end the so-called "Lamb War" between France and Great Britain. New Zealand, from which France imported large quantities of lamb, would be permitted to export only 20 000 t (22,050 T) per year of sheepmeat to EC countries. New Zealand farmers, however, were promised higher revenues for their animals. After attending the South Pacific Forum in Australia in late July, Muldoon went to India for a regional Commonwealth Conference and then to China in September. In October, he attended the annual meetings of the World Bank and the International Monetary Fund (IMF) in Washington and concluded a dairy agreement with Mexico.

Domestic Affairs. Public opinion polls showed that the opposition Labour Party slightly trailed the governing National Party in popularity. However Social Credit, holding at about 20%, scored an astounding by-election victory, taking a safe National seat and increasing its representation in parliament to two for the first time. The triennial local body elections in October were marked by a low turnout, a decline in Labour strength, and the defeat of Sir Dove-Myer Robinson, six-term mayor of Auckland City. According to the polls, inflation, the economy, and unemployment were the most worrisome issues to more than 60% of citizens.

On October 23, an attempt to oust Prime Minister Muldoon by cabinet ministers and backbenchers in his own National Party collapsed when Brian Talboys, the deputy prime minister and foreign minister, refused to join the revolt at a party caucus. Muldoon had come under attack for his style of leadership and handling of the economy.

In January, Soviet Ambassador V. N. Sofinsky was expelled for interfering in domestic politics. He was accused of transferring funds from the Soviet government to the tiny Socialist Unity (pro-Moscow Communist) Party.

In May, Paul Reeves, bishop of Auckland, was appointed Anglican archbishop of New Zealand. He is the youngest person and first part-Maori to be chosen.

GRAHAM BUSH, *University of Auckland*

NIGERIA

The civilian government of President Alhaji Shehu Shagari, which assumed power from the military on Oct. 1, 1979, did little in 1980 to arouse serious opposition or to offend the former military leaders.

Politics. The president attempted to further compromise with other parties by convening meetings to discuss Nigeria's problems. These were boycotted by Chief Obafemi Awolowo and the United Party of Nigeria (UPN). Except for the UPN, there was little resistance to Shagari's moderate program. Wage and price controls were announced in April establishing a minimum wage of 100 Naira (N 100 or U.S.$185) per month and a ceiling on income increases of between 10% and 15% through 1982. In July a new

---
—— NEW ZEALAND • Information Highlights ——

Official Name: New Zealand.
Location: Southwest Pacific Ocean.
Area: 103,736 sq mi (268 676 km²).
Population (1980 est.): 3,200,000.
Chief Cities (March 1979): Wellington, the capital, 349,-900; Auckland, 805,900; Christchurch, 327,300.
Government: Head of state, Elizabeth II, queen, represented by Sir Keith Holyoake, governor general (took office Oct. 1977). Head of government, Robert Muldoon, prime minister (took office Dec. 1975). Legislature (unicameral)—House of Representatives.
Monetary Unit: New Zealand dollar (1.0186 N.Z. dollars equal U.S.$1, Aug. 1980).
Manufactures (major products): Processed foods, wood products, cement, fertilizer, beverages, domestic appliances.
Agriculture (major products): Wheat, corn, barley, potatoes, dairy products, wool.
GNP (1979 est., U.S.$): $17,140,000,000.
Foreign Trade (1979, U.S.$): Imports, $4,542,000,000; exports, $4,694,000,000.

Nigerian President Alhaji Shagari (left) meets with UN Secretary General Kurt Waldheim on October 6 at UN headquarters. Shagari called for immediate action to set up free elections in Namibia.

UPI

census was proposed. Previous censuses have been very divisive and the National Party of Nigeria (NPN) government planned for a year of preparation before launching this difficult task. The central government acquired 14 000 ha (35,-000 acres) of land in each state which is to be devoted to grain production. Shagari hoped this would begin a green revolution, based on Western technology, which would relieve Nigeria from dependence on imported food which in 1979 cost Nigeria ₦ 1,000,000,000. The most serious crisis facing Shagari's government was the "Oilgate" scandal, in which the Nigerian National Petroleum Commission was accused of misappropriation of ₦ 2,800,000,000 during the military regime. There was a public outcry. Students took to the streets and invaded the National Assembly in April demanding an investigation. The report of a commission of inquiry appointed by Shagari, while pointing out poor management, exonerated the former military regime of misappropriation of funds.

Economics. Profits from the export of "sweet" (low sulfur) crude continued to climb, providing the largest percentage of Nigeria's estimated $50,000,000,000 gross national product. The United States alone imported more than 1 million barrels of Nigerian oil each day. Petroleum income, which has made Nigeria the richest state in black Africa, has mixed blessings. Inflation is high and migrants still pour into the cities at an alarming rate. Lagos has had a fourfold population increase since the mid-1960s. Previous military regimes have overspent and Shagari's first budget anticipated a deficit of ₦ 2,830,000,000. Once a major food exporter, Nigeria now imports food. Nevertheless, the government income for 1980, estimated at ₦ 11,800,000,000, allowed for major road, harbor, and water improvements, maintenance of an armed force of 150,000 men, the expansion of education at all levels, and government sponsorship of industry and major agricultural development.

Foreign Policy. Nigeria was a dominant force at the Organization of African Unity (OAU) meeting in Freetown in July. Shagari recommended a plan for mediating the situation in the Western Sahara and largely was responsible for convincing Sgt. Samuel Doe to moderate the excesses of the Liberian revolution. A Liberian delegation visited Lagos in August. In Lagos in July U.S. Vice-President Walter Mondale and Nigeria's Vice-President Alex Ekwueme signed two economic accords. Relations with Britain, strained over the Rhodesia (Zimbabwe) problem, improved considerably, although a major point of contention, Britain's economic interests in South Africa, continued. Shagari declared his unequivocal support of Robert Mugabe's government and sent ₦ 10 million to Zimbabwe in April. He has also demanded that Namibia be free of South African control by 1981. Even before his state visit to the United States and the United Nations in October he had made it clear that his primary foreign policy objective was the overthrow of the white-dominated government in South Africa and he did not rule out the use of petroleum as a weapon to change the direction of U.S. and British policies.

HARRY A. GAILEY
San Jose State University

NIGERIA • Information Highlights

Official Name: Federal Republic of Nigeria.
Location: West Africa.
Area: 356,669 sq mi (923 773 km²).
Population (1980 est.): 77,100,000.
Chief Cities (1976 est.): Lagos, the capital, 1,100,000; Ibadan, 850,000; Ogbomosho, 435,000; Kano, 400,-000.
Government: *Head of state and government,* Alhaji Shehu Shagari, president (took office Oct. 1979). *Legislature*—Senate and House of Representatives.
Monetary Unit: Naira (0.53891 naira equals U.S.$1, July 1980).
Manufactures (major products): Petroleum, textiles, cement, food products, footwear, metal products, lumber.
Agriculture (major products): Cocoa, rubber, palm oil, yams, cassava, sorghum, millet, corn, rice, cotton.
GNP (1980 est., U.S.$): $50,000,000,000.
Foreign Trade (1978, U.S.$): *Imports,* $12,763,000,000; *exports,* $9,865,000,000.

In Greensboro, NC, in February 1980, black youths hold a unity march against the Ku Klux Klan.

NORTH CAROLINA

Political surprises and a long trial provided the year's leading stories.

Politics. James B. Hunt, Jr., became the first governor to be elected to a second four-year term, but his overwhelming vote of confidence was overshadowed by the stunning upset of Democratic Sen. Robert Morgan by a political science professor, John P. East. Other Democratic candidates won their statewide races, but Congressmen Richardson Preyer and Lamar Gudger were defeated by Republicans. Harry L. Bridges, longtime state auditor, retired, but the dean of American secretaries of state, Thad Eure, was elected for his twelfth four-year term. Richard C. Erwin was the first black to be appointed a federal judge in North Carolina in the 20th century.

Trials and Court Rulings. The longest trial in the state's history ended with a jury's 36-page verdict of not guilty for four members of the Ku Klux Klan and two Nazis who had been accused of shooting five supporters of the Communist Workers Party (CWP) at an anti-Klan rally in Greensboro in November 1979. CWP members refused to testify. During the trial Governor Hunt became the object of threats both in and out of state, and the jury's verdict set off protest demonstrations on several college campuses.

The three life-in-prison terms given in 1979 to Dr. Jeffrey R. MacDonald for the alleged murder of his wife and two daughters at Fort Bragg in 1970 were overturned by a federal court of appeals. The court of appeals also ruled unconstitutional the printing of a motorist's prayer on maps issued by the state. Marine PFC Robert R. Garwood became the only Vietnam war serviceman to be placed on trial for desertion and collaboration with the enemy.

Economy. Holding its own in relation to the rate of inflation, the state's tax collection from all sources increased by 12.91% over that of the previous fiscal year. Reduced driving was reflected in a 3% drop in highway fund collections. Capi-

tal investments in new and expanded industry continued at record levels, particularly in the electronics-related industries. The governor announced plans for a novel microelectronics research and development center in the Research Triangle Park. The state became active also in promoting the making of motion pictures within its borders. The lengthy litigation between the Amalgamated Clothing and Textile Workers Union and J. P. Stevens Company ended with a recognition of the union as bargaining agent at the company's Roanoke Rapids plant.

Education. The ten-year battle between the federal government and the University of North Carolina over control of higher education continued. The state produced impressive figures of progress away from a dual racial system, but federal officials sought the transfer of some established programs from one campus to another as a means of speeding integration. The North Carolina School of Mathematics and Science for exceptional students was opened in Durham, and work began on a school of veterinary science at North Carolina State University.

"Jamscam." Revelation that the North Carolina Junior Chamber of Commerce had diverted funds, raised from the sale of jams and jellies for a burn center, to payment of national dues for

— **NORTH CAROLINA · Information Highlights** —

Area: 52,586 sq mi (136 198 km^2).
Population (Jan. 1980 est.): 5,628,000.
Chief Cities (1976 est.): Raleigh, the capital, 136,883; Charlotte, 281,696; Greensboro, 157,324.
Government (1980): *Chief Officers*—governor, James B. Hunt, Jr. (D); lt. gov., James C. Green (D). *General Assembly*—Senate, 50 members; House of Representatives, 120 members.
Education (1979–80): *Enrollment*—public elementary schools, 796,033 pupils; public secondary, 354,020; colleges and universities, 269,065 students. *Public school expenditures,* $2,210,120,000 ($1,686 per pupil).
State Finances (fiscal year 1979): *Revenues,* $5,537,-000,000; *expenditures,* $5,249,000,000.
Personal Income (1979): $41,399,000,000; per capita, $7,385.
Labor Force (June 1980): *Total labor force,* 2,819,400; *unemployed,* 208,800 (7.4% of total force).

"memberships" in bogus chapters led to the resignation of President J. Harold Herring and to his withdrawal as the unopposed candidate for the national presidency of the Jaycees. The organization began restoring the funds, and the center opened in Chapel Hill in November.

Names in the News. John R. Jordan, Jr., was elected chairman of the university system's board of governors, and Christopher C. Fordham III was installed as chancellor of the Chapel Hill campus.

H. G. JONES, *University of North Carolina*

NORTH DAKOTA

Weather dominated events in North Dakota in 1980. Politics and energy development also were major news stories.

Weather. Farmers and ranchers lost in excess of $1,300,000,000 due to weather. More than 52,000 crop disaster loan applications were filed as damage from drought, hail, wind, and unseasonable rain equaled one half of the previous year's total farm income. A statewide drought emergency was declared in June, and National Weather Service officials reported that spring 1980 had been the driest since 1936. In midsummer, violent hail and windstorms destroyed maturing crops on 535,000 acres (217 000 ha) and caused $9.6 million damage to farm and ranch buildings. Prolonged rain at harvest time left standing and cut cereal grains with sprout damage, discoloration, and little market appeal. Agricultural producers received more than $150 million from federal disaster and emergency feed and forage programs in partial redress of farm and ranch losses. Overall crop production fell 33% below 1979 and farmers abandoned 17.5% of planted small grain acreage and 12% of row crop acreage due to weather. Normally, weather causes abandonment of about 3% of total acreage.

Politics. State Attorney General Allen I. Olson was the first Republican to be elected governor since 1960. Voters filled most state offices with Republicans and continued the GOP's legislative dominance. Republican Rep. Mark Andrews was chosen to succeed fellow Republican Milton R. Young, who was retiring from the Senate after 35 years. Tax Commissioner Byron Dorgan, a Democrat, was picked to fill the state's lone House seat. North Dakotans approved a 6.5% tax on oil extraction in addition to the current 5% production tax, passed a mortgage loan plan for low-income residents, changed the primary election date back to June from September, approved the prohibiting of the legislature from levying a real or personal state property tax, and eliminated the office of county judge (effective in 1983). Voters nullified legislation to acquire 10,000 acres (4 000 ha) of ranch land for a park and rejected changes in election laws.

In an effort to increase employment and economic development, in 1980 North Dakota started a Beginning Farmer Project, which provides income tax incentives to land owners for selling or leasing land to farmers who are just starting out in that business.

Energy. Major energy industry events were start of construction on a $1,500,000,000 coal gasification plant and start-up of a 1,100-megawatt electric generating plant. Both are part of a huge mine-mouth energy-producing complex in coal-rich western North Dakota, representing investments of more than $4,000,000,000. The gasification plant is the first commercial-size synthetic fuel project in the nation. The generating plant is the largest lignite coal-fed one in the nation and one of six in the state exporting power to the Midwest. The state's oil and gas industry set exploration and development records in 1980, drilling 550 wells—100 more than the 1958 high—and producing 40 million barrels of oil.

Environment. Expanding energy development brought new environmental conflicts, and an old controversy over Garrison Diversion irrigation project continued. The Public Service Commission rejected a U.S.-approved gas pipeline route through the state's Badlands and substituted a less scenic and more costly route. A lawsuit challenging the state's right to make the change was pending at year-end.

Congress authorized $9.7 million for work on the Garrison project and ordered the Interior Department to restore $3 million previously appropriated but diverted by the Carter administration to other projects. Canadian officials and citizens, the Audubon Society, and area landowners continued to oppose the plan and one county in the Conservancy District won a yearlong legal fight to withdraw.

U.S. Courts. Federal judges struck down two state abortion laws and a law that required display of the Ten Commandments in all public school classrooms. Regarding the abortion laws, the federal court judge ruled that provisions prohibiting advertisement of abortion services and requiring a 48-hour wait, informed consent, and parental notice for minors were in violation of the private relationship between a physician and patient.

NORTH DAKOTA • Information Highlights

Area: 70,665 sq mi (183 022 km²).

Population (Jan. 1980 est.): 658,000.

Chief Cities (1970 census): Bismarck, the capital, 34,703; Fargo, 53,365; Grand Forks, 39,008.

Government (1980): *Chief Officers*—governor, Arthur A. Link (D); lt. gov., Wayne G. Sanstead (D). *Legislative Assembly*—Senate, 50 members; House of Representatives, 100 members.

Education (1979–80): *Enrollment*—public elementary schools, 75,542 pupils; public secondary, 42,146; colleges and universities, 31,904 students. *Public school expenditures*, $248,041,000 ($1,916 per pupil).

State Finances (fiscal year 1979): *Revenues*, $823,000,000; *expenditures*, $777,000,000.

Personal Income (1979): $5,408,000,000; per capita, $8,231.

Labor Force (June 1980): *Nonagricultural wage and salary earners*, 250,600; *unemployed*, 16,200 (5.0% of total force).

A U.S. appeals court declared unconstitutional two state election laws that imposed restrictions on ballot access for independent candidates. The court indicated that the laws' 15,000 required signatures (more than those required in most states) and early filing deadlines (90 days before the primary) were unnecessarily oppressive.

Sports News. The University of North Dakota, located in Grand Forks, won the National Collegiate Athletic Association (NCAA) ice hockey title on March 29.

STAN CANN, *"The Forum," Fargo*

NORTHWEST TERRITORIES

Discussion of a possible division of the Northwest Territories (NWT) into two jurisdictions and hearings into a proposed oil pipeline from Norman Wells south to Alberta were major developments on the political and economic fronts in 1980.

Politics. One of the first moves of the 22-member Territorial Council (legislative assembly) of the NWT, elected in October 1979, was to establish a committee to determine the means by which a public consensus could be reached on political development. The committee's report was extensively debated at the assembly's fall 1980 session, and its recommendations were adopted, with amendments. Basically, the assembly gave commitment in principle to the division of the existing NWT into an eastern and a western territory; recommended a plebiscite on the division question; and called for the formation of a constitutional development committee to make recommendations concerning the political future of the western NWT. The pressure for division came from the eastern part of the Territories, in conjunction with proposals from the Inuit Tapirisat of Canada (an organization negotiating Inuit land claims), but the final decision rests with the federal government. In December 1980, two assembly members from the Arctic regions were appointed to the executive committee, or territorial cabinet.

Economy. Canada's National Energy Board held hearings into a proposed pipeline project that would transport crude oil from Imperial Oil's field in Norman Wells to Zama in northern Alberta. The project would have significant economic impact in the Mackenzie region of the NWT. The territorial government and native associations called for a delay in the project until certain conditions could be met regarding aboriginal rights, establishment of a northern-based control agency, arrangements for resource revenue sharing, and guarantees on energy supplies for northern residents.

ROSS M. HARVEY
*Assistant Director of Information
Government of the Northwest Territories*

NORWAY

Rising income from offshore oil and gas fields prevented Norway from feeling the full effects of the international recession.

Economy and Trade. The country continued to enjoy modest prosperity and high employment levels in 1980, but some export industries, particularly iron ore, steel, and ferroalloys, were hit by world trends. Prices rose when controls on wages and prices, which had been in effect for 15 months, were relaxed in January. Wage bargaining between the national trade union federation and the employers' association in the spring resulted in a national settlement that granted generous increases to lower paid workers, while the overall rise averaged only 5.2%. The government contributed to the package by granting tax concessions and increasing allowances for children.

The hope of the Labor government was to hold down inflation in spite of the end of the freeze, but this proved difficult. Some regulation of domestic prices continued, most seriously affecting the profits of companies producing for the domestic market. At the same time, higher import prices pushed up living costs. The North Sea unions, which had not taken part in the national spring bargaining, called for large wage increases and backed their demands by going on strike in the summer. A stoppage by 2,000 production workers lasted 16 days, after which the government intervened and ordered compulsory arbitration. A strike by 2,000 seamen and officers on floating platforms lasted much longer,

─────── NORTHWEST TERRITORIES · ───────
Information Highlights

Area: 1,304,903 sq mi (3 379 700 km²).
Population (1980 est.): 46,063.
Chief City (1979 est.): Yellowknife, the capital, 9,918.
Government (1980): *Chief Officers*—commissioner, John H. Parker; chief justice, Court of Appeal, William A. McGillivray; judge of the Supreme Court, C.F. Tallis. *Legislature*—Territorial Council, 22 elected members.
Education (1980–81 est.): *Enrollment*—public elementary and secondary schools, 12,484 pupils. *Public school expenditures* (1979–80), $48,591,000.
Public Finance (fiscal year 1979–80): *Revenues*, $307,-530,000; *expenditures*, $301,744,000.
Mining (1980 est.): Production value, $515,116,000. (All monetary figures are in Canadian dollars.)

─────── NORWAY · Information Highlights ───────

Official Name: Kingdom of Norway.
Location: Northern Europe.
Area: 125,181 sq mi (324 219 km²).
Population (1980 est.): 4,100,000.
Chief Cities (Jan. 1979): Oslo, the capital, 457,446; Bergen, 210,405; Trondheim, 134,683.
Government: *Head of state,* Olav V, king (acceded Sept. 1957). *Head of government,* Odvar Nordli, prime minister (took office Jan. 1976). *Legislature*—Storting: Lagting and Odelsting.
Monetary Unit: Krone (5.199 kroner equal U.S.$1, Dec. 1980).
Manufactures (major products): Pulp and paper, ships, oil and gas, food products, aluminum, ferroalloys.
Agriculture (major products): Potatoes, barley, wheat, apples, pears, dairy products, livestock.
GNP (1979 est., U.S.$): $46,000,000,000.
Foreign Trade (1979, U.S.$): *Imports*, $13,818,000,000; *exports*, $13,271,000,000.

however, upsetting oil company exploration programs. The striking unions were members of the powerful LO federation, which opposed any compulsory settlement and was an important political ally of the ruling Labor Party. After nearly five weeks, the employers agreed to voluntary arbitration. The final agreement was for a 23% increase.

By autumn, it was clear that cost of living increases for the year likely would exceed 11%, against a rise of only about 4% in 1979, when the freeze was in force. The government's $25,000,000,000 budget for 1981, proposed in October, did nothing to curb the trend. It proposed subsidy cuts and large increases in indirect taxes, which together were expected to increase living costs by another 2.5%. It provided, moreover, for a continued high level of public spending, financed by record oil revenues. In his budget speech, Finance Minister Ulf Sand conceded that the liberal use of oil money in the domestic economy would be inflationary, but said that it was necessary to maintain employment.

Government revenues from the petroleum industry increased sharply in 1980, partly because of higher oil and gas prices and partly because the state tax on oil company profits was raised from 70% to 82%.

On March 27, the Alexander L. Kielland floating oil platform on Norway's Ekofisk field in the North Sea capsized in high winds and turbulent waters, killing 123 persons. One of the worst disasters in the history of offshore oil operations, it stirred a national debate on safety standards in the industry. The government earmarked extra funds for safety training and the staffing of supervisory bodies. Tougher regulations were drafted and scheduled for implementation in January 1981.

Government and Politics. The political scene was affected by heightening East-West tension following the Soviet Union's intervention in Afghanistan. Norway's sports federation decided to join the boycott of the summer Olympics in Moscow, a decision that was unpopular with sports fans. There was dissent within the Labor Party over a government proposal to stockpile U.S. military equipment for use by American forces during a crisis.

Early in October, the ministers of labor, oil and energy, and justice resigned from the cabinet of Prime Minister Odvar Nordli. Their resignation, coming less than a year before the September 1981 parliamentary elections, was interpreted by many Norwegians as a sign of dissatisfaction with Nordli's leadership.

THØR GJESTER
Editor, "Øknomisk Revy," Oslo

NOVA SCOTIA

The year 1980 saw further expansion of the Nova Scotian economy. Unemployment declined, while real income per capita improved modestly. On the energy front, the federal-provincial dispute over the ownership of oil and gas reserves continued, while the province made further advances in the development of alternative sources of energy.

Legislation and Government. During its second year in office, the Conservative government of Premier John Buchanan decided to develop a new hospital complex, a cancer treatment and research foundation, and a new school for the blind in Halifax. A major reorganization of government departments was carried out, creating departments of manpower planning, transportation and energy, and mines and resources.

On the legislative front, the government debated 111 bills, of which 90 became law. The subjects included protection of single-parent families, energy conservation, municipal government, trade unions, health, religion, and recreation.

Economy. Against the backdrop of a sagging Canadian economy, the provincial economy made significant gains in various sectors. In the primary sector, coal production was up, while significant oil and gas exploration off the coast of Nova Scotia pointed to continued growth. The volume of fish landings also showed an increase, and farm cash receipts rose significantly. Growth in the production of petroleum, coal products, and transportation equipment maintained a buoyant manufacturing sector, which expected added stimulus from a decision by Michelin to locate a third plant at Waterville.

The government presented a budget of $1,700,000,000 for fiscal 1980–81, with a projected deficit of $16.2 million.

Energy. Overall, Nova Scotia has efficiently managed its existing energy resources, while alternative sources are being developed. The Energy and Mineral Resources Conservation Board was created to control pollution, appraise energy production capacity, and regulate the construction of gas pipelines. A second coal-fired, 150,000-megawatt power generating plant was brought on line at Lingan, while work on a tidal power project on the Annapolis River began.

R. P. SETH
Mount St. Vincent University, Halifax

—— NOVA SCOTIA · Information Highlights ——

Area: 21,425 sq mi (55 490 km²).
Population (1980 est.): 851,600.
Chief Cities (1976 census): Halifax, the capital, 117,882; Dartmouth, 65,341; Sydney, 30,645.
Government (1980): *Chief Officers*—lt. gov., John E. Shaffner; premier, John Buchanan (Progressive Conservative). *Legislature*—Legislative Assembly, 52 members.
Education (1979–80 est.): *Enrollment*—public elementary and secondary schools, 189,960 pupils; private schools, 1,340; Indian (federal) schools, 730; postsecondary, 21,420 students.
Public Finance (1980–81 est.): *Revenues,* $1,554,796,000; *expenditures,* $1,571,030,000.
Personal Income (average weekly salary, May 1980): $264.68.
Unemployment Rate (Aug. 1980, seasonally adjusted): 10.1%.
(All monetary figures are in Canadian dollars.)

MEANY, George

U.S. labor leader: b. New York City, Aug. 16, 1894; d. Washington, DC, Jan. 10, 1980.

George Meany died at the age of 85, less than two months after relinquishing the presidency of the American Federation of Labor and the Congress of Industrial Organizations (AFL-CIO). He had led the federation of 14 million members without serious challenge since its founding 24 years earlier.

Under Meany's leadership, the two union groups put aside 20 years of bitter rivalry to unite and, against all predictions, stayed united, to become the largest and most influential labor movement in the free world. The gruff, cigar-smoking, one-time Bronx plumber was often portrayed as the ultimate "labor boss," a misconception of both the federation and its president.

The AFL-CIO is a voluntary federation of unions. Under Meany's presidency, three unions, including the Teamsters, were expelled; two of them later reentered. Only the United Automobile Workers (UAW) dropped out—in 1968. With a few exceptions, the other 105 national unions followed Meany's lead year after year because he shared their attitudes, understood their needs, and had the energy to do his homework on the issues. Besides ability—and a photographic memory—Meany had personal integrity and was dedicated to two causes, workers' welfare and human freedom.

Background. George Meany was born in New York City, Aug. 16, 1894. His father, Michael Meany, was president of a plumber's local union. When family circumstances forced him to leave high school, Meany apprenticed in his father's trade, getting his journeyman's papers in 1915. Seven years later his local union elected him its full-time business agent. In 1934 he was elected president of the New York State Federation of Labor. Success in Albany led in 1939 to Meany's election as secretary-treasurer of the American Federation of Labor.

On the death of William Green in 1952, the AFL Executive Council elevated him to the presidency. His first goal was to end the civil war between the labor movements. Three years later the AFL and CIO merged.

President Dwight D. Eisenhower twice named Meany U.S. delegate to the UN General Assembly, the first labor leader so honored.

When the battle for civil rights for black Americans began again after the election of President John F. Kennedy, Meany took his stand as an ally in that struggle. When Dr. Martin Luther King needed bail money, the AFL-CIO put it up. When the battle moved to the floor of Congress Meany was there, insisting that the Civil Rights bill include Title VII, prohibiting job discrimination. With Meany's encouragement, mi-

UPI

nority participation in apprenticeship programs increased from 3% to 20%. According to the U.S. Bureau of Labor Statistics, proportionally more black workers than white are now union members.

During the Meany years, union organization and collective bargaining were extended to public sector employees and to professionals. Meany is credited with persuading President Kennedy to sign an executive order giving collective bargaining rights to federal workers. Meany collaborated with President Lyndon B. Johnson on a host of social issues.

In 1972, Meany kept the AFL-CIO neutral in the presidential race between Richard M. Nixon and George McGovern. Notwithstanding, many national unions endorsed McGovern for president. One year later, at the height of the Watergate scandal, Meany led the AFL-CIO, at its annual convention, in calling for the resignation of President Nixon. At the same convention, with Meany presiding, the AFL-CIO reversed its traditional position of support for protective legislation to endorse the Equal Rights Amendment.

Meany attracted the most controversy in foreign affairs. He was a determined foe of all police states—fascist, Communist, and Nazi. He supported the Vietnam war to the bitter end.

Meany is survived by three daughters and 14 grandchildren. His wife, Eugenia, whom he courted while she walked a picket line and married in 1919, had died nine months before him.

GORDON H. COLE

[1] Arranged chronologically by death date

UPI

DOUGLAS, William Orville

Associate Justice, U.S. Supreme Court; b. Maine, MN, Oct. 16, 1898; d. Washington, DC, Jan. 19, 1980.

William O. Douglas, the U.S. Supreme Court's most outspoken defender of citizens' rights and the justice with the longest tenure—36½ years—on that tribunal, died of pneumonia and kidney failure at age 81 on Jan. 19, 1980.

A "lion-like defender of individual liberty," according to President Jimmy Carter, Douglas served under five chief justices and with one third of all the justices ever to sit on the court. He was the author of 1,306 opinions (550 expressing the majority view, 583 in dissent, and 173 others) and some 20 books. Writing with blunt clarity, Douglas espoused a "strict constructionist" view of the federal constitution. The purpose of the Bill of Rights, he wrote, is to "keep the government off the backs of the people." He advocated "full and free discussion even of ideas we hate"; fought against unreasonable search and seizure, intrusions upon privacy, and curtailment of the privilege against self-incrimination; and was an activist on questions of minority rights and equal opportunity.

Douglas' indomitable personality, identification with the poor, and gut reaction against injustice were molded early in life. He was the son of a Presbyterian minister who preached in frontier communities and died when the boy was six. The family was left impoverished, and his mother moved it to Yakima, WA, where William contracted poliomyelitis. By climbing and hiking through the state, Douglas overcame the effects of the disease and developed a passion for the outdoors. He would later become a noted environmentalist and world traveler.

He was graduated Phi Beta Kappa from Whitman College (Walla Walla, WA) in 1920 and made his way across the country as a freight hand and hobo. Douglas' later antipathy for vagrancy statutes was perhaps based on that experience. He attended Columbia University Law School, graduating second in his class in 1925. After a few years in private practice on Wall Street, he joined the law faculty at Columbia but in 1929 moved to Yale, where he built a reputation as a financial law expert.

In 1934, Douglas was appointed to the staff of the newly-formed Securities and Exchange Commission (SEC). In 1936, he became a member of the commission and in 1937 was chosen its chairman. While at the SEC, he became a friend and poker companion of Franklin Roosevelt and was brought into FDR's inner circle of advisers.

In 1939, Roosevelt nominated him to the Supreme Court, succeeding the retiring Justice Louis Brandeis. The Senate confirmed his nomination by a vote of 62 to 4, and he joined the court April 17, 1939. The four legislators who voted against him believed he was reactionary and biased in favor of the financial community. To the contrary, Douglas, like his predecessor, had a mistrust of corporate bigness. His background in finance law enabled him to write the court's opinions in the fields of corporate finance, rate-making, taxation, and antitrust law.

With friend and colleague Justice Hugo Black, Douglas worked to incorporate most of the guarantees of the Bill of Rights as protections against the states through the "due process" clause of the Fourteenth Amendment. He eventually got the court to acknowledge that the constitution requires all persons charged with a serious crime to be provided with an attorney. A champion of the First Amendment, Douglas favored the protection of "symbolic speech," such as mass demonstrations and the burning of draft cards; on freedom of the press, he was a strong advocate of the unfettered right to publish.

In 1946, both Douglas and Black dissented when the court refused to overturn legislative malapportionment. Sixteen years later, they joined a majority decision which recognized the right to judicial remedy if there was a denial of the "one person, one vote" principle. Douglas also dissented in the Smith Act prosecution of top U.S. Communists and opposed Cold War loyalty oaths and passport restrictions.

In 1944, FDR briefly considered Douglas for his running mate. Years later, the justice would say, "Elective office was never in my bloodstream." Three times during his career, Congressional opponents of his liberal views sought Douglas' impeachment and removal from the court. However, only a stroke could remove him from the bench where, for more than 36 years, he had maintained an intense schedule and a reputation as the fastest worker among the justices. He resigned in November 1978.

MARTIN GRUBERG

DURANTE, Jimmy

American comedian: b. New York, NY, Feb. 10, 1893; d. Santa Monica, CA, Jan. 29, 1980.

One of America's most beloved comedians, Jimmy Durante—whose career in show business spanned more than six decades—was the master of a distinctive comic style that brought him millions of fans among vaudeville, nightclub, theater, motion picture, radio, and television audiences. Nicknamed "Schnozzola" because of his formidable nose, Durante was noted for his mock hard-boiled, yet good-natured manner, his raffish appearance, his slaughter of standard English, his self-deprecating comic routines, his honky-tonk style of piano-playing, his gravelly voice and delivery, and songs of his own creation, such as *Inka Dinka Doo* and *I'm Jimmy, That Well-Dressed Man.*

A native of Manhattan's Lower East Side, James Francis Durante was encouraged by his father to take up the piano. After dropping out of school in the seventh grade, Jimmy worked at various jobs, and at 17 began playing the piano in saloons on the Bowery-Chinatown-Coney Island circuit. Eventually he organized his own band, and in 1923 he opened a nightclub-speakeasy with Eddie Jackson and Lou Clayton, who became his partners in a vaudeville comedy act. By the mid-1930s he had met with success on Broadway in *Jumbo* (1935) and *Red, Hot and Blue* (1936). Between 1930 and 1951 he also appeared in 29 films. In the mid-1940s he began a series of radio broadcasts and from 1950 to 1956 attained new popularity with a TV program.

Noted for his generosity, Mr. Durante raised millions of dollars for various causes. At 68 he and his second wife adopted an infant daughter.

HENRY S. SLOAN

LONGWORTH, Alice Roosevelt

American socialite: b. New York, NY, Feb. 12, 1884; d. Washington, DC, Feb. 20, 1980.

Known as "Princess Alice" or "Washington's other monument," Mrs. Alice Roosevelt Longworth, the elder daughter and last surviving child of President Theodore Roosevelt and the widow of House Speaker Nicholas Longworth, was a leading figure in Washington social circles for nearly eight decades. Noted for her charm, patrician elegance, and barbed wit, she was acquainted with virtually every major Washington political figure from Benjamin Harrison to Gerald Ford, and few were spared her caustic comments. Calvin Coolidge, for example, looked, she said, "as if he had been weaned on a pickle" and Thomas E. Dewey reminded her of "the bridegroom on a wedding cake." A favorite subject of the social columns in her youth, she inspired the popular song *Alice Blue Gown*. Her independence once prompted Teddy Roosevelt to tell a visitor: "I can be president of the United States, or I can control Alice. I cannot possibly do both."

Two days after Alice Roosevelt's birth, her mother died. She was brought up by an aunt, and later by her stepmother, spending much of her childhood at Sagamore Hill in Oyster Bay, NY. In 1901, when Vice-President Theodore Roosevelt became the 26th president following the assassination of William McKinley, she moved to the nation's capital. In a White House ceremony in 1906, Alice Roosevelt married Nicholas Longworth, Ohio congressman and the House Speaker from 1925 until his death in 1931. A Republican, she remained active politically until her death.

HENRY S. SLOAN

FROMM, Erich

Psychoanalyst and social philosopher: b. Frankfurt, Germany, March 23, 1900; d. Muralto, Switzerland, March 18, 1980.

A prolific author, effective lecturer, and much sought-after teacher, Erich Fromm was regarded as one of the most influential social philosophers of the 20th century. His twenty books—including *Escape From Freedom* (1941), *The Sane Society* (1955), *The Art of Loving* (1956), and *To Have or To Be* (1961)—reached a vast general audience and often attained bestseller status. No area of human experience was outside his interest, and his writings ranged over subjects from the alienation of the individual to faith and sanity in modern society. He lectured all over the world and held university teaching positions in his native Germany, the United States—where he emigrated in 1941 to escape Hitler's National Socialism—and Mexico. Developing his own neo-Freudian analysis, Dr. Fromm was a distinguished therapist.

Abandoning orthodox Jewish convictions and practices at age 26, Fromm saw historic man rejecting a God requiring submission and finding release in a nameless God symbolizing the universe. Yet he enjoyed reading the scriptures of the major Eastern and Western faiths and valued the mystical elements of the religious experience. On the earthly plane, man's freedom of choice seemed to lead to the peaceful society envisioned by Karl Marx; he regarded the militant Communism of the Soviet Union as a misinterpretation. Through the practice of psychoanalysis, Fromm discovered in the human condition positive and negative drives and a tension between freedom and biological needs.

ERNST ROSE

OWENS, James Cleveland

American athlete: b. Oakville, AL, Sept. 12, 1913; d. Tucson, AZ, March 31, 1980.

Jesse Owens' four gold medals in the 1936 Berlin Olympics made him probably the greatest and most famous track and field athlete in history. His performances in the 100-m and 200-m dashes, long jump, and 400-m relay set or equaled four Olympic records. And although no other track and field athlete has ever won as many golds in one Games, Owens' triumphs were as significant politically as they were athletically. One of what the Nazis had called "America's black auxiliaries," Owens made a mockery of the Nazi "master race" ideology and was snubbed by the embarrassed Adolph Hitler. In later years, Owens became known as an inspirational and energetic public speaker. "Re-

SARTRE, Jean-Paul

French author and philosopher: b. Paris, France, June 21, 1905; d. Paris, April 15, 1980.

Existential philosopher, playwright, novelist, biographer, essayist, and leftist revolutionary, Jean-Paul Sartre was regarded as a master among French intellectuals and literati for more than 40 years. His ever-shifting and developing ideas covered every topic from meaning and existence to art, sexuality, and politics. At times attacked by both the left and right, Sartre was highly respected by serious intellectuals. His death, caused by an edema of the lung at age 74, left a gaping void in the Western philosophical and literary community.

As he wrote in the caustic memoir of his childhood, *Les mots* (The Words, 1964), Jean-Paul was reared by his mother, her parents, and

HITCHCOCK, Alfred

Motion picture director: b. London, England, Aug. 13, 1899; d. Los Angeles, CA, April 29, 1980.

Filmdom's unrivaled "master of suspense," Alfred Hitchcock—who directed 54 feature films in a career that spanned nearly 60 years—was perhaps more popular among motion picture viewers than any other director of his time. In his meticulously crafted, taut melodramas, with their occasional touches of whimsical humor and romance, he skillfully used the camera and the soundtrack to create the appropriate combination of tension and relaxation in his audiences. Rejecting interpretations of critics who claimed to find profound philosophical meaning in his work, "Hitch" preferred to view himself as a storyteller and entertainer. In the 1950s and 1960s, he became something of a celebrity in his

gardless of his color," he told audiences, "a man who becomes a recognized athlete has to learn to walk 10 feet tall. But he must have his dignity off the athletic field, too."

The son of a sharecropper and grandson of slaves, Owens picked cotton in rural Alabama until age 9, when the family moved to Cleveland, OH. While still only a senior at East Technical High School, he tied the world record (9.4 seconds) for the 100-yard dash. Although he is best remembered for his triumphs in Berlin, probably his greatest performance came during his sophomore year at Ohio State. In the 1935 Big Ten meet in Ann Arbor, MI, Owens hobbled onto the track with a painful back injury, and in a span of 45 minutes set three world records (long jump, 220-yard dash, 220-yard low hurdles) and tied a fourth (100-yard dash).

When the U.S. Olympic team returned from Berlin, Owens was the main attraction in enormous ticker tape parades in New York, Cleveland, and Chicago. In 1936, however, there were no dollars for black athletes in professional sports, commercials, or endorsements. Two weeks after his hero's welcome, Owens was still suffering financially and was once again riding at the back of buses. To support himself, Owens took a job as a playground janitor and ran exhibition races against horses and dogs.

Even during his lean years, Owens' faith in himself and his country did not diminish. Having studied speech at Ohio State, he decided to put his speaking skills to work. Promoting patriotism, personal pride, charity, and the Olympic movement, Owens spoke at clubs and corporations across the United States. He devoted much of his time to several religious and youth organizations. He was awarded the Presidential Medal of Freedom in 1976.

MARTY GLICKMAN

---

a stepfather in a "hotbed of bourgeois hypocrisy." A brilliant student, Sartre entered the prestigious Ecole Normale Supérieure at age 20 and was graduated first as an agrégé in philosophy. It was at the school that he met Simone de Beauvoir, his mistress and companion for almost 50 years. His teaching in French lycées and studies in Berlin with German phenomenologists Edmund Husserl and Martin Heidegger were interrupted by World War II.

By 1945, however, Sartre was well known in France for his writings and his activity in the Resistance. Although his success as a novelist was not undisputed, *La nausée* (Nausea, 1938) is considered one of the best philosophical novels of the century. The anti-hero, Roquentin, is seized with the horrors of existing in an absurd, alien reality. Existential terror is also the major theme in Sartre's numerous plays—among them *Huis clos* (No Exit, 1944) and *Les mouches* (The Flies, 1942)—which many consider his most lasting works. Highly valued in literary circles are his biographies of Baudelaire, Jean Genêt, and Gustave Flaubert. In 1945, Sartre founded the influential monthly review *Les temps modernes* (Modern Times), which carried many of his essays. Sartrian existentialism, as developed in *L'être et le néant* (Being and Nothingness, 1943) emphasizes freedom of choice, moral responsibility, and *engagement* (involvement); it is summarized by the famous formula "Existence precedes essence." In *Les mots,* however, Sartre rejected these concepts as "aristocratic idealism."

A maverick political leftist, Sartre broke with formal Communist parties and followed his own revolutionary conscience. His active militancy led to numerous arrests. In 1964, he rejected the Nobel Prize for literature because he did not wish to be "transformed into an institution."

PIERRE E. BRODIN

---

role of the genially cynical host of the popular weekly television series *Alfred Hitchcock Presents* and the *Alfred Hitchcock Hour.*

Nominated five times for Academy Awards as best director, Hitchcock won the 1967 Irving G. Thalberg Memorial Award of the Academy of Motion Picture Arts and Sciences and the 1979 Life Achievement Award of the American Film Institute. He exercised a profound influence on a younger generation of filmmakers, including director François Truffaut. Although he had long been a U.S. citizen, Queen Elizabeth II of Great Britain knighted him in 1980.

Background. Born the son of a poultry dealer and fruit importer, Alfred Joseph Hitchcock studied engineering at the Jesuit St. Ignatius College and art at the University of London. He entered the motion picture industry in 1920 as a title writer, and by 1925 he had become a full-fledged director with *The Pleasure Garden,* filmed in Germany. He directed *Blackmail* (1929), the first successful British sound film, and won international acclaim with such spy thrillers as *The Man Who Knew Too Much* (1934), *The 39 Steps* (1935), *Sabotage* (1936), *The Secret Agent* (1937), and *The Lady Vanishes* (1938).

At the invitation of producer David O. Selznick, Hitchcock went to Hollywood, where his first film, *Rebecca* (1940), won an Academy Award as best picture and earned him an Oscar nomination as best director, as did his *Lifeboat* (1944), *Spellbound* (1945), *Rear Window* (1954), and *Psycho* (1960). Other of his films include *Suspicion, Shadow of a Doubt, Notorious, Strangers on a Train, Dial M for Murder, To Catch a Thief, Vertigo, North by Northwest, The Birds, Marnie, Topaz, Frenzy,* and *Family Plot.*

Hitchcock is survived by his wife Alma, daughter Patricia, and three grandchildren.

HENRY S. SLOAN

Liaison

MARSHAL TITO (Josip Broz)

President of Yugoslavia: b. Kumrovec, Austro-Hungarian Empire, May 7, 1892; d. Ljubljana, Yugoslavia, May 4, 1980.

Josip Broz, known by the revolutionary nickname Tito since the 1930s, was a man whose pride, strength, and personal luck elevated him from an itinerant metal worker to one of the most influential and durable leaders of post-World War II Europe. Surviving wounds in both world wars and years of clandestine guerrilla fighting, Tito ruled Yugoslavia with absolute authority for 35 years. He defied Stalin by resisting subservience to the Soviet Union and instituted a more moderate form of communism, which became known as Titoism. As president of Yugoslavia and its ruling League of Communists of Yugoslavia (LCY), Tito's aim was to build and maintain a strong federated republic. In a balancing act between the Western democracies and the Soviet Communist bloc, he championed the cause of underdeveloped nations and helped found the "nonaligned" movement.

Born the seventh of 15 children, Josip grew up in a modest but not poor peasant family in the Croatian village of Kumrovec. His father was a Croat, his mother a Slovene. After working as a journeyman metalworker, Broz was called to the Austro-Hungarian army in 1913. During World War I he distinguished himself as a noncommissioned officer and spent time in Serbia with the invading forces. Transferred to the Eastern front, he was seriously wounded and captured by the Russians.

Broz escaped from prison in 1917, and although his sympathy was with the Bolsheviks, he played no significant role in the ensuing civil war and returned to Yugoslavia in 1920. In the early 1920s, he joined the Communist underground and became an active Communist Party (CPY) member and strike organizer. After five years in jail (1929–34), he went abroad and resumed political activity, survived Stalinist purges in the Soviet Union, and in 1937 was appointed secretary of the CPY by the Communist International in Moscow. Back again in Yugoslavia, he succeeded in building a new party leadership.

The dismemberment of Yugoslavia by the Axis powers in April 1941 gave the CPY a unique chance for effective action. Following the Nazi attack on the Soviet Union and Stalin's appeal for help, the CPY launched, in July 1941, its Partisan "people's liberation" struggle against the occupiers. The architect of this campaign, Tito made preparations for seizing political power at the end of the war. Benefiting from Anglo-American military and political aid beginning in mid-1943 and the capture of Belgrade by the Red Army (with the Partisans' help) in October 1944, Tito became the undisputed ruler of a devastated Yugoslavia in 1945.

Tito's postwar Yugoslavia was radical in every respect. Domestically, he introduced the essential features of the Soviet Communist model. In foreign policy, he pursued a militant policy which displeased Stalin. On June 28, 1948, to the astonishment of the entire world, Tito was excommunicated from the new Communist international body—the Cominform—by the explicit fiat of Stalin. The CPY and its leader were accused of every political and ideological deviation, but Tito refused to capitulate. A ferocious conflict ensued, leading to the first breach in the emerging Soviet-led, Communist bloc. The unwanted battle with Stalin forced the Yugoslav to make changes, giving birth to Titoism.

This new brand of Communism was characterized by four main elements: 1) a system of worker self-management extended institutionally to all economic and social organizations of Yugoslav society; 2) decentralization of the federal government, with the six constituent republics and two autonomous regions of Yugoslavia granted expanded administrative powers; 3) a combination of market and planning mechanisms ("socialist market economy"); and 4) the organization of "nonaligned" states.

The "rampant consumerism" spawned by the socialist free-market forces of Titoism was perhaps a reflection of Josip Broz's own taste for luxurious living. Still, Tito never relinquished his monopoly of political power in the LCY and was the supreme arbiter in all intraparty conflicts. In later years, he relied on the Yugoslav Army as the ultimate bulwark of his regime. He did leave many problems unresolved, and it remained to be seen whether his "collective leadership" formula for succession would prove adequate to cope effectively with these problems in a complex country that for so long depended on the authority of one man.

MILORAD M. DRACHKOVITCH

PAHLAVI, Mohammed Reza

Shah of Iran: b. Tehran, Iran, Oct. 26, 1919; d. El Maadi, Egypt, July 27, 1980.

The life of the late shah of Iran dramatically illustrated the classical theme of the transience of power and the vanity of human ambition. Born to the purple, he came to supreme power at an early age and exercised it in dignity and splendor for almost four decades. But fortune deserted him, and he spent the last year and a half of his life a sick and harassed exile.

Mohammed Reza Pahlavi was the eldest child of Reza Shah Pahlavi, who replaced the last of the Kajar dynasty on the Peacock Throne in 1925. Mohammed Reza was educated partly in Tehran but mostly in Switzerland, which he continued to visit frequently throughout his life. His European education made him a Westerner by culture and preference, thereby alienating him in some measure from his more conservative Muslim countrymen.

Mohammed Reza was catapulted onto the throne on Sept. 16, 1941, when joint Anglo-Russian pressure forced the pro-German shah to abdicate. During the first several years of his reign, Shah Mohammed Reza Pahlavi was no more than an inexperienced young man feeling his way in international politics. In November 1943, Tehran was the site of a conference of the "Big Three"—Roosevelt, Stalin, and Churchill—and, as the shah recounted in his memoirs 37 years later, Stalin was the only one who observed the normal diplomatic courtesies to the ruler of the host country. This bitter memory doubtless strengthened the shah's later determination to turn Iran into a genuinely independent power.

The shah's first great success came in resolving a crisis with the Soviet Union in 1945–46. By rallying his government and employing skillful diplomacy in the new United Nations, he forced the reluctant Soviets to evacuate the occupied province of Azerbaijan. After strengthening his authority in the late 1940s, the shah faced a serious threat to his reign in the early 1950s. On March 15, 1951, the parliament voted to nationalize the oil industry and named the popular Dr. Mohammed Mossadegh prime minister. After a two-year struggle for power, a showdown finally came. The shah formally dismissed Mossadegh and named a replacement, but the prime minister stood his ground and announced that Pahlavi had been deposed. The shah was forced to flee for one week (Aug. 16–22, 1953), but the tide of Mossadegh's popularity had ebbed and there still was wide support for the shah. With the help of the U.S. Central Intelligence Agency, Pahlavi engineered a triumphant return to power.

The great watershed of the shah's reign was January 1963, when he launched a major effort to modernize Iran. Far-reaching plans for social and economic development, called the White Revolution, were announced. A major part of

UPI

the program was the redistribution of land, affecting latifundia of both private owners and the Islamic clergy. The reform effort also involved the emancipation of women, the creation of a "literacy corps," and the expansion of education at all levels. Anti-shah riots were firmly put down in 1963 and 1965, and for about ten years there was little effective opposition to him. There was enormous economic and social development, but the transformation of traditional Iranian society was not universally welcomed.

Once he believed the reforms were effectively under way, the shah held his coronation—26 years after his accession—in 1967. With a sharp increase in oil revenues in 1973, the shah's plans became more ambitious. Western technology was imported on a large scale, and the military was equipped with expensive arms.

In October 1971, the ancient city of Persepolis was the scene of a lavish celebration of the 2,500th anniversary of the founding of the Persian Empire and the shah's 30th year in power. Sixty-nine countries were represented, most by their heads of state. If this was *hubris,* it was punished. Nothing ever again went quite right. Oil prices leveled off, demand fell, and revenues did not meet expectations. Discontent with the activities of the secret police (Savak) and with the unequal distribution of wealth became widespread. Worst of all, though it was a well-kept secret, in about 1973 the shah began to suffer from the lymphatic cancer that was eventually to kill him.

Faced with the revolutionary fervor of Shiite Muslim fundamentalists and radical student leftists, the shah fled Iran on Jan. 16, 1979. The rest of his life was a pathetic shuttling from one country to another. He is survived by Farah Diba, his third wife, by whom he had two daughters and two sons, including Crown Prince Reza.

ARTHUR CAMPBELL TURNER

PIAGET, Jean

Psychologist: b. Neuchâtel, Switzerland, Aug. 9, 1896; d. Geneva, Sept. 17, 1980.

For his ideas on how children learn, Jean Piaget, the Swiss psychologist, ranked as one of the 20th century's most original thinkers. Where others saw only childish mistakes, Jean Piaget saw intelligence at work. His classic, simple experiments, sometimes done with his own three children, include one employing two containers, one tall and thin, the other short and bulky. Young children first think the tall, thin flask holds more water. Then at age six or seven the same child sees that the shape does not matter and that each flask holds the same amount. Piaget theorized that children learn by passing through distinct intellectual stages. They are their own significant agents in learning.

Piaget took a middle position in the nature/nurture, heredity/environment controversy. In the United States, where stimulus-response advocates and environmentalists dominated, his ideas did not win favor until the 1950s.

He was a rather reserved, fatherly figure, seen smoking his pipe and walking or bicycling along Geneva streets, where he headed the Jean Jacques Rousseau Institute and later the Institute for Educational Science, Geneva University.

The son of a historian, Piaget began his scientific pursuits as a naturalist. His first paper, published when he was not quite 11, described a rare part-albino sparrow. He was offered a job in a Geneva museum, but declined it to finish high school. After completing his Ph.D. in biology at age 22, he experimented briefly with psychoanalysis in Zurich and worked with Théodore Simon in the Alfred Binet Laboratory at the Sorbonne.

FRANKLIN PARKER

McCORMACK, John W.

U.S. congressman and House Speaker: b. Boston, MA, Dec. 21, 1891; d. Dedham, MA, Nov. 22, 1980.

A product of rough-and-tumble big-city politics, Boston Irishman John W. McCormack—Democratic congressman from Massachusetts for 43 years and speaker of the U.S. House of Representatives from 1962 to 1971—was one of the most influential American political figures of his era. A master of the art of compromise, he was a conscientious legislator whose imprint is on many of the key measures of the time. A Roman Catholic, he enjoyed a good rapport with his Jewish constituents. For more than a year following the death of President Kennedy, House Speaker McCormack was a "heartbeat" away from the presidency.

One of the 12 children of a bricklayer, of whom only three reached maturity, John William McCormack grew up amid poverty in South Boston. At 13, after the death of his father, he left school to support the family. While working as an office boy for a law firm, he was persuaded by his employer to study law independently. After passing his bar examinations at age 21 he became a skilled trial lawyer and active in Democratic politics. He served in the Massachusetts legislature (House, 1920–22, and Senate, 1923–26). After an unsuccessful first bid for a U.S. congressional seat in 1926, he was elected in 1928. A champion of the New Deal, he was a protégé of John N. Garner and Sam Rayburn. In January 1962, after Speaker Rayburn's death, he was elected the 45th speaker of the house.

His wife of 51 years, the former Harriet Joyce, died in 1971.

HENRY S. SLOAN

WEST, Mae

U.S. actress/playwright: b. Brooklyn, NY, Aug. 17, 1893; d. Los Angeles, Nov. 22, 1980.

The epitome of the "sex goddess," ageless Mae West maintained her glittering image as a performer on stage and screen for more than 60 years. With her hourglass figure, flamboyant wardrobe, sultry voice, mock-sophisticated delivery of sexy double entendres, easy-going nonchalance, and earthy wit, she won immense popularity that made her the highest-paid performer in Hollywood films in the 1930s and earned her such honors as having a World War II life jacket named after her. Her material, which she often wrote, included such lines as "It's not the men in my life that count, it's the life in my men."

The oldest of the three children of a livery stable owner and former boxer, Mae West began to perform on stage as a small child, and at 13, with only minimum schooling, she entered the national vaudeville circuit. Beginning in 1911 she met with success as a performer in Broadway musicals. The first play that she wrote and produced, *Sex* (1926), became a Broadway hit but brought her a brief jail sentence on a morals charge. She had her greatest triumph with her play *Diamond Lil* (1928). Arriving in Hollywood in 1932, Miss West starred in its screen version, *She Done Him Wrong* (1933), with the young Cary Grant, who also appeared with her in *I'm No Angel* (1933). In all, she made 12 films. In 1944 she made another appearance on Broadway in the revue *Catherine Was Great*. She also performed in nightclubs and appeared on radio and television.

Once briefly married, she was a teetotaler and health food addict.

HENRY S. SLOAN

LENNON, John

English pop musician; b. Liverpool, England, Oct. 9, 1940; d. New York City, Dec. 8, 1980.

John Lennon was the founding member and driving force of the Beatles, the most popular rock group of its time, and one that influenced the course of pop music and culture wherever it emerged. His death at the hands of a deranged fan for many marked the end of an era.

John Winston Lennon was born to working class parents, Alfred and Julia Lennon, but was reared by an aunt from age 4½. His mother died when he was 16, and the pain of their relationship colored much of his music. The Beatles grew from Lennon's first band, the Quarrymen, formed in 1955. Later that year, John teamed with Paul McCartney. Writing together, the two became the brains and heart of the Beatles. As the band evolved, absorbing the influence of American rock 'n' roll, George Harrison, and later Ringo Starr, joined. By then the group had avid fans in Hamburg, Germany and at Liverpool's Cavern club. Brian Epstein, who became their manager in 1961, created four lovable moptops from the leather-clad rockers and set the stage for worldwide Beatlemania. In all the quartet sold more than 200 million records.

The output of the inventive Lennon-McCartney team was prodigious. The balance of Lennon's acerbic wit and McCartney's melodic genius was a brilliant combination which culminated in *Sgt. Pepper's Lonely Hearts Club Band*. However, a rift between the two, which first had appeared back in 1965, eventually contributed to the group's disbandment.

Lennon's youthful cheekiness turned to harshness as he began examining openly his own turmoil and growing social and political conscience. It was he who led the Beatles in their experimentation with drugs and Eastern mysticism and who first made political statements (he returned his Member of the Order of British Empire award in protest of British policies).

Many wrongly blamed the band's demise on Yoko Ono, the avant-garde artist whom Lennon married in 1969. In the post-Beatles decade, both with her and as a solo artist, Lennon produced albums dealing with politics, the self, and old-time rock 'n' roll. In 1975, Lennon dropped out of public life to become a "househusband," caring for his and Ono's child, Sean. He emerged after five years with *Double Fantasy*, a paean to familial love. This album and the interviews he granted just before his death painted a picture of a man who had achieved, at 40, a sane, healthy maturity. He left his wife, two sons—Julian, from his first marriage, and Sean—a legacy of more than 30 recordings, a few books and films, and a multimillion-dollar estate.

PAULETTE WEISS

KOSYGIN, Aleksei Nikolayevich

Soviet premier: b. St. Petersburg, Russia, Feb. 21, 1904; d. Moscow, USSR, Dec. 18, 1980.

Dour, well-mannered Aleksei N. Kosygin held the Soviet premiership for 16 years (1964–1980), longer than any other premier in Soviet history. Prior to that, he served for a quarter century in the USSR cabinet. His 41 years in top government posts were, if nothing else, a political feat. Known for many years primarily as a capable industrial executive, specializing in production of consumer goods, his political savvy allowed him to survive in high positions under three Soviet leaders: Joseph Stalin, Nikita Khrushchev, and Leonid Brezhnev. It was in 1964 that Kosygin helped Brezhnev remove Premier Khrushchev from power in the first coup in post-revolutionary Soviet history.

After taking over the premiership from Khrushchev, Kosygin also distinguished himself as a diplomat, mediating a 1966 cease-fire in an undeclared war between India and Pakistan. In 1967, during his only visit to the United States, Kosygin and then U.S. President Lyndon Johnson agreed that their two countries should soon conclude a treaty limiting proliferation of nuclear weapons. The treaty was signed in 1968.

Background. Of worker parentage, Kosygin at the age of 15 joined the Red Army to fight in the Russian Civil War which erupted after the Bolshevik Revolution. When the war ended, Kosygin enrolled in a retail trade school, graduating in 1924. For the next five years, he managed Siberian consumer cooperatives, joining the Communist party in 1927. Returning to his native St. Petersburg (by then named Leningrad), he completed his education at the Leningrad Textile Institute in 1935. Beginning as a textile factory engineer in 1936, he became a fabric factory director in 1937, mayor of Leningrad in 1938, minister of textile industry in 1939, vice premier in 1940, alternate member of the Politburo in 1946, and full Politburo member in 1948.

Then he briefly fell from favor. Stalin removed him from the Politburo in 1952, and the post-Stalin collective leadership demoted him from vice premier to minister of consumer goods industry in 1953. But with Khrushchev's support, Kosygin regained his vice-premiership in 1954, his alternate membership on the Politburo in 1957, and his full Politburo membership by 1960. His reward for helping Brezhnev oust Khrushchev was the premiership.

During his final two years in office, Kosygin's health deteriorated badly, forcing him to miss many important public meetings. On Oct. 23, 1980, he resigned as premier and was replaced by Nikolai Tikhonov. (*See* USSR.) Within two months, Kosygin suffered heart failure and died.

ELLSWORTH RAYMOND

The following is a selected list of prominent persons who died during 1980. Articles on major figures appear in the preceding pages.

Adamson, Joy (69), Austrian author and wildlife conservationist; best known for her book *Born Free* (1960): d. Kenya, Jan. 3.

Allon, Yigal (61), Israeli military and political figure; leader of Palmach, a commando force that operated before the establishment of Israel. Following entry into parliament in 1955 he held a series of cabinet posts, including deputy prime minister and foreign minister in the last Labor government, headed by Yitzhak Rabin: d. Afula, Israel, Feb. 29.

Amerasinghe, Hamilton Shirley (67), Sri Lankan diplomat; became Sri Lanka's chief delegate to the United Nations in 1967. Served as president of the General Assembly (1976) and in recent years headed the Conference on the Law of the Sea: d. New York City, Dec. 4.

Anson, Jay (58), author; his book, *The Amityville Horror*, about supernatural occurrences in a Long Island home, became a best seller: d. Palo Alto, CA, March 12.

Arnold, Elliott (67), author; he wrote some two dozen novels and other books about the Western Indian frontier and about World War II confrontations, including *Blood Brother* (1947) and *A Night of Watching* (1967): d. New York City, May 13.

Aronson, Boris (81), stage designer, who did more than 100 productions for the Broadway theater. Born in Russia, he studied in Moscow, Kiev, and Paris. Early in his career he was involved in the Group Theater in New York. He won Tony awards for his designs for Broadway productions of *The Rose Tattoo, Pacific Overtures, Cabaret, Zorba, Company,* and *Follies:* d. near Nyack, NY, Nov. 16.

Lord Ballantrae (né Bernard Edward Fergusson) (69), British soldier and author of 13 books, who was governor general of New Zealand (1962–67). He was a member of the Black Watch regiment, retiring in 1958 as a brigadier. He served in the Middle East and Burma in World War II. Knighted in 1962, he was created a life peer in 1972: d. London, Nov. 28.

Bates, L(ucius) C(hristopher) (79), newspaper publisher and civil-rights leader; he was a key figure in the 1957 desegregation of Central High School in Little Rock, AR. His respected newspaper, *Arkansas State Press,* boycotted by segregationists, eventually folded: d. Little Rock, AR, Aug. 22.

Bateson, Gregory (76), British anthropologist, author, and philosopher; he early studied primitive cultures and in his later life explored advanced western cultures. In the 1930s he married Dr. Margaret Mead and they collaborated on an extensive study of the people of Bali. They were divorced after 14 years of marriage. In addition to his anthropological studies, Dr. Bateson led the antipsychiatric movement. He contributed to psychology the "double-bind" hypothesis, which holds that individuals may be sent contradictory messages of love and rejection by their parents, resulting in schizophrenia in some cases. Other of his interests included cybernetics and communications, the peace movement, and ecology: d. San Francisco, July 4.

Baxter, Richard Reeve (59), Harvard law professor (1954–80) and judge of the International Court of Justice at The Hague (1979–80). He wrote numerous articles and several books. He served in The Hague as a member of the Permanent Court of Arbitration (1968–75), and was a member of the U.S. State Department's Advisory Committee on the Law of the Sea (1973–78) and of its Advisory Panel on International Law (1970–75): d. Boston, Sept. 26.

Beaton, Sir Cecil (76), photographer and designer, well known as a photographer of the British royal family and of the famous. He was the stage designer for the Broadway show *My Fair Lady* (1956) and won two Academy Awards. He was knighted in 1972: d. near Salisbury, England, Jan. 18.

Benedictos I (88), Greek Orthodox Patriarch of Jerusalem; elected in 1957. Made a member of the Holy Synod in 1946; from 1951 until 1957 he was archbishop of Tiberias: d. Jerusalem, Dec. 10.

Bigard, Barney (74), jazz clarinetist, who learned his music from the New Orleans school of jazz musicians. He was one of the last exponents of the Albert system of clarinet playing: d. Culver City, CA, June 27.

Bitar, Salah el (68), former prime minister of Syria and cofounder of the Baath political party. He served four times as prime minister during the 1960s and was exiled on several occasions during his political career: d. Paris, July 21.

Blanshard, Paul (87), writer and critic of the Roman Catholic Church, who began his criticism of the Church while a Vatican correspondent for *The Nation* magazine. He was in the ministry briefly, but charged that Christianity was "full of fraud." He then became involved in the labor movement and the Socialist Party. He wrote 15 books and was coauthor, along with Norman Thomas, of *An Outline of the British Labor Movement:* d. St. Petersburg, FL, Jan. 27.

Bonelli, Richard (91), American operatic baritone; he made his American debut in 1925 with the Chicago Civic Opera, following vocal study and performances in Europe. He sang with the Chicago company until its demise in 1931, then joined the Metropolitan Opera in New York City in 1932. He sang there for 12 sea-

Wide World Photos   UPI
JOY ADAMSON   **MARCELLO CAETANO**

sons before moving to the New York City Opera company. He taught at the Curtis Institute in Philadelphia (1941–55) and was a founding member of Los Angeles' Music Academy of the West in 1947: d. Los Angeles, June 7.

Bonham, John (32), drummer for the English rock group Led Zeppelin; he had been with the group since 1968: d. Windsor, England, Sept. 25.

Prince Boun Oum na Champassak (68), pro-Western Laotian prime minister (1949–50, 1960–62). After he signed an independence agreement with France in 1949, he became Laos' first prime minister. In 1962, after a government of national union led by Souvanna Phouma established Laos as a neutral state, Boun Oum became inspector general of Laos. He left Laos in 1974: d. Paris, March 17.

Breslow, Alexander (52), pathologist who developed a test used in the diagnosis and care of many cases of the skin cancer known as melanoma: d. Washington, July 20.

Burpee, David (87), head of the W. Atlee Burpee Company, the world's largest mail-order seed supplier. He took over the company from his father in 1915 at the age of 22: d. Doylestown, PA, June 24.

Burrows, Millar (91), Yale University professor (1934–55) and author of several works on the Dead Sea Scrolls: d. Ann Arbor, MI, April 29.

Caetano, Marcello (74), right-wing prime minister of Portugal from 1968 until 1974, when he was ousted by a military group headed by General António de Spinola: d. Rio de Janeiro, Oct. 26.

Cámpora, Héctor J. (71), president of Argentina in 1973, he was elected as a stand-in for Juan Perón and resigned after 49 days to allow for a new election in which Perón and his wife Isabel Martínez de Perón could be elected president and vice-president. Dr. Cámpora, a former dentist and longtime Peronist, was then made ambassador to Mexico. Earlier in his political career he had served nine years in the Chamber of Deputies, including seven as president of that body: d. Mexico City, Mex., Dec. 19.

Champion, Gower (59), dancer, choreographer, and theatrical director. He started dancing professionally at age 15 as half of the Gower and Jean dance team. Later he teamed with Marjorie Belcher, whom he married in 1947; they performed as Marge and Gower Champion. The Champions appeared in several Hollywood film musicals of the 1940s and early 1950s and on television variety shows. He directed theatrical musicals, including *Bye, Bye Birdie, Carnival,* and *Hello, Dolly!*. He won seven Tony Awards. His last Broadway show, *42d Street,* opened just hours after his death: d. New York City, Aug. 25.

Cheney, Sheldon Warren (94), theater critic, author, and art historian; his work was regarded as an important influence on the Modernist Movement in American drama in the 1920s and 1930s: d. Berkeley, CA, Oct. 10.

Chervenkov, Vulko (80), former head of the Bulgarian Communist Party, who fell from power after Joseph Stalin's death in 1953. In 1961 he was ousted from the Politburo but was politically rehabilitated in 1969: d. Bulgaria, Oct. 21.

Clurman, Harold (78), theater director, critic, author, and teacher; in 1931 he helped found the Group Theater, which expounded the acting method of Russian director Konstantin Stanislavsky. In 1941 the Group disbanded and Clurman went to Hollywood to work as a producer and to direct one film. During the 1940s he directed four Broadway plays; none was successful. In 1949 he coproduced *All My Sons* and later directed *Member of the Wedding* on Broadway. His last stage directing effort was in 1969 when he did *Uncle Vanya* in Los Angeles. He began writing theater criticism, first for *The New Republic* and after 1953 for *The Nation:* d. New York City, Sept. 9.

Cochran, Jacqueline (70 or 74), American aviatrix; she was the first woman to fly faster than the speed of sound: d. Indio, CA, Aug. 9.

Connelly, Marc (90), American writer; famed as the Pulitzer Prize-winning author of *The Green Pastures*, a stunning play that made theater history when it was debuted on Broadway in 1930. The play in its first five years was performed 1,642 times, with 640 performances in New York. It had numerous revivals, and a motion picture also was made later. In addition Connelly collaborated on several plays with George S. Kaufman and was an important member of the Algonquin Round Table, a nearly daily gathering during the 1920s of New York's literary wits: d. New York City, Dec. 21.

Day, Dorothy (83), social activist, founder of the Catholic Worker Movement. As a social radical committed to nonviolence, she influenced a generation of American priests and laymen. Born in Brooklyn, she lived in both Chicago and California before returning to New York (1916). In 1914 she joined the Socialist Party. She worked for various socialist newspapers and magazines and joined the Industrial Workers of the World (Wobblies) union. She entered a common-law marriage in the mid-1920s. From this relationship a daughter was born. It was her desire to have the child baptized that led to her conversion to Catholicism. Through the editor of *Commonweal*, a liberal Catholic magazine for which she wrote, Miss Day met Peter Maurin. Together they started the *Catholic Worker* in 1933. Through the Catholic Worker Movement many refuges for the poor and homeless were established. Her social philosophy included promotion of a decentralized, cooperative social order, pacifism and conscientious objection, disarmament, and just race relations. In her later years, she sided with those who opposed the Vietnam War: d. New York City, Nov. 29.

Dennison, Robert Lee (78), admiral, U.S. Navy. He served as a naval aide to President Harry Truman (1948–53) and for three years, until his retirement in 1963, he was Atlantic Fleet commander and Supreme Allied Commander of the Atlantic forces for the North Atlantic Treaty Organization: d. Bethesda, MD, March 14.

Doenitz, Karl (89), grand admiral in Hitler's naval force, he commanded Germany's U-boat campaign against Allied shipping during World War II. He presided over Germany's surrender in World War II, and thereafter served ten years in confinement after his conviction at Nuremberg for war crimes: d. West Germany, Dec. 24.

Douglas, Helen Gahagan (79), actress and U.S. Representative from California (1945–51); in 1950 she ran unsuccessfully for a California Senate seat against Richard Nixon. Miss Douglas' acting career began in 1922. She also studied singing and performed in opera in Europe: d. New York City, June 28.

Dragonette, Jessica (about 75), American soprano; famed as a radio singer of operetta and semiclassical music: d. New York City, March 18.

Duvoisin, Roger (79), author-illustrator of children's books. He also illustrated greeting cards for the United Nations Children's Fund and magazine covers for *The New Yorker* magazine. His awards included the American Library Association's Caldecott Medal: d. Morristown, NJ, June 30.

Erim, Nihat (68), prime minister of Turkey (1971–72); a professor of international law, in 1945 he was with the Turkish delegation in San Francisco that helped to draw up the United Nations Charter. From 1956 to 1962 he was a member of the European Human Rights Commission, and from 1961 until 1970 he represented the Turkish Parliament in the European Council: d. near Istanbul, July 19.

Evans, Bill (51), jazz pianist. He joined the Miles Davis sextet in 1959, and six months later formed his own trio. He won five Grammy Awards and the *Downbeat* critics poll five times: d. New York City, Sept. 15.

Fallon, George Hyde (77), Democratic Congressman from Maryland (1945–71): d. Baltimore, March 21.

Finletter, Thomas K. (86), former Secretary of the U.S. Air Force and a long-time activist in New York politics; in 1948 he was the primary author of a report "Survival in the Air Age," which led to his appointment as Air Force Secretary during the Korean War. However, he favored a strong defense only as a deterrent. He helped found an antiwar organization, and also appealed in book and newspaper articles for universal disarmament: d. New York City, April 24.

Fogarty, Anne (60), designer, prominent in the fashion world during the 1950s; her specialty was tiny-waisted, full-skirted dresses: d. New York City, Jan. 15.

Fox, Virgil (68), concert organist. In his 55-year career he gave concerts all over the world. He was the organist at New York's Riverside Church for 19 years, where he played the five-manual Aeolian-Skinner, a 10,561-pipe organ, considered one of the five best in the world: d. West Palm Beach, FL, Oct. 25.

Frank, Otto (91), father of Anne Frank, the Jewish girl whose diary became renowned throughout the world. He was the sole survivor in his family of the Nazi holocaust. A decorated German officer of World War I, he had been a Frankfurt businessman before fleeing Germany with his family after the Jewish prosecutions began in the 1930s: d. Basel, Switzerland, Aug. 19.

Froman, Jane (72), actress-singer; she appeared in the Broadway musicals *Ziegfeld Follies* (1934), *Keep Off the Grass* (1940), and *Artists and Models* (1943). She was injured in a plane crash during a U.S.O. tour in 1943: d. Columbia, MO, April 22.

Galindez, Victor (31), boxer; he was the World Boxing Association's light-heavyweight champion between 1974 and 1979: d. Argentina, Oct. 26.

Gandhi, Sanjay (33), member of the Indian parliament. (*See also* India.): d. New Delhi, India, June 23.

Gardiner, Reginald (77), English-born actor. He went to the United States in 1935 at the urging of Beatrice Lillie and appeared in her revues. He made his motion picture debut in 1936: d. Westwood, CA, July 7.

Gary, Romain (né Roman Kacew) (66), French novelist and former diplomat; he wrote more than 17 books and wrote and directed films. A World War II French war hero, he at first flew for the British Royal Air Force, later joining the Free French forces. As a diplomat he served in the French delegation to the United Nations and as Consul General in Los Angeles. He married actress Jean Seberg in the 1960s: d. Paris, Dec. 2.

Giri, Varahagiri Venkata (85), president of India (1969–74); he was an opposition candidate, but Prime Minister Indira Gandhi supported his election against the old-guard leadership of the Congress Party, resulting in Mrs. Gandhi's expulsion from the party and its subsequent split. He was denied renomination for president in 1974: d. Madras, India, June 24.

Griffith, Hugh (67), Welsh film, stage, and television actor; he was probably best known for the role of Squire Western in the film *Tom Jones* (1963). He appeared in about 50 films and won an Academy Award in 1959 as best supporting actor for his work in *Ben Hur*: d. London, May 14.

Guston, Philip (66), Abstract Expressionist painter; he had gained some attention in the 1940s as a representational painter before taking up the abstract expressionist style for which he became best known. Around 1970 he returned to figurative paintings, producing works of cartoon-like imagery: d. Woodstock, NY, June 7.

Halberstam, Michael J. (48), physician, journalist, and novelist. Clinical professor of medicine at George Washington University, a senior medical editor of *Modern Medicine* magazine, and a diplomat of the American Board of Internal Medicine, he also wrote three books, one a novel, and numerous journalistic articles. He was shot to death when he surprised a burglar in his home: d. Washington, DC, Dec. 5.

GOWER CHAMPION

MARC CONNELLY

HELEN GAHAGAN DOUGLAS

DICK HAYMES

Haymes, Dick (61), singer and actor; a popular singer in the Big Band era of the 1940s and a soloist for such band leaders as Tommy Dorsey, Harry James, Benny Goodman, and Bunny Berrigan. He also appeared in 35 motion pictures: d. Los Angeles, March 28.

Hecht, George J. (84), publisher; founded *Parents' Magazine* in 1926 and later started *Humpty Dumpty's Magazine*, *Children's Digest*, and *Baby Care*: d. New York City, April 23.

Heller, Ott (70), hockey player; was a New York Rangers defenseman for 15 years (1931–46) and was captain of the team from 1942 to 1945: d. Kitchener, Ontario, June 16.

Howard, Elston (51), baseball player. He joined the New York Yankees club in 1955, and in his career played the outfield, first base, and catcher. He was a dependable hitter, averaging .274 with 167 home runs over 14 seasons, and was the American League's most valuable player in 1963. He played one season with the Boston Red Sox before retiring in 1968. He then returned to the Yankees as a coach: d. New York City, Dec. 14.

Iturbi, José (84), Spanish-born pianist and conductor. In 1928, he made his debut as a concert pianist in London and rapidly gained fame throughout Europe. His New York debut in 1929 was favorably hailed by music critics. He began conducting in 1933 and for the following eight years led the Rochester Philharmonic. In 1959 he conducted his first opera in the United States at the City Center in New York. A flamboyant personality, he appeared as himself in motion pictures in the 1940s. Although he said he was "a musician and not a politician," he would not perform in Spain from 1933 to 1948: d. Hollywood, CA, June 28.

Jackson, Eddie (84), entertainer; best known as the sidekick to Jimmy Durante. He first appeared with Durante in a five-piece Dixieland band. In 1923 the team of Clayton (Lou), Jackson, and Durante was formed. During the 1950s, Jackson appeared on TV variety shows with Durante: d. Los Angeles, July 16.

Janssen, David (né David Harold Meyer) (49), television and motion picture actor; probably best known as the title character from the long-running television series *The Fugitive* (1963–67): d. Malibu, CA, Feb. 13.

Johnson, Gerald W. (89), reporter, historian, author, educator. He published more than 30 books, including several biographies of U.S. presidents. After a two-year teaching stint he joined *The Baltimore Sun* in 1926, becoming friends with H.L. Mencken. In 1954 Johnson became a contributing editor for *The New Republic*. He was also a contributing book critic for *the New York Times* and *The New York Herald Tribune*. Under the pen name of Charles North, he wrote mystery novels. An admirer of Adlai Stevenson, he wrote some of his campaign speeches: d. Baltimore, MD, March 22.

Jones, Edward (71), architect; working with three First Ladies—Pat Nixon, Betty Ford, and Rosalynn Carter—he did restoration and interior design for the White House. He also worked at the U.S. Department of State, where he recreated a Palladian room in the department. As a consultant to the Metropolitan Museum of Art in New York, he designed several rooms, including the Greek Revival parlor of the new American Wing: d. Albany, GA, Oct. 1.

Jones, Howard Mumford (88), professor and historian; he was a professor of English at Harvard (1936–62). He wrote more than 30 books and in 1965 won the Pulitzer Prize for general nonfiction with his *O Strange New World*, the first of a trilogy in which he traced the formative years of American culture in the 1840s. He held 15 honorary degrees: d. Cambridge, MA, May 11.

Kaminska, Ida (80), actress of the Yiddish stage, whose greatest recognition outside the Yiddish theater was in Jan Kadar's film *The Shop on Main Street* (1966): d. New York City, May 21.

Kaufman, Boris (83), cinematographer; born in Poland, he went to Paris at the age of 21 where he studied at the Sorbonne. His early work was with the French filmmaker Jean Vigot: d. New York City, June 24.

Kean, Robert (86), U.S. congressman from New Jersey (1939–59): d. Livingston, NJ, Sept. 21.

Keeney, Barnaby C. (65), president of Brown University (1955–66); he served as the 12th president of the university: d. Providence, RI, June 18.

Khama, Sir Seretse (59), president of Botswana (1966–80); he was the hereditary chief of the Bamangwato tribe. In 1950 he was exiled from the then British protectorate of Bechuanaland for his insistence upon marriage to a white British woman. In order to return to the protectorate he was forced to renounce all claims to the tribal throne for himself and his heirs. He took a lesser post as secretary of the tribe. In 1961 he was elected to Bechuanaland's legislature, and in 1965 he was elected prime minister. Sir Seretse became president upon independence of the country in 1966, when the name was changed to Botswana. He was knighted by Queen Elizabeth II: d. Botswana, July 13.

Kokoschka, Oskar (93), painter, writer, illustrator, and teacher; was a major figure of the Expressionist art movement: d. Montreux, Switzerland, Feb. 22.

Kostelanetz, Andre (78), musical conductor, equally at ease with symphonic and popular music. He was hired in 1930 by CBS to conduct its symphony orchestra and made it part of the *Chesterfield Hour*, one of the most successful radio programs of the 1930s. In 1963 he was invited by the New York Philharmonic to start a spring series which he dubbed the "Promenades": d. Port-au-Prince, Haiti, Jan. 13.

Kris, Marianne (80), psychoanalyst and teacher; along with Anna Freud, a pioneer in the field of child psychoanalysis: d. London, Nov. 23.

Kronenberger, Louis (75), critic, author, and anthologist. He was the drama critic for *Time* magazine (1938–61) and concurrently for *PM* magazine (1940–48). In addition he wrote books on 18th century England: d. Brookline, MA, April 30.

Lamarsh, Judy (55) former Canadian cabinet minister and a Liberal member of Canada's parliament. She served as Minister of Health and Welfare from 1963 until December 1965, when she was appointed Secretary of State. She left politics in 1968: d. Toronto, Oct. 27.

Lauck, Chester A. (78), actor, who portrayed "Lum" of the *Lum 'n' Abner* radio show for 24 years. With Norris Goff, who played "Abner," he made six feature films: d. Hot Springs, AR, Feb. 21.

Law Yone, U (69), Burmese newspaper editor. Following the independence of Burma in 1948, he founded *The Nation*, an English-language newspaper, and became a recognized leader of a free press in Asia. When the military seized power in 1962, he was imprisoned for five years, and his newspaper was nationalized. He attempted to organize a rebellion and failed. He settled in the United States and translated U Nu's autobiography, *Saturday's Son*: d. Kensington, MD, June 27.

Léger, Jules (67), French Canadian governor-general of Canada (1974–79); during his tenure he oversaw the transfer from Britain of authority to sign war and peace treaties and to accredit diplomats abroad: d. Ottawa, Nov. 22.

Lesage, Jean (68), premier of Quebec (1960–66). He was active in federal politics from 1945 until 1970 and head of the Liberal Party from 1958 until 1970: d. near the city of Quebec, Dec. 11.

Levene, Sam (né Levine) (75), actor; he appeared in more than 100 movies and Broadway plays. One of his legendary roles was as Nathan Detroit in the Broadway musical *Guys and Dolls*: d. New York City, (found dead) Dec. 28.

Levenson, Sam (68), teacher and humorist; he taught school from 1934 to 1945, then took a five-year leave of absence to test his abilities as a full-time entertainer. In 1951 he had his own television show which lasted a year and a half, and in 1959 he replaced ailing Arthur Godfrey with his *Sam Levenson Show*, which was so successful he was given a five-year contract with CBS. He also wrote several books: d. Brooklyn, NY, Aug. 27.

Libby Willard F. (71), chemist, he developed the radio-carbon atomic clock which dated archeological artifacts thousands of years old to an exactness of 120 years. For this development, Dr. Libby won the 1960 Nobel Prize in chemistry: d. Los Angeles, Sept. 8.

Lloyd, Norman (70), musical composer and author; in 1965 he designed the arts program at the Rockefeller Foundation, serving as its director for 12 years. From 1946 to 1949 he was director of the Juilliard School of Music and for 14 more years was a faculty member at Juilliard: d. Greenwich, CT, July 31.

Longley, James Bernard (56), governor of Maine (1975–79); he was Maine's only independent governor. He called himself a liberal, but was an opponent of feminism, President Carter's welfare reforms, and the White House study group's proposals regarding compensation to the Penobscot and Passamaquoddy Indians: d. Lewiston, ME, Aug. 16.

Longo, Luigi (80), Italian Communist party leader; he was secretary general of the party from 1964 until his retirement in 1972: d. Rome, Oct. 16.

Lowenstein, Allard K. (51) lawyer, former professor, and former member of the U.S. House of Representatives; he was long active in liberal political causes: d. New York City, March 14.

McDonnell, James S., Jr. (81), chairman of McDonnell Douglas Corporation and a pioneer in spacecraft. He worked for the

ELSTON HOWARD **SAM LEVENSON**

Photos UPI

HERBERT MARSHALL McLUHAN

ANNUNZIO PAOLO MANTOVANI

HENRY MILLER

Photos UPI

A. C. NIELSEN

Glenn L. Martin Company until 1939 when he formed the McDonnell Aircraft Corporation. The company began missile research in 1943 and in 1946 delivered the FH-1 Phantom, the world's first carrier-based jet fighter. McDonnell began work in 1958 on a manned orbital craft, and in 1959 was awarded the prime contract for the Mercury spacecraft. In 1961 the company won the prime contract for Gemini, the first two-man spacecraft. McDonnell merged with the financially troubled Douglas Aircraft Corporation in 1967: d. Ladue, MO, Aug. 22.

McEwen, Sir John (80), political leader of Australia; he became a caretaker prime minister of Australia from Dec. 19, 1967 (upon the death by drowning of the prime minister, Harold Holt) until Jan. 10, 1968. First elected to the House of Representatives in 1934, he had been a leader of the Country Party since 1958. He was knighted in 1971: d. Melbourne, Australia, Nov. 20.

McLuhan, Herbert Marshall (69), communications theorist. Born in Canada, he studied at the University of Manitoba, intent on becoming an engineer; however he said that he read himself "out of engineering and into English literature" and so took a bachelor of arts degree in 1933 and a master's degree in 1934. He then studied at Cambridge in England, taking a B.A. in 1936 and a doctorate in 1942. He taught briefly at the University of Wisconsin and from 1937 to 1944 at St. Louis University. Returning to Canada he soon began teaching at the University of Toronto. He won wide recognition in 1962 for his book *The Gutenberg Galaxy*, in which he discussed effects on Western European culture of the invention of movable type. He theorized that the resulting importance of print accounted for linear development in musical and serial thinking, in mathematics and sciences. In his 1964 book *Understanding Media: The Extensions of Man* he took on the electronic media, teaching that "the medium is the message," or that the way people receive information is more important than the information or content itself. In 1967, along with Quentin Fiore, he produced *The Medium Is the Massage*. In 1966 he was named to the Albert Schweitzer Chair in Humanities at Fordham University in New York: d. Toronto, Dec. 31.

McQueen, Steve (né Terrence Stephen) (50), actor; first gained attention when he replaced Ben Gazzara in the 1956 Broadway production of *A Hatful of Rain*. In 1958 he began the three-year television series *Wanted—Dead or Alive* which established him as a star. His main work, however, was in motion pictures: d. Juarez, Mexico, Nov. 7.

Mandelstam, Nadezhda (81), wife of Russian poet Osip Mandelstam; instrumental in preserving his writings after his arrest (and subsequent death) during Stalinist purges: d. Moscow, Dec. 29.

Mantovani, Annunzio Paolo (né Annunzio Paolo) (74), musical conductor; he performed with 40- or 50-piece orchestras and produced a pseudo-symphonic, easy-to-listen-to type of music. Audience favorites included his rendition of *Charmaine, Misty, Greensleeves, Streets of Laredo, Three o'Clock in the Morning*, and *Donkey Serenade*. In the United States between 1951 and 1966, 18 of his recordings sold 500,000 copies: d. Tunbridge Wells, Kent, England, March 29.

Marini, Marino (79), Italian sculptor and painter, famous for his equestrian figures: d. Viareggio, Italy, Aug. 6.

Marquard, Richard (Rube) (90), Hall of Fame baseball pitcher. He set a major league record which still stands by pitching 19 consecutive victories. In his 18 years in the major leagues, he played for the New York Giants, Brooklyn Dodgers, Cincinnati Reds, and Boston Braves, winning 205 games and losing 177, and appearing in five World Series: d. Baltimore, MD, June 1.

Martinez, Maria Povera (94), American Indian potter. She and her husband, Julian, revived the technique of making black ware in 1918. Her pottery is world famous and among the most desired of all Indian art: d. San Ildefonso Pueblo, NM, July 20.

Medford, Kay (59) actress, well known for her stage performance in *Paint Your Wagon, A Hole in the Head, Bye, Bye Birdie*, and *Funny Girl*: d. New York City, April 10.

Milestone, Lewis (né Milstein) (84), motion picture director; his more famous films include *Two Arabian Knights* (1928) and *All Quiet on the Western Front* (1930)—both of which won Oscars. He directed more than 30 films: d. Los Angeles, Sept. 25.

Miller, Henry (88), American writer; his most famous book, the sexually-explicit *Tropic of Cancer* (1934), written in Paris, was banned in the United States until 1964. Other of his books included *Tropic of Capricorn* and *Sexus, Plexus*, and *Nexus*, written as the trilogy, *The Rosy Crucifixion*. A strong individualist, known as an eclectic anarchist, he influenced Jack Kerouac and other members of the so called "Beat Generation." Miller's *The Colossus of Maroussi* was the result of a year in Greece at the start of World War II, and *Big Sur and the Oranges of Hieronymus Bosch* and *Quiet Days in Clichy* were written during his sojourn at Big Sur. Late in his life he took up painting, creating about 150 pictures a year. In 1975 the French government awarded Miller the Legion of Honor: d. Pacific Palisades, CA, June 7.

Monroney, A(lmer) S(tillwell) (Mike) (77), Democratic Representative (1939–51) and Senator (1951–69) from Oklahoma. He is known for cosponsoring the Legislative Reorganization Act of 1946, the only major Congressional overhaul in 50 years, and for introducing legislation in 1956 that led to the establishment of the Federal Aviation Agency. He actively supported federal aid to education, civil rights, foreign aid, and most of President Lyndon Johnson's anti-poverty legislation: d. Rockville, MD, Feb. 13.

Morgenthau, Hans J. (76), author, teacher, and political scientist; he was a leading opponent of U.S. involvement in Vietnam. A respected foreign policy analyst, he was also a critic of Soviet treatment of Jews and an advocate of nuclear arms control and of détente with the Soviet Union. Born in Germany, he practiced law there until 1932, when he began teaching in Geneva. After Hitler's rise to power, he decided not to return to Germany. He was professor of international law in Madrid before going to the United States in 1937. He taught at a number of American universities and authored several books: d. New York City, July 19.

Muñoz Marín, Luis (82), governor of Puerto Rico (1948–64); he was the island's first elected governor. He served as president of the Puerto Rican Senate for eight years. In his early life he vacillated between a career in politics and one in letters. He counted among his acquaintances many major American poets of the 1920s, and moved back and forth between New York and Puerto Rico before finally settling in Puerto Rico in 1931. He raised Puerto Rico to the status of an economically developing land, starting Operation Bootstrap, the program which gave tax incentives to American companies which opened branch factories there. He founded the Popular Democratic Party: d. San Juan, April 30.

Nenni, Pietro (88), leader of the Italian Socialist Party (1949–1969): d. Rome, Jan. 1.

Nielsen, A(rthur) C(harles) (83), founder and former chairman of the A.C. Nielsen Company (f. 1923), the largest marketing research organization in the world: d. Chicago, June 1.

Ohira, Masayoshi (70), prime minister of Japan (1978–80) and leader of the Liberal Democratic Party. He started his political career in 1936 by entering the ministry of finance, a post he held through World War II. In 1949 he was appointed private secretary to the finance minister, Hayato Ikeda, and in 1952 he was elected to the House of Representatives. In 1960 Ohira was selected as chief cabinet secretary to then Prime Minister Hayato Ikeda. In 1962 he became Ikeda's foreign secretary, and in 1964 deputy secretary general of the Liberal Democratic Party. He served in other governmental ministries until he became prime minister in December 1978. Following a no-confidence vote on May 16, 1980, he set elections for June 22. He was hospitalized on May 31, suffering from exhaustion and a heart ailment: d. Tokyo, June 12.

Okun, Arthur (51), economist; chairman of the Council of Economic Advisers (1968–69); known for his contributions to economic forecasting, analysis, and policymaking. He served as an economic adviser to presidents John Kennedy and Lyndon Johnson, and then joined the Brookings Institution as a senior fellow. In 1972, along with George Perry, he founded a weekly journal *Brookings Papers on Economic Activity*, which he coedited. He was well known for "Okun's Law": d. Washington, March 23.

KATHERINE ANNE PORTER

UPI
FINN RONNE

UPI
HARLAND SANDERS

UPI
C. P. SNOW

Paasio, Rafael (76), former prime minister of Finland and leader of the Social Democratic Party; he presided over his party's return to government by means of a coalition in 1966. The coalition lasted two years. In 1972 Paasio formed a minority government which lasted six months. He was a member of Parliament (1948–75) and chairman of the Foreign Affairs Committee (1949–66): d. Turku, Finland, March 17.

Page, Joe (62), baseball pitcher. He pitched in 278 games for the New York Yankees from 1944 through 1950, winning 57 games, losing 49, and saving 76. He was a great relief pitcher and inspired other major league clubs to train pitchers strictly for relief: d. Latrobe, PA, April 21.

Patrick, Gail (née Margaret Fitzpatrick) (69), motion picture actress; she appeared in about 50 pictures, including *My Man Godfrey, Death Takes a Holiday, Stage Door*, and *My Favorite Wife*. She later gave up her film career to produce the Perry Mason television series: d. Hollywood, July 6.

Pehrson, Wilfred R. (53), Penobscot Indian governor 1978–80; he helped negotiate the Maine Indian land claims settlement signed by President Carter just four days prior to Pehrson's death: d. Indian Island, ME, Oct. 14.

Pignedoli, Sergio Cardinal (70), cardinal of the Roman Catholic church, was appointed archbishop in 1950, and was sent as papal nuncio to Bolivia and then to Venezuela: d. Reggio Emilia, Italy, June 15.

Porter, Katherine Anne (90), author, widely acclaimed for her short stories and novelettes (most of them written between 1922 and 1940). In 1966 she won both the Pulitzer Prize and the National Book Award for *The Collected Stories of Katherine Anne Porter* (1965). Other works include *The Days Before*, a collection of her criticism (1952), and *Ship of Fools* (1962). Her last published book was *The Never-Ending Wrong* (1977), in which she gave her version of the trial of Nicola Sacco and Bartolomeo Vanzetti: d. Silver Spring, MD, Sept. 18.

Powers, John A. (Shorty) (57), lieutenant colonel, U.S. Air Force; known as the "voice of the astronauts" during the U.S. Mercury space flights. He resigned in 1963 following a dispute with NASA: d. Phoenix, Jan. 1.

Raft (né Ranft), **George** (85), motion picture actor whose specialty was bad-guy roles. In a career spanning the years from 1931 until about 1967, he appeared in at least 60 motion pictures, mostly "B-type" melodramas: d. Hollywood, Nov. 24.

Reed, Stanley (95), U.S. Supreme Court justice (1938–57); a descendant of one of Kentucky's founding families. He studied law at the University of Virginia, Columbia, and the University of Paris. He served in the Kentucky legislature (1912–16). In 1924 he was admitted to practice before the Supreme Court. He was appointed a Supreme Court justice by Franklin D. Roosevelt and wrote more than 300 opinions on issues including social welfare, civil rights, and the regulatory authority of the federal government. He was identified with the thinking of New Deal politics, although his voting record was not always in line with that philosophy: d. Huntington, NY, April 3.

Renaldo, Duncan (76), film and television actor; best known for his role as the Cisco Kid. He made seven Cisco Kid feature films and 156 television episodes: d. Santa Barbara, CA, Sept. 3.

Rhine, J(oseph) B(anks) (84), psychologist; pioneered in the field of parapsychological research, joining Duke University in 1930, and in 1940 becoming director of its Parapsychology Laboratory. In 1965, following his retirement from Duke, he established his own research center. His books include *Extra Sensory Perception* (1934), *New Frontiers of the Mind* (1937), and *The Reaches of the Mind* (1947): d. Hillsborough, NC, Feb. 20.

Ribla, Gertrude (née Ribler) (62), opera singer and teacher; in 1949 she made her debut with the Metropolitan Opera in the title role of Verdi's *Aïda*. Prior to her debut, she had sung with the New York City Opera, the New York La Scala Opera, the San Carlo Opera, and the Fortune Gallo Opera Company: d. Bloomington, IN, March 20.

Roberts, Rachel (53), Welsh-born actress; her most famous screen roles were in *Saturday Night and Sunday Morning* (1960) and *This Sporting Life* (1963). She also appeared on the British stage: d. Los Angeles, Nov. 26.

Roberts, Richard (69), physicist and microbiologist. In his work as a physicist, he confirmed discovery of uranium fission. He was the main contributor to the discovery of delayed neutrons. After World War II, he began a career in microbiology and discovered the major chemical synthetic mechanisms by which cell duplication occurs: d. Washington, DC, April 4.

Robinson, Francis (70), opera executive; in 1948 he began working for the Metropolian Opera in New York. He worked first as a tour manager, a position he held throughout his tenure there. He was head of the box office and subscription department (1950–62), press director (1954–77), and assistant manager (1952–76): d. New York City, May 14.

Ronne, Finn (80), Norwegian-born explorer, traveled to Antarctica nine times. He accompanied Adm. Richard E. Byrd on his second Antarctic expedition (1923): d. Bethesda, MD, Jan. 12.

Roth, Lillian (69), actress, singer, and author. At age eight she won a featured role in the Broadway production of *Shavings*. In 1929 Miss Roth went to Hollywood where she performed in several motion pictures. In 1954 her best-selling autobiography, *I'll Cry Tomorrow*, was published: d. New York City, May 12.

Rukeyser, Muriel (66), American poet; her concerns revealed political and social commitments to causes ranging from the Scottsboro trial of 1932 to the plight of Iran's Kurdish Socialists in 1979. She attended Vassar College and was the literary editor of an undergraduate journal, the *Student Review*, but left without graduating. She published poetry in numerous periodicals and turned out several volumes of poetry. A comprehensive collection of her work, *The Collected Poems of Muriel Rukeyser*, was issued in 1979: d. New York City, Feb. 12.

Runnels, Harold Lowell (56), Democratic Representative from New Mexico's second district (1971–80): d. New York City, Aug. 5.

Sá Carneiro, Francisco (46), prime minister of Portugal; he founded the Popular Democratic Party (later renamed the Social Democratic Party) in 1974. Following the 1976 legislative election, the party was the second largest group, after the Socialists, in the legislature. Prime Minister Sá Carneiro was a liberal reformer under Marcello Caetano and moved politically to the right after the 1974 coup in Portugal. In 1979 he put together a majority rightist coalition. In the October 1980 election, the coalition gained a greater majority: d. Lisbon, Dec. 5.

Sanders, Harland (90), founder of the Kentucky Fried Chicken Corporation and honorary colonel of Kentucky; he first sold fried chicken in 1929 at the Corbin, KY, Sanders' Cafe, located in the rear of a service station. In 1939, after some years of refining a method for cooking fried chicken, he found a quick and easy method by means of the recently invented pressure cooker. He flavored his chicken with a mixture of 11 spices and herbs. At the age of 66 he sold his Corbin restaurant and shortly thereafter established the chicken franchise business which made him famous: d. Shelbyville, KY, Dec. 16.

Schary, Dore (74), playwright and motion picture producer; he produced or supervised production of more than 250 films. He also directed and produced Broadway plays and wrote *Sunrise at Campobello*, which opened during the 1957–58 Broadway season: d. New York City, July 7.

Sellers, Peter (54), British comedian and actor. He was born into a theatrical family, and following service in World War II received some exposure at the Windmill Theater, a London vaudeville house, before attracting the interest of a British Broadcasting Corporation radio producer who cast him in the *Goon Show* series, which ran for seven years. Following his success in radio he appeared on the stage and in several motion pictures before becoming internationally known in the film *I'm All Right, Jack*. He was known for his abilities in creating different voices and accents: d. London, July 24.

Sherrill, Henry Knox (89), Presiding Bishop of the Episcopal Church (1946–58). He supported the causes of birth control, racial justice, church flexibility toward divorce, and ecumenism. In 1950 he began the first two-year term as president of the National Council of Churches, and he helped establish the World Council of Churches, serving as one of its six presidents from 1954 to 1961: d. Boxford, MA, May 11.

Silverheels, Jay (62), actor; best known as the Lone Ranger's sidekick Tonto in *The Lone Ranger* television series which ran from 1949 to 1957, before being widely syndicated: d. Woodland Hills, CA, March 5.

Simpson, Gen. William Hood (92), commander of the Ninth Army during World War II; he served on the German front. A graduate of West Point, he spent two years in the Philippines and in 1916 was in Gen. John J. Pershing's punitive expedition into Mexico against Mexico's Pancho Villa. He served in France during World War I: d. San Antonio, TX, Aug. 15.

Smith, Anthony Peter (Tony) (68), sculptor; an architect by profession, he was noted for large-scale monochromatic Minimalist structures: d. New York City, Dec. 26.

Smythe, Conn (85), Canadian founder of the Toronto Maple Leafs ice hockey team and a member of the National Hockey League (NHL) Hall of Fame; he also built the Maple Leafs Garden hockey arena: d. Toronto, Nov. 18.

Snow, C(harles) P(ercy) (74), British novelist, playwright, and scientist; he was educated at Cambridge University as a physicist, taking his Ph.D. in 1930. Shortly thereafter he became a tutor at Christ's College where he remained until 1940, while simultaneously developing his skills as a writer. His first and last works of fiction, *Death Under Sail* (1932) and *A Coat of Varnish* (1979), were murder mysteries. His masterwork was *Strangers and Brothers*, a series of 11 novels, the first of which came out in 1940. A highly versatile man, he held various civil posts and was director of the English Electric Company and a member of the House of Lords (knighted in 1957). He was also a popular lecturer. His work includes 25 books of fiction and nonfiction, five plays, and numerous articles: d. London, July 1.

Somoza Debayle, Anastasio (54), former ruler of Nicaragua and member of a family which came to power in 1936 when his father, Anastasio Somoza Garcia, seized power and ruled as a dictator. Following his father's death by assassination in 1956, his brother, Luis, took over as president, serving until 1963. General Somoza, during his brother's rule, headed Nicaragua's National Guard. He promoted himself through the ranks, eventually becoming a five-star general. From 1963 until 1967, the country was ruled by a Somoza puppet government. In 1967 General Somoza took direct control of the government when he won election to the presidency amid charges of fraud and repression. He ruled until 1972 when he stepped down (although without relinquishing control) from the presidency in order to have the country's constitution rewritten. He began a new presidential term in 1974 and served until 1979, when the Sandinist revolutionary forces took control: d. Asunción, Sept. 17.

Stein, William H. (68), biochemist; he joined Rockefeller Institute after receiving his doctorate from Columbia University in 1938. He was elected to the National Academy of Sciences in 1960, and in 1972 shared the Nobel Prize in Chemistry for his studies on the chemical structure of a pancreatic enzyme: d. New York City, Feb. 2.

Still, Clyfford (75), American painter who rejected the European tradition and worked to create an authentic American expression. Although some art historians rank him among the founders of the Abstract Expressionist school, he saw himself as set apart. A large body of his work, which he kept all his life, was completed by 1934: d. Baltimore, June 23.

Stone, Milburn (74), actor; he became famous in the role of Doc Adams on *Gunsmoke*, the television series which had a 20-year run: d. La Jolla, CA, June 12.

Summerskill, Baroness (Edith Clara) (78), member of the House of Commons (1938–61); she was a chairman of the Labour Party (1954–55). She moved to the House of Lords in 1961 after having been made a life peer: d. London, Feb. 4.

Sutherland, Graham (76), British artist; commissioned by Parliament to create a portrait of Sir Winston Churchill on the occasion of Sir Winston's 80th birthday in November 1954. The portrait was so disliked by Churchill and his family that it was ordered destroyed by Lady Spencer-Churchill. Mr. Sutherland also created the tapestry "Christ the King" for the rebuilt Coventry Cathedral in central England: d. London, Feb. 17.

Tarnower, Herman (69), physician of cardiology and internal medicine; he became well known as the author of *The Complete Scarsdale Medical Diet* (1979): d. of gunshot wounds, Purchase, NY, March 10.

Thang, Ton Duc (91), president of Vietnam; he was elected to that office (largely ceremonial since the death of Ho Chi Minh) following the unification of Vietnam in 1976: d. Vietnam, March 30.

Thomas, Billy (49), actor; from 1934 to 1944 he played the role of "Buckwheat" in the "Our Gang" movie series: d. California, Oct. 10.

Tolbert, William R., Jr. (66), president of Liberia (1971–80). He brought about some reforms during his tenure as president and encouraged participation in business and government of the more than 95% of the population who are not descended from the American slaves who were Liberia's founders. Liberian Army enlisted men, charging "rampant corruption," staged a coup in which he was killed: d. Monrovia, Liberia, April 12.

Tynan, Kenneth (53) British drama critic; regarded by many as the greatest theater critic since George Bernard Shaw. In 1952–53 he was drama critic for the *London Evening Standard*, and from 1954 until 1963 he was drama critic for *The Observer*. In 1958 he became a drama critic for *The New Yorker*, a position he held for two years. In 1963 he became literary manager for Britain's National Theatre and from 1969 until 1973 he was a literary consultant to the company. Suffering from emphysema, he moved to California in 1976 and, during his last years, wrote profiles for *The New Yorker*: d. Santa Monica, CA, July 26.

Vagnozzi, Egidio Cardinal (74), cardinal of the Roman Catholic church; he served as Apostolic Delegate to the United States (1958–67) at a time when the Second Vatican Council (1962–65) brought great changes to the Roman Catholic church. He was made a cardinal in 1967, and at the time of his death he was the Vatican's Prefect of Economic Affairs: d. Rome, Dec. 26.

Van, Bobby (né Robert King) (47), actor, comedian, and dancer; he appeared in nine motion pictures, on numerous television variety shows, and in the 1971 stage revival of *No, No, Nanette.* He also did a nightclub act with Mickey Rooney for seven years: d. Los Angeles, July 31.

Van Vleck, John Hasbrouck (81), professor emeritus of Harvard University and 1977 Nobel laureate for physics. Dr. Van Vleck won the Nobel Prize for work he did during the 1930s, which described the magnetic properties of solids: d. Cambridge, MA, Oct. 27.

Vodopyanov, Mikhail (80), Soviet Arctic flier and author; he was a pioneer of new polar air routes and took part in a rescue flight of the Soviet ship *Chelyuskin* which became stuck in the ice in 1934, a feat for which he received the title Hero of the Soviet Union. He is credited with the idea of establishing a base camp on the ice at the North Pole, and he landed an expedition on a suitable floe in 1937. He rose to the rank of major general during service as commander of an Air Force division in World War II. After military retirement in 1946 he published his autobiography and several novels and stories based on his Arctic flights: d. Moscow, reported Aug. 14.

Wagner, Winifred (82), British-born daughter-in-law of German composer Richard Wagner and director of the Bayreuth festival of Wagner's operatic works (1930–44): d. Bayreuth, West Germany, March 5.

Walsh, Stella (née Stanislawa Walasiewicz) (69), Olympic track star. She competed in the 1932 and 1936 Olympics for her native Poland, winning gold and silver medals. In the 1932 Olympics she set a record for the 100-meter dash. She became a U.S. citizen in 1947: d. Cleveland, Dec. 4.

Warren, Shields (82), Harvard University pathologist; he was an early specialist in the biological effects of radiation. He worked for more than 50 years at the New England Deaconess Hospital in Boston—for 36 years as its chief pathologist. Warren wrote nine medical textbooks: d. Mashpee, MA, July 1.

Wilder, Alexander L. C. (Alec) (73), composer; he wrote both popular and classical music. His formal music included compositions for operas, operettas, choral works, and concert songs, for full orchestra and wind ensembles. His great love was chamber music: d. Gainesville, FL, Dec. 24.

Wright, James (52), poet; professor of English at Hunter College since 1966. He was highly regarded as a visionary poet. He won the 1972 Pulitzer Prize for Poetry for *Collected Poems* (1971): d. New York City, March 25.

Yahya Khan, Agha Mohammad (63), Pakistan's military ruler (1969–71). General Yahya was forced to resign after the 1971 war with India over Bangladesh and was sentenced to five years' house arrest: d. Rawalpindi, Pakistan, Aug. 8.

MILBURN STONE

JOHN VAN VLECK
Photos UPI

OCEANIA

With political independence in effect almost throughout Oceania, attention focused on economic well-being in light of spiraling energy costs. Important conferences were held in Honolulu ("Development the Pacific Way") in March, and on Tarawa, Kiribati (the 11th meeting of the South Pacific Forum), in July. General levels of economic growth were sustained in the area. There was increasing realization that economic dependence persisted even after political independence. Trade prospects were brightened with the acceptance of a South Pacific regional trade and economic agreement allowing island countries to send a wider range of products to Australia and New Zealand on especially-favorable terms.

Four U.S. territorial entities in Micronesia clarified their future status, accepting continued fragmentation rather than possible statehood. The emergence of Sir Julius Chan as prime minister of Papua New Guinea (PNG) marked that nation's first change in direction since independence. The Anglo-French Condominium of New Hebrides became the Melanesian nation of Vanuatu (*see* page 567).

Region-wide Cooperation. The four-day Honolulu conference brought together leaders from nine island mininations and other island entities, including Hawaii and Guam; only PNG was unrepresented. Diverging factors of political independence and matters of economic well-being were discussed. A consensus view developed that there was need for a stronger regional pooling of knowledge. A survey presented at the meeting showed that almost three out of four people in the area remained in agriculture yet per capita food output was falling. Meanwhile the islands' import bills for food were rising. Larger fuel import bills were endangering development programs.

At the forum held in Tarawa, Australian Prime Minister Malcolm Fraser stressed the merits of an enhanced sense of regionalism. His call was backed strongly by Fiji's Prime Minister Ratu Sir Kamisese Mara.

Fiji's proposal for a regional development fund to supplement lending by other agencies was endorsed for further study.

The forum expressed opposition to proposals for the disposal of nuclear waste in the Pacific. Subsequently a "nuclear-free Pacific" seminar was held in Sydney, Australia. Hilda Lini, sister of Vanuatu's prime minister, led in the condemning of French nuclear testing and of Japan's proposal to dump nuclear waste in the Pacific.

PNG. PNG's change of government followed Michael Somare's defeat in a parliamentary vote in March. Sir Julius Chan, 41-year-old leader of the People's Progress Party (PPP), became prime minister. In his first national administration (1975), Somare had the support of Chan and the PPP; by 1978 a clear divergence in economic and social aims was evident. The PPP espoused free enterprise, and Somare's Pangu Party showed Socialist leanings. The PPP broke away and Somare promoted a new coalition; but parliamentary support eroded steadily until Somare was defeated in a crucial March vote. Chan, a businessman, promised to foster investment from abroad and to make PNG more self-sufficient. In foreign policy he moved away from Somare's neutralist stance. Chan also promised greater attention to defense. The new government quickly eased wage-setting rules to permit a progressive raising of the minimum wage for both rural and urban workers.

Micronesia. In the strategically-located islands of Micronesia, constitutional developments moved forward with the initialing in January of the long-negotiated Compact of Free Association to replace the U.S. trusteeship granted by the Security Council in 1947. The territory includes 2,100 islands covering an area of nearly 3,100,000 sq mi (8 000 000 km²). The compact arose from the 1977 Statement of Agreed Principles for Free Association, itself an outcome of the decision of the disparate island peoples of the Trust Territory not to unite. The compact laid down the terms under which the Commonwealth of the Northern Mariana Islands, the Federated States of Micronesia (Truk, Ponape, Kosrae, and Yap), and the republics of Palau and the Marshall Islands would attain new status. Each state would gain local autonomy and the United States would control foreign affairs and defense. It also provided for substantial U.S. assistance over the 15-year free association relationship.

Later, in the UN Trusteeship Council, the Federated States of Micronesia sought to have trusteeship extended beyond the 1981 termination planned by the United States.

R. M. YOUNGER

OCEANOGRAPHY

The Global Weather Experiment (GWE), the largest scientific experiment ever held, ended on Nov. 30, 1979. It obtained data from orbiting satellites such as NOAA-6 and TIROS-N, as well as from geostationary satellites, meteorological balloons, a network of 368 drifting buoys, remote automatic stations, and research vessels. From the data, scientists from some 70 nations can now determine the practical limits to weather forecasting and begin to design a global forecasting system. The satellite information covered large ocean areas that act as storm-generating centers but lack permanent weather stations. All data were relayed to the French National Space Center in Toulouse, processed, and fed into the World Weather Watch's Global Telecommunications system.

The instrumented buoys used for GWE proved so successful that some 30 buoys were used in October 1980 by a joint United States-

Canada effort in the northeast Pacific, to observe an area crucial to North American weather but without conventional data sources. Many other technological advances used in GWE, such as a prototype aircraft-to-satellite data relay (ASDAR), were adopted for an improved weather reconnaissance system for storm observations.

The GWE with its frequent satellite observations also offered an ideal opportunity for an ocean survey of the Somali Current and western equatorial Indian Ocean during the onset of the southwest monsoon, which was termed the Indian Ocean Experiment (INDEX). In this area, the surface currents change with the annual cycle of monsoon winds but the transitional seasons have not been examined previously because of the practical problems of mapping rapid changes over a wide area. INDEX ran from February to August 1979. It was found that the Somali Current does not grow continuously but appears to extend itself northward in a series of steps. A clockwise eddy developed near 4°N in late May or early June and was swept away by the main current migrating through to the northeast in August. There was evidence of a deep countercurrent under the southern part of the Somali Current, connected near the Equator to the westward flow at about 700-m (2,300-ft) depth. In addition, two areas of upwelling were observed near the coast, one near 10°N and one near 5°N, both with high concentrations of surface nutrients and increased phytoplankton productivity.

To resolve argument about deep undercurrents on the western boundary of ocean basins, a High Energy Benthic Boundary Layer Experiment (HEBBLE) was designed to study how swift currents near the bottom interact with the surface of the sediments. Data were gathered in 1979 from two cruises on the outer slope of Georges Bank, south of Nova Scotia, and from instruments left on the bottom. The results show that currents can surge to high speeds, abate rapidly, and swing through different directions over only a few weeks. Large variations in the turbidity of the water were noted and strong currents were measured intermittently between 4 800 and 5 000 m (15,750 and 16,400 ft), where they form meterwide, 15 cm (6 inch) high ripples parallel to the current. It is thought that a relationship of the undercurrents with the surface movement of the Gulf Stream system may exist, but conclusive details are lacking. The most immediate need is for a longer record of current speeds and directions to delineate the ripple-forming currents which leave their imprint on the bottom features.

The Deep Sea Drilling Program (DSDP), with the research vessel *Glomar Challenger,* began using a new hydraulic poston corer, which recovers deep sea sediment without disturbing the minute layering. Shipboard scientists were thus able to collect from the Caribbean Sea and the eastern Pacific Ocean a detailed, continuous record of magnetic and biological events for the past eight million years. The information would help to confirm the time of the rising of the isthmus of Panama that now blocks oceanic circulation from the Atlantic Ocean to the Pacific. A later cruise concentrated on exploration of the Costa Rica rift in the Gulf of Panama, midway between the Panama Canal and the Galapagos Islands. The later expedition used a new downhole sonic camera to photograph lava flows and cracks in the wall of the hole drilled in the sea floor, and a Russian device for measuring the magnetic field inside the hole. The geothermal interaction of the overlying water filtering into the seabed lavas is extensive and similar to such systems on land, where they are responsible for many of the world's major metallic deposits and for much of the available geothermal energy.

The DSDP also conducted observations on the sea floor plateau near the Falkland Islands and other areas of the Argentine Shelf near the Antarctic Convergence or polar front, which marks the boundary of cold, nutrient-rich surface water flowing northward from Antarctica into the Atlantic Ocean. The sediment data and the fossil plant remains indicated shifting of this front with time. It was south of its present position some three million years ago.

In 1980 DSDP activity also was centered on the Rio Grande rise in the southwest Atlantic, off Brazil, and on the Walvis Ridge, extending from near the island of Tristan da Cunha on the mid-Atlantic ridge to the coast of South Africa. A series of holes were drilled across the top of the Walvis Ridge and down its northern slope into the Angola Basin, as a means to determine the history and structure of the ridge. The fossil remains indicate that the ridge has sunk gradually since the last outpourings of lava completed its formation 70 million years ago.

DSDP data recovered at other sites traced the evolution of the Antarctic ice cap from its beginning some 30 or 40 million years ago. Preliminary studies indicated that highly saline waters generated by the freezing of the ice cap began actively to flow through this part of the South Atlantic some 4.5 million years ago. Before that time, the bottom waters of the eastern South Atlantic varied in carbon dioxide as the remains of surface organisms collected on the ocean bottom. Intervals of peak organic supply were 10 to 12 million years ago, just following the buildup of the large ice cap on Antarctica, and 3 to 6 million years ago, just prior to the ice ages of the northern hemisphere. Scientists from numerous institutions in the United States, Brazil, France, West Germany, Austria, the United Kingdom, and the Soviet Union participated in these DSDP activities, which were planned by the Joint Oceanographic Institutions for Deep Earth Sampling (JOIDES).

DAVID A. MCGILL
U.S. Coast Guard Academy

Many steelworkers in Youngstown were laid off as 1980 began. The economy, particularly the employment outlook, was a prime concern to Ohioans during the year.

OHIO

Ohio was considered a pivotal state in what was expected to be a tight presidential race. Consequently, the candidates visited its cities numerous times. When the count was in, Gov. Ronald Reagan carried the state, winning 52% of the vote. The victory of Norwalk's Clifford F. Brown brought the total number of supreme court justices named Brown to three.

Sen. John H. Glenn, Jr., a Democrat, won re-election easily. He obtained nearly 2.8 million votes, a record for any candidate in Ohio. Thirteen Republicans and 10 Democrats, the same ratio as in 1978, were elected to the U.S. House of Representatives. Republicans took control of the Ohio Senate, 18–15, which had been the Democratic margin.

Two statewide measures were on the ballot. A constitutional amendment won; a citizens' initiative amendment lost. The first will create two classes of real estate property for tax purposes— industrial-commercial and residence-farm. Tax increases on residences and farms now will not be so precipitous as reappraisals had forced them to be. "Windfall" tax credits for business properties will be eliminated. The second amendment would have restructured state levies on personal income, real estate, corporations, and personal property. Low income families would have benefited. Foes of this proposal said it would have added $1,000,000,000 in taxes, much of it from sales and use taxes on transactions of unfinished products now exempted.

Overspending. Unemployment, principally caused by cuts at automobile-related factories, slashed state income tax revenues while falling sales, especially of vehicles, stifled sales tax collections. Welfare costs rose.

Although he promised not to raise taxes when elected to his fourth four-year term in 1978, Gov. James A. Rhodes (R) on December 19 signed a hurried law which raised the 4% sales tax to 5%, effective January 1, to help keep public schools open. Cigarette and beer taxes also were increased. About $395 million added revenue was expected.

Earlier, the legislature had trimmed spending to prevent a $266 million budget deficit, and Governor Rhodes ordered a 3% reduction in spending. Prices at state-controlled liquor stores were raised. In November, acting on the threat of a $403 million deficit by the June 30, 1981, end of the fiscal year, Rhodes ordered another 3% slash in spending.

Yen for Business. Efforts to interest Japanese automobile companies in manufacturing vehicles in Ohio were successful. In January Honda Motor Co. announced that it would build cars at Marysville, near Columbus, where it has been making motorcycles. Two thousand jobs were expected to result by 1983, when a $200 million plant was to be completed.

By the end of 1980 Ohio was reported to have edged ahead of Missouri to become the number 2 car-producing state in the nation, building 644,187 in the 1980 model year despite numerous layoffs. Michigan is first.

Seasonally adjusted unemployment in Ohio was about 453,000, 8.8%, in November, down from 502,500, 9.7%, in June.

OHIO • Information Highlights

Area: 41,222 sq mi (106 765 km²).
Population (Jan. 1980 est.): 10,743,000.
Chief Cities (1976 est.): Columbus, the capital, 533,075; Cleveland, 625,643; Cincinnati, 410,441.
Government (1980): Chief Officer—governor, James A. Rhodes (R). General Assembly—Senate, 33 members; House of Representatives, 99 members.
Education (1979–80): Enrollment—public elementary schools, 1,219,745; public secondary, 805,511; colleges and universities, 463,548 students. Public school expenditures, $3,839,100,000 ($1,770 per pupil).
State Finances (fiscal year 1979): Revenues, $11,435,-000,000; expenditures, $9,762,000,000.
Personal Income (1979): $93,517,000,000; per capita, $8,715.
Labor Force (November 1980): Nonagricultural wage and salary earners, 4,459,000; unemployed, 453,000 (8.8% of total force).

Efforts to arrange a 1981 reopening of steel facilities at McDonald, near Youngstown, which closed in 1979, apparently were successful after a November out-of-court settlement of a lawsuit.

Boundary Dispute. Ohio gained square footage though probably not much stature through resolution of a 14-year tilt with Kentucky on where their borders in the Ohio River should be. The U.S. Supreme Court on January 21 ruled that the 1792 low-water mark should be the dividing line, not the current mark as Kentucky contended. This shunted the line about 80 to 100 ft (24–30.5 m) farther south, within the river. Some taxes from fishing and boating licenses and over-water restaurants were involved.

Schools. The state board of education adopted guidelines for erasing public school racial discrimination, after the board was found liable for not doing enough to ensure desegregation in Columbus and Cleveland. The guidelines permit the board to cut off funds to any offending district.

Other. Probate Judge James V. Barbuto of Summit county was convicted of sex-related crimes on June 13. He was sentenced to a one- to ten-year prison term, but later was released and placed on shock probation because of illness.

Gold fever was reported in southern Ohio, where the Illinoisan glacier once passed. A few ounces of gold were reported found.

The state stepped up attempts to lure tourists with an "Ohio's for you" slogan.

JOHN F. HUTH, JR.
Reporter, "The Plain Dealer," Cleveland

OKLAHOMA

In the November elections, 59% of Oklahoma's voting age population went to the polls. In the presidential race, former Gov. Ronald Reagan won the state's eight electors with 60.5% of the popular vote. President Jimmy Carter received 35%, John Anderson (I) 3.3%, and Ed Clark (L) 1.2%. Democratic party leaders conceded Oklahoma to Reagan early in the campaign, and neither candidate visted the state.

Elections. In the U.S. Senate race to replace outgoing Sen. Henry Bellmon (R), 30-year-old first-term state Sen. Don Nickles (R) won a surprise victory over Oklahoma County Dist. Att. Andy Coats (D). Nickles, a Catholic, received conservative support and the backing of moral majority forces in defeating both Coats and Republican primary opponent Harold Zink, a Tulsa businessman. In the Democratic runoff, Coats had defeated Robert S. Kerr, Jr., the eldest son of the former U.S. senator.

Incumbent congressional Democrats James R. Jones (first district), Mike Synar (second district), Wes Watkins (third district), and Glenn English (sixth district) were reelected, and Republican incumbent Mickey Edwards (fifth district) easily defeated his Democratic opponent, David Hood. In the fourth district, where veteran Congressman Tom Steed (D) retired after 32 years in office, 30-year-old Norman attorney David McCurdy (D) defeated 53-year-old retired Navy captain and former Vietnam prisoner of war Howard Rutledge (R).

A constitutional amendment allowing the state legislature to call itself into special session was approved by Oklahoma voters. Seven amendments were defeated, however, including five which would have permitted authorization of special tax levies by counties, by school districts, or for transportation purposes.

Legislation. The Oklahoma legislature convened on January 8 and adjourned on June 16, meeting for 80 of the 90 allowable legislative days. A record $1,200,000,000 was appropriated during the regular session. In July, Gov. George Nigh called a special session to consider and approve an additional $62 million in surplus funds for highways and bridges, thus reducing the estimated surplus to $21 million. Republican leaders instead supported a measure to exempt food and drugs from state sales tax.

Major legislation enacted during the year included state sales tax exemptions on electric and natural gas utility bills, as well as on television, radio, and some newspaper advertising. The state minimum wage was increased to $3.10 per hour. State employees received an average 10% annual salary increase. Public school teachers received an annual salary increase of $1,612, bringing minimum salaries to a range of $9,675–$13,675. Public employee and teacher retirement systems were changed to permit retirement, with increased benefits, at age 58 after 30 years of service. Retirement systems for police and firefighters also were changed and benefits increased. Tuition and fee increases were approved for institutions of higher education, and record appropriations were made for a 12% average salary increase in colleges and universities. University hospitals were transferred to the state department of human services, permitting them to use as operating funds money from state sales tax. Legislation was passed to allow voluntary prayer in public schools. The state transportation

--------- **OKLAHOMA • Information Highlights** ---------

Area: 69,919 sq mi (181 090 km²).

Population (Jan. 1980 est.): 2,914,000.

Chief Cities (1976 est.): Oklahoma City, the capital, 369,-438; Tulsa, 333,765; (1970 census): Lawton, 74,470; Norman 52,117.

Government (1980): *Chief Officers*—governor, George Nigh (D); lt. gov., Spencer Bernard (D). *Legislature*—Senate, 48 members; House of Representatives, 101 members.

Education (1979–80): *Enrollment*—public elementary schools, 325,252 pupils; public secondary, 258,206; colleges and universities, 152,683 students. *Public school expenditures*, $1,143,000,000 ($1,771 per pupil).

State Finances (fiscal year 1979): *Revenues*, $2,966,-000,000; *expenditures*, $2,733,000,000.

Personal Income (1979): $24,607,000,000; per capita, $8,509.

Labor Force (June 1980): *Nonagricultural wage and salary earners*, 1,137,900; *unemployed*, 57,500 (4.3% of total force).

department was given authorization to purchase abandoned railroads. Welfare recipients were granted a $100 one-time bonus. And the minimum coverage for automobile liability insurance was increased.

Natural Disasters. Following a prolonged summer drought, the entire state was declared a federal disaster area. Water was rationed in most cities, and many small towns encountered severe shortages.

JOHN W. WOOD, *The University of Oklahoma*

OLDER POPULATION

The greater longevity of its members continues to challenge American society. In 1980 there were 34.2 million persons in the United States aged 60 and over, surpassing the number of children under age 11, and the youths from 11 to 19. During the 1970s the older population increased by at least 10% in most states, with the South and the West having the most pronounced gains. In 1980 the federal government strove to ensure that this growing segment of the population received adequate social services and medical care.

Programs and Services. Regulations were issued in 1980 to implement Title III of the Older Americans Act Amendments of 1978. Title III authorizes formula grants to state agencies on aging and expands the role of state and local area agencies in developing comprehensive systems of services for older persons. Included under Title III, which had an appropriation of $652 million for fiscal 1980, are nutrition programs, the establishment of multipurpose senior centers, and other social services.

Currently, there are about 5,000 senior centers nationwide, generating programs and activities that encourage older persons to maintain their health and to engage in productive tasks that benefit themselves and their communities.

A serious problem facing many older people is a nationwide lack of adequate noninstitutional care for persons with chronic disabilities. It is now widely accepted that prolonged institutional living, for those who do not need it, can be a damaging and debilitating experience. Government effort, therefore, is directed at providing care and services in the home and in other community settings for disabled persons who are eligible for Medicare and Medicaid.

The Administration on Aging (AOA), within the Department of Health and Human Services, issued final regulations for a new program for older Indians. The program, authorized by Title VI of the Older Americans Act, as amended, is intended to provide social and nutrition services to Indians aged 60 and over. Eligible tribal organizations will receive direct funding to pay the costs of the services, which are comparable to those provided through the State and Community Programs on Aging and include the acquisition and maintenance of senior centers.

Older Volunteers. As the 1980s began, it appeared that the vast resources of the older population were beginning to be effectively used. Older persons have made a great contribution to the expansion and provision of services to the elderly. In 1980 about 180,000 older volunteers served in nutrition programs and another 25,000 worked in the 586 Area Agencies on Aging that are the backbone of the national effort. More than 16,000 volunteers served as Foster Grandparents to provide personal, sustained attention for especially needy children. Approximately 3,600 Senior Companions filled a similar need for frail elderly or handicapped persons. A quarter of a million older persons worked an average of one day a week as members of the Retired Senior Volunteer Program. Volunteers also worked in neighborhood service centers; in the Senior Corps of Retired Executives; in the developing Nursing Home Ombudsman program; in neighborhood watches aimed at protecting lives and property; and as teachers' aides. Volunteer work has helped many elderly feel useful and needed by society. Another 3 million people aged 65 and over are engaged in paid employment.

White House Conference on Aging. Plans were underway for the third White House Conference on Aging, to be held in Washington, DC, Nov. 30–Dec. 4, 1981, under the aegis of the U.S. Department of Health and Human Services. The conclusions of the two previous conferences, held in 1961 and in 1971, led to increased social security benefits and helped to generate Medicare and Medicaid, the National Institute on Aging, and the Older Americans Act.

Participation began at local levels, and communities nationwide were organizing small-scale conferences on aging to identify issues and concerns that affect the lives of the elderly. These will become the basis for the agenda of the 1,800 conference delegates in 1981. Delegates will be chosen from each state.

President Carter appointed 81-year-old Dr. Sadie Alexander to chair the conference. She is the first black woman in the United States to earn a doctor of law degree.

CELIA B. WEISMAN, *Director Gerontological Institute, Yeshiva University*

ONTARIO

During 1980, Ontario emerged as one of the few provinces to support firmly Prime Minister Elliott Trudeau's various proposals for patriating the Canadian constitution. At the September constitutional discussions among Trudeau and the ten provincial premiers, and then again in October, Premier William Davis endorsed the entrenchment of a Bill of Rights, with guarantees of language rights, in any new constitution. As leader of Canada's most industrialized province, Davis also strongly favored effective federal authority over the economy and natural resources.

Speculation about a fall election ended in September, when Premier Davis decided against a dissolution and when New Democratic Party leader Michael Cassidy indicated that he would support the minority Conservative government in any nonconfidence motion moved by the opposition Liberal Party.

In May, the first jury trial conducted in French opened in the Ontario Supreme Court. On January 1, the attorney general had guaranteed that trials at any level would be conducted in either English or French. In the throne speech of March 11, it was announced that the use of French would be extended to small claims courts and that a French language agricultural college would be opened at Alfred in the eastern part of the province. Under pressure created by the Quebec referendum, permission finally was given for the building of a French high school at Penetanguishene, a move the cabinet previously had opposed.

As the center of the Canadian automobile industry, Ontario was a party to the efforts of the Canadian and U.S. governments to help the ailing Chrysler Corporation, which has 14,000 employees in the province. Ontario refused to provide C$50 million in loan guarantees unless it received a promise from Chrysler regarding employment in the province. The promise was not forthcoming, but Ontario and Chrysler each agreed to contribute $10 million toward a new research facility in the province.

The budget submitted to Treasurer Frank Miller in April called for no tax increases. Grants to municipalities were raised by 12.4%, to C$4,000,000,000. Tax refunds were provided to senior citizens, and credits were extended to small businesses. The sales tax was removed from energy-saving supplies and vehicles fueled by hydrogen, propane, alcohol, natural gas, or electricity. A C$940 million deficit was forecast.

Legislation going into effect on Jan. 1, 1980, required motorists to carry liability insurance. A bill introduced in June provided for the mandatory checkoff of union dues for all members of a bargaining unit. In return, all members of the

Canadian Consulate General

Ontario's Premier Bill Davis supported Prime Minister Trudeau in Canada's constitutional debate.

unit, whether union members or not, would be eligible to vote in strike or ratification ballots. The province also permitted the establishment of what is believed to be the largest nongovernment lottery in North America. The lottery would be run jointly by, and for the benefit of, the Ontario Association for the Mentally Retarded, the Kidney Foundation, the Crippled Children's Society, and the Multiple Sclerosis Society.

On April 22, the film censorship board refused to permit public screening of the Academy Award-winning movie, *The Tin Drum,* unless certain cuts were made. Controversy over the decision raged throughout the year and there was growing agitation for the abolition of the board and the substitution of a movie rating system. Frank Drea, the minister responsible for the board, refused to take any action, however, claiming that the board enjoys public confidence.

PETER J. KING, *Carleton University*

OREGON

In June, Gov. Victor Atiyeh announced an anticipated state revenue crisis. The shortfall projected was $204 million from a total state budget of $1,600,000,000, approximately 12.8%. Remedies proposed appeared to have identified higher education as the most likely candidate for budget cutting. Early in the summer, the State Board of Higher Education proposed the closing of three of the state's institutions, Oregon College of Education, Oregon Institute of Technology, and the University of Oregon's Health Sciences Center, the state's only medical and dental school. By September conditions were such that

---

——— **ONTARIO · Information Highlights** ———

Area: 412,582 sq mi (1 068 587 km²).
Population (1980 est.): 8,558,200.
Chief Cities (1976 census): Toronto, the provincial capital, 633,318; Ottawa, the federal capital, 304,462.
Government (1980): *Chief Officers*—lt. gov., Pauline McGibbon; premier, William G. Davis (Progressive Conservative); chief justice, Supreme Court, High Court of Justice, Gregory T. Evans. *Legislature*—Legislative Assembly, 125 members.
Education (1979–80 est.): *Enrollment*—public elementary and secondary schools, 1,885,250 pupils; private schools, 63,700; Indian (federal) schools, 7,530; postsecondary, 226,280 students. *Total expenditures,* $7,-154,457,000.
Public Finance (1980–81 est.): *Revenues,* $16,160,000,-000; *expenditures,* $17,121,000,000.
Personal Income (average weekly salary, May 1980): $306.05.
Unemployment Rate (July 1980, seasonally adjusted): 6.9%.
(All monetary figures are in Canadian dollars.)

no institutions were closed, but funding for all state colleges and universities was cut to minimum maintenance levels. Left unfunded were accounts for the hiring of new and replacement faculty, library acquisitions, travel, and others. Other state agencies suffered curtailment as well.

At the root of the problem was Oregon's dependence upon the forest products industry for a significant share of state revenues. The imposition of a tight money policy as a weapon against national inflation caused interest rates to soar, and building starts to plummet. With the closure or curtailment of lumber and plywood mills, Oregon's unemployment rates rivaled those of Michigan and other hard-hit industrial states. State revenues depend entirely upon the income tax—Oregon has no sales tax—so fluctuations in the forest products industry are quickly reflected in the state's income.

Recent interregional shifts within the plywood industry have exaggerated the fiscal woes of the Pacific Northwest generally, and of Oregon especially. In the mid-1960s scientists developed a technique for processing southern pine into plywood. Thus, the plywood mills of the Pacific Northwest, with a virtual national monopoly in plywood until the 1970s, have seen their share of the market fall to approximately 50%. As a result, logs are now being exported to Japan and processed by Japanese labor in Japanese mills to Japanese specifications. Georgia Pacific Corporation, a giant in the industry, announced that it would move its corporate headquarters from Portland to Atlanta, GA, by 1982.

Election. Seventy-two percent of Oregon's registered voters turned out for the general election. Ronald Reagan won the state's electoral votes, and long-time Democrat Congressman Al Ullman, chairman of the House Ways and Means Committee, was defeated by Denny Smith. Democrats Les Au Coin and James Weaver maintained their congressional seats and a newcomer, Ron Wyden (D), was elected in the third district. Republican Sen. Bob Packwood won reelection and incumbent Republicans were returned to the offices of secretary of state and state treasurer. Ballot measure six, a second attempt to limit local property taxes, was defeated. The Oregon legislature remained under Democratic control with majorities of 33–27 and 22–8 in the lower and upper houses, respectively.

Environment. A series of eruptions of Washington's Mount St. Helens, some 30 mi (48 km) from the Oregon border, dumped significant volumes of ash upon Portland and other portions of the Willamette Valley. Portland suffered extensive clogging of its storm sewer system, which could cause problems during the winter rainy season.

L. CARL BRANDHORST
Oregon College of Education

OTTAWA

Downtown development was the major preoccupation of Canada's capital city during 1980. The demolition of World War II federal office buildings in Cartier Square started a lively controversy between the federal government on the one hand, and the city and citizen groups on the other. The federal government proposed that the site be used for a provincial courthouse and a new U.S. embassy. The city government and various community groups objected to putting the embassy there; the community groups favored a new National Art Gallery and a park. When the U.S. government opted for an alternative site on Sussex Drive, the Canadian federal government decided to proceed with an office complex and park space. In another downtown area, an attempt by the city to expropriate land to build a new police station was thwarted by its owner, the University of Ottawa. Less controversial was the proposed $36 million convention center, part of a $250 million redevelopment plan for the Rideau Street area. In July, the province agreed to contribute $11.5 million, and work on the project was begun.

A relatively snowless winter in 1979–80 left a large surplus in the snow-removal budget, allowing the city to limit its tax increase for the subsequent year to 4.8% and to reduce borrowing. In the fall, a new general hospital was opened in the University of Ottawa's health sciences complex.

A strike by film projectionists during the summer closed almost all of Ottawa's movie theaters for 13 weeks. In August, the Ottawa *Journal*, one of the city's two English language dailies, ceased publication.

In March, the province decided to give the towns of Gloucester and Nepean an extra seat on the regional council. The two additional seats would deprive Ottawa of its council majority, much to the annoyance of Mayor Marion Dewar. Because of declining student enrollments, the Ottawa Board of Education was ordered by the provincial cabinet to transfer one of its high schools to the Carleton board.

PETER J. KING
Carleton University

─────── **OREGON • Information Highlights** ───────

Area: 96,981 sq mi (251 181 km^2).
Population (Jan. 1980 est.): 2,570,000.
Chief Cities (1970 census): Salem, the capital, 68,856; Eugene, 78,389; (1976 est.): Portland, 379,826.
Government (1980): *Chief Officers*—governor, Victor Atiyeh (R); secy. of state, Norma Paulus (R). *Legislative Assembly*—Senate, 30 members; House of Representatives, 60 members.
Education (1979–80): *Enrollment*—public elememtary schools, 281,472 pupils; public secondary, 185,656; colleges and universities, 154,597 students. *Public school expenditures,* $1,163,200,000 ($2,281 per pupil).
State Finances (fiscal year 1979): *Revenues,* $3,499,-000,000; *expenditures,* $2,906,000,000.
Personal Income (1979): $22,587,000,000; *per capita,* $8,938.
Labor Force (May 1980): *Nonagricultural wage and salary earners,* 1,032,600; *unemployed,* 104,000 (8.3% of total force).

PAKISTAN

In 1980 General or President Zia ul-Haq ruled Pakistan with as iron a hand as he could wield. He was beset by continuing domestic turmoil over his execution of former President Zulfikar Ali Bhutto in 1979. His own version of Pakistani democracy involved jailing political opponents and postponing elections. But, in addition, Pakistan was threatened by the Soviet occupation of Afghanistan and was forced to accept huge numbers of Afghan refugees.

Domestic Affairs. In February the U.S. Department of State released its annual survey on "human rights conditions" in the world community; Pakistan was singled out in the report: ". . . President Zia indefinitely postponed national elections, dissolved all political parties, expanded the jursidiction of military courts, and imposed formal censorship of newspapers." The report continued by asserting that many of the political associates of Bhutto were still being held, without charge or trial. At the time the prisoners included the wife and daughter of Bhutto; the two were relased from house arrest in April. Bhutto's daughter, Benazir, immediately defied a ban on political speeches by telling the Karachi Bar Association that Pakistanis wanted "democracy and not an illegal government." She was arrested again in November.

Indeed, considerable proscribed political activity took place in the late spring. Among the most uncompromising of Zia's opponents was former Air Marshal Asghar Khan who publicly referred to Zia as "slippery, shifty, unpopular, and disliked, a man with no credibility." Asghar Khan's reward for this was a return to house arrest. Repeated reports of an Army coup surfaced in March. Although no coup occurred, at least one general on the active list was arrested for trying to mount one. There was a consensus that the armed forces were characterized by disenchantment with Zia and a growing readiness to bring him down.

Very serious problems, some of which were the product of the international scene, confronted Zia on every hand. There were the continual, never-ending separatist sentiments,

Liaison

Pakistan's Zia ul-Haq confronted continued domestic turmoil and the Soviet invasion of Afghanistan.

voiced by the Baluchi (almost certainly encouraged by the Russians). Then there was Zia's dedication to "Islamization" in a country whose Islam is a bit heterogeneous. In July demonstrations by the Shiites (other Pakistanis are Sunnites) were marked with violence. The religious fervor resulting from Pakistani events acquired a life of its own and generated more problems than anyone had imagined. The presence in the Northwest Frontier Province of hundreds of thousands of Afghans (largely Pathan; ethnically identical with the Pakistanis in that region) produced a huge task of feeding, clothing, and rearming individuals to fight in Afghanistan. Perhaps as a result, President Zia, while calling for national unity, trust, and faith, postponed elections indefinitely.

On August 9 former Gen. Agha Mohammed Yahya Khan (known as General Yahya) died. He had taken over control of Pakistan from Field Marshal Mohammad Ayub Khan in 1969. He himself lost power in the aftermath of the civil war in East Pakistan (Bangladesh) in 1971, when Bhutto became the ruler of Pakistan.

Foreign Affairs. It was a dangerous and chaotic year for Pakistan in terms of foreign affairs. Indira Gandhi returned to power in India; Gandhi's long-run goal is almost certainly the dismemberment of Pakistan. Pakistan has every reason to fear her and the Indians. Partially for this reason, Pakistan has labored to achieve nuclear capability. Although by late 1980 Pakistan had not exploded a nuclear device, there were many who believed that it now had at least a simple bomb or two. The United States, although traditionally an ally of Pakistan, permitted this nuclear effort to poison its relations with

---
PAKISTAN · Information Highlights

Official Name: Islamic Republic of Pakistan.
Location: South Asia.
Area 310,403 sq mi (803 943 km²).
Population (1980 est.): 86,500,000.
Chief Cities (1974): Islamabad, the capital, 250,000; Karachi, 3,500,000; Lahore, 2,100,000.
Government: *Head of state and government,* Mohammed Zia ul-Haq, president (took power Sept. 1978). *Legislature*—Parliament: Senate and National Assembly (dissolved July 1977).
Monetary Unit: Rupee (9.90 rupees equal U.S.$1, Aug. 1980).
Manufactures (major products): Textiles, processed foods, tobacco, chemicals, natural gas.
Agriculture (major products): Wheat, cotton, rice.
GNP (1978 est., U.S.$): $18,500,000,000.
Foreign Trade (1979, U.S.$): *Imports,* $4,061,000,000; *exports,* $2,036,000,000.

Pakistan. Late in the year the United States approved the shipment of enriched uranium to India, an act not only contrary to established U.S. policy on nuclear nations but one almost designed to drive Pakistan to fury.

In January 1980 the United States offered Pakistan $400 million in military and economic aid. It was rejected by Zia as "peanuts." Then, in the aftermath of the Soviet Union's invasion of Afghanistan, Pakistan felt the full weight of the Soviet threat. It supported the Afghan "rebels" (those who were fighting the Soviet troops) at great cost to itself. Its own armed forces were too weak to defend against invasion from either India or the Soviet Union. Pakistan remained friendly with China, but the connection was not very valuable. Its relations with its neighbor to the southwest, Iran, suffered from the ambiguity that characterized all Iranian policy in 1980. With the Iraqi-Iranian conflict, General Zia attempted to play the role of Islamic mediator, but was rebuffed. Thus, Pakistan was surrounded by enemies or untrustworthy friends.

In the early spring, relations with the United States thawed a bit. In early February, National Security Adviser Zbigniew Brzezinski visited Pakistan and the Khyber Pass (into Afghanistan). The visit seemingly had little effect. But by the late summer, Zia was urging the United States to take a stronger role in the Indian Ocean and by fall was displaying a greater readiness to accept U.S. aid. By the canons of international politics, both Pakistan and the United States needed each other.

CARL LEIDEN, *University of Texas, Austin*

PARAGUAY

The political environment in Paraguay during 1980 was no different from that which has prevailed since 1954, when Alfredo Stroessner seized control of the government. Under this longest-lived dictator in modern Latin America, a state of siege (semi-martial law), a common but temporary aberration in other Latin American nations, had been the normal political condition. Opposition forces have been, and still were, se-

────── PARAGUAY • Information Highlights ──────

Official Name: Republic of Paraguay.
Location: Central South America.
Area: 157,047 sq mi (406 752 km²).
Population (1980 est.): 3,300,000.
Chief Cities (1978 est.): Asunción, the capital, 463,735; Caaguazú, 72,630; Coronel Oviedo, 66,621.
Government: *Head of state and government,* Gen. Alfredo Stroessner, president (took office Aug. 1954). *Legislature*—Congress: Senate and Chamber of Deputies.
Monetary Unit: Guarani (126 guaranies equal U.S.$1, Aug. 1980).
Manufactures (major products): Processed foods, wood products, consumer goods, cement, hydroelectric power.
Agriculture (major products): Wheat, corn, manioc, sweet potatoes, beans, rice, sugarcane, fruits.
GNP (1978 est., U.S.$): $2,140,000,000.
Foreign Trade (1979, U.S.$): *Imports,* $432,000,000; *exports,* $305,000,000.

verely curtailed. A censored press and other restrictions regarding human rights continued.

On March 28, a group of tenant farmers, members of a nonviolent agrarian cooperative, on their way to Asunción to protest attempts by landlords to drive them from their lands, hijacked a bus and demanded to be taken to the capital. They fled the bus when it was stopped by the police. The next day the government mounted a 5,000-man military search for the men. Amnesty International reported the deaths of 18 and the arrest of 300 more and their detention in a torture center. The peasants had been led by longtime activist Victoriano Centurion, who had been arrested in 1972 and had served three years in jail. He eventually took refuge in the Panamanian Embassy. The government protested to the Panamanian government.

The assassination on September 17 in Asunción of former Nicaraguan President Anastasio Somoza, while embarrassing to the government, gave it an excuse for cracking down on the opposition. By September 30, the police had arrested 200 persons, including a group of businessmen, and had deported 100 Argentine "guerrillas."

Economy. Workers won a 15% increase in wages in January after a series of ani-inflation demonstrations. Paraguay experienced a 10.9% growth in the gross domestic product (GDP), as compared with 6.4% annually during 1971–74. UNC Resources Inc. reached an agreement with the government to explore a 55 million acre (22.2 million ha) region in western Paraguay for uranium and other minerals. The corporation has a five year contract. The government announced plans to build an international airport at Ciudad Presidente Stroessner. Japan would provide a loan of $80 million to cover 70% of the cost.

Brazil was experiencing some financial difficulties in the construction of the huge hydroelectrical complex being built jointly with Paraguay at Itaipu. The Brazilians assumed almost total financial responsibility for the project from the outset. In 1980 Brazil expressed hope that Paraguay would raise money in the Eurocurrency market to help finance the project. Paraguay was reluctant to do so since the government told its people that not only would the project cost Paraguay nothing but it would bring benefits.

LEO B. LOTT, *University of Montana*

PENNSYLVANIA

Voters in traditionally Republican strongholds turned out in relatively large numbers in the November election to give GOP national and state candidates comfortable margins over their Democratic opponents. The Republican swing was spurred by reaction to the Carter administration's economic policies, which were blamed for widespread unemployment in the state's major industries, especially steel. In addition to giving the Reagan-Bush ticket a clear endorsement, the electorate chose a Republican, Philadelphia lawyer Arlen Specter, to succeed the GOP's retiring U.S. senator, Richard Schweiker. The GOP also narrowed the Democrats' edge in the House congressional delegation to one and gained control of both houses of the legislature.

Abscam Indictments and Other Crime. U.S. Rep. Michael J. "Ozzie" Myers, a Philadelphia Democrat, became the first congressman since Civil War days to be expelled from the House, following his conviction on bribery charges in the nation's first Abscam trial. Myers subsequently was defeated in a bid for reelection in November, but Raymond Lederer, a second Philadelphia Democratic congressman awaiting trial under an Abscam indictment, won another term. In a subsequent case, a jury found three Philadelphia city councilmen guilty of accepting Abscam bribes, but on appeal a federal judge overturned the convictions of George Schwartz and Harry Jannotti, ruling that the FBI had overstepped its bounds in setting up an elaborate payoff scheme.

In an unrelated trial, a member of the state senate, a former senate majority leader, and a turnpike commissioner were convicted of placing ghost workers on the legislative payroll.

The ambush slaying of Philadelphia crime boss Angelo Bruno in March touched off gangland murders and the disappearance of several mobsters in a war for control of the Mafia family. The state Crime Commission reported that organized crime figures, using legitimate business as a front, held paving and defense contracts. In October, six persons were charged with rigging the State Lottery's Daily Number Game on April 24 to cash in on heavy bets.

Three Mile Island. Twenty-one months after a reactor malfunctioned at the Three Mile Island generating station south of Harrisburg, most of the problems arising from the nation's worst nuclear power accident remained. The massive cleanup job, expected to take seven years and cost $1,000,000,000, had been confined to venting krypton gas and removing a limited amount of radioactive water from the system. A plethora of hearings and reports by federal and state agencies wrestled with questions related to safety procedures and who would pay for the cleanup.

Meanwhile, the plant's owners filed a $4,000,-000,000 claim against the Nuclear Regulatory Commission, charging that agency negligence was largely responsible for the accident. The operators also sought permission to reactivate the plant's other nuclear generating unit, which was not involved in the accident. Antinuclear groups generally were opposed. The company estimated the total cost of the 1979 mishap at more than $3,100,000,000. In addition, thousands of legal claims against the utility and its insurers were pending in court.

Cuban Refugees. Fort Indiantown Gap, near Harrisburg, was pressed into service as a processing center for 19,000 Cuban refugees. Although 88% were resettled with sponsors during a five-month period, the program was plagued by unrest among the refugees and incidents that alienated residents of the surrounding area. On August 5, rioting erupted inside the camp, resulting in one death and more than 60 injuries. In October, the remaining 2,000 inhabitants were airlifted to Fort Chaffee, AR.

The Economy and Business. By midsummer the recession drove the unemployment rate in chronically depressed areas to double-digit figures. The steel and apparel industries, hard-hit by foreign competition, unsuccessfully pressed for import controls. By December, the employment picture had brightened in most areas. The Pennsylvania-based Bethlehem Steel Corp. was fined $325,000 in August after pleading guilty to a million-dollar bribery scheme designed to generate business for its ship-repair yards.

Weather. A severe summer drought in the eastern part of the state extended into winter, prompting Gov. Richard L. Thornburgh to authorize water rationing in 50 counties. Agriculture suffered considerable economic loss. Paradoxically, flash floods in the western section in August claimed seven lives and caused property damage in excess of $50 million.

Historic Sites. The farm home of the late President Dwight D. Eisenhower near Gettysburg was opened to the public in June as a national historic site.

RICHARD ELGIN, *State Desk*
"The Patriot, The Evening News, and The Sunday Patriot-News," Harrisburg

---

PENNSYLVANIA • Information Highlights

Area: 45,333 sq mi (177 412 km²).

Population (Jan. 1980 est.): 11,723,000.

Chief Cities (1970 census): Harrisburg, the capital, 63,-061; (1976 est.): Philadelphia, 1,797,403; Pittsburgh, 449,092.

Government (1980): *Chief Officers*—governor, Richard L. Thornburgh (R); lt. gov., William W. Scranton, III (R). *General Assembly*—Senate, 50 members; House of Representatives, 203 members.

Education (1979–80): *Enrollment*—public elementary schools, 930,658 pupils; public secondary, 1,038,-143; colleges and universities, 481,347 students. *Public school expenditures,* $5,288,939,000 ($2,351 per pupil).

State Finances (fiscal year 1979): *Revenues,* $12,757,-000,000; *expenditures,* $11,575,000,000.

Personal Income (1979): $100,398,000,000; per capita, $8,558.

Labor Force (May 1980): *Nonagricultural wage and salary earners,* 4,830,500; unemployed, 381,800 (7.2% of total force).

PERU

The major political event of 1980 was a return to elected civilian rule with the inauguration on July 28 of Fernando Belaúnde Terry as Peru's 85th president.

Belaúnde Inaugurated. Ousted by the military in October 1968, Belaúnde Terry surprised many observers by winning 43.6% of 4,064,292 valid votes in May 18 elections. Armando Villanueva del Campo of the American Popular Revolutionary Alliance (APRA) received 26.6%, Luis

Francisco Morales Bermúdez, president of Peru's military junta, congratulates Belaúnde Terry, winner of the May presidential elections.

UPI

Bedoya Reyes of the Popular Christian Party received 11.2%, while twelve leftists received only 18% of the votes. Belaúnde's Popular Action Party won 100 of 180 seats in the Chamber of Deputies and 26 of 60 Senate seats, compared with APRA's 17 senators and 50 deputies.

A new cabinet, headed by Manuel Ulloa Elias, a prominent businessman, was composed of 13 civilians and three retired military officers. Among its first actions, the new government freed all political prisoners, rehired thousands of public school teachers fired during a four-month-long 1979 strike, ended press censorship, and returned newspapers and radio and television stations to their former owners. Although the Popular Action Party was supported in November municipal elections, leftists won control of six provinces.

Foreign Policy. Belaúnde Terry asked Argentina's President Jorge Rafael Videla not to attend the inauguration ceremonies at which four heads of state and Rosalynn Carter were present, because of the June 16 kidnapping of five Argentines in Lima by Argentine agents aided by Peruvian military officers. Peru joined Colombia, Ecuador, and Venezuela in denouncing the military coup ousting Bolivia's President Lydia Gueiler Tejada.

Diplomatic relations with Cuba were strained when more than 10,000 Cubans camped within the Peruvian Embassy compound in Havana in early April. (*See also* REFUGEES.)

Before the military left office, Peru acquired two squadrons of Soviet Sukhol-22 swept-wing fighter bombers as part of a buildup related to ongoing political tensions with Chile. President Francisco Morales Bermúdez asserted May 26 that he favored uniting with Bolivia in ceremonies marking the 100th anniversary of a battle in the 1879–1880 War of the Pacific.

Economic Matters. Potatoes, rice, cotton, grain, and sugar crops suffered $400 million losses in the worst drought in 70 years. Peru was forced to import sugar for the first time ever.

New contracts were signed by PETRO-PERU, the state oil monopoly, with Occidental Petroleum and Belco Petroleum of the United States on April 30. The agreements assured Peru 84% of the oil produced on concessions in the Amazon and Northern Coast. Peru expected to earn $1,200,000,000 in 1980, compared with 1979 earnings of $900 million. Continued high prices for copper and silver were expected to provide $1,500,000,000 in foreign exchange in 1980.

Mining and Energy Minister Pedro Pablo Kuczynski announced in September that oil reserves were expected to last only three more years, necessitating additional exploration and probable import by 1984. At that time the country would owe an estimated $1,500,000,000 in annual foreign debt payments.

The Peruvian sol continued to decline in value. Inflation dropped to an estimated 50%, compared with 66.7% in 1979 and 73.8% in 1978. While the Morales Bermúdez government raised minimum wages in January to $72 a month from the previous $60 a month, it was estimated that Peruvian workers earned only 64% of 1973 real income. Strikes and demonstrations occurred in January and September when the prices of bus rides, electricity, gasoline, and several basic foodstuffs were increased.

NEALE J. PEARSON, *Texas Tech University*

―――――――― **PERU · Information Highlights** ――――――――

Official Name: Republic of Peru.
Location: West coast of South America.
Area: 496,223 sq mi (1 285 216 km²).
Population (1980 est.): 17,600,000.
Chief City (1972 census): Lima, the capital, 3,350,000 (met. area).
Government: *Head of state,* Fernando Belaúnde Terry, president (took office July 1980). *Head of government,* Manuel Ulloa, prime minister (took office July 1980). *Legislature*—Congress: Senate and Chamber of Deputies.
Monetary Unit: Sol (317.12 soles equal U.S.$1, Nov. 1980).
Manufactures (major products): Mineral and petroleum products, fish meal, textiles.
Agriculture (major products): Cotton, sugar, coffee.
GNP (1978 est., U.S.$): $12,400,000,000.
Foreign Trade (1979, U.S.$): *Imports,* $2,022,000,000; *exports,* $3,533,000,000.

PHILIPPINES

A new kind of violence erupted in the Philippines in the latter half of 1980. It threatened President Ferdinand E. Marcos' eight-year-old rule by martial law and the Filipino leader's promised end to authoritarian government.

Politics. The first local elections in nine years were held in January. President Marcos' "New Society Movement" party gave its limited opposition only 30 days' notice of the voting. The Marcos party emerged victorious in balloting for 73 governors, 1,500 mayors, and local councils. Most of the government's opponents boycotted the elections, which were accompanied by widespread charges of fraud.

President Marcos, who spoke publicly of ending martial law in 1981 if the country's Muslim rebellion could be contained and economic conditions improved, allowed his chief rival, 47-year-old former Sen. Benigno Aquino, Jr., to go to the United States for heart surgery. Aquino, jailed after Marcos established martial law in 1972, had been under detention for seven years and eight months. Aquino, however, did not return to the Philippines after his operation. Remaining in the United States, he not only spoke out against the Marcos regime but also warned, on August 4, of a coming wave of urban terrorism.

The first of the predicted political bombings occurred August 22, and four such incidents took place in the following two months. The Manila press called the September 12 bombings of seven government and business offices, in which an American woman was killed, the "worst terrorist strike" in the eight years of martial law. On October 19 the annual convention of the American Society of Travel Agents, which had gathered 3,500 delegates in Manila, was bombed immediately following an address by President Marcos. Bombings also occurred in Manila on October 4 and 11. The Philippine leader accused Senator Aquino of masterminding the bombings, for which a body calling itself the "April 6 Liberation Movement" claimed credit. The government detained former Sen. Jovito Salonga and

promised to arrest 29 other Marcos foes—most of them in exile in the United States.

The bombings were not the only expressions of growing opposition to the Marcos government. Leaders of the "Light a Fire Movement," which practiced anti-Marcos political arson, went on trial before a military tribunal in June. In July, 10,000 students staged the biggest youth demonstration against the Marcos regime in the eight years of martial law, protesting stricter political control of universities. Former Sen. Eva Estrada Kalaw and several retired military officers were charged in midyear with plotting a coup. And, in late August, eight moderate opposition parties signed a "national covenant for freedom"—calling for the "immediate and absolute termination" of the "Marcos dictatorship."

Rebellions. The eight-year Muslim insurrection continued in central Mindanao and Sulu in the southern Philippines. Some 50,000 persons have been killed or wounded and hundreds of thousands have been uprooted from their homes in the internal war. Rebel strength was estimated at 10,000 fighting men.

Maoist "New People's Army" insurrectionists in central Luzon numbered from 3,000 to 5,000 armed men. The Communist rebellion, which fed primarily on agrarian dissatisfaction, also existed in more limited form on Samar and Mindanao.

Economy. Economic progress continued despite the two insurrections and the new threat of urban terrorism. The gross national product (GNP) increased 6%, and the Philippines exported 300 000 t (330,000 T) of rice (worth $100 million). Sugar prices rose impressively. And tax revenues (40,000,000,000 pesos) were eight times what they were in 1972, when martial law was proclaimed.

At the same time, however, the annual inflation rate was 20%. International prices dropped for such key Filipino exports as bananas and coconut oil. Unemployment—and, no less important, underemployment—grew. Some 600,000 new workers joined the labor market in 1980—a faster rate apparently than the Philippines economy could absorb. The external debt rose to a new high of $11,000,000,000. The birthrate—4.5% a year in 1972—dropped to 3.4%.

Foreign Relations. President Marcos traveled to Hawaii, his first visit to the United States in 16 years. Although Marcos' foes accused the Carter administration of helping to keep him in power, the Philippine president increasingly criticized the United States for permitting his opponents to use its soil to plot against his government.

Libya continued its financial and other support of the Muslim rebellion in Mindanao and Sulu, but the willingness of the Conference of Islamic States to mediate differences between the government and the Moro National Liberation Front stimulated renewed hope for a settlement of the eight-year conflict.

RICHARD BUTWELL, *Murray State University*

—————— **PHILIPPINES** • Information Highlights ——————

Official Name: Republic of the Philippines.
Location: Southeast Asia.
Area: 115,830 sq mi (300 000 km²).
Population (1980 est.): 47,700,000.
Chief Cities (May 1975): Manila, the capital, 1,479,116; Quezon City, 956,864; Cebu, 413,025.
Government: *Head of state and government,* Ferdinand E. Marcos, president and prime minister. *Legislature* (unicameral)—National Assembly.
Monetary Unit: Peso (7.56 pesos equal U.S.$1, Nov. 1980).
Manufactures (major products): Processed foods, tobacco, beverages, rubber products, cement, glass, textiles.
Agriculture (major products): Rice, corn, sugar, copra, coconut oil.
GNP (1979 est., U.S.$): $29,060,000,000.
Foreign Trade (1979, U.S.$): *Imports,* $6,142,000,000; *exports,* $4,601,000,000.

PHOTOGRAPHY

Despite wildly fluctuating silver prices, confusing changes in international monetary rates, rampant inflation, and a recession, photography flourished in the United States in 1980. Photographers snapped more than 10,000,000,000 pictures, according to Eastman Kodak, which celebrated its 100th anniversary, and the retail value of the photographic consumer markets hovered at around $7,000,000,000.

The medium that had fought for and acquired full-fledged art-form status by the end of the previous decade was now undisputedly accepted as such in major museums and by important collectors. The electronics revolution that had automated a different part of the camera during each year of the late 1970s had stabilized into a steady evolution by the onset of the 1980s. No major breakthrough occurred in hardware technology in 1980. The revolutionary activity switched to the software arena, where the introduction of a black-and-white "silverless" film was the year's major technological story.

Hardware. The professional photographers who might have felt neglected during the recent boom of automatic, compact, lightweight 35mm single-lens reflex cameras directed at the amateur market now had several such cameras worth their attention: Nikon's F3, 20% lighter and smaller than its predecessor, with full-exposure automation, interchangeable screens and viewfinders, and liquid crystal display of exposure data; Pentax's first systems camera ever, the LX; and the Contax 137-MD Quartz SLR from Yashica, with a built-in motor winder, flash metering at the film plane, and the first use of quartz timing for more accurate exposures. Fuji's new Auto-5 gave clues to the future with a film cartridge that automatically sets the film speed; it also features automatic film advance and auto rewind of the film back into the cartridge.

Among new 110-format "pocket-size" cameras were Tasco's Bino/Cam 8000, the world's first camera and binocular, featuring three interchangeable lenses that together give it a greater reach than most 110s; and Minolta's Weathermatic A, the world's first underwater 110.

At the annual Photographic Manufacturers Association trade show, held for the first time in Las Vegas instead of Chicago, interchangeable lenses for 35mm SLRs, as well as new brand names, including Kiron, Tosner, and Rokina, proliferated. Many independent companies had decided to make their own lines while continuing to supply lenses under existing brand names, resulting in apparently identical lenses under several labels.

While the telephoto zoom lens remained most popular, the wide-angle zoom was coming up fast. Light weight, compactness, and fast speed continued to be prominent characteristics, with shorter focal-length zooms—mostly from 35mm to 70mm and 70mm to 150mm—especially popular.

Independent flash makers also were attempting to expand their business by signing with camera companies to make "dedicated" units (which are electronically synchronized with camera exposure), or by sidestepping patents held by the companies. A few independents did show entries, including Berkey, marketing three Sunpak units with interchangeable feet to allow for the differing locations of hot shoe contacts on popular cameras from Canon, Nikon, Minolta, and Olympus. Also on the flash scene was a proliferation of two-headed units with fill light plus bounce capability.

In movie cameras, the major development was Sony's working model (not expected to be marketed until 1985) of a video movie unit, a complete self-contained color video camera and recorder that uses a single-chip, charge-coupled device (CCD) as image sensor, and a 20-minute micro cassette. And Canon introduced its AF514XL-S sound camera that makes use of a totally new kind of auto-focusing system called Solid State Triangulation (SST).

Software. With the price of silver fluctuating between $5 and $50 an ounce in 1980 and silver recovery an increasingly common darkroom procedure, the introduction by Ilford and Agfa of a black-and-white "silverless" film, based on the principles of color technology, was timely. The film uses silver, but what is used is released during processing and can be recycled. Known as XP1 400, the ASA 400 film and related chemistry, which was launched at photokina, became available in 35mm 36-exposure size in West Germany and was expected to be available in the United States and Canada in 1981. Unlike the conventional black-and-white emulsion, the image of the new film consists of varying densities of translucent dye formed during development by a dye-coupling action; conventional film forms its image by varying densities of developed silver grains.

Ilford, celebrating its founding in England in 1879, also introduced a conventional black-and-white film with 72 exposures (twice the normal), called HP5 Autowinder Film, that reflects the unswerving popularity of motor drives and winders. In color emulsions, Fujichrome 400 is a new color slide film that gives Kodak competition in the daylight-balance, high-speed arena.

In instant films, Polaroid brought out Polacolor 3, its newest peel-apart variety with greatly improved color fidelity and saturation, and began to market its Time-Zero Supercolor SX-70 Film, which develops virtually as it leaves the camera, with a full image in 30 seconds and full development in 1 minute.

Exhibitions. A *New York Times* headline, "The Trend Is a Backward Look," summarized the continuing retrospective nature of exhibitions in New York. "Photography of the Fifties:

International Center of Photography

Lisette Model's "Larry's Bar" (left) and William Klein's "Gun 1" were shown at "Photography of the Fifties: An American Perspective." The exhibit was to travel throughout the United States.

an American Perspective," curated by Helen Gee in conjunction with the Center for Creative Photography, opened at the International Center of Photography; at the Metropolitan Museum of Art, "Masters of 19th Century Photography from the Bibliothèque Nationale" comprised 200 daguerreotypes and prints from the 1840s to 1880s; and "Before Photography" was the Museum of Modern Art's (MoMA's) first attempt to integrate photography into the larger history of painting. The Smithsonian's National Museum of History and Technology organized a show called "Western Views and Eastern Visions." Scheduled to travel to small and mid-size museums, it demonstrates the role of photography in winning the West.

Large one-person retrospectives were held in New York, including widely differing styles of street photography by Helen Levitt and William Klein. Also exhibited were works by Jerry Uelsmann, America's best known photographic surrealist, and 76 prints of "Earthly Bodies," nudes photographed in the 1950s by fashion photographer Irving Penn.

The trend continued to hold an exhibition in conjunction with the release of a book from an independent publisher. Master black-and-white photographer Harry Callahan had two books released along with two simultaneous exhibits, both containing many previously unexhibited color selections.

Nine young photograhers using both color to convey concepts and states of mind, and the nightflash photography so popular in the Bay Area, participated in "Beyond Color" at the San Francisco Museum of Art.

Books and Periodicals. While Britain's long-time photographic book publisher, Focal Press, disbanded in 1980, general U.S. publishers brought out long essays in book form, including Janet Beller's *Street People* from Macmillan and Ellen Land-Weber's *The Passionate Collector* from Simon & Schuster. Joel Meyerowitz rhapsodized in colored light and shadow on *St. Louis & the Arch* from the New York Graphic Society.

Among periodicals, Ziff-Davis brought out a new magazine, *Camera Arts,* which is clear confirmation that photography-as-art has arrived, and a new journal, *Image Plane,* devoted to the holographic art, was in the works.

Other. Polaroid founder and head Dr. Edwin Land retired at age 70, becoming consulting director of basic research. Stagnating sales in instant photography in the consumer market led Polaroid to expand into scientific, technical, and commercial applications. And other photographic companies continued to develop their office photocopier lines. In the spring, Canon was reported to have 47% of its business in cameras and 44% in office machines.

Ben Rose died on June 8 at age 64. Noted for his work in stroboscopic lighting, multiple imaging, motion studies, and computer applications, he was an innovator in the use of modern technology prior to photography's dawning age of electronics.

BARBARA LOBRON
Free-lance Writer and Photographer

PHYSICS

Exciting new results were obtained in the physics of neutrinos; there was rapid growth in microscience and technology; and significant developments occurred in controlled fusion.

Neutrinos. New experiments questioned basic assumptions concerning neutrinos. Enrico Fermi formulated a theory of electron decay in 1934, which involved a new particle called the neutrino (small neutral particle). The neutrino was assumed to have zero rest mass, to travel always at the speed of light, and to interact extremely weakly with matter. The neutrino (the electron neutrino) was first observed by the American physicists Frederick Reines and George Cowan in 1956. Subsequently another type of neutrino, the muon neutrino, which is associated with the decay of muons, was discovered. After the discovery of the tau particle, the existence of a corresponding tau neutrino was assumed. There are three members of the lepton family (electron, muon, and tau), three corresponding neutrinos, and an antineutrino for each type (flavor) of neutrino.

In 1980 an experiment at Savannah River, SC, by Reines and collaborators suggested that the assumptions that neutrinos were massless particles with separate identities were wrong. A detector full of heavy water was placed near a reactor. The electron antineutrinos from the reactor struck the deuterium nuclei of the heavy water and led to reactions which produced either two neutrons and a positron or one neutrino, one proton, and an antineutrino. Physicists call these reactions charged current and neutral current processes. Reines eliminated many experimental uncertainties by measuring the ratio of the rate for the charged and neutral current reactions and comparing this ratio to the theoretical ratio. The result was 0.43 instead of the expected value of one. One possible explanation for the finding is that the neutrinos do not maintain fixed identities but instead oscillate between electron and muon neutrinos. If neutrinos have a rest mass, then a significant fraction of the mass of the universe, possibly enough to slow down the expansion of the universe, could go undetected. These results might also explain the so-called solar neutrino problem, the fact that the measured solar neutrino flux is much less than predicted.

Particle Physics. Elementary particles called hadrons (protons, neutrons, mu mesons) are thought to consist of subparticles called quarks. Initially there were thought to be three quarks, but in 1974 a fourth (charmed) quark was found necessary, and in 1978 a fifth (bottom) quark was added. A sixth (top) quark is now expected. Quarks have remarkable properties, including fractional electric charge. Further, the strength of the interaction between quarks is almost zero when they are very close together but is very strong when the quarks are separated. Thus, quarks can never be directly observed.

The general theory is called quantum chromodynamics (QCD), analogous with quantum electrodynamics (QED). Just as there is a quantum of electromagnetism (the photon), there should be a quantum of the strong interaction. Since this quantum can be considered the "glue" that holds quarks together, it is called the gluon. Gluons also cannot be observed directly. In the collision of high energy electrons and positrons (antielectrons), quarks and antiquarks are created and move in opposite directions. Other pairs of quarks and antiquarks are created along the path, and some decay to form observable particles. Since all of these particles tend to move in the original directions, the tracks appear close together. Two streams or jets of particles are expected; another jet would indicate existence of the gluon. Three-jet events have been observed at PETRA, a particle accelerator of the storage ring design at Hamburg, West Germany.

Microscience. A new field, microscience, serves as the basis for microelectronics technology. As electronic devices have shrunk dramatically in size, so have costs. This development has provided the impetus for astonishing growth in both quantity and quality of applications. Further size reduction is in the offing, but as the scale shrinks, so does the scientific basis. The result is the rapid growth of the new, interdisciplinary field called microscience.

The developments rest on small circuits. A wafer of silicon is cut from a single crystal, oxidized, and then coated with a photosensitive material. The pattern of a circuit is formed by some beam in this top layer (the resist), and the exposed area is now soluble to a solvent. After etching away the oxide, the circuit remains on the chip. As the size shrinks, and the complexity grows, various advantages appear. The smaller devices work much faster, use less power and less material, can perform more complicated functions, and still cost less. Although the applications have snowballed, the limits of ordinary or ultraviolet light eventually will be reached. The next step is X-ray printing or lithography, perhaps using synchrotron radiation from a high-energy storage ring. Particles (electrons or ion beams) can also be used. The real question, for the era of very large-scale integration, with millions of connections on a chip, is whether the technology will still have a firm scientific basis. The recent increase in microscience research is a response to that concern.

Controlled Thermonuclear Fusion. Fusion remains an appealing long-term solution to the energy problem—unlimited fuel, few radioactive wastes, no nuclear proliferation. The root problem is the exceptionally high temperature required to initiate fusion (10 to 100 million degrees Kelvin). Reaching these high temperatures and obtaining a high enough density in the plasma for a sufficiently long time remained key problems. By late 1980 they had been solved separately, but not simultaneously. The two basic approaches are magnetic confinement and inertial confinement (implosion).

The more popular approach is magnetic confinement with a toroidal (doughnut) shaped magnet system. A large torus at Princeton, NJ, has achieved plasma conditions close to those needed for a fusion reaction. An alternative design, a straight magnet with magnetic mirrors at the ends, has proven quite promising at Lawrence Laboratory, Livermore (CA). The alternate approach of inertial confinement involves an implosion technique. One method uses a collection of high-powered, well-focused laser beams. Other similar schemes utilize ion beams. A particle beam fusion accelerator is under construction at Sandia Laboratories (NM). The U.S. Department of Energy has established a new U.S. Institute for Fusion Studies at the University of Texas at Austin. The institute is to serve as a center for magnetic fusion studies. Physicists agree that practical fusion reactors are at least a generation or two in the future.

GARY MITCHELL
North Carolina State University

POLAND

Major political and economic upheaval in Poland during 1980 culminated in the replacement of top party and government leaders and the initiation of far-reaching institutional reforms. Massive strikes by Polish workers beginning in July led to the ouster of Premier Edward Babiuch on August 24 and of the First Secretary of the Polish United Workers Party (PZPR), Edward Gierek, on September 6. They also forced the government to agree to a system of independent trade unions with the right to strike. The concession was without precedent among Communist block countries.

Labor Unrest. The crisis began when Premier Babiuch announced on July 1 that the government would end its subsidy of meat prices, estimated at about $3,300,000,000 annually. Having incurred a foreign debt of more than $20,000,000,000, the regime was hard-pressed just to pay the interest, let alone repay the capital. The financial plight appeared to be brought about by a combination of circumstances, including an over-ambitious and ineffective industrialization program, several poor harvests, increased world prices for fuel, and a drop in demand for Polish exports in the wake of an economic recession in the West. The immediate consequence of ending the meat subsidy was to increase the cost to consumers by 40 to 60%. As in December 1970, when the regime of party leader Wladyslaw Gomulka attempted to economize by raising food prices, a wave of strikes and labor unrest swept the country. In the course of the summer, work stoppages spread to all parts of Poland and virtually every major industrial center, including Warsaw. By mid-August, at least 800,000 workers and miners were on strike, and the nation's industry was close to being fully shut down. At least 150 separate industrial locations were affected by work stoppages.

The strike activity was centered in the northern seaports of Gdansk, Gdynia, Szczecin, and Elblag. At the Lenin shipyards in Gdansk, the workers elected a strike committee led by 37-year-old electrician Lech Walesa. (*See* BIOGRAPHY.) During the month of August, Walesa and his committee emerged as the spokesmen for the nationwide strike movement.

Unlike 1956 and 1970, the government's response to the strikes was cautious. At first, government spokesmen urged workers to return to their jobs; warned against the economic consequences of the strike; vaguely promised to undo the errors of the past; hinted at possible Soviet intervention if the bases of the "socialist system" in Poland were threatened; and attempted to justify the price increases on grounds of dire economic necessity. Punitive action was taken against members of dissident organizations, such

Marc Bulka, Liaison

Deputy Premier Mieczyslaw Jagielski (center, facing camera) led a Polish government commission in discussions with an inter-company strike committee in Gdansk. The late August talks resulted in major gains for the workers, including the right to form independent unions and the right to strike.

as the Committee of Social Self-Defense, the Committee for the Defense of Human Rights, and the Confederation of Independent Poland. A number of dissidents, including Jacek Kuron, Adam Michnik, Jan Litynski, Seweryn Blumsztajn, and Leszek Moczulski, were arrested for allegedly inciting and abetting the labor unrest. But when all its appeals and threats proved fruitless, the government agreed to negotiate with the strikers. It sought first to negotiate separately with representatives of each plant and thus divide the strike movement, but the offer was rebuffed. Essentially nationwide negotiations were begun in August at the Gdansk shipyard.

The strikers presented the regime with a list of 21 demands, including the right to establish unions independent of the government's Central Council of Trade Unions; the right to strike; the abatement of censorship; increased rights for the Catholic Church (such as the right to broadcast Sunday Mass over the state radio network); the release of all arrested dissidents; substantial wage increases to offset the government's price hikes; and a variety of other industrial and labor reforms.

On August 31, the government capitulated and agreed to most of the demands. It did not give in to the demand for an immediate across-the-board wage increase equivalent to about $65 per month, but it did agree to wage increases, especially for the lowest-paid workers, as soon as financially feasible. It also consented to a price freeze on many foods and other consumer necessities. But even after the agreement, strikes were

Stanislaw Kania replaced an ailing Edward Gierek as first secretary of the Communist party.

UPI

held throughout Poland for about two weeks. A variety of grievances were cited. Working conditions in Silesia, for example, where 62 miners had died in accidents in 1979, figured in the demands of thousands of strikers.

Soviet Reaction. As in the crises of 1956 and 1970, there was concern in Poland and the West about possible Soviet military intervention to crush the strikes and thwart any reforms. The unease was further heightened by official Soviet statements alleging foreign intervention and antisocialist activities in Poland. The statements were reminiscent of those issued from Moscow before the invasion of Czechoslovakia in 1968. There were also reports of Warsaw Pact military maneuvers in East Germany within 60 miles (96 km) of the Polish frontier and Soviet troop concentrations in other nearby areas. Even after the Gdansk settlement, the Soviet press continued to attack Polish dissidents and charge that foreign interference and antisocialist agitation were responsible for the strikes. The Soviet attitude led to speculation about a possible rollback of some of the concessions made to the workers.

Changes in Leadership. The strike wave brought the most substantial personnel changes in the Polish ruling elite since the advent of Wladyslaw Gomulka in 1956 and Edward Gierek in 1970. The principal change came on September 6 with the ouster of 67-year-old PZPR First Secretary Edward Gierek—who was said to have suffered a heart attack. Gierek's leadership had been compromised not only by the crippling wave of strikes but also by a personal scandal. Shortly before Gierek's ouster, it was officially revealed that his old friend and protégé, Maciej Szczepanski, head of the Polish radio-television network, had misappropriated large sums of money to provide lavish entertainment and luxurious accommodations for various bureaucrats and cronies. Gierek was replaced by 53-year-old Stanislaw Kania. The new party leader had been a relatively obscure member of the Politburo since 1975. His previous responsibilities included the supervision of the police and military-security apparatus. Since 1971 he had also served as a secretary of the party's Central Committee. In a series of meetings with workers and a televised speech to the nation, Kania promised to honor the agreements concluded with the strikers and to overhaul the country's economy. He also reaffirmed Poland's ties to the Soviet Union and pledged to oppose antisocialist elements in Poland. Appearing before the party's Central Committee on September 6, Kania said that the strikes had been "a protest not against the principles of socialism but against the mistakes of the party."

Among other leaders who were purged as a result of the strikes were Premier Edward Babiuch; Deputy Premier Tadeusz Pyka, an early negotiator at Gdansk; Jan Szydlak, a Politburo member and head of the discredited state trade unions; Jerzy Lukaszewicz, party propagandist and ideologist; and three officials closely associated with the regime's disastrous economic policies—Eugeniusz Grochal, chairman of the state price committee, Tadeusz Wrzaszczyk, director of planning, and Stanislaw Kuzinski, head of the economic statistical office.

Among the more significant promotions in the party-state apparatus was the elevation of Josef Pinkowski, 51, to the premiership. An economist who had joined the party's Politburo only in February, Pinkowski's highest previous post had been chief inspector of the Grain Control Commission. On November 21, Jerzy Ozdowski, a Catholic political leader, was appointed one of six deputy premiers, an unprecedented broadening of the government to persons outside the ruling party or its official adjuncts. In meetings in Warsaw, December 1-2, the party's Central Committee made further personnel changes. One of these was the elevation of former Interior Minister Mieczyslaw Moczar, who had been purged by the Gierek regime, to full Politburo status. On the whole, the new party appointments favored the liberal and moderate segments of the party organization.

Other Consequences. In early September, Deputy Premier Henryk Kisiel promised economic reforms to avert a repetition of the 1980 disaster. The main principle of the reforms was decentralization, with more authority being delegated to local officials in such fields as retail trade, housing, services, and transportation. A 20-member commission was said to be formulating concrete changes. This time, the regime indicated, it would meet its austerity needs by reducing government spending, not by cutting off the people's food subsidies. The government also promised to increase its investment in health and housing; increase paid maternity leaves; assure freedom of expression and religion; and give workers employment and promotion opportunities without regard to party membership.

On September 17, some 300 representatives of regional and local worker committees met in Gdansk to establish a united free labor confederation under the name "Solidarity." The delegates adopted a resolution criticizing the government for obstructing the foundation of the union movement and spreading false information about it. Throughout September, Lech Walesa and other labor activists attempted to organize the new unions and comply with government requirements for their registration.

On October 3, the union federation called a one-hour general strike, alleging that the government was not meeting its Gdansk commitments in three respects: by failing to grant adequate wage increases; by failing to give the federation access to the media; and by interfering with the work of independent union organizers. The government responded by accusing the federation of bad faith.

A Warsaw district court officially registered the organization on October 24 but inserted a clause subjecting the 10 million-member "Solidarity" to the control of the party. The trade union federation condemned the decision and threatened another major strike. On October 30, Polish party leaders traveled to Moscow for consultations with the Soviets. On November 10, the Polish Supreme Court reversed the lower court decision, thus averting a general strike and a major confrontation between the regime and the unions. Later in November, the government was threatened by a strike when Jan Narozniak, a Solidarity volunteer, was arrested in Warsaw. The threat was relieved by Narozniak's release.

In late December, the government announced that 1981 would see the first deficit budget since the Communist regime had been established. Rationing of meat and butter would continue for at least the first three months of 1981. Meanwhile, the independent Farmers Union, representing millions of private farm owners, sought legal representation similar to that of Solidarity. The farmers threatened a nationwide strike in case of official refusal. On December 29, the Polish Supreme Court postponed its decision. Uncertainty with respect to internal political and economic development as well as the possibility of armed Soviet intervention continued at year's end.

Church and State. Church-state relations, always strained, were further complicated by the labor unrest. The Catholic Church was sympathetic to the grievances and goals of the strikers but exhibited caution. On August 14, at the height of the crisis, Cardinal Wyszynski, the primate of Poland, addressed 150,000 religious pilgrims in Czestochowa on the anniversary of Poland's 60th victory over the Soviet Union. He reminded his listeners of the heroism that Poles had displayed when "freedom was endangered." Within two weeks, however, the cardinal was calling for restraint and realism. His latter remarks were widely interpreted as a call for a halt to the strike and were aired on state television. Nevertheless, the primate celebrated a private Mass for Lech Walesa and his associates on September 7. On Sunday, September 21, the Church

---

POLAND • Information Highlights

Official Name: Polish People's Republic.
Location: Eastern Europe.
Area: 120,727 sq mi (312 683 km²).
Population (1980 est.): 35,500,000.
Chief Cities (Dec. 1980): Warsaw, the capital, 1,552,-300; Łodz, 825,200; Cracow, 693,200.
Government: *Head of state,* Henryk Jabłonski, president of the Council of State (took office 1972). *Head of government,* Josef Pinkowski, chairman of the Council of Ministers (Aug. 1980). *First secretary of the United Polish Workers' Party,* Stanislaw Kania (Sept. 1980). *Legislature* (unicameral)—Sejm.
Monetary Unit: Złozoty (33.20 złotys equal U.S.$1, 1980).
Manufactures (major products): Iron and steel, chemicals, textiles, processed foods, ships, transport equipment.
Agriculture (major products): Grains, sugar beets, potatoes, hogs, livestock.
GNP (1979 est., U.S.$): $146,100,000,000.
Foreign Trade (Jan.-June 1980, U.S.$): *Imports,* $8,547,-000,000; *exports,* $8,645,000,000.

enjoyed probably its greatest benefit of the strikers' victory: the first Mass ever broadcast nationwide on Polish state radio.

On December 20, a 130-ft (40-m) monument, topped by three crosses, was unveiled in Gdansk to commemorate the killing of workers by government troops in 1970. Lech Walesa and leaders of both the church and government participated in the commemorative ceremonies. Peace, internal harmony, and reconciliation were prominent themes in their speeches. Pope John Paul II sent a message of remembrance of the 1970 unrest.

Foreign Affairs. Several Eastern European countries—including Rumania, Czechoslovakia, and East Germany—expressed apprehension over the Polish developments. East Germany curtailed tourist travel to and from Poland. Given its critical economic situation, Poland sought financial assistance from abroad. On September 12, the U.S. Department of Agriculture extended $670 million in new credits for the purchase of agricultural commodities. West Germany extended nearly $700 million in additional credits and the Soviets $1,300,000,000. East Germany, Czechoslovakia, Hungary, Bulgaria, and Rumania all accelerated their food shipments to Poland.

At a summit meeting in Moscow on December 5, the Warsaw Pact declared that the Polish Communist Party and the Polish people "can firmly count on the fraternal solidarity and support of all pact members." On December 7, U.S. officials reported that Soviet preparations for an invasion of Poland had been completed. Concern over a possible invasion led to a NATO meeting in Brussels on December 11, and grave Western warnings were sent to the Soviets. In a statement from Moscow on December 26, Soviet President Leonid Brezhnev and visiting Polish Foreign Minister Czyrek agreed to let Poles solve Polish problems but also denounced "imperialist subversion" in the country.

ALEXANDER J. GROTH
University of California, Davis

POLAR RESEARCH

Antarctic. During the 1979–1980 season, more than 300 investigators traveled to Antarctica to conduct 80 science projects.

A major geological and glacial study was conducted in the Ellsworth Mountains of the Antarctic from December 1979 through January 1980. Forty-two scientists from eight countries, the largest field party ever to investigate this region, used motorized toboggans, helicopters, and airborne remote sensing instruments to supplement investigations conducted on foot. Geologists made new studies of fossil animals and landforms to increase understanding of the evolutionary, environmental, and geological changes that the continent has undergone. Their findings suggested that an uplift of the area occurred about 160 million years ago. Based on analyses of soil development and rock weathering, they also concluded that most of the southern peaks were probably covered with an ice sheet about 18,000 years ago.

Because the Ellsworth Mountains act as a barrier between the interior ice sheet and the coast, glacial geologists were able to investigate and map two aspects of glacial development—erosion and deposition. Alpine glaciation, produced by local glaciers moving down the sides of mountains, formed the first phase of the region's glacial history. During the second phase, the mountains were partially submerged by a westward-moving ice sheet. From the data acquired in this study, scientists obtained a greater understanding of global climate changes.

At the South Pole, U.S. and Swedish scientists used a 30-cm (12-inch) heliostat in combination with a 20-cm (8-inch) lens to make solar observations. Their work confirmed the existence of solar global oscillations (pulsations of the surface of the sun) with 5-minute periods. Preliminary analysis also suggested the possibility of oscillations with 160-minute periods. The 5-minute oscillations are attributed to activity in the sun's outer layers, while the 160-minute oscillations may come from deep within. Their findings upset the previously accepted theory that the sun is composed of defined layers.

Oceanographers collected current meters from the Weddell Sea and completed analyses of temperature and salinity data accumulated during the International Weddell Sea Oceanographic Expedition. They also measured ice thickness in various locations to determine its effect on heat and other exchanges between the air and sea. Off the South Georgia Islands in the southwest Atlantic Ocean, U.S. and British investigators monitored the diving behavior of seals and penguins to gain more data on anatomical and physiological adaptations of warm-blooded vertebrates.

Arctic. Scientists from the United States, Denmark, and Switzerland continued their investigation of the Greenland ice sheet. At the close of the season (August 1980), ice cores had been retrieved from a depth of 901 m (2,956 ft). At the drilling site, the ice is 2 200 m (7,218 ft) thick, with the bottom layers possibly deposited 100,000 years ago. The retrieved core is believed to be composed of ice deposited before the birth of Christ. Core analysis was performed at the site, but additional laboratory tests (analysis for oxygen isotope ratios, chemical composition, particle content, conductivity and mechanical properties) would be accomplished at the participants' home institutions. Bound in these ice cores are the records of changes in temperature, precipitation, and atmospheric composition over the last 100,000 years.

Studies of marine ecosystems in the Bering Sea entered the fourth year of a 6-year project. Scientists discovered two distinctly different food webs in the two existing interfront zones. In the outer shelf zone, primary production is directly tied to secondary production, resulting in an efficient transfer to the open sea food chain. However, the midshelf zone processes are not so closely linked, creating a relatively low transfer of energy to bottom-dwelling species.

WINIFRED REUNING
National Science Foundation

PORTUGAL

Portuguese voters demonstrated their support for a moderate-conservative coalition in parliamentary elections, confirming a shift to the right six years after leftist military leaders overturned one of Western Europe's oldest dictatorships. However, the future of Portugal's nascent democracy was put in doubt when Premier Francisco Sá Carneiro, leader of the Democratic Alliance (AD), died in a plane crash December 4.

Government and Politics. The Democratic Alliance (AD), composed of Social Democrats, Center Democrats, and the tiny monarchist party, scored an impressive victory in the October 5 legislative election, increasing its majority in the 250-member parliament from 128 to 134. This triumph came mainly at the expense of the Moscow-oriented Communist party whose share of the popular vote, which had steadily risen from 12.5% in 1975 to 19% in December 1979, fell to only 16.7% as its number of seats declined from 47 to 41. Especially impressive were AD gains in such Communist strongholds as the working-class suburbs of Lisbon and Oporto and the country's chief grain-producing area, Alentejo.

Although the once-dominant Socialists registered a slight gain in capturing 28% of the votes cast, former Premier Mário Soares resigned as head of the party after the balloting. He announced his decision when Socialist leaders rejected his proposal that the party oppose Gen. Antonio Ramalho Eanes, who won 55% of the vote in the Dec. 7, 1980, presidential contest.

Francisco Sá Carneiro, premier since late 1979, had spearheaded the AD legislative campaign. He largely ignored personal attacks—the left accused him of both financial irregularities and immorality for leaving the Portuguese mother of his five children to live with a Danish divorceé (who died with him)—while promoting controversial constitutional reforms. He urged elimination of the Council of the Revolution, a self-appointed body of left-wing officers, empowered by the 1976 constitution to supervise Portugal's "transition toward socialism"; recommended curtailing such presidential prerogatives as the right to remove a government, even if it enjoys a parliamentary majority; and advocated reopening nationalized sectors of the economy to private enterprise.

To accomplish these changes, AD would need the backing of two thirds of the deputies. This majority would be difficult to muster because President Eanes, whom Sá Carneiro had excoriated, has opposed all changes, and the Socialists, while disposed to disband the Council of the Revolution, have resisted the resurgence of capitalism championed by AD. The prospect of deadlock and drift encouraged Sá Carneiro to suggest holding a referendum to alter the two-thirds rule to a simple majority.

On December 22, the president designated Francisco Pinto Balsemão, a 43-year-old journalist and lawyer and a cofounder with Sá Carneiro of the Social Democratic Party, premier. The new government was to take office in 1981.

Economy. The electoral success of the AD indicated confidence in Sá Carneiro's economic program. On May 21, the Council of the Revolution, acting as a constitutional watchdog, blocked legislation designed to denationalize such strategic sectors of the economy as steel, armaments, and petrochemicals. Angered at this rebuff, the premier continued his effort to achieve short-term economic improvements to demonstrate that his policies could work despite the military council's obstructionism.

He curbed government spending and froze the recruitment of personnel in moves that helped reduce the inflation rate from 25% to 19%. Although charges for auto licenses and telephone rentals were raised, he lowered the income tax. He also broadened social security coverage, boosted the minimum wage, and increased pensions. He worked to improve the trade balance. Continued growth in national income attended these changes.

Portugal planned to press ahead with its application to join the European Community. Negotiations over membership were suspended in midyear because the nine EC nations could not agree on a common position on agriculture and fishing. The fact that the Common Market countries have provided $3.3 million in assistance to Lisbon demonstrates a commitment to Portugal's accession. A 7- to 10-year transition to full EC membership was to begin in 1983.

A brief visit by U.S. President Carter to Lisbon on June 26 reaffirmed the close relations.

GEORGE W. GRAYSON
College of William and Mary

─────── **PORTUGAL · Information Highlights** ───────

Official Name: Republic of Portugal.
Location: Southwestern Europe.
Area: 35,553 sq mi (92 082 km²).
Population (1980 est.): 9,900,000.
Chief Cities (1979 est.): Lisbon, the capital, 1,100,000; Oporto, 350,000.
Government: *Head of state,* António Ramalho Eanes, president (took office July 1976). *Head of government,* Francisco Pinto Balsemão, prime minister-designate (Dec. 1980). *Legislature* (unicameral)—Assembly of the Republic.
Monetary Unit: Escudo (51 escudos equal U.S.$1, Oct. 1980).
Manufactures (major products): Textiles, clothing, cork products, chemicals, transport equipment.
Agriculture (major products): Wine, grapes, tomatoes, wheat, olives, fruit, rice, cereals.
GNP (1979 est., U.S.$): $21,800,000,000.
Foreign Trade (1979, U.S.$): *Imports,* $6,086,000,000; *exports,* $3,468,000,000.

POSTAL SERVICE

From the U.S. Postal Service (USPS) in 1980 there was good news and bad news, both tempered by considerable uncertainty.

Operations. Mail volume rose 4%, topping 100,000,000,000 pieces for the first time. This also helped revenues. Productivity, the highest in the world, also rose, though more slowly, by 2-3%. A survey by the respected Poje consulting firm concluded that "first-class mail is getting better." New marketing experiments involving discounts to high-volume customers who agree to presort their bulk mail were successful, and electronic mail was finally on its way.

Nevertheless, there were still problems with the network of bulk mail handling centers established in the mid-1970s, and the United Parcel Service and others were cutting more and more into USPS package business. Late in 1980, USPS marketing experiments to reverse this trend remained tied up in the courts by its opponents. There were serious charges of USPS failure to maximize safety precautions. Continued trouble with new highly-mechanized operations in New York City caused widespread complaints about mail delivery in the Northeast.

In a controversial move to assist productivity further, the service planned to adopt a nine-digit ZIP code in 1981. The plan would permit new automated equipment to arrange mail in bundles sorted to individual city blocks. When fully operational in 1986, the system could cut mail processing manpower needs in half. Use of the new code would be voluntary, but the USPS planned to provide rate incentives for large mailers to participate.

Finances. The impact of inflation on a fixed-rate structure turned the fiscal year (FY) 1979 surplus of $469 million into a nearly $600 million deficit for FY 1980. The 1979 surplus had been the first since 1945.

As predicted, the USPS filed with the independent Postal Rate Commission on April 21, 1980, for new postal rates to go into effect early in 1981. If approved, as expected, first class rates would rise from 15 to 20 cents for the first ounce and from 13 to 17 cents for each additional ounce. Postal cards would go from 10 to 13 cents. The concept of reduced rates for mailers who ease the postal work load by presorting would be expanded. The USPS also said it would be filing for a holiday season discount for nonbusiness mail deposited between December 1 and 10, effective in 1981, to allow more effective use of the work force at this peak mailing time. "I think," said Postmaster General William F. Bolger, "that holding prices from 1978 to 1981 is an excellent record." Even at 20 cents the U.S. first class rate would be the second lowest in the world, under priced only by the 17-cent Canadian rate.

In October a U.S. House-Senate conference committee acting on appropriations for FY 1981 proposed to reduce the postal subsidy of nearly $1,000,000,000 a year by $250 million. Passage of the Postal Reform Act of 1970 assumed a gradual reduction in this subsidy, but such will not simplify the financing of the USPS.

Electronic Communications. Between late 1978 and the summer of 1980 efforts of the USPS to enter this communications sector, involving nearly 80% of all transmitted messages, were stymied by two agencies. The Postal Rate Commission refused to approve the USPS initial proposals and the Federal Communications Commission (FCC), asserting jurisdiction over all such communications, also balked. However, on Aug. 15, 1980, the USPS Board of Governors decided to accept, though under protest, a compromise proposal by the commission which had prospects of approval by the FCC.

As a result, the USPS revived its 1978 plans in modified form. First, it joined with Canada on Sept. 22, 1980, to apply the Canadian-British INTELPOST (International Electronic Post) system, inaugurated on June 17, 1980, to the United States. This system, aimed at business users, permits the sending of facsimile messages by land lines from either Washington, DC, or New York to Toronto, Canada, in less than two minutes at a cost of $5 a page.

On September 24 the USPS invited bids on a contract to design and install an advanced electronic message system for large-volume domestic mailers, to be known as E-COM (Electronic Computer Originated Mail). Planned to function by Jan. 4, 1982, the system would permit mailers to transmit computer-generated messages to 25 SPOs (Serving Post Offices) located so as to assure two-day delivery anywhere in the United States. Upon receipt, the messages would be printed, then automatically separated, folded, inserted and sealed in envelopes, and delivered as first class mail. Meanwhile the USPS was appealing to the courts a commission action that would limit E-COM to an experimental trial period ending on Oct. 1, 1984, and was awaiting FCC permission to expand INTELPOST to other countries.

In addition, on May 2, 1980, the postmaster general wrote President Carter, charging the chairman of the Postal Rate Commission, A. Lee Fritschler, with a series of ethical and other rules violations. An investigation was promised by presidential counselor Lloyd N. Cutler.

Canada. In Febraury the Canada Post concluded its first settlement with the Letter Carrier Union without third party assistance. By late 1980 it appeared almost certain that the Canadian Parliament would make the Canada Post, now a department, into a Crown corporation somewhat on U.S. and British lines. It was also expected that the legislation would update and clarify many of the provisions of the Post Office Act.

PAUL P. VAN RIPER
Texas A&M University

PRINCE EDWARD ISLAND

Decentralization of provincial government services emerged as a major political issue, with one of the Conservative administration's own members of the Legislative Assembly sparking a row on the question. Work began on a new federal office complex in Charlottetown. And Daniel MacDonald, one of Prince Edward Island's (P.E.I.) best-known politicians, died.

Government Operations. Peter Pope, the Conservative member of the provincial legislature for Prince 5th, caused a political stir when he publicly urged the immediate transfer of Holland College headquarters and the P.E.I. Hospital Services Commission from Charlottetown, the capital, to Summerside. Pope called a press conference in Summerside on September 15 to urge greater decentralization of government operations. He noted that he had often criticized the former Liberal government on the same issue. Prime Minister J. Angus MacLean tartly retorted that Summerside was not the only town deserving consideration.

Federal Election. In the February 18 national elections, the Liberals gained two seats at the expense of the Conservatives. Each party won two of the island's four House of Commons seats; previously the Tories held all four.

David MacDonald, a prominent member of Joe Clark's short-lived Conservative government, lost Egmont to Liberal George Henderson.

Daniel MacDonald won back the Cardigan seat he had lost in the 1979 election, and was appointed to his former federal cabinet job as veterans affairs minister. MacDonald, who lost an arm and a leg while serving as a sergeant in the Canadian Army in Europe in World War II, died in Charlottetown on September 30. He had been admitted to the hospital four days earlier with suspected influenza. Death was attributed to acute blood clotting.

Conservatives Tom McMillan and Mel Gass won reelection.

Federal Move. The first sod was turned for a new $16 million headquarters building for the

---

PRINCE EDWARD ISLAND • Information Highlights

Area: 2,184 sq mi (5 657 km²).
Population (1980 est.): 124,000.
Chief Cities (1976 census): Charlottetown, the capital, 17,063; Summerside, 8,592.
Government (1980): *Chief Officers*—lt. gov., Gorden L. Bennett; premier, J. Angus MacLean (Progressive Conservative); chief justice, Supreme Court, John Paton Nicholson. *Legislature*—Legislative Assembly, 32 members.
Education (1979–80 est.): *Enrollment*—public elementary and secondary schools, 26,840 pupils; Indian (federal) schools, 60; post-secondary, 2,360. *Total expenditures,* $87,933,000.
Personal Income (average weekly salary, May 1980): $223.30.
Unemployment Rate (July 1980, seasonally adjusted): 10.7%.
(All monetary figures given in Canadian dollars.)

Veterans Affairs Department in Charlottetown. Veterans Affairs Minister MacDonald performed the ceremonial function. MacDonald told the large crowd assembled for the occasion: "This is a major step in the federal government's decentralization program. It is important that all areas of this country share in the benefits of federalism." Construction is to be completed in 1983. Moving the headquarters from Ottawa will mean 500 new jobs in Charlottetown.

Oil Drilling Halted. The issue of oil exploration permits for P.E.I. was frozen pending a government review. Provincial Energy Minister Barry Clark said no more permits would be issued until existing resource legislation had been changed, possibly in 1981.

JOHN BEST, *Chief, Canadian World News*

PRISONS

The number of prisons in the United States increased to a new high in 1980 but could not keep pace with an even sharper rise in inmate population. Conditions, especially at the state and local levels, continued to deteriorate. Overcrowded and understaffed, the prisons and jails throughout the country were frequently the scenes of deadly violence. Prison officials were challenged by a growing number of lawsuits protesting inadequate and even inhumane conditions. Because of the extremely high costs of incarceration, little relief was in sight.

The more than 600,000 Americans detained behind bars are held in a variety of penal institutions. According to the most recent figures, there are more than 6,500 facilities nationwide. These include 3,921 jails for those awaiting trial and those serving short sentences (generally less than a year); 1,277 private juvenile detention and correctional facilities, often run by voluntary agencies; 697 public juvenile detention and correctional facilities (not including halfway houses); 592 state prisons; 68 federal prisons; and 46 military detention facilities. A majority— 57%—of persons behind bars were awaiting trial, having failed for various reasons to have made bail. A large number—nearly 25%—were jailed on charges of public inebriation. In some jurisdictions, even mentally ill persons end up in jail. In San Francisco, for example, about one inmate in twelve is classified as mentally ill.

Because almost every city and county in the United States has a jail, it is impossible to offer a single description that applies to all. One report, however, came particularly close when it noted that U.S. jails "are, for the most part, dirty, dangerous, overcrowded, unhealthy and stupefyingly dull." Most jails contain a mixture of drunk drivers, petty thieves serving short sentences, criminals awaiting trial on serious charges, and, no doubt, a number of innocent people. Because the inmate's stay is usually short, there often are no recreational programs, organized activities, or exercise facilities. It is no

A group of inmates is held at bay by National Guardsmen at the New Mexico State Penitentiary in Santa Fe after 36 hours of rioting in early February. By the time order was restored, there were 33 deaths and an estimated $60 million in damages.

UPI

surprise that overcrowding has produced volatile conditions, with frequent violent eruptions.

The total number of prisoners—314,083—held in U.S. federal and state prisons in 1980 was a record high for the sixth year in a row. The number of federal prisoners actually declined because of a policy decision not to prosecute at the federal level persons crossing a state line in a stolen car. About 96% of the prisoners in state and federal facilities were serving sentences of more than one year.

Overcrowding. Over the past decade, there has been a gradual but steady rise in the percentage of persons convicted who are sentenced rather than paroled. The lengths of sentences also have increased. The results of that policy shift, intended or not, have become more evident each year. The U.S. prison population in 1980 was 58% above safe capacity. Half the state prisons hold more than they were built for. William Nagel, head of the American Foundation and a former warden, noted that overcrowding "puts pressure on eating, housing, and programs. It raises the fear level, and it increases the turnover of the staff." In many cases, control of the facility passes from the understaffed officials into the hands of the inmates themselves.

Violence. Although no one prison should be singled out as typical of the thousands of lock-up facilities in the country, Attica Correctional Facility in New York State, because it was the scene of the bloodiest prison uprising in American history in 1971, has had a special notoriety. And, like so many prison facilities that go unnoticed by the media, Attica had its share of tension and violence in 1980. In January, 16 guards and two inmates were injured in several fights and stabbings in the prison mess hall. After the 1971 outburst, which left 43 persons dead, the inmate population at Attica had been reduced to 1,200. By January 1980, however, it was back to 1,862. Almost any prison official would agree that when the number of inmates grows, prison programs and activities must be cut back because of the added security problems. More lock-up time and idleness frequently lead to violent confrontations, both between guards and prisoners and among the prisoners.

The New Mexico State Penitentiary in Santa Fe was built in 1957 to house 850 prisoners. On Feb. 2, 1980, it housed 1,100 inmates, guarded by 18 officers. On that day, a rampage broke out, resulting in 33 deaths and property damage estimated at $60 million. Unsatisfactory conditions at the prison had been apparent to officials for some time, and law suits had been filed two years earlier by the American Civil Liberties Union (ACLU) charging that the overcrowding fostered homosexual rape and other violence. What began as a confrontation between officers and inmates—two prisoners had overpowered a guard who had caught them drinking liquor and then were joined by other inmates—soon turned into a horror-filled bloodbath. For 36 hours, authorities looked on as prisoners turned on prisoners, using blow torches and axes, beating, beheading, and burning. Initial reports, later proven unfounded, suggested a frenzy brought about through drugs. Later explanations were that an "execution squad" of prisoners was seeking vengeance against purported informers. A report issued in September criticized a hard-line corrections policy that eliminated incentives and diminished inmate self-esteem. A riot in July heavily damaged the State Penitentiary of Idaho. As in New Mexico, no shots were fired in the retaking of the prison, but new places to house 500 prisoners had to be found, and costly reconstruction was required.

The events of 1980 again suggested that U.S. penal institutions, no matter how massive, can be destroyed as a result of inmate unrest. With the construction cost of a maximum security prison at more than $50,000 per bed, the more difficult question is whether more rational, safe, and humane alternatives can be implemented.

See also CRIME; LAW.

DONALD GOODMAN
John Jay College of Criminal Justice
City University of New York

PRIZES AND AWARDS

NOBEL PRIZES

Chemistry ($212,000 shared): Dr. Paul Berg, professor of biochemistry, Stanford University ($106,000); Dr. Walter Gilbert, professor of molecular biology, Harvard University ($53,000); Dr. Frederick Sanger, professor of molecular biology, Cambridge University ($53,000); honored for their investigations of the "chemical basis of the genetic machinery in living organisms."

Economics ($212,000): Lawrence R. Klein, economics professor, University of Pennsylvania; "the leading research worker within the field of the economic science which deals with the construction and analysis of empirical models of business fluctuations."

Literature ($210,000): Czeslaw Milosz, Polish émigré poet and novelist (*see* Literature).

Medicine or Physiology ($210,000 shared): Dr. Baruj Benacerraf, chairman, Pathology Dept., School of Medicine, Harvard University; Dr. George D. Snell, scientist, Jackson Laboratory, Bar Harbor, ME; Dr. Jean Dausset, head, Department of Immunology, University of Paris; cited for their work on the genetic regulation of the body's immune responses.

Peace Prize ($212,000): Adolfo Pérez Esquivel, Argentine human rights activist (*see* Biography).

Physics ($212,000 shared): Dr. James W. Cronin, University of Chicago; Dr. Val L. Fitch, Princeton University; cited "for the discovery of violations of fundamental symmetry principles in the decay of neutral K mesons. The new truth reached by the discovery of violations of the laws of symmetry in nature recently also has been incorporated as an important ingredient in cosmological speculations. The aim has been to try to understand how a universe, originally very hot and symmetric, could avoid that matter and antimatter almost immediately annihilated each other. In other words, efforts have been made to describe how the matter we are made of was once created in a big bang and how it could have survived the birth pains."

ART

American Academy and Institute of Arts and Letters Awards
Academy-Institute Awards ($4,000 ea.): art—Richard Anuszkiewicz, Edward Dugmore, Marion Lerner Levine, Howard Newman, Charmion Von Wiegand; music—Donald Grantham, Eugene O'Brien, Malcolm Peyton, Lawrence L. Widdoes
Arnold W. Brunner Memorial Prize in Architecture ($1,000): Michael Graves
Charles Ives Scholarships in Music ($4,000 ea.): Thomas Barker, Laura Clayton, Lowell Lieberman, William Maiben, Mario Pelusi, George Tsontakis
Charles Ives Award ($11,000): Charles Ives Society
Goddard Lieberson Fellowships ($10,000 ea.): David Chaitkin, Robert Xavier Rodriguez
Richard and Hinda Rosenthal Foundation Award ($3,000): Dolores Milmoe (in art)

American Institute of Architects 25-Year Award: Skidmore, Owings, & Merrill

Avery Fisher Prize ($5,000): Richard Goode

Capezio Award: Walter Terry, *The Saturday Review*

Dance Magazine Awards: Patricia McBride, Ruth Page, Paul Taylor; Award of distinction—Herbert Ross, Nora Kaye

John F. Kennedy Center for the Performing Arts Awards for lifetime achievement in the performing arts: Leonard Bernstein, James Cagney, Agnes de Mille, Lynn Fontanne, Leontyne Price

National Academy of Recording Arts and Sciences Grammy Awards for excellence in phonograph records
Album of the year: *52nd Street*, Billy Joel
Classical album: *Brahms: Symphonies Complete*, Sir Georg Solti, conductor, Chicago Symphony Orchestra
Country song: *You Decorated My Life*, Bob Morrison, Debbie Hupp, songwriters
Jazz vocal performance: *Fine and Mellow*, Ella Fitzgerald

New artist: Rickie Lee Jones
Record of the year: *What a Fool Believes*, Doobie Brothers
Song of the year: *What a Fool Believes*, Kenny Loggins, Michael McDonald, songwriters
1980 Hall of Fame awards: *Ballad for Americans*, Paul Robeson; *In a Mist*, Bix Beiderbecke; *Jelly Roll Morton: The Saga of Mr. Jelly Lord*, Ferdinand "Jelly Roll" Morton

National Endowment for the Humanities 1980 Jefferson Lecturer ($10,000): Barbara W. Tuchman

National Gold Medal of Merit Award of the National Society of Arts and Letters: George Balanchine

Pritzker Architecture Prize ($100,000): Luis Barragán

Pulitzer Prize for Music: David Del Tredici, *In Memory of a Summer Day*

JOURNALISM

George Polk Memorial Awards
Book: William Shawcross, *Sideshow: Kissinger, Nixon, and the Destruction of Cambodia*
Commentary: *The New Yorker* magazine, "Notes and Comment"
Film documentary: Jack Willis, Saul Landau, New Time Films
Foreign reporting: John Kifner, *New York Times*
Local reporting: Ed Petykiewicz, *Saginaw* (MI) *News*
Metropolitan reporting: Walt Bogdanich, Walter Johns, Jr., *The Cleveland Press*
National reporting: Brian Donovan, Bob Wyrick, Stuart Diamond, *Newsday*
National television reporting: WRC-TV, Washington DC
News photography award: United Press International
Regional reporting: Jim Adams, Jim Detjen, *Louisville Courier-Journal*
Special interest reporting: *Angolite* editors (*Angolite* magazine is published by inmates of the Angola State Prison in Louisiana)
Television reporting from abroad: Ed Bradley, CBS

National Magazine Awards
Essays and criticism: *Natural History*
Fiction: *Antaeus*
Public service: *Texas Monthly*
Reporting excellence: *Mother Jones*
Service to the individual: *The Saturday Review*
Single topic issue: *Scientific American*
Specialized journalism: *IEEE Spectrum*
Visual excellence: *GEO*

Overseas Press Club Awards
Book on foreign affairs: Peter Wyden, *Bay of Pigs*
Business news reporting from abroad: William J. Holstein, United Press International
Cartoon on foreign affairs: Don Wright, *Miami News* and *New York Times* Syndicate
Daily newspaper or wire service reporting from abroad: Sajid Rizvi, United Press International
Magazine interpretation of foreign affairs: Sidney Zion, Uri Dan, *The New York Times Magazine*
Magazine reporting from abroad: Walter Isaacson, Donald Neff, *Time*
Photographic reporting from abroad: David Burnett, Contact Press Images
Radio interpretation of foreign news: CBS radio news network, "Iran: the Critical Days"
Radio spot news from abroad: Philip Till, NBC Radio
Television interpretation of foreign affairs: CBS news team of Ed Bradley, Andrew Lack, Howard Stringer, Greg Cooke, Ian Wilson for a report on Pulau Bidong
Television news reporting from abroad: Bill Stewart (posthumously), Jack Clark, ABC
Bob Considine Memorial Award: Ray Vicker, *The Wall Street Journal*
Robert Capa Gold Medal: Kaveh Golestan, *Time*
Madeline Dane Ross Award: Jean-Pierre Laffont, Sygma
Reporting which describes human rights abuses and supports the principles of human rights: Paul Heath Hoeffel, Juan Montalvo, *The New York Times Magazine*

Pulitzer Prizes
Commentary: Ellen H. Goodman, *The Boston Globe*
Criticism: William A. Henry 3d, *The Boston Globe*
Editorial cartooning: Don Wright, *The Miami News*

Editorial writing: Robert L. Bartley, *The Wall Street Journal*

Feature photography: Erwin H. Hagler, *The Dallas Times Herald*

Feature writing: Madeleine Blais, *The Miami Herald*

General local reporting: *The Philadelphia Inquirer* staff for reportage of the nuclear reactor accident at Three Mile Island

International reporting: Joel Brinkley, Jay Mather, *The Louisville Courier-Journal*

National reporting: Bette Swenson Orsini, Charles Stafford, *The St. Petersburg* (FL) *Times*

Public service: John M. Hanchette, William F. Schmick, Carlton Sherwood, The Gannett News Service

Special local reporting: Stephen A. Kurkjian, Alexander B. Hawes, Jr., Nils Bruzelins, Joan Vennochi, Robert Porterfield, *The Boston Globe*

Spot news photography: UPI photographer for ''Firing Squad in Iran'' (name withheld because ''present unrest in Iran'' could endanger him)

LITERATURE

Academy of American Poets Fellowship Award ($10,000): Mona Van Duyn

Academy of American Poets Walt Whitman Award ($1,000 and publication of the award-winning book): Jared Carter, *Work, for the Night is Coming*

American Academy and Institute of Arts and Letters Awards

Academy-Institute Awards ($4,000 ea.): Ann Beattie, William Dickey, Paul Fussell, Maxine Kumin, George Oppen, Robert Pinsky, Lewis Thomas, Larry Woiwode

American Academy in Rome Fellowship in Creative Writing ($2,000): Mary Morris

Award of Merit Medal for Poetry ($1,000): Richard Howard

Witter Bynner Prize for Poetry ($1,350): Pamela White Hadas

The Gold Medal for Drama: Edward Albee

The Gold Medal for Graphic Art: Peggy Bacon

William Dean Howells Medal for Fiction: William Maxwell

Sue Kaufman Prize for First Fiction ($1,000): Jayne Anne Phillips

Richard and Hinda Rosenthal Foundation Award ($3,000): Stanley Elkin (in writing)

Harold D. Vursell Memorial Award ($5,000): Tom Wolfe

Morton Dauwen Zabel Award ($2,500): Donald Finkel

The American Book Awards ($1,000)

Autobiography (hardcover): *By Myself*, Lauren Bacall

Autobiography (paperback): *And I Worked at the Writer's Trade*, Malcolm Cowley

Biography (hardcover): *The Rise of Theodore Roosevelt*, Edmund Morris

Biography (paperback): Max Perkins: *Editor of Genius*, A. Scott Berg

Children's Books (hardcover): *A Gathering of Days: A New England Girl's Journal, 1830–32*, Joan W. Blos

Children's Books (paperback): *A Swiftly Tilting Planet*, Madeline L'Engle

General Fiction (hardcover): *Sophie's Choice*, William Styron

General Fiction (paperback): *The World According to Garp*, John Irving

General Nonfiction (hardcover): *The Right Stuff*, Tom Wolfe

General Nonfiction (paperback): *The Snow Leopard*, Peter Matthiessen

History (hardcover): *White House Years*, Henry Kissinger

History (paperback): *A Distant Mirror: The Calamitous 14th Century*, Barbara W. Tuchman

Mystery (hardcover): *The Green Ripper*, John D. MacDonald

Mystery (paperback): *Stained Glass*, William F. Buckley, Jr.

Poetry: *Ashes*, Philip Levine

Bancroft Prizes for best books in American history or diplomacy ($4,000 ea.): Robert Dallek, *Franklin D. Roosevelt and American Foreign Policy, 1932–1945*; Thomas Dublin, *Women at Work: The Transformation of Work and Community in Lowell, Massachusetts, 1826–1860*; Donald E. Worster, *Dust Bowl: The Southern Plains in the 1930s*

Canada's Governor General's Literary Awards

English fiction: Jack Hodgins, *The Resurrection of Joseph Bourne*

French fiction: Marie-Claire Blais, *Le Sourd dans La Ville*

English nonfiction: Maria Tippett, *Emily Carr: A Biography*

French nonfiction: Dominique Clift, Sheila McLeod Arnopolous, *Le Fait Anglais au Quebec*

English poetry and drama: Michel Ondaatje, *There's a Trick with a Knife I'm Learning to Do*

French poetry and drama: Robert Melancon, *Peinture Aveugle*

National Medal of Literature ($15,000): Eudora Welty

Pulitzer Prizes

Biography: Edmund Morris, *The Rise of Theodore Roosevelt*

Fiction: Norman Mailer, *The Executioner's Song*

General nonfiction: Douglas R. Hofstadter, *Gödel, Escher, Bach: An Eternal Golden Braid*

History: Leon F. Litwack, *Been in the Storm So Long: The Aftermath of Slavery*

Poetry: Donald Rodney Justice, *Selected Poems*

MOTION PICTURES

Academy of Motion Picture Arts and Sciences ("Oscar") Awards

Actor: Dustin Hoffman, *Kramer vs. Kramer*

Actress: Sally Field, *Norma Rae*

Cinematography: Vittorio Storaro, *Apocalypse Now*

Costume design: Albert Wolsky, *All That Jazz*

Director: Robert Benton, *Kramer vs. Kramer*

Film: *Kramer vs. Kramer*

Foreign language film: *The Tin Drum*

Music—adaptation score: Ralph Burns, *All That Jazz*

Music—original score: George Delerue, *A Little Romance*

Music—original song: *It Goes Like It Goes*, music by David Shire, lyric by Norman Gimbel

Original screenplay: Steven Tesich, *Breaking Away*

Screenplay based on material from another medium: Robert Benton, *Kramer vs. Kramer*

Supporting actor: Melvyn Douglas, *Being There*

Supporting actress: Meryl Streep, *Kramer vs. Kramer*

Academy Award of Merit: Mark Serrurier

Jean Hersholt Humanitarian Award: Robert Benjamin

Honorary Awards: Hal Elias, Sir Alec Guinness

Special Achievement Award: Alan Splet, *The Black Stallion*

Irving G. Thalberg Award: Ray Stark

American Film Institute's Life Achievement Award: James Stewart

Cannes Film Festival Awards

Best actor: Michel Piccoli, *Salto nel Vuoto*

Best actess: Anouk Aimée, *Salto nel Vuoto*

Best director: Krzysztof Zanussi, *Constans*

Best film (shared): *All That Jazz* (United States); *Kagemusha* (Japan)

Special jury prize: Alain Resnais, *Mon Oncle d'Amérique*

PUBLIC SERVICE

Albert Einstein Peace Prize ($50,000): Alva Myrdal

The American Institute for Public Service Jefferson Awards ($5,000)

Public service by an elected official: Cyrus R. Vance

Public Service performed by an individual 35 or under (shared): 1980 U.S. Olympic hockey team

Public service benefiting the disadvantaged: Allard K. Lowenstein (posthumously)

Public service by a private citizen: Dr. Norman Borlaug

Public service benefiting communities ($1,000 ea.): John Carpenter, Elaine Griebenow, Tilda Kemplen, Lee Klein, Dr. Louis Mattucci

Rockefeller Public Service Awards ($10,000 ea.)

Community revitalization: Sister Isolina Ferre, director, Center for Orientation and Services, Ponce Playa, PR

Health: Eula Bingham, assistant secretary of Labor for Occupational Safety and Health

International development: James P. Grant, executive director of UNICEF, United Nations

Opportunities for youth: Dr. James P. Comer, professor, Yale Child Study Center; associate dean, Yale Medical School

Public service: William Hensley, president, NANA Development Corporation; Henry R. Richmond, executive director, 1000 Friends of Oregon

Templeton Prize for Progress in Religion ($206,000): Ralph Wendell Burhoe

U.S. Medal of Honor (presented by President Jimmy Carter on July 19, 1980): Lieut. Col. Matt Urban for "limitless bravery" under enemy fire in World War II

U.S. Presidential Medal of Freedom (presented by President Jimmy Carter on June 9, 1980): Ansel Adams, Lucia Chase, Archbishop Iakovos, Clarence Mitchell, Jr., Roger Tory Peterson, Hyman Rickover, Beverly Sills, Robert Penn Warren, Eudora Welty, Tennessee Williams; posthumous awards to Rachel Carson, Hubert Humphrey, Lyndon B. Johnson, John Wayne

SCIENCE

Albert Lasker Awards ($15,000):

Basic medical research (shared): Dr. Paul Berg, Dr. Stanley N. Cohen, Dr. A. Dale Kaiser, all of Stanford University; and Dr. Herbert W. Boyer, University of California, San Francisco

Clinical medical research: (shared): Dr. Vincent J. Freda, Dr. John Gorman, Columbia University; Dr. William Pollack, Columbia and Ortho Diagnostics, Inc.; Professor Sir Cyril A. Clarke, University of Liverpool; Dr. Ronald Finn, Royal Liverpool Hospital, England

Public health award: National Heart, Lung and Blood Institute of the National Institutes of Health

Bristol-Myers Award ($25,000): Dr. Howard Skipper, Southern Research Institute, Birmingham, AL

Columbia University's Louisa Gross Horwitz Prize for research in biology and biochemistry ($22,000): Dr. Cesar Milstein, Medical Research Council, University of Cambridge, England

General Motors Cancer Research Foundation Awards ($100,000 ea.):

Charles F. Kettering Prize: Elwood V. Jenson

Charles S. Mott Prize: James and Elizabeth Miller

Alfred P. Sloan, Jr., Prize: Isaac Berenblum

National Academy of Sciences Public Welfare Medal: Walter Sullivan, *The New York Times*

TELEVISION AND RADIO

Academy of Televison Arts and Sciences ("Emmy") Awards

Actor—comedy series: Richard Mulligan, *Soap* (ABC)

Actor—drama series: Ed Asner, *Lou Grant* (CBS)

Actor—limited series or special: Powers Boothe, *Guyana Tragedy: The Story of Jim Jones* (CBS)

Actress—comedy series: Cathryn Damon, *Soap* (ABC)

Actress—drama series: Barbara Bel Geddes, *Dallas* (CBS)

Actress—limited series or special: Patty Duke Astin, *The Miracle Worker* (NBC)

Children's programs—individual achievement: Bob O'Bradovich, *The Halloween That Almost Wasn't* (ABC)

Classical program in the performing arts: *Live from Studio 8H: A Tribute to Toscanini* (NBC)

Comedy series: *Taxi* (ABC)

Drama series: *Lou Grant* (CBS)

Individual achievement—special class: Geof Bartz, *Operation Lifeline: Dr. James "Red" Duke, Trauma Surgeon* (NBC)

Informational program: "The Magic Sense," *The Body Human* (CBS)

Limited series: *Edward & Mrs. Simpson* (SYN)

Program Achievement: *Fred Astaire: Change Partners and Dance* (PBS)

Special—drama or comedy: *The Miracle Worker* (NBC)

Supporting actor—comedy series: Harry Morgan, *M*A*S*H* (CBS)

Supporting actor—drama series: Stuart Margolin, *Rockford Files* (NBC)

Supporting actress—comedy series: Loretta Swit, *M*A*S*H* (CBS)

Supporting actress—drama series: Nancy Marchand, *Lou Grant* (CBS)

Governors' Award: Johnny Carson

George Foster Peabody Awards

Radio: WCBS radio, New York, for an investigative report on New York City taxicab drivers; WGBH radio, Boston, for a dramatic presentation about the life of Charlotte Brontë; Children's Radio Theatre, Washington, for a series of performances of original play scripts by children ages 5 to 13; Canadian Broadcasting Corporation for a documentary on the development of a fetus; KSJN-Minnesota Public Radio, St. Paul, for a study of the legal process governing commitment to mental institutions in Minnesota.

Television: KTVI-TV, St. Louis, for satiric commentaries on current issues; WMAQ-TV, Chicago, for an investigative report on police strip-searches of women arrested on minor charges; CBS News, New York, *CBS News Sunday Morning;* ABC-TV, New York, *Valentine;* ABC-TV, New York, *Friendly Fire;* NBC-TV, New York, *Dummy;* NBC-TV, New York, *When Hell Was in Session;* KOOL-TV, Phoenix, AZ, *The Long Eyes of Kitt Peak;* NBC and British Broadcasting Corporation, *Treasures of the British Crown;* ABC-TV, New York, *A Special Gift;* KRON-TV, San Francisco, for a report on health problems caused by herbicide sprayings in northern California; WTTW-TV, Chicago, for a documentary about age discrimination; WTTW-TV, Chicago, for a program about a high school in the years following a desegregation crisis; KNXT, Hollywood, CA, for a look at the jazz greats who performed at Hollywood's Dunbar Hotel; WGBH-TV, Boston, for international documentaries; CBS News, New York, for coverage of the Boston Symphony's trip to China

Individual Awards: Sylvia Fine Kaye, Roger Mudd, Robert Trout

Humanitas Prizes

Two-hour category ($25,000): Stephen Kandel, Suzi Lyte Kaufman, Barry Neil Kaufman for *Son-Rise.*

One-hour category ($15,000): Sally Robinson for "Thanksgiving," *Family*

One-half-hour category ($10,000): Alan Alda, James Rubinfier for "Dreams," *M*A*S*H*

THEATER

Antoinette Perry ("Tony") Awards

Actor (drama): John Rubinstein, *Children of a Lesser God*

Actor (musical): Jim Dale, *Barnum*

Actress (drama): Phyllis Frelich, *Children of a Lesser God*

Actress (musical): Patti LuPone, *Evita*

Choreography: Tommy Tune, Thommie Walsh, *A Day in Hollywood/A Night in the Ukraine*

Costume design: Theoni V. Aldredge, *Barnum*

Director (drama): Vivian Matalon, *Morning's at Seven*

Director (musical): Harold Prince, *Evita*

Featured actor (drama): David Rounds, *Morning's at Seven*

Featured actor (musical): Mandy Patinkin, *Evita*

Featured actress (drama): Dinah Manoff, *I Ought to Be in Pictures*

Featured actress (musical): Pricilla Lopez, *A Day in Hollywood/A Night in the Ukraine*

Musical: *Evita*

Play: *Children of a Lesser God*

Score: Andrew-Lloyd Webber, Tim Rice, *Evita*

Special awards: Actors Theater of Louisville, Goodspeed Opera House, Richard Fitzgerald, Mary Tyler Moore, Hobe Morrison

Lawrence Langer Award for distinguished lifetime achievement in the theater: Helen Hayes

New York Drama Critics' Circle Theater Awards

American play: *Talley's Folly*

Musical: *Evita*

Foreign play: *Betrayal*

Special citation: Peter Brook's Le Centre International de Créations Théâtrales

Pulitzer Prize for Drama: Lanford Wilson, *Talley's Folly*

PUBLISHING

The growth in publishing, evident during the 1970s, continued into 1980. Despite an uneven economy, record revenues were reported in book sales, the newspaper industry, and magazine advertising. As anticipated, publishing costs climbed; however, more books were printed, new magazines flooded the markets, and newspaper circulation edged upward. Technological advances, foreshadowing a predicted electronic news era, challenged the newspaper industry.

BOOKS

Revenues and Costs. Book sales for 1980 were expected to reach $6,700,000,000, a continuation of the trend noted in 1979. New titles expanded in 1979, and "a steady and increasing demand for general trade books (and) professional, religious, and other books" was observed. *Publishers Weekly* warned of inflation and rising interest rates, but noted that postal hikes were moderate.

According to *Publishers Weekly,* the number of new book titles for 1979 totaled 36,112, while the number of new editions reached 9,070. This 45,182 total was nearly 4,000 more than that of 1978. The publishers' export business in 1979 reached $439 million, up 18.5% over 1978's figure; imports reached $268 million, up 15.7%.

By its 50th anniversary, the *Better Homes & Gardens New Cook Book* reached sales of 21 million copies. Harlequin paperbacks sold more than 160 million volumes in 1979, becoming the most successful line of fiction ever published. Aided by television evangelists, the sale of religious books was expected to reach $300 million.

Miscellaneous News. About 16,500 people attended the American Booksellers Association convention in June. Discussions were held on the needs, and advantages, of the small publisher and the marketing and distribution of books dealing with homosexual rights and feminist views. The Association of American University Presses focused attention on economics and the marketplace, and changing campus attitudes.

Publishers prepared a record 550 different types of calendar for 1981; the "Miss Piggy Cover Girl Fantasy" was a best-seller.

The famed fictional character Nancy Drew celebrated her 50th anniversary and, along with the Hardy Boys, maintained a wide reading public.

Readership among youth was stimulated by the Multiple Sclerosis Society's READ-a-thon, which raised $30 million through the participation of two million students in 19,000 schools.

Large book chains, such as Dalton and Waldenbooks, expanded. Doubleday & Company purchased the New York Mets baseball team, and Newhouse Publications acquired Random House. Mergers declined in 1980.

Best-sellers. Kurt Vonnegut's *Jailbird* topped early 1980 fictional offerings, followed by John le Carré's *Smiley's People,* Frederick Forsyth's *The Devil's Alternative,* Robert Ludlum's *The Bourne Identity,* and Sidney Sheldon's *Rage of Angels.*

Among leading nonfictional offerings were Bob Woodward and Scott Armstrong's *The Brethren: Inside the Supreme Court* and Gay Talese's *Thy Neighbor's Wife.* Milton and Rose Friedman were on the list for weeks with *Free to Choose: A Personal Statement.* Shelley Winters' *Shelley: Also Known as Shirley* was an autumn leader, along with Alvin Toffler's *The Third Wave* and Douglas R. Casey's *Crisis Investing.* Erma Bombeck's audience enjoyed *Aunt Erma's Cope Book.* Truman Capote's latest book, *Music for Chameleons,* drew mixed reactions from literary critics. Three books recalled the Nixon era: Richard Nixon's *The Real War,* Henry Kissinger's *White House Years,* and G. Gordon Liddy's *Will: The Autobiography of G. Gordon Liddy.* Norman Cousins' *Anatomy of an Illness as Perceived by the Patient* was a success, as was *Donahue: My Own Story* by television talk show host Phil Donahue. Books on taxes, real estate, investing, diets, and exercising sold well.

Successful paperback editions included Taylor Caldwell's *Bright Flows the River,* Lauren Bacall's *Lauren Bacall By Myself,* Stephen King's *The Stand* and *The Dead Zone,* John Jakes' *The Americans,* Herman Tarnower's *The Complete Scarsdale Medical Diet,* Herman Wouk's *War and Remembrance,* Donald F. Glut's *The Empire Strikes Back,* Trevanian's *Shibumi,* V.C. Andrews' *Petals on the Wind,* William Styron's *Sophie's Choice,* Harold Robbins' *Memories of Another Day,* Dana Ross' *Texas!,* and James Clavell's *Shōgun.*

MAGAZINES

Amid warnings of economic difficulties for new publications, magazines increased their circulation and advertising revenues in 1980. By midyear 57 magazines each had a circulation of more than one million. Advertising revenues reached a record $2,670,000,000 in 1979, with $3,290,000,000 expected in 1980. Another $2,000,000,000 came from U.S. and Canadian newsstand buyers. Specialization continued, with the appearance of new publications directed to the interests of science fans, senior citizens, sports enthusiasts, and women.

The Leaders. *TV Guide* retained its circulation leadership, although it dropped to 18.8 million. Regional competition, especially in the cable industry, created problems for the magazine.

Reader's Digest, second in circulation with 18.1 million, appealed a government fine of $1.75 million, based on Federal Trade Commission charges of deceptive advertising in the use of simulated checks in sweepstakes.

National Geographic reached 10.5 million, the third magazine in the United States to exceed a circulation figure of 10 million. Other mid-1980 leaders were *Better Homes & Gardens,* 8 million; *Woman's Day,* 7.5; *Family Circle,* 7.3; *Modern Maturity,* 6.7; *McCall's,* 6.2; *Playboy,*

5.7; *Ladies' Home Journal,* 5.4; and *Good House-keeping,* 5.1. *Parade's* circulation surpassed that of all other Sunday newspaper supplements, with 21.8 million; *Family Weekly* had a circulation of 12 million. *National Enquirer* sold more than 5 million weekly.

Folio magazine reported statistics of 400 periodicals. The top ten accounted for 32% of all reported dollars. *Folio's* revenue leaders included *TV Guide,* $566 million; *Time,* $356 million; *Reader's Digest,* $261 million; *Newsweek,* $254 million; *Sports Illustrated,* $188 million; *People,* $171 million; *Playboy,* $170 million; *Family Circle,* $166 million; *Better Homes & Gardens,* $162 million; and *Woman's Day,* $153 million. The report estimated that *Time,* with $228 million in advertising revenues, surpassed *TV Guide,* with $220 million. *Business Week,* with 5,107 pages, led in consumer magazine advertising pages, while *Travel Agent,* with 7,384, led business periodicals.

New Magazines. The advent of *Dial,* the Public Broadcasting System's new monthly magazine, drew criticism from *Washingtonian* publisher Phil Merrill. He objected to government funds being used in commercial publishing in competition with private periodicals. *Reader's Digest* introduced *Families.* The first issue featured Alex Haley, Erma Bombeck, and James Michener. Time Inc. started *Discover* as a "newsmagazine of science." *Science Digest* was revamped, while *Scientific American, Science 80, Omni,* and others enjoyed a boom. *Prime Time* entered the senior citizen interest area presently dominated by *Modern Maturity, NRTA Journal,* and *Dynamic Years. Slimmer* was started by *Playgirl,* and *Cosmopolitan* added a German edition as well as *Cosmopolitan Living. Intro* arrived for singles. Other special-interest periodicals included *New Shelter, Photoshow, Magazine Age, Next, Feelings, Frequent Flyer, Output, Alcoholism—The National Magazine,* and *Rod, Wire, & Fastener. Newsweek* expanded to a new area with *Inside Sports.* In all, several hundred new periodicals were marketed.

Milestones. *The Atlantic Monthly, Harper's Magazine,* and *Saturday Review* acquired new owners. Fiftieth anniversaries were celebrated by *Fortune, Business Week, Advertising Age,* and *Electronics. Sports Illustrated* observed its 25th year. *Smithsonian* and *Essence* passed their tenth anniversaries. *Natural History* observed its 80th year. *Town & Country,* founded in 1846, printed its 5,000th issue in 1980.

NEWSPAPERS

Katharine Graham, the first woman president of the American Newspaper Publishers Association, urged better use of new communications aids, as she visualized the sending of wire service reports, advertisements, and other materials via satellite. The "electronic newspaper," a process utilizing telephone hookups or cable connections, was predicted.

Business Data. The Commerce Department reported receipts of $16,100,000,000 for the industry in 1979, up 11% over revenues of 1978. Industry employment reached 420,000, plus 652,-000 carriers. However, with newsprint selling at $440 a metric ton, rising paper costs blurred the outlook. To offset costs, publishers turned to lightweight paper and closer editing, and provided less space for pictures and comics.

Circulation gains were slight. *Editor & Publisher 1980 International Year Book* reported 1,-763 dailies with a total circulation of 62,223,040. The 720 Sunday papers reached a total circulation of 54,379,923. The United States' 7,954 weeklies reported a record total circulation of 42 million. U.S. residents spent nearly $5,000,000,-000 on newspapers.

The California-based Times-Mirror Company reported a volume of $1,650,000,000 in 1979, attributed in part to the *Los Angeles Times'* 25th consecutive year of advertising leadership. Gannett, the leading newspaper group in number of dailies (82), topped the billion-dollar figure. Knight-Ridder, group leader in total circulation, approached the billion-dollar mark.

Expansion. The trend toward morning papers continued, as did the growth of all-day editions. The "war of the tabloids" exploded in New York when the morning *New York Daily News* earmarked $20 million for the planned publication of an afternoon edition which would compete with the *New York Post. Post* executives indicated that they might counter with a morning edition.

The *Los Angeles Times* earmarked $215 million for expansion. The Times-Mirror Company reached an agreement in principle to buy *The Denver Post.* Dow Jones & Company, which publishes *The Wall Street Journal,* expanded to 17 plants. The *Journal* approached a circulation of two million daily. U.S. and Canadian publishers spent $670 million for modernization.

Milestones. The *Berkeley Barb,* pioneer alternative newspaper, died in 1980. *Family Weekly,* which appears in 353 Sunday newspapers, was sold to CBS Inc. for $50 million. The *Kansas City Star* observed its 100th anniversary.

Miscellaneous News. Publishers continued their fight to hold down postal rates and to maintain First Amendment protection. Editors wanted clearer access to trials, and reporters refused to reveal news sources. Merger talks between the Newspaper Guild and International Typographical Union bogged down. Guild membership fell to 32,698 after *The Montreal Star* closed and two Cincinnati dailies merged. Five strikes occurred through mid-1980.

Canada. Canada's 117 dailies reached a total circulation of 5,150,000 and its 34 Sunday papers attained 4 million. Canadian residents spent $400 million for them. Two major Canadian newspapers, the *Ottawa Journal* and *The Winnipeg Tribune,* folded in August.

WILLIAM H. TAFT, *University of Missouri*

PUERTO RICO

The island's first U.S. presidential primary elections, an unresolved gubernatorial race, the death of a seminal political figure, the issue of statehood, and controversy over a new refugee camp made 1980 an eventful year in Puerto Rico.

Elections. In Puerto Rico's first party primaries for the U.S. presidency, George Bush easily won the support of island Republicans on February 17. Because all the Republican candidates had vowed support for statehood, the large voter turnout was regarded as a victory for that cause. The Democratic vote, however, was closely contested. The governing pro-statehood New Progressive Party (PNP) backed President Carter, while the opposition pro-Commonwealth Popular Democratic Party (PPD) supported Senator Kennedy. Although Carter narrowly won the March 16 vote, a strong showing by the PPD in this and local primaries suggested that the November gubernatorial and legislative elections would be close.

The PNP, led by Gov. Carlos Romero Barceló, put on a strong campaign, stressing reliable government and a commitment to move directly toward statehood if reelected. The PPD, led by former Gov. Rafael Hernández Colón, defended the existing Commonwealth status and attacked the government for mismanagement and an inability to deal with worsening economic problems.

Gov. Carlos Romero Barceló votes for President Carter in Puerto Rico's first Democratic primary.

UPI

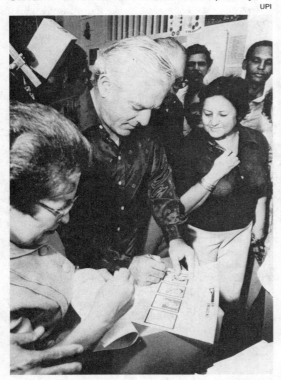

Despite the intense campaign and sometimes vicious personal criticisms by both candidates, Puerto Rico's first election with open polling went smoothly. The results of the gubernatorial contest, however, were too close for an official winner to be declared without a recount. With 1.5 million ballots cast, Romero Barceló held a mere 2,000-vote lead, with 18,000 ballots disputed. The recount was completed in mid-December, and Barceló was declared the winner. However, his PNP had failed to get a mandate for statehood, and there was a stalemate in the legislature, pending a court decision on one seat. Also noteworthy was the fact that the two small parties favoring independence together won less than 10% of the total vote.

Resident Commissioner Baltasar Corrado of the PNP was reelected to his post in Washington.

Independence Movement. The image of the PNP was damaged on April 25 by a federal grand jury decision not to prosecute four policemen who shot and killed two young advocates of independence in 1978. The case sparked criticism of the governor, who originally said that he had no prior knowledge of the attack but then admitted that he had.

Eight members of the Fuerzas Armadas de Liberacion Nacional (FALN), a terrorist independence group, were arrested in Chicago on April 4 and convicted on July 30 of conspiring to commit armed robbery and of illegal possession of weapons.

Refugee Camp. On September 18, the Carter administration announced a unilateral decision to establish a refugee resettlement camp at Fort Allen, a deserted army base near Ponce. The camp would be used to house 5,000 Cuban and Haitian refugees who had arrived in Florida. On September 30, Puerto Rico filed suit against the U.S. government to block the plan. On October 24, U.S. Supreme Court Justice William Brennan issued a temporary restraining order against the transfer of refugees to the camp.

Death. Luis Muñoz Marín, who had dominated the political scene in Puerto Rico since the 1930s, died on April 30, 1980, at the age of 82. Muñoz was perhaps best known as the creator of Puerto Rico's Commonwealth status with the United States. He also was the island's first elected governor, a post to which he was elevated four times, and the original organizer of the PPD. (*See* OBITUARIES.)

THOMAS MATHEWS, *University of Puerto Rico*

PUERTO RICO · Information Highlights

Area: 3,421 sq mi (8 860 km²).
Population (1980 est.): 3,500,000.
Chief Cities (1978 est.): San Juan, the capital, 544,596; Bayamon, 231,456; Ponce, 206,282.
Government (1980): *Chief Officers*—governor, Carlos Romero Barceló (New Progressive Party); secretary of state, Pedro R. Vázquez. *Legislative*—Senate, 27 members; House of Representatives, 51 members.
Manufactures (major products): Rum, distilled spirits, beer, cement, electricity.
Agriculture (major products): Sugarcane, coffee, tobacco, pineapples, molasses.

Groups opposing sovereignty-association put on a major advertising campaign prior to the May 20 referendum. Their vandalized billboard in Quebec reads: "Here I am, here I stay, for my liberty."

Ponopresse, Liaison

QUEBEC

The May 20 referendum on sovereignty-association was at the core of the province's political life and public debate in 1980. The Parti Québécois (PQ) provincial government sought a mandate to negotiate independence from the Canadian federation. In the event of a "yes" answer on the referendum, a plebiscite was to be held after the negotiations to confirm the verdict. However, provincial voters soundly defeated the proposal by a margin of 58.2% to 41.8%. It was voted down in 96 of the province's 110 electoral districts. The high voter turnout—84.3% of 4.3 million eligible voters—indicated the intense passions aroused by the issue.

On the "no" side, the prereferendum period was marked by a huge advertising campaign by the Canadian government. The federalists rallied to their cause members of the Quebec Liberal Party, the Union Nationale, and the Social Credit. During the campaign, Prime Minister Pierre Elliott Trudeau promised to interpret a "no" vote as "a vote for the rebuilding of the Canadian federation." An estimated 80% of English-speaking Quebecers were joined by 54% of the French-speaking community and other ethnic groups in voting "no." For the separatists, an important historical chance had been lost. A day after the referendum, Trudeau announced a new round of talks with provincial and territorial leaders on rewriting the federal constitution. (*See* special report, page 172.)

At the federal-provincial constitutional conference September 8–13 in Ottawa, Quebec Prime Minister René Lévesque adopted an approach that conformed both to the negative results of the referendum as well as to Quebec's autonomous tradition. Although the provinces all agreed in principle with patriating the constitution, the sharing of power with the federal government was disputed in specific areas of education, culture, economy, and social services. The discussions ended without agreement on any point.

On September 18, Trudeau decided unilaterally to impose patriation of the Canadian Constitution (the 1967 British North America Act). Although the formula contains a charter on human rights and freedoms for all Canadians, it was rejected in Quebec for not respecting the fundamental and historical principles on which the Canadian Confederation was founded in

Quebec Liberal leader Claude Ryan encouraged provincial voters to cast their ballots for the "no."

CP Picture Service

449

Provincial Prime Minister René Lévesque (left), leader of the Parti Québécois, tried to convince the mining industry that independence would be to its advantage.

CP Picture Service

1867. At its fall orientation congress, the Parti Québécois decided to postpone a new referendum on sovereignty (its party goals being unchanged after the May defeat) and to campaign for "good government" in upcoming provincial elections. This approach was expected to reap rewards, as the PQ government had been acclaimed in the previous four years as being one of the province's best ever. But on October 16, Lévesque confused political analysts when he announced that fall elections would not be held. It would have been unwise, said Lévesque, to let Quebec stay in a political vacuum while a fundamental constitutional change was being made in Canada.

Meanwhile, the political map was being redrawn somewhat, as several Parti Québécois members of parliament and ministers announced their resignations and the former leader of the Union Nationale, Rodrigue Biron, joined the PQ. Camille Samson, the legendary Social Credit leader, joined Claude Ryan's Quebec Liberal Party.

Economic and Social Trends. While the public eye was on political events, the Quebec economy slowed down and in some sectors even declined. Unemployment was very high, and the cost of newly-adopted social policies underscored the need for higher tax revenues and limits on state spending.

The economic and social life of the province was also affected by a population decline. A decrease in immigration, a low birth rate, and a high mortality rate caused Quebec to lose some 10,000 inhabitants in one year. The numerical importance of the adult population and its educational needs brought about the formation of a public commission to study continuing education. The recommendations of the commission,

to be made public in 1981, were expected to call for better access to educational services, more state investments, and programs that will correspond to the present and future needs of Quebec society.

Foreign Ties. Continuing its policy of representation in foreign countries, the Quebec government decided to open a new general delegation in Mexico. The decision was prompted by the longtime cultural links between Quebec and Mexico, that nation's important role in Latin American affairs, and the fact that it has become a major oil-producing and exporting country. In the same vein, the Université du Québec initiated the Panamerican Association of Universities, with its headquarters in Quebec City. The association's first congress was held in October, with more than 300 intellectual and academic personalities gathered in the provincial capital for the occasion.

FERNAND GRENIER
Télé-université du Québec

QUEBEC · Information Highlights

Area: 594,860 sq mi (1 540 687 km²).
Population (1980 est.): 6,298,000.
Chief Cities (1976 census): Quebec, the capital, 177,082; Montreal, 1,080,546; Laval, 246,243.
Government (1980): *Chief Officers*—lt. gov., Jean-Pierre Coté; premier, René Lévesque (Parti Québécois). *Legislature*—Legislative Assembly, 110 members.
Education (1979–80 est.): *Enrollment*—public elementary and secondary schools, 1,108,150 pupils; private schools, 72,120; Indian (federal) schools, 4,820; postsecondary, 204,160 students. *Total expenditures,* $5,670,467,000.
Public Finance (1980–81 est.): *Revenues,* $14,850,000,000; *expenditures,* $17,150,000,000.
Personal Income (average weekly salary, May 1980): $312.64.
Unemployment Rate (July 1980, seasonally adjusted): 9.9%.
(All monetary figures are in Canadian dollars.)

RECORDINGS

Rapidly developing technology and an unpredictable economy were the dominant concerns of the U.S. recording industry in 1980. Home video recording reached the consumer level. Incompatible formats, high prices, and rapid obsolescence merely delayed the inevitable mass market explosion. Although movies were the mainstay of video software, major recording labels geared up for an audio/video union. Audiophile recordings entered the mainstream. It appeared that digital encoding, vastly superior to analog, would become the recording standard of the future.

Classical. Despite important personnel changes within the classical record industry, classical records maintained their steady 5% total record sales in the United States. Globally, the sales of a particular classical record or artist could be impressive. In 1980 the Lasalle Quartet sold their one-millionth record on the Deutsche Grammophon label. Antal Dorati received a gold medal for the worldwide sale of two million records on which he had been the conductor.

Opera continued to account for a large percentage of classical record sales. Especially prominent in 1980 were soprano Renata Scotto and tenors Luciano Pavarotti and Placido Domingo.

London Records was absorbed by the German conglomerate PolyGram, which now markets London classics along with Deutsche Grammophon and Philips records. CBS and Angel were active in applying the new digital recording technology.

Popular Music. The pop music sector was still reeling from its first recession. Sales were up from the 11% decline of 1979, but shifting demographics, less cash for leisure pursuits, and the development of more sophisticated tastes changed the familiar habits of the pop audience. Early in 1980, record and tape prices rose between 4% and 9%, and sales declined. However, blank tape sales escalated. Counterfeiting of records and tapes assumed massive proportions. Spearheaded by the Recording Industry of America Association, the industry called for stringent government legislation and developed protective devices like the laser-etched pattern on the "Tru Colours" disk by Split Enz.

Rock was still the bread and butter of the industry, but its audience was more selective. Record companies extended their mid-price lines. In the hope of improving the record sales market, Nu-Disk, a smaller 33⅓ record designed to carry two compositions on each side, was introduced by Epic Records in June.

It was the year of the soundtrack. Three of them—*Urban Cowboy, Fame,* and *Xanadu*—held the Top Ten simultaneously. Broadway show music was alive and well, captured in recordings of *Evita* and *Barnum*.

The unprecedented success of *Urban Cowboy* helped make country music second only to rock in popularity. Country fans in the South and Midwest still clung to their eight-track tapes despite the phasing out of this format.

With earnings of $500 million, black music was resurging, while disco faded from the top-seller charts. Major recording companies formed new black music departments.

Small independent labels catered to the special desires of the followers of New Wave, blues, and jazz. Although many regarded Clash's *London Calling* as the finest rock album of 1980, New Wave disks had not developed strong commercial appeal. While projects like Prestige's 12-disk package of all its Miles Davis material still were essayed, jazz recording grew more reliant for its survival on the independent labels.

Superstars like Elton John, Stevie Wonder, Paul McCartney, Linda Ronstadt, Diana Ross, and Bob Seger dominated the top-seller charts. The Rolling Stones' *Emotional Rescue* was the longest sustained chart topper of that group's career. The Kinks made news with *One for the Road,* the first audio recording released simultaneously on videocassette.

Elvis remained "The King." To mark his 25th year of RCA releases, the company produced *Elvis Aron Presley,* an eight-disk limited edition, priced at $69.95.

PAULETTE WEISS, *"Stereo Review"*

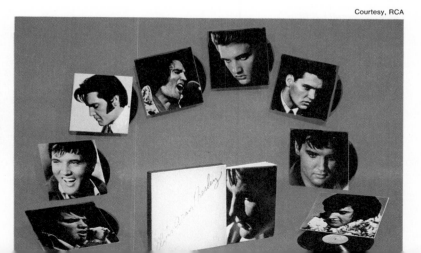

"Elvis Aron Presley," an eight-disk limited edition, was the first massive multiple album to enter the top-seller charts.

RECORDINGS OF 1980

CLASSICAL

BEETHOVEN: *Piano Concerto No. 1;* Michelangeli, Giulini, Vienna Symphony (Deutsche Grammophon).

BELLINI: *Norma;* Scotto, Troyanos, Giacomini, Plishka, Levine, National Philharmonic Orchestra (Columbia).

BERG: *Lulu;* Stratas, Minton, Schwartz, Riegel, Mazura, Boulez, Paris Opera Orchestra (Deutsche Grammophon).

DEBUSSY: *Images pour Orchestre;* André Previn, London Symphony Orchestra (Angel).

DELIBES: *Coppélia;* David Zinman, Rotterdam Philharmonic Orchestra (Philips).

LAGOYA: *Spanish Guitar;* Alexandre Lagoya (Columbia).

LISZT: *Piano Music;* Jorge Bolet (L'Oiseau-Lyre).

MAHLER: *Songs of a Wayfarer;* Frederica Von Stade, Andrew Davis, London Philharmonic Orchestra (Columbia).

MAHLER: *Symphony No. 4;* Elly Ameling, André Previn, Pittsburgh Symphony Orchestra (Angel).

MASSENET: *Le Roi de Lahore;* Sutherland, Pavarotti, Milnes, Ghiaurov, Bonynge (London).

MOZART: *Mostly Mozart, Vol. IV;* Alicia de Larrocha (London).

MOZART: *Piano Concertos No. 8 and No. 22;* Murray Perahia, English Chamber Orchestra (Columbia).

MOZART: *Die Zauberflöte;* Mathis, Araiza, van Dam, Ott, Hornik, von Karajan, Berlin Philharmonic (Deutsche Grammophon).

RUGGLES: *Complete Works;* Michael Tilson Thomas, Buffalo Philharmonic Orchestra (Columbia).

SCARLATTI: *Sonatas;* Aldo Ciccolini (Angel).

SCHUBERT: *Drei Klavierstücke, Piano Sonata D. 840;* Gilbert Kalisch (Nonesuch).

VERDI: *Rigoletto;* Cappuccilli, Cotrubas, Domingo, Giulini, Vienna Philharmonic Orchestra (Deutsche Grammophon).

VIVALDI: *The Four Seasons;* Iona Brown, Academy of St. Martin-in-the-Fields (Philips).

WHITE: *Danny Boy;* Robert White, Charles Gerhardt, National Philharmonic Orchestra (RCA).

WILLIAMS: *Pops in Space;* John Williams, Boston Pops Orchestra (Philips).

JAZZ

ART ENSEMBLE OF CHICAGO: *Full Force* (ECM/Warner Bros.).

RON CARTER: *NY Slick* (Milestone).

AL DiMEOLA: *Splendido Hotel* (Columbia).

SCOTT HAMILTON: *Tenorshoes* (Concord Jazz).

THE HEATH BROTHERS: *Live at the Public Theater* (Columbia).

AL JARREAU: *This Time* (Warner Bros).

CHUCK MANGIONE: *Fun and Games* (A&M).

ART PEPPER: *Landscape* (Galaxy).

SARAH VAUGHAN: *Duke Ellington Songbook One* (Pablo T.).

MUSICALS, MOVIES

BARNUM: original cast (Columbia).

THE BLUES BROTHERS: soundtrack (Atlantic).

COAL MINER'S DAUGHTER: soundtrack (MCA).

NEIL DIAMOND: THE JAZZ SINGER: soundtrack (Capitol).

THE EMPIRE STRIKES BACK: soundtrack (RSO).

EVITA: original cast (MCA).

FAME: soundtrack (RSO).

42ND STREET: original cast (RCA).

HONEYSUCKLE ROSE: soundtrack (Columbia).

THE ROSE: soundtrack (Atlantic).

PAUL SIMON: ONE TRICK PONY (Warner Bros.).

URBAN COWBOY: soundtrack (Asylum).

XANADU: soundtrack (MCA).

POPULAR

AC/DC: *Back in Black* (Atlantic).

HERB ALPERT: *Beyond* (A&M).

JOAN ARMATRADING: *Me Myself I* (A&M).

JEFF BECK: *There and Back* (Epic).

PAT BENATAR: *Crimes of Passion* (Chrysalis).

GEORGE BENSON: *Give Me the Night* (Warner Bros.).

B-52's: *The B-52's* and *Wild Planet* (Warner Bros.).

BLONDIE: *Autoamerican* and *Eat to the Beat* (Chrysalis).

DAVID BOWIE: *Scary Monsters* (RCA).

JACKSON BROWNE: *Hold Out* (Asylum).

CAMEO: *Camoesis* (Chocolate City)

CHEAP TRICK: *All Shook Up* (Epic).

CHIC: *Real People* (Atlantic).

ERIC CLAPTON: *Just One Night* (RSO).

THE CLASH: *London Calling* (Epic).

THE COMMODORES: *Heroes* (Motown).

CHRISTOPHER CROSS: *Christopher Cross* (Warner Bros.).

LACY J. DALTON: *Lacy J. Dalton* and *Hard Times* (Columbia).

CHARLIE DANIELS BAND: *Full Moon* (Epic).

THE DOOBIE BROTHERS: *One Step Closer* (Warner Bros.).

BOB DYLAN: *Saved* (Columbia).

THE EAGLES: *Live* (Asylum).

EARTH, WIND AND FIRE: *Faces* (ARC/Columbia).

ARETHA FRANKLIN: *Aretha* (Arista).

CRYSTAL GAYLE: *These Days* (Columbia).

J. GEILS BAND: *Love Stinks* (EMI/America).

GENESIS: *Duke* (Atlantic).

THE GRATEFUL DEAD: *Go to Heaven* (Arista).

HALL & OATES: *Voices* (RCA).

EMMYLOU HARRIS: *Roses in the Snow* (Warner Bros.).

THE ISLEY BROTHERS: *Go All the Way* (T-Neck).

JERMAINE JACKSON: *Let's Get Serious* (Motown).

WAYLON JENNINGS: *Music Man* (RCA).

JETHRO TULL: *A* (Chrysalis).

ELTON JOHN: *21 at 33* (MCA).

JOURNEY: *Departure* (Columbia).

CAROLE KING: *Pearls—Songs of Goffin and King* (Capitol).

THE KINKS: *One for the Road* (Arista).

GLADYS KNIGHT & THE PIPS: *About Love* (Columbia).

JOHN LENNON & YOKO ONO: *Double Fantasy* (Geffen).

LIPPS, INC.: *Mouth to Mouth* (Casablanca).

KENNY LOGGINS: *Alive* (Columbia).

THE MANHATTANS: *After Midnight* (Columbia).

BOB MARLEY & THE WAILERS: *Uprising* (Island).

MARSHALL TUCKER BAND: *Tenth* (Warner Bros.).

PAUL McCARTNEY: *McCartney II* (Columbia).

JONI MITCHELL: *Shadows and Light* (Asylum).

VAN MORRISON: *Common One* (Warner Bros.).

ANNE MURRAY: *Somebody's Waiting* and *Greatest Hits* (Capitol).

TED NUGENT: *Scream Dream* (Epic).

GARY NUMAN: *Telekon* (Atco).

THE OAK RIDGE BOYS: *Greatest Hits* (MCA)

THE O'JAYS: *The Year 2000* (The Sound of Philadelphia).

DOLLY PARTON: *Dolly, Dolly, Dolly* (RCA).

TEDDY PENDERGRASS: *T.P.* (Philadelphia Int'l.).

THE POLICE: *Zenyatta Mondatta* (A&M).

ELVIS PRESLEY: *Elvis Aron Presley* (RCA).

PRETENDERS: *Pretenders* (Sire).

QUEEN: *The Game* (Elektra).

EDDIE RABBITT: *Horizon* (Elektra).

THE ROCHES: *Nurds* (Warner Bros.).

BOBBI ROGERS: *Tommy Wolf Can Really Hang You Up the Most* (Focus).

KENNY ROGERS: *Gideon* (United Artists) and *Greatest Hits* (Liberty).

ROLLING STONES: *Emotional Rescue* (Rolling Stones)

LINDA RONSTADT: *Mad Love* (Asylum).

DIANA ROSS: *Diana* (Motown).

ROSSINGTON COLLINS BAND: *Anytime, Anyplace, Anywhere* (MCA).

BOB SEGER & THE SILVER BULLET BAND: *Against the Wind* (Capitol).

CARLY SIMON: *Come Upstairs* (Warner Bros.).

FRANK SINATRA: *Trilogy; Past, Present, & Future* (Reprise).

S.O.S. BAND: *S.O.S.* (Tabu).

SOUTHSIDE JOHNNY & THE ASBURY JUKES: *Love is a Sacrifice* (Mercury).

THE SPINNERS: *Love Trippin'* (Atlantic).

SPLIT ENZ: *True Colours* (A&M).

BRUCE SPRINGSTEEN: *The River* (Columbia).

SQUEEZE: *Argy Bargy* (A&M).

BARBRA STREISAND: *Guilty* (Columbia).

DONNA SUMMER: *The Wanderer* (Geffen).

TALKING HEADS: *Remain in Light* (Sire).

PETE TOWNSHEND: *Empty Glass* (Atco).

UTOPIA: *Deface the Music* (Bearsville).

VAN HALEN: *Women and Children First* (Warner Bros.).

DIONNE WARWICK: *No Night So Long* (Arista).

DON WILLIAMS: *I Believe in You* (MCA).

STEVIE WONDER: *Hotter Than July* (Tamla).

YES: *Drama* (Atlantic).

Susan Greenwood, Liaison

Cuban-Americans show their support for their relatives and friends leaving the Caribbean island.

REFUGEES

Burgeoning refugee problems in 1980 underscored the view that immigration and refugee issues may prove to be among the most important and troubling world problems in the forthcoming decade. For Americans the major drama was the sudden exodus in April and May of more than 100,000 Cubans from the port of Mariel and their arrival in southern Florida aboard a makeshift fleet of fishing vessels and private yachts. But elsewhere in the world, there were even more massive flows of people escaping strife and persecution. An estimated 1 million Afghans fled their country after the Soviet invasion of December 1979 and sought refuge in neighboring Pakistan. More than a million have left Ethiopia's war-torn Ogaden province over

the past few years and settled temporarily in Somalia and the Sudan. Three decades after the Arab-Israeli war of 1948–49, some 1.8 million Palestinians are still scattered throughout the Arab world. And although 750,000 Indochinese refugees have been resettled in the United States, China, Canada, Australia, and Europe since 1975, more than 250,000 remain in camps in Southeast Asia.

The Office of the United Nations High Commissioner for Refugees (UNHCR) estimates the population of refugees and displaced persons at 10-12 million. An official of the Federation for American Immigration Reform, a group seeking to tighten U.S. immigration laws, puts the figure at 14 million. In addition to the highly publicized Cuban, Afghan, and Indochinese outflows, there are many other refugee problems, smaller in

A refugee camp in Chad. As the result of a 14-year-old civil war in the African nation, some 100,000 refugees looked for a new life in Cameroon.

UPI

number, but no less tragic in dimension. Thousands of Central Americans have fled the violence and bloodshed that have overtaken such countries as El Salvador and Guatemala. Following the 1979 overthrow of the Somoza government in Nicaragua, more than 10,000 Nicaraguans asked for exile in the United States. In Africa, some 100,000 refugees from Chad and Equatorial Africa have sought shelter in Cameroon. Tanzania has taken in more than 150,000 victims of chronic strife in Rwanda and Burundi. A U.S. Senate study states that as many as 3.5 million Africans from 14 different countries may be living in exile, forced out of their homelands.

One of the least known refugee situations is in East Timor, a small island 350 mi (560 km) north of Australia in the eastern end of the Indonesian archipelago. Once a Portuguese colony, East Timor was annexed by Indonesia in 1976. Since that date, an estimated 150,000 persons of a population of 650,000 have died from starvation and disease. The island has experienced severe civil unrest and, according to some reports, "hundreds of thousands" of East Timorese have been rounded up by government troops and relocated in Indonesian refugee camps.

Relief Organizations. The UNHCR is the lead agency in international refugee relief work, coordinating refugee aid, appealing for food, clothing, and tents, and supervising their distribution. In 1980, it became clear that the world agency was in danger of being overwhelmed by the magnitude of refugee problems around the earth. In January, for example, the UNHCR issued an appeal for $55 million to care for the then 500,000 Afghans in Pakistan. As the year wore on, the refugee flow continued unabated, doubling to 1 million, and as it drew to a close no end of the flow was in sight. Similarly, Cambodians continued to pour into camps along the border with Thailand. In Somalia, Western countries and the UNHCR spent more than $130 million in refugee relief in 1980 alone.

The UNHCR is not itself an operational agency. Virtually all its relief work is carried out through governments and private voluntary organizations. Funds for UNHCR (and its companion agency, the UN Relief and Works Agency for Palestine Refugees in the Near East) come from the voluntary contributions of UN members, a system that often makes for precarious budgeting for refugee relief efforts.

Many of the groups working with the UNHCR are religious organizations, some with worldwide operations, such as Catholic Relief Services (CRS) and Church World Service (CWS), an affiliate of the National Council of Churches. Some concentrate their activities in a few nations. Lutheran World Relief, for one, confines its work to a select group of countries. Some focus on a single group of countries. American Near East Refugee Aid (ANERA) and the American Fund for Czechoslovak Refugees (which began working in Czechoslovakia and has now extended its programs to Uganda and Indochina as well) are examples.

Other sizable relief agencies include the Hebrew Immigrant Aid Society (HIAS), the International Rescue Committee, the Tolstoy Foundation, and Caritas Internationalis (International Conference of Catholic Charities—ICCC). The Intergovernmental Committee for European Migration (ICEM), established in 1951 to assist European émigrés, has become global in scope, helping refugee populations in Asia and the Far East, Eastern Europe, Latin America and the Caribbean, Africa, and the Middle East.

Among governments supporting the work of the UNHCR, the United States is one of the most active. The United States is by far the largest recipient of refugees for permanent settlement. Other nations have been more heavily impacted by refugee masses—Pakistan, for example, and Thailand. But the policy of such countries has generally been to afford only temporary shelter and to return refugees to their countries of origin when conditions improve, or, if they do not improve, to transfer the refugees to new homes in other parts of the world. In 1978, the last year for which official statistics are available, over 600,000 legal immigrants and refugees were admitted for permanent residence in the United States, far more than were accepted for permanent residence by any other country. (An equal number of illegal immigrants are believed to have eluded apprehension by authorities.) The 1980 total was undoubtedly much higher than that of 1978, owing to the heavy inflow of Cubans and other Caribbean nationals, and the continuing immigration of Indochinese refugees under special quotas.

Cuban Refugees. More than 800,000 Cuban refugees have been admitted to the United States since Fidel Castro came to power on New Year's day 1959. The refugee crisis of 1980 began on April 4, when Peruvian authorities refused to hand over six Cubans who had forced their way into the Peruvian embassy in Havana. Cuba retaliated by withdrawing security forces around

From their new shelter of Pakistan, Muslim refugees, escaping war in Afghanistan, pray to Allah.
UPI

the embassy. With the gates open, Cubans began flocking to the embassy, seeking asylum. By April 6, more than 7,000 had jammed into the half-acre embassy compound.

At first Castro agreed to permit those within the embassy to leave Cuba by airlift to Costa Rica. But when fewer than 700 had flown out, Castro closed that route and opened the port of Mariel, 30 mi (48 km) west of Havana, to a rag-tag fleet of private vessels from Florida. All Cubans who wanted to leave the country were free to go, he said, not just those in the Peruvian embassy. There was a proviso, however: any Cuban exile who came to Mariel to collect a relative had to take out several others designated by the Cuban government. Early in the sealift, it became apparent that Castro was using the so-called "freedom flotilla" to rid Cuba of dissidents, criminals, and other undesirables.

During the rest of April, throughout May and the early part of June, hundreds of small boats made the 90 mi (144 km) voyage across the Florida Strait to Mariel and returned with Cubans seeking asylum in the United States. As

As a child waves a Cuban flag in farewell, part of the "freedom flotilla" prepares to leave Mariel.
Susan Greenwood, Liaison

many as 4,000 refugees a day were landed, straining reception and processing facilities. By mid-June, over 120,000 had arrived, more than 1% of Cuba's total population of 9.9 million. The federal government set up temporary refugee centers at Eglin Air Force Base in northern Florida; Fort Chaffee, AR; Indiantown Gap, PA; and Fort McCoy, WI. Later, the government said it would open another center at Fort Allen, PR. The protests and objections of the Puerto Rican government forced the project to be canceled.

U.S. policy appeared to change several times during the crisis. Initially, the government sought to discourage the sealift and to regularize the refugee flow through diplomatic channels. Early in May, President Carter announced an "open arms" policy toward the refugees. He declared southern Florida a disaster area and released $10 million for refugee relief. On May 14 the administration reversed its position again, ordering an end to the sealift and ordering the Coast Guard to seize vessels and levy fines against boat owners participating in the freedom flotilla. Finally, on June 20, the government granted provisional entrant status to all Cubans who entered the United States between April 21 and June 19. These "parolees" were made eligible for public assistance and emergency aid.

During the next few months, Cubans continued to arrive at an average of 200 a day. In September, the Cuban government closed the port of Mariel and ordered the remaining boats of the freedom flotilla to leave. Nonetheless, Cubans found other ways to make the trip. In an unexpected backlash, Dade County (including Miami) voted in November to make it illegal to spend county funds for the use of any language but English, effectively ending the use of Spanish as a second official language. Reaction was also apparent in cities near the temporary processing centers. Some Cubans, impatient at long delays in resettlement, rioted in the camps. The government said it had found convicted criminals and homosexuals among the refugees.

Haitian Refugees. Compounding the government's problems was the parallel arrival of thousands of "boat people" from Haiti, the poorest country in the Western Hemisphere. While their numbers never reached the proportions of the Cubans, the total number of Haitian boat people in the United States was estimated at between 30,000 and 35,000 by year's end. On one weekend in April, authorities said that nearly 1,000 Haitians had waded ashore from decrepit sail boats, fishing craft, and even rowboats.

Like the Cubans, the Haitians were technically illegal immigrants. But the federal government, initially at least, refused to relax immigration laws, as it had done for the Cubans. For several years, the Immigration and Naturalization Service had routinely rejected Haitian requests for refugee status, claiming the boat people were fleeing poverty, not persecution, as required by law for refugee status.

UPI

Young Vietnamese appear pleased to be aboard the ''M.V. Megalohari'' in the Philippines.

The differential treatment of the Haitians and Cubans raised charges that the United States was pursuing a "racist" policy. Legal suits were filed on behalf of the Haitians, and several American black leaders publicly criticized the government's stand. On June 20, Haitians were given the same provisional entrant status granted the Cubans. In July, a federal judge found that the government had indeed practiced "wholesale discrimination" and ordered new deportation hearings for Haitians who had been ordered out.

New Immigration Law. Ironically, the Cuban and Haitian refugee waves hit the United States only a few months after passage of a law making major changes in U.S. refugee policy. The Refugee Act of 1980 (PL 96-212) declared that "it is the historical policy of the United States to respond to the urgent needs of persons subject to persecution in their own homelands." The act permitted entry of refugees not only from communist countries, but from all political oppression. The act set a "normal flow" of 50,000 a year, but the president is empowered, in consultation with the Congress, to raise the limit "for humanitarian concerns" or "in the national interest." President Carter set a fiscal year 1980 quota of 234,200 refugees, including 168,000 from Indochina but only 19,500 from Cuba and 1,000 from the rest of the hemisphere. The influx of Cubans and Haitians two months after passage of the law clearly rendered parts of it obsolete. The 1981 refugee quota was set at 217,000.

Study Commission. Congress has made periodic adjustments in immigration law since the enactment of the Immigration and Nationality Act of 1952. In recent years, though, there has been an increasing consensus on the need for wholesale reform of policies on immigration and refugee problems. In 1977 an interagency Task Force on Immigration Policy was established, composed of representatives of the departments of state, justice, and labor, to assess current immigration laws and to develop recommendations for future legislation. A year later, Congress created a Select Commission on Immigration and Refugee Policy, made up of four members from each house of Congress, four cabinet members, and four public members appointed by the president. Its task was to propose a basic rewriting of immigration laws and to examine such questions as how many immigrants should be admitted each year, from where they should come, under what criteria, and through what processes. The commission was also to study the phenomenon of increased illegal immigration and recommend how to deal with illegal immigrants already in the United States. The commission was scheduled to complete its studies by the end of 1980 and to present a final report by March 1, 1981. The impending change of administration in 1981 made it unclear at year's end what steps the United States would take to cope with refugee problems and immigration.

RICHARD C. SCHROEDER

Visiting France in the spring, Pope John Paul II joins President Giscard in a ride through Paris.

RELIGION

Survey

Pope John Paul II of the Roman Catholic Church made news in 1980 with strategic pastoral visits that included a twelve-day tour of the world's most populous Roman Catholic nation, Brazil. Christianity continued to grow in Africa with gains of more than six million a year. The growth and increasingly reactionary mood of the world's Islamic community were highlighted by the holding of American hostages in the U.S. Embassy in Tehran, Iran, and the selection of the Ayatollah Khomeini as *Time* magazine's Man of the Year for 1979. The Rt. Rev. Robert Runcie became the 102d archbishop of Canterbury and titular head of the world's 65 million Anglicans. The Orthodox Eastern Church showed signs of renewal in areas of the Soviet Union.

The Mormon Church at 150. In December 1979, Sonia Johnson of Sterling, VA, was excommunicated from the Church of Jesus Christ of Latter-Day Saints. An ardent supporter of women's rights, a policy which is against the basic tenets of Mormonism, Ms. Johnson was charged with spreading false doctrine. The event can be considered a sign of the coming-of-age of the Mormon religion. It indicates that the movement has become sufficiently a part of the mainstream of American life and that the Mormon church will have to contend increasingly with the influence of values that are not Mormon. The church plans to build seven new temples in the near future, six of which are to be outside the United States. The building program is a measure of the recent success of the Latter-Day Saints as they celebrate 150 years of institutional existence. There are currently nearly 4.5 million Mormons in more than 60 countries, and the church is growing at a rapid rate, particularly in the United States and in Latin American nations.

It was in April 1830 that the prophet, Joseph Smith, Jr., and five of his followers founded the new church in Fayette, NY. During the ensuing decades the Latter-Day Saints have existed as a kind of "established sect" on the American religious scene. That is to say, they have existed long enough to gain acceptance. They have always been identified strongly with American destiny, but many of their doctrines and practices run counter to those of the Christian consensus, with its predominantly Protestant stamp. To some extent Mormonism is a new religion. It speaks of itself as the "restored" true Church of Jesus Christ, which implies that prior Christian history from the second century onward has been apostate. This accounts in large measure for the divergence of Mormon belief and practice from the rest of the Christian tradition.

The Saints believe that America is the Promised Land. They see themselves as a chosen people, called to be the vanguard for the return of Christ which will take place on the North American continent. That is partly because, according to Mormon belief, Christ made a post-resurrection appearance in North America with the intention of organizing His church. This fact had been lost to history until it was revealed to Joseph Smith by the angel Moroni, who was formerly the last prophet of Christ's original church, destroyed in the second century. Together with the Bible as a scriptural text, the Saints emphasize the *Book of Mormon,* which is Smith's translation of ancient gold tablets shown to him by Moroni. The book is a biblical account set in North America, dealing with the years 600 B.C. to 421 A.D. It begins with the migration of a small group of Hebrews who wish to escape the Babylonian invasions.

What is unique about Mormon teaching is its basis in philosophical materialism. Matter is all that exists; even God is material and subject to the laws of matter. Everything that is has always existed; therefore there is no creation. God, too, preexisted in another world and achieved godhood. In like manner, human beings were brought into existence from preexistent forms. They have the potential to achieve godhood.

This emphasis on matter tends to make Mormon morality an affair of rigorous and legalistic emphasis on outward behavior. Mormons are ardent believers in free enterprise and close community ties. Mormons practice clean living, self-reliance, devotion to family, and obedience to ecclesiastical authority. Family life is central to their morality because they are imitators of a material God who procreates with a female counterpart as humans do. Marriage, procreation, and parenthood are what life is all about in present and future existence.

The present dilemma facing the Latter-Day Saints is: How will their unique enterprise fare in a world that holds different values? Coming-of-age is a mixed blessing. Mormon scholars are beginning to engage in dialogue with outsiders. The educational experience of young Mormons fashions a world that raises deep and unsettling questions about a religion that is very authoritarian and traditionalist. While the Mormon doctrine of revelation makes changes in doctrine a relatively easy process, the changes wrought may presage the end of America's most successful and exotic religious invention.

RICHARD E. WENTZ
Arizona State University

From its headquarters in Salt Lake City, the Mormon Church marked its 150th anniversary in 1980.
Porterfield, Photo Researchers

Far Eastern

The People's Republic of China may well become the scene of new and vital religious impulses in the Far East. Nearly 200 Chinese bishops and priests of the Catholic Church met in synod for the first time in nearly two decades. The Church in China considers itself independent of Rome, a policy made expedient by the government's regulation of all religious activity. Clergy are paid by the state, which is also permitting the publication of Bibles. There were some reports of mass conversions to Christianity among youth in rural communes.

Scholars of religion were interested in the fact that the new Academy of Social Sciences in Peking includes an Institute of World Religion. China has always been the home of unique and diverse religious movements that include a thriving Muslim community which reflects its existence in a Chinese environment since the Tang Dynasty (7th-10th centuries).

Dialogue between Christian theologians and Buddhist thinkers continued in Japan. One of the difficulties in such dialogue is that Western theologians tend to be philosophically speculative while Buddhist thinkers tend to be philosophically experiential.

There was considerable speculation over the background of the resignation of Daisaku Ikeda as president of the powerful Buddhist lay organization Sōka Gakkai. Ikeda had led the organization to a membership of nearly 8 million and had become a figure whose influence apparently challenged the authority of the priesthood of the parent organization, Nichiren Shōshū. According to reliable reports, some of the members of the Sōka Gakkai had begun to deify Ikeda, to consider him to be the "true Buddha." This idea is part of the tradition of Nichiren Shōshū itself, which was begun in the 13th century by a Buddhist monk, Nichiren, when it was affirmed that he was "true Buddha" with Gautama as precursor. Nichiren Shōshū is a conservative sect, and it was rumored that Ikeda and Sōka Gakkai sought to effect change in the doctrine. It was expected that Sōka Gakkai under its new president, Hōjō Hiroshi, would be more withdrawn and less aggressive.

RICHARD E. WENTZ

Judaism

The dimming of hopes for a lasting peace in the Middle East and outbreaks of open anti-Semitism in various parts of the world caused grave concern among Jews in 1980. Against a background of virulent Arab terrorism in Israel and widespread assaults on Jews elsewhere, world Jewry witnessed an erosion of international support for Israel and a deterioration of the "normalization process" with Egypt.

Arab-Israeli Relations. Normalization of Israeli-Egyptian relations continued early in the year with the official opening of the border in late January and the exchange of ambassadors in late February. However, the construction of Jewish settlements in Judea and Samaria and Israel's firm stand on "undivided Jerusalem," both of national-religious importance to Israel, caused Egypt to suspend the peace process and much of the international community to voice protest.

The controversy was precipitated when the Knesset (Israeli parliament) adopted the "Jerusalem Law," which states that undivided Jerusalem is the capital of Israel. In response, Egypt suspended normalization proceedings, Saudi Arabia called for a "holy war" against Israel, the United Nations Security Council passed a resolution denouncing Israel "for changing the status of the Holy City," 13 nations reversed their support for Jerusalem as the nation's capital by removing their embassies, and the Vatican issued a warning against modifications in "the overall character of Jerusalem as a sacred heritage." In a countermove, more than 1,000 evangelical Christians from 20 countries gathered in Jerusalem to demonstrate solidarity with Israel.

Perhaps inspired by the "Islamic Revolution," Arab terrorism assumed religious overtones and escalated from kidnapping to direct assaults on Jewish life. A predominant number of victims were pious Jews identifiable by their skullcaps. A worshipper was murdered near the Western Wall in Jerusalem, Yeshiva students were massacred in Hebron, and a group of vacationing orthodox Jewish children was attacked in Antwerp, Belgium.

Neo-Nazism and Anti-Semitism. The rise in scope and violence of neo-Nazi activities was an echo of the Holocaust to world Jewry. While deepening sympathy with Jewish suffering during the Nazi era was manifested in a proliferation of Holocaust memorials and growing public interest in books, films, and study courses on the subject, vandalism of these memorials and the publication of literature denying the Holocaust were also on the increase. Destruction or defacement of monuments with swastikas and anti-Semitic slogans in Italy, Switzerland, and the United States was compounded by bodily assaults on prominent Jews in Brazil and Argentina, a flood of anti-Semitic publications in Uruguay, and the growth of paramilitary neo-Nazi groups in West Germany.

The most violent outbreak of anti-Semitism, however, occurred in France. In October, neo-Nazi agitation culminated in a series of knifings of Jewish individuals, machine gun attacks on Jewish schools, and the bombing of the largest synagogue in Paris. Four persons were killed and 30 others injured in the bombing. Massive demonstrations were held by French Jews and gentiles alike to protest the government's anti-Israel policies, which were blamed for the outbreaks. Demonstrations against anti-Semitism were organized by various Jewish organizations abroad. In New York, the Legal Coalition for Syrian Jewry was formed to defend the rights of that beleaguered group, and the Society for Iranian Jewry was organized in response to the growing threat to the Jewish community in that country. More than 100 Iranian Jews were imprisoned and several executed on charges of having "U.S. and Zionist" loyalties.

Religious Issues. Several controversial religious issues reemerged during the year. In Israel, the Knesset abrogated a clause in its abortion law which had permitted abortion for socio-economic reasons. In the United States, reformed Rabbi Alexander Schindler proposed that a child of mixed marriage be considerd Jewish. Both chief rabbis of Israel rejected the proposal, and the Rabbinical Council of America—the association of orthodox rabbis—took an official stand against intermarriage. In another development, the Rabbinical Assembly, the association of conservative rabbis, for the first time endorsed women as rabbis.

LIVIA E. BITTON JACKSON
Herbert H. Lehman College, CUNY

Orthodox Eastern

During 1980 the Orthodox Church in America (OCA) celebrated its tenth anniversary as the fifteenth autocephalous (self-governing) unit in the world family of orthodox churches. At a council in Detroit in November 1980, participants from dioceses in the United States (including the original diocese in Alaska), Canada, and Mexico had recommitted the church to the effort to unite all Orthodox administratively into one ecclesiastical body. The OCA is currently comprised of dioceses of the original Russian, Albanian, Rumanian, and Bulgarian Orthodox in America.

Valerian Trifa, the OCA bishop of Detroit, gave up his American citizenship in September 1980. The leader of the church's Rumanian episcopate, who was accused by the U.S. Department of Justice of "concealing his activities as a student leader of the Fascist and Nazi-supporting Iron Guard of Rumania" during the 1940s and of thus entering the United States illegally, denied that he had participated in anti-Jewish activities during his student days in Bucharest. Bishop Trifa said that he could not receive a fair trial, and that he did not wish to continue his episcopal work in the United States as long as the charges stood. The Detroit diocese elected the Rev. Nathanial Popp as its auxiliary bishop.

A Greek Orthodox clergy-laity congress was held in Atlanta in June. Although by charter the church remains administratively dependent on the Ecumenical Patriarchate of Constantinople, the congress affirmed its commitment to a unified American Orthodoxy.

Official dialogue between the Eastern Orthodox Churches and the Roman Catholic Church was held in Rhodes and Patmos, Greece, May 29–June 4, 1980. A five-year plan of theological study and discussion was agreed to. The Ortho-

Marc Bulka, Liaison

Violent acts of anti-Semitism in France brought massive demonstrations in the streets of Paris.

dox delegation, which failed to include Americans, was called formal and unrepresentative. Certain Orthodox, including the Council of the Monks of Mount Athos and the Theological Faculty of Athens, also criticized the dialogue itself. The inflexible Catholic position on papal infallibility and statements by Pope John Paul II in support of Uniatism (recognition of papal authority by an Eastern church) led to the criticism. The Catholic delegation included Eastern Rite Uniates.

In the USSR two Orthodox priests were among the many dissidents arrested during 1980. The Rev. Dmitri Dudko, author of *Our Hope,* was imprisoned and was forced to recant his crimes against the state on Moscow television on June 20. In July, the Rev. Gleb Yakunin, longtime organizer of Orthodox dissent, especially among the youth, was given five years at hard labor, to be followed by five years of internal exile. In the USSR, it remains a criminal offense to propagate Christianity outside the walls of a government-sanctioned church. The Rev. George Calciu received a five-year sentence in Rumania.

Archbishop Paul of Kuopio, leader of Finnish Orthodoxy, continued to call for autocephaly for his church and for greater administrative unity among the Orthodox in Western Europe and North America. His church hosted an International Conference of Orthodox Youth Movements.

THE REV. THOMAS HOPKO
St. Vladimir's Seminary

461

Protestantism

It may not be another Great Awakening in the religious life of the United States, as some historians have suggested, but there is little doubt that renewed interest in politics by conservative Christians is having its impact on American life, religious and political. Presidential politics made "born-again" a familiar term in the public media since all three major candidates identified themselves as evangelical Christians who could point to a specific moment of conversion in their lives.

President Jimmy Carter had benefited from his identification with evangelical Christians in the 1976 election, but in losing his bid for re-election to Ronald Reagan, he was affected, many observers felt, by the anti-Carter mood among conservative Christians. Certainly the influence of conservative Christians was felt in other parts of the political process as Religious Roundtable, a group favoring a politically conservative posture, conducted a major rally in Dallas, TX, in September, to urge Protestant and Roman Catholic clergy to become active in politics. Television evangelists, including Jerry Falwell, who headed Moral Majority, and Pat Robertson, president of the Christian Broadcasting Network, each reached over 100 million listeners with their blend of preaching and conservative politics.

Major issues of concern to these groups focused primarily on personal life-styles and family life. Conservative evangelical Christians were reacting to what they felt was too much government toleration of immoral behavior. They objected, for example, to the rise in pornography, abortion, homosexuality, and portrayals of sex and violence on television. In addition, they argued against the Equal Rights Amendment on the grounds that it is anti-family. Other religious groups supported the ERA.

In previous decades conservative Christians, some of whom were in the anti-Baptist tradition of "shunning the evils of the world," insisted that religion had no place in politics. But 1980 was a year when the conservative attitude shifted. Further involvement in national and local politics could be expected, as the public reacted against changes in life-styles from the more traditional family-oriented value systems. On the other hand, liberal church people protested the conservative participation, saying that their own earlier liberal activity had been aimed at changing society. According to the liberals the conservatives—often called the New Religious Right—

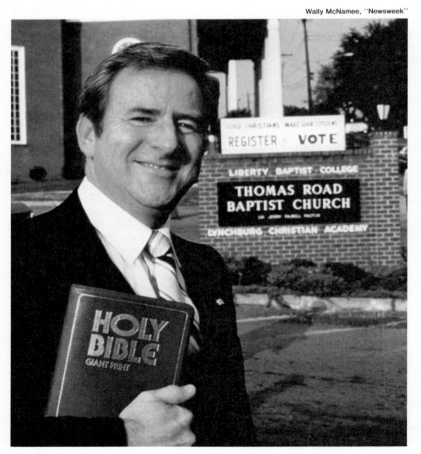

Wally McNamee, "Newsweek"

As leader of Moral Majority, a political action organization, television evangelist Jerry Falwell played an active part in the 1980 U.S. election campaign. His aim was the election of Republican presidential candidate Ronald Reagan and other conservatives. According to the 47-year-old host of the "Old-Time Gospel Hour," the moralists in America had "had enough" and were "joining hands for the changing, the rejuvenating of a nation."

Paul Wigboldy, Robert Schuller Ministries

Wheaton College

The Crystal Cathedral (above) in Garden Grove, CA, which was dedicated in September 1980, is to serve the congregation of the Rev. Robert H. Schuller, a television evangelist. Philip Johnson and John Burgee designed the $18 million building. At right, visitors view an exhibit at the new $13.5 million Billy Graham Center at Wheaton College, Wheaton, IL. The facility at the liberal arts college includes a library, archive, and museum on evangelism.

Some 200,000 evangelical Christians attended a "Washington for Jesus" rally in the nation's capital in late April.

Les Moore, Uniphoto

were seeking to affect personal life decisions through the government.

Both sides quoted biblical sources to defend their positions. And within conservative circles there was strong disagreement over the inerrancy question. Some Christians insisted that each word of the Bible is literally true; others argued that even though the Bible is a final authority for the believer, it is not necessary to accept each word literally.

A group of younger evangelicals, the Evangelicals for Social Action, urged fellow conservatives to become active in politics, but cautioned that while the Bible does say many things about personal morality, it also contains considerable guidance on matters of social justice and care for the poor. *Christianity Today,* a conservative publication, faulted Moral Majority and similar organizations for limiting their concern for biblical mandates to only pro-family and pro-life issues: "Too narrow a front in battling for a moral crusade, or for a truly biblical involvement in politics, could be disastrous."

One denomination that also struggled over conservative-liberal issues was the United Methodist Church. Meeting in its quadrennial session in April 1980, the church debated the sensitive topic of homosexuality and reached an ambiguous conclusion: in its Social Principles statement, the denomination reaffirmed its opposition to homosexuality but then left the way open for local conferences to ordain "self-avowed, practicing homosexuals" if they seek to become clergypersons.

The United Methodists were also caught in the national conflict over how the country should respond to the crisis of 52 American citizens being held hostage in Iran. An eight-member delegation went to the White House to urge President Carter not to use force in resolving the crisis. They reported back to the General Conference that they were satisfied with the president's attitude, only to discover the next morning that a rescue mission had been attempted, and American lives were lost in the effort.

Ecumenism, which appeared to be popular among Protestants in the 1960s and 1970s, now seemed a lower priority as the Consultation on Church Union (COCU) celebrated its 20th anniversary in December 1980 with little progress toward actual merger of the ten denominations which originally came together in the Consultation. At its plenary meeting during the year, however, COCU delegates moved ahead by adopting a seven-chapter document which would be studied by the churches. A final chapter, on the ministry of Christ, that called for a three-part structure of bishops, presbyters (ministers of word and sacrament), and deacons (ministers of service to the world), was adopted.

Tension continued between Christians and Jews over U.S. attitudes toward Israel. The National Council of Churches adopted a report which attempted a balanced perspective, but which was criticized by Jewish leaders as "tilted" in favor of the Palestinian call for a separate state in the Middle East. And the Mennonite Church, with a long record of service in the Arab world, complained that one of its clergy, the Rev. Paul Quring, had been prevented from returning to work in the West Bank of the Jordan River because he had testified before the U.S. Congress regarding Israeli practices in the occupied area.

JAMES M. WALL, *"The Christian Century"*

Roman Catholicism

For Roman Catholicism, 1980 was a year of settling in for Pope John Paul II as he began devoting more attention to "in-house" matters such as liturgy reform, seminary education, the family, and the role of clergy in politics. It was also a year of growing dissent and turmoil.

The year was one of Synods: the Dutch Synod, called by the pope to mediate the rift between theologically conservative and progressive bishops in the Netherlands, and the world Synod of Bishops, devoted to establishing new directions and support for the Catholic family.

Pope John Paul journeyed to six nations of Africa and to France, Brazil, and West Germany. During the latter trips, he combined pastoral direction with calls for social reform and new initiatives to end poverty and violence.

Controversy continued to stir the Church. Dissent grew over the beliefs and practices of certain theologians, including the Rev. Edward Schillebeeckx, a Dutch Dominican; over the ouster of the Rev. Hans Küng, a Swiss theologian, from his Catholic faculty post in Germany; and over the direct papal order that led the Rev. Robert F. Drinan (see Biography), a Jesuit, not to run for a sixth term in the U.S. Congress.

Church ties to politics were even more significant in Latin America. Several Nicaraguan priests, participants in the 1979 overthrow of strongman Anastasio Somoza, joined the revolutionary regime and even held cabinet posts. Archbishop Oscar Romero of El Salvador, an outspoken critic of government repression, was assassinated as he celebrated Mass.

Carolyn Farrell, a 44-year-old nun, is mayor of Dubuque, IA. Nuns were unaffected by the Vatican order banning priests from serving in public office.
UPI

During the pope's Brazil trip, in which he openly criticized oppressive elements in the Brazilian government, John Paul was confronted with a statement signed by 1,500 Latin American clergymen which termed the struggle for liberation from poverty "an imperative of the Gospel."

In Iran, where Vatican efforts ensued in behalf of U.S. hostages and were instrumental in gaining the release of bodies of Americans killed in the abortive rescue attempt, a bishop and several priests were jailed and then exiled.

As the debate over priestly celibacy mounted, a group of Indonesian bishops asked the Vatican to allow ordination of married men to the priesthood. In the United States, bishops announced that they had received permission to admit married Episcopal Church clergy to the Catholic priesthood. Pope John Paul indicated that he had relaxed restrictions on the laicization of priests.

Vocations to the priesthood continued to decline, particularly among diocesan clergy, and new efforts were mounted for the training of lay persons in a variety of Church ministries. The Vatican asked the world's bishops to contemplate a major redistribution of clergy.

In the United States and Italy, especially, anti-abortion movements increased in effectiveness as support for voter and legislative efforts to bar abortion continued to surface. Pro-family and right-wing political movements attracted conservative Catholics in the United States, spilling over into the 1980 political campaigns. Humberto Cardinal Medeiros of Boston caused considerable controversy when he urged Catholics not to vote for candidates favoring abortion. Catholic non-profit groups and publications challenged an Internal Revenue Service ruling barring "single issue" voter education efforts.

On the social justice front, Catholic leaders backed efforts worldwide for a more just standard of living. Particularly significant was the Church's support of the Polish workers' strike. Pope John Paul and other bishops around the world also spoke out against the proliferation of nuclear arms, and in the United States, many dioceses set up draft counseling centers following enactment of draft registration.

William Cardinal Baum became the top American at the Vatican when he was named Prefect of the Sacred Congregation for Catholic Education. He was succeeded as archbishop of Washington, DC, by Bishop James Hickey of Cleveland. John Cardinal Dearden of Detroit resigned, and the Apostolic Delegate in the United States, Archbishop Jean Jadot, was named to head the Vatican Secretariat for Non-Christians. Also in the United States, the bishops voted to hold a meeting in 1982, similar in format to the 1979 Puebla, Mexico, conference, to discuss their roles, and approved a TV magazine-type program for prime-time viewing.

ROBERT L. JOHNSTON
Editor, "The Catholic Review"

Korvettes, once a leading U.S. discount retailing chain, suffered bad times and decided to close its stores.

Vic DeLucia, NYT Pictures

RETAILING

In 1980, U.S. retailers had a difficult, pressure-ridden year, as growing inflation and deepening recession forced millions of Americans to cut their buying. Merchants found their profits shrinking despite their cost-cutting efforts and offerings of special "values."

Rising interest rates and higher overhead and merchandise costs eroded profits in the first half, although there was some improvement in the second half. But the imposition of the Credit Controls Act by President Carter in mid-March limited credit sales for more than five months.

Aimed at curbing inflation, the credit controls forced large retail chains to raise minimum monthly payments and interest charges. As a result, many consumers decided that their normal rate of credit buying would be unwise and perhaps unpatriotic. Credit-card applications declined by one third, and credit sales dropped by almost half.

Irked by its reduced earnings, Sears, Roebuck & Company, the largest U.S. retail chain, restructured itself along the lines of a holding company to help its main businesses reach their potential. With a $72 million loss in the first half, Montgomery Ward, owned by Mobil Corporation since 1974, purchased a number of Two Guys store sites in the East for its Jefferson Ward discount chain and announced the conversion of 100 conventional Ward stores to the more profitable and productive Jefferson chain.

The problems of these companies, as well as of the J.C. Penney Company, were related to the fact that the nation's more moderate earners—families with incomes of $20,000 or less—were being hardest hit in the troubled economy. Even run-of-the-mill discounters, who should have thrived in such a situation, were suffering as they tried to cope with slower sales and higher costs.

Virtually regardless of income level, Americans appeared to want clearly identifiable value for their money no matter how high the price tags. This was clearly reflected in the significantly higher sales and profits of "upscale" discounters who stress better-grade national brands at discount prices, such as the Caldor and Target and Venture chain stores. As if to emphasize this point, the K Mart Corporation, the fastest growing discounter of the 1970s, announced that it would test more fashionable apparel and improved presentation in its more than 2,500 stores.

It was also apparent, however, that affluent shoppers remained relatively unscathed by the recession, buying freely in such stores as Bloomingdale's, Saks Fifth Avenue, Bergdorf Goodman, Neiman-Marcus, and Lord and Taylor. Department stores catering to middle- and upper-income customers fared relatively well compared to the large retail-catalog chains.

The year's most dramatic development came in the virtual dismemberment of Korvettes Inc. by the Agache-Willot Group of France. After less than a year of disappointment over the failing health of the discount chain, the French owners reduced the number of stores from 50 to 15, discharged about 10,000, or 90%, of the employees, and turned operations over to a liquidator until the remaining store sites were sold. A victim of four mergers in less than 15 years, Korvettes underwent abrupt changes in merchandising policy, which only confused the buying public.

Despite the liquidation of Korvettes, the trend toward large investment for eventual takeover continued. Interstate Properties, a shopping center developer, acquired 18% of the stock of Vornado Inc., operator of the Two Guys discount chain, and took control of the board. Lane Bryant Inc., which had sought vainly to buy Beeline Inc., the direct-selling company, found itself the target of a potential takeover move by Hatleigh Corporation, a Canadian holding company. And Alexander's Inc., the New York retailer, became the unhappy target of sizable investments by financiers openly hinting at eventual takeover.

Suburban shopping centers generally recovered from the reluctance of consumers to drive long distances. But retailers began to eye sites in urban areas which might be more accessible for new branch stores because of returned middle-income residents and federally-funded housing projects.

ISADORE BARMASH, "The New York Times"

RHODE ISLAND

Politics took center stage in the state during much of 1980, with both state and national contests attracting keen interest.

The Elections. A vigorous effort to promote Edward Kennedy for the Democratic nomination began long before the June 3d presidential primary. Organizations supporting various Republican aspirants also sprang up. A small primary turnout heavily endorsed Kennedy over President Jimmy Carter. On the Republican side, Ronald Reagan won overwhelmingly.

In the November election President Carter carried the state, 48% to 37% for Reagan, with 14% for John Anderson.

Republican Mayor of Providence Vince A. Cianci, Jr.'s challenge to incumbent Democratic governor, J. Joseph Garrahy, highlighted state contests. The mayor was beset by mounting financial woes and scandals in Providence and lost to the governor by a massive three-to-one margin. For Congress, while Rep. Fernand St. Germain, a Democrat, had little trouble winning an 11th term in the first district, Edward P. Beard faced tough fights in the second. He won a close primary but lost to Republican Claudine Schneider (whom he had narrowly defeated in 1978) in the fall. Rep. Beard's defeat gave the state an even partisan division in its Senate and House delegations for the first time in decades. Democrats won all the other state-level races and retained wide margins in the General Assembly.

The Economy. Employment in Rhode Island held up fairly well through April, but factory jobs dropped by 2,700 in May, signaling the onset of recession in the state. The June unemployment rate was 7.3%, exceeded in New England only by Maine's. Fall figures showed some improvement, with September employment totals below those of September 1979, but an unemployment rate down to 6.1% (5.8% in September 1979). These trends were major campaign issues. July through September sales tax revenues were under the amount estimated.

On the other hand, tourism in Rhode Island was up 24% over 1979, due in part to Newport's busy summer and particularly to the America's Cup races. The year's gross from tourism was predicted at $400 million. Electric Boat announced plans in July for 500 more hirings at Quonset, up to a total employment of 4,800.

The Environment. Pollution of Narragansett Bay by Providence's antiquated and inadequate sewer treatment plant has long caused concern. During its 1980 session, the state legislature established a sewer authority to take over, rebuild, and run the plant. In November the voters approved the necessary $87.7-million bond issue. Disposal of toxic waste was an urgent concern.

General Assembly. The state's legislators voted a balanced budget with a $10-per-person income tax rebate, and in two steps raised the drinking age to 20. Near the start of the January session Speaker Edward P. Manning resigned and was succeeded by House Finance Chairman Matthew J. Smith. The end-of-session acceptance of judgeships by the House and Senate majority leaders meant a major reshuffle for 1981.

Other Developments. Preliminary 1980 census figures showed a tiny decrease in the state's population, but major internal shifts. Coastal towns and those on the fringe of the metropolitan areas saw sharp growth while the old central cities declined, with a 13% drop in Providence.

Providence voters approved the city's first home rule charter in November, to take effect in January 1983.

ELMER E. CORNWELL, JR., *Brown University*

In the North Providence school district, teachers join the picket lines in support of striking janitors.
Providence Journal Company

—— **RHODE ISLAND • Information Highlights** ——

Area: 1,214 sq mi (3 144 km²).

Population (Jan. 1980 est.): 928,000.

Chief Cities (1976 est.): Providence, the capital, 164,989; (1970 census): Warwick, 83,694; Pawtucket, 76,984.

Government (1980): *Chief Officers*—governor, J. Joseph Garrahy (D); lt. gov., Thomas R. DiLuglio (D). *Assembly*—Senate, 50 members; House of Representative, 100 members.

Education (1979–80): *Enrollment*—public elementary schools, 78,348 pupils; public secondary, 75,750; colleges and universities, 64,435 students. *Public school expenditures*, $331,603,000 ($2,096 per pupil).

State Finances (fiscal year 1979): *Revenues*, $1,211,-000,000; *expenditures*, $1,171,000,000.

Personal Income (1979): $7,906,000,000; per capita, $8,510.

Labor Force (June 1980): *Total labor force*, 461,500; *unemployed*, 33,900 (7.3% of total force).

RUMANIA

Despite apprehension over the potential consequences of the passing of President Tito in Yugoslavia and massive labor unrest in Poland, Rumania experienced a relatively quiet year.

Domestic Affairs. A nationwide celebration in January marked the 62nd birthday of President and Secretary General of the Communist Party Nicolae Ceauşescu. In the July observance of the 2,050th anniversary of a "centralized and independent Dacian state," Ceauşescu was hailed as a "true successor" of the first Dacian ruler, Burebistas. On March 29, Elena Ceauşescu, the president's wife, was named first deputy premier and charged with the leadership of Rumania's nine other deputies.

At the 12th Communist Party Congress in late November 1979, 2,664 delegates elected a 408-member Central Committee. In his address to the Congress, Ceauşescu announced a party card exchange, aimed at purification and revitalization of membership, in 1980. He also called for a European disarmament conference; expressed hope for cooperation among all socialist countries; wished success for Sino-Soviet talks; and, in domestic matters, praised "collective leadership."

As a result of the energy crisis, overinvestment in industry—particularly oil-consuming petrochemicals—overcentralization of labor, and low productivity, Rumania's gross national product in 1979 fell far below projections.

In September 1980, the Executive Committee of the Communist Party decided to reduce the military budget by 16% in an effort to raise the standard of living. In January, provisions for increased worker self-management went into ef-fect. The government also decreed new restrictions on foreign travel, the most severe in any communist country.

Several Rumanians, including diplomats, defected to the West. In February, Nicolae Ion Horodnica, a third secretary at the Rumanian Embassy in Washington, asked for asylum after receiving orders to return home. In July, 20 Rumanians escaped to Austria in a state-owned cropduster plane.

Although some strikes were reported, the Polish workers' upheaval appeared to have little impact in Rumania. The events in Poland were ignored by the Rumanian mass media.

Foreign Affairs and Trade. On July 28, Rumania became the first member of the COMECON bloc to enter into a trade agreement with the European Community (EC). Accords were reached on organizational structures, mode of payments, and allowable credits. The Rumanian government and press urged the COMECON countries to enter into a similar agreement as a collective body.

As a result of the Soviet Union's drastically reduced oil exports, Rumania became dependent on other oil-producing states for its yearly import requirement of approximately 130 million barrels. Several agreements with the United Arab Emirates, Libya, Iraq, and Iran were concluded.

In May, Prime Minister Ilie Verdet made an "official friendship visit" to Moscow. In July, President Ceauşescu traveled to France, returning President Valéry Giscard d'Estaing's March visit. State and party officials made increasingly frequent exchange visits with leaders of China, Great Britain, and African, Asian, and Scandinavian nations, as well as with members of COMECON. In May, U.S. President Jimmy Carter recommended to Congress that Rumania's most favored nation trade status be continued.

The death of Yugoslav President Tito on May 4 received wide publicity in Rumania. His "historic role" in the causes of independence, national socialism, and international nonalignment was extolled in the media.

JAN KARSKI, *Georgetown University*

President Nicolae Ceauşescu (right) named his wife, Elena (third from right), first deputy premier.

Eastfoto

RUMANIA · Information Highlights

Official Name: Socialist Republic of Rumania.
Location: Southeastern Europe.
Area: 91,700 square miles (237 500 km²).
Population (1980 est.): 22,300,000.
Chief Cities: (July 1978): Bucharest, the capital, 1,987,-872; Iaşi, 278,545; Timişoara, 277,779.
Government: *Head of state,* Nicolae Ceauşescu, president and secretary general of the Communist Party (took office 1965). *Head of government,* Ilie Verdet, premier (took office March 1979). *Legislature* (unicameral)—Grand National Assembly.
Monetary Unit: Leu (4.47 leu equal U.S.$1, May 1980).
Manufactures (major products): Power; mining, forestry, and construction materials; metal products; chemicals; machines; processed foods; textiles.
Agriculture (major products): Corn, potatoes, wheat, oil seeds.
GNP (1979 est., U.S.$): $91,200,000,000.
Foreign Trade (Jan.-March 1980, U.S.$): *Imports,* $3,-104,000,000; *exports,* $2,843,000,000.

Government of Saskatchewan

Lt. Gov. Irwin McIntosh reads greetings from Queen Elizabeth at a 75th anniversary ceremony.

SASKATCHEWAN

Celebrations welcoming the new year were of particular significance to Saskatchewan, as 1980 marked the province's 75th year as a member of the Canadian federation. To commemorate the jubilee, a theme of "Celebrate Saskatchewan" was adopted to recognize the province's heritage and celebrate its potential for further growth and development. Community activities were planned and carried out across the province. Saskatchewan's official admission into the Canadian federation on Sept. 4, 1905 was reenacted in Regina's Victoria Park on Sept. 4, 1980. Prime Minister Pierre Elliott Trudeau, Governor-General Edward Schreyer, provincial Premier Allan Blakeney, and other government officials attended the ceremony.

Government. While cultural activities focused on Saskatchewan's past, the provincial government was equally concerned with economic and social development in the 1980s. The 61-seat house was dominated by the New Democratic Party (NDP), which held 44 seats. The Conservative party acted as the official opposition, holding 15 seats. The Conservatives lost two members to the newly formed Unionest Party, which split from its parent body to promote the union of the prairie provinces with the United States. The throne speech delivered by Premier Blakeney indicated government's intention of reforming the court system, initiating drainage

and flood control, extending seat belt legislation, and strengthening legislation regarding employee pension rights. The legislature was prorogued July 17 after a record 81-day sitting and passage of 137 bills.

The government broke a three-year cycle of deficit financing with a $2,000,000,000 balanced budget based on projected initiatives in energy security, conservation, grain transportation, and health care. No major social legislation was initiated by the government, although plans were finalized for an urban native program encouraging initiatives in education, job training, and employment. Steps also were taken to establish a Saskatchewan government office in Ottawa to enhance federal-provincial relations.

── SASKATCHEWAN • Information Highlights ──

Area: 251,700 sq mi (651 900 km²).
Population (1980 est.): 967,400.
Chief Cities (1976 census): Regina, the capital, 149,593; Saskatoon, 133,750; Moose Jaw, 32,581.
Government (1980): *Chief Officers*—lt. gov., C. Irwin McIntosh; premier, Allan Blakeney; chief justice, Court of Appeal, E. M. Culliton; Queen's Bench, F. W. Johnson. *Legislature*—Legislative Assembly, 61 members.
Education (1979–80 est.): *Enrollment*—public elementary and secondary schools, 207,790 pupils; private schools, 1,830; Indian (federal) schools, 7,300; postsecondary, 17,740 students. *Total expenditures,* $706,565,000.
Personal Income (average weekly salary, May 1980): $301.35.
Unemployment Rate (July 1980, seasonally adjusted): 4.8%.
(All monetary figures are in Canadian dollars.)

Agriculture and Resources. Below-average rainfall in the winter and spring resulted in severe drought conditions by early summer. Wheat farmers and cattle ranchers were hardest hit, with the poor agricultural conditions also affecting farm implement manufacturers. A welcome break in the dry weather later in the year was accompanied by a joint federal-provincial drought relief program. But because of the poor grain crop, the province's gross domestic product was down.

The pace of heavy oil-drilling accelerated, with lease sales maintaining record prices. The Canpotex Corporation concluded a major three-year contract with China for the export of potash. Uranium exploration and development continued, although environmental hearings delayed mine openings at Key Lake. Saskatchewan Power and Northern Telecom continued to expand their respective interests in the province with a 300-megawatt coalfield and a new optical systems division.

JENNIFER JOHNSON
Regina Public Library

SAUDI ARABIA

High production of oil kept Saudi Arabia prosperous in 1979–80 despite the dangers posed by revolution and war in the Persian Gulf.

Oil and Finance. Although the Saudi government said that it wished to produce only 8.5 million barrels of oil per day, production remained at 9.5 million barrels and even increased following the outbreak of war between neighboring Iraq and Iran in September 1980. Saudi Arabia became the second largest producer of oil in the world, exceeded only by the Soviet Union.

Prices for Saudi light crude oil were increased in stages from $24 per barrel in November 1979 to $30 per barrel in September 1980. In order to force the Organization of Petroleum Exporting Countries (OPEC) to agree on a uniform oil pricing policy, Saudi Arabia held its level of production high and its prices relatively low. By September 1980, the Saudis had achieved some success in restoring OPEC's pricing unity, but the disruption of oil production in Iran and Iraq threatened the stability of the world market.

An economic development plan announced in May 1980 called for spending $236,000,-000 during the following five years, plus a $50,-000,000,000 allowance for inflation. The new plan reflected the Saudi desire for increased spending on industry and agriculture after the completion of most infrastructure projects.

Saudi holdings of foreign assets increased sharply to about $77,000,000,000 in 1979, while the inflation rate was held to a modest 10%. Saudi revenue from oil was expected to be $90,-000,000,000 in 1980. More than one million foreign workers provided the basic work force in construction and service industries.

Foreign Affairs. Saudi opposition to the Egyptian-Israeli peace process brought the kingdom closer to Iraq, Libya, and Jordan, which also were against establishing ties with Israel. In August, Crown Prince Fahd asked for a holy war by all Muslims against Israel because of its continued occupation of East Jerusalem. However, the United States and Saudi Arabia remained close allies despite America's role in the peace process. Saudi Arabia still did not have diplomatic relations with the Soviet Union. Saudis condemned the Soviet invasion of Afghanistan and, on January 6, Saudi Arabia became the first country to withdraw from the 1980 summer Olympics in Moscow.

Zbigniew Brzezinski, U.S. President Jimmy Carter's chief adviser on foreign policy, conferred with Prince Fahd in Riyadh on February 4. Saudi oil minister Ahmed Zaki Yamani opposed the use of Saudi oil for the building up of U.S. energy reserves. Saudi pressure contributed to the American decision to stop adding to its oil reserve.

Saudi complaints about the television film "Death of a Princess," which depicted the execution of a Saudi princess for adultery, were not sufficient to stop its airing in Great Britain and the United States. The U.S. State Department opposed the broadcast from the beginning, and the British Foreign Office later officially apologized to the Saudis for the film.

Saudi Arabia was cautiously favorable to Iraq in its war against Iran but did not become involved in the fighting. Saudi financial aid to friendly countries remained generous; more than $600 million was given to Turkey.

Government and Military. The seizure of the Grand Mosque of Mecca on Nov. 20, 1979, initially seemed to threaten the stability of the Saudi government. By early December, Saudi troops had regained control of the mosque from tribal and religious dissidents and had suppressed Shiite Muslim riots in the Persian Gulf region. The mosque was reopened for worship by King Khalid on Dec. 6, 1979. Sixty-three of those involved in the November attack were beheaded on Jan. 9, 1980.

In 1980, four new provincial governors were installed, a shake-up of military officers took

---
SAUDI ARABIA · Information Highlights

Official Name: Kingdom of Saudi Arabia.
Location: Arabian peninsula in southwest Asia.
Area: 830,000 sq mi (2 149 690 km²).
Population (1980 est.): 8,200,000.
Chief Cities (1976 est.): Riyadh, the capital, 667,000; Jidda, 561,000; Mecca, 367,000.
Government: *Head of state and government,* Khalid ibn Abd al-Aziz al-Saud, king (acceded March 1975).
Monetary Unit: Riyal (3.31 riyals equal U.S.$1, Oct. 1980).
Manufactures (major products): Petroleum products, cement, fertilizers.
Agriculture (major products): Dates, vegetables, grains.
GNP Per Capita (1978 est., U.S.$): $8,040.
Foreign Trade (Jan.–June 1979, U.S.$): *Imports,* $11,-526,000,000; *exports,* $25,529,000,000.

place, and a consultative council and constitution were promised, but few basic changes actually were made in Saudi politics as a result of the mosque seizure. Since the chief demands of the rebels in Mecca had been for greater enforcement of Islamic religious strictures, the government increased pressure to restrict further the number of women working in public places and to close shops at times of prayer. More money was given to the tribes, but the constitution and advisory council were not acted upon.

Crown Prince Fahd retained the chief responsibility for governing because of the poor health of King Khalid, who was hospitalized in Riyadh during February and March. No major changes were made in the Saudi cabinet.

Saudi Arabia's exclusive dependence on U.S. armaments was somewhat lessened by purchases of naval vessels and tanks from France. Saudi Arabia requested from the United States additional equipment to increase the range and effectiveness of the 60 F-15 aircraft already purchased, but the request was opposed by 68 U.S. senators who feared the military impact on Israel. Saudi Arabia opposed the creation of permanent U.S. military bases on Saudi territory. The kingdom did request and receive aircraft that remained under U.S. control and that were used to increase Saudi radar capability during the Iran-Iraq fighting.

In 1980, the Saudi leadership felt that military interventions, foreign policy changes, and government reforms were too risky, given the heightened diplomatic tensions in the Middle East following the Iranian Revolution and Soviet intervention in Afghanistan.

WILLIAM OCHSENWALD
Virginia Polytechnic Institute

SINGAPORE

Continuing prosperity, which permitted increased industrial and commercial growth, was accompanied by doubts about the labor force. Singapore also saw the promotion of new leaders and general elections in December.

Economy. To strengthen the nation's role as a world leader in petroleum refining, the Japanese firm Sumitomo began construction of a major petrochemical complex. Major building projects, which would transform the crowded commercial center of Singapore city, were being undertaken in conjunction with Americans. The largest of these projects, Raffles City, was to include the tallest hotel in the world. Relief was expressed when it became apparent that the project is to preserve much of the famous 19th century colonial hotel, the Raffles.

Transportation remained a major issue as the government increased efforts to discourage private commuting, especially in the central city. One proposed solution, a multibillion dollar mass-transit rail system, faced delays as technocrats debated a study by American consultants calling for a less costly bus and restructured highway system.

For the second year, the National Wage Council gave substantial increases to Singapore workers as part of the officially sponsored "second industrial revolution." It seeks to encourage high-technology, capital-intensive industrialization in the labor-scarce nation. The Council, however, shared the concern of Prime Minister Lee Kuan Yew that Singapore workers were becoming complacent and urged that monetary incentives be awarded to productive workers.

Immigration was proposed as a means to meet manpower needs and stimulate greater dedication from Singapore workers. Lee said that "skilled and disciplined" workers from abroad would be allowed permanent residence to challenge Singaporeans. Permanent residence is already offered to individuals willing to invest substantial sums of money in the nation's development.

Politics. As part of its projected ten-year transition to a new generation of leaders, the ruling People's Action Party (PAP) elevated two heirs-apparent to full cabinet positions. Suppiah Dhanabalan was made minister of foreign affairs and Tony Tan Keng Yam became education minister. They took the places of two of the nation's founding elder statesmen, S. Rajaratnam and Dr. Goh Keng Swee, who were named second and first deputy prime ministers, respectively. While the younger ministers assumed greater responsibilities, it was clear that the elders remained fully involved in directing Singapore's government.

For the fourth consecutive time since independence in August 1965, the PAP won all parliamentary seats in the general election and 75% of the popular vote in December 1980.

Foreign Affairs. Singapore maintained its support of the Association of Southeast Asian Nations (ASEAN) as the focus of its policies. It also emphasized its anti-communism as both Lee Kuan Yew and Rajaratnam repeatedly condemned the Vietnamese invasion of Thailand and continued occupation of Cambodia (Kampuchea).

K. MULLINER, *Ohio University*

——— **SINGAPORE** • Information Highlights ———

Official Name: Republic of Singapore.
Location: Southeast Asia.
Area: 224 sq mi (580 km²).
Population (1980 est.): 2,400,000.
Chief City (1974 est.): Singapore, the capital, 1,327,500.
Government: *Head of state,* Benjamin H. Sheares, president (took office Jan. 1971). *Head of government,* Lee Kuan Yew, prime minister (took office 1959). *Legislature* (unicameral)—Parliament.
Monetary Unit: Singapore dollar (2.08 S. dollars equal U.S.$1, Oct. 1980).
Manufactures (major products): Refined petroleum, processed rubber.
Agriculture (major products): Tobacco, vegetables, fruits, rubber and coconut palms.
GNP (1978 est., U.S.$): $8,100,000,000.
Foreign Trade (1979, U.S.$): *Imports,* $17,635,000,000; *exports,* $14,233,000,000.

SOCIAL WELFARE

Global economic stagnation, inflation, and continued population growth stimulated both social welfare concerns and action during the year.

The World Bank and IMF. The World Bank's joint meeting with the International Monetary Fund (IMF) in late September featured Robert S. McNamara's farewell address. The retiring World Bank president called for an increased commitment of loans (up to $5,800,000,000) for food, energy, and educational projects in the poor nations of the world. The Bank estimated that at least 780 million people were subsisting in absolute poverty, spending at least 80% of meager incomes on food alone. The IMF pledged to increase its loans to Third World nations.

Political tensions between rich and poor nations grew with greater disparities of income. The "Group of 77" nations, which actually numbered 119 by December, called for tariff reductions that would give them access to export markets and thereby the opportunity to solve their own welfare problems.

The World Bank and the United Nations joined the World Health Organization to declare the 1980s a "Decade for Drinking Water Supply and Sanitation." In October, Dame Barbara Ward stressed that 90 million deaths each year were caused by dirty water or lack of water, with more than three of every five children in many Third World nations dying from diseases associated with dirty water—dysentery, cholera, bilharzia, and malaria. Only 22% of the world's rural areas have adequate water supplies, and it would cost from $20,000,000,000 to $30,000,000,000 annually to deal properly with this need in the 1980s.

The current account fiscal deficits of non-oil-producing, developing nations worsened rapidly. Such deficits totaled $36,000,000,000 in 1978, $53,000,000,000 in 1979, and about $70,000,000,000 in 1980, debts which these countries could not finance without cutting welfare programs further. Poor nations joined with Arab oil states in pressing for a larger voice in both the World Bank and the IMF, while opposition grew in the U.S. Congress to increases in American aid contributions, still the largest of any nation.

Mexico's booming oil and gas exports enabled the government to restore cuts in welfare and to launch a massive effort to improve the lot of the rural poor.

World Problems. In Africa and Cambodia, famine took as great a toll as in previous years. Efforts to feed the hungry in Cambodia were frequently thwarted by bureaucratic tangles between relief agencies and a suspicious regime. The worst drought in East Africa since 1973 compounded the seventh year of famine in the Sachel. In large parts of Africa, the problems were exacerbated by war, violence, and growing numbers of refugees.

A conference of 36 delegations from the "Great Cities of the World," held in Boston in September, provided many reports of ever-mounting problems associated with poverty, pollution, and rapid populaton growth.

The Vatican became a center of controversy when Pope John Paul II personally led a campaign to overturn Italy's recently enacted, liberal abortion law. The church's traditional position on this and related matters was reaffirmed and strengthened by the Fifth World Synod of Bishops, convened in Rome in late September. In Ireland, church-led groups pressured druggists not to sell the contraceptive devices which legislation made legal there for the first time.

The major welfare concerns in much of Europe were unemployment and inflation. The British government under Prime Minister Margaret Thatcher adhered to a course of fiscal austerity in spite of mounting criticisms and a jobless rate exceeding 7.5%. The government also began implementing recommendations of the Royal Commission on the National Health Service for a full reorganization of the system on a district and regional basis.

The ceremonies for the investiture of the Netherlands' new queen on April 30 were overshadowed by riots in Amsterdam. Thousands rampaged through the streets demanding housing, which has been critically scarce for some time. At about the same time, Sweden was paralyzed by major labor disputes, putting pressures on a national budget in which welfare programs already were slashed heavily. Staid Switzerland also confronted violent protests in Zurich, where pitched battles erupted during the spring and summer between police and mobs of enraged young people, protesting the closing of a youth center and the high cost of housing. Labor unrest of a more conventional type, though also associated with demands for better housing and a voice in work place affairs, came on a large scale, virtually revolutionary in its implications, to Poland, and on a smaller scale to the auto assembly plants of the Volga basin in the Soviet Union, where public discontent was endemic over shortages of milk and meat resulting at least in part from the American grain embargo.

The United States. Welfare issues were central during the U.S. elections. During the presidential primary campaign President Carter set a cautious course. His opponent for the Democratic nomination, Sen. Edward M. Kennedy, called for federal programs at or above current spending and for additional programs in the New Deal tradition. Carter won the nomination in August, but Kennedy supporters won much of the struggle over the party platform, pushing through strong plans in support of the Equal Rights Amendment (ERA) and federally funded abortions for needy women. Ronald Reagan's landslide winning of the presidency came with pledges by his party to cut sharply welfare programs and to reverse fully the tendencies toward liberal abortion legislation. The GOP platform called for tighter eligibility requirements for food stamps, termination of aid to the "voluntarily unemployed" and aliens, rejection of any guaranteed annual income, and a constitutional amendment to protect "the rights to life for unborn children." Some conservative organizations, such as those headed by evangelical Protestant leaders, rated the voting record of candidates on welfare and other issues. Several key Senate victories gave the Republicans control of that body after contests in which these new political pressure groups played large roles.

Just before the election, however, the National Advisory Council on Economic Opportunity, in its annual report to the president and the Congress, warned that the "politics of negativism sweeping the United States would, if unchecked, thrust millions of Americans into the ranks of the poor." It attributed the reduction by 11 million since 1964 in the number of people whose incomes were below the "poverty line" not to the growth of the private sector, but rather to such welfare programs as food stamps, representing a real transfer payment. The current poverty line for a nonfarm family of four is an annual income of $7,450; nearly 25 million Americans were below it, and another 40 million near it, claimed the commission. The report also asserted that Congressional pressure to reduce welfare programs contributed to the three-day riot in the black ghetto of Miami.

Economic stagnation and anticipated cuts in federal welfare aid forced state and local governments, especially those that were most vulnerable to contractions in auto sales and construction, to curtail spending. Struggling with rising demands for welfare services, city governments also were very sensitive to the potential reductions in their share of shrinking state and federal help that the 1980 census counts would bring. Even with liberal allowances for an undercount, the old cities of the Northeast and Middle West suffered major losses of population in the 1970s. According to a U.S. Conference of Mayors estimate, the allocation of $50,000,000,000 a year in grant programs for local jurisdictions was based in good part on census figures. The mayors waged an impassioned campaign to make the Census Bureau count every overlooked person. To keep welfare costs under control, New York, Connecticut, and New Jersey began pressing their urban welfare agencies to find jobs for as many welfare recipients as possible.

In providing medical care, cities were confronted with cost problems apparently out of control. One solution for high costs that hospital administrators pushed was decentralization through more care in the home and in neighborhood health centers. Another proposal, opposed by most hospitals, was state or federal regulation of hospital rates. Six states created agencies that set maximum rates hospitals could charge, reducing the average annual increase in charges from 14% to 11%. With costs of medical care soaring, the movement for a national health insurance program slowed considerably. Another problem in health care was the growing shortage of nurses and greater militancy by nurses' unions, shown by an increasing number of strikes.

Continued immigration, along with an influx of refugees, strained welfare and educational facilities. Continued housing shortages for the elderly and poor were met in part by the Housing and Community Development Act, authorizing $31,200,000,000 for low and moderate income housing programs, and some funds for community development block grants. Abortion questions brought new cases to the Supreme Court. One decision reaffirmed the constitutionality of the Hyde Amendment that prevents federal funding of abortions. An outcry developed over the disposal of toxic wastes from chemical plants, acknowledged as the nation's most important new major health problem. (*See* feature article, page 47.)

The use of marijuana by schoolchildren raged at epidemic rates amid mounting evidence of both short-term and long-term damage, particularly since new varieties were more potent. In many communities parents organized campaigns against "head shops" and smoking by children. A bumper crop of poppies in the Orient and Near East sent record amounts of heroin and its derivatives to the United States. Alcoholism continued to run rampant in high schools and in society as a whole, and the spread of licensed gambling to New Jersey led to the opening of four new chapters of Gamblers Anonymous to deal with what is now listed as the mental disorder of "pathological gambling."

The most important single issue was the future of Social Security. During the winter, energy assistance payments under Supplementary Security Income (SSI) went to about 3.9 million recipients. The national commission on the system recommended that no reduction be made in the scheduled increase in taxes for 1981 and that authority be granted for the Old Age and Survivors Insurance (OASI) trust fund to borrow from other funds in the system to keep benefit payments from exceeding contributions. The basic problem is that the pool of workers paying into the fund is shrinking and the number of retirees is growing and living longer after retirement. During the presidential campaign, Reagan pledged not only to protect the system, but to press for repeal of the current limitations on earnings by recipients. A special task force recommended that coverage be extended to all federal civil service employees and other groups outside the system. Mid-November saw a Joint Economic Committee of the Congress study conclude that a long-term redesign of the system was imperative.

MORTON ROTHSTEIN
University of Wisconsin-Madison

Violence was widespread throughout South Africa during 1980. At left, supporters of black nationalist guerrillas, convicted in connection with a raid on a police station, demonstrate in front of the Palace of Justice in Pretoria.

SOUTH AFRICA

The extraordinary rise in the price of gold and the demand for South Africa's other minerals ensured that 1980 would be a boom year for the nation's economy. This was reflected in the budget. But for much of South Africa, 1980 was another year of frustration, tension, unrest, and deteriorating race relations.

The high expectations of significant change in racial legislation, with which the year began, proved illusory. Although the expectations may have been unrealistic, they rested on Prime Minister P. W. Botha's own 1979 statements and the emphasis he placed on the need for urgency. At year-end, the promise of impending change was once more heralded in the government's new constitutional arrangements, Botha's major cabinet shuffle, and his references to radical change. But by then the public's expectations were more realistic and disillusionment more widespread. It seemed clear both that the process was to be a slow one and that the essential power and decision-making structure of the Nationalist government would not be touched. Furthermore, it still remained to be seen whether or not, after more than two years in office, the prime minister had the will and the means to override those *verkrampte* (rigidly conservative) elements in his party who opposed any weakening of the existing apartheid controls. Even the most modest of reform programs would now demand this. Botha had contrived for another year to avoid an open breach with the verkramptes. At the same time he had reaffirmed the view that whatever changes were necessary to ensure the security of the republic, the National Party was the only vehicle for their realization.

Meanwhile, a rising tide of unrest in the nonwhite urban centers confronted the government. Botha barely had absorbed the shock of Prime Minister Robert Mugabe's runaway election victory in Zimbabwe—he had supported Bishop Abel Muzorewa—before he faced a powerful protest movement by schoolchildren. The protests escalated to countrywide violence. This was followed by boycotts, strikes, and continued labor unrest. The worst violence occurred in June—the fourth anniversary of the Soweto rebellion—when some 40 persons were killed and many more were injured. The year also saw the most serious act of sabotage so far—a successful raid on the two major synthetic fuel plants and an oil refinery on June 1.

Internal Affairs. The 1980 parliamentary session dimmed the hopes for major reform but witnessed some interesting developments. The most important was the government's attempt to push through its long-awaited constitutional proposals. The Senate was to be abolished as of the end of the year, and the House of Assembly was to be increased by the addition of 12 nominated members of parliament (MPs). Crucial was the creation of new consultative institutions to accommodate leaders from other ethnic groups. The government's decision first to exclude blacks, then to set up a separate black council to advise the proposed state president's advisory council—whose task it would be to make new constitutional proposals—resulted in the plans being rejected by most leading blacks and Coloured and Indian leaders, as well as by the official opposition party. The Progressive Federal Party, however, expelled Japie Basson, one of its senior MPs, for his readiness to serve on the council. At the same time, the three MPs of the South African Party, led by John Wiley, joined the National Party.

On October 2, Botha announced the composition of the council which, predictably, was dominated by the National Party. There were no black members and the Coloureds and Asians could hardly be described as leaders of their communities. The council consisted of 54 nominees, five committee chairmen (appointed by the government), and a state vice-president who would head the council. The same week Botha's close ally, Alwyn Schlebusch, was chosen the country's first vice-president. Earlier, Botha prepared for his forthcoming struggle with his verkrampte rival, the Transvaal leader A. P. Treurnicht, with a major shakeup of his cabinet.

While Botha could not remove Treurnicht, the prime minister brought in seven new ministers, including four members of the president's council, and removed five. Of the new ministers, three were drawn from outside Parliament, including Gen. Magnus Malan, the former chief of the defense force, who became minister of defense, and Gerrit Viljoen, the former administrator-general of Namibia (South-West Africa).

Generally speaking, the changes were regarded as providing Botha with the kind of cabinet support he required for his reform program. Significantly, Professor Gerrit Viljoen was the man who defeated Treurnicht for the leadership of the powerful Afrikaner Broederbond society. The new Cabinet took office on October 6.

The Disturbances. The school boycotts which became the youth revolts of 1980 began with isolated protests during February and March by students and parents at one or two Coloured schools near Cape Town over the poor conditions and quality of teaching. The rejection of their complaints led to sporadic walkouts and boycotts which spread to Coloured schools elsewhere. By April 21 Coloured and Indian schools in many parts of the country had agreed, under the leadership of a group which met in Cape Town, to conduct a full-scale boycott and present a list of grievances to the Minister of Coloured Affairs. It soon was estimated that 100,000 students were participating. Protest marches were broken up by police.

The minister alleged that agitators were responsible, threatened reprisals, but made no move to address the grievances. Police action was stepped up as support for the boycott spread. The boycott entered a new phase when it was joined by African students in their schools and universities. Fort Hare University and the University of the North were closed. On May 24 some 3,000 young persons disrupted the shopping centers of Cape Town. The police arrested more than 100 of them. It was clear by now that what was being protested was the whole discriminatory education system.

In June these protests were caught up in the violence precipitated by the government's ban on all meetings of more than ten persons. Intended to prevent demonstrations and confrontations on the fourth anniversary of the Soweto protest, the ban led to riots, violence, stonings,

looting, arson, and bloodshed. Most of the Coloured and Asian children returned to school by the end of July, but there were still some 60,000 African children out of school in October.

From these events emerged a sense of both the alienation of the Coloured youth and their cohesion. In addition an atmosphere of tension was increased by the unprecedented wave of strikes at a time when the government claimed it was instituting major labor reforms. In most cases the increased labor unrest was caused by dissatisfaction with low wages, but it also stemmed from management's refusal to accept the system of representation chosen by the non-white workers. The widespread pattern of calling in the police often led to violent confrontation.

The year also saw several incidents of urban guerrilla activity by members of the banned African National Congress. The attack on the oil-from-coal plants was the most spectacular, but they included the seizing of hostages at a Pretoria bank, hit and run attacks on police stations, and the setting of explosive charges along the main Johannesburg-Soweto railway line.

The Homelands. The prime minister told the Transvaal National Party Congress in September that at present none of the tribal homelands, whether independent or not, was economically viable and that all of them would need to be integrated into the government's development program. An independent commission, appointed by Chief Lennox Sebe, reported the same finding with regard to the Ciskei and recommended that the chief not move to join the independent territories of Transkei, Bophuthatswana, and Venda. However, Chief Sebe held a referendum and opted for independence.

The Budget. Sweeping tax concessions, the abolition of loan levies, and pay increases and benefits for public servants (including teachers and nurses) marked the government's budget, which was presented in March. Defense spending and education spending for all groups rose.

Namibia. Since 1978, when South Africa agreed in principle to internationally supervised elections and the transfer of power to an internationally approved government in Namibia, the government systematically has questioned the impartiality of the UN arrangements. At the same time the government has done everything possible to strengthen a white-led multiracial political assembly. In 1980 UN proposals called for a pre-implementation conference for all parties, including the South-West Africa People's Organization (SWAPO) guerrillas, to be held Jan. 7-14, 1981. Foreign Minister R. F. Botha continued to reiterate that a UN solution is not the republic's only option.

During the last three weeks of June, South African forces carried out their largest assault against SWAPO guerrilla forces in Angola in the 14-year-old war. The UN Security Council censured South Africa for "aggression."

R. B. Ballinger, *Rhode Island College*

─────SOUTH AFRICA • Information Highlights─────

Official Name: Republic of South Africa.
Location: Southern tip of Africa.
Area: 471,445 sq mi (1 221 043 km²).
Population (1980 est.): 28,400,000.
Chief Cities (1970 census): Pretoria, the administrative capital, 543,950; Cape Town, the legislative capital, 691,296; Johannesburg, 642,967; Durban, 495,458.
Government: *Head of state,* Marais Viljoen, president (took office June 1979). *Head of government,* P. W. Botha, prime minister (took office Sept. 1978). *Legislature*—Parliament: Senate and House of Assembly.
Monetary Unit: Rand (0.7553 rand equals U.S.$1, Dec. 1980).
GNP (1979 est., U.S.$): $54,300,000,000.

SOUTH CAROLINA

Unexpectedly, Ronald Reagan carried South Carolina by a small margin. For the first time, two congressional districts, the second and the fourth, elected Republicans, giving the GOP a 4-2 representation in the U.S. House. U.S. Sen. Ernest (Fritz) Hollings was reelected by a wide margin.

A state constitutional amendment permitting the governor to be elected for two consecutive terms was approved. The Republicans gained two seats in both the House and the Senate. There now would be 107 Democrats and 17 Republicans in the House, while in the Senate the Democrats would have 41 members and the Republicans 5. Fifteen blacks were elected to the House, but none to the Senate.

President-elect Reagan named former Gov. James B. Edwards secretary of energy.

Government. The General Assembly had a very long session. Some of the most important legislation passed included: increasing the gas tax by 1 cent, relating the rate of income taxes to inflation, permitting income tax deductions for the installation of energy-saving devices, establishing a pretrial intervention program for persons charged with nonviolent crimes, providing collection methods for defaulted education loans, revising the membership and power of the insurance commission, authorizing the use of marijuana for medical purposes, requiring proof of payment of property taxes on motor vehicles before a license may be renewed, and strengthening the regulations pertaining to bingo games.

Education. The teacher-student ratio was reduced by one—1 to 23. Adjustments were made in the funding formulas of the minimal educational foundation finance act. South Carolinians improved their SAT scores. Readiness tests were given to all first grade students. By 1983 tests measuring the effectiveness of education would be required for students in grades 1, 2, 6, 8, and 11. Sixty-five percent of all high school students were enrolled in some type of vocational educational program. Programs for gifted and talented students doubled, and classes on how parents can aid their children were emphasized. Contrary to national trends, higher education enrollment increased.

Economy. Although about $1,500,000,000 was invested in new industries, tax revenues leveled off. As a result state agencies would be asked to reduce their personnel by 7%. The textile industry spent large sums modernizing plants. Highly technical electronics equipment plants increased significantly. Foreign investment amounted to about 15% of the funds invested. The unemployment rate was 8%, nearly double that of a year earlier.

The economy was hampered seriously by a long, dry summer and the state was declared a disaster area. The dry weather reduced production of all major crops, except peaches. Tobacco was not hurt as badly as corn and soybeans. The latter continued as the chief cash crop. The number of small farms decreased by about 1,000.

Social and Cultural. The Spoleto Festival had another very successful year. Many performances were held in several cities outside of Charleston. The state university was given a multimillion-dollar collection of Movietone News films. Programs in art, theater, and music continued to improve and increase. Historic preservation received special interest in Charleston and Columbia.

Mental health institutions battled to keep their accreditation. Restitution payments were authorized for criminals who had not committed a violent crime.

ROBERT H. STOUDEMIRE
University of South Carolina

— SOUTH CAROLINA • Information Highlights —

Area: 31,055 sq mi (80 432 km²).
Population (Jan. 1980 est.): 2,948,000.
Chief Cities (1976 est.): Columbia, the capital, 112,779; (1970 census): Charleston, 66,945; Greenville, 61,-436.
Government (1980): *Chief Officers*—governor, Richard W. Riley (D); lt. gov., Nancy Stevenson (D). *General Assembly*—Senate, 46 members; House of Representatives, 124 members.
Education (1979–80): *Enrollment*—public elementary schools, 326,397 pupils; public secondary, 298,399; colleges and universities, 131,459 students. *Public school expenditures,* $937,378,000 ($1,306 per pupil).
State Finances (fiscal year 1979): *Revenues,* $3,169,-000,000; expenditures, $3,007,000,000.
Personal Income (1979): $20,690,000,000; per capita, $7,057.
Labor Force (May 1980): *Nonagricultural wage and salary earners,* 1,200,100; (June 1980): *unemployed,* 110,-800 (8.4% of total force).

SOUTH DAKOTA

The abandonment of rail service in several parts of South Dakota inspired Gov. William Janklow to propose that the state government purchase Milwaukee Railroad property and let contracts for the operation of trains to transport agricultural products to market. Following rigorous debate, the governor and the legislature reached an agreement to authorize expenditures up to $25 million for tracks and right-of-way, but not to become involved with the acquisition and operation of rolling stock.

To fund the core railway system, the legislature voted a 1¢ increase in sales tax. To raise funds for road repairs, the legislators added 3¢ per gallon to the gasoline tax. To generate additional money for other purposes, they levied about $6.7 million in taxes on the gold production of the Homestake Mining Company. Finally, to balance the budget, the legislature limited general fund expenditures to about $240 million—the anticipated level of state revenues for the fiscal year 1980–81.

The governor and the legislature also took steps to stimulate employment and economic growth by inviting the transfer of Citicorp's

Master Charge and Visa services from Long Island to South Dakota. Attracted by license to charge 24% interest on credit card balances instead of the 18% allowed in New York, the corporation's managers opened an office in Sioux Falls.

Economy. The economy faltered. Personal income and employment levels slumped in the professions as well as in financial, real estate, service, and manufacturing industries. Receipts at tourist facilities declined because nonresident vacation traffic was diminished by the high cost of gasoline as well as by the inflation of other costs. Ranchers lost money due to sagging prices in cattle and hog markets. Farmers were devastated by hailstorms and droughts, which reduced the production of corn and some small grains by one third and caused a loss estimated at more than $500 million. Tax revenues fell below the projected level as a result, and the governor ordered a 5% cut in spending for all major programs to maintain a balanced budget.

Elections. South Dakotans encountered five proposed constitutional amendments and two referenda. Responding, they approved the hunting of mourning doves, altered the length of legislative sessions, and curbed the governor's power to fill vacancies in the state circuit and supreme courts. But they rejected a proposition to limit real estate taxes. They refused to endorse a measure to require approval from the electorate as well as from the state Department of Water and Natural Resources for uranium mining and processing, nuclear plant construction, or nuclear waste disposal in the state. They voted against two instruments that would have limited legislative authority over issues previously decided by initiative and referendum.

The electorate followed national conservative trends in every way except in the reelection of popular one-term Congressman Thomas D. Daschle (D) in the first district. South Dakotans cast their four electoral votes for the Reagan-Bush ticket, by a margin of about two to one. They returned strong Republican majorities to both houses in the state legislature (Senate: 25R–10D; House: 49R–21D). They elected for-

mer state Secretary of Agriculture Clint Roberts (R) to Congress from the second district, replacing James Abdnor. And they chose Abdnor (R), former lieutenant governor and four-term congressman, over George McGovern in the race for the seat in the U.S. Senate.

Since George McGovern can perhaps be considered, along with the progressive Governor-Senator Peter Norbeck, one of South Dakota's most effective politicians, his defeat marked the end of an era. In 1956, historian McGovern left a professorial position to run successfully for the U.S. House of Representatives. He soon thereafter breathed life into a state Democratic Party that had been nearly defunct since the 1930s. Under his leadership, through his three terms in the U.S. Senate (1963–81), McGovern's party gained strength equal to that of the Republicans.

HERBERT T. HOOVER
The University of South Dakota

SPACE EXPLORATION

The year 1980 saw a new manned spaceflight endurance record of 185 days set by the USSR, which continued its very active space program. The USSR launched almost seven times the number of spacecraft as the United States. The U.S. space shuttle moved significantly closer to its first test flight, scheduled for March 1981.

In planetary space exploration, U.S. President Carter hailed the Voyager-1 encounter of Saturn as "a superb scientific achievement." The spacecraft returned many exciting images and scientific measurements of the planet, including its 15 moons and more than 100 rings.

Manned Space Flight. The USSR continued to employ the Salyut 6 Space Station for manned scientific and earth observation experiments, while breaking their previous manned spaceflight endurance record of 175 days. Once again, an international group of cosmonauts was used to carry out the six-month mission.

The new manned spaceflight record of six months (185 days) in orbit was set by cosmonauts Valery Ryumin and Leonid Popov of the USSR aboard the Salyut 6 Space Station. The cosmonauts arrived at Salyut 6 on April 10, after a flight aboard Soyuz 35. They remained until October 11, returning in Soyuz 37. The cosmonauts had a hero's welcome upon their return. Ryumin received the Order of Lenin and his second gold medal for having flown one year in space, while Popov was proclaimed Hero of the Soviet Union. The previous record of 175 days was set in 1979 by Valery Ryumin and Vladimir Lyakhov aboard the same space station.

Three unmanned Soviet tanker-transport satellites, Progress 9, 10 and 11, were used to resupply Salyut 6 during the six-month mission. In addition, four pairs of cosmonauts joined Ryumin and Popov for short periods during their lengthy stay. Valery Kubasov of the USSR and

---

— SOUTH DAKOTA • Information Highlights —

Area: 77,047 sq mi (199 552 km²).
Population (Jan. 1980 est.): 689,000.
Chief Cities (1970 census): Pierre, the capital, 9,699; Sioux Falls, 74,488; Rapid City, 43,836.
Government (1980): *Chief Officers*—governor, William J. Janklow (R); lt. gov., Lowell C. Hansen II (R). *Legislature*—Senate, 35 members; House of Representatives, 70 members.
Education (1979–80): *Enrollment*—public elementary schools, 87,387 pupils; public secondary, 45,440; colleges and universities, 31,294 students. *Public school expenditures,* $280,450,000 ($1,856 per pupil).
State Finances (fiscal year 1979): *Revenues,* $656,000,-000; *expenditures* $642,000,000.
Personal Income (1979): $5,137,000,000; per capita, $7,455.
Labor Force (June 1980): *Nonagricultural wage and salary earners,* 247,100; *unemployed,* 16,400 (4.6% of total force).

Soviet cosmonauts Leonid Popov (right) and Valery Ryumin face newsmen after spending a record 185 days in space. The team completed extensive experiments aboard the Salyut 6-Soyuz complex.

Bertalan Farkas of Hungary were orbited in Soyuz 36 and linked up with Salyut 6 on May 27, returning in Soyuz 35 on June 3. Yuri Malyshev and Vladimir Aksyonon of the USSR flew Soyuz T-2 on its first manned flight, arriving at Salyut 6 on June 6 and returning on June 9. The new Soyuz T series manned spacecraft are improved versions of existing manned spacecraft containing solar panels for electric power supply and progress-type cargo carrying capabilities. Viktor Gorbatko of the USSR and Pham Tuan of Vietnam used Soyuz 37 to link up with Salyut 6 on July 24, returning in Soyuz 36 on July 31. The next group of cosmonauts to visit Salyut 6 was Yuri Romanenko of the USSR and Arnaldo Tamayo Mendez of Cuba. They arrived on September 19 in Soyuz 38 and returned on September 26.

In late November, Leonid Kizim, Oleg Makarov, and Gennady Strekalov linked up with the orbiting lab in order to make the necessary repairs to extend its life. The three-man crew returned to earth in their Soyuz T-3 spacecraft on December 10 following a 13-day flight.

Many scientific and technological experiments were conducted aboard Salyut 6, including earth resources photographic studies, biomedical investigations, and material processing in space experiments. The latter experiments included growth of gallium arsenide, gallium antimonide, and gallium bismuth crystals in the weightless environment and return to earth. These materials are important as possible replacements for silicon in the manufacture of microelectronic chips and in microprocessors.

The cosmonauts returned to earth in excellent health after adhering to a daily regimen of exercise, a balanced diet, and nine hours of sleep. The Salyut 6 has been maintained in orbit since its launch on Sept. 29, 1977. By year-end, a total of 15 cosmonaut teams aboard Soyuz spacecraft had docked with the space station. The U.S. manned spaceflight program, which has been inactive since the flight of the Apollo-Soyuz test program in 1975, was scheduled to resume with the first orbital flight of the space shuttle.

Planetary Probes. Viking, Pioneer Venus, and Voyager spacecraft continued during 1980 to gather valuable information on the origin and evolution of the solar system.

Viking Lander 1 remained operational on Mars and continued to transmit images and meteorological and engineering data to earth following periodic interrogation. It was designed to continue operating until 1994. Viking Lander 2 completed its mission in April after four years of operation and achieved all of its objectives. Viking Orbiter 1 ran out of attitude control gas and was deactivated on August 7. More than 9,700 pictures were collected to identify future mission landing sites and 97% of the surface of Mars was mapped at higher resolutions than were available previously. The Viking biological experiments produced no conclusive evidence that living organisms exist in the Martian soil. However, 2-3% nitrogen was detected in the thin Martian atmosphere, which is composed principally of carbon dioxide. This discovery is important because nitrogen is an essential part of the protein molecules of living cells.

Pioneer Venus Orbiter completed the planned exploration of Venus, including topographic altimeter measurements of 93% of the cloud-covered surface of the planet. The orbit of the spacecraft was permitted to rise as a result of propellant limitations. The higher orbit will allow more sensitive measurements of the planet's mass distribution since the spacecraft's orbital motion will not be affected by atmospheric drag. In addition, the higher orbit will carry the spacecraft to the region behind Venus in the "wake" of its passage through the solar wind and permit this region to be studied for the first time. Studies of the composition of the atmosphere of Venus with comparisons to Mars and earth are providing insight into the formation and evolution of all three terrestrial planets. In addition, studies in planetary geology with the radar altimeter have provided elevation contour maps of much of the surface. Evidence of major tectonic activity has been discovered, which may parallel tectonic processes fundamental to the geology of our own planet.

Three new satellites of Jupiter were discovered as a result of the highly successful Voyager spacecraft encounters with the planet. These moons were discovered in the fall of 1979, spring 1980, and summer of 1980, respectively, through analysis of images returned from Jupiter. The number of known Jovian satellites is now 16. The 16th moon is estimated to be 25 mi (40 km) in diameter. The Galileo orbiter and probe spacecraft, to be launched in 1984, will explore Jupiter further.

The two Voyager spacecraft, launched on Aug. 20 and Sept. 5, 1977, continued their journeys toward Saturn. Voyager 1 made its closest approach, within 78,125 mi (125 000 km), on November 12, and Voyager 2 is scheduled to pass within 63,125 mi (101 000 km) on Aug. 25, 1981. Voyager 2 is then scheduled to continue on to encounter Uranus in January 1986 and possibly even reach Neptune in 1989. The November encounter of Saturn was at a distance of more than ten times the maximum distance from the earth to the sun, resulting in a transmission time delay of approximately 1½ hours.

Saturn's moons differ from those of Jupiter in that only one moon, Titan, compares with the size of Jupiter's four Galilean moons. Titan, which is about the size of the planet Mercury, may be the largest moon in the solar system and the only one to have an atmosphere. Excellent images of Titan were obtained from a pathfinder spacecraft, Pioneer 11, in 1979. Initial findings indicated that Titan's atmosphere is as thick as the earth's and is composed mainly of nitrogen. The infrared and ultraviolet spectrometers on Voyager made the nitrogen measurements. Although nitrogen is associated with life on earth, the extremely low temperatures of approximately $-250°$ F ($-157°$ C) preclude any form of life as we know it.

Planetary radio astronomy experiments have obtained data that indicate that the rotation period of Saturn is 10 hours and 39.9 minutes. This is almost 25 minutes longer than the previously estimated period derived from earth-based observations. In addition to observations of the planet, more than 100 of Saturn's rings or distinct concentric features orbiting the planet were observed.

Earth Observation Satellites. Environmental observations from the Nimbus series of satellites have yielded a significantly improved understanding of ozone processes in the earth's upper atmosphere. Data from the Nimbus 4 Backscatter Ultraviolet Experiment, Nimbus 7 Scanning Backscatter Ultraviolet and Total Ozone Monitoring Spectrometer, and Nimbus 7 Limb Infrared Monitor of the Atmosphere experiments have been analyzed to provide information on the long-term global diurnal distribution and variability of ozone. Ozone is an important trace gas in the stratosphere, which protects the earth by filtering ultraviolet sunlight. The Stratospheric Aerosol and Gas Measurement Experiment (SAGE), launched in 1979, continued to provide information on the distribution of dust-like particles or aerosols in the stratosphere. Extensive measurements were made in the vicinity of the Mount St. Helens volcanic eruption.

SAGE also yielded the surprising result that an almost unnoticed Galapagos Island volcano eruption in 1979 injected three times more material into the atmosphere than did the St. Vincent Island volcano seven months prior. On a short-term basis, major volcano eruptions are felt to have a much larger effect on global surface temperatures than do carbon dioxide increases.

The polar orbiting NOAA-B weather satellite was launched into an improper orbit as a result of a Delta launch vehicle failure on May 29. It had been called up as a result of TIROS-N command-control system failures. As a result, NOAA-C was prepared for launch. NOAA-5 and 6 and TIROS-N continued to provide full weather coverage in the interim.

GOES-D was launched on September 9 into a geostationary orbit to complement two orbiting geostationary weather satellites in providing

In August the Jet Propulsion Laboratory released this Viking Lander 1 photo of Mars. The boulder, nicknamed Big Joe, and dust drifts near the lander are the largest visible features.

continuous mesoscale data, which are important for monitoring severe storms. GOES-D was performing a research and operational mission by testing the first Visible and Infrared Spin-Scan Radiometric Atmospheric Sounder (VAS), which records temperature and water vapor profile or sounding information. Existing GOES satellites do not contain sounding capability.

Resource observation satellites continued to supply global synoptic data on the earth's resources. Landsat 2, which was launched in 1975, experienced attitude control problems. By June these were corrected so that dual satellite coverage was reestablished with Landsat 3, which was launched in 1978. The Landsat user community continues to rely on data from these satellites until Landsat D, with the proven Multispectral Scanner and the experimental Thematic Mapper, is available in the early 1980s. Landsat data are now being used to supply resource information for many federal, regional, and private users on a quasi-operational basis. In addition, international reception and use of Landsat data have resulted in establishment of nine direct receiving stations operating outside the United States.

The Landsat system has been operated by the National Aeronautics and Space Administration (NASA) in an experimental mode to date. However, the demand for operational continuity of data resulted in a 1979 presidential directive to provide the framework for the implementation of a civil operational land remote sensing satellite system. The National Oceanographic and Atmospheric Administration (NOAA) was given the charge to study the issues and options related to the implementation of such a system.

A major agricultural research and development program, based on Landsat data, was initiated with NASA, the U.S. Department of Agriculture (USDA), NOAA, the U.S. Department of the Interior, and the Agency for International Development. The Agriculture and Resources Inventory through Aerospace Remote Sensing (AgRISTARS) Program is a joint six-year effort. It will determine the extent to which aerospace remote sensing can be used to meet USDA information needs.

In geologic mapping, analysis of Heat Capacity Mapping Mission and Seasat data, which were launched in 1978, has shown that thermal infrared and microwave techniques can provide information about crustal structure that cannot be obtained by analysis of visible multispectral imagery alone. The earth's magnetic field data also were valuable for mineral exploration, in order to identify crustal magnetic anomalies and update current models of large-scale crustal structure and composition. The Magnetic Field Satellite (Magsat), launched in 1979, reentered the earth's atmosphere on June 11 after obtaining a complete survey of the earth's magnetic field, including vector field measurements.

Earth observation satellites launched by the USSR included an ocean monitoring satellite (Cosmos 1151) on January 23, a geophysics satellite (Cosmos 1180) on May 15, a natural resources satellite (Cosmos 1201) on July 15, and a Meteor 2 series weather satellite on September 9. The USSR has cited significant economic return on its space program in such areas as weather forecasting, mineral and petroleum exploration, and agricultural and forest mapping.

Scientific Satellites. High Energy Astronomical Observatories (HEAO) 2 and 3 continued to provide provocative results in their wide field surveys of the X Ray and Gamma Ray Universe. Previous hypotheses concerning the origin of stellar atmospheres and supernovae or exploding stars were being modified to conform with the HEAO observations. The International Ultraviolet Explorer (IUE), a cooperative mission with Great Britain and the European Space Agency (ESA), continued to support guest observers for the third year. Ultraviolet spectra observations in the solar system were emphasized.

The Solar Maximum Mission (SMM) was launched on February 14 and by year-end had detected more than 1,000 solar flares. SMM instruments provided data on the storage and release of magnetic energy thought to power flares, acceleration of particles resulting from this release, and heating and cooling of the surrounding gas. Variations in total solar radiative output also were being monitored. These variations appear to be related to solar activity and sunspot numbers, but are not large enough to have a detectable effect on weather.

International Sun-Earth Explorers (ISEE) 1, 2, and 3, a collaborative effort with ESA, continued to provide information on the structure and time variability of the solar wind–magnetosphere interface. These data are provided routinely to NOAA as a warning for geomagnetic disturbances, shortwave fadeouts, and similar local manifestations of solar activity.

Communication Satellites. The United States launched four geostationary communication satellites in 1980, while the USSR launched nine. U.S. satellites included Fleet Sat Com C and D, launched January 17 and October 30 with Atlas Centaur launch vehicles from the Eastern Space and Missile Center (ESMC). These satellites form the Navy part of the Department of Defense satellite communication system. In the commercial sector, Intelsat-V A was launched on December 4 by an Atlas Centaur launch vehicle from ESMC, while Satellite Business Systems (SBS)-A was launched by a Delta launch vehicle on November 15. Intelsat-V A is the first of a new series of international communication satellites, while SBS-A is the first satellite supplying domestic communications services to be provided by the SBS Corporation. The nine USSR communication satellites launchings included Molniya 1–46, 1–47, and 1–48; Raduga 6; Gorizant 4 and 7; Molniya 3; and two EKRAN satellites, launched on July 15 and December 26.

MICHAEL A. CALABRESE

SPAIN

Amid an economic crisis and escalating attacks from political opponents on his left and right, Premier Adolfo Suárez González sought to consolidate his political base in 1980 in order to dispel charges of incompetence and preserve Spain's five-year experiment in democracy.

Politics and Government. On September 8, Suárez moved to shore up his sagging popularity and restore public confidence in the government by replacing his foreign minister and reshuffling other ministers. A major factor in the cabinet change—the fifth since Suárez took office in 1976—was the departure of Deputy Premier Fernando Abril Martorell, a Suárez confidant who attracted criticism from across the political spectrum for his lackluster performance as minister of economic planning. He was succeeded by Leopoldo Calvo Sotelo, who had previously guided Spain's effort to join the European Community (EC). Sotelo's close ties to the business community and his reputation as a "progressive centrist" capable of independent judgment have stirred rumors that he eventually would succeed Suárez.

Of the seven new ministers, five had served in previous Suárez cabinets. The selections appeared based on the competence of the nominees as well as the premier's desire to neutralize critics within the governing Union of the Democratic Center Party (UDC) by giving them responsibility for national affairs. This attempt at co-optation may have been intended to convert the party from a coalition of disparate interests into a unified political organization.

Once the cabinet was renewed, Suárez moved to bolster his position in the national parliament (Cortés) where the UDC holds 166 of 350 seats. The Spanish Socialist Workers' Party, led by Felipe González, constitutes the major force on the left, with 121 seats. On the right, the magnetic Manuel Fraga Iribarne, a minister under Franco and present leader of the Democratic Coalition, boasts few votes but has emerged as the government's most articulate detractor. His support comes from Francoists in the judiciary, bureaucracy, and army, and from citizens who yearn for the stability of the old order. The premier obtained backing from Catalan nationalists and the Andalusian party, both of which received pledges of greater autonomy for their regions, before calling for a vote of confidence on September 16. By 180 votes to 164, he won parliament's approval for his new cabinet. The crucial test followed extended debates in which the government linked the confidence motion to a series of new economic and political proposals.

Economic Conditions. Deteriorating economic conditions nourished discontent among Spaniards, prompting some to insist "things were better under Franco." Unemployment, which afflicts 1.5 million Spaniards (11.4% of the work force), encourages street crime in Madrid, and by 11 P.M. the capital appears almost deserted. The standard of living for most Spaniards declined in 1980 as the inflation rate surpassed 15%. At the same time, massive energy imports gave rise to a $12,000,000,000 oil bill—twice that of 1979. Higher domestic energy prices sparked labor unrest, featuring a nationwide strike by taxi drivers. Such labor activism must not be confused with the relentless terrorism practiced by Basque separatists and other extremists.

The government fashioned a new economic plan to uplift the economy. It includes (1) a target of 4% growth in national income by 1983, (2) major public investment in agriculture, rural housing, transportation, and services to generate 500,000 new jobs in four years, (3) implementation of a national scheme to conserve energy and develop such alternative sources as nuclear power and coal, and (4) facilitation of Spain's entry into the EC.

French President Valéry Giscard d'Estaing dealt a blow to Spain's aspirations when, on June 5, he insisted that the admission of new members into the Community await the resolution of existing problems. Fear that French farmers could not compete with fruit, wine, and olive oil produced in Spain inspired this statement. Giscard was also concerned lest the flow of Spanish workers into his and other countries exacerbate unemployment. Before the French leader's ominous statement, Spain had looked forward to 1983 when it was scheduled to begin a 7- to 10-year transition period to full EC membership. Suárez views such membership as offering economic opportunities, while enhancing the legitimacy of his nation's fledgling democracy.

Foreign Affairs. During a June 25 visit to Madrid, President Carter endorsed Spain's accession to the Common Market because it "will strengthen the Community, just as the Community strengthens Europe." He also urged Spain to join the North Atlantic Treaty Organization (NATO)—a step that Suárez has agreed to take at a time convenient to his country. Spain agreed to receive 500 Cuban refugees who asked to leave their country early in the year.

GEORGE W. GRAYSON
College of William and Mary

SPAIN • Information Highlights

Official Name: Spanish State.
Location: Iberian Peninsula in southwestern Europe.
Area: 195,270 sq mi (505 750 km²).
Population (1980 est.): 37,800,000.
Chief Cities (1975 est.): Madrid, the capital, 3,500,000; Barcelona, 2,000,000; Valencia, 700,000.
Government: *Head of state,* Juan Carlos I, king (took office Nov. 1975). *Head of government,* Adolfo Suárez González, prime minister (took office July 1976). *Legislature*—Cortés: Senate and Chamber of Deputies.
Monetary Unit: Peseta (74.18 pesetas equal U.S.$1, Oct. 1980).
Manufactures (major products): Textiles, footwear, petrochemicals, steel, automobiles, ships, cement.
Agriculture (major products): Cereals, vegetables, citrus fruits, feed grains, wine, olives and olive oil, livestock.
GNP Per Capita (1978 est. U.S.$): $3,520.
Foreign Trade (1979 est., U.S.$): *Imports:* $25,432,000,000; *exports:* $17,903,000,000.

SPORTS
The Year in Review

On and off the field, the 1980 sports year was one of excesses. It had more than its share of dramatic moments, memorable performances, and unprecedented feats. At the same time, international affairs, investigations and indictments, labor disputes, rule changes, and even proposed federal legislation crowded the sports pages.

The victory of the U.S. Olympic hockey team surpassed even the players' own wildest dreams. Eric Heiden seemed superhuman in taking five gold medals, and the Pittsburgh Steelers went after their fifth Super Bowl win. In baseball, George Brett flirted with .400 and wound up with the highest batting average in 39 years; the National League playoff championship was considered by many the most exciting series ever. The NBA playoffs were a magic show, and the first Leonard-Duran bout may live up to its billing as "The Fight of the Decade." The fighter of the century, Muhammad Ali, fought one fight too many, and hockey bid goodbye to *its* great-est, Gordie Howe. The tennis world marveled at McEnroe and Borg, and a U.S. yacht won the America's Cup for an unbelievable 25th time in a row.

As if that weren't enough, there were outside influences. The tension between politics and amateur sports reached a breaking point, and the summer Olympics suffered the consequences. Baseball players threatened to strike, prompting many fans to say they'd gone too far. Unethical practices in college sports reached an excess by anyone's standards, and the penalties were stiff. Hockey violence got out of hand, and penalties were made even stiffer. Rep. Donald M. Mottl (D-OH) felt that sports violence had gone beyond the pale and proposed legislation calling for a $5,000 fine and a year in prison for any professional athlete who uses "excessive force."

It was a lot for one year.

See also feature article, page 62.

JEFF HACKER

Freedom, left, *skippered by Dennis Conner, sailed to an easy America's Cup victory.*

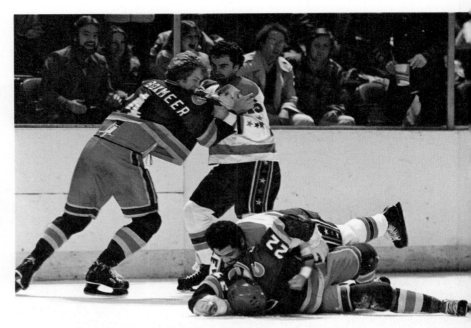

Fighting in the National Hockey League led to sweeping rule changes following the 1979–80 season.

Jerry Wachter, Focus on Sports

UPI

Spain's Severiano Ballesteros, age 23, became the youngest golfer ever to win the Masters. Genuine Risk was the first filly to win the Kentucky Derby in 65 years.

UPI

Duncan Raban, Duomo

Focus on Sports

Giorgio Chinaglia (left) led the New York Cosmos to a win in Soccer Bowl. George Brett (above) tore up American League pitching. And Larry Holmes dashed Muhammad Ali's title hopes.

UPI

Johnny Rutherford, driving a Pennzoil Chaparral, finished ahead of the pack in the Indy 500.

Evonne Goolagong Cawley used a variety of shots to defeat Chris Evert Lloyd at Wimbledon.

The sensational running of rookie Billy Sims helped bring respectability to the Detroit Lions.

AUTO RACING

Johnny Rutherford of the United States won the Indianapolis 500-mile race for the third time and went on to capture his first national driving championship.

It was another season of turmoil and discontent in the world of open cockpit auto racing. The United States Auto Club (USAC) and Championship Auto Racing Teams (CART) began 1980 under a truce, but the fragile knot came untied in July and USAC canceled the remainder of its schedule.

In Europe, Formula One organizers and constructors continued at loggerheads, with the constructors announcing at the end of the season that they would form a separate sanctioning body in 1981.

Alan Jones of Australia continued the surge that nearly earned him the 1979 crown and captured the 1980 World Driving Championship. Jones won five of the 14 Grand Prix events. He also took the Spanish Grand Prix but a rules controversy nullified the race.

It was a year of new stars on the Formula One circuit. Nelson Piquet of Brazil won three races. René Arnoux of France won two in a row early in the season, and France's Didier Peroni brought the tricolor home in front in the Belgium Grand Prix.

Buddy Baker, one of the superstars in the National Association for Stock Car Racing (NASCAR), gained just about the only gem that had eluded him in a 19-year career by starting from the pole position and winning the Daytona 500-mile race. Bobby Unser of the United States won four races, including the Pocono and Ontario, but Rutherford finished ahead in five and was a model of consistency, finishing all of 1,332 laps in the first 10 races. A spinout at Mexico City broke his string.

Formula One veteran Patrick DePallier of France was killed in a practice run at Hockenheim, West Germany. Jody Scheckter retired after the 1980 season.

BOB COLLINS, *"The Indianapolis Star"*

BASEBALL

The 1980 baseball season almost was short-circuited by five months when the players threatened to strike over free-agent compensation and other issues. A last-minute compromise on May 22, however, delaying the matters in question until 1981, enabled the season to go on as scheduled. The owners won the right to impose whatever form of compensation they deemed fair in 1981 after a bipartisan study committee has rendered its findings. The players retained the right to strike in 1981 if they do not agree with the owners' proposal.

With a strike looming, the caliber of play early in the season was uncertain. But after the threat was averted, some remarkable happenings occurred. Of the most interest was the quest for a .400 batting average pursued by George Brett, Kansas City Royals third baseman. No batsman since Boston's Ted Williams in 1941 had hit .400. (Williams hit .406 that year.) Brett soared above that plateau in August and had a chance to finish there before falling off late in the season. Yet, Brett wound up at .390, the highest batting average in major league baseball since Williams. Brett also drove in 118 runs in the 117 games he played, marking the first time that a player (in 100 or more games) had driven in more runs than games played since Boston's Walt Dropo had 144 RBIs in 136 games in 1950.

Play-offs and Series. The Royals, thanks to Brett, 230 hits by Willie Wilson, and 33 saves by reliever Dan Quisenberry, won the American League Western Division title in a romp, defeating second-place Oakland by 14 games. Then they won their first American League pennant by defeating their longtime nemesis, the New York Yankees, in three straight games in the championship series. New York had beaten Kansas City in the 1976, 1977, and 1978 play-offs but Brett's three-run homer off Rich Gossage gave the Royals a 4–2 win in the third game. The Yankees had won 103 games to outdistance runner-up Baltimore by three games in the AL East but could score only six runs in three games against the Royals.

But in the Royals' first appearance in the World Series, they were six-games losers to the Philadelphia Phillies, who posted their first World Series title in their 98-year history. The Phillies had survived two grinding struggles to reach the World Series. First they edged the Montreal Expos by one game in the National League East and then they won baseball's most exciting play-off series ever, defeating the Houston Astros in five games, with the final four games going extra innings.

AUTO RACING—1980 CHAMPIONS

World Champion: Alan Jones, Australia
CART: Johnny Rutherford, U.S.
NASCAR: Dale Earnhardt, U.S.
Can-Am: Patrick Tambay, U.S.
Formula Atlantic: Jacques Villeneuve, Canada

Major Races

Indianapolis 500: Johnny Rutherford
California 500: Bobby Unser, U.S.
Pocono 500: Bobby Unser
Daytona 500: Buddy Baker, U.S.

Grand Prix for Formula One Cars, 1980

Argentina: Alan Jones
Brazil: René Arnoux, France
South Africa: René Arnoux
U.S. West: Nelson Piquet, Brazil
Belgium: Didier Peroni, France
Monaco: Carlos Reutemann, Argentina
France: Alan Jones
Britain: Alan Jones
Germany: Jacques Laffite, France
Austria: Jean-Pierre Jabouille, France
Netherlands: Nelson Piquet
Italy: Nelson Piquet
Canada: Alan Jones
U.S. East: Alan Jones

Mike Schmidt, who was named the National League's Most Valuable Player and the Most Valuable Player of the World Series as well, gave the Phillies the Eastern Division pennant when his 11th-inning home run beat the Expos on the next-to-last day of the season. Meanwhile, Houston was forced into the first divisional play-off in National League history when the Los Angeles Dodgers swept a three-game series on the season's last weekend to force a tie for first place in the West. But the Astros won the play-off game, 7–1, to gain their first National League title.

Houston took a 2–1 lead in the championship series on an 11-inning 1–0 victory and had a two-run lead entering the eighth inning of what would have been the decisive fourth game. But the Phillies, whose manager, Dallas Green, was completing his first major league season, rallied to win that game, 5–3, in 10 innings. The next day, Houston had a three-run lead entering the eighth inning, but the Phils again rallied to pull out an 8–7, 10-inning triumph.

The World Series began with the Phillies winning twice on home ground, 7–6 in the first game, despite two home runs and four runs batted in by Kansas City's Willie Mays Aikens, and 6–4 in game two. Philadelphia, keyed by Del Unser's pinch-double, assaulted Royals ace Quisenberry for four runs in the eighth inning to overcome a 4–2 deficit in the second game.

A 10th-inning single by Aikens gave the Royals their first triumph, a 4–3 victory in the third game, and then Aikens swatted two more home runs in a 5–3 Kansas City victory in the fourth game. The Royals had only three more outs to nail down in game five, at Kansas City, but another double by Unser sparked a two-run ninth inning that gave the Phillies a 4–3 verdict and the upper hand.

Lefthander Steve Carlton, the National League Cy Young Award winner with 24 regular-season victories, combined with reliever Tug McGraw for a 4–1 Phillies win in game six at Philadelphia, and the season that seemed in so much jeopardy finally had ended.

Brett's performance was the most significant individual accomplishment, overshadowing a 25-victory season by Baltimore's Steve Stone, the American League Cy Young Award winner, and the .352 average, 25 home runs, and 122 runs batted in by Milwaukee's Cecil Cooper.

Schmidt was the majors' home run leader with 48, and he led the National League with 121 runs batted in. Reggie Jackson of the Yankees and Ben Oglivie of Milwaukee both had 41 home runs in the American League.

Two veteran pitchers, whose best days were thought to be behind them, Don Sutton and Rudy May, captured the earned run average (ERA) crowns. Sutton, 35, of the Dodgers, had a 2.21 ERA, and May, 36, of the Yankees, won the American League ERA championship with a 2.47 reading.

The most significant team accomplishment probably belonged to the Oakland A's, who improved by 29 games under new manager Billy Martin. The A's pitching staff completed 94 games, a record for post-expansion baseball. The most frightening occurrence of the season was the stroke suffered by Houston pitcher J. R. Richard, who had compiled a 10–4 mark and 1.89 ERA before being stricken. Richard was lost for the season after July 30 but was expected to try to come back in 1981.

Two old mavericks departed the baseball scene, Charles O. Finley in Oakland and Bill Veeck in Chicago. After numerous misfires, the cantankerous Finley finally sold his A's for $12.7 million to three members of the family that founded the Levi Strauss & Co. clothing firm. Almost simultaneously, Veeck sold the White Sox for $20 million to Edward DeBartolo, Sr., a Youngstown, OH, developer. However, a

Steve Sutton, Duomo

Philadelphia Phillies fans cheered the club's first World Series triumph in the 98-year history of the franchise. Relief pitcher Tug McGraw was a special heartthrob.

wrench was thrown into that transaction when American League owners failed to give the necessary ten-vote approval for the sale, putting the White Sox back in limbo. Early in the year, the New York Mets were sold to Doubleday and Co., a New York publisher. The company's chairman is a descendant of the reputed inventor of baseball, Abner Doubleday.

The St. Louis Cardinals went through the most managers (four) in the season, and after it was over, named Whitey Herzog manager and general manager, marking the first time in nearly ten years that one man had held both rolls. The Astros shockingly changed general managers, firing popular Tal Smith and replacing him with former Yankee general manager Al Rosen. Seattle hired Maury Wills as its manager, making him the third black manager.

Outfielders Duke Snider (Brooklyn) and Al Kaline (Detroit) were elected to the Baseball Hall of Fame. Chuck Klein (Philadelphia Phillies) and Boston Red Sox owner Tom Yawkey joined the Hall posthumously. Death claimed Hall of Famer Rube Marquard at age 90. Marquard, former New York Giants pitching ace, holds the record of 19 consecutive victories in one season. Ernie Shore, who as a relief pitcher for the Boston Red Sox in 1917 retired 27 batters in a row, died at age 89. Former Yankees relief ace Joe Page, 62, Yankees catcher Elston Howard, 51, and veteran American League umpire, Bill McKinley, 70, also died.

RICK HUMMEL, *"St. Louis Post-Dispatch"*

Kansas City could not keep Mike Schmidt down for long. The Phillies third baseman went on to win World Series and National League MVP honors.

Focus on Sports

BASEBALL

Professional—Major Leagues

AMERICAN LEAGUE
(Final Standings, 1980)

Eastern Division	W	L	Pct.	Western Division	W	L	Pct.
New York	103	59	.636	K. C.	97	65	.599
Baltimore	100	62	.617	Oakland	83	79	.512
Milwaukee	86	76	.531	Minnesota	77	84	.478
Boston	83	77	.519	Texas	76	85	.472
Detroit	84	78	.519	Chicago	70	90	.438
Cleveland	79	81	.494	California	65	95	.406
Toronto	67	95	.414	Seattle	59	103	.364

NATIONAL LEAGUE
(Final Standings, 1980)

Eastern Division	W	L	Pct.	Western Division	W	L	Pct.
Philadelphia	91	71	.562	Houston	93	70	.571
Montreal	90	72	.556	Los Angeles	92	71	.564
Pittsburgh	83	79	.512	Cincinnati	89	73	.549
St. Louis	74	88	.457	Atlanta	81	80	.503
New York	67	95	.414	San Fran.	75	86	.466
Chicago	64	98	.395	San Diego	73	89	.451

Play-off—American League: Kansas City defeated New York, 3 games to 0; National League: Philadelphia defeated Houston, 3 games to 2.

World Series—Philadelphia defeated Kansas City, 4 games to 2. First Game (Veterans Stadium, Philadelphia, Oct. 14, attendance 65,791): Philadelphia 7, Kansas City 6; Second Game (Veterans Stadium, Oct. 15, attendance 65,775): Philadelphia 6, Kansas City 4; Third Game (Royals Stadium, Kansas City, Oct. 17, attendance 42,380): Kansas City 4, Philadelphia 3; Fourth Game (Royals Stadium, Oct. 18, attendance 42,363): Kansas City 5, Philadelphia 3; Fifth Game (Royals Stadium, Oct. 19, attendance 42, 369): Philadelphia 4, Kansas City 3; Sixth Game (Veterans Stadium, Oct. 21, attendance 65,838): Philadelphia 4, Kansas City 1.

All-Star Game (Dodger Stadium, Los Angeles, July 8, attendance 56,088): National League 4, American League 2.

Most Valuable Players—American League: George Brett, Kansas City; National League: Mike Schmidt, Philadelphia.

Cy Young Memorial Awards (outstanding pitchers)—American League: Steve Stone, Baltimore; National League: Steve Carlton, Philadelphia.

Managers of the Year—American League: Billy Martin, Oakland; National League: Bill Virdon, Houston.

Rookies of the Year—American League: Joe Charboneau, Cleveland; National League: Steve Howe, Los Angeles.

Leading Hitters—(Percentage) American League: George Brett, Kansas City (.390); National League: Bill Buckner, Chicago (.324). (Runs Batted In) American League: Cecil Cooper, Milwaukee (122); National League: Mike Schmidt, Philadelphia (121). (Home Runs) American League: Ben Oglivie, Milwaukee, and Reggie Jackson, New York (41); National League: Schmidt (48). (Runs) American League: Willie Wilson, Kansas City (134); National League: Keith Hernandez, St. Louis (111).

Leading Pitchers—(Earned run average) American League: Rudy May, New York (2.47); National League: Don Sutton, Los Angeles (2.21); (Victories) American League: Steve Stone, Baltimore (25); National League: Steve Carlton, Philadelphia (24); (Strikeouts) American League, Len Barker, Cleveland (187); National League: Carlton (286).

No-Hit Games—Jerry Reuss, Los Angeles, against San Francisco, June 27.

Professional—Minor Leagues, Class AAA

American Association (play-offs): Denver
International League (Governor's Cup): Columbus
Pacific Coast League (play-offs): Albuquerque

Amateur

NCAA Division I: Arizona; Division II: Cal Poly (Pomona); Division III: Ithaca
Little League World Series: Taiwan

BASKETBALL

An interim coach, Paul Westhead, and the unlikeliest of substitute centers, Earvin "Magic" Johnson, rose to the top of the professional basketball world when the Los Angeles Lakers beat the Philadelphia '76ers, four games to two, to capture the 1979-80 National Basketball Association (NBA) championship. It was the Lakers' first time at the top since 1972. In the collegiate world, Louisville beat UCLA in a memorable NCAA men's final, and Old Dominion successfully completed its defense of the women's crown.

THE PROFESSIONAL SEASON

Westhead replaced Jack McKinney as the Lakers' head coach barely one month into the season, when McKinney was badly injured in a bicycle accident. The Lakers went on to win 60 of 82 regular season games, a record second only to Boston's 61–21. When Philadelphia (59–23) upset Boston, four games to one, in the semifinal round, a dramatic '76er-Laker final was set.

Those who wondered why Earvin Johnson, the 20-year-old who led Michigan State to the NCAA title the year before, was called "Magic" discovered the answer in the championship series. He was named most valuable player (MVP) of the play-offs.

Los Angeles' Kareem Abdul-Jabbar, who won a record sixth MVP for the regular season, sparked Los Angeles to a Game 1 victory, 109–102, in the Forum in Inglewood, CA, the Lakers' home court. The 7'2" (2.18 m) center scored 33 points and had 14 rebounds and 6 blocked shots.

In Game 2, also at the Forum, Philadelphia gained a 107–104 victory, as Darryl Dawkins scored 25 points and Julius "Dr. J" Erving added 23. The Sixers zoomed to an 89–71 advantage at the end of three quarters. The Lakers sliced the deficit to 99–98 and were within reach in the final moments when the Sixers' Bobby Jones hit a jump shot with 7 seconds to play.

The Lakers went ahead 2–1 in games with a 111–101 win in the Philadelphia Spectrum. Abdul-Jabbar hit 33 points and grabbed 14 rebounds. Los Angeles took command late in the first half, scoring nine straight points for a 58–44 lead.

In Game 4, at the Spectrum, the Sixers held Abdul-Jabbar to 23 points for a 105–102 win. Dawkins and Maurice Cheeks headed a 20–7 surge in the third period to send Philadelphia ahead, 81–74. Dawkins had 26 points in all, and Erving finished with 23.

Abdul-Jabbar suffered a sprained ankle in the third quarter of Game 5, in Inglewood, but he returned in the final period to score 14 of his game-high 40 points. A 3-point play late in the game enabled Abdul-Jabbar to break a 103-all tie and put the Lakers up, three games to two.

The Lakers elected to rest their star center for Game 6, in the Spectrum. While Kareem

Reibel, Focus on Sports

L. A. Laker center Kareem Abdul-Jabbar (33) and teammate Earvin "Magic" Johnson (32) rose above the Philadelphia '76ers in the NBA playoff finals.

watched on television from his L.A. home, Westhead started Johnson at center. The 6'8" (2.03 m) rookie thus played all three positions—center, forward, and guard—in the series. Magic responded by hitting 14 of 23 field goal attempts and all 14 of his free throws for 42 points in the series-clinching, 123–107 triumph. Magic's play, which included 15 rebounds and 7 assists, overshadowed that of teammate Jamaal Wilkes, who had 37 points.

To reach the final, L.A. had defeated Phoenix (4 games to 1) and defending champion Seattle (4–1), while the Sixers had ousted Atlanta (4–1) and Boston (4–1).

San Antonio's George Gervin became the fifth man in the league's 34-year history to win three straight scoring crowns; he averaged 33.1 points per game. San Diego's Swen Nater won the rebounding honors with a 15.0 average. Houston's Rick Barry won his sixth free throw title, making 93.5% of his tries. New York's Michael Ray Richardson won two titles, assists (10.1) and steals (3.23). In a new category, 3-point field goal accuracy, Seattle's Fred Brown won with a mark of 44.3%. Boston's Larry Bird (*see also* Biography) edged Magic Johnson as rookie of the year. Bill Fitch, whose Boston team improved its record from 29–53 in 1978–79 to 61–21 in 1979–80, was named coach of the year.

Off the court, the league approved the addition of the Dallas Mavericks for 1980–81, raising the number of NBA teams to 23.

Louisville's Darrell "Dr. Dunkenstein" Griffith streaks past Kiki Vandeweghe of UCLA on the way to an NCAA title and tournament MVP honors.

Louisville Cardinal

PROFESSIONAL BASKETBALL

National Basketball Association
(Final Standings, 1979–80)

Eastern Conference

Atlantic Division	W	L	Pct.
*Boston Celtics	61	21	.744
*Philadelphia '76ers	59	23	.720
*Washington Bullets	39	43	.476
New York Knickerbockers	39	43	.476
New Jersey Nets	34	48	.415
Central Division			
*Atlanta Hawks	50	32	.610
*Houston Rockets	41	41	.500
*San Antonio Spurs	41	41	.500
Cleveland Cavaliers	37	45	.451
Indiana Pacers	37	45	.451
Detroit Pistons	16	66	.195

Western Conference

Midwest Division	W	L	Pct.
*Milwaukee Bucks	49	33	.598
*Kansas City Kings	47	35	.573
Chicago Bulls	30	52	.366
Denver Nuggets	30	52	.366
Utah Jazz	24	58	.293
Pacific Division			
*Los Angeles Lakers	60	22	.732
*Seattle SuperSonicss	56	26	.683
*Phoenix Suns	55	27	.671
*Portland Trail Blazers	38	44	.463
San Diego Clippers	35	47	.427
Golden State Warriors	24	58	.293

*Qualified for play-offs

Play-offs
Eastern Conference

First Round	Philadelphia	2 games	Washington	0
	Houston	2 games	San Antonio	1
Semifinals	Philadelphia	4 games	Atlanta	1
	Boston	4 games	Houston	0
Finals	Philadelphia	4 games	Boston	1

Western Conference

First Round	Seattle	2 games	Portland	1
	Phoenix	2 games	Kansas City	1
Semifinals	Los Angeles	4 games	Phoenix	1
	Seattle	4 games	Milwaukee	3
Finals	Los Angeles	4 games	Seattle	1
Championship	Los Angeles	4 games	Philadelphia	2

All-Star Game: East 144, West 136

Individual Honors
Most Valuable Player: Kareem Abdul-Jabbar, Los Angeles
Most Valuable Player (play-offs): Earvin Johnson, Los Angeles
Rookie of the Year: Larry Bird, Boston
Coach of the Year: Bill Fitch, Boston
Leading Scorer: George Gervin, San Antonio; 2,585 points; 33.1 per game
Leading Rebounder: Swen Nater, San Diego; 15.0 per game

The New York Stars won the Women's Professional Basketball League (WBL) championship with a 125–114 victory over the Iowa Cornets in the fourth game of their best-of-five title series. Earlier in the series, New York won by scores of 128–96 and 119–99 before Iowa got its only victory, 119–112.

THE COLLEGE SEASON

Irony enveloped the two finalists, Louisville (33–3) and UCLA (22–10) at the NCAA championships in Market Square Arena, Indianapolis. Cardinal Coach Denny Crum had played at UCLA and had been an assistant coach there under the legendary John Wooden. In 1975, however, he was the Louisville coach when the Cards lost to UCLA, 75–74, in the NCAA semi-

George Tiedemann, "Sports Illustrated"

Nancy Lieberman's second player of the year award showed she was more than a passing fancy.

finals. UCLA, meanwhile, was a late selection for the tournament field, which was expanded to 48 teams. The Bruins reached the final despite having lost nine games.

Louisville gained its first title ever by beating UCLA, 59–54, with a 9–0 burst at game's end. Darrell Griffith, considered by most the nation's top college senior, led the Cards with 23 points, on 9 for 16 field goal shooting. Griffith, a 6′4″ (1.93 m) guard, was the tournament's MVP. Ex-

cept for the last spurt, the game was close all the way.

Louisville, the Metro Conference titlist, reached the final by beating Iowa, 80–72. UCLA, which finished only fourth in the Pacific 10, won its semifinal, 67–62, over Purdue. The Bruins pulled several upsets along the tournament trail, including the elimination of top-ranked DePaul, 77–71. The DePaul squad was led by 6′7″ (2.00 m) sophomore forward Mark Aguirre, who won the Adolph Rupp Trophy as the top player in men's college basketball. He was coached by the venerable Ray Meyer, who won Coach of the Year honors.

Indiana had started the season with the No. 1 ranking but lost it a month into the campaign when Kentucky tipped the Hoosiers, 69–58. Duke took over the lead in mid-December, only to lose it to DePaul after successive losses to Clemson and North Carolina. DePaul finally lost, 76–74, to Notre Dame, but the Blue Demons retained their No. 1 position until the UCLA upset.

An Atlantic Coast Conference (ACC) team, Virginia, won the National Invitation Tournament (NIT) in New York City's Madison Square Garden. The Cavaliers beat Minnesota's Gophers, 58–55.

Old Dominion (37–1) of Norfolk, VA, reigned again in women's play, beating Tennessee (33–5), 68–53, for the Association of Intercollegiate Athletics for Women (AIAW) title. Inge Nissen, the tournament MVP, scored 20 points. Her Lady Monarchs' teammate, Nancy Lieberman, who won her second straight Margaret Wade Trophy as the women's collegiate player of the year, added 12.

GREG HEBERLEIN, *"Seattle Times"*

COLLEGE BASKETBALL

Conference Champions*

Atlantic Coast: Duke
Big East: Georgetown
Big Eight: Kansas State
Big Sky: Weber State
Big Ten: Indiana
East Coast: La Salle
Eastern Athletic: Villanova
Ivy League: Pennsylvania
Metro: Louisville
Mid-American: Toledo
Missouri Valley: Bradley
Ohio Valley: Western Kentucky
Pacific-10: Oregon State
Pacific Coast Athletic: San Jose State
Southeastern: Louisiana State; Kentucky won regular season championship.
Southern: Furman
Southland: Lamar
Southwest: Texas A&M
Southwestern: Alcorn State
Sun Belt: Virginia Commonwealth
West Coast Athletic: (tie) San Francisco, St. Mary's (Moraga, CA)
Western Athletic: Brigham Young

*Based on post-season conference tournaments, where applicable.

Tournaments

NCAA: Louisville
NIT: Virginia
NCAA: Div. II: Virginia Union
NCAA Div. III: North Park College
NAIA: Cameron College
AIAW (Women): Old Dominion

In what had been promoted as "The Fight of the Decade," Panamanian welterweight Roberto Durán (left) took the WBC title from Sugar Ray Leonard, June 20 in Montreal. In a rematch on November 25 at the New Orleans Superdome, Leonard regained the crown with an eighth round technical knockout.

UPI

BOXING

Despite a classic welterweight confrontation in which Roberto Durán dethroned Sugar Ray Leonard for the World Boxing Council (WBC) title, the heavyweight division held the limelight in 1980. The reason was Muhammad Ali, who tried to regain the heavyweight title for a fourth time. Ali had already become the only man to regain the heavyweight crown three times when he took the World Boxing Association (WBA) version from Leon Spinks on Sept. 15, 1978. He formally gave up the title by retiring in 1979. Then in the summer of 1980, he signed to challenge Larry Holmes, the WBC champion and Ali's former sparring partner.

The bout on October 2, at Las Vegas, NV, drew a gate of $6.2 million, a record for a heavyweight title bout. A crowd of 24,790, paying $500 for ringside seats, and a huge closed-circuit television audience were sorely disappointed and saddened. Ali was a pathetic figure as Holmes hit him at will. After Ali took a steady, humiliating pounding for 10 rounds, his trainer, Angelo Dundee, signaled that his fighter would not answer the bell for the 11th round. It went into the books as a knockout, the first of Ali's career. During his retirement, Ali had bloated to 256 lbs (116 kg). For the Holmes fight he trimmed to 217.5 lbs (99 kg). However, after the fight it was revealed that he had taken an overdose of medication that might have contributed to his rapid weight loss and the subsequent weakness he claimed he felt during the bout. Ringside experts said Ali threw only about 15 punches over 10 rounds. For the unbeaten Holmes, who had stopped Lorenzo Zanon of Italy, Leroy Jones, and Scott LeDoux during the year, the triumph was his eighth straight by a knockout in a title defense, breaking a record set by Joe Louis. Ali was assured $8 million for the fight.

John Tate, who claimed the WBA title (vacated when Ali retired) by beating Gerrie Coetzee in South Africa in 1979, was the victim of a stunning upset before a hometown crowd in Knoxville, TN, on March 31. Mike Weaver of Gatesville, TX, knocked him out in the 15th round after Tate, unbeaten in 20 previous bouts, was ahead on the scorecards of all officials. Tate inexplicably walked into a smashing hook and lost the title virtually on one punch.

In one of the most publicized fights in boxing history, at Montreal's Olympic Stadium on June 20, Durán, fighting in a heavier class after giving up the lightweight crown in February 1979, took a unanimous decision from Leonard in a classic contest. The Panamanian and the former Olympic champion slugged for 15 rounds in a throwback to the great lighter-weight fights of the 1930s and 1940s. Leonard retook the crown in a late November rematch.

With more than 100 title bouts in all divisions, boxing enjoyed unprecedented success during the year, as revenues from television buoyed promotions and created widespread interest. Among the welterweights a newcomer with devastating punching power, Thomas Hearns of Detroit, wrested the WBA title from José (Pipino) Cuevas of Mexico, a clever veteran who had held the crown since 1976 and was making his 13th defense. Hearns won on a second-round knockout. Another veteran, Danny (Little Red) Lopez, the WBC featherweight titleholder since 1976, was stopped by Salvador Sanchez of Mexico in the 13th round in February.

Marvin Hagler of Brockton, MA, long regarded as the uncrowned champion, finally emerged as the middleweight titleholder, inflicting severe punishment on Alan Minter of England to score a knockout in a September bout at Wembley.

GEORGE DE GREGORIO

BOXING

World Boxing Champions

(Year of achieving title in parentheses)

Junior Flyweight—Yoko Gushiken, Japan (1976), World Boxing Association (WBA); Hilario Zapata, Panama (1980), World Boxing Council (WBC).

Flyweight—Peter Mathebula, South Africa (1980), WBA; Shoji Oguma, Japan (1980), WBC.

Bantamweight—Jeff Chandler, Philadelphia (1980), WBA; Lupe Pintor, Mexico (1979), WBC.

Junior Featherweight—Sergio Palma, Argentina (1980), WBA; Wilfredo Gomez, Puerto Rico (1977), WBC.

Featherweight—Eusebio Pedroza, Panama (1978), WBA; Salvador Sanchez, Mexico (1980), WBC.

Junior Lightweight—Yasutsune Uehara, Japan (1980), WBA; Bazooka Limon, Mexico (1980), WBC.

Lightweight—Hilmer Kenty, Detroit (1980), WBA; James Waat, Scotland (1979), WBC.

Junior Welterweight—Aaron Pryor, Cincinnati (1980), WBA; Saoul Mamby, New York City (1980), WBC.

Welterweight—Thomas Hearns, Detroit (1980), WBA; Ray Leonard, Palmer Park, MD (1980), WBC.

Junior Middleweight—Ayud Kalule, Uganda (1979), WBA; Maurice Hope, England (1979), WBC.

Middleweight—Marvin Hagler, Brockton, MA (1980), WBA and WBC.

Light Heavyweight—Eddie Mustafa Muhammad, Gutenberg, NJ (1980), WBA; Matthew Saad Muhammad, Philadelphia (1979), WBC.

Heavyweight—Mike Weaver, Gatesville, TX (1980), WBA; Larry Holmes, Easton, PA (1978), WBC.

FOOTBALL

Before 75,500 fans in the Superdome in New Orleans, the Oakland Raiders defeated the Philadelphia Eagles, 27-10, in Super Bowl XV. Raiders' quarterback Jim Plunkett was the game's most valuable player. The University of Georgia finished the college season as Number 1.

THE PROFESSIONAL SEASON

Super Bowl XV brought together the Philadelphia Eagles, who fulfilled Coach Dick Vermeil's preseason prediction, and the Oakland Raiders, who arrived unexpectedly, thanks to a quarterback no other team had wanted in 1978.

The ebullient Vermeil told the Eagles at training camp what he expected of them, and they responded with winning performances from the start. They held or shared first place in their division all season. The Eagles finally attained Vermeil's objective when they beat their perennial rivals, the Dallas Cowboys, in the National Conference (NFC) title showdown, 20-7. The victory over Dallas put them in the NFL championship game for the first time since 1960, when Philadelphia beat the Green Bay Packers, 17-13.

The Eagles' best season in 20 years revolved around quarterback Ron Jaworski and running back Wilbert Montgomery on offense. With 6′8″ (2.03 m) Harold Carmichael his prime target, Jaworski threw for 3,529 yards and 27 touchdowns, to top all other NFC passers in the statistical rating. Montgomery, one of the league's premiere running backs, was burdened with injuries, missing four games, but he still managed to rush for 778 yards.

Philadelphia's defense proved to be the league's stingiest, yielding only 222 points. Tackle Charlie Johnson was the key man in the front three, and Bill Bergey and Jerry Robinson led a first-rate linebacking corps. A solid secondary featured Randy Logan at strong safety.

After hurting his knee in practice, Montgomery was a doubtful starter for the NFC final. But

Mitchell B. Reibel, Focus on Sports

Wide receiver Harold Carmichael was Philadelphia quarterback Ron Jaworski's favorite target. The duo helped lead the Eagles to New Orleans and their first Super Bowl appearance.

he erased all doubts when he took off on a 42-yard touchdown scamper on the game's second play from scrimmage. He wound up with 194 yards, only two shy of the NFL record for a play-off game, set by another Eagle, Steve Van Buren, in 1949.

With the score tied, 7-7, at halftime, the Eagles shut down the Cowboys' attack in the second half. Dallas was limited to a total of 86 yards on the ground, and Tony Dorsett, who had rushed for 1,185 yards during the season, was able to gain only 41. Philadelphia clinched the victory on a nine-yard touchdown run by Leroy Harris and two field goals by Tony Franklin.

While the Eagles had a successful quarterback in Jaworski, the Raiders expected to have a losing season, enjoyed a sudden turnaround because of the surprising performance of their own passer, Jim Plunkett. Plunkett was a discarded quarterback on whom no team was willing to risk the $100 waiver fee when he was cut by the San Francisco 49ers two years before. A Heisman Trophy winner at Stanford, Plunkett was battered and bruised, and his confidence was shattered, in five trying years with the New England Patriots and two with the 49ers.

Al Davis, the controversial managing general partner of the Raiders, who is noted for his reclamation projects, picked up Plunkett as a free agent. After two years on the bench healing his physical and psychic wounds, Plunkett was ready when the call came. Dan Pastorini, obtained in a trade with the Houston Oilers for Ken Stabler, suffered a broken leg in the fifth game of the season. Oakland's record was 2-3 when Plunkett took over. He compiled an amazing 9-2 record as the starting quarterback and piloted the Raiders to a wild card play-off spot in the American Conference (AFC).

The Raiders then defeated the AFC's other wild card team, the Oilers, 27-7, in the first play-off matchup. Only days after the game, Houston Coach Bum Phillips was fired because of a disagreement with team owner Bud Adams over the need for an offensive coordinator.

The Raiders' resurgence was nearly stopped by the Cleveland Browns in the semifinal round. Playing in arctic conditions—with the wind-chill factor the temperature was −30°F (−49°C)—Oakland tried to hold on to a 14-12 lead in the final minute. The Browns were on the Oakland 12-yard line when Coach Sam Rutigliano made what was to become a much-debated decision. He called for a pass on second down rather than a run to set up a short field goal. Mike Davis intercepted Brian Sipe's throw in the end zone to end the Cleveland season. It was a sad finish for Sipe, who had a spectacular campaign, leading the Browns to the AFC central division title by passing for 4,132 yards.

The Raiders then confronted the aerial circus of the San Diego Chargers, coached by Don Coryell, for the AFC title. Dan Fouts had passed for a record 4,715 yards with the help of the No. 1 pass-receiving trio in the NFL—John Jefferson, Charlie Joiner, and Kellen Winslow. Chuck Muncie added muscle to the running attack.

The passing pyrotechnics started immediately, but by Oakland. The Raiders scored on a bizarre 65-yard toss from Plunkett to Raymond Chester after the ball was deflected off the hands of running back Kenny King. By midway in the second quarter, Oakland had built a 28-7 lead, but the dangerous Chargers rallied their offense.

PROFESSIONAL FOOTBALL

National Football League
Final Standings

AMERICAN CONFERENCE

Eastern Division

	W	L	T	Pct.	Points For	Agst.
Buffalo	11	5	0	.688	320	260
New England	10	6	0	.625	441	325
Miami	8	8	0	.500	266	305
Baltimore	7	9	0	.438	355	387
Jets	4	12	0	.250	302	395

Central Division

	W	L	T	Pct.	Points For	Agst.
Cleveland	11	5	0	.688	357	310
Houston	11	5	0	.688	295	251
Pittsburgh	9	7	0	.563	352	313
Cincinnati	6	10	0	.375	244	312

Western Division

	W	L	T	Pct.	Points For	Agst.
San Diego	11	5	0	.688	418	327
Oakland	11	5	0	.688	364	306
Denver	8	8	0	.500	310	323
Kansas City	8	8	0	.500	319	336
Seattle	4	12	0	.250	291	408

Play-offs

Oakland 27, Houston 7
San Diego 20, Buffalo 14
Oakland 14, Cleveland 12
Oakland 34, San Diego 27

NATIONAL CONFERENCE

Eastern Division

	W	L	T	Pct.	Points For	Agst.
Philadelphia	12	4	0	.750	384	222
Dallas	12	4	0	.750	454	311
Washington	6	10	0	.375	261	293
St. Louis	5	11	0	.313	299	350
Giants	4	12	0	.250	249	425

Central Division

	W	L	T	Pct.	Points For	Agst.
Minnesota	9	7	0	.563	317	308
Detroit	9	7	0	.563	334	272
Chicago	7	9	0	.438	304	264
Green Bay	5	10	1	.344	231	371
Tampa Bay	5	10	1	.344	271	341

Western Division

	W	L	T	Pct.	Points For	Agst.
Atlanta	12	4	0	.750	405	272
Los Angeles	11	5	0	.688	424	289
San Francisco	6	10	0	.375	320	415
New Orleans	1	15	0	.063	291	487

Play-offs

Dallas 34, Los Angeles 13
Philadelphia 31, Minnesota 16
Dallas 30, Atlanta 27
Philadelphia 20, Dallas 7

Super Bowl: Oakland 27, Philadelphia 10

and scored three of the next four times they had the ball. With seven minutes left in the final quarter, the Chargers closed the gap to 34–27. With reliable fullback Mark van Eeghan carrying much of the load, however, Oakland managed to control the ball for most of the remaining time and came away with the 34–27 win and a trip to Super Bowl.

The 1980 season also saw the end of a dynasty, as old age and a horrendous series of injuries caught up with the Pittsburgh Steelers. The winner of the previous two Super Bowls and of a record four in all, the Steelers finished with a 9–7 record and missed the play-offs for the first time in eight years.

Rookie-of-the Year honors in the NFC went to Billy Sims after the league's top draft pick turned things around for the Detroit Lions. The former Oklahoma All-American and Heisman Trophy winner led the conference in touchdowns with 16, rushed for 1,303 yards, and helped Detroit improve its record from 2–14 the previous year to a respectable 9–7.

Another rookie running back who made an impressive debut was Joe Cribbs of the Buffalo Bills. The former Auburn star gained 1,178 yards and was the only rookie to make the AFC Pro Bowl squad. He also helped the Bills reach the play-offs for the first time since 1974.

Still unparalleled among running backs, however, was Houston's Earl Campbell, who ran for 1,934 yards, again tops in the league.

THE COLLEGE SEASON

The arrival of Herschel Walker, the heralded freshman running back, at the University of Georgia created great expectations among Bulldogs fans. The team had compiled a 6–5 record the previous year, but not even the most optimistic loyalists could have envisioned that Georgia would finish the season as the only major undefeated and untied team in the nation. Walker lived up to all expectations. A rugged 6'2" (1.88 m), 220 lbs (100 kg), Walker displayed the speed of a sprinter and the power of a shot putter (track and field events at which he earned Georgia state titles in high school). The perfect tailback for Coach Vince Dooley's I-formation, he rushed for 1,616 yards, establishing a national collegiate mark for freshmen.

So outstanding was Walker's performance that he was often mentioned in preballoting speculation on the Heisman Trophy winner, a rare compliment for a first-year player. While George Rogers, South Carolina's hard-running senior tailback, was voted the prestigious award, Georgia's favorite peach placed third. It was the highest-ever finish for a freshman.

In addition to Walker, Georgia's top offensive threats were the passing of Buck Belue and the consistent field-goal kicking of Rex Robinson, the all-time leading scorer in the Southeast Conference. The Bulldogs finally achieved the Number 1 ranking in the weekly polls—their

In a midseason upset, Mississippi State hands Alabama its first defeat since 1978.

Dusty Perkins, "Sports Illustrated"

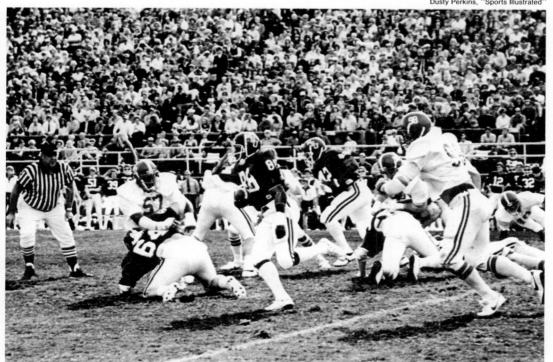

first time in 38 years—after posting their ninth victory, 26–21, over Florida. By defeating Auburn, 31–21, the following week, the Bulldogs captured the conference championship and earned a ticket to the Sugar Bowl.

Notre Dame accepted a bid to oppose Georgia on New Year's Day after edging Alabama, 7–0, at Birmingham. (Alabama Coach Bear Bryant suffered only his second home field shutout in 23 years.) Except for a 3–3 tie against Georgia Tech and a 20–3 loss to the University of Southern California (USC), Notre Dame played inspired football in posting a 9–1–1 record.

In the Sugar Bowl, Georgia scored a 17–10 win, giving them the unofficial national championship for the first time in the school's history. But the victory didn't come easy against the aroused Irish, whose two crucial mistakes in the first half lost them the game. Herschel Walker was virtually the entire Georgia offense. Although Notre Dame set its defense to stop him, the freshman All-American slashed his way for 150 yards and scored both Georgia touchdowns. The Irish, noted for comebacks in bowl games, took command in the second half, but interceptions blunted their late scoring threats.

After five Pac-10 Conference teams, including USC and UCLA, were declared ineligible for the Rose Bowl because of academic violations involving athletes, officials of the Pasadena classic were fearful of having to settle for a weak West Coast team. But little-regarded Washington (9–2) came to the rescue. Paced by quarterback Tom Flick, the Huskies put on a late-season spurt and won the Pac-10 crown outright. Michigan (9–2) made its fourth Rose Bowl appearance in five years by capturing the Big Ten championship with a 9–3 win over Ohio State.

Michigan Coach Bo Schembechler savored his first bowl triumph after a total of seven defeats, as the Wolverines set back Washington, 23–6. Butch Woolfolk rushed for 182 yards and one touchdown, while quarterback John Wangler connected on 12 of 20 passing attempts for 145 yards, including a 7-yard scoring pass to his favorite receiver, Anthony Carter.

Florida State, which had its undefeated season spoiled by Oklahoma in the Orange Bowl the previous year, got the opportunity to even matters by posting a 10–1 record. In order to return to the Orange Bowl, Oklahoma again had to defeat Nebraska in the customary tussle for the Big Eight title. The Sooners nearly did not make it. Nebraska went ahead, 17–14, late in the final quarter, but Oklahoma staged an 80-yard drive in the closing minutes to squeak out a 21–17 win.

In Miami, Florida State again was thwarted, as Oklahoma scored a two-point conversion in the final 1 minute and 27 seconds for an 18–17 triumph. Sooner quarterback J.C. Watts, who had fumbled three times, went from goat to hero on the last touchdown drive.

The Cotton Bowl confrontation between Alabama and Baylor was surprisingly one-sided, as the Crimson Tide notched a 30–2 decision for Coach Bear Bryant's 306th career victory, just eight short of Alonzo Stagg's all-time record.

LUD DUROSKA

COLLEGE FOOTBALL

Conference Champions

Atlantic Coast—North Carolina State
Big Eight—Oklahoma
Big Sky—Boise State
Big Ten—Michigan
Ivy League—Yale
Mid-American—Central Michigan
Missouri Valley—Tulsa
Pacific Coast Athletic—Long Beach State
Pacific Ten—Washington
Southeastern—Georgia
Southern—Furnam
Southwest—Baylor
Southwestern—Jackson State
Western Athletic-Brigham Young

Heisman Trophy—George Rogers, South Carolina
Lombardi Trophy—Hugh Green, Pittsburgh

NCAA Champions

Division I-AA—Boise State
Division II—California Poly—San Luis Obispo
Division III—Dayton

NAIA Champions

Division I—Elon
Division II—Pacific Lutheran

Major Bowl Games

Independence (Shreveport, LA, Dec. 13)—Southern Mississippi 16, McNeese State 14
Garden State (East Rutherford, NJ, Dec. 14)—Houston 35, Navy 0
Holiday (San Diego, CA, Dec. 19)—Brigham Young 46, Southern Methodist 45
Tangerine (Orlando, FL, Dec. 20)—Florida 35, Maryland 20
Blue-Gray Classic (Montgomery, AL, Dec. 25)—Blue 24, Gray 23
Fiesta (Tempe, AZ, Dec. 26)—Penn State 31, Ohio State 19
Hall of Fame (Birmingham, AL, Dec. 27)—Arkansas 35, Tulane 15
Liberty (Memphis, TN, Dec. 27)—Purdue 26, Missouri 25
Sun Bowl (El Paso, TX, Dec. 27)—Nebraska 31, Mississippi State 17
Gator (Jacksonville, FL, Dec. 29)—Pittsburgh 37, South Carolina 9
Bluebonnet (Houston, TX, Dec. 31)—North Carolina 16, Texas 7
Cotton (Dallas, TX, Jan. 1)—Alabama 30, Baylor 2
Orange (Miami, FL, Jan. 1)—Oklahoma 18, Florida State 17
Rose (Pasadena, CA, Jan. 1)—Michigan 23, Washington 6
Sugar (New Orleans, LA, Jan. 1)—Georgia 17, Notre Dame 10
Peach (Atlanta, GA, Jan. 2)—Miami 20, Virginia Tech 10

Final College Rankings

	AP Writers	UPI Coaches		AP Writers	UPI Coaches
1	Georgia	Georgia	6	Alabama	Alabama
2	Pittsburgh	Pittsburgh	7	Nebraska	Nebraska
3	Oklahoma	Oklahoma	8	Penn State	Penn State
4	Michigan	Michigan	9	Notre Dame	North Carolina
5	Florida State	Florida State	10	North Carolina	Notre Dame

The Crisis in College Athletics

Intercollegiate sport never had a year like it and would not want to have another. Disclosures of misconduct, coming one after another like hammer blows, rocked some of the most respected educational institutions in the United States—the University of Southern California, UCLA, Purdue, Oregon, and others—and caused even the most sanguine of administrators to wonder what had suddenly gone so wrong. By sheer volume, the scandalous revelations were suffocating enough. What made them even more demoralizing was that they involved academic cheating: fraudulent grades; bogus credits; altered transcripts; coaches, administrators, and academicians conspiring to undermine the educational process itself.

What had gone wrong was not sudden, however. It was the predictable consequence of a long and shameful neglect.

Traditionally, the custodians of big-time college sports have had a painfully difficult time administering the procedures that bring their athletes into school and keep them eligible for play. Big-time college recruiting, primarily for talented basketball and football players, has long been a ritual of bribery, much of it within the rules of the National Collegiate Athletic Association (NCAA). In recent years, more liberal attitudes and admissions policies that opened the door to increasingly large numbers of deprived and undereducated youngsters, though well intended, only exacerbated the problem. Potential for abuse was always great; it became massive.

The occasional penalties meted out by the NCAA did little to stem the tide of underqualified collegians or discourage the cheaters. For good reason. Big-time college sport is a high-profile, high-priced, high-pressure business, not lacking in modern business practices. Illegal benefits given talented athletes are easily rationalized when the vested interest in an athletic program is more fiscal than moral. The rewards are great: stadiums and arenas full of paying customers, profitable television appearances, invitations to prestigious post-season contests. The risk is minimal. No cheating coach has ever been barred from coaching; no cheating school has ever been drummed out of the NCAA.

Penn State football coach Joe Paterno, a vigorous critic of the bottom-line mentalities that spawned this condition, said in mid-1980: "My feeling has been for many years that the university presidents and the faculties of many institutions have just walked down the halls and looked at the ceilings. They didn't want to see anything. They evaded responsibility and compromised themselves. . . ."

By the end of the year, even the most insouciant college presidents had been forced to bring their gazes down from the ceiling. Into the laps of administrators had been dumped evidence of improprieties they could not tolerate. Some reacted swiftly. On the west coast, the punishment was especially severe. Half the membership of the Pacific Ten Conference—Southern California, UCLA, Oregon, Oregon State, and Arizona State—was ruled ineligible for post-season play (including the Rose Bowl) on findings ranging from the falsifying of transcripts to phony credits given by junior colleges for "correspondence" courses.

The lengths to which some cheating went were bizarre. Eight Arizona State football players received credits for a class which they never attended and for which they completed none of the required work. The class was taught not in a classroom in Arizona but in a garage in California and was administered by Rocky Mountain College in Montana. Five New Mexico basketball players were ruled ineligible for receiving credits for an extension course taught in California but provided by a school in Kansas (Ottawa University).

The granting of false credits to athletes was also uncovered by the University of Utah, California Poly at Pomona, and San Jose State. Others uncovered a good deal more. The football coach at the University of Arizona was indicted for tampering with airline tickets and expense accounts. The Portland State basketball coach was accused by the university of paying players with school funds and then taking kickbacks from them.

University of Oregon athletes were indicted on felony charges involving telephone credit cards and airline tickets; four were indicted on charges of sodomy and coercion. Athletes at New Mexico were charged with a number of crimes, including armed robbery, aggravated assault, misappropriation of city funds, credit card fraud, and rape. Athletes at Kentucky were involved in 15 arrests over a five-year period; the charges ranged from burglary to rape.

In the wake of the problems at his school, University of Oregon President William B. Boyd resigned. When Boyd took the job in 1975, he announced that he would seek "athletic excellence" as a benefit to the university. Upon resigning, he said, "I did not know the price we were going to pay."

In the larger sense, price is exactly what the crisis in college sports is all about. Throughout the United States, collegiate athletic programs are being squeezed by the worst money crunch in their histories. As they moved into the new decade, even the most successful programs were facing serious financial difficulties. For those who had to watch their pennies, the problem was crit-

YOU CAN PLAY BALL WITH
ME KID! I'M ON YOUR
SIDE!

ADULT
PRESSURE

ALUMNI

COLLEGE
RECRUITING

Copyright 1978 by Hy Rosen, The Times-Union

Rosen, Rothco

ical. The inflationary spiral, heavy competition from professional sports leagues for the entertainment dollar, and the need to comply with federal legislation (Title IX) demanding equal opportunity for women in intercollegiate participation, together threatened to price them out of existence.

Typical of the complaints was that of University of Maryland Athletic Director Jim Kehoe. Kehoe maintained that the cost of running his department had increased 25% in two years; the price of a football helmet, he said, now was what an entire uniform cost a few years earlier. The consequence, he feared, could be the abolishing of some sports at his school and "the severe reduction in travel and squad sizes" in others. "There is no way in the world we can generate an extra 12% revenue every year," he said. Even University of Michigan Athletic Director Don Canham, with one of the most affluent intercollegiate programs, saw "bad times ahead" due to the desperate financial conditions.

Desperate conditions make desperate coaches and, as the events of 1979 and 1980 proved, desperate administrators. The results are desperate acts that corrupt sport. By the autumn of 1980, the impact of the scandals and the gravity of the situation had prompted widespread outrage and a cry for reform that was remarkable in its unanimity.

It was the coaches themselves who spoke out first and loudest. Basketball coach Tex Winter of California State at Long Beach charged that the rules and regulations that govern intercollegiate athletics "are made by people in ivory towers who haven't been on the waterfront or battle line. They haven't seen things in the proper perspective. . . ." Syracuse football coach Frank Maloney called for a "summit conference" to "redefine the aims and objectives of NCAA sports."

The American Football Coaches Association (AFCA), meeting in Dallas earlier in the year, called for stricter academic requirements and the closing of loopholes in the recruiting process. The Rev. Edmund Joyce, chairman of the faculty board in control of athletics at Notre Dame, said to the AFCA: "I believe that most knowledgeable people would agree that the intercollegiate athletic establishment today is suffering from a serious malaise. . . . In the past our chief concern has been directed toward unscrupulous coaches who conspired with alumni or others to offer illegal inducement to prospective players. Today, academic cheating has reared its ugly head. To my mind, this is a far more insidious and unpardonable transgression. To reverse this situation is going to take more than rhetoric."

The football coaches adopted a resolution that challenged the NCAA to raise admission standards. They asked that a uniform "normal progress" rule be established, whereby the classroom work of student-athletes would be monitored and each school would be required to meet national minimum standards. University of Tennessee football coach Johnny Majors called for an end to the "hypocrisy" of year-round recruiting and for strict limitations on the time college coaches would have to visit high school athletes. The NCAA's committee on academic testing and requirements announced that it was moving to crack down on credits for extension and correspondence courses and the processing of transcripts.

These steps were recognized by the more visible college leaders as a beginning, but only a beginning. Said Father Joyce: "In the final analysis, meaningful reform is going to come about only if college administrators make it a matter of conscience that no student-athlete is going to be exploited."

JOHN UNDERWOOD

GOLF

For the fourth straight year, Tom Watson was the leading money-winner on the PGA tour, this time with a record $530,808. Watson led the tour with six victories and added his third British Open crown in a runaway at Muirfield, Scotland. He was named the Professional Golfers Association's Player of the Year, again for the fourth consecutive time.

But Watson, even though he recorded his finest scoring average ever at 69.95, lost a chance to win his fourth straight Vardon Trophy when Lee Trevino averaged 69.73, the lowest since 1950. Trevino, 41, won three tournaments, finished second in three others, and was second on the money list with a career-high $385,814.

Perhaps the biggest news of the year was the return of Jack Nicklaus, who had slumped virtually out of sight in 1979. Nicklaus outdueled Japan's Isao Aoki to win the U.S. Open at Baltusrol with a tournament-record 272, then walked off with the PGA championship at Oak Hill in Rochester, NY, with a record score of 274. Nicklaus now has tied Willie Anderson, Ben Hogan, and Bobby Jones with four U.S. Open victories and equaled Walter Hagen's five PGA championships. He became only the third golfer in history to win the Open and the PGA in the same year and, at age 40, had an unmatched total of 19 major championships.

Curtis Strange, a fourth-year professional, won two tournaments and finished third on the money chart with $271,400 to earn *Golf Digest's* most improved male professional award. Gary Hallberg, who won $64,244 plus another $11,600 in unofficial money in less than half a season, was named *Golf Digest's* rookie of the year.

Spaniard Severiano Ballesteros led all the way in romping to a four-stroke victory in the Masters, his first major triumph on U.S. soil.

Even Arnold Palmer struck back at the age of 50, thrilling his Army by winning the Canadian PGA championship, a nontour event, by a stroke over Aoki. It was Palmer's first victory since 1975.

On the Ladies Professional Golfers Association tour, second-year player Beth Daniel cracked Nancy Lopez-Melton's two-year domination by winning four tournaments and $231,000 to become the first woman professional to break the $200,000 earnings barrier. Rookie of the Year in 1979, Daniel was named *Golf Digest's* most improved female professional.

She was challenged for the top money spot by Donna Caponi Young, who won five tournaments and $220,619, by Amy Alcott with four victories and $219,887, and by Lopez-Melton with three wins and $209,078. JoAnne Carner also won five times in 1980.

Alcott won the U.S. Women's Open and Sally Little took the LPGA Championship.

GOLF

PGA 1980 Tournament Winners

Bob Hope Desert Classic: Craig Stadler (343)
Phoenix Open: Jeff Mitchell (272)
Andy Williams-San Diego Open: Tom Watson (275)
Bing Crosby National Pro-Am: George Burns (280)
Hawaiian Open: Andy Bean (266)
Joe Garagiola-Tucson Open: Jim Colbert (270)
Glen Campbell-Los Angeles Open: Tom Watson (276)
Bay Hill Classic: Dave Eichelberger (279)
Jackie Gleason Inverrary Classic: Johnny Miller (274)
Doral-Eastern Open: Ray Floyd (279)
Tournament Players Championship: Lee Trevino (278)
Heritage Classic: Doug Tewell (280)
Masters Tournament: Seve Ballesteros (275)
MONY-Tournament of Champions: Tom Watson (276)
Greater New Orleans Open: Tom Watson (273)
Houston Open: Curtis Strange (266)
Byron Nelson Classic: Tom Watson (274)
Colonial National Invitation: Bruce Lietzke (271)
Memorial Tournament: David Graham (280)
Kemper Open: John Mahaffey (275)
Atlanta Classic: Larry Nelson (270)
U.S. Open: Jack Nicklaus (272)
Canadian Open: Bob Gilder (274)
Danny Thomas-Memphis Classic: Lee Trevino (272)
Western Open: Scott Simpson (281)
Sammy Davis-Hartford Open: Howard Twitty (266)
Philadelphia Classic: Doug Tewell (272)
PGA Championship: Jack Nicklaus (274)
Westchester Classic: Curtis Strange (273)
World Series of Golf: Tom Watson (270)
B.C. Open: Don Pooley (271)
Pleasant Valley Jimmy Fund Classic: Wayne Levi (273)
Hall of Fame: Phil Hancock (275)
Texas Open: Lee Trevino (265)
Anheuser-Busch Classic: Ben Crenshaw (272)

LPGA 1980 Tournament Winners

Whirlpool: JoAnne Carner (282)
Elizabeth Arden Classic: Jane Blalock (283)
Bent Tree Ladies Classic: JoAnne Carner (280)
Sun City Classic: Jan Stephenson (275)
Sunstar: JoAnne Carner (207)
Honda Civic Golf Classic: JoAnne Carner (279)
LPGA National Pro-Am: Donna Young (286)
Women's Kemper Open: Nancy Lopez Melton (284)
Colgate-Dinah Shore Winners Cir.: Donna Young (275)
American Defender: Amy Alcott (206)
Florida Lady Citrus: Donna White (283)
Birmingham Classic: Barbara Barrow (210)
CPC Women's International: Hollis Stacy (279)
Coca-Cola Classic: Donna White (217)
Corning Classic: Donna Young (281)
Golden Lights Classic: Beth Daniel (287)
LPGA Championship: Sally Little (285)
Boston Five Classic: Dale Lundquist (276)
Lady Keystone Open: JoAnne Carner (207)
Sarah Coventry: Nancy Lopez Melton (283)
Mayflower Classic: Amy Alcott (275)
U.S. Women's Open: Amy Alcott (280)
WUI Classic: Sally Little (284)
Peter Jackson Classic: Pat Bradley (277)
Patty Berg Classic: Beth Daniel (210)
Columbia Savings LPGA Classic: Beth Daniel (276)
Rail Charity Golf Classic: Nancy Lopen Melton (275)
World Series of Women's Golf: Beth Daniel (282)
United Virginia Bank Classic: Donna Young (277)
ERA Real Estate Classic: Donna Young (283)
Mary Kay Classic: Jerilyn Britz (139)
Inamori Golf Classic: Amy Alcott (280)
Japan Classic: Tatsuko Ohsako (213)

Other Tournaments

U.S. Men's Amateur: Hal Sutton
U.S. Women's Amateur: Juli Simpson Inkster
U.S. Men's Public Links: Jodie Mudd
U.S. Women's Public Links: Lori Castillo
USGA Senior Men's Amateur: Bill Campbell

USGA Senior Women's Amateur: Dorothy Porter
U.S. Senior Open: Roberto de Vicenzo
World Amateur Cup, Men's: Hal Sutton
World Amateur Cup, Women's: Patti Rizzo

Myra Van Hoose, with $40,924 in winnings, was named rookie of the year by *Golf Digest.*

The burgeoning senior professional tour gained credibility in 1980 when the U.S. Golf Association staged its first U.S. Senior Open at Winged Foot in Mamaroneck, NY. Argentina's Roberto De Vicenzo won the event.

LARRY DENNIS, *Senior Editor, "Golf Digest"*

HORSE RACING

In 1980, Spectacular Bid ruled as Horse of the Year, and Genuine Risk became only the second filly ever to win the Kentucky Derby.

Spectacular Bid, ridden by Bill Shoemaker, won all nine of his starts in 1980. His triumphs came in the Malibu Stakes, San Fernando Stakes, Charles H. Strub Stakes, Santa Anita Handicap, Mervyn LeRoy Handicap, Californian Stakes, Washington Park Stakes, Amory L. Haskell Handicap, and Woodward Stakes. In the Woodward, the three other entries scratched, and Spectacular Bid ran alone.

Owned by the Hawksworth Farm and trained by Grover "Bud" Delp, Spectacular Bid won 26 of 30 career starts and retired with record earnings of $2,781,607. The former record of $2,393,818 was held by Affirmed. Spectacular Bid set another record earlier in the year, when on March 11 he was syndicated for stud for $22 million, the highest price ever paid for stud.

Genuine Risk, the first filly since Regret in 1915 to win the Kentucky Derby, also ran in the two other legs of thoroughbred racing's Triple Crown, the Preakness and Belmont Stakes. The talented filly placed second in both races. Representing Mrs. Bert Firestone and trained by LeRoy Jolley, Genuine Risk compiled a record of four victories, three seconds, and one third in eight races during 1980.

Another outstanding three-year-old filly was Bold n' Determined, who captured 9 of 12 races in 1980. Bold n' Determined won the Maskette by a nose over Genuine Risk in the only meeting between the two horses.

Temperence Hill, which wasn't nominated to run in the Kentucky Derby, won the Belmont Stakes, Travers, and Jockey Club Gold Cup, to earn recognition as the champion among three-year-old colts and geldings. Temperence Hill won 8 of 17 starts during the year and earned a total of $1,130,452.

In the second leg of the Triple Crown, the Preakness, Codex was the winner by almost five lengths over Genuine Risk.

HORSE RACING

Major U.S. Thoroughbred Races

Beldame: Love Sign, $160,500 (value of race)
Belmont Stakes: Temperence Hill, $293,700
Brooklyn Handicap: Winter's Tale, $217,000
Californian Stakes: Spectacular Bid, $319,450
Champagne Stakes: Lord Avie, $142,250
Charles H. Strub Stakes: Spectacular Bid, $209,500
Jockey Club Gold Cup: Temperence Hill, $549,000
Kentucky Derby: Genuine Risk, $339,300
Man o' War: French Colonial, $140,500
Marlboro Cup Handicap: Winter's Tale, $300,000
Maskette: Bold 'n Determined, $81,900
Mervyn LeRoy Handicap: Spectacular Bid, $210,400
Preakness Stakes: Codex, $250,600
Ruffian Handicap: Genuine Risk, $136,500
Santa Anita Handicap: Spectacular Bid, $350,000
Spinster Stakes: Bold 'n Determined, $172,650
Suburban Handicap: Winter's Tale, $163,200
Travers: Temperence Hill, $168,300
Turf Classic: Anifa, $300,000
Washington DC International: Argument, $250,000
Washington Park Stakes: Spectacular Bid, $259,800

Major U.S. Harness Races

Cane Pace: Niatross, $321,365
Fox Stake: Slapstick, $173,648
Hambletonian: Burgomeister, $293,570
Kentucky Futurity: Final Score, $100,000
Kentucky Pacing Derby: French Chef, $200,000
Levy Memorial: Pat's Gypsy, $200,000
Little Brown Jug: Niatross, $207,361
Meadowlands Pace: Niatross, $1,011,000
Messenger Stake: Niatross, $173,522
Roosevelt International: Classical Way, $250,000
Woodrow Wilson Memorial: Land Grant, $2,011,000
Yonkers Trot: Nevele Impulse, $261,040

UPI

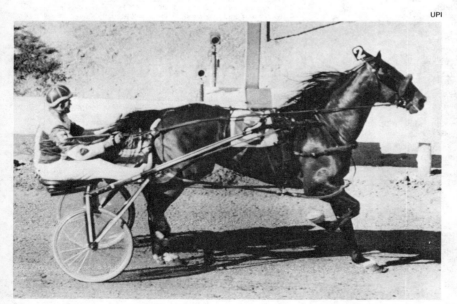

Niatross, driven by Clint Galbraith, easily wins the Little Brown Jug pacing classic in September. The three-year-old colt was the toast of harness racing in 1980, winning more than $2 million.

Harness Racing. Niatross, hailed by many racing experts as the greatest harness horse of all time, paced one mile in the incredible time of 1:49$^1/_5$ in a time trial at The Red Mile in Lexington, KY, to lower the world record by almost three seconds. Niatross finished 1980 with a record of 37 triumphs in 39 starts. His earnings of $2,019,212 were the highest in harness racing history.

Quarter Horse Racing. Higheasterjet won the All American Futurity at New Mexico's Ruidoso Downs.

JIM BOLUS, *Sports Department*
"The Louisville Times," Louisville, KY

ICE HOCKEY

The 1979–80 National Hockey League (NHL) season was notable for three reasons. It marked the end of a dynasty, the end of a rival league, and the end of the most successful—and the longest—career in the history of the game. The four-year stranglehold which the Montreal Canadiens had on the Stanley Cup was finally loosened in a play-off upset by the Minnesota North Stars. The team that went on to win the Stanley Cup, the New York Islanders, had never won it before. The World Hockey Association (WHA) was dissolved, and its four surviving members—Quebec, Edmonton, Winnipeg, and Hartford—were absorbed by the NHL. And Gordie Howe, 52 years old and a grandfather, retired after returning to the NHL for one last season with Hartford. Howe began his career in 1946 in Detroit, went to the WHA in 1973, and finished with a career total of 2,121 goals, by far the most of any pro player.

Among the most stunning achievements of the season was the 137 points registered by 19-year-old Wayne Gretzky of the Edmonton Oilers. It was Gretzky's first NHL season after only one year in the WHA. He tied Marcel Dionne of the Los Angeles Kings for most points and became the youngest player in the history of the league to win the Hart Trophy as most valuable player. Billy Smith of the New York Islanders scored only one goal, but it was as shocking as any of Gretzky's. Smith became the first goalie in NHL history to be credited with a goal, when an errant pass by Colorado's Rob Ramage trickled the length of the ice into his team's empty net. But most of the attention during the regular season was focused on the Philadelphia Flyers, who led the league with 116 points and assembled a record 35-game unbeaten streak.

The Flyers were able to breeze through the play-offs to the final round while other well-heeled teams were ousted quickly in the quarterfinals. The Flyers defeated the New York Rangers, finalists the year before, in five games. The New York Islanders beat the Boston Bruins, semifinalists the year before, also in five games. The biggest upset of all was managed by the North Stars. They beat the Canadiens in the first two games of their best-of-seven series, both in the Montreal Forum, then lost three straight games. But Minnesota won the next game to even the series and clinched the round by edging the Canadiens, 3–2, in the final game—again in Montreal. It was the earliest the Canadiens had been eliminated in six years, and it was a disappointing close to a tumultuous season and to their string of four straight championships.

Former Canadien star Boom-Boom Geoffrion started the season as the new Montreal coach, but with the team struggling, Geoffrion resigned in December. He was replaced by assistant coach Claude Ruel. Montreal regrouped but could not march through the play-offs without star Guy Lafleur, who missed the decisive seventh game against Minnesota because of a knee injury. But just as the Canadiens' dynasty ended so too did the North Stars' dramatic rise. They were eliminated by the Flyers in only five games in the semifinals while the Islanders required six games to defeat the Buffalo Sabres, the team that had finished second to Philadelphia in overall points during the regular season. That set up a final between the two Patrick Division rivals.

Thinned by injuries to star players and wracked by dissension, the Islanders had wallowed under .500 for much of the season, plunging into fourth place in the division at one stage. The New Yorkers finished 25 points behind the Flyers, but ended the season with a 12-game unbeaten streak and two new players—center Butch Goring, who was acquired from Los Angeles, and defenseman Ken Morrow, who joined the team after playing for the victorious U.S. Olympic team.

With Denis Potvin scoring an overtime goal on a power-play, the Islanders won the opener in Philadelphia, 4–3. The Flyers, however, rallied for an 8–3 victory in the second game. The series moved to Nassau Coliseum and the Islanders won the next two games by scores of 6–2 and 5–2, pushing the Flyers to the edge of elimination. Back in Philadelphia, the Flyers rallied for a 6–3 win and the teams returned to Long Island for the sixth game. Two disputed goals helped the Islanders to a 4–2 lead after two periods, but the Flyers tied the score in the third period on goals by Bob Dailey and John Paddock, sending the game into overtime. With just over seven minutes gone in the extra period, however, Lorne Henning fed John Tonelli with a pass at mid-ice. Tonelli passed ahead to Bobby Nystrom, and Nystrom deflected the puck behind goalie Pete Peeters at 7:11, giving the Islanders their first Stanley Cup ever and giving New York its first since the Rangers' championship in 1940.

But while the victory over Philadelphia delighted the Islanders and coach Al Arbour, it cost them dearly. Islander Assistant Coach Bill Mac-Millan left the club to take over as coach of the Colorado Rockies, the team with the worst record during the season. In other changes, Chi-

Bobby Nystrom of the New York Islanders scores against Philadelphia Flyers goalie Pete Peeters in overtime of the sixth game of the NHL championship play-off series at the Nassau (Long Island) Coliseum. The goal gave the Islanders a 5-4 victory and their first Stanley Cup.

UPI

ICE HOCKEY

National Hockey League
(Final Standings, 1979–80)

Campbell Conference

Patrick Division

	W	L	T	Pts	Goals For	Goals Against
*Philadelphia	48	12	20	116	327	254
*N.Y. Islanders	39	28	13	91	281	247
*N.Y. Rangers	38	32	10	86	308	284
*Atlanta	35	32	13	83	282	269
Washington	27	40	13	67	261	293

Smythe Division

	W	L	T	Pts	Goals For	Goals Against
*Chicago	34	27	19	87	241	250
*St. Louis	34	34	12	80	266	278
*Vancouver	27	37	16	70	256	281
*Edmonton	28	39	13	69	301	322
Winnipeg	20	49	11	51	214	312
Colorado	19	48	13	51	234	308

Wales Conference

Adams Division

	W	L	T	Pts	Goals For	Goals Against
*Buffalo	47	17	16	110	318	201
*Boston	46	21	13	105	310	234
*Minnesota	36	28	16	88	311	253
*Toronto	35	40	5	75	304	327
Quebec	25	44	11	61	248	313

Norris Division

	W	L	T	Pts	Goals For	Goals Against
*Montreal	47	20	13	107	328	240
*Los Angeles	30	36	14	74	290	313
*Pittsburgh	30	37	13	73	251	303
*Hartford	27	34	19	73	303	312
Detroit	26	43	11	63	268	306

*Made play-offs

Stanley Cup: New York Islanders

INDIVIDUAL HONORS

Hart Trophy (most valuable player): Wayne Gretzky, Edmonton Oilers
Ross Trophy (leading scorer): Marcel Dionne, Los Angeles Kings
Norris Trophy (best defenseman): Larry Robinson, Montreal Canadiens
Lady Byng Trophy (sportsmanship): Wayne Gretzky
Vezina Trophy (top goaltender, shared): Bob Suave and Bob Edwards, Buffalo Sabres
Selke Trophy (best defensive forward): Bob Gainey, Montreal Canadiens
Calder Trophy (rookie of the year): Ray Bourque, Boston Bruins
Conn Smythe Trophy (most valuable in play-offs): Bryan Trottier, N.Y. Islanders
Coach of the Year: Pat Quinn, Philadelphia Flyers

cago hired former player Keith Magnuson to coach, while Pittsburgh hired Eddie Johnston, formerly the Chicago mentor. Quebec general manager Maurice Filion decided to coach the team himself, and Boston goalie Gerry Cheevers retired to become coach of that team. No team made a bigger move than the Atlanta Flames, however. After the season ended, the club was sold for $20 million to industrialist Nelson Skalbania, who announced plans to move the Flames to Calgary for the 1980–81 season.

The league made several rule changes to cut down on fighting among players. The biggest fight of the season involved spectators and members of the Boston Bruins who brawled after a game against the New York Rangers at Madison Square Garden. As a result, four men filed a $7 million lawsuit against the Bruins and the NHL. Three Bruins—Terry O'Reilly, Mike Milbury, and Peter McNab—were suspended by NHL president John Ziegler for a total of 20 games in one of the harshest decisions ever handed down.

See also feature article, page 70.

PAT CALABRIA, *"Newsday"*

SOCCER

As the decade of the 1980s began, soccer continued to establish itself as one of the top sports in the United States. And, in the North American Soccer League (NASL), a state of normality returned.

NASL. After being dethroned by Vancouver as league champion in 1979, the New York Cosmos reestablished themselves as the premier team in the NASL by blanking the Fort Lauderdale Strikers, 3–0, in Soccer Bowl–80 before 50,-768 fans at Kennedy Stadium in Washington, DC, on September 21. Julio Cesar Romero scored the first goal, and Giorgio Chinaglia capped an incredible season by scoring the last

SOCCER

North American Soccer League
(Final Standings, 1980)

National Conference

East

	W	L	G.F.	G.A.	Pts.
New York	24	8	87	41	213
Washington	17	15	72	61	159
Toronto	14	18	49	65	128
Rochester	12	20	42	67	109

Central

Dallas	18	14	57	58	157
Minnesota	16	16	66	56	147
Tulsa	15	17	56	62	139
Atlanta	7	25	34	84	74

West

Seattle	25	7	74	31	207
Los Angeles	20	12	61	52	174
Vancouver	16	16	52	47	139
Portland	15	17	50	53	133

American Conference

East

Tampa Bay	19	13	61	50	168
Ft. Lau'dale	18	14	61	55	163
New England	18	14	54	56	154
Philadelphia	10	22	42	68	98

Central

Chicago	21	11	80	50	187
Houston	14	18	56	69	130
Detroit	14	18	51	52	129
Memphis	14	18	49	57	126

West

Edmonton	17	15	58	51	149
California	15	17	61	67	144
San Diego	16	16	53	51	140
San Jose	9	23	45	68	95

NASL Champion: New York Cosmos
NASL MVP: Roger Davies, Seattle Sounders

ASL Champion: Pennsylvania Stoners
MISL Champion: New York Arrows
European Cup: Nottingham Forest
European Nations Cup: West Germany
NCAA Champion: University of San Francisco

two, as the Cosmos earned their third NASL title in four years.

Chinaglia was the biggest name in the league in 1980. Giorgio won the league scoring title with 77 points, including 32 goals, and then scored an amazing 18 more goals in seven play-off matches. Counting his 11 tallies in five international games, Chinaglia totaled 61 goals. His May 16th score against the California Surf was No. 103 of his NASL career, breaking the league record formerly held by Ilija Mitic. Chinaglia was named the most valuable player (MVP) of both the play-offs and Soccer Bowl–80.

The only major award to elude Chinaglia was the league's most valuable player award, which went to Roger Davies of the Seattle Sounders. Other major award winners were Rookie of the Year Jeff Durgan of the Cosmos; North American Player of the Year Jack Brand of Seattle; and Coach of the Year Alan Hinton of Seattle, who led his team to a 25–7 record, the best regular season mark in the league.

Seattle, the National Conference Western Division champion, was eliminated in the play-offs by regular season runner-up Los Angeles. The Aztecs then were knocked out by East

champion New York, which also took care of Central champion Dallas. In the American Conference, the Tampa Bay Rowdies, Chicago Sting, and Edmonton Drillers won division titles (East, Central, and West, respectively), but all were eliminated in the second round of the play-offs. Fort Lauderdale, the runner-up to Tampa Bay in the East, earned its berth in Soccer Bowl by beating San Diego, the last team to qualify for the play-offs. The Sockers knocked out both Chicago, the best team in the American Conference during the regular season with a 21–11 record, and Tampa Bay.

ASL. The American Soccer League (ASL) crowned a new champion in the Pennsylvania Stoners, who beat the Sacramento Spirit, 2–1, in the September 18 championship game at Allentown, PA. Mal Roche of Sacramento won the ASL scoring championship, and defender George Gorleku of Pennsylvania was the MVP.

MISL. In the Major Indoor Soccer League (MISL), Steve Zungul led the New York Arrows to their second straight title. Zungul won the scoring championship with 136 points, including 90 goals, and also was the league's MVP.

International. In the year's major international tournament, West Germany won the European Nations Cup June 22 in Rome, Italy. It also was a big year for the United States. The U.S. Olympic team qualified for a berth among the final 16 in Moscow but stayed home because of the U.S. boycott of the Games. Yugoslavia won the gold medal.

JIM HENDERSON, *"Tampa Tribune"*

SWIMMING

American swimmers were disappointed that a U.S.-led boycott prevented them from competing in the 1980 Summer Olympics in Moscow. They competed instead in the combined Olympic Trials and National Outdoor championships at Irvine, CA, the American version of the Olympics. The meet began 48 hours after the conclusion of Olympic swimming events. Organizers of the U.S. Olympic Trials tried to hype the competition by displaying a huge scoreboard showing the times made at Moscow, as if to spur the young Americans by simulating head-to-head competition against the clock. Instead, the meet lost its competitive edge. The American youngsters were all too aware that they were not participating in the real thing. Still, they managed to register three world records and lowered six American marks. The times, however, were generally considered slow, prompting some criticism that the swimmers had lost incentive and were not up to their best efforts.

Mary T. Meagher, the 15-year-old sensation from Louisville, KY, bettered her 200-meter butterfly world mark of 2:07.01, set in 1979, with a clocking of 2:06.37. Bill Barrett of Cincinnati lowered the world standard in the men's 200 individual medley with a time of 2:03.24, and 19-

year-old Craig Beardsley of Harrington Park, NJ, shattered Mike Bruner's world record of 1:59.23 in the 200 butterfly preliminary heat by more than a second with a 1:58.21 clocking. Then he won the final, beating Bruner.

Tracy Caulkins of Nashville, TN, took four gold medals. She set American records in the 100 breaststroke (1:10.40) and the 400 individual medley (4:40.61). Brian Goodell established an American and U.S. Open mark of 7:59.66 in the 800 freestyle. Following the meet a team of 43 men and women was selected as the official U.S. Olympic team that would have competed in Moscow had there been no boycott.

The indoor championships at Austin, TX, produced three world records. Miss Meagher scored in the 100 butterfly (0:59.26), Rowdy Gaines broke the 200 freestyle mark (1:49.16) and Par Arvidsson of Sweden and the University of California snapped the 100 butterfly record (0:54.15). Seven individual American records also fell in the meet.

On the international scene, Petra Schneider of East Germany broke Miss Caulkin's world mark, set in January, in the 200-individual medley by .69 of a second, with 2:13. Miss Schneider later broke her own mark in the 400-individual medley by 1.52 seconds, with a time of 4:38.44 in the East German national championships at Magdeburg. The men's 400 world freestyle mark fell to Peter Szmidt of Canada, whose 3:50.49 at Etobicoke, Ont., clipped .71 of a second off the record set earlier in the year by Vladimir Salnikov of the Soviet Union.

GEORGE DE GREGORIO

TENNIS

The year 1980 reestablished some old values in tennis and threatened others. The sport's direction historically has swirled unpredictably, responding neither to trends nor common sense. The game's incredible growth rate of the 1970s has slowed down, because a beginner's enthusiasm often wanes when it is discovered that a reasonable amount of expertise is needed to enjoy tennis. If tennis was losing novices as regular participants, it was gaining spectators.

Björn Borg tightened his hold on the world's number one ranking by winning the Masters and his fifth French and Wimbledon opens. His jinx at the U.S. Open continued, however, with John McEnroe upsetting the nonpareil Swede in a five-set final in which both were below their best. But at Wimbledon, where the same pair faced each other in the championship round, the standard was magnificent, particularly the fourth-set, 18-16 tie-breaker, causing several scribes to record it as the greatest match ever.

Shortly after Wimbledon, Borg was married to Rumanian professional Mariana Simionescu and thereafter went into a slump, not winning a tournament for three-and-a-half months. He finally emerged victorious at the Stockholm Open in November which, ironically, he had never won, and fortunately for his record (and pride), scored a straight set triumph over McEnroe, who had captured his rival's homeland title the two previous years. McEnroe established himself as the clear challenger to Borg's throne.

The Ratings. Just below Borg and McEnroe in the rankings stood Jimmy Connors, who has never regained his 1974 form and who seemed resigned to a role as understudy to the main characters. But Connors had enough fire left to put distance between himself and the rest of the field. The biggest drop in the rankings was suffered by Vitas Gerulaitis, who plunged to ninth from fourth despite his whipping McEnroe in three early-season encounters. Unhappily, Vitas' three best performances, the Masters, the Pepsi Grand Slam, and the Tournament of Champions at Forest Hills, in which he won more than $200,000, did not count on the ATP computer rankings whose weird machinations listed Gene Mayer fifth and which may be a compelling reason why Gerulaitis refuses to join the ATP (players' union). However, the computer clearly had the proper programming in shooting Ivan Lendl up to sixth. Lendl, with a glorious serve and groundstroke, has the magic bond of discipline and flair to soar one day to Borg's and McEnroe's lofty parapet. The 20-year-old Czech narrowly lost to McEnroe at the U.S. Open and then beat fourth-ranked Guillermo Vilas in the Davis Cup on his foe's home Argentine turf. For an encore he smashed Borg in Europe in late season and then terrorized the Asian circuit.

Another youngster, Frenchman Yannick Noah, also 20, whom the pundits pick as a future superstar, reached the final of the Italian Open against Vilas but showed tendencies to be sidetracked by the temptations of the circuit.

The Women. The women pros completely reshuffled the top of their deck. Whereas Martina Navratilova finished 1979 as number one, she could do no better than third in world rankings at 1980's end. Some felt that she was lucky to finish that high. Although the 1979 U.S. Open winner, Tracy Austin, was tapped as the clear choice to pick up the pieces left by Chris Evert Lloyd and Navratilova, she did not. She was attacked from all sides. Evert Lloyd whipped her at the U.S. Open, veteran Evonne Goolagong Cawley ambushed her at Wimbledon, and upstart Andrea Jaeger (15) bushwhacked Austin at Mahwah, NJ, the tune-up to the U.S. Open.

Whatever Austin had done to establish her credentials as the ranking woman pro during the winter tour by winning the Avon championships, she was upstaged later by Cawley, who won Wimbledon, Evert Lloyd, Jaeger, and yet another Czech wonder-kid, Hana Mandlikova. The latter crushed Navratilova and Jaeger to reach the U.S. Open finals, where she also won the first set against Evert Lloyd.

Evert Lloyd, who in 1979 was distracted by her marriage to John Lloyd and lost titles she was not accustomed to losing, came back like a person who had a score to settle. Chris won the Italian and French opens, reached the Wimbledon finals, captured the U.S. Open, and won both her Wightman Cup singles—more than 40 wins with but a single loss to reposition herself at the top.

Prize Money. The prize money in tennis continued to climb. Almost 50 men and women earned $100,000 on the court alone in 1980, but prize money is only half the picture. Borg and McEnroe turned down $2 million for a one-night challenge in South Africa because of political

Steven Sutton, Duomo

John McEnroe was second to Björn Borg in world tennis rankings but beat him at the U.S. Open.

pressures. Borg made almost $1 million for endorsing the Donnay racquet and another million for wearing Fila tennis clothes. Even Rod Laver, Ken Rosewall, and Fred Stolle, all over 40, were enjoying the proceeds from their former glory years by playing a new circuit called the Living Legends, a band of elite pros competing in weekend tournaments.

EUGENE L. SCOTT
Publisher, "Tennis Week"

TENNIS

Major Team Competitions

Davis Cup: Czechoslovakia.
Federation Cup: United States.
Wightman Cup: United States.

Major Tournaments

U.S. Open—men's singles: John McEnroe; women's singles: Chris Evert Lloyd; men's doubles: Bob Lutz and Stan Smith; women's doubles: Billie Jean King and Martina Navratilova; men's 35 singles: Colin Dibley; women's 35-singles: Judy Alvarez; junior men's singles: Mike Falberg; junior women's singles: Susan Mascarin; Hall of Fame doubles: Ham Richardson and Owen Davidson.
U.S. Open Clay Court Championships—men's singles: Jose-Luis Clerc; women's singles: Chris Evert Lloyd; men's doubles: Kevin Curren and Steve Denton; women's doubles: Anne Smith and Paula Smith.
U.S. National Indoors—men's singles: John McEnroe; men's doubles: John McEnroe and Brian Gottfried.
National Men's 35 Clay Court Championships—men's singles: Fred Stolle; men's doubles: Fred Stolle and Eugene L. Scott.
U.S.T.A. Women's Clay Court Championships—women's 35 singles: Judy Alvarez; women's 35 doubles: Judy Alvarez and Charlene Hillebrand; women's 45 singles: Jane Crofford; women's 45 doubles: Jane Crofford and Olga Palafox; women's 55 singles: Betty Pratt; women's 55 doubles: Dodo Cheney and Phyllis Adler; women's 65 singles: Wilma Smith; women's 65 doubles; Margo Mahony and Mercina Parker.
National Boy's 18s—singles: Scott Davis; doubles: Scott Davis and Ben Testerman.
National Girl's 18s—Kathy Horvath.
Volvo Grand Prix Masters—singles: Björn Borg; doubles: John McEnroe and Peter Fleming.

U.S. Collegiate Championships

NCAA (Division I)—singles: Robert Van't Hof, Southern California; doubles: Mel Purcell and Rodney Harmon, Tennessee; team: Stanford.
NAIA—singles: John Mattke, Gustavus Adolphus; team: University of Redlands.
AIAW—singles: Wendy White, Rollins; doubles: Trey Lewis and Anne White, Southern California; team: Southern California.

Professional Championships

U.S. Pro Championships—men's singles: Eddie Dibbs; men's doubles: Gene Mayer and Sandy Mayer.
World Championship Tennis Tour—men's singles: Jimmy Connors; men's doubles: Brian Gottfried and Raul Ramirez.

Other Countries

Wimbledon—men's singles: Björn Borg; men's doubles: Peter McNamara and Paul McNamee; women's singles: Evonne Goolagong Cawley; women's doubles: Kathy Jordan and Anne Smith; mixed doubles: John Austin and Tracy Austin.
Australian Open—men's singles: Guillermo Vilas; men's doubles: Peter McNamara and Paul McNamee; women's singles: Barbara Jordan.
French Open—men's singles, Björn Borg; men's doubles: Victor Amaya and Hank Pfister; women's singles: Chris Evert Lloyd; women's doubles: Kathy Jordan and Anne Smith; mixed doubles: Anne Smith and Billy Martin.
Italian Open—men's singles: Guillermo Vilas; men's doubles: Mark Edmonson and Kim Warwick; women's singles: Chris Evert Lloyd.
Canadian Open—men's singles: Ivan Lendl; men's doubles: Bruce Manson and Brian Teacher; women's singles: Chris Evert Lloyd; women's doubles: Andrea Jaeger and Regina Marsikova.

TRACK AND FIELD

World records in track and field tumbled like tenpins in 1980. Six were set at the Summer Olympics in Moscow, but 15 others were broken either before or after the Games.

The glamour record, the one-mile run, was shattered by 24-year-old Steve Ovett of Britain at Bislet Stadium in Oslo, Norway, on July 1. Ovett clocked a blistering 3 minutes 48.8 seconds to break the mark of 3:49 set by Sebastian Coe, also of Britain, on the same track July 17, 1979. Earlier in the day, before Ovett broke the mile mark, Coe set a world record for 1,000 meters with a time of 2:13.40, making him the holder, if only briefly, of four world records at one time— the mile, 1,500, 1,000, and 800. Ovett's performance in the mile took one of those marks from Coe, and on July 15, again at Oslo, Ovett gained a share of the 1,500 mark by equaling Coe's time of 3:32.1.

The performances at Oslo by Coe and Ovett, who chose to run at the Moscow Olympics despite a U.S.-led boycott, stirred anticipation that they would engage in a dramatic showdown at the Games. They ran against each other but did not produce any startling times. But in an international meet at Koblentz, West Germany, on August 27, a week after the Olympics, Ovett took sole possession of the 1,500 record, with a time of 3:31.4.

Edwin Moses of the United States, the holder of the 400-meter hurdles mark since 1976, who did not compete in the Games, lowered his previous mark of 0:47.45 to 0:47.13 at Milan, Italy, on July 3.

An interesting progression took place in the decathlon. Daley Thompson of Britain, who won the Olympic gold medal, broke the mark held by Bruce Jenner of the United States with 8,622 points in May at Goetzis, Austria. Jenner's mark, set at the Montreal Olympics in 1976, was 8,618. In June, Guido Kratschmer of West Germany set the world record with 8,649 points at Filderstadt, West Germany. Thompson's winning score at Moscow was 8,495, fourth highest in the history of the event.

Although Gerd Wessig of East Germany set the world high jump mark of 7' 8¾" at Moscow, two jumpers during the year bettered the mark of 7' 8" held since 1978 by Vladimir Yashchenko of the Soviet Union. Jacek Wszola of Poland leaped 7' 8½" on May 25 at Eberstadt, West Germany, and Dietmar Meogenburg, a 19-year-old West German, tied that mark at Rehlingen, West Germany.

Before Wladyslaw Kozakiewicz of Poland pole vaulted to an 18' 11½" world standard in the Olympics, he and several other vaulters took turns bettering the existing record. First, on May 11, Kozakiewicz shattered the record of 18' 8¼", held by Dave Roberts of the United States since 1976, with a vault of 18' 9¼". On June 1 in Paris, Thierry Vigneron of France surpassed that with 18' 10¼", a mark he equaled again on June 29 at Lille. Then on July 17, two days before the Olympics, Philippe Houvion of France went 18' 11".

On April 23, at Tata, Hungary, Ferenc Paragi of Hungary threw the javelin 317' 4" for the world standard.

Mary Decker of the United States set a world mark of 4:21.7 in the mile at Auckland, New Zealand, on January 26, breaking the 4:22.1 standard of Natalia Maracescu of Rumania set in 1979, and leading the women's assault on the record book.

Marathons. For a third consecutive time, Bill Rodgers won the 1980 Boston Marathon. Jacqueline Garreau captured the ladies' event. In the New York marathon in October, Alberto Salazar, 22-year-old senior at the University of Oregon, and Grete Waitz, 27-year-old Norwegian school teacher, emerged victorious.

GEORGE DE GREGORIO

YACHTING

For the 25th time over a span of 129 years the United States proved invincible in America's Cup sailing in 1980. The 12-Meter yacht *Freedom,* representing the New York Yacht Club and skippered by Dennis Conner, a San Diego land developer, defeated *Australia,* skippered by Jim Hardy, a Sydney winemaker, four to one, in the four-of-seven-race series sailed off Newport in the Rhode Island Sound.

Freedom, backed by $2.1 million in computer technology and sporting strong mainsails, clinched the cup with her fourth victory on September 25. Designed for strong breezes, she took advantage of 12-to-16-knot winds and clipped through for a winning margin of 3 minutes 38 seconds in the fifth and deciding race, leaving no doubt about her superiority. In each of her victories, *Freedom* led at all the turning marks on the 24.3-mi (38.8-km) course.

The Australian syndicate was headed by Alan Bond, who over three challenges, the previous one in 1977, directed the spending of $8 million in the Australians' attempt to wrest the cup from the United States. The Australians had relied heavily on an innovative bending mast and prior to the final series had changed mainsails to the stronger Kevlar-Mylar fabric. They hoped that this change in strategy and their innovative bending mast would overcome and defeat the Americans.

Freedom had gained the right to become the defender by outsailing *Courageous,* owned by Ted Turner of Atlanta, and *Clipper.* In the process, *Freedom* won 47 of 52 races in the trials and finals. *Australia* beat out three nations who sailed their yachts in the trials. They were England, represented by *Lionheart;* France, with *France 3,* owned by Marcel Bich; and Sweden, with *Sverige.*

Freedom won the opening race by a margin of 1:52. In the second race, *Australia* was leading but could not finish the course within the 5½ hour time limit. The race had to be resailed. In the resail, the Australians, getting an assist from light winds for which their yacht was designed, indicated that the United States might face a strong challenge after all. Hardy sent his 12-Meter to a 28-second victory, nosing out *Freedom* by three boat lengths and finishing eight minutes before the time limit, tying the series at 1–1. It was the first victory by a challenger since 1970. *Freedom* took a 2–1 lead with a 53-second triumph the next time out and thereafter it was all clear sailing. *Freedom* easily won by 3:48, her widest margin, for a 3–1 lead and then gained a clear-cut triumph by 3:38 to assure the New York Y.C. retention of the Victorian silver ewer.

Holger Danske, skippered by Richard Wilson of Boston, was declared the winner of the 1980 Newport-Bermuda Race.

GEORGE DE GREGORIO

UPI

Tracee Talavera won the women's all-around title at the American Cup international gymnastics meet.

SPORTS SUMMARIES[1]

ARCHERY—United States Champions: men: Rich McKinney, Glendale, AZ; women: Judi Adams, Phoenix, AZ.
BADMINTON—World Champions: men: Rudy Hartono, Indonesia: women: Wiharjo Verawaty, Indonesia.
BILLIARDS—World Champions: men's pocket: Nick Varner, Owensboro, KY; women's pocket: Jean Balukas, Brooklyn, NY.
BOWLING—Professional Bowling Association: leading money winner: Wayne Webb, Rehoboth, MA. **American Bowling Congress:** Regular Division: singles: Mike Eaton, Grand Rapids, MI (782); doubles: Bob Bures and Ron Thacker, Cleveland, OH (1,-378); all-events: Steve Fehr, Cincinnati, OH (2,076); team: Stroh's Beer, Detroit, MI (3,119). Masters Division: singles: Neil Burton, St. Louis, MO. **Women's International Bowling Congress:** Open Division: singles: Betty Morris, Stockton, CA (674); doubles: Carole Lee and Dawn Raddatz, Long Island, NY (1,247); all-events: Cheryl Robinson, Van Nuys, CA (1,848); team: All Japan, Tokyo (3,014).
CRICKET—West Indies-England: West Indies.
CROSS-COUNTRY—World Champions: men: Craig Virgin, United States; women: Grete Waitz, Norway. **NCAA:** Suleiman Nyambui, Texas-El Paso. **AIAW (women):** Julie Shea, North Carolina State.
CURLING—World Champion: Canada; men: Saskatoon, Saskatchewan; women: Regina, Saskatchewan. **United States Champions:** men: Hibbing, MN; women: Washington.
CYCLING—Tour de France: Joop Zoetemelk, Netherlands. **World Pro Champions:** sprint: Koichi Nakano, Japan; pursuit: Tony Doyle, England; road: Bernard Hinault, France; points: Stan Tourne, Belgium. **United States Road Racing Champions:** men: Dale Stetina, Indianapolis, IN; women: Beth Heiden, Madison, WI.
DOG SHOWS—Westminster (New York): best: Ch. Innisfree's Sierra Cinnar, Siberian husky owned by Kathleen Kanzer, Accokeek, MD. **International** (Chicago): best: Ch. Thrumpton's Lord Brady, Norwich terrier owned by George and Sally Bell, Washington, DC.
FENCING—United States Champions: men's foil: Greg Massialas, San Jose, CA; men's épée: Leonid Dervbinsky, Bronx, NY; men's saber: Pete Westbrook, New York City; women's foil: Nikki Franke, Philadelphia, PA; women's épée: Jane Littman, Columbia, SC. **NCAA:** foil: Ernie Simon, Wayne State; épée: Gil Pezza, Wayne State; saber: Paul Friedberg, Pennsylvania; team: Wayne State. **Intercollegiate Women's Fencing Association:** individual: Gina Farkashazy, Wayne State; team: Penn State.
GYMNASTICS—World Cup: men: all-around: Bogdan Makuz, USSR; floor exercise: Bogdan Makuz; pommel horse: Roland Bruckner, East Germany; rings: Yubin Huang, China, and Bogdan Makuz; vault: Roland Bruckner; parallel bars: Yueliu Li, China; horizontal bar: Koji Gushiken, Toshiomi Nishikii, Japan, and Bogdan Makuz; team: USSR. Women: all-around: Stella Zakharova, USSR; floor exercise: Maxi Gnauck, East Germany; balance beam: Elena Naymoushina, USSR; uneven parallel bars: Maxi Gnauck; vault: Stella Zakharova; team: USSR. **United States Gymnastics Federation Champions:** men's all-around: Peter Vidmar, Los Angeles, CA; women's all-around: Tracee Talavera, Eugene, OR. **NCAA:** all-around: Jim Hartung, Nebraska; team: Nebraska. **AIAW (women):** all-around: Sharon Shapiro, UCLA; team: Penn State.
HANDBALL—United States Handball Association Champions: 4-wall men: singles: Naty Alvarado, Hesperia, CA; team: Blicks All Stars; collegiate team: West Point; women: singles: Rosemary Bellini, New York City; team: Midwest Orange; collegiate team: West Point.

HORSESHOE PITCHING—World Champions: men: Walter Ray Williams, Chino, CA; women: Opal Reno, Lucasville, OH.
HORSE SHOWS—World Cup: Conrad Homfeld, Pinehurst, NC, riding Balbuco.
ICE SKATING, FIGURE—World Champions: men: Jan Hoffman, East Germany; women: Anett Poetzsch, East Germany; pairs: Marina Cherkosova and Sergei Shakrai, USSR; dance: Krisztina Regoczy and Andras Sallay, Hungary. **United States Champions:** men: Charles Tickner; women: Linda Fratianne; pairs: Tai Babilonia and Randy Gardner; dance: Stacey Smith and John Summers.
ICE SKATING, SPEED—World Champions: men: Hilbert Van Der Duim, Netherlands; women: Natalia Petruseva, USSR. **World Sprint Champions:** men: Eric Heiden, Madison, WI; women: Karin Enke, East Germany. **United States Outdoor Champions:** men: Greg Oly, Minneapolis, MN; women: Shari Miller, Butte, MT. **United States Indoor Champions:** men: Barth Levy, Lakewood, OH; women: (tie) Pam Mercer, Wyandotte, MI, and Debbie Carlstrom, Des Plaines, IL.
LACROSSE—NCAA: Div. I: Johns Hopkins; Div. II: Maryland-Baltimore County; Div. III: Hobart. **AIAW (women):** Penn State.
PLATFORM TENNIS—United States Champions: men: singles: Doug Russell, New York City; doubles: Steve Baird, Port Chester, NY, and Rich Maier, Allendale, NY; women: singles: Robin Fich, Fairfield, CT; doubles: Yvonne Hackenberg, Kalamazoo, MI, and Hilary Hilton, Glen Ellyn, IL.
POLO—Gold Cup: Retama, San Antonio, TX; **World Cup:** Hallal of Nigeria; **America Cup:** Macondo, Colombia; **U.S. Open:** Retama.
RACQUETBALL—United States Champions: men's open: Brett Hartnett, Las Vegas, NV; women's open: Susie Dugan, Dallas, TX.
RODEO—Professional Rodeo Cowboy Association: all-around: Paul Tierney, Rapid City, SD.
ROLLER SKATING—United States Champions: figure: men's singles: Michael Glatz, San Diego, CA; women's singles: Kathleen O'Brien DiFelice, Brighton, MI; pairs: Tina Kneisley and Paul Brice, Brighton, MI; dance: Harvey White, Newark, CA, and Beth Wahlig, Del Vista, CA; speed: men: Robb Dunn, Farmington Hills, MI; women: Linda Swaim, High Point, NC; 2-man relay: Robb Dunn and Chuck Jackson; 2-woman relay: Sandra Dulaney and Sandra Johnson.
ROWING—United States Collegiate Champions: men: pair with coxswain: Washington State; pair without coxswain: Wisconsin; four with coxswain: Wisconsin; four without coxswain: Dartmouth; eight: Navy; women's elite: single: College Boat Club; quad: College Boat Club, Yale, Long Beach Rowing Assoc.; Princeton; pair without coxswain: Vesper; four with coxswain: College Boat Club; double: College Boat Club; eight: Oregon State.
RUGBY—United States Champion: Old Blues, Berkeley, CA; **Test Match:** Canada 16, United States 0.
SKIING—Alpine World Cup Champions: men: overall: Andreas Wenzel, Liechtenstein; downhill: Peter Mueller, Switzerland; slalom: Ingemar Stenmark, Sweden; giant slalom: Ingemar Stenmark; women: overall: Hanni Wenzel, Liechtenstein; downhill: Marie-Theres Nadig, Switzerland; slalom: Perrine Pelen, France; giant slalom: Hanni Wenzel. **NCAA:** Vermont. **AIAW (women):** 4-event: Middlebury; Alpine: Vermont; Nordic: Middlebury.
SOFTBALL—World Champion: fast pitch: Home Savings, Aurora, IL. **United States Amateur Softball Association:** men: fast pitch: Peterbuilt Western, Seattle, WA; slow pitch: Campbell's Carpets, Concord, CA; 16-inch slow pitch: Har-Crest Whips, Chicago, IL; industrial slow pitch: Sikorsky, Stratford, CT; Class A fast pitch: S.H. Good, New Holland, PA; Class A slow pitch: Houston (TX) Wreckers; women: fast pitch: Raybestos Brakettes, Stratford, CT; slow pitch: Howard Rubi-Otts, Graham, NC.
SQUASH RACQUETS—World Champion: pro: Clive Caldwell, Toronto, Canada. **United States Squash Racquets Association:** singles: Michael Desaulniers, Montreal, Canada; North American Open: Sharif Khan; U.S. pro singles: Sharif Khan. **United States Women's Squash Racquets Association:** singles: Barbara Maltby, Philadelphia, PA; singles 35s: Joyce Davenport, King of Prussia, PA; singles 40s: Marigold Edwards, Pittsburgh, PA.
SQUASH TENNIS—United States Open Champion: Pedro Bacallao, Miami, FL.
TABLE TENNIS—World Cup Champion: men: Guo Yuehua, China. **United States Open Champions:** men: singles: Mikael Appelgren, Sweden; doubles: Danny Seemiller and Ricky Seemiller, Pittsburgh, PA; team: United States; women: singles: Kayoko Kawahigashi, Japan, doubles: Kyung-Ja Kim and Soo-Ja Lee, South Korea; team: South Korea.
VOLLEYBALL—United States Champions: U.S.V.B.A. Open: San Francisco (CA) Olympic; U.S.V.B.A. Women's Open: ANVA, Fountain Valley, CA; **NCAA:** Southern California; **AIAW (women):** Hawaii.
WRESTLING—AAU Freestyle: 105.5-lb class: Bob Weaver, New York Athletic Club (NYAC); 114.5: Joe Gonzales, Sunkist Kits W.C.; 125.5: Joe Corso, Hawkeye W.C.; 136.5: Ricky Dellagatta, NYAC; 149.5: Jim Humphrey, Oklahoma Underdogs W.C.; 163: Bruce Kinseth, Hawkeye W.C.; 180.5: Chris Campbell, Cyclone W.C.; 198: Ben Peterson, Wisconsin W.C.; 220: Russ Hellickson, Wisconsin W.C.; Heavyweight: Bruce Baumgartner, NYAC; team: NYAC. **AAU Greco-Roman:** 105.5: Mark Fuller, San Francisco Peninsula Grapplers; 114.5: John Hartupee, Michigan W.C.; 125.5: Bruce Thompson, Rosemount, MN; 136.5: Abdurrahim Kuzu, Nebraska Olympic Club; 149.5: Doug Keats, Canada; 163: John Mathews, Michigan W.C.; 180.5: Louis Santerre, Canada; 198: Laurent Soucie, Wisconsin W.C.; 220: Brad Rheingans, Minnesota W.C.; heavyweight: Jeff Blatnick, Adirondack W.C. **NCAA:** 118: Joe Gonzales, California State; 126: Joe Azevedo, California State; 134: Randy Lewis, Iowa; 142: Lee Roy Smith, Oklahoma State; 150: Andy Rein, Wisconsin; 158: Ricky Stewart, Oklahoma State; 167: Matt Reiss, North Carolina State; 177: Ed Benach, Iowa; 190: Noel Loben, Clemson; heavyweight: Howard Harris, Oregon State; team: Iowa.

SRI LANKA

In 1980, Sri Lanka continued to gain recognition not only for its natural beauty but also for its quality of life, relatively stable political system, relatively low cost of living, and generally favorable social climate, including one of the lowest crime rates of any developing country. These features tended to overshadow the less encouraging developments of the year.

Politics. In February, President Junius R. Jayewardene effected a major reshuffling of his cabinet. The new body comprised 35 ministers and 35 deputy ministers, with the 74-year-old leader of the United National Party (UNP) himself taking the defense, plan implementation, state plantation, and higher education portfolios.

In March, the president appointed a commission to examine the long-standing problem of stateless Indian Tamils in Sri Lanka. In response to a general strike throughout the country in July, the government proclaimed a state of emergency and banned strikes in essential services. By the end of the year, the government's program for the establishment of village development councils was virtually completed.

The most controversial and potentially explosive development of the year was the removal from parliament of former Prime Minister Sirimavo Bandaranaike for abuses of power during her 1970–77 term. On October 16, on the recommendation of a presidential commission of inquiry, parliament voted (139 to 18) to expel Mrs. Bandaranaike and her nephew, former Minister of Finance Felix Dias Bandaranaike, and to revoke their civil rights. Two days earlier, the government called a state of emergency to prevent a "bloodbath" allegedly planned by the former prime minister's Freedom Party.

Economy. The generally favorable economic picture was somewhat marred by widespread drought, a power crisis, and frequent strikes. As in many other countries, however, the most serious problem was inflation. The cost of imported oil alone amounted to about 45% of the country's total foreign exchange earnings. The estimated budget deficit of about $600 million was only slightly larger than the foreign aid pledged by an international aid consortium in July. President Jayewardene listed as national development priorities the Mahaveli River valley project, the investment promotion zones, housing, population control, and exports. Private foreign investment increased phenomenally during the year. In February, it was announced that all remaining food subsidies would be abolished.

Foreign Policy. In June, Colombo hosted a conference of the Afro-Asian People's Solidarity Organization commemorating the historic Bandung (Afro-Asian) Conference of 1955. President Jayewardene played a leading role in a five-day conference of leaders of the Asian and Pacific Commonwealth Nations, held in New Delhi in early September.

NORMAN D. PALMER, *University of Pennsylvania*

STAMPS AND STAMP COLLECTING

The year in stamps was punctuated by various U.S. Postal Service actions that brought widespread protest from the philatelic community. A stamp to "honor W.C. Fields as an outstanding performing artist" was announced in 1979, but lawyers for the Fields estate waited until its release on Jan. 29, 1980, to demand a royalty for the use of the actor's name and portrait "because both are protected by copyright." Instead of scrapping the stamp, Washington went through with its tribute.

A second controversial action came on March 11, when Postmaster General William F. Bolger withdrew from sale six stamps, two postal cards, a stamped envelope, an aerogramme, and a $7.50 album, all commemorating the 1980 Summer Olympics in Moscow and staggered into circulation since September 1979. The withdrawal was "in support of President Jimmy Carter's decision to boycott the Games unless the Soviets withdrew occupation troops from Afghanistan." It led to a stampede by speculators, who paid up to $65 for material that had cost $15.50 in post offices. In June, Mr. Bolger told a columnist for *Linn's Stamp News* that "if this profiteering continues, I'll dump our stored

─────── **SRI LANKA • Information Highlights** ───────

Official Name: Democratic Socialist Republic of Sri Lanka.
Location: Island off the southeastern coast of India.
Area: 25,332 sq mi (65 610 km²).
Population (1980 est.): 14,800,000.
Chief City (1977 est.): Colombo, the capital, 616,000.
Government: *Head of state,* Junius R. Jayewardene, president (took office Feb. 1978). *Head of government,* Ranasinghe Premadasa, prime minister (took office Feb. 1978). *Legislature* (unicameral)—National State Assembly.
Monetary Unit: Rupee (16.795 rupees equal U.S.$1, Aug. 1980).
Manufactures (major products): Consumer goods, textiles, chemicals and chemical products.
Agriculture (major products): Tea, rubber, rice, coconuts, spices.
GNP (1978 est., U.S.$): $2,800,000,000.
Foreign Trade (1979, U.S.$): *Imports,* $1,441,000,000; *exports,* $890,000,000.

SELECTED U.S. COMMEMORATIVE STAMPS, 1980

Subject	Denomination	Date
Winter Olympics	14¢ postal card	Jan. 15
Winter Olympics	4x15¢	Feb. 1
Windmills	5x15¢	Feb. 7
Benjamin Banneker	15¢	Feb. 15
Letter Writing Week	6x15¢	Feb. 25
Mormon Temple	10¢ postal card	April 5
Frances Perkins	15¢	April 10
Bicycling	15¢ envelope	May 16
Dolley Madison	15¢	May 20
Emily Bissell	15¢	May 31
Helen Keller	15¢	June 27
Gen. Rochambeau	10¢ postal card	July 11
VA Jubilee	15¢	July 21
Gen. Galvez	15¢	July 23
Coral Reefs	4x15¢	Aug. 26
Edith Wharton	15¢	Sept. 5
American Education	15¢	Sept. 12
America's Cup	15¢ envelope	Sept. 16
Indian Masks	4x15¢	Sept. 25
King's Mountain	10¢ postal card	Oct. 7
American Architecture	4x15¢	Oct. 9
Honey Bee	15¢ envelope	Oct. 10
Philip Mazzei	40¢	Oct. 13

stocks on the market to kill it." This infuriated the traders, who maintained that they were merely reacting to the law of supply and demand. On July 30, Mr. Bolger ordered all Olympic material again put on sale "to honor American athletes in general and Jesse Owens, hero of the 1936 Berlin Olympics, in particular."

Another tempest began on January 15, five days after the death of George Meany. It was announced that the former labor leader would be honored with a new 15¢ stamp, to be issued on his August 16 birthday. Despite a policy that only presidents could be so honored before they had been dead ten years, "an exception would be made because of his influence on American life." The gesture was widely regarded as an attempt by the government to mollify organized labor, which had expressed opposition to the Carter administration. Because of the same policy, a new stamp commemorating the 1927 flight of Charles Lindbergh did not bear the name or portrait of the aviator. On August 8, Bolger announced that a stamp honoring "Organized Labor" would be issued on Labor Day. There was no mention of an actual Meany commemorative, and none appeared.

Most important of the year's seven international exhibitions was LONDON 1980. The show attracted about 100,000 visitors, including Queen Elizabeth II, some of whose stamp collection treasures were displayed.

The market highlight of 1980 was the sale of the 1856 British Guiana one-cent magenta. Considered to be the most valuable object on earth for its size and weight, the stamp was bought by a private collector for a record $850,000. Previous owner Irving Weinberg, a Pennsylvania dealer, put it up for sale at New York's Robert A. Siegel Auction Galleries on April 5.

ERNEST A. KEHR
Director, Stamp News Bureau

STOCKS AND BONDS

For the U.S. stock market, 1980 was the year of the bull. Prices of a broad range of stocks, from old blue-chip oils traded on the New York Stock Exchange to new issues just arriving on the over-the-counter market, climbed with a force rarely seen since the soaring 1960s. Trading volume broke records in all the major markets. And while a steep business recession was sending such major industries as autos and housing into a tailspin, the brokers of Wall Street enjoyed by far their best year ever.

In mid-November, the Dow Jones average of 30 industrials touched the 1,000 mark for the first time since the end of 1976. It subsequently retreated in the face of some year-end selling, but still wound up New Year's eve at 963.99, up 125.25 from the end of 1979.

While the Dow, a relatively small sample of old-line issues, remained below its all-time high of 1,051.70 reached in January 1973, most other, broader indicators established record highs. They included the NYSE's composite index, which finished the year up 15.91 at 77.86; the American Stock Exchange market value index, up 101.92 at 348.99, and the NASDAQ composite index for the over-the-counter market, up 51.20 at 202.34.

Big Board volume for the year topped 11,-350,000,000 shares, far outstripping the previous record of 8,160,000,000 set in 1979.

Though many people might not have fully recognized it until the fireworks really started in the summer of 1980, the rising trend in stock prices actually had begun several years before.

A compilation, published by *Barron's* magazine in late November, of the performance of 10 market indexes since the depths of late 1974 showed some truly spectacular results. The Value Line composite index, one of the broadest measures, was up 216%; the Amex index up 521% and *Barron's* own index of low-priced stocks up 653%.

In some of the wildest days of 1980, including the November 5 post-election session in which an unprecedented 84.08 million shares were traded, it seemed as though all types of investors, big and small, had fallen in love with stocks again. The large institutions, with billions to manage, appeared to have little choice. Bonds, the other traditional mainstay of their portfolios, simply were no longer attractive in an era of rapid, persistent inflation.

In fact, the performance of bond prices during 1980 was almost exactly the reverse of what stocks did. In the waning days of the year, many a seasoned, top-quality bond was trading at its lowest level ever. Henry Kaufman, a Salomon Brothers economist, issued a study in the fall that found that bonds actually had become more volatile in price than stocks.

With their sheer size, institutions shying away from this hazardous market had few other

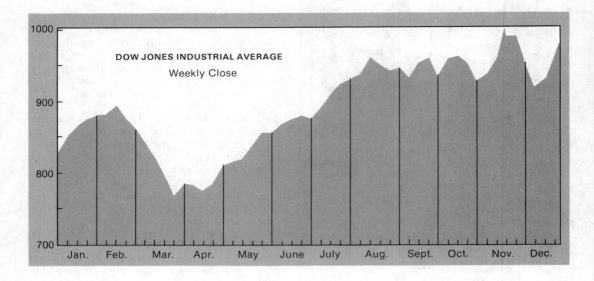

places to turn but the trillion-dollar-plus pool of wealth that the stock market represented. The small investor was back as well, perhaps drawn into the game by nothing more than the smell of money to be made. This was evident in revived interest in mutual funds, notably those that took the biggest risks in search of "maximum capital gains." This same breed of fund had fallen into great disfavor at the end of the 1960s. Since the mid-'70s, however, funds' performance had improved dramatically.

If any further evidence of the small investor's return was needed, it was provided in December by the results of a "shareholder census," taken by the NYSE every five years. The exchange found that 29.8 million Americans owned shares of stock or stock mutual funds, up 18% from 1975 and not far short of the record of 30.85 million in 1970.

That was sweet news, naturally, for Wall Street, which had undergone a great upheaval in the 1970s. In 1975 brokers had been ordered to drop their long-standing fixed commission rates, opening the way to price competition. By the end of the decade, regulators were continuing to press them and the exchange to prepare to cope with ever-rising volume. All this produced more than a little moaning and groaning within the industry. No complaints were heard, however, about the profitability of the business in 1980. In a December estimate, the Securities Industry Association projected brokers' pre-tax income of $2,100,000,000 for the year, almost double what they had earned in 1979. The trade group listed heavy trading volume as the main source of the surge. But it also cited diversification by many firms into new types of services—insurance, real estate, and others.

One notable success story was the money-market fund, a vehicle that began to appear in the early 1970s as a means of allowing small in-

vestors access to the high returns available on short-term securities, including Treasury bills, large bank certificates of deposit, and commercial paper issued by corporations. Fund assets, which jumped from $8,000,000,000 to $40,000,000,000 in 1979, climbed further in 1980 to about $75,000,000,000.

The United States was by no means the only place where markets rose during the year. A study by analyst William LeFevre in New York found December-to-December gains of 71% in Hong Kong, 38% in Singapore, and 42% in Australia. The depressed Italian market approximately doubled, while British, Canadian, and Japanese markets showed more modest gains.

Though the year produced many more pluses than minuses for Wall Street, it was by no means all clear sailing. In late March, the stock and commodities markets were jolted by a near-collapse in the price of silver. (*See* special report, page 288.)

And there was precious little to like in the economic outlook. The 1980 recession came and went without making a perceptible dent in the continuing problem of inflation, which continued to run at or close to two-digit levels. At year-end, fears were mounting of another, possibly worse business slump in 1981 with the Federal Reserve once again tightening credit. The bank prime lending rate, which hit a once-unthinkable 20% early in 1980, reached 21½% in December. It was clearly not the state of the economy that encouraged investors to buy stocks in 1980. Rather, it was evident that the markets were pinning their hopes on the prospect that new government policies in coming years would restore the vitality of American industry. That optimism coincided with the political tide that swept Ronald Reagan and other conservatives to victory in November.

CHET CURRIER, *The Associated Press*

SUDAN

Following the third national congress of the ruling Sudanese Socialist Union in January, Sudan's political system was reformed with the implementation of a federal system of government. Designed to put an end to long-standing political problems arising out of Sudan's diverse ethnic and religious composition, the plan divided the country into six self-governing regions under the national government at Khartoum. Southern Sudan, which has operated under an autonomy statute since 1972, retained that status, but northern Sudan was divided into five regions.

In February, President Jaafar al-Nemery dissolved the National People's Assembly and the regional council of the South to make way for April elections to the new assemblies. Gen. Joseph Lagu, chairman of the regional council of the South and former leader of the southern separatist movement during the 17-year civil war, stepped down when the legislative body was dissolved. Abel Alier, ruler of the southern region from 1972–78, was elected president and head of the southern government in May.

In June, Nemery dismissed from his cabinet Vice-President and Foreign Minister Rashid al-Tahir and Minister of Parliamentary Affairs Galal Ali to allow them to take up the positions of speaker and deputy speaker, respectively, in the new assembly, which opened in mid-June. Nemery took over the vacated posts and also created the Ministry of Internal Affairs, headed by Ahmed Abdel-Rahman Mohammed.

Economy and Foreign Relations. With an economy suffering from severe balance of payments problems, an inflation rate estimated at above 40%, a foreign debt of more than $2,000,000,000, and a serious shortage of foreign exchange, Sudan was anticipating the start of oil production and refining in the southwest within two years. In October, Sudan's $600 million debt to five major foreign banks was rescheduled, and it was hoped that its 200 other creditors would follow suit. The Sudanese government reached an agreement with the International Monetary Fund (IMF) in October for an annual $200 mil-

----

SUDAN • Information Highlights

Official Name: Democratic Republic of Sudan.
Location: Northeast Africa.
Area: 967,500 sq mi (2 505 825 km²).
Population (1980 est.): 18,700,000.
Chief Cities (April 1973): Khartoum, the capital, 333,906; Omdurman, 299,399.
Government: *Head of state*, Gen. Jaafar Mohammed al-Nemery, president (took office Oct. 1971). *Legislature* (unicameral)—People's Assembly.
Monetary Unit: Pound (0.50 pound equals U.S.$1, Aug. 1980).
Manufactures (major products): Cement, textiles, pharmaceuticals, shoes, processed foods.
Agriculture (major products): Cotton, sesame seeds, peanuts, gum arabic, sorghum, wheat, sugarcane.
GNP Per Capita (1978 est., U.S.$): $320.
Foreign Trade (1978, U.S.$): *Imports*, $1,198,000,000; *exports*, $533,000,000.

lion loan in addition to the $260 million obtained in 1979.

Sudan followed an IMF prescription by shifting economic priorities to the production of cash crops, such as cotton, groundnuts, and sugar. The World Bank agreed in February to provide a $65 million credit to revive agricultural production, $30 million of which was allocated to the Gezira scheme where most of the country's cotton is grown.

A reconciliation was achieved between Nemery and Ethiopian leader Col. Mengistu Haile Mariam in May after three years of tensions. Sudan's backing of Eritrean rebels fighting for independence from Ethiopia had soured relations and Nemery, as part of the agreement with Mengistu, offered to mediate in the Eritrea-Ethiopia dispute. He also pledged to resettle Eritrean refugees away from the border with Ethiopia.

See also REFUGEES.

MARGARET A. NOVICKI, *"African Report"*

SWEDEN

In October 1979, a new three-party, center-right coalition government was presented to the Swedish parliament by returning Prime Minister Thorbjörn Fälldin of the Center Party. The new cabinet comprised eight Moderate, seven Center, and five Liberal ministers. One year later, the government faced a no-confidence vote—the first ever held in Sweden—and won by only a single vote.

National Affairs. The year 1980 brought a whole new set of laws, including provisions for higher child support, higher state residence aid for families with children, and increased rights for parents who stay home from work to care for sick children. Self-employed farmers and fishermen would have the right to partial retirement pay if they chose to cut their work time at least in half. Summer time (daylight savings) was introduced for the first time, and certain positions in the Air Force were opened to women.

A nationwide referendum, the fourth in Sweden's history, was held March 23 on the question of nuclear energy. Given the choice of three proposals, Swedish voters gave qualified support (by a 3–2 margin) to the continued use of nuclear energy. Sweden's six nuclear reactors would continue operating and six others would be loaded, but a 25-year limit was established for such development.

The largest labor dispute in Sweden's history left the country virtually paralyzed for two weeks beginning May 2. The crisis in the private sector began when the employers association (SAF) locked out some 770,000 employees—about half of all working people in the nation—after the Trade Union Confederation (LO) had refused to call off wildcat strikes or end a ban on overtime. The LO in turn responded to the lockout by ordering strikes by more than 100,000 workers. The LO originally had asked for an

During a two-week general strike in May—the largest in Sweden's history—union patrols saw to it that only white collar employees were admitted to company premises.

Sica, Liaison

11.3% wage increase for its blue-collar members, but received a counteroffer of only 2.3% from the SAF. Prime Minister Fälldin prevailed on both sides to accept a 6.8% increase. A separate dispute in the public sector ended with both sides accepting a 7.3% increase.

A nationwide poll in September revealed that Fälldin's Center Party had the support of only 13% of Swedish voters, while the opposition Social Democrats had increased their support to 48%. On October 22, the Communists joined with the Social Democrats in an attempt to oust Fälldin in a vote of no-confidence. The opposition charged that the government's economic programs had deviated from Sweden's traditional policy of full employment and also had broken commitments to pensioners. When the ballots were counted, however, Fälldin had survived by a vote of 175–174.

An opinion poll conducted on behalf of Swedish television showed that a clear majority of Swedes regarded alcohol abuse as the country's most serious social problem. Another poll revealed that avoiding tax payments by paying out or working for "black" money was becoming more common among wealthy Swedes.

——— **SWEDEN · Information Highlights** ———

Official Name: Kingdom of Sweden.
Location: Northern Europe.
Area: 173,000 sq mi (448 068 km²).
Population (1980 est.): 8,300,000.
Chief Cities (1978 est.): Stockholm, the capital, 653,929; Göteborg, 436,985; Malmö, 236,716.
Government: *Head of state,* Carl XVI Gustaf, king (acceded Sept. 1973). *Head of government,* Thorbjörn Fälldin, prime minister (took office Oct. 1979). *Legislature* (unicameral)—Riksdag.
Monetary Unit: Krona (4.29 kronor equal U.S.$1, Nov. 1980).
Manufactures (major products): Machinery, instruments, metal products, automobiles, aircraft.
Agriculture (major products): Dairy, grains, sugar beets, potatoes, wood.
GNP (1979 est., U.S.$): $103,000,000,000.
Foreign Trade (1979, U.S.$): *Imports,* $28,488,000,000; *exports,* $27,240,000,000.

Economy. The nation's inflation rate went from 7% in 1979 to an estimated 13% in 1980, as the consumer price index rose steadily. First National Bank of Chicago, one of Sweden's international loan underwriters, rated the nation's credit worthiness the lowest among the Nordic countries. Higher taxes on oil, gas, alcohol, and tobacco were levied in 1980. An increase of 1.9% in the value-added tax (VAT) on September 6 brought the levy to a total of 19%, increasing retail prices by 2.35%. The budget deficit reached 10,000,000,000 kronor, and the national debt rose by about 50,000,000,000 kronor during the 12-month period ending in January 1980, to a total of more than 135,000,000,000 kronor (about $45,000,000,000 U.S.). Wage increases totaling about 45% in 1975 and 1976 and the consequent rise in prices have caused Sweden to lose about 15% of its share in world markets. This represents about $5,000,000,000 annually, roughly equal to the amount the country has borrowed from foreign banks to finance its deficit.

On May 22, Mexican President José López Portillo arrived in Sweden for a three-day visit. It was agreed that by the end of the year, Sweden would be allowed to buy about 11% of its annual oil needs—some 70,000 barrels per day—from Mexico. The two countries also worked on details of joint projects in steel production, mining, petrochemicals, pulp and paper manufacture, port development, and electric power.

Royal Family. King Carl XVI Gustaf and Queen Silvia made their first visit to the United States for the XIII Olympic Winter Games in Lake Placid, NY, during February. The royal couple made a state visit to Japan in April and attended the America's Cup yachting races in Newport, RI, in August. Because of a constitutional change, their eldest child, Victoria, became crown princess on Jan. 1, 1980, while eight-month-old Carl Philip, previously crown prince, became prince.

MAC LINDAHL, *Harvard University*

SWITZERLAND

Youth riots, church-state relations, and involvement in international affairs dominated Swiss concerns in 1980.

Social Unrest. On May 30, some 8,000 young people rioted in Zurich, smashing storefront windows and shouting obscenities. Police reaction was swift and forceful, but youth unrest manifested itself in Bern, Basel, Lausanne, and Geneva during the year. On July 12–13, another major outbreak in Zurich resulted in 124 arrests; more than 50 persons were treated for injuries. New demonstrations in September and early October brought more arrests and fines.

The catalyst for the discontent was an announcement on May 30 that the Zurich city government planned to spend $38 million to renovate the municipal opera house. For three years, the city's youth had sought support for an "alternative culture" center, only to be told that the city had no funds. In the wake of the May riots, a site was made available, but on September 7 municipal officials ordered the center closed down, citing a multitude of problems.

Referenda. In the 300th national referendum since the founding of the Swiss Confederation in 1848, the nation's voters overwhelmingly defeated a proposal that would have prohibited all ties between church and state at the cantonal level. On the same day, March 2, voters approved a provision allowing the government to suspend normal commerce and trade regulations during a domestic crisis in order to allow the stockpiling of strategic materials, a practice previously possible only in time of war.

Nuclear Policy. Agreements by Swiss firms to supply major elements of nuclear technology to Argentina and Pakistan brought protests from the United States that such actions violated the spirit, if not the letter, of the Nuclear Nonproliferation Act of 1978. At the same time, irritated by Canadian demands for formal assurance that uranium purchases would be used only for peaceful purposes, the Swiss government on May 29 suspended a tentative sale agreement reached in 1979.

——— SWITZERLAND • Information Highlights ———

Official Name: Swiss Confederation.
Location: Central Europe.
Area: 15,943.4 sq mi (41 923.2 km²).
Population (1980 est.): 6,300,000.
Chief Cities (1979 est.): Bern, the capital, 142,900; Zurich, 376,400; Basel, 183,000.
Government: *Head of state,* Georges-André Chevallaz, president (took office Jan. 1980). *Legislature*—Federal Assembly: Council of States and National Council.
Monetary Unit: Franc (1.73 francs equal U.S.$1, Nov. 1980).
Manufactures (major products): Watches, clocks, precision instruments, machinery, chemicals, pharmaceuticals, textiles, generators, turbines.
Agriculture (major products): High-quality cheese and other dairy products, livestock, fruits, grains, potatoes, wine.
GNP (1979 est., U.S.$): $96,500,000,000.
Foreign Trade (1979, U.S.$): *Imports,* $29,354,000,000; *exports,* $26,507,000,000.

Foreign Affairs. Despite tension over nuclear issues, Switzerland represented U.S. interests in two major hot spots, Iran and Cuba, during 1980. The Swiss played a major role in attempts to secure the release of the 52 American embassy personnel being held hostage in Tehran. Swiss authorities also helped in the negotiations for and transfer of the bodies of the U.S. servicemen killed in the unsuccessful April 24 attempt to free the hostages. In Havana, the Swiss embassy became the center of demonstrations and riots when, on May 2, 387 armed Cubans waited outside to seek information about emigration to the United States. The United States and Cuba did not have formal diplomatic ties, but a U.S. "interests section" was maintained at the Swiss embassy.

Economy. In an effort to increase demand for the Swiss franc, all restrictions on deposits of francs in Swiss banks by nonresident foreigners were lifted. Also, banks were given permission to offer interest on time deposits made by foreign banks. Exports during the first half of 1980 increased by 17.3% to $14,791,000,000, but imports rose by 35.5% to $18,324,000,000.

PAUL C. HELMREICH
Wheaton College, MA

SYRIA

Syria's President Hafez al-Assad, the target of an assassination attempt on June 26, 1980, was forced by internal political and economic decay and Syria's growing isolation in Middle Eastern affairs to take two unexpected gambles in an effort to strengthen his regime domestically and internationally. Assad's isolation, caused initially by his break with Egypt over the 1978 Camp David accords and intensified by his failure to align with longtime rival Iraq, was exacerbated by the outbreak of the Iran-Iraq war in September and a Syrian-Jordanian near-conflict in late November.

Unrest. The assassination attempt, believed to be by political extremists, came in spite of Assad's efforts early in the year to reform his government. In January, he replaced 14 cabinet ministers, released more than a hundred political prisoners, granted pay raises to public employees, and instituted a series of measures to slow inflation and root out official corruption.

The ruling Baath Socialist Party blamed the assassination attempt and general domestic unrest on the Muslim Brotherhood, a fundamentalist Sunni sect critical of the party's secular policies and the predominance of Assad's Alawite co-religionists in the government and military. The opposition continued its two-year series of hit-and-run assassination attempts on government leaders, pro-government clergymen, and Soviet technical and military advisers.

In November, Syria threatened to send troops into Jordan to destroy camps of the Muslim Brotherhood. Accusing Jordan of aiding the

Syrian President Assad (center) is welcomed in Tripoli, September 8, as Col. Qaddafi (right) looks on.

Brotherhood, Assad amassed troops on the border and demanded a written statement from Jordan that it did not support the group. The situation was defused after about two weeks, however, on Soviet advice to Syria to withdraw.

Union with Libya. Assad's failure to rally popular support at home, combined with the breakdown of reconciliation talks with Iraq in August, were major reasons for his surprising announcement on September 2 that Syria would join Libya in a total constitutional merger.

On September 8, Assad flew to Tripoli and, two days later, signed an agreement to establish an "unconditional" union with Libya's unpredictable leader, Muammar el-Qaddafi. The agreement called for a political, economic, military, and cultural merger with one capital, one head of state, and one foreign policy. Few details had been agreed upon, and it was clear that a long negotiating process would be required to satisfy the concerns of both nations. (*See also* Libya.)

While Assad hoped the merger would boost his domestic popularity, there were perhaps more critical economic and political reasons for the bold move. Not only did Assad believe that the merger would provide a way out of his regional isolation, but he also hoped that access to Qaddafi's oil revenues would pay for modernizing the Syrian armed forces and revitalizing the ailing economy.

Despite receiving a $1,600,000,000 subsidy from the Arab oil states, Syria experienced a severe hard currency shortage in midsummer, forcing the delay of several development projects and repayment of some foreign debts. To offset the loss of Iraq's $300-million contribution to the

subsidy, Qaddafi immediately sent $1,000,000,000 to the Soviet Union to finance Syrian arms purchases and $600 million directly to Damascus. Despite the early motions toward unity, mutual caution and the outbreak of the Iran-Iraq war delayed a subsequent meeting between Assad and Qaddafi.

Treaty With USSR. On October 7, Syria blamed Iraq for its war on Iran and assailed Assad's longtime rival, Iraqi President Saddam Hussein Takriti as "an agent of imperialism." One day later, in a far more important move for Syria's strategic interests, Assad was in Moscow to sign a 20-year treaty of "friendship and cooperation" with the Soviets.

Similar to a treaty the Soviet Union had with Iraq, the pact called for political, economic, scientific, technical, and cultural cooperation. The sections on defense and "mutual consultation" in the event of a threat to each other's security ulti-

----

SYRIA · Information Highlights

Official Name: Syrian Arab Republic.
Location: Southwest Asia.
Area: 71,500 sq mi (185 184 km²).
Population (1980 est.): 8,600,000.
Chief Cities (1975 est.): Damascus, the capital, 1,042,-245; Aleppo, 778,523; Homs, 267,132.
Government: Head of state, Lt. Gen. Hafez al-Assad, president (took office March 1971). Head of government, Abdel Raouf al-Kasm, prime minister (took office Jan. 1980). Legislature (unicameral)—People's Council.
Monetary Unit: Pound (3.92 pounds equal U.S.$1, Aug. 1980).
Manufactures (major products): Petroleum, textiles, cement, glass, soap, processed foods, phosphates.
Agriculture (major products): Wheat, barley, sugar beets, tobacco, sheep, goats, grapes, tomatoes.
GNP Per Capita (1978 est., U.S.$): $930.
Foreign Trade (1979, U.S.$): Imports, $3,307,000,000; exports, $1,634,000,000.

mately pointed to a new and large arms deal, which Assad hoped Qaddafi would finance.

Arab-Israeli Conflict. As apparently planned, the Libyan merger and the pact with the Soviet Union offered President Assad the opportunity to break Syria's diplomatic isolation and make it the primary Arab counterweight to Israel and the senior member of the so-called Steadfastness and Confrontation Front. Assad, long a foe of the Camp David process, sought to refocus Arab concern on Israel rather than on Iran.

F. NICHOLAS WILLARD, *Georgetown University*

TAIWAN (Republic of China)

As its economic growth continued in 1980, Taiwan paid increased attention to the improvement of the material life of its people. Social security programs were expanded and farmers' income raised. Unity and stability were stressed after riots in Kaohsiung in December 1979. Although some indirect trade was carried on with the Chinese mainland, Taiwan adhered to its anti-Communist policies. Progress was made in economic, trade, and cultural relations with the United States, despite the continued lack of formal U.S. recognition.

Domestic Policy. Taiwan's basic policy, said President Chiang Ching-kuo, was to build a "prosperous and equalitarian economic system as well as a peaceful and happy society." He stressed the importance of rule of law and emphasized stability as imperative to national and social progress.

To promote a happy society, Taiwanese officials spoke of narrowing the gap between rich and poor. They planned to augment public health facilities, increase housing construction, and expand social security. In 1980, $930 million was allocated for social welfare programs. This represented 13.3% of the total government budget and an increase of 37.45% over the preceding year.

Anti-Communism. Taiwan continued its opposition to Chinese Communism on the mainland. In a statement on February 22, Premier Sun Yun-suan reiterated that "coexistence" between Taiwan and the People's Republic of China was impossible unless Peking threw out Marxism-Leninism and all other Communist trappings. Nevertheless, there was indirect trade between Taiwan and China through Hong Kong middlemen. The People's Republic stopped shelling Quemoy and other offshore islands held by the Nationalists and helped rescue numerous Taiwanese fishermen in distress. This show of goodwill seemed to suggest that the neighborly status quo would continue, at least for a time.

Sedition Trial. In March, eight defendants were tried for sedition for their role in an antigovernment demonstration that turned into a riot in the city of Kaohsiung in December 1979. All eight were connected with the outlawed magazine *Formosa*, which had served as the center of Taiwan's opposition movement. The riot had ended in a clash with police, injuring 182 security personnel.

A military court found the eight defendants guilty of plotting the forcible overthrow of the government and of promoting independence for Taiwanese residents of the island. Shih Ming-teh, the leader of the demonstration, was sentenced to life imprisonment. Huang Hsin-chieh, the magazine's publisher, received a 14-year term. The others were each given 12 years.

Economy. Despite worldwide recession, Taiwan continued its economic growth. The government set a target of 8% growth for 1980, with special attention to agricultural production. The price of rice was to be maintained at a high enough level to keep farmers' profits at not less than 20%. Fertilizer prices were kept down, and low-interest loans were provided to help reduce farming costs.

The government also encouraged investment in technological and sophisticated industries. It stepped up the search for oil and gas and expedited construction of nuclear power plants. Taiwan's gross national product in the first half of 1980 registered an increase of 7.2%, with manufacturing industries making the largest contribution. Unemployment was held under 2%, but urban consumer prices in the first eight months rose by 17% over the corresponding period in 1979.

Foreign trade in the first eight months of 1980 totaled $25,800,000,000, an increase of 31.2% over the same period a year earlier. But a continuing rise in the price of imported oil and massive purchases of American goods led to a trade deficit of $423 million in the first eight months.

To reduce its trade deficit, the Taiwanese government expanded exports to Japan and Western Europe. Exports to Europe in the first four months of 1980 rose to $1,006,000,000, while imports came to $641 million.

Foreign Affairs. In January 1980, the United States announced that it would sell to Taiwan $280 million worth of antiaircraft missiles and other defensive weapons. It rejected, however,

---

TAIWAN (Republic of China) • Information Highlights

Official Name: Republic of China.
Location: Island off the southeastern coast of mainland China.
Area: 13,885 sq mi (35 961 km^2).
Population (1980 est.): 17,800,000.
Chief Cities (Dec. 1978): Taipei, the capital, 2,163,605; Kaohsiung, 1,063,797; Taichung, 579,726.
Government: *Head of state,* Chiang Ching-kuo, president (installed May 1978). *Head of government,* Sun Yun-suan, premier (took office May 1978). *Legislature* (unicameral)——Legislative Yüan.
Monetary Unit: New Taiwan dollar (38 NT dollars equal U.S.$1, Nov. 1980).
Manufactures (major products): Textiles, electronic equipment, light manufactures, cement.
Agriculture (major products): Sugarcane, sweet potatoes, rice, vegetables.
GNP Per Capita (1978 est., U.S.$): $1,400.

Taiwan's request for advanced aircraft which could attack the Chinese mainland.

The January arms sale was the first one approved by the Carter administration since the United States had severed diplomatic relations with Taiwan in December 1978. At that time, President Carter declared that the United States would continue to sell defensive weapons to Taiwan after the expiration of the Mutual Defense Treaty on Dec. 31, 1979.

In the spring, Taiwan was expelled from the International Monetary Fund, and China was admitted. The Nationalists protested but to no avail. Blessed with constant trade surpluses, Taiwan had not requested financial aid from the fund in many years.

On March 9, Premier Sun Yun-suan left Taiwan for a two-week tour of four African countries. He signed agreements with South Africa, Malawi, Lesotho, and Swaziland on cooperation in agriculture, industry, and transportation.

Because most of the countries with which Taiwan maintains formal diplomatic relations are in Latin America, it spared no efforts to strengthen its ties in that area. In August, Premier Sun Yun-suan paid an official visit to Costa Rica, Panama, and the Dominican Republic. Taiwan and the three countries agreed to expand trade and cooperation in the economic, technical, and cultural fields.

Saudi Arabia remained a close friend of Taiwan. Its increased supply of oil was a great help to the island's industry.

See also China, People's Republic of.

CHESTER C. TAN, *New York University*

TANZANIA

Continued military and economic involvement in Uganda and a faltering economy were the main concerns in Tanzania in 1980.

Uganda. Nearly one and a half years after the overthrow of Ugandan dictator Idi Amin, Tanzania still had almost 10,000 troops in that country. Tanzanian soldiers remained the only organized force in that devastated land. The war and subsequent occupation cost Tanzania more than

--------- **TANZANIA • Information Highlights** ---------

Official Name: United Republic of Tanzania.
Location: East Africa.
Area: 364,900 sq mi (945 087 km²).
Population (1980 est.): 18,600,000.
Chief City (1980 est.): Dar es Salaam, the capital, 520,-000.
Government: *Head of state,* Julius K. Nyerere, president (took office 1964). *Head of government,* Edward Moringe Sokoine, prime minister (took office Feb. 1977). *Legislature* (unicameral)—National Assembly.
Monetary Unit: Shilling (8.17 shillings equal U.S.$1, Aug. 1980).
Manufactures (major products): Textiles, cement, refined petroleum products.
Agriculture (major products): Sugar, maize, rice, cloves, cotton, coffee, sisal, cashew nuts, tea, tobacco.
GNP (1979 est., U.S.$): $3,900,000,000.
Foreign Trade (1979, U.S.$): *Imports,* $1,084,000,000; *exports,* $523,000,000.

$500 million, cut the nation's foreign exchange holdings by three fourths, and caused a $640 million trade deficit, leaving Tanzania almost 18 months in arrears to its foreign creditors. In addition to the war's impact, a severe drought reduced production of major cash crops by 15%, thus reducing Tanzanian ability to pay its debts.

That the economic crisis did not lead to political turmoil is due largely to the efforts and example of President Julius K. Nyerere, who instituted strict controls on prices, limited government and ruling party spending, and restricted the sale of "luxury" items. Gasoline was sold only on four days of the week, and automobile driving was banned totally on Sundays. In order to preserve the integrity of the nation's socialist system, Nyerere also refused a loan of $300 million from the World Bank, which would have required severe cuts in social services and a sharp devaluation of the currency. However, most observers agreed that Tanzania could not support the military effort in Uganda much longer. Tanzania could play a major political role, nevertheless; it was certain that Tanzanian support was behind the ouster of Ugandan President Godfrey Binaisa, whose removal apparently paved the way for a return to power of Nyerere's close friend, former President Milton Obote.

Politics. Tanzania continued its policy of "villagization," moving people into rural villages from both small settlements and from the cities. The program was designed to make it easier to provide basic services (such as running water), improve agriculture, and end the flood of rural unemployed to the towns. By 1980, almost 15 million of Tanzania's 18 million people had been relocated and almost 1,000 (of 7,000) villages had piped water and other utilities. However, the 3% yearly population growth threatened to undermine the whole scheme.

President Nyerere was reelected in October to another five-year term, despite his announced desire to retire. All agreed that the entire Tanzanian political system rested on his continued service, and Nyerere consented to another term, while expressing admiration for the two-term limit for a U.S. president.

Nyerere expelled from the ruling party, Chama Cha Mapinduzi, 2 cabinet ministers and 13 party officials on charges of corruption and for opposing the continued involvement in Uganda. Nyerere further ordered high-level studies of the role of the party and the government vis-à-vis the people. He was said to fear that the party's total control of the nation was leading to abuses of power and alienation, and that over-regulation was stifling productivity, thus adding to Tanzania's economic woes.

Other Foreign Affairs. Tanzania continued to keep its border with Kenya closed. It also agreed to accept massive food gifts from the West totaling nearly $600 million, with no conditions attached or repayment required.

ROBERT GARFIELD, *DePaul University*

TAXATION

Tax policy decisions in 1980 mirrored the concern of most industrial nations over problems stemming from a new economic recession and continued high inflation.

THE UNITED STATES

Congressional Action. Congress cleared the Crude Oil Windfall Profits Tax Bill of 1980, which was signed by President Jimmy Carter on April 2, 1980. Proposed by the president in April 1979, when he announced the decontrol of oil prices, the tax was expected to yield $227,300,-000,000 in the 1980s. It is a severance or excise tax on the production of domestic crude oil, and applies at different rates according to the type of oil, discovery date, producing method, and producer. For tax purposes, the oil is classified in three tiers. (*See also* ENERGY.)

Two significant provisions of the law were unrelated to energy. Most important of them was repeal of a law, scheduled to take effect Jan. 1, 1981, which would have changed the basis for taxing inherited property. Under the new law, the capital gain to be taxed was to have been based on the difference between the original purchase price of the asset and the price when it is sold by the heir. Repeal left standing present law, which imposes the tax on the difference between the value of property when it is inherited and when it is sold. The other major non-energy provision of the new law increased from $100 to $200 ($200 to $400 for married couples) the exclusion from taxable income of dividends and broadened the exclusion to include interest.

Congress approved several other tax changes, including the acceleration of estimated income tax payments for large corporations, for 1980 a $1,000 one-time exemption from the windfall profit tax to royalty owners, and a provision that an employer's payment of an employee's Social Security tax would result in additional taxable income to the employee.

Supreme Court. Two of the major tax cases before the court dealt with the recurring issue of state powers to tax certain income of large corporations that conduct only part of their business within the taxing state. In both cases, the court's decision strengthened the taxing powers of states. In *Mobil Oil Corp. v. Commissioner of Taxes of Vermont,* the company challenged the state's tax on foreign source dividend income from Mobil's subsidiaries and affiliates, most of which were foreign corporations. For the three years at issue, 1970 through 1972, the company computed its tax, excluding the dividend income, at $1,871. Vermont recalculated the tax, including foreign source dividend income in the base, and assessed the tax at $76,419. After the Vermont Supreme Court decided in favor of the state, Mobil appealed to the Supreme Court, arguing that the tax violated the due process and

commerce clauses of the Constitution. The court said that the company had failed to establish that its subsidiaries and affiliates engage in business activities unrelated to its sale of petroleum products in Vermont, and therefore had failed to sustain its burden of proving that its foreign source dividends are exempt, as a matter of due process, from income taxable by Vermont. The appellant's claim that the tax imposes a burden on interstate or foreign commerce, the justices said, understates the courts' power to correct discriminatory taxation of foreign commerce that results from multiple state taxation. The issue in question, generally known as the "foreign source dividend problem," has long been a matter of controversy, because the majority of states tax dividends earned by out-of-state companies under a variety of formulas. The court's ruling means that states have a constitutional right to tax some of the foreign source dividend income of corporations. The decision left unanswered the validity of Vermont's particular formula for apportioning such income to the state.

In *Exxon Corp. v. Wisconsin Department of Revenue,* the court relied heavily on the Mobil case in upholding the power of Wisconsin to base its corporate income tax on a multistate corporation's entire income rather than just the income earned from local operations. Exxon conducts only marketing operations in the state and maintains separate accounting records for its exploration and development, refining, and marketing activities, treating them as separate profit centers. In view of these considerations, the company argued that Wisconsin should not tax its income from operations other than marketing. In the tax years at issue, 1965 through 1968, Exxon determined that it owed no tax to Wisconsin based on its marketing operations. The state revenue department recomputed the tax on a unitary basis and assessed a tax of $316,000 for the four years. In a decision applicable to most large corporations with nationwide or worldwide operations, the court held that Exxon operated a "unitary business," with all of its operations interdependent and subject to taxation wherever the company chooses to conduct any of them.

In its only significant case involving a federal tax, *U.S. v. Euge,* the court decided that the legal summons power of the Internal Revenue Service (IRS) includes the power to compel the execution of handwriting exemplars. The case involved a taxpayer, an income tax preparer, who had not filed his income tax returns for the years 1973 through 1976. In estimating the taxpayer's income and tax liability for those years, the IRS agent in the case discovered 20 bank accounts maintained under different names that he suspected belonged to the taxpayer. The agent issued a summons requiring the taxpayer to appear and execute exemplars of the various signatures on the bank signature cards. When the taxpayer refused to comply, the government brought suit to enforce the summons. The district court granted enforcement, but the circuit court reversed the decision. The Supreme Court's ruling dealt only with interpreting the extent of the power that Congress meant to give the IRS under Section 7602 of the Internal Revenue Code. That section authorizes the IRS to summon a person "to appear . . . and to produce such books, papers, records, or other data and to give such testimony, under oath, as may be relevant or material to such an inquiry." An obligation to "appear," the court held, necessarily entails the display of physical features to the summoning authority, including one's handwriting.

State and Local Revenue. Despite a slowing in revenue growth in many states, overall state and local tax yields increased somewhat from the previous fiscal year. State and local tax collections totaled $221,000,000,000 in 1980, a rise of $18,000,000,000 or 9% over 1979. Restrained by the influence of California's Proposition 13, tax revenues in 1979 had increased by only 6% over 1978. In previous years during the 1970s, gains had averaged 11% annually.

In an effort to ease fiscal strains, the legislatures in 16 states approved tax increases totaling $850 million annually. The increases largely were in higher levies on gasoline and corporate income. The tax increases partially were offset by reductions of $430 million in seven states. Thus the estimated net yearly increase attributable to 1980 legislative decisions was $420 million. This was the first time in three years that statutory tax increases in the states had outweighed reductions.

In the five states where a Proposition 13-type tax reduction was on the November ballot, voters rejected the change. In Massachusetts, however, a measure limiting property taxes to 2.5% of full value and introducing other changes was approved.

INTERNATIONAL

Canada. Budget plans of the Canadian government, announced in October, placed heavy emphasis on higher revenues from petroleum resources, both through new taxes and a new energy policy aimed at direct government acquisition of some foreign-owned oil companies. New levies were imposed on oil and gas production revenues, refinery stocks, and natural gas sales. The rate of tax on net oil and gas production, payable by both individuals and corporations, was set at 8% initially, and is to be reviewed as domestic energy prices rise. The refinery levy would initially add 80 cents a barrel to the basic domestic oil price, and the tax would rise by $2.50 a barrel annually over the next several years. On natural gas sales, the tax was imposed at the rate of 30 cents per 1,000 cubic feet. In an unexpected move, the government decided to continue the system of adjusting personal income taxes for inflation, to save individuals an estimated $1,580,000,000 in taxes during 1981. Earlier in the year Canada had imposed a 5%

surtax on corporate income, effective for 1980 and 1981.

Europe. The British government in September announced tax increases totaling almost $5,000,-000,000 and hinted that there would be others in the spring of 1981. Almost half of the revenue increase—$2,350,000,000 a year—would come from a new tax on North Sea oil, to take effect at the beginning of 1981. It was expected that the tax would be levied at the rate of 20% on gross revenue, less certain allowances. The government also proposed an increase of one percentage point in employee social security contributions, starting in April 1981, to raise more than $2,000,000,000 annually. In March the government had announced a rise in the current tax on North Sea oil revenue from 60% to 70%, as well as increases in excise duties on alcohol, tobacco, most types of oil, and automobiles. Personal income taxes were adjusted for inflation, by a factor of 18% for lower incomes and 11% at higher levels.

The West German government eased income taxes by raising the threshold at which the lowest rate (22%) applies and by increasing various exemptions—including employee tax exemptions for Christmas bonuses and employment expenses. The deduction system was revised to include personal deductions in a basic taxfree amount now equal to $2,190 for single taxpayers and $4,380 for married couples.

The French government adjusted personal income taxes for inflation, generally allowing a 13.3% adjustment factor, except for the highest income bracket, where the adjustment was only 8%. The 1981 budget, approved in September, also provided a 19% investment tax rebate for businesses during 1981 through 1985, increased alcohol excises by 9.5%, and imposed an additional tax on oil companies amounting to about $400 million. The 1980 budget, published in January, had levied a temporary special tax on oil companies.

Italy's new tax provisions include reductions in income taxes through increased deductions or allowances for children, employment income, the aged, and married persons.

Far East. The Japanese government adopted a tax revision bill calling for a substantial revenue increase, primarily by repealing a number of business tax credits and raising electricity tax rates.

China's rulers announced new income taxes on individuals and businesses. Individuals will be taxed on income above about $6,500 a year, generally at rates ranging from 5% to 45%. Since the average Chinese worker earns far less than the taxable minimum, the levy would apply almost entirely to foreigners. The income tax on business applies to income of joint ventures with Chinese and to foreign investment in China and is to be levied at a rate of 33%.

ELSIE M. WATTERS
Tax Foundation, Inc.

Walter Cronkite (left) discusses the vice-presidency with Gerald and Betty Ford at the GOP convention.

TELEVISION AND RADIO

It was fitting that John B. Anderson, the independent presidential candidate in 1980, presented his "solo debate" on cable television while President Jimmy Carter and former Gov. Ronald Reagan battled it out on the network airwaves. Like Anderson, cable television has not yet shaken the foundations of what might be called television's established party system—ABC, CBS, and NBC—but it is on the ballot and fast becoming America's favorite entertainment alternative.

The number of cable television subscribers trebled in the 1970s, and in 1980 it grew by an estimated 12%, to 17 million. The industry's pre-tax profits soared by more than 45% during the year. Still, cable does not create much programming—software, as it is called in the trade—so the networks and the movie studios, who sell their films to the pay-cable channels, "Home Box Office" and "Showtime," are virtually unchallenged in software. Who else but one of the Big Three could dream up, package, and promote a national madness like "Who Shot J.R."?

The Ratings Race. As anyone not in seclusion on a Tibetan mountaintop must have known, the catch-phrase "Who Shot J.R.?" referred to the unexplained crime that concluded the 1979–80 season of *Dallas*. Some 83 million Americans—and untold numbers of fans around the world (particularly in Great Britain)—were curious enough to know who had plugged the Texas ty-

coon, played by Larry Hagman, to give the November 21 episode that launched the 1980–81 season the highest Nielsen ratings in history. (J.R. was shot by his sister-in-law and former mistress, Kristin Shepard.)

And the *Dallas* feat did not hurt the Columbia Broadcasting System (CBS), which returned to its historical ratings preeminence in 1980 after a five-year interregnum dominated by the American Broadcasting Company (ABC). It was the closest ratings race ever, with CBS scoring a 19.6 rating (percentage of all households with television sets) for the period of September 1979 to April 1980, compared with 19.5 for ABC and 17.4 for the beleaguered National Broadcasting Company (NBC).

The ratings race was distorted somewhat by a three-month strike by the American Federation of Television and Radio Artists, which forced the networks to phase in their new fall programs on a staggered schedule.

Programs. ABC's stable of dependable comedies like *Three's Company* hardly lost any ground, and the innovative 11:30 P.M. newscast *Nightline* with Ted Koppel began to unseat the perennial late-night king, Johnny Carson of NBC. But CBS produced outstanding dramatic specials with big names—such as *Gideon's Trumpet* with Henry Fonda and *Little Lord Fauntleroy* with Alec Guinness—and tapped what appeared to be a growing audience hunger for more investigative news and more social realism in their entertainment, as demonstrated by the success of *Lou Grant, The White Shadow,* and the still-growing *60 Minutes.*

Despite two early shots in the arm—World Series coverage and *Shōgun,* the admirable mini-series set in 17th-century Japan—NBC did not realize the bold prediction of its president, Fred Silverman, that it would return to the top of the ratings in 1980. But among its programs that failed in the ratings were some critically-acclaimed innovations. *Skag,* starring Karl Malden as a steelworker, and a witty adult comedy called *United States* never got off the ground. *NBC Magazine with David Brinkley* had the bad fortune to be scheduled against the racy *Dallas.*

Raciness is a mild term for much of the innuendo and subject matter that continued to fill the tube. Two nearly-identical 1980 programs were built on the premise of divorced fathers moving in next door to their young daughters, putting a cramp in their sex lives.

Public Television. Lack of funds endangered local news production on many affiliates of the Public Broadcasting Service (PBS), but that network's cultural programming continued to be as lavish as ever, with British imports and a new series of television adaptations called *The American Short Story. The MacNeil/Lehrer Report* news analysis program began to gain wide recognition, and *3-2-1 Contact* blazed trails in teaching science to youngsters.

Television and International Affairs. Even as critics everywhere derided the lack of taste in much of commercial television, the medium proved as never before that it not only has a profound influence on public perception of events, but that it often *is* the event itself, having power to shape national and international affairs. *Death of a Princess,* a British film dramatizing the 1977 execution of a Saudi noblewoman for adultery, portrayed modern Islamic law and morality in such an unfavorable light that Saudi Arabia expelled the British ambassador, James Craig, on April 23. Similar repercussions were feared when PBS aired the "docu-drama" in the United States in May. There were no major incidents, but several PBS affiliates refused to carry it.

The casting of Vanessa Redgrave, a Palestinian sympathizer, as a Jewish concentration camp inmate in the CBS dramatic special *Playing for Time* enraged Jews around the world. Fania Fenelon, who played in an all-woman orchestra at Auschwitz and the character portrayed by Redgrave, denounced the drama. It was Fenelon's own memoirs that were the basis of Arthur Miller's teleplay. The air date, September 30, was marked by peaceful demonstrations at CBS affiliates across the United States, but the program, and Redgrave's performance in particular, received critical acclaim and a 41% audience share, extraordinary for a serious drama.

The U.S. boycott of the 1980 Summer Olympics in Moscow spelled a $20-million loss for hapless NBC, which had paid $95 million for exclusive broadcast rights.

Television and Politics. There were no great coups or humiliating gaffes to spice up the October 28 debate between President Carter and Ronald Reagan, televised from Cleveland's Convention Center on the three commercial networks and PBS. The candidates reaffirmed familiar positions and suffered no difficulties on the scale of the loss of sound transmission in the 1976 debate between then President Gerald Ford and Jimmy Carter. As many analysts saw it, however, the Republican may have been the winner. Though the harsh lights showed all his facial creases in unflattering relief, Reagan was seen as far more animated and spontaneous ("There you go again," he sighed when he believed the president was distorting an issue), while to many the chief executive's demeanor seemed chilly and tight-lipped. Many analysts believed that his on-camera performance lost him the 1% lead he held over Reagan in an October 23 *CBS News-New York Times* poll.

In dramatic terms, election night coverage was little more than an entr'acte. Tom Brokaw of NBC declared Reagan the projected winner at 8:15 P.M., the earliest announcement of a winner by a news organization since Theodore Roosevelt's 1904 victory.

What constitutes a political message and what entitles a political spokesman to exercise his legal right to "equal time" on the airwaves became even more confused in 1980. A group of television stations owned by *Washington Post-Newsweek* refused to air a British Broadcasting Company (BBC) production which had been offered for syndication by the Mobil Showcase Network—*Edward and Mrs. Simpson*—because they regarded the advertisements for Mobil Oil Corporation as politically slanted. The elaborately-produced ads were in the form of fables illustrating the burden of government regulation on free enterprise—the major oil companies, in particular—and consumer groups demanded equal time from stations that aired the program.

Presidential candidate Ronald Reagan also requested, but was refused, equal network time following a September 18 news conference by President Carter which Reagan termed a "political commercial." And the president tried, but failed, to keep off the air a March 2 segment of *60 Minutes* which dealt with the hostage crisis in Iran. The White House feared that the report, which examined the admission of Shah Mohammed Reza Pahlavi into the United States for medical treatment, would be "inflammatory" or would "strengthen the hand" of the Iranian militants.

Personalities. Johnny Carson appeared to be toying with his fans' emotions—and Fred Silverman's pocketbook—when he dropped his previously-announced plans to leave the *Tonight* show and accepted a three-year contract with NBC at an estimated $5 million annually. One of

THE 1980 TELEVISION SEASON

—Some Sample Programs

American Short Story—Series includes the dramatization of Ring Lardner's *The Golden Honeymoon*, Willa Cather's *Paul's Case*, James Thurber's *The Greatest Man in the World*, Nathaniel Hawthorne's *Rappaccini's Daughter*, Katherine Anne Porter's *The Jilting of Granny Weatherall*, Mark Twain's *The Man That Corrupted Hadleyburg*, William Faulkner's *Barn Burning*, Ernest Gaines' *The Sky is Gray*, Flannery O'Connor's *The Displaced Person*, Stephen Crane's *The Blue Hotel*, and John Updike's *The Music School*. PBS, Feb. 4 Debut.

Arthur Miller on Home Ground—Playwright Arthur Miller reminisces about his life and work. PBS, Oct. 8.

Baryshnikov on Broadway—Ballet star Mikhail Baryshnikov salutes the American musical theater; with Liza Minnelli and Nell Carter. ABC, April 24.

Bernstein Conducts Bernstein—A series of six weekly concerts featuring Leonard Bernstein and some world-famous orchestras. Independent, Jan. 28.

Big Blonde—Dramatization of Dorothy Parker's short story of a 1920s flapper; with Sally Kellerman. PBS, Dec. 1.

Bob Hope—Around the World with the Troops—Two-part television special presenting film footage of Bob Hope's USO tours at Christmastime. NBC, Feb. 3.

The Body Beautiful—A telecast of *The Body Human* series which explores the world of reconstructive surgery. CBS, April 16.

Body in Question—A 13-part series on the workings of the human body; with Jonathan Miller. PBS, Sept. 30.

A Cameraman's Vietnam War Memoir—Film footage of combat soldiers of the Vietnam War taken in Indochina by Australian cameraman Neil Davis from 1964 to 1975. PBS, May 27.

La Cenerentola (Cinderella)—A *Live From Lincoln Center* telecast of Gioacchino Rossini's opera; sung by the New York City Opera company. PBS, Nov. 6.

Cosmos—Thirteen-part series on the cosmos; with astronomer Carl Sagan. PBS, Sept. 28 Debut.

Crime and Punishment—*Masterpiece Theatre* presents this four-part adaptation of Fyodor Dostoevsky's novel; with John Hurt. PBS, Sept. 28.

Death in a Southwest Prison—An *ABC News Closeup* report on the insurrection at the New Mexico State Penitentiary near Santa Fe. ABC, Sept. 23.

Der Rosenkavalier—A *Great Performances* telecast of Richard Strauss' comic opera; sung in German by the Bavarian State Opera. PBS, Dec. 8.

The Diary of Anne Frank—A 1980 made-for-television movie based on the play of the same name which recounts two years in a Jewish teenager's life, spent hiding in an attic to avoid discovery by the Nazis during World War II; with Melissa Gilbert, Joan Plowright, Maximilian Schell. NBC, Nov. 17.

Disraeli: Portrait of a Romantic—*Masterpiece Theatre's* four-part biography of Benjamin Disraeli; with Ian McShane. PBS, June 1.

Edward & Mrs. Simpson—A six-part series on the love affair and subsequent marriage of Edward VIII of Great Britain and Wallis Simpson; with Edward Fox and Cynthia Harris. Independent, Jan. 23.

Fred Astaire: Puttin' on His Top Hat—Fred Astaire special which traces the famed dancer's career; Joanne Woodward is the narrator. PBS, March 10.

Gauguin the Savage—This 1980 made-for-television movie dramatizes the life of Paul Gauguin, who in his middle years left his job, his wife, and his children for a career as a painter, mostly in the South Sea islands; with David Carradine, Lynn Redgrave, Edwige Taie. CBS, April 29.

Gideon's Trumpet—A 1980 made-for-television movie based on the true story of Clarence Earl Gideon, who brought about a landmark decision of the U.S. Supreme Court; with Henry Fonda, José Ferrer, John Houseman, Sam Jaffe, Dean Jagger, Fay Wray. CBS, April 30.

Guyana Tragedy: The Story of Jim Jones—The true-life tragedy of murder/suicide which occurred in Jonestown, Guyana, in November 1978; with Powers Boothe, Meg Foster, Diane Ladd, Colleen Dewhurst. CBS, April 15.

Happy Days—A *Great Performances* telecast of this 1961 Samuel Beckett play; with Irene Worth. PBS, June 25.

Live From Lincoln Center—Isaac Stern, Itzhak Perlman, and Pinchas Zukerman perform in concert with Zubin Mehta and the New York Philharmonic. PBS, Sept. 24.

Lulu—A *Live from the Met* telecast of the complete version of Alban Berg's 1937 opera; with Teresa Stratas. PBS, Dec. 20.

Carl Sagan discusses the Rosetta Stone in "Cosmos," a 13-part series on the stars and universe.

Bill Ray

UPI

In "Playing for Time," Vanessa Redgrave (center) starred as an orchestra pianist at Auschwitz.

Marilyn: The Untold Story—A 1980 made-for-television movie based on Norman Mailer's biography of Marilyn Monroe; with Catherine Hicks. ABC, Sept. 28.

Martian Chronicles—Three-part miniseries based on Ray Bradbury's science fiction classic; with Rock Hudson. NBC, Jan. 27.

The Most Happy Fella—A *Great Performances* telecast of Frank Loesser's Broadway musical. PBS, March 5.

Moviola—Three-part dramatization of Hollywood's golden era. Part I—"This Year's Blonde"; Part II—"The Scarlett O'Hara War"; Part III—"The Silent Lovers." NBC, May 18 Debut.

A Musical Tribute to Toscanini—A New York Philharmonic concert dedicated to Arturo Toscanini; conducted by Zubin Mehta. NBC, Jan. 9.

Mysteries of the Mind—National Geographic documentary on the human brain. PBS, Feb. 4.

Nonfiction Television—A 13-part series of documentaries. PBS, April 4 Debut.

The Oldest Living Graduate—This drama, starring Henry Fonda, was telecast live from a theater on the campus of Southern Methodist University in Dallas; with Cloris Leachman, George Grizzard. NBC, April 7.

Pavarotti in Concert—A *Live From Lincoln Center* telecast with tenor Luciano Pavarotti, the New York Philharmonic, and Zubin Mehta conducting. PBS, Jan 14.

Picasso—A Painter's Diary—Documentary which combined newsreels, home movies, and photographs to present this portrait of artist Pablo Picasso. PBS, June 2.

Playing for Time—Dramatization of the memoirs of Fania Fenelon, adapted by Arthur Miller, the play is set in 1944 at the Auschwitz concentration camp; with Vanessa Redgrave, Jane Alexander, Shirley Knight, Marisa Berenson, Viveca Lindfors. CBS, Sept. 30.

Pride and Prejudice—A five-part *Masterpiece Theatre* telecast of the Jane Austen novel. PBS. Oct. 26.

Requiem for a Heavyweight—A *Golden Age of Television* telecast of one of the classic plays from CBS's anthology series *Playhouse 90*. The teleplay, written by Rod Serling, starred Jack Palance, Keenan Wynn, Ed Wynn, and Kim Hunter. PBS, Aug. 22.

The Shadow Box—A television adaptation of Michael Cristofer's Pulitzer Prize-winning play; with Joanne Woodward, Christopher Plummer, Valerie Harper, Sylvia Sidney. ABC, Dec. 28.

Shakespeare Plays—The second season of this six-year series, presenting *Twelfth Night, Richard II, Henry IV* (Parts I and II), and *Hamlet*. PBS, Feb. 27; March 19, 26; April 9; Nov. 10.

Shogun—A five-part miniseries based on the novel by James Clavell about the adventures of a 17th-century shipwrecked English navigator who is brought ashore in Japan; with Richard Chamberlain and Yoko Shimada. NBC, Sept. 15.

A Tale of Two Cities—A 1980 made-for-television dramatization of Charles Dickens' novel, with Chris Sarandon, Alice Krige. CBS, Dec. 2.

Tannhäuser—A *Great Performances* telecast of Richard Wagner's opera. PBS, June 4.

Testament of Youth—*Masterpiece Theatre* telecast based on Vera Brittain's 1933 autobiography. PBS, Nov. 30.

This Shattered Land—An *ABC News Closeup* on the Cambodian refugee problem. ABC, March 29.

Tinker, Tailor, Soldier, Spy—A six-part dramatization of the John le Carré spy novel; with Alec Guinness. PBS, Sept. 29.

Verdi's Requiem—A *Live From Lincoln Center* telecast of Giuseppe Verdi's choral work; with Montserrat Caballé, Bianca Berini, Placido Domingo, and Paul Plishka, the New York Philharmonic and Zubin Mehta. PBS, Oct. 22.

The Voyage of Charles Darwin—A seven-part docudrama about Charles Darwin. PBS, Jan 27.

What Shall We Do About Mother?—A *CBS Reports* documentary on the problems of aging parents. CBS, Aug. 2.

White Mama—A made-for-television movie about a poor white woman and a black paroled juvenile offender and their attempts to survive in a rundown New York neighborhood; with Bette Davis. CBS, March 5.

The Women's Room—A 1980 made-for-television movie based on the novel by Marilyn French; with Lee Remick, Colleen Dewhurst, Patty Duke Astin. ABC, Sept. 14.

Carson's conditions was a trimming of his show from 90 minutes to one hour, with the slack to be taken up by an expanded *Tomorrow* show, with Tom Snyder. The blunt-spoken Snyder promptly started his new format by feuding with—and banishing, at least temporarily—gossip columnist Rona Barrett, who had been lured from ABC to serve as co-host.

On February 15, CBS ended two years of speculation by naming Dan Rather, the combative, 48-year-old correspondent for *60 Minutes,* to succeed, beginning in 1981, the venerated Walter Cronkite as anchorman on *The CBS Evening News.* Roger Mudd, passed up for the key post after a tough, revealing interview with presidential hopeful Edward M. Kennedy, switched to NBC News along with several seasoned CBS correspondents.

Regulation. The U.S. Federal Communications Commission (FCC) stunned many in the broadcast industry on January 24, when it voted not to renew three television licenses owned by one of the most venerable names in the industry, RKO General. The commission cited its concern over the close tie between RKO's management and the parent company, General Tire, which had been charged with making illegal payoffs and pressuring its clients to advertise on RKO stations. In a related move, the commission voted November 6 to move one of the three stations, WOR-TV in New York, to New Jersey. Because of its position between the clusters of New York and Philadelphia stations, New Jersey was one of only two states without its own VHF station. At year's end, the move across the Hudson River was pending RKO's appeal of the FCC ruling.

One of the quieter FCC actions, but one that could have a profound impact on the whole communications industry in the future, was its proposal to allow Communications Satellite Corporation (Comsat) to provide direct satellite signals to subscribers with small antenna dishes attached to their homes. Theoretically, such a configuration could bypass broadcast stations and cable systems set up on the ground to amplify and deliver the satellite signals.

Cable Television. The burgeoning cable television industry entered a new phase June 1 with the inauguration of the Cable News Network, a 24-hour news service initially available to more than 2 million viewers in 30 states. For nearly a year, the ambitious nature of the Atlanta-based operation and the flamboyant personality of its founder, sports and communications entrepreneur Ted Turner, raised eyebrows throughout the established news media. The service, however, which hired away many big names from the other media, got high marks for content as well as originality.

As if cable television were not already growing fast enough, most of the year's actions by the FCC seemed to improve its competitive stance versus over-the-air television. A July 22 ruling lifted an eight-year-old ban on the importing of broadcast signals from distant to local markets—for example, bringing a Boston station into New York—by cable systems. Cable operators also no longer would be prevented from presenting a syndicated program that already was being shown by an over-the-air station in the same market. The National Association of Broadcasters challenged the FCC and in November obtained a temporary stay on the ruling.

The up-and-coming cable company appeared to be Warner-Amex, which won franchises to wire Dallas, Pittsburgh, and Cincinnati, partly on the strength of such sophisticated features as the Qube two-way viewer-response keypad.

Video Disks and Cassettes. In 1980, the commercial networks appeared to adopt a new strategy toward the emerging television technologies, which for much of the 1970s they had viewed with indifference. The new strategy basically was, "If you can't beat 'em, join 'em." ABC made plans to convert some of its news and sports archives—including coverage of the 1980 Winter Olympics and Pope John Paul II's 1979 visit to the United States—into video cassettes. In general, however, the television networks were behind the pace of the motion picture studios—Warner Brothers, in particular—in the production of video cassette software.

Aware that at the present only they have the resources to produce glossy programming for a mass audience, the networks continued to study when and where they should forcefully enter the new video marketplace. Two ancient rivals, CBS and RCA (the parent company of NBC) became overnight bedfellows on January 10, when they agreed to produce jointly video disks designed for RCA's SelectaVision disk player. This venture, like so many others in the new technologies, was tinged with risk. The RCA player began to appear on the market slightly behind its rival, Magnavox. The latter has an incompatible—and, some analysts say, superior—technology, in that it uses a laser rather than a stylus to "read" the grooves on the disk, allowing the player to "freeze frame." Many in the television industry were skeptical that two incompatible systems could survive, while others felt that the marketplace would prove to be big enough for all.

Radio. The death rattle of disco as radio format was heard in 1980. The year's strongest new format was country-and-western, particularly "crossover," containing elements of rock and pop music—as evidenced by the abrupt change of New York City's WRVR-FM from jazz to country despite protest rallies throughout the city.

The FCC also cleared the way for AM radio to adopt stereo technology, which some broadcasters hoped would stem the flow of music listeners to FM.

DAN HULBERT
"The New York Times"

TENNESSEE

In a close contest decided by about 5,000 votes out of 2 million cast, Gov. Ronald Reagan won Tennessee's ten electoral votes. It was the sixth time since 1952 that Tennessee, traditionally Democratic in state politics, had voted Republican in a presidential election. All incumbent congressmen were reelected.

Late in October, former governor Ray Blanton and two of his aides were indicted by a federal grand jury on charges of mail fraud and receiving payoffs. Blanton, also charged with tax evasion and falsifying income tax returns, became the first former governor in the state's history to be indicted for a criminal offense.

A decrease in revenue but an increased demand for services continued as major governmental problems. State Commissioner of Finance Lewis Donelson estimated that sales tax collections would be several million dollars less than the amount budgeted—the first sales tax decline in 19 years. Conditions have resulted in an impoundment of budgeted funds, with higher education sustaining the major impact.

Problems in Nashville rose to fever pitch during the late spring when more than 1,000 firemen struck after failing to win their requested wage increases. Firemen returned to work after a few of their demands were met.

Education. In Nashville, district judge Thomas A. Wiseman ordered the school board to abandon busing for racial balance in the elementary grades—a practice which had been in force for more than a decade. In the field of higher education, the number of students enrolled in colleges and universities was the highest in the state's history, despite the recession and an increase in tuition which ranged from 18% in most undergraduate programs to 42% at the East Tennessee State University School of Medicine. Two university presidents, Billy Mac Jones of Memphis State and Arthur DeRosier of East Tennessee State, resigned to take positions elsewhere.

Agriculture and Industry. Severe drought conditions in much of the state curtailed crop pro-

duction, after a wet spring had hindered early planting. In July, temperatures soared for a week or more to well over 100°F (38°C). Soybeans continued to be the major money crop, but drought conditions were such that production, which exceeded 70 million bushels in 1979, was estimated at less than 50 million bushels in 1980. Cotton—the smallest crop since 1967—corn, and tobacco also were curtailed by drought conditions. Cattle numbers continued to decline for the fifth straight year.

Nissan Motors of Tokyo announced in October plans to build a $300 million Datsun truck assembly plant near Smyrna. The largest single capital investment by a private industry in Tennessee, Nissan should place at least 2,200 workers on a $40 million payroll.

Names in the News. John King resigned as commissioner of revenue, and was replaced by Martha Olsen. Her appointment marks the first time in the state's history that three women have served at the same time in a governor's cabinet. The others are Sammie Lynn Puett and Ann Tuck.

Joe Henry, state Supreme Court justice; Charles H. Smith, III, publisher of the *Knoxville Journal;* Jesse Beasley, national known sculptor; the historian Stanley Horn; Maxey Jarman, chairman of the board of Genesco; and D. F. Fleming, political scientist, radio commentator, and authority on international affairs, died during 1980.

Odell Horton, appointed in Memphis during the summer, became the first black to sit on the federal bench in Tennessee.

ROBERT E. CORLEW
Middle Tennessee State University

TEXAS

Politics, energy, the weather, and urban concerns dominated the news in Texas in 1980.

Politics and Government. With the enthusiastic backing of Gov. William Clements, former Gov. John Connally, and Sen. John Tower, Ronald Reagan carried Texas by a substantial margin in the 1980 presidential election. George Bush, Reagan's vice-presidential running mate and a former Texas oil businessman, strengthened the Republican ticket in the state. Although President Carter and his supporters, including Sen. Edward Kennedy, campaigned strenuously among the state's black and Hispanic voters, Reagan's strength in the cities and among suburban voters proved decisive.

The Republican presidential blitz in Texas carried over into the U.S. House of Representatives as longtime liberal Congressman Bob Eckhardt was defeated by newcomer Jack Fields. The latter's campaign was financed heavily by major oil companies based in the Houston area. The new Texas state legislature also tilted somewhat to the conservative side, particularly with the defeat of A. R. "Babe" Schwartz of the Galveston district.

TENNESSEE • Information Highlights

Area: 42,244 sq mi (109 412 km²).

Population (Jan. 1980 est.): 4,405,000.

Chief Cities (1976 est.): Nashville, the capital, 430,941; Memphis, 667,880; Knoxville, 185,649.

Government (1980): *Chief Officer*—governor, Lamar Alexander (R). *General Assembly*—Senate, 33 members; House of Representatives, 99 members.

Education (1979–80): *Enrollment*—public elementary schools, 610,435 pupils; public secondary, 255,682; colleges and universities, 199,654 students. *Public school expenditures,* $1,200,749,000 ($1,220 per pupil).

State Finances (fiscal year 1979): *Revenues,* $3,615,-000,000; *expenditures,* $3,361,000,000.

Personal Income (1979): $32,162,000,000; per capita, $7,343.

Labor Force (May 1980): *Nonagricultural wage and salary earners,* 1,789,700; *unemployed,* 135,100 (6.7% of total force).

The trial, coded Brilab (bribery-labor), of Billy Clayton, speaker of the Texas House of Representatives, generated a great deal of state-wide interest. Moved from Austin to Houston after a change of venue plea, the trial featured the testimony of a government informer who testified that he had paid Speaker Clayton a bribe of $5,000 to secure a lucrative contract insuring state employees. Clayton testified in his own defense and gained an acquittal. Following the verdict, Clayton immediately announced his intention to run for an unprecedented fourth term as speaker in 1981. Upon the conclusion of the unsuccessful prosecution, U.S. Attorney Tony Canales resigned his position.

Energy. *The Wall Street Journal* reported that, due to the optimism generated by the deregulation of oil and gas prices, there was more drilling activity in the Lone Star state than ever before. So great was the potential for profit that many wells which earlier had been abandoned were now being reworked. Local majors such as Texaco and Transco were also very active in bidding for offshore leases in the Gulf of Mexico and the "Baltimore Canyon" fields off the Maryland and Virginia coastlines.

Urban Problems. Settled originally by pioneers seeking farmland and characterized by an agrarian emphasis until recent times, Texas today is experiencing the force of urbanism. The 1980 census indicated that San Antonio had passed Dallas to become the second largest city in the state. Houston, the fifth largest city in the United States, continued to attract more than 1,000 newcomers each month. The city's economy was among the strongest in the United States and the prospect of employment explained the steady lure of the Bayou City. An enlarged City Council that included black, Hispanic, and women members was forced to deal with a strike by garbage workers and insistent demands by police and firemen for substantial pay hikes. A public referendum to guarantee pay raises for all city employees failed to pass. Mayor Jim McConn came under increased attacks for his frequent absences from the city and inattention to routine duties. The mayor and the council were blamed

James R. LaCombe, Houston Chamber of Commerce

Although Houston, TX, experienced typical urban problems during 1980, the city continued to grow.

for traffic snarls and a dearth of city services. However, all Houstonians took pride in the Houston Astros baseball team, which captured the National League's western division.

Heat Wave. Dallas and Fort Worth experienced more than 30 days of temperatures exceeding 100°F (38°C) as the state was struck by a record-breaking summer heat wave. More than 100 persons lost their lives, the livestock industry suffered heavy losses, and President Carter declared a state of emergency in Texas.

Education. Faced with ever-increasing costs, the Coordinating Board of Texas Colleges and Universities recommended an increase in state college tuition for Texas residents. Legislative reaction was less than enthusiastic, however, though considerable sentiment was manifested for raising tuition for out-of-state and foreign students. Taking note of the increased number of distinguished faculty who have been lured away from Texas universities because of higher salaries elsewhere, the coordinating board also called for substantial increases in legislative funding for faculty salaries. Public school teachers also pressed similar demands and threatened affiliation with the American Federation of Labor teachers union as a last resort.

STANLEY E. SIEGEL, *University of Houston*

--------- **TEXAS · Information Highlights** ---------

Area: 267,338 sq mi (692 405 km²).
Population (Jan. 1980 est.): 13,552,000.
Chief Cities (1976 est.): Austin, the capital, 313,009; Houston, 1,455,046; Dallas, 848,829.
Government (1980): *Chief Officers*—governor, William P. Clements (R); lt. gov., William P. Hobby (D). *Legislature*—Senate, 31 members; House of Representatives, 150 members.
Education (1979–80): *Enrollment*—public elementary schools, 2,004,301 pupils; public secondary, 869,053; colleges and universities, 676,047 students. *Public school expenditures* (1978–79), $5,003,401,000 ($1,387 per pupil).
State Finances (fiscal year 1979): *Revenues,* $11,049,000,000; *expenditures,* $9,665,000,000.
Personal Income (1979): $117,585,000,000; per capita, $8,788.
Labor Force (June 1980): *Nonagricultural wage and salary earners,* 5,779,600; *unemployed,* 385,500 (6.0% of total force).

THAILAND

Inflated consumer prices led to an early change in government. The new Thai cabinet faced problems associated with the more than 200,000 Indochinese refugees in the country, an invasion by Vietnam, and soaring prices.

Politics. Sparked by February increases of 33–50% in fuel prices and by a declining economy, Prime Minister Kriangsak Chamanan shuffled his cabinet in an unsuccessful attempt to save his government. With disaffection among supporting parties and a pending parliamentary confidence vote, he resigned in March.

Commander-in-Chief of the Army Gen. Prem Tinsulanonda was the royal and the popular choice to head a new cabinet. Prem easily defeated former prime minister and perennial challenger Kukrit Pramoj, 399–80. The new cabinet included leaders of the major parties, headed by Bank of Bangkok President Boonchu Rojarasthien as deputy prime minister for economic affairs and veteran Thanat Khoman as deputy prime minister for foreign affairs. Air Marshal Sithi Sawetawila remained foreign minister. The coalition assured a broad base of support but the cabinet became the focus of party disputes.

Refugees. In late 1979 Kriangsak yielded to international pressure and adopted an "open door" policy for refugees. Facing starvation at home, Cambodians (Kampucheans) flooded the border area. Refugee centers that were intended to serve the destitute became armed camps as anti-Vietnamese rightist and leftist forces competed for international aid. Devastating battles among and within the diverse factions in March and April decimated some camps, stimulating resettlement away from the border, as well as greater interest in repatriation.

Invasion. In mid-June, the Thai government acquiesced in, if it did not encourage, a voluntary repatriation program which offered food, medicine, and agricultural supplies to Cambodian refugees wishing to return. Vietnam opposed what it saw as refreshed recruits for opposition armies. On June 23, Vietnamese forces attacked Thailand, capturing three villages. The Thais counter-attacked on the following day, dislodging and scattering the invaders.

Foreign Relations. The invasion coincided with a meeting of foreign ministers of the Association of Southeast Asian Nations (ASEAN) in Malaysia. The ministers united in condemning the Vietnamese aggression and voicing support for Thailand. The United States accelerated delivery of previously promised military supplies.

Throughout the year the borders with Cambodia, to which the Vietnamese moved a number of divisions, and with Laos remained tense and subject to sporadic clashes. Thailand retaliated to a Laotian incident by stopping shipments of fuels and supplies to that landlocked nation.

Internal Security. The armed struggle within Thailand led by the Thai Communist Party abated as the party split between Vietnamese-Soviet and Chinese factions, as well as between the communists and students who had joined the struggle following the return to military rule in 1976.

Renewed activity by irredentist Malay-Muslims in southern Thailand included bombings in Bangkok as well as in the south and at least partially successful efforts to gain backing from Middle Eastern militants.

K. MULLINER, *Ohio University*

THAILAND · Information Highlights

Official Name: Kingdom of Thailand.
Location: Southeast Asia.
Area: 198,000 sq mi (514,000 km^2).
Population (1980 est.): 47,300,000.
Chief Cities (1980 est.): Bangkok, the capital, 4,870,509; Chiang Mai, 105,230.
Government: *Head of state,* Bhumibol Adulyadej, king (acceded June 1946). *Head of government,* Gen. Prem Tinsulanonda, prime minister (took office March 1980).
Monetary Unit: Baht (20.50 baht equal U.S.$1, Aug. 1980).
Manufactures (major products): Processed foods, textiles, wood, cement.
Agriculture (major products): Rice, rubber, tapioca, corn, sugar, pineapple.
GNP (1978 est., U.S.$): $21,900,000,000.
Foreign Trade (1979 est., U.S.$): *Imports,* $7,156,000,-000; *exports,* $5,308,000,000.

UPI

The Thai prime minister, Gen. Prem Tinsulanonda, inspects the front lines at the scene of the Vietnamese invasion in June.

Phyllis Frelich and John Rubinstein share a scene from "Children of a Lesser God," a drama about the romance of a deaf girl and her non-handicapped lover. Miss Frelich (who is deaf) and Mr. Rubinstein received "Tony" awards for their performances, and the drama won a "Tony" as best play of 1980.

Martha Swope

THEATER

The New York theater in 1980 furnished a virtual cross section and summation of its recent history. The three leading living U.S. dramatists, Arthur Miller, Tennessee Williams, and Edward Albee, who in recent years seldom had been represented on Broadway, were all heard from this year. However, not one of them made a notable contribution to his reputation. Broadway's box-office champion Neil Simon contributed a new play, as did Jean Kerr, one of Broadway's more occasional commercial champions. While Albert Innaurato, a young dramatist who had recently made the leap to Broadway, tried but failed to repeat his *Gemini* success, new hopefuls—Mark Medoff, Samm-Art Williams, and Lanford Wilson (with two plays)—made their first appearances on Broadway; all three made a considerable impression. Revivals indicated a quickened interest in the nation's theatrical past as plays by Paul Osborn, Philip Barry, and Lillian Hellman were staged out of genuine interest and not out of that sense of duty that stimulated revivals in the U.S. bicentennial year. Foreign plays reached Broadway in abundance and in a pattern that suggested a diplomatic zeal for representativeness. There were two plays each from Britain and Canada, and one each from France, Italy, East Germany, Russia, Ireland, and South Africa. Not only did dramatists reappear but that long-absent institution, the Vivian Beaumont Theater of Lincoln Center, reopened after several years of disuse. Likewise, the most flamboyant and cantankerous of Broadway producers, David Merrick, surfaced to present Broadway's most successful musical.

Plays. The most admired living U.S. dramatists disappointed even their most hopeful adherents. In *The American Clock,* Arthur Miller offered what seemed to be an essentially undramatic interpretation of his own family's life during the great American depression. In a drama that seemed to be going only where chronology led it, the parents (played by John Randolph and Joan Copeland, Miller's sister) were more vivid than their son, the nominal protagonist and narrator. Striking events of these years, drawn from Studs Terkel's volume of interviews, *Hard Times,* and seen through the eyes of Miller's characters, comprised half the evening but failed to create the documentary atmosphere they were apparently intended to contribute. In *The Lady from Dubuque,* some of the trivial but relentless chatterboxes who people Edward Albee's recent plays are measured against the high seriousness of the mysterious lady of the title, who has come to minister to a dying woman. Tennessee Williams undertook, in *Clothes for a Summer Hotel,* his first biographical play, which takes a curious view of Zelda and Scott Fitzgerald's lives as seen through the perspective of Zelda's recollections in her latter years as a mental patient.

Some of the newer dramatists gave more cause for hope about the future of drama on Broadway. The hero of Samm-Art Williams' *Home,* which first was presented at the Negro Ensemble Company, is a young black who leaves a farm in North Carolina to experience the characteristic crises of our time but returns home at last, well satisfied to indulge his love of the land. Its humor is casual, and its staging (by Douglas Turner Ward) is ingenious in its deployment of three actors, two of them women who play a number of participants in the young farmer's life.

Not surprisingly, other new plays of interest concerned themselves with members of minorities—a deaf girl, a Jewish refugee, a homosexual. Mark Medoff's *Children of a Lesser God,* from the Mark Taper Forum in Los Angeles, showed both wit and spirit in chronicling the stormy romance and marriage of a deaf girl and the instructor who teaches her to communicate (played most attractively by Phyllis Frelich, who has been deaf since birth, and John Rubinstein). Lanford Wilson's off-Broadway success of 1979,

527

Talley's Folly, won a new audience on Broadway for its sensitive representation of the courtship of a Missouri girl by a Jewish refugee; it ran as long as its popular star, Judd Hirsch, could stay away from his television commitments in Hollywood. It was followed by Wilson's *Fifth of July,* an earlier play recording a later chapter in the history of the same Missouri homestead. The central issue this time was the fate of the family estate, but particular attention was given to a homosexual descendant of the Talley family who has been crippled in Vietnam. Some actors from an earlier off-Broadway version were in the Broadway production as well, but the public showed more interest in Christopher Reeve, who had won fame in the title role of the film *Superman* but seemed less assured as the homosexual veteran, and in Swoosie Kurtz, who was spectacular in the role of a pop singer.

Neil Simon somewhat muted his comic one-liners in *I Ought to Be in Pictures,* a study of a daughter who seeks out the father who, after abandoning her as a child, became a seedy Hollywood scriptwriter. It was given a remarkable amount of life by Dinah Manoff's skillful performance as the awkward but spirited daughter. Gilda Radner, best known as a television performer, gave a broadly comic portrait of awkwardness in Jean Kerr's more obviously commercial comedy of marriage and infidelity, *Lunch Hour.*

Paul Osborn's 1939 comedy drama *Morning's at Seven,* a loving study of a peculiar family, got an attractive revival in which Maureen O'Sullivan and Nancy Marchand won particular praise. A bright production of Philip Barry's comedy of the same year, *The Philadelphia Story,* in which Blythe Danner excelled as a Philadelphia heiress, auspiciously opened the Vivian Beaumont Theater for its new management. On the other hand, Lillian Hellman's anti-Nazi drama of 1941, *Watch on the Rhine,* which came from New Haven's Long Wharf Theater, quickly closed.

Some of Broadway's quick flops were written by playwrights of whom better things were expected. Howard Sackler's anti-Castro drama, *Goodbye Fidel,* was criticized for its lack of clarity. Steve Tesich, never a universal favorite as a writer for the stage, aroused hopes with the script he wrote for the enormously popular comic film *Breaking Away,* but his farcical play *Division Street* proved inadequate to the serious ideas he hoped to convey. In *Passione,* Albert Innaurato tried but failed to exploit again the Italo-American family comedy materials he had used in *Gemini.* The dramatist Tom Topor made a promising start with his courtroom comedy *Nuts.*

This year's two British plays on Broadway were Harold Pinter's *Betrayal* and Peter Shaffer's *Amadeus,* both of which were directed by Peter Hall, who had originally staged them in London. Displaying the authentic Pinterian oddity, Pinter's ambiguous comedy of infidelity gave the critics their first opportunity of the year to celebrate the cheering presence of Blythe Danner. *Amadeus,* which saw Ian McKellen in the role of Mozart's jealous rival Salieri, who presides over the ironic drama of Mozart's life and death, gave clear indications that it would repeat its London success.

Among the many other foreign plays on Broadway, the Russian and South African entries drew particular notice because they assailed their respective governments. Nikolai Erdman's *The Suicide* had been staged in Moscow in 1932, but the censors banned it after the dress rehearsal and it has never played there. The comedy centers on an early dissident who threatens suicide and is urged to proclaim that he is killing himself for any of several good causes. The Broadway production, which benefited greatly from the performance of the British actor Derek Jacobi in the title role, was directed by Jonas Jurasas, a refugee from Soviet Lithuania. Jurasas' elaborate and inventive interpretation rather overpowered the play (and incidentally suggested that the entire incident was a dream). More straightforward versions of the same play were to be seen in Chicago, New Haven, and London, England (the last of which had premiered in 1979 in Stratford-on-Avon). Athol Fugard's *A Lesson from Aloes* (presented in 1979 at the National Theatre in London) explored the difficulty of social action and interracial communication in South Africa.

Among the other foreign plays on Broadway, only Hugh Leonard's *A Life,* from Ireland, won any notable measure of popular esteem. The British actor Roy Dotrice (who had enjoyed a *succès d'estime* earlier in the season playing a U.S. president in the one-man show *Mister Lincoln*) gave a moving portrait of a dour, dying man who examines his past life. A modern stage classic, *Filumena,* by the Neapolitan dramatist Eduardo de Filippo arrived in what was originally a British production. First directed by Franco Zeffirelli and then revamped by Laurence Olivier, it featured Frank Finlay as a wealthy Neapolitan who must decide whether to marry his longtime mistress, played by Joan Plowright. The American public did not take kindly to Britons impersonating Italians. Nor did it take kindly to Frenchmen impersonating furry beasts. TSE, a French company of Argentinian origin, presented *Heartaches of a Pussycat,* based on a sentimental fable by Honoré de Balzac. After warm receptions in Paris and London (where the actors spoke French), this visually stunning show owed its Broadway failure in some measure to the American public's hostility to the sound of French-accented English. Throughout Europe, a considerable success was scored by the East German Peter Hacks' play in which Goethe's mistress, Charlotte von Stein, delivers a monologue to her silent husband. Retitled *Charlotte,* directed by Herbert Berghof, acted by Uta Hagen, and translated by this husband and wife team, it showed again that inter-

BROADWAY OPENINGS OF 1980

MUSICALS

Barnum, book by Mark Bramble, music by Cy Coleman, lyrics by Michael Stewart; directed by Joe Layton; with Jim Dale; April 30–.

Brigadoon, book and lyrics by Alan Jay Lerner, music by Frederick Loewe; directed by Vivian Matalon; Oct. 16–.

Camelot, book and lyrics by Alan Jay Lerner, music by Frederick Loewe; directed by Frank Dunlop; with Richard Burton; July 9–August 23.

Canterbury Tales, book by Martin Starkie and Nevill Coghill, music by Richard Hill and John Hawkins, lyrics by Mr. Coghill; directed by Robert Johanson; Feb. 12–24.

Charlie and Algernon, book and lyrics by David Rogers, music by Charles Strouse; directed by Louis W. Scheeder; Sept. 14–28.

A Day in Hollywood/A Night in the Ukraine, book and lyrics by Dick Vosburgh, music by Frank Lazarus; directed by Tommy Tune; with Priscilla Lopez, David Garrison, Frank Lazarus, Stephen James, Peggy Hewett, Kate Draper, Niki Harris, Albert Stephenson; May 1–.

Fearless Frank, book and lyrics by Andrew Davies, music by Dave Brown; directed by Robert Gillespie; with Niall Toibin; June 15–26.

42nd Street, songs by Harry Warren and Al Dubin, lead-ins and crossovers by Michael Stewart and Mark Bramble; directed by Gower Champion; with Jerry Orbach, Tammy Grimes, Wanda Richert; August 25–.

Happy New Year, based on *Holiday,* by Philip Barry, adapted and directed by Burt Shevelove, songs by Cole Porter; April 27–May 10.

It's So Nice to Be Civilized, book, music, and lyrics by Micki Grant; directed by Frank Corsaro; June 3–8.

Musical Chairs, book by Barry Berg, Ken Donnelly, and Tom Savage, music and lyrics by Tom Savage; directed by Rudy Tronto; May 14–25.

The Music Man, book, music, and lyrics by Meredith Willson, book in collaboration with Franklin Lacey; directed by Michael Kidd; June 5–22.

Onward Victoria, book and lyrics by Charlotte Anker and Irene Rosenberg, music by Keith Herrmann; directed by Julianne Boyd; Dec. 14.

Reggae, concept and production by Michael Butler; story by Kendrew Lascelles, book by Melvin Van Peebles, Mr. Lascelles, and Stafford Harrison, music and lyrics by Lascelles, Harrison, and others; March 27–April 10.

West Side Story, book by Arthur Laurents, music by Leonard Bernstein, lyrics by Stephen Sondheim; directed by Jerome Robbins and Gerald Freedman; with Ken Marshall, Jossie De Guzman, Debbie Allen; Feb. 14–Nov. 30.

Your Arms Too Short to Box with God, conceived from the "Book of St. Matthew" by Vinnette Carroll, music and lyrics by Alex Bradford, additional music and lyrics by Micki Grant; directed by Miss Carroll; June 2–Oct. 12.

PLAYS

Amadeus, by Peter Shaffer; directed by Peter Hall; with Ian McKellen, Tim Curry; Dec. 17–.

The American Clock, by Arthur Miller; directed by Vivian Matalon; with Joan Copeland, John Randolph, William Atherton; Nov. 20–30.

The Bacchae, by Euripides; translated and directed by Michael Cacoyannis; with Irene Papas, Christopher Rich; Oct. 2–Nov. 23.

Betrayal, by Harold Pinter; directed by Peter Hall; with Raul Julia, Blythe Danner, Roy Scheider; Jan. 5–May 31.

Billy Bishop Goes to War, written, composed, and directed by John Gray in collaboration with Eric Peterson; with Eric Peterson; May 29–June 7.

Censored Scenes from King Kong, by Howard Schuman; directed by Colin Bucksey; with Carrie Fisher, Chris Sarandon; March 6–9.

Charlotte, by Peter Hacks; directed by Herbert Berghof; with Uta Hagen; Feb. 28–March 1.

Children of a Lesser God, by Mark Medoff; directed by Gordon Davidson; with John Rubinstein, Phyllis Frelich; March 30–.

Clothes for a Summer Hotel, by Tennessee Williams; directed by José Quintero; with Geraldine Page, Kenneth Haigh; March 26–April 6.

Division Street, by Steve Tesich; directed by Tom Moore; with John Lithgow; Oct. 8–25.

Fifth of July, by Lanford Wilson; directed by Marshall W. Mason; with Christopher Reeve, Swoosie Kurtz; Nov. 5–.

Filumena, by Eduardo de Filippo (English version by Willis Hall and Keith Waterhouse); directed by Laurence Olivier; with Joan Plowright, Frank Finlay; Feb. 10–March 4.

Goodbye Fidel, by Howard Sackler; directed by Edwin Sherin; with Jane Alexander; April 23–26.

Harold and Maude, by Colin Higgins; directed by Robert Lewis; with Janet Gaynor; Feb. 7–10.

Heartaches of a Pussycat, adapted by Genevieve Serreau and James Lord from a story by Honoré de Balzac; directed by Alfredo Rodriguez Arias; March 19–23.

Hide and Seek, by Lezley Havard; directed by Melvin Bernhardt; with Elizabeth Ashley; May 4–11.

Home, by Samm-Art Williams; directed by Douglas Turner Ward; May 7–.

Horowitz and Mrs. Washington, by Henry Denker; directed by Joshua Logan; with Sam Levene; April 2–6.

I Ought to Be in Pictures, by Neil Simon; directed by Herbert Ross; with Dinah Manoff; April 3–.

John Gabriel Borkman, by Henrik Ibsen (translated by Rolf Fjelde); directed by Austin Pendleton; with E. G. Marshall, Irene Worth, Rosemary Murphy; Dec. 18–.

The Lady from Dubuque, by Edward Albee; directed by Alan Schneider; with Irene Worth; Jan. 31–Feb. 9.

A Lesson from Aloes, by Athol Fugard; directed by Mr. Fugard; with James Earl Jones; Harris Yulin, Maria Tucci; Nov. 17–.

A Life, by Hugh Leonard; directed by Peter Coe; with Roy Dotrice; Nov 2–.

Lunch Hour, by Jean Kerr; directed by Mike Nichols; with Gilda Radner, Sam Waterston; Nov. 12–.

Major Barbara, by George Bernard Shaw; directed by Stephen Porter; Feb. 26–March 30.

The Man Who Came to Dinner, by George S. Kaufman and Moss Hart; directed by Stephen Porter; with Ellis Rabb; June 26–Sept. 7.

Mister Lincoln, by Herbert Mitgang; directed by Peter Coe; with Roy Dotrice; Feb. 25–March 9.

Mixed Couples, by James Prideaux; directed by George Schaefer; with Geraldine Page, Julie Harris, Rip Torn, Michael Higgins, John Stewart; Dec. 28–.

Morning's at Seven, by Paul Osborn; directed by Vivian Matalon; with Teresa Wright, Nancy Marchand, Maureen O'Sullivan; April 10–.

Nuts, by Tom Topor; directed by Stephen Zuckerman; with Anne Twomey; April 28–July 21.

Of the Field, Lately, by David French; directed by Jamie Brown; May 27–June 1.

Passione, by Albert Innaurato; directed by Frank Langella; with Jerry Stiller; Sept. 23–Oct. 5.

Past Tense, by Jack Zeman; directed by Theodore Mann; with Barbara Feldon, Laurence Luckinbill; April 24–June 1.

The Philadelphia Story, by Philip Barry; directed by Ellis Rabb; with Blythe Danner; Nov. 14–.

The Roast, by Jerry Belson and Garry Marshall; directed by Carl Reiner; May 8–11.

The Suicide, by Nikolai Erdman; directed by Jonas Jurasas; with Derek Jacobi; Oct. 9–Nov. 29.

Talley's Folly, by Lanford Wilson; directed by Marshall W. Mason; with Judd Hirsch; Feb. 20–Oct. 19.

Tricks of the Trade, by Sidney Michaels; directed by Gilbert Cates; with George C. Scott; Nov. 6.

Watch on the Rhine, by Lillian Hellman; directed by Arvin Brown; with Jan Miner; Jan. 3–Feb. 3.

REVUES

Ballet National de Marseille; August 20–Sept. 21.

Banjo Dancing, devised by Stephen Wade with Milton Kramer; directed by Mr. Kramer; with Stephen Wade; Oct. 21–Nov. 30.

Black Broadway, orchestrations and musical arrangements by Dick Hyman; musical direction by Frank Owens; May 4–24.

Blackstone! The Magnificent Musical Magic Show, directed and choreographed by Kevin Carlisle; with Harry Blackstone; May 19–August 17.

Contemporary Ballet Company; Nov. 25–30.

Dance Theatre of Harlem; Jan. 9–27.

Insideoutsideandallaround Shelley Berman; Oct. 2–25.

Makarova and Company; Oct. 7–Nov. 2.

Perfectly Frank, revue of songs by Frank Loesser, with other music by various composers; directed by Fritz Holt; with Jo Sullivan; Nov. 30–Dec. 14.

Radio City Music Hall revues—Acrobats of Canton, Nov. 4–16; **It's Spring,** March 14–April 13; **The Magnificent Christmas Spectacular,** Nov. 21–; **A Rockette Spectacular,** with Ginger Rogers (May 4–June 1), with Carol Lawrence (June 2–22).

Shanghai Acrobatic Theater; March 25–April 13.

Tintypes, conceived by Mary Kyte, with Mel Marvin and Gary Pearle; directed by Mr. Pearle; Oct. 23–.

Twyla Tharp and Dancers; March 24–April 12.

Wanda Richert, who plays a young unknown who becomes an "overnight" success, is spotlighted in this scene from "42nd Street," the smash Broadway musical about making a Broadway musical. The hit is a David Merrick production and was the last work of the director and choreographer Gower Champion; Mr. Champion died hours before the show opened.

national success is likely to end at the water's edge. Two Canadian plays presented on Broadway, *Of the Fields, Lately* and *Billy Bishop Goes to War,* were not successful.

The Circle in the Square, which has been, in the absence of the Vivian Beaumont, the only permanent theater to enjoy Broadway status, had five openings during the year: George Bernard Shaw's *Major Barbara;* Jack Zeman's *Past Tense;* the 1939 comedy, *The Man Who Came to Dinner,* by George S. Kaufman and Moss Hart; *The Bacchae,* by Euripides; and Henrik Ibsen's *John Gabriel Borkman.*

Musicals. David Merrick returned to Broadway by presenting the most spectacularly publicized, most lavishly produced musical of the season, *42nd Street,* a tap-dancing extravaganza based on the old movie about the girl from the chorus line who replaces a star and makes good on Broadway. The songs came from the earlier film and from other Warner Brothers musicals of the 1930s. This show's boldly fake show-business pathos was augmented by the real thing when director/choreographer Gower Champion died a few hours before the opening. Although it originated in London, *A Day in Hollywood/A Night in the Ukraine* made good use of Hollywood nostalgia as its chief stock in trade. *Barnum* provided what was in effect a miniature circus on stage, highlighted by Jim Dale's performance in the title role. The movie *Charly* (1968) (and the novel on which it was based, *Flowers for Algernon*), the life of the Victorian author Frank Harris, the songs of Frank Loesser, and Philip Barry's play *Holiday* inspired other musicals. Revivals were numerous; they included *Camelot* (with Richard Burton in his original role), *Brigadoon, West Side Story, The Music Man, Canterbury Tales,* and *Your Arms Too Short to Box with God.*

Off Broadway. The most celebrated event of the off-Broadway season had a tenuous connection with off Broadway. In Central Park during the summer Joseph Papp presented an entertaining production of Gilbert and Sullivan's The

Pirates of Penzance, with a notable cast led by two pop singers, Linda Ronstadt and Rex Smith. With most of the original cast intact, it was set to reopen on Broadway in January 1981. Papp's regular productions at the Public Theater included JoAnne Akalaitis' *Dead End Kids* (created by Mabou Mines), a revue about nuclear power; Thomas Babe's *Salt Lake City Skyline,* about the labor organizer Joe Hill; Wallace Shawn's *Marie and Bruce,* about a troubled marriage; Elizabeth Swados' *Alice in Concert,* based on *Alice in Wonderland,* with Meryl Streep in the lead; and Sam Shepard's *True West,* a play concerning the deep hostility between two brothers.

At the Brooklyn Academy of Music, the British director David Jones founded the new BAM repertory company. The company revived two American plays (Charles MacArthur's *Johnny on a Spot* and Rachel Crothers' *He and She*), but asserted repertory's more traditional function with *The Winter's Tale.*

Other off-Broadway plays included John Ford Noonan's *A Coupla White Chicks Sitting Around Talking,* about a cultural confrontation in a Westchester kitchen; James Lapine's *Table Settings,* a stylized comedy of Jewish family life; *Really Rosie,* adapted by Maurice Sendak from his book for children; and David Rimmer's *Album,* about teenagers in the 1960s.

Canada and Great Britain. At the Stratford Festival of Stratford, Ontario, it was artistic director Robin Phillips' last season. A committee of four was appointed to succeed Phillips but was abruptly fired and replaced by the British director John Dexter, who was denied permission to work in Canada. Finally, a Canadian, John Hirsch, became the new head of the festival. (*See also* CANADA: The Arts.)

Probably the most striking news of the London season was made by the Royal Shakespeare Company, first with *The Greeks* and then with *Nicholas Nickleby.* (*See also* GREAT BRITAIN: The Arts.)

HENRY POPKIN
State University of New York at Buffalo

THIRD WORLD

What little unity had existed among countries of the Third World was further eroded in 1980 by a series of events that included the Iran-Iraq conflict and the Soviet aggression in Afghanistan.

The death in May of Yugoslav President Tito (Josip Broz) had a special symbolism. Tito had tried to create a nonaligned coalition of Third World states which would not only be independent of the superpowers but which also would have a major say in international affairs. At the time of Tito's death, however, the nonaligned movement was in disarray and virtually powerless.

Invasion of Afghanistan. The nations of the nonaligned movement had special reason to be concerned about the Soviet invasion of Afghanistan in December 1979. Traditionally, Afghanistan had been a sort of model Third World country which maintained its independence by carefully following a nonaligned policy. Events in Afghanistan in 1980 showed that nonalignment means nothing to Moscow when the interests of Soviet expansionism are at stake.

Most nonaligned member states did band together in January to support a United Nations General Assembly resolution condemning the Soviet invasion. There were some notable defections, however, including such Soviet allies as Cuba, Ethiopia, and South Yemen. Cuba, a leader of the nonaligned movement, saw its prestige plummet as a result of the invasion. The Castro regime was unable to muster enough Third World support at the UN in January to get a two-year term on the Security Council. Nevertheless, nonaligned opposition to the invasion was not monolithic; even India abstained on the resolution. Nonaligned foreign ministers meeting in September during the regular General Assembly session either out of fear of Moscow or indifference did not show the same intense concern for Afghanistan that had been shown in January.

Iran-Iraq War. The nonaligned movement proved to be particularly ineffective in the Iran-Iraq conflict, which pitted two of its member states. Some Third World states took sides in the dispute. Others tried to ignore it.

The war in the Persian Gulf showed once again that the Third World is rife with disputes and conflicts that can lead to very dangerous situations. Although the United States and the Soviet Union had provided arms for the combatants, neither Moscow nor Washington could be blamed for the war. Their military support demonstrated, however, that such Third World conflicts could drag the superpowers into a confrontation.

Nuclear Development. In light of the Iran-Iraq conflict, it was ominous that a number of Third World nations were embarking on nuclear development programs. India had already set the pattern with its "peace bomb"—a nuclear explosion for so-called peaceful purposes. Pakistan, India's archenemy, seemed on the path to developing nuclear weapons. Iraq, with the help of France, has a nuclear reactor program which Israel and others claim will enable it to join the nuclear weapons club. Other Third World countries which may be on the threshold of acquiring nuclear weapons capability include Brazil, Argentina, Taiwan, and South Korea. It was no wonder that Third World states, led by Iraq, helped undermine a UN conference on strengthening the Nuclear Non-Proliferation Treaty. The Third World states charged that the nuclear powers were using the treaty to prevent the export of nuclear technology for peaceful purposes.

New Economic Order. In 1980, Third World countries used various international forums to call for a "new economic order." A special session of the UN General Assembly held in late August and early September broke down when agreement could not be reached between the West and Third World states on a new international system. Among the Third World demands were more economic aid from the West, higher prices for Third World raw material exports, and a greater say in such international aid agencies as the World Bank and the International Monetary Fund (IMF).

At the fall meeting of the World Bank and the IMF in Washington the bitter debate continued over aiding the Third World have-not states, which were severely hurt by rising food prices as well as soaring oil prices. Robert McNamara, the outgoing World Bank president, sharply criticized his own country, the United States, for not doing enough to help the poor countries. The World Bank and the IMF pledged more aid to the poor states, but the Third World said this was not enough. The richer Third World members of the Organization of Petroleum Exporting Countries (OPEC) again proved not to be particularly generous to poor countries.

Other Issues. Other arenas of dispute between the Third World and the West were UNESCO (UN Educational, Scientific and Cultural Organization) and the UN Law of the Sea Conference. The West was unhappy with Third World demands in UNESCO, but in October agreed to a resolution on the basic principles of a new world information order. The major problem at the Sea Conference was how to divide up undersea mineral wealth.

World Bank and IMF reports on the economic prospects for poor countries in the 1980s made very grim reading. The problem of oil supply and prices actually worsened in 1980 because of the Persian Gulf conflict. Add to this the question of Afghanistan, the feuds between Third World states, and the apparent rush into nuclear weapons development, and the Third World picture took on an aura of impending catastrophe.

AARON R. EINFRANK, *Free-lance writer*

TRANSPORTATION

For U.S. transportation, 1980 was a banner year in terms of new federal legislation, but the industry suffered the effects of another economic recession.

A Banner Legislative Year. The year 1980 will be remembered for the enactment of an unusual amount of federal legislation affecting transportation. Although an omnibus bill dealing with both the regulatory and promotional aspects of merchant-marine policy failed to be reported out for floor action, significant legislation was passed in the rail, motor, freight forwarder, and urban transit areas. While not entirely to the liking of several industry groups, transportation leaders generally believed that they could live with the new laws. On the other hand, the new regulatory statutes will certainly be challenged, as they are interpreted and applied, in some significant respects. Indeed, by late 1980 several court actions already were pending. But the legislative steps taken marked the culmination of several years of intense congressional effort and, so far as U.S. domestic transportation is concerned, set a pattern which is likely to persist for a number of years to come.

The circumstances under which domestic surface transportation will be conducted were fundamentally changed. The thrust of the legislation was to enhance competition, increase reliance on market forces, and lessen interference by the regulatory authorities. The Motor Carrier Act of 1980, signed by President Carter on July 1, significantly eases the entry of new trucking companies into the business and simplifies the extension of the route patterns of existing carriers. The legislation directed the Interstate Commerce Commission (ICC) to eliminate rules that require carriers to stop at specific points or take circuitous routes. It requires the ICC to encourage the amendment of existing certificates and permits to eliminate gateway restrictions,

lack of backhaul authority, unduly narrow commodity authority, and other restraints which have held down the efficiency of many motor carriers. It provides a zone within which carriers can adjust their rates, both upward and downward, without interference by the ICC. It encourages independent, competitive rate-making and curtails the permissible activities of rate bureaus, which operate with antitrust immunity. For freight forwarders the act confers a right, long sought, to purchase rail service wholesale under contract rates. Some expansion in freight forwarder activities may be anticipated. Finally, private carriers may now haul for compensation for subsidiaries that are 100% owned by the parent company. A speedup of private trucking is likely to result.

The railroad regulatory policy act of 1980, the Staggers Rail Act, signed by the president on October 14, concentrates heavily on rate-making aspects of rail regulation. Entry of new carriers is not to be expected in the rail industry except as states, shippers, or employee groups take over light-traffic lines of existing carriers through newly incorporated short-line companies. The act encourages this sort of change as an alternative to abandonment of lines which, though burdensome to the carriers, may have some importance to the local economy and to shippers located on the lines. The legislation also extends and increases authorized funding through preferred stock purchases by the U.S. Treasury for the rehabilitation of run-down lines whose continued operation is considered to serve a public purpose.

The act defines rates that are free of ICC intervention by providing statutory percentages of variable costs permissible until Sept. 30, 1984, and a cost-recovery level thereafter which includes a return on equity equivalent to the embedded cost of capital. A zone of freedom for rate increases pegged to a base adjusted by an index of rail cost is also provided. Contract rates

The Motor Carrier Act of 1980, signed by President Carter in the White House Rose Garden on July 1, substantially eased government restraints on the U.S. trucking industry.

are given specific statutory authorization so that for the first time railroads may become contract as well as common carriers. Such contracts are open to few challenges on grounds of discrimination unless agricultural, forest, or paper products are involved. Like the Motor Carrier Act the rail statute curtails the antitrust immunity of rate bureaus. Since the cost-finding procedures employed by the ICC in the past have been open to much criticism, a Railroad Accounting Standards Board, headed by the U.S. comptroller general, is provided for.

Not all aspects of the new laws reduce the impact of regulations. The ICC gained authority to require through routes and joint rates among motor carriers, which it had long sought. In addition it may require reciprocal switching among railroads when certain conditions are observed. The commission must also require written contracts between owner-operators and their employers or customers in the trucking business to provide a measure of protection to such operators. Finally the Department of Transportation (DOT) must prescribe minimum insurance requirements within statutory limits for all interstate haulers of goods, including private carriers.

Important changes occurred in federal government participation in the financing of urban transportation. Formula funding, which could be used to help fund operating deficits as well as for capital projects, became available to cities. Modest allocations from the windfall-profit tax on oil increased the available funding.

The Recession. Motor carriers of general commodities began to feel the effects of a faltering economy in the fourth quarter of 1979. By June their traffic was some 25% below that of June 1979 and, while the decline flattened thereafter, traffic remained depressed. Stimulated by lack of business and the rate-making freedom accorded by 1980 legislation, a number of carriers began to offer reduced rate and discounts. Nonunion carriers in particular precipitated this type of action. Three large carriers failed early in the year, and many others saw their operating ratios move above 100%. Carriers sought to reopen the master contract with the International Brotherhood of Teamsters with the particular object of deferring the cost of living increase due in the autumn. The union, however, refused concessions, except through negotiation with individual locals.

Railroad traffic as a whole held up surprisingly well. During the first half of the year it showed levels higher than a year earlier. It then lost ground. Trailer-on-flatcar traffic was down, but not so sharply as motor-carrier traffic. The severe impact of recession on the automobile, truck and trailer manufacturing, farm equipment, iron and steel, and related industries struck a sharp blow at rail traffic. Coal and grain, on the other hand, moved at substantially higher levels than in 1979. Hence the impact of the economic slowdown was largely regional, affecting the railroads of the northeast most seriously.

Conrail's carloadings were off by some 20% and its deficit widened. The railroads as a whole suffered declining earnings, but individual carriers geographically positioned to benefit from the coal and grain traffic did well.

Gathering recession in the industrialized world boded ill for the ocean-line carriers. Both the Pacific and North Atlantic trade areas were experiencing an excess of sailings, and rate pressures were severe. The participation of independent lines in competition with members of the rate-setting conferences grew. Allegedly because the Japanese-flag lines exerted bloc-voting power and the conferences were unresponsive to the need to adjust rates, Sea-Land, the largest carrier in the trade, withdrew from 12 eastward Pacific conferences. On the Atlantic a growing imbalance of trade eastward produced disparities in rates with some eastward rates as much as six times as high as their westward counterparts. American exporters complained of discrimination and the Federal Maritime Commission undertook an investigation. It appeared that the weakness of the American dollar during part of 1978–79 may have generated a sharp excess of exports to Europe in comparison with imports from the same area. The future prospect was poor. Since a substantial number of containerships are under construction, an excess of ships will doubtless increase, and trade volume may fall as the European recession curtails American exports.

Airlines suffered more severely than other forms of transport. Both passenger and cargo volumes were down, more seriously in domestic than in international markets. In the face of deregulation carriers continued to invade one another's territories. Most notable was the entry of Eastern Airlines into the transcontinental routes. The result was depressed fares on a number of the most important long-haul segments. Though the general level of rates and fares was increasing rapidly, important volumes of traffic were involved on the sharply competitive routes. Most major trunk lines chalked up big losses.

Congestion and Bottlenecks. Recession is ordinarily accompanied by ample transport capacity. In 1980, car supply generally eased and surpluses of plain box cars developed. Despite an embargo on export of grain to the USSR, however, high foreign demand continued to place pressure on port elevators. Heavy grain traffic in particular produced unparalleled congestion and delays at Lock and Dam 26 on the upper Mississippi near Alton, IL. Construction of a new lock, in controversy for a number of years because of railroad and environmental opposition, would not relieve this condition for four or five years.

U.S. coal exports always have been confined largely to metallurgical grades. With worldwide depression in the steel industry, such exports were off. But a sudden sharp growth in steam coal exports produced by a shift from oil to coal in other countries caught U.S. ports with grossly inadequate capacities. The principal export center is the Hampton Roads ports of Norfolk and Newport News, VA. The ports' 1980 tonnage would be about double that of the prior year. Through the summer and autumn large numbers of ships were delayed awaiting access to the piers for loading. The piers are owned by the railroads and the sudden change in demand caught them by surprise. Various expansion plans were under consideration. Relief is essential lest the United States lose a competitive position in the coal trade to Australia, Canada, and South Africa.

The continued growth of domestic coal traffic, running nearly a million tons a week above 1979, augmented the pressure on a number of rail lines. The heavy flow of Wyoming coal both eastward and southeastward began in the early 1970s as Environmental Protection Agency restrictions required a shift to low-sulfur coal in generating plants. Burlington Northern, whose constituent lines originated almost no coal in 1970, now loads more coal than any other railroad. Its lines were not constructed with a view to handle large volumes of bulk traffic, hence upgrading and expansion of capacity are the order of the day. In the southeast an unprecedented southbound movement of coal has developed over difficult profile and lines of limited capacity.

Fuel Supply and Cost. Except for a very limited mileage of electrified railways and a slowly growing mileage of light-rail and heavy-rail transit lines in a few major metropolitan areas, American transportation is wholly based on petroleum-derived fuels. The doubling of fuel prices in 1979 hit all forms of for-hire transportation severely, especially as recession and reduced regulation made it more difficult to pass increased costs for fuel to rates and fares. Fuel costs represent some 30% of airlines' operating expenses. Ocean-lines operating containerships devote as much as 50% of voyage cost to fuel. Concern about supply over the longer run has been endemic, while the Iraq-Iran war raised the possibility of short-term deficiences.

Efforts to improve fuel economy are under way in all forms of transportation. Carriers seek not only improved mileage, but the ability to use a greater variety of fuels. The availability of high-specification fuels is especially in doubt, hence a desire for propulsion units that can perform well on inferior grades. Inadequate earnings prevent airlines from rapidly replacing their fleets with more fuel-efficient aircraft. Yet progress has been made. The long-standing propensity of U.S. steamship lines to rely upon steam turbines finally was breached. Sea-Land was putting into service ten foreign-built containerships propelled by slow-speed diesels with a prospective saving of 30% in fuel consumption. In late August the first American-built high-horsepower, low-speed marine diesel was completed by Allis Chalmers under Sulzer license for American President Lines. As many as 70 old ships may be converted to this form of power.

Motor carriers, assisted by the innovative work of truck manufacturers, have made significant progress in fuel economy. Improved engines and drive trains, radial tires, and intermittent fan operation have made major contributions. Attention is paid to the reduction of air resistance which is important even at speeds below 55 mph (88 km/h). The more economical diesel is rapidly being substituted for the gasoline engine in small road rigs and in city vehicles. Railroads are moving to improve power-tonnage relationships, reduce tare weight, and improve aerodynamics. Tests are underway to increase the range of fuel specifications usable in the diesel locomotive with or without engine modifications. On electrified lines regenerative braking is being extended.

Railroads. The year was noteworthy for the beginnings of liquidation of the Chicago, Rock Island & Pacific Railroad and discontinuance of operation over some 4,600 mi (6 400 km) of the bankrupt Milwaukee Railroad. Important portions of both railroads were being taken over by other lines, non-rail companies, and operators under contract to states. The year was also marked by major merger developments. Merger

Bill Grimes, Black Star

On September 18, a $500 million airport passenger terminal, the largest in the world, was opened at the Atlanta International Airport.

To qualify for federal funding, U.S. urban transit systems must meet Department of Transportation requirements regarding accommodations for the handicapped. Although buses can be equipped with such conveniences as a wheelchair lift, right, some cities insisted that they cannot afford the expense.

GMC

of the Chessie System and the Seaboard Coast Lines was completed. Grand Trunk Western got a green light to acquire Detroit, Toledo and Ironton. A Norfolk & Western-Southern merger was pending. And Union Pacific applied for merger with Missouri Pacific and Western Pacific. Some ten years earlier there were 104 Class I railways; there were 39 in 1980.

Adverse economic developments clouded the future of Conrail. Some would argue this system is too large to be managed effectively. But its immediate problems trace to traffic declines. More than $3,200,000,000 of government funding has been appropriated, and Conrail estimated that as much as $900 million more may be required to bring the system to a break-even point.

Airlines. The strategies of airlines as they have tried to adapt to deregulation have differed sharply. Braniff, which took advantage of the opportunity to expand more than any other carrier, was forced to curtail its route pattern drastically and dispose of a large number of aircraft. Nevertheless its position remained precarious. United was abandoning many of its short-haul routes and the success of its concentration in principal long-haul markets remained to be proved. Pan Am's acquisition of National did not give it as strong a U.S. feeder system as might have been desired. Continental and Western, once turned down, were again seeking a merger as a means to stem losses. American and TWA were burdened with an excessive number of old, fuel-inefficient aircraft. Pacific Southwest, having expanded outside California, was hit by a strike by pilots seeking pay and fringes more nearly equivalent to those provided by the large interstate carriers. Eastern turned aggressive in the transcontinental markets from which it was formerly barred.

Fare plans have multiplied to the point where neither travel agents nor airline ticket counter personnel can be sure of the applicable fare. Many communities have lost trunk airline service but, in most cases, commuter airlines have provided a substitute. The safety of such lines has been in doubt and the Federal Aviation Agency (FAA) strengthened its regulatory efforts. Shortage of space on prime-time flights, overbooking, and loss of service to small communities have stimulated the growth of corporate fleets.

Urban Transit. The year saw San Francisco's Bay Area Rapid Transit District retreat from the plan of computer-controlled automatic operation after years of unsatisfactory performance. it saw the prospect of rehabilitation of the subway and surface lines of the Philadelphia area and continued progress with Buffalo's transit system. It saw the state of California assume responsibility for the losses of Southern Pacific's peninsular suburban service, an expansion of San Diego transit prospects and Amtrak services, and the promise of rapid transit development in Los Angeles. Increased reliance on foreign manufacturers for transit equipment seemed unavoidable as Pullman, faced with possible heavy liability in connection with cars built for the New York Transit Authority, contemplated retirement from the transit car business. The bus design imposed by the DOT was plagued with service failures, and some municipalities elected to sacrifice federal funding and purchase their own designs.

In the autumn the New York Transit Authority decided to risk loss of federal funding by defying the DOT requirements in respect of transport of the handicapped. This is an issue of no small importance, since it would require diversion of funds badly needed to maintain a rapidly deteriorating system to the installation of elevators and ramps in all subway and elevated stations and the equipping of all new buses with mechanisms to load wheelchairs. The proposition that the limited number of handicapped can be better and much more cheaply served by assigned vehicles on a dial-a-bus basis was summarily rejected at the federal level.

ERNEST W. WILLIAMS, JR., *Columbia University*

TRAVEL

Some years, it is said, do not "travel" well, and 1980 was a serious disappointment to many segments of the travel and resort industry. The battered U.S. dollar, which failed to recover the equilibrium lost in 1979, continued to fluctuate on world money markets under pressure from forces domestic and foreign. Inflation, rising oil prices, and recession became a negative combination that ultimately was responsible for changing traditional patterns of tourism.

Though countries, airlines, and travel agents had varying experiences—and bottom lines—depending on factors such as economic conditions at specific destinations, routes served, and class of clients or areas where based, neither rose-colored glasses nor lowered expectations could make 1980 a very good year.

As early as January, a forum sponsored in Washington by the U.S. Travel Data Center (nongovernmental) and the Travel Research Association had predicted that the overall increase in travel costs in the United States would average about 13.5% above 1979. By September the actual increase was about 23%. Contributing to travelers' budget problems and inviting consumer resistance in 1980 was a 35% boost in U.S. air fares, despite increased competition spurred by deregulation. (The airlines pointed out that a one-cent-per-gallon rise in the price of jet fuel added $115 million to their annual operating costs.) An approximate 12% increase in restaurant prices and 15% higher rates for hotel and motel accommodations in the United States, compared with 1977, were also significant. And what was true for the estimated $150,000,000,000-a-year U.S. travel industry, with about 7 million dependent jobs, was true to some extent for the $350,-000,000,000-a-year international travel market.

Most Americans did not stop planning their getaways trips. But many did change the destination, the duration, the class of accommodations or the mode of transportation—and sometimes *all* of these choices. They still wanted a vacation, but they felt that price had limited their options. Of course, the blue-chip clients and other affluent (or simply less-concerned) tourists were still buying big-money tours to faraway places. But instead of flying across oceans, or even driving across the United States, many Americans decided to settle instead for a vacation near home.

Travel has always been an integral part of the American lifestyle, yet by spring the refrain about "go now, it will cost more later," began to be replaced by "maybe we better start thinking about tomorrow." Though gasoline was available at the pumps during the summer high season, the volatile price per gallon—not to mention the already substantial charges for motel rooms and meals along the highway—caused many motorists to scale down their itineraries.

Travel is one of the top three industries in almost all of the 50 states. Resorts, restaurants, amusement parks, and other tourist attractions began to concentrate on markets within a limited radius. For those advantageously located near major population centers, business was good. Naturally, business travel constituted a distinct category. While not unaffected by higher costs—many corporations had long since cut out or reduced first-class travel by executives—business travelers comprised about 55% of airline passengers and remained important customers for the industry.

Thus, despite heavy promotional spending by the tourism offices of many European countries and emphasis on legitimate savings that were still available through prepaid tours, the percentage of Americans sightseeing overseas failed to approach comfortable levels. (Actually, U.S. travel to Europe and the Pacific had been far from booming for some time.) In some instances, international political developments such as revolutions, invasions, riots, and bombings strongly affected tourism. Iran, torn by religious fanaticism and holding American diplomatic personnel hostage, and Afghanistan, invaded by the Russian army, were crossed off itineraries. The U.S.-led boycott of the Moscow Summer Olympics was followed by a severe slump in visitors to the Soviet Union. In contrast, regularly scheduled air service between Tel Aviv and Cairo began with fanfare in March, before hopes for a Mideast peace dimmed, and the People's Republic of China continued to cater to wide-eyed Americans while scoring public relations gains and earning foreign exchange.

Cruise ships, despite some softness in advance bookings and some cancellations, reported a steady demand by sea-loving passengers who could afford to pay an average of $140 a day for a vacation afloat. A few big ships that seemed destined for the scrap heap because of fuel, labor, and other expenses prepared to sail again. The *S.S. France*, largest passenger ship in the world, was refitted as the *Norway* and began regular cruises to the Caribbean from Miami. Plans to remodel the *S.S. United States* and offer longer voyages and time-sharing vacations were going forward, despite problems in arranging financing. A number of cruise lines were either preparing to build new ships or "stretching" existing vessels by adding midsections to increase passenger capacity.

There was also a bright side to the dollar's decline. It was responsible for further encouraging a heavy influx of foreign visitors with healthy currencies for whom travel in America was still a great bargain. The trend not only provided profits for the travel industry but it also helped to improve the U.S. balance of payments picture. The combination of Visit U.S.A. arrivals, cruise ship sailings, business travelers, close-in vacationers, and weekend short-trippers helped keep 1980 travel from losing all flavor and excitement.

MORRIS D. ROSENBERG
Travel Editor, "The Washington Post"

──────── TRINIDAD AND TOBAGO · ────────
Information Highlights

Official Name: Republic of Trinidad and Tobago.
Government: *Head of state,* Ellis Clarke, president (took office Dec. 1976). *Head of government,* Eric Williams, prime minister (took office Oct. 1956). *Legislature*— Parliament: Senate and House of Representatives.
Monetary Unit: Trinidad and Tobago dollar (2.40 TT dollars equal U.S.$1, Aug. 1980).
Manufactures (major products): Petroleum, cement, cigarettes, rum, beer.
Agriculture (major products): Sugar, cocoa, coconuts, citrus fruits.
GNP Per Capita (1978 est., U.S.$): $2,910.
Foreign Trade (1979, U.S.$): *Imports,* $1,946,000,000; *exports,* $2,476,000,000.

TRINIDAD AND TOBAGO

The political fragmentation that has afflicted the Caribbean in recent years reached the oil-producing nation of Trinidad and Tobago in 1980. On November 24, the residents of the small island of Tobago, located to the northeast of Trinidad, voted for members to the first island parliament in 90 years. Apparently favoring autonomy, Tobagon voters gave a solid victory to the Democratic Action Congress (DAC) party, led by Arthur Napoleon Raymond Robinson. Robinson earlier had resigned his seat in the Trinidad-Tobago legislature to dramatize his struggle for self-government for the smaller island. Although the DAC had only two seats in the Trinidad-Tobago legislature, it succeeded in capturing 8 of the 12 seats in the Tobago parliament. The remaining seats are held by the representatives of the People's National Movement, led by Prime Minister Eric Williams, the dean of Caribbean politicians, with 25 years as head of government. The setback for Williams' party was not regarded as serious, however, since the prime minister was expected to win easily his sixth term of office in elections early in 1981.

The oil-backed economy of Trinidad-Tobago has given the population of more than 1 million persons an affluent way of life in comparison with their poverty-stricken island neighbors. However, inflation and a lethargic bureaucracy have stirred rumblings of discontent.

THOMAS MATHEWS, *University of Puerto Rico*

TUNISIA

A period of instability followed the January commando raid on Gafsa and the sudden departure from political life of Hedi Nouira in February, due to a cerebral hemorrhage.

On the anniversary of the January 1978 general strike, a guerrilla force calling itself the Tunisian Resistance Army launched an armed attack on the phosphate mining town of Gafsa, striking at the army barracks, gendarmerie headquarters, and police station. The 50-member group, allegedly formed in opposition to President Habib Bourguiba's rule, was routed by government forces after heavy fighting in which many casualties occurred on both sides.

──────── TUNISIA · Information Highlights ────────

Official Name: Republic of Tunisia.
Location: North Africa.
Area: 63,170 sq mi (163 610 km²).
Population (1980 est.): 6,500,000.
Chief City (1975 census): Tunis, the capital, 550,404.
Government: *Head of state,* Habib Bourguiba, president-for-life (took office 1957). *Chief Minister,* Mohamed Mzali, prime minister (took office April 1980). *Legislature* (unicameral)— National Assembly.
Monetary Unit: Dinar (0.402 dinar equals U.S.$1, Aug. 1980).
Manufactures (major products): Crude oil, phosphates, olive oil, textiles, construction materials.
Agriculture (major products): Wheat, olives, grapes, citrus fruits.
GNP (1979 est., U.S.$): $6,990,000,000.
Foreign Trade (1979, U.S.$): *Imports,* $2,830,000,000; *exports,* $1,766,000,000.

The Tunisian government claimed the commandos were trained in and assisted by Libya and used Algeria as a launching point from which to destabilize the government and jeopardize relations between Algiers and Tunis.

French military equipment and personnel were dispatched to guard the area on Bourguiba's bidding. The Tunisian state security court sentenced 15 people to death for their participation in the raid. The government followed up the attack with an investigation of the region's security situation, culminating in the replacement of Internal Minister Othman Kechrid by Driss Guiga, ambassador to West Germany and former director of internal security.

Prime Minister Hedi Nouira, long regarded as Bourguiba's successor, was replaced in April by former Education Minister Mohamed Mzali, 55. A cabinet shake-up coincided with Mzali's appointment. Three former ministers who departed from the government in 1978 in protest over the ruling Socialist Destour Party's (PSD) harsh treatment of unionists were brought back into the government. Mohammed Sayah, PSD director and a hard-liner with regard to union policies, was replaced by Mongi Kooli and demoted to head the supplies and housing ministry. A ministry of economy was formed to replace the industry and commerce ministries.

Labor Relations. Continuing with his policy of wooing the opposition unionists, Bourguiba released two trade union leaders, jailed following the January 1978 unrest. Abderrazak Ghorbal, former deputy secretary of the powerful General Union of Tunisian Workers (UGTT), and Salah Brour, former head of its training program, were the last of the union leaders to be held in prison.

Other liberalization measures included Mzali's May announcement of a 10% increase in the minimum wage. Social security, old age, and invalid pension laws were also amended in the workers' favor. The government promised union elections early in 1981 to allow for a change in the Nouira-appointed UGTT leadership. But in September, Bourguiba announced that none of the labor leaders jailed following the 1978 events would be allowed to take up new union posts.

MARGARET A. NOVICKI, *"Africa Report"*

TURKEY

The year 1980 in Turkey was marked by continued domestic violence which at times threatened to reduce the republic to a state of anarchy. The economy seemed on the road to ruin. Compromise and cooperation between Prime Minister Süleyman Demirel of the Justice Party (AP) and former Prime Minister Bülent Ecevit of the Republican People's Party (CHP) was essential for solving the country's problems, but this was not forthcoming and governmental paralysis barred any progress. It was not surprising, therefore, that on September 12, the Turkish Army, which had repeatedly warned the political parties that they were failing to deal with the economic difficulties and social unrest, took over the country in an apparently bloodless coup.

Politics and Terrorism. With the seven-year term of President Fahri Korutürk due to expire on April 6, parliament was faced with electing a successor. But because there were no candidates, the initial March 22 vote was postponed. Beginning two days later, there were 25 unsuccessful ballots in three weeks, and Senate Speaker Ihsan Sabri Caglayangil became acting president.

The seven-month-old government of Prime Minister Demirel survived a vote of confidence July 2 but was dealt a severe blow when parliament later censured Foreign Minister Hayrettin Erkmen and expelled him from that body by a vote of 200–2.

Former Prime Minister Nihat Erim was assassinated in a suburb of Istanbul, July 19. Eight members of an urban guerrilla group called Dev Sol were arrested for the crime October 3. In a trial of 835 persons for "armed insurrection and massacre" in December 1978, a military court August 8 sentenced 22 defendants to the death penalty and 424 others to prison terms of varying lengths. Two convicted terrorists were hanged on October 8; the executions were the first in Turkey since 1972.

Continued violence by political extremists on the left and right by midyear cost the lives of between 20 and 30 persons daily. By the end of 1980, it was estimated that up to 5,000 persons had been killed by political violence since 1977.

TURKEY · Information Highlights

Official Name: Republic of Turkey.
Location: Southeastern Europe and southwestern Asia.
Area: 306,870 sq mi (794 793 km²).
Population (1980 est.): 45,500,000.
Chief Cities (1979 est.): Ankara, the capital, 2,106,076; Istanbul, 2,882,579; Izmir, 730,692.
Government: *Head of state,* Gen. Kenan Evren, chairman of National Security Council (took power Sept. 1980). *Head of government,* Bülent Ulusu, prime minister (took office Sept. 1980). *Legislature*—Grand National Assembly: Senate and National Assembly.
Monetary Unit: Lira (84.80 liras equal U.S.$1, Nov. 1980).
Manufactures (major products): Textiles, processed foods, minerals.
Agriculture (major products): Cotton, tobacco, cereals, sugar beets, fruit, nuts.
GNP (1980 est., U.S.$): $49,000,000,000.
Foreign Trade (1979, U.S.$): *Imports,* $4,946,000,000; *exports,* $2,261,000,000.

Economy. Second only to Turkey's political problems was the state of the economy. During 1978–80, Turkey had the highest inflation rate of any member of the Organization of Economic Cooperation and Development (OECD)—nearly 100%. By 1980, the nation's economic problems included an external debt of $12,000,000,000, a lack of foreign exchange, and 20% unemployment. The gross national product (GNP) was $49,000,000,000, or $1,120 per capita. Expenditures for 1980 were expected to total some $15,700,000,000—an 82% increase over 1979. Labor remittances for 1980 were estimated at $1,300,000,000, with $970 million coming from Turkish workers in West Germany, a primary trading partner. The 1980 balance of payments was expected to show a deficit of $3,500,000,000. By 1979–80 it was clear that Turkey could not carry forward its economic plans without assistance from its NATO allies. On Jan. 25, 1980, Prime Minister Demirel announced an "Economic Stablization Program" designed to boost exports and reduce imports. During the year, the International Monetary Fund (IMF), OECD, and the European Community (EC) made arrangements for major assistance to Turkey. On March 29, the United States and Turkey signed an agreement allowing the former to continue to use 12 military bases in Turkey in return for military and economic aid estimated at $400 million annually for five years.

Coup. Meanwhile, with the continuing deterioration of the internal situation, the Turkish armed forces, under the command of Chief of Staff Gen. Kenan Evren and five other high-ranking officers, seized control of the government on September 12. Some 500 prominent officials, including Prime Minister Demirel and Bülent Ecevit, were placed under temporary house arrest. The military junta, which assumed the designation of the Turkish National Security Council, had informed the United States of the coup some days before the takeover. After the junta swore themselves in on September 18, General Evren called for new elections, the framing of a new constitution, and the return to civilian authority as soon as possible. Close ties with NATO and a general pro-Western orientation were to be maintained. A new, 27-member cabinet was announced on September 20, with retired Adm. Bülent Ulusu as prime minister and Turgut Ozal, author of Demirel's economic austerity program, as deputy prime minister. The next day, the junta announced changes in the martial law code, tightening censorship rules and control over labor activities. Prime Minister Ulusu stated that the main goals of his government would be to end the widespread terrorism and implement economic austerity programs. By adopting necessary security measures, readjusting state institutions, and amending the law, the new government would prepare the ground for a smoothly functioning parliamentary democracy. Prime Minister Ulusu promised a wide range of changes in the legal system, education, finance, and labor relations.

On October 27, the junta approved a stringent new constitution that gave it unlimited power until a new charter is drawn up. They did not say when that would be. On October 30, 18 days after being released from detention, Bülent Ecevit resigned as leader of the CHP to protest the new regime's ban on political activities.

HARRY N. HOWARD, *Middle East Institute*

UGANDA

Political instability together with continuing economic and social collapse were dominant trends in Uganda in 1980, as the nation tried with little success to recover from the horrors of the Idi Amin era and its violent end.

Political Unrest. In May 1980, President Godfrey Binaisa, the second president since the overthrow of Idi Amin, was removed from power in a military coup. The action was prompted by the president's refusal to consult senior military men about government policy, by removals of key army men from important ministries, and by fears that Binaisa was showing favoritism to a few of Uganda's rival tribes, especially those in the south. The new head of state was Paulo Muwenga, a former interior minister, and at the time labor minister in Binaisa's cabinet. Muwenga, a Ganda, was widely viewed as a front man designed to mollify Ganda opposition to the new regime, and as a means of easing the return to power of former president Milton Obote.

Real power appeared to rest in the hands of a Military Commission. The commission delayed the proposed elections from September to December 1980, but agreed to allow any political party to contest them, and also permitted Obote to return immediately to Uganda from exile in Tanzania. This prompted speculation that Tanzania's President Julius Nyerere was behind the coup, since Obote is his close friend and the Tanzanian army is the only effective military force in Uganda. Nyerere, it appeared, favored Binaisa's removal, but had opposed a coup, preferring that it be done by the interim Ugandan legislature.

Elections were held in mid-December and Obote's People's Congress Party was declared the winner. Obote, 55, was sworn in for a second term. Immediately, the Democratic Party called the elections unfair and demanded new ones. However, a Commonwealth observation group accepted the overall voting procedure. Following announcement of the results, brief fighting broke out in the streets of Kampala.

Economy. The economic collapse of Uganda, a legacy of the Amin years, continued without letup. Industry was functioning at about 5% capacity, due to a lack of raw materials, a worthless currency, and a physical insecurity that led to the theft of almost anything produced or shipped. The Uganda shilling, nominally worth 7.5 to the U.S. dollar, was being traded at 29 and more to the dollar. So worthless had Ugandan money become that Kenya shillings, at a stable 7.45 to the dollar, became the actual medium of exchange. As a partial remedy, the government, in late 1979, called in all old Uganda notes (supposedly because they bore Idi Amin's picture) and issued a new currency. This also had the effect of making all old notes worthless, thus striking at currency hoarders, profiteers, and at Amin, who is supposed to have billions in cash with him in exile to be used to finance a possible return to power. The government also put a 5,000-shilling limit on the amount of Kenyan currency that could be exhanged for the new Uganda shilling, hoping to destroy the flourishing financial black market. It seemed, however, that these actions had little effect in restoring economic stability.

Further deterioration was seen in the appearance of widespread starvation in Uganda. By mid-1980, it was estimated that 100 persons a day were dying of starvation, mostly in the north among the Karamojong. So critical was the food situation that tribesmen were raiding United Nations food convoys and even attacking villages in Kenya in search of food. It was estimated that some 20,000 persons had died and thousands of others were victims of nutritional disease. Even in Kampala, scarcity caused suffering. Inflation was at 200%, eggs cost $1 each, a loaf of bread cost $6, and an average monthly wage (for those who were working at all) was $85. Uganda also could not pay for its imports, since its main cash crop, coffee, was effectively in the hands of smuggling gangs. Tanzanian troops were implicated in such activities. The country needed at least $2,000,000,000 in immediate aid.

Social Chaos. The total collapse of the rule of law and of basic civilized behavior continued in Uganda. More than 25 murders and hundreds of robberies occurred nightly in Kampala, and the numbers elsewhere were even higher. Foreign embassies had become armed camps, and few diplomatic personnel went out on the street unarmed. Thefts and robberies had in fact become the main form of economic exchange, while armed gangs easily defied the efforts of the nation's 5,000 troops and police. The "kondos" (armed robbers) were so brazen that even daylight was considered an unsafe time to be on the streets of the capital. The city itself was virtually functionless, without water, power, sewage, garbage collection, or effective administration.

ROBERT GARFIELD, *DePaul University*

UGANDA · Information Highlights

Official Name: Republic of Uganda.
Location: East Africa.
Area: 91,134 square miles (236 037 km²).
Population (1980 est.): 13,700,000.
Chief City (1980 est.): Kampala, the capital, 500,000.
Government: *Head of state,* Milton Obote, president (elected Dec. 1980). *Head of government,* Otema Alimadi, prime minister (appointed Dec. 1980). *Legislature*—Parliament, 126 members.

Aleksei Kosygin, who resigned as premier in October, died in December and was given a state funeral.

USSR

The most embarrassing development for Soviet foreign policy during 1980 was the failure of the Red Army to defeat the ill-armed Afghan nationalists rebelling against Kabul's Communist government. Besides being condemned by most of the world's non-Communist governments, the Soviet military intervention in Afghanistan caused the United States to stop further sales of grain and high technology to the USSR. The U.S. grain embargo worsened a Soviet food shortage, originally created by a poor grain harvest due to bad weather. Meanwhile, the Soviet industrial recession that had begun in 1979 continued throughout 1980, mainly because of a labor shortage.

While failing in agriculture, industry, and war, the USSR won the most medals of any country at the Summer Olympic Games in Moscow. But the invasion of Afghanistan also had its effect in the sports arena, as more than 60 countries refused to send their athletes to the Games. (*See* feature article, page 62.) Another achievement was a new world record of 185 days in space by two Soviet cosmonauts.

Late in the year, continued unrest in Poland prompted the USSR to mount troops at the border, creating fears of military intervention.

FOREIGN AFFAIRS

United States. When, in December 1979, Soviet troops invaded Afghanistan to help overthrow Afghan President Hafizullah Amin and replace him with their own puppet, Babrak Karmal, the Kremlin apparently did not anticipate

the magnitude of the U.S. oppposition. On Jan. 4, 1980, U.S. President Jimmy Carter delayed the opening of an American consulate in the Ukrainian city of Kiev and of a Soviet consulate in New York City; postponed most planned U.S.-USSR cultural exchanges; reduced Soviet fishing privileges in U.S. territorial waters; ended further sale of American high technology to the USSR; and stopped the shipment of 17 million t (18.7 million T) of American grain already ordered by the Soviet government. During February, the U.S. government forced the USSR to reduce the number of Soviet trade-mission personnel stationed in the United States. Under strong pressure from President Carter, the U.S. Olympic Committee on April 12 decided not to send a team to the XXII Olympic Games in Moscow.

A number of other incidents also created friction in U.S.-Soviet relations during 1980. On January 13, a bomb, apparently detonated by anti-Castro Cubans, destroyed the front windows of the New York City office of Aeroflot, the Soviet airline. On February 21, an unknown rifleman fired a shot at the New York building of the Soviet mission to the United Nations.

In the spring, the U.S. government queried the USSR about an alleged explosion of a bacteriological warfare plant in the Ural city of Sverdlovsk in 1979. At issue was Soviet adherence to a 1975 multinational treaty banning germ warfare. On March 20, the Soviet government replied that the outbreak of anthrax in Sverdlovsk in 1979 was caused by impure meat, not a factory explosion.

On September 15, the U.S. government complained to the USSR that a Soviet underground nuclear test a day earlier had violated a 1974 treaty limiting such tests to an explosive power of 150 kilotons.

Europe. Soviet relations with West European nations were marred by several incidents. During February, Spain expelled the head of the Aeroflot office in Madrid and a first secretary of the Soviet embassy for engaging in espionage. In April, a Soviet frigate rammed the stern of a Danish minelayer that was observing Warsaw-Pact naval maneuvers near the coast of Denmark. On May 2, Ilya G. Dzhirkvelov, a Soviet intelligence agent, deserted his post in Switzerland and sought asylum in England. In August, Portugal expelled four Soviet diplomats for interfering in domestic politics.

On a more peaceful note, France in March began receiving Soviet natural gas from a pipeline originating in the Ural Mountains, and West Germany during the summer signed an economic cooperation treaty with the USSR. Besides exchanging technical aid with all the Communist countries of Eastern Europe except Albania, the USSR gave assistance to the economies of Cyprus, Finland, Greece, Iceland, Portugal, and Spain.

On August 1, the USSR claimed that it had completed the withdrawal of 20,000 Soviet soldiers and 1,000 tanks from East Germany, but some 190,000 Soviet troops reportedly were still there.

From May to September 1980, the USSR granted hard currency loans totaling $550 million to Poland, which was suffering economic difficulties. Though Polish leaders constantly consulted the Kremlin, the USSR officially did not intervene in Polish affairs during August and September, when nationwide strikes forced the Polish government to permit the formation of free trade unions. But the official Soviet press repeatedly stated its disapproval of unions not under complete Communist control, and the continued inability of the Polish regime to quell labor unrest led many to believe that the Soviets would forcibly intervene.

On November 11, the 35-nation review meeting of the 1975 Helsinki accords on European security and cooperation was opened in Madrid, with the Soviet Union and United States among the participants. While the conference was intended for the evaluation of each nation's compliance with the pact, the USSR and its Eastern European satellites fought to limit the amount of time devoted to human rights provisions and to silence Western criticism of the Soviet military occupation of Afghanistan. So uncooperative was the attitude of the USSR that the U.S. delegation publicly questioned the Soviet desire for peace.

Middle East and South Asia. The 1979 invasion of Afghanistan was intended not only to install a new puppet ruler, Babrak Karmal, but admittedly also to save Afghanistan's government from being overthrown by a nationwide Islamic rebellion. The Kremlin apparently believed that the Soviet troops would win a fast victory and convince world public opinion that Afghan Communism was permanent. But the 85,000-man Soviet army in Afghanistan was inadequately trained for guerrilla combat and could gain control only of cities and major highways. The countryside was ruled by rebel nationalists.

Meanwhile, the Soviet adventure in Afghanistan was being condemned by the Communist countries of China, Albania, and Yugoslavia, as well as the majority of the world's non-Communist nations. On Jan. 14, 1980, the United Nations General Assembly voted (104–18) in favor of a resolution calling for the removal of all "foreign" troops from Afghanistan. A similar resolution was adopted (111–22) by the assembly on November 20. On January 29, 36 Muslim governments at an Islamic Conference in Islamabad, Pakistan, issued a resolution demanding the im-

Soviet President Leonid Brezhnev (right) welcomes Stanislaw Kania, the new secretary general of the Polish Workers' Party, in Moscow on October 30. Kania and Polish Premier Josef Pinkowski, who accompanied him, returned to Poland the same day with Soviet support for their handling of the country's labor problems.

mediate withdrawal of all Soviet troops from Afghanistan. The demand was repeated at a second Islamic conference May 22.

The USSR, however, sought to strengthen its influence in Afghanistan through nonmilitary means. Early in the year, Soviet engineers began building a railway and highway bridge across the Amu Darya River between Soviet Central Asia and Afghanistan. On February 1, the USSR and Afghanistan concluded an annual trade pact, increasing mutual commerce by 70% over the 1979 level. On April 4, the two countries also signed a treaty regulating the alleged temporary presence of Soviet troops on Afghan territory.

At the same time, the USSR was attempting to befriend the new Islamic government of Iran. A Soviet-Iranian treaty on June 20 provided for improvement of sea and land communications between the two countries, increased mutual trade, and committed the USSR to helping Iran in the construction of 142 economic projects. Iran, however, remained basically unfriendly toward the USSR. In February, the flow of Iranian natural gas by pipeline to the USSR was reduced by two thirds, and the price was raised by 500%. When the USSR refused to pay the inflated price, Iran discontinued all gas shipments. Also during 1980, Iran closed a Soviet consulate, forced the Soviet embassy to send home most of its staff, and openly armed the nationalist rebels in Afghanistan.

In 1980, the USSR contracted to sell $1,600,-000,000 worth of arms to India, concluded additional technical aid treaties with South Yemen, and on October 8 signed a 20-year friendship pact with Syria. All together, 14 Near Eastern and South Asian countries received technical aid from the Soviet Union.

When war broke out between Iran and Iraq in September, the Soviet Union proclaimed its neutrality and continued to send technical aid to both countries.

Far East. Sino-Soviet relations continued to be poor. In July, a Soviet citizen, Nikolai P. Zhang, was sentenced by a Chinese court to seven years' imprisonment for espionage. During October, Chinese soldiers shot and killed a Soviet fisherman sailing on the Argun, the border river.

While cruising in Japanese territorial waters in late August, a Soviet nuclear submarine caught fire, killing nine crew members. After receiving assurances from the USSR that the submarine carried no nuclear weapons and was not leaking radiation, Japan permitted a Soviet tug to tow it through Japanese waters. Though both countries were still arguing over the terms of a peace treaty never concluded after World War II, Japan in February loaned to the USSR $2,-600,000 for the purchase of textile machinery.

The USSR rendered technical aid to nine Communist and non-Communist countries in the Far East. The Soviet Union and Cambodia concluded treaties for trade, cultural exchanges, and technical aid. The USSR also agreed to help Vietnam search for oil and gas deposits below that country's coastal waters.

Africa. In 1980, the Soviet Union provided technical aid to 40 African countries, of which about half were receiving Soviet munitions. In addition, Moscow openly admitted that it was arming rebel guerrillas in South Africa. Because of alleged subversive activities by the Soviets, the Central African Republic broke diplomatic relations in January.

Latin America. In an effort to weaken U.S. influence, the USSR gave technical aid to 12 Latin American nations. The chief recipient continued to be Cuba, whose Soviet aid amounted to $3,-000,000,000 per year. In March, the USSR concluded trade and technical aid pacts with Nicaragua. During July, a treaty with Argentina called for the USSR to purchase 22.5 million t ($24.8 million T) of Argentine grain and soybeans in the following five years.

Soviet leaders attend celebrations in Red Square marking the 63rd anniversary of the October Revolution.

UPI

Canada. Despite good trade relations, friction developed between the USSR and Canada. As a protest against the Soviet invasion of Afghanistan, the Canadian government canceled more than 100 planned cultural exchanges with the USSR. In January, Canada expelled two Soviet military attachés and a Soviet embassy chauffeur for espionage against the United States. In retaliation for the Soviet expulsion of a Canadian military attaché, Canada in February expelled a trade official of the Soviet embassy.

DOMESTIC AFFAIRS

Government and Politics. Top-level changes in Soviet government and Communist Party personnel took place in the fall. On October 21, Mikhail S. Gorbachov, 49, a national party secretary in charge of agriculture, was promoted from alternate to full Politburo membership, thus becoming the youngest full member of that all-powerful body.

Because of ill health, Aleksei N. Kosygin, 76, resigned from the post of premier, which he had held for 16 years, on October 23. He was replaced by Nikolai A. Tikhonov, 75, who had been serving as first vice-premier. On December 18, Kosygin died of heart failure. (*See* OBITUARIES, page 413.)

Meanwhile, Leonid I. Brezhnev, 74, remained the top Soviet leader, simultaneously holding the positions of president and secretary general of the Communist Party.

Armed Forces. In 1980, the Soviet armed forces comprised about 4.3 million men. The USSR ranked first in the world in number of tanks, artillery, intercontinental ballistic missiles, submarine-based and medium-range missiles, medium-range bombers, and submarines. But the Soviet arsenal lagged behind that of the United States in number of aircraft carriers, long-range bombers, tactical atomic weapons, and total nuclear warheads. Of the conscripts serving in the Soviet armed forces, about 70% were urban youths and only 30% peasants.

In September, Warsaw Pact land, air, and amphibious forces conducted joint maneuvers in East Germany and nearby Baltic Sea waters.

Carefully watching the U.S. naval buildup in the Arabian Sea was the Indian-Ocean Soviet fleet of about 25 vessels, one third of which were combat ships.

Space. A series of spectacular space flights began on April 9, 1980, when Soyuz 35 was launched in Kazakhstan with Leonid I. Popov and Valery V. Ryumin on board. On April 10, Soyuz 35 docked with the Salyut 6 space station, where Popov and Ryumin stayed for six months and received several visitors from earth. These included Valery Kubasov and a Hungarian, Bertalan Farkas, May 26–June 3; Yuri Malyshev and Vladimir Aksyonov, June 5–9; Col. Viktor V. Gorbatko and Vietnamese Lt. Col. Pham Tuan, July 23–31; and Yuri V. Romanenko and a Cuban, Arnaldo T. Mendez, September 18–26.

The non-Soviet cosmonauts were the first from their respective countries to travel in space. The Salyut 6 space station also received fuel and other supplies from four unmanned rockets, which were then let loose to disintegrate in space. On October 11, Popov and Ryumin returned safely to earth after a record 185 days in space.

On November 27, Soyuz T-3 was launched with three cosmonauts on board. The next day, it docked with the Salyut 6 space station, where the cosmonauts stayed until their return to earth December 10.

Population. In 1980, the total population of the Soviet Union was 265.5 million. The total labor force numbered 135 million, of which 51% were women, and there were 49 million pensioners.

Among the largest public organizations of the country were the Communist Party, with 17.2 million members; the consumer cooperatives, with 60 million; sport societies, with 80 million; and trade unions, with 127 million.

Emigration was officially authorized for about 20,000 Soviet Jews, as compared with the 51,000 who left legally in 1979. Several thousand Armenians also were permitted to emigrate permanently in 1980.

Dissidents. During 1980, many dissidents were imprisoned for demanding freedom of religion, full political rights for non-Russian minorities, or the release of political prisoners from mental hospitals. In January, the distinguished dissident scientist, Andrei D. Sakharov, was exiled with his wife from Moscow to the Volga city of Gorki, where he lived under virtual house arrest. Sakharov was publicly accused of revealing state secrets to Western governments and of urging them to interfere in Soviet internal affairs.

In February, Sulamith M. Messerer, 71, a ballet instructor, and her son Mikhail, 31, a solo dancer with the Bolshoi Ballet, defected while on a visit to Japan and found asylum in the United States. Several Soviet writers who wished to stay

---

USSR • Information Highlights

Official Name: Union of Soviet Socialist Republics.
Location: Eastern Europe and northern Asia.
Area: 8,649,540 sq mi (22 402 308 km^2).
Population (1980 est.): 265,500,000.
Chief Cities (Jan. 1979): Moscow, the capital, 8,011,000; Leningrad, 4,588,000; Kiev, 2,144,000.
Government: *Head of state,* Leonid I. Brezhnev, president (took office June 1977). *Head of government,* Nikolai A. Tikhonov, premier (took office Oct. 1980). *Secretary general of the Communist party,* Leonid I. Brezhnev (took office 1964). *Legislature*—Supreme Soviet: Soviet of the Union, Soviet of Nationalities.
Monetary Unit: Ruble (0.64 ruble equals U.S.$1, 1980—noncommercial rate).
Manufactures (major products): Iron and steel, steel products, building materials, electrical energy, textiles, domestic and industrial machinery.
Agriculture (major products): Wheat, rye, corn, oats, linseed, sugar beets, sunflower seeds, potatoes, cotton and flax, cattle, pigs, sheep.
GNP (1979 est., U.S.$): $650,000,000,000.
Foreign Trade (1979, U.S.$): *Imports,* $57,773,000,000; *exports,* $64,762,000,000.

in the USSR were forced to leave. In July, three feminists—Tatyana Goritscheva, Tatyana Mamonova, and Natalya Nalachoskaya—and their families were exiled to the West for issuing an illegal journal urging Soviet men not to fight in Afghanistan. After unsuccessfully challenging government censorship, novelist Vasily P. Aksyonov, 47, decided that it was useless for him to remain in the USSR and emigrated to the West with his family. Fearful of being imprisoned for publishing his memoirs abroad, the scholarly Lev Kopelev went with his wife in November to West Germany.

On November 11, exiled dissident Andrei A. Amalrik, author of the book *Will the Soviet Union Survive Until 1984?* died in an auto accident in Spain.

ECONOMY

Trade. The USSR, which continued to be the world's largest exporter of raw materials, conducted trade with 131 nations in 1980. Soviet foreign trade increased by about 21% over 1979, the largest rise of any year in the 1976–1980 Five-Year Plan. Because of the U.S. embargo on the sale of grain and high technology, however, Soviet-American trade declined by 40% compared with the 1979 level.

Soviet foreign aid continued to be extensive, with 469 economic projects in 81 Communist and non-Communist countries.

Nuclear Power. In 1980, the USSR operated 29 nuclear power stations, with 29 others under construction. The share of total electricity production from nuclear power was planned to rise

Dissident scientist Andrei Sakharov and his wife were placed under virtual house arrest in Gorki.

Liaison

from 3% in 1980 to 25% by 1990. Most new nuclear power stations under construction were located near cities in European USSR, which faced a growing shortage of energy.

Standard of Living. The standard of living in the Soviet Union remained mediocre. There were admitted store shortages of meat, milk, butter, cheese, fruit, fish, soap, toothbrushes, toothpaste, needles, thread, medicines, cotton clothes, furs, and furniture. Housing was overcrowded, and there were not enough restaurants and stores. The average urban yearly wage was 2,016 rubles ($3,226), while a collective farmer earned 1,428 rubles ($2,285).

Agriculture. The 1980 grain harvest of 181 million t (200 million T) was little better than the poor 1979 crop of 179 million t (197 million T) and far below the planned 235 million t (259 million T). The U.S. embargo on most grain sales prevented the Soviets from importing 17 million t (18.7 million T) of American wheat and corn. Though Soviet purchases from other capitalist countries partially covered this import loss, USSR grain supplies for livestock feed had to be reduced.

In an attempt to effect fast farm improvements, the Soviet budget for 1981 called for slightly increased investments in industry and railway transport, somewhat reduced funds for retail trade, and sharply cut expenditures for the construction of urban public works. The 15,000,000,000 rubles ($24,000,000,000) saved from these areas would be added to the already large appropriation for farm modernization.

Transportation. Because of pay raises for railwaymen, the Soviet railroads, which haul 70% of all internal freight, performed better in 1980 than in 1979. But Soviet leaders still complained that railway freight was not delivered to industry on time.

Labor. For the first time since World War II, the Soviet Union suffered a shortage of urban labor. The shortage was said to have resulted from a low birthrate. Although some 90% of able-bodied women were employed and one fifth of all pensioners still worked, the USSR had two million vacant jobs, mostly in industry.

Industry. Because of weak railways and the national labor shortage, the industrial recession of 1979 continued throughout 1980. Output of the following products failed to surpass 1978 levels: iron ore, iron, crude and finished steel, coal, machine tools, power-station generators, cement, reinforced concrete, tractors, pesticides, caustic soda, electric locomotives, railway freight cars, motorcycles, radios, refrigerators, paper, knitwear, and shoes.

As a result, the industrial Five-Year Plan of 1976–1980 fell far short of fulfillment. The plan called for a total industrial output of 720,000,000,000 rubles in 1980, but the actual output was 623,000,000,000—only 86%.

ELLSWORTH RAYMOND
New York University

The Security Council on January 7 voted for the withdrawal of "foreign" troops from Afghanistan.

UNITED NATIONS

In its 35th anniversary year, the United Nations found itself frustrated, unable to come to grips with the increasing political tensions in the world or deal effectively with the major crises confronting it—the American hostages in Iran, the Iran-Iraq war, the Soviet invasion of Afghanistan, the Arab-Israeli dispute, and the economic frictions between rich and poor nations.

Part of the problem was that the issues themselves were so intractable. But another factor was the decline in cooperation between the superpowers, so necessary for accommodation on most international problems. As a result of these stresses, 1980 saw a deterioration in the functioning of the prime UN organs—consensus-building in the General Assembly, peacemaking in the Security Council, and private mediating by the secretary general.

There were, however, some encouraging successes by the UN. The leverage of UN political organs was used to promote a relatively successful relief operation in famine-stricken Cambodia. Secretary General Kurt Waldheim moved painstakingly toward agreement with South Africa on UN-supervised elections and independence for the territory of Namibia. A diplomatic breakthrough was achieved in the decade-long negotiations on a comprehensive sea law treaty. Intercommunal talks between Greek and Turkish Cypriots were resumed under a UN mediator on August 9 after a year's hiatus.

These scattered achievements provided "some reason for celebration," said Waldheim in his annual report. But, he admitted, 1980 had in the main produced tension and disorder, a lack of direction and "a growing mistrust among the nations of the world."

General Assembly. In addition to its regular three-month meeting in the autumn, the General Assembly held three special sessions during the year 1980.

The emergency session on Afghanistan (January 10–14) made use of the UN's "Uniting for Peace" safety valve, under which the assembly can take up an issue if a veto (in this case by the Soviet Union) creates a deadlock in the Security Council. The 40 nations of the Islamic Conference, led by Pakistan, asked for the meeting and sponsored a resolution which called for the immediate, total, and unconditional withdrawal of "foreign troops" from Afghanistan. The vote was 104–18 in favor of the resolution, with 18 abstentions. Although there was no expectation that Moscow would comply, the UN action dramatized the outrage of the international community over the invasion. It served as a severe setback to Soviet relations with the Third World, which the Russians have long wooed as their "natural ally."

Several actions by the regular assembly session demonstrated the depth and continuity of the Soviet–Third World split.

Despite intensive lobbying and threats from Moscow, a second demand for troop withdrawal from Afghanistan, somewhat milder in tone, was adopted on November 20 by an even larger majority of 111–22, with 12 abstentions.

Three weeks later, the assembly called, by a 62–17 vote, for an impartial UN investigation of charges that chemical and biological weapons had been used by the Soviets in Afghanistan and by their allies, the Vietnamese, in Cambodia.

On October 13, the assembly voted down (74–35, with 32 abstentions) a motion by Moscow and Hanoi to reject the credentials of delegates sent to the assembly by the Pol Pot regime, which had been ousted from power in Cambodia

ORGANIZATION OF THE UNITED NATIONS

THE SECRETARIAT

Secretary-General: Kurt Waldheim (until Dec. 31, 1981)

THE GENERAL ASSEMBLY (1980)

President: Rüdiger von Wechmar (Federal Republic of Germany). The 154 member nations were as follows:

Afghanistan
Albania
Algeria
Angola
Argentina
Australia
Austria
Bahamas
Bahrain
Bangladesh
Barbados
Belgium
Belorussian SSR
Benin
Bhutan
Bolivia
Botswana
Brazil
Bulgaria
Burma
Burundi
Cambodia
Cameroon
Canada
Cape Verde
Central African
   Republic
Chad
Chile
China, People's
   Republic of
Colombia
Comoros
Congo
Costa Rica
Cuba
Cyprus
Czechoslovakia
Denmark
Djibouti
Dominica
Dominican Republic
Ecuador
Egypt
El Salvador
Equatorial Guinea
Ethiopia
Fiji
Finland
France
Gabon
Gambia
German Demo-
   cratic Republic

Germany, Federal
   Republic of
Ghana
Greece
Grenada
Guatemala
Guinea
Guinea-Bissau
Guyana
Haiti
Honduras
Hungary
Iceland
India
Indonesia
Iran
Iraq
Ireland
Israel
Italy
Ivory Coast
Jamaica
Japan
Jordan
Kenya
Kuwait
Laos
Lebanon
Lesotho
Liberia
Libya
Luxembourg
Madagascar
Malawi
Malaysia
Maldives
Mali
Malta
Mauritania
Mauritius
Mexico
Mongolia
Morocco
Mozambique
Nepal
Netherlands
New Zealand
Nicaragua
Niger
Nigeria
Norway
Oman

Pakistan
Panama
Papua New Guinea
Paraguay
Peru
Philippines
Poland
Portugal
Qatar
Rumania
Rwanda
Saint Lucia
Saint Vincent and
   the Grenadines
São Tomé and
   Principe
Saudi Arabia
Senegal
Seychelles
Sierra Leone
Singapore
Solomon Islands
Somalia
South Africa
Spain
Sri Lanka
Sudan
Surinam
Swaziland
Sweden
Syria
Tanzania
Thailand
Togo
Trinidad and Tobago
Tunisia
Turkey
Uganda
Ukrainian SSR
USSR
United Arab Emirates
United Kingdom
United States
Upper Volta
Uruguay
Venezuela
Vietnam
Western Samoa
Yemen
Yemen, Democratic
Yugoslavia
Zaire
Zambia
Zimbabwe

COMMITTEES

General. Composed of 29 members as follows: The General Assembly president; the 21 General Assembly vice presidents (heads of delegations or their deputies of Bahrain, Bolivia, China, Ecuador, France, Greece, Honduras, Malaysia, Mauritius, Mongolia, Niger, Oman, Rumania, Senegal, Thailand, Tunisia, USSR, United Kingdom, United States, Zaire, Zimbabwe); and the chairmen of the following main committees, which are composed of all 154 member countries:

First (Political and Security): Niaz Naik (Pakistan)

Special Political: Leonardo Mathias (Portugal)

Second (Economic and Financial): Abdelhadi Sbihi (Morocco)

Third (Social, Humanitarian and Cultural): Ivan Garbalov (Bulgaria)

Fourth (Decolonization): Noel Sinclair (Guyana)

Fifth (Administrative and Budgetary): Enrique Buj-Flores (Mexico)

Sixth (Legal): Abdul Koroma (Sierra Leone)

THE SECURITY COUNCIL

Membership ends on December 31 of the year noted; asterisks indicate permanent membership.

Japan (1982)
China*
France*
German Dem. Rep.
   (1981)
Panama (1982)

Mexico (1981)
Niger (1981)
Ireland (1982)
Philippines (1981)
Spain (1982)

Tunisia (1981)
USSR*
United Kingdom*
United States*
Uganda (1982)

Military Staff Committee: Representatives of chief of staffs of permanent members.

Disarmament Commission: Representatives of all UN members.

THE ECONOMIC AND SOCIAL COUNCIL

President: Andreas Mavrommatis (Cyprus). Membership ends on December 31 of the year noted.

Algeria (1981)
Argentina (1983)
Australia (1982)
Bahamas (1982)
Bangladesh (1983)
Barbados (1981)
Belgium (1982)
Belorussian SSR (1983)
Brazil (1981)
Bulgaria (1982)
Burundi (1983)
Cameroon (1983)
Canada (1983)
Chile (1982)
China (1983)
Cyprus (1981)
Denmark (1983)
Ecuador (1981)
Ethiopia (1982)

Fiji (1983)
France (1981)
German Democratic
   Republic (1981)
Germany, Federal
   Republic of (1981)
Ghana (1981)
Indonesia (1981)
India (1983)
Iraq (1982)
Ireland (1981)
Italy (1982)
Jordan (1982)
Kenya (1983)
Libya (1982)
Malawi (1982)
Mexico (1982)
Morocco (1981)

Nepal (1982)
Nicaragua (1983)
Nigeria (1982)
Norway (1983)
Pakistan (1981)
Peru (1983)
Poland (1983)
Senegal (1981)
Spain (1981)
Sudan (1983)
Thailand (1982)
Turkey (1981)
USSR (1983)
United Kingdom (1983)
United States (1982)
Venezuela (1981)
Yugoslavia (1982)
Zaire (1982)
Zambia (1981)

THE TRUSTEESHIP COUNCIL

President: Albert Turot (France)

China[2]

France[2]
USSR[2]

United Kingdom[2]
United States[1]

[1] Administers Trust Territory. [2] Permanent member of Security Council not administering Trust Territory.

THE INTERNATIONAL COURT OF JUSTICE

Membership ends on February 5 of the year noted.

President: Sir Humphrey Waldock (United Kingdom, 1982)
Vice President: Taslim O. Elias (Nigeria, 1985)

Isaac Forster (Senegal, 1982)
André Gros (France, 1982)
Manfred Lachs (Poland, 1985)
Platon Dmitrievich-Morozov
   (USSR, 1988)
José Maria Ruda (Argentina,
   1982)
Hermann Mosler (Fed. Rep. of
   Germany, 1985)
Nagendra Singh (India, 1982)

Shigeru Oda (Japan, 1985)
Roberto Ago (Italy, 1988)
Abdullah Ali El-Erian (Egypt,
   1988)
José Sette Câmara (Brazil, 1988)
Stephen M. Schwebel (United
   States, 1988)
Abdullah Fikri al-Khani (Syria,
   1985)

INTERGOVERNMENTAL AGENCIES

Food and Agricultural Organization (FAO); General Agreement on Tariffs and Trade (GATT); Intergovernmental Maritime Consultative Organization (IMCO); International Atomic Energy Agency (IAEA); International Bank for Reconstruction and Development (World Bank); International Civil Aviation Organization (ICAO); International Fund for Agricultural Development (IFAD); International Labor Organization (ILO); International Monetary Fund (IMF); International Telecommunication Union (ITU); United Nations Educational, Scientific and Cultural Organization (UNESCO); Universal Postal Union (UPU); World Health Organization (WHO); World Intellectual Property Organization (WIPO); World Meterological Organization (WMO).

by the Vietnamese. The following week, a resolution was adopted (97–23, with 22 abstentions) calling on Vietnam to withdraw its troops from Cambodia and proposing an international conference in 1981 to set up free elections in that country.

Another Soviet ally, Cuba, for the second straight year lost its bid to win a Security Council seat. On November 13, the General Assembly voted by secret ballot to give the seat to Panama, after Havana had demonstrated its residual power by blocking the candidacy of Costa Rica.

A drive by the Palestine Liberation Organization (PLO) to have the assembly reject the credentials of the Israeli delegation and force a vote on economic sanctions against Israel fizzled out in the face of Arab disunity resulting from the Iran-Iraq war.

The effort began at an emergency session of the assembly, which opened July 22. Seven days later, the body adopted (112–7, with 24 abstentions) a resolution setting a November 15 deadline for unconditional Israeli withdrawal from "all the Palestinian and other Arab territories occupied since June 1967, including Jerusalem." The resolution also reaffirmed the Palestinians' right to their own independent state. Israel and the United States rejected the resolution and maintained that the special session had been convened illegally.

By the time the deadline—ignored by Israel—rolled around, the intra-Arab split had become so wide that no agreement could be reached on specific follow-up measures. A number of resolutions were adopted by the regular assembly session on various aspects of the Arab-Israeli dispute, including one reaffirming the demand for withdrawal and asking the Security Council to consider sanctions against Israel. But there was no time set for compliance and no attempt to reject Israeli credentials.

The third of the assembly's special sessions (August 25–September 15) was called to set an agenda and agree on ground rules for new negotiations between the Third World and the industrialized nations on economic issues. Objections by the United States, Great Britain, and West Germany prevented a consensus on the key issue—whether the ultimate power for international decision-making should lie with a new forum dominated by the Third World or with such agencies as the World Bank and International Monetary Fund (IMF), in which the industrial nations hold blocking votes. The dispute was still under negotiation as 1980 came to an end.

The 35th regular session of the General Assembly opened on September 16, with an agenda of 120 items. Baron Rüdiger von Wechmar, the West German ambassador, was elected president. General Assembly membership was increased to 154 with the admission of Zimbabwe and a new Caribbean nation, St. Vincent and the Grenadines. Resolutions were adopted on disar-

UPI
Newly-elected General Assembly President Rüdiger von Wechmar (right) opens the 35th regular session, September 16. Kurt Waldheim looks on.

mament, the disputes in Belize, East Timor, and Western Sahara, the protection of diplomats, refugee problems, various aspects of human rights, and a proposal to increase the Security Council from 15 to 21 members.

Security Council. As the year began, Soviet vetoes blocked council action on the hostage crisis (January 13) and Afghanistan (January 7). As 1980 ended, the intransigence of both Iran and Iraq prevented the council from defining principles upon which the Persian Gulf war could be resolved. In between, the council dealt with southern Africa, Cyprus, and a Malta-Libya squabble, but spent most of its time on the Arab-Israeli dispute.

From March 1 through December 19, the Security Council voted on nine separate resolutions criticizing Israel for its West Bank settlements, its interventions in Lebanon, its rejection of Palestinian rights, its treatment of West Bank mayors, and its legislative action formally making Jerusalem its capital.

The first resolution, adopted unanimously on March 1, caused a political uproar in the United States when President Carter disavowed the American vote. Secretary of State Cyrus A. Vance took the blame for a "communications failure" with the UN delegation. The resolution criticized Israeli settlements in "Palestinian" territories, "including Jerusalem."

The United States subsequently used its veto power to defeat a resolution defining Palestinian rights and calling for Israeli withdrawal from all occupied Arab territories, including Jerusalem. The vote on April 30 was 10–1, with the four western European members abstaining.

The American representative abstained on all but one of the subsequent resolutions against Israel—May 8 and 20, on the expulsion of two Arab mayors; June 5, on bomb attacks on three West Bank mayors; and June 30 and August 20, on Jerusalem. The intensity of the Arab campaign at the UN was cited as a reason for the defiant response by the Israeli parliament in adopting the law on Jerusalem.

The United States voted for the final draft, December 19, which again called on Israel to admit the two exiled mayors. The two then staged a five-day hunger strike inside the UN to promote their cause.

After the Iran-Iraq war erupted in September, the Security Council issued two statements (September 23 and November 5) and adopted one unanimous resolution (September 28) calling for an end to the fighting. On the basis of these, Secretary General Waldheim on November 11 named former Swedish Prime Minister Olof Palme as a mediator. But as the year ended, Palme's efforts—like those of the Islamic Conference and the nonaligned nations—had failed to end the fighting.

Secretariat. Secretary General Waldheim began his year in Tehran in a fruitless effort to arrange a "package deal" with the Iranian government—freedom for the U.S. hostages in return for the creation of an international forum to air Iranian grievances.

A second attempt, which came agonizingly close to success, began on February 20, when Waldheim named an inquiry panel of five jurists from Algeria, France, Sri Lanka, Syria, and Venezuela. The panel visited Tehran from February 23 to March 11, but, because of Ayatollah Ruhollah Khomeini's support for the militant students, Iran's Revolutionary Council was unable to fulfill its pledges to take the hostages out of the hands of the militants or even to allow the UN panel to visit the captives.

After the World Court ruled on May 24 that the hostages should be freed, Waldheim made one last effort, sending Abid Daoudy, the Syrian member of his panel, to Tehran. But Daoudy, too, was stymied, and the UN faded from the center of the hostage negotiations.

Waldheim and his aides also were active throughout the year in negotiating the terms of independence for Namibia. Agreement was reached on June 20 for the establishment of a demilitarized zone between the territory and neighboring Angola and Zambia. In a report to the Security Council on November 25, Waldheim announced agreement on a multi-party conference in January 1981 to resolve final details. He also announced agreement in principle on the dispatch of a UN peace force in March 1981 to supervise a cease-fire, elections, and independence for Namibia before the end of the year. But there was no certainty that South Africa would give final agreement to the deal.

The UN staff protested the arrest and detention of various Secretariat officials stationed abroad. Especially vehement was the reaction to a seven-year jail term handed down by a Polish court March 7 to a UN employee, Alicja Wesolowska, on charges of spying. A number of UN bodies adopted resolutions affirming the sanctity of UN personnel.

Several UN agencies joined together on November 10 to launch a decade-long drive to provide safe drinking water and sanitation in the Third World. The object is to end water-borne diseases that threaten three out of five people in developing countries and claim millions of victims each year.

Economic and Social Council. The council dealt extensively with refugee problems in Indochina, Afghanistan, Latin America, and Africa. It convened a conference on May 26, at which $116 million were raised to cover most of the outstanding costs of the international relief operation in Cambodia.

On June 27, the UN Conference on Trade and Development reached agreement after four years on the establishment of a "common fund" to help stabilize the price of global commodities.

Several agencies, led by the UN Environmental Program, joined on March 5 to launch a global strategy for the conservation and management of natural resources and wildlife.

The Human Rights Commission, meeting in Geneva, adopted resolutions on Cambodia, Soviet "aggression" in Afghanistan, and human rights violations by Israel, Guatemala, South Africa, and Equatorial Guinea.

Trusteeship and Decolonization. On June 12, the Trusteeship Council, with the Soviet Union dissenting, accepted the concept of "free association" between the United States and various regions of Micronesia when the latter achieve self-determination in 1981.

The decolonization committee reaffirmed Puerto Rico's right to independence from the United States and urged "the full transfer of all powers to the people." The vote was 12–0, with 11 abstentions. The United States rejected UN jurisdiction, saying Puerto Rico had already achieved self-government.

Legal Activities. The UN Conference on the Law of the Sea ended its work for 1980 on August 29, after achieving a breakthrough on a unique voting formula for the regulation of deep-sea mining. The major unresolved issue was the criteria for settling disputes on maritime boundaries. The conference had hoped to complete its work in 1980, but it was forced to schedule its 10th session for March 1981 in the hope that the remaining issues could be resolved and the final treaty signed before the end of the year.

MICHAEL J. BERLIN
"New York Post"

Dennis Brack, Black Star

Flags fly in Heritage, PA, in special remembrance of the American hostages in Iran.

UNITED STATES

The penultimate decade of the twentieth century was ushered in by a frustrating and disquieting year for the United States. The prolonged captivity of the American hostages in Iran loomed large in the national consciousness as a symbol of new limits on U.S. power in the world. An erratic economy slumped, then began a sluggish recovery amid a dangerous resurgence of inflation. Members of Congress were embroiled in an ugly scandal and racial tensions appeared to be on the rise. The defeat of President Jimmy Carter and many of his fellow Democrats in the Congress seemed to reflect public dissatisfaction with the national condition. And the election of Republican Ronald Reagan as president and the first Republican-controlled Senate in 26 years at least held out the hope of new approaches to long-festering problems. (*See* feature article, page 10.)

DOMESTIC AFFAIRS

The Administration. President Carter's chief problems, apart from his effort to gain reelection, were international tensions, exacerbated by anxiety over the fate of the hostages in Iran and the Soviet invasion of Afghanistan, and the twin economic evils of recession and inflation.

"It has never been more clear that the state of our union depends on the state of the world," the president declared in his State of the Union address on January 23. In response to the Soviet move into Afghanistan the president had already, in a televised speech on January 4, embargoed future grain sales to the Russians. He had also threatened to boycott the 1980 Summer Olympics in Moscow, a threat which ultimately was fulfilled. In the State of the Union speech he called for reestablishing registration for the military draft to back up his pledge that the United States would go to war if necessary to protect its interests in the Persian Gulf region. Carter told the nation that he hoped it would not become necessary actually to resume induction into the military. But he contended that resumption of registration was necessary so that the nation could move rapidly to deal with any future threat to its security.

The president's plans for draft registration, as subsequently revealed on February 8, called for registration of women as well as men. The idea of female registration was rejected by Congress which, however, did provide for male registration. Despite protests from peace groups and a lawsuit contending that the exclusion of women was unconstitutional, registration of 19- and 20-year-old men went ahead as planned. On September 4 Bernard D. Rostker, director of the Selective Service System, announced that 93% of those eligible, 3,593,187, had registered.

Carter's domestic program of necessity was concerned mainly with the economy and energy. "Restraining inflation remains my highest domestic priority," the president declared in his State of the Union address. He also reiterated hopes for a comprehensive energy policy, stressing conservation, which would lessen U.S. dependence on foreign oil. In addition, Carter sought movement toward such other previously stated objectives as national health insurance

According to census figures released at year-end, there were 226,504,825 Americans in 1980.

and welfare reform. But he set few new legislative goals for Congress to reach.

Adding to the administration's problems during the year was controversy over the methods used in computing the 1980 census. An organization called the Federation for American Immigration Reform, together with 28 members of Congress, filed suit to bar the Census Bureau from counting illegal aliens in the population figures used for the reapportionment of Congress. The suit was dismissed by a three-judge federal court.

A number of big cities charged that the conduct of the census, which affects the distribution of federal financial aid as well as Congressional representation, had resulted in an under-counting of their population, particularly of members of minorities. On September 25, U.S. District Judge Horace Gilmore of Detroit ruled that the census figures had to be revised upward before they could be released. But then the U.S. Supreme Court stayed Gilmore's ruling pending appeal, thus allowing the census count of 226 million people to stand, at least for a while.

The Economy. In his budget message to Congress on January 28, President Carter stressed the need to control inflation, even at the cost of undergoing a recession. The federal budget for the 1981 fiscal year, which began Oct. 1, 1980, was based on the forecast of a relatively mild recession during the first half of 1980, with unemployment rising to 7.5% by the fourth quarter of the year. Charles Schultze, chairman of the president's Council of Economic Advisers, said this was the first time any administration had actually forecast a recession.

But the slump hit harder and sooner than the president's economic advisers had anticipated. In April unemployment jumped to 7%, an .8% climb from the previous month and the highest figure since August 1977. And in May the jobless rate increased again to 7.8%, bringing total unemployment in the nation to 8.2 million. The rising unemployment was accompanied by a drop in the gross national product and in other key economic indicators, signaling a recession.

The president acknowledged on June 6 that the recession, which most economic experts attributed at least in part to efforts to curb inflation by tightening interest rates and other monetary controls, was "a serious problem." But he said: "We're taking the proper action to minimize the damage to our people." And he claimed: "We have turned the corner on inflation."

In July, the consumer price index did not show any increase over the previous month, the first time there had been no monthly rise in the cost of living since March 1967. By September, the economy was showing signs of recovery. The unemployment rate had dropped to 7.5% in that month and it registered 7.4% in December. Meanwhile, real gross national product grew by .9% in the third quarter, compared with a 9.6% decline in the second quarter.

On August 28 the president announced a new economic program designed to revive the economy without spurring inflation. He proposed $26,700,000,000 in tax cuts for individuals and business in 1981, along with a $4,290,000,000 increase in federal spending during the 1981 and 1982 fiscal years. The proposed tax cuts were intended partly to offset the rise in Social Security taxes scheduled for 1981. Carter said these proposals would make the economy "more productive, more competitive, and more prosperous." But critics pointed out that this was the fifth different plan for improving the economy that Carter had introduced during his presidency and accused him of inconsistency in his economic policies. And the partisan climate of the presidential campaign doomed chances for Congressional approval.

Meanwhile, the recession, by cutting federal tax receipts and boosting outlays for unemployment compensation, pushed the government deeper into the red. The $36,500,000,000 deficit Carter had forecast in his March 31 budget message for fiscal 1980 climbed to more than $60,000,000,000.

Moreover, the apparent relief from inflation's toll proved to be short-lived. In August the consumer price index rose .7% and in September and October it jumped a full percentage point. In December the index climbed 1.1%, bringing the estimated annual inflation rate for 1980 to 12.4%.

Congress. Like the executive branch, the lawmakers had to reckon with the pressures of the troubled economy and of the political campaign. An understandable reluctance to avoid costly and controversial action resulted in a relatively modest output for the second session of the 96th Congress.

The most significant Congressional action was in the areas of energy and business deregulation, where a number of administration proposals from previous years were improved. In March Congress passed the windfall profits tax, which was expected to give the government more than $227,000,000,000 in revenues by 1990 from taxes on decontrolled oil prices. This was about $70,000,000,000 less than the president had sought when he originally proposed the measure as part of his April 1979 energy package. About 60% of the revenues would be used to reduce business and personal taxes. The rest would go to help finance energy development and mass transit, and to help the poor meet energy costs.

Another part of the president's energy package, the synthetic fuels bill creating the U.S. Synthetic Fuels Corporation, was approved by Congress in June. The corporation's purpose was to stimulate development of alternative energy sources, with a goal of raising domestic production of synthetic fuels to 2 million barrels daily by 1992. Included in the measure was a special bank to help finance development of solar fuel.

Congress allowed to become law a standby gasoline rationing plan submitted by the president. The plan called for gasoline rationing to begin if a 20% shortage of oil supplies existed, or was likely to exist. Congress would have to give further approval before the president actually could impose rationing.

But the Congress rejected another major component of the president's energy package, a proposed Energy Mobilization Board, intended to cut through governmental red tape to expedite projects designed to help foster U.S. energy independence. The board proposal passed the Senate but was defeated in the House. Also rejected was a Carter proposal to impose a $4.62-per-barrel fee on imported oil.

On the deregulation front, Congress endorsed two key measures designed to increase competition in the trucking and railroad industries. The trucking bill, signed in July, was intended to encourage new companies to enter the field, to curb regulations restricting service, and to give companies more freedom to raise or lower their rates without approval of the Interstate Commerce Commission (ICC). The railroad deregulation bill, given final approval in October, similarly gave the nation's railroads more authority to set their own rates, which have been regulated tightly by the ICC.

Because the Congress had failed to complete action on a number of major proposals before its preelection recess, October 2, the Democratic leadership resolved to schedule a post-election session beginning November 12, only the sixth such lame duck session since 1945. But the defeat of President Carter, and the turnover of Senate control in the next Congress to the Republicans reduced activity in the lame duck session. One significant accomplishment was approval of the Alaska Lands Act, which designated about 105 million acres (42.5 million ha) of land, an area larger than the state of California, for national parks, wildlife refuges, and conservation areas. While the measure did not totally satisfy environmentalists, they decided to give it their backing because they feared similar legislation would face trouble in the new Reagan administration.

Also in the environmental field, Congress passed legislation creating a $1,600,000,000 "su-

'WELCOME BACK, CONGRESSMAN.'

© 1980 Oliphant

perfund" to clean up toxic waste dump sites and spills, similar to New York's Love Canal, across the country. The chemical industry would finance most of the fund through taxes, with the government paying the rest.

Congress also passed a $632,400,000,000 federal budget spending ceiling for fiscal 1981, which in theory, at least, included enough spending cuts to give the new president room for $35,000,000,000 to $40,000,000,000 in tax cuts in 1981.

Disputes over two civil rights issues—an unsuccessful attempt to ban the Justice Department from seeking court-ordered busing in school desegregation, and a fair housing bill which failed to pass—delayed the adjournment of the special session, which had been scheduled for December 5, until December 16. In one of its final acts, the 96th Congress decided not to increase salaries of congressmen and other government employees. Other measures that were allowed to die were President Carter's proposals for welfare reform, unemployment benefits extension, youth employment, and national health insurance. (*See also* LEGISLATION, page 558.)

Scandals. In the wake of previous disclosures of Congressional wrongdoing, notably the Koreagate affair, 1980 produced a shattering new scandal, Abscam. It involved not only seven members of Congress but also a number of state and local officials in Pennsylvania and New Jersey. The allegations of bribery and corruption first came to light in February, following a two-year investigation by the Federal Bureau of Investigation (FBI). FBI agents had posed as representatives of Arab sheikhs and sought to bribe the targets of the probe to use their official influence for such favors as special immigration legislation and gaining building permits and gambling casino licenses. Tens of thousands of dollars were allegedly accepted by the officials. Abscam was a contraction of Abdul Enterprises, a fictitious business used by the FBI as a cover for its probe, and the word scam.

The FBI's evidence, including videotapes of Congressional members' bribe-taking, was presented to federal grand juries and resulted in the indictments of Democratic Sen. Harrison Williams of New Jersey, five Democratic House members—Michael O. (Ozzie) Myers and Raymond Lederer of Pennsylvania, Frank Thompson, Jr., of New Jersey, John M. Murphy of New York, and John W. Jenrette, Jr., of South Carolina—and one Republican lawmaker, Rep. Richard Kelly of Florida.

On August 31 Myers was convicted of bribery and conspiracy, and on October 2 he was expelled from the House of Representatives, the first member in the history of the House ever expelled for official corruption. On October 7 Representative Jenrette was also convicted of bribery and conspiracy, and on December 3 Representative Thompson was convicted of bribery and conspiracy and Murphy of conspiracy.

While legal proceedings were going forward against the accused legislators, their constituents imposed a stern political verdict on most of those implicated in Abscam who sought reelection. In the Republican primary in Florida, Representative Kelly lost his bid to retain his seat. And Thompson, Murphy, Myers, and Jenrette were defeated in the general election. Of the six House members indicted only Lederer escaped the wrath of the voters and was reelected. Senator Williams was not up for reelection.

Though the conduct of the congressmen found no defenders, the disclosure of the allegations against them long before the indictments were handed down stirred criticism, and so did the tactics used by the FBI in gathering evidence against the congressmen and other public officials. Some civil liberties advocates contended that in their efforts to crack down on official corruption the FBI had gone too far, enticing the defendants into wrongdoing. This view gained support from District Judge John Fullam of Philadelphia who, on November 26, dismissed Abscam convictions against two Philadelphia councilmen. The judge ruled that the investigation of these defendants had violated "the rights of all citizens not to be led into criminal activity by government over-reaching." It was not clear immediately what effect, if any, the judge's ruling in this case would have on the charges against the other defendants involved in Abscam.

Another sort of scandal involved Rep. Robert E. Bauman of Maryland, a prominent conservative leader in the House. After disclosures of alcoholism and homosexual soliciting he was defeated for reelection.

The suspicion of scandal also embarrassed the White House during the year as a result of disclosures that the president's brother, Billy, had accepted $220,000 from the Libyan government. Billy Carter claimed that the money was a loan and ultimately registered as a foreign agent.

But the president himself acknowledged that his brother's business dealings were "inappropriate." And the fact that the White House had sought to use Billy Carter as a go-between to seek Libyan aid in gaining the release of the American hostages held in Iran prompted a Congressional inquiry by a special subcommittee of the Senate Judiciary Committee.

With the episode attracting increasing attention in the midst of the presidential campaign, President Carter called a press conference on August 4 in which he denied any wrongdoing and said that his brother had had no influence on U.S. policy toward Libya. President Carter also sent a 13,000-word report on the episode to the Senate investigating committee.

In its report, issued October 2 at the close of a nine-week inquiry, the committee supported the president's claim that there had been no illegal or clearly unethical activity by federal officials. But the report concluded that Billy Carter had

acted in a way "contrary to the interests of the president and the United States and merits severe criticism." It also criticized the president for using his brother as a contact with the Libyans on the hostage affair, and said that he should have made it clear to the Libyans that they could not expect to influence U.S. policy as a result of their dealings with Billy Carter.

Meanwhile, the Justice Department's Office of Professional Responsibility conducted its own inquiry into the case, and on November 1 issued a report complaining that the White House had failed to cooperate sufficiently in providing investigators with presidential documents bearing on the case. The White House claimed that it had cooperated in trying to provide documents relevant to the case.

Race Relations. In January the National Urban League, one of the oldest U.S. civil rights groups, delivered a report that called the decade of the 1970s a "time of retreat, retrenchment,

—— UNITED STATES · Information Highlights ——

Official Name: United States of America.
Location: Central North America.
Area: 3,615,123 sq mi (9 363 169 km²).
Population (1980 est.): 226,504,825.
Chief Cities (1977 est.): Washington, DC, the capital, 684,891; New York, 7,297,787; Chicago, 3,062,881; Los Angeles, 2,761,222; Philadelphia, 1,778,345.
Government: *Head of state and government,* Jimmy Carter, president (took office Jan. 1977). *Legislature*—Congress: Senate and House of Representatives.
Monetary Unit: Dollar.
Manufactures (major products): Motor vehicles, aircraft, ships and railroad equipment, industrial machinery, processed foods, chemicals, electrical equipment and supplies, fabricated metals.
Agriculture (major products): Wheat, rye, corn, barley, oats, soybeans, tobacco, cotton, cattle, fruits.
GNP (1979 est.): $2,368,800,000,000.
Foreign Trade (1979): *Imports,* $217,664,000,000; *exports,* $178,578,000,000.

and lost opportunities" for black Americans. Citing a decline in black income relative to whites, and a rise in black unemployment, the report warned that racism is "alive and well in the American body politic."

Evidence supporting the League's contentions was provided in mid-May in Miami, where violence erupted in the black community. In three days, 18 persons were killed, more than 400 injured, and nearly 1,000 arrested. The rioting was touched off when an all-white jury in Tampa found not guilty four former Miami police officers who had been charged in the fatal beating of a black insurance executive. On November 30 a committee appointed by Florida Governor Bob Graham blamed the May 17–19 riots on racism and the perception of racism by blacks in the Miami area.

In July, the acquittal by an all-white jury in Chattanooga, TN, of two Kentucky Klu Klux Klan members charged in the shooting of four black women led to violence in that southern city. There were firebombings, lootings, and sniping at police officers before order was restored.

Blacks found further cause for concern in the acquittal in November in Greensboro, NC, of four Klansmen and two members of the American Nazi party who had been charged with killing four whites and one black who were members of the Communist Workers Party. The shootings took place at an anti-Klan rally in Greensboro in November 1979. About 500 persons, mostly black, staged a protest march, and the U.S. Department of Justice launched an investigation to determine if any of the acquitted defendants could be charged with violations of the federal civil rights laws.

ROBERT SHOGAN, *"Los Angeles Times"*

The Federal Trade Commission

The U.S. Federal Trade Commission (FTC) has had a unique history. In the past, because it was thought by many to be an outmoded and ineffectual bureaucracy, many referred to it as the "little old lady on Pennsylvania Avenue." After the publication of an extremely critical study of the FTC by seven young law students under the direction of Ralph Nader, President Richard Nixon asked the American Bar Association (ABA) to make a thorough study of the agency. The ABA's equally critical study prompted the president to act. New blood was injected into the leadership of the FTC; additional authority was given it by Congress; and more importantly, the FTC commissioners began interpreting more broadly the laws under which they were operating.

The result? The business community and a majority in Congress thought the FTC had become too aggressive. In 1980 Congress, which had once considered allowing the FTC to cease functioning because of its inability to act, debated whether the agency should be dismantled because of its aggressiveness. The turnaround in attitude was so significant that Congress, under tremendous pressure from the business community, almost allowed the agency to terminate by not appropriating funds. Twice during 1980 the FTC had to shut down (for a total of three days) because of a lack of congressional funding. Such a shutdown of a federal agency was believed to be a first in the history of the U.S. government.

The FTC was established by Congress in 1914 and was organized as an independent administrative agency in 1951. It was given authority to move against unfair trade practices occurring in commerce wherever such action was deemed to be in the public interest. The basic objective of the FTC has been to maintain free competitive enterprise—to prevent such enterprise from being stifled by monopoly or corrupted by unfair or deceptive trade practices.

The Congress, by passing the Magnuson-Moss Warranty FTC Improvement Bill in 1974, gave the commission the power to issue trade regulation rules for an entire industry. This new power incurred the wrath of the business community. Prior to 1974, the FTC was required to issue rules on a company-by-company basis. This procedure was very slow and generally ineffective. Following enactment of the 1974 act, the FTC drew up 18 industry-wide trade regulation rules to curb what were felt to be unfair and/or deceptive trade practices of business. Two of those rules—one removing the restraints on price advertising of eyeglasses and another requiring marketers of franchises to disclose certain information to prospective investors—were in effect in 1980. Some of the other trade regula-

tion rules in process covered funerals, mobile homes, hearing aids, home insulation, and television commercials aimed at children. Representatives of the industries concerned, particularly those involved with funerals and children's television commercials, lobbied to curb FTC activity and were successful in securing passage of the FTC Improvements Act of 1980. President Carter signed the bill on May 28, 1980, after threatening to veto any bill he believed would unduly restrict the FTC.

The most significant section of the 1980 act grants Congress a two-house veto right of any FTC trade regulation rule. President Carter called the provision "unwise and unconstitutional" but said that he signed the bill because the "very existence" of the FTC was "at stake." The president added that "under the bill, a suit to test the legislative veto provision can be expedited" and that he looked "forward to such a court challenge."

The rule to regulate television commercials directed at children generated tremendous opposition in the business community. The act as passed states that no further action by the FTC may be based on advertising practices directed at children that are merely "unfair." The FTC may only investigate "deceptive" advertising practices. The act also allows the FTC to adopt a rule requiring price disclosures and preventing abuses in the funeral industry, but it blocks any continuation of the FTC investigation of the insurance industry unless it is requested to do so by either the Senate or House Commerce Committees. (*See also* CONSUMER AFFAIRS: The Funeral Industry)

FTC Chairman Michael Pertschuk stated that he does not believe that the 1980 act makes the FTC ineffective, but that it forces the agency to develop even stronger cases against industry abuses than it had in the past. Shortly after passage of the act, the FTC moved into discussions with executives of food manufacturing companies and supermarket chains concerning a joint government-industry advertising program to educate the public on the nutritional values of foods.

In the past few years, the effectiveness of the FTC in performing a very necessary service for consumers and business has been improving. In one nine-month period it obtained more than $86 million in restitution for consumers. The total was more than its annual budget of $70 million. Nevertheless the Congress sent the FTC a clear message in 1980: its ongoing responsibility is still to help make the U.S. economic system work better for all, but the agency cannot simply "run roughshod through the private sector."

STEWART M. LEE

The Reagan Cabinet

In selecting his cabinet, President-elect Ronald Reagan seemed to favor people with personal and political backgrounds similar to his own—fellow conservative Republicans. But Reagan also added some variety and balance by naming a black lawyer, Samuel Pierce, as secretary of Housing and Urban Development and a woman political scientist, Jeane Kirkpatrick (D), as his ambassador to the United Nations.

Probably Reagan's most controversial cabinet choice appeared to be that of Alexander Haig for secretary of state. A number of Democratic Senators vowed to question Haig closely about his role as White House chief of staff during the Watergate scandal and the final days of the Nixon administration. But Haig's defenders pointed out that no wrongdoing ever had been proved against the retired general. And they cited his foreign policy experience as deputy to former National Security Adviser Henry Kissinger and later as commander of NATO forces. Haig was born in Philadelphia Dec. 2, 1924, and was graduated from the U.S. Military Academy.

Also controversial was the choice of James Watt, born Jan. 31, 1938, and a graduate of the University of Wyoming, to head the Department of the Interior. Watt, who had served in the Interior Department under Presidents Nixon and Ford, had, as president of a Denver organization called the Mountain States Legal Foundation, antagonized conservationists by his efforts to promote economic development on public lands.

To head the Department of Defense Reagan chose Caspar Weinberger, who had been state finance director of California during Reagan's first term as governor. Weinberger, born Aug. 18, 1917, and a Harvard graduate, served as director of the Office of Management and Budget (OMB) from 1972 until 1973, and as secretary of Health, Education, and Welfare (1973–75).

Another Californian, William French Smith, was picked as attorney general. A Los Angeles lawyer, Smith had been Reagan's personal attorney and a close adviser for more than 15 years. He was born Aug. 26, 1917, in Wilton, NH, and obtained his law degree from Harvard.

To deal with economic policy Reagan chose a seasoned executive, Donald T. Regan, as treasury secretary, and an intellectually inclined young Republican Congressman from Michigan, David Stockman, as director of OMB. Regan, who was born in Cambridge, MA, Dec. 21, 1918, and graduated from Harvard, was chairman of Merrill Lynch, the nation's largest brokerage firm. Stockman, the youngest cabinet-level nominee, had served two terms in the House. He was born Nov. 10, 1946, and attended Michigan State.

Retiring Republican Sen. Richard Schweiker of Pennsylvania was picked to head the Department of Health and Human Services. Schweiker, born June 1, 1926, and a Pennsylvania State graduate, had been Reagan's choice to be his vice-presidential running mate in 1976 when Reagan unsuccessfully sought the Republican presidential nomination.

To head the Transportation Department Reagan turned to another Pennsylvanian, Andrew (Drew) Lewis, Jr., who was born Nov. 31, 1931. The head of a management consultant firm, Lewis, a Harvard Business School graduate, had long been active in Pennsylvania Republican politics.

Connecticut industrialist Malcolm Baldrige, designated as commerce secretary, is a longtime friend of vice-president-elect George Bush. He was born on Oct. 4, 1922, and is a Yale graduate.

John R. Block, selected to be agriculture secretary, was director of the Illinois Department of Agriculture, and managed his 3,000-acre (1 200-ha) family farm in Gilson, IL. He was born Feb. 15, 1935, and attended West Point.

Pierce, a New York lawyer who was born Sept. 8, 1922, had served in the Eisenhower administration as under secretary of labor and then as general counsel to the Treasury Department under Nixon. The only black in Reagan's cabinet was graduated from Cornell University.

For Labor Secretary, Reagan selected Raymond J. Donovan, a New Jersey contractor who had helped to raise funds and win labor support for Reagan's presidential candidacy. He was born in Bayonne on Aug. 31, 1930, and attended Notre Dame Seminary in New Orleans.

Two of Reagan's cabinet nominees, James Edwards as secretary of energy and Terrel H. Bell as secretary of education were expected to have only limited tenures because Reagan had promised during the campaign to abolish both departments and transfer their functions.

Edwards, who was born June 24, 1927, has been a supporter of nuclear power development. The former South Carolina governor earned a dental degree from the University of Louisville.

T. H. Bell, Utah's commissioner of education, was born Nov. 11, 1921, and was graduated from the universities of Idaho and Utah. A spokesman said that Bell would "agree" with the incoming president regarding the department's future.

Chosen to the cabinet level post of Central Intelligence Agency director was William J. Casey. A New York lawyer who served in the Office of Strategic Services during World War II, Casey, who was born March 13, 1913, managed Reagan's presidential campaign.

Mrs. Kirkpatrick has been a Georgetown University political science professor since 1967. She was born Nov. 19, 1926, and studied at Barnard College and Columbia University.

GOP chairman William E. Brock 3d, who was born Nov. 23, 1930, and studied at Washington and Lee University, was named special representative for trade.

ROBERT SHOGAN

SENATE MEMBERSHIP

(As of January 1981: 53 Republicans, 47 Democrats)

Letters after senators' names refer to party affiliation—D for Democrat, R for Republican. Single asterisk (*) denotes term expiring in January 1983; double asterisk (**), term expiring in January 1985; triple asterisk (***), term expiring in January 1987; (1) ran as independent; (2) appointed in 1980 to fill vacancy.

ALABAMA
**H. Heflin, D
***J. Denton, R

ALASKA
**T. Stevens, R
***F. H. Murkowski, R

ARIZONA
***B. Goldwater, R
*D. DeConcini, D

ARKANSAS
***D. Bumpers, D
**D. Pryor, D

CALIFORNIA
***A. Cranston, D
*S. I. Hayakawa, R

COLORADO
***G. Hart, D
**W. Armstrong, R

CONNECTICUT
*L. P. Weicker, Jr., R
***C. J. Dodd, D

DELAWARE
*W. V. Roth, Jr., R
**J. R. Biden, Jr., D

FLORIDA
*L. M. Chiles, Jr., D
***P. Hawkins, R

GEORGIA
**S. Nunn, D
***M. Mattingly, R

HAWAII
***D. K. Inouye, D
*S. M. Matsunaga, D

IDAHO
**J. A. McClure, R
***S. D. Symms, R

ILLINOIS
**C. H. Percy, R
***A. J. Dixon, D

INDIANA
*R. G. Lugar, R
***D. Quayle, R

IOWA
**R. Jepsen, R
***C. E. Grassley, R

KANSAS
***R. J. Dole, R
**N. Kassebaum, R

KENTUCKY
*W. Huddleston, D
***W. H. Ford, D

LOUISIANA
***R. B. Long, D
**J. B. Johnston, D

MAINE
**W. Cohen, R
*G. Mitchell, D (2)

MARYLAND
***C. M. Mathias, Jr., R
*P. S. Sarbanes, D

MASSACHUSETTS
*E. M. Kennedy, D
**P. Tsongas, D

MICHIGAN
*D. W. Riegle, Jr., D
*C. Levin, D

MINNESOTA
*D. Durenberger, R
**R. Boschwitz, R

MISSISSIPPI
*J. C. Stennis, D
**T. Cochran, R

MISSOURI
***T. F. Eagleton, D
*J. C. Danforth, R

MONTANA
*J. Melcher, D
**M. Baucus, D

NEBRASKA
*E. Zorinsky, D
**J. Exon, D

NEVADA
*H. W. Cannon, D
***P. Laxalt, R

NEW HAMPSHIRE
*G. Humphrey, R
***W. Rudman, R

NEW JERSEY
*H. A. Williams, Jr., D
**W. Bradley, D

NEW MEXICO
**P. V. Domenici, R
*H. Schmitt, R

NEW YORK
*D. P. Moynihan, D
***A. D'Amato, R

NORTH CAROLINA
**J. Helms, R
***J. P. East, R

NORTH DAKOTA
*Q. N. Burdick, D
***M. Andrews, R

OHIO
*J. H. Glenn, Jr., D
*H. M. Metzenbaum, D

OKLAHOMA
**D. Boren, D
***D. Nickles, R

OREGON
**M. O. Hatfield, R
***B. Packwood, R

PENNSYLVANIA
*H. J. Heinz, III, R
***A. Specter, R

RHODE ISLAND
**C. Pell, D
*J. H. Chafee, R

SOUTH CAROLINA
**S. Thurmond, R
***E. F. Hollings, D

SOUTH DAKOTA
*L. Pressler, R
***J. Abdnor, R

TENNESSEE
**H. H. Baker, Jr., R
*J. Sasser, D

TEXAS
**J. G. Tower, R
*L. M. Bentsen, D

UTAH
***J. Garn, R
*O. Hatch, R

VERMONT
**R. T. Stafford, R
***P. J. Leahy, D

VIRGINIA
*H. F. Byrd, Jr., D (1)
**J. Warner, R

WASHINGTON
*H. M. Jackson, D
***S. Gorton, R

WEST VIRGINIA
**J. Randolph, D
*R. C. Byrd, D

WISCONSIN
*W. Proxmire, D
***R. W. Kasten, Jr., R

WYOMING
*M. Wallop, R
**A. Simpson, R

HOUSE MEMBERSHIP

(As of January 1981: 242 Democrats, 191 Republicans, 1 Independent, 1 Vacant)

"At-L." in place of Congressional district number means "representative at large." * Indicates elected Nov. 4, 1980; all others were reelected in 1980.

ALABAMA
1. J. Edwards, R
2. W. L. Dickinson, R
3. W. Nichols, D
4. T. Bevill, D
5. R. Flippo, D
6. *A. Smith, R
7. R. Shelby, D

ALASKA
At-L. D. Young, R

ARIZONA
1. J. J. Rhodes, R
2. M. K. Udall, D
3. B. Stump, D
4. E. Rudd, R

ARKANSAS
1. W. V. Alexander, Jr., D
2. E. Bethune, Jr., R
3. J. P. Hammerschmidt, R
4. B. Anthony, Jr., D

CALIFORNIA
1. *E. Chapple, R
2. D. H. Clausen, R
3. R. Matsui, D
4. V. Fazio, D
5. J. L. Burton, D
6. P. Burton, D
7. G. Miller, D
8. R. V. Dellums, D
9. F. H. Stark, Jr., D

10. D. Edwards, D
11. *T. Lantos, D
12. P. N. McCloskey, Jr., R
13. N. Y. Mineta, D
14. N. Shumway, R
15. T. Coelho, D
16. L. E. Panetta, D
17. C. Pashayan, R
18. W. Thomas, R
19. R. J. Lagomarsino, R
20. B. M. Goldwater, Jr., R
21. *B. Fiedler, R
22. C. J. Moorhead, R
23. A. C. Beilenson, D
24. H. A. Waxman, D
25. E. R. Roybal, D
26. J. H. Rousselot, R
27. R. K. Dornan, R
28. J. Dixon, D
29. A. F. Hawkins, D
30. G. E. Danielson, D
31. *M. Dymally, D
32. G. M. Anderson, D
33. W. Grisham, R
34. D. Lungren, R
35. *D. Dreier, R
36. G. E. Brown, Jr., D
37. J. Lewis, R
38. J. M. Patterson, D
39. W. Dannemeyer, R
40. R. E. Badham, R
41. *B. Lowery, R
42. *D. Hunter, R
43. C. W. Burgener, R

COLORADO
1. P. Schroeder, D
2. T. E. Wirth, D
3. R. Kogovsek, D
4. *H. Brown, R
5. K. Kramer, R

CONNECTICUT
1. W. R. Cotter, D
2. *S. Gejdenson, D
3. *L. DeNardis, R
4. S. B. McKinney, R
5. W. Ratchford, D
6. T. Moffett, D

DELAWARE
At-L. T. B. Evans, Jr., R

FLORIDA
1. E. Hutto, D
2. D. Fuqua, D
3. C. E. Bennett, D
4. W. V. Chappell, Jr., D
5. *B. McCollum, R
6. C. W. Young, R
7. S. M. Gibbons, D
8. A. P. Ireland, D
9. B. Nelson, D
10. L. A. Bafalis, R
11. D. Mica, D
12. *C. Shaw, R
13. W. Lehman, D
14. C. D. Pepper, D
15. D. B. Fascell, D

GEORGIA
1. R. B. Ginn, D
2. *C. Hatcher, D
3. J. Brinkley, D
4. E. H. Levitas, D
5. W. F. Fowler, Jr., D
6. N. Gingrich, R
7. L. P. McDonald, D
8. B. L. Evans, D
9. E. L. Jenkins, D
10. D. D. Barnard, Jr., D

HAWAII
1. C. Heftel, D
2. D. K. Akaka, D

IDAHO
1. *L. Craig, R
2. G. V. Hansen, R

ILLINOIS
1. *H. Washington, D
2. *G. Savage, D
3. M. A. Russo, D
4. E. J. Derwinski, R
5. J. G. Fary, D
6. H. J. Hyde, R
7. C. Collins, D
8. D. Rostenkowski, D
9. S. R. Yates, D
10. *J. Porter, R
11. F. Annunzio, D
12. P. M. Crane, R
13. R. McClory, R

14. J. N. Erlenborn, R
15. T. J. Corcoran, R
16. *L. Martin, R
17. G. M. O'Brien, R
18. R. H. Michel, R
19. T. Railsback, R
20. P. Findley, R
21. E. R. Madigan, R
22. D. Crane, R
23. C. M. Price, D
24. P. Simon, D

INDIANA
1. A. Benjamin, Jr., D
2. F. J. Fithian, D
3. *J. Hiler, R
4. *D. Coats, R
5. E. H. Hillis, R
6. D. W. Evans, D
7. J. T. Myers, R
8. H. Deckard, R
9. L. H. Hamilton, D
10. P. R. Sharp, D
11. A. Jacobs, Jr., D

IOWA
1. J. A. S. Leach, R
2. T. Tauke, R
3. *C. Evans, R
4. N. Smith, D
5. T. R. Harkin, D
6. B. W. Bedell, D

KANSAS
1. *P. Roberts, R
2. J. Jeffries, R
3. L. Winn, Jr., R
4. D. Glickman, D
5. R. Whittaker, R

KENTUCKY
1. C. Hubbard, Jr., D
2. W. H. Natcher, D
3. R. L. Mazzoli, D
4. G. Snyder, R
5. *H. Rogers, R
6. L. Hopkins, R
7. C. D. Perkins, D

LOUISIANA
1. R. L. Livingston, Jr., R
2. C. C. Boggs, D
3. W. J. Tauzin, D
4. *C. Roemer, D
5. J. Huckaby, D
6. W. H. Moore, R
7. J. B. Breaux, D
8. G. W. Long, D

MAINE
1. D. F. Emery, R
2. O. Snowe, R

MARYLAND
1. *R. Dyson, D
2. C. D. Long, D
3. B. A. Mikulski, D
4. M. S. Holt, R
5. G. N. Spellman, D
6. B. Byron, D
7. P. J. Mitchell, D
8. M. Barnes, D

MASSACHUSETTS
1. S. O. Conte, R
2. E. P. Boland, D
3. J. D. Early, D
4. *B. Frank, D
5. J. Shannon, D
6. N. Mavroules, D
7. E. J. Markey, D
8. T. P. O'Neill, Jr., D
9. J. J. Moakley, D
10. M. M. Heckler, R
11. B. Donnelly, D
12. G. E. Studds, D

MICHIGAN
1. J. Conyers, Jr., D
2. C. D. Pursell, R
3. H. Wolpe, D
4. Vacant
5. H. S. Sawyer, R
6. *J. Dunn, R
7. D. E. Kildee, D
8. B. Traxler, D
9. G. A. Vander Jagt, R
10. D. Albosta, D
11. R. Davis, R
12. D. E. Bonior, D

13. *G. Crockett, D
14. *D. Hertel, D
15. W. D. Ford, D
16. J. D. Dingell, D
17. W. M. Brodhead, D
18. J. J. Blanchard, D
19. W. S. Broomfield, R

MINNESOTA
1. A. Erdahl, R
2. T. M. Hagedorn, R
3. B. Frenzel, R
4. B. F. Vento, D
5. M. Sabo, D
6. *V. Weber, R
7. A. Stangeland, R
8. J. L. Oberstar, D

MISSISSIPPI
1. J. L. Whitten, D
2. D. R. Bowen, D
3. G. V. Montgomery, D
4. J. Hinson, R
5. T. Lott, R

MISSOURI
1. W. L. Clay, D
2. R. A. Young, D
3. R. A. Gephardt, D
4. I. Skelton, D
5. R. Bolling, D
6. E. T. Coleman, R
7. G. Taylor, R
8. *W. Bailey, R
9. H. L. Volkmer, D
10. *B. Emerson, R

MONTANA
1. P. Williams, D
2. R. Marlenee, R

NEBRASKA
1. D. Bereuter, R
2. *H. Daub, R
3. V. Smith, R

NEVADA
At-L. J. D. Santini, D

NEW HAMPSHIRE
1. N. E. D'Amours, D
2. *J. Gregg, R

NEW JERSEY
1. J. J. Florio, D
2. W. J. Hughes, D
3. J. J. Howard, D
4. *C. Smith, R
5. M. Fenwick, R
6. E. B. Forsythe, R
7. *M. Roukema, R
8. R. A. Roe, D
9. H. C. Hollenbeck, R
10. P. W. Rodino, Jr., D
11. J. G. Minish, D
12. M. J. Rinaldo, R
13. J. Courter, R
14. F. Guarini, D
15. *B. Dwyer, D

NEW MEXICO
1. M. Lujan, Jr., R
2. *J. Skeen, R

NEW YORK
1. W. Carney, R
2. T. J. Downey, D
3. *G. Carman, R
4. N. F. Lent, R
5. *R. McGrath, R
6. *J. LeBoutillier, R
7. J. P. Addabbo, D
8. B. S. Rosenthal, D
9. G. Ferraro, D
10. M. Biaggi, D
11. J. H. Scheuer, D
12. S. A. Chisholm, D
13. S. J. Solarz, D
14. F. W. Richmond, D
15. L. C. Zeferetti, D
16. *C. Schumer, D
17. *G. Molinari, R
18. S. W. Green, R
19. C. B. Rangel, D
20. T. Weiss, D
21. R. Garcia, D
22. J.B. Bingham, D
23. P. Peyser, D
24. R. L. Ottinger, D
25. H. Fish, Jr., R
26. B. A. Gilman, R
27. M. F. McHugh, D

28. S. S. Stratton, D
29. G. Solomon, R
30. *D. Martin, R
31. D. J. Mitchell, R
32. *G. Wortley, R
33. G. Lee, R
34. F. Horton, R
35. B. B. Conable, Jr., R
36. J. J. LaFalce, D
37. H. J. Nowak, D
38. J. Kemp, R
39. S. N. Lundine, D

NORTH CAROLINA
1. W. B. Jones, D
2. L. H. Fountain, D
3. C. O. Whitley, Sr., D
4. I. F. Andrews, D
5. S. L. Neal, D
6. *E. Johnston, R
7. C. Rose, D
8. W. G. Hefner, D
9. J. G. Martin, R
10. J. T. Broyhill, R
11. *B. Hendon, R

NORTH DAKOTA
At-L. *B. Dorgan, D

OHIO
1. W. D. Gradison, Jr., R
2. T. A. Luken, D
3. T. Hall, D
4. T. Guyer, R
5. D. L. Latta, R
6. *B. McEwen, R
7. C. J. Brown, R
8. T. N. Kindness, R
9. *E. Weber, R
10. C. E. Miller, R
11. J. W. Stanton, R
12. *B. Shamansky, D
13. D. J. Pease, D
14. J. F. Seiberling, D
15. C. P. Wylie, R
16. R. Regula, R
17. J. M. Ashbrook, R
18. D. Applegate, D
19. L. Williams, R
20. M. R. Oakar, D
21. L. Stokes, D
22. *D. Echart, D
23. R. M. Mottl, D

OKLAHOMA
1. J. R. Jones, D
2. M. Synar, D
3. W. W. Watkins, D
4. *D. McCurdy, D
5. M. Edwards, R
6. G. English, D

OREGON
1. L. AuCoin, D
2. *D. Smith, R
3. *R. Wyden, D
4. J. Weaver, D

PENNSYLVANIA
1. *T. Foglietta, I
2. W. Gray, D
3. R. F. Lederer, D
4. C. Dougherty, R
5. R. T. Schulze, R
6. G. Yatron, D
7. R. W. Edgar, D
8. *J. Coyne, R
9. B. Shuster, R
10. J. M. McDade, R
11. *J. Nelligan, R
12. J. P. Murtha, D
13. L. Coughlin, R
14. *W. Coyne, D
15. D. Ritter, R
16. R. S. Walker, R
17. A. E. Ertel, D
18. D. Walgren, D
19. W. F. Goodling, R
20. J. M. Gaydos, D
21. D. Bailey, D
22. A. J. Murphy, D
23. W. Clinger, Jr., R
24. M. L. Marks, R
25. E. Atkinson, D

RHODE ISLAND
1. F. J. St Germain, D
2. *C. Schneider, R

SOUTH CAROLINA
1. *T. Hartnett, R
2. F. D. Spence, R

3. B. C. Derrick, Jr., D
4. C. Campbell, Jr., R
5. K. Holland, D
6. *J. Napier, R

SOUTH DAKOTA
1. T. Daschle, D
2. *C. Roberts, R

TENNESSEE
1. J. H. Quillen, R
2. J. J. Duncan, R
3. M. L. Bouquard, D
4. A. Gore, Jr., D
5. W. H. Boner, D
6. R. L. Beard, Jr., R
7. E. Jones, D
8. H. Ford, D

TEXAS
1. S. B. Hall, Jr., D
2. C. Wilson, D
3. J. M. Collins, R
4. *R. Hall, D
5. J. A. Mattox, D
6. P. Gramm, D
7. B. Archer, R
8. *J. Fields, R
9. J. Brooks, D
10. J. J. Pickle, D
11. J. M. Leath, D
12. J. C. Wright, Jr., D
13. J. E. Hightower, D
14. *W. Patman, D
15. E. de la Garza, D
16. R. C. White, D
17. C. Stenholm, D
18. M. Leland, D
19. K. Hance, D
20. H. B. Gonzalez, D
21. T. Loeffler, R
22. R. Paul, R
23. A. Kazen, Jr., D
24. M. Frost, D

UTAH
1. *J. Hansen, R
2. D. D. Marriott, R

VERMONT
At.-L. J. M. Jeffords, R

VIRGINIA
1. P. S. Trible, Jr., R
2. G. W. Whitehurst, R
3. *T. Bliley, R
4. R. W. Daniel, Jr., R
5. D. Daniel, D
6. M. C. Butler, R
7. J. K. Robinson, R
8. *S. Parris, R
9. W. C. Wampler, R
10. *F. Wolf, R

WASHINGTON
1. J. M. Pritchard, R
2. A. Swift, D
3. D. L. Bonker, R
4. *S. Morrison, R
5. T. S. Foley, D
6. N. D. Dicks, D
7. M. Lowry, D

WEST VIRGINIA
1. R. H. Mollohan, D.
2. *C. Benedict, R.
3. *M. Staton, R.
4. N. J. Rahall, D

WISCONSIN
1. L. Aspin, D
2. R. W. Kastenmeier, D
3. *S. Gunderson, R
4. C. J. Zablocki, D
5. H. S. Reuss, D
6. T. E. Petri, R
7. D. R. Obey, D
8. T. Roth, R
9. F. J. Sensenbrenner, Jr., R

WYOMING
At-L. R. Cheney, R

PUERTO RICO
Resident Commissioner
B. Corrada

DISTRICT OF COLUMBIA
Delegate, W. E. Fauntroy, D

AMERICAN SAMOA
Delegate, Fofo Sunia

Major Legislation Enacted During Second Session of 96th Congress

SUBJECT	PURPOSE
Refugees	See page 457. Signed March 17. Public Law 96-212.
Banking	See page 144. Signed March 31. Public Law 96-221.
Oil Windfall Profits Tax	See page 219. Signed April 2. Public Law 96-223.
Federal Trade Commission	See page 554. Signed May 28. Public Law 96-252.
Adoption Assistance	Reforms the federal children's foster care program, and reinforces the child welfare services program. Signed June 17. Public Law 96-272.
Military Draft	Authorizes the military-draft registration of some 4 million men aged 19–20. Signed June 27. Public Law 96-282.
Synthetic Fuels	See page 218. Signed June 30. Public Law 96-294.
Trucking Industry	See page 532. Signed July 1. Public Law 96-296.
Olympic Team	Authorizes the presentation of a special medal to members of the 1980 U.S. Summer Olympic team. Signed July 8. Public Law 96-306.
Central Idaho Wilderness	Adds more than 2.3 million acres (931,500 ha) to the national wilderness system and designates 125 miles (200 km) of the Salmon River in Idaho as a wild and scenic river. Signed July 23. Public Law 96-312.
Wildlife	Establishes a program to manage non-game animals or those that were hunted for sport, food, fur, or pelt. Signed September 29. Public Law 96-366.
Mental Health	See page 352. Signed October 7. Public Law 96-398.
Housing	See page 270. Signed October 8. Public Law 96-399.
National Historic Sites	Establishes the Martin Luther King, Junior, National Historic Site in Atlanta, GA, and a Boston African American National Historic Site. Signed October 10. Public Laws 96-428 and 96-430.
Privacy Protection	Establishes safeguards to protect a free press and protects the first amendment activities of authors and scholars. Signed October 14. Public Law 96-440.
Railroad Deregulation	See page 532. Signed October 14. Public Law 96-448.
Household Moving	Reduces federal regulation of and improves consumer protection in the household moving industry. Signed October 15. Public Law 96-454.
Judicial Behavior	Outlines procedures for disciplining federal judges for misconduct. Signed October 15. Public Law 96-458.
Foreign Service	Revises the personnel legislation for the U.S. Foreign Service. Signed October 17. Public Law 96-465.
Veterans Education	Provides a 10% cost-of-living increase for veterans receiving GI Bill education assistance and a 17% living allowance for disabled veterans enrolled in vocational rehabilitation programs. Signed October 17. Public Law 96-466.
Alaska Lands	Designates more than 105 million acres (42.5 million ha) of Alaska lands as national parks, wildlife refuges, and wilderness areas. Signed December 2. Public Law 96-487.
Recreation	Promotes good health and public safety in skiing and other outdoor winter recreational activities. Signed December 1. Public Law 96-489.
Agriculture	Establishes a reserve of food grain to be held by the U.S. government to help alleviate world hunger. Signed December 3. Public law 96-494.
Budget	Reduces through reconciliation the 1981 federal budget deficit by more than $8,200,-000,000. Signed December 5. Public Law 96-499.
Juvenile Justice	Continues for four years the Juvenile Justice and Delinquency Prevention Act and the Runaway and Homeless Youth Act. Signed December 8. Public Law 96-509.
Paperwork Reduction	Creates within the Office of Management and Budget an office to oversee federal agencies' requests for information from the public. Signed December 11. Public Law 96-511.
Historic Preservation	Seeks to clarify the responsibilities of all federal agencies with respect to historic preservation, and gives local governments a role in the effort. Signed December 12. Public Law 96-515.
Foreign Service	Provides for the settlement and payment of claims of U.S. civilians and military personnel against the United States for losses resulting from acts of violence directed against the U.S. government or its representatives in a foreign nation. Signed December 12. Public Law 96-519.

THE ECONOMY

The economy was on everyone's mind throughout 1980. How could it have been otherwise, when consumer prices rose steadily all year long, when interest rates scaled heights not seen before in the 20th century, when debts and taxes worked their way relentlessly higher, when the means of paying the rent or mortgage or heating bills came right out of the vacation money?

Repeated frustrations with the family budget, and the White House budget too, seemed at times to depress spirits close to despair, and the phrase "something has to be done" was heard again and again. The tired economy was failing, and despite continued big profits for oil companies and a renewed interest in the stock market, some of the biggest companies in the United States were drowning in red ink.

At times it seemed that the economy was beyond President Carter's ability to deal with, and that impression was underscored by announcements of at least four separate revitalization plans during his term, the final one just two months before the November 4 elections. Taking matters into their own hands, voters concluded that President Jimmy Carter, despite his repeated promises and new beginnings, was not doing that something. They voted him out of office in a manner reminiscent of the defeat 48 years before of President Herbert Hoover.

And so too, it was said, the Keynesian economic era, which dated from the Great Depression of the 1930s and which placed great reliance on spurring demand, had come to a close. Replacing it would be "supply side" economics, in which taxing and other policies would seek instead to stimulate saving and investment, to make the nation's production facilities—the supply side of the supply-demand equation—more efficient and less inflationary. Most people called the new challenge "reindustrialization," a word generally attributed to Professor Amitai Etzioni. They applied to it their own versions of what needed to be done, but generally they agreed that after four decades of seeking to fulfill consumer demands the production machinery was burned out and needed to be rebuilt. And that if productivity was not raised, inflation would remain a constant threat.

Inflation, the U.S. Budget, Interest Rates. There was much reason to fear. In the first month of the year the consumer price index spurted 1.4%, or at an annual rate of about 17%, the sharpest one-month rise since August 1973, and it continued at that rate before declining slightly in April. The tendency of some Carter administration officials was to blame the situation on high oil prices, but that excuse no longer was acceptable to an increasingly large segment of the people. January's underlying rate of inflation, which excluded such volatile prices as those of energy, housing, food, and mortgage interest, rose to an annual rate of 10%, compared with 8.6% in the preceding quarter, and 7.9% in the third quarter of 1979.

Business blamed government spending more than rising oil prices. As the year began, the

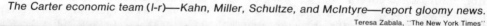

The Carter economic team (l-r)—Kahn, Miller, Schultze, and McIntyre—report gloomy news.

Teresa Zabala, "The New York Times"

president's initial estimate of spending was $532,000,000,000, which would have produced a budget deficit of about $30,000,000,000. He was far off the mark. When the fiscal year ended on September 30 the deficit was $59,000,000,000, the second largest (after President Ford in 1976), on record. Carter's estimate of spending was $47,000,000,000 too little; the final total was $579,000,000,000, and that did not include many billions for "off-budget" items such as rural electrification and railroad improvement projects. "On-budget" spending rose to 23% of gross national product in 1980 from 21.3% a year earlier. And for fiscal 1981, when spending was expected to reach at least $636,000,000,000, and the budget deficit at least $30,000,000,000, government spending would almost certainly consume an even larger share of the national product.

Business productivity, meanwhile, continued to fall, meaning products were being produced less efficiently and at great cost, adding inexorably to the nation's inflation problem. But despite the cost of goods and money, demand remained high.

Reflecting that strong demand, as well as a shortage of lendable funds, interest rates continued to move higher. By February, the prime rate to the best corporate borrowers edged close to 16%, and reached 20% in April. Henry Kaufman, whose comments on the financial markets attracted a growing audience, declared that the nation was nearing "a national economic emergency" that would require "substantial risks and pain to avert." The credit-wise partner in the investment firm of Salomon Brothers said demand, from business and government, was too great for the limited supply of lendable funds. Paul Volcker, chairman of the Federal Reserve Board, grew increasingly unhappy, and he called for less government spending to reduce the burden of demand. Some Congressional Democrats spoke of wage-price controls, a notion that Charles Schultze, chairman of the Council of Economic Advisers, rejected as "neither a quick nor a sure way to reduce inflation." The underlying problem, he said, was declining productivity, or output per man-hour. It was a problem for which there was no quick solution, especially with unemployment already around 7.5%. If the jobless rate were lower, some short-term productivity improvement might be expected from layoffs. But those already had occurred.

Downturn. While the nation battled with high prices, high interest rates, unemployment, and lagging productivity, fears also grew about "the long-delayed recession." Some prominent economists persistently had forecast a downturn for almost a year, and still it had not come. It finally did, in the second quarter, and by some measures it was sudden enough to be called a collapse, a word that until now many commentators had avoided using because of its association with the vast economic debacle of a half-century earlier. It followed the imposition in March of credit restraints, primarily on consumer borrowing. By May 22 the economic shock was so great that the Fed, the nation's central bank, sought to ease the restraints, and on July 3 it abandoned the program altogether. When the second quarter statistics arrived they were received with disbelief; the nation's output of goods and services had slid at an annual rate of 9.6% for the three months of April, May, and June, the steepest quarterly production decline on record. It was as if a train had braked.

While some government officials and economists defended the combined White House-Federal Reserve credit restraints, many retailers and scholars criticized them as having dealt with symptoms rather than causes. The biggest criticism of all, however, came from the consumer price index, which remained at an annual rate of about 12% through June. The collapse had helped little or not at all to lower prices.

By this time, two of the biggest industries in America, housing and automobiles, were in deep trouble from rising fuel prices and high interest rates—and in the case of cars, from foreign competition. They would remain in trouble throughout the year.

Housing and Autos. Volatile, unpredictable interest rates were probably the chief villain. After declining to 10.75% from a record-setting 20% in April, the prime resumed climbing late in the year, and by late December it hit 21.5%. Housing was devastated. Potential buyers withdrew from the market because they could not qualify for loans, and those who could qualify at the higher rates decided they could not afford them. Housing starts fell to an annual rate of less than 1 million units as the year ended, compared with an estimated 2 million starts a year if shelter were to be provided for a record 42 million Americans who would reach age 30 in the 1980s. Even so, prices fell only slightly late in the year, and in some areas they continued to rise almost without interruption.

For those who already owned houses, the price increases became the source of equity loans for education, travel, or just paying the bills. In fact, said some, the house was a bank; the swift appreciation in values provided as much warmth and security as the fireplace. Robert Parry, president of the National Association of Business Economists, commented that he really wondered if Americans wanted inflation to end. "When you go to a cocktail party," he said, "the first thing people say to you is 'Isn't this inflation terrible?' And the second thing is 'Do you know how much the value of my house has gone up in the past year?'" If you wanted to dishevel the suburban *élégantes* at such a party you needed only to bring up the subject of "the coming collapse of real estate prices." That possibility, though undocumented, struck fear into the hearts of the "house rich."

The biggest change was the beginning of the end for the standard, fixed-rate, long-term home mortgage, in which a buyer could obtain possession of a house for just 10% down and an agreement to pay regular monthly installments for the next 20 or 30 years. It had been a standby since the 1930s, helping push homeownership in America to more than 65% of households. But with rates so erratic, lenders declared they were unable to commit funds for 20 years into the future. They suggested various other mortgages, but the most popular were the variable rate mortgage and the renegotiable, rollover mortgage. Though different in many respects, they shared a common component: Interest rates would rise or fall, to some extent at least, with changes in the overall cost of money. Gone was the security of knowing what your monthly mortgage costs would be for a score or more years. After nearly five decades, the standard or conventional mortgage seemed gone for good. Commentators said the person who held an 8 or 9%, fixed-rate mortgage with 15 or 20 years to maturity, while the nation's biggest corporations paid 21% for their money, was among the luckiest people on earth.

Little luck could be discerned in the automotive industry, once the nation's strongest. As always, automakers began the model year with high hopes, but reality dashed them. The industry's new, trimmer, more fuel-efficient cars did not sell nearly so well as expected, and imports continued to account for a quarter of domestic sales. Between July 1 and September 30 no less than 504 automobile dealers went out of business, bringing to a record-high 1,643 the number who closed their doors during the 1980 model year. Their misery was matched at Detroit headquarters. In the first nine months of the year, General Motors, Ford, and Chrysler suffered a combined loss of $3,500,000,000, a debacle never equaled in the annals of U.S. industry. For GM it made certain the first annual deficit in nearly 60 years. For Ford the losses resurrected worries that it might have to join Chrysler in seeking federal aid.

Chrysler was barely afloat, and only because the federal government had propped it up with $1,500,000,000 in loan guarantees. All through the year Chairman Lee Iacocca was a presence on radio and television and in newspapers, appearing optimistic, aggressive, and even tough. The words varied, the message did not: "Does Chrysler have a future? You bet it does." Its future would be a new line of cars for which he forecast an enthusiastic reception that would give the company a fourth-quarter profit. Neither came. What came instead were higher interest rates that destroyed sales. A discouraged Iacocca called the nation's monetary policy "madness," closed some plants and laid off workers, and sought a wage freeze from workers and a price freeze from suppliers.

Positive Signs. At times, and in places, and depending sometimes upon your point of view, there were things to cheer about in 1980.

Though it remained in deficit, the U.S. trade balance improved through much of the year. Commerce Department officials said the total deficit might be only $2,000,000,000, down from $37,290,000,000 in 1979 and a record $39,560,-000,000 in 1978. It was a surprising achievement, especially since the oil import bill soared. In the first ten months of the year it came to $65,080,-000,000, $17,000,000,000 more than in the same period of 1979, and it would have caused the deficit to rise sharply had exports not been so strong.

The dollar held its own against major European currencies, but whether that was considered good news or bad was a matter of perspective. Almost all analysts attributed its strength not to belief in the future of the American economy but to the attraction of the extraordinarily higher interest rates.

The stock market went through the gyrations that had become common in recent years, but it also showed pockets of strength late in the year. Merrill Lynch Pierce Fenner and Smith noted that from their early spring lows to mid-August the Dow Jones Industrial Average moved up 27% or 200 points to more than 900; the Standard & Poor's 500 gained 34%; and the Value Line Index, a very broad measure of many stocks, jumped 47%. It observed that hundreds of issues more than doubled in price in a year.

Commodities, too, rose through much of the year—and then collapsed in a heap on December 11. Said Nelson Chang, commodity research director of Shearson Loeb Rhoades Inc.: "It's the biggest decline, I believe, in the history of commodities trading." Many prices rose again the next day, but even after that the price of sugar was 32% lower than its high of just three weeks before, followed by silver with a loss of 30%, soybeans, 23%, and gold, the wonder metal that magnetized so many people earlier in the year, 15%.

On the same day prices plunged on the bond market, with some declines reaching 3 points, or $30 on the face amount of $1,000. Those who had the guts to buy bonds found themselves able to obtain 13% on some U.S. government issues and 15% on top-rated corporate bonds. But when interest rates rise, the market value of bonds declines. "It really is awful. People are very, very nervous," said Edwin Kantor, a top executive with Drexel Burnham Lambert Inc. Prices recovered considerably before the end of the year, but the nervousness remained.

As the year ended even the president-elect, Ronald Reagan, was said to be considering scrapping some of his earlier economic plans because an emergency existed. It was a situation that ordinary Americans understood well because, with inflation averaging better than 12% a year, they had seen the buying power of their paychecks shrink relentlessly.

See also STOCKS AND BONDS.

JOHN CUNNIFF, *The Associated Press*

FOREIGN AFFAIRS

The United States achieved few successes in foreign affairs, faced a series of challenges, suffered a number of setbacks, and committed several blunders in 1980. Shifts in policy concerned the Persian Gulf and Indian Ocean, and foreign affairs became a major issue in the presidential campaign.

General Policy. In his State of the Union message to Congress in January, President Jimmy Carter focused on "the most important challenges facing our country" abroad. He stressed five traditional goals: building military strength; resolving disputes peacefully; preventing the spread of nuclear weapons; solving international economic problems; and promoting democratic institutions and protecting human rights, including ratification of five pending human rights conventions.

The president also emphasized future action. "Prosperity, progress, and . . . peace," he said, "cannot be had by standing still" and the need for the United States is "to assert a leading role in a world undergoing the most extensive and intensive change in history." He cautioned that the challenges of this decade will test "our toughness and willingness to sacrifice for larger goals, our courage, and our vision," and he sounded his battle cry for the 1980s: "We must rise above our narrow interests" and forge "a new national consensus and sense of purpose."

Referring in his accompanying State of the Union address to "the abhorrent acts" in Iran and Afghanistan, he warned: "The United States will not yield to blackmail." He then proclaimed what came to be called the Carter Doctrine: "An attempt by any outside force to gain control of the Persian Gulf region will be regarded as an assault on the vital interests of the United States . . . and will be repelled by any means necessary, including military force."

American Malaise. The new sense of national purpose failed to materialize. Instead, the United States was constantly on the defensive: the Iranian hostage and Afghan crises festered; the attempted rescue of the hostages in Tehran failed; Secretary of State Cyrus Vance resigned abruptly; terrorist attacks on diplomatic missions were repeated in Latin America; the Arab-Israeli settlement stalemated; several thousand Soviet troops remained in Cuba; and the Vietnamese invasion of Cambodia and its threat to Thailand continued.

In addition, the price of imported oil mounted; the value of the dollar slipped while the price of gold reached record highs; authoritarianism and leftism continued to spread; two false nuclear alerts of Soviet ICBM launchings were sounded; and the government publicly acknowledged that it voted contrary to its intent on a resolution condemning Israel in the UN Security Council. U.S. credibility in foreign affairs was questioned, and the American people manifested their mounting anxiety at the polls in November.

Conduct of Foreign Affairs. The family of nations increased to 165 when Zimbabwe (Rhode-

U.S. diplomatic affairs were in the hands of Cyrus Vance (left) and Edmund Muskie in 1980. The Persian Gulf, the hostage crisis in Iran, and the Soviet invasion of Afghanistan were of special concern.

Photos UPI

sia) gained independence in April and Vanuatu (New Hebrides) followed in July; Syria and Libya announced a merger in September. The United States maintained 265 diplomatic and consular missions in 1980—151 diplomatic agencies and 114 consular establishments. Because of widespread attacks on diplomats, the Department of State increased the security force of its missions in 15 troubled areas.

President Carter signed an executive order in January to reorganize U.S. international trade machinery. A special trade representative for policymaking was appointed, while implementation was turned over to an expanded Commerce Department. The president also pressed Congress for a new "charter" to define the legal status of intelligence agencies. Secretary of State Cyrus Vance resigned on April 28, and Sen. Edmund Muskie was sworn in May 8 to replace him. (*See also* BIOGRAPHY.) In July, when the Justice Department investigated unauthorized disclosure of classified national security information, the president requested his senior aides to sign sworn statements of innocence.

On Jan. 1, 1980, the United States was a party to 7,142 treaties and agreements, and more than 400 new accords were signed during the year. The government participated in nearly 1,000 international conferences and meetings, including two sessions of the Law of the Sea Conference and the Madrid conference on security in Europe. In February the United States rejoined the International Labor Organization.

Some 16 summit visits were made to Washington during the year. President Carter went abroad twice—to attend a memorial service for Prime Minister Masayoshi Ohira of Japan and to undertake an eight-day, five-nation visit to Europe and attend the Venice Western summit meeting. In Venice the powers condemned the Iranian seizure of American hostages and Soviet aggression in Afghanistan, and pledged reduction of the use of imported oil by 15 million to 20 million barrels per day by 1990. Vice-President Walter Mondale went abroad twice—to attend the funeral of Yugoslavia's President Tito and to visit four African countries—and the secretaries of state ventured abroad four times. (Vance went to Canada and major European capitals, and Muskie traveled to two NATO meetings).

Western Hemisphere. American policy continued to promote human rights, democratization, economic development, and nonintervention in Latin America. The massive flight of Cuban and Haitian refugees to the United States, political violence and authoritarianism in Central America, and Cuban adventurism in the Caribbean constituted major challenges to the United States during 1980. (*See also* CUBA; CENTRAL AMERICA; REFUGEES.)

In February militant leftists assaulted the Spanish embassy in El Salvador and Colombian terrorists seized more than 60 hostages at a Dominican embassy reception in Bogota, including U.S. Ambassador Diego C. Asencio, who was released two months later. In both cases the terrorists demanded the freeing of leftist political prisoners. When armed forces assumed control in Bolivia in July to prevent a "Communist assault" and established a military junta, the United States suspended its military and economic aid and reduced its embassy staff.

Movement toward leftism and authoritarianism mounted in Central America. Only Honduras and Costa Rica remained free of Castro-backed insurgencies. In Nicaragua, the Sandinistas ruled through their revolutionary junta and the United States became their principal foreign financial supporter. The economy of El Salvador deteriorated, in part because of leftist guerrilla violence; its government came under siege, and an army coup instituted a military junta in October. As the government sought to restrain a leftist insurgency in Guatemala, the United States criticized its human rights record and cut military and economic aid.

The Middle East. The major problems confronting the United States in the Middle East included the American hostage crisis with Iran, the Iraqi-Iranian war, the Soviet threat to the Persian Gulf, and the negotiation of an Arab-Israeli settlement. (*See* feature articles, pages 28–46.)

During the hostage crisis, it took months for the Iranian revolutionary governmental system to stabilize, and direct, genuine negotiations proved to be impossible during most of the year. The United States instituted diplomatic and economic sanctions and succeeded in diplomatically isolating Iran but failed in its forceful attempt to rescue the hostages in April. Only in November, a year after their seizure, did the Iranian parliament lay down specific conditions for the hostages' release.

The Soviet invasion of Afghanistan, viewed by the United States as a threat to Iran and the Persian Gulf, resulted in the promulgation of the Carter Doctrine. The outbreak of the Iraqi-Iranian war complicated Mideast geopolitical stability and, although the United States opposed the Iraqi aggression, it had little alternative but to remain neutral.

The Egyptian-Israeli settlement proceeded, with the withdrawal of Israel's forces from the Sinai and the return of the area to Egypt, the opening of their mutual border, the formal exchange of ambassadors, and the inauguration of commercial aviation. Although President Anwar el-Sadat and Menahem Begin agreed in April to maximize their efforts to reach agreement on Palestinian autonomy by May 26, little progress was made.

President Carter declared that the United States would not recognize the Palestine Liberation Organization (PLO) until after the latter "recognizes Israel's right to exist," and Israel refused to negotiate with the PLO. Negotiations also were hindered by Israel's establishment of new settlements in the West Bank, the expropria-

Jimmy Carter visited Italy during an eight-day, five-nation visit to Europe. At left, accompanied by Sandro Pertini, Italy's head of state, the U.S. president inspects the honor guard in Rome.

tion of Arab-owned lands, the annexation of East Jerusalem, and the Israeli determination to make united Jerusalem the Israeli capital. The United States opposed Israel's decisions on Jerusalem; the UN General Assembly called again for the creation of an independent Palestinian state; and the Security Council condemned Israel for its actions in the West Bank and Jerusalem.

Asia and the Pacific. The president called the Soviet invasion of Afghanistan "the most serious threat to the peace since the Second World War," and declared that the USSR "must pay a concrete price" for its aggression. In addition to suspending ratification of SALT II, he imposed sanctions and strengthened the American posture in the Indian Ocean area.

The United States recalled Ambassador Thomas J. Watson from Moscow and suspended the opening of new consulates in Kiev and New York City. Economic sanctions consisted of refusing permits for Soviet fishing in American waters, cutting Soviet access to high technology equipment and agricultural products, and limiting other commerce with the Soviet Union. The United States also called for a boycott of the Moscow Summer Olympics.

Responding to the geopolitical challenge of the Soviet invasion, the president enunciated the Carter Doctrine. National Security Adviser Zbigniew Brzezinski indicated that U.S. forces would help defend Pakistan against Soviet attack, and the United States offered Pakistan substantial economic aid. President Carter issued plans to demothball four battleships, ordered additional ships and marines to the Indian Ocean, accelerated the establishment of military facilities in the area (especially in Diego Garcia, Kenya, Oman, and Somalia), and launched a new military draft registration in July. At the end of the year, Soviet forces remained in Afghanistan, but the United States had enlarged its commitments in the Persian Gulf and western Indian Ocean.

In Southeast Asia the Indochina tragedy persisted. Vietnam continued its invasion of Cambodia and threatened Thailand, a U.S. ally. The United States issued direct warnings to the USSR and Vietnam and increased military and economic aid to Thailand. The plight of Cambodia worsened, with thousands falling to warfare and famine, and others taking refuge in Thailand. The United States joined other countries in providing economic assistance and sanctuary to thousands of Southeast Asian refugees.

In January the United States initialed an agreement providing for the limited independence of the Marshall Islands in the western Pacific, while retaining military and security rights in the islands. The Immigration and Naturalization Service announced in March that residents of the northern Mariana Islands would be regarded as aliens but would be exempt from visa and passport requirements.

Africa. The United States opposed the political violence and human rights violations that flourished in a number of African countries and supported efforts to promote peaceful transition to majority rule in southern Africa. It backed British negotiations among contending groups in Rhodesia and cooperated in attempting to achieve independence and a majority system in Namibia.

As agreement was reached late in 1979 on a cease-fire and a method of autonomous governance in Rhodesia, the United States lifted its economic sanctions. On April 18, 1980, following elections and the creation of a new government, Rhodesia became the independent state of Zimbabwe, with full membership in the British Commonwealth. The United States opened its embassy in Salisbury the same day, signed a foreign aid agreement, and supported Zimbabwe's admission as the 153rd member of the UN.

ELMER PLISCHKE
Adjunct Professor, Gettysburg College

Assistant to the President
National Security Affairs

Under the U.S. system of government the president possesses undivided executive authority, but to function effectively he needs readily available, high-level advisers and assistants who are able to function cooperatively as his integrated inner team. In matters of foreign affairs, the assistant to the president for national security affairs is central to the process.

Development of the Office. When the National Security Council (NSC) was established in 1947, President Harry S Truman named Sidney W. Souers (later succeeded by James S. Lay, Jr.) executive secretary of the council staff of the NSC system. In 1950 he also appointed Averell Harriman his special assistant for foreign relations.

The NSC system was formally institutionalized by President Dwight D. Eisenhower. He distinguished between foreign-policy planning and operations and appointed two assistants. Operations came under Paul T. Carroll and later Andrew J. Goodpaster, staff aides to brief the president and manage the implementation of NSC determinations. Robert Cutler was named special assistant for national security affairs to oversee NSC policy planning.

President John F. Kennedy eliminated the distinction between planning and operations and appointed McGeorge Bundy to head a small staff of independent experts, with direct access to sources of information and increased foreign relations responsibility. Bundy served the president directly rather than the NSC, paving the way for conflict with the secretary of state. In 1966 President Lyndon B. Johnson selected Walt W. Rostow to succeed Bundy. Johnson relied more on his operational officers for policy planning. He also introduced the informal "Tuesday Lunch"—consisting of the president, the secretaries of state and defense, and the special assistant—to deal primarily with the Vietnam war.

At the start of the Nixon administration, Henry Kissinger was appointed assistant to the president for national security affairs. Kissinger converted the office into a major foreign relations power center. His position encompassed the roles of Eisenhower's special assistants—servicing a structured policy-planning process—and those of Bundy and Rostow—managing the day-to-day policy process—as well as that of the president's personal, sometimes secret, envoy. Supported by a large staff (more than 50 professionals), Kissinger emerged as the architect of foreign-relations strategy. In 1973 Kissinger also became secretary of state. Under Gerald Ford, Kissinger continued as secretary of state, but in 1975 NSC deputy Brent Scowcroft succeeded him as presidential assistant.

President-elect Jimmy Carter appointed Zbigniew Brzezinski presidential assistant for national security affairs. Initially, Carter assumed great control over the immediate management of foreign relations. Brzezinski sought to emulate Kissinger as strategist and spokesman. Conflict between him and Secretary of State Cyrus Vance arose over access to the president, information flow, and especially over policy guidance and promulgation. Differences involved not only policy substance, but also the manner in which decisions were made. In April 1980, Vance resigned, ostensibly over the White House decision to attempt the forceful rescue of the American hostages in Tehran.

Functions. The principal functions of the presidential assistant include: (1) identifying issues requiring presidential attention; (2) coordinating the flow of information and intelligence reports to the president; (3) providing independent advice and staff analysis concerning policy options; (4) facilitating liaison with cabinet officers and other high officials on foreign-policy making and implementation; (5) aiding presidential participation in the NSC process by preparing agendas, briefing the president, supervising the flow of recommendations and decision papers, and managing the substructure of the system; (6) communicating presidential decisions and instructions to executive agencies; and (7) monitoring governmental operations to promote coordination and responsiveness to presidential interests and determinations.

The presidential assistant is a staff aide to the chief executive but, unlike other executive officers, his relationship is more immediate and direct. He is not an operational officer. His functions are primarily advisory (for policy planning) and managerial (for the NSC system). He is not the official policy spokesman, nor is he the principal decision-maker.

Problems and Difficulties. The presidential assistant possesses a limited, though central policy role at a high level, the breadth of which depends on the operating style of the president and the interrelations of the White House with the secretaries of state and defense. If the president permits his assistant to create his own White House State Department, he is courting difficulty. When both the presidential assistant and the secretary of state are forceful individuals, build opposing centers of bureaucratic power, acquire high visibility, and compete for presidential attention, conflict is inevitable. For an administration to be effective, the president must balance authority and influence between both offices.

ELMER PLISCHKE

URUGUAY

In 1980, the military regime in power in Uruguay since 1973 took its first serious steps toward a return to constitutional government. Meanwhile, activity of the country's illegal but still functioning political parties was intensified.

Government and Politics. On June 10, the military-controlled government of figurehead President Aparicio Méndez Manfredini announced plans for a constitutional plebiscite on November 30 and for general elections on Nov. 29, 1981. In the latter, one presidential candidate would be agreed upon by all the parties. The regime also indicated, however, that if the proposed new constitution were rejected, plans for a return to elected government would be postponed indefinitely.

The proposed constitution, published on November 2, would give the military a permanent share of power. The military would be allowed to appoint a nine-member tribunal with the power to remove government and party officials for "ethical, moral, or civic reasons." Freedom of expression would be limited to what is deemed "true, objective, and well-founded"; Marxist and certain other political parties would be outlawed; and congressional authority to restore powers taken away during national emergencies would be limited.

Jorge Batlle Ibáñez of the traditional Colorado Party and leaders of other political groups denounced the proposal. Batlle insisted that the parties be given full freedom immediately. He added that if they were not allowed to function freely, he would urge the public to vote "no" in the plebiscite. Batlle and several colleagues were arrested several times in the weeks preceding the vote.

The proposed return to constitutional government also included a new law regarding the status of political parties, issued in late September. The law provided that all parties except the traditional major ones, the Colorado Party and the National Party, would have to show a membership of at least 2% of eligible Uruguayans in order to obtain legal status. In the first general election, these parties would have to obtain at least .5% of the total vote in order to maintain their legal status. The law also provided that no party could have in its leadership anyone "dedicated to destroying the political structure by violence" and that no party could have ties with a foreign state or organization. Also, the new political parties law did not end the 1976 decree that all politicians who had participated in the 1966 and 1971 elections would lose their civil rights for 15 years.

The November 30 plebiscite, however, resulted in an overwhelming rejection of the regime's proposals. Voting for the first time in seven years, Uruguayans defeated the proposed constitution by a margin of 58% to 42%. At the heart of the opposition was a rejection of the continuing military rule prescribed in the new charter. After the plebiscite, the regime once again prohibited political activity.

The military regime had dealt harshly with its opponents throughout the year. On January 3, the Council on Hemispheric Affairs in Washington denounced the regime for continuing abuses of human rights. In July, a member of the Supreme Military Tribunal announced that the government still was holding 1,272 political prisoners. In September, the government announced that it had broken up the underground organization of the Socialist Party and had arrested its secretary general, José Pedro Cardozo.

ROBERT J. ALEXANDER, *Rutgers University*

UTAH

Ronald Reagan easily carried the state with approximately 72% of the vote to win Utah's four electoral votes. Sen. Jake Garn (R) defeated Democratic challenger Dan Berman by the highest percentage of popular vote gained by a Senate candidate in Utah's history. In the Congressional race in the second district, incumbent Dan Marriott (R) won decisively over Salt Lake County Treasurer Arthur Monson (D). In the first Congressional district, the Republican challenger, James V. Hansen, unseated five-term veteran Gunn McKay (D) in a very close race.

The exception to the national trend was the reelection of Gov. Scott M. Matheson (D). He defeated former Republican chairman Robert Wright in a tight battle. All other state and major county offices went to Republicans. In addition, both the new state Senate and House of Representatives would be under Republican control.

Utah voters rejected two tax initiatives, one for removing the sales tax from food and a California-type property tax limitation.

The MX Missile System. The deployment of an elaborate, expensive mobile missile system (MX) became a major issue in Utah during 1980. This giant missile system, as proposed by the Air Force, called for the deployment of 200 missiles to be secretly shuttled among 4,600 launch shel-

---

URUGUAY • Information Highlights

Official Name: Eastern Republic of Uruguay.
Location: Southeastern coast of South America.
Area: 68,536 sq mi (177 508 km²).
Population (1980 est.): 2,900,000.
Chief City (1975 census): Montevideo, the capital, 1,229,-748.
Government: *Head of state,* Aparicio Méndez Manfredini, president (took office Sept. 1976). *Head of government,* Lt. Gen. Luis Vicente Quevedo, head of the military junta. *Legislature*—General Assembly (suspended June 1973).
Monetary Unit: Peso (9.63 pesos equal U.S.$1, Nov. 1980).
Manufactures (major products): Processed meat, textiles, wools and hides, shoes, handbags and leather wearing apparel, cement, fish, refined petroleum.
Agriculture (major products): Livestock, grains.
GNP (1978 est., U.S.$): $3,700,000,000.
Foreign Trade (1979, U.S.$): *Imports,* $1,206,000,000; *exports,* $788,000,000.

──────── **UTAH · Information Highlights** ────────

Area: 84,916 sq mi (219 932 km^2).
Population (Jan. 1980 est.): 1,394,000.
Chief Cities (1976 est.): Salt Lake City, the capital, 168,-667; (1970 census): Ogden, 69,478; Provo, 53,131.
Government (1980): *Chief Officers*—governor, Scott M. Matheson (D). *Legislature*—Senate, 29 members; House of Representatives, 75 members.
Education (1979–80): *Enrollment*—public elementary schools, 191,641 pupils; public secondary, 141,408; colleges and universities, 90,398 students. *Public school expenditures,* $665,029,000 ($1,518 per pupil).
State Finances (fiscal year 1979): *Revenues,* $1,605,-000,000; *expenditures,* $1,464,000,000.
Personal Income (1979): $9,838,000,000; per capita, $7,197.
Labor Force (June 1980): *Nonagricultural wage and salary earners,* 568,700; *unemployed,* 38,400 (6.2% of total force).

ters across thousands of acres of public land in western Utah and eastern Nevada. The estimated cost of this "racetrack" mode of deployment was between $34,000,000,000 and $50,000,-000,000. U.S. strategists insisted that the MX system was vital to the national interest; it would supplement existing stationary ICBMs which had become vulnerable to a Soviet attack.

The deployment issue became a subject of major debate throughout Utah. At issue were such questions as: (1) was the MX an appropriate weapons system, and would it deter or invite holocaust? (2) could Utah (Nevada) accommodate history's largest public works project? (3) had defense planners considered all possible alternatives? (4) was the danger of fallout a neglected MX issue? and (5) were the actual costs realistically assessed in terms of environmental impact, social disorder, and actual dollar cost? Some analysts concluded that the dollar cost would exceed $100,000,000,000, rather than the Air Force's estimate of $34,000,000,000.

Utah's Gov. Scott Matheson and Nevada's Gov. Robert List appeared before the House Appropriations Subcommittee on Military Construction in April and attacked the administration's deployment proposal as possibly doing considerable harm to both states. They argued that the project would irreparably damage the fragile ecosystem of the entire area and would increase an already severe water shortage. Further, Matheson argued that the influx of construction and maintenance crews would change forever the life in Utah's rural communities.

Although these arguments were rebutted immediately by the Defense Department, by year's end none of the vital questions had been answered to the satisfaction of the people of Utah.

LORENZO K. KIMBALL, *University of Utah*

VANUATU

At midnight on July 30, British and French flags were lowered to mark the end of the Anglo-French Condominium of New Hebrides and the birth of the South Pacific's new nation of Vanuatu. Inauguration of the regime led by

President Ati George Sokomanu and Prime Minister Walter Lini, an Episcopalian minister, began at a minute past midnight with a simple induction ceremony.

The drive for independence began in the late 1970s with the emergence of a "national" political party, Lini's Vanuaaku Pati, which boycotted the Representative Assembly in 1977 after declaring that the assembly's composition favored expatriate groups. The party's uncompromising stand steadily overcame British inertia and French opposition to full independence.

Early in 1980 a secessionist movement was fanned on Espiritu Santo, the group's largest island, by "rebel" leader Jimmy Stevens, who seized control with financial backing and arms supplied by foreigners—mainly, it was reported, Americans interested in land holdings and some French-speaking planters—and with the support of Santo tribesmen armed with bows and arrows. The revolt that flared on May 28 received worldwide attention. The secessionists believed they would face discrimination under the government of the Anglophone majority in the emerging nation. The outgoing colonial powers failed to end the revolt, and in mid-July the multination South Pacific Forum backed Lini's call to Britain and France to live up to the independence timetable and to hand over a united nation to the elected government.

Independence did not end the violence, however. Early in August Lini arranged with Papua New Guinea to supply a well-trained police contingent; on Santo, Stevens' 24-year-old son was killed in a skirmish, and the rebellion continued until hundreds were disarmed. On August 31 Stevens was captured with his main supporters, including four Frenchmen.

Economic development revolves around agriculture and fishing and, in Vila, professions associated with banking and finance. Some manganese is mined. The new nation hoped to expand food output and diversify beyond the export crops—copra, coffee, and cocoa—and local food items—yams, manioc, bananas, cattle, and pigs. Communications and transport will be improved. Modern health care has been established but malaria remains a serious disease.

A Spanish "crusader" group led by Ferdinand Quiros arrived in 1606 to plant a Christian community in what Quiros believed to be the Great South Land. Captain Cook named the group New Hebrides in 1774. In 1888 an Anglo-French compact created a joint protectorate, and Condominium rule was set up in 1906.

R. M. YOUNGER

──────── **VANUATU · Information Highlights** ────────

Official Name: Vanuatu.
Location: Islands in the south-west Pacific.
Area: 5,700 sq mi (14 763 km^2).
Population (1979 est.): 112,596.
Chief City (Dec. 1975 est.): Vila, the capital, 16,604.
Monetary Unit: New Hebrides franc (65.68 NH francs equal U.S.$1, Feb. 1980).
GNP Per Capita (1978 est., U.S.$): $540.

VENEZUELA

Political scandal, economic doldrums, rising inflation, and maritime disputes afflicted Venezuela in 1980.

Domestic Affairs. Former President Carlos Andrés Pérez was censured by Congress in May for being politically responsible for the purchase of the ship, *Sierra Nevada,* at a cost of $8.1 million more than its owners were asking. All formal charges against him were dropped in July, however. The incident caused considerable dissension in Acción Democratica (AD), a party already in a bitter leadership struggle between the forces supporting Pérez and former President Romulo Betancourt. It also caused bad feeling between AD and the ruling Christian Democratic (COPEI) party.

President Luis Herrera Campins' government was harshly criticized by Fedecámaras, the powerful business organization, which called upon it to practice austerity in government spending and to put an end to the "distorting influence of oil export income." An August poll indicated that only 14% of Venezuelans thought the regime was performing positively. An investigation into charges, brought by Andrés Pérez, of CIA involvement in the internal affairs of Venezuela was authorized by Congress in May.

In October, 60,000 students took to the streets in a peaceful protest over a $183 million university allocation. The students demanded double the amount to fund the 60-odd state universities. Some 10,000 peasants using 7,000 vehicles blocked roads to call attention to their demands for $160 million in compensation for low prices for their products.

A Venezuelan court ruled that Creole and Mobil Oil corporations owed $240 million in back taxes at the time of their nationalization in 1976. Claims totaling $600 million were pending against 30 more foreign companies. Charges that Bethlehem Steel paid $400,000 to Venezuelan naval officers to secure ship repair contracts brought demands for investigation.

Economic Affairs. Venezuela's economy seemed to be in a sluggish state. Its gross domestic product rate of growth declined to 4% in 1979. The rate of inflation rose from 7.2% in 1978 to 12.2% in 1979. Predictions for 1980 ranged from 15% to 30%.

Early in 1980 Venezuela announced it would cut oil production by 6% in 1980. The higher prices were expected to produce $3,500,000,000 in additional revenue. Oil revenues now provide 95% of the total export revenue. Domestic demands for oil products grew by 10% in 1980. To meet these and foreign demands the government planned to invest $2,500,000,000 in new refining facilities. The government also increased its oil prices during the year.

Some 546 million T (500 million t) of bauxite, the principal ingredient in aluminum, were discovered in 1980. Venezuela is now the seventh largest aluminum producer in the world. The metal has become its second largest source of foreign exchange.

The national debt at the end of 1979 was $13,300,000,000. The government secured a $100 million line of credit from 17 international banks to assist it in consolidating its short-term obligations. At the same time, international banks expressed alarm over the failure of several state corporations to meet their interest payments.

Foreign Affairs. Venezuela condemned the military takeover in Bolivia in July, but it adhered to its support of the civilian-military regime in El Salvador. Former President Pérez represented Venezuela in Nicaragua on the anniversary of the overthrow of Somoza. President Herrera visited seven OPEC countries in February but failed to get them to agree on a unified oil price policy. He was in France in April and Costa Rica in August to discuss oil matters. He was invited to visit China.

The government announced it would move its embassy in Israel from Jerusalem to Tel Aviv.

The maritime dispute with Colombia over territory in the Gulf of Venezuela was not settled. A new effort began in September but it showed no signs of success. Colombians accused Venezuela of expelling more than 10,000 settlers from the disputed border region in a six-week period. Venezuela closed four of its seven consulates in Colombia.

Relations with Cuba deteriorated in 1980 over the issue of diplomatic asylum involving many Cubans seeking refuge in the Venezuelan embassy. Later, 1,200 Cubans were admitted to Venezuela.

The government bought 32,760 T (30 000 t) of sugar from the Dominican Republic in 1980 and planned to buy an additional 218,400 T (200 000 t) over the next three years. Mexico and Venezuela will supply 160,000 barrels of oil a day to the Central American and Caribbean countries at world prices, but with a loan at 4% for five years to help them pay for 30% of the costs. Venezuela and the United States signed a technological cooperation agreement.

LEO B. LOTT, *University of Montana*

VENEZUELA · Information Highlights

Official Name: Republic of Venezuela.
Location: Northern coast of South America.
Area: 352,143 sq mi (912 050 km²).
Population (1980 est.): 13,900,000.
Chief Cities (1976 est.): Caracas, the capital, 2,576,000; Maracaibo, 792,000; Valencia, 439,000.
Government: *Head of state and government,* Luis Herrera Campins, president (took office March 1979). *Legislature*—Congress: Senate and Chamber of Deputies.
Monetary Unit: Bolivar (4.29 bolivares equal U.S.$1, Oct. 1980).
Manufactures (major products): Refined petroleum products, iron and steel, paper products, textiles, transport equipment, consumer goods.
Agriculture (major products): Coffee, bananas, sugar, rice, corn, livestock, dairy products.
GNP (1978 est., U.S.$): $39,300,000,000.
Foreign Trade (1979 est., U.S.$): *Imports,* $9,456,000,-000; *exports,* $13,111,000,000.

VERMONT

Despite legislative criticism of the 1980 census as an unwarranted invasion of privacy, the counting of the Vermont population was completed without incident. The final figures revealed a gain of 67,000 persons (15%) since 1970. It was the state's largest decennial gain since the 1880 census and the first time since 1830 that every county shared in the increase. However, Vermont's largest communities—Burlington, Rutland, St. Johnsbury, Montpelier, and Brattleboro—all showed a reversal of the past growth trends, while neighboring towns recorded large increases. The greater Burlington area subsequently was designated a "standard metropolitan statistical area," the first such district in Vermont.

State Government. Taxes and budgets dominated the 1980 legislative session. The legislature made permanent the one-year, 8% income tax reduction instituted in 1979. It rejected, however, Gov. Richard A. Snelling's proposal either to rebate to income taxpayers the $21-million surplus of 1979 or to use it to cover the anticipated highway fund deficit. The legislature instead held the surplus as a reserve in the Property Tax Relief Fund. The House made history by defeating the entire 1980–81 appropriation bill and forcing a rewrite. Nevertheless, tax cuts and recessionary conditions—worsened by a poor season for the ski industry—led to a deficit of $7 million by June 30. The Senate acted to restrict abortions and funding for Planned Parenthood, but the House rejected these moves. Unresolved controversies were the alleged maintenance of secret personnel files by the state police and the governor's veto of a bill tightening legislative oversight of administrative rule making. The long-standing issue of a state-owned whey processing plant apparently was settled by the approval of a subsidy to a Dublin company to operate the facility. More than 15 alternatives to the Miller Formula, by which Vermont distributes its state aid to local education funds, were rejected as even less equitable. After a six-year controversy, the legislators approved the split-

Office of Senator Leahy

Sen. Patrick Leahy (D-VT) narrowly won reelection.

ting of the rate-setting and planning functions of the Public Service Board.

Elections. In the March "beauty contest" presidential primaries, President Jimmy Carter easily won the Democratic balloting, while former Gov. Ronald Reagan scored a narrow victory over John Anderson among Republicans. In the April caucuses to determine the actual delegate count, however, Sen. Edward Kennedy upset President Carter, while Reagan won complete control of the Republican delegation. In a six-man senatorial primary in September, Banking Commissioner Stewart Ledbetter was nominated by state Republicans to challenge incumbent Patrick Leahy (D). In a close Democratic primary for governor, three-term Att. Gen. M. Jerome Diamond defeated three-term House Speaker Timothy O'Connor.

In the November elections, 80% of registered voters went to the polls, reversing a 20-year decline. The State's three electoral votes went to Governor Reagan, who won 44% of the popular vote; President Carter took 39% and Anderson 15%. Governor Snelling was reelected with a 59% plurality, thus becoming the first three-term Republican governor in Vermont history. Democrat Madeleine Kunin recaptured the lieutenant governorship with 56% of the vote, and Republican James Jeffords, Vermont's sole U.S. representative, ran unopposed except for minor parties. The closest contest was for the U.S. Senate, in which Leahy beat Ledbetter only by about 2,000 votes. The Democrats gained four seats in the Senate, though the Republicans still held a 16–14 majority. The Republicans picked up four House seats, increasing their margin to 85–65.

ROBERT V. DANIELS and SAMUEL B. HAND
University of Vermont

—— VERMONT · Information Highlights ——

Area: 9,609 sq mi (24 887 km²).

Population (1980 census, preliminary count): 511,299.

Chief Cities (1980 census, preliminary count): Montpelier, the capital, 8,249; Burlington, 37,727; Rutland, 18,427; Bennington, 15,772.

Government (1980): *Chief Officers*—governor, Richard A. Snelling (R); lt. gov., Madeleine M. Kunin (D). *General Assembly*—Senate, 30 members; House of Representatives, 150 members.

Education (1979–80): *Enrollment*—public elementary schools, 52,053 pupils; public secondary, 46,285; colleges and universities, 29,550 students. *Public school expenditures,* $178,433,000 ($1,701 per pupil).

State Finances (fiscal year 1979): *Revenues,* $640,000,000; *expenditures,* $612,000,000.

Personal Income (1979): $3,613,000,000; per capita, $7,329.

Labor Force (May 1980): *Nonagricultural wage and salary earners,* 197,400; *unemployed,* 13,400 (5.6% of total force).

VETERANS

On July 21, 1980, the U.S. Veterans Administration (VA) celebrated its golden anniversary. During its 50 years, the administration expanded veteran assistance into a comprehensive aid program with an annual price tag of $21,000,000,-000. While not all veterans sought assistance, the potential clientele of the VA comprised 30.1 million veterans. Together with their 63 million dependents and the survivors of deceased veterans, they accounted for about 4 out of every 10 Americans.

By the end of 1980, nearly 2.3 million veterans, 240,000 surviving spouses, and 83,000 children of deceased veterans were receiving compensation totaling some $7,500,000,000. Compensation paid to veterans is contingent on the degree of service-connected disability, ranging from monthly benefits of $54 for 10% disability to $1,016 for 100% disability. The average monthly payment is $224. Seriously disabled veterans with 30% or more impairment receive added compensation for the support of dependents. For example, a veteran who is 40% disabled and has a spouse receives $25 per month more than the $206 regular entitlement. Additional amounts—up to $2,898 per month—are paid for certain specific disabilities, such as the loss of eyesight or an organ.

Many veterans are poor/aged. Beyond protecting disabled veterans and their dependents against loss of income, the government offers support to indigent veterans and their needy survivors. In fiscal 1980, the VA distributed $2,300,-000,000 to 1 million veterans and $1,400,000,000 to 1.2 million dependents. Pensions paid to poor veterans, as distinguished from compensation paid to veterans with service-connected disabilities, have been on the rise because of the aging of World War II veterans. In fiscal 1980, the VA qualified 90,100 newly-indigent veterans and dependents to receive pensions. Any disabled or aged single veteran with an annual income of less than $4,460 ($5,884 for a veteran with one dependent, with an additional $755 added for each dependent) is qualified to receive a pension. The maximum assistance is reduced if a veteran has other income. Dependents of deceased veterans also qualify for pensions if they are indigent.

The VA also provides care to veterans who are considered medically indigent, regardless of the cause of their illness. Veterans who are more than 65 years of age or who are pensioners are accepted without an indigency claim, as are veterans with service-connected disabilities who seek treatment for nonservice-connected ailments. To meet that need, the Veteran's Administration operated 172 hospitals in 1980. A total of 1.3 million veterans were admitted to these hospitals; in addition, 226 outpatient clinics registered 18 million visits. Most of the veterans receiving medical care did not have any service-connected disabilities. The VA also operated 109 nursing homes, providing domiciliary facilities to 78,000 aged veterans who were not in need of hospital care. In fiscal 1980, the VA health care budget amounted to $6,200,000,000.

For veterans who cannot find a job, the government provides aid in the search and some temporary income, while veterans who opt for further education or professional training receive stipends. The maximum weekly benefits vary from state to state, and the federal government reimburses the states for their outlays. In 1980, nearly 238,000 veterans collected unemployment compensation for an average duration of 14 weeks at a total cost of $323 million.

The most significant aid the government offers to young veterans is education and training assistance. By the end of 1980, about two out of every three Vietnam veterans had taken advantage of this program. Some 1.1 million veterans, dependents of disabled veterans, and survivors of those whose deaths were service-connected, received GI benefits in fiscal 1980 at a cost of $2,300,000,000.

Disabled veterans receive special attention. In 1980, Congress expanded available services to veterans with service-connected disabilities to include training in skills essential to independent living. Until the legislation was enacted, vocational rehabilitation services for disabled veterans were confined to skills directly related to employment. Vocational rehabilitation is generally limited to 48 months, and eligibility was extended in 1980 to 12 years after discharge. Disabled veterans undergoing vocational rehabilitation are entitled to the same subsistence allowance as any other veteran attending an education or training course.

The VA offers many other services to veterans. It guarantees home loans up to a maximum of $27,500 and sells life insurance valued in excess of $100,000,000,000 to more than 8 million veterans. Finally, the VA takes care of the veteran even after death by providing burial facilities in 198 cemeteries throughout the country. In 1980, the number of burials exceeded 40,000.

To provide all these services and many others, the Veterans Administration employed 218,000 persons. Of these, only 16,000 were employed in the delivery of nonmedical services; the rest were assigned to hospitals and nursing homes. All together, some 3% of every VA dollar was spent on operating expenses and the rest on providing income or medical services.

In 1980, the U.S. Congress considered allegations of physical disabilities—including sperm damage, resulting in deformed offspring—by veterans exposed to a herbicide used in Vietnam. Named Agent Orange, the herbicide was contaminated with minute quantities of the toxic chemical dioxin. Congress rejected the claim pending further study. Meanwhile, the VA was collecting data on the effects of the substance.

SAR A. LEVITAN
The George Washington University

VIETNAM

Vietnam experienced few successes in 1980—economic or diplomatic. There were, however, widespread celebrations in 1980 marking the 50th anniversary of the founding of the Vietnamese Communist Party.

Politics. A generational change of the political guard took place. Vo Nguyen Giap, 68-year-old hero of the decisive battle of Dienbienphu that ended French colonial rule in 1954, was replaced as defense minister. His successor was Gen. Van Tien Dung, 62, who led the final offensive against Saigon in 1975 to end the Vietnam war in which the United States played such a prominent part. Dung also was in charge of Vietnam's lightning-like assault against Cambodia in 1978–79 that replaced anti-Hanoi Premier Pol Pot with Vietnamese puppet Heng Samrin.

Nguyen Co Thach, 54, de facto chief in the foreign office the previous two years, became foreign minister. He replaced 79-year-old Nguyen Duy Trinh. Nguyen Lam, also 54, took over from Le Thanh Nghi, 70, as chairman of the state planning commission. Trinh, who along with Giap remained a deputy premier, was a founding member of the Vietnamese Communist Party in 1930. In another major change, Deputy Prime Minister Pham Hung assumed the interior portfolio from Tran Quoc Han.

Vietnam's two top government officials, Premier Pham Van Dong and Truong Chinh, chairman of the National Assembly's Standing Committee, retained their posts, together with Party Secretary Le Duan. Ton Duc Thang, national hero Ho Chi Minh's successor as president, died in March.

As 1980 drew to a close, a new constitution calling for a collective presidency—a council of state headed by a chairman—was adopted.

War in Cambodia. The war in Cambodia that began in late 1978 and resulted in the overthrow of the pro-Chinese Pol Pot regime in early 1979 continued indecisively in 1980. The Vietnamese moved half of their 200,000 troops in Cambodia to the far western portion of the country, bordering Thailand. In that area remnants of both Pol Pot's Communist "Khmer Rouge" and the revived right-wing "Khmer Serei" persisted in opposing the invaders. The dry season offensive that began in February fell far short of defeating the Cambodian resistance forces.

Vietnam's frustration over the failure of its military operations against the anti-Hanoi Cambodians expressed itself in a late June border crossing by the Vietnamese into Thailand. This short-lived invasion caused the Chinese to place troops on alert along their troubled frontier with Vietnam. It also prompted the United States to warn the Vietnamese that Thailand was an American ally. The Thais (as well as China) had variously aided the Cambodian resistance forces—which both angered Hanoi and prevented it from attaining its military goals.

Worldwide opposition to the Vietnamese occupation of most of Cambodia underlay the October 13 vote to continue to seat the Pol Pot government in the UN General Assembly. The vote was 74-35 (with 32 abstentions). A subsequent "peace in Cambodia" motion introduced by the five ASEAN (Association of Southeast Asian Nations) governments—Indonesia, the Philippines, Thailand, Malaysia, and Singapore—carried overwhelmingly. It called for Vietnam's withdrawal from Cambodia, a UN peace-keeping force in the country, and free elections.

Economy. The cost of the war in Cambodia and of maintaining a 250,000-300,000-man standing army along the Chinese frontier placed a major burden on the economy, which was by no means yet recovered from the Vietnam war that ended in 1975. Natural disasters and a reduction in non-Communist trade and aid—reflecting opposition to Vietnam's occupation of most of neighboring Cambodia—added to economic difficulties.

The inflation rate was 100% generally and a staggering 350% in southern Ho Chi Minh City (formerly Saigon). Unemployment was 20%. Rice and other foods were rationed, and a "black market" not only flourished but was tolerated openly. The country's exports declined, largely because of the diversion of resources to Cambodia and the cost of fortifying the border with China, and foreign exchange holdings dropped.

Midyear monsoons flooded nearly 1.2 million acres (486 000 ha) and destroyed nearly 16,000 buildings in the process. The rains left 3 million persons homeless.

Foreign Relations. Vietnam's increasing international isolation deepened its dependence upon the USSR. Moscow's aid reached the level of $3 million a day, there were 6,000 Soviet advisers in the country, and the Soviets occupied former American bases at Cam Ranh Bay, Danang, Bien Hoa, and Tan Son Nhut. Premier Pham Van Dong and Party Secretary Le Duan visited Moscow, and the premier also traveled to India.

UN Secretary General Kurt Waldheim visited Hanoi and Bangkok in August and failed to mediate differences between the two nations.

RICHARD BUTWELL, *Murray State University*

VIETNAM · Information Highlights

Official Name: Socialist Republic of Vietnam.
Location: Southeast Asia.
Area: 127,246 sq mi (329 566 km^2).
Population (1980 est.): 53,300,000.
Chief Cities (1976 est.): Hanoi, the capital, 1,443,500; Ho Chi Minh City, 3,460,500; Haiphong, 1,191,000; Da Nang, 500,000.
Government: *Head of state*, president (vacant). *Head of government*, Pham Van Dong, premier (took office 1954). *First secretary of Communist Party*, Le Duan. *Legislature* (unicameral)—National Assembly.
Monetary Unit: Dong (2.02 dongs equal U.S.$1, Feb. 1980).
Manufactures (major products): Phosphate fertilizer, cement, electric energy, processed foods.
Agriculture (major products): Rice, sugarcane, tea, sweet potatoes, cassava, rubber, corn, fruits.
GNP (1979 est., U.S.$): $8,500,000,000.

VIRGINIA

Republican Gov. John Dalton cajoled a leery Democratic-controlled General Assembly into adopting a higher gasoline tax, the most controversial issue of the year.

Ronald Reagan easily outdistanced President Carter in the November elections. At the same time, Republicans swept to victory in 9 of Virginia's 10 Congressional seats. Republicans achieved a stunning gain of three House seats, capturing the Richmond district and the two seats in northern Virginia. Dan Daniel of Danville, a right-wing conservative, remained the only nominal Democrat in the delegation.

Independent Sen. Harry F. Byrd, Jr., clashed with President Carter during the year over federal judgeship nominations. A commission appointed by Byrd at Carter's suggestion submitted a list of nominees which Carter criticized for failing to include women or blacks. Subsequently, Carter substituted the name of a prominent Virginia black when he made his four formal nominations to the Senate. Byrd stuck by his commission's list. Even before Reagan's victory, the president's nomination appeared to have foundered. Parenthetically, Byrd broke his customary silence on presidential politics to endorse Reagan over Carter.

Early in the year, in a move somewhat contradictory to his general record as a financial conservative, Governor Dalton boldly proposed a four-cent-per-gallon increase in the state's tax on gasoline. As justification, he cited lagging revenues and inflationary costs. Though inclined initially toward outright rejection of an increment, the Assembly eventually accepted a compromise two-cent raise. Dalton also supported another successful Assembly move to give northern Virginia localities the right to add additional gasoline taxes earmarked for support of the area's metropolitan transport system.

Democrats did triumph, however, in a campaign to amend the Virginia constitution to permit a short "veto session" of the Assembly to convene after the governor had acted on bills sent up from the regular session. Generally op-posed by Republicans, the proposal nevertheless passed the Assembly for the requisite second time. It was approved by the people in referendum.

In other financial matters, the Assembly defeated or tabled proposals to repeal the sales tax on food or drugs, to assess trucks higher taxes for road maintenance, and to establish fixed spending limits for state government. However, another constitutional amendment was approved to lower the maximum legal indebtedness of local governments.

For the eighth consecutive year, the Assembly declined to ratify the federal Equal Rights Amendment. The lawmakers once again turned down collective bargaining for state employees; killed a bill to give students the right to elect a member to the governing boards of state colleges; took no action on a proposal to establish the initiative as a populist political process; and turned aside two separate moves to establish judicial nominating and legislative ethics commissions.

Virginia farmers suffered from a severe drought that especially paralyzed eastern counties. In a frantic search for water, coastal metropolitan cities attempted to drill emergency wells.

WILLIAM LARSEN

VIRGINIA • Information Highlights

Area: 40,817 sq mi (105 716 km²).
Population (Jan. 1980 est.): 5,213,000.
Chief Cities (1976 est.): Richmond, the capital, 226,639; Norfolk, 284,033; Virginia Beach, 224,595.
Government (1980): *Chief Officers*—governor, John Dalton (R); lt. gov., Charles Robb (D). *General Assembly*—Senate, 40 members; House of Delegates, 100 members.
Education (1979–80): *Enrollment*—public elementary schools, 630,300 pupils; public secondary, 401,103; colleges and universities, 270,599 students. *Public school expenditures*, $1,963,468,000 ($1,675 per pupil).
State Finances (fiscal year 1979): *Revenues*, $5,136,-000,000; *expenditures*, $4,876,000,000.
Personal Income (1979): $44,628,000,000; per capita, $8,587.
Labor Force (June 1980): *Nonagricultural wage and salary earners*, 2,130,700; *unemployed*, 147,200 (5.8% of total force).

VIRGIN ISLANDS

The U.S. census of 1980 showed a 52% increase in the population of the Virgin Islands since 1970. The population of St. Croix was 48,-916; St. Thomas, 43,828; and St. John, most of which is a national park, 2,470. The total of 95,-214 was far below the estimate of 120,000 used by the government for federal funding.

Constitution. Early in 1980, Gov. Juan Luis called for the election of a new constitutional convention for the territory. It was the fourth such convention to be convened in the islands, and it met from March 24 to July 25. The previously proposed constitution had been apathetically rejected by island voters in a referendum held in March 1979. The proposed constitution drawn up by the 1980 convention was taken to Washington and presented to President Carter, who, after study, recommended some minor modifications and sent it to Congress for approval. If approved by Congress, the constitution then would be placed before the citizens on the islands for approval in a referendum. The new proposal creates a less elaborate bureaucratic structure than previously had been proposed.

Elections. In November, islanders elected a new legislature and the resident commissioner to the U.S. Congress. The incumbent resident commissioner, Dr. Melvin Evans (R), a former governor, was defeated in his bid for reelection by Ron de Lugo (D), himself a former resident commissioner. De Lugo had resigned the post to run for governor of the islands against incumbent Governor Luis.

Elections for the 15 seats in the unicameral legislature produced some surprises. Five incumbents seeking reelection were defeated, and no Republicans were elected. Five Democrats from St. Croix and five from St. Thomas were voted into office, as well as two independents from each of these two larger islands. The fifteenth, at-large seat went to an independent, Dr. Gilbert Spauve, a professor at the College of the Virgin Islands and a native of St. John. Sen. Ruby Rouss was selected by her peers to serve as the first woman president of the legislature.

The three extremist candidates of the United Caribbean Association Movement failed to receive any popular backing.

Social Unrest. Crime and racial violence continued to plague the Virgin Islands, particularly St. Croix. Early in the year, citizens marched in protest of the rising incidence of violence. The political fervor stirred up by the election year increased the feelings of racial tension. The governor put the National Guard on "partial alert" prior to and during the elections, but there were no major acts of violence.

THOMAS MATHEWS, *University of Puerto Rico*

WASHINGTON

During the third week of March, after lying quiet since 1857, Mount St. Helens began to generate disquieting tremors and on March 27 its superheated gases blew steam and volcanic ash high into the sky, opening a small, red-glowing crater at the summit. This relatively small initial eruption was followed by more than seven weeks of intermittent shocks, avalanches, and smaller eruptions. Suddenly, at 8:32 A.M. on May 18, the 9,677-ft (2 903-m) mountain exploded in the most violent volcanic eruption on the North American continent in recorded history. Cities and other parts of the state were plunged into mid-day darkness and covered with ash as much as 7 inches (18 cm) deep. A state of emergency was proclaimed. Airports were closed over a wide area. Because of precautions and forced evacuations following the earlier activity, the toll of dead and missing was under 75. The major eruption of May 18 was followed by a series of less devastating ones. (*See also* special report, page 248).

Corruption. In April, federal racketeering charges were filed against John Bagnariol, co-speaker of the state House of Representatives, Gordon Walgren, majority leader of the Senate, and Patrick Gallagher, lobbyist. The three men had been contacted, through Gallagher, by FBI agents posing as officers of companies purported to be controlled by persons associated with organized crime and involved in gambling activities on the West Coast. The contacts between the parties, most of which were electronically monitored, covered a period from July 1978 to January 1980. When the charges were filed, Bagnariol was launching a campaign for governor and Walgren was organizing a campaign for attorney general. On October 4, after many weeks of trial, which was dubbed the "Gam-Scam" trial, and 11 days of deliberations on the 28-count indictment, the jury found all three guilty of racketeering and a number of lesser charges. In addition, Bagnariol and Gallagher were found guilty of conspiracy, extortion, mail fraud,

---

WASHINGTON • Information Highlights

Area: 68,192 sq mi (176 617 km²).
Population (Jan. 1980 est.): 3,997,000.
Chief Cities (1970 census): Olympia, the capital, 23,111; (1976 est): Seattle, 490,586; Spokane, 175,751; Tacoma, 153,621.
Government (1980): *Chief Officers*—governor, Dixy Lee Ray (D); lt. gov., John A. Cherberg (D). *Legislature*—Senate, 49 members; House of Representatives, 98 members.
Education (1979–80): *Enrollment*—public elementary schools, 399,331 pupils; public secondary, 365,548; colleges and universities, 303,469 students. *Public school expenditures*, $2,271,898,000 ($2,208 per pupil).
State Finances (fiscal year 1979): *Revenues*, $5,660,000,000; *expenditures*, $4,860,000,000.
Personal Income (1979): $37,552,000,000; per capita, $9,565.
Labor Force (June 1980): *Total labor force*, 1,964,800; unemployed, 167,600 (8.5% of total force).

UPI

Washington state suffered from the effects of the eruption of Mount St. Helens in 1980. As a result, some patrol cars were equipped with homemade breathing devices to prevent volcanic ash from entering the engines.

As 1981 began, the U.S. capital was preparing for a presidential inauguration. Bleachers were being installed along the parade route on Pennsylvania Avenue.

UPI

and crossing state lines to promote bribery and extortion.

The Election. More than normal interest was shown in the primary election, particularly in the races for governor and U.S. Senate. Democrat Gov. Dixy Lee Ray's unhappy relations with the press and legislative leaders and her forthright but often-controversial stand on a number of issues led to her primary defeat by state Sen. Jim McDermott. Many Republicans crossed party lines to express their disapproval of her administration. This crossover was evident in the general election when King County Executive John Spellman (R) easily defeated Jim McDermott.

Equally stunning was the defeat of U.S. Sen. Warren G. Magnuson (D), by three-time state Attorney General Slade Gorton (R). After six terms, Senator Magnuson was not only the Senate's senior member, he was chairman of the Appropriations Committee and president pro tempore. Magnuson's age, 75, and the general Republican landslide served to hand the senator his first election defeat in a public office career that began in 1932.

Six of the seven incumbent U.S. Representatives, 5 Democrats and 1 Republican, were returned to office. The Republican tide swept the other incumbent, Rep. Mike McCormack (D), out of office and Sid Morrison (R) to Washington from the fourth district. An initiative to keep nonmedical nuclear waste from entering the state after July 1, 1981, was approved overwhelmingly.

WARREN W. ETCHESON
University of Washington

WASHINGTON, DC

Politics was the dominant theme in the nation's capital in the election year. Citizen initiatives to legalize some forms of gambling and to direct the district toward statehood dominated the political discussions and campaigns. Proponents of the initiatives considered them possible solutions to the city's worsening budget crisis.

Legalized Gambling. City-run lottery and numbers games, with profits going directly into the district's treasury, were approved by voters in the November 4 general election. The initiative measure also legalized raffles and bingo games conducted for charitable purposes. A lottery and charitable games control board would be created to regulate gambling activities.

The initiative was a modified version of one defeated in the May primary election. The original measure proposed to legalize parimutuel betting on jai alai and dog racing, as well as lottery and daily numbers, with profits passing through an independent gaming control board before being allotted to special education programs and service-oriented nonprofit agencies. Social gambling, such as poker games in private homes, also would have been legalized.

Statehood. Voters approved an initiative to begin a drive to become the nation's 51st state. It was the initial step in a lengthy process that requires a state constitution to be written by delegates elected to a special convention and, if accepted by voters, submitted to Congress as a statehood bill. As a state, Washington would have full voting representation in Congress and control over its legislative and fiscal affairs.

Elections. Voters returned five councilmembers to office: John L. Ray (D) and Jerry A. Moore (R), as at-large members; and John A. Wilson (D), Charlene Drew Jarvis (D), and Wilhemina J. Rolark (D), representing individual wards. H.R. Crawford (D) was elected to the ward-based post vacated by Willie J. Hardy.

Walter E. Fauntroy, who has served as the nonvoting delegate in Congress since the post was created in 1971, was reelected.

In the presidential race, Washington's three electoral votes went to President Jimmy Carter.

Constitutional Amendment. Legislatures in Wisconsin, Maryland, and Hawaii raised to nine the number of states that have ratified the proposed constitutional amendment giving the district full voting representation in Congress.

MORRIS J. LEVITT, *Howard University*

WEST VIRGINIA

Except for two Congressional races, West Virginia retained its usual Democratic complexion in November 1980 elections. Gov. John D. (Jay) Rockefeller 4th, whose campaign expenses totaled nearly $11.6 million, won reelection over former Gov. Arch Moore. President Jimmy Carter carried the state with 50% of the vote. All incumbents in major state races—Commissioner of Agriculture Gus R. Douglass, Secretary of State A. James Manchin, Attorney General Chauncey H. Browning, Auditor Glen B. Gainer, Jr., and Treasurer Larrie Bailey—easily defeated challengers.

In Congressional races, Mick Staton defeated Democrat John Hutchinson, giving the third district its first GOP representative in 50 years, and Procter and Gamble heir Cleveland Benedict defeated Pat Hamilton in the second, which had been Harley Staggers' domain since 1948. Staton had lost to Charleston Mayor Hutchinson in a special June election to fill the vacancy created by the death of John Slack on March 17. Democratic incumbents Robert Mollohan and Nick Joe Rahall easily retained their seats.

Two amendments were approved. In one, which had been debated since 1950, bingo for nonprofit groups was approved by a 2-1 margin. However, local referenda on the issue are required. In the other, elderly and disabled citizens were given an additional break in real estate taxes.

Legislation. The 1980 legislative session generated a great deal of heated debate, well-attended public hearings, demonstrations by various pressure groups, but very little constructive legislation. After 20 years of frustration, proponents of beer with more than 3.2 alcoholic content finally got their measure adopted, but only after Governor Rockefeller's veto was overridden. A related drive to get the state out of the liquor business failed. A measure that would have permitted branch banking and another that would have called for compulsory automobile insurance occupied much of the session but collapsed in last-minute scrambling.

The legislators did enact changes that brought the state's strip mining laws into closer conformity with federal standards. The measure was supported by the ailing coal industry, pivot of West Virginia's economy and marked for the third straight year by increased layoffs and slumping production. The license fee for out-of-state bear hunters was raised to $1,000, a move to stop the slaughter of the state animal.

Public school salaries, always a major legislative issue, received the usual long and loud attention. Teachers gained a 7.7% increase, non-teaching school personnel an 11% raise, and elective officials 20%. The state minimum wage was increased from $2.20 to $2.75 per hour.

Miscellaneous. Unemployment leveled off at 7.7% by Thanksgiving (after a July high of 7.9%). Deregulation of airlines cost the state some 100 flights. On November 7 in Madison, a methane explosion, the worst in West Virginia in more than a decade, claimed five lives. Forest fires were devastating in the south in November.

DONOVAN H. BOND, *West Virginia University*

WISCONSIN

The conservative sweep throughout the country had its effect in Wisconsin, though not with the force it had in the other states. The major result was the defeat of Sen. Gaylord Nelson, a popular liberal who in his 18 years in office had embodied Democratic liberalism and had been called the "conscience of the Senate." Nelson had stood almost alone against the initial funding of the Vietnam War, had founded Earth Day, and had led in other environmental battles. Seeking his fourth term, Nelson, 64, was defeated for a variety of reasons: his age; the feeling on the part of some that he had lost touch with the state; a campaign that did not recognize the strength of his opponent. The winner was Robert W. Kasten, Jr., 38, a conservative former congressman from the 9th district who had given up his seat in 1978 to wage an unsuccessful primary campaign for governor.

Republicans also gained a seat in the House, with Steve Gunderson, a 29-year-old former assemblyman, defeating Alvin J. Baluds, 54, a Democrat seeking his fourth term in the 3rd district. All other Congressional incumbents won. Despite the efforts of Republican Gov. Lee Dreyfus to win more GOP seats in the legislature, Democrats held their own. Ronald Reagan carried the state.

Legislative Session. A spring legislative session that was supposed to deal with energy and criminal justice matters proved frustrating. Observers said that Governor Dreyfus did not push his proposals hard enough, but also that the majority Democrats brushed his bills aside and did not come up with their own. The results included a major revamping of bail procedures; increased penalties for some crimes; the first steps toward pretrial detention of some persons without bail; legislation to cope with teenage alcohol abuse; an improved approach to mental patient commitments; a two-cent increase in the gasoline tax; and strict standards for auto emission tests. The legislature battled over the site for the state's third prison, finally settling on Portage, in south-central Wisconsin.

Cuban Refugees. Fort McCoy, in central Wisconsin, used mostly in recent years for summer training of military reservists, was designated as a site for Cuban refugees who arrived in Florida in the spring. Governor Dreyfus at first objected, wanting assurances that the federal government would pay the costs. And during the summer, the tensions among refugees waiting for release to sponsors resulted in many incidents that caused concern—stabbings, fights, escapes, near-riots. But the fact remained that nearly 15,000 refugees had arrived at the camp and by summer's end, when those left were transferred to Fort Chaffee, AR, 9,986 had found new U.S. homes.

Economy. Wisconsin's economy faltered in 1980 as a result of the nationwide recession. Manufacturing employment was down about 6.5% from record levels of 1979, when the state ranked third in the creation of new manufacturing jobs. Total employment was off about 4.2% from the year before; still, unemployment, at about 7.1%, was below the national levels.

Tourism, while perhaps showing a slight gain in receipts, was down slightly in the number of people visiting the state. Agriculture, led by higher milk and grain prices, had a good year.

PAUL SALSINI, *"The Milwaukee Journal"*

WOMEN

As might be expected in an election year, politics dominated the list of women's concerns in 1980. Many feminists expressed a wait-and-see attitude toward president-elect Ronald Reagan who, while claiming to support equal rights for women, ran on a Republican platform that did not endorse the Equal Rights Amendment (ERA).

Although 1980 was not a good year for incumbent Democrats, it was a good year for women in the Democratic Party. Under a rule adopted in 1976, half of the voting delegates to the 1980 Democratic Convention were women. The delegates approved the strongest ERA and abortion rights planks in the party's history.

Women made notable gains in the 1980 congressional elections: the 97th Congress would include 21 women, the greatest number ever to serve in a federal legislature. Among the victors was Paula Hawkins, a Florida Republican who became the second woman in the U.S. Senate, joining Nancy Landon Kassebaum, a Kansas Republican. Four other women who sought Senate seats in 1980 were defeated.

In a year when incumbency was hardly a political advantage, all 15 women running for reelection to the House won. They were joined by four newcomers, all Republicans. Three of these—Claudine Schneider of Rhode Island, Marge Roukema of New Jersey, and Bobbi Fiedler of California—defeated incumbent Democrats. Lynn Martin of Illinois replaced fellow Republican John B. Anderson.

Women candidates did reasonably well at the state level. More than 1,400 women ran for state legislator—879 made it. According to the National Women's Political Caucus, there were about three times as many women state legislators as there were in 1970. At the year's end there were no longer any women governors—Dixy Lee Ray of Washington lost in her state's primary, and Connecticut's Ella Grasso, stricken with cancer, resigned as of December 31.

ERA. Even before the November election, the outlook for passage of ERA was bleak. ERA supporters suffered a serious blow June 18 when the Illinois House of Representatives defeated the amendment for the second time in two years. Although a majority of the legislators voted for ERA, state rules required a three-fifths vote. Two other states—Georgia and Virginia—also voted down ERA in 1980. By late 1980, 35 of the necessary 38 states had ratified the amendment.

The U.S. Supreme Court on October 6 refused to hear Missouri's appeal of a ruling by the 8th Circuit Court of Appeals that an economic boycott of states whose legislatures have not ratified ERA does not constitute a violation of the Sherman Antitrust Act.

Women in Business. Office politics became news when two high-level women executives were forced to resign. The most publicized case involved Mary E. Cunningham, who resigned October 9 as vice-president for strategic planning at the Bendix Corporation because of controversy surrounding her rapid promotions and her relationship with her boss, Bendix chairman William Agee. Cunningham, a graduate of Harvard Business School, had joined Bendix in June 1979.

Jane Cahill Pfeiffer, often called the most powerful woman in corporate America, formally resigned as chairman of the National Broadcasting Corporation on July 10. She reportedly had major disagreements with Edgar H. Griffiths, chairman of RCA, NBC's parent corporation.

The avalanche of press coverage of the Cunningham and Pfeiffer resignations focused attention on the growing number of women in high-level management jobs. According to the Equal Employment Opportunity Commission, there were 688,645 women managers and officers in companies with more than 100 employees in 1978. By contrast, there were just 260,921 women managers in 1970.

Another sign of women's rising status in the corporate world is the growing number of women serving on boards of directors. Women were on the boards of more than a third of the 552 manufacturing, financial, and retail companies surveyed in 1980 by Kern/Ferry International, a New York-based executive search firm. That was more than three times the number reporting female representation in 1973.

Although women managers are no longer oddities, few have made it to the top echelons of management. A survey conducted by Heidrick & Struggles, the executive search firm, found that in 1980 there were only 497 women officers in the nation's largest business organizations, up from 325 in 1977. No woman was listed in *Forbes* magazine's 1980 annual survey of the chief executive officers of the largest U.S. corporations.

For many women, job discrimination does not end once they make it to the executive suite. On average, women in managerial and administrative jobs earn only 60% of what their male colleagues make, according to a 1980 salary survey conducted by *Working Woman* magazine.

UN Decade for Women Conference. Some 1,000 delegates (about 900 of them women), representing 136 countries, met in Copenhagen July 14–31 for the second world conference of the United Nations Decade for Women. The purpose of the conference was twofold: (1) to review and appraise progress in meeting the goals of the World Plan of Action adopted in Mexico City in 1975 at the first international women's year conference, and (2) to develop a Program of Action for the second half of the UN Decade for Women.

UN Secretary Kurt Waldheim opened the conference on July 14. Several speakers con-

UPI
The U.S. Naval Academy's first woman graduate.

tended that, since the 1975 conference, the status of women had deteriorated, especially in Third World countries.

To the chagrin of many delegates, discussions of women's issues often took a back seat to debates over such issues as apartheid in South Africa and the Israeli occupation of Arab territory. The conference ended July 31 with adoption of a detailed Program of Action that included a number of politically controversial statements. The plan was approved by a roll call vote of 94 in favor to four against, with 22 abstentions. Voting against were the United States, Canada, Australia, and Israel.

The United States was among the 53 nations that signed the UN Convention on the Elimination of All Forms of Discrimination Against Women. Approved by the UN General Assembly in December 1979 and considered by many to be an international version of the ERA, the accord had been signed by 12 nations before the Copenhagen ceremony. The women's rights convention must be approved by the U.S. Senate.

SANDRA STENCEL, *Editorial Research Reports*

WOMEN—SPECIAL REPORT:

Women in the Military

The 1980 graduation ceremonies at the U.S. service academies were a familiar scene, except that, for the first time, 227 of the graduates were women. Adm. Thomas Hayward declared in front of the Annapolis graduating class that "They have met the test; they have proven themselves in an environment that was far more stress-filled than that endured by most of their male counterparts." The graduation of these women by the institutions that so long barred their entry is symbolic of the growing participation of women in the military. The 1980 graduates joined nearly 20,000 other women already commissioned as officers in the military. The number of women in the military has jumped from 43,000 in 1972 to 150,000 in 1980.

The participation of women in the military is crucial to the All Volunteer Force. A 1977 Defense Department report stated that "The success of the volunteer force may well depend on the number of women who join the military and how they are used." Their impact has been such that civilian leaders of the Pentagon have pressed the services into setting recruitment goals that would increase the number of women in the military by more than 50% by 1985, to about 235,000.

The increased participation of women in the armed forces has sparked a renewed debate about just what role they should play. Should military women have equal rights and opportunities in addition to their responsibilities in national defense? Or do classic role model and physical differences impose limitations on the mission of women in the armed forces? These questions were highlighted in 1980 by the issue of whether women should be required to register for the draft (*see* page 365).

An Army personnel newsletter released in December 1979 stated that "women soldiers are a fully integrated part of the Army." Indeed, all branches of the military have made efforts to give women greater opportunities in a broad variety of fields. Women share in control of the Titan II intercontinental missiles and are undergoing the Marine Corps' rugged bootcamp training. They are chief instructor pilots and are helping to create the MX missile. These women are highly qualified personnel.

Because the numerical quotas for women are lower than for men, however, the services are able to impose more restrictive requirements on their entry. Women must have a score of at least 59 on the Mental Aptitude Test, compared with a required 31 for men. In addition, women must have a high-school diploma before they can be admitted into the armed forces, while only 75% of the monthly quota of male enlistees must meet the same requirements.

In spite of the level of success women have achieved in the military, all aspects of military service are not open to them. The most significant area closed to women is combat duty. For although the Defense Department has recommended that the combat ban be dropped, present federal law prevents women from serving on combat missions in the Navy and Air Force. The Army imposes similar restrictions in policy directives. Those opposed to women in combat contend that women are not psychologically or physiologically equipped to cope with the rigors of combat duty. They cite the greater physical size and power of the male, and evidence that men are more aggressive, competitive, and willing to take risks. James Webb, a much-decorated Marine officer in Vietnam, writes that the mere presence of women at the service academies "has sterilized the whole process of combat leadership training, and our military forces are doomed to suffer the consequences." Navy Cmdr. Richard Hunter refutes this view as nonsense: "Just substitute the word 'woman' for 'black' and it's the same stuff I heard 20 years ago."

In addition, combat duty is nothing new to American women. During the American Revolution and the Civil War, women participated in intense combat situations. They also played significant roles in the combat that took place dur-

Keza, Liaison

These women troops getting their basic training are among some 150,000 women in the U.S. military services.

ing the expansion of the country westward. Claims that women are not physically capable are also refuted as women recruits must go through much the same physical training as male recruits. Additionally, there are many combat jobs that require little physical strength. The issue of combat duty is especially important to women, as assignment to combat positions is a prerequisite for promotion to many upper-level jobs.

Military women indicate that sexual harassment is another barrier to full participation in military life. While such harassment is not limited to the armed forces, it is a serious problem and an everyday part of the lives of many military women. "When I first drove on to the post, I thought there was something wrong with my car," recalled Lt. Ann Clawson. "Guys just stopped what they were doing and stared, like they'd never seen a female before." Women complain of unsolicited and unwelcome advances by male soldiers that often go unpunished, and of mess hall stares that force them to eat off base. Military policy expressly forbids such behavior, but as retired Air Force Gen. Jeanne Holm says, "There's still this feeling that this is a man's army. Deep down there's this feeling that women are asking for it." A poll taken in 1978 indicated that two thirds of the men at Pendleton Army base felt perfectly comfortable serving with the opposite sex. Nevertheless such harassment will probably continue until women are fully accepted as equal and able members of the armed forces.

REP. PATRICIA SCHROEDER (D-CO)

WYOMING

The accelerating demand for Wyoming's energy resources sustained economic and population growth in the state. Major energy companies continued to develop extensive coal reserves in the Powder River basin. Along the Overthrust Belt, a geological formation in western Wyoming, intensive exploration indicated an oil and gas potential of major dimensions. Vast strip mines, mobile-home boom towns, and the ubiquitous oil drilling rig were new, high-visibility elements of the state's image.

Economic and Demographic Developments. Wyoming's economy largely escaped the recession of 1980. The state's labor force grew by 4% and its unemployment rate remained near 3%, one of the nation's lowest. As the price of energy minerals rose and their production in the state increased, state tax revenues went up proportionately. Wyoming's share of mineral royalties from federal lands within its borders, from which the state received about $80 million in 1980, also rose. The deregulation of oil prices in 1981 would mean for Wyoming an estimated increase in tax and royalty revenues of about $300 million annually.

Preliminary 1980 census figures indicated that between 1970 and 1980 the state population increased by 41.1%. Only Nevada's grew faster. But with a total population of 468,090, Wyoming remained the state with fewer persons than any other except Alaska. All of the state's 23 counties gained population, several at remarkable rates. Coal-rich Campbell county showed an 88% increase, and on the Overthrust Belt, Sweetwater county had a population of 41,662, an increase of 126% since 1970.

Legislation. The 45th Legislature met in biennial budget session in February, with Republicans in control, 42–20, in the House and 19–11 in the Senate. Democrats again worked to increase the state mineral severance tax; a dozen such bills failed to pass. Adopted, however, was a law ordering quarterly rather than annual severance tax payments. Local governments, pressed by rising operating costs and unprecedented demand for services, failed to persuade legislators of their plight. Bills to increase the local share of the state sales tax and to distribute to local governments a portion of the mineral royalty income both failed. The legislature did, however, substantially increase state aid to public schools. Endorsing a hallowed bit of "state's rights" dogma, the lawmakers passed a "Sagebrush Rebellion" bill. The measure asserted Wyoming's claim to most of the federal lands within its borders, but left unsaid how this would be established. Other legislation increased the number of district judges from 15 to 17, and raised district judges' salaries to $46,000 and those of Supreme Court judges to $48,000.

In action surrounded by controversy, the legislature provided Cheyenne with a $31 million loan from state funds plus an outright grant of $16 million, the money to underwrite a project that would divert stream water from south-central Wyoming to the city's reservoir system.

Politics. In the November elections, Wyoming voters favored Reagan over Carter by a 2–1 margin. Incumbent Rep. Dick Cheney (R) carried 64% of the vote, easily defeating Jim Rogers. With 181,004 votes cast in the election, Wyoming's voter turnout rate was 82.5%, a new state record as well as one of the nation's highest.

H. R. DIETERICH, *University of Wyoming*

――――― **WYOMING** · Information Highlights ―――――

Area: 97,914 sq mi (253 597 km²).
Population (1980 census, preliminary count): 468,954.
Chief Cities (1980 census, preliminary count): Cheyenne, the capital, 47,207; Casper, 50,704; Laramie, 24,339; Rock Springs, 19,415.
Government (1980): *Chief Officers*—governor, Ed Herschler (D); secy. of state, Thyra Thomson (R). *Legislature*—Senate, 30 members; House of Representatives, 62 members.
Education (1979–80): *Enrollment*—public elementary schools, 53,067; public secondary, 42,438; colleges and universities, 19,490 students. *Public school expenditures,* $273,108,000 ($2,267 per pupil).
State Finances (fiscal year 1979): *Revenues,* $789,000,000; *expenditures,* $633,000,000.
Personal Income (1979): $4,465,000,000; per capita, $9,922.
Labor Force (June 1980): *Nonagricultural wage and salary earners,* 219,700; *unemployed,* 9,500 (3.9% of total force).

THE YEMENS

"Events in South Yemen, not to mention those in North Yemen, can be rather obscure," wrote a British authority in April 1980. The year's developments in the two Yemens—the Yemen Arab Republic, also known as North Yemen or Yemen (San'a), and the People's Democratic Republic of Yemen, also known as South Yemen or Yemen (Aden)—illustrated the point. The facts were often uncertain, the interpretations even more so.

North Yemen. In 1979, it had appeared briefly that North Yemen would become closely aligned with Saudi Arabia and the United States, while Marxist South Yemen was becoming more and more dominated by thousands of so-called advisers from the Soviet Union and other Communist-bloc countries. The lines became clearly drawn during the three-week war between the two states in early 1979, as South Yemen relied on Soviet arms and North Yemen was the beneficiary of military and economic support from Saudi Arabia and the United States (channeled through Saudi Arabia). However, puzzling trends emerged almost immediately. No sooner had a cease-fire ended the war than the North and the South, amazingly, began to discuss a unification plan.

The talk of union upset Saudi Arabia, which had regarded the more capitalistic San'a government as a buffer against the radical Aden regime. The Saudis reduced the flow of U.S. arms to the North and attempted to influence San'a policy by withholding its own economic support in December 1979 and January 1980. Saudi aid had been running at about $250 million per year and was vital to deficit-ridden North Yemen.

Resentful, the North Yemenis, who had already been receiving Soviet as well as U.S. military aid, welcomed more than ever new Soviet materiel in the second half of 1979. Analysts estimated that by the middle of 1980 the San'a regime had received about half of a promised 60 warplanes, as well as about 500 tanks and rocket-launchers and other Soviet arms. About 230 Soviet military advisers were reported to be working in North Yemen by mid-1980, as against perhaps two dozen Americans (down from about 70 in 1979.)

On Jan. 14, 1980, North Yemen abstained on the UN General Assembly vote condemning Soviet intervention in Afghanistan. Friendly relations with the Soviet Union and South Yemen continued, although the unification project with Aden did not seem to make much progress. In March, Saudi Arabia managed to pressure North Yemen into refusing any further military support from the Soviet Union and sending home Soviet advisers. The Saudis then resumed economic aid, but there was little indication that the Yemeni promises had been kept. The political leaders in San'a insisted that their country was merely continuing its nonaligned policy, but the West detected a distinct and ominous drift leftward.

In other matters, a dispute between North Yemen and Great Britain over a legal action in the British courts that led to the detention of a Yemeni airliner was eased when the plane was released on January 17. A project for the vast expansion of the port of Hodeida was announced. Two Japanese firms won a $113 million contract to build a cement plant at Amram, 25 mi (40 km) south of San'a. And Yemeni Jews, once about 60,000 in number but almost all emigrated to Israel, were encouraged to return.

South Yemen. On April 23, President and Secretary General of the Yemeni Socialist Party Abdel Fattah Ismail resigned from office, allegedly for health reasons. He was replaced by his prime minister, Ali Nasser Mohammed. Western and Arab observers speculated that Ismail actually had been ousted in a power struggle over the unification proposal. It was also suggested that Mohammed was elevated as a result of Soviet influence. Analogies were drawn with the 1979 coup in Afghanistan, in which the more flexible Babrak Karmal was installed over Hafizullah Amin, who was unsatisfactory to Moscow. An unusual feature of the Aden change, therefore, was that Ismail not only stayed alive but was given the honorary post of chairman of the party. The new president immediately took steps to improve relations with other Arab states, including Saudi Arabia—an interesting, if confusing, turn in tactics.

ARTHUR CAMPBELL TURNER
University of California, Riverside

— **NORTH YEMEN** · Information Highlights —

Official Name: Yemen Arab Republic.
Location: Arabian peninsula in southwest Asia.
Area: 75,000 sq mi (194 000 km²).
Population (1980 est.): 5,600,000.
Chief City (1975 census): San'a, the capital, 447,898.
Government: *Head of State*, Ali Abdullah Saleh, president. *Head of government*, Abdel Aziz Abdel Ghani, prime minister. *Legislature* (unicameral)—Constituent People's Assembly.
Monetary Unit: Rial (4.56 rials equal U.S.$1, Aug. 1980).
Manufactures (major products): Textiles, aluminum, cement.
Agriculture (major products): Wheat, barley, maize, sorghum, potatoes.
GNP (1977 est., U.S.$): $1,500,000.

— **SOUTH YEMEN** · Information Highlights —

Official Name: People's Democratic Republic of Yemen.
Location: Arabian peninsula in southwest Asia.
Area: 112,000 sq mi (290 078 km²).
Population (1980 est.): 1,900,000.
Chief City (1977 est.): Aden, the capital, 271,590.
Government: *Head of state*, Ali Nasser Mohammed, president and secretary general of the Yemeni Socialist Party. *Legislature* (unicameral)—People's Supreme Assembly.
Monetary Unit: Dinar (.3454 dinar equals U.S.$1, Aug. 1980).
Manufactures (major products): Fuel oils, processed foods.
Agriculture (major products): Millet, wheat, barley, sesame.
GNP (1978 est., U.S.$): $500,000,000.

Rampant consumerism, as in the Slovenian capital of Ljubljana, above, is a legacy of Tito.

YUGOSLAVIA

The most important political event of the year in Yugoslavia was the death on May 4 of Marshall Tito (Josip Broz), head of the Socialist Federal Republic of Yugoslavia (SFRY), president of the League of Communists of Yugoslavia (LCY), and supreme commander of the Yugoslav People's Army (YPA). (*See* OBITUARIES, page 410.) Although the mechanism for Tito's succession was firmly in place upon his death and the transition took place without controversy or infighting, the new collective leadership faced difficult policy decisions left unresolved by the former leader.

Succession. Despite his own exclusively personal rule for more than 35 years, Tito had carefully worked out a plan of succession whereby he would be replaced by rotating collective leaderships on both the state and LCY levels. A collective state presidency composed of eight persons (one from each of the six SFRY constituent republics—Serbia, Croatia, Slovenia, Bosnia and Herzegovina, Montenegro, and Macedonia—and two autonomous provinces—Vojvodina and Kosmet) was in place at the moment of Tito's death. The vice-president of that body, Lazar Koliševski, a Macedonian, immediately became president of the collective state presidency. Because of the yearly rotating system, however, Koliševski was replaced on May 15 by a Serb from Bosnia, Cvijetin Mijatović. Mijatović would exercise the same function for a full year, after which he would be replaced by the current vice-president, Sergej Kraigher, a Slovene. All

the members of the state presidency are also powerful figures in the ruling Communist party, the LCY.

In a similar vein, the supreme leadership of the Communist party is the collective presidium of the LCY's central committee, composed of 23 persons (three from each of the republics, two from each of the autonomous provinces, and a representative of the YPA). As in the state system, alternative presidents will head the presidium for one year each. Stevan Doronjski, a Serb from Vojvodina, exercised that function until Oct. 20, 1980, when he was replaced by a Macedonian, Lazar Mojsov.

While Tito's succession went smoothly, and there were no signs of internal conflicts within the supreme state and party bodies, the YPA, Tito's most trusted overall Yugoslav entity, took on added authority. A few days after Tito's demise, a new Council for Territorial Defense was created in the Federal Secretariat for National Defense. The functions of the new council are to supervise and centralize Yugoslavia's nationwide defense system. Gen. Stane Potočar, a Slovene and chief-of-state of the YPA until 1979, was appointed chairman of the council.

Domestic Policies. On October 29, after several months of public discussions, the Federal Council of the Yugoslav Assembly adopted seven amendments which in April 1981 would alter the established (1974) Yugoslav Constitution. The aim of the amendments is to limit the tenure of officials in organs of self-management at all levels. The amendments implement Tito's own last ideas regarding such institutions. They bar

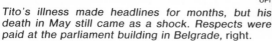

UPI

Tito's illness made headlines for months, but his death in May still came as a shock. Respects were paid at the parliament building in Belgrade, right.

UPI

any individual from holding office for more than two consecutive four-year terms.

Throughout the year, the new collective leadership demonstrated its reluctance to liberalize the political life of the country. A petition to revise the criminal code by dropping Article 133 (concerning "hostile propaganda"), a request for amnesty for political offenders, and an application by prominent and mainly neo-Marxist intellectuals and writers to launch an independent magazine, all were refused by the authorities. A change in the law on universities adopted June 5 threatened eight prominent professors of the Faculty of Philosophy in Belgrade with the loss of their academic jobs. Some were editors of, and all were active collaborators in, the internationally-noted review *Praxis,* whose publication was forbidden by the authorities in 1975. At that time, the eight professors were suspended from teaching but not from research at specialized institutes. Another leading dissident, Milovan Djilas, was vehemently assailed in the press for publishing in the foreign press articles and a book critical of Tito. Still, signs of oppositional attitudes throughout the country remained persistent though for the time being ineffective.

A deepening of Yugoslavia's economic crisis, in particular serious shortages of some food and items of general consumption—such as coffee, meat, edible oil, detergents, and medicines—created an atmosphere of social dissatisfaction. A decrease in the standard of living (in July, real personal income was 7% lower than in 1979)

contributed to a pervasive feeling of uncertainty. The upheaval in Poland opened the possibility of pressure for reform, which certainly added to the mute worries of the new collective leadership.

Economy. If the immediate post-Tito phase did not bring any serious political challenge to the regime, the country's economy was facing an across-the-board crisis. Its main manifestations were an inflation rate that exceeded 30% by the end of the year; foreign indebtedness of about $13,000,000,000, of which almost 70% was to Western countries; only a slight decrease in the 1979 balance of payment deficit of more than $4,000,000,000; and an unemployment rate of more than 12%.

In an extremely frank and revealing interview given in early September, Veselin Djuranović, president of the Federal Executive Council (i.e., prime minister) enumerated and tried to explain the "many shortcomings" of the Yugoslav economy. Although he did cite the negative impact of general world economic disturbance, Djuranović also blamed essentially domestic weaknesses for the fact that economic stabilization was more elusive than ever since the reform of 1965. Quoting the late chief theoretician of Titoism, Edvard Kardelj, Djuranović spoke of a "deepening of economic disproportions" in a country in which the transition from dominance by the state in the overall sphere of social reproduction to dominance by associated labor has not yet been achieved. Djuranović also made the key admission that the basic tenet of Yugoslav socialism—the system of self-management—was "incompletely implemented and insufficiently developed," and that "bureaucratic-technocratic interests" had the upper hand in a country in which at the present time "we spend much and work little."

Identified as a particularly detrimental phenomenon by the prime minister were irresponsible and excessive investments over the years. "Up to 50% of the necessary funds may be lacking," he said. Djuranović then specified other deficiencies: low labor productivity and a general slowing of economic growth; exports below the planned figures and imports exceeding the permitted limits; illiquidity of many enterprises; a "practically nonfunctioning market"; new conflicts between the republics and provinces (tendencies toward local autarchy); shortages in supplies of raw materials, agricultural products, and food; an increase in the cost of living; and a real fall in earnings.

To combat the negative economic trends, the government on June 6 introduced a 30% devaluation of the national currency, raising the exchange rate of the U.S. dollar to 27.3 dinars from its previous level of 20.9. At the same time, the government ordered an overall price freeze. The essential aim of the devaluation was to make imports more expensive and exports cheaper, especially at a time when new and more favorable economic arrangements with the Economic Community (EC) were taking effect (July 1). A five-year agreement between Yugoslavia and the EC had been signed April 2, assuring a freer access to EC markets of Yugoslav industrial and agricultural goods.

Hopes to improve the country's financial situation rested also on new foreign credit arrangements. The International Monetary Fund (IMF) approved $460 million in support of the stabilization programs of 1980 and 1981. Banks in Kuwait agreed to provide $750 million in loans between 1980 and 1982; Austrian banks agreed to a $100 million loan; and other borrowings were being negotiated from institutions in other Arab and European countries. Untapped potentials in agricultural production and tourism also were seen as promising for the future.

On October 31, the government announced various new regulations, including the free formation of prices for some nonessential industrial goods, stricter conditions for obtaining consumer goods, and imposition of a national ceiling on retail meat prices. The Iran-Iraq war was expected to cause oil shortages during the winter because Yugoslavia had been importing one third of its total fuel needs from these countries.

Foreign Relations. As expected, the foreign policy line pursued by the new leadership was of pure Tito vintage. Official state delegations from 121 countries, as well as the highest representatives from Communist parties and other political movements around the world, attended Tito's elaborate funeral in Belgrade on May 8. The funeral became an occasion for informal discussions between and among world leaders. Besides paying their respects to the late Yugoslav leader, such prominent foreign dignitaries as Soviet President Leonid Brezhnev, Chinese Chairman Hua Guofeng, British Prime Minister Margaret Thatcher, Indian Prime Minister Indira Gandhi, premiers Raymond Barre of France, Francesco Cossiga of Italy, and Masayoshi Ohira of Japan, Chancellor Helmut Schmidt of West Germany, as well as kings, presidents, and party leaders, used the occasion for a large number of informal

Arthur Grace, Sygma

Upon his arrival in Belgrade, June 24, U.S. President Jimmy Carter pledged the continued "friendship and support of the United States." Yugoslav President Cvijetin Mijatović welcomed both the visitor and his remarks.

In 1980, the people of Yugoslavia faced shortages of agricultural products, food, and other commodities.

UPI

diplomatic meetings. Notable absentees from the funeral were U.S. President Jimmy Carter, French President Valéry Giscard d'Estaing, and Cuban head of state and government Fidel Castro.

Despite Yugoslavia's condemnation of the Soviet invasion of Afghanistan and its vote in the United Nations General Assembly for the withdrawal of Soviet troops from that country, Yugoslav-Soviet relations were as intensive and outwardly friendly and cooperative in the economic and political fields as they were during the last years of Tito's life. Still, the LCY boycotted the Soviet-inspired conference on peace and disarmament, sponsored by the French and Polish Communist parties and held in Paris, April 28–29.

The confrontation in Poland between the workers' movement and the central government and Communist party was widely reported and commented on in the Yugoslav press. Insistence on the failure of central planning and manage-

——— YUGOSLAVIA · Information Highlights ———

Official Name: Socialist Federal Republic of Yugoslavia.
Location: Southwestern Europe.
Area: 98,650 sq mi (255 504 km^2).
Population (1980 est.): 22,400,000.
Chief Cities (1974 est.): Belgrade, the capital, 845,000; Zagreb, 602,000; Skopje, 389,000.
Government: *Head of state*, collective state presidency, Cvijetin Mijatović, president (took office May 1980). *Head of government*, Veselin Djuranović, prime minister (took office March 1977). *Legislature*—Federal Assembly: Federal Chamber and Chamber of Republics and Provinces.
Monetary Unit: Dinar (27.45 dinars equal U.S.$1, Aug. 1980).
Manufactures (major products): Processed food, machinery, textiles, nonferrous metals, wood.
Agriculture (major products): Corn, wheat, sugar beets, tobacco.
GNP (1978 est., U.S.$): $45,000,000,000.
Foreign Trade (1979, U.S.$): *Imports*, $12,862,000,000; *exports*, $6,491,000,000.

ment of the Polish economy, as well as the absence of working people from the decision-making process, were common themes in the Yugoslav press. But by the same token, some of the aspirations and achievements of Polish workers were hailed as the beginnings of a genuine workers' democracy along the lines of Yugoslavia's own self-management system. Other aspects of the events in Poland, however, such as the demand for the lifting of censorship, the role of the Catholic Church, and the activities of dissident intellectuals, often were not covered or discussed. Threats of a Soviet invasion of Poland were categorically denounced.

Despite his absence from Tito's funeral, president Carter visited Yugoslavia on June 24. Upon his arrival, Carter declared that the United States "supports and will continue to support the independence, territorial integrity, and unity of Yugoslavia."

Cautiously but persistently, Yugoslav diplomatic representatives and press expressed concern over the weakening of the nonaligned movement. Deeply regretted by Yugoslavia were the Cuban-led shift toward the Soviet Union and the movement's further debilitation by conflict among its members, such as Iran and Iraq. And while Tito's absence naturally diminished Yugoslavia's prestige among the nonaligned nations, a number of state visits were exchanged and important financial agreements were reached in Belgrade and other Third World capitals.

In Central Europe and the Balkans, there was an improvement in Yugoslav relations with Austria, a rapprochement with Albania, a lull in disputes with Bulgaria, and a continuation of close cooperation with Rumania.

MILORAD M. DRACHKOVITCH
The Hoover Institution
Stanford University

YUKON

A dispute at federal-provincial constitutional talks over the status of the territory, a major new mineral discovery, and a modern-day gold rush were events of significance in the Yukon Territory. An $89.7 million budget with a $3 million deficit was presented to the legislature in March.

Government and Politics. The federal Liberal government's offer to the Yukon government to attend the constitutional talks as observers only precipitated a boycott by Yukon government leader Chris Pearson, who demanded permission to speak and table documents at the constitutional conference. (*See also* special report, page 172).

A federal report recommended to the Trudeau cabinet that the Yukon's constitutional status as initiated by the former federal Conservative government remain unchanged.

Renewable Resources Minister Swede Hanson resigned following disclosures of his involvement with a native Indian organization and subsequent legal action against him and the Yukon government.

Economy and Energy. The discovery of a new ore body at the Yukon's largest producing mine in Faro extended the projected life of the operation beyond the year 2000. Prior to the discovery, the Cyprus Anvil lead-zinc mine was expected to exhaust its mineral base by the mid-1980s.

Gold mining continued at an accelerated rate because of the record high prices for precious metals on the world market. A major coal deposit discovered in the remote Bonnet Plume region gave promise of a future thermoelectric generating plant.

Natural gas wells in southeastern Yukon came on stream, and a number of political and financial hurdles were cleared for the Alaska Highway natural gas pipeline. Clearing of the right-of-way began during the summer, and the final route of the pipeline corridor was established. The pipeline will run from Prudhoe Bay, AK, through the Yukon, and eventually to the southern United States.

Tourism continued to play a key role in the economy, generating in excess of (C.) $30 million.

A labor dispute interrupted production at the United Keno Hills Mines in Elsa. It was the only strike in the territory during the year.

ANDREW HUME
Free-lance writer, Whitehorse, Yukon

─────── YUKON · Information Highlights ───────

Area: 207,076 sq mi (536 327 km²).
Population (1980 est.): 21,400.
Chief City (1980 est.): Whitehorse, the capital, 16,649.
Government (1980): *Chief Officers*—commissioner, vacant; administrator, Douglas Bell; government leader, Christopher Pearson; chief justice, Court of Appeal, and judge of the Supreme Court, H. C. B. Maddison. *Legislature*—16 member legislative assembly.
Education (1980 est.): *Enrollment*—public elementary and secondary schools, 5,120 pupils.

ZAIRE

Zaire's fiscal situation remained precarious as fears of foreign-based intervention receded. Despite pessimistic prediction of lingering political instability, President Mobutu Sese Seko governed unchallenged amidst cabinet reshuffles and modest reforms. Pope John Paul II visited the nation in May.

No Follow-up Invasions. In spite of Western concern following the 1977 and 1978 rebel invasions of the southern province, Shaba looked secure. Agreement by Angola, Zambia, and Zaire not to harbor one another's dissidents was helping to guarantee the peace. Prior to early 1980, Mobutu had spent much time in Shaba trying to strengthen the hold of the army and to publicize renewed safety.

The Zairian army, once as much inclined toward looting as the rebels, was retrained. But armed gangs still threatened life and property.

Economy and Mining. Copper volume and income were still low due to a continued slump in world prices as well as a lack of the spare parts and expertise needed to extract the ore. Yet the decline was less than anticipated. The shortest export route, across Angola by the Benguela railway, continued to be inoperative because of guerrilla fighting against the Angolan government. Cobalt and industrial diamond output were sizable, with Zaire producing a high percentage of the world's supply. Timber and tobacco production were rising, but transportation remained poor.

Once again, the government devalued the zaire, this time by 30%. The International Monetary Fund (IMF) dictated this devaluation to align the official exchange rate with the market value. The hope was to boost official export trade and reduce smuggling. In return the IMF agreed to another disbursement of credit, and Western creditors assented to reschedule some of Zaire's external debt in return for Mobutu's intention to cut budget deficits.

Domestic Affairs. Neither Mobutu's foreign creditors' pressure for political liberalization nor his troubles in Shaba weakened his position. A major reshuffling of his cabinet in January confirmed his strength as well as his benign policy toward former opponents, two of whom were named to the new cabinet.

Mobutu promised two popular reforms. The army was being returned to the barracks in the interest of public safety; the state police was to be inspected for corruption. Although there was no convincing evidence of a united rebel opposition, there was widespread disenchantment with pervasive corruption in the government and police force, along with dissatisfaction with low wages ($150 per month is the average), high prices (the inflation rate was estimated at 200%), and lack of electricity, running water, and passable roads. Kinshasa university students staged a strike to protest conditions.

François Lehr, Liaison

Zaire's income from copper was low, due to a slump in world prices and a shortage of mining equipment.

Another announced reform sought to change the educational curricula in favor of vocational and agricultural training at the expense of purely academic degrees. In the past the latter led to salaried occupations in the government or business. Parents and educators were displeased by this change. Mobutu also announced the promotion of women's rights. The mobilization of women into the president's party, the Popular Revolutionary Movement, could strengthen the regime.

The spontaneous and rapturous celebrations during the pope's visit in May provided brief respite from Zairian troubles. Unfortunately, seven women and two children were crushed to death while attempting to attend a mass celebrated by the pontiff.

――――― **ZAIRE • Information Highlights** ―――――

Official Name: Republic of Zaire.
Location: Central equatorial Africa.
Area: 905,365 sq mi (2 344 895 km²).
Population (1980 est.): 29,300,000.
Chief Cities (1976 est.): Kinshasa, the capital, 2,443,876; Kananga, 704,211.
Government: *Head of state,* Mobutu Sese Seko, president (took office Nov. 1965). *Head of government,* Nguza Karl-I-Bond, prime minister (took office Aug. 1980). *Legislature* (unicameral)—National Legislative Council.
Monetary Unit: Zaire (2.88 zaires equal U.S. $1, June 1980).
Manufactures (major products); Processed and unprocessed minerals, consumer products, metal and chemical products, construction materials, steel.
Agriculture (major products): Palm oil, coffee, rubber, tea, cotton, cocoa beans, manioc, plantains, corn, rice, vegetables, fruits, sugarcane.
GNP Per Capita (1978 est., U.S.$): $210.
Foreign Trade (Jan.-June 1979 , U.S.$): *Imports,* $271,-000,000; *exports,* $520,000,000.

Foreign Affairs. Although the nature of its economic woes makes for closer ties with Western nations, Zaire maintained relations with both East and West. Mobutu, who has been courted by the Chinese since the mid-1970s, visited China, where he signed a cultural agreement. China also agreed to assist in the training of commando units.

The United States continued to help Zaire despite criticism in the House of Representatives Subcommittee on Africa about Zaire's lack of progress in political reforms and human rights. American officials continued to regard Mobutu's leadership as Zaire's best hope for stability.

Although relations with neighboring Angola and Zambia remained good, Zaire and the People's Republic of the Congo hurled charges against each other. The Zairian government claimed that an unsuccessful rebel plot was hatched across the Zaire (Congo) River. In January, the Congo government repatriated a number of Zairians living there. The two actions point up the strained relations between the two capitals.

Contrary to policies elsewhere in the continent, Mobutu seeks to increase the number of European resident workers and entrepreneurs. By so doing, he hopes to boost the ailing agricultural and small business sectors. Mobutu discussed with Portugal's president an increase in Portuguese immigration.

See also AFRICA.

THOMAS H. HENRIKSEN
Hoover Institution on War, Revolution and Peace

Prince Charles and Lord Soames watch as the British flag is lowered for the final time in Zimbabwe.

ZIMBABWE

For Zimbabwe 1980 was the year of independence, the *annus mirabilis* of the black Rhodesian independence movement. It brought to a conclusion a momentous chapter in the history of the former British colony. After more than 20 years of sustained opposition to white supremacy and seven years of bitter and bloody guerrilla conflict, the militant and "external" black nationalist leaders emerged as the victors in a British-supervised general election based on universal franchise. They inherited a British-style parliamentary system and effective control of the military forces, the police, and all the various departments of government. International sanctions aimed at Prime Minister Ian Smith's illegal Rhodesian governments since his unilateral declaration of independence in 1965 had been lifted following the success of the London Conference in December and the resumption of direct British rule. Now, international recognition followed swiftly as Zimbabwe became the 153d member of the UN and the 50th state in the Organization of African Unity.

Internal Affairs. The first half of 1980 was dominated by the general election in February, the preparations for independence, and the inauguration of the new government in April. The election, which was marked by violence and bloodshed, took place in two stages. The first was confined to the 20 seats reserved by the new constitution for whites. These seats were swept by Smith's Rhodesian Front party.

The second occupied the last three days of February. The leaders of the Patriotic Front alliance, Robert Mugabe and Joshua Nkomo, contested the election separately as the heads of their respective movements. The other main contestant was the former prime minister in Smith's short-lived internal settlement, Bishop Muzorewa. At stake were the remaining 80 parliamentary seats. In all, nine political groups took part. Under the British governor-general, Lord Soames, the security arrangements consisted of a small British and Commonwealth contingent of troops and police and official observers. Some 14 truce assembly camps were set up across the country for the guerrilla forces.

Rarely has an election been watched so closely by press corps and interested external groups. While most reported on the intimidation practiced, they generally were agreed that it was not enough to explain the decisive results of the voting. Mugabe's Zimbabwe African National Union-Patriotic Front (ZANU-PF) captured 57 seats and, therefore, an absolute majority in the Parliament; his erstwhile ally Nkomo won 20 for the Zimbabwe African People's Union-Patriotic Front (ZAPU-PF), while Bishop Muzorewa's United African National Council (UANC) succeeded in winning only 3. The 2.7 million votes cast constituted something close to a 94% turnout of the electorate. Mugabe's share was 63%. The

Zimbabweans mark the election victory of Robert Mugabe (above). He formed a government in the spring.

results were announced amid loud cries of foul play on all sides.

Independence. The extent of Mugabe's landslide victory took the British government—and many others—by surprise. It also relieved Lord Soames of the need for what might have been very difficult choices fraught with disruptive consequences. Reportedly, he had been considering a coalition government. But on the same day as the official announcement of the election results, March 4, he invited Mugabe to become prime minister-designate and to form a government pending a speedy transition to full independence and the withdrawal of the British government. The British authorities made it clear that this would be delayed no longer than it took to fulfill the constitutional requirements, namely, the announcement of the new government, the election of the Senate, and the choice by electoral college of the ceremonial state president. The Senate, a 40-member chamber with power to delay but not veto legislation, gives half the seats to the parliamentary majority while the other half are chosen by whites and traditional chiefs. All this done, Lord Soames was to depart immediately. As expected, Mugabe's party dominated the Senate. On April 11, his close ally, the Rev. Canaan Banana, was chosen president-elect. Finally, the independence celebrations were set for April 17–18.

With Prince Charles presiding, the handing over of sovereignty took place at midnight. The Union Jack was lowered and the new Zimbabwe flag raised in its place to the accompaniment of a 21-gun salute. Representatives of more than 100 states were present at the ceremonies. The United States, which became the first country to open an embassy in the new state, was represented by Averell Harriman and Andrew Young. Former Prime Minister Ian Smith was not present; he had left for a lecture tour of South Africa. There were a few incidents but nothing like those which led *Time* to describe the two months of electioneering as "marked by political violence, brutality, and intimidation, perhaps the worst in the history of the continent's turbulent independence movements." Most observers would have echoed the words attributed to Lord Soames: "this has been nothing less than a series of miracles."

The New Government. There is no space to catalogue the anxieties, suspicions, hostility, and fears—of violence, resumption of warfare, treachery, rejection of the election results or the refusal by one party or another to abide by them, or of a coup—which threatened the path of independence. But few were more pervasive than the doubts raised by the reputation of Mugabe. A self-professed Marxist, he generally was regarded by those not his supporters as a radical extremist, the most intractable of the nationalist leaders, and the head of guerrilla forces whose behavior in the war, against black and white civilians, had been ruthless and brutal.

In his first post-election address to the country Mugabe showed himself well aware of his image. He called for peace, moderation, and reconciliation. "Today, white or black, we are all Zimbabweans," he said. And he promised to bring the other parties into the government, to give the constitution a fair trial, and not to impose any sweeping program of nationalization or appropriation. He also said that Zimbabwe would seek membership in the Commonwealth and pursue a nonaligned foreign policy.

His first actions gave some substance to his words. He turned first to his former partner and rival, Joshua Nkomo, and invited him to join a coalition government. Nkomo agreed, refusing the presidency and settling for the ministry of home affairs. Three of Nkomo's supporters were appointed to minor cabinet posts and two more as deputy ministers. Mugabe also persuaded two prominent Rhodesian Front (RF) whites to join him. Former Finance Minister and Deputy Prime Minister David Smith became minister of commerce and industry, while the leader of the country's white farmers, Dennis Norman, became minister of agriculture. As expected, the 22-member cabinet remained firmly in the hands of Mugabe's party, 14 of whom came from its powerful central committee.

But as important as any other of his early moves was his decision to ask Lt. Gen. Peter Walls to retain the supreme military command and to preside over the integration of the former Rhodesian army and the guerrilla forces in a new national army.

Again and again throughout the year Mugabe gave evidence of his readiness to temper his ideology with a pragmatic recognition of the problems confronting the country. In practical terms this involved the need to retain and reassure the country's skilled white industrial and commercial manpower, and above all its vital white agriculture, while at the same time satisfying those of his followers who increasingly were demanding rapid change and the fruits of victory. Then there was the continued rivalry and periodic violence between the Mugabe and Nkomo guerrilla forces, most of whom at the end of the year were still heavily armed and far from demobilization or assimilation into either the new army or the country's work force. Nor was Mugabe's task made any easier by two heavily publicized crises in the government, both of which intimately affected the various armed groups in the country as well as the whites.

The Armed Forces. The first of these crises concerned General Walls, whose reappointment by Mugabe was seen by the whites as some guarantee of continuity and security. Walls resigned as of July 29 and went on leave pending his retirement by the end of the year. He was said to have been frustrated and defeated by the conflicts between the two rival guerrilla forces, whose leaders, Rex Nhongo and Dumiso Dabengwa, were appointed with him to a new Joint Command and by the failure to speed up the formation of the new army. On leave, he made a series of statements which brought down a storm of controversy on himself and on the country. He revealed that he had asked Britain's Prime Minister Margaret Thatcher to reject the election results on the ground of widespread intimidation by ZANU-PF. Prime Minister Mugabe was outraged. He condemned the behavior as disloyalty and stated that Walls could not be allowed to re-

Robert Mugabe and other officials welcome Prince Charles to Salisbury for independence ceremonies.
Jordan, Liaison

Guerrillas overturn a bus in the town of Rusape in February. Such terrorist activity was common throughout the election campaign.

UPI

main in the country. Finally on September 17 Mugabe dismissed him and General Walls ultimately was forbidden to return to Zimbabwe.

Mugabe's hopes of slowing white emigration received yet another blow when on August 6 his minister of manpower planning and development, and the secretary-general of his party, Edgar Tekere, guerrilla commander and hero, was arrested and charged with the murder of a 68-year-old white farmer. Mugabe sent word to Parliament that justice would be done. He had ordered the arrest—which also included six of Tekere's bodyguards who were with him during the attack on the farm—but after bail was at first refused Mugabe felt compelled to give his personal assurances to the court that his minister would appear at the trial. Tekere had been a consistent and outspoken critic of Mugabe's moderation toward both the whites and Nkomo's party. There were popular demonstrations in his favor in the capital and the guerrilla

camps. On December 8, he was acquitted. The white judge was overruled by two black magistrate-assessors who held in terms of the 1975 Indemnity and Compensation Act covering ministers that Tekere had acted "in good faith" to suppress terrorism.

Meanwhile by the end of the year white emigration had risen once again to close to 2,000 a month. No attempt to disarm the guerrilla groups had been made, and the new integrated army consisted of only a few battalions.

External Affairs. The election results took the South African government by surprise; Prime Minister P. W. Botha confined himself to a warning that Pretoria would not interfere unless Zimbabwe became a base for guerrilla warfare against his republic. Mugabe reiterated his intention of avoiding a confrontation with South Africa. However, he did not invite South Africa to the independence celebrations and it was known that he would break official diplomatic relations—which he announced July 4—but maintain the vital economic and transportation links through a trade office as Mozambique did.

On August 4 Mugabe welcomed his ally, Mozambique's President Samora Machel, as the country's first state visitor. On August 20 he left with a 27-member delegation for a week-long visit to the United States, officially to address the UN. A main concern of his government was the question of U.S. economic aid and investment in Zimbabwe. The United States had promised $20 million in 1980 and $30 million for 1981. Britain had promised $172 million over five years. But these figures made up but a fraction of the sum needed to repair the ravages of seven years of war.

R. B. Ballinger, *Rhode Island College*

ZIMBABWE · Information Highlights

Official Name: Republic of Zimbabwe.
Location: Southern Africa.
Area: 150,673 sq mi (390 245 km²).
Population (1980 est.): 7,400,000.
Chief Cities (Dec. 1978): Salisbury, the capital, 616,000; Bulawayo, 357,000.
Government: *Head of state,* Canaan Banana, president (took office April 1980). *Head of government,* Robert Mugabe, prime minister (took office March 1980). *Legislature*—Parliament: Senate and House of Assembly.
Monetary Unit: Zimbabwe dollar (0.694 Z. dollar equals U.S.$1, March 1980).
Manufactures (major products): Textiles, machinery, fertilizers.
Agriculture (major products): Tobacco, sugar, tea, groundnuts, cotton, corn, millet, sorghum, wheat.
GNP Per Capita (1978 est., U.S.$): $480.
Foreign Trade (1979, U.S.$): *Imports,* $937,000,000; *exports,* $1,164,000,000.

ZOOLOGY

Concern for animal welfare continued to be newsworthy in the popular press, but the impact of human land use on rare and endangered species often only made page two. Orchestrated campaigns to save threatened animal life were conducted by various groups in Europe and America. In the United States, the Research Modernization Act (HR 4805) was introduced in Congress to create a Center for Alternative Research to curb research on live animals. The proposed center could cut off funds to any federal project using live animals if it judged that "mathematical models, isolated organs, tissue or cell cultures ... mechanical models, computer simulation or lower organisms" would serve the same purpose. Even congressmen not connected with the bill received many supporting letters. One congressman revealed that "we got ten letters on windfall profits and something like 600 so far on research modernization."

Discoveries. Eric G. Barham of the National Marine Fisheries Services in La Jolla, CA, reported that the primitive chordate group Larvacea occurs in large numbers in the deep ocean. Further, these relatively large (3 inches or 76 mm), tadpolelike animals secrete "houses" of mucus up to 39 inches (100 cm) in diameter. These structures serve as elaborate feeding structures, directing the flow of water into restricted areas where food materials are trapped by a sieve. They are temporary structures that are abandoned when damaged or clogged with debris. New houses can be rapidly secreted, and some larvacea apparently form new feeding structures every two to four hours.

New Species. Several hundred new animal species were named during the year. Canadian zoologists Robert G. B. Reid and Frank R. Bernard reported a new species of gutless clams from the northeastern Pacific Ocean. Landis L. Hinesley named a new species of grasshopper mouse from New Mexico.

Paleontology. The discovery of the remains of a giant bird from fossil beds near Buenos Aires, Argentina, was given popular press coverage. The remains are from the Pliocene Epoch and are about 5 million years old. These condor-like birds, called teratorns, had wingspreads of about 25 ft (7.6 m) and probably weighed 160 to 170 lbs (73 to 77 kg). The find was made by Eduardo P. Tonni and Rosendo Pascual of Argentina's La Plata Museum.

Today, penguins occur only in southern hemisphere regions, but paleontologists have discovered remains of a new family of flightless birds that lived in the north Pacific. These giant diving birds, like penguins, used their wings as underwater propulsion devices. Starrs L. Olson of the Smithsonian Institution in Washington, DC, and Yoshikazu Hasegawa of the National Science Museum of Japan reported that some of the birds grew to nearly 7 ft (2m) long. They

In January 1980, the U.S. Department of the Interior issued a new list of the ten most endangered species in North America. Among the animal species on the list were the dusky seaside sparrow, the snail darter, and the red wolf.

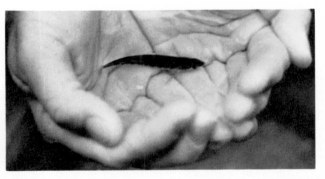

Photos US Fish & Wildlife Service; Tennessee Valley Authority (snail darter)

The new endangered species list also included the Houston toad, left, and Kemp's Ridley sea turtle.

lived 25 to 40 million years ago and may have become extinct because seals and porpoises evolved to fill their food niche.

Behavior. One group of tropical spiders never spins its own webs but survives by eating insects trapped in the webs of various other, orb-weaving spiders. The kleptoparasitic species has a long, fine thread leading from the host's orb to its own hiding place. Fritz Vollrath of the Smithsonian Tropical Research Institute in the Canal Zone, Panama, reported how vibrations through this thin thread communicate detailed information concerning the location and activities of the orb spider and of prey on the web.

For several years, zoologists have been reporting that higher primates such as apes can use signs as language. In 1980, however, the conclusion was disputed by several scientists who maintained that the ape response is simply a mimicking of signs made by trainers and not a spontaneous attempt to communicate. (*See* Anthropology.)

The relative heat-absorbing and reflecting qualities of black and white surfaces have long been known. Various zoologists have proposed that plumage coloration in birds may play an important role in body temperature regulation. However, Sheldon Lustick and his associates at The Ohio State University showed that dark herring gulls can, by changing their posture, become "white" as far as heat absorption is concerned. Body position in relation to the heat source, and not feather color, appears to be the controlling factor.

Christopher W. Clark and Jane M. Clark of the State University of New York at Stony Brook reported the results of experiments in which recorded sounds were played back to Southern Right Whales. Their results indicated that these whales recognize recordings of sounds made by their own species but not sounds made by other species or various other tones and sounds.

Concealing colors and other adaptations for escaping notice are well documented, but Robert Silberglied and Annette Aiello of the Smithsonian Tropical Research Institute in Panama reported a rather extreme example. Exoskeletons of most insects shed water. However, certain bark-inhabiting bugs have evolved surface layers that become wet. Thus, when tropical rains wet the bark of trees and change the reflectivity of the surface, the "wettable" surface of the bug permits an automatic compensation.

Important new books in the field of behavioral zoology included Bern Henrich's *Bumblebee Economics,* in which biological energy is analyzed in terms of costs and benefits; and *Behavioural Ecology,* edited by J. R. Krebs and N. B. Davies, which evaluates current theories of genetics, ethology, and ecology.

Evolution. Zoologists continued to be inundated by books and articles on Darwinian evolution. The year included four new books concerned with the paleobiological view. M. R. House edited *The Origin of Major Invertebrate Groups;* Jasen A. Lillegraven and associates edited *Mesozoic Mammals: The First Two-Thirds of Mammalian History;* George Gaylord Simpson authored *Splendid Isolation: The Curious History of South American Mammals;* and Frederick S. Szalay and Eric Delsen wrote *Evolutionary History of the Primates.*

Other new books on evolution included *Herbivores: Their Interaction with Secondary Plant Metabolites,* edited by Gerald A. Rosenthal and Daniel H. Janzen; *Diversity of Insect Faunas,* edited by L. A. Mound and N. Waloff, which attempts to explain the evolutionary success of insects; and Michael Ruse's thoughtful *The Darwinian Revolution: Science Red in Tooth and Claw* which focuses more on the history of evolutionary ideas and concepts than on the details of the theory.

E. Lendell Cockrum
University of Arizona

INDEX

Main article headings appear in this index as bold-faced capitals; subjects within articles appear as lower-case entries. Both the general references and the subentries should be consulted for maximum usefulness of this index. Illustrations are indexed herein. Cross references are to the entries in this index.

A

ABC: see American Broadcasting Company
Abdul-Jabbar, Kareem (Amer. athl.) 489
ABMs: see Antiballistic Missiles
Abortion 55, 189, 321, 473, 576
  Catholicism 465
  Israel 461
  Italy 472
  Massachusetts 347
  North Dakota 402
  Presidential Campaign 472
  South Dakota 403
Abscam Investigation 552
  New Jersey 394
  Pennsylvania 429
Abu Dhabi, UAE 33
Academy Awards 444
Access, Right of (U.S. law)
  Shopping Centers 322
  Trials 321
ACCIDENTS AND DISASTERS 98
  Atlanta Day-Care Center Explosion 252
  Earthquakes 247, 299
  MGM Grand Hotel Fire 392
  Michigan Storm Damage 357
  Mount St. Helens Eruption 248, 274, 573
  Nebraska 390
  North Dakota Weather 402
  North Sea Oil Platform 404
  Tampa Bay 235
  Titan Missile Silo Explosion 125
  Toxic Waste Explosion 181
  U.S. Drought and Heat Wave 275, 308, 390, 402, 424, 525

Vietnam Monsoons 571
  West Virginia Methane Explosion 575
Acid Rain 174, 223
Acupuncture (med.) 137
Adamson, Joy (Aus. nov., conservationist) 414
Adaptation (zool.) 592
Administration on Aging (U.S.) 424
Adoption Assistance and Child Welfare Act (1980) 58
ADVERTISING 99
  Federal Trade Commission 554
  Magazines 446, 447
  Mobil Oil Advertising Controversy 520
  Olympic Games 67
  Public Utilities 322
Affirmative Action Programs (U.S.) 227
AFGHANISTAN 100, 134, 361
  China 187
  India 278
  Islam 46
  Mining 366
  Pakistan 427, 428
  Refugees 453
  Third World 531
  United Nations 545, 547
  United States 564
  USSR 540, 541
  Illus. 82
AFL-CIO: see American Federation of Labor–Congress of Industrial Organizations
AFRICA 104
  Agriculture 112
  Food Shortages and Famine 236, 472
  Refugees 454
  United States 564
  USSR 542

African Development Bank 104
AFT: see American Federation of Teachers
Aged: see Older Population
Agent Orange (herbicide) 570
AGRICULTURE 110
  Agriculture and Resources Inventory 480
  Archaeology 119, 120
  Chemicals Output 282
  European Community 262
  Food 236
  Genetics 243
  Green Revolution 106
  International Trade and Finance 287
  Maine Potato Farmers' Protest 345
  Mount St. Helens Effects 251
Agriculture, Department of (U.S.) 555
Aid India Consortium 278
Ailey, Alvin (Amer. choreog.) 205
Air Conditioners 284
Aircraft Industry 282, 284
Airplane (film) 372
  Illus. 376
Airplane Crashes 98, 264, 390
Air Pollution:
  Chemical Waste Disposal 50
  Mount St. Helens Eruption 274
  Illus. 355
Air Transportation 533 fol.
  Accidents 98, 264, 390
  Business Travel 164
Aksyonov, Vasily P. (Russ. nov.) 544
ALA: see American Library Association
ALABAMA 113
ALASKA 113
  Alaska Lands Act 218, 551, 558
  Archaeology 120

Alaska Highway Natural Gas Pipeline, U.S.–Can. 115, 171, 585
ALBANIA 115
  Ecuador 208
  Yugoslavia 584
Albee, Edward (Amer. dram.) 527
ALBERTA 116, 170 fol., 174
Alcohol (chem.):
  Alcohol-Powered Vehicles 162
  Biomass Synfuels 219
Alcoholism 352, 473
  Pregnancy 350
  Sweden 512
Alexander, Sadie (Amer. law.) 424
ALGERIA 116, 105
  Earthquake 247
  Tunisia 537
  Illus. 246
Algiers Pact (1975) 35
Ali, Muhammad (Amer. athl.) 492
Aliens, Illegal: see Illegal Aliens
Allen, Woody (Amer. writ., act., dir.) 374
Allon, Yigal (Isr. pol. leader) 298, 414
Altman, Robert (Amer. film dir.) 373, 375
Aluminum 366
  Venezuela 568
Amadeus, play (Shaffer) 528
Amalgamated Clothing and Textile Workers 315, 401
Amaluza Dam, Ecua. 221
Amerasinghe, Hamilton Shirley (Sri Lankan dipl.) 414
American Academy and Institute of Arts and Letters Awards 443, 444
American Association of Petroleum Geologists 247
American Ballet Theatre 204, 205
American Book Awards, The 329, 333, 444

Put The World At Your Fingertips . . .

ORDER THIS EXQUISITELY DETAILED LENOX GLOBE

The world's never looked better! Why? Because this Lenox Globe — the most popular raised-relief model made by Replogle — is as stunning to look at as the living planet it represents.

Handsomely crafted and easy-to-use, the Lenox is the latest word in the state of the mapmaker's art — an ingenious marriage of classic, antique styling with clean, modern readability.

The Lenox is a giant 12-inch globe, beautifully inscribed with eye-catching "cartouches" and colorful compass "roses" . . . solidly-mounted on an elegantly sturdy, 18-inch Fruitwood stand . . . and covered with three dimensional "mountain ranges" children love to touch!

Five pounds light, the Lenox comes complete with a 32-page **STORY OF THE GLOBE** — a richly-illustrated, full-color handbook you and your whole family will refer to over and over again.

TO ORDER, simply send us your name and address, along with a check or money order for $29.95* to:

> Grolier Yearbook, Inc.
> Lenox Globe
> Sherman Turnpike
> Danbury, Connecticut 06816

*Please note: New York and Connecticut residents must add state sales tax.

THE LENOX GLOBE . . . by Replogle. Make it yours *today.*